New American World
A Documentary History of North America to 1612

NEW
AMERICAN
WORLD

A Documentary History of
North America to 1612

IN FIVE VOLUMES

VOLUME III

English Plans for North America. The Roanoke Voyages. New England Ventures.

Edited, with a Commentary by

DAVID B. QUINN

With the Assistance of

Alison M. Quinn and Susan Hillier

ARNO PRESS
A New York Times Company

and

HECTOR BYE, INC.
New York, 1979

Copyright © David Beers Quinn, Alison Moffat Quinn, 1979

Library of Congress Cataloging in Publication Data
Main entry under title:

English plans for North America.

   (New American world ; v. 3)
    1. Virginia—History—Colonial period, ca. 1600-1775
—Sources. 2. New England—History—Colonial period,
ca. 1600-1775—Sources. I. Quinn, David Beers.
II. Quinn, Alison M. III. Hillier, Susan.
E101.N47 vol. 3 [F229]   970.01s [975.5'02] 78-23464
ISBN 0-405-10762-5

Library of Congress Cataloging in Publication Data
Main entry under title:

New American world.

   Includes bibliographies and indexes.
    1. America—Discovery and exploration—Sources.
2. America—History—To 1810—Sources. I. Quinn,
David Beers. II. Quinn, Alison M. III. Hillier,
Susan.
E101.N47   970.01   77-20483
ISBN 0-405-10759-5

Printed in the United States of America

Contents

PART XII.   THE ROANOKE VOYAGES, 1584–1590

PART XIV. THE ESTABLISHMENT OF A DUTCH PRESENCE IN NORTH AMERICA

Chapter Sixty-eight.   Hudson's Voyage

Maps
List of Plates

(Notes on the Maps will precede the plate section in each volume.)

VOLUME III

Preface

VOLUME III DIFFERS again from volumes one and two. Volume I has its sights on distant lands, but was mainly focused on defining a limited range of coasts and inlets with only one major incursion into the interior in the East (the St. Lawrence) and one (that of Coronado) into the West. Volume II concerns itself mainly with the major attempts to insert European influence into the interior of southern North America from the East, one achieving the first crossing of the continent, another (that of Soto) making a major attempt to do so. It also brings onto the stage the European rivalry of France and Spain, fought out for the first time on American soil in Florida, showing that North America was no longer merely marginal to affairs in the Old World. Volume III is, in some ways, a step backward. More than anything else it is concerned with what people wrote about colonization in North America without any practical achievement.

The English were most active in this writing. They start with theories about the Northwest Passage, and they go on to consider almost every other aspect of the theoretical possibilities for colonization opened up by North American discovery. They are not so effective in practice. Sir Humphrey Gilbert failed: Ralegh and the Hakluyts inspired Roanoke colonies, which interesting though they are, did not work out. Francis Drake's California exploit excited attention but led to no follow-up whatever. The same was true to some extent of the English New England ventures of the early seventeenth century. They, like their sixteenth-century precursors, produced valuable observation and theory but little in the way of practical result over six years of effort from 1602 to 1608. They fit into a sixteenth rather than a seventeenth-century context.

We know a great deal more than we used to about English activities in Norumbega (known as North Virginia from 1600 to 1614, and as New England after 1616) during the period it became known as North Virginia. The English explorations were extensive, and we still do not understand fully why they did not master before 1612 the art of establishing English communities there. This volume is more about the English than about anyone else, although it leaves for a later volume their actual attempts to discover a Northwest Passage, their most vigorously pursued American enterprise of the earlier period.

Introduction

THE ENGLISH DOCUMENTATION from about 1565 onward is more varied in character and diverse in the areas it represents than for the period immediately preceding. There are perhaps no narratives quite as extended or as dramatic as those for the great expeditions into the interior or the Franco-Spanish clash in Florida. They do include, however, the very significant and interesting documentation of the earliest English colonial plans and attempted settlements. Sir Humphrey Gilbert's plans are important if only to illustrate a type of land speculation that was not to be unknown in later America: the selling sight unseen of vast acreages which had never even been explored by the operators themselves. His formal annexation of Newfoundland in 1583 and his death at sea on the return voyage make dramatic episodes which highlight the fairly numerous attempts by the two great colonial theorists of the Elizabethan period— Richard Hakluyt, lawyer, the elder cousin, and Richard Hakluyt, preacher, the younger—to work out from 1578 onward what claims the English monarch should be able to make to America, to estimate the economic advantages it should be possible to obtain from English settlements in North America, and also to provide a battery of inducements to English settlers to uproot themselves from their homeland and install themselves in the empty (it seemed) and undeveloped lands of North America. These plans were not always realistic, partly because details of the climate and natural resources of North America were insufficient, and partly because they almost wholly ignored the occupants of North America—the American Indians were thought of mainly as passive factors in the European intrusion who might be of some assistance to the settlers but whose own right to occupy the lands coveted by Europeans and possible resistance was virtually disregarded.

The Roanoke voyages under the auspices of Sir Walter Ralegh, the half-brother of Sir Humphrey Gilbert, were of great importance as the first systematic attempt by Englishmen to settle in any part of North America.

The narratives of the expeditions of 1584 to 1590 were interesting and full in most respects (though of course they leave some episodes unexplained). If well known, they also require continuing study if we are to understand what the English tried to do, what they achieved, and why they failed. The 1584 narrative of Arthur Barlowe introduces us to "Virginia"—the northern section of the North Carolina coastlands—while the settlement on Roanoke Island in 1585–1586 is brought before us by Ralph Lane, by the summary of the results of a survey of the area's resources by Thomas Harriot, and by the drawings of John White. The colony's experience demonstrated that this was healthy country for Europeans since the settlers survived and returned in good physical shape to England in 1586. But it also showed that it was a mistake to underestimate the Indians' attachment to their land and to rely too much on the limited help they could or would give to intrusive settlements. It also showed how difficult it was to keep male settlers, mainly soldiers by trade, occupied in a situation where exploration was almost the only activity open to them. The French had already found this to be true in 1564–1565. The material Thomas Harriot and John White brought back provided the first report on conditions in North America available to Europeans (since it was so widely circulated between 1588 and 1600). Even if it is not as full as we might have hoped, it was and has remained an essential basic source of information on North American resources and inhabitants. The bringing back of the colonists by Drake in 1586, with no gold or jewels, disillusioned some Englishmen who thought of America only in terms of Mexico or Peru, but it encouraged others to seek for a real community settlement and led to the installation of John White's little group of families on Roanoke Island in 1587. The fact that they were then neglected (largely owing to the war with Spain in European waters) and that they disappeared brought the brief run of experiments to an end, but left behind the hope and expectation that the colonists, containing in themselves the seeds for their own survival, had flourished in their isolation. This helped to keep interest alive until the wars were over and settlements could start afresh.

Viewed from the longer term, the fullest and most interesting contribution the English made to the understanding of North America lay in a long series of projects, some of them comprised in published pamphlets, others remaining in the collections of those important persons to whom they had been directed. Most of them represented a reasonably coherent approach to some or all of the problems of combined economic exploitation and settlement, with some consideration of the Amerindian peoples and at least a token objective of turning them into Europeanized Christians. From the academic and dusty *Discourse* of Sir Humphrey Gilbert (written in 1566, later revised, but the first to suggest for over a generation a continuing English settlement in North America) to the sophistication of the younger Richard Hakluyt's "Particuler discourse" (*Discourse of Western Planting*) of 1584, and in the elaborate plan of Edward Hayes written about 1592–1593 (with the apparent collaboration of Christopher Carleill), there is a considerable development. The elder Richard Hakluyt, obsessed with the need an overpopulated England had for new markets and new sources of raw materials, made several brief but cogent pleas for the exploitation of various parts of eastern North America by English settlers during the years 1578 to 1585. His cousin, the younger Richard Hakluyt, compiled a great treatise for the guidance of Queen Elizabeth I in 1584 (though it is not certain she ever read it closely), summing up diplomatic, economic, social, and cultural reasons why Englishmen should take a hand in the settlement and exploitation of North America, preferably on a large scale (as indeed Gilbert had contemplated in 1582–1583) and with royal support as well as connivance. The difficulty with such plans was that they were based on little or no local knowledge of North American conditions; they assumed that soil and climate would be identical with those of Europe in similar latitudes, and they wholly underestimated the magnitude of the task of getting even a relatively small English population established in a territory in which they had to learn almost everything, and to do so in the face of a thickly settled, indigenous, and quite probably hostile population. The Hakluyts were especially keen on settlements in areas where "Mediterranean" conditions and crops might be found and favored latitudes around 48°N. But Christopher Carleill was more realistic. In 1583 he commended small trading and agricultural settlements rather farther north where climates more like those of England itself might be found, and from which gradual expansion into other areas might be contemplated. Edward Hayes, after a phase of hoping almost everything for an English settlement in Newfoundland which would control the international fishery, turned in the early 1590s (in apparent collaboration with Carleill) to more realistic plans for what we know as New England and the Maritimes. But, although the pamphlets of Christopher Carleill and Sir George Peckham in 1583 were linked with attempts to raise subscriptions for voyages, they did not have any great immediate impact.

Thomas Harriot's *Briefe and true report* (1588) had rather more. It was the fruit of an actual stay in parts of what are now North Carolina and Virginia, and his description of plant and animal products was more specific and not uncritical in its commentary (although we can regard it as rather optimistic in its view of future prospects). The narratives of the Roanoke colonies of 1584–1587 did provide some means of checking the pamphleteers, as did the published accounts of the Bartholomew Gosnold (1602) and George Waymouth (1605) voyages later—as will be shown in a succeeding volume. Yet the ground which the promotional literature covered was very wide; it represented much thinking—at least some of it constructive—on how to begin the settlement and exploitation of a great, new, and—from the European point of view if not that of the Amerindian inhabitants—unpeopled territory across the Atlantic (the crossing of which was becoming gradually a less fearsome thing to contemplate even for women and children).

The revival of English interest in Norumbega, which at the beginning of the seventeenth century came to be known as North Virginia (it was not New England until 1616), is treated as being very much in line with earlier English efforts to plan and settle various parts of North America in the sixteenth century. The narratives and discussions associated with the voyages of Bartholomew Gosnold, Martin Pring, and George Waymouth, with much of the surviving matter on the unsuccessful colony on the Kennebec in 1607–1608 (although much has also been lost), are very like those inspired by Richard Hakluyt in the sixteenth century and attempted under the auspices of Gilbert and Ralegh. The lack of success of all these men in establishing viable colonies of settlement is striking, but on the other hand the buildup of information they achieved on the areas explored did much to lay firm foundations (built on in 1614–16 by John Smith) for the wave of exceptionally successful colonization that began in 1620 and accelerated so amazingly in the 1630s. There is a case for considering them in parallel with the French activities in their Acadia (which comprised the later New England as well as the later Maritimes) between 1604 and 1607, but these were more integral with the eventual concentration of the French on the St. Lawrence Basin (with an outpost in Acadia) than with the

English ventures which led on, if rather farther in the future, to the colonization of New England.

Early English New England ventures should also not be considered wholly apart from what went on in what was at the opening of the century known as South Virginia. The Virginia Company 1606 charter envisaged the two sets of ventures running in double harness, but the three-year experiment from 1606 to 1609 showed clearly their whole impetus and function was to proceed on quite distinctive lines. Virginia was something unique, a prestige venture, which could not be allowed, at whatever the cost, to fail. What happened farther north was more a matter of empirical enterprise and speculation by much less influential bodies of men. The English colony in Newfoundland, begun in 1610, lay somewhere between the two. It showed that English men and women could settle on what had been thought to be an inhospitable island and could conduct a small settlement there with some success. But, although greater efforts were made to colonize there after 1612, the end result was to show that settlements in Newfoundland had little chance of permanence and, even when they became rooted, lacked the capacity to grow. The mainland was to be the hope of the future.

Finally, as a presage of things to come, we have Henry Hudson's discovery of the Hudson River in 1609 and the beginnings of an active Dutch movement to take part in the trade, if not yet the settlement, of the more temperate parts of the North American continent.

Note on Presentation
of Materials

SOME INDICATIONS of editorial methods must necessarily be given. We have modernized, except in a very few cases (where explanations are given), usages of "u," "v," "i," and "j." We have kept "yᵉ" although we are well aware that the bastardized thorn it contains annoys linguistic purists. Since we have retained "yt" or "yᵗ" meaning "it," we have expanded on grounds of possible confusion "yᵗ" meaning "that."

From 1582 onward continental dating was ten days ahead of English dating. For French and Spanish documents this must be kept in mind and, also, when relating English documents to continental. Where confusion is likely to arise, double dating has been given.

We have not been afraid to expand contracted words, without indication, in either printed or manuscript sources, except where there is a genuine ambiguity. We have capitalized proper names where we have thought fit to do so. We have added full points to complete sentences and occasionally used either the comma or full point for the slash (/) (where ambiguity might arise from its retention).

Sidenotes are frequent in sixteenth-century published works and less frequently in manuscripts. Usually, they simply form a running index to the contents of the document. Where they do so they have been omitted. But from time to time they either convey additional information or express the point of view of the contemporary editor. In such cases they have been added as footnotes.

Square brackets have been used to fill lacunae conjecturally, although usually with a question mark. They also comprise words or phrases in non-English languages that may not be conveyed clearly in the translation or where the exact words of the document appear important. Occasionally, but only occasionally, they are included to explain a word, or a place name, which otherwise might be wholly unintelligible.

Almost all documents have been printed in full, although where omissions have been made they are indicated in the headnotes. In a few cases where the text was not suitable for transcription in full, abstracts have been made.

For each document or closely associated group of documents bibliographical references have been given. In the case of major sources, of which there have been many editions, this has been expanded in the introduction to the appropriate section. The editors have been generous with their own writing. The introductions to each volume attempt to point to the major characteristics of the selection in that volume and to bring out major comparative points of relationship. Longish introductory passages have been given for main sections where it was felt that headnotes alone might not be sufficient. Subsections have been knit together by brief introductory summaries. Finally, individual headnotes have tried to throw light on the nature of the particular document without trying, however, to summarize its contents in detail. Precise consistency in producing introductory matter of these kinds has not been aimed at or achieved. What assistance appeared to be required for each group of documents was given, rather than attempt to follow a completely consistent plan. Over such a wide range of materials it would be surprising if some discrepancies in treatment, which were not intended, will be observed. A broad measure of uniformity has, it is hoped, been maintained. We believe that, within the terms of our brief, this is the best selection on this scale that we could make. We see many ways in which it could have been improved, but we profoundly believe it will be useful, although it cannot within its scale be definitive. Another generation of editors may perhaps put together on film, after spending unlimited time and money, the complete documentary record of earliest European contacts with America. We hope they do so, but we also wish the users of this present set many interesting and productive hours, reading from a well-printed set of books much of what remains on an endlessly stimulating and engrossing topic.

Abbreviations
Used in the Text

A.G.I., Seville. Archivo General de Indias, Seville

A.G. Simancas. Archivo General de Simancas

B.L. British Library, Reference Division (formerly British Museum Library)

Biggar, H.P. *Precursors of Jacques Cartier.* H.P. Biggar, *The Precursors of Jacques Cartier, 1497–1534.* Publications of the Public Archives of Canada, no. 5. Ottawa, 1911.

Calendar of State Papers, Spanish. (a) *Letters, Despatches and State Papers Relating to the Negotiations Between England and Spain, 1485–1558.* 14 vols., London, 1862–1954; (b) *Letters and State Papers Relating to English Affairs, Preserved Principally in the Archives of Simancas, 1558–1603.* 4 vols. London, 1892–1899.

Colección de documentos inéditos de Indias. Colección de documentos inéditos relativos al descubrimiento, conquista y colonización de las posesiones Española en América y Oceanía, edited by Joaquin F. Pacheco, Francisco de Cárdenas, and Luís Torres de Mendoza. 1st series. 42 vols. Madrid, 1864–1889.

Hist. MSS Comm. Historical Manuscripts Commission, *Reports,* London, 1868-.

N.Y.P.L. New York Public Library.

P.R.O. Public Record Office, London.

Quinn, D.B., *Gilbert.* D.B. Quinn, *The Voyages and Colonising Enterprises of Sir Humphrey Gilbert.* 2 vols. London, Hakluyt Society, 1940.

Quinn, D.B., *North American Discovery.* D.B. Quinn, *North American Discovery, c. 1000–1612.* New York, 1971.

Quinn, D.B., *Roanoke Voyages.* D.B. Quinn, *The Roanoke Voyages, 1584–1590.* 2 vols. Cambridge, Eng., Hakluyt Society, 1955.

Taylor, E.G.R., *Hakluyts*. Eva G.R. Taylor, *The Original Writings and Correspondence of the two Richard Hakluyts*. 2 vols. London, Hakluyt Society, 1935.

T.L.S. The Times Literary Supplement. London.

Williamson, J.A., *The Cabot Voyages* (1962). James A. Williamson, *The Cabot Voyages and Bristol Discovery under Henry VII*. Cambridge, Eng., Hakluyt Society, 1962.

Williamson, J.A., *The Voyages of the Cabots* (1929). James A. Williamson, *The Voyages of the Cabots and the English Discovery of North America in the Reigns of Henry VII and Henry VIII*. London, 1929.

VOLUME III

English Plans for North America. The Roanoke Voyages. New England Ventures.

X

English Colonial Plans and Projects, 1576–1602

THE MOST ORIGINAL contribution that Englishmen made to the long-term exploitation of North America in the later sixteenth century was not so much in action as in discussion. In a long series of reports, pamphlets, and books they discussed, with much variety but also much repetition, why England should take a part in the commerce, settlement, and exploitation of the area. They fortified these plans not only by experiments in exploration and settlement but also by publishing informative documents about French, English, and Spanish voyages and colonizing enterprises. Such collections were made in 1553, 1555, 1577, 1582, 1589, and 1598–1600 (as the general introduction to volume I indicates), and they were reinforced by a number of volumes containing translations of accounts of individual enterprises.

The colonial plans fall into a number of groups and phases. The first is dominated by Sir Humphrey Gilbert's *A discourse of discoverie of a new passage to Cataia* (1576) (355). This is a highly academic treatise using traditional and novel geographical arguments—not many of them based on actual experience—to establish that the seas to the north of North America were open to shipping and provided a Northwest Passage to the Pacific Ocean and thence to Asia. It also contained the first specific proposals for an English settlement in the most northerly part of North America, as a halfway house between the Atlantic and the Pacific. Written in 1566 in the course of a debate as to the respective merits of Northeast and Northwest passages (Vol. IV, nos. 652–653), the *Discourse* was revised in the early 1570s and published in 1576 when plans were being put in hand for a series of expeditions under Martin Frobisher to the Northwest (Vol. IV, nos. 457–463).

1

Richard Hakluyt the elder opened the colonizing phase directly in his "Notes" in 1578 (356) setting out North America as a field for direct exploitation by English settlers, and raising for the first time the idea that colonies there should act as a complementary economy to that of England and so free her from foreign-based imports. When his younger cousin of the same name was promoting Gilbert's ventures by publishing documents on America, he included the "Notes" in *Divers voyages* in 1582. Christopher Carleill's *A breef and sommarie discourse,* published in April, 1583, follows the broad lines of the elder Hakluyt's 1578 prescriptions, but narrows them down largely to trade in furs, timber, and cloth, and making the proposed colony a large trading post which would only gradually involve itself in agricultural experiments. It was designed to appeal to established business interests. That it had an appeal was seen by the appearance of a second edition, probably early in 1584, but it did not create enough confidence to produce a viable venture.

Sir George Peckham's *A true reporte of the late discoveries . . . by . . . Sir Humphrey Gilbert* (1583) capitalized on the interest Gilbert's ventures had produced to combine late in 1583 some account of what had happened on the voyage with a nationalistic manifesto in favor of an oppressive colonizing policy which would be "good for" the Amerindians and profitable for England. This was an ambitious but somewhat prosaic set of headlines of Elizabethan imperialism. At the end the proposal came down to earth with a prospectus inviting subscriptions and setting out the supposed benefits to be expected from investment. If the pamphlet appears to have had a fairly wide circulation, it produced no positive results, and the Peckham venture fell by the wayside early in 1584, some months before Carleill set out. The elder Richard Hakluyt's two sets of "Inducements" of 1584–1585 follow on from Carleill rather than from Peckham since they are concerned with what can be extracted from or grown in North America rather than with what kind of estates colonists can hope for. They are concerned both with things to be done to provide employment for settlers and with the kind of settler required. Like Peckham and unlike Carleill, they envisage a large settler population as the main object of the exercise and agricultural exploitation as its prime purpose.

It is probable that the two sets of "Inducements" straddle the much larger and more systematic exposition of the English case for colonizing North America prepared by the younger Richard Hakluyt between July and October 1584: "A particuler discourse concerninge the greate necessitie and manifolde comodyties that are like to growe to this Realme of Englande by the Westerne discoveries lately attempted," which has been known by various short titles and now usually as *Discourse of Western Planting*—a document about which there has been much misunderstanding. It was not published at the time and was never intended to be published. It was a confidential report written for Queen Elizabeth I and intended to be seen, apart from her, by a small number of people intimately concerned with planning voyages and colonizing expeditions under the terms of Walter Ralegh's patent of March 25, 1584 (427), possibly only Sir Francis Walsingham and Ralegh himself. As such it could be fuller and more frank—and also more academic in its use of materials—than a document prepared for publication. But if it was not intended directly as promotion material for intending colonists, it was nonetheless biased in its attempt to convince the queen that she must in her country's interests support the colonizing ventures which were under way. It was a brief for Ralegh in this respect, even though Hakluyt presented it to her in his official character as chaplain and secretary to the English ambassador in Paris. But if it was written as an official report intended to convince the queen of the need for a substantial change in external policy (in which it failed) it also, and deliberately, contained much ammunition for Walsingham and Ralegh for the propagation of the view that colonization in Virginia was not only patriotic but also practical and potentially highly profitable. This played an appreciable, although indirect, part in the preparation of the first serious English colonizing expedition, that of 1585.

Thomas Harriot's celebrated *A briefe and true report of the new found land of Virginia* (1588) was the first piece of English promotion material to be based on actual experience in America. As such it had both a range and an authority not previously experienced in this sequence. Just as Hakluyt's *Discourse of Western Planting* was more than a simple piece of promotion and was a serious treatise on English external policy as well, so Harriot's little book was more than an advertisement in that it was also an authoritative sketch of what a segment of North America was really like, based on a serious survey of resources and an intelligent study of Amerindian society. It had limitations in this latter respect, due to its being basically in the form of a prospectus for future settlers. It also contained a considerable polemic against those who had gone to Roanoke Island in 1585 and had returned in 1586 with bad reports about the place and its prospects. Although this was mainly of short term relevance, it was not wholly so, as its arguments were to be revised in a different context by the Virginia Company as late as 1610. Virginia was to be sold to investors and intending settlers on its merits as seen by a perceptive intellectual, optimistic, perhaps, but not just an academic or a theorist building a colonial future on precedents and conjectures. Harriot's tract, too, was to last and to be a standby for promoters for more than a generation.

Shortly after his return from Gilbert's voyage in 1583 Edward Hayes wrote up "A report of the voyage and successe thereof, attempted in the yeare of our Lord, 1583, by Sir Humphrey Gilbert knight" (Vol. IV, no. 536). Hayes includes a strong promotional boost for Newfoundland, notably in the section "A briefe relation of the Newfoundland," but this was not published until it was included by Hakluyt in *Principall navigations* (1589) pp. 679-697, and it remained there and in *Principal navigations*, III (1600), 143-165, a powerful argument for future English intervention in the island. His approaches to Lord Burghley in 1586 (362-364) are based on his own ambitions to be concerned in a corporation that would take over control of the Newfoundland inshore fishery, probably by garrison colonies there and partly by means of coastal patrol vessels. Newfoundland's own potential resources were also stressed. He had added to his experience gained during his visit in 1583 an impressive amount of material on the fishery which is invaluable as evidence.

His proposals for exploiting the island and the fishery were, however, those of the pure promoter. Too elaborate, too detailed to be even remotely practical, they represented the "projecting" impulse which carried Hayes forward into many other plans for industrial or commercial enterprises, many but not all of them impracticable, over the next twenty years.

The plan for a further American venture was prepared about 1592 by Edward Hayes and, probably, Christopher Carleill (366). It focused attention on the temperate lands between 40° and 49°N rather than on Newfoundland. The keypoint was: "It is not mines of gold and silver which make a commonweal and state to flourish . . . but a temperate and wholesome land, well peopled, replenished with commodities albeit gross yet needful for mans use, aptly situated for concourse and recourse of nations to the maintenance of trade." All this these lands would provide, even subsistence for 20,000 colonists. There were many ingenious suggestions on how a company could build up such a colony, but also characteristic overelaboration, especially on developing a transcontinental trade by way of the St. Lawrence to the Pacific. In spite of its extravagance this plan showed that the kind of arguments that were later focused on the settlement of New England were already emerging in the 1590s.

The author of a commentary on the Hayes-Carleill plan (367) is very much more skeptical about the prospects of a colony in the region than were the original projectors. He drew attention particularly to the slow development an agricultural colony in a cool climate was likely to require and to the problem of maintaining a capital flow in the absence of early profits. But he recommended that an experiment be made, although with some help from the queen. When an attempt was made to settle the Magdalen Islands in 1597, no such help was forthcoming. Realism, it seemed, was gradually penetrating the rather cloudy optimism of the early 1580s. Hakluyt, however, in his *Principal navigations*, III (1600) reprinted only the older promotion literature and not the newer, more realistic material.

The first New England voyage of the new century, that of Bartholomew Gosnold, took place in 1602. John Brereton's narrative *A briefe relation . . . of the north part of Virginia* (1602) included a number of other documents bearing on the area. Among them was an abbreviated version attributed to Edward Hayes (368) of the Hayes-Carleill plan. In it the more ambitious and unrealistic arrangements were toned down or eliminated and the emphasis was placed on what was known of the French fur trade, mineral discoveries, and exploration of the preceding twenty years. It was intended with the other material to lead on to an attempt at settlement, although this was not to be made for a further five years.

The series of documents that have been surveyed are significant of a growing and varied English attempt to come to terms with the problem of settlement in North America. Often poorly informed, unrealistically elaborate, or hopelessly optimistic, they yet covered many of the topics, national and economic, social and religious, that were to be raised in a more concrete form during the years after 1603, and they also contained at least the germ of many of the real problems and their solutions; although so far as we know, they were never studied as a single body of material by any of the persons vitally involved with English colonization after 1606.

Chapter Forty-two
Sir Humphrey Gilbert's Early Projects

355. Sir Humphrey Gilbert. *A discourse of a discoverie for a new passage to Cataia* (London, 1576).

At the time it was first drafted, in 1566, the Discourse *had little general relevance. When it was finally published, on April 12, 1576, under the auspices of the poet and occasional writer George Gascoigne, it was very much in the van of current thought. When Michael Lok was writing his own treatise on the Northwest Passage (Vol. IV, no. 655) in 1578, he was careful to stress that in 1576 Gilbert's views had not influenced him in the promotion of the expedition. Martin Frobisher was about to make a search for the Northwest Passage, but Gilbert's statements and proposals were taken seriously at the time and later on. His manner and matter were pedantic, but this alone made his arguments respectable in a way that straight promotion would not have done, and his recommendations at the end, however promotional in fact, took on weight and authority from their context. Gilbert's tract, too, came at the end of a period of intense colonization promotion—if little tangible achievement—in Ireland in which Gilbert had had a hand, and in the lull that followed, Englishmen, Gilbert again among them, began to turn seriously toward the possibility of colonizing some parts of America, a movement that got under way with the granting of Gilbert's patent in June, 1578 (370). The small book is, therefore, of exceptional interest for its timing as well as for its content. It was "Imprinted at London by Henry Middleton for Richarde Jhones, Anno. Domini. 1576. Aprilis 12," and reprinted by Richard Hakluyt in* Principall navigations *(1589), pp. 597–610; and* Principal navigations, *III (1600), 11–24. It has several times been reprinted (e.g., in D. B. Quinn, Gilbert, I, 129–164) in modern times.*

George Gascoigne
Esquire to the Reader.

Every man that is of judgment, and hath a reasonable disposition to the atteining of anie vertue, together with a discretion to use the benefites of nature, will confesse, that we are by as great reason bounde to encourage and commend the industrie of the diligent, as to dispraise and punish the slouth or abuse of the negligent: For if princes doe not aswell rewarde and cherish the well deserving subjecte, as their Judges and Magistrates are readie to correct the offendour, the Common Wealth might then quickly be deprived both of the one and the other: I meane that as fast as the sword of Justice should weede out the one, so fast the scourg of ingratitude woulde chase out the other. And so thereby their dominions might (in the end) become naked and altogether unfurnished.

We see the good huswife is no lesse curious to decke her bees hive, to rub and perfume it with sweete herbes, to cover and defend it from raine with clay and boordes, and to place it in the warme Sunshine safe from the Northerly blastes: then Shee is readie to wreck her malice on the drones, to smoke and smoulder them with Bunte and Brimstone, to fray and chase them out by soudain noyse, and to kill them and caste them away, as unprofitable members in her Microcosmos. Yea, and with melodie of Basons and Timbrils will shee welcome home her swarme, if at anye time they doe (waspishly) goe astray, and yet at last retourne to their former abyding.

Thus muche (gentle reader) I have thought good (Allegorically) to write in the behalfe of the right worshipful and my very frend Sir Humfrey Gilbert Knight, the true authour of this little (yet profitable) Pamphlet, intituled A Discourse of a Discoverie for a newe passage to Cataia, etc. In whose Commendation I woulde fayne write as-muche as hee deserveth, were I not afrayde to bee condemned by him of flatterie: which blame (with my friendes) I use not to deserve. But surely, over and besides that, hee is a gentleman wel and worshipfully borne and bredde, and well tryed to bee valiant in martiall affayres, whereby hee hath worthely beene constituted a Coronell and gener-all in places requisite, and hath with sufficiencie discharged the same, both in this Realme, and in forreigne Nations: hee is also indued with sundrie great gyftes of the minde, and gen-erally well given to the advauncemente of knowl-edge and vertue. All whiche good partes I rather set downe constrained by the present occasion, then prompted by any vaine desire to currie favoure with my friende: For his vertues are sufficient to praise themselves. And it shalbe a sufficient conclusion for my prayses, to wishe that our realme had store of suche Gentlemen.

But as the good Gardener doth cover his tender herbes in winter, and cherishe them also in sum-mer: so have I thought my selfe bounden some-what to say in the commendation of this present Treatise, and somewhat to answere unto the ob-jections that might bee made by such as list to cavill at everie commendable enterprise.

And surely I cannot chuse, but highly prayse the noble minde and courage of the Authour, who more respecting the publique profit that might ensue by this Discoverie, then the delicate life of a Courtier, well countenanced and favoured both by his Prince and all the Nobilitie, had prepared his owne bodie to abide the malice of the windes and waves, and was even ready to have per-fourmed the voyage in proper person, if he had not beene by her Majestie otherwise commanded and imployed in martiall affaires, aswell in Ire-land, as sithence in other places.

You must herewith understand (good Reader) that the authour havinge a worshipfull Knight to his brother, who abashed at this enterprise (as-well for that he himselfe had none issue, nor other heier whome he ment to bestow his lands upon, but onely this Authour, and that this voyage then seemed strang and had not beene commonly spo-ken of before, as also because it seemed unpossi-ble unto the common capacities) did seeme partly to mislike his resolutions, and to disuade him from the same: thereupon he wrote this Treatise unto his saide Brother, both to excuse and cleare him-

selfe from the note of rashnesse, and also to set downe such Authorities, reasons, and experi-ences, as had chiefly encouraged him unto the same, as may appeare by the letter next follow-ing, the which I have here inserted for that pur-pose. And this was done about vii. yeares now past, sithence which time the originall copies of the same have lien by the authour as one rather dreading to hazarde the Judgements of curious perusers, then greedie of glorie by hasty publica-tion.

Now it happened that my self being one (amongst manie) beholding to the said Sir Hum-frey Gilbert for sundrie curtesies, did come to visit him in Winter last passed at his house in Limehowse, and beeing verie bolde to demaunde of him howe he spente his time in this loytering vacation from martiall stratagemes, he curte-ously tooke me up into his Studie, and there shewed me sundrie profitable and verie com-mendable exercises, which he had perfected painefully with his owne penne: And amongst the rest this present Discoverie. The which as well because it was not long, as also because I under-stoode that M. Fourboiser (a kinsman of mine) did pretend to travaile in the same Discoverie, I craved at the saide Sir Humfreyes handes for two or three dayes to reade and to peruse. And hee verie friendly granted my request, but stil seming to doubt that thereby the same might, contrarie to his former determination, be Imprinted.

And to be plaine, when I had at good leasure perused it, and therwithall conferred his allega-tions by the Tables of Ortelius, and by sundrie other Cosmographicall Mappes and Charts, I seemed in my simple judgement not onely to like it singularly, but also thought it very meete (as the present occasion serveth) to give it out in publike. Wherupon I have (as you see) caused my friendes great travaile, and mine owne greater presumption to be registred in print.

But since I have thus adventured both his rebuke, and mine owne reproofe, let me thus muche alledge in both our defences.

1. First it is but a Pamphlet and no large discourse, and therefore the more to be borne withall: since the faults (if any be) shalbe the fewer, because the volume is not great.

2. Also it was ment by the autour, but as a private Letter unto his Brother for his better satisfaction: and therefore his imperfections

therein (if any were) are to be pardoned, since it is very likely that if he had ment to publish the same, he would with greater heede have observed and perused the worke in everie parte.

3. Againe, it commeth foorth without his consent: So that he had neither warning nor time to examine, nor yet to amende anie thing that were worthie misliking.

4. Furthermore it treateth of a matter whereof no man hath heretofore written particularly, nor shewed ani approved reason for the same. So that not onely his travaile and paine are very commendable (who out of sundrie Authorities woulde gather one reasonable conjecture) but also the worke is not to be thought bareine, although it doe not fully proove somuch as may be expected, since he that plougheth in a flintie fielde, speedeth well if he reape but an indifferent crop.

5. And last of all it is to bee considered, that of things uncertaine, the greatest Clerke that ever was could write but probably.

Herewithall, as I have preposterously answered such objections as might be made against it, So now let mee say that a great learned man (even M. Dee) doth seeme very well to like of this Discoverie and doth much commende the Authour, the which he declareth in his Mathematical preface to the english Euclide. I refer thee (Reader) to peruse the same, and thinke it not strange though I be encouraged by so learned a foreleader, to set forth a thing which hee so well liked of.

To conclude, whereas other Cosmographical workes doe but shew us things already knowen and treated of, this Discoverie doeth tend to a very profitable and commendable practise of a thing to bee discovered. So that I thought it my part, both for great good will to the authour, and for publike perfourmance of a common duetie, to commend a little Bee somuch commendable, to defend it from the stormes of objections, with boords and clay of direct answers: To set it in the sunshine (as you see) and to ring it out with my best basons, for the better expressing of such joye and comfort, as I have therein conceived.

All whiche, together with the frendly constructions of the authours travaile and my boldnes, I commend (gentle reader) unto thy curteous consideration, wishinge unto thee, much profite by perusing this treatise, unto the authour, much prayse according to his deserts, to my kinsman

(who nowe attempteth to prove the same discovery) happy returne, and to my selfe, some thankes and none ill will, for my presumption.

So that the Authour being thereby incouraged, may be the more willing hereafter to publishe some other well worthy which he hath in readinesse, and whereof hee hath made me alreadie an eyedwitness. Farewell.

From my lodging where I march amongst the Muses for lacke of exercise in martiall exploytes, this 12. of April. 1576. A friend to all well willing Readers.

[signed:] George Gascoine.

A Prophetical Sonnet of the same George Gascoine, upon the commendable travaile which Sir Humfrey Gilbert hath disclosed in this worke.

Men praise Columbus for the passing skil
Which he declared, in Cosmographie,
And nam'd him first (as yet we cal him stil)
The 2. Neptune, dubd by dignity.
Americus Vesputius, for his paine,
Neptune the 3. ful worthely was named,
And Magellanus, by good right did gaine,
Neptune the 4. ful fitly to be famed.
But al those three, and al the world beside,
Discovered not, a thing of more emprice,
Then in this booke, is learnedly descride,
By vertue of my worthie friendes device.
If such successe, to him (as them) then fall,
Neptune the 5. we justly may him call.

Tam Marti quam Mercurio.

A letter of Sir Humfrey Gilbert, Knight, sent to his Brother, Sir John Gilbert, of Compton, in the Countie of Devon Knight, concerning the discourse of this Discoverie.

Sir, you might justly have charged mee with an unsetled head if I had at any time taken in hand, to discover Utopia, or any countrey fained by imagination: But Cataia is none such, it is a countrey, well knowen to be described and set foorth by all moderne Geographers, whose authoritie in this art (contrarie to all other) beareth most credit, and the passage thereunto, by the Northwest from us, through a sea which lieth on the Northside of Labrador, mentioned and prooved, by no smal number of the most expert, and best learned amongst them. By whose authoritie, if I (amongst others) have beene moved, to hope of that passage, who can justly blame me? sith everie man is best to be credited and beleeved, in his owne professed art and science, wherin he doth most excell.[1]

And if I would not give that credit, to those authours which they deserve, but were so wedded unto my owne ignorance, that neither the authoritie of learned Geographers, the reasons of wise Philosophers, nor the experience of painfull Travellers, might persuade me to believe a trueth: Then might I justly be accompted selfe willed (which a learner ought chiefly to eschewe) holding for a Maxime, that, Discentem oportet credere. And knowing you to be one that may easily be induced to hearken, and yeelde to reason, I will briefly open unto you, some fewe of the grounds of mine opinion, to the ende you may the better understand, that my hope of this discoverie and passage, was not so rashe, or foolishe, as you heretofore have deemed: but contrariwise, grounded upon a very sure foundation, and that not unadvisedly, but after long consideration and great conference, had with such as I knew to be both wise, learned, and of great experience, as well touching this passage, as the wonderfull welth and commodities, which might, and would ensue thereby, it being once discovered: whose abundance of riches and treature, no man of learning, and judgement doubteth, for that the countreys themselves, and their commodities, are apparently knowen by sundrie mens experience.

But as it is one thing to speak, and an other by reason to confirme, so I wil briefly do my indevour to prove the same. And have herewithall sent you, for your better understandinge, a rough draught, of a universall Map in the end of the boke, sufficient to explane the matter, with those names only in effect which are mencioned in this discourse: to the ende that by resorting to this general Mappe, etc. finding without difficultie, everie particular place mencioned herein, you may the better gather my meaning, and conceive my reasons, alledged for the proofe of this passage, nowe in question: which I wil prove three wayes.

Al which, I have divided into severall chapters, which may fully deliver unto you the whol con-

tents of this worke, by their severall titles: as followeth. Fare you well from my lodging the last of June, Anno D. 1566.

Your loving Brother
    [signed:] Humfrey Gilbert.

The Table of the matters conteyned in everie Chapter of this Booke.

Capitulo 1.

To proove by authoritie a passage to be on the Northside of America, to goe to Cataia, China, and to the East India.

Capitulo 2.

To proove by reason, a passage to be on the Northside of America, to goe to Cataia, the Mulluccae, etc.

Capitulo 3.

To proove by experience of sundrie mens travails the opening of some parte of this Northwest passage, whereby good hope remaineth of the rest.

Capitulo 4.

To proove by Circumstance, that the Northwest passage hath bene sayled through out.

Capitulo 5.

To proove that suche Indians as have bene driven upon the coastes of Germanie came not thither by ye Southeast, Southwest nor from any part of Afrik or America.

Capitulo 6.

To proove that the Indians aforenamed came not by the Northeast, and that there is no thorow passage Navigable that way.

Capitulo 7.

To proove that these Indians came by the Northwest, which induceth a certaintie of this passage by experience.

Capitulo 8.

What severall reasons, were alledged before the Queenes Majestie, and certaine Lordes of her Highnes privie Counsell, by a Gentleman of great travaile and experience, to proove this passage by

---

1. Sidenote: "Cuique in sua arte credendum est."

the Northeast, with my severall answeres then alledged to the same.

Capitulo 9.

How that this passage by the Northwest, is more commodious for our traffike, then the other by the Northeast, if there were any such.

Capitulo 10.

What commodities would ensue, this passage being once discovered.

Finis.

To prove a passage by authoritie to be on the Northside of America, to goe to Cataia, China, and the East India. etc.

When I gave my self to the studie of Geographie, after I had perused and diligently scanned the descriptions of Europe, Asia, and Afrike, and conferred them with the Mappes and Globes both Antique and Moderne: I came in fine to the fourth part of the worlde, commonly called America, which by al descriptions I founde to be an Islande environed round about with the Sea, having on the southside of it, the frete, or strayte of Magellan, on the West side Mare de sur, which Sea runneth towardes the North, separating it from the East parts of Asia, where the dominions of the Cataians are, On the East part our Weste Ocean, and on the Northside the sea that severeth it from Grondland, thorow which Northern seas, the passage lyeth, which I take now in hande to discover.

Plato in Timeo, and in the Dialogue called Critias, discourseth of an incomparable great Ilande, then called Atlantis, being greater than all Affrik, and Asia, whiche laye Westward from the Straits of Gibraltar, Navigable round aboute: affirming also that the Princes of Atlantis, did aswel enjoye the governaunce of all Affrik, and the most part of Europe, as of Atlantis it selfe.

Also to proove Platoes opinion of this Ilande, and the inhabyting of it in auncient tyme, by them of Europe, to be of the more credit: Marineus Siculus, in his Chronicle of Spayne, reporteth that there hath been found by the Spaniardes, in the Golde Mynes of America, certeine peeces of Money, ingraved with the Image of Augustus Caesar: which peeces were sent unto the Pope, for a testimonie of the matter, by John Rufus, Archebishop of Cosentinum.

Moreover, this was not onely thought of Plato, but by Marsilius Ficinus, an excellent Florentine Philosopher, Crantor the Graecian, Proclus,[2] and also Philo the famous Jewe, (as appeareth in his booke De Mundo, and in the Commentaries upon Plato) to be overflowen, and swallowed up with water, by reason of a mightie Earthquake, and streamyng downe of the heavenly Fludgates. The like whereof happened unto some part of Italie, when by the forciblenes of the Sea, called Superum, it cut of Cicilia from the Continent of Calabria, as appeareth in Justine, in ye beginning of his fourth boke.[3] Also there chaunced the like in Zelande and part of Flaunders.

And also the cities of Pyrrha, and Antissa, aboute Meotis palus: and also, the Citie Burys, in the Corynthian bosome, commonly called Sinus Corynthiacus, have bene swallowed up with the sea, and are not at this day to be discerned:[4] By which accident, America grew to be unknowen of long time, unto us of the later ages, and was lately discovered again, by Americus Vespucius, in the yere of our Lord, 1497. which some say to have bene first discovered, by Christopherus Columbus, a Genuest. Anno. 1492.

The same calamity hapned unto this Isle of Atlantis 600. and od yeres before Plato his time, which some of ye people of the southeast parts of ye world accompted as 9000. yeres: for the manner then was to recone the moone, her Period of the Zodiak for a yere, which is our usuall moneth, depending a Luminari minore.

So that in these our dayes there can no other mayne or Islande bee founde, or judged to be parcell of this Atlantis, then those Westerne Islandes, which beare now the name of America: countervailing thereby the name of Atlantis, in the knowledge of our age.

Then, if when no part of the said Atlantis was oppressed by water, and earthquake, the coastes rounde about the same were navigable: a far greater hope now remaineth of the same by the Northwest, seeing the most parte of it was, since that time, swalowed up with water, which coulde not utterly take away the olde deepes and chanels, but rather, be an occasion of the inlarging of the olde, and also an inforcing of a great

---

2. Sidenote: "Proclus pag. 24."
3. Sidenote: "Justine Lib. 4."
4. Sidenote: "Plinie."

many new[5]: why then should we nowe doubte of our Northwest passage and navigation from Englande to India? etc. seeing that Atlantis, now called America, was ever knowen to be an Islande, and in those days navigable round about, which by accesse of more water coulde not be diminished.

Also Aristotle in his boke De Mundo, and the learned Germane, Simon Gryneus in his annotations upon the same, saith that the whole earth (meaning thereby as manifestly doth appeare, Asia, Afrik and Europe, being al the countreis then knowen) to be but on Islande, compassed about with ye reach of the Sea Atlantine: which likewise approveth America to be an Islande, and in no parte adjoyning to Asia, or the rest.

Also many Auncient writers, as Strabo[6] and others, called both the Ocean sea (which lieth East of India) Atlanticum pelagus, and that Sea also on the west coasts of Spayne and Afrik, Mare Atlanticum: the distance betweene which two coastes, is almost halfe the compasse of the earth.

So that it is incredible, as by Plato appeareth manifestly, that the East Indian sea had the name Atlanticum pelagus, of the Mountaine Atlas in Afrik, or yet the Sea adjoining to Afrik had name Oceanus Atlanticus, of the same mountaine: but yet those Seas and the mountaine Atlas, were so called of this great Islande Atlantis,[7] and that the one and the other, had their names for a memoriall of the mightie prince Atlas, sometime King thereof, who was Japhet youngest sonne to Noah, in whose time the whole earth was divided betweene the three bretherne, Sem, Cam, and Japhet.[8]

Wherefore I am of opinion that America by the Northwest, wilbe founde favorable to this our enterprise, and am the rather imboldened to beleeve the same, for that I finde it not onely confirmed by Plato, Aristotle, and other auncient Philosophers: but also by al the best moderne Geographers, as (Gemma Frisius, Munsterus, Appianus, Hunterus, Costaldus, Guyzardinus, Michael Tramesinus, Franciscus Demongenitus, Barnardus Puteanus, Andreas Vavasor, Tramontanus, Petrus Martyr, and also Hortelius) who

doth coaste out in his generall Mappe (set out Anno 1569.) al ye countreys and capes, on the Northwestside of America, from Houchelaga to C. De Paramantia: describing likewise ye sea coasts of Cataia and Grondland, towardes any part of America, making both Grondland and America, Ilands disjoyned by a great sea, from any part of Asia.

Al which learned men and painful travellers have affirmed, with one consent and voice, that America was an Iland: and y[t] there lyeth a great Sea betweene it, Cataia, and Grondland, by the which any man of our countrey, that wil give the attempt, may with smal danger passe to Cataia, the Moluccae, India, and al other places in ye East, in much shorter time, then either the Spaniard, or Portingale doth, or may do, from the neerest part of any of their countreis within Europe.

What mooved these learned men to affirme thus much, I know not,[9] or to what end so many and sundrye travellers, of both ages, have allowed the same: But I conjecture that they would never have so constantly affirmed, or notified their opinions therein to the world, if they had not had great good cause, and many probable reasons, to have lead them thereunto.

Now least you should make smal accompt of ancient writers or of their experiences, which travelled long before our times, reconing their authority amongst fables of no importance: I have for the better assurance of those proofes, set down some part of a discourse, written in the Saxon tongue, and translated into English by M. Nowel Servaunte to Maister Secretarie Cecill,[10] wherein there is described a Navigation, which one Ochther made, in the time of Kinge Alfred, Kinge of Westsaxe Anno. 871.[11] the wordes of which discourse were these: He sayled right North, having alwayes the desert land on the Starborde, and on the Larbord, the mayne sea, continueing his course, untill he perceived that the coaste bowed directly towardes the East, or else the Sea opened into the land he could not tel how far, where he was compelled to staye, until he had a westerne winde, or somewhat upon the

5. Sidenote: "A minore ad maius."
6. Sidenote: "Strabo lib. 15."
7. Sidenote: "Valerius Anselmus in Catalogo annorum et principum, fol. 6."
8. Sidenote: "Genesis the 9, and 10."

9. Sidenote: "We ought by reasons right to have a reverent opinion of worthy men."
10. Sidenote: "Now Lord Burleighe & highe Treasurer of England."
11. Sidenote: "A Navigation, of one Ochther made in king Alfreds time."

North, and sayled thence directly East, alongst the coast, so farre as he was able in foure dayes, where he was againe inforced to tary, until he had a North wind, because the coast there bowed directly towardes the South, or at least opened, he knew not how far into the land, so that he sayled thence along the coaste continually ful South, so farre as he could travel in the space of five dayes, where he discovered a mightie river, whiche opened farre into the lande, and in the entrye of this river he turned backe againe.[12]

Wherby it appeareth, that he went the verye same waye, that we now do yearely trade by S. Nicholas into Muscovia, whiche way no man in our age knewe, for certeintie to be sea, untill it was since discovered by our English men, in the time of King Edwarde the sixt:[13] but thought before that time that Grondlande had joyned to Normoria Byarmia, and therfore was accompted a newe discoverie, being nothing so in deede, as by this discourse of Ochthers it appeareth.

Nevertheles if any man shoulde have taken this voiage in hand, by the incouragment of this onely author, he should have beene thought but simple: consideringe that this Navigation was written so many yeares past, in so barbarous a tongue by one onely obscure author, and yet wee in these our dayes finde by our owne experiences, his former reports to be true.

How much more then, ought we to beleve this passage to Cataia to be, being verified by the opinions of all the best, both Antique, and Moderne Geographers, and plainly set out in the best and most allowed Mappes, Charts, Globes, Cosmographicall tables, and discourses, of this our age, and by the rest, not denyed, but left as a matter doubtfull.

To prove by reason, a passage to be on the North-side of America: to goe to Cataia, etc.

Cap. 2.

First, al seas are mainteined by the abundance of water, so that ye nearer the end, any River, Baye or Haven is, the shallower it waxeth, (although by some Accidental barre, it is sometime found otherwise) But the farther you saile West,

from Island, towardes ye place, wher this fret is thought to be, the more deeper are the seas:[14] which giveth us good hope, of continuance of ye same sea, with Mare de Sur, by some frete that lyeth betweene America, Grondlande, and Cataia.

2. Also, if that America were not an Iland, but a part of the continent adjoining to Asia, either the people which inhabite Mangia, Anian, and Quinzay, etc. being borderers upon it, would before this time, have made some roade into it: hoping to have found some like commodities to their owne.

3. Or els the Scythians, and Tartarians, (which oftentimes heretofore, have sought far and nere, for new seates, driven thereunto, through the necessitie of their colde, and miserable countreys) would in al this time, have found the way to America, and entred ye same, had the passages bene never so strayte, or difficult:[15] the countrie beeing so temperate, pleasaunte and fruitfull, in comparison of their owne. But there was never any such people found there, by any of the Spaniardes, Portingals, or Frenchemen, who firste discovered the Inlande of that Countrie: which Spaniardes, or Frenchemen, must then of necessitie, have seene some one Civil man in America, consideringe how full of civil people in Asia is: But they never sawe so muche as one token, or signe, that ever any man of the knowen part of the worlde, had beene there.

4. Furthermore, it is to be thought, y^t if by reason of mountains, or other craggy places, ye people neither of Cataia, or Tartarie could enter ye countrie of America, or they of America, have entred Asia, if it were so joyned: yet some one savage, or wandring beast wold in so many yeres, have passed into it: but there hath not at any time been found any of ye beasts proper to Cataia, or Tartarie etc. in America: nor of those proper to America, in Tartarie, Cataia, etc. or ani part of Asia.

Which thing proveth America, not only to be one Iland, and in no part adjoyning to Asia, But also that the people of those Countreyes, have not had any traffyke with each other.

5. Moreover, at the leaste some one of those painefull travellors, which of purpose have passed the Confines of both countreys, with intent only

---

12. Sidenote: "A perfect Description of our Muscovia voyage."
13. Sidenote: "By Sir Hugh Wyllowbe, Knight, Chauncellor and borough."

14. Sidenote: "Experimented by our english fishers."
15. Sidenote: "Neede makes the olde wife to trotte."

to discover, would, (as it is most likely) have gone from the one to the other: if there had bene any piece of lande, or Ismos, to have joyned them together, or else have declared some cause to the contrary.

6. But neither Paulus venetus, who lyved, and dwelt a long time, in Cataia, ever came into America, and yet was at the Sea coastes of Mangia, over against it, where he was imbarked, and perfourmed a great Navigation along those Seas: Neither yet Verarzanus, or Franciscus vasques de Coronado, who travelled the North parte of America by lande, ever founde entrye from thence by land, to Cataia, or any part of Asia.

7. Also it appeareth to be an Iland, insomuche as the Sea runneth by nature circularly, from the East to the West,[16] following the Diurnal motion of Primum Mobile, and carieth with it all inferiour bodies moveable, aswel celestial, as elemental: which motion of ye waters, is most evidently seene in the Sea, which lyeth on the Southside of Afrik, where the currant that runneth from the East to the West, is so strong (by reason of such motion) that the Portingales in ye voiages, Eastward to Callecute, in passing by Cap. De buona speranca, are enforced to make divers courses, the currant there being so swift, as it str... striketh from thence, all along Westward, upon the fret of Magellan, being distant from thence, nere the fourth parte of the longitude of the earth: and not having free passage and entrance, thorow that fret towardes the West, by reason of the narrownesse of the said straite of Magellan, it runneth to salve this wrong (Nature not yelding to accidental restraintes) all along the Easterne coasts of America, Northwardes, so farre as Cap. Fredo, beeing the farthest knowen place of the same continent, towardes the North: which is about, 4800. leagues, reconing therewithal the trending of the land.

8. So that this Currant, being continually mainteined with such force, as Jaques Cartier affirmeth it to be, who mette with the same being at Baccalaos, as he sailed alongst the coastes of America, then, either it must of necessitie, have way to passe from Cap. Fredo, thorowe this frete, Westwarde towardes Cataia, being knowen to

come so farre, onely to salve his former wronges, by the authoritie before named: or els it must needes strike over, upon the coast of Island, Lappia, Finmarke, and Norway, (which are East from the said place, about 360. Leagues) with greater force, then it did from Cap. de buona Speranca, upon the fret of Magellan, or from the frete of Magellan to Cap. Fredo, upon whiche coastes, Jaques Cartier mette with the same, considering the shortnes of the Cut, from the said C. Fredo, to Island, Lappia, etc. And so the cause Efficient remaining, it would have continually followed along our coastes, through the narrowe seas, which it doth not, but is disgested about the North of Labrador, by some through passage there, thorow this fret.[17]

The like course of the water, in some respect, happeneth in the Mediterrane Sea (as affirmeth Conterenus)[18] whereas the currant, which commeth from Taniis, and the sea Euxinus, running along al the coasts of Greece, Italie, Fraunce, and Spaine, and not finding sufficient way out through Gibralter, by meanes of the straitnes of the fret, it runneth back againe, alongst the coasts of Barbarie, by Alexandria, Natolia, etc.

It may (peradventure) be thought, that this couse of the sea, doth sometimes surcease, and therby impugne this principle, because it is not discerned all along the coast of America, in such sort as Jaques Cartier found it:[19] Whereunto I answere this: that albeit, in everie parte of the Coaste of America, or els where, this Currant is not sensibly perceived, yet, it hath evermore such like motion, either in the uppermost, or nethermost parte of the sea: as it may be proved true, if ye sinke a sayle by a couple of ropes, nere the ground, fastening to ye nethermost corners, two gun chambers, or other weights: by the driving whereof you shal plainly perceive, the course of the water, and Currant, running with such like course in the bottome.[20]

By the like experiment, you may finde the ordinarie motion of the sea, in the Ocean: how farre soever you be of the land.

9. Also there commeth another Currant from out the Northeast from the Scythian Sea (as M.

16. Sidenote: "The Sea hath three motions 1 Motum ab oriente in occidentem. 2 Motum fluxus et refluxus. 3 Motum circularem. Ad caeli motum elementa omnia (excepta terra) moventur."

17. Sidenote: "Posita causa, ponitur effectus."
18. Sidenote: "Conterenus."
19. Sidenote: "An Objection answered."
20. Sidenote: "The Sea doth evermore performe this circular motion, either in Suprema, or concava superficie aquae."

Jynkinson a man of rare vertue, great travaile and experience, told me) which runneth Westwarde towardes Labrador, as the other did, which commeth from the South: so that both these Currants, must have way thorowe this our frete, or else incounter together and runne contrary courses, in one line, but no suche conflictes of streames, or contrary courses are found about any parte of Labrador, or Terra nova, as witnesse our yerely fishers, and other saylers that way, but is there disgested, as aforesaid, and founde by the experience of Barnard de la Tore, to fall into Mare del Sur.[21]

10. Furthermore, the Currant in the great Ocean, coulde not have beene mainteined to runne continually one way, from the beginning of the world, unto this day had there not bene some thorow passage by the frete aforesaide, and so by circular motion, be brought againe to mainteine it selfe:[22] For the Tides, and courses of the Sea, are maintained by their interchangeable motions: as freash rivers are by springes, and ebbing and flowing, by rarefaction and condensation.

So that it resteth not possible (so farre as my simple reason can comprehend) that this perpetual currant, can by any means be maintained, but only by continual reaccesse of the same water, which passeth thorow the fret, and is brought about thither againe, by suche Circular motion as aforesaid. And the certaine falling thereof by this fret, into Mare de sur, is proved by the testimonie and experience, of Barnarde del la Torre, who was sent from P. del la Nativita, to the Mulluccae, Anno. Dom. 1542. by commandement of Anthonie Mendoza, then Viceroy of Nova Hispania, which Barnarde, sayled 750. Leagues, on the Northside of the Aequator, and there mette with a currant, which came from the Northeast which drove him backe againe to Tidore.[23]

Wherefore, this currant being proved to come from C. de buona Speranca, to the fret of Magellan, and wanting sufficient entrance there, by narrownes of the straite, is by ye necessitie of natures force, brought to Terra de Labrador, where Jaques Cartier met ye same, and thence certainly knowen, not to strike over upon Island, Lappia, etc. and founde by Barnarde de la Torre, in Mare del Sur, on the backeside of America, therefore, this currant (having none other passage) must of necessitie, fall out thorow this our fret into Mare del Sur, and so trending by the Mulluccae, China, and C. De buona, speranca, maintaineth itself by circular motion which is all one in nature, with Motus ab Oriente in Occidentem.

So that it seemeth, we have now more occasion to doubt of our returne, then whether there be a passage that way, yea or no: which doubt, hereafter shalbe sufficiently removed. Wherefore, in mine opinion, reason it selfe, grounded upon experience, assureth us of this passage, if there were nothing els to put us in hope thereof. But least these might not suffise, I have added in this Chapiter followinge, some further proofe hereof, by the experience of such as have passed some part of this discoverie: and in the next adjoyning to that, the authoritie of those, which have sayled wholy, thorowe everie part thereof.

To prove by experience of sundrie mens travels, the opening of some part of this Northwest passage: wherby good hope remaineth of the rest.

Cap. 3.

Paulus Venetus, who dwelt many yeres in Cataia, affirmed that he sailed, 1500 myles, upon the coastes of Mangia, and Anian, towards the Northeast: always finding the Seas open before him, not onely as farre as he went: but also as far as he could discerne.

2. Also, Franciscus Vasques de Coronado, passing from Mexico by Cevola, through the countrey of Quivir, to Sierra Nevada, found there a great Sea, where were certaine Ships laden with Merchandize, the mariners wearing on their heades the pictures of certaine birdes, called Alcatrarzi, part whereof were made of golde, and parte of silver: who signified by signes, that they were 30. dayes comming thither: whiche likewise proveth, America by experience, to be disjoyned from Cataia, on that part, by a great Sea, because they coulde not come from any parte of America, as Natives thereof: for that, so far as it is discov-

---

21. Sidenote: "Ex Nihilo, nihil fit."
22. Sidenote: "One, and the self same place in the earth, may be both East and West in sundry respects: so that this Oriental motion of the water, is brought to be circular (without repugnancie) by the regular course of Primum Mobile."
23. Sidenote: "The flowing is occasioned by reason that the heate of the moone boyleth, and maketh the water thinne by way of rarefaction. And the ebbing commeth for want of that heate, which maketh the water to fal againe by way of condensation. An experience to proove the falling of this Currant, into Mare del Sur."

ered, there hath not bene founde there, any one Shippe of that Countrey.

3. In like maner, Johan.Baros,[24] testifieth y^t the Cosmographers of China (where he himself had bene) affirme y^t the Sea coast, trendeth from thence, Northeast, to 50. degrees, of Septentrional latitude, being the farthest parte that way, whiche the Portingals had then knowledge of: And that the said Cosmographers, knewe no cause to the contrarie, but that it might continue further.

By whose experiences, America is proved to be seperate from those partes of Asia, directly against the same. And not contented with the judgements of these learned men only, I have serched, what might be further said, for the confirmation hereof.

4. And I found, that Franciscus Lopes de Gomara,[25] affirmeth, America to be an Iland, and likewise Grondland: and that Grondland is distant from Lappia. 40. leagues, and from Terra de Labrador, 50.

5. Moreover, Alverus Nunnius, a Spaniarde and learned Cosmographer, and Jacobus Cartier, who made two voyages, into those partes, and sayled 500. myles, upon the Northeast coasts of America.

6. Likewise, Hieronimus Fracastorius, a learned Italian, and Traveller, in the North parts of the same land.

7. Also Verarsannus, a Florentine, having done ye like, heard say at Houchelaga in Nova Francia, how yt there was a great Sea at Saguinay, whereof the ende was not knowen: which they presupposed to be the passage to Cataia.

8. Furthermore, Sebastian Gabota, by his personall experience, and travell, hath set foorth, and described this passage,[26] in his Charts, whiche are yet to bee seene, in the Queenes Majesties privie Gallerie, at White hall, who was sent to make this discoverie by King Henrie the seaventh, and entred the same fret: affirming, that he sailed very far westward, with a quarter of the North, on the Northside of Terra de Labrador, the eleventh of June, until he came to the Septentrional latitude of 67½ degrees and finding

the Seas still open, said, that he might, and would have gone to Cataia, if the Mutinie of the Maister and Mariners, had not ben.

Now, as these mens experience, have proved some parte of this passage: so the Chapter following, shal put you in full assurance of ye rest, by their experiences which have passed thorow every part thereof.

To prove by circumstance, that the Northwest passage, hath beene sayled thorough out.

Cap. 4.

The diversity betwene bruite beastes and men, or betweene the wise and the simple, is that the one judgeth by sense onely, and gathereth no suertie of anye thing that he hath not sene, fealt, heard, tasted, or smelled:[27] And the other not so onely, but also findeth the certaintie of thinges by reason, before they happen to be tryed. Wherefore, I have added proofes of both sortes, that the one and the other might thereby be satisfied.

1. First, as Gemma Frisius reciteth, there went from Europe, 3 brethren through this passage: whereof it tooke the name, of Fretum trium fratrum.

2. Also, Plinie affirmeth, out of Cornelius Nepos,[28] (who wrote 57. yeres before Christ) that there were certain Indians driven by tempest, upon the coast of Germanie which were presented by ye King of Suevia, unto Quintus Metellus Celer, then Proconsul of Fraunce.

3. And Plinie, upon the same, saith that it is no marvel, though there be Sea by the North, where there is such abundance of moisture: which argueth, that he doubted not of a Navigable passage that way, thorow which those Indians came.

4. And for the better profe, that the same authoritie of Cornelius Nepos, is not by me wrested, to proove my opinion of the Northwest passage: you shal finde the same affirmed more plainely in that behalfe, by the excellent Geographer, Dominicus Marius Niger,[29] who sheweth how many wayes the Indian Sea stretcheth it selfe, making in that place, recitall of certaine

---

24. Sidenote: "Baros lib. 9. Of his first Decas. cap. I."
25. Sidenote: "Lopes in his hystorie of India."
26. Sidenote: "Writen in the discourse of Navigation."
27. Sidenote: "Quinque sensus. 1 Visus. 2 Auditus. 3 Olfactus. 4 Gustus. 5 Tactus. Singularia sensu, universalia vero mente percipiuntur."
28. Sidenote: "lib. 2. cap. 66."
29. Sidenote: "Pag. 590."

Indians, that were likewise driven through the North Seas from India, upon the coasts of Germanie, by great tempest, as they were sayling in trade of Merchandize.

5. Also, whiles Frederic Barbarossa raigned Emperour, Anno D. 1160. there came certeine other Indians, upon the coaste of Germanie.[30]

6. Likewise, Othon, in the storie of the Gothes affirmeth, that in the time of the Germane Emperours, ther were, also certain Indians cast by force of weather, upon the coast of the said Countrey: which foresaid Indians, coulde not possiblie have come by the Southeast, Southwest, nor from any part of Afrik, or America, nor yet by the Northeast: therfore they came of necessity, by this our Northwest passage.

To proove that these Indians aforenamed, came not by the Southeast, Southwest, nor from any other part of Afrik, or America.

Cap. 5.

First, they coulde not come from the Southeast, by C. de buona Speranca, because ye roughnes of the Seas there, are such (occasioned by the Currants, and great windes, in that part) that the greatest Armados, the King of Portingale hath, cannot without great difficulty passe that way: much lesse than a Canoa of India coulde live in those outragious Seas, without Shipwracke (beeing a vessell but of verie small burden) and have conducted themselves to the place aforesaide, beeing men unexpert in the Art of Navigation.

2. Also, it appeareth plainely, that they were not able, to come from alongest the coast of Afrik aforesaide, to those partes of Europe, because the winds do (for the most part) blow ther Easterlie, of from the shore, and the Currante running that way, in like sort, should have driven them Westward, upon some part of America, for such windes and Tydes, coulde never have led them from thence, to the said place where they were found, Nor yet could they have come from any of the Countries aforesaid keeping the Seas alwayes without skilfull Mariners, to have conducted them such like courses, as were necessarie, to perfourme such a voyage.

3. Presupposing also, if they had bene driven to the west (as they must have beene comming that way) then they should have perished, wanting supplie of victuals, not having any place (once leaving the coaste of Afrik) until they came to America: nor from America, until they arrived upon some part of Europe, or the Ilandes adjoyning to it, to have refreshed themselves.

4. Also, if (notwithstanding such impossibilities) they might have recovered Germanie, by comming from India, by the Southeast, yet must they, without al doubt, have striken upon some other part of Europe, before their arrival there, as the Iles of Madera, Portingal, Spaine, Fraunce, England, Ireland, etc. which if they had done, it is not credible, that they should, or would have departed, undiscovered of the inhabitants: but there was never found in these dayes, any such Ship or men, but onely upon the coasts of Germanie, where they have bene sundrie times, and in sundrie ages cast a land: Neither is it like, that they woulde have committed themselves againe to Sea, if they had so arrived, not knowing wher they were, nor whither to have gon.

5. And by the Southwest it is as unpossible, because the currant aforesaide, which commeth from the East, striketh with such force upon the fret of Magellan, and falleth with such swiftnes and furie, into Mare de Sur, that hardly any ship (but not possible a Canoa, with such unskilfull Mariners) can come into our westerne Ocean, thorow that fret, from the west Seas of America, as Magellans experience hathe partly taught us.[31]

6. And further, to prove that these people, so arriving upon the coast of Germanie, were Indians, and not inhabiters of anye part, either of Africa, or America, it is manifest: because the Natives both of Africa and America, neither had, or have, at this day (as is reported) other kinde of boates, then such as do beare neither masts, nor sayls, (except onely upon the Coastes of Barbarie and the Turks Shippes) but do carie themselves from place to place, neere the shore, by the ore onely.[32]

To proove that those Indians came not by the

---

30. Sidenote: "Avouched by Franciscus Lopes de Gomara in his historie of India."

31. Sidenote: "Why the Indians coulde not come by the Southwest."
32. Sidenote: "That the Indians coulde not be natives either of Africa or of America."

Northeast, and that ther is no thorow Navigable passage that way.

Cap. 6.

It is lykelie that there should be no thorowe passage by the Northeast, whereby to goe rounde about the world: because al seas (as aforesaide) are maintained by the abundance of water, waxing more shallow and shelffie towardes the end, as we finde, it doth by experience, in Mare Glaciali, towardes the East, which breedeth smal hope of any great continuance, of that Sea, to be Navigable towardes the East, sufficient to sayle thereby, rounde about the worlde.

2. Also, it standeth scarcely with reason, that the Indians dwelling under Torrida Zona, could indure the injurie of the colde ayre, about the Septentrional latitude of 80 degrees, under which elevation, the passage by the Northeast, cannot be (as the often experience had of al the South parts of it sheweth) seeing that some of the inhabitants of this colde Climat (whose summer is to them an extreame winter) have bene stroken to death, with the colde damps of the ayre, about 72 degrees, by an accidental mishappe: and yet the ayre in such like Elevation is always colde, and to colde for suche as the Indians are.[33]

3. Furthermore, the pearcing colde of the grose thicke ayre so neere the Pole, will so stiffen and furre the sayles, and shippe tackling, that no Mariner can either hoise or strike them (as our experience farre nerer the South, then this passage is presupposed to be, hath taught us) without the use whereof no voyage can be perfourmed.

4. Also, the ayre is so darkened, with continual mysts, and fogges, so neere the Pole, that no man can well see, either to guide his shippe, or direct his course.

5. Also the compasse at such elevation, doth verie sodenly varie: which thinges must of force, have bene their destructions, although they had beene men of muche more skil then the Indians are.

6. Moreover al Bayes, Gulffes and rivers[34], doe receive their increase upon the fludde, sensibly to be discerned, on the one side of the shoare, or the other, as many wayes as they be open to any maine sea, as Mare Mediterraneum, Mare Rubrum, Sinus Persicus, Sinus Bodicus, Thamisis, and al other knowen Havens, or rivers in any part of the world: and eche of them opening but on one part to ye mayne sea, do likewise receive their encrease upon the fludde, the same way, and none other, which Mare Glaciale doth, onely by the West (as M. Jynkinson affirmed unto me) and therefore it followeth that this Northeast sea, receiving increase but onely from the West, cannot possibly open to the maine Ocean, by the East.

7. Moreover, the farther you passe into any sea, towards the end of it, on that parte which is shutte up from the mayne Sea (as in all those above mentioned) the lesse and lesse the Tydes rise and fall.[35] The like whereof also happeneth in Mare Glaciale, which proveth but small continuance of that sea, toward the East.

8. Also, the farther ye goe towarde the East, in Mare Glaciale, the lesse salte the water is: whiche coulde not happen, if it were open to the salte Sea towardes the Easte, as it is to the Weste onely, seeing (Everie thinge naturally ingendereth his lyke) and then must it bee like salte throughout, as all the Seas are, in such like Climate, and Elevation.

And therfore it seemeth, that this Northeast sea is maintained by the river Oby, and such like fresshets as Mare Goticum, and Mare Mediterraneum, in ye uppermost parts thereof, by ye river Nilus, Danubius, Neper, Tanais. etc.

9. Furthermore, if there were any such sea at that elevation, of like it should be alwayes frosen throughout (there being no tydes to hinder it) because the extreame coldnes of the ayre in the uppermost part, and the extreame coldnes of the earth in the bottome, the sea there being but of small depth, whereby the one accidental coldnes doth meete with the other, and the sunne not having their reflection so neere the Pole, but at verie blunt angles, it can never bee dissolved after it is frosen, notwithstandinge the great length of their day: for that the sunne hath no

---

33. Sidenote: "Quicquid naturali loco privatur, quam citissimè corrumpitur. Qualis causa talis effectus."
34. Sidenote: "Similium similis est ratio."

35. Sidenote: "It may perhaps be found otherwise in some one ryver, by reason of a bare in the entrance or some other like accident. Quicquid corrumpitur a contrario corrumpitur. Omne simile gignit sui simile."

heate at al in his light, or beams, but proceding only by an accidentall reflection, whiche there wanteth in effect.

10. And yet if the sunne were of sufficient force in that elevation, to prevaile against this Ise, yet must it be broken before it can be dissolved, which cannot be but through the long continuance of the sunne above their Horizon, and by that time the summer woulde be so farre spent, and so great a darkenes and colde insue, that no man could be able to endure so colde, darke, and discomfortable a Navigation, if it were possible for him then, and there to live.

11. Further, the Ise being once broken, it must of force, so drive with the windes and Tydes, that no ship can sayle in those Seas, seeing our fishers of Island, and the Newe found Land, are subject to daunger, thorowe the great Ilandes of Ise, whiche fleete in the Seas, (to the saylers great daunger) farre to the South of that presupposed Passage.

12. And it cannot be, that this Northeast passage should be any nerer the South, then before recited, for then it shoulde cut of Ciremissi, and Turbi, Tartarii, with Uzesucani, Chisani, and others from the Continent of Asia, which are knowen to be adjoyning to Scythia, Tartaria, etc. with the other part of the same Continent.

And if there were any thorough passage by the Northeast, yet were it to small purpose for our traffike, because no shippe of great burden, can Navigate in so shallowe a Sea: and shippes of small burden are very unfit and unprofitable, especially towardes the blusteringe North, to perfourme suche a voyage.

To proove that the Indians afore named, came onely by the Northwest, which induceth a certeintie of our passage by experience.

Cap. 7.

It is as likely, that they came by the Northwest, as it is unlikely that they should come, ether by the Southeast, Southwest, Northeast, or from any other parte of Africa, or America, and therefore this Northwest passage, having bene already so many wayes proved, by disproving of the others, etc. I shal the lesse nede in this place, to use many wordes otherwise then to conclude in this sort, That they came onely by the Northwest

from England: havinge these many reasons to leade mee thereunto.

1. Firste, the one halfe of the windes of the compasse, might bring them by the Northwest, bearinge alwayes betweene two sheats, with which kinde of saylinge ye Indians are only acquainted, not having any use of a bowe, line, or quarter winde, without ye which no ship can possibly come either by the Southeast, Southwest, or Northeast, having so many sundrie capes to double, whereunto are required such chaunge and shift of windes.

2. And it seemeth likely, that they should come by the Northwest,[36] because the Coast whereon they were driven, lay East from this our passage, And all windes, do naturally drive a Shippe to an opposite point, from whence it bloweth, not beeing otherwise guided by Art, which the Indians do utterly want. And therefore it seemeth, that they came directly thorowe this our fret, which they might doe with one winde.

3. For if they had come by Cap. de buona Speranca, then must they (as aforesaid) have fallen upon the South partes of America.

4. And if by the fret of Magellan, then upon the coastes of Afrik, Spaine, Portingal, Fraunce, Ireland, or England.

5. And if by the Northeast, then upon the coasts of Cerecinissi Tartarii, Lappia, Island, Terra de Labrador, etc. and upon these coasts, (aforesaid) they have never bene found.

So that by all likelyhood, they coulde never have come, without shipwracke, upon the coasts of Germanie, if they had first striken upon the coastes of so manie countreys, wanting both Art and shipping, to make orderly discoverie: and altogether ignorant both in the Art of Navigation, and also of the Rockes, Flats, Sands, or Havens of those parts of the world, which in most of these places are plentifull.

6. And further it seemeth very likely, that the inhabitants of the most parte of those countries, by which they must have come, any other way besides, by the Northwest, being for the most part Anthropophagi, or men eaters, woulde have devoured them, slaine them, or (at the leaste wise) kept them as wonders for the gaze.

36. Sidenote: "True, both in ventis obliquè flantibus as also, in ventis ex diametro spirantibus."

So that it plainly appeareth, that those Indians (which, as you have heard, in sundrie ages were driven by tempest, upon the shore of Germanie) came onely through our Northwest passage.

7. Moreover, the passage is certeinely prooved, by a Navigation that a Portingal made, who passed thorow this fret: giving name to a Promontorie far within the same, calling it after his owne name, Promontoria Corterialis, neere adjoyning unto Polisacus fluvius.

8. Also one Scolmus a Dane, entred and passed a great part thereof.

9. Also there was one Salva Terra, a Gentleman of Victoria, in Spaine, that came by chaunce out of the West Indians, into Ireland, Anno, 1568. who affirmed the Northwest passage from us to Cataia, constantly to be beleeved in America, Navigable. And further said, in the presence of Sir Henry Sidney (then Lord Deputie of Ireland) in my hearing, that a Frier of Mexico, called Andro Urdaneta, more then viii. yeares, before his then comming into Ireland, tolde him there, that he came from Mare de Sur into Germanie, through this Northwest passage, and shewed Salva Terra (at that time beeing then with him in Mexico) a Sea Carde made by his owne experience, and travel, in that voyage: wherin was plainly set downe and described, this Northwest passage: agreeing in al pointes with Hortelius Mappe.

And further, this Frier, tolde the King of Portingal, (as he returned by that countrey homewarde) that there was (of certaintie) suche a passage, Northwest from England, and that he ment to publishe the same: which done, the King most earnestly desired him, not in any wise to disclose, or make the passage knowen to any Nation: For that (said the King) If England had knowledge, and experience thereof, it would greatly hinder both the King of Spaine, and me.[37] This Frier (as Salva Terra reported) was the greatest Discoverer by sea, that hath bene in our age. Also Salva Terra, beinge perswaded, of this passage by the Frier Urdaneta, and by the common opinion of the Spaniardes, inhabiting America, offered most willingly to accompanie me

in this Discoverie: which of like hee woulde not have done, if he had stoode in doubt thereof.

And now as these moderne experiences, cannot be impugned: So, least it might be objected,[38] that these thinges (gathered out of auncient writers, which wrote so many yeres past) might serve little to prove this passage, by the North of America, because both America and India, were to them then utterly unknowen to remove this doubt, let this suffise: That Aristotle, (who was 300. yeres before Christ) named Mare Indicum.[39] Also Berosus (who lived 330 yeres before Christ) hath these words, e Ganges in India. Also in the first Chapter of Hester be these words, In the dayes of Assuerus which ruled from India, to Aethiopia: which Assuerus lived 580 yeres before christ. Also Quintus Curtius (where he speaketh of the Conquests of Alexander) mencioneth India. Also, Arianus Philostratus, and Sidrach in his discourses of the warres of the king of Bactria, and of Garaab, who had the most part of India under his government. Al which assureth us, that both India, and Indians were knowen in those dayes.

These things considered, we may (in my opinion) not only assure our selves of this passage, by ye Northwest, but also yt it is navigable, both to come and goe, as hath beene proved in part and in al, by the experience of divers, as Sebastian Gabota, Corterialis, the three brethren above named, the Indians, and Urdaneta the Frier of Mexico, etc.

And yet notwithstanding al which, there be some that have a better hope of this passage to Cataia, by ye Northeast, then by ye west: whose reasons, with my severall answeres, ensue in the Chapter following.

Certaine reasons, alledged for the proving of a passage by the Northeast, before the Queenes Majestie, and certaine Lordes of the Counsell, with my severall answeres, then used to the same.

Cap. 8.

Because you may understande, aswell those thinges alledged against me, as what doth serve

---

37. Sidenote: "The wordes of the King of Portingal, to Andro Urdaneta a Frier, touchinge the concealing of this Northwest passage From England to Cataia."

38. Sidenote: "An Objection."
39. Sidenote: "Aristotle, lib. de mundo, cap. secund. Berosus lib. 5."

for my purpose, I have here added the reasons of a worthy Gentleman, and a great traveller, who conceived a better hope of the passage to Cataia, from us, to bee by the Northeast, then by the Northwest: whom I have not named in this place, because I seeke to impugne his opinions, as followeth.

He first said, that he thought not to the contrarie, but that there was a passage by the Northwest,[40] according to mine opinion: But assured he was, that there might be founde a Navigable passage, by the Northeast from England, to go to al the East partes of the worlde: which he endevoured to proove three wayes.

The first[41] was, that he heard a fisherman of Tartaria say, in hunting the Morce, that he sayled very far towards the Southeast, finding no ende of the Sea: whereby hee hoped a thorowe passage to bee that way.

Whereunto I answered, that the Tartarians were a barbarous people, and utterly ignorant in the Art of Navigation, not knowing the use of the sea, Carde, compasse, or starre, which he confessed true: and therefore they coulde not (saide I) certainly know the Southeast, from the Northwest, in a wide sea, and a place unknowen, from the sight of the land.

Or if he sailed any thing nere the shore, yet he (being ignorant) might be deceived by the doubling of many points and Capes, and by the trending of the land:[42] Albeit he kept continually alongst the shore.

And further, it might be, that the poore fisherman through simplicitie, thought that there was nothing that way but sea, because he saw no land: which proofe (under correction) giveth smal assurance of a Navigable sea by the Northeast, to goe round about the worlde, For that he judged by the eye onely,[43] seeinge wee in this our cleare ayre doe accompt 20 myles a ken at Sea.

His second reason[44] is, that there was a Unicornes horne founde upon the coaste of Tartaria, which could not come (saide he) thither, by any other meanes, then with the Tides, through some fret in the Northeast of Mare Glaciale, there being no Unicorne in any parte of Asia, saving in India, and Cataia: which reason (in my simple judgement) forceth as litle.

First it is doubtful,[45] whether those barbarous Tartarians doe know an Unicorns horne, ye, or no: and if it were one, yet it is not credible, that the sea could have driven it so farre, being of such nature that it will not swimme.

Also the Tydes running to and froe, would have driven it as farre backe with the ebbe, as it brought it forwarde with the fludde.

There is also a beast called Asinus Indicus (whose horne most like it was) whiche hath but one horne, like an Unicorne, in his forehead, whereof there is great plentie, in al the North parts thereunto adjoyning:[46] as in Lappia, Norvegia, Finmarke, etc. as Jacobus Zeiglerus writeth, in his historie of Scondia.

And as Albertus saith, there is a fishe, which hath but one horne in his forehead like to an Unicorne, and therfore it seemeth very doubtful,[47] both from whence it came, and whether it were an Unicornes horne, yea, or no.

His thirde and last reason[48] was, that there came a continual streame, or currant through Mare Glaciale, of such swiftnesse (as a Colmax tolde him) that if you cast anything therin, it would presently be caried out of sight, towards the West.

Wherunto I answered,[49] that there doth the like from Maeotis Palus, by Pontus Euxinus, Sinus, Bosphorus, and along the coaste of Graecia, etc. As it is affirmed by Contarenus, and divers others, that have had experience of the same: and yet that sea, lieth not open to any maine sea that way, but is maintained by fresshets, as by Taniis, Danubius, etc.

In like maner is this currant in Mare Glaciale increased, and maintained, by the Volgo, the river Oby, etc.

Now as I have here briefly recited the reasons alledged, to proove a passage to Cataia, by the Northeast, with my severall answeres thereunto:

---

40. Sidenote: "The Northwest Passage assented unto."
41. Sidenote: "The first reason. The Morce, is a kinde of fish which the Tartarians do often hunt by water, and greatly seeke to kill."
42. Sidenote: "The 'answere', or resolution."
43. Sidenote: "Visus nonnunquam fallitur in suo objecto."
44. Sidenote: "The second reason or allegation."

45. Sidenote: "The answere, or resolution."
46. Sidenote: "Omne simile, non est idem."
47. Sidenote: "Nulla ratio, ab Ambiguo certa sed fallax."
48. Sidenote: "The thirde and last reason or Assertion. Colmaxes are a people inhabiting the North part of Asia."
49. Sidenote: "The answere, or resolution."

so will I leave it to your judgement, to hope or dispaire of either, at your pleasure.

How that the passage by the Northwest, is more commodious for our traffik, then the other by the East: if there were any such.

Cap. 9.

First, by the Northeaste (if your windes doe not give you a marveylous speedie, and luckie passage) you are in daunger (being so nere the Pole) to be benighted, almost the one halfe of the yeare, and what miserie and daunger that were, to live so long comfortlesse, voyde of light, (if the colde killed you not) eche man of reason or understanding may judge.

2. Also Mangia, Quingit, and the Molluccae, are neerer unto us by the Northwest, then by the Northeast, more then 2/5 parts which is almost by the halfe.

3. Also wee may have by the West, a yerely returne, it being at al times Navigable, wheras you have but six moneths, in the whole yere, to goe by the Northeast: the passage beinge at such elevation, as it is formerly expressed, for it cannot be any neerer the South.

4. Furthermore, it cannot be finished without divers wintrings by the way, having no havens in any temperate Climate, to harbour in ther. For it is as much as we can well sayle, from hence to S. Nicholas, in the trade of Muscovia, and return in the Navigable season of the yeare, and from S. Nicholas to Cerimissi Tartarii, which standeth at 80 degrees of the Septentrional latitude, it is at the least 400 Leagues, which amounteth scarce to the thirde part of the way, to the ende of your voyage by the Northeast.

5. And yet after you have doubled this Cape, if then there might be found a navigable sea, to cary you Southeast, according to your desire, yet can you not winter conveniently, until you come to 60 degrees, and to take up one degree running Southeast, you must sayle 24 leagues 3/4 which amounteth to 495 leagues.

6. Furthermore, you may by the Northwest, saile thither with al Easterly winds, and returne with any westerly windes, wheras you must have by the Northeast sundrie windes, and those proper, accordinge to the lying of the coastes and capes, you shalbe inforced to double, which

windes are not always to be had, when they are looked for: wherby your journey should be greatly prolonged, and hardly endured so nere the Pole. As we are taught by Sir Hugh Wiloughbie, who was frosen to death far nerer the South.

7. Moreover, it is very doubtfull, whether we should long injoy that trade by ye Northeast, if there were any such passage that way, the commodities therof once knowen to the Muscovite, what privilege soever he hath graunted, seeing policie with the Maze of excessive gaine, to the enriching (so greatly) of himselfe and all his dominions, would persuade him to resume the same, having so great opportunitie, to utter the commodities of those countreys by the Narve.

But by the Northwest, wee may safely trade without daunger, or annoyance, of any prince living, Christian, or heathen, it being out of al their trades.

8. Also ye Queenes Majesties dominions, are nerer the Northwest passage, then any other great princes that might passe that way, and both in their going and returne, they must of necessitie succour themselves and their shippes, upon some parte of the same, if any tempestious weather shoulde happen.

Further, no Princes Navie of the world, is able to encounter the Queenes Majesties Navie, as it is at this present: and yet it should be greatly increased, by the traffike ensuing upon this discoverie, for it is the long voyages, that increase and maintaine great shipping.

Now it seemeth necessarie, to declare what commodities would grow thereby, if al these things were, as we have heretofore presupposed, and thought them to be: which next adjoyning are briefly declared.

What commodities woulde ensue, this passage once discovered.

Cap. 10.

First, it were the onely way for our princes, to possesse ye welth of all the East partes (as they tearme them) of the worlde, which is infinite: as appeareth by the experience of Alexander the great, in the time of his conquest of India, and other the East partes of the worlde, alledged by Quintus Curtius, which would be a great advauncement to our Countrie, wonderfull inriching to our Prince, and unspeakeable commodities to all the inhabitants of Europe.

2. For through the shortnesse of the voyage, we should be able to sell all maner of Merchandize, brought from thence, far better cheape, then either the Portingal, or Spaniarde doth, or may doe: And further, share with the Portingal in the East, and the Spaniarde in the West, by trading to any part of America, through Mare de Sur, wher they can no maner of way offend us.

3. Also we may saile to divers marveilous riche Countries, both Civil and others, out of both their jurisdictions, trades and traffiks, where ther is to be found great aboundance of gold, silver, precious stones, Cloth of golde, silkes, all maner of Spices, Grocery wares, and other kindes of Merchandize, of an inestimable price: which both the Spaniarde, and Portingal, through the length of their journeys, can not well attaine unto.

4. Also we might inhabite some parte of those Countreys, and settle there suche needie people of our Countrie, which now trouble the common welth, and through want here at home, are inforced to commit outragious offences, whereby they are dayly consumed with the Gallowes.

5. Moreover, we might from all the aforesaid places, have a yerely retourne, inhabiting for our staple some convenient place of America, about Sierra Nevada, or some other part, wheras it shal seeme best for the shortening of the voyage.

6. Beside the uttering of our Countrie commodities, which the Indians, etc. much esteeme: as appeareth in Hester[50] where the pompe is expressed, of the great King of India, Assuerus, who matched the coloured clothes, wherewith his houses and tents, were apparelled, with golde and silver, as part of his greatest treasure: not mencioning either velvets, silkes, cloth of golde, cloth of silver, or suche like, being in those countreys most plentiful: wherby it plainly appeareth, in what great estimation, they woulde have the clothes of this our country, so that there would be founde a farre better vent for them, by this means, then yet this realme ever had: and that without depending, either upon Fraunce, Spaine, Flaunders, Portingal, Hamborowe, Emdem, or any other part of Europe.

7. Also, hereby we shall increase, both our shippes, and mariners, without burdening of the state.

8. And also have occasion, to set poore mens children, to learne handie craftes, and therby to make trifles and such like, which the Indians and those people doe muche esteeme: By reason whereof, there should be none occasion, to have our countrey combred with loyterers, vagabonds, and such like idle persons.

All these commodities would growe, by following this our Discoverie, without injurie done to any Christian prince, by crossing them in any of their used trades, whereby they might take any just occasion of offence.

Thus have I briefly shewed you, some part of the groundes of mine opinion, trusting that you wil no longer judge me fantastike in this matter: seeing I have conceived no hope of this voyage, but am persuaded thereunto, by the best Cosmographers of our age, the same being confirmed, both by reason and certaine experiences.

Also this discoverie, hath bene divers times heretofore by others, both offered attempted, and perfourmed.

It hath bene offred by Stephen Gomes unto Carolus the fifth Emperour, in the yere of our Lord God 1527, as Alphonso Ulloa testifieth, in ye story of Carolus life: who would have set him forth in it (as the storie mencioneth) if ye great want of money, by reason of his long warres, had not caused him to sucresse the same.

And the King of Portingal, fearing lest the Emperour woulde have persevered in this his enterprise, gave him, to leave the matter unattempted, the sum of 350000 Crownes:[51] and it is to be intended that the King of Portingal, would not have given to the Emperour, sich summes of money for egges in mooneshine.

It hath bene attempted by Corterialis the Portingal, Scolmus the Dane, and by Sebastian Gabota, in the time of King Henry the seventh.[52]

And it hath beene perfourmed, by the three brethren, the Indians aforesaid, and by Urdaneta, the Frier of Mexico.[53]

Also divers have offered the like, unto the

---

50. Sidenote: "Hester. cap. I."

51. Sidenote: "This discoverie offered."
52. Sidenote: "This discoverie attempted."
53. Sidenote: "This discoverie performed."

Frenche King, who hath sent two or three times to have discovered the same. The discoverers, spending and consuming their victuals, in searching the gulfes, and bayes, betweene Florida, and Terra de Labrador, whereby the Ise is broken to the after commers.

So that the right way, may now easily be founde out, in short time: and that with litle joperdie and lesse expences.

For America is discovered, so farre towards the North as Cape Fredo,[54] which is at 62 degrees, and that part of Grondland next adjoyning, is knowen to stand but at 72. So that we have but 10 degrees, to sayle North and South, to put the worlde out of doubt hereof: and it is likely, that the King of Spaine, and the King of Portingal, would not have sate out al this while, but that they are sure to possesse to themselves, all that trade they now use, and feare to deale in this Discoverie, least the Queenes Majestie, having so good opportunitie, and finding the commoditie, which thereby might ensue to the common welth: woulde cutte them of,[55] and enjoye the whole traffique to her selfe, and thereby the Spaniardes and Portingals, with their great charges, should but beate the bushe, and other men catche the birds: which thinge they forseeing, have commaunded, that no Pylate of theirs, upon payne of death, shoulde seeke to discover to the Northwest, or platte out in any sea carde, any thorowe passage that way, by the Northwest.

Now, and if you wil indifferently, compare the hope that remaineth, to animate me to this enterprise, with those likelihoodes which Columbus alledged before Ferdinando, the King of Castilia, to proove that there were such Ilands in the west Ocean, as were after, by him and others discovered, to the great commoditie of Spaine and all the worlde: you will thinke then this Northwest passage, to be most worthy travell therein.

For Columbus had none of the west Ilands set forth unto him, either in globe, or card, neither yet once mencioned of any writer, (Plato excepted, and the commentaries upon the same) from 942 yeres before Christ, until that day.

Moreover, Columbus himself, had neither seene America or any other of the Ilands about it, neither understoode he of them, by the report of any other that had seene them, but onely comforted himself with this hope, that the land had a beginninge, where the sea had an ending: For as touching that, which the Spaniards doe write of a Biscaine, which shuld have taught him ye way thither, it is thought to be imagined of them, to deprive Columbus of his honour, beeing none of their countreymen, but a stranger borne.

And if it were true of the Biscaine, yet did he but rove at the matter, or (at the least) gathered the knowledge of it, by conjectures onely.

And albeit, my selfe have not seene this passage, or any part thereof, but am ignorant of it as touching experience, (as Columbus was before his attempt made) yet have I, both the report, relation, and authoritie, of divers most credible men, which have both seene and passed through some, and everie part of this discoverie: besides sundrie reasons, for my assurance thereof: all which Columbus wanted.

These things considered, and indifferently wayed together, with the wonderful commodities which this discoverie may bring, especially to this realme of England: I must needes conclude with Hieronimus Fracastorius, and divers other learned men, who said, that this discoverie hath beene reserved, for some noble Prince, or worthy man, therby to make himselfe rich, and the world happie: desiringe you to accept in good part, this briefe and simple discourse, written in hast, which if I may perceive, that it shal not sufficiently satisfie you in this behalfe, I will then imparte unto you a large discourse, which I have written only of this discoverie.

And further, because it sufficeth not, onely to know that such a thing there is, without abilitie to perfourme the same, I wil at more leasure make you partaker, of another simple discourse of Navigation, wherein I have not a litle travelled, to make my selfe as sufficient, to bring these things to effect, as I have bene readie to offer my selfe therein.

And therein I have devised to amende the errours of usuall sea cardes, whose common fault is, to make the degrees of longitude, in everie latitude, of one like bignes.

And have also devised therein, a Spherical

54. Sidenote: "The labour of this discoverie shortened by other mens travel."
55. Sidenote: "Why the king of Spaine and Portingal would not persever in this discoverie."

instrument, with a compasse of variation, for the perfect knowing of the longitude.

And a precise order to prick the sea carde, together with certaine infallible rules for the shortening of any discoverie, to know at the first entring of any fret, whether it lye open to the Ocean, more wayes then one, how farre soever the sea stretcheth it selfe, into the land.

Desiring you hereafter, never to mislike with me, for the taking in hand of any laudable and honest enterprise, for if through pleasure or idlenes we purchase shame, ye pleasure vanisheth, but the shame remaineth for ever.

And therefore to give me leave without offence, alwayes to live and die in this minde, That he is not worthie to live at all, that for feare, or daunger of death, shunneth his countrey service, and his owne honour, seeing death is inevitable, and the fame of vertue immortall. Wherefore in this behalfe, Mutare vel timere sperno.[56]

356. 1578. Notes prepared by Richard Hakluyt the elder for Sir Humphrey Gilbert.

Richard Hakluyt the elder was a lawyer of the Middle Temple who had come to act as a business adviser to merchants and others engaging in overseas voyages and trading ventures. Probably under the stimulus of the Northwest Passage voyages which began in 1576, he developed an interest in the possibilities of American colonization. While Sir Humphrey Gilbert was casting around for an attractive overseas objective, Hakluyt became one of his advisers. Probably before Gilbert received his patent from the queen in June, 1578, Hakluyt drafted these notes for him. They are significant as the first attempt (so far as we know) to set out the advantages to Englishmen of settlement in temperate climates in eastern North America. There is much practical advice on what type of site it is best to choose and how to build up a firm hold on it. Most important, it is a flexible scheme to exploit the existing resources of the country by commerce and extraction together

with an emphasis on the use of the soil to grow crops or graze animals. Stress is laid on growing, if the climate is suitable, grapes, olives, citrus fruits, and dye stuffs, while timber, salt, and fishing may also be valuable. The general emphasis is practical, with the basic premise being the need to exploit America in order to reduce England's dependence on products that it must at present import from Europe. Its pragmatic tone was to set a pattern for those tracts that followed.

It was first published (with his own heading) by Richard Hakluyt the younger, a cousin of the elder Hakluyt, a clergyman and a senior member of an Oxford college, when he was making a promotion collection of materials for Gilbert's second expedition in Divers Voyages touching the discoverie of America *(London, 1582). Sig. K1–K3v.*

Notes framed by a Gentleman heretofore to bee given to one that prepared for a discoverie. and went not: And not unfitt to be committed to print, considering the same may stirre up considerations of these and of such other thinges, not unmeete in such new voyages as may be attempted hereafter.

That the first seate be chosen on ye seaside so as (if it may be) you may have your owne Navie within Bay, river or lake, within your seat safe from the enemie. And so as the enemie shalbe forced to lie in open rode abroad without, to be dispersed with all windes and tempests that shall arise. Thus seated you shall bee least subjecte to annoy of the enemie, so may you by your Navie within, passe out to all partes of the worlde, and so may the shippes of Englande have accesse to you to supply all wantes, so may your commodities be caried away also. This seate is to bee chosen in temperate Climat, in sweete ayre, where you may possesse a[l]wayes sweete water, wood, seacoles, or turfe, with fish, flesh, grayne, fruits, herbes and rootes, or so many of those, as may suffice very necessitie for the life of such as shall plant there. And for the possessing of mines of golde, of silver, copper, quicksilver, or of any such precious thing, the wantes of divers of those needfull things may be supplied from some other place by sea, &c.

Stone to make Lyme of.
Slate stone to tyle withall
  or such clay as
    maketh tyle,
Stone to wall withal if
  Brycke may not bee
  made,
Timber for building
  easely to be conveied
  to the place,
Reede to cover houses or
  such like, if tile or
  slate be not.
} are to be looked for as thinges without which no Citie may bee made nor people in civill sorte be kept together.

The people there to plant and to continue are eyther to live without trafficke, or by trafficke and by trade of marchandize. If they shall live without sea trafficke, at the first they become naked by want of linen and wollen, and very miserable by infinite wantes that will otherwise ensue, and so will they be forced of them selves to depart, or els easely they will bee consumed by the Sp[aniards] by the Fr[ench] or by the naturall inhabithantes of the countrey, and so the inter-price becomes reprochfull to our nation, and a lett to many other good purposes that may be taken in hande.

And by trade of marchandize they can not live, excepte the sea or the lande there may yeelde commoditie for commoditie. And therefore you ought to have most speciall regarde of that point, and so to plant, that the naturall commodities of the place and seate, may draw to you accesse of Navigation for the same, or that by your owne Navigation you may carie the same out, and fetche home the supplye of the wantes of the seate.

Such navigation so to bee employed, shall be-sides the supply of wantes, bee able to encounter with forreyne force.

And for that in the ample vente of suche thinges as are brought to you out of Engl[and] by sea, standeth a matter of great consequence, it be-hoveth that all humanitie and curtesie and much forbearing of revenge to the inland people be used, so shall you have firme amitie with your neyghbours, so shall you have their inland com-modities of maintayne trafficke, & so shall you waxe rich and strong in force. Divers & severall commodities of the inland are not in great plentie to be brought to your handes, without the ayde of some portable or Navigable ryver, or ample lacke, and therefore to have the helpe of such a

one is most requisite: And so is it of effecte for the dispersing of your owne commodities in exchange into the inlandes.

Nothing is more to be indevoured with the Inland people then familiaritie. For so may you best discover al the naturall commodities of their countrey, and also all their wantes, all their strengthes, all their weakenesse, and with whome they are in warre, and with whome con-fiderate in peace and amitie, &c. whiche knowen, you may woorke many great effectes of greatest consequence.

And in your planting the consideration of the climate and of the soyle bee matters that are to bee respected. For if it be so that you may let in the salt sea water, not mixed with the fresh into flattes, where the sunne is of the heate that it is at Rochell, in the Bay of portingall, or in Spaine, then may you procure a man of skill, and so you have wonne one noble commoditie for the fishing, and for trade of marchandize by making of Salt.

Or if the soyle and clymate bee such as may yeelde you the Grape as good as that at Burdeus, as that in Portingale, or as that about Sivi [Se-ville] in Spaine, or that in the Ilands of the Can-aries, then there resteth but a woorkeman to put in execution to make wines, and to dresse Resings of the sunne and other, &c.

Or if you finde a soyle of the temperature of the South part of Spaine or Barbarie, in whiche you finde the Olif tree to growe: Then you may bee assured of a noble marchandize for this realme, considering that our great trade of clothing doth require oyle, and weying howe deere of late it is become by the vent they have of that commoditie in the West Indies, and if you fine the wilde olif there it may be graffed.

Or if you can find the berrie of Cochenile with whiche wee colour Stammelles, or any Roote, Berrie, Fruite, wood or earth fitte for dying, you winne a notable thing fitt for our state of clothing. This Cochenile is naturall in the west Indies on that firme.

Or if you have hides of beastes fit for sole Lether, &c. It wilbe a marchandize right good, and the savages there yet can not tanne Lether after our kinde, yet excellently after their owne maner.

Or if the soyle shall yeelde Figges, Almondes, Sugar Canes, Quinces, Orenges, Lemons, Potatos, &c. there may arise some trade and trafficke by figges, almonds, sugar, marmelade, Sucket &c.

Or if great woods bee founde, if they be of Cypres, chests may bee made, if they bee of some kinde of trees, pitche and tarre may be made, if they bee of some other then they may yeelde Rasin, Turpentine, &c. and al for trade and trafficke, and Caskes for wine and oyle may be made; likewise ships and houses, &c.

And because trafficke is a thing so materiall, I wish that great observation be taken what every soyle yeeldeth naturally, in what commoditie soever, and what it may be made to yeeld by indevour, and to send us notice home, that thereuppon we may devise what meanes may be thought of to rayse trades.

Nowe admit that we might not be suffered by the savages to enjoy any whole countrey or any more then the scope of a Citie, yet if wee might enjoy trafficke and be assured of the same, wee might bee inriched, our Navie might be increased, & a place of safetie might there be found, if change of religion or civill warres shoulde happen in this realme, which are thinges of great benefite. But if we may injoy any large Territorie of apt soyle, we might so use the matter, as we should not depende upon Spaine for oyles, sacks, resinges, orenges, lemons, Spanish skinnes, &c. Nor uppon Fraunce for woad, baysalt, and gascoyne wines, nor on Estlande for flaxe, pitch, tarre, mastes, &c. So we shoulde not so exhaust our treasure, and so exceedingly inriche our doubtfull friendes, as we doe, but shoulde purchasse the commodities that we want for halfe the treasure that now we do: but should by our owne industries & the benefits of the soile there cheapley purches oyles, wines, salt, fruits, pitch, tarre, flaxe, hempe, mastes, boordes, fishe, gold, silver, copper, tallowe, hides and many commodities: besides if there be no flatts to make salt on, if you have plentie of wood you may make it in sufficient quantitie for common uses at home there.

If you can keepe a safe haven, although you have not the friendship of the neere neyghbours, yet you may have trafficke by sea upon one shore or other, upon that firme in time to come, if not present.

If you finde great plenty of tymber on the shore side or upon any portable river, you were best to cut downe of the same the first wynter, to bee seasoned for shippes, barkes, botes and houses.

And if neere such wood there be any river or brooke upon the which a sawing mill may be placed, it woulde doe great service, and therefore consideration woulde bee had of suche place.

And if such port & chosen place of setling were in possession & after fortified by art, although by ye land side our Englishmen were kept in, and might not injoy any traffick with the next neighbours, nor any vittel: yet might they vittel themselves of fishe to serve verie necessitie, and enter into amitie with the enemies of their next neighbours, & so have vent of their marchandize of England and also have vittel, or by meanes hereupon to be used to force the next neighbours to amitie. And keeping a navie at the setling place, they shoulde finde out along the tracte of the lande to have trafficke, and at divers Ilandes also. And so this first seate might in time become a stapling place of the commodities of many countreys and territories, and in tyme this place myght become of all the provinces round about the only governour. And if the place first chosen should not so wel please our people, as some other more lately founde out: There might bee an easie remove, and that might be rased, or rather kept for others of our nation to avoyde an ill neyghbour, &c.

If the soyles adjoyning to such convenient haven and setling places be found marshie and boggie, then men skilful in draining are to be caried thither. For arte may worke wonderfull effectes therein, and make the soyle rich for many uses.

To plante uppon an Ilande in the mouth of some notable river, or upon the poynt of the lande entring into the river, if no such Iland be, were to great ende. For if such river were navigable or portable farre into the lande, then would arise great hope of planting in fertil soyles, and trafficke on the one or on thother side of the river, or on both, or the linking in amitie with one or other petie king, contending there for dominion.

Such rivers founde, both barges and boates may bee made for the safe passage of such as shall perce ye same. These to bee covered with doubles of course linnen artificially wrought, to defend the arrow or the dart of the savage from the rower.

Since every soyle of the world by arte may be made to yeelde things to feede and to cloth man, bring in your returne a perfect note of the soyle without and within, and we shall devise if neede require to amende the same, & to draw it to more perfection. And if you finde not fruits in your planting place to your liking, we shall in v. drifats furnish you with such kinds of plants to be caried thither ye winter after your planting, as shall the very next summer following, yeeld you some fruite, and the yere next folowing, as much as shal suffice a towne as bigge as Callice, and that shortly after shall be able to yeeld you great store of strong durable good sider to drinke, & these trees shalbe able to increase you within lesse then vii yeres as many trees presently to beare, as may suffice the people of divers parishes, which at the first setling may stand you in great steade, if the soyle have not the commoditie of fruites of goodnesse already. And because you ought greedily to hunt after thinges that yeelde present reliefe, without trouble of cariage thither, therefore I make mencion of these, thus specially, to the ende you may have it specially in mynde.

Chapter Forty-three
Projects Deriving from Sir Humphrey Gilbert's Last Voyage

357. April, 1583. Christopher Carleill's
A breef and sommarie discourse upon the entended voyage to the hethermoste partes of America.

Christopher Carleill, Walsingham's stepson, comes into the colonizing picture at a point when Sir Humphrey Gilbert's enterprise seemed to be in jeopardy after his failure to get to sea in 1582. He could not attract big business either in London or in Bristol to support him, and Carleill set out to do just this and take over from Gilbert the economic development of America in the area north of modern southern New England—it is impossible to be more precise about the area. The first edition of his promotion pamphlet came to light comparatively recently, when copies were located in Westminster Abbey Library and Dulwich College Library. The title page stated that the scheme was launched in April, 1583, and it included a set of articles that we know from another source (see D. B. Quinn, Gilbert, II, 365) were drawn up on May 9, arranging for the support of the influential Muscovy Company, which claimed in right of its charter of 1555 (165) to have monopoly rights over voyages to the Northwest. The emphasis throughout was on commerce—"the Merchandizing . . . the matter especially looked for." Furs and timber were to be bought, English cloth to be sold, a passage through America to the Pacific found, some Mediterranean-type products to be developed by settlers, though he aimed, he says, at a latitude of about 40°N (which was to bring him into direct competition with Gilbert). Nevertheless, all his examples of potential trade rest on French activity in the St. Lawrence Valley from Cartier to their most recent fur trading exploits. He wanted a small compact colony to build up commerce and one that would only gradually involve itself in agriculture. Gilbert's preparations and depar-
ture led to a wait-and-see attitude on the part of Carleill's supporters. The news of Gilbert's failure to reach Norumbega and of his own probable loss at sea appears to have scared off large investors. But about the end of the year or very early in 1584 he was on the move again. In the first four months of 1584 his agents were trying to raise subscriptions of £100 from town corporations. Most probably it was to help them that he had his pamphlet reprinted, without change, except for a different title, A discourse upon the extended voyage to the nethermost partes of America: written by Captain Carleill. A unique copy of this with no title page is in the John Carter Brown Library. Somehow he raised enough money to set out in July, 1584, but went no further than Ireland. His tract is original in that he makes a very specific economic appeal, contrasting with the extravagant range of Gilbert's offers.

A breef and sommarie discourse upon the entended Voyage to the hethermoste partes of America: Written by Captaine Carleill in Aprill 1583. for the better inducement to satisfie suche Marchauntes of the Moscovian Companie and others, as in disburcyng their money towardes the furniture of the present charge: doe demaunde forthwith a present returne of gaine: albeit their saied perticuler disburcements are required but in verie slender sommes: The highest beeyng twentie and five pounde. The seconde at twelve pound ten shillynges. And ye lowest at six pound five shillinges.

Captaine Carleills discourse

When the Goldsmith desireth to finde the certaine goodnesse of a peece of golde, which is newly offered unto hym, he presently bryngeth the same to the Touchstone: whereby comparyng the showe or touche of this newe peece with the touch or shewe of that whiche he knoweth of olde, he forthwith is able to judge what the valewe is of that, which is newly offered unto hym. After the exsample wherof I have thought it good to make some briefe repetition of the perticuler estate of many other forraine Voyages and trades alreadie frequented and knowne unto us, wherby you may be the better able to conceive and judge what certaine likelihood of good there is to be expected in the Voyage, whiche is presently recommended unto your knowledge and resolution.

And first to lay doune that of Moscovia, whose beginnyng is yet in the remembrance of many. It is well knowne that what by the charges of the first discoverie, and by the greate giftes bestowed on the Emperor and his Nobilitie, together with the leaud dealing of some of their servauntes, who thought themselves safe enough from orderly punishment. It cost the Companie above fower skore thousande poundes, before it could be brought to any profitable reckoning. And now that after so long a pacience, and so greate a burthen of expences, the same beganne to frame to some good course and commodity: It faleth to very ticklish tearmes, and to as slender likelihood of any further goodnesse as any other trade that may be named. For first the estate of those Countreis and the Emperours dealinges, are thinges more fickle then are by every bodie understoode. Next, the Dutchmen are there so crept in, as they daely augment their trade thether, which may well confirme that uncertentie of the Emperours disposition to keepe promise with our Nation. Thirdly, the qualitie of the voyage, suche as it may not bee performed but once the yere. Fourthly, the charges of all Ambassadours betweene that Prince & her Maiestie, are alwayes borne by the Marchants stocke. And lastly, the daunger of the Kyng of Denmarke, who besides that presently he is like to enforce a tribute on us, hath likewise an advauntage upon our Shippes in their voyage, either homewardes or outwardes whensoever he listeth to take the opportunitie.

The bad dealynges of the Esterlynges are sufficiently knowne to be suche towardes our Marchauntes of that trade, as they do not onely offer them many injuries overlong to be written, but doe seeke all the meanes they can, to deprive them wholy of their occupiyng that way: and to the same purpose have of late, cleane debarred them their accustomed and auncient privileges in all their greate Townes.

The traffiques into Turkie, besides that by some it is thought a harde poinct to have so muche familiarity with the professed and obstinate Enemie of Christ: It is likewise a voyage whiche can not bee made but at the devotion, and as it were in the daunger of many States, who for sondrie respectes are apt to quarrell with us uppon sudden occasions. And the presentes to be given away in Turkie this yere cost litle lesse then two thousande poundes.

As for the trades into all the partes of Italie, it may easely be considered by every one of judgement, that the same standeth in the like termes touching the passages, as that of Turkie, and that many tymes our Shippes beeyng taken in the way by the Galleis of Barbary, our poore Mariners after the losse of their goodes and travaile, are sett at such excessive Raunsomes before they can be freed of their slaverie: as for the most parte they are no way able to discharge: as for Example at this instaunt there are some prisoners poore ordinary Mariners, for whose releasing there must be paied two hundred Duckets the man, for some three hundred, yea, fower or five hundred Duckets the man for some of them. And how enviously they doe already oppose them selves against our frequenting into their partes, may appeare by the late customes which they have imposed aswell uppon our English Marchaundize whiche wee bryng them, as also upon suche their Marchaundize whiche we fetche from them.

The trade into Barbary groweth likewise to worse tearmes then before tymes: and when it was at the best our Marchauntes have beene in daunger of all their goodes thei had there, whensoever it happened the Kyng to die. For untill a new were chosen, the liberty of al discordered persons is such, as they spoile & wrong whom they list without any redresse at al.

Touchyng Spaine and Portugall, with whom wee have very greate trade, and muche the greater, by meanes of their ventyng a good parte of our wares into their Indies, as also of the provision they have from the same, wherwith are made manye of our returnes from them againe. It falleth out that twise the yere ordinarily we sende our Flates into those partes: So that whensoever the Kyng of Spaine listeth to take the opportunity, he may at these seasons deprive us not only of a greate nomber of our very good Shippes, but also of our honestest, and ablest sort of Marriners that are to be found in our whole Realme againe: which is a matter of no small consequence: for it is to bee noted, that when he shall take a quarrell in hande, though it be but his owne perticulerly, yet hath he the meanes to put in hazarde aswell those of our Shippes which are in his owne Countreis of Spaine and Portugall, as also all others whiche shall be bounde to any the partes of all Italie or of Turkie either. And further whosoever ne bee that is but so meanly affected in Religion, as of necessitie becommeth every ordinarie man and good Christian to be, can not but be agreeed in his harte to consider, that his childred and servaunts whom he desireth to have well brought up, are in these trades of Spaine and Portugall and all Italie, forced to deny their owne profession, and made to acquaint them selves with that which the Parentes and Maisters doe utterly denie and refuse, yea which many of them doe in their own hartes abhorre as a detestable and most wicked doctrine.

But who shall looke into the quality of this voyage, beyng directed to the latitude of 40. degrees, or there aboutes of that hithermost part of America, shal finde it hath as many poinctes of good moment belonging unto it, as may almost be wished for. As first it is to be understoode, that it is not any long course, for it may be performed to and fro in fower monethes, after the first discovery thereof: Secondly, that one wind suffiseth to make the passage; wheras most of your other voyages of like length, are subject to three or fower winds. Thirdlie, that it is to be performed at all tymes of the yere. Fowerthly, that the passage is upon the high sea, wherby you are not bound to the knowledge of daungers, on any other coast, more then of that Countrey, and of ours here at home. Fiftlie, that those partes of Englande and Irelande, whiche lye aptest for the proceedyng outward, or homeward upon this voyage, are verie well stored of goodlie Harbourghes. Sixtly, that it is to be accompted of no daunger at al, as touching the power of any foraine Prince or State, when it is compared with any the best of all the other voyages before recited.

And to the godlie mynded, it hath this comfortable commoditie, that in this trade, their Factours, bee they their servauntes or children, shall have no instruction or confessions of Idolatrous Religion enforced upon them, but contrarily shall bee at their free libertie of conscience, and shall finde the same Religion exercised, whiche is most agreable unto their parentes and Maisters.

As for the Merchandizyng, which is the matter especially looked for, albeit that for the present, we are not certainly able to promise any suche like quantitie, as is now at the best tyme of the Moscovian trade brought from thence: So likewise is there not demaunded any suche proportion of daily expences, as was at the first, and as yet is consumed in that of Moscovia and other. But when this of America shall have been haunted and practized, thirtie yeres to an ende, as the other hath been, I doubte not by Gods grace, that for the tenne Shippes, that are now commonly employed once the yere into Moscovia, there shall in this voyage twise tenne be imployed well, twise the yere at the least. And if for the present tyme, there dooe fall out nothyng els to bee founde, then the bare Fishyng, yet doubte I not after the first yeres planting, but by that matter only to serve half a dozen of your best sort of shippes, although my supplie of people doe not followe me so substancially, as in all reason may be well looked for.

But when it is asked what may bee hoped from thence after some yeres, it is first to bee considered, that this situation in 40. degrees, shalbe verie apte to gather the commodities, either of those partes whiche stande to the Southward of it, as also of those whiche are to the Northward.

In the Northerlie may be expected, not onely an especiall good fishing for Salmon, Codde, and Whales, but also any other suche commodities, as the Easterne Countreis doe yeeld us now: as Pitche, Tarre, Hempe, and therof Cordage, Mastes, Loshe hides, riche Furres, and other suche like, without beyng in any sort beholdyng to a Kyng of Denmarke, or other Prince or State, that shalbe in such sort able to commaund our shippes at their pleasure, as those dooe at this day, by meanes of their straight, passages, and strong Shippyng.

As for those partes which lye West, and to the Southwardes, it may well be hoped they will yeeld wines with a small helpe, since the grapes doe grow there of themselves already very faire, and in great abundance. Olives beyng once planted, will yeeld the like Oile as Spain and Italy. The

Countrey people beyng made to know, that for Waxe and Honie, we will give them suche triflyng thynges, as they desire of us, and shewyng them once the meanes, how to provide the same, the labour thereof beyng so light, no doubt but in short tyme they will earnestly care to have the same in good quantitie for us. Besides what greate likelihoode there is of good meanes to make Salt, which may serve for ye fishing of those partes, may well enough appeare unto them, who can judge the quality of such places, as are required to make ye same in.

Thus muche for the beginnyng, because they may be had with an easie kinde of travaill. But when it may have pleased God, to establishe our people there any suche tyme, as they may have planted amongeste them, in sondrie partes of the Countrey, and that by gentle and familiar entreatyng them, they bee made to see, what is better for them, then they doe as yet understande of, and that in so many sortes of occasions, as were infinite to be set doune. It is to be assuredly hoped, that they will daiely by little & little, forsake their barbarous, and savage livyng, and grow to suche order and civilitie with us, as there may be wel expected from thence no lesse quantitie, and diversity of Marchandize, then is now had out of Dutchlande, Italie, Fraunce, or Spaigne. And as the borderyng neighbours, are commonly the aptest to fall out with us,[1] so these partes, beyng so these partes, beyng somewhat further remote, are the liker to take, or give lesse occasion of disquiet. But when it is considered, that they are our owne kindred, and esteemed our owne Countrey Nation whiche have the governement: meanyng by those who shalbe there planted, who can looke for any other then the dealyng of most loving, and moste assured freendes.

There are further to be considered, these twoo pointes of good importaunce, concernyng the matter of trade. The one is, that by the good prosperyng of this action, there muste of necessitie fall out, a verie liberall utteraunce of our Englishe Clothes, into a maine Countrey, described to be bigger then all Europe, the larger parte whereof bendyng to the Northward, shall have wonderfull greate use of our saied Englishe Clothes, after they shall once come to knowe the commoditie thereof. The like will be also of many other thinges, overmany to be reconed, which are made here by our Artificers & labouryng people, and of necessity must be provided from hence.

The other is, if there bee any possible meanes, to finde a Sea passage, or other freshe water course, whiche may serve in some reasonable and convenient sorte, to transporte our Marchandize into the East Indian Sea, through any of these Northerly partes of America, it shalbe sonest and moste assuredly performed by these who shall inhabite, and first grow into familiaritie with the Inlande people.

What Minerall matter may fall out to be founde, is a thing leaft in suspence, until some better knowledge, because there be many menne, who having long since, expected some profites herein, upon the great promises that have been made them, and beyng as yet in no poincte satisfied, doe thereupon conceive, that they bee but woordes pourposely caste out, for the inducyng of menne to bee the more willyng to furnishe their money, towardes the charge of the first discoverie.

But now to aunswere some others, who beginne with an other objection, saiyng: That it is not for the Marchauntes purse, to continue the charges of transportyng and plantyng: and that since these hundred menne, whiche are now to bee planted, will coste fower thousande pounde, it is then to bee thought, that the charge of a farre greater nomber, will be also a farre greater some of money. Whereunto I annswere, that in all atemptes unknowne, especially suche a one as is this, wherewith wee are presently in hande, the first charges are commonly adventured in more desperate kind, then those that folowe uppon some better knowledge: and therewith it falleth out, that whereas one adventureth in the firste enterprise, an hundred for that one will of them selves bee willyng, and desirous to adventure in the next, if there be never so little more apparaunce, that the entended matter is by some knowledge of our owne, found true in some poinctes of our firste presumption.[2] The examples are many, and may

1. Sidenote: "This is spoken upon the opinion which by some is conceived that Irelande is not suffered to be reduced to that perfection whiche it might be, least one day by chaunce revoltyng from the Crowne it might prove an overstrong partie to be so nere an enemie unto England."

2. Sidenote: "The ewer of Mettall brought by Maister Frobisher, caused two severall Supplies the two yeares next followyng, whereof the latter was of xiiij. tall Shippes."

easily bee remembred by those who bee Marchantes, even in their ordinarie and daiely trades, as well as in extraordinarie attemptes, whiche of late yeres, have fallen into those tearmes of some likelihoode, as is above saied. So then no doubt, but when certaine reportes shalbe brought by them, who directly come from thence: that such a Countrey and people, they have themselves seen, as is by us spoken of, but that then there will come forwarde a greater nomber of those, who now neither have hard any thing of the matter, as also of others, who presently make suche frivolous scruple, as will not otherwise be satisfied, then by the reporte of saincte Thomas. I speake not this by the Marchauntes, whom for their freedomes of trade, I would not have pressed to any further charge, then this first preparacion, but rather by suche as have great affection, to hazarde the chaungyng of their estates, and would be well content to goe in the Voyage, if they might onely bee assured that there is suche a Countrey, and that their money should not be wasted to nothyng in the preparations.[3] The right examination of this poincte, must bee the contrary sequell of the common Proverbe, *Nothyng venture, nothyng have*, so on the other side by venturyng, many greate good proffites are found out, to the wonderful benefite of the common weale, and to those especially in private, who take on the hazarde of their life and travaill, or substance in the first attemptes, and therefore I would wishe that they who (God bee thanked) are well able to spare that, whiche is required of eche one towardes the undertakyng of this adventure, bee well content and willyng to employe the same, since the sequell in good and substanciall reason dooeth promise, not onely a greate commoditie in perticuler to the Marchaunte, who shall here at home exercise the trade of Marchaundize: But also to an infinite nomber of other, who presently live in poore estate, and may by takyng the opportunitie of this discoverie, alter the same to a farre better degree. Wherefore to make some conclusion upon this poincte of the Marchauntes misdoubt, who suspecteth least this first disburcement, without returne of present gaine, should not bee all his

charge, but that afterwardes he might yet further bee urged to continue the like againe, as hath happened in the discoverie of the Moscovian trade. It may suffice to consider, that this is not an action, whiche concerneth onely the Marchauntes perticulerly, but a great deale more the generall sorte of people throughout all Englande: And that when suche relation shalbe returned, as that it maie bee founde a matter worthie the folowyng, the whole generalitie will not refuse to contribute towardes the furtherance thereof, rather then it should sincke, for wante of any reasonable supplie. But as it is a very little tyme, since I have been throughlie resolved, to trie my fortune in the matter, so is it more then tyme, the preparation were in hande already, and therefore no fit tyme now, to make any nomber of ignoraunt men to understande with reason, the circumstance that belongeth to a matter of so greate consideration and importance.

To those who have any forwarde myndes in wel doyng, to the generalitie of mankinde, I say this muche more, that Christian charitie doeth as greatly perswade the furtherance of this action, as any other that may bee laied before us, in as muche as thereby, wee shall not onely dooe a moste excellent worke, in respect of reducyng the savage people, to Christianitie and civilitie, but also in respect of our poore sorte of people, whiche are verie many amongst us, livyng altogethere unprofitable, and often tymes to the great disquiet of the better sorte. For who knoweth not, how by the long peace, happie health, and blessed plentifulnesse, wherewith GOD hath endewed this Realme, that the people is so mightely encreased, as a great nomber beyng brought up, duryng their youth in their parentes houses, without any instruction how to gett their livinges, after their parents decease, are driven to some necessitie, whereby verie often, for want of better education they fall into sondrie disorders, and so the good sorte of people, as I saied before, are by them ordinarily troubled, and themselves ledd on, to one shamefull ende or other, wheras if there might bee founde some suche kinde of imploymente, as this would bee no doubt but a greater part of them would be with held, from fallyng into suche vile deedes: and insteade thereof, prove greatly serviceable in those affaires, where they might be so imploied. This I speake of myne owne experience, havyng seen

3. Sidenote: "Sir Fraunces Drake his passedge only through the Iles of Molucca, was cause of a preparation thither of seventeene thousande poundes, whereof there was not above five or six thousand in Marchaundize, the rest in other charges of Shippyng and expensive provision."

divers come over to the warres of the lawe Countries, duryng my residence in the same, who here
had been verie evill and idle livers, and by some
little continuance with us, have growne to bee
verie industrious in their facultie, whiche I can
assure you, was a more painfull maner of living,
then in this action is like to fall out, and withall to a
purpose of farre lesse valew, in respect of their
perticuler recompence, then with an assured
kinde of good hope is loked for in this.

Thus you see in every poincte, that may be
wished for, in a good action and voyage, there is
matter and reason enough to satisfie the well
disposed. But now to growe somwhat nerer the
quicke, and to showe you some greater apparaunce, then hath been yet spoken of touching
the trade whiche is the onely subject wherwith I
doe meane to entermeddle at this tyme, because
my addresse hereby is cheifly to men of such like
faculty: you may understande by that foloweth,
the circomstance of a little discourse, whiche
doeth concerne these matters very directly.

In the yere 1534. James Carthier of Deepe,
made his first discoverie of those partes of
America, whiche lye to the Westwardes, and as it
were on the backside of newfounde land. In
whiche voyage his principall intention was to
seeke out the passage, whiche he presumed might
have been founde out, into the East Indian sea,
otherwise called the passage to Cathayo, but this
yere he went no higher, then the Islandes of the
assumption in the greate Bay of S. Laurence, and
so returned backe into Fraunce.

The next yere followyng he went with greater
provision into the grand Bay againe, where he
keeping the Northerly shore, ranne up the greate
River that comes doune from Canada and other
places, untill at laste with his small Pinaces, having lefte his greate Shippyng by the way, he
arived at Hochelaga Toune, beeyng five hundred
leagues within the entrance of the grande Bay. In
whiche travaill he had spent so muche of the yere,
that it was now the moneth of October, and therefore thought it convenient, for the better enfor-
myng hymself at large in this discoverie, to
Winter it out in those partes, which he did at a
place called by himself holy Crosse. This Winter
fell out to bee a verie long and hard Winter, as
many tymes the like happeneth with us in these
partes, and the savage people who for the moste
parte, make but a slender kinde of provision, even

as it were from hand to mouth fell into some
scarcitie of victualles; yet did they not refuse to
serve the Frenchmen, with any thyng they had all
the Winter long, albeit at somewhat higher prices
towardes the end, when the neede was moste, as
with our selves the like happeneth at suche
tymes. But when the Frenche had had their
wantes served all the yere, and that as yet they
sawe not, any apparance of their entended matter, whiche was the discoverie of the passage, and
yet imaginyng by the signes wherwith the
willyng people, endevoured to declare their
knowledge in that poinct, that some good matter
might bee had from them, if they might have been
well understoode, they resolved with themselves,
to take some of the sufficientest men of that
Countrey home into Fraunce, and there to keepe
them so long, as that havyng once achieved the
Frenche tongue, thei might declare more substancially their mynd, and knowledge in the saied
passage, concludyng this to be the meane of least
charge, of least travaile, and of least hazarde.
And when they came to bethinke themselves,
who might bee meetest for it, they determined to
take the King, as the person who might bee best
enformed of suche partes, as were somewhat
remote from his owne Countrey, as also that for
the respect of hym, the people would be alwaies
readie, and content to doe them any further service, when if should happen them to retourne
thether againe about the discoverie. Thus the
poore Kyng of the Countrey, with two or three
others of his chief companions commyng aboard
the Frenche Shippes, being required thether to a
bancket, was traiterously caried away into
Fraunce, where he lived fower yeares, and then
dyed a Christian there, as Thevet the French
Kynges Cosmographer doeth make mention. This
outrage and injurious dealyng, did put the whole
countrey people into suche dislike with the
Frenche, as never since they would admit any
conversation, or familiaritie with them, untill of
late yeres, the olde matter beginnyng to growe
out of mynd, and beyng the rather drawen on by
giftes of many triflyng thynges, whiche were of
greate value with them, they are (as I said) within
these two or three yeares[4] content againe to
admitte a traffique, whiche two yeares since, was
begonne with a small Barke of thirtie tunnes,

4. Sidenote: "The yere 1581."

whose retourne was founde so profitable, as the next yere followyng, beyng the last yeare, by those Marchauntes, who meant to have kept the trade secrete unto them selves, from any others of their owne Countrey men, there was hired a Shippe of fower score tunnes out of the Ile of Jersey, but not any one Mariner of that place, saving a Shipboye. This Shippe made her retourne in suche sorte, as that this yeare they have multiplied three Shippes to bee one of nine score tunnes, an other of an hundred tunnes, and a third of fower score tunnes: whiche reporte is given by very substanciall and honest men of Plymouth, who sawe the saied Shippes in readinesse to departe on their Voyage, and were aboarde of some of them. Here is at this instant in the towne a man of Gernesey, Lewis de Vicke: who reporteth to have credibly heard, that by this last yeares Voyage the Frenchmen got foreteene or fifteene hundred for every one hundred. But how soever it bee, it carieth good likelihoode, of some notable profite, in asmuche as they doe so greatly, and thus suddenly encrease the burthen and number of their Shippes this present yeare. Now, if in so little as two yeares tymes this voyage of the Northerne partes bee growne to such good passe as hath been declared unto you: it is worthe the thinkyng on to consider what may bee hoped for, from the Sotherne parte: whiche in all reason may promise a greate deale more. And so as one who was never touchd with any indirect meanyng, I presume to wishe and perswade you to some better takyng of this matter to harte, as a thing which I doe verely thinke wil turne to your greater and more assured commoditie, then you receive by any other Voyage, as yet frequented of so shorte and safe a course as this hath: dealyng herein no otherwise with you for your several smal sommes, then I doe with my self, bothe for more of myne owne, then is required of any one of you: besides the hazard and travell of my person, and the total imployment of my poore credite, whiche (I thanke God) hath hetherto passed clere and unspotted in matters of greater importaunce and difficultie, then is like to fall out in this betweene you and mee.

Articles set doune by the Comitties[5] appointed in

5. Sidenote: "The Comitties. Maister Alderman Hart. Maister Alderman Spencer. M. Hoddesden. Mai. Willyam Burrowgh. Mai. Slany. M. Towerson. Ma. Stapers. Maister Jhon Castelyn. Mai. Leake."

the behalfe of the Companie of Moscovian Marchaunts, to conferre with Maister Carleill, upon his entended discoveries and attempt into the hethermost parties of America.

First, the Committies are well perswaded that the Countrey whereunto this action pretendeth is very fruitfull, Inhabited with savedge people of a middle & tractable disposition. And that of all other places whiche are unfrequented at this day, it is the onely most fittest and most commodious for us to entermeddle withall.

The convenientest maner of attemptyng this enterprise, is thought to be thus: That there should be one hundred men conueied thether to remaine there one whole yeare: who with freendly entreatie of the people, may enter into better knowledge of the particuler estate of the Countrey, and thereby gather what Commoditie may be hereafter or presently looked for.

The charge to transporte these hundred men, to victuall them, and to furnishe them of Munition and other needefull thynges, will not bee lesse then fower thousande poundes: whereof hath beene very readily offered by the Citie of Bristoll one thousande poundes, the residewe beeyng three thousande poundes, remaineth to bee furnished by this Citie of London: or any others who will adventure their money in this first preparation.

The Comitties thinke it convenient that a Priviledge should be procured by Maister Carleill from her Maiestie, by vertue whereof these Conditions and Articles followyng, maie be effectually provided for.

First, that they who shall disburce their money for the first preparation, shall bee named Adventurers, and shall have the one halfe of all suche Landes, Territories, Townes, Mynes of golde and silver, and other Mettalles whatsoever that shal be found, gotten, obtained, and conquered by this discoverie: yeeldyng to her Maiestie one fift parte of all their part golde and silver, as shall happen to be had out of any Mynes that so shall be founde.

That those parties which doe employ themselves personally in the present discoverie, shall be named Enterprisers, and shall have the other halfe of all the Landes, Territories, Townes, Mynes of golde and silver, and other Mettalles, yeeldyng to her Majestie the fift part of the golde and silver, as the Adventurers doe: The same to bee distributed by the Generall, with the consent of the greatest part of twelve discreete persons to bee chosen out of the whole number of Enterprisers.

Also, that all trade of Marchaundize whiche shall be used to and from those partes, whiche by this discoverie shall bee founde out, shall appertaine onely to the Adventurers whiche first shall disburce their money for this discoverie, with prohibition to all other her Majesties Subjectes and other Marchauntes to deale in the saied partes, without the consent of the first Adventurers, upon losse of Shippe and goodes, and punishment of their persons, that so shall adventure in trade of Marchaundize: or otherwise by imprisonment at the Companies pleasure.

That no person shall hereafter adventure in this discoverie, as Adventurers for the profites mentioned in the first Article, but suche onely as doe disburce their money in this first preparation: and they shall not adventure hereafter any greater somme then ratablie accordyng to their proportion of this their first adventure.

Also, the profite whiche by this discoverie shall be attained unto, either by lande whiche may be conquered, or otherwise gotten: as also suche profite whiche by this discoverie shal be obtained by Mynes, or otherwise gotten, that eache one shall have his parte rate and rate like: according to the proportion of their first adventure, and not otherwise.

The Adventurers in this first preparation, shall at their owne free will and libertie, choose whether they will supplie hereafter any further charge or not: if there doe fall out any suche occasion to require the same. And yet withall shall for ever holde to them the freedome of the trade whiche shall growe in any of these partes. Notwithstandyng their saied refusall to beare any further charge.

That in the Patent whiche is to be obtained, be graunted that all her Majesties subjectes, may transporte themselves thether that shall be contented to goe. And that the patented or his assignes may shippe thether from tyme to tyme, so many and suche persons, men, women and children, as they shall thinke meete. And the same persons to inhabite or remaine there at their pleasure, any law to the contrarie notwithstandyng, with expresse prohibition as is mentioned in the third Article, against all others whiche [shall goe thether] without the license of the patented or his assignes [first obtained].

That it shall not be lawfull for any of her Majesties subjectes, or any other to enhabite or traffique within twoo hundred Leagues any way of the place, where the Generall shal have settled his cheefest beyng or residence.

358. 1583. Sir George Peckham's *True reporte of the late discoveries . . . by . . . Sir Humphrey Gilbert.*

Sir George Peckham and his son, George, were leading members in the group of Catholic gentlemen who purchased rights to land in America in and around Verrazzano's "Refugio" (Narragansett Bay) from Sir Humphrey Gilbert in 1582 (394–397,400). That year they hoped to send out a reconnaissance, but do not appear to have been able to get a ship to sea. By 1583 they had lost many of their Catholic supporters so the Peckhams, in association with Sir Philip Sidney, attempted to put their venture on a wider nonsectarian basis. They apparently held back their main propaganda effort until they learned the result of Sir Humphrey Gilbert's expedition of 1583 (Vol. IV, nos. 534–538), but it is probable that much of the pamphlet published late in 1583 was written much earlier. On September 22 the Golden Hind *alone returned and her captain, Edward Hayes, reported that contact with Gilbert was lost on the way back and he had perhaps drowned while his flag ship had been wrecked in American waters (536). The Peckhams, in spite of this bad news, went ahead and wrote up their interview with Hayes on Gilbert's achievements in Newfoundland. The George Peckham who dated the dedication to Sir Francis Walsingham on November 12, 1583, may well have been the son rather than the father. There were ten dedicatory poems from verse writers as unlikely as Sir Francis Drake and Anthony Parkhurst (three different states of these verses are known, suggesting that the tract was assembled in small batches as needed). It had a long and complex title:* A true reporte of the late discoveries and possession, taken in the right of the Crown of Englande, of the Newfound Landes: by that valiant and worthye gentleman, Sir Humphrey Gilbert knight. Wherein is also breafly sett downe her highnesse lawfull tytle thereunto, and the great and manifolde commodities, that is likely to grow thereby, to the whole realm in generall, and to the adventurers in particular. Together with the easiness and shortness of the voyage *(London, 1583). It began by skillfully combining an account of Gilbert's voyage with the justification of planting in America on national, economic, and humanitarian grounds–the last since it would be beneficial to "the Savages." Successive chapters showed close contacts with the two Hakluyts and their circle, but also, most probably to focus Catholic interest on his projects, the author attempts to use Spain's experience in America to justify English emulation of her achievements. He justified, on Biblical, classical, and renaissance authority, the legitimacy of conquest as a right and duty of Christians. He asserted, with such precedents as he had, the priority of English and Welsh claims to discovery. His main stress is on economic advantage. His appeal was primarily to noblemen and gentlemen who would find profitable and pleasing the wide acres they would acquire with little effort. He included great lists of products—vegetable, animal, and mineral—to be gathered, extracted, or grown, and gave promise of wealth such as had indeed been acquired by the Spaniards in other parts of America. At the end he published the terms on which subscriptions would be received and showed that he aimed at a fully diversified English population, although one dominated by great landholders.*

To the Right Honourable Sir Fraunces Walsingham Knight, principall Secretarie to the Queene, her most excellent Majestie.

How much more happie might I account my selfe, (right honourable Sir) if I had so well applied my time in this Universitie, as through my more dilligent studye, I were able to handle the matter, (which I have in this treatise taken uppon me) as the worthynes thereof dooth meryte.

Truely Sir I was for a time, drawen into a doubtfull ballaunce, whether I should proceede therein, as my affection intised me, or leave it off, as good discretion advised mee. Eftsoones have I righte hartely wished that some of those rype, and perfect witts, adorned with like judgement, (wherewith God hath plentifully blessed this our age) woulde have imploied their pennes, learnedly to have sette foorth thys cause: But seeing that in wishing, I doo fynde nothing, but to wish, and that the case so standeth, as eyther the thyng, right woorthye bothe knowledge, and practise, shall styll lie in a slumber, or rather rest buryed in the grave of oblivion, unlesse I doo make publique my weaknesse and insufficiencye, and therby subject my selfe to the diversitye of mens judgements, I have made choyse, rather to indure the disgrace of the one, then that my Countrey shoulde sustaine the inconvenience of the other, trusting that your honour (who hath hetherto beene a principall Patron of this Action) will upon my humble sute vouchsafe your favourable protection heerof. For wee doo reade (right honourable) that Archimedes in respecte of his gravitie and wisedome helde that reputation amongst the Syracusans, that whatsoever he allowed, was accounted for good: which historye, if I shoulde apply unto your honour perticularlie, as both aptlie and truely I could, I might (in the opinion of some men) incurre the suspition of flattery, and receive from your Honour but the like answer, which King Theseus made unto blind Oedipus.

I doo not (quoth hee) O Oedipus, honour my selfe with other mens words, but with mine owne works. In silence therefore will I passe your ready and vertuous disposition, bothe honourably to favour, and favourably to further all such attemptes as seeme pleasing to God and profitable to your Countrey, both which (by the testimony of good writers, the opinion of wise men, and experience of great travailors, these Westerne Discoveries doo certainly promise. In regarde whereof, I doo the rather presume to preferre this Pampflet to bee Patronized by so woorthy a personne, whereby my escapes may bee the more easilye excused, my willing paynes the better accepted, and the voyage more effectually supplyed.

Thus beeing lothe any longer to detayne your honour from your weightye affayres, I humblye take leave, beseeching God manie yeeres to

lengthen your life, with much encrease of honour.
From my lodging in Oxforde, the twelvth of
November.

Your Honours poore Scholler, in all service to use
    G. P.

Sir William Pelham Knight, in commendation of the discourse following.

Like as the Fishes, breeding in the deepe,
    Through all the Ocean are allowed to raung:
    Nor forst in any certaine boundes to keepe,
But as their motions carry them to chaung.
    To men like libertie, dooth reason give:
    In choise of soile, through all the world to live.

To valiaunt mindes each land is a native soile,
    and vertue findes no dwelling place amis.
Regard of honour measures not the toyle,
    To seeke a seat wherein contentment is.
        That seat, that soile, that dwelling place of
        rest:
        In this discourse, most livelie is exprest.

Our forren neighbours bordring hard at hand,
    Have found it true, to many a thousands gaine:
And are inricht by this abounding land,
    While pent at home, like sluggardes we
    remaine.
        But though they have, to satisfie their will:
        Inough is left, our cofers yet to fill.

Then England thrust among them for a share,
    Since title just, and right is wholie thine:
And as I trust the sequell shall declare,
    Our lucke no worse, then theirs before hath
    beene.
        For where the attempt, on vertue dooth
        depend:
        No doubt but God, will blesse it in the ende.
                William Pelham.

Sir Fraunces Drake Knight in commendation of this Treatise.

Who seekes, by worthie deedes, to gaine
    renowme for hire:
Whose hart, whose hand, whose purse is prest: to
    purchase his desire
If anie such there bee, that thristeth after Fame:
Lo, heere a meane, to winne himselfe an
    everlasting name.
Who seekes, by gaine and wealth, t'advaunce his
    house and blood:

Whose care is great, whose toile no lesse, whose
    hope, is all for good
If anie one there bee, that covettes such a trade:
Lo, heere the plot for common wea[l]th, and
    private gaine is made.
Hee, that for vertues sake, will venture farre and
    neere:
Whose zeale is strong, whose practize trueth,
    whose faith is void of feere,
If any such there bee, inflamed with holie care.
Heere may hee finde, a readie meane, his purpose
    to declare:
So that, for each degree, this Treatise dooth
    unfolde:
The path to Fame, the proofe of zeale, and way to
    purchase golde.
                Fraunces Drake.

M. John Hawkins, his opinion of this intended Voyage.

If zeale to God, or countries care, with private
    gaines accesse,
Might serve for spurs unto th'attempt this
    pamflet doth expresse.
One coast, one course, one toile might serve, at ful
    to make declard
A zeale to God, with countries good, and private
    gaines regarde.
And for the first this enterprise the name of God
    shall founde,
Among a nation in whose eares the same did
    never sounde.
Next as an endles running streame, her Channels
    doth discharge:
That swell above theyr boundes, into an Ocean
    wide and large.
So England that is pestered nowe, and choakt
    through want of ground
Shall finde a soile where roome inough, and
    perfect doth abounde.
The Romains when the number of their people
    grewe so great,
As neither warres could waste, nor Rome suffice
    them for a seate.
They led them forth by swarming troupes, to
    forraine lands amaine
And founded divers Colonies, unto the Romaine
    raigne.
Th'athenians us'de the like devise, the Argives
    thus have doone,

And fierce Achilles Myrmidons when Troy was
    over runne.
But Rome nor Athens nor the rest, were never
    pestered so,
As England where no roome remaines, her
    dwellers to bestow,
But shuffled in such pinching bondes, that very
    breath dooth lacke:
And for the want of place they craule one ore
    anothers backe.
How noblie then shall they provide that for
    redresse heerein,
With ready hand and open purse this action dooth
    beginne.
Whence glory to the name of God, and countries
    good shall spring,
And unto all that further it, a private gaine shall
    bring.
Then noble youthes couragiously this enterprise
    discharge,
And age that cannot mannage Armes, let them
    support the charge.
The yssue of your good intent, undoubted will
    appeare,
Both gratious in the sight of God, and full of
    honour heere.

               John Hawkins.

    Maister Captaine Bingham, his commenda-
        tion uppon this Treatise.

If honour and reward, may moove the minde,
    By noble actions, highlie to aspire:
The forward man in this discourse shall finde,
    Reward and honour, propos'd for hire.
      Which meede, no right renowmed hart
      mislikes:
      Though gaind by passing, through ten
      thousand pikes
The white whereat wee levell, well is knowen,
    The plot and place, with finger poynted out:
The name thereof through all the world is blone,
    To put the hard beleevers out of doubt.
      Our forren neighbours, like it to their gaine:
      And sucke the sweete, while sleeping we
      remaine.
The jorney is but easie to bee gonne,
    The frozen Pole disjoyned farre dooth lye:
We shape our course, farre from the burning
    Zonne,

The soile is subject to a milder skye.
    And by proofe, of many recordes tride:
    The Paradise, of all the world beside:
Then launch ye noble youthes into the maine,
    No lurking perrils lye amidde the way:
Your travell shall retourne you treble gaine,
    and make your names renoumed another day.
      For valiaunt mindes, through twentie Seas
      will roome:
      And fish for lucke, while sluggardes lye at
      home.

               Richard Bingham.

    Maister Captaine Frobisher, in commenda-
        tion of the voyage.

A pleasaunt ayre, a sweete and firtell soile,
    A certaine gaine, a never dying praise:
An easie passage, voide of lothsome toile,
    Found out by some, and knowen to mee the waies.
      All this is there, then who will refraine to trie:
      That loves to live abroade, or dreades to die.

               Martin Frobisher.

    Maister Captaine Chester, his commenda-
        tion of this Treatise.

Marke well this booke when you to reade beginne,
And finde you shall great secretes hid therein.
For with your selves you may imagine thus,
That God hath left this honour unto us.
The journey knowne, the passage quicklie runne,
The land full rich, the people easilie wunne.
Whose gaines shalbe the knowledge of our faith,
And ours such ritches as the country hath.
Pinche not for pence to set this action out,
Poundes will returne, thereof be not in doubt.
Your countrey shall be bounde due thankes to
    give,
For that the poore heereby you may relieve.
Unto your Prince good service you shall doo,
And unto God, a worke right gratefull to.

               John Chester.

    Mathew Roydon maister of Arte to his fel-
        lowe Student.

To prayse thy booke because I am thy freende,
Though it be common and thy due indeede:
Perhaps it may some daintie eare offende,
    Reproofe repines that vertue hath her meede.
    Yet neverthelesse how ever thinges succeede,

Sith to no other ende thy booke was made:
All that I wish, is that thou mayest perswade.

Mathew Roydon.

Maister Anthony Parkhurst in commenda-
tion of this Treatise.

Beholde a worke that dooth reveale,
  The ready way to welth and fame.
  Commodious to the common weale.
And just without impeache of blame.
  Which followed as the course doth lie,
  May make all Englande thrive thereby.

It is not fond surmisde report,
Nor phantasie vaine heades to feede:
The mention of the trueth, coms short,
And lesser then the thing indeede.
  Of recorde many thousandes are,
  That can all this and more declare.

Howe happy were our England then,
(Sith neither men nor shipping want)
Some good and well disposed men,
An other England there would plant:
  And so employ a number there,
  Whose persons may be spared heere.

Th'atempt coulde never faile his fame,
Nor proofe returne without effect:
For commonlie all actions frame,
Where Christian cause hath cheefe respect.
  And he that in the heavens above doth raigne,
  (No doubt) will blesse the sequell of theyr
    payne.

Anthonie Parkhurst.

Arthur Hawkins in commendation of this
Treatise.

My freendes, if at Th'exchaunge a man shoulde
    goe and tell,
that such, and such commodities he had to sell.
Whereof we stood in neede and scarcelie to be
    founde,
Whereby a quicke returne with profit woulde
    redounde.
I doubt not ere I past, but you would crave the
    sight,
Of these commended wares, and buy them if you
    might.
Y'are proferd at this time, fayre Grapes to make
    your wine,
The pleasaunt fruites of Spaine, the Figs and
    Orenge fine.

The speckled Russian Furres, that Esterlings us
    sendes,
The Rosen, Pitch, and Deales that Dansk and
    Denmarke lendes.
The Mettall heere is showne that with a quenchles
    fire,
Inflames our thirsting hartes unstaunched in
    desire.
A bargaine may you have, t'is put into your
    handes,
Of all commodities you have from other landes.
And at so easie price you can not choose but gaine:
A trifle is the most, together with your paine,
But what is that some sayes? our Englishmen
    gives eare,
Onelie to gaine, God shielde it shoulde be true I
    heare.
If we religious be, lets rigge our shippes with
    speede,
And carry Christ to these poore souls, that stande
    in neede,
Why pause yee thereupon? the fraight will quite
    the charge,
For what is doone for God, dooth finde rewarde
    full large.

A. H.

John Achelley Cyttyzen and Marchantailour
of London, for conclusion.

If truth and praise have power, to make this
    matter gratious:
What neede we then extoll the thing, hath beene
    commended thus.
And by the better sorte that wright, of truth and
    knowledge so:
As nothing of this worke, they promised further
    then they know.
Beleeve them for they be our freendes, and with
    our Counties weale:
Let us imbrase that God and truth, so loovinglie
    reveale.
Whereof the merrit is no lesse, then is the bruted
    Fame:
Aske straungers and that noble minde, that did
    attempt the same:
To whom we owe the titles, that to Vertues
    Nimpes are due:
So good a Knight whom English men, in vertue
    should persue.
No doubt but God will blesse th'atempt, succeed
    him roundly then:

And in this Voyage follow fast, you that bee
    English men.
With such supplie from time to time, as what is
    well begonne:
Bee not for want of men and aide, through
    slackfulnes undoone.
So shall you harbour in your hartes, the seedes of
    magnanimitie:
A vertue where with all, the Romaines did
    enlarge their Empery.
Be you prepared for every foe, and be couragious
    then:
For that you slippe through negligence, will fall to
    other men.
Envie hath eyes to see afarre, your new attempt
    will whet:
A number more to seeke therefore, if you your
    selves forget.
Send foorth with speede, get footing there and
    make provision:
Tis ill for us to linger thus, and talke thereof so
    longe.

              John Achelley.

The Table of the Chapters, containing the
principall matters in this Booke.

1. The first Chapiter, wherein the Argument of
the Booke is contayned.

2. The seconde Chapiter, sheweth that it is
lawfull and necessary, to trade and traficke with
the Savages. And to plant in theyr Countreys.
And devideth planting into two sortes.

3. The third Chapiter, dooth shewe the lawfull
Title, which the Queenes most excellent Majestie
hath unto those Countreys, which through the
ayde of almighty God are to be inhabited.

4. The fourth Chapiter sheweth, how that the
trade, traficke and planting in those Countreys, is
likely to proove very profitable to the whole
Realme in generall.

5. The fift Chapiter, sheweth that the trading
and planting in those Countreys, is likely to proove
to the perticuler profit of all the Adventurers.

6. The sixt Chapiter, sheweth that the traficke
and planting in those Countryes, shall bee unto
the Savages themselves very beneficiall and gainfull.

7. The seaventh Chapiter, sheweth that the
planting there is not a matter of such charge or
diffyculty, as many woulde make it seeme to bee.

8. The Contents of Articles of Assuraunce,
between the Principal assignes of Sir Humfrey
Gilbert Knight, and the foure sortes of Adventur-
ers, with them in the voyage for the Westerne
Discoveries.
The ende of the Table.

The first Chapter, wherein the Argument
of the Booke is Contayned.

It was my fortune (good Reader) not many
dayes past, to meete with a right honest and
discrete Gentleman, who accompanied that valiant and worthy Knight Sir Humfry Gilbert, in
this last journey for the Westerne discoveries.[1]
And is owner and Captaine of the onelie Vessell
which is as yet returned from thence:

By him I did understande, that Sir Humfrey
departed the coaste of Englande the eleventh of
June last past, with five sayle of Shippes from
Caushenbay neere Plimmouth, wherof one of the
best forsooke his companie, the thirteenth day of
the same moneth, and returned into England.

The other foure (through the assistaunce of
almightye God) did arrive at Saint Johns Haven,
in Newfounde Lande, the thyrd of August last.[2]
Upon whose arrivall all the Maisters and cheefe
Mariners of the English Flete, which were in the
sayd Haven before, endevouring to fraughte
themselves with Fysh, repayred unto Sir Humfrey, whom he made acquainted with the effect of
his commission: which being doone, he promised
to intreate them and their goods well and honourably as dyd become her majesties Lieftennaunt.
They did all welcome him in the best sorte that
they coulde, and shewed him and his, all such
courtesies as that place coulde affoorde or yeelde.

Then he went to viewe the Countrey, being wel
accompanied with most of his Captaines and Soldiers. They found the same very temperate, but
somewhat warmer then Englande at that season
of the yeere, replenished with Beastes[3] and great
store of Fowle of divers kindes: And Fish of
sundry sortes, both in the salte water and in the
fresh, in so great plentie as might suffice to
victuall an Armie, and they are verie easilie
taken. What sundrie other commodities for this

1. Sidenote: "Maister Edward Hay"
2. Sidenote: "Sir Humfrey Gilbert did arrive at S. Johns haven in
Newfounde Land, the 3. of August. Anno. Do. 1583."
3. Sidenote: "Among these there was founde the tract of a beast of 7.
inches and a halfe over."

Realme, right necessarie the same dooth yeelde, you shall understande in this treatise heereafter, in place more convenient.

On munday being the fift of August, the Generall caused his Tent to be set upon the side of an hill, in the viewe of all the Flete of Englishmen and Straungers, which were in number betweene thirty and fortie sayle, then being accompanied with all his Captaines, Maisters, Gentlemen and other Soldiers, he caused all the Maisters, and principall Officers of the Shippes, as well Englishmen as Spaniardes, Portingals, and of other nations to repayre unto his Tent: And then and there, in the presence of them all, he did cause hys commission, under the great seale of England to bee openlie and solempnlie reade unto them, whereby were graunted unto him his heyres, and assignes, by the Queenes most excellent Majestie, manie great and large royalties, liberties, and priviledges. The effect whereof being signified unto the Straungers by an Interpretor, he tooke possession of the sayd land in the right of the Crowne of England by digging of a Turfe and receiving the same with an Hasell wande, delivered unto him, after the manner of the lawe and custome of England.[4]

Then he signified unto the company both strangers and others that from thence forth, they were to live in that Land, as the Territories appertayning to the Crowne of England, and to be governed by such Lawes as by good advise shoulde bee set downe, which in all poyntes (so neere as might be) shold be agreeable to the Lawes of England: And for to put the same[5] in execution, presentlie he ordeined and established three Lawes.

Fyrst, that Religion publiquely exercised, should be such and none, other then is used in the Church of England.

The seconde, that if any person should bee lawfully convicted of any practise against her Majestie, her crowne and dignity, to be adjudged as traytors according to the Lawes of Englande.

The thyrd, if any shoulde speake dishonourably of her Majestie, the partie so offending, to loose his eares, hys Shippe and goods, to be confiscate to the use of the Generall.

All men did verie willingly submit themselves to these Lawes. Then he caused the Queenes majesties Armes, to be engraved, sett uppe, and erected, with great solempnity. After this, divers English men, made sute unto Sir Humfrey to have of him by inheritaunce, theyr accustomed Stages, standinges and drying places, in sundry partes of that Land for theyr Fish, as a thing that they doo make great accompte off, which he graunted unto them, in fee farme. And by thys meanes, he hath possession mayntained for him, in many partes of that Country. To be briefe, he dyd lette, sette, give and dispose of many thinges, as absolute governour there, by vertue of her majesties letters pattents.[6]

And after theyr Shippes were repayred, whereof one, hee was driven to leave behinde, bothe for want of men sufficient to furnish her, as also to carrie home such sicke persons as were not able to proceede any further: He departed from thence the 20 of August, with the other three, namelie, the Delight, wherein was appointed Captaine in Maister William Winters place, (that thence returned immediatlie for Englande) Maister Morries Browne: the Golden Hynde, in which was Captaine and owner, Maister Edwarde Hay: and the little Frigat where the Generall himselfe did goe, seeming to him most fitt to discover and approche the Shoare.

The 21. day they came to Cape Rase, towarde the South partes whereof, lying a while becalmed, they tooke Codd in largenes and quantitie, exceeding the other parts of Newfound Lande, where any of them had beene. And from thence, trending the Coast West, towarde the Bay of Placencia. The Generall sent certain men a Shoare, to view the countrey, which to them as they sayled along, seemed pleasaunt. Whereof his men at theyr returne gave great commendation, likeing so well of the place, as they would willinglie have stayed and wintred there. But having the winde fayre and good, they proceeded on theyr course towards the fyrme of Ameryca, which by reason of continuall Fogges, at that time of the yeere especially: they coulde never see, till Cox Maister of the Golden Hinde did discerne Lande, and presently lost sight thereof againe, at

4. Sidenote: "Sir Humfrey tooke possession of the New found lande in the right of the crowne of Englande."
5. Sidenote: "Three lawes established there by Sir Humfrey."

6. Sidenote: "Sundry persons, became Tennants to Sir Humfrey, and doo maintaine possession for him in divers places there."

what time they were all upon a breache in a great and outragious storme, having under 3. fadome water. But God delivered the Frigat and the Golden Hinde, from this great daunger. And the Delight in the presence of them all was lost, to theyr unspeakable greefe, with all theyr cheefe victuall, munition, and other necessary provisions, and other thinges of value not fitt heere to be named. Whereuppon, by reason also that Winter was come upon them, and fowle wether increased with Fogges and Mysts that so covered the Land, as without daunger of perishing they coulde not approche it: Sir Humfrey Gilbert and Maister Hays, were compelled much against theyr wills to retyre homewardes. And beeing 300. Leagues on theyr way, were afterwarde by tempestious weather, seperated the one from the other, the 9. of September last, since which time, Maister Hay with his Barke, is safelie arrived, but of Sir Humfrey as yet, we heare no certaine newes.

Uppon this reporte (together with my former intent, to write some briefe discourse in the commendation of this so noble and woorthy an enterprise) I did call to my remembraunce, the Historie of Themystocles the Grecian,[7] (who beeing a right noble and valiant Captaine) signified unto hys Countrimen, the cittizens of Athens, that hee had invented a devise for theyr common wealth very profitable, but it was of such importaunce and secrecie, that it ought not to be revealed, before private conference had with some perticuler prudent person of their choise.

The Athenians knowing Aristides the Philosopher, to be a man indued with singuler wisedome and vertue, made choyse of him to have conference with Themystocles, and thereuppon to yeelde his opinion to the Cittizens concerning the sayd device: which was, that they might set on fire the Navie of theyr enemies, with great facilitie as hee had layde the plotte: Aristides made relation to the Cittizens, that the stratageme (devised by Themystocles) was a profitable practise for the common wealth but it was dishonest. The Athenians (without further demaunde what the same was) dyd by common consent rejecte and condemne it, preferring honest and upright dealing before profite.

By occasion of this historie, I drewe my selfe into a more deeper consideration, of thys late undertaken voyage, whether it were as well pleasing to almightie God, as profitable to men? as lawfull as it seemed honourable. As well gratefull to the Savages, as gainfull to the Christians. And upon mature deliberation, I founde the action to bee honest and profitable, and therefore allowable by the opinion of Aristides if he were nowe alive, which beeing by me heerein sufficiently prooved, (as by Gods grace I purpose to doo) I doubt not but that all good mindes, wyll endevour themselves to be assistauntes to this so commendable an enterprise, by the valiant and woorthy Gentlemen our Countrimen alreadie attempted and undertaken.

Nowe whereas I doo understande that Sir Humfrey Gilbert, his adherents, associates, and freendes doo meane with a convenient supplie (with as much speede as may bee) to maintaine, pursue and followe, this intended voyage already in part performed,[8] and (by the assistaunce of almightie God) to plant themselves and theyr people in the continent of the hether part of America, betweene the degrees of 30. and 60. of septentrionall latitude. (Within which degrees by computation Astronomicall and Cosmographicall are doubtles to be founde, all things that be necessarie profitable, or delectable for mans life. The climate mylde and temperate, neither too hotte nor too colde, so that under the cope of heaven there is not any where to be founde a more convenient place to plant and inhabite in: which manie notable Gentlemen, bothe of our owne nation and straungers (who have beene traveilers)[9] can testifie: and that those Countries are at this day inhabited with Savages who have no knowledg of God) Is it not therfore (I say) to be lamented, that these poore Pagans, so long living in ignoraunce and Idolatry, and in sorte, thirsting after christianitie, (as may appeare by the relation of such as have travailed in those partes,) that our heartes are so hardned, that fewe or none

8. Sidenote: "Apparation in hand for a newe supply."
9. Sidenote: "Englishmen. Ma. John Hawkins Sir Fraunces Drake Ma. William Winter. Ma. John Chester. Ma. Martin Furbisher. Anthony Parkelhurst. William Batts. John Lowell David Ingram. Strangers French. Sir John Ribaulte. Jacques Cartier. Andrew Thevet. Mounser Gourden. Mounser Popellynere John Verasanus. Italian. Christopher Columnus."

7. Sidenote: "Plutarch."

can be found which wil put to theyr helping hands, and applie themselves to the relieving of the miserable and wretched estate of these sillie soules?

Whose Countrey dooth (as it were with arme advaunced) above the climats both of Spayne and Fraunce, stretche out it selfe towardes England onelie. In manner praying our ayde and helpe, as it is not onelie set foorth in Mercators generall Mappe, but it is also founde to bee true by the discovery of our nation, and other straungers, who have often times travailed upon the same Coastes.

Christopher Columnus of famous memorie the firste instrument to manifest the great glorie and mercy of almightie God in planting the Christian Faith, in those so long unknown regions, having in purpose to acquaint (as he did) that renowmed Prince, the Queenes Majesties Grandfather, King Henry the seventh, with his intended voiage for the Westerne Discoveries, was not onely derided and mocked generally even heere in Englande, but afterward became a laughing stocke to the Spaniardes themselves, who at thys day (of all other people) are moste bounden to laude and prayse God, who first sturred uppe the man to that enterprise.[10]

And while he was attending there to acquaint the King of Castile (that then was) with his intended purpose, by howe many wayes and meanes was hee derided? Some scorned the pildnes of his garments, some tooke occasion to jest at his simple and silly lookes, others asked if this were he, that lowts so lowe,[11] which did take uppon him to bring men into a Country that aboundeth wyth Gold, Pearle, and Precious stones? If hee were any such man (sayd they) he would carrie another manner of countenaunce with him, and looke somewhat loftier. Thus some judged him by his garments and others by his looke and countenaunce, but none entered into the consideration of the inward man.

In the ende, what successe his voyage had, who list to read the Decades. The Historie of the West Indies, the conquest of Hernando Cortese about Mexico, and those of Francisco Pizare in

Peru about Casamalcha and Cusco, may knowe more perticulerly.[12] All which their discoveries travells, and conquests, are extant to be had in the English tongue. This device was then accounted a fantasticall imagination, and a drowsie dreame.

But the sequel thereof, hath since awaked out of dreames thousandes of soules to knowe theyr Creator, being thereof before that time altogether ignoraunt. And hath since made sufficient proofe, neyther to be fantasticke, nor vainely imagined.

Withall, how mightely hath it inlarged the dominions of the Crowne of Spayne, and greatly enritching the subjectes of the same, let all men consider. Besides, it is well knowne, that sithence the time of Columnus his first discoverie, through theyr planting, possessing, and inhabiting those partes, there hath beene transported and brought home into Europe, greater store of Golde, Silver, Pearle, and Pretious stones, then heeretofore hath beene in all ages, since the creation of the worlde.

I doe therefore hartelie wish, that seeing it hath pleased almighty God, of hys infinite mercie at the length, to awake some of our worthy Countrey men, out of that drowsie dreame, wherein we all have so long slumbered.

That wee may nowe not suffer it to quaile for want of maintenance, that by these valiant Gentlemen our Countreymen is so nobly begun and enterprised. For which purpose, I have taken upon me to write this simple shorte treatise, hoping that it shall be able to perswade such as have beene, and yet doo continue detractors and hinderers of this journey, (by reason perhappes that they have not deliberately and advisedly entered into the judgment of the matter) that yet now upon better consideration they will become favorable furtherers of the same. And that such as are already well affected there unto, will continue theyr good dispositions And with all, I most humbly pray all such as are no Nyggardes of their purses, in buying of costly and rich apparell, and liberall Contributors, in setting foorth of games, pastimes, feastings and banquettes, (whereof the charge being past, there is no hope of publique profit or private commoditie) that henceforth

---

10. Sidenote: "God doth not alwaies begin his greatest workes by the greatest persons."

11. Sidenote: "His custome was to bow himselfe very lowe in making of curtesie."

12. Sidenote: "Hernando Cortese. Francisco Pyzare."

they will bestowe and employe theyr liberalitie (heeretofore that way expended) for the furtherance of these so commendable purposed proceedings.[13]

And to this ende have I taken penne in hande, as in conscience thereunto mooved, desiring much rather, that of the great multitude, which this Realme dooth nourish, farre better able to handle this matter then I my selfe am, it woulde have pleased some one of them to have undertaken the same. But seeing they are silent, and that it falleth to my lott to put penne to the paper, I will indevour my selfe, and doo stande in good hope (though my skill and knowledge be simple, yet through the assistaunce of almighty God) to proove that this voyage, late enterprised, for trade, traficke, and planting, in America, is an action tending to the lawfull enlargement of her Majesties dominions, commodious to the whole Realme in generall. Profitable to the adventurers in perticuler, beneficial to the Savages, and a matter to be attained without any great daunger or difficultie.[14]

And lastlye (which moste of all is) A thing likewise tending to the honor and glory of almighty God: And for that the lawfulnes to plant in those Countreyes, in some mens judgements, seemeth very doubtfull, I will beginne with the proofe of the lawfulnesse of trade, traficke, and planting.

The second Chapiter, sheweth that it is lawfull and necessarye to trade and traficke with the Savages. And to plant in their Countries. And devideth planting into two sortes.

And firste for traficke, I say that the Christians may lawfully travaile into those Countries and abide there whom the Savages may not justly impugne and forbidde, in respect of the mutuall society and fellowship betweene man and man prescribed by the Lawe of Nations.

For from the first beginning of the creation of the world and from the renuing of the same after Noes floode, all men have agreed, that no violence shoulde be offered to Ambassadours. That the Sea with his Havens should bee common. That

such as should fortune to be taken in warre, should be servauntes or slaves And that Straungers sholde not be dryven away from the place or Countrey whereunto they doo come.

If it were so then, I demaunde in what age, and by what Lawe is the same forbidden or denied since? For who doubteth but that it is lawfull for Christians to use trade and traficke with Infidels or Savages, carrying thether such commodities as they want, and bringing from thence some parte of theyr plentie.

A thing so commonly and generally practised, bothe in these our dayes, and in times past, beyonde the memory of man, both by Christians and Infidels, that it needeth no further proofe.

And for as much as the use of trade and traficke, (bee it neever so profitable) ought not to bee preferred before the planting of Christian fayth. I will therefore somewhat entreate of planting (whythout which, Christian Religion can take no roote, be the Preachers never so carefull and diligent) which I meane to devide in two sortes.[15]

The first, when Christians by the good likeing and willing assent of the Savages, are admitted by them to quiet possession.

The seconde, when Christians beeing unjustly repulsed, doo seeke to attaine and maintaine the right for which they doo come.

And thoughe in regarde of the establishment of Christian Religion, eyther of bothe maye bee lawfullye and justlye exercised. Whereof manye examples may bee founde, as well in the tyme of Moises and Josua, and other Rulers before the byrth of Christ.[16] As of many vertuous Emperours and Kinges sithence his incarnation: yet doo I wish, that before the second be put in practise, a proofe may bee made of the firste, saving that for theyr safety as well against the Savages as all other forraine enemies, they should first well and stronglie fortefie themselves, which beeing doone, then by all fayre speeches, and every other good meanes of perswasion to seeke or take away all occasions of offence.

As letting them to understand, howe they came not to theyr hurt, but for theyr good, and to no other ende, but to dwell peaceably amongst them,

13. Sidenote: "A reasonable request."
14. Sidenote: "The argument of the Booke."

15. Sidenote: "The principall causes why thys viage is undertaken."
16. Sidenote: "The first kinde of Planting."

and to trade and traficke with them for theyr owne commoditie, without molesting or greeving them any way, which must not be doone by wordes onely but also by deedes.

For albeit, to maintaine right and repell injurie, be a just cause of warre, yet must there heereof be heedefull care had, that whereas the Savages be fearefull by nature, and fonde otherwise, the Christians shoulde doo theyr best endevour to take away such feare as may growe unto them by reason of theyr straunge apparrell, Armour, and weapon, or such like, by quiet peaceable conversation, and letting them live in securitie and keeping a measure of blameles defence, with as little discommoditie to the Savages as may bee, for this kinde of warre woulde be onely defensive and not offensive.

And questionles there is great hope and likelyhoode that by this kinde of meanes, we should bring to passe all effectes to our desired purposes: Considering that all straunge creatures, by constitution of nature, are rendred more tractable and easilier wunne for al assayes, by courtesie and myldnes, then by crueltie and roughnes: and therefore beeing a principle taught us by naturall reason, it is first to be put in ure.

For albeit as yet the Christians are not so throughlye furnished with the perfectnes of theyr language, either to expresse theyr mindes to them, or againe to conceive the Savages intent. Yet for the present opportunitie, such pollicie may be used by freendly signes, and courteous tokens towards them, as the Savages may easily perceive, (were theyr sences never so grosse) as an assured freendship to be offered them and that they are encountered with such a nation as bring them benefite, commoditie, peace, tranquillity and safetie. To further this, and to accomplish it in deedes, there must be presented unto them gratis, some kindes of our prittie merchaundizes and trifles: As looking Glasses, Bells, Beades, Braceletts, Chaines, or Collers of Bewgle, Christall, Amber, Jett, or Glasse etc. For such be the things, though to us of small value, yet accounted by them of high price and estimation: and soonest will induce theyr Barbarous natures to a likeing and a mutuall society with us.

Moreover, it shall be requisite, either by speeche, if it bee possible, either by some other certaine meanes, to signifie unto them. That once league of freendshippe, with all loving conversation, beeing admitted betweene the Christians and them: that then the Christians from thence forth will alwayes bee ready with force of Armes to assiste and defende them in theyr just quarrelles, from all invasions, spoyles and oppressions, offered or to bee offered them by any Tyraunts, Adversaries, or theyr next borderers: and a benefit is so much the more to be esteemed, by how much the person uppon whome it is bestowed standeth in neede thereof.

For it appeareth by the relation of a countreyman of ours, namely David Ingram,[17] (who travelled in those countries xi. monethes and more) That the Savages generally for the most part, are at continuall warres wyth their next adjoyning neighbours, and especially the Canniballs, beeing a cruell kinde of people, whose foode is mans flesh, and have teeth like dogges, and doo pursue them with ravenous myndes to eate theyr flesh, and devoure them.

And it is not to be doubted, but that the Christians may in this case justly and lawfully ayde the Savages against the Canniballs. So that it is very likelie that by this means wee shall not onely mightely stirre and inflame theyr rude myndes gladly to embrace the loving companye of the Christians, proffering unto them bothe commodities succor, and kindnes. But also by theyr francke consents, shall easily enjoy such competent quantity of Lande, as every way shall be correspondent to the Christians expectation, and contentation, considering the great aboundance that they have of Lande, and howe small account they make thereof. Taking no other fruits thereby then such as the ground of itselfe dooth naturally yeelde. And thus much concerning the first sort of planting, which as I assuredly hope, so I most hartelie pray may take effect and place.

But if after these good and fayre meanes used, the Savages nevertheles will not be heerewithall satisfied, but barbarously wyll goe about to practise violence either in repelling the Christians from theyr Portes and safe Landinges or in withstanding them afterwardes to enjoye the rights for which both painfully and lawfully they have adventured themselves thether.[18]

Then in such a case I holde it no breache of

---

17. Sidenote: "This David Ingram was in this last journey with Sir Humfrey and is very desirous to be imployed thether againe."
18. Sidenote: "The second kinde of Planting."

equitye for the Christians to defende themselves, to pursue revenge with force, and to doo whatsoever is necessary for the attayning of theyr safety: For it is allowable by all Lawes in such distresses, to resist violence with violence. And for theyr more securitie to increase their strength by building of fortes, for avoyding the extremities of injurious dealing.

Wherein if also they shall not be suffered in reasonable quietnes to continue, there is no barre (as I judge) but that in stoute assemblies, the Christians may issue out, and by strong hande pursue theyr enemies, subdue them, take possession of theyr Townes, Cities, or Villages, (and in avoyding murtherous tyranny) to use the Lawe of Armes, as in like case among all nations at thys day is used: and most especially to the ende they may with securitye holde theyr lawfull possession, least happily after the departure of the Christians, such Savages as have beene converted, shoulde afterwardes through compulsion and enforcment of theyr wicked Rulers, returne to theyr horrible Idolatry (as did the children of Israell, after the decease of Josua)[19] and continue theyr wicked custome of most unnaturall sacrificing of humaine creatures.

And in so dooing, doubtles the Christians shall no whitt at all transgresse the bondes of equitie or civillity, for as much as in former ages, (yea before the incarnation of Christ) the like hath beene doon by sundry Kings and Princes, Governers of the children of Israell: cheefely in respect to beginne theyr Planting, for the establishment of Gods word: as also since the nativity of Christ, myghty and puissaunt Emperours and Kinges have performed the like, I say to plant, possesse, and subdue. For proofe whereof, I wyll alledge you examples of bothe tymes.

We read in the olde testament, howe that after Noes fludde was ceased, restoration of mankinde began onely of these few of Noes children and family as were by God prelected to be saved in the Arke with him, whose seede in processe of time, was multiplyed to infinite numbers of nations, which in divers sortes devided themselves to sundry quarters of the earth. And forasmuch as all the posteritie being mightely encreased followed not the perfect lyfe of Noe theyr predicessor, God chose out of the multitude, a peculiar

people to himselfe, to whome afterwardes beeing under the governement of Moises in Mount Synay, hee made a graunt to inherite the Lande of Canaan, called the Land of Promise, with all th'other rich and fertile Countryes next adjoyning thereunto. Neverthelesse, before they came to possession thereof, having beene afflicted with many greevous punishments and plagues for theyr sinnes, they fell in dispayre to enjoy the same.

But beeing encouraged and comforted by theyr Rulers, (men of God) they proceeded, arming themselves with all patience, to suffer what soever it shoulde please God to sende: and at last attaining to the Lande, they were encountered with great numbers of strong people and myghtye Kinges.

Notwithstanding Josua theyr leader, replenished with the spirite of God, beeing assured of the justnes of his quarrell, gathered the cheefe strength of the children of Israell together, to the number of 40000, with whom he safely passed the huge River Jourden,[20] and having before sent privie spyes for the discovery of the famous Cittie Jerico, to understand the certaintie of the Cittizens estate, he foorthwith came thether, and environed it rounde aboute, with his whole power the space of sveen dayes.[21]

In which respite, perceiving none of the Gentiles disposed to yeeld or call for mercie, he then commaunded (as God before had appointed) that both the Cittie Jericho should be burned, yea, and all the inhabitaunts, as well olde as young, with all their cattell, should be destroied, onelie excepted Rahab, her kindred and Familie, because she before had hid secretly the messengers of Josua, that were sent thether as spies. As for all their golde, silver, precious stones, or vesselles of brasse, they were reserved and consecrated to the Lords treasurie.

In like manner he burned the cittie Hay, slew the inhabitants thereof, and hanged up their King.[22] But for so much as the Gebionites (fearing the like event) sent Ambassadors unto Josua, to intreate for grace, favour, and peace: he commaunded that all their lives should be saved, and that they should be admitted to the companie of

19. Sidenote: "Judges. 6."

20. Sidenote: "Josua. 4."
21. Sidenote: "Josua. 6."
22. Sidenote: "Josua. 8."

the children of Israel.[23] Yet understanding afterwards they wrought this by a pollicie, he used them as drudges to hewe wood and to carie water, and other necessaries for his people. Thus beganne this valiaunt Captaine his conquest, which he pursued and never left till he had subdued all the Hethites, Amorites, Cananites, Pheresites, Hevites, and Jebusites, with all their Princes and Kings, being thirtie and one in number, and divers other straunge Nations besides, whose lands and dominions, he wholie devided among Gods people.[24]

After that Josua was deceased, Juda was constituted Lord over the Armie, who receiving like charge from God pursued the proceedings of the holie Captaine Josua, and utterlie vanquished many Gentiles, Idolaters, and adversaries to the children of Israel, with all such Rulers or Kings, as withstoode him,[25] and namely, Adonibezek, the most cruell tyraunt: whose thombes and great toes he caused to be cut off, for so much as he had doon the like before unto seventy Kings, whome being his prisoners, he forced to gather up their victualles underneath his Table. In this God shewed his justice to revenge tyranny.[26] We reade likewise, that Gideon a most puissant and noble warrier, so behaved himself in following the woorthy actes of Josua and Juda, That in short time he not onely delivered the children of Israel from the hands of the multitude of the fierce Madianites, but also subdued them and their Tyrants, whose landes he caused Gods people to possesse and inherite.[27]

I could recite divers other places out of the Scripture, which aptly may be applied heerunto were it not I do endevour my selfe by all meanes to be breefe. Now in like manner will I alledge some few of Inductions out of the autenticall writings of the Ecclesiasticall Historiographers, all tending to the like argument. And first to begin with all, we doo reade That after our saviour Jesus Christ had suffered his passion. The apostles being inspired with the holy Ghost, and the knowledge of all straunge languages, did immediatly dispearse themselves to sundrie partes of the world, to the preaching of the Gospell. Yet

not in so generall manner, but that there remained some farre remote Countries unvisited by them, among which is reported that India the great, called the uttermost India, as yet had received no light of the word.[28] But it came to passe, that one Metrodorus, a verie learned and wise Philosopher in that age, being desirous to search out unknowne landes, did first discover the same, finding it wonderful populous and rich, which uppon his returne being published, and for certaine understoode, there was another grave Philosopher of Tyrus called Meropius,[29] being a christian, who did resolve himselfe (folowing the example of Metrodorus) to travaile thether, and in a short time assisted but with a fewe, in a small Vessell arrived there, having in his company two young youthes, Edesius, and Frumentius, whome (being his schollers)[30] he had throughly instructed, both in lyberall Sciences and christian Religion. Now after that Meropius somewhile staying there, had (as he thought) sufficient understanding of the Indians whole estate. He determined to depart, and to bring notice thereof unto the Emperor, whom he meant to exhort to the conquest of the same. But by misfortune he was prevented, for being in the middest of his course on the Sea homeward, a sore tempest arose, and perforce drove him backe againe, to an unknowne Port of the saide lande: where he by the most cruell barbarous Indians on the suddaine was slaine with all his company, except the two young schollers aforesaide, whome the barbarous Indians, by reason they were of comely stature and beautifull personages, tooke foorthwith and presented them to theyr King and Queene: which both being verie well lyked of, the King courteously entreated, and ordeined Edesius to be his Butler, and Frumentius his Secretary, and in few yeeres by reason of their learning and civill gouvernement, they were had in great favour, honour and estimation with the Princes. But the King departing this life, left the Queene his wife with her young sonne to governe, and gave free scope and lybertie to the two christians, at their best pleasure to passe to their native soyles, allowing them all necessaries for the same. Yet

23. Sidenote: "Josua. 9."
24. Sidenote: "Judg. 11. 13."
25. Sidenote: "Judg. 1."
26. Sidenote: "A good note for all Conquerers to be mercifull."
27. Sidenote: "Judges. 6. 7."

28. Sidenote: "India the great, not preached unto by the Apostles. Metrodorus the Philosopher, first discovered that India."
29. Sidenote: "Meropius."
30. Sidenote: "Edesius and Frumentius."

the Queene who highly favoured them, was verie sorowful they should depart, and therefore most earnestlie intreated them to tarie and assist her in the government of her people, tyll such tymes as her young Sonne grewe to rype yeeres, which request they fulfilled.

And Frumentius excelling Edesius farre in all wisedome, ruled both the Queene and her subjects at his discretion,[31] whereby he tooke occasion to put in practise privilie, that the foundation of christian religion might be planted in the hearts of such as with whome he thought his perswasion might best prevaile, and that soonest would give eare unto him, which being brought to passe accordingly, he then with his fellow Edesius, tooke leave of the Queene to returne to his native countrie. And so soone as he was arrived there, he revealed to the Emperor Constantine, the effect of all those events: who both commending his deeds and wholie allowing thereof, by the advise and good liking of Athanasius then Bishop of Alexandria, did arme and set foorth a convenient power for the aide of Frumentius, in this his so godlie a purpose. And by this meanes came the Emperor afterwardes by faire promises, and by force of Armes together, unto the possession of all the Indians countrie. The aucthor of this storie Ruffinus received the trueth heerof, from the verie mouth of Edesius companion to Frumentius.[32]

Moreover, Eusebius in his Historie Ecclesiasticall in precise termes, and in divers places maketh mencion how Constantine the great, not onelie enlarged his Empire by the subduing of his next neighbours, but also endevored by all meanes, to subject all such remote Barbarous and Heathen nations, as then inhabited the fowre quarters of the world. For (as it is written) the Emperor throughlie aided with a puissaunt armie of valiaunt souldiers whom he had before perswaded to christian religion, in proper person himselfe, came even unto this our native Countrie of England, then called the Island of Brittaines, bending from him full west, which he wholie conquered, made tributarie, and setled therein christian faith, and left behinde him such Rulars thereof, as to his wisedome seemed best. From

thence he turned his force towards the North coast of the world, and there utterlie subdued the rude and cruell Nation of the Scithians, whereof part by freendly perswasions, part by maine strength, he reduced the whole to christian Faith. Afterwardes he determined with himselfe to search out what straunge people inhabited in the uttermost partes of the South. And with great hazard and labour, making his jorney thether, at last became victor over them all, even to the countrie of the Blemmyans, and the remote Etheopians, that now are the people of Presbiter John, who yet tyl this daie, continue and beare the name of christians.[33]

In the East likewise, what Nation soever at that time he could have notice off, he easilie wunne and brought in subjection to the Empire. So that to conclude, there was no region in any part of the world, the inhabitaunts wherof being Gentiles, though unknowne unto him. But in time he overcame and vanquished.

This woorthy beginning of Constantine, both his sonnes succeeding his roome, and also divers other Emperors afterward to their uttermost endevor followed and continued, which all the Bookes of Eusebius more at large setteth foorth. Theodoritus likewise in his Ecclesiasticall historie[34] maketh mencion how Theodosius the vertuous Emperour, emploied earnestlie all his time, as well in conquering the Gentiles to the knowledge of the holie Gospel, utterlie subverting the prophane Temples and abhominable Idolatry. As also in extinguishing of such usurping tiraunts, as with Paganisme withstoode the planting of christian religion. After whose decease his sonnes, Honorius, and Arcadius, were created Emperors, the one of the East, the other of the West, who with all stoutly godlines, most carefully imitated the foresteps of their Father, eyther in enlarging their territories, or increasing the christian flocke.[35]

Moreover, it is reported by the saide aucthor, that Theodotius Junior the Emperour, no whit inferiour in vertuous life to any of the above named Princes, with great study and zeale pur-

31. Sidenote: "Frumentius in great favour with the Queene of the Indians."
32. Sidenote: "An other great work of God begun by a man of meane birth. Ruffinus. the Author of this storye."
33. Sidenote: "Euseb. in ecclesiasticall history testifieth howe that Constantine the great, did enlarge his dominions by subduing of Infidels and Idolatrous nations. Eusebius lib I. de vita Constant. Cap. 4. et Cap. 3 Eu. eod. lib. Cap. 39."
34. Sidenote: "Theodarit in Ecclesiast. Hist. lib. 5. Cap. 20."
35. Sidenote: "Theodaritus cap. 26 eod. libro."

sued, prosecuted the Gentiles, subdued theyr Tyraunts and Countries, and utterly destroied all their Idolatry, converting their soules to acknowledge their onelie Messias and Creator, and their countries to the enlargement of the Empire. To be breefe, who so listeth to reade Eusebius, Pamphilus, Socrates Scolasticus, Theodoritus, Hermia, Sozomen, and Eragrius Scolasticus, which all were most sage Ecclesiastical writers, shall finde great store of examples of the woorthy lives of sundry Emperors, tending all to the confirmation of my former speeches.

And for like examples of latter time (yea, even in the memory of man) I shall not neede to recite any other then the conquest made of the West and East Indies, by the Kings of Spaine and Portugall, whereof there is particular mencion made in the last chapter of this Booke. Heerein have I used more copy of examples, then otherwise I would have doone, saving that I have beene in place where this maner of planting the christian Fath, hath beene thought of some to be scarce lawfull, yea, such as doo take uppon them to be more then meanely learned. To these examples could I joyne many more but whosoever is not satisfied with these fewe, may satisfie himselfe in reading at large the aucthors last above recited Thus have I (as I trust) prooved that we may justly trade and traffique with the Savages, and lawfullie plant and inhabite theyr Countries.

The third Chapter dooth shewe the lawfull tytle, which the Queenes most excellent Majestie hath unto those Countries, which through the ayde of almightie God are mente to be inhabited.

And it is very evident that the planting there shall in time right amplie enlarge her Majesties Territories and Dominions (or I might rather say) restore her to her Highnesse auncient right and interest in those Countries, into the which a noble and woorthy personage, lyneally descended from the blood royall, borne in Wales, named Madocke ap Owen Gwyneth,[36] departing from the coast of England, about the yeere of our Lord God. 1170. arrived and there planted himselfe, and his Colonies, and afterward returned himselfe into England, leaving certaine of his people there, as

appeareth in an auncient Welch Chronicle, where he then gave to certaine Ilandes, Beastes, and Fowles, sundrie Welch names, as the Iland of Pengwyn,[37] which yet to this day beareth the same.

There is lykewise a Fowle in the sayde Countries, called by the same name at this daye, and is as much to saye in Englishe, as Whiteheadde, and in trueth, the sayde Fowles have white heads.

There is also in those Countries a fruite called Gwynethes which is likewise a welch word. Moreover, there are divers other welch wordes at this dite in use, as David Ingram aforesaid reporteth in his relations.[38] All which most strongly argueth, the saide Prince with his people to have inhabited there. And the same in effect is confirmed by Mutuzuma that mightie Emperor of Mexico, who in an Oration unto his subjects, for the better pacifying of them, made in the presence of Hernando Curtese, used these speeches following.[39]

My kinsemen, freends, and servaunts, you do well know that eigteene yeeres I have been your King, as my Fathers and Grandfathers were, and alwaies I have beene unto you a loving Prince, and you unto me good and obedient subjects, and so I hope you will remaine unto me all the daies of my life. You ought to have in remembraunce, that eyther you have heard of your Fathers, or else our divines have instructed you that we are not naturallie of this Countrie, nor yet our Kingdome is durable, because our Forefathers came from a farre countrie, and their King and Captaine who brought them hither, returned againe to his natural countrie, saying, that he would send such as should rule and governe us, if by chaunce he himselfe returned not, etc.

These be the verie words of Mutuzuma, set downe in the Spanish Chronicles, the which being throughlie considered,[40] because they have relation to some straunge noble person, who long before had possessed those Countries, doo all sufficientlie argue, the undoubted title of her

36. Sidenote: "Owen Gwyneth, was then Prince of Northwales."

37. Sidenote: "This Iland was discovered by Sir Humfrey and his company, in this his last jorney."
38. Sidenote: "Who hath also seene berded men there, which can not bee naturall cuntrimen, for that the Americans are voide of beardes."
39. Sidenote: "Mutuzuma his Oration to his subjects in presence of Hernando Curtese. which Oration was made about the yeere 1520."
40. Sidenote: "Looke the conquest of West Indias fol. 231."

Majestie: For as much as no other Nation can truelie by any Chronicles they can finde, make prescription of time for themselves, before the time of this Prince Madocke. Besides all this, for further proofe of her highnes title sithence the arrivall of this noble Britton into those partes (that is to say) in the time of the Queenes Majesties Grandfather, of worthy memorie, King Henry the seventh, Letters pattents were by his Majestie graunted to John Gabota an Italian, to Lewes, Sebastian, and Sansius, his three sonnes, to discover remoate, Barbarous and Heathen Countries, which discovery, was afterwards executed to the use of the crown of England, in the sayd Kings time, by Sebastian and Sansius his sonnes, who were borne heere in Englande: In true testimony whereof, there is a fayre Haven in Newfounde Land, knowne and called until this day, by the name of Sansius Haven, which prooveth that they firste discovered upon that Coast, from the heyght of 63. unto the Cape of Florida, as appeareth in the Decades.[41]

And this may stande for another title to her Majestie, but any of the foresayde titles is as much, or more then any other Christian Prince can pretende to the Indies before suche time as they had actuall possession thereof, obteyned by the discovery of Christopher Columnus, and the conquest of Vasques Numes de Balboa, Hernando Cortese, Francisco Pysare, and others, And therefore I thinke it needeles to write any more touching the lawfulnes of her Majesties title.

> The fourth Chapiter sheweth, howe that the trade traficke and planting in those Countries, is likely to proove very profitable to the whole Realme in generall.

Now to shewe howe the same is most likely to proove very profitable and beneficiall generallie to the whole Realme. It is verye certaine, that the greatest Jewell of this Realme, and the cheefest strength and force of the same, for defence or offence, in martiall matter and manner is the multitude of Shippes, Maisters and Marriners, ready to assist the most stately and royall Navie of her Majestie, which by reason of this voyage shall have, both increase and maintenaunce. And it is well knowne, that in sundry places of this Realme, Shippes have beene built and sette foorth of late dayes for the trade of fishing onely: Yet not withstanding the fishe which is taken and brought into England by the English Navie of Fishermen, will not suffice for the expence of this realme foure moneths, if there were none els brought of straungers.[42] And the cheefest cause why our Englishmen doo not goe so farre westerly, as the especiall fishing places doo lie, both for plenty and greatnes of fish, is for that they have no succour and known safe harbour in those partes. But if our nation were once planted there, or neere thereaboutes: whereas they now fish but for two monethes in the yeere, they myght then fish so long as pleased themselves or rather at theyr comming find such plenty of Fish readie taken, salted and dryed, as might be sufficient to fraught them home without long delay, (God graunting that salt may be found there) whereof David Ingram (who travelled in those Countries as aforesayde) saith that there is great plentie: and withall the Climate dooth give greate hope, that though there were none naturallye growing, yet it might aswell be made there by arte, as it is both in Rochell and Bayon, or els where. Which beeing brought to passe, shall encrease the number of our ships and Marriners, were it but in respect of fishing onelie: but much more in regarde of the sundry Marchaundises and commodities which are there founde and had in greate aboundance.

Moreover, it is wel known that all Savages, as wel those that dwell in the South, as those that dwell in the North, so soone as they shall begin but a little to taste of civillitie, will take mervailous delight in any garment be it never so simple: As a shirt, a blewe, yellow, redde, or greene Cotton cassocke, a Cappe or such like, and will take incredible paynes for such a trifle.

For I my selfe have heard this reporte made sundrye times, by divers of our Countreymen, who have dwelt in the sotherly partes, of the West Indies, some 12. yeeres together, and some of lesse time: That the people in those partes, are easily reduced to civilitie bothe in manners and garments. Which beeing so, what vente for our English clothes will thereby ensue, and howe

41. Sidenote: "Ma. Oliver Dalbony. Ma. Edward Reow. Ma. R. H. Ma. J. A."

42. Sidenote: "Cox the Maister."

greate benefit to all such persons and Artificers whose names are coated in the margent,[43] I doo leave to the judgment of such as are discrete.

And questionles heereby it will also come to passe, that all such Townes and Villages, as bothe have beene and nowe are utterlye decayed and ruinated (the poore people thereof beeing not sette a worke by reason of the transportation of rawe Wooll of late dayes, more excessively then in tymes past) shall by this meanes be restored to theyr pristinate wealth and estate, all which doo likewise tende to the enlargement of our Navie and mayntenaunce of our navigation.

To what ende neede I endevour my selfe by arguments to proove that by this voyage, our navie and navigation shall be enlarged, when as there needeth none other reason then the manifest and late example of the neere Neighbours to this Realme, the Kings of Spayne, and Portingall who since the first discovery of the Indias, have not onelye mightily enlarged theyr dominions, greatly enritched themselves and theyr subjectes: but have also by just account trebbled the number of theyr Shippes, Maysters and Marriners, a matter of no small moment and importaunce.

Besides this, it will proove a generall benefite unto our Country, that through this occasion, not onely a greate number of men which doo nowe live ydlely at home, and are burdenous, chargeable and unprofitable to this Realme, shall heereby be sette on worke, but also children of 12. or 14. yeeres of age or under, may bee kept from ydlenes, in making of a thousand kindes of trifeling things, which will be good Marchandize for that Country.[44] And moreover, our ydle women, (which the Realme may well spare) shal also bee imployed on plucking, drying, and sorting of Feathers, in pulling, beating, and working of Hempe,[45] and in gathering of Cotten, and dyvers things right necessary for dying. All which thinges are to bee found in those Countries most plentifully. And the men may imploy themselves in draging for Pearle, working for Mynes, and in matters of husbandry, and likewise in hunting the Whale for traine, and making Caskes to put the same in: besides, in fishing for Codde, Salmon and Herring, drying, salting, and barrelling the same, and felling of Trees, hewing and sawing of them, and such like woorke, meete for those persons as are no men of arte or science.

Many other thinges may be founde to the greate reliefe and good emploiem[e]nts of no small number, of the naturall subjectes of this Realme, which doo nowe live heere ydlelie to the common annoy of the whole state. Neither may I heere omitte the great hope and likelyhoode of a passage by the Graunde bay, into the South Seas,[46] confirmed by sundrie Aucthors to be founde leading to Cataia, the Moluccos and Spiceries, whereby may ensue as general a benefite to the Realme or greater, then yet hath beene spoken off, without eyther such charges, or other inconveniences, as by the tedious tract of time and perrill, which the ordinarie passage to those partes at this day doth minister. And to conclude this argument withall, it is well knowne to all men of sounde judgement, that this voyage is of greater importaunce, and will be founde more beneficiall to our Countrey, then all other voyages at this day in use and trade amongst us.

The fift Chapiter sheweth, that the trading and planting in those Countries is likely to proove, to the perticuler profit of all the Adventurers.

I must nowe according to my promise shew forth some probable reasons, that the adventurers in this journey, are to take perticuler profite by the same. It is therefore convenient that I doo devide the Adventurers into two sortes: The Noble men and Gentlemen by themselves, and the Marchaunts by themselves. For as I doo heare, it is meant that there shalbe one societie of the Noble men and Gentlemen, and another societie of the Marchants. And yet not so devided, but that eache society may freely and franckly trade and traficke one with the other.

And first to bende my speeche to the Noblemen and Gentlemen, who doo cheefely seeke a tem-

---

43. Sidenote: "Clothiers. Wolmen. Carders. Spinners. Weavers. Fullers. Sheremen. Diers. Drapers. Clothiers. Cappers Hatters. etc. And many decayed townes repayred."
44. Sidenote: "The ydle persons of this Realm shall by occasion of this journey be wel employed and sette on worke."
45. Sidenote: "Hempe doth growe neere Saint Lawrence River naturally."
46. Sidenote: "Reade the beginning of the boke intituled, divers voyages touching the discovery of America."

perate climate, holesome ayre, fertile soyle, and a strong place by nature, whereupon they may fortifie, and there either plant themselves, or such other persons as they shall thinke good to sende to be Lordes of that place and Country: To them I say that all these thinges are very easye to be founde within the degrees of 30. and 60. aforesayde, eyther by Southe or North, both in the Continent, and in Islands thereunto adjoyning at theyr choyse: But the degree certaine of the elevation of the Pole and the very Climate where these places of force and fertilitie are to be founde, I omitte to make publique, for such regarde as the wiser sort can easily conjecture: the rather because I doo certainly understand, that some of those which have the managing of this matter, knowe it as well or better then I my selfe, and doo meane to reveale the same when cause shall require, to such persons whom it shall concerne and to no other: So that they may seate and settle themselves in such Climate as shal best agree with their owne nature, disposition, and good likeing: and in the whole tract of that land, by the discription of as many as have beene there, great plentie of minerall matter of all sortes, and in verye many places bothe stones of price, Pearle, and Christall, and great store of Beastes, Byrdes, and Fowles both for pleasure and necessarie use of man is to be founde.

And for such as take delight in hunting, there are Stagges, Wild Bores, Foxes, Hares, Conneys, Badgers, Otters, and divers other such like for pleasure.[47] Also for such as have delight in Hawking, there are Hawkes of sundry kindes, and great store of game, both for Land and River, as Feazaunts, Partridges, Cranes, Heronshawes, Duckes Mallardes, and such like. There is also a kinde of Beaste, much bigger then an Oxe, whose hyde is more then 18. foote long, of which sorte a Countriman of ours, one Walker a Sea man, who was uppon that Coast, did for a trueth reporte, in the presence of divers honourable and worshipfull persons, that he and his company did finde in one Cottage above 240. Hides. which they brought away and solde in Fraunce for xl. shillinges an hyde, and with this agreeth David Ingram, and discribeth that beast at large, supposing it to be a certaine kinde of Buffe: there are likewise beastes

and fowles of divers kindes, which I omitte for brevities sake, great store of fish both in the salt water and in the fresh, plentie of Grapes as bigge as a mans thombe, and the most delicate Wine of the Palmetree, of which wine there be divers of good credit in this realm have tasted:[48] and there is also a kind of graine called Maize, Potato rootes, and sundry other fruites naturall growing there: so that after such time as they are once setled, they shall neede to take no great care for victuall.

And nowe for the better contentation and satisfaction of such worshipful, honest minded, and wel disposed Marchants, as have a desire to the furtherance of every good and commendable action, I wil first say unto them, as I have doon before to the Noble men and Gentlemen, that within the degrees above sayde, is doubtles to be founde, the moste holesom and best tempature of ayre, fertillitie of soile, and every other commoditie or marchaundize, for the which, with no smal perril we doo travaill into Barbery, Spayne, Portingall, Fraunce, Italie, Muscovie and Dansike. All which may be either presently had, or at the least wise in verye shorte time, procured from thence with lesse danger then now we have them. And yet to the ende my argument shall not altogether stand uppon likelihoodes and presumptions, I say that such persons as have discovered and travailed those partes doo testifie, that they have founde in those Countries, all these thinges following, namelie.

Of Beastes for furres:
Martens.
Beavers.
Foxes blacke and white.
Leopardes.

Of Wormes:
Silkeworms great and large

Of Byrdes:
Hawkes.
Bitters.
Curlewes.
Herons.
Partridges.
Cranes.
Mallards.
Wildgeese.
Stockdoves.

47. Sidenote: "Beastes for pleasure."

48. Sidenote: "Hides solde for xl. shillings apece. Great Grapes. Wine of the Palmtree."

Margaus.
Blackbirds.
Parrotts.
Pengwyns.

Of Fishes:
Codd.
Salmon.
Seales.
Herrings.

Of Trees:
Palme trees yeelding sweete wines.
Cedars.
Fyrres.
Sasafras.
Oake.
Elme.
Popler.

And sundry other strange Trees, to us unknowne.

Of Fruites:
Grapes, verie large.
Muskemellons.
Limons.
Dates great.
Orrenges.
Figges.
Prounes.
Reisons, great and small.
Pepper.
Almonds.
Citrons.

Of Mettalles:
Golde.
Sylver.
Copper.
Leade.
Tinne.

Of Stones:
Turkeis.
Rubies.
Pearles, great and faire.
Marble, of divers kinds.
Jasper.
Christall.

Sundry other commodities of all sortes:
Rosen.
Pitch.
Tarre.
Turpentine.
Frankensence
Honny.
Waxe.

Rubarbe.
Oyle Oliffe.
Traine Oyle.
Musk codde.
Salte.

Tallowe.
Hydes.
Hempe:
Flaxe.
Chuchenelle and Dies of divers sortes.

Feathers of sundry sorts, as for pleasure and
filling of Featherbeddes.

And seeing that for small costes, the truth of these thinges may be understoode (wherof this intended supply wil give us more certaine assuraunce) I doo find no cause to the contrarie, but that all wel minded persons should be willing to adventure some convenient portion, for the furtheraunce of so good an enterprise.

Now for the triall heereof, considering that in the Articles of the Societie of the adventurers in this voiage, there is provision made, that no adventurer shalbe bound to any further charge then his first adventure: and yet notwithstanding keepe styl to himselfe, his children, his apprentises and servants, his and their freedome for trade and traficke which is a priviledge that Adventurers in other voiages have not: and in the saide articles it is likewise provided, that none other then such as have adventured in the first voiage, or shall become adventurers in this supply, at any time heerafter are to be admitted in the said society, but as Redemptionaries, which wil be very chargeable: Therefore generally I say unto all such according to the old Proverb, Nothing venture, Nothing have. For if it do so fal out, according to the great hope and expectation had (as by Gods grace it wil) the gaine which now they reape by traffique into other farre Countries, shall by this trade returne with lesse charge, greater gaine, and more safety: Lesse charge I say, by reason of the ample and large deepe Rivers at the verie banke, whereof there is many, wherby both easily and quietly they may transport from the innermost partes of the maine land, all kind of merchandize, yea, in Vessels of great burden, and that three times, or twise in the yeere at the least. But let us omit all presumptions how vehement soever, and dwel upon the certainty of such commodities as were discovered and found by Sir Humfrey Gilbert, and his assistants in Newfoundland, in August last.[49] For there may be very easily made, Pitch, Tarre, Rosen, Sope ashes, in great plenty, yea, as it is thought inough to serve the whole Realme of every of these kindes. And of Traine Oyle such quantity, as if I should set downe the value that they doo esteeme it at, which have been there, it would seeme incredible.

It is heerby intended, that these commodities in this aboundaunt manner, are not to be gathered from thence, without Planting and setling there. And as for other thinges of more value, and that of more sortes and kinds then one or two, (which were likewise discovered there) I doo hold it for some respects, more meet for a time to be concealed and uttered.

Of the Fishing I doo speake nothing, because it is generally known: And it is not to be forgotten, what very trifles they be that the Savages doo require in exchaunge of these commodities: yea for Pearle, Gold, Silver, and precious stones. All which are matters in trade and traffique of great moment. But admit that it shold so fal out, that the above specified commodities, shall not happely be found out within this first yeere. Yet it is very cleere that such and so many may be found out as shall minister just occasion to thinke al cost and labor well bestowed. For it is very certaine, that there is one seate fit for fortification, of great safety, wherin these commodities following, especially are to be had, that is to say, Grapes for wine, Whales for oyle, Hempe for cordage and other necessary thinges, and Fish of farre greater sise and plenty, then that of Newfoundland, and of all these so great store as may suffise to serve our whole Realme.

Besydes all this if credite, may be given to the Inhabitaunts of the same Soyle, a certaine River dooth thereunto adjoyne, which leadeth to a place abounding with ritch substaunce: I doo not heereby meane the passadge to the Moluchos, whereof before I made mencion.

And it is not to be omitted, howe that about two yeeres past, certaine Marchaunts of S. Mallowes in Fraunce, dyd hire a Shippe out of the Island of Jersey, to the ende that they would keepe that trade secrete from theyr Countreimen, and they would admit no Mariner other then the Ship boy belonging to the sayd Shippe to goe with them.

which Ship was about 70. Tunne. I doo knowe the Ship and the boy very well, and am familiarly acquainted with the Owner, which voyage prooved very beneficiall.

To conclude, this which is already saide, may suffice any man of reasonable disposition to serve for a taste, untyll such tyme as it shall please almightie God through our owne industrie, to send us better tydings. In the meane season, if any man well affected to this journey, shal stand in doubt of any matter of importance touching the same, he may satisfie himselfe with the judgement and lyking of those of good calling and credite, as are principall dealers herein. For it is not necessary in this treatise, publickly to sette foorth the whole secretes of the voyage.

The sixt Chapter, sheweth that the Traffique and Planting in those Countries, shall be unto the Savages themselves verie beneficiall and gainefull.

Now to the end it may appeare, that this voiage is not undertaken altogether for the peculiar commoditie of our selves, and our Countrie, (as generallie other trades and journeies be) it shall fall out in proofe, that the Savages shal heerby have just cause to blesse the howre, when this enterprise was undertaken.

First and cheefly, in respect of the most happy and gladsome tydings of the most gracious Gospel of our Saviour Jesus Christ, whereby they may be brought from falsehood to truth, from darknes to lyght, from the hieway of death, to the path of life, from superstitious idolatry, to sincere Christianity, from the devill to Christ, from hell to Heaven. And if in respect of all the commodities they can yeeld us (were they many moe) that they should but receyve this only benefite of christianity, they were more then fully recompenced.

But heerunto it may be objected, that the Gospel must be freely preached, for such was the example of the Apostles, unto whom although the aucthorities and examples before alledged, of Emperors, Kings, and Princes, as wel before Christes time as since, might sufficiently satisfie: Yet for further aunswer, we may say with Saint Paule. If we have sowen unto you heavenlie thinges, doo you thinke it much that we should reape your carnall thinges?[50] And withall, The

49. Sidenote: "Commodities found in August last."

50. Sidenote: "2. Cor. 9."

workman is worthy of his hier. These heavenly tydings which those labourers our countreymen (as messengers of Gods great goodnes and mercy) wyl voluntarily present unto them, dooth farre exceed their earthly ritches. Moreover, if the other inferior worldlie, and temporall thinges, which they shal receive from us, be waied in equal balance, I assure my selfe, that by equall judgement of any indifferent person, the benefites which they then receive, shall far surmount those which they shall depart withall unto us. And admitte that they had (as they have not) the knowledge to put theyr land to some use: Yet being brought from brutish ignoraunce, to civility and knowledge, and made them to understand how the tenth part of their land may be so manured and emploied, as it may yeeld more commodities to the necessary use of mans life, then the whole now dooth: What just cause of complaint may they have? And in my private opinion, I doo verily think that God did create lande, to the end that it shold by Culture and husbandrie, yeeld things necessary for mans lyfe.

But this is not all the benefit which they shall receive by the christians, for, over and beside the knowledge how to tyl and dresse their grounds, they shalbe reduced from unseemly customes, to honest maners, from disordred riotous rowtes and companies, to a wel governed common wealth, and withall shalbe taught mecanicall occupations, artes, and lyberal Sciences: and which standeth them most upon, they shalbe defended from the cruelty of their tyrannicall and blood sucking neighbors, the Canniballes, wherby infinite number of their lives shalbe preserved. And lastly, by this meanes many of their poore innocent children shalbe preserved from the bloody knife of the sacrificer, a most horrible and detestable custome in the sight of God and man, now and ever heertofore used amongst them.[51] Many other thinges could I heere alledge to this purpose, were it not that I doo feare least I have already more then halfe tired the Reader.

The seaventh Chapter sheweth that the Planting there, is not a matter of such charge or diffycultie, as many would make it seeme to be.

51. Sidenote: "The bargaine can not be unjust, where both parties are gainers."

Now therefore for proofe, that the Planting in these parts is a thing that may be doone without the aide of the Princes power and purse, contrarye to the allegation of many malicious persons, who will neither be actors in any good action themselves, nor so much as afoord a good word to the setting forward thereof: and that wurse, is they wyl take upon them to make Molehylles seeme Mountaines, and flies Elephants, to the end they may discourage others, that be verye well or indifferently affected to the matter, being like unto Esoppes Dogge which neither would eate haie himself, nor suffer the poore hungry asse to feede thereon.

I say and affirme that God hath provided such meanes for the furtheraunce of this enterprise, as doth stande us in steede of great treasure: for first by reason that it hath pleased God of his great goodnesse, of long time to holde his merciful hand over this Realme, in preserving the people of the same, both from slaughter by the sword, and great death by plague, pestilence, or otherwise, there is at this day great numbers (God he knoweth) which live in such penurie and want, as they could be contented to hazarde their lives, and to serve one yeere for meate, drinke, and apparel, onely without wages, in hope thereby to amend theyr estates: which is a matter in such lyke journeis, of no small charge to the Prince. Moreover, thinges in the lyke journeis of greatest price and cost, as victual (whereof there is great plenty to bee had in that countrye without money) and powder, great artillery, or Corselets, are not needful, in so plentiful and chargeable manner, as the shew of such a journey, may present, for a smal quantity of all these to furnish the Forte onely wyl suffice, untyl such time as divers commodities may be found out in those parts, which may be thought wel woorthy a greater charge. Also the peculiar benefite of Archers which God hath blessed this land withal, before al other nations, will stand us in great stede amongst those naked people.

Another helpe we have also, which in such lyke cases is a matter of mervailous cost, and wil be in this journey procured very easily (that is to say) To transport yeerely as wel our people, as al other necessaries, needful for them into those parts by the Fleete of Merchaunts, that yeerely venture for Fish in Newfound Land, being not farre distaunt from the countrey, meant to be inhabited, who commonly go with empty Vesselles in effect, saving some lyttle fraught with Salt. And thus it appeareth that the Souldiers wages, and the transportation may be defrayed for farre lesse summes of money, then the detractors of this enterprise have given out. Againe, this intended voiage for conquest, hath in lyke manner many other singular priviledges, wherewith God hath as it were, with his holy hand blessed the same before all others. For after once we are departed the coast of England, we may passe straight way thether, without the daunger of being driven into any the countries of our enimies, or doubtfull freends, for commonly one winde serveth to bring us thether, which sildome faileth from the middle of Januarie, to the middle of Maie, a benefite which the Mariners make great account off, for it is a pleasure that they have in few or none of the other journies. Also, the passage is short, for we may go thither in thirty of forty daies at the most, having but an indifferent winde, and returne continually in sixteene or twenty dayes at the most. And in the same our journey, by reason it is in the Occean, and quite out of the way from the intercourse of other countries: we may safely trade and traffique, without perill of pyracie, neither shal our Ships, people, or goods, ther be subjecte to the arrest or molestation of any Pagan Potentate, Turkishe Tyrant, yea, or christian Prince, which heertofore, sometimes upon slender occasion in other parts, have staied our Shippes and marchaundizes, whereby great numbers of our Countrimen have beene utterly undoone, dyvers put to raunsome, yea and some lost their lives: a thing so fresh in memory as it needeth no proofe, and well worthy of consideration.

Besides, in this voyage, we doo not crosse the burnt line, whereby commonly both beverage and victuall are corrupted, and mens health very much impaired, neither doo we passe the frozen Seas, which yeelde sundrye extreme daungers: but have a temperate Climate at all times of the yeere, to serve our turnes. And lastly, there neede no delayes by the way, for taking in of freshwater and Fewell, (a thing usually doone in long journeys) because as I said above, the voyage is not long, and the fresh waters taken in there, our men heere in England, at theyr returne home, have found so holesome and sweete, that they have made choise to drinke it before our Beere or Ale.

Beholde heere good Countreimen, the manifolde benefites, commodities and pleasures heeretofore unknowne, by Gods especiall blessing not onelie revealed unto us, but also as it were infused into our bosomes, who though hetherto like Dormise have slumbered in ignoraunce thereof, beeing like the Cattes that are lothe for theyr praye to wette their feete, yet if now therefore, at the last we would awake, and with willing mindes (setting frivolous imaginations aside) become industrious instruments to our selves, Questionles we shoulde not onely heereby set foorth the glorie of our heavenlie Father, but also easily attaine to the ende of all good purposes, that may be wished or desired.

And may it not much encourage us to hope for good successe in the countrey of these Savages, beeing a naked kinde of people, voyde of the knowledge of the discipline of warre, seeing that a Noble man, beeing but a subjecte in this Realme, (in the time of our King Henrie the second) by name Strangbowe, then Earle of Chepstowe in South Wales, by himselfe and his Alleis and assistaunts, at their owne proper charges, passed over into Ireland, and there made conquest of the nowe Countrey, and then kingdom of Lympster, at which time it was verie populous and strong; which historie, our owne Chronicles doo witnes. And why should we be dismaide. more then were the Spaniardes, who have beene able within these fewe yeeres, to conquer, possesse and enjoy, so large a tracte at the earth, in the west Indies, as is betweene the two Tropicks of Cancer and Capricorne, not onely in the maine firme lande of America, which is 47. degrees in latitude from South to North, and doth contain 2820. English miles at the least, that the King of Spayne hath there, in actual possession, besides many goodly and rich Islands, as Hispaniola, now called Sa. Domingo, Cuba, Jamica, and divers other, which are bothe beautiful and full of treasure, not speaking anie whitt at all, how large the saide Lande is from East to West, which in some places is accounted to be 1500. English miles at the least, from East to West, betweene the one Sea and the other.

Or why should our Noble nation be dismaide, more then was Vasques Numes de Balboa, a private Gentleman of Spayne, who with the number of 70. Spaniardes at Tichiri, gave an overthrow unto that mightie King Chemacchus, having an Armie of an hundred Canoas and 5000. men, and the sayde Vasques Numes not long after, with his small number, did put to flight King Chiapes his whole Armie.[52]

Likewise Hernando Cortese, beeing also but a private Gentleman of Spayne, after his departure from the Islands of Cuba and Acusamill, and entring into the firme of America, had many most victorious and triumphant conquests,[53] as that at Cyntla, where beeing accompanied with lesse then 500. Spanish footemen, thirteene Horsemen, and six peeces of Ordenaunce onely he overthrewe 40000 Indians The same Cortese with his sayde number of Spaniardes, tooke prisoner that mightie Emperour Metezuma in his most cheefe and famous Cittie of Mexico, which at that instant had in it above the number of 500000. Indians at the least, and in short time after, obteyned not onelie the quiet possession of the saide Cittie, But also of his whole Empire.[54]

And in like manner in the Country of Peru, which the King of Spayne hath nowe in actual possession, Francisco Pysare, with the onelie ayde of Diego de Almagro, and Hernando Luche, beeing all three but private Gentlemen was the principall person that first attempted the discoverie and conquest of the large and rich Countrye of Peru, which through the ayde of the almighty, he brought to passe and atchived, in the Tambo of Casstamalcha, (which is a large place of ground, enclosed with walles) in which place he tooke the great and mightye Prince Attabalipa prisoner, amidest the number of 60000. Indians his subjectes, which were ever before that day accounted to bee a warlike kinde of people, which his great victory it pleased God to graunt unto him in the yeere of our Lorde 1533.[55] he not having in his company above the number of 210. Spaniardes, whereof there was not past 60. horsemen in all: After the taking of which Prince, Attabalipa, he offered unto Pyzare for his raunsome, to fill a great large Hall ful of Golde and Silver, and such Gold and Silver vessels as they then used, even as hie as a man might reache with his arme. And the sayd Prince caused the same Hall to be marked rounde about at the sayde

height, which raunsome Pyzara graunted to accept. And after when as thys mightie Prince had sent to his vassals and subjects to bring in Golde and Silver for the filling of the Hal, as aforesaid, as namelie to the Citties or Townes of Quito, Pacyacama and Cusco, as also to the Caloa of Lyma, in which Towne, as their owne writers doo affyrme, they founde a large and fayre house, all slated and covered with Golde: and when as the said Hal was not yet a quarter full, a mutenye arose amongst the Spaniardes, in which it was commonly given out, that the said Prince had politiquely offered this great raunsome under pretence to rayse a much more mightie power, whereby the Spaniardes should bee taken slayne, and overthrowne: whereuppon they grewe to this resolution, to put the sayd Prince to death, and to make particion of the gold and silver already brought in, which they presently put in execution. And comming to make perfect Inventory of the same, as well for the Emperor then King of Spayne, his fift parte as otherwise there was founde to be already brought in into the sayde Hall, the number of 132425. pounde weight of silver, and in golde the number of 1828125. pezos,[56] which was a ritches never before that nor since seene of any man together, of which there did appertaine to the Emperor for his fyft parte of Golde 365625. pezos, and for his fift parte of silver 26485. pound weight, and to every Horseman 8000. pezos of gold, and 67. pounde weight of silver. Every Soldier had 4550. pezos of golde, and 280. pounde weight of silver. Every Captain had, some 30000. some, 20000. pezos of golde and of silver, proportionally aunswerable to theyr degrees and calling, according to the rate agreed upon amongst them. Fraunces Pizare as their General, according to his degree and calling proportionally, had more then any of the rest, over and besides the Massie table of gold, which Attabalipa had in his Lyttier, which wayed, 25000. pezos of Golde: never was there before that day, Soldiers so riche in so small a time, and with so little danger. And in this journey for want of Iron, they did shoe theyr Horsses some with Gold, and some with silver. This is to be seene in the generall Historye of the west Indies, whereas the

---

52. Sidenote: "2. Decad. lib 5. fo. 77. of the West Indes, in English Canoas is a kinde of boate."
53. Sidenote: "3. Decad. lib. I. fol. 97. About the yeere of our Lord, 1511."
54. Sidenote: "Conquest of the West Indes fol. 43 and 45. in English."

55. Sidenote: "A mervelous victorie."
56. Sidenote: "A pezo is worth viis. vi d. English."

dooings of Pizare, and the conquest of the Peru is more at large set foorth.[57]

To this may I adde the great discoveries and conquestes, which the Princes of Portingall have made rounde about the West, the South, and the East partes of Africa, and also at Calicute and in the East Indies, and in America, at Brasilia and elswhere, in sundry Islandes, in fortefying, peopling, and planting all along the sayd Coastes, and Islandes, ever as they discovered, which beeing rightly wayed and considered, dooth minister just cause of incouragement to our countrymen, not to account it so harde and difficult athing for the subjectes of this noble Realme of Englande, to discover people, plant and possesse the like goodly lands and rich Countries not farre from us, but neere adjoyning and offering it selfe unto us (as is aforesayde) which have never yet heeretofore, beene in the actuall possession of any other Christian Prince, then the Princes of this realm All which, (as I thinke) shoulde not a little animate and encourage us, to looke out and to adventure abroade, understonding what large Countries and Islandes the Portingals with theyr small number have within these fewe yeeres discovered, peopled, and planted, some part wherof I have thought it not amisse, breefely in perticuler to name, bothe the Townes, Countries, and Islandes, so neere as I coulde upon the suddaine call them to remembraunce, for the rest I doo referre this Reader to the Histostories [sic], where more at large the same is to be seene. Fyrste they did winne and conquere from the Princes of Barbary the Island of Geysera and towne of Arzilla, not past 140 myle distaunt from their Metrapolitane and cheefe Cittie of Fesse: and after that they wunne also from the sayde Princes the Townes of Tangier, Seuta, Mazigam Azamore and Azaffie, all alongst the Sea Coostes. And in the yeere of our Lorde 1455. Alouis de Cademoste a gentleman Venetian, was he that first discovered for theyr use Cape Verd, with the Islandes adjoyning, of which hee then peopled and planted those of Bonavista and Santiago discovering also the River Senega, otherwise called Niger and Cape Rouge and Sere Leone, and in a fewe yeeres after they did discover the Coast of Ginea, and there peopled and built the Castell of

Myne: then discovered they further, to the countreys of Melegettes, Benyn, and Manicongo, with the Islandes of Principe, Anobon, Saint Mathew, and Saint Thomas, under the Equynoctial lyne, which they peopled and built in the sayd Island of Saint Thomas, the Haven Towne or Port of Panosan. After that, about the yeere of our Lorde 1494. one Bartholomew Dias was sent foorth, who was the first man that discovered and dobled that great and large Cape called Bon, Esperance, and passing the Curraunts that runne uppon the sayd coast, on the Southest parte of Africa, betweene the sayde maine Land and the Island of S. Lawrence, otherwise called of the auncients, Madagascar, he discovered to the harbor named the River of Infants. After that since the yeere of our Lorde God 1497. and before the full accomplishment of the yeere of Christ 1510 through the travails and discoveries of Vasques de Game, Peeter Alvares, Thomas Lopes, Andrew Corsale, John de Empolie, Peeter Sinter, Sancho Detoar, and that noble and woorthy Gentleman Alonso de Alburqueque, they did discover people and plant at Ceffala, beeing upon the East side of Affrica, in 20. degrees of latitude of the South pole, and direct West from the Islande of S. Lawrence, (at which Port of Ceffala,[58] divers doo afirme that King Salomon did fetch his golde) As also upon the sayd East side of Affrica, they did afterwarde discover people, and plant at Monzanbique, Quiloa Monbaza and Melinde 2. degrees of sotherly latitude, and so uppe to the streight of Bubell, Mandell at the entring of the Redde sea, all uppon the East coast, of Affrica, from whence they put off at the Cape of Garda Funi, and past the great gulfe of Arabia, or Indian Sea East to Sinus Persicus, and the Island of Ormus, and so passing the large and great River Indus, where he hath his fall into the mayne Occean, in 23. degrees, and di. under the tropick of Cancer, of Septentrionall latitude, they made theyr course againe directly towards the South, and began to discover people, and plant upon the west side of the hether India at Goa, Mangallor, Cananor, Calecute, and Chochyn, and the Island of Zeylam.

And heere I thinke good to remember to you, that after theyr planting upon this coaste, their forces grewe so great, that they were able to

57. Sidenote: "Se the History of the West Indies in French, the xiii. booke. fol. 138. some part whereof is translated into English."

58. Sidenote: "Ceffala is accounted to be the place where the Noble and wise King Salomon did fetch his golde."

compell all the Mores, the subjectes of the mighty Emperor of the Turks to pay tribute unto them, ever as they passed the Gulfe of Arabia, from the porte of Mecca in Arabia filice, where Mahomet lyeth buried, or any of the other portes of the sayd Land, ever as Cananor, and by theyr martiall manner of discipline, practised in those partes, the great and mightye Prince the Sophie Emperor of the Persians, and professed enemie to the Turck, came to the knowledge and use of the Caliver shotte, and to interlace and joine footemen with his Horsemen, sithence which time the Persians, have growen to that strength and force, that they have given many mighty and great overthrowes to the Turke, to the great quiet of all Christendome.

And from the Island of Zeylam aforesayde, they also discovered more East, in passing the Gulfe of Bengala, and so passed the notable and famous River of Ganges, where he hath his fall into the maine Occean, under the tropicke of Cancer, and to the Cape of Malaca, and unto the great and large Islands of Sumatro, Java major, Java minor, Mindano, Palobane, Celebes, Gilolo, Tydore, Mathin, Borneio, Machian, Terranette,[59] and all other the Islandes of Molucques and Spiceries, and so East, alongst the coasts of Cataia, to the Ports of China, Zayton, and Quinsay, and to the Islandes of Zipango, and Japan, situate in the East, in 37. degrees of septentrionall latitude and in 195. of longitude. Their noble and worthy discoveries heere also is not to be forgotten, that in the yeere of our Lorde 1501. that famous and woorthy gentleman Americus Vespusne, did discover people and plant to theyr use the Holdes and fortes which they have in Brasillia, of whom hee beeing but a private Gentleman, the whole Conntry or firme Land of the West Indies, is commonly called and knowne by the name of America.

I do greatlie doubt least I seeme overtedious in the recitall of the perticuler discoveries and conquestes of the East and west Indies, wherein I was the more bolde to urge the patience of the Reader, to the ende it might most manifestly and at large appeare, to all such as are not acquainted with the Histories, howe the King of Portirgall, whose Country for popularity and number of people, is scarce comparable to some three shires of Englande. And the King of Spayne likewise, whose naturall Countrey dooth not greatly abounde with people. Both which Princes, by meanes of theyr discoveries, within lesse then 90. yeeres past, have as it appeareth, both mightely and mervailouslie enlarged theyr territories and dominions through theyr owne industrie, by the assistance of the omnipotent, whose ayde we shall not neede to doubt, seeing the cause and quarrell which we take in hand tendeth to his honour and glory, by the enlargement of the Christian fayth.

To conclude, since by christian duety we stand bounde cheefely to further all such acts as doo tende to the encreasing the true flocke of Christ, by reducing into the right way those loste sheepe which are yet astray. And that wee shall therein followe the example of our right vertuous predicessors of renowmed memory, and leave unto our posteritie, a device memoriall of so godly an enterprise. Let us I say for the considerations alledged, enter into judgement with ourselves, whether this action may belong to us or no. The rather for that this voyage through the mighty assistaunce of the omnipotent God, shal take our desired effect (whereof there is no just cause of doubt) Then shall her Majesties dominions be enlarged, her highnes auncient titles justly confyrmed, all odious ydlenes from this our Realme utterly banished. Divers decayed Townes repayred, and many poore and needy persons relieved, and estates of such as nowe live in want shalbe embettered. The ignorant and barbarous Idolaters taught to knowe Christ. The innocent defended from their bloodie tyrannicall neighbours. The diabolicall custome of sacrifycing humaine Creatures abolished.

All which (no man doubteth) are thinges gratefull in the sight of our Saviour, and tending to the honour and glory of the Trinitie: Be of good cheere therefore, for he that can not erre hath sayd: That before the ende of the world, his word shall bee preached to all nations. Which good worke, I trust is reserved for our Nation to accomplish in these partes: Wherefore my deere Countrimen, be not dismayed, for the power of God is nothing diminished, nor the love that he hath to the preaching and planting of the Gospell any whitt abated. Shall we then doubt he will be lesse ready, most mightily and miraculously to

---

59. Sidenote: "These are the furthest parts of the world from Englande. At these Islands hath Sir Fraunces Drake beene, wher the fame of the Qu. most excellent Majestie was renowned."

assist our Nation in this quarrel, which is cheefely and principally undertaken for the enlargement of the christian fayth abroad, and the banishment of ydlenes at home, then he was to Columnus, Vasques Numes, Hernando Cortese, and Fraunces Pyzare in the west: and Vasques de Game, Peter Alvares, and Alonso de Alburqueque in the East.

Let us therefore with cheerfull mindes and couragious hearts, give the attempt, and leave the sequell to almightye God, for if he be on our part, what forceth it who be against us. Thus leaving the correction and reformation unto the gentle Reader, whatsoever is in this Treatise too much or too little, or otherwise unperfect, I take leave and so ende.

The Contentes of the Articles of Assuraunce, betweene the Principall assignes of Sir Humfrey Gilbert Knight, and the foure sortes of adventurers, with them in the voyage for the Westerne Discoveries.

Assocyates.
Assystants.
Adventurers in the first degree.
Adventurers in the second degree.
which be such as adventure.
C. li.
L. li.
XX. v. li.
Xii. li. x. s.

The ratyficatyon of former Adventurers.

Every person which hath adventured with Sir Humfrey Gilbert Knight, or with any principall assigne from him, shall have and enjoy all such Lands, Liberties, Freedomes, Priveleges and commodities as to any of them hath beene graunted, or covenaunted by the said Sir Humfrey, or by any principall assigne, in writing to bee shewed under his or theyr handes and seales.

Rewards to such as have adventured in person in the last voyage. Assocyats.

And every person which hath adventured himselfe in the last voyage, and continued in the same, until such time as the admirall of the sayd voyage was lost, and will adventure himselfe in this next voeage, shall in recompence have his rate doubled.

1. Everie person, that shall adventure in this next voyage, in money or commodityes, the some

of one hundreth poundes and receyved by the treasurer, or agent to be kept in a Storehouse, provided for that purpose: shal beare the name of an associate, he, his heires and fower of his servaunts serving him seven yeeres, to have free libertie to trade and trafique in the said Countries. And shall have a just portion accordyng to the quantity of his adventure, of all commodities gotten and retourned into England, by any the Vessels which shall be set forth by the sayde principall assigne, before the twenteth of March next, in Anno 1583.

2. He shall have to him and his heyres for ever, sixteene thousand acres of Land, there to bee peopled and manured at his pleasure, holding the same in socage tenner by Fealtie onely, with aucthoritie to keepe Court Leete, and Court Barron uppon the same, at his pleasure, with as great roialties in as large and ample maner as any Associate there, or other Subject in this Realme now enjoyeth any landes in England.

3. Hee to bee chosen for one of the cheefest persons for making of Lawes there. And shall be free from all arrestes, tortures, and execution by Marshall Lawe.

4. Yeelding and paying yeerely, tenne shillinges for everye thousand acres after the same shall bee possessed and occupied one whole yeere and to the Queenes majestie the fift part of Golde and Sylver Ower, which shall bee cleerely gotten, one other fift part of Golde, Sylver, Ower, Pearle and Precious stones, to Sir Humfrey Gylbert and his heires, and to the principall assigne the like fift part, and also one fift part of Christall to the said principal assigne to be found and clearely gotten upon the same sixteene thousand acres.

5. There shalbe levied within three yeeres after the sayd Land shalbe inhabited, for every acre manured on halfepeny yeerely for the building of Fortes, Townes, Churches Shippes, maintenaunce of learning and Soldiers, and releeving of maimed persons etc., to bee bestowed and imployed at the discretion of the principall Assigne and his heyres, the Lieftenaunt and Associate, there for the time beeing.

Assystants.

1. Every person adventuring as aforesayde the some of fifty poundes, shall beare the name of an Assistant he and his heires males, and three of his servauntes serving him seven yeeres, to have

free liberty to trade, as in the first Article of Associates.

2. He shal have to him and his heires for ever eight thousand acres of Lande, to bee peopled and manured as aforesayd, holding the same as aforesayd, with free liberty to keepe Court Leete, and courte Baron at his pleasure, and to take the commodities thereunto belonging.

3. Yeelding and paying as in the fourth Article of the Associates.

4. To be levied one halfpeny yeerelie for everie acre, as in the fift Article of the Associates.

Adventurers in the first degree.

1. Every person adventuring as aforesaid; the some of xxv. pound shalbe an adventurer of the first degree he and his heires males, and two of his servauntes, serving him seaven yeeres, to be free of trade etc. as in the first Article of the Associates.

2. He shall have to him and his heires for ever, four thousand acres of Lande, to be peopled and manured as aforesaide, holding the same as aforesaid, with free liberty to keepe Court Barron at his pleasure, and to take the commodities thereunto belonging.

3. Yeelding and paying as aforesaid, and over and above to the principall assigne the tenth part of Copper.

4. To be levied one halfpeny yeerely as aforesaid.

Adventurers in the second degree.

1. Every person adventuring, as aforesaid of some of xii. pound x. shillings, shalbe an adventurer of the second degree, hee and his heires males and one of his servauntes servinge him seven yeeres, to be free of trade, etc. as in the first article of the associates.

2. He shall have to him and his heires for ever two thousand acres of land, to bee peopled and manured as aforesaid, holding the same as aforesaid.

3. Yeelding and paying as aforesaid, in the third article of the adventurers of the first degree.

4. To be levied one halfpeny yeerelie as aforesaid.

Generall.

The generall and admirall in this voyage, shall have in all thinges as an associate, with double quantity of Land, the Leiftenaunt and Viceadmirall in quantity of Land as an associate, and in priviledges as an assistant.

Captains and Maysters.

Every Captaine, and Maister of a ship in the said voyage, shall have as an assistant.

Every Ma. his mate, Ma. Carpenter and Ma. Gonner, and quarter Ma shall have in Land as an assistant, and in priviledges as an adventurer of the first degree.

Every skilfull man in trying of minerall matters, and every apoticarie skilful in choise of drugges, shall have in Land as an assistant, and in priviledges as an adventurer of the first degree.

Every Gunners and Carpenters mates, Steward, Surgion, Boteswane, Purser, Trumpeter and other Officer and necessarie artificer, having their necessary instrumentes and tooles, shall have according to the rate of Landes as an adventurer of the first degree, and in previledges as an adventurer of the second degree.

Soldiours.

Every Soldiour and Mariner shall have in all thinges as an adventurer of the second degree.

Every Person that shall winter and remaine in those Countries, one whole yeere shall have double the quantity of Land, as by this rate hee ought to have, if hee did not stay one yeere as aforesaid.

These rewardes to be extended to those persons only, which shall travell in the sayd voyage for, their thirds or shares uppon their owne adventures without wages and not to any others.

Every person, who shalbe willing to adventure in commodities, as aforesaid under the some of xii. pound x. shillinges shall have freedome of trad, land and liberties rated, according to the proporcion of his adventure.

Every person which hath, or shall adventure in this voyage in money or commodities as aforesaid, and will also adventure his person in this next voyage, shall have in respect of his person according to the rate aforesaid, over and above his adventure.

Chapter Forty-four
Two Contributions by Richard Hakluyt
the Elder to North American Colonizing
Objectives, 1584–1585

RICHARD HAKLUYT the elder may well have been consulted by Gilbert in 1583. Although we have no specific evidence to this effect, a set of promotion considerations he formulated ("Inducements" I, Document 359) are found in a manuscript along with a copy of David Ingram's "True discourse" (in B. L., Sloane MS 1447, fols. 12–15v., first printed in P. C. G. Weston, *Documents Connected with the History of South Carolina* [1856], and reprinted in E. G. R. Taylor, *The Original Writings and Correspondence of the Two Richard Hakluyts*, 2 vols. [London, Hakluyt Society, 1935].) It may be that they were composed early in 1584 (see D. B. Quinn, *Roanoke voyages*, I, 5) when Walter Ralegh was sending out his first expedition. They are designed for lands between 34° and 36°N although they also applied farther north. The Inducements are primarily promises of profitable employment for colonists through a wide range of means of exploiting the land, mainly by agriculture and use of native peoples. A profusion of objectives is set out with productive tasks to be assigned specifically to settlers. He clearly expected a great deal of North America, and his inducements were therefore prolific. It may, however, belong to the period between September, 1584, and March, 1585, with somewhat less likelihood. The second set of promotion proposals, also called "Inducements" (hence "Inducements" II), was almost certainly prepared in the latter period. The heading ("Inducements to the liking of the voyage intended towards Virginia in 40. and 42. degrees of latitude, written 1585, by Mr. Richard Hakluyt the elder") was added to fit in with the objectives of the editors of John Brereton's *A briefe and true relation of the discoverie of the north part of Virginia* (1602), and its limitation to these latitudes is not implicit in the text itself, although it suited the objectives of the 1602 collection (360). It does, however, state that the expedition envisaged was to be directed toward 40°N. Very similar to "Inducements" I, it argued more fully the case for assuring that the economic resources and potentialities of eastern North America were what was claimed. The main difference is that, instead of concentrating on the employment that would be found for settlers, it was concerned with what sort of men should be selected to perform tasks ("Sorts of men which are to be passed in this voyage"), so that it is clearly concerned with the planning stages of the 1585 Virginia voyage. It is, in this respect, very close to the final section of Richard Hakluyt the younger's "Particuler discourse" and so may reflect some cooperation between the cousins, probably during the period in 1584 when the younger man was in England. The two sets of "Inducements" indicate continuing, even growing optimism about North American resources, together with an approach to the practical selection of colonists in the context of an expedition designed not for reconnaissance but settlement.

359. "Inducements to the lykinge of the voyadge intended to that parte of America which lyethe betwene 34. and 36. degree."

1. The Countrye wherunto we dyrecte our voyadge lyinge as aforesaid conteynethe the Clymates of Barbary, Spayne, Portingale, Fraunce, Germany, Englande, Danske, Norway and Moscovia.

2. And we maye make our voyadge to and from thence in three monethes and soe make 2. or 3. retornes yearlie, a matter in trade of greate moment.

3. The Soyle is moste exelente and fruitfull garnished with woodes of dyvers sortes of trees with many lardge and deepe Ryvers replenished with great plentye of Beastes, fowle, fyshe, fruictes, and mynes of dyvars kyndes, and all other Comodyties for the lyef of men.

4. The people be well proportyoned in there Lymbes, well favored, gentle, of a mylde and tractable disposition, apte to submytte them selves to good government, and ready to imbrace the christian faythe.

5. By inhabyting of Countreyes with Englishe people of dyvers Comodyties will ensue: as:

Firste the glorye of god by plantinge of christian Religion among the Gentilles there.

Item the inlarged domynions, power, Revenewes, and honnor of the Quenes moste exelent majestie her heires and successours.

Item the increase of Shippinge and mariners and the mayntenance of much navigacion which is the strengthe of the Realme.

Item the poore and Idle persons which nowe are ether burdensome or hurtefull to this Realme at home maye hereby become profytable members by ymployinge them ether at home. viz.

Item ymployinge them in those Countryes in mynes of goulde, sylver, copper etc.

In dregginge of Pearle etc.

In plantinge of sugar canes in the moste southerlie partes.

In mayntenance and increasinge of silke wormes for sylke and dressinge of the same.

In gatheringe of Cotton whereof there is great store.

In Tyllinge of the Soyle there for grayne etc.

In plantinge of Vynes for wyne.

Ollives for oyle.

Trees for orrenges, leomandes, Almondes, fygge and other fruictes.

In sowinge oade and madder for dyvers.

Hempe and flaxe for Clothes Cordage etc.

In dressinge of rawe hydes of dyvers kindes of Beastes.

In makinge of Salte as in Rochell or Bayion.

In killinge the whale, wherpole, seale, and porpose etc. for Trayne oyle.

Fyshinge saltinge and dryinge Lynge Codd Salmon etc.

In makinge of Ropes and other Cordages.

In makinge and gatheringe Honye, waxe, Pitche, Tarre, Rosen, and Turpentyne.

In hewinge and shapinge of Stone as marble, gete, Christall, freestone etc. which wilbe good Balest for our Shippes homewardes and after serve for noble buildinges.

In felling of Timber, hewinge and sawinge the same for buildinge of howses and shippes etc.

In makinge of Caske owers and all other manner of staves.

In buildinge of Churches Townes fortes etc.

In powdringe and barellinge of fyshe and fowles which wilbe noble provytion for sea and lande.

In dryinge sortinge and packinge of feathers whereof there may be had great quantytie.

6. Soe as by reason of the varyable Climates in the saide Countryes and excellent Soyle with the industrye aforesaide we may retorne from thence all the Comodyties which we nowe receave from Barbarye, Spayne, Portugale, Italy, Danske, Norway and Muscovia better cheape than nowe we have them and not inrytche our doubtfull frendes and infydelles as nowe by our ordynary trade we doe.

7. Our ladinge and unladynge there wilbe boathe easye and cheape, by reson the Ryvars be soe deepe.

8. The passage to and froe is nether by the Coaste of Fraunce, nor throughe the streighte of Juberaltar, nor by the Streighte of Denmarke. Soe as we shall not be in daunger of the frencheman, nor the Spanyarde, nor Turke, nor of any State of Italye, nor of the kinge of Denmarke, nor any other Prince or Potentate in the northe nor in the northe Easte partes of the worlde.

9. In this voyadge we are not to pass the burnt lyne nor to passe the frosen Seas but in a temperate Clymate at all tymes of the yeare, and yt requireth not as longe voyadges doethe the

takinge in of water in dyvers places by reson yt maye be sayled in v or vi weekes, whereby the merchaunt maye make yearly 2. or 3. retornes.

10. In this trade by the waye in passage to and froe, we have in Tempestes and other happes all the portes of Ireland to our ayde and noe nearer Coaste of any Enimye.

11. By this ordinarye trade we may injoye the Enimyes to Ireland and succoure the Queenes Ma^tes frendes there and in shoarte tyme we maye from these Coastes yealde them whatsoever Comodyties they nowe receave from Spayne, and so the Spanyard shall wante the ordynary victualles that they receave yearlie from thence wherby they cannot contynewe trade nor fall so aptly to practize against this government as nowe by there trade thither they maye and doe.

12. In tradinge to those Countreyes we shall not neade (for to feare the Spanishe Inquisition) to throwe out our Bibles and prayer bookes into the Seas before arryvall nor yet take suche horrible othes offred by the Spanishe searchers to such daylie wilfull and highe offence of the Almightye as daylye we doe in followinge our Trades into Spayne.

13. In this voyadge having settled our factorye in some convenyent place fortyfyed by nature or arte, our Shippes men and goodes shall not be subjecte to the daunger of our Auncyent Enemyes or doubtfull ffrendes as in other forren places of usuall trade they have bynne and yet are, in which respecte we shalbe in more safetye and quiett then before.

14. Yf our nacion doe not make any Conqueste there but onlye use trafique and chaunge of Comodyties by meane the Countrye is not so mightie a nacion as ether ffraunce or Spayne, they shall not dare to offer us any anoye but suche as we maye easylie revenge with sufficient Chastisement to the unarmed people there.

15. Yf they will not suffer us to have any Comodyties of theres without Conqueste which doethe require long tyme, yet maye we maynteyn our firste voyadges by the Sea fyshinge on the Coastes there, and by retorne of that Comodyties the Chardges shalbe defrayed which is a matter of consyderacion in enterprises of Chardge.

16. Yf we fynde any kinges readye to defende their Tirratoryes by warre and the Countrye populous desieringe to expell us that seeke but juste and lawfull Traffique, then by reason the Ryvers be lardge and deepe and we lordes of navigacion, and they without shippinge, we armed and they naked, and at continuall warres one with another, we maye by the ayde of those Ryvars joyne with this kinge here or with that kinge there at our pleasure and soe with a fewe men be revenged of any wronge offered by them and consequentlie maye yf we will conquere fortefye and plante in soyles moste sweete, most pleasaunte, moste fertill and strounge. And in the ende to bringe them all in subjection or scyvillitie for yt is well knowen they have bynne contented to submytte them selves and all that which they possesse to suche as hathe defended them againste there Enemyes speciallie againste the caniballes.

17. From the northe partes of these Countreyes there is great hope to sayle into the Southe Sea, whereby unspeakable honnor and benyfitt maye aryse by the trades to ensue aswell in Caytaia the Islandes of Malucos and other landes and Islandes in thother Hemispherie for Spice, drugges, goulde, sylver, pearle, pretious stones and other ritche marchaundizes for the which we maye have large and ample vente not only of our wolleyn Clothes of Englande but also of the labor of our poore people at home by sale of Hattes, Cappes, and a thousande kynde of other wrought ware that in tyme may be brought in use amounge the people of those Countryes to the great relief of the multitude of our pore people, and to the wounderfull inrytchinge of this Realme, and in tyme such league and entercourse maye aryse, betwene our Staplynge Seate there and all the portes of Ameryca that incredible thinges may followe tendinge to the ympeachment of our myghtye Enimyes and to the comon good of all the Domynions of this noble government.

18. And to conclude by reason of the great increase of wolles in Spayne the like in the weste Indyes and the great ymployment of the same into Cloathe in both those places with the great decaye of our usuall Trades in all places in Europe at this tyme, And the wounderfull increase of our people here in Englande and a great nomber of them voyde of any good trade or ymployement to gete their lyvinge maye be a sufficient cause to move not onlye the marchaunts and Clothiers but alsoe all other sortes and degrees of our nacion to seeke newe dyscovereyes of peopled regions for

vente of our Idle people, otherwyse in shourte tyme many mischeifs maye ensue.

360. "Inducements to the Liking of the Voyage intended towards Virginia in 40. and 42. degrees."

1. The glory of God by planting of religion among those infidels.

2. The increase of the force of the Christians.

3. The possibilitie of the inlarging of the dominions of the Queenes most excellent Maiestie, and consequently of her honour, revenues, and of her power by this enterprise.

4. An ample vent in time to come of the Woollen clothes of England, especially those of the coursest sorts, to the maintenance of our poore, that els sterve or become burdensome to the realme: and vent also of sundry our commodities upon the tract of that firme land, and possibly in other regions from the Northerne side of that maine.

5. A great possibilitie of further discoveries of other regions from the North part of the same land by sea, and of unspeakable honor and benefit that may rise upon the same, by the trades to ensue in Iapan, China, and Cathay, &c.

6. By returne thence, this realme shall receive (by reason of the situation of the climate, and by reason of the excellent soile) Oade, Oile, Wines, Hops, Salt, and most or all the commodities that we receive from the best parts of Europe, and we shall receive the same better cheape, than now we receive them, as we may use the matter.

7. Receiving the same thence, the navie, the humane strength of this realme, our merchants and their goods shal not be subiect to arrest of ancient enemies & doubtfull friends, as of late yeeres they have beene.

8. If our nation do not make any conquest there, but only use trafficke and change of commodities, yet by meane the countrey is not very mightie, but divided into pety kingdoms, they shall not dare to offer us any great annoy, but such as we may easily revenge with sufficient chastisement to the unarmed people there.

9. Whatsoever commodities we receive by the Steelyard merchants, or by our owne merchants from Eastland, be it Flaxe, Hempe, Pitch, Tarre, Masts, Clap-boord, Wainscot, or such like; the like good may we receive from the North and Northeast part of that countrey neere unto Cape Briton, in returne for our course Woollen clothes, Flanels and Rugges fit for those colder regions.

10. The passage to and fro, is thorow the maine Ocean sea, so as we are not in danger of any enemies coast.

11. In the voyage, we are not to crosse the burnt Zone, nor to passe thorow frozen seas encombred with ice and fogs, but in temperate climate at all times of the yeere: and it requireth not, as the East Indie voiage doth, the taking in of water in divers places, by reason that it is to be sailed in five or six weeks: and by the shortnesse, the merchant may yeerely make two returnes (a factory once being erected there) a matter in trade of great moment.

12. In this trade by the way in our passe to and fro, we have in tempests and other haps, all the ports of Ireland to our aid, and no neere coast of any enemy.

13. By this ordinary trade we may annoy the enemies to Ireland, and succour the Queenes Maiesties friends there, and in time we may from Virginia yeeld them whatsoever commoditie they now receive from the Spaniard; and so the Spaniards shall want the ordinary victual that heertofore they received yeerely from thence, and so they shall not continue trade, nor fall so aptly in practise against this government, as now by their trade thither they may.

14. We shall, as it is thought, enioy in this voyage, either some small Islands to settle on, or some one place or other on the firme land to fortifie for the saftie of our ships, our men, and our goods, the like whereof we have not in any forren place of our trafficke, in which respect we may be in degree of more safetie, and more quiet.

15. The great plentie of Buffe hides, and of many other sundry kinds of hides there now presently to be had, the trade of Whale and Seale fishing, and of divers other fishings in the great rivers, great bayes, and seas there, shall presently defray the charge in good part or in all of the first enterprise, and so we shall be in better case than our men were in Russia, where many yeeres were spent, and great summes of money consumed, before gaine was found.

16. The great broad rivers of that maine that we are to enter into so many leagues navigable or

portable into the maine land, lying so long a tract with so excellent and so fertile a soile on both sides, doe seeme to promise all things that the life of man doth require, and whatsoever men may wish, that are to plant upon the same, or to trafficke in the same.

17. And whatsoever notable commoditie the soile within or without doth yeeld in so long a tract that is to be carried out from thence to England, the same rivers so great and deepe, do yeeld no small benefit for the sure, safe, easie and cheape cariage of the same to shipboord, be it of great bulke or of great weight.

18. And in like sort whatsoever commoditie of England the Inland people there shall need, the same rivers doe worke the like effect in benefit for the incariage of the same, aptly, easily, and cheaply.

19. If we finde the countrey populous, and desirous to expel us, and iniuriously to offend us, that seeke but iust and lawfull trafficke, then by reason that we are lords of navigation, and they not so, we are the better able to defend our selves by reason of those great rivers, & to annoy them in many places.

20. Where there be many petie kings or lords planted on the rivers sides, and by all likelihood mainteine the frontiers of their severall territories by warres, we may by the aide of this river ioine with this king heere, or with that king there, at our pleasure, and may so with a few men be revenged of any wrong offered by any of them; or may, if we will proceed with extremitie, conquer, fortifie, and plant in soiles most sweet, most pleasant, most strong, and most fertile, and in the end bring them all in subiection and to civilitie.

21. The knowen abundance of Fresh fish in the rivers, and the knowen plentie of Fish on the sea coast there, may assure us of sufficient victuall in spight of the people, if we will use salt and industrie.

22. The knowen plentie and varietie of Flesh, of divers kinds of beasts at land there, may seeme to say to us, that we may cheaply victuall our navies to England for our returnes, which benefit every where is not found of merchants.

23. The practise of the people of the East Indies, when the Portugals came thither first, was to cut from the Portugals their lading of Spice: and heereby they thought to overthrow their purposed trade. If these people shall practise the

like, by not suffering us to have any commoditie of theirs without conquest, (which requireth some time) yet may we mainteine our first voyage thither, till our purpose come to effect, by the sea-fishing on the coasts there, and by dragging for pearles, which are said to be on those parts; and by returne of those commodities, the charges in part shall be defraied: which is a matter of consideration in enterprises of charge.

24. If this realme shall abound too too much with youth, in the mines there of Golde, (as that of Chisca and Saguenay) of Silver, Copper, Yron, &c. may be an imployment to the benefit of this realme; in tilling of the rich soile there for graine, and in planting of Vines there for Wine; or dressing of those Vines which grow there naturally in great abundance, Olives for Oile; Orenge trees, Limons, Figs and Almonds for fruit; Oad, Saffron, and Madder for Diers; Hoppes for Brewers; Hempe, Flaxe; and in many such other things, by imploiment of the soile, our people void of sufficient trades, may be honestly imploied, that els may become hurtfull at home.

25. The navigating of the seas in the voyage, and of the great rivers there, will breed many Mariners for service, and mainteine much navigation.

26. The number of raw Hides there of divers kindes of beasts, if we shall possesse some Island there, or settle on the firme, may presently imploy many of our idle people in divers severall dressings of the same, and so we may returne them to the people that can not dresse them so well; or into this realme, where the same are good merchandize; or to Flanders, &c. which present gaine at the first, raiseth great incouragement presently to the enterprise.

27. Since great waste Woods be there, of Oake, Cedar, Pine, Wall-nuts, and sundry other sorts, many of our waste people may be imploied in making of Ships, Hoies, Busses and Boats; and in making of Rozen, Pitch and Tarre, the trees naturall for the same, being certeinly knowen to be neere Cape Briton and the Bay of Menan, and in many other places there about.

28. If mines of white or gray marble, Jet, or other rich stone be found there, our idle people may be imploied in the mines of the same, and in preparing the same to shape, and so shaped, they may be caried into this realme as good balast for our ships, and after serve for noble buildings.

29. Sugar-canes may be planted aswell as they are now in the South of Spaine, and besides the imploiment of our idle people, we may receive the commodity cheaper, and not inrich infidels or our doubtful friends, of whom now we receive that commoditie.

30. The daily great increase of Woolles in Spaine, and the like in the West Indies, and the great imploiment of the same into Cloth in both places, may moove us to endevour, for vent of our Cloth, new discoveries of peopled regions, where hope of sale may arise; otherwise in short time many inconveniences may possibly ensue.

31. This land that we purpose to direct our course to, lying in part in the 40 degree of latitude, being in like heat as Lisbone in Portugall doth, and in the more Southerly part as the most Southerly coast of Spaine doth, may by our diligence yeeld unto us besides Wines and Oiles and Sugars, Orenges, Limons, Figs, Resings, Almonds, Pomegranates, Rice, Raw-silks such as come from Granada, and divers commodities for Diers, as Anile and Cochenillio, and sundry other colours and materials. Moreover, we shall not onely receive many precious commodities besides from thence, but also shal in time finde ample vent of the labour of our poore people at home, by sale of Hats, Bonets, Knives, Fish-hooks, Copper kettles, Beads, Looking-glasses, Bugles, & a thousand kinds of other wrought wares, that in short time may be brought in use among the people of that countrey, to the great reliefe of the multitude of our poore people, and to the woonderfull enriching of this realme. And in time, such league & entercourse may arise betweene our Stapling seats there, and other ports of our Northern America, and of the Islands of the same, that incredible things, and by few as yet dreamed of, may speedily follow, tending to the impeachment of our mightie enemies, and to the common good of this noble government.

The ends of this voyage are these:
1. To plant Christian religion.
2. To trafficke.
3. To conquer.
Or, to doe all three.

To plant Christian religion without conquest, will bee hard. Trafficke easily followeth conquest: conquest is not easie. Trafficke without conquest seemeth possible, and not uneasie. What is to be done, is the question.

If the people be content to live naked, and to content themselves with few things of meere necessity, then trafficke is not. So then in vaine seemeth our voyage, unless this nature may be altered, as by conquest and other good meanes it may be, but not on a sudden. The like whereof appeared in the East Indies, upon the Portugals seating there.

If the people in the Inland be clothed, and desire to live in the abundance of all such things as Europe doth, and have at home all the same in plentie, yet we can not have trafficke with them, by meane they want not any thing that we can yeeld them.

Admit that they have desire to your commodities, and as yet have neither Golde, Silver, Copper, Iron, nor sufficient quantitie of other present commoditie to mainteine the yeerely trade: What is then to be done?

The soile and climate first is to be considered, and you are with Argus eies to see what commoditie by industrie of man you are able to make it to yeeld, that England doth want or doth desire: as for the purpose, if you can make it to yeeld good Wine, or good Oile, as it is like you may by the climat, (where wilde Vines of sundry sorts doe naturally grow already in great abundance) then your trade may be mainteined.[1] But admit the soile were in our disposition (as yet it is not) in what time may this be brought about?

For Wine this is to be affirmed, that first the soile lying in 36 or 37 degrees in the temperature of South Spaine, in setting your Vine-plants this yeere, you may have Wine within three yeeres. And it may be that the wilde Vines growing there already, by orderly pruning and dressing at your first arrivall, may come to profit in shorter time.

And planting your Olive trees this yeere, you may have Oile within three yeeres.

And if the sea shores be flat, and fit for receipt of salt water, and for Salt making, without any annoy of neere freshes, then the trade of Salt onely may mainteine a yeerely navigation (as our men now trade to the isle of Maio, and the Hollanders to Terra Firma neere the West end of the isle of Margarita.)

But how the naturall people of the countrey may be made skilfull to plant Vines, and to know the use, or to set Olive trees, and to know the

---

1. Sidenote: "Meanes to breed a speedie trade."

making of Oile, and withall to use both the trades, that is a matter of small consideration: but to conquer a countrey or province in climate & soile of Italie, Spaine, or the Islands from whence we receive our Wines & Oiles, and to man it, to plant it, and to keepe it, and to continue the making of Wines and Oiles able to serve England, were a matter of great importance both in respect of the saving at home of our great treasure now yeerely going away, and in respect of the annoyance thereby growing to our enemies. The like consideration would be had, touching a place for the making of Salt, of temperature like those of France, not too colde, as the Salts of the Northern regions be; nor too too firy, as those be that be made more Southerly than France. In regard whereof, many circumstances are to be considered; and principally, by what meane the people of those parties may be drawn by all courtesie into love with our nation; that we become not hatefull unto them, as the Spaniard is in Italie and in the West Indies, and elswhere, by their maner of usage: for a gentle course without crueltie and tyrannie best answereth the profession of a Christian,[2] best planteth Christian religion; maketh our seating most void of blood, most profitable in trade of merchandise, most firme and stable, and least subiect to remoove by practise of enemies. But that we may in seating there, not be subiect wholly to the malice of enemies, and may be more able to preserve our bodies, ships, and goods in more safetie, and to be knowen to be more able to scourge the people there, civill or savage, than willing to offer any violence. And for the more quiet exercise of our manurance of the soiles where we shall seat, and of our manuall occupations, it is to be wished that some ancient captaines of milde disposition and great iudgement be sent thither with men most skilfull in the arte of fortification; and that direction be taken that the mouthes of great rivers, and the Islands in the same (as things of great moment) be taken, manned, and fortified; and that havens be cut out for safetie of the Navie, that we may be lords of the gates and entries, to goe out and come in at pleasure, and to lie in safetie, and be able to command and to controle all within, and to force all forren navigation to lie out in open rode subiect to all weathers, to be dispersed by tempests and

flawes, if the force within be not able to give them the encounter abroad.

1. The Red Muscadell grape, that bishop Grindall procured out of Germanie; the great White Muscadell; the Yellow grape: the cuts of these were woont yeerely to be set at Fulham; and after one yeeres rooting to be given by the bishop, and to be sold by his gardener. These presently provided, and placed in earth, and many of these so rooted, with store of cuts unrooted besides, placed in tubbes of earth shipped at the next voyage, to be planted in Virginia, may begin Vineyards, and bring Wines out of hand.

2. Provision great of wilde Olive trees may be made out of this citie so then to be caried, to encrease great store of stocks to graffe the best Olive on: and Virginia standing in the same degree that The Shroffe the Olive place doth in Spaine, we may win that merchandise, graffing the wilde.

3. Sugar-canes, if you can not procure them from the Spanish Islands, yet may you by your Barberie merchants procure them.

4. There is an herbe in Persia, whereof Anile is made, and it is also in Barbarie: to procure that by seed or root, were of importance for a trade of merchandise for our clothing countrey.

5. Oad by the seeds you may have; for you may have hundreds of bushels in England, as it is multiplied: and having soile and labor in Virginia cheape, and the Oad in great value, lying in small roome, it will be a trade of great gaine to this clothing realme: and the thing can not be destroyed by Salvages. The roots of this you may have in plenty and number comming in the trade: so this may grow in trade within a yeere ready for the merchant.

6. Figge trees of many good kinds may be had hence in barrell, if now presently they be provided; and they in that climat will yeeld noble fruit, and feed your people presently, and will be brought in frailes home as merchandise, or in barrell, as Resings also may be.

7. Sawed boords of Sassafras and Cedar, to be turned into small boxes for ladies and gentlewomen, would become a present trade.

8. To the infinite naturall increase of Hogs, to adde a device how the same may be fed by roots, acornes, &c. without spoiling your corne, would be of great effect to feed the multitude continually imployed in labour: and the same cheaply bred

2. Sidenote: "A gentle course best to be held."

and salted, and barrelled there and brought home, will be well solde for a good merchandise; and the barrels after, will serve for our home Herring-fishing; and so you sell your woods and the labour of your cooper.

9. Receiving the salvage women and their children of both sexes by courtesie into your protection, and imploying the English women and the others in making of Linnen, you shal raise a woonderfull trade of benefit, both to carie into England and also into the Islands, and into the maine of the West Indies, victuall and labour being so cheape there.

10. The trade of making cables and cordage there, will be of great importance, in respect of a cheape maintenance of the Navie that shall passe to and fro; and in respect of such Navie as may in those parties be used for the venting of the commodities of England to be brought thither. And Powldavies, &c. made for sailes of the poore Salvages, yeeld to the Navie a great helpe, and a great gaine in the trafficke.

But if seeking revenge on every iniurie of the Salvages we seeke blood & raise war, our Vines, our Olives, our Figge trees, our Sugar-canes, our Orenges and Limons, Corne, Cattell, &c. will be destroyed, and trade of merchandise in all things overthrowen; and so the English nation there planted and to be planted, shalbe rooted out with sword and hunger.

Sorts of men which are to be passed in this voyage

1. Men skilfull in all Minerall causes.
2. Men skilfull in all kinde of drugges.
3. Fishermen, to consider of the sea fishings there on the coasts, to be reduced to trade hereafter: and others for the fresh water fishings.
4. Salt-makers, to view the coast, and to make triall how rich the sea-water there is, to advise for the trade.
5. Husbandmen, to view the soile, to resolve for tillage in all sorts.
6. Vineyard-men bred, to see how the soile may serve for the planting of Vines.
7. Men bred in the Shroffe in South Spaine, for discerning how Olive trees may be planted there.
8. Others, for planting of Orenge trees, Figge trees, Limon trees, and Almond trees; for iudging how the soile may serve for the same.
9. Gardeners, to proove the severall soiles of the Islands, and of our setling places, to see how the same may serve for all herbs and roots for our victualling; since by rough seas sometimes we may want fish, and since we may want flesh to victuall us, by the malice of the naturall people there: and gardeners for planting of our common trees of fruit, as Peares, Apples, Plummes, Peaches, Medlers, Apricoes, Quinces for conserves, &c.
10. Lime-makers, to make lime for buildings.
11. Masons, Carpenters, &c. for buildings there.
12. Bricke-makers and Tile-makers.
13. Men cunning in the art of fortification, that may chuse out places strong by nature to be fortified, and that can plot out and direct workemen.
14. Choise Spade-men, to trench cunningly, and to raise bulwarks and rampiers of earth for defence and offence.
15. Spade-makers, that may, out of the Woods there, make spades like those of Devonshire, and of other sorts, and shovels from time to time for common use.
16. Smithes, to forge the yrons of the shovels and spades, and to make blacke billes and other weapons, and to mend many things.
17. Men that use to breake Ash trees for pikestaves, to be imploied in the Woods there.
18. Others, that finish up the same so rough hewd, such as in London are to be had.
19. Coopers, to make caske of all sorts.
20. Forgers of pikes heads and of arrow heads, with forges, with Spanish yron, and with all maner of tooles to be caried with them.
21. Fletchers, to renew arrowes, since archerie prevaileth much against unarmed people: and gunpowder may soone perish, by setting on fire.
22. Bowyers also, to make bowes there for need.
23. Makers of oares, since for service upon those rivers it is to great purpose, for the boats and barges they are to passe and enter with.
24. Shipwrights, to make barges and boats, and bigger vessels, if need be, to run along the coast, and to pierce the great Bayes and Inlets.
25. Turners, to turne targets of Elme and tough wood, for use against the darts and arrowes of Salvages.
26. Such also as have knowledge to make targets of horne.

27. Such also as can make armor of hides upon moulds, such as were woont to be made in this realme about an hundred yeeres since, and were called Scotish jacks: such armor is light and defensive enough against the force of Salvages.

28. Tanners, to tanne hides of Buffes, Oxen, &c. in the Isles where you shall plant.

29. White Tawyers of all other skinnes there.

30. Men skilfull in burning of Sope ashes, and in making of Pitch, and Tarre, and Rozen, to be fetched out of Prussia and Poland, which are thence to be had for small wages, being there in maner of slaves.

The severall sorts of trees, as Pines, Firres, Spruses, Birch and others, are to be boared with great augers a foot or halfe a yard above the ground, as they use in Vesely towards Languedock and neere Bayona in Gascoigne: and so you shall easily and quickly see what Gummes, Rozen, Turpentine, Tarre, or liquor is in them, which will quickly distill out cleerely without any filthie mixture, and will shew what commoditie may be made of them: their goodnesse and greatnesse for masts is also to be considered.

31. A skilfull painter is also to be caried with you which the Spaniards used commonly in all their discoveries to bring the descriptions of all beasts, birds, fishes, trees, townes, &c.

Chapter Forty-five
Richard Hakluyt the Younger's *Discourse of Western Planting*, 1584

IT BECAME EVIDENT in 1583 to Sir Francis Walsingham, after his stepson Christopher Carleill had taken up the American enterprise, that existing English knowledge of North America was quite inadequate. One way of remedying the situation was to send an intelligence mission to the continent. The younger Richard Hakluyt was chosen for this in the summer of 1583. He went to France as chaplain and secretary to the English ambassador in Paris and spent his time collecting information from interviews, manuscripts, and books on what Frenchmen had done and were doing in North America, and assembling any printed materials that came his way on Spanish and Portuguese knowledge of the area. He sent suggestions home for the benefit of Carleill and Ralegh and in July, 1584 came to England to report his findings. Ralegh, after dispatching his reconnaissance expedition, had come to the conclusion, apparently supported by Walsingham, that some degree of royal involvement was necessary if North American colonizing plans were to succeed. Hakluyt therefore wrote up his report in a form that stressed the need for participation by the queen. He completed his long "A particuler discourse" in September after the first of Ralegh's reconnaissance vessels returned with favorable reports of its mission. He covered such themes as the English title to North America, the importance of preventing its occupation by non-English powers, the nature of published information on North American resources, and much on French fur trading and other activities. Throughout, he is concerned to stress in detail the economic resources and potentialities of North America and to develop the theme of how settlement would lead to complementary, supplementary, and novel products being acquired from there and how the English cloth trade and other crafts could benefit from sales to Amerindians. North America, he saw, offered prospects and employment to many misfit or dissatisfied Englishmen. The queen must sponsor the enterprise, protect it, and give the kind of lead which would bring it mass support. He concluded with the assumption that colonization would in fact be attempted on a large scale and proceeded to specify what kind of men should be selected. Essentially his approach was similar to the three papers by his elder cousin (356, 359–360), but he was much better informed and wrote at much greater length. He could consider the problem, too, in a context of foreign relations, which his cousin could not. He was able, on account of his official status, to make recommendations for the participation of the Crown that would not have come so effectively from outside the official hierarchy. Although he was very optimistic about North American prospects, his greater knowledge and expertise made his recommendations much more authoritative than those of his cousin could have been. The result was in many respects a masterly performance. But, it must be stressed, it was a confidential report by a minor official, which might or might not bear any practical fruits.

The original manuscript, presented to the queen in October, 1584, has disappeared. The surviving fair copy, in an elaborate binding which may be strictly contemporary, cannot be traced to any of the participants. It is most likely to have been Sir Francis Walsingham's, but this cannot be firmly established. When it was in the Phillipps collection it was first published by Charles Deane and Leonard Woods as "A Discourse on Western Planting," both as volume II of *Documentary History of the State of Maine* (Collections of the Maine Historical Society, Second Series, II, 1877) and separately (Cambridge, Mass., 1877), and subsequently, from the manuscript by E. G. R. Taylor, *Hakluyts*, II (1935), 211–326. The manuscript is now in the New York Public Library. The text has been prepared from the published versions with a very few amendments from the manuscript.

361. "A particuler discourse concerninge the greate necessitie and manifolde comodyties that are like to growe to this Realme of Englande by the Westerne discoveries lately attempted, Written in the yere 1584."

1. That this westerne discoverie will be greately for thinlargement of the gospell of Christe whereunto the Princes of the refourmed relligion are chefely bounde amongest whome her ma^tie ys principall.

2. That all other englishe Trades are growen beggerly or daungerous, especially in all the kinge of Spayne his Domynions, where our men are dryven to flinge their Bibles and prayer Bokes into the sea, and to forsweare and renownce their relligion and conscience and consequently theyr obedience to her Majestie.

3. That this westerne voyadge will yelde unto us all the commodities of Europe, Affrica, and Asia, as far as wee were wonte to travell, and supply the wantes of all our decayed trades.

4. That this enterprise will be for the manifolde imploymente of nombers of idle men, and for bredinge of many sufficient, and for utterance of the greate quantitie of the commodities of our Realme.

5. That this voyage will be a great bridle to the Indies of the kinge of Spaine and a meane that wee may arreste at our pleasure for the space of tenne weekes or three monethes every yere, one or twoo hundred saile of his subjectes shippes at the fysshinge in Newfounde lande.

6. That the mischefe that the Indian Threasure wrought in time of Charles the late Emperour father to the Spanishe kinge, is to be had in consideracion of the Queenes moste excellent Majestie, leaste the contynuall commynge of the like threasure from thence to his sonne, worke the unrecoverable annoye of this Realme, whereof already wee have had very dangerous experience.

7. What speciall meanes may bringe kinge Phillippe from his high Throne, and make him equal to the Princes his neighbours, wherewithall is shewed his weakenes in the west Indies.

8. That the lymites of the kinge of Spaines domynions in the west Indies be nothinge so large as ys generally ymagined and surmised, neither those partes which he holdeth be of any such forces as ys falsly geven oute by the popishe Clergye and others his fautors, to terrifie the Princes of the Relligion and to abuse and blynde them.

9. The Names of the riche Townes lienge alonge the sea coaste on the northe side from the equinoctiall of the mayne lande of America under the kinge of Spayne.

10. A Brefe declaracion of the chefe Ilands in the Bay of Mexico beinge under the kinge of Spaine, with their havens and fortes, and what commodities they yelde.

11. That the Spaniardes have executed most outragious and more then Turkishe cruelties in all the west Indies, whereby they are every where there, become moste odious unto them, whoe woulde joyne with us or any other moste willingly to shake of their moste intollerable yoke, and have begonne to doo it already in dyvers places where they were Lordes heretofore.

12. That the passage in this voyadge is easie and shorte, that it cutteth not nere the trade of any other mightie Princes, nor nere their Con-

tries, that it is to be perfourmed at all tymes of the yere, and nedeth but one kinde of winde, that Ireland beinge full of goodd havens on the southe and west sides, is the nerest parte of Europe to yt, which by this trade shall be in more securitie, and the sooner drawen to more Civilitie.

13. That hereby the Revenewes and customes of her Majestie bothe outwardes and inwardes shall mightely be inlarged by the toll, excises, and other dueties which withoute oppression may be raised.

14. That this action will be greately for thincrease, mayneteynaunce and safetie of our Navye, and especially of greate shippinge which is the strengthe of our Realme, and for the supportation of all those occupations that depende upon the same.

15. That spedie plantinge in divers fitt places is moste necessarie upon these luckye westerne discoveries for feare of the daunger of being prevented by other nations which have the like intentions, with the order thereof and other reasons therwithall alleaged.

16. Meanes to kepe this enterprise from overthrowe and the enterprisers from shame and dishonour.

17. That by these Colonies the Northwest passage to Cathaio and China may easely quickly and perfectly be searched oute aswell by river and overlande, as by sea, for proofe whereof here are quoted and alleaged divers rare Testymonies oute of the three volumes of voyadges gathered by Ramusius and other grave authors.

18. That the Queene of Englande title to all the west Indies, or at the leaste to as moche as is from Florida to the Circle articke, is more lawfull and righte then the Spaniardes or any other Christian Princes.

19. An aunswer to the Bull of the Donacion of all the west Indies graunted to the kinges of Spaine by Pope Alexander the vi[th] whoe was himselfe a Spaniarde borne.

20. A brefe collection of certaine reasons to induce her Majestie and the state to take in hande the westerne voyadge and the plantinge there.

21. A note of some thinges to be prepared for the voyadge which is sett downe rather to drawe the takers of the voyadge in hande to the presente consideracion then for any other reason for that divers thinges require preparation longe before the voyadge, withoute which the voyadge is maymed.

1

That this westerne discoverie will be greately for thinlargemente of the gospell of Christe, whereunto the Princes of the refourmed Relligion are chefely bounde, amongeste whome her Majestie ys principall.

Seinge that the people of that parte of America from 30. degrees in Florida northewarde unto 63. degrees (which ys yet in no christian princes actuall possession) are idolaters, and that those which Stephen Gomes broughte from the coaste of Norumbega in the yere 1524 worshipped the Sonne, the Moone, and the starres, and used other idolatrie, as it ys recorded in the historie of Gonsalvo de Oviedo, in Italian, fol. 52. of the thirde volume of Ramusius: and that those of Canada and Hochelaga in 48. and 50. degrees worshippe a spirite which they call Cudruaigny, as we reade in the tenthe chapiter of the seconde relacion of Jaques Cartier: whoe saieth, This people beleve not at all in God but in one whome they call Cudruaigny. They say that often he speaketh with them, and telleth them what weather shall followe, whether goodd or badd, &c. And yet notwithstandinge they are very easie to be perswaded, and doo all that they sawe the Christians doo in their devine service with like imitation and devotion, and were very desirous to become christians, and woulde faine have been baptized as Verarsanus wittnesseth in the laste woordes of his relacion, and Jaques Cartier in the tenthe chapiter before recited: It remayneth to be throughly weyed and considered by what meanes and by whome this moste godly and Christian work may be perfourmed, of inlarginge the glorious gospell of Christe, and reducinge of infinite multitudes of these simple people that are in errour into the righte and perfecte waye of their salvacion: The blessed Apostle Paule the converter of the Gentiles, Rom. 10. writeth in this manner: Whoesoever shall call on the name of the Lorde shall be saved: But howe shall they call on him in whom they have not beleved? And howe shall they beleve in him of whom they have not hearde? And howe shall they heare withoute a preacher? and howe shall they preache excepte they be sente? Then it is necessarie for the salvation of those poore people which have sitten so longe in darkenes and in the shadowe of deathe, that preachers should be sent unto them: But by whome shoulde these preachers be sente? By them no doubte which have taken upon them the protection and defence of the Christian faithe: Nowe the Kinges and Queenes of England have the name of Defendors of the Faithe:[1] By which title I thinke they are not onely chardged to maynteyne and patronize the faithe of Christe, but also to inlarge and advaunce the same: Neither oughte this to be their laste worke but rather the principall and chefe of all others, accordinge to the comaundemente of our Saviour Christe. Mathewe 6. Firste seeke the kingdome of god and the righteousnes thereof, and all other thinges shalbe mynistred unto you: Nowe the meanes to sende suche as shall labour effectually in this busines ys by plantinge[2] one or twoo Colonies of our nation uppon that fyrme, where they may remaine in safetie, and firste learne the language of the people nere adjoyninge (the gifte of tongues beinge nowe taken awaye), and by little and little acquainte themselves with their manner, and so with discrecion and myldenes distill into their purged myndes the swete and lively liquor of the gospell: Otherwise for preachers to ronne unto them rashly with oute some suche preparacion for their safetie, yt were nothinge els but to ronne to their apparaunte and certaine destruction, as yt happened unto those Spanishe Fryers that before any plantinge withoute strengthe and company landed in Florida, where they were miserablye massacred by the Savages: On the other side by meane of plantinge, firste the small nation of the Portingales towardes the southe and easte have planted the Christian faithe accordinge to their manner: and have erected many Bisshoprickes and Colledges to traine upp the youthe of the Infidells in the same: Of which acte they more vaunte in all their histories and Chronicles, then of anythinge els that ever they atchieved. And surely if they had planted the gospell of Christe purely as they dyd not, they mighte justly have more rejoyced in

1. Sidenote: "The Prynces of England called the defendors of the faithe."
2. Sidenote: "Plantinge fyrste necessarye."

that deede of theirs then in the conqueste of the whole Contrie or in any other thinge whatsoever. The like may be saied of the Spaniardes, whoe (as yt is in the preface of the last edition of Osorius *de rebus gestis Emanuelis*) have established in the West Indies three Archebisshopricks, to witt, Mexico, Lima, and Cusco, and thirtene other Bisshopricks there named, and have builte above CC. houses of Relligion in the space of fyftie yeres or thereaboutes: Now yf they, in their superstition, by meanes of their plantinge in those partes, have don so great thinges in so shorte space, what may wee hope for in our true and syncere Relligion, proposinge unto ourselves in this action not filthie lucre nor vaine ostentation as they in deede did, but principally the gayninge of the soules of millions of those wretched people, the reducinge of them from darkenes to lighte, from falshoodde to truthe, from dombe Idolls to the lyvinge god, from the depe pitt of hell to the highest heavens. In the 16. of the Actes of the Apostles when Paule soughte to preache in Asia and to goo into Bithinia, the holy ghoste suffred him not: But at Troas a vision appered unto him by nighte: There stoode a man of Macedonia and prayed hym, sayenge: Come into Macedonia and helpe us: And after he had seene the vysion, ymmediatly he prepared to goe into Macedonia, beinge assured that the Lorde had called him to preache the gospell unto them: Even so wee whiles wee have soughte to goo into other Contries (I woulde I might say to preache the gospell) God by the frustratinge of our actions semeth to forbydd us to followe those courses, and the people of America crye oute unto us their nexte neighboures to come and helpe them, and bringe unto them the gladd tidinges of the gospell. Unto the Prince and people that shalbe the occasion of this worthie worke, and shall open their cofers to the furtheraunce of this most godly enterprise, God shall open the bottomles treasures of his riches and fill them with aboundance of his hidden blessinges: As he did to the goodd Queene Isabella, which beinge in extreme necessitie, laied her owne Jewells to gage for money to furnishe oute Columbus for the firste discovery of the weste Indies: And this enterprice the Princes of the Relligion (amonge whome her Majestie ys principall) oughte the rather to take in hande, because the papistes confirme themselves and drawe other to theire side, shewinge that they are the true Catholicke Churche because they have bene the onely converters of many millions of Infidells to Christianitie: Yea, I my selfe have bene demaunded of them howe many Infidells have beene by us converted?[3] Whereunto albeit I alleaged the example of the mynisters which were sente from Geneva with Villegagnon into Bresill, and those that wente with John Ribault into Florida, as also those of our nation that went with Frobisher, Sir Fraunces Drake, and Fenton, yet in very deede I was not able to name any one Infidell by them converted: But god quoth I hath his tyme for all men, whoe calleth some at the nynthe, and some at the eleventh hower. And if it please him to move the harte of her Majestie to put her helpinge hande to this godly action she shall finde as willinge subjectes of all sortes as any other prince in all christendome: And as for the boastinge of your conversion of such multitudes of Infidells, yt may justly be coumpted rather a perversion, seeinge you have drawen them as yt were oute of Sylla into Charibdis, that is to say from one error into another. Nowe therefore I truste the time ys at hande when by her Majesties forwardnes in this enterprise not onely this obiection and suche like shalbe aunswered by our frutefull labor in godds harvest amonge the Infidells, But also many inconveniences and strifes amongest ourselves at home in matters of Ceremonies shalbe ended: For those of the Clergye which by reason of idlenes here at home are nowe alwayes coyninge of newe opynions, havinge by this voyadge to sett themselves on worke in reducinge the Savages to the chefe principles of our faithe, will become lesse contentious, and be contented with the truthe in Relligion alreadie established by aucthoritie: So they that shall beare the name of Christians shall shewe themselves worthye of their vocation, so shall the mouthe of the adversarie be stopped, so shall contention amongest Brethren be avoyded, so shall the gospell amonge Infidells be published.

2

That all other englishe trades are growen beggerly or daungerous especially daungerous in all the kinge of Spayne his dominyons, where our men are dryven to flinge their bibles and prayer bookes into the sea, and to forsweare and renownce their Relligion and conscience, and consequently their obedience to her Majestie.

Wee are nowe to consider the qualitie and condition of all the trades which at this day are frequented by our nation: And firste to begynne southwarde and so come to the Northe, leavinge Bresill and Guynea where wee have little to doe: Let us firste speake of our trade in Barbarie: If any of our shippes tradinge thither be dryven upon the coaste of Spaine, and that proofe may be made that wee have bene there, they make it a very sufficient cause of confiscation of shippe and goodds, and so they thruste our men into the Inquisition, chardginge them that they bringe armour, munition, and forbidden marchandize to strengthen the Infidells againste these partes of Christendome: which thinge is committed to printe and confessed by all our marchantes tradinge thither: And thoughe our men escape the Spaniardes tyrannie, yet at the deathe of the Prince in Barbary, all our mennes goodds there are subjecte to the spoile, the custome of the Contrie permittinge the people to robbe and rifle until an nother kinge be chosen withoute making any kinde of restitution. Besides that inconvenience, the trafficque groweth daily to worse termes then heretofore. I omytt to shewe here howe divers have bene undon by their servauntes which have become Renegadoes, of whome by the custome of the Contrie their Masters can have no manner of recoverye, neither call them into Justice. In all the kinge of Spaines domynyons[4] our men are either inforced with wounded consciences to playe the dissemblinge hipocrites, or be drawen to mislike with the state of Relligion mainteyned at home, or cruelly made away in the Inquisition: Moreover he being our mortall enemye, and his Empire of late beinge encreased so mightely, and our necessitie of oiles and of coulours for our clothinge trade being so greate, he may arreste almoste the one halfe of our navye, our traficque and recourse being so greate to his domynyons. For the new trade in Turky[5] besides the greate expences in mayneteyninge a kind of Embassador at Constantinople, and in sendinge

---

3. Sidenote: "A question of the adversary."

4. Sidenote: "The Domynions of the Kinge of Spayne."
5. Sidenote: "The trade of Turky."

of presentes to Selym the graunde Segnior and to divers of his insatiable Bassaes, our marchantes are faine with large rewardes to gratifie the Knightes of Malta in whose daunger their shippes muste often passe: Moreover that trade is so moche to the detrymente of the state of Venice, and all the other states of Italie, that they are dayly occupied in seekinge howe they may overthrowe the same. Neither is it the leaste incommoditie that our shippes are contynually assaulted by the Corsaries and pirates and gallies of Algiers by which they had a rich shippe, called the Mary Martin soncke this yere; and the last yere another was taken at Trypoly in Barbary, and the Master with another hanged, and the reste made slaves: Besides the barke Reynoldes was arrested at Malta, and at lengthe with moche adoe delivered. To leave the Levant and to come to Fraunce,[6] the traficque there of myne owne knowledge is growen to such decaye partly by the ympositions and taxes which are daily devised by the kinge partly by their subtill sleights and devises to confiscate our clothes for insufficient workemanshippe, and partly by their owne labour in makinge more and better clothe then heretofore they were accustomed, that our men for the moste parte are wearye of the Contrie, and some of them utterly undone by their subtill and unconcionable wranglinge. As for all Flaunders[7] and the lowe Contries, these eightene yeres moste cruell civill warres have so spoiled the traficque there, that there is nothinge but povertie and perill, and that which is worse, there is no hope of any spedy amendemente. To come to the Esterlinges[8] and the trades with the cities within the sounde of Denmarke, they beinge deprived of the olde priviledges of the Stilliarde here in London, have not only offred our men at home many injuries in their Cities, but seeke all the meanes they can devise wholy to cutt of all our occupienge that way: And to the same purpose have lately cleane debarred our men of their accustomed and auncient priviledges in all their greate Townes: Also the exactions of the kinge of Denmarke[9] at our passage in and oute by the sounde to Lubecke, Danske, Elvinge, Rye, Revell, and the Narve, besides the power that he hath to arreste all our

shippes within the sounde at his pleasure, are twoo no small inconveniences and myschefes: Our trade into Muscovye[10] ys the laste, which was so chardgeable in the begynnynge, what with the coste of the discoverie, what with presentes to the Emperor, together with the disorderly dealinge of their factors, that it stoode them in fourscore thousande poundes before they broughte it to any goodd passe. And nowe after longe hope of gayne, the Hollanders as also the men of Depe are entred into their trade by the Emperours permission, yea whereas at the firste our men paid no custome, of late yeres contrarie to their firste priviledge they have bene urged to pay yt: Also the chardges of bringinge the Emperours Embassador hither, and mayneteyninge him here, and the settinge furthe of her Majesties Embassadour thither with presentes to the Emperour, lyenge all upon the poore Marchantes neckes, is no easie burden unto their shoulders. And to encrease the same, the kinge of Denmarke requireth a tribute of them thoughe they touche not upon any of his domynions: And nowe the Empero[r] of Russia beinge late deade, yt is greately feared that the voyadge wilbe utterly overthrowen, or els become not worthe the contynuaunce. Thus havinge regarde unto the premisses, yt behoveth us to seeke some newe and better trade of lesse daunger and more securitie, of lesse dommage, and of more advauntage. The rather to avoide the wilfull perjurie of suche of our Englishe nation as trade to Spaine and other of kinge Phillipps domynions, where this oathe followinge ys usually ministred unto the Master of our shippes. Firste he willeth the Master to make a crosse with his fore finger and his thombe layenge one over the other crossewise, This beinge don, he saieth these wordes followinge: You shall sweare to speake the truthe of all thinges that shalbe asked of you, and yf you doo not, that god demaunde yt of you; and the Englishe Master muste saye Amen. You shall sweare by that crosse that you bringe no man in your shippe but suche as are goodd christians, and doo beleve as our Catholicke churche of Rome dothe beleve. Nexte that you bringe no manner of bookes but suche as are allowed by our Catholicke Churche of Rome. And that you use no manner of prayers but suche as are allowed by our Churche of Rome. What

6. Sidenote: "Fraunce."
7. Sidenote: "Flaunders."
8. Sidenote: "Estlande."
9. Sidenote: "Denmarke."

10. Sidenote: "Russye."

marchandize bringe you, suche and suche. Wee will and commaunde you and your Companie to come on lande to masse every sonday and holyday upon paine of discommunicacion. Then they open their chestes and looke if the Master and maryners bringe any bookes with them in their chests. This don the officers that come with the preestes aske of the Master and maryners, chese, butter, befe, bacon, and candles as beggers, and they give it to them for feare they have of them, and so they goe from the shippes with their walletts full of victualls. The Master doth pay 4. Ryalls of plate for the Barke that bringeth them aboorde to visite them. Thus is wilfull perjurye permitted by the governours if they knowe it. Thus the covetous marchante wilfully sendeth headlonge to hell from day to day the poore subjectes of this Realme. The marchant in England cometh here devoutly to the communyon, and sendeth his sonne into Spaine to here masse. These thinges are kepte secrete by the marchantes, and suche as depende upon the trade of marchandize are lothe to utter the same.

3

That this westerne voyadge will yelde unto us all the commodities of Europe, Affrica and Asia, as farr as wee were wonte to travell, and supplye the wantes of all our decayed trades.

The nexte thinge ys that nowe I declare unto you the commodities of this newe westerne discoverie, and what marchandize are there to be had, and from thence to be expected: wherein firste you are to have regarde unto the scituacion of the places, which are left for us to be possessed. The Contries therefore of America whereunto we have just Title[11] as being firste discovered by Sebastian Gabote at the coste of that prudente prince kinge Henry the Seaventh from Florida northewarde to 67. degrees, (and not yet in any Christian princes actuall possession) beinge aunswerable in clymate to Barbary, Egipte, Siria, Persia, Turky, Greece, all the Ilandes of the Levant sea, Italie, Spaine, Portingale, Fraunce, Flaunders, highe Almayne, Denmarke, Estland, Poland, and Muscovye, may presently or within a shorte space afforde unto us for little or nothinge and with moche more safetie eyther all or a greate

parte of the commodities which the aforesaide Contries doo yelde us at a very dere hande and with manifolde daungers.

Firste therefore to begyn at the southe from 30. degrees, and to quote unto you the leafe and page of the printed voyadges of those which personally have with diligence searched and viewed these contries, John Ribault[12] writeth thus, in the firste leafe of his discourse extant in printe bothe in frenche and englishe: Wee entred (saieth he) and viewed the Contrie, which is the fairest, frutefullest, and pleasauntest of all the world, aboundinge in honye, waxe, venison, wilde fowle, Forrestes, woodds of all sortes, palmetrees, cipresses, cedars, bayes,[13] the highest and greatest with also the fairest vines in all the worlde with grapes accordinge which naturally withoute arte or mans helpe or trymmynge will growe to toppes of oakes and other trees that be of wonderfull greatenes and heighte. And the sighte of the faire meadowes is a pleasure not able to be expressed with tongue, full of herons, curlues, bitters, mallardes, egriphts, woodcockes, and all other kinde of small birdes, with hartes, hindes, bucks, wilde swyne, and all other kynde of wilde beastes,[14] as wee perceaved well bothe by their footinge there, and also afterwardes in other places by their crye and roaringe in the nighte: Also there be conies, and hares, silkewormes in marvelous nomber, a greate deale fairer and better then be our silkewormes.[15] Againe in the sixte leafe and seconde page, they shewed unto us by signes that they had in the lande golde and silver and copper, whereof wee have broughte some home.[16] Also leade like unto ours which wee shewed them: Also turqueses and greate aboundaunce of perles which as they declared unto us they tooke oute of oysters, whereof there is taken ever alonge the Rivers side, and amongest the reedes, and in the marishes in so marvelous aboundaunce as it is scante credible. And wee have perceaved that there be as many and as greate perles founde there as in any contrie in the worlde: In the seaventh leafe it followeth thus: The scituation is under 30. degrees, a goodd clymate, healthfull,

11. Sidenote: "In the firste volume of Ramusius, fol. 374 pag. 2."

12. Sidenote: "John Ribault."
13. Sidenote: "Hony, venison, palmetrees, ceders, cipresses, vynes,"
14. Sidenote: "Herons, curlues, bitters, mallardes, egripthes."
15. Sidenote: "Sylkewormes exceedinge faire."
16. Sidenote: "Fol. 6. pag. 2. Golde. silver. copper. Turqueses. perles in aboundaunce."

and of goodd temperature, marvelous pleasaunte, the people goodd and of a gentle and amyable nature, which willingly will obey,[17] yea be contented to serve those that shall with gentlenes and humanitie goo aboute to allure them, as yt is necessarie for those that be sente thither hereafter so to doo: In the 8. leafe: It is a place wonderfull fertile and of strong scituation, the grounde fatt, so that it is like that it woulde bringe forthe wheate and all other corne twise a yere.[18] In the 9. leafe yt followeth: Wee founde there a greate nomber of pepper trees the pepper beinge yet greene and not ready to be gathered: In the 10. leafe:[19] There wee sawe the fairest and the greatest vines with grapes accordinge, and younge trees and small wooddes very well smellinge that ever weare sene: Thus have you brefely the somme of the commodities which were founde by John Ribault and his Companye on the coaste of America from 30. to 34. degrees.

Moreover, Doctor Monardus that excellent phisition of Civill writing of the trees of the west Indies in his booke called *Joyfull Newes out of the newfounde worlde*, maketh mention of a tree called Sassafras[20] which the Frenchmen founde in Florida, fol. 46. of his Booke in manner followinge: From the Florida they bringe a woodde and roote of a tree that groweth in those partes of greate vertues and excellencies, healinge therewith grevous and variable diseases: It may be three yeres paste that I had knowledge of this tree, and a frenche man that had bene in those partes shewed me a pece of yt and tolde me marvells of the vertues thereof, and howe many and variable diseases were healed with the water which was made of it, and I judged that which nowe I doo fynde to be true and have seene by experience. He tolde me that the frenchemen which had bene in the Florida at the time when they came into those partes had bene sicke the moste of them of grevous and variable diseases, and that ye Indians did shewe them this tree and the manner howe they shoulde use yt, and so they did and were healed of many evills, which surely bringeth admiration that one onely remedy shoulde worke so variable and marvelous ef-

fectes. The name of this tree as the Indyans terme yt is called Paranne, and the Frenchemen called it Sassafras: To be brefe the Doctor Monardus bestoweth xi leaves in describinge the sovereinties and excellent properties thereof: The nature and commodities of the reste of the coaste unto Cape Briton I will shewe unto you oute of the printed Testymonies of John Verarsanus and Stephen Gomes bothe which in one yere 1524, discovered the said Contries, and broughte home of the people Verarsana into Fraunce, and Gomes into Spaine.

Verarsana fallinge in the latitude of 34. degrees, describeth the scituation and commodities in this manner: Beyonde this wee sawe the open Contrie risinge in heighte above the sandie shoare with many faire feeldes and plaines full of mightie greate wooddes some very thicke and some very thynne, replenished with divers sortes of trees and plesaunte and delectable to beholde as ys possible to ymagine. And your Majestie may not thinke that these are like the wooddes of Hyrcinia or the wilde desertes of Tartaria and the northerne coastes full of fruteles trees, but full of palme, date trees, bayes, and highe cypresses, and many other sortes of trees to us unknowen in Europe which yelde moste swete savours farr from the shoare; neyther doo wee thincke that they partakinge of the easte worlde rounde aboute them are altogether voyde of drugs and spicerye,[21] and other riches of golde, seinge the colour of the lande dothe altogether argue yt. And the lande is full of many beastes as redd dere, fallowe dere, and hares, and likewise of lakes and pooles of freshe water with greate plentie of fowles convenient for all plesaunte game. This lande is in latitude of 34. degrees[22] with goodd and holesome ayre, temperate betwene hote and colde, no vehement winds doo blowe in these Regions, &c. Againe, in the 4. leafe as it is in Englishe speakinge of the nexte Contrie, he saieth: Wee sawe in this contrie many vines growinge naturally, which springinge upp tooke holde of the trees as as they doe in Lumbardye, which, if by husbandmen they were dressed in goodd order, withoute all doubte they woulde yelde excellent wynes,[23] for having oftentymes

---

17. Sidenote: "30. degrees. The gentlenes of the people."
18. Sidenote: "Harvest twise yn the yere."
19. Sidenote: "Pepper groweth here; yt is longe pepper."
20. Sidenote: "Sassafras."

21. Sidenote: "Druggs. spycery. golde."
22. Sidenote: "34. degrees."
23. Sidenote: "Vynes excellent."

seene the frute thereof dryed, which was swete and pleasaunte and not differinge from oures, wee thinke they doo esteme of the same because that in every place where they growe, they take away the under braunches growinge rounde boute, that the frute thereof may ripen the better: Wee founde also roses, violetts, lyllies and many sortes of herbes and swete and odoriferous flowers.[24] And after in the 6. leafe he saithe: Wee were oftentimes within the lande v. or vi. leagues, which wee founde as pleasaunte as is possible to declare, apte for any kinde of husbandrye of corne, wine, and oile.[25] For therein there are plomes 25. or 30. leagues broade, open and with-oute any impedymente of trees of suche frutefulnes that any seede beinge sowen therein will bringe furthe moste excellente frute. Wee entred afterwardes into the wooddes, which wee founde so greate and thicke that an armye (were it never so greate) mighte have hydd it selfe therein, the trees whereof were okes, cypresses, and other sortes unknowen in Europe: Wee founde *pomi appii*,[26] plomes and nuttes and many other sortes of frutes to us unknowen: There are beastes in greate aboundaunce as redd dere and fallowe dere, leopardes and other kindes which they take with their bowes and arrowes, which are their chefeste weapons: This lande is scituate in the paraclete of Rome in 41. degrees and 2. terces.[27] And towardes the ende he saieth: Wee sawe many of the people weare earinges of cop-per[28] hanginge at their eares. Thus farr oute of the relacion of Verarsana.

Nowe to come to Stephen Gomes[29] which by the commaundemente of the Emperor Charles the fyfte discovered the coaste of Norumbega: These are the wordes of Gonsalvo de Oviedo in his *Summarye of the Weste Indies* translated into Italian concerninge him. fo. 52. Dapoi che vostra majestà è in questa città di Toledo, arrivà qui nel mese di Novembre il piloto Stephano Gomez, il quale nel anno passato del 1524. per comman-damento di vostra majestà navigò alla partè di tramontana e trovò gran partè di terra continuata a quelle che si chiama dellos Bacallaos discorrendo ill occidente: et giace in 40. et 41. grado et cosi poco piu et meno; del qual luogo menò alcuni Indiani, et ne sono al presente in questa città, li quali sono di maggior grandezza di quelli di terra ferma, secondo chè communemente sono: perche anchora il detto piloto disse haver visto molti, che sono tutti di quella medesima grandezza: il color veramente è come quelli di terra ferma; sono grandi arcieri, et vanno coperti di pelle d'animali salvatici, et altri animali.[30] Sono in questa terra eccellenti martori et zibilini, et altrè ricche fo-derè, delle quali ne portò alcune pelle il detto pilotto: Hanno argento et rame: et secondo che dicono questi Indiani et con segni fanno inten-dere, adorano il sole et la luna, anche hanno altro Idolatrie et errori come quelli di terra ferma.

An other Frenche Capitaine of Diepe[31] which had bene alongest this coaste geveth this tes-tymonie of the people and Contrie from 40. to 47. degrees as it is in the thirde volume of viages gathered by Ramusius fol. 423. pag. secunda: Gli habitatori di questa terra sono genti trattabili, amichevoli, et piacevoli. La terra abondantissima d'omni frutto:[32] vi nascono aranci, mandorle, vua salvatica, et molte altre sorti d'arbori odoriferi: la terra è detta da paesani suoi Norumbega.

This coaste from Cape Briton CC leagues to the south west was againe discovered at the chardges of the Cardinall of Burbon by my frende Stephen Bellinger[33] of Roan the laste yere 1583: whoe founde a Towne of fourscore houses covered with the Barkes of Trees upon a Ryvers side aboute C leagues from the aforesaide Cape Briton, he re-porteth that the Contrie is of the temperature of the coaste of Gascoigne and Guyan: He broughte home a kinde of mynerall matter supposed to holde silver whereof he gave me some, a kynde of muske called Castor,[34] divers beastes skynnes, as bevers, otters, marternes, lucernes, seales, buf-fes dere skynnes all dressed and painted on the Innerside with divers excellent colours, as redd, tawnye, yellowe, and vermillyon:[35] All which thinges I sawe and divers other marchandize he hath which I sawe not: But he tolde me that he had

---

24. Sidenote: "Roses. violetts. lyllies."
25. Sidenote: "Corne. wine. oyle."
26. Sidenote: "These apples growe in Italy and are yellowe like a pippon."
27. Sidenote: "41 degrees & 2 terces."
28. Sidenote: "Copper."
29. Sidenote: "Stephen Gomez."

30. Sidenote: "Martores. sables. rich furres. silver and copper."
31. Sidenote: "A capitaine of Diepe."
32. Sidenote: "Oranges. almonds. grapes."
33. Sidenote: "Stephen Bellinger."
34. Sidenote: "Muske called castor."
35. Sidenote: "Excellent colours for dyenge."

CCCC and xl. Crownes for that in Roan, which in trifles bestowed upon the savages stoode him not in fortie Crownes: And this yere 1584 the Marques de la Roche[36] wente with three hundreth men to inhabite in those partes, whose voyadge was overthrowen by occasion that his greatest shippe of CCC Tonnes was caste away over againste Burwage, and so the enterprize for this yere ceseth.

The nature and qualitie of thother parte of America from Cape Briton, beinge in 46 degrees unto the latitude of 52. for iij C leagues within the lande even to Hochelaga is notably described in the twoo voyadges of Jaques Cartier:[37] In the fifte Chapter of his seconde Relacion thus he writeth: ffrom the 19. till the 28. of September wee sailed upp the Ryver never loosinge one houre of tyme, all which space wee sawe as goodly a Contrie as possibly coulde be wisshed for, full of all sortes of goodly trees, that is to say oakes, elmes, walnut-trees, cedars, fyrres, asshes, boxe, willoughes, and great store of vynes[38] all as full of grapes as coulde be, that if any of our fellowes wente on shoare they came home laden with them: There are likewise many cranes, swannes, geese, mallardes, fesauntes, partridges, thrusshes, black-birdes, turtles, finches, reddbrestes, nightingales, sparrowes, with other sortes of birdes even as in ffraunce, and great plentie and store. Againe in the 6. chapter of the said relation there ys mention of silver and golde to be upon a ryver that is three monethes saylinge navigable south-warde from Hochelaga: and that redde copper[39] is yn Saguynay: All that contrie is full of sondire sortes of woodde and many vines. There is greate store of stagges, redd dere, fallowe dere, beares, and other suche like store of beastes, as conies, hares, marters, foxes, otters, bevers, squirrells, badgers and rattes excedinge greate, and divers other sortes of beastes for huntinge. There are also many sortes of fowles, as cranes, swannes, outardes, wilde geese, white and graye, duckes, thrusshes, blackbirdes, turtles, wilde pigeons,[40] lynnetts, finches, redd brestes, stares, nightin-gales, sparrowes and other birdes even as in Fraunce. Also, as wee have said before, the said ryver is the plentifullest of fyshe that ever hath bene seene or hearde of, because that from the heade to the mouthe of yt you shall finde all kinde of freshe and salte water fyshe accordinge to their season. There are also many whales, porposes, sea horses and adhothins which is a kinde of fishe which wee have never seene nor hearde of before. And in the xii[th] chapter thus: We understoode of Demaconna and others that there are people cladd with clothe as wee are very honest, and many inhabited townes, and that they had greate store of golde and redde copper.[41] And that within the lande beyonde the said ryver unto Hochelaga and Saguynay ys an Iland envyroned rounde aboute with that and other ryvers, and that there is a sea of freshe water[42] founde, and as they have hearde say of those of Saguynay, there was never man hearde of that founde oute the begynnynge and ende thereof. Finally in the postscripte of the seconde relation wee reade these wordes: They of Canada saye that it is a moones sailinge to goe to a land where cynamonde and cloves[43] are gathered. And nowe because hitherto I have spoken of the outewarde coaste, I will also alledge the commodities of the Inlande in the latitude of 37. degrees, about the Citie of Cevola usinge the very wordes of Vasques de Coronado[44] in the thirde chapter of his relation written to Don Antonio di Mendoza Viceroy of Mexico, which sente him thither with many Spaniardes and iiii C horses and a thousande Indians to discover those Contries: He speakinge there of the Citie of Cevola[45] procedeth in this manner: In questo dove Io sto hora allogiato possono asservi qualche dugento case tutte circondate di muro, et parmi con le altrè che non sono cosi, possono arrivare a cinquecento fuochi, v' è uni altra terra vicina che è una delle sette, et è alquanto maggiore di questa, et una altra della medesima grandezza di questa, et le altre quattro sono alquanto minori, et tutte Io le mando depinte a vostra segnioria con ill viaggio: et pergamino dove va la pittura si trova qui con altri pergamini: Hanno mantelli depinti della maniera che Io

---

36. Sidenote: "The Marques de la Roche 1584."
37. Sidenote: "Jaques Cartier."
38. Sidenote: "Vynes."
39. Sidenote: "Silver, golde, redd copper."
40. Sidenote: "Staggs. dere. beares. conies. hares. marters. foxes. otters. bevers. squirrells. badgers. Cranes. swannes. outardes. wild geese. mallards. thrushes. blackbirds. turtles. wilde pigeons."

41. Sidenote: "Golde and redd copper."
42. Sidenote: "A sea of freshe water."
43. Sidenote: "Cynamon. cloves."
44. Sidenote: "Vasques de Coronado."
45. Sidenote: "Cevola a toune of CC houses."

mando a vostra segnioria: Non raccolgono bombaso pero ne portano mantelli, come ella vedrà per la mostra: et è vero che si ritrovo nelle lor case certo bombaso filato: et hanno delle turchine penso in quantità, si trovaron in una charta due punte di smeraldi[46] et certe picciole pierte rotte, che tirano al color di granata et altre pietre di christallo. Si trovaron galline: sono bonissime et maggiori che quelle di Mexico. Si trovo bonissima herba una quarta lega di quà: Mangiano le miliori tortelle che io habbia veduto in alcuna parte: Hanno bonissimo sale[47] in grano, che levano dè un Lugume che è lunghe di quà una jornata: Vi sono di molti animali, orsi, tigri, leoni, porci spinosi, lepri, conigli, et certi castrati della grandezza d' un cavallo con corni molto grandi e code picciole:[48] Vi sono delle capre salvatice, delequali io ho vedato le teste, et le pelli de i cingialli. Vi sono cacciagoni di cervi, pardi, cavrioli molto grandi: fanno otto jornate verso le compagne al mare di settentrione:[49] Quivi sono certe pelli ben concie, et la concia et pittura si dan dove uccidon le vacche.[50] In the last chapiter he addeth: Mando a vostra Segnioria una pelle di vacca, certe turchine et duoi pendenti d'orecchie delle medesime, et quindici petini degli Indiani, et alcune tavolette guarniti di queste turchine, &c. And for a conclusion he endethe sayenge: In questo luogo si e trovato alquanto oro et argento,[51] che quei che si intendono di miniera non l'han reputato per cattivo. And Franciscus Lopez de Gomera in his Generall Historie of the Indies fol. 297 and 298. intreatinge of the seconde voyadge of Franciscus Vasques de Coronado from Cevola to Tigues, from Tigues to Cicuic, and from Cicuic to Quivera, saieth firste of the contrye about Tigues: Ci sono in quel paese melloni et cottone bianco e rosso, del quale fanno piu larghi mantelli, che in altre bande delle Indie. And of Quivera he saieth: è Quivera in quaranta gradi, è paese temperato di bonissime aque, di molto herbatico, prugne, more, noci, meloni et une che maturano benissimo; e vescono pelle di vacche e caprioli, viddero per la costa navi che portavano Alcatrarzes de oro et argento per le proe con mercantie: e credettero ch'eravo del Cataio et China: per chè accennavano, che havevanono navigato trenta di. Touchinge newefounde lande, because no man hath better searched it oute and all the commodities thereof then those that were there the laste yere 1583 the space of eightene daies on lande with Sir Humfry Gilbert I will make rehersall thereof, as I finde it committed to printe in a learned discourse intituled *A True Reporte of the late discoveries and possessyon taken in the righte of the Crowne of England, of the Newfounde landes, &c.* The wordes are these in the firste leafe: Then Sir Humfry wente to viewe the Contrie, beinge well accompanied with moste of his capitaines and souldiers. They founde the same very temperate but somwhat warmer then England at that time of the yere, replenished with beastes and greate store of fowle of divers kyndes, and fisshes of sondrye sortes bothe in the salte water and in the freshe, in so greate plentie as mighte suffice to victuall an armye, and they are very easely taken. And in the fifte chapter of the said discourse I reade in this manner: But let us omitte all presumptions, howe vehemente soever, and dwell upon the certentie of suche commodities as were discovered and founde by Sir Humfry Gilbert and his assistantes in Newfounde lande, in Auguste laste; ffor there may very easely be made pitche, tarr, rosen, sope asshes in greate plentie, yea as it is thoughte ynoughe to serve the whole realme of every of these kindes, and of trayne oyle[52] suche quantitie as if I shoulde [set] downe the value that they doo esteme it at which have bene there, it woulde seme incredible. To this in effecte agreeth that which one Stephanus Parmenius[53] a learned hungarian borne in Buda and lately my bedfelowe in Oxforde wrote unto me oute of Newfounde lande[54] beinge of Sir Humfryes companye: Piscium (saieth he writinge in Latin) inexhausta copia, inde huc comeantibus magnus questus; vix hamus fundum attigit, ilicò insigni aliquo onustus est: Terra universa montana et sylvestris: arbores ut plurimùm pinus, et abietes.[55] Herbæ omnes proceræ, sed rarò à nostris diversæ: Natura videtur velle niti etiam ad generandum frumentum. Inveni enim gramina et spicas in similitudinem secales: Et facilè cultura et sacione

46. Sidenote: "Bombase. turchine. smeraldè."
47. Sidenote: "Excellent salt."
48. Sidenote: "Shepe exceeding greate apes."
49. Sidenote: "The northe sea."
50. Sidenote: "Oxen."
51. Sidenote: "Golde and silver."

52. Sidenote: "Pitche, tarr, rosen, sopeasshes, trayne oyle."
53. Sidenote: "Stephanus Parmenius of Buda."
54. Sidenote: "Letters the last yere in latin out of Newfounde lande."
55. Sidenote: "Pynes and fyrres."

in usum humanum assuefieri posse videntur. Rubi in silvis vel potiùs fraga arborescentia magna suavitate: ursi circa tiguria nonnunquam apparent et conficiuntur. Ignotum est an aliquid metalli subsit montibus, etsi aspectus eorum mineras latentes preseferat. Nos admiralio authores fuimus sylvas incendere,[56] quô ad inspiciendum regionem spacium pateret, nec displicebat illi consilium, si non magnum incommodum allaturum videretur: Confirmatum est enim ab idoneis hominibus, cum casu quopiam, in alia nescio qua statione id accidisset, septennium totum pisces non comparuisse, exacerbata maris unda ex terebinthina quæ conflagrantibus arboribus per rivulos defluebat. Cœlum hoc anni tempore ita fervidum est[57] ut nisi pisces qui arefiunt ad solem assidui invertantur, ab adustione defendi non possint: Aer in terra mediocriter clarus est. Ad orientem supra mare perpetuæ nebulæ, &c. Nowe, to passe from Newfounde lande to 60 degrees I finde it beste described by Jasper Corterealis[58] in the thirde volume of the voyadges gathered by Ramusius fol. 417. There I reade as followeth: Nella parte del mondo nuovo che corre verso tramontana et maestro all' incontro del nostro habitabile del Europa, v' hanno navigato molti capitani et il primo (per quel che si sa) fù Gasparo Cortereale Portoghese, che del 1500. v' andò con due caravelle, pensando di trover qualche stretto di mare donde per viaggio piu breve, che non è l' andare attorno l'Affrica potesse passare all' Isole delle Spicerie. Esso navigò tanto avanti, che venue in luogo dove erano grandissimi freddi, et in gradi 60.[59] di latitudine trovò un fiume carrico di neve, dalla quali detta il nome chiamandalo Rio Nevado, nè li bastò l'animo di passar più avanti. Tutta questa costa che corre dal detto rio nevado[60] insu [insino] al porto di Maluas leghe 200. ilquale è in gradi 56. La vidde piena di genti et molto habitato: sopra laqual dismontato preso alcuni per menarli seco. Scoperse ancho molte Isole per mezo la detta costa tutte populate, a ciascuna delle quali diede il nome. Gli habitanti sono homini grandi, ben proportionati, ma alquanto berretini, et si dipingono

la faccia et tutto il corpo con diverso colori per galanteria. Portono manigli d' argento et di rame, et si cuoprono con pelli cucite insieme di martori et di altri animali diversi. Il verno le portono col peto di dentro, et la state di fuori. Il cibo loro per la magior parte è di pesce piu che d'alcuna altera cosa, massimamente di salmoni,[61] che v'hanno in grandissima copia: et anchora che visiano diversi sorti d'uccelli et di frutti non dimeno, non fanno conto se non di pesce, le loro habitationi sono fatte di legni deiquale hanno abondantia, per esservi grandissimi et infiniti boschi, et in luogo di tegole le cuoprono con pelli di pesce,[62] che ne pigliano grandissimi, et le scorticano. Vidde molti uccelli et altri animali massimamente ursi tutti bianchi. The reste of this coaste from 60. to 63. is described by Frobisher and in freshe memorye so that I shall not nede to make repetition thereof. Thus, havinge alleaged many printed testymonies of these credible persons which were personally betwene 30. and 63. degrees in America as well on the coaste as within the lande, which affirmed unto the princes and kinges which sett them oute that they founde there golde, silver, copper, leade, and perles in aboundaunce, precious stones, as turqueses and Emrauldes, spices and druggs, as pepper, cynamon, cloves, rubarb, muske called Castor, Turpentine, Silke wormes fairer then ours of Europe, white and redd cotten, infinite multitudes of all kinde of beastes, with their tallowe and hides dressed and undressed, Cochenilio founde last yere by the men of St. John de Luze and many other kindes of coulours for clothinge,[63] millions of all kindes of fowles for foode and fethers, salte for fisshinge, excellent vines in many places for wines, the soile apte to beare olyves for oile, all kindes of frutes as oranges, almondes, filberdes, figges, plomes, mulberies, raspis, pomi appij, melons, all kinde of odoriferous trees and date trees, Cipresses, Cedars, bayes, sapines, hony and waxe, and in new founde lande aboundaunce of pynes and firr trees, asshes, and other like to make mastes and deale boordes, pitche, tarr, rosen, and hempe for cables and cordage, and, upp within the Graunde Baye excedinge quantitie of all kynde of precious

---

56. Sidenote: "Afterwardes they sett the woodds on fire which burnte three weekes together."
57. Sidenote: "Greate heate in Newfounde lande in sommer."
58. Sidenote: "Jasper Corterealis."
59. Sidenote: "60. degrees."
60. Sidenote: "Rio Nevado."

61. Sidenote: "Dyvers colours. sylver. copper. martori et altri animali diversi. pesce. salmoni."
62. Sidenote: "mightie & huge woodds. mightie fishe."
63. Sidenote: "A singuler commoditie for dyenge of englishe clothe."

furres, (whereof I sawe twentie thousande frenche Crownes worthe the laste yere broughte to Paris to Valeron Perosse and Mathewe Grainer the kinges skynners) also suche abboundaunce of trayne oile to make sope,[64] and of fishe as a third part of Europe ys furnished therewith: I may well and truly conclude with reason and aucthoritie that all the commodities of all our olde decayed and daungerous trades in all Europe, Africa, and Asia haunted by us may in shorte space for little or nothinge and many for the very workemanshippe in a manner be had in that parte of America which lieth betwene 30. and 60. degrees of northerly latitude, if by our slackness wee suffer not the frenche or others to prevente us.[65]

4

That this enterprize will be for the manifolde ymployment of nombers of idle men, and for bredinge of many sufficient, and for utteraunce of the greate quantitie of the commodities of our Realme.

It is well worthe the observacion to see and consider what the like voyadges of discoverye and planting in the easte and weste Indies hath wroughte in the kingdomes of Portingale and Spayne. Bothe which Realmes beinge of themselves poore and barren and hardly able to susteine their inhabitaunts by their discoveries have founde suche occasion of employmente, that these many yeres wee have not herde scarcely of any pirate of those twoo nations: whereas wee and the frenche are moste infamous for our outeragious, common, and daily piracies. Againe when hearde wee almoste of one theefe amongest them. The reason is that by these their new discoveries they have so many honest wayes to sett them on worke as they rather wante men than meanes to ymploye them: But wee for all the Statutes that hitherto can be devised, and the sharpe execution of the same in poonishinge idle and lazye persons for wante of sufficient occasion of honest employmente cannot deliver our common wealthe from multitudes of loyterers and idle vagabondes. Truthe it is that throughe our longe peace and seldome sicknes (twoo singuler blessinges of almightie god) wee are growen more populous than

ever heretofore: So that nowe there are of every arte and science so many, that they can hardly lyve one by another, nay rather they are readie to eate upp one another: yea many thousandes of idle persons are within this Realme, which havinge no way to be sett on worke be either mutinous and seeke alteration in the state,[66] or at leaste very burdensome to the common wealthe, and often fall to pilferinge and thevinge and other lewdnes, whereby all the prisons of the lande are daily pestred and stuffed full of them, where either they pitifully pyne awaye, or els at lengthe are miserably hanged, even xx[ti]. at a clappe oute of some one Jayle: whereas yf this voyadge were put in execution, these pety theves mighte be condempned for certen yeres in the westerne partes,[67] especially in Newfounde Lande in sawinge and fellinge of tymber for mastes of shippes and deale boordes, in burninge of the firres and pine trees to make pitche tarr rosen and sope asshes, in beatinge and workinge of hempe for cordage: and in the more sowtherne partes in settinge them to worke in mynes of golde, silver, copper, leade and yron, in dragginge for perles and currall, in plantinge of suger canes as the Portingales have done in Madera, in mayneteynaunce and increasinge of silke wormes for silke and in dressinge the same: in gatheringe of cotten whereof there is plentie, in tillinge of the soile there for graine, in dressinge of vines whereof there is greate aboundaunce for wyne, olyves whereof the soile is capable for oyle, trees for oranges, lymons, almondes, figges, and other frutes all which are founde to growe there already: in sowinge of woade and madder for diers as the Portingales have don in the Azores, in dressinge of raw hides of divers kindes of beastes, in makinge and gatheringe of salte as in Rochel and Bayon which may serve for the Newe Lande fisshinge, in killinge the whale, seale, porpose, and whirlepoole for trayne oile, in fisshinge, saltinge, and dryenge of linge, codde, salmon, herringe, in makinge and gatheringe of hony, wax, turpentine, in hewinge and shapinge of stone, as marble, jeate, christall, freestone, which will be goodd balaste for our shippes homewardes, and after serve for noble buildinges, in making of

---

64. Sidenote: "plancks for shipps oares. Thinges incident to a navy. sope asshes."
65. Sidenote: "prevention to be taken hede of."

66. Sidenote: "Idle persons mutynous and desire alteration in the state."
67. Sidenote: "A remedy to all these inconveniences."

caske, oares, and all other manner of staves; in buildinge of fortes, townes, churches; in powderinge and barrellinge of fishe, fowles, and fleshe, which will be notable provision for sea and lande: in dryinge, sortinge and packinge of fethers whereof may be had there marvelous greate quantitie. Besides this, such as by any kinde of infirmitie cannot passe the seas thither, and now are chardgeable to the Realme at home, by this voyadge shalbe made profitable members by employinge them in England in makinge of a thousande triflinge thinges, which will be very goodd marchandize for those Contries where wee shall have moste ample vente thereof. And seinge the savages of the graunde Baye and all alonge the mightie Ryver that ronneth upp to Canada and Hochelaga are greately delighted with any cappe or garment made of course wollen clothe, their Contrie beinge colde and sharpe in the winter, yt is manifeste wee shall finde greate utteraunce of our clothes, especially of our coursest and basest northerne doosens and our Irishe and Welshe frizes, and rugges: whereby all occupacions belonginge to clothinge and knittinge shalbe freshly sett on worke, as cappers, knitters, clothiers, wollmen, carders, spynners, weavers, fullers, sheremen, dyers, drapers, hatters and such like, whereby many decayed townes may be repaired: In somme this enterprice will mynister matter for all sortes and states of men to worke upon: namely all severall kindes of artificers, husbandmen, seamen, marchauntes, souldiers, capitaines, phisitions, lawyers, devines, Cosmographers, hidrographers, Astronomers, historiographers, yea olde folkes, lame persons, women, and younge children by many meanes which hereby shall still be mynistred unto them, shalbe kepte from idlenes, and be made able by their owne honest and easie labour to finde themselves withoute surchardginge others. For proofe of the last part of my allegation, I will use but onely this one example followinge.

In the yere of our Lorde 1564 at what tyme the flemishe nation were growen as yt were to the fulnes of their wealthe and to the heighte of their pride, and not remembringe what wonderfull gaine they had yerely by the wolles, clothes and comodities of England, beganne to contempne our nation and to rejecte our clothes and commodities: A subjecte of the then twoo Erles of Emden a man of greate observacion wrote a notable discourse to

the younge Erles to take occasion of that present tyme by offer of large priviledges in Emden to the Englishe men. In which discourse the said subjecte for the better inducemente of the said twoo younge Erles dothe write of his owne knowledge, as he in his discourse affirmeth, and as also by his reporte appereth in the 22th booke of *Sleydans Commentaries*, That, anno 1550 Charles the fifte then Emperour would have had the Spanishe Inquisition broughte into Andwerpe and into the Netherlandes: whereaboute there was moche adoe, and that neither the sute of the Towne of Andwerpe, nor the requeste of their frendes could perswade the Emperour from it, till at the laste they tolde him playnely that if the Inquisicion came into Andwerpe and the netherlandes, that the Englishe marchantes woulde departe oute of the Towne and out of his Contries: And upon declaration of this suggestion, searche was made what profite there came and commoditie grewe by the haunte of the englishe marchantes: Then was it founde by searche and enquirie that within the Towne of Andwerpe alone there were fourtene thousande persons fedde and mayneteyned onely by the workinge of englishe commodities, besides the gaines that marchantes and shippers with other in the sayd Towne did gett, which was the greatest parte of their lyvinge which were thoughte to be in nombre half as many more, and in all other places of his netherlandes by the indrapinge of englishe woll into clothe and by the workinge of other englishe commodities, there were thirtie thousande persons more mayneteyned and fedd, which in all amounteth to the nomber of li.M. persons. And this was the reporte that was geven to this mightie Emperour whereby the towne of Andwerpe and the Netherlandes were saved from the Inquisition: And in the ende of the 45th article of the same discourse, also he setteth down by particuler accompte howe the subjectes of the same Emperour in the netherlandes dyd gaine yerely onely by the woll and wollen clothe that came eche yere oute of England almoste vi.C.M.li.: I say almoste six hundreth thousande poundes sterling,[68] besides the gaines they had for sondry other thinges that were of marvelous sommes: Nowe if her Majestie take these

68. Sidenote: "Six hundred thousand pounde gayned yerely by Englishe wolles."

westerne discoveries in hande and plante there, yt is like that in shorte time wee shall vente as greate a masse of clothe yn those partes as ever wee did in the netherlandes, and in tyme moche more: which was the opinion of that excellent man Master Roberte Thorne extante in printe in the laste leafe savinge one of his discourse to Doctor Lea Embassador for King Henry the eighte in Spaine with Charles the Emperour whose wordes are these: And althoughe (saieth he) wee wente not into the said Ilandes of Spicerye for that they are the Emperours or kinges of Portingale, wee shoulde by the way and commynge once to the lyne equinoctiall finde landes no lesse riche of golde and spicerie, as all other landes are under the said lyne equinoctiall: And also shoulde yf wee may passe under the northe enjoye the navigacion of all Tartarye: which should be no lesse profitable to our commodities of clothe, then those spiceries to the Emperour and kinge of Portingale.

This beinge soe, yt commeth to passe that whatsoever clothe wee shall vente on the tracte of that firme, or in the Ilandes of the same, or in other landes, Ilandes, and territories beyonde, be they within the circle articke or withoute, all these clothes I say are to passe oute of this Realme full wroughte by our naturall subjectes in all degrees of labour. And if it come aboute in tyme that wee shall vente that masse there that wee vented in the base Contries, which is hoped by great reason, then shall all that clothe passe oute of this Realme in all degrees of labour full wroughte by the poore naturall subjectes of this Realme, like as the quantitie of our clothe dothe passe that goeth hence to Russia, Barbarie, Turkye, Persia, &c. And then consequently it followeth that the like number of people alleaged to the Emperour shalbe sett on worke in England of our poore sujectes more then hath bene: And so her Majestie shall not be troubled with the pitefull outecryes of Cappers, knytters, spynners, &c. And on the other side wee are to note that all the commodities wee shall bringe thence, wee shall not bringe them wroughte as wee bringe now the commodities of Fraunce and Flaunders, &c., but shall receave them all substaunces unwroughte to the ymploymente of a wonderfull multitude of the poore subjectes of this Realme in returne: And so to conclude what in the nomber of thinges to goe oute wroughte, and to come in unwroughte, there nede not one poore creature to steale, to sterve,

or to begge as they doo: And to aunswer objections,[69] where fooles for the swarminge of beggars alleage that the realme is toto populous: Salomon saieth that the hono^r and strengthe of a Prince consisteth in the multitude of the people: And if this come aboute that worke may be had for the multitude, where the Realme hath nowe one thousande for the defence thereof, the same may have fyve thousande: For when people knowe howe to lyve, and howe to maynetayne and feede their wyves and children, they will not abstaine from mariage as nowe they doe: And the soile thus aboundinge with corne, fleshe, mylke, butter, cheese, herbes, rootes, and frutes, &c. and the seas that envyron the same so infynitely aboundinge in fishe, I dare truly affirme that if the nomber in this Realme were as greate as all Spaine and ffraunce have, the people beinge industrious, industrious I say, there shoulde be founde victualls ynoughe at the full in all bounty to suffice them all: And takinge order to cary hence thither our clothes made in hose, coates, clokes, whoodes, &c., and to returne thither hides of their owne beastes tanned and turned into shoes and bootes, and other skynnes of goates whereof they have store into gloves &c. no doubte but wee shall sett on worke in this Realme besides sailers and suche as shalbe seated there in those westerne discovered Contries, at the leaste C. M. subjectes to the greate abatinge of the goodd estate of subjectes of forreine Princes enemyes or doubtfull friends, and this *absque injuria* as the lawyers say albeit not *sine damno*: And having a vente of lynnen as the Spaniardes have in the rest of that firme, wee may sett our people in making the same infinitely on worke, and in many other thinges besides which time will bringe aboute, thoughe nowe for wante of knowledge and full experience of this trade wee cannot enter into juste accompte of all particulers.

5

That this voyage will be a great bridle to the Indies of the Kinge of Spaine, and a meane that wee may arreste at our pleasure for the space of tenne weeks or three monethes every yere one or twoo C. saile of his subjectes shippes at the fyshinge in Newfounde Lande.

69. Sidenote: "Objection. Aunswer."

The cause why the Kinge of Spaine these three or foure yeres last paste was at suche intollerable chardges in furnishinge oute so many navies to wynne Tercera and the other small Ilandes of the Azores adjacent to the same, was the oportunitie of the places in interceptinge his West Indian flete at their returne homewarde as a matter that toucheth him indeede to the quicke: But the plantinge of twoo or three strong fortes upon some goodd havens (whereof there is greate store) betweene Florida and Cape Briton woulde be a matter in shorte space of greater dommage as well to his flete as to his westerne Indies, for wee shoulde not onely often tymes indaunger his flete in the returne thereof, but also in fewe yeres put him in hazarde in loosinge some parte of Nova Hispania: Touchinge the fleete, no man (that knoweth the course thereof comynge oute betwene Cuba, and the Cape of Florida alonge the gulfe or Straite of Bahama) can denye that it is caried by the currant northe and northeaste towardes the coaste which wee purpose god willinge to inhabite: which hapned to them not twoo yeres past as Master Jenynges and Master Smithe the master and masters mate of the shippe called the Toby belonginge to Bristowe infourmed me and many of the chefest merchauntes of that Citie, whereof they had particuler advertisement at Cadiz in Spaine a little before by them that were in the same flete the selfe same yere, and were in person driven upon the same coaste and sawe the people which they reported to be bigge men somewhat in makinge like the hollanders, and lighted on a Towne upon a ryvers side which they affirmed to be above a quarter of a mile in lengthe. Besides the current, it is also a thinge withoute controversie that all southerne and southeasterne windes inforce the Spanish flete returninge home nere or upon the aforesaide coaste and consequently will bringe them into our daunger after wee shalbe there strongly setled and fortified: wee are moreover to understande that the Savages of Florida are the Spaniardes mortall enemyes and wilbe ready to joyne with us againste them, as they joyned with Capitaine Gourgues a Gascoigne, whoe beinge but a private man and goinge thither at his owne chardges by their aide wonne and rased the three small fortes which the Spaniardes aboute xx$^{ti.}$ yeres agoe had planted in Florida after their traiterous slaughter of John Ribault; which Gourgues slewe and hanged upp divers of them on the same trees whereon the yere before they had hanged the Frenche. Yea one Holocotera brother to one of the kinges of the Savages leapinge upp on an highe place with his owne handes slewe a Spanishe Canonier as he was puttinge fire to a pece of ordynaunce, which storye is at large in printe sett furthe by Monsieur Poplynier in his book intituled *Trois Mondes*.

Also within the lande on the northe side of Nova Hispania there is a people called Chichimici which are bigg and stronge men and valiaunte archers which have contynuall warres with the Spaniardes and doo greatly annoye them: The Spanishe histories which I have reade and other late discourses make greate mention of them: Yea Myles Phillipps whoe was xiiii. yeres in those partes, and presented his whole travell in writinge to her Majestie, confesseth this to be moste certaine. Nowe if wee (being thereto provoked by spanishe injuries) woulde either joyne with these Savages, or sende or give them armour as the Spaniardes arme our Irishe Rebells, wee shoulde trouble the kinge of Spaine more in those partes, then he hath or can trouble us in Ireland, and holde him at suche a Bay, as he was never yet helde at: For if (as the aforesaide Miles Phillipps writeth) yt be true that one negro which fledd from his cruell spanishe Master is receaved and made Capitaine of multitudes of the Chichimici and daily dothe grevously afflicte them, and hath almoste enforced them to leave and abandon their silver mynes in those quarters, what dommage mighte divers hundreds of englishe men doo them being growen once into familiaritie with that valiaunte nation: And this is the greatest feare that the Spaniardes have, To witt our plantinge in those partes, and joyninge with those Savages their neighbours in Florida and on the northe side of Nova Hispania. Which thinge an englishe gentleman Capitaine Muffett whoe is nowe in Fraunce, tolde divers tymes this laste winter in my hearinge and others of credite, namely that when he was in Spaine prisoner not longe since, he hearde the Threasurer of the west Indies say, that there was no suche way to hinder his Master, as to plante upon the coaste nere unto fflorida, from whence by great ryvers any man mighte easely passe farre upp into the lande and joyne with his enemyes, whereof he stoode in contynuall feare, and said moreover that that was the occasion why suche crueltie was used towardes John Ribaulte and his Companie upon his seekinge to settle there: Fynally if wee liste not to come so nere Florida this is a matter of no small momente, that if wee fortifie ourselves about Cape Briton nere Newfounde land[70] partely by the strengthe of our fortificacion and partely by the aide of our navye of ffishermen which are already commaunders of others there, havinge our double forces thus joyned together, wee shalbe able upon every soodden to cease upon one or twoo hundreth Spanishe and Portingale shippes, which for tenne weekes or three monethes are there on fisshinge every yere. This I say will be suche a bridle to him and suche an advauntage unto us, as wee cannot possibly ymagine a greater: And thus the Frenche served them in the time of Mounsieurs being in Flaunders, caryenge awaye oute of some harborowes three or foure spanishe and portingale shippes at ones, and more they woulde have taken, if our Englishmen and namely one of myne acquaintaunce of Ratclife had not defended them. And hither of necessitie they must yerely repaire beinge not able to make their provision for land and sea of fishe in any place els excepte on the coaste of Ireland and at Cape Blancke in Africa, which twoo are nothinge worthe in comparison to this thirde place: So shall wee be able to crye quittaunce with the King of Spaine if he shoulde goe aboute to make any generall arreste of our navye, or rather terrifie him from any such enterpryse, when he shall bethincke himself that his navye in Newfounde Lande is no lesse in our daunger then ours is in his domynions wheresoever.

6

That the mischefe that the Indian Treasure wroughte in time of Charles the late Emperour father to the Spanishe kinge is to be had in consideracion of the Queenes most excellent Majestie leaste the contynuall comynge of the like treasure from thence to his sonne, worke the unrevocable annoye of this Realme, whereof already we have had very daungerous experience.

It is written in the xxxth. article of the discourse before specified dedicated to the twoo younge Erles of Emden as followeth *verbatim*: With this greate treasure did not the Emperour Charles gett from the Frenche kinge the kingdome of Naples, the Dukedome of Myllaine, and all other his domynions in Italy, Lombardy, Pyemont, and Savoye? with this treasure did he not take the Pope prisoner: and sacked the sea of Rome? With this treasure did he not take the frenche kinge prisoner and mayneteyne all the greate warres with Fraunce since the yere of o[r] lorde 1540 to the yere of our lorde 1560 as is declared in the 12. and 13. article of his booke? With this treasure hath he not mayneteyned many Cities in Italie as well againste the Pope as againste the frenche kinge, as Parma, Florence and such other? With this treasure did he not overthrowe the Duke of Cleave, and take Gilderland, Groyninge lande and other Domynions from him? which oughte to be a goode warninge to you all, as it shall be most plainely and truly declared hereafter? With this treasure did he not gett into his handes the Erldome of Lingen in westfalia? With this treasure did he not cause the Erle of Esones, your subjecte to rebell againste your graces father and againste you? the cause you knowe best: And what worke this treasure made amongest the Princes and Townes in Germany when the Duke of Saxony and the Launtzgrave van Hessen were taken, Sleydan our owne countryman by his chronicle declareth at large. And did not this treasure, named the Burgundishe asse, walke and ronne in all places to make bothe warr and peace at pleasure? And tooke he nothinge from the Empire then? yes truly to moche as you shall heare: When the Emperour Charles was firste made Empero[r], what were the Townes and Contries in the netherlandes that justly or properly came to him by birthe and inheritaunce? There was Brabant, Flaunders, Holland, Zeland, Artoys, and Henego: And yet there is a greate question concerninge Holland howe the Emperour Charles and his progenitours came by yt, and what homage and duetie they oughte to doo for the same: Because thereby the house of Burgundy hath the mouthe of the River Rhene at their commaundemente, which is to the greate losse, domage, and daunger of Germanye as hereafter shalbe declared. Here be all the Contries that belonged to the house of Burgundie when the Emperour Charles was made Emperour. But howe moche hath bene added to the

70. Sidenote: "The benefite of plantinge aboute Cape Bryton or Newfounde lande."

netherlandes since by him contrary to his oathe made? That are these Townes and Contries as yt appereth in Sleydans Chronicle, viz., Lutzenburge, Lymeburge, Gelderlande, the Erldome of Sutphen, the Citie and straite of Utright with all the landes in over Isel, West Frizeland, the Citie of Groninge, and Groininge lande. And as before it is saied he hath by pollicie gotten into his handes the Erldome of Lingen standinge in Westfalia: and by the like pollicie with money he is become the defendour of the Erledome of Esons which is parcell of your graces Countrie of East frizeland. All these Contries and Townes with the treasure of the netherlandes hath he taken from the Empire.

Thus farr procedeth this excellent man in describinge howe Charles the Emperour employed his treasure to the afflictinge and oppressinge of moste of the greatest estates of Christendome. The effecte of these treasures which he had oute of the west Indies, Peter Martir of Angleria in the epistle dedicatory of his Decades to the said Emperour Charles truly prognosticated in the begynnynge before hand, where he writeth thus unto him: Come therefore and embrace this newe worlde and suffer us no longer to consume in desire of your presence. From hence, from hence (I say) moste noble younge Prince shall instrumentes be prepared for you whereby all the worlde shalbe under your obeysaunce: And in very deede it is moste apparaunte that riches are the fittest instruments of conqueste, and that the Emperour turned them to that use. To leave the father and to come to the sonne, hath not Kinge Phillippe employed his treasure as injuriously to all Princes and potentates of Europe?[71] Is it not he that with his Indian treasure corrupted the *Quinqueviri* in portingale that in the interregnum were appointed overseers of the common wealthe and so hath joyned that kingdome to his, with all the Ilandes, Townes, and domynions belonginge to that Crowne? Is it not he that with his treasure hath gon aboute to hier some ungodlye murderer to make away with Don Antonio one while by open proclamacion, and another while *sotto capo*, under hande? Is it not he that by his treasure hathe hired at sondry times the sonnes of Beliall to bereve the Prince of Orange of his life? And hath he not suborned by hope of rewarde other moste ungodly persons to lay violent handes upon other Christian princes? Hath not he these many yeres geven large pensions to nombers of englishe unnaturall rebelles? Doth he not support the Semynaries of Rome and Rhemes to be thornes in the sides of their owne common wealthes? Hath not he divers tymes sente forren forces into Ireland furnished with money, armour, munition, and victualls? Hath not he sente rounde sommes of money into Scotland bothe to the Kinge and those that are aboute him to alter the estate there and to trouble oures? And is it not knowen that this Spanishe asse ronneth upp and downe laden throughe all Fraunce, and when it coulde not enter into the papistes gates, yt hath soughte to enter into the Courtes of the princes of the Rellig-ion to renewe the late intermitted civile warres? What it hath don and nowe dothe in all the Empire and the lowe Contries and is like to worke in other places unlesse spedy order be taken to hinder it, is described at large by Mounsieur de Aldegonnde a germaine gentleman in a pithie and moste earnest exhortation (extant in latine, Italian, frenche, englishe, and duche) concerninge the estate of Christendome, together with the meanes to defende and preserve the same, dedicated to all christian kinges, princes, and potentates.

7

What speciall meanes may bringe kinge Phillippe from his highe Throne and make him equall to the Princes his neighboures: wherewith all is shewed his weakenes in the west Indies.

Firste it is to be considered that his Domynions and Territories oute of Spaine lye farr distant from Spaine his chefest force, and farr distante one from another, and are kepte by greate tyrannie, and *quos metuunt oderunt*. And the people kepte in subjection desire nothinge more then freedome. And like as a little passage geven to water it maketh his owne way, so give but a small meane to suche kepte in tyranie, they will make their owne way to libertie, which way may easely be made. And entringe into the consideracion of the way how this Phillippe may be abased, I meane firste to begynne with the west Indies as there to laye a chefe foundation for his over-throwe. And like as the foundation of the strongest holde undermyned and removed, the mightiest and strongest walles fall flatt to the

---

71. Sidenote: "Kinge Phillipps injuries offred by his Treasures."

earthe, so this prince spoiled or intercepted for a while of his treasure, occasion by lacke of the same is geven that all his Territories in Europe oute of Spaine slide from him, and the Moores enter into Spaine it selfe, and the people revolte in every forrein territorie of his, and cutt the throates of the proude hatefull Spaniardes their governours. For this Phillippe already owinge many millions, and of late yeres empaired in credite, bothe by lacke of abilitie of longe tyme to pay the same, and by his shamefull losse of his Spaniardes and dishonour in the Lowe Contries, and by lacke of the yerely Renewe of his Revenewe, he shall not be able to wage his severall garrisons kepte in his severall frontiers, territories, and places, nor to corrupte in princes Courtes, nor to doo many feates. And this weyed, wee are to knowe what Phillip ys in the west Indies. And that wee be not abused with Spanishe braggs, and made to beleve what he is not, and so drawen into vain feare suffer fondly and childishly our owne utter spoile. And therefore wee are to understande that Phillippe rather governeth in the West Indies by opinion, then by mighte. For the small manred of Spaine of itselfe being alwayes at the best slenderly peopled was never able to rule so many Regions, or to kepe in subjection such worldes of people as be there, were it not for the error of the Indian people, that thincke he is that he is not, and that doo ymagine, that Phillippe hath a thousande Spaniardes for every single naturall subjecte that he hath there. And like as the Romaynes allured hither into Britaine perced the Iland and planted here and there in the mouthes of Rivers and upon straites, and kepte Colonies, as at Westchester upon the River of Dee, at Yorke upon the River of Owse, and upon the Rivers of Thames and Severne, and yet in truthe never enjoyed more of the contries rounde aboute, then the Englishe planted at Bulloine and Calice did of the frenche soile adjoyninge, nor in effecte had the Brittishe nation at commaundement: Even so hath the Spaniarde perced the Indies and planted here and there very thinlye and slenderlye withoute havinge the Indian multitude in subjection, or in their Townes and fortes any nomber to holde any of them againste the meanest force of a Prince: So as in truthe the Spaniarde ys very weake there. And it is knowen to Sir Fraunces Drake and to Master Hawkins, and Miles Phillipps (which Miles lyved xiiii yeres

in Nova Spania) and to dyvers others of her Majesties subjectes besides that have been there: That the Ilandes there abounde with people and nations that rejecte the proude and bluddy governemente of the Spaniarde, and that doo mortally hate the Spaniarde: And they also knowe that the Moores and suche as the Spaniardes have broughte thither for the mynes and for slavery have fledd from them into the Inlandes, and of them selves maineteine in many places frontier warres againste the Spaniarde, and many tymes so prevaile and especially of late, that the Spaniardes have bene inforced to sende the Spanishe marchauntes themselves into the warres, althoughe yt be againste the speciall priviledges graunted by Charles the late Emperour to the marchauntes, as may plainely appere by Spanishe marchauntes letters taken by Sir Fraunces Drake passinge in the sea of Sur towarde Panama to be conveyed into Spaine: And it is thoughte that Sir Fraunces Drake and some other Englishe are of so greate credite with the Symerons and with those that mayneteyne those frontier warres, that he mighte, bringinge thither a fewe Capitaines and some of our meaner souldiers late trayned in the base Contries, with archers and lighte furniture &c. bringe to passe that joyninge with those Inland people, Kinge Phillippe mighte either be deprived of his governmente there, or at the leaste of the takinge of his yerely benefite of the mynes. Thus with small chardge and fewe men nowe and then renewinge this matter by a few sailes to be sent thither for the comforte of suche as shalbe there residente, and for the incouragemente of the Symerons, greater effecte may followe then by meetinge with his golden flete, or by takinge of his treasures once or twise at the sea: For by this meanes, or by a platforme well to be sett downe, England may enjoye the benefite of the Indian mynes, or at the leaste kepe Phillippe from possessinge the same.

Hereunto yf wee adde our purposed westerne discoveries, and there plante, and people ryally, and fortifie strongly, and there builde shippes and maineteine a navy in special porte or portes, wee may by the same either encounter the Indian fleete, or be at hande as it were to yelde freshe supplye, courage, and comforte by men or munition to the Chichimici and the Symerons and suche other as shalbe incited to the spoile of the mynes, which in tyme will if it be not looked to bringe all Princes to weake estate that Phillippe, either for religion or other cause dothe hate, as the aforesaide Monsieur de Aldegond in his pithie and moste earneste exhortation to all Christian kinges, Princes, and Potentates to beware of kinge Phillipps ambitions growinge, dothe wisely and moste providently forwarne.

To this may be added (the Realme swarming wth lustie youthes that be turned to no profitable use) there may be sente bandes of them into the base Contries in more rounde nombers then are sente as yet. For if he presently prevaile there at o^r doores, farewell the traficque that els wee may have there (whereof wise men can say moche). And if he settle there, then let the Realme saye adewe to her quiet state and safetie. If these enter into the due consideration of wise men, and if platformes of these thinges be sett downe and executed duelye and with spede and effecte, no doubte but the Spanishe Empire falles to the grounde, and the Spanishe kinge shall be lefte bare as Aesops proude Crowe, the peacocke, the perot, the pye, and the popingey and every other birde havinge taken home from him his gorgeous fethers, he will in shorte space become a laughinge stocke for all the worlde, with such a mayme to the Pope and to that side, as never hapned to the sea of Rome by the practise of the late kinge of famous memory her Majesties father, or by all the former practises of all the protestant princes of Germanie, or by any other advise layde downe by Monsieur de Aldegond here after by them to be put in execucion. If you touche him in the Indies, you touche the apple of his eye, for take away his treasure which is *nervus belli*, and which he hath almoste oute of his West Indies, his olde bandes of souldiers will soone be dissolved, his purposes defeated, his power and strengthe diminished, his pride abated, and his tyranie utterly suppressed.

8

That the lymites of the Kinge of Spaines domynions in the west Indies be nothinge so large as is generally ymagined and surmized, neither those partes which he holdeth be of any such forces as is falsly geven oute by the popishe Clergie and others his fautors to terrifie the Princes of the Relligion and to abuse and blynde them.

As the Secretary of Don Antonio kinge of Portingale called Custodio Etan tolde me lately at Paris that the Portingales never had in Guinea, Bresill, and all the Easte Indies above twelve thousande Portingale souldiers whensoever they had moste, which was confirmed by one of the kinges Capitaines borne in Goa then presente, and that they governed rather by gevinge oute of greate rumors of power and by secrecie then by any greate force which they had in deede: So the like is to be proved of the kinge of Spaine in his west Indies. For he beinge in those partes exedinge weake hath nothinge such nombers of people there as ys geven oute: neither doo his domynions stretche so far as by the ignoraunte ys ymagined: which hereby easely may appere, seinge he hath no one Towne or forte in actuall possession in all Nova hispania to the northe of the Tropick of Cancer, which standeth in 23. degrees and an halfe, excepte the Towne of St. Helen and one or twoo small fortes in Florida: ffor as it is in the mappe of Culiacan sett oute twoo yeres paste with all diligence by Ortelius, Saincte Michael ys the furthest Towne northwarde on the backside of America, and Panuco, and Villa Sancti Jacobi are the moste northerly Colonies upon the Bay of Mexico that the Spaniardes inhabite, as the aforesaide Ortelius witnesseth in his mapp of those partes sett oute this presente yere 1584, which three Townes above named are under or within the Tropicke of Cancer. And so the kinge of Spaine hath no footinge beyonde the said Tropicke which is contrary to the opinion of the vulgar sorte which ymagine and by some are borne in hande that all is his from the equinoctiall as farr as the lande stretcheth towardes the Pooles: Againe that parte from the equinoctiall to the southe ys not inhabited by the Spaniarde any further then unto the Tropicke of Capricorne, as ys to be seene by the mappe of Peru this presente yere 1584 published by Ortelius: neither is it peopled by the Spaniardes to any purpose savinge onely alonge the sea coaste. And howe weake they are there and what simple shippinge they have, and howe dayly they be afflicted by the Inhabitauntes, Sir Fraunces Drake can tell and the letters by him intercepted doo declare. One Peter Benzo de Millano which was fourtene yeres in those partes writeth that they holde greate Townes, some with tenne, some with sixe, some with foure, and some with twoo souldiers, and that they commaunded that all the Italians, whome they called Levantines in contempte, shoulde departe those Contries, fearinge they shoulde reveale their nakednes to the worlde, and encourage others to sett in footinge there: Seeinge then they suffer no people of Europe to inhabite there savinge onely Spaniardes, any reasonable man that knoweth the barenes, desolacion and wante of men in Spaine together with these eightene yeres civill warres that hath wasted so many thousandes of them in the Lowe contries must nedes confesse that they have very simple forces there. The provinces which he holdeth are indeede many, yet more denuded than ever was any Empire since the creacion of the worlde. Some of his Contries are dispeopled, some barren, some so far asonder also held by Tyranie, that in deede upon the due consideracion of the matter, his mighte and greatenes is not suche as *prima facie* yt may seme to be: And weare yt not that he doth possesse suche a masse of treasure oute of the Indies, the frenche kinge of one onely kingdome with his onely people of Fraunce were able to drive him oute of all his domynions that he hath in the worlde.

It is written that Antigonus beinge to fighte againste certaine of his enemyes, they appered a farr of to be so huge and mightie, that his souldiers were halfe afraied to encounter them, but beinge incouraged by his valo^r, they easely overthrewe them in a conflicte, whereof he stripped one or twoo, which beinge turned oute of their bombasted and large apparell, were in deede but very weakelinges and shrimpes, which when he had shewed unto his souldiers, they were ashamed of themselves that ever they had bene afraied of suche wretches. So when wee shall have looked and narrowly pried into the Spanishe forces in America, wee shalbe doubtles ashamed of ourselves that wee have all this while bene afraied of those dissemblinge and feble scarr crowes. This wch I say concerninge the weakenes of the Spaniardes in America, may more easelie appere by this note followinge gathered by an excellent Frenche capitaine moste experte and privie to the state and force of the Islandes, havens, Townes, and fortes of all that parte of America which lieth upon our Ocean, which excedinge large coaste beinge so rarely and simply manned and fortified, wee may well assure ourselves that the Inlande is moche more weake and unmanned.

9

The names of the riche Townes lienge alonge the sea coaste on the north side from the equinoctiall of the mayne lande of America under the Kinge of Spaine.

1. Over againest the ilande of Margarita there is a Towne called Cumina wherein is great store of perle. There be divers boates belonginge to the Towne which onely dragge perles: This Towne is the farthest eastwarde which the kinge hath on the north side of India: It is environed with their enemyes viz. the Indyans and Caribes. The victualls come from this Towne to Margarita.

2. The nexte Towne westwarde is Carakas which is very riche of golde. This Towne standeth upon the sea and hath some victualls, but not plentie, and is environed likewise wth the Indians their mortall enemyes.

3. The towne Burborowate was destroyed by 50. Frenchemen and the treasure taken aweye.

4. The nexte Towne to the westwarde is called Coro which hath greate plentie of golde and victualls, this standeth upon the sea. This is a Civill Contrie, and some of the Indians broughte to a civill governemente.

5. At Rio de Hacha there is a Towne çalled Hacha, where is greate store of perle and silver but no golde, and not farr from thence there is a perle house: There is plentie of victualls, the Contrie civill, and some of the Indians at the Spaniardes comaundement. Master John Hawkins told me he wan this Towne and was master of yt three daies in his laste voyadge.

6. Further westwarde is a Towne called Santa Maren alias Marta where is greate store of golde but little victualls. This is envyroned with Indians enemyes to the Spaniardes.

7. The nexte Towne is Carthagena where is greate store of silver, golde, and precious stone. This Towne hath a nomber of Indians and Symerons to their enemyes, there is also greate store of victualls.

8. The nexte Towne thereunto is Nombro di Dios. To this towne cometh all the golde, perle, stone, and Jewells that cometh from Chile, Peru, and Panama oute of the southe sea. To this towne cometh halfe the fleete which taketh in halfe their treasure, and goeth to Havana, and so throughe the Gulfe of Bahama unto the Ilandes of Corvo, Flores, and the Azores and from thence into Spaine: This towne hath no victualls but such as

cometh from Panama and the ilandes by sea: By this Towne is a gulfe called Guluata, where the Cymerons and Indians have certaine Townes and kepe warres dayly with the Spaniardes as well as the Indians. At the southende of the gulfe there is not paste five legues over lande into the South sea.

9. The nexte towne is called Vraga alias Var, where is moche golde and small store of victualls, this is a civill Contrie nere to the Towne, the nexte is Nicaragua.

10. At Nicaragua is moche golde that cometh out of the Southe Sea, and there is a place where they make their frigotts: there ys little victualls, the people are civill.

11. In the Bay of Hondoras is a Towne called Hondoras alias Tres Islas, where is golde and hides and greate store of victualls: This Towne standeth upon an hill very strongly, and is but simply manned. This Towne hath within a mile great plentie of Indians, which are at warr with the Spaniardes.

12. Then there is a towne called Porto de Cavallos where is store of silver, stones, perles, and jewells made and sett with precious stones and perles: To this Towne come yerely twoo shippes that goo from thence to the Havana, and so into Spaine with all their riches. This Towne is full of victualls. This porte of Cavallos adjoyneth to the gulfe Dowse.

13. All the Bay of Mexico is full of Indian Townes and full of victualls. There is one Towne named Vera Crux to which Towne cometh all their Treasure from the Citie of Mexico, and from thence to the porte of St. John de Ulloa, from thence to Havana and so into Spayne.

Florida

In Florida the Spaniardes have one Towne called Sancta Helena where they have perles, silver, and greate store of victualls: The Floridians be a gentle sorte of people, and use somtymes to heade their arowes with silver.

There is one principall place called Rio de Jordan alias Rio de Maio where in an iland standeth a forte which was Ribaults, which River ronneth throughe the Lande into the southe sea from whence greate plentie of Treasure is brought thither: There are small pynnesses that use the same river: It is also thoughte that shippes come from Cathaio to the southwest ende of the said River: This is very full of victualls: There was by

Peter Melanda[72] a River cutt from the Citie of Mexico to Rio de Maio, so that moche treasure is broughte from thence to this forte with small pynnesses.

All that parte of America eastwarde from Cumana unto the River of St. Augustine in Bresill conteyneth in lengthe alongest to the sea side xxi C miles, In whiche compasse and tracte there is neither Spaniarde, Portingale nor any Christian man but onely the Caribes, Indians, and salvages. In which places is greate plentie of golde, perle, and precious stones.

On the coaste of Bresill is one goodly Ile called Trinidada conteyninge C xx[ti.] miles in lengthe, and lxxv. miles in bredthe, and is onely inhabited by gentle Indians and Savages borne in the said Ilande. In this ilande is great plentie of maiz, venison, fishe, wooddes, and grasse, with divers faire frutes and other commodities: Yt hath also divers goodly havens to harborowe yn, and greate stoare of tymber for buildinge of shippes. With the kinge[73] of this Ilande wee are in league.

10
A brefe declaration of the chefe Ilandes in the Baye of Mexico beinge under the Kinge of Spaine with their havens and fortes and what commodities they yelde.

There ys one Ilande as the fleete cometh into the Baye named Margarita wherein is greate store of perle: a riche Ilande full of Maiz (which is their corne), oxen, shepe, goates, fowle and fishe, greate store of frutes, grasse and woodds.

Over againste the said Iland northewarde, there is one other Iland named St. John de porto ricco which hath store of all manner of victualls and suger.

The nexte is a faire Iland called Hispaniola, in some parte well inhabited havinge one Citie called Sancto Domingo, which hath a faire haven whereunto many of the shippes of the kinges fleete come and there devide themselves, some goo to St. John de Leu, and some to Nombro di Dios and other portes of the mayne lande: This is a frutefull Iland for all manner of victuall hides and suger.

The nexte Ilande is called Jamaica and hath in it great store of victualls.

The nexte is a faire greate and long Iland called

---

72. Sidenote: "A speciall note of a passage."
73. Sidenote: "The Frenche."

Cuba: this Iland hath a forte and haven in it called the Havana, which is the key of all India: It is called the key of India for that the Spaniardes cannot well returne into Spaine, but that they muste touche there for victualls, water, woodde, and other necessaries. It lieth at the mouthe and entraunce into the gulfe of Bahama. This Ilande hath great plentie of victualls, but it is not greately inhabited.

There be divers other Ilandes riche for victualls, as Aeriuba, Corsal, Marigalante, &c., havinge not in them some xx. some x. Spaniardes a pece.

Thus you see that in all those infinite Ilandes in the gulfe of Mexico whereof Cuba and Hispaniola are thoughte to be very nere as bigge as England and Ireland, wee reade not of past twoo or three places well fortified, as St Sancto Domingo in Hispaniola and Havana in Cuba: I may therefore conclude this matter with comparinge the Spaniardes unto a dromme or an emptie vessell, which when it is smitten upon yeldeth a greate and terrible sound and that afarr of, but come nere and looke into them, there ys nothinge in them, or rather like unto the asse which wrapte himselfe in a lyons skynne and marched farr of to strike terror into the hartes of the other beastes, but when the foxe drewe nere he perceaved his longe eares and made him a jeste unto all the beastes of the forrest. In like manner wee (upon perill of my life) shall make the Spaniarde ridiculous to all Europe, if with percinge eyes wee see into his contemptible weakenes in the west Indies, and with true stile painte hym oute *ad vivum* unto the worlde in his fainte colours. And if any man woulde objecte that if by his weakenes he had loste the Treasure of the west Indies, yet the riches of the easte Indies woulde holde upp his heade: I answer that those Contries beinge so farr of, and suche naturall malice beinge betweene the portingale and the Spaniarde as greater cannot be, that it is not possible for him to holde those partes no more than the other, wantinge the treasure of the west Indies to supporte his garrisons both there and in Christendome againste his manifolde and mightie enemyes.

11

That the Spaniardes have exercised moste outragious and more then Turkishe cruelties in all the west Indies, whereby they are

every where there become moste odious unto them, whoo woulde joyne with us or any other moste willinglye to shake of their moste intollerable yoke, and have begonne to doe yt already in divers places where they were lordes heretofore.

So many and so monstrous have bene the Spanishe cruelties, suche straunge slaughters and murders of those peaceable, lowly, milde, and gentle people together with the spoiles of Townes, provinces, and kingdomes which have bene moste ungodly perpetrated in the west Indies, as also divers others no lesse terrible matters, that to describe the leaste parte of them woulde require more than one chapter especially where there are whole bookes extant in printe not onely of straungers but also even of their owne contrymen (as of Bartholmewe de las Casas a Bisshoppe in Nova Spania), yea such and so passinge straunge and excedinge all humanitie and moderation have they bene that the very rehersall of them drave divers of the cruell Spanishe which had not bene in the west Indies, into a kinde of extasye and maze, so that the sayenge of the poet mighte therein well be verified.

  Quis talia fando;
  Myrmidonum Dolopumve aut duri miles Ulisses,
  Temperet a lachrimis?

Nevertheles I will repeate oute of that mightie masse and huge heape of massacres some fewe, that of them you may make an estymate of the rest, and consider what cause the small remainder of those moste afflicted Indians have to revolte from the obedience of the Spaniardes and to shake of from their shoulders the moste intollerable and insupportable yoke of Spaine, which in many places they have already begonne to doo of themselves withoute the helpe of any christian Prynce.

This being so I leave it to the depe consideration of the wise, what greate matters may be broughte aboute by our nation if her Majestie (beinge a mightie prince at sea) woulde put in a foote in that enterprise, and assiste the revolted Indians, Symerons and Chichimici after one or twoo yeres planting there, and growinge into acquaintance and familiaritie with those oppressed nations.[74]

---

74. This paragraph marked for deletion.

Nowe because these moste outeragious and infinite massacres are put downe by Don Bartholmewe de las Casas the Bisshoppe above mentioned and dedicated to Kinge Phillippe that nowe ys, which author testifieth that to his inspeakable grefe he was an eye witnesse of many of them, therefore it semeth best unto me to bringe him in, which in his firste chapiter describeth the same in manner followinge. Upon these lambes (meaninge the Indians) so meke, so qualified and endewed of their maker and creator as hath bene saied, entred the spanishe, incontinent as they knew them, as wolves, as lyons, and as Tigres moste cruell of longe tyme famished: and have not don in those quarters these 40. yeres be paste, neither yet doo at this presente oughte els, then teare them in peces, kill them, martir them, afflicte them, tormente them and destroye them by straunge sortes of cruelties, never either seene or reade or hearde of the like, (of the which some shalbe sett downe hereafter) so farr forthe as of above three millions of soules that were in the Ile of Hispaniola, and that wee have seene there, there are not nowe twoo hundreth natives of the Contrie. The Ile of Cuba which is as farr in lengthe as from Valladolid untill Rome, ys at this day as it were all waste. St. John's Isle, and that of Jammaica bothe of them very greate, very fertile, and very faire are desolate. Likewise the Iles of Lucayos nere to the Ile of Hispaniola, and of the northside unto that of Cuba, in nomber beinge above three score Ilandes, together with those which they call the Isles of Geant, one with another greate and little whereof the very worste is fertiler then the kinges garden at Civill, and the Contrie the helthsomest in the worlde: There were in some of these Isles more then five hundred thousande soules, and at this day there is not one only creature, for they have bene all of them slaine after that they had drawen them oute to labor in their myneralls in the Ile of Hispaniola, where there were no more lefte of the Inborne natives of that Iland: A shippe ridinge for the space of three yeres betwixte all these Ilandes to thende that after the wyninge of this kinde of vintage to gleane and cull the Remainder of these folke (for there was a goodd Christian moved with pitie and compassion to converte and wynne unto Christe suche as mighte be founde) there were not founde but eleven persons which I sawe. Other Iles more than thirtie nere to the Ile of St.

John, have likewise bene despeopled and massacred. All those Iles conteyne above twoo thousande leagues of lande and are all dispeopled and laid waste.

As touchinge the mayne firme lande wee are certaine that for Spaniardes by their cruelties and cursed doinges have dispeopled and made desolate more then tenne Realmes greater then all Spaine comprisinge therein also Arragon and Portingale, and twise as moche or more lande than there is from Civill to Jerusalem, which are above a thousand leagues: which Realmes as yet unto this presente day remain in a wildernes and utter desolation, havinge bene before time as well peopled as was possible.

Wee are able to yelde a goodd and perfecte accompte that there is within the space of 40. yeres by these said tyranies and devilishe doinges of the Spaniardes don to deathe unjustly and tyranously more then xij millions of soules men women and children.

And I verely doe beleve and thinke I doo not mistake therein there are deade more then fiftene millions of soules: Thus havinge hearde of the multitudes of soules slayne, you shall heare the manner of their slaughter. In the chapiter of Hispaniola it thus followeth:

Nowe after sondry other forces violences and tormentes which they wroughte againste them, the Indians perceaved that those were no men descended from heaven. Some of them therefore hidd their victualls, others hidd their wives and their children, some other fledd into the mountaines to seperate themselves afarr of from a nation of so harde natured and ghastly conversation: The Spaniardes buffeted them with their fistes and bastianadoes, preasinge also to lay their handes on the Lordes of the Townes: And these cases ended in so greate an hazarde and desperatnes, that a Spanishe capitaine durste adventure to ravishe forcibly the wife of the greatest kinge and Lorde of this Ile: Since which time the Indians began to searche meanes to caste the Spaniardes oute of their landes and sett themselves in armes: But what kinde of armes? Very weake and feble to withstande or resiste, and of lesse defence: Wherefore all their warres are no more warres then the playenge of children when as they play at *jogo de cane* or reedes. The Spaniardes with their horses, speares, and launces began to comitt murders and straunge cruelties: They entred into Townes, Burroughes, and villages sparinge neither children, nor olde men, noyther women with childe, neither them that laye in, but they ripped their bellies and cutt them in peces as if they had bene openinge of lambes shutt upp in their folde: They laied wagers with suche as with one thruste of a sworde woulde paunche or bowell a man in the middest, or with one blowe of a sworde most readily and most deliverly cut of his heade, or yt woulde best perce his entralls at one stroke. They tooke the little soules by the heeles rampinge them from their mothers brestes and crusshed their heades against the cliftes. Others they caste into the Rivers, laughinge and mockinge, and when they tombled into the water, they saied, nowe shifte for thy selfe suche a ones corps: They put others together with their mothers and all that they mett to the edge of the sworde. They made certaine gibbetts longe and toughe in such sorte that the feete of the hanged on touched in a manner the grounde, every one enoughe for thirtene, in the honour and worshippe of our saviour and his xii Apostles (as they used to speake), and setting to fire, burned them all quicke that were fastened. Unto all others whome they used to take and reserve alive cuttinge of their twoo handes as nere as mighte be, and so lettinge them hange, they saied, Go you with these letters to cary tydinges to those which are fled by the mountaines: They murdred commonly the Lordes and nobilitie on this fasshion, they made certen grates of perches laid on pitchforkes, and made a little fire underneathe to the intente that by little and little yellinge and despairinge in these tormentes they mighte give up the ghoste.

One time I sawe foure or five of the principall Lordes roasted and broyled upon these gredyrons: also I thincke that there were twoo or three of the said gredyrons garnished with the like furniture. And for that they cried oute piteously, whiche thinge troubled the Capitaine that he coulde not then slepe, he comaunded to strangle them: The serjeant which was worse then the hangman that burned them, (I knowe his name and frendes in Civill) woulde not have them strangled, but hymselfe puttinge bulletts in their mowthes to the ende they shoulde not crye, put to the fire until they were softly roasted after his desire. I have seene all the aforesaide thinges

and others infinite:[75] And forasmoche as all the people that coulde flee, hidd themselves in the mountaines and mounted on the toppes of them, fledd from the men so withoute all manhodde, emptie of all pietie, behavinge themselves as savage beastes, the slaughterers and murderers of mankinde, they taughte their houndes, fierce doggs, to tear them in peces at the first viewe, and in the space that one might say a *Credo* assailed and devoured an Indian as if it had bene a swine: These doggs wroughte greate destructions and slaughters. And forasmoche as somtymes (thoughe seldome) the Indian put to deathe some Spaniardes upon goodd righte and lawe of due Justice, they made a lawe betwene them, that for one Spaniarde they had to slaye an hundred Indians.

And thus farr oute of the large volume of Don Bartholomewe de las Casas Byshoppe of the citie of Chiape in the west Indies, where he lyved many yeres.

Will you nowe heare one Testymonie of Johannes Metellus Sequanus,[76] whoo was a papiste and favoured the spanishe superstition, yet he writes as followeth in the preface of the Historie of Osorius *de rebus gestis Emanuelis*, fol. 16: At vero ut semel intelligatur quid Indos toties ad res novas contra hispanos moliendas, et seditiones tanta pertinacia favendas impulerit, et quid causæ fuerit cur duo illa christianæ reipublicæ summa capita Indicæ nationis libertatem, frementibus quibusdam et invitis dubio procul militibus hispanis, sanctissimo suo calculo comprobarint, paucis novorum dominorum in miseras immanitatem, deinde quorundam inexplebilem avaritiam, et ex hijs graviores quosque tumultus, vnde novi orbis pene totius nunquam satis deploranda vastitas est sequuta, perstringam. Principio quidem illud apud plerosque milites hispanos, pessimo sane exemplo, in more positum fuit, uti ab oculatis et fide dignis testibus perscriptum est, ut servos suos gravissime punirent, si mercedem diurnam aut non attulissent, aut pensum in auro argentove effodiendo non absoluissent, aut si quid levioris denique delicti perpetrassent. Etenim vesperi reduces, cœnæ

---

75. Sidenote: "Bishop Bartholomew de las Casas an eye wytnes of these cruelties."
76. Sidenote: "Johannes Metellus Sequanus."

loco, primùm vestimentis exuebant, manibus dein pedibusque in transverso palo revinciebant: mox chorda bubalove nervo dirissime verberabant. Sic tractatos, pice oleove ferventi guttatim perfundebant; salita post aqua corpus obluebant, et in mensa tamdiu relinquebant, quamdiu dolorem ferre posse putarentur. Qui mos animadvertendi ipsis etiam in Christianos servos domi familiaris esse dicitur: post carnificium hujusmodi, si durior dominus illis contigerat, vivos in totam noctem collo tenus defodiebant, presentissimum illud ad plagas remedium esse ludibrio dicitantes. Si quis ex illis præ dolore moreretur, id quod non raro accidit, dominus singula servorum capita regi in occisorum locum sufficiens, ab homicidij pœna liberabatur. Hanc crudelitatem lege Baiona, quam dicunt, quidem excusant. Sed omnibus impia merito videtur, tanquam omnis pietatis expers: Quamobrem diabolicæ nomen inter Indos jure quidem obtinuit: Ad hanc autem immanitatem in miseros Indos excercendam nonnullos ingenita quædam naturæ sævities, multis iam bellis exasperata, plerosque habendi sitis impulit. Hinc hispanus miles quasi ad aucupium aut venationem, sic ad prædas hominum agendas, jam inde ab invento novo orbe ferri cœpit. Aut igitur bello captos in servitutem abripiebat, aut ex eorum mancipio, magnam sibi pecuniæ vim conflabat, aut eos ad diurnas operas mittebat, quarum mercedem ab ijs quotidie perquam importunus exigebat: fuere qui servos fodinis manciparent, in quibus insolito labore fractæ servorum myriades periere. Alij mercibus illos permutare soliti sunt alione modo distrahere: Idque tam inclementer et amare nonnulli fecerunt, ut christianæ omnis humanitatis prorsus obliti, e continente abreptos utriusque sexus homines, nulla nec ætatis nec valetudinis habita ratione, navibus in vicinas Insulas transportarent. Eorum non pauci qui mari non assueverant, et in sentinam abdebantur, et fame, fœtore, et squallore crudeliter obsorpti sunt. Quid? Quod fæminæ complures ex hispanis gravidæ, una cum innoxio fœtu pro ancillis sunt venditæ? Atque hijs quidem modis, militum aliqui ad summas opes pervenerunt: Alij magnas dignitates domi forisque sunt consequuti: Alij rem pecuniariam plurimorum damnis sic auxerunt, ut inventi sint, qui octo pecudum millia possiderent. Hanc tam insignem novorum hominum injustitiam atque tyrannidem

fieri non potuit, quin magni statim motus et bella, tam ab ipsis inter se, quam ab incolis in illos excitata sequerentur. After a longe beade roll of moste monstrous cruelties of the spanishe nation in every place of the west Indies moste heynously committed, he concludeth yt thus: Tanta ergo fuit Hispani militis in India tyrannis, ut ea non solum Indos, verum etiam servorum maurorum animos ad rebellionem impulerit. Dicuntur enim in exigua quadam Insula ad septem millia defecisse: Quos hispani initio securos et incautos facilime trucidassent, nisi suo malo vigilantiores factos precibus et pacifica legatione expugnare potius, quam armis frustra tentassent: Multi denique fugitivi Mauri in nominis dei provinciæ silvis habitant: qui initia cum incolis amicitia, ferro, flammaque hispanos ubicunque persequuntur, et inventos frustratim dilacerant.

This, therefore, I gather of the premisses that those Contries whereof the Spaniarde ys Lorde, are partly ruinated, dispeopled, and laid waste by their incredible and more then barbarous and savage endeles cruelties, and partly grevously infested by the Indians, Symerons, Moores, Chichimici revolted, and consequently he is easie to be driven thence; and turned out of all with moche lesser force then is commonly ymagined: for, *Nullum violentum est diuturnum, et malus diuturnitatis custos est metus.*

And surely the more I thinke of the spanishe monarchie, the more me thinketh it is like the Empire of Alexander the greate,[77] which grew upp sooddenly and sooddenly vpon his deathe was rente and dissolved for faulte of lawfull yssue. In like manner the kinge of Spaine nowe 59. yeres of age as beinge borne in the yere of our Lorde 1526 in the moneth of May, and beinge subjecte to the fallinge sicknes, in common reason can be of no longe life, and leavinge no fitt yssue to wealde so greate a governemente, and a question risinge whether his younge weake sonne by his sister's daughter be lawfull heire, they are like upon his deathe to fall together by the eares amongest themselves, and then as men moste odious not onely to the people of the west Indies, but also to all Christendome and all the worlde beside, ys it not likely that every province will seke their

77. Sidenote: "The Spanishe monarchy is like unto the monarchy of Alexander the greate."

libertie? And to say the truthe what nation I pray you of all Christendome loveth the Spaniarde the scourge of the worlde, but from the teethe forwarde and for advauntage? The Italians which sometime were Lordes of the earthe in greate parte nowe broughte under his vile yoke, doo many wayes shewe the utter mislike of their satanicall arrogancie and insolencies, and in all their playes and commodies bringe in the spanishe souldier as a ravisher of virgins and wives, and as the boastinge Thraso and *miles gloriosus*: notinge to the worlde their insupportable luxuriousnes, excessive pride and shamefull vaineglorie. The Citie of Rome beinge sackt by Charles the Emperour, the Pope and Cardinalls taken and ymprisoned cannot brooke their doinges in their hartes. The Venecians stande daily in feare of them almoste as moche as of the Turke, and doubte that if they be not with spede restrained they will inclose them and use them at their pleasure beinge on bothe sides become almoste lordes of the mouthe of the Straites of Giberaulter: The Frenche remembringe the takinge of their kinge prisoner, their crueltie in Florida, the late overthrowe of Strozzi and their fleete, their takinge of Tercera, and other disgraces, hate them for the moste parte worse then Scorpions: The Princes of Germanie, the Duke of Saxonie, the Lantsgrave of Hassia, the Duke of Cleve, the Duke Cassimere have susteyned wronges sufficient to make them his mortall enemies: His innumerable outrages in the netherlandes have inforced the flemynges to those termes which nowe they stande at: Their manifolde practises to supplant us of England give us moste occasion to bethincke ourselves howe wee may abate and pull downe their highe myndes: The poore oppressed Prince and people of Portingale doo watche nighte and day when to finde a convenient occasion of defection. In fine there is almoste no nation of Europe that may not say againste the Spaniarde with the poet: *Distulerat-que graves in idonea tempora pœnas:* And so *eum multos metuere necesse est, quem multi metuunt:* And *multorum odijs nulla respublica stare diu potest.*

12

That the passage in this voyadge is easie and shorte, that it cutteth not nere the trade of any other mightie princes, or nere their

Contries, that it is to be perfourmed at all times of the yere, and nedeth but one kinde of winde: that Ireland beinge full of goodd havens on the southe and weste side, is the nerest parte of Europe to yt, which by this trade shalbe in more securitie, and the sooner drawen to more Civilitie.

In this voyadge wee may see by the globe that wee are not to passe the burnte zone nor to passe throughe the frozen seas, but in a temperate climate unto a Contrie muche like to those partes of Gascoigne and Guyen, where heretofore our nation for a longe tyme have inhabited. And it requireth not as longe voyadges doe the takinge in of freshe water by the way in divers places, by reason it may be sailed in five or sixe weekes, whereby the marchant nede to expecte twoo or three yeres for one returne, as in the voyadge of Sir Fraunces Drake, of Fenton and William Hawkins, but may receave twoo returnes every yere in the selfe same shippes I saye, and well repose themselves at their arryvalls, which thinge I my selfe have seene and understoode in Fraunce this presente yere don by the frenchemen: whoe, settinge furthe in January broughte their bankefishe which they tooke on the bancke forty or threescore leagues from Newefoundelande to Roan in greate quantitie by the ende of May, and afterwarde returned this yere againe to the fisshinge and are looked for at home towardes the fine of November. To the spedy perfourmaunce of which voyadge this is a speciall furtheraunce, that whereas moste of our other voyadges of like lengthe require twoo or three sortes of windes at the leaste, one onely winde suffiseth to make this: which was no doubte the cause of the quicke returne of my frende Stephen Bellinger of Roan, whoo departed from Newhaven in January was twelve monethes, arryved at Cape Briton in xx[ti] daies space, and from thence discouered very diligently CC leagues towardes Norumbega, and had traficque with the people in tenne or twelve places, founde a Towne conteyninge fourescore houses, and returned home with a diligent description of the coaste in the space of foure monethes, with many commodities of the contrie which he shewed me. Moreover this passage is neither by the straites of Giberaulter, nor on the coastes of Spaine, Portingall, Fraunce, nor Flaunders, neither by the sounde of Denmarke nor Wardhouse in Norwey, so as in takinge our course on the highe seas wee shall not be in daunger of the Cursaries in the levant, nor of the Gallies of Barbarie, nor of the Turke, nor of any state of Italie, neither of the Spaniarde, the frenche, nor the Dane, nor of any other Prince nor Potentate within the sounde in the northe or in the northeaste partes of the worlde: Wee may also travell thither and perfourme the same at all tymes of the yere with the like facilitie as our marchantes of Bristowe, Weymouthe, and other partes of the west Contries travell for woade to the iles of St. Mighell and Tercera (which are halfe the way thither) all the yere longe. For this coaste ys never subjecte to the Ise, which is never lightly seene to the southe of Cape Razo in Newfounde Lande. Besides this in our way as wee passe to and froe wee shall have in tempestes and other necessities the portes of Ireland to our aide and no nerer coaste of any enemye. Moreover by the ordinary entercourse wee may annoye the enemyes to Ireland and succour the Queenes Majesties faithfull subjects, and drawe the Irishe by little and little to more civilitie, and in shorte tyme wee may yelde them from the coastes of America whatsoever commodities they nowe receave at the handes of the Spaniardes: So the Spaniardes shall wante the ordinarye victualls they receave every yere from thence, whereby they cannot contynue traficque, nor fall so aptly to practize againste our governemente there, as heretofore by their trade thither they have don and doo daily, to the greate expences of her Majestie, and no small indaungeringe and troublinge of our state. And to conclude in tradinge to these Contries wee shall not nede for feare of the Spanishe bloudy Inquisition to throwe our Bibles and prayer bookes over boorde into the sea before our arryvall at their portes, as these many yeres wee have don and yet doe, nor take suche horrible oathes as are exacted of our men by the spanishe searchers to suche dayly wilfull and highe offence of almightie God, as wee are driven to contynually in followinge our ordinary trafficque into the Kinge of Spaines dominyons whereof at large wee have spoken before in the seconde Chapiter.

13

That hereby the Revenewes and Customes of her Majestie bothe outewarde and inwarde shall mightily be inlarged by the Toll excises, and other dueties which withoute oppression may be raysed.

The manifolde Testimonies verbatim alleaged by me in the thirde chapiter of John Ribault, John Verarsanus, Stephen Gomes, Vasques de Coronado, Jaques Cartier, Gasper Corterialis and others which all were the discoverers of the coaste and Inlande of America betwene 30. and 63. degrees prove infallibly unto us, that Golde, silver, copper, perles, pretious stones, and Turqueses, and Emraldes, and many other commodities have bene by them founde in those Regions. To which testimonies I coulde have added many moe yf I had not feared to be tedious: Nowe the fyfte parte of all these aforenamed commodities cannot choose but amounte to a greate matter beinge yerely reserved unto her Majestie accordinge to the tenor of the Patent graunted by King Henry the Seaventh in the xi^{th.} yere of his raigne to John Gabott and his three sonnes Lewes, Sebastian, and Sancius. The wordes whereof it shoulde not be amiss here to sett downe as they are printed in my booke of voyadges: these are the wordes: Ex omnibus fructibus, proficuis, emolumentis, commodis, lucris, et obventionibus ex hujusmodi navigatione provenientibus, prefatus Johannes et filij ac heredes et eorum deputati teneantur et sint obligati nobis pro omni viagio suo, toties quoties ad portum nostrum Bristolliæ applicuerint (ad quem omnino applicare teneantur et sint astricti) deductis omnibus sumptibus et impensis necessarijs per eosdem factis, quintam partem capitalis lucri sive in mercibus sive in pecuniis persolvere.

What gaines this imposition may turne unto the Crowne of England in shorte tyme wee may more then gesse havinge but an eye to the Kinge of Spaines revenewes, which he nowe hath oute of all his domynions in all the west Indies. The like in all respectes may be saied of the revenewes of the Crowne of Portingale which beinge of itselfe one of the smallest and poorest kingdomes of all Christendome became in shorte space so riche and honourable soone after their entringe into their southesterne discoveries, traficques, and conquestes, that before the deathe of their late younge kinge Sebastian, their Embassadors woulde strive and chalenge for the chefest place with the Embassadores of the greatest kinges of Christendome, as I have hearde it dyvers tymes spoken at Paris at my Lordes table by men of greate hono^r and experience, in which Citie moste princes and states of Christendome have their Embassadors commonly resident. To leave them and to come to our nation I say that amonge other meanes to encrease her Majesties customes this shalbe one, especially that by plantinge and fortifieinge nere Cape Briton, what by the strengthe of our shipps beinge harde at hande and bearinge the sway already amongest all nations that fishe at Newfoundelande, and what by the fortes that there may be erected and helde by our people, wee shall be able to inforce them havinge no place els to repaire unto so convenient, to pay us suche a contynual custome as shall please us to lay upon them: which Imposition of twoo or three hundred shippes laden yerely with sondry sortes of fish, trane oyle, and many kyndes of furres and hides, cannot choose but amounte to a greate matter beinge all to be levied upon straungers. And this not onely wee may exacte of the Spaniardes and Portingales but also of the frenche men our olde and auncient enemyes: What shoulde I speake of the customes of the greate multitudes of course clothes, welshe frise, and Irishe ruggs that may be uttered in the more northerly partes of the Lande amonge the Esquimawes of the graunde Bay and amonge them of Canada, Saguynay, and Hochelaga wch are subjecte to sharpe and nippinge winters, albeit their Sommers be hotter moche then oures. Againe the multitudes of small yron and copper workes wherewith they are excedingly delighted, will not a little encrease the customes being transported oute of the lande: I omitt the rehersall of a Thowsande other triflinge wares, which besides they may sett many women, children, and ympotent persons on worke in makinge of them woulde also helpe to the encreasinge of the customes: Lastly whatsoever kind of commodyties shoulde be broughte from thence by her Majesties subjectes into the Realme, or be thither transported oute of the Realme, cannot choose but inlarge the Revenewes of the Crowne very mightely and inriche all sortes of subjectes ingenerally.

14

That this action will be for the greate increase, mayneteynaunce and safetie of our navie, and especially of greate shippinge which is the strengthe of our Realme, and for the supportation of all those occupations that depende upon the same.

In the Statutes moste providently ordeyned for increase and mainteynaunce of o^r navigation in the Raignes of Kinge Richarde the Seconde, Kinge Henry the seaventh, Kinge Henry the viii^th., and her Majestie that nowe ys thoughe many and sondry rewardes were proposed to encourage our people unto the sea, yet still I fynde complaintes of decaye of the navye, notwithstandinge so many goodly priviledges to mayneteine fisshermen the ordeyninge of Wendisday to be a newe fishe day for the better utteraunce of their fishe that they shoulde take at sea. Yea albeit there hath bene graunted a certene proportionable allowaunce oute of Thexchequer to suche as woulde builde any shippes of burden to serve the prince in tyme of warr, yet very little hath bene done in that behalfe: For setting the Citie of London aparte, goe your waye into the west parte of England and Wales, and search howe many shippes of CC tonnes and upwardes those partes can affoorde, and you shall finde (god wotteth) no such nomber as at firste you did ymagine: At this day I am assured there are scarce twoo of CC Tonnes belonginge to the whole Citie of Bristowe, and very fewe or none of the like burden alonge the Channell of Severne from Glocester to the Landes ende on the one side, and Milfordehaven on the other: Nowe to remedie this greate and unknowen wante no enterprise possibly can be devised more fitt to increase our great shippinge then this Westerne fortifienge and planting. For in this action wee are not to cutt over the narrowe seas in a day or a nighte betwene Flaunders, Fraunce, or Ireland in small barkes of xx^ti. or xxx^ti. Tonnes, but wee are to passe over the breste of the maine Ocean and to lye at sea a moneth or six weekes together, whereby wee shall be constrayned of our selves withoute chardginge of the Prince to builde greate shippes as well to avoide the daunger of tempest, as also for the commoditie of portage whereunto the greater shippes in longe voyadges are moste conveniente, which the Portingales and Spaniardes have founde oute by longe experience. Whoe for that cause builde shippes of v. vi. vii. viii. C. and a M. Tonnes to sende into their easterne and westerne Indies. The like whereof wee shalbe the rather invited to doe, since by this voyadge wee shall have many thinges for little or nothinge that are necessarie for the furniture of greate shippinge. For beinge possessed of New-founde lande which the last yere was seazed upon in her Majesties name, wee may have tarr, rosen, mastes, and cordage for the very workeman-shippe of the same. All which commodities cannot choose but wonderfully invite our men to the buildinge of greate shippinge, especially havinge store of the best shipwrightes of the worlde, whereof some for wante of employmente at home, have bene driven to flye into forren partes as into Denmarke: Moreover in the judgemente of those that are experte in sea causes, yt will breed more skilfull, connynge, and stowte pilotts and maryn-ers then other belonginge to this lande: ffor it is the longe voyadges (so they be not to excessive longe, nor throughe intemperate Clymates as those of the portingales into their West Indies) that harden seamen and open unto them the se-cretes of navigation, the nature of the windes, the currentes and settinge of the Sea, the ebbinge and flowinge of the mayne Ocean, the influence of the sonne, the moone, and of the rest of the celestiall planetts, and force which they have at sondry seasons upon that mightie body: whiche skill in sea causes the Emperour Charles the fyfte knowinge howe moche yt did ymporte his state, to the intente it mighte better encrease amongest the Spaniardes, in great providence erected a lecture of the arte of navigation[78] in Civill, and ordeyned that no man shoulde take chardge to the west Indies that had not hearde the Reader of the same for a certaine space, and upon due examyna-cion were allowed as sufficient by him and others adjoyned unto him as assistantes to examyn mat-ters of experience: wch order if it had bene estab-lished in england such grosse and insufficient felowes as he that caste away the Admirall of Sr Humfryes company with an C. persons in her to the west of Newfounde lande this tyme twelve monethes, had not bene admitted to take so greate a chardge: But to returne to the increase and mayneteynaunce of our shippes and shippmen, I say this is not as the voyadge to Muscovy which is open not paste foure monethes, but may be passed and repassed at our pleasure at all tymes of the yere, and so our maryners may be sett on worke all the yere longe: Neither is the trade

likely to prove so small as that of Muscovy, wherein not past tenne shippes at the moste are employed ones a yere: For here there is a greate hope the Contrie beinge as bigge as all Europe and nothinge in frutefulnes inferiour to yt, as I have proved before at large in the thirde chapiter, that wee shall have twoo fleetes as bigge as those of the kinge of Spaine to his west Indies imployed twise in the yere at the leaste, especially after our fortifienge in the Contrie, the certen place of our factory beinge there established, whereby yt muste nedes come to passe that our navye shalbe mightely increased and mayneteyned: which will not onely be a chefe strengthe and suertie in tyme of warres, as well to offende as defende, but will also be the mayneteynaunce of many Masters, maryners, and seamen, whereby they their wyves and children shall have their lyvinges, and many Cities, Townes, villages, havens, and Creekes nere adjoyninge unto the seacoaste, and the Queenes subjectes, as Brewers, Bowchers, Smithes, ropers, shipwrights, Tailours, shoe-makers, and other victuallers and handicraftes men inhabitinge and dwellinge nere thereaboutes shall also have by the same great parte of their lyvinge. For proofe hereof wee nede not to seeke any further then unto oure neighboures of Spaine and Portingale, whoe since the firste discoverie of their Indies have not onely mightely inlarged their domynions, marveilously inriched themselves and their subjectes, but have also by juste accompte trebled the number of their ship-pes, Masters, and maryners, a matter of no small momente and importaunce. In so moche that nowe of late kinge Phillippe hath made the Mar-ques de La Cruz,[79] which laste yere wanne Ter-cera graunde Admirall of the Ocean sea, and Prince d'Oria of Genoa Admirall in the Levant. A taste of this increase wee have had in our owne selves even by our trade of fisshinge in New-founde Lande which as yt is well knowen hath bene occasion that in sondry places of this Realme divers tall shippes have bene builte and sett furthe even of late daies, and more would be if whereas nowe havinge but twoo monethes or tenne weekes of fisshinge, by this newe plantinge they mighte be drawen more south westerly where the speciall fisshing places are bothe for plentie and greatenes of fishe, and beinge out of daunger

---

78. Sidenote: "A lecture of the arte of navigation."

79. Sidenote: "Marques de la Cruz Admyrall of the Ocean."

and ympedimente of yse, they mighte fishe there safely the greatest parte of the yere, and by their nerenes unto our fortes there builte aboute Cape Briton, they mighte yelde succour unto them, and likewise by their neighbourhoode be themselves in more securitie. ffynally their shippes, their goodds, and their persons shoulde not be subjecte to soodden arrestes of straungers[80] as they are in all other trades of Christendome: but shoulde enjoye as greate freedome, libertie, and securitie as they usually doo in their native Contrie, the havens, Townes, and villages in those partes beinge occupied and possessed by their fellowe subjectes. Which freedome and libertie will greatly incourage them to contynewe constantly in this newe traficque.

15

That spedie plantinge in divers fitt places is moste necessarie upon these laste luckye westerne discoveries for feare of the danger of beinge prevented by other nations which have the like intention: with the order thereof and other reasons therew[th]all alleaged.

Havinge by gods goodd guidinge and mercifull direction atchieved happely this presente westerne discoverye, after the seekinge the advauncemente of the kingedome of Christe, the seconde chefe and principall ende of the same is traficque, which consisteth in the vent of the masse of our clothes and other commodities of England, and in receiving backe of the nedeful commodities that wee nowe receave from all other places of the worlde. But forasmoche as this is a matter of greate ymportaunce and a thinge of so greate gaine as forren princes will stomacke at, this one thinge is to be don, withoute which it were in vaine to goe aboute this, and that is the matter of plantinge and fortificacion, withoute due consideracion whereof in vaine were it to thinck of the former. And therefore upon the firste said viewe taken, by the shippes that are to be sente thither, wee are to plante upon the mouthes of the greate navigable Rivers which are there, by stronge order of fortification, and there to plante our Colonies. And so beinge firste setled in strengthe with men, armour and munition, and havinge our navy within our Bayes, havens, and

Roades, wee shall be able to lett the entraunce of all subjectes of forren princes, and so with our freshe powers to encounter their shippes at the sea, and to renewe the same withe freshe men as the soodden feightes shall require. And by our fortes shalbe able to holde faste our firste footinge, and readily to annoye suche weary power of any other that shall seke to arryve. And shalbe able with our navye to sende advertisemente into England upon every soodden whatsoever shall happen. And these fortifications shall kepe the naturall people of the Contrye in obedience and goodd order. And these fortes at the mowthes of those greate portable and navigable Ryvers, may at all tymes sende upp their shippes, Barkes, Barges, and boates into the Inland with all the commodities of England, and returne unto the said fortes all the commodities of the Inlandes that wee shall receave in exchange, and thence at pleasure convey the same into England: And thus settled in those fortes yf the nexte neighboures shall attempte any annoye to our people, wee are kepte safe by our fortes; and wee may upon violence and wronge offred by them, ronne upon the Rivers with our shippes, pynnesses, Barkes and boates and enter into league with the petite princes their neighboures that have always lightly warres one with an other, and so entringe league nowe with the one, and then with the other wee shall purchase our owne safetie and make ourselves Lordes of the whole.

Contrarywise withoute this plantinge in due tyme wee shall never be able to have full knowledge of the language manners and customes of the people of those Regions, neither shall wee be able thoroughly to knowe the riches and commodities of the Inlandes with many other secretes whereof as yet wee have but a small taste. And althoughe by other meanes wee mighte attaine to the knowledge thereof, yet beinge not there fortified and strongly seated, the french that swarme with multitude of people, or other nations mighte secretly fortifie and settle themselves before us hearinge of the benefite that is to be reaped of that voyadge, and so wee shoulde beate the bushe and other men take the birdes: wee shoulde be at the chardge and travell, and other men reape the gaine. To make this plaine by example in the vi[th] leafe of the Italian edition of the *Historie of ffernando Cortes* written by ffranciscus Lopez de

---

80. Sidenote: "A meane to avoide the sodden arrests of our navy."

Gomera is lively described the folly of John Grigalva for his not inhabitinge that goodd and riche Contrie of Jucatan, which ymmediatly after he had neglected, the same Fernando Cortes tooke in hande and perfourmed and gott all the hono^r and commoditie from him, leaving greate wealthe and hono^r to his posteritie, and to himself an everlastinge name. The storye is thus: Giovan di Grigalva se n'ando a Jucatan combattere con quelli Indiani di Cimpoton, et se ne ritorno ferito entro nel fiume di Tanasco che per questo si chiama ora Grigalva, nel qual riscatto o cambio per cose di poco valuto molto oro, robbe et cottone, et bellissime cose di penne. Statte in San Giovanni di Ullua, piglio possessione di quel paese per il re, in nome del Governatore Diego Velasques: et cambio la sua merciaria per pezzi di oro, coperte di cottone et penne. Et si havesse conosciuto la ventura sua, haveria fatto populatione in paese cosi ricco, come lo preganano i suoi compagni et lui saria stato quello che dipoi il cortes. Ma tanta ventura non era riservata per chi non la conosceva, ancora che si scusana che lui non andana per populare, se non per riscattare o permutare le cose che levana del governatore: et discoprire, se quella terra di Jucatan era Isola o terra ferma.

And if any man liste to knowe what intertainement he had of his uncle at his returne for not inhabitinge upon the present occasion, yt followeth in the ende of the same Chapiter in these wordes: Et quando arrivo non lo volse videre il governatore suo zio, che li fece quello che lui meritana.

The like story wee have fol. 298. of Franciscus Lopes de Gomera his *generall historie of the west Indies* of Vasques de Coronado, which after excedinge greate chardges bestowed for his royall furnishinge furthe upon his voyadge to Cevola and Quivera for wante of courage and for other private respectes neglected plantinge there had as colde welcome at his dastardly and unconsiderate returne of Don Antonio de Mendoza viceroy of Mexico, as Grigalva had of his uncle above mentioned. It is written thus of him after his returne from Quivera:—

Cascò del Cavallo in Tiguez Francisco Vasques, e con il colpo usci di Cervello et disvariana. Questo caso alcuni credettero che fusse finto, altri n'hebbero grandissimo dolore: Quelli che l'intendevano a mala parte stavano male con lui per che non si

metteva a popolare. And a little afterwarde: molto dispiagne a Don Antonio di Mendoza che fussero ritornati, per che havena speso piu di sessanta milla pesi d'oro in quella impresa, molti volevano restare l'a, ma Francesco Vasques di Coronado, che ricco era et nuovamente maritato con una bellissima donna non volse, dicendo che non si poteriano sustentarsi ne defendere in cosi povero paesa et tanto lontani del soccorso. Caminarono presso a tre milla miglia di longo in questa Giornata.

Notwithstandinge these colourable excuses and dispraisinges of the Contrie yt is described by relation of his owne companions in this manner in the same leafe: E Quivera in quaranta gradi. E paesa temperato, di bonissime acque, di molto herbatico, prugne, more, noci, et melloni, et une, che naturano bonissimo, non vi `e cottone, et vestono pelle di vacche e capriole.

The greate inconvenience of the delaye and neglecte of plantinge with spede of goodd Contries newe discovered beinge well weyed and foreseene by John Ribault, made him to plante and fortefie at his firste voyadge thoughe it were but with thirtie men: which that you may the better understande together with the wise course and choice of place which oughte to be had in plantinge and seatinge at the firste, I will alleage his owne wordes which are in the laste leafe of his firste printed voyadge: Wherefore (my Lorde) saith he I truste you will not thincke it amisse (consideringe the commodities that may be broughte thence) yf wee leave a number of men there, which may fortifie and provide themselves of thinges necessarie. For in all newe discoveries it is the chefest thinge[81] that may be don at the begynnynge to fortifie and people the Contrie. I had not so soone set furthe this to our Companie, but many of them offred to tary there, yea with suche a goodd will and jolly courage, that suche a nomber did offer themselves as wee had moche to doe to stay their importunitie. And namely of our shippe Masters and pilotts and suche as wee woulde not spare. Howebeit wee lefte there but to the nomber of 30. men in all gentlemen, souldiers, and maryners and that at their owne sute and prayer and of their owne free willes, and by the advise and deliberation of the gentlemen sent on the behalfe of the Prince and yours. And I have

81. Sidenote: "The chefest pointe in all newe discoveries."

lefte unto them for heade and ruler, followinge therein your pleasure, Capitaine Albert de la Pierria, a souldier of longe experience and the firste that from the begynnynge offred to tary, and further by their advise choice and will inscaled and fortified them in an Iland on the northe side thereof, a place of stronge scituation and commodious upon a River which wee named Chevonceau, and the habitation and fortres Charlesforte. After wee had instructed and duely admonished them of what they should doe, as well for their manner of procedinge, as for the goode and lovinge behaviour of them, the xi^th. day of the moneth of June last paste wee departed from porte royall, &c.

Nowe to leave the Spaniardes and frenche and to come to ourselves, Seinge it hath pleased almightie god at this instant to reveale unto her Majestie and the Realme that once againe afreshe, which was in part discovered by Sebastian Gabota and other the subjectes of this lande to her moste famous Grandfather Kinge Henry the Seaventh,[82] and was then lefte of and caste aside and not sufficiently regarded by occasion of the warres of Scotland as Sebastian himself writes, and so hath bene intermitted for the space of aboute foure score and sixe yeres: If nowe the Queene her Counsell and other subjectes shall never so little delaye the throughe managinge of the cause and entringe effectually into the action, let them assure themselves that they will come to late and a day after the faire. ffor as the wise man saieth *post est occasio calva.* For to speake nothinge of the laste yeres preparation of the Marques de la Roche to inhabite and plante in those partes nowe discovered by our men which preparation was luckely overthrowne in respecte of us by reason that his greatest shippe was cast away upon the travers of Burwage, the men of St. John de Luze sent the laste yere to sollicite the frenche kinge and his Counsell to plante there, And nowe our neighboures the men of St. Maloe in Brytaine in the begynnynge of Auguste laste paste of this yere 1584 are come home with five shippes from Canada and the Contries upp the Bay of St. Laurence and have brought twoe of the people of the Contrie home, and have founde suche swete in that newe trade that they are preparinge tenne

shippes to returne thither in January nexte, as one John de la Marche and Master Pryhouse of Garnesey affirme, which Master Pryhouse beinge yet in London was at St. Malowe within these five weekes, and sawe the twoe savages, the five shippes and the riche commodities and understoode of the greate preparation, And lieth nowe at London in philpott lane at the stonehouse there. And that it may be knowen that not onely the ffrenche affecte this enterprize, but even the duche longe since thoughte of yt, I can assure you that Abraham Ortelius the great Geographer told me at his laste beinge in England 1577 that if the warres of Flaunders had not bene, they of the Lowe Contries had meant to have discovered those partes of America, and the northwest straite before this tyme. And yt semed that the chefe cause of his comynge into England was to no other ende but to prye and looke into the secretes of Frobishers voyadge, for yt was even then when Frobisher was preparinge for his first returne into the north west. To conclude yf wee doe procrastinate the plantinge, (and where our men have nowe presently discovered and founde it to be the best parte of America that is lefte and in truthe more agreable to our natures, and more nere unto us then Nova hispania), the frenche, the Normans, the Brytons, or the duche, or some other nation will not onely prevente us of the mightie Baye of St. Laurence where they have gotten the starte of us already, thoughe wee had the same revealed to us by bookes published and printed in Englishe before them, but also will deprive us of that goodd lande which nowe wee have discovered. Which if they doe (as god defende they shoulde), then it falleth oute that wee shall have our enemyes or doubtfull frendes rounde aboute us, and shall not onely loose a singuler commoditie and inestymable benefite, but also incurr greate daunger and inconvenience in suffringe papistes by plantinge rounde aboute us to take from us all succours, and to lett them enriche themselves under our noses to be better able to supplant or overronne us.

16
Meanes to kepe this enterprise from overthrowe and the enterprisers from shame and dishonour.

Every newe enterprise is in the begynnyinge burdenous, chardgeable and heavie, and moste

---

82. Sidenote: "The cause why these discoveries went not forward in Kinge Henry the Seavenths tyme."

commonly hath many greate enemies: which is the cause that many goodd men much affected to the Contrie in wittie excellent enterprises, sincke and fainte under their burden. And because that this enterprise which wee have in hande or in purpose (besides that it is much maliced specially by our mightie faction of the papistes), is an enterprize that requireth beside the favour of the prince no small chardge, Therefore wee are to devise howe the burden may leste tyme reste on the backe of the bearer of the same, that he sincke not under the same, but that he maye stande upp in full strengthe, and goe throughe with ease, fame, and profitt withoute shame of all the bymedlers and fauters of the same. And entred into consideracion hereof, this cometh to mynde, that the firste chardge of the navye to be admitted as for the present deade chardge for the tyme, howe supply of the chardges followinge may be mayneteyned, and borne, for in that standeth one greate matter that ymporteth honour, credite, profite and the whole sequele of the enterprize: Wee are induced by late plaine examples of the Frenche, that have traficqued in those partes with greate profite, to beleve that upon our plantinge wee shall as yt were defraye as well the firste chardges as the chardges followinge by the commodities in trafficque that wee shall receave by passinge into the Inland by River and otherwise: But admittinge the worse that the people will neither receave our commodities, nor yelde us theirs againe; Then wee are to devise of our selves howe wee may otherwise at the firste countervaile our chardges and become greate gayners will or nill the naturall inhabitantes of those Regions or others: And that is by enjoyinge certaine naturall commodities of the landes infinitely aboundinge in no accompte with them and with us of greate price, which is this way to be broughte aboute.

The soiles there upon the seacoaste and all alonge the tracte of the greate broade mightie Ryvers all alonge many hundreth miles into the Inland are infinitely full fraughte with swete wooddes of Fyrr, cedars, cypres, and with divers other kindes of goodly trees: And settynge upp mylles to sawe them,[83] suche as be commen in poland and in all the northeaste regions, wee may with spede possesse infinite masses of boordes of

83. Sidenote: "Sawe milles."

these swete kindes, and those frame and make ready to be turned into goodly chestes, cupboordes, stooles, tables, deskes &c. upon the returne. And consideringe the present wante of tymber in the Realme, and howe derely the Cipres chestes are solde that come from the Ilandes of the levant seas, and lately from the Azores to Bristoll and the westerne havens, these may be bothe amply and derely vented in all the portes of the Realme and of the Realmes adjoyninge, consideringe that in this age every man desireth to fill his house with all manner of goodd furniture. So that were there no other peculier commodities, this onely I say were ynoughe to defraye all the chardges of all the begynnynge of the enterprize, and that oute of hande, for suche mylwrightes may easely be procured from suche places where they abounde, and some suche (possible) be in England, for I have herde of a frende of myne, that one suche mill within these xxxti. yeres was sett upp in Worcestershere by a knighte of that Contrie. And one man onely were able to directe a thousande of our common milwrightes in that trade, and Carpinters and Joyners, the realme may spare thousandes for a nede. And wth like ease and shortenes of time wee may make of the wooddes there pitch and tarr which are thinges fitt for or navie and marchandizes of goodd vente and of common neede.

And with like ease wee may make of the wooddes there plentie of sope asshes a commoditie very dere and of greate and ample vent with us and elswhere in forren kingdomes of Europe. Also wee may there prepare for pikes, chasinge staves, oares, halberts, and the like for cullen cleftes for sondry uses, &c. And also wee may there withoute payeng for the same, have tymber to builde greate navies, and may bringe them into this Realme, and have goodd sale of the same.

All this I say may be broughte to passe, if wee wisely plante upon our arryvall aboute the mouthes of greate Rivers and in the Ilandes of the same: and so wee shall have the starte before the frenche and all others, and our people sente thither for the purposes afore, shall be ready to man our shippes to give repulse at the firste to all suche as shall come thither to sett foote to our annoye.

Thus all thinges removed that mighte bringe discouragement, The firste that tooke the enterprise in hande have wonne greate honor and highe estymation with all degrees in England, and havinge by these former meanes wonne to defraye all the chardges of the brunte of thenterprize, they stande full able to followe the same withoute cravinge aide of the lingringe marchaunte, and have the possibilitie onely to themselves of the trades of traficque with the people, which they may bringe aboute eyther with curtesie or by pollicie and force, as by joyninge now wth this petite kinge and nowe with that, &c.

And this once plainely founde and noted in England, what noble man, what gentleman, what marchante, what citizen or contryman will not offer of himselfe to contribute and joyne in the action, forseeinge that the same tendeth to the ample vent of our clothes, to the purchasinge of riche commodities, to the plantinge of younger brethren, to the employment of our idle people, and to so many noble endes, and great joyninge in contribution upon so happy begynnynges geveth abilitie to fortifie, to defende all forren force in divers commodious places even at the firste.

17

That by these colonies the northwest passage to Cathaio and China may easely quickly and perfectly be searched oute as well by River and overlande as by sea, for proofe whereof here are quoted and alleaged divers rare Testymonies oute of the three volumes of voyadges gathered by Ramusius and other grave authors.

In the thirde volume of Navigations and voyadges, gathered and translated into Italian by Master John Baptista Ramusius fol. 417. pag. 2. I reade of John Verarsanus as followeth: This unhappy ende had this valiaunte gentleman, whoe if this misfortune had not happened unto him (with the singuler knowledge that he had in sea matters and in the arte of navigation, beinge also favoured with the greate liberalitie of kinge Fraunces), woulde have discovered and opened unto the worlde that parte also of Lande even to the poole. Neither woulde he have contented himselfe with the outeside and sea coaste onely, but woulde have passed further upp within the lande so farr as he coulde have gon. And many that have knowen him and talked with him have told me that he saied he had in mynde to perswade the frenche kinge to sende oute of Fraunce a goodd number of

people to inhabite certaine places of the said coaste which be of ayre temperate and of soile moste fertile, with very faire ryvers and havens able to receave any navie: The inhabitants of which places mighte be occasion to bringe to passe many goodd effectes, and amongest other to reduce those poore rude and ignoraunte people to the knowledge of God and true relligion, and to shewe them the manner of husbandrie for the grounde, transportinge of the beastes of Europe into those excedinge large and champion Contries: And in time mighte discover the partes within lande, and see if amongest so many Ilandes there be any passage to the southe sea, or whither the firme lande of Florida contynewe still even to the pole. Upon occasion of these laste wordes I thincke it not amisse to alleage those Testimonies tendinge to the proofe of this longe desired northwest passage, which with no small care these many yeres I have observed in my readinges and conferences concerninge the same matter.

1. My firste aucthoritie is in the seconde volume of Ramusius in the discourse of the discoverie of the Ilandes ffreseland, Iseland, Estotiland, Engroneland, Drogeo, and Icaria made in the northe by Sir Nicholas Zeny Knighte and Master Anthony his brother in the yere 1380. In which discourse amonge many other thinges tendinge to the proofe of this passage, I finde this recorded: Scoprirono vna Isola detta Estotilanda posta in ponente lontana da Frislanda piu che mille miglia, whereof I gather that whereas still he calleth Estotiland an Ilande and that it is distant westwarde from Frislande more then a thousande miles, that the sea is open above five hundreth miles further then ffrobisher and his companie discovered: For he himself confesseth that he never sailed paste five or six hundreth miles to the weste of Friselande and here is mention made that those fishermen that discovered the iland of Estotiland founde it to be more then a M. miles to the weste of the same.

2. The seconde testimonie to prove this northwest passage is in the preface of the aforesaide Ramusius before his thirde volume where he alleageth in manner followinge that which Sebastian Gabote wrote unto him concerning this matter: Many yeres paste I was written unto by Sebastian Gabote our contryman a Venecian and a man of greate experience and very singuler in

the arte of navigation and in the knowledge of Cosmographie, whoe sailed alonge and beyonde Nova Francia, at the chardges of kinge Henry the seaventh kinge of England, and he signified unto me that havinge sailed a longe tyme west and by northe beyonde these Ilandes unto the latitude of 67. degrees and [an halfe] under the north pole, on the xjth day of June, and findinge the sea open and withoute any manner of ympedymente, he thoughte verely that he mighte have passed by that way unto Cathaia which is in the easte: and he woulde have done yt, if the mutinie of the shipm^r and unruly mariners had not inforced him to returne homewardes from that place; But it semeth (saith Ramusius) that god doth yet reserve to some greate prince the discoverie of this voyadge to Cathaio by this way, which for the bringinge of the spicerie from India into Europe woulde be the moste easie and shortest of all others hitherto founde oute. And surely this enterprize woulde be the moste glorious and of moste importaunce of all other that any coulde ymagine to make their name moche more eternall and ymmortale amonge all ages to come, then these so greate tumultes and troubles of warres which are to be seene contynually in Europe amonge the miserable and unhappy Christians.

3. Thirdly the reporte which the people of Hochelaga made to Jacques Cartier, in the viij$^{th.}$ chapter of his seconde relation of the River three monethes navigable to the southewarde dothe not a little confirme the same.

4. Fourthly the relation of the people of Canada in the xij$^{th.}$ Chapiter followinge on this manner. Moreover they tolde us and gave us to understande that there are people cladde with clothe as wee are, and that there are many inhabited Townes and goodd people, and that they have greate store of golde and redd copper, and that upp into the lande beyonde the River firste above mentioned even to Hochelaga and Saguynay there is an Ile environed aboute with that and other Rivers which beyonde Saguenay entereth into twoo or three greate lakes. Also that there is founde a sea of freshe water the heade and ende whereof there was never man founde that had throughly searched as farr as they have hearde say of them of Saguenay, for they (as they signified unto us) had not bene there themselves.

5. Fyftly in the ende of that seconde relation this postscripte is added as a speciall pointe. To witt that they of Canada say that it is the space of a moone (that is to saye a moneth) to saile to a lande where Cynamon and cloves are gathered, and in the Frenche originall which I sawe in the kinges Library at Parris in the Abbay of St. Martines yt is further put downe that Domaconna the Kinge of Canada in his barke had traveled to that contrie where Cynamon and cloves are had, yea and the names whereby the Savages call those twoo spices in their owne language are there put downe in writinge.

6. Sixtly this passage is likewise proved by the double reporte of Vasques de Coronado. For firste he beinge at Cevola, which standeth in 37. degrees and an halfe of northerly latitude within the lande, he had this informacion of the people of that place fanno otto giornate verso le campaigne al mare di settentrione: whereby I gather that some parte of the northerne sea ys wthin viij. daies journey of Cevola. Againe when he was afterwardes at the Towne of Quivera, which is scituated by the sea side in the latitude of 40. degrees he founde there shippes with maryners wch had the picture of a birde called Alcatraizzi in silver upon their bonnetts and on the forepartes of their shippes which signified that they were thirtie daies sailinge to that place, where it is saied that they muste nedes be of Cathaio or China seinge that there is none but spanishe shippinge upon all the coaste of the backside of Nova Spania.

7. Seaventhly the people of Florida at the River of May in 30. degrees signified to John Ribault and his Company that they mighte saile in boates from thence through the Contrie by Ryver to Cevola in xx$^{ti.}$ daies: These are the wordes: viz. As wee nowe demaunded of them concerninge the Towne of Cevola (whereof some have written that it is not farr from thence and is scituated within the lande and towardes the sea called mare del sur) they shewed us by signes which wee understoode well ynoughe that they mighte goe thither with their boates by Rivers in xx$^{ti.}$ daies.

8. Eightly Don Antonio di Castillo Embassador to her Majestie from Henry the kinge of Portingale, tolde me here in London the yere before his departure, that one Anus Corteriall Capitaine of the Ile of Tercera, in the yere 1574. sente a shippe to discover the northwest passage which arryvinge on the coaste of America in 57. degrees of latitude founde a greate entraunce very depe and broade withoute impedimente of Ise unto which

they passed above xx^{ti.} leagues and founde it alwayes to tende towardes the southe, the lande lay lowe and plaine on either side, they woulde have gon further but their victualls drawinge shorte, and beinge but one shippe, they returned backe, with hope at another tyme to make a full searche of the passage whereof they sawe not small likelyhoodde.

9. Nynthly Don Antonio Kinge of Portingale shewed me in Paris this present sommer a greate olde rounde carde (out of which Postellus tooke the forme of his mappe) that had the northwest straite plainely sett downe in the latitude of 57. degrees.

10. Tenthly there is a mightie large olde mappe in parchemente made as yt shoulde seme by Verarsanus, traced all alonge the coaste from fflorida to Cape Briton with many Italian names, which laieth oute the sea making a little necke of lande in 40. degrees of latitude, much lyke the streyte necke or Istmus of Dariena. This mappe is nowe in the custodie of Master Michael Locke.

11. Eleventhly there is an olde excellent globe in the Queenes privie gallory at Westminster which also semeth to be of Verarsanus makinge havinge the coaste described in Italian which laieth oute the very selfe same streite necke of lande in the latitude of 40. degrees with the sea joyninge harde on bothe sides as it dothe on Panama and Nombre di Dios which were a matter of singuler importaunce yf it shoulde be true as it is not unlikely.

12. Twelvethly the judgemente of Gerardus Mercator that excellent Geographer, which his sonne Rumolde Mercator shewed me in a letter of his and drewe oute for me in writinge, of wise men is not lightly to be regarded: These were his wordes: Magna tametsi pauca de nova navigatione scribis, quam miror ante multos annos non fuisse attentatam. Non enim dubium est quin recta et brevis via pateat in occidentem Cathaium vsque. In quod regnum si recte navigationem instituant, nobilissimas totius mundi merces colligent, et multis gentibus adhuc Idololatris Christi nomen communicabunt. You write (saieth he to his sonne) greate matters thoughe very brefely of the newe voyadge, whereat I wonder that it was not these many yeres heretofore attempted: For there is no doubte but there is a streighte and shorte waye open into the west even to Cathaio. Into which kingdome if they governe their voyadge well, they shall gather the moste noble marchandize of all the worlde and shall make the name of Christe to be knowen to many Idolaters and heathen people.

13. Hereunto agreeth the relation of Monsieur de Leau an honest gent of Morleux in Britaine which tolde me this springe in the presence of divers Englishe men at Paris that a man of St. Malowe this laste yere discovered the sea on the backside of Hochelaga.

14. Moreover the relation of David Ingram confirmeth the same, for as he avowcheth and hath put it downe in writinge, he traveled twoo daies in the sighte of the north sea.

15. Againe the prohibition which Kinge Philippe hath made that none of his pilotts shall discover to the northewardes of 45. degrees may seme chefely to procede of these twoo causes: The one leaste passinge further to the northe, they mighte fall upon the open passage from Mare del Sur into our northerne sea: The other because they have not people ynoughe to possesse and kepe the same, but rather in tyme shoulde open a gappe for other nations to passe that waye.

16. Lastly I will ende with the earnest peticion and constant assertion of Ramusius, in his firste Volume fol. 374. where speakinge of the severall waies by which the spicery bothe of olde and of late yeres hath bene broughte into Europe, he useth these speaches in the person of another: Why doo not the princes (saieth he) which are to deale in these affaires sende furthe twoo or three Colonies to inhabite the Contrie and to reduce this savage nation to more civilitie considering what a battle and frutefull soile it is, how replenished with all kinde of graine, howe it is stored with all kinde of birdes and beastes, with such faire and mightie Rivers that Capitaine Cartier and his Companie in one of them sailed upp an C. and iiij^{xx.} leagues findinge the Contrie peopled on bothe sides in greate aboundaunce: And moreover to cause the governours of those Colonies to sende furthe men to discover the northe landes aboute Terra de Labrador and west northwest towardes the seas, which are to saile to the Contrie of Cathaio and from thence to the Ilandes of Molucka. These are enterprises to purchase ymmortal praise which the Lord Antony de Mendoza viceroy of Mexico willinge to put in execution sente furthe his Capitaines bothe by sea and lande

upon the northwest of Nova Spania and discovered the kingdomes of the seaven Cities aboute Cevola: And Franciscus Vasques de Coronado passed from Mexico by lande towardes the northwest 2850. miles, in so moche as he came to the sea which lieth betwene Cathaio and America where he mett with the Cathaian shippes: And no doubte if the frenche men in this their Nova Francia woulde have discovered upp further into the lande towardes the west northwest partes they shoulde have founde the sea and have sailed to Cathaio: Thus farr Ramusius.

God which doth all thinges in his due tyme, and hath in his hande the hartes of all Princes, stirr upp the mynde of her Majestie at lengthe to assiste her moste willinge and forwarde Subjectes to the performance of this moste godly and profitable action which was begonne at the chardges of Kinge Henry the vii[th.] her grandfather, followed by Kinge Henry the eighte her father, and lefte as it semeth to be accomplished by her (as the three yeres golden voyadge to Ophir was by Salomon) to the makinge of her Realme and subjectes moste happy, and her selfe moste famous to all posteritie. Amen.

18
That the Queene of Englandes Title to all the west Indies or at the leaste to as moche as is from Florida to the Circle articke is more lawfull and righte then the Spaniardes or any other christian Princes.

To confute the generall claime and unlawfull title of the insatiable Spaniardes to all the west Indies, and to prove the justenes of her Majesties title and of her noble progenitors if not to all yet at leaste to that parte of America which is from Florida beyonde the Circle articke, wee are to sett downe in true order accordinge to the juste observation of tyme, when the west Indyes with the Ilandes and continent of the same were firste discovered and inhabited, and by what nation, and by whome. Then are wee to answer in generall and particulerly to the moste injurious and unreasonable donation graunted by Pope Alexander the sixte a spaniarde borne of all the West Indies to the kinges of Spaine and their Successors, to the greate prejudice of all other christian Princes but especially to the domage of the kinges of England.

For the firste pointe wee of England have to shewe very auncient and aucenticall Chronicles written in the welshe or brittishe tongue, wherein wee finde that one Madock ap Owen Guyneth a Prince of North Wales beinge wearye of the civill warres and domesticall dissentions in his Contrie, made twoo voyadges oute of Wales and discovered and planted large Contries which he founde in the mayne Ocean south westwarde of Ireland, in the yere of our Lord 1170. This historie is also to be seene in englishe in printe in the booke sett furthe this yere of the Princes of Wales, dedicated to Sir Henry Sidney. And this is confirmed by the language of some of those people that dwell upon the continent betwene the Bay of Mexico and the graunde Bay of Newfoundelande, whose language is said to agree with the welshe in divers wordes and names of places by experience of some of o[r] nation that have bene in those partes. By this Testimonie it appereth that the west Indies were discovered and inhabited 322. yeres before Columbus made his firste voyadge which was in the yere 1492.

Secondly the acceptation of Columbus his offer of the West Indies by Kinge Henry the Seaventh at the very firste maketh moche for the title of the kinges of England althoughe they had no former interest: which I will here putt downe as I finde it in the eleventh Chapiter of the historie of Ferdinandus Columbus of the Relation of the life and doinges of his father. This practise saieth he of the kinge of Portingale (which was secretly to deprive him of the honour of his enterprice) beinge come to the knowledge of the Admyrall and havinge lately buried his wife, he conceaved so greate hatred againste the citie of Lysbone and the nation, that he determyned to goe into Castile with a younge sonne that he had by his wife called Diego Colon, which after his fathers deathe succeded in his state. But fearinge yf the kinges of Castile also shoulde not consente unto his enterprise he shoulde be constrayned to begynne againe to make some newe offer of the same to some other Prince, and so longe tyme shoulde be spente therein, he sente into England a brother of his which he had with him named Bartholmewe Columbus: Nowe Bartholmewe Columbus beinge departed for England, his fortune was to fall into the handes of pyrates which robbed him and his other Companions that were in his shippe of all that they had: By which occasion and meanes of his povertie and sicknes which cruelly afflicted him in a strange Contrie, he deferred for a longe space his Embassage, till havinge gotten upp a little money by makinge of seacardes, he began to practize with kinge Henry the seaventhe the father of kinge Henry the viii^{th} which nowe reigneth: to whome he presented A general Carde wherein these verses were written, which I will rather here put downe for their antiquitie then for their elegancie:

Terrarum quicunque cupis fœliciter oras
Noscere, cuneta decens doct`e pictura docebit:
Quam Strabo affirmat, Ptolomæus, Plinius atque
Isodorus: non una tamen sententia cuique.
Pingitur hîc etiam nuper sulcata carinis
Hispanis Zona illa, priùs incognita genti
Torrida, quæ tandem nunc est notissima multis.

And somewhat more beneath he saied:

Pro authore sive pictore.

Janua cui patria est, nomen cui Bartholomæus
Columbus, de terra rubra, opus edidit istud
Londonijs, Anno Domini 1480 atque insuper anno
Octavo, decimáque die cùm tertia mensis
Februarij: Laudes Christo cantentur abundè.

But to returne to the kinge of England I say that after he had sene the generall Carde, and that which the Admyrall Columbus offred unto him, he accepted his offer with a cherefull countenaunce, and sente to call him into England. These thinges beinge so, wee nede not to be our owne Judges, but are able to prove as you see by a forren Testimonie of singuler greate aucthoritie that Christopher Columbus beinge in Portingale before he wente into Castile sente his brother Bartholmewe into England to practise with kinge Henry the seaventh aboute the discovery of the West Indies, and that his said brother made his generall seacarde of this secrete voyadge in London in the yere of our lorde 1488. the xiiith. of February, above foure yeres before Christopher was sett oute upon his firste voyadge by the Princes of Spaine fferdinando and Isabella, which was the thirde of Auguste 1492. It appereth also that the onely cause of his slowe dispatche was his fallinge into the handes of pyrates which spoiled him and his Companie of all that they had, whereby he was inforced a longe tyme to worke in London in makinge instrumentes and sea cardes to get somwhat aboute him that he mighte come in some honest furniture to the kinges presence. Also that there was no delaye nor wante of goodd will of the kinges parte to sett furthe the action, whoe willingly condescended to all Columbus de-

maundes, as is further to be seene in the 60. chapiter of the same historie: where I reade y^t Bartholmewe Columbus, havinge agreed with the kinge of England upon all Capitulations, and returninge into Spaine by ffraunce to fetche his brother, when he hearde newes at Paris that he had concluded in the meane season with the kinge of Spaine and was entred into the action for him, was not a little vexed for his brothers abusinge the kinge of England which had so curteously graunted all his requestes and accepted of his offer. But Christofer not receavinge so spedy aunswer as he hoped for from his brother oute of England by reason of his fallinge into pirates handes as is aforesaide, and not by reason of any slacknes or unwillingnes of the kinge, in the meane season for feare of beinge prevented by the portingales which once before in secrete manner had gon aboute to take the honor of the action oute of his handes, was stirred contrary to honesty to play on bothe handes, and to deal with the Princes of Spaine before he had receaved the kinge of Englandes resolucion. But leavinge this abuse offered to the kinge of England either by Christopher Columbus or the kinges of Spaine in takinge that enterprise oute of his handes which was first sente to him and never refused by him, and to put the case that Columbus firste discovered parte of the Ilandes of Hispaniola and Cuba, yet wee will prove most plainely, that a very greate and large parte as well of the continent as of the Ilandes was firste discovered for the kinge of England by Sebastian Gabote an Englishe man borne in Bristoll, the sonne of John Gabote a Venesian, in the yere of o^r Lorde 1496 as an Italian gentleman a greate philosopher and mathematitian witnesseth which harde the same of his owne mouthe and there were many then also lyvinge which wente with him in that voyadge, which coulde have proved him a liar yf it had bene otherwise: These be the very wordes of this gent which he uttered to certen noblemen of Venyce upon the disputation concerninge the voyadges of the spicerye: Know yee not (quoth he) to this effecte to goe to finde the easte Indies by the northwest, that which one of your Citie hath done: which is so skilfull in the arte of navigacion and Cosmographie, that he hath not his like in Spaine at this day? And this sufficiencie hath so greatly advaunced him, that the kinge hath geven him the oversighte of all the pilotts that saile to the west

Indies, so that withoute his licence they cannot meddle in this arte, by reason whereof they call him the graund pilott. This was segnior Sebastian Gabote which I wente to see beinge myselfe in Cyvill certen yeres paste, whome I founde to be a moste curteous and gentle person. After he had made very moche of me, and geven me good entertainment he shewed me many singularities which he had, and amonge the rest a greate mappe of the worlde, wherein were marked and described all the particuler navigations as well of the portingales as of the Castilians. And he declared unto me that his father beinge departed from Venyce, he wente to dwell in England for trade of marchandize, and caried him with him to the Citie of London, thoughe he were very younge: yet for all that not so younge but that he had studied of humanitie and the sphere: Moreover that his father died aboute the tyme that the newes came that Christopher Colon had discovered the coaste of the west Indies and there was no other talke but of that in the Courte of kinge Henry the vii[th.] which reigned then in England. Whereof every man saied that yt was rather a thinge devine then humaine to have founde out that way never knowen before, to goe by the west into the easte: This brute of Segnior Columbus did so inflame my harte, that I determyned also to doe some notable thinge. And knowinge by the reason of the Sphere that, in directinge my course righte towarde the northweste I shoulde shorten the way greatly to goe to the east Indies, withoute delaye I gave the kinges Majestie to understande of myne opinion, which was marveylously well pleased: and he furnished me of twoo shippes with all thinges necessarie: and this was in the yere 1496. in the begynnynge of sommer: And I began to saile towardes the northwest thinckinge to finde no lande savinge that where Cathaio is, and from thence to turne towardes the Indies. But after certaine daies I discouered lande which ronneth towardes the northe, wherewithall I was excedingly agreved: notwithstandinge I ceassed not to ronne alonge that coaste towardes the northe to see yf I coulde finde any gulfe which turned towardes the northweste, until I came to the heighte of 65. degrees of our pole. Beinge there I sawe that the coaste turned towarde the easte and beinge oute of hope to finde any straite, I turned backe againe to searche out the said coaste towarde the equinoctiall with intention always to finde some passage to the Indies, and in followinge this coaste I sailed as farr as that parte w[ch] at this present they call Florida: and nowe my victualls failinge and fallinge shorte I sailed no further, but lefte the coaste there and sailed into England, where I was no sooner arryved, but I founde greate troubles of the people that were upp in armes, by reason of the warres in Scotland: whereby the voyadge to those partes was laide aside for that time,[84] and had in no further consideration: Upon this Relation Monsieur Popiliniere being a Frencheman in his seconde booke *Des Trois Mondes* inferreth these speaches: This then was that Gabote which firste discovered Florida for the kinge of England, so that the Englishemen have more righte thereunto then the Spaniardes, yf to have righte unto a Contrie it sufficeth to have firste seene and discovered the same: Howbeit Gabota did more then see the contrie, for he wente on lande on divers places, tooke possession of the same accordinge to his patente which was graunted to his father John Gabot, to Lewes, himselfe, and Sancius his brethren, beinge to be sene in the Rolles and extant in printe, and moreover he broughte home three of the Savages of the Indies as Fabian in his auncient Chronicle dothe write declaringe their apparell, feedinge, and other manners, which he saieth he observed himselfe in the Courte at Westminster, where he sawe twoo of them two yeres after they were broughte into England in englishe apparell: Nay that which is more Gabota discovered this longe tracte of the firme lande twoo yeres before Columbus ever sawe any parte of the continente thereof. For the firste parte of the firme Land called Paria and Bocca di Dragone that is to say the Dragons mouthe, lienge to the southe of the Iland of Hispaniola was discovered by him in his thirde voyadge, which as Peter Martir de Angleria which was one of the Councell of the west Indies wryteth, was in the yere 1498, which is confirmed by Ferdinandus Columbus his owne sonne which was with his father in the voyadge as Oviedo confesseth libr. 19. cap. I., and wrote a journall of that voyadge, shewinge in the 67. chapter of his historie that his father firste sawe the firme lande the firste of Auguste in the yere 1498. But Gabote made his greate discoverie in

84. Sidenote: "The reason why the discovery was lefte of in Kinge Henry the Seaventh's tyme."

the yere 1496. as he testifieth in his relation above mentioned. And the day of the moneth is also added in his owne mappe which is yn the Queenes privie gallorie at Westminster, the copye whereof was sett oute by Master Clemente Adams and is in many marchantes houses in London: In which mappe in the Chapiter of Newfoundelande there in Latyn is put downe besides the yere of our Lorde even the very day, which was the day of St. John Baptiste, and the firste lande which they sawe, they called prima visa or prima vista, and Master Roberte Thorne in his discourse to doctor Ley kinge Henry the eights embassador to Charles the Emperour, affirmeth that his father and one Hughe Elliott of Bristoll were the firste persons that descried the lande. This case is so clere that the Spaniardes themselves thoughe full sore againste their willes are constrained to yelde unto us therein: For Franciscus Lopez de Gomera in the 4. Chapiter of his seconde booke of his *generall historie of the Indies* confesseth that Sebastian was the firste discoverer of all the coaste of the west Indies from 58. degrees of northerly latitude to the heighte of 38. degrees towardes the equinoctiall: He whiche broughte moste certeine newes of the Contrie and people of Baccalaos, saieth Gomera, was Sebastian Gabot a Venesian, which rigged up ij. shippes at the coste of kinge Henry the seaventh of England havinge greate desire to traficque for the spices as the portingales did: he caried with him CCC. men and tooke the way towardes Island from beyonde the Cape of Labrador untill he founde himselfe in 58. degrees and better. He made relation that in the moneth of July it was so colde and the Ise so greate, that he durste not passe any further, that the daies were very longe in a manner withoute any nighte, and for that shorte nighte that they had it was very clere. Gabot feelinge the colde turned towardes the west, refreshinge himselfe at Baccalaos: and afterwardes he sailed alonge the coaste unto 38. degrees, and from thence he shaped his course to returne into England: Moreover this Fraunces Lopez de Gomera acknowledgeth in his firste booke and xxi[th.] Chapiter of his *generall historie of the Indies* that Columbus on his thirde voyadge, sett oute from St. Lucar of Barameda in Spaine in the ende of May, Anno 1497. In which thirde voyadge at lengthe after many greate dangers by the way he arryved in the firme lande of the Indies towardes the province called Paria, which all the Spanishe authors confesse to have bene the firste of the continent that was discovered for the kinges of Spaine. So to conclude whether wee beleve the Testimonie of Peter Martir and fferdinandus Columbus which affirme that Christopher Columbus discovered the firme firste in Anno 1498. a greate and large tracte of the continente of the Indies was discovered by Gabote and the englishe above twoo yeres before, To witt in the yere 1496 in the monethes of June and July: Or whether wee be contente to yelde to Gomera which saieth Columbus sett furthe of the discovery of the firme lande 1497, yet wee of England are the firste discoverers of the continent above a yere and more before them: To witt 1496. or as Clement Adams saith 1494. in the Chapiter of Gabbotts mapp *de terra nova*, which is above three yeres before the Spaniarde or any other for the kinges of Spaine had any sighte of any parte of the firme lande of the Indies. At leaste wise by Gomera his owne confession from 58. degrees of northerly latitude to 38. towardes the equinoctiall wee have beste righte and Title of any Christian. As for the discovery of John Ponce de Leon beinge in Anno 1512. yt cannot be prejudiciall to our Title as beinge made sixtene yeres after Gabotes voyadge.

19

An aunswer to the Bull of the Donacion of all the west Indies graunted to the kinges of Spaine by Pope Alexander the vi[th] whoe was himselfe a spaniarde borne.

Whereas Fraunces Lopez de Gomera, in the 19. Chapiter of his firste booke of his *generall historie of the Indies* putteth downe that Pope Alexander the vi[th] of his proper will and of his owne mere motion with the consente of his Cardinalls gave of his free grace to the kinges of Spaine all the Iles and firme landes which they shoulde discover towardes the west, and therewithall alledged the Bull itselfe: I aunswer that no Pope had any lawfull aucthoritie to give any such donation at all: For proofe whereof I say that if he were no more then Christes vycar, as Gomera calleth him in that place, then he must nedes graunte that the vicar is no greater then his Master. Nowe our saviour Christe beinge requested and intreated to make a lawfull devision of inheritaunce betwene one and his brother, refused to do yt, sayenge *Quis me constituit judicem inter vos*? Whoe made me a judge betwene you? What meaneth then the

Pope not beinge spoken to nor entreated of his owne proper will and of his owne mere motion to meddle in those matters that Christe in no wise, no not beinge thereunto instantly requested woulde not have to deale in? Againe oure saviour Christe confessed openly to Pilate that his kingdome was not of this worlde, Why then doth the Pope that woulde be Christes servaunte take upon him the devision of so many kingdomes of the worlde? If he had but remembred that which he hath inserted in the ende of his owne Bull, To witt that god is the disposer and distributer of kingdomes and Empires, he woulde never have taken upon him the devidinge of them with his line of partition from one ende of the heavens to the other. The historie of the poore boye whome god stirred upp to confounde and deride the Spaniardes and Portingales, when they were devidinge the worlde betwene themselves alone, is so well knowen as I nede not stand to repeate it: But it is the Popes manner always to meddle as in this matter, so in other thinges, where they have nothinge to doe, and to intrude themselves before they be called: They mighte rather call to mynde the counsell of the goodd Apostle, who tolde godly Tymothe the Bisshoppe of Ephesus, that no man that warreth intangleth himself with the affaires of this presente life, because he woulde please him that hath chosen him to be a souldier, and then they woulde learne to kepe themselves within the lymites of that vocation and ecclesiasticall function whereunto they are called: which ecclesiasticall function hath nothinge to doe with absolute donation and devidinge of mere Temporalties and earthly kingdomes: St. Chrisostome in his dialogue *de dignitate sacerdotali* saieth that the mynisterie is a chardge geven by God to teache withoute armes or force, and that the same is no power to give or to take kingdomes nor to make lawes for the politique governemente. St. Hillary writes as moche to the Emperour Constantine againste Auxentius Bisshoppe of Milan: Our saviour Christe himselfe saieth to his disciples that while they were in the worlde they shoulde be broughte before kinges and pollitique magistrates for his names sake. So then they shoulde not be Judges and magistrates themselves especially in the devisions of kingdomes, and to leave all spirituall men an example, he paid tribute and toll for himselfe and Peter, and submitted himselfe and his Apostles under the civill magistrate and politique gov-

ernemente: yet the Pope whoe saieth he is Peters successor will be a disposer of civill causes and temporall domynions: The Apostle saieth Romaines the 13. Let every soule be submitted unto the higher powers: Nowe if the Popes will not beleve the worde of god withoute the exposition of the fathers of the Churche, at leaste let them beleve St. Chrisostome and give eare to that which he hath written upon this place: That these thinges be commaunded to all men saieth he bothe to prestes and monckes, and not onely to secular or laymen the Apostle declareth even in the very begynnynge when he saieth in this manner: Let every soule be subjecte unto their higher powers, thoughe thou were an Apostle, thoughe thou were an Evangeliste, thoughe thou were a prophet, or thoughe thou were any other whatsoever. For obedience dothe nothinge hinder godlines: But the Popes woulde prove that they may give and bestowe kingdomes upon whome they please, by Samuels example that annointed David and deposed Saul: of Elyas that annoynted Hazaell kinge of Siria in steade of Benhadad, and Jehu kinge of Israell in steade of Jehoram; as also by the example of Jehoida the highe preste that put the Queene Athalia to deathe, and placed Joas the younge sonne of Ochosias in the kingdome.

All those examples make nothinge at all in the worlde for them: for neither Samuell, nor Elias, nor Elizeus did any thinge in that matter withoute an expresse commaundement and all circumstances from the mouthe of God himselfe, as appereth moste evidently by their severall histories in the Bible: Samuell also did his commission full sore againste his will, and Elias, and Elizeus with greate feare of their lyves: As for Athalia she was an usurper and had cruelly murdered as many of the lawfull inheritours of the kingdome as she coulde possibly lay handes on, and therefore Jehoiada the highe preste not of his owne absolute aucthoritie, but by the helpe of the kinges officers and joyfull consente of all the people caused her moste justely to be deposed and put to deathe. He was also uncle to the younge kinge by mariage of his wife Jehosheba which was sister to Ahasia the father of the younge kinge, and therefore bounde in conscience and affinitie to helpe him to his righte and succour him in his mynoritie.

Nowe when the Popes have the like excellent spirites of prophecie, and the like chardges and expresse commaundementes from Gods owne mouthe in the behalf of some one by name againste some one which God by name woulde have deposed, then they may ymitate them in pronouncinge unto them that God will rente their kingdomes from this or that kinge for his synnes. But none of the prophetts made Bulls or donations in their palaces under their handes and seales and dates, to bestowe many kingdomes which they never sawe nor knewe, nor what nor howe large they were, or to say the truthe whether they were extant *in rerum natura,* as the Pope hath done in gevinge all the west Indies to the kinges of Spaine: He shoulde firste have don as the prophetts dyd, that is he shoulde firste have gon himselfe and preached the worde of God to those Idolatrous kinges and their people, and then if they woulde not by any meanes have repented, he mighte have pronounced the severe and heavie judgemente of God againste them shewinge oute of the worde of God that one kingdome is translated from another for the sinnes of the Inhabitantes of the same, and that God in his justice woulde surely bringe some nation or other upon them to take vengeaunce of their synnes and wickednes. And thus moche not onely Popes but also any other godly and zealous Bisshoppe or mynister may doo beinge called thereunto by God extraordinarily, or havinge the ordinarye warrante of his worde. Yea but the Popes can shewe goodd Recordes that they have deposed Emperors, that they have translated Empires from one people to another, as that of the Easte unto the Germaines, and that they have taken kingdomes from one nation and geven them to another. In deede in some respectes they have done so: But how? They never gave that which was in their actuall possession yf by any meanes possible they mighte have kepte it themselves. It is an easie matter to cutt large thonges as wee say of other mens hides, and to be liberall of other mens gooddes. Neither ys it any marvaile thoughe (as Gomera saieth) the Pope gave all the west Indies of his free grace to the kinge of Spaine, for they never coste him a penye: But he that will be in deede and truthe liberall, he muste give of his owne and not of other mens: ffor to take from one that which is his to give it to another to whom it is not due, ys plaine injurie and no liberalitie, thoughe the gifte were bestowed upon him that were in nede: For as one saieth *Eripere alteri fraudulenter quod alteri des misericorditer, in-*

justitia quidem est et non eleemosyna. To take from one fraudulently to give to an other mercifully is no almes nor charitie, but plaine iniquitie: The Pope shoulde rather have sent into the West Indies store of godly pastors of his owne coste freely, then to have geven them and their gooddes wrongfully to be eaten upp and devoured of such insatiable and gredy wolves: He should have remembred the worde of our savio[r] whoe saieth: *Beatius est dare qûam accipere:* It is a blessed thinge to give rather then to receave. The Popes say they gave Ireland to kinge Henry the seconde and his successors, and indeede they have don it in wordes: But when gave they yt unto him, forsoothe after he had faste footinge in it, and when Dermutius the King of Leynester had firste offred to make the kinge his heire: And for all their donation yf the kinge had not by his force more then by their gifte holpe himselfe the Popes donation had stoode him in small stede: neither did the kinges of Ireland admitt and allowe of the Popes donation: If they had, they woulde never have rebelled so ofte againste the Crowne of England: To conclude this pointe thoughe wee confesse that the Popes have don this or that, yet yt is no goodd argumente to say that they did it and therefore it is lawfull, unless they coulde shewe that they did it rightfully: *de facto constat, de jure non constat.* And they themselves are driven to confesse that their medlinge on this sorte with kingdomes ys not directly but indirectly. But suche indirecte dealinge is warranted neither by lawe of God nor men.

Nowe to the donation it selfe wee are firste to consider whoe it was that was the author thereof, secondly unto whome it was made, thirdly what were the causes and inducementes that moved the Pope thereunto, fourthly the fourme and manner of donation, fyftly the inhibition of all other christian Princes, and the penaltie of all them that shoulde doo the contrarye: Lastly the recompence of the kinges of Spaine to the sea of Rome for so greate a gifte.

1. Touchinge the firste the Author hereof was Pope Alexander the vi[th.] whoe as Platina, and Onuphrius and Bale doo write was himselfe a Spaniarde and borne in Valencia of the familie called Burgia, and therefore no marvell thoughe he were ledd by parcialitie to favour the spanishe nation, thoughe yt were to the prejudice and dommage of all others. Whiche foule faulte of his

may hereby appere, that havinge in all the tyme of his Popedome created sixe and thirtie Cardinalles of those xxx^{tie}vj. he made xviij. to witt the one halfe spaniardes as Bale dothe testifie writinge of his life: Nowe let any man be judge whether that were extreame parcialitie and ambition to make Spaine equal in that pointe with all the rest of Christendome: No marvaile therefore thoughe as in this, so in his donacion he was beyonde all reason caried away with blynde affection to his nation, which faulte of his had bene more to be borne withall yf it had bene in a private or small matter: But in this so generall and common cause, yt cannot choose but be altogether intollerable: If any man liste to see this man painted oute farther in his colours, let him reade John Bale in his eighte Centurye where he shall finde so many of his badd partes as a man woulde thincke he coulde not be a fitt man to make a goodd and uprighte judge in so weightie a matter as this.

2. The persons to whome he made this donation were Ferdinando and Isabella Princes of Spaine, to whome and to their heires and successors for ever he confirmed the same excludinge all other Christian Princes: These Princes thoughe otherwise very vertuous and commendable, yet at the time of the makinge of this donacion were more unable then divers other kinges of Christendome to accomplishe and bringe the same to effecte, as beinge greately ympoverished with the warres of Granadoe so farr furthe that they were constrained to seke for helpe of kinge Henry the vij^{th.} of England to subdue the Moores in their owne Contrie. Yea Queene Isabella was so poore and bare that she was faine to offer her owne Jewells to gage to borowe money to sett furthe Columbus in his firste voyadge, as it is to be seene in the 14. chapiter of the historye of Ferdinandus Columbus his owne sonne. It is also well knowen that the Spaniardes for wante of people of their owne Contrie, have not bene able nowe, in the space of $\frac{xx}{iiii}$ and xii. yeres to inhabite a thirde or fourthe parte of those excedinge large and waste Contries which are as greate as all Europe and Africke.

3. The inducementes that moved his holines to graunt these unequall donations unto Spaine were firste (as he saieth) his singuler desire and care to have the Christian Relligion and Catholicque faithe exalted, and to be enlarged and spredd abroade throughoute the worlde especially in his

daies, and that the salvation of soules shoulde be procured of every one, and that the barbarous nations shoulde be subdued and reduced to the faithe &c.

To this I aunswer that if he had ment as in deede he saieth he shoulde not have restrayned this so greate and generall a worke belonginge to the duetie of all other Christian Princes unto the kinges of Spaine onely, as thoughe god had no servauntes but in Spaine. Or as thoughe other Christian kinges then lyvinge had not as greate zeale and meanes to advaunce gods glory as they. Or howe mente he that every one shoulde put their helpinge hande to this worke, when he defended all other Christian princes, in paine of his heavie curse and excomunicatyon to meddle in this action, or to employe their subjectes thoughe yt were to the conversion of thinhabitauntes in those partes. And whereas to colour that his donacion he addeth that the kinges of Spaine had bene at greate chardges in that discoverie, in respecte whereof he was induced to deale so franckly with them, yt is evident that the Bull was graunted in the yere 1493. the iiii^{th.} of the moneth of May at what time Columbus had made but one voyadge, wherein he was furnished onely with one small shippe and twoo little Caravells, and had in all his Companie but foure score and tenne men, and the whole voyadge stoode the kinge of Spaine in 2500. Crownes only. So these 2500. Crownes were the greate chardges that the Pope speaketh of that induced him to graunte so large a donacion, for that was the uttermoste that Columbus desired, as is to be redd in the 14. Chapter of his owne sonnes historie: Moreover where the Pope confesseth he was informed before the donation of his Bull, That the kinges of Spaine had purposed by the aide of God to subdue and reduce unto the faithe all those landes and Ilandes with their inhabitantes whiche Columbus had founde in his firste discovery, in commendinge highly of this their intention, he semeth to confesse that they mighte have pursued that godly action very lawfully wthoute makinge of him privy to their enterprice, which they did not in their firste sendinge furthe of Columbus: And with what righte he builded and lefte men in Hispaniola at the firste before the Popes donation, with the selfe same righte he mighte have subdued all that he shoulde afterwardes discover. So then the Popes gifte was of no more force, then of that which they mighte have chalenged by their former righte and interest of discoverie: and as for their former zeale and resolucion to publishe the christian faithe in those quarters which the Pope confesseth to have bene in them before his donation, whoe seeth not that he stirres them uppe to nothinge but to that which he acknowledgeth to have bene in them already, and so he did nothinge but *actum agere*. Againe in that he saieth that in no other respecte but moved onely by his mere and francke liberaltie, *And for certeine secrete causes* he gave unto them all the Ilandes and firme landes which already have bene founde and which shoulde afterwardes be founde, which were then discovered or afterwardes to be discovered, towardes the west and the southe, drawinge a straighte line from the Pole articke to the Pole antarticke, whether the ilandes or firme landes founde or to be founde were towardes the Indies or towardes any other quarter, intendinge nevertheles that this line be distant an hundred leagues towardes the west and the southe from the Iles which are commonly called the Azores, or those of Cape Verd: To this wee aunswer that here wee are firste to consider that yt was no marvell that his holines beinge a Spaniarde borne sett aparte all other respectes of justice and equitie and of his mere motion and francke liberalitie was ready to raise and advaunce his owne nation with doinge secrete wronge and injurie as moche as in him laye and more unto all other Princes of Christendome: For what els can those wordes importe that he did it also for certen secrete causes, but give us juste cause to suspect that there wanted uprighte indifferent and sincere dealinges? And surely if he had ment uprightly, he woulde have delte more plainely, for truthe seketh no secrete corners. But if you will have me to reveale those secrete causes, to say as the thinge was, they were nothinge else but the feare and jelousie that he had that kinge Henry the vii[th.] of England withe whome Bartholmewe Columbus had bene to deale in this enterprice and even aboute this time had concluded with the kinge upon all pointes and articles, whoe even nowe was readie to sende him into Spaine to call his brother Christopher into England, shoulde put a foote into this action, which if he had don, he shoulde bothe have share with the Spaniardes in the profitt, and greatly ecclips their hono[r] and glorie. Also he coulde not choose but be privie to the longe conference that Christopher Columbus had before time with the kinge of Portingale and offer which he made firste of all to the said kinge of this discovery, whoe thoughe at the firste delte doubly with Columbus, and sent other to finde oute that thinge which Columbus offred, yet they missinge of their purpose, the kinge of Portingale woulde have employed Columbus and delte effectually with him to that ende, but he conceavinge a greate displeasure againste the kinge and his nation for his secrete seekinge to defraude him of his hono[r] and benefite of his offer, stole prively oute of his Realme into Castile. But the Pope fearinge that either the kinge of Portingale mighte be reconciled to Columbus, or that he mighte be drawen into England by interposinge of his usurped aucthoritie, thoughte secretly by his unlawfull division to defraude England and Portingale of that benefite: Loe, these were indeede those secrete causes sodenly withoute makinge the other kinges privie, to make his generall and universall donation of all the west Indies to the kinges of Spaine, by drawinge a lyne of partition from one Pole unto another passinge a hundred leagues westwarde of the Iles of Azores, which division howe God caused to be deryded by the mouthe of a poor simple childe, Fraunces Lopes de Gomera one of the Spaniardes owne Historiographers dothe specially note in manner followinge: Before I finishe this Chapiter (saieth he) I will recite to recreate the Reader that which happened upon this partition to the Portingales: As Fraunces de Melo, Diego Lopes of Sequeria and others came to this assembly and passed the River by Quidiana a little Infant that kepte his mothers clothes which she had washt and honge abroade to drye, demaunded of them whither they were those that shoulde come to devide the worlde with the Emperour? and as they aunswered yea, he tooke up his shirte behinde and shewed them his buttocks, sayenge unto them, Drawe your Lyne throughe the middest of this place: This saieth the Author was published in contempte all abroade bothe in the towne of Badayos and also in the assemblye of these Committies. The Portingales were greatly angrie therewithall, but the rest turned yt to a Jest and laughed yt oute. But what wiseman seeth not that God by that childe laughed them to scorne and made them ridiculous and their partition in the eyes of the worlde and in their owne consciences, and caused the childe to reprove them, even as the dombe beaste speakinge with mans voyce, reproved the foolishnes of Balam the prophett.

4. The fourthe pointe which I purpose to touche is the forme and manner of the stile of the donation itselfe, after a large preface and connynge preamble, and that begynneth in this manner:

Wee therefore by the aucthoritie of God almightie which is geven to us in the person of Saincte Peter, and which wee enjoye in this worlde as the vicar of Jhesus Christe, give unto you all the Ilandes and firme landes with their seigniories, Cities, Castells, &c. In which repetition of his donation the seconde time for failinge he woulde shewe unto the world by what aucthoritie and warrant he gave away from all the Indians their landes, Contries, seigniories, Cities, Castells, places, villages, rightes, jurisdictions, and all other appurtenaunces and thinges belonginge to the same to the kinges of Spaine onely, and to their heires and successors for ever. This usurped aucthoritie as I have plainely confuted and denied in the begynnynge, so nowe in a worde or twoo I will shewe that God never gave unto the Popes any suche aucthoritie. The chefest and greatest aucthoritie that ever was geven by Christe to Peter is mentioned in the 16. Chapiter of St. Mathewe[85] where Christe saieth unto him, I will give unto thee the keyes of the kingdome of heaven, and whatsoever thou shalte binde in earthe, shalbe bounde in heaven, and whatsoever thou shalte loose in earthe shalbe loosed in heaven: St. Hierome expoundinge of this place saieth that the Priestes or Bisshopps duetie and aucthoritie of the keyes, to binde or loose, is to knowe and declare by the holy scripture and by the judgemente of the Catholicque Churche, when and whoe he is that hath offended againste the will of god, and whoe beinge once a Christian, is fallen from the societie, or gone astraye oute of the pathe and waye of the Churche: These are the trewe keyes and twoo swordes which God hath put into prestes handes: And Peter Lombarde the Master of the Sentences one of their owne Doctors is of St. Hieromes opinion. And what aucthoritie in the place above recited Christe comitted unto Peter, the same gave he also unto all the rest of his Apostles, John 20. vers. 21. sayenge to them all, Whosoever synnes yee remitte they

85. Sidenote: "Matth: 16."

are retained. But that either Peter or any of the Apostles did teache or affirme that they had aucthoritie to give awaye kingdomes of heathen Princes to those that were so farr from havinge any interest in them, that they knewe not whether there were any suche Contries in the worlde or noe, I never reade nor hearde, nor any mane else as I verely beleve: Which moste unjuste and wrongfull dealinge of the Pope was notably confuted by Atabalipa beinge an Infidell: For after Fryer Vincent of Valverde of the companie and traine of Pisar had made an oration to him, the somme whereof was that he shoulde become a Christyan and that he shoulde obey the Pope and the Emperor to whome the Pope had geven his kingdome: Atabalipa beinge greately insensed replied that seeinge he was nowe free he woulde not become tributarye, nor thincke that there was any greater Lorde then himselfe, but that he was willinge to be the Emperours frende and to have his acquaintaunce, for that he muste nedes be some great Lorde that sente so many armies abroade into the worlde: He aunswered moreover that he woulde not in any wise obey the Pope seinge he gave away that which belonged to another, moche lesse that he woulde leave his kingdome that came unto him by inheritaunce to one which he had never seene in his life. And whereas Fryer Vincent beinge displeased at his replye was gladd to seeke any waye to wreake his anger upon him, in somoche as when Atabalipa lett his portesse fall to the grounde, he was so testye, that he sett Pisar and his souldiers forwardes cryenge, vengeaunce Christians vengeaunce, give the chardge upon them, whereby many Indians withoute resistaunce or any stroke stricken on their partes were moste pitefully murdred and massacred, and Atabalipa himselfe taken, and afterwardes trecherously put to deathe: This ffrier himselfe by gods juste judgemente was afterwardes beaten to deathe with clubbes by the Inhabitantes of Puna as he fledd from Don Diego de Almagre, as Fraunces Lopes de Gomera precisely and of purpose noteth libro. 5. cap. 85. of his *generall historie of the Indies,* and besides him all the reste of the chefe that were the executioners of his rashe counsell and of the Popes donation came to moste wretched and unfortunate endes, as the aforesaide Author there setteth downe in twoo severall Chapiters of considerations as he calleth them. Moreover since the fourme of the donation ronneth not absolutely but with this condition and chardge moste straightly enjoyned, viz., That the kinges of Spaine shoulde sende thither sober and godly men, and cause the Inhabitantes of those Contries discovered or to be discovered to be instructed in the catholique faithe, and noseled in goodd manners, and that they shoulde carefully applye themselves thereunto: Wee aunswer that these conditions have bene wonderfully neglected, and that neither the people have bene carefully instructed in relligion nor manners: and consequently that the conditions beinge not perfourmed the donation oughte of righte to be voide: For the kinges of Spaine have sent suche helhoundes and wolves thither as have not converted but almoste quite subverted them, and have rooted oute above fiftene millions of reasonable creatures as Bartholmewe de Casas the Bisshoppe of Chiapa in the west Indies, a Spaniarde borne dothe write at large in a whole volume of that argumente. And Gonsalvo de Oviedo another of their owne historiographers and Capitaine of the Castle of Sancto Domingo in Hispaniola affirmeth the like. For there hath Spaniardes come into these contries, saieth he, which havinge lefte their consciences and all feare of God and men behinde them, have plaied the partes not of men but of dragons and infidells, and havinge no respecte of humanitie, have bene the cause that many Indians that peradventure mighte have bene converted and saved, are deade by divers and sondrie kindes of deathes. And althoughe those people had not bene converted, yet if they had bene lett to live, they mighte have bene profitable to your Majestie and an aide unto the Christians, and certaine partes of the Lande shoulde not wholy have bene disinhabited, wch by this occasion are altogether in a manner dispeopled. And they that have bene the cause of suche destruction call this contrie thus dispeopled and wasted, the Contrie conquered and pacified. But I call it quoth Gonsalvo the contrie wch is destroyed and ruyned: yea so farr have they bene of from drawinge the Indians to the likinge of Christianitie and true Relligion, that the sentence of the Apostle may moste truly be verified of them, whoe saieth, The name of God is blasphemed amonge the Gentiles throughe you. ffor proofe whereof you shall not nede to reade but that which Peter Benzo of Milan hath written

whoe remayned in these Indies and served in the warres with the Spaniardes againste the Indians for the space of fourtene yeres: This Benzo saieth that the Indians not havinge studied Logicke concluded very pertinently and categorically that the Spaniardes which spoiled their Contrie, were more dangerous then wilde beastes, more furious then Lyons, more fearefull and terrible then fire and water, or any thinge that is moste outeragious in the worlde. Some also called them the fome of the sea, others gave them names of the beastes which are moste cruell and lyvinge of praye which they have in their Contrie: There were some likewise that called them Tuira, as one would say, the Devills goodd grace.

Those thinges beinge thus, whoe seeth not that the Pope is frustrated of the ende which he intended in his donacion, and so the same oughte not to take effecte.

5. Fiftly yf yt be true and that the Pope mente goodd earnest that all Emperours and kinges which should sende their subjectes or others to discover withoute the kinge of Spaines leave shoulde be excommunicated by him: Why did he not first excommunicate kinge Henry the seaventh for sendinge furthe Sebastian Gabota with three hundred englishemen, whoe by Gomera his owne confession discovered from 58. degrees in the northe to 38. degrees towardes the equinoctiall? Why did he not the like to kinge Henry the eighte for sendinge to discover westwarde in the xix^th. yere of his reigne while he was yet in obedience to the Churche of Rome? Why was he not offended and incensed againste Queene Mary whoe suffered her subjectes in the yere 1556. to seke oute by the northeaste the way to Cathaio and China, which are bothe within the pretended lymites of his donation as John Gaetan and other Spaniardes doo write? Why did he not exercise his censures ecclesiasticall againste the kinge of ffraunce, ffraunces the firste for sendinge furthe Verarsanus twise or thrise, Iaques Cartier twise, and Robervall once towardes the southwest and northwest? Why was not Henry the seconde of Fraunce excomunicated for sendinge Villegagnon to inhabite in Brasill under the Tropicke of Capricorne? Or Charles the ix^th. for aidinge Ribault firste and after Ladoniere, and a thirde tyme Ribault to fortifie and inhabite in Florida? Or why did he not thunder againste Emanuell kinge of Portingale for sufferinge Gasper Corterealis

twise to seke to finde oute the northweste passage, and one of his brothers another time afterwarde? Or wherefore did he not openly rebuke the kinge of Denmarke for suffringe his subjecte John Scolno a dane in the yere 1500. to seke the straighte by the northweste, of whome Gemma Frisius and Hieromy Gerava a Spaniarde make mention? Or what shoulde be the reason that all these kinges of England, Fraunce, Portingale and Denmarke beinge otherwise all at these times in obedience of the Churche of Rome, shoulde withoute consente as yt were disanull and never make accompte of this Bull of the Pope? Which thinge doubtles they woulde never have don yf they had bene fully perswaded in their consciences, that if any prince or Emperoʳ of what estate or condition soever shoulde attempte the contrary, as it is in the conclusion of the said Bull, he shoulde be assured to incurr the indignation of Almightie God, and of the Apostles St. Peter and St. Pawle: But nowe seinge all the kinges aforesaide sente all their subjectes to discover beyonde the Popes partition lyne withoute the leave or permission of the Spaniarde, they seme with one accorde to testifie unto the worlde, that they made no reconynge of the breache of that Bull as of an acte moste unjuste, moste unreasonable, and moste prejudiciall to all other Chrisitan Princes of the worlde. Againe yt were small charitie in the Popes, to curse those princes that have bene or are willinge to employe their treasures and people in advauncinge the honoʳ and glory of god, and the lawfull enrichinge and benefite of their people. And whatsoever Pope shoulde excommunicate or curse any Christian prince for seekinge to reduce to the knowledge of god and to civill manners those infinite multitudes of Infidells and heathen people of the west Indies, which the Spaniardes in all this time have not so moche as discovered moche less subdued or converted, his curse woulde lighte upon his owne heade, and to those which he cursed undeservedly woulde be turned to a blessinge.

To be shorte thoughe Pope Alexander the vjᵗʰ· by his unequall division hath so puffed upp and inflamed with pride his moste ambitious and insatiable contrymen that they are growen to this high conceite of themselves that they shall shortly attaine to be Lordes and onely seigniors of all the earthe, insomoche as Gonsalvo de Oviedo sticketh not to write to Charles the Emperoʳ sayenge, God

hath geven you these Indies *accio che vostra majesta sia uniuersale et unico monarcha del mondo*, to the intente that your Majestie shoulde be the universall and onely monarch of the world: yet god that sitteth in heaven laugheth them and their partitions to scorne, and he will abase and bringe downe their proude lookes, and humble ther faces to the duste, yea he will make them at his goodd time and pleasure to confesse that the earthe was not made for them onely, as he hath already shewed unto the Portingales, which not longe since takinge upon them to devide the worlde with lynes, doo nowe beholde the line of gods juste judgemente drawen over themselves and their owne kingdome and possessions: And nowe no doubte many of them remember that the threateninge of the prophet hath taken holde upon them, whoe pronounceth an heavie woe againste all suche as spoile, because they themselves shall at length be spoiled.

6. ffinally to come to the sixte and laste pointe, yf you consider what recompence the kinges of Spaine have made to the Popes for this so greate a benefite bestowed upon them, you shall easely see and acknowledge with me that they were either moste ungratefull or, which is moste likely, that they never thoughte that they helde the Indies as the Popes gifte unto them, or that their Title unto those Regions depended upon his francke almes or liberalitie: ffor if they had don soe, they coulde have done no lesse but have geven him the presentation of all Archebisshopricks and Bisshoprickes, and other greate ecclesiastical promotions in recompence of their former and large curtesie: Wherein they have don the flatt contrary, reservinge onely unto themselves the presentation and patronage of all the Archebisshopricks and Bisshopricks that they have erected in the west Indies: For as Gomera saieth in his 6. booke and 23. Chapiter of his *generall historie of the Indies*, The kinge of Spaine is patrone of all the Archebisshopricks, Bysshoprickes, dignities, and Benefices of the west Indies, and so he onely appointeth and presenteth them, so that he is absolute lorde of the Indies.

This argueth that the kinges of Spaine never made any greate accompte of the Popes' donation, but onely to blinde the eyes of the worlde with the sea of Rome; ffor doubtles if they had acknowledged their tenure to depende as I saied of the

Popes mere liberalitie, they woulde have don otherwise, and woulde have requited them farr otherwise then by excludinge them quite oute, and makinge themselves absolute Patrones of all ecclesiasticall dignities whatsoever.

20

A brefe Collection of certaine reasons to induce her Majestie and the state to take in hande the westerne voyadge and the plantinge there.

1. The soyle yeldeth and may be made to yelde all the severall commodities of Europe, and of all kingdomes domynions and Territories that England tradeth withe, that by trade of marchandize cometh into this Realme.

2. The passage thither and home is neither to longe nor to shorte, but easie and to be made twise in the yere.

3. The passage cutteth not nere the trade of any Prince, nor nere any of their contries or Territories and is a safe passage, and not easie to be annoyed by Prince or potentate whatsoever.

4. The passage is to be perfourmed at all times of the yere, and in that respecte passeth our trades in the Levant seas within the straites of Juberalter, and the trades in the seas within the kinge of Denmarkes straite, and the trades to the portes of Norwey and of Russia &c., for as in the southwest straite there is no passage in sommer by lacke of windes, so within the other places there is no passage in winter by yse and extreme colde.

5. And where England nowe for certen hundreth yeres last passed by the peculiar commoditie of wolles, and of later yeres by clothing of the same, hath raised it selfe from meaner state to greater wealthe and moche higher honour, mighte and power then before, to the equallinge of the princes of the same to the greatest potentates of this parte of the worlde, It commeth nowe so to passe that by the greate endevo^r of the increase of the trade of wolles in Spaine and in the west Indies nowe daily more and more multiplienge, That the wolles of England and the clothe made of the same, will become base, and every day more base then other, which prudently weyed, yt behoveth this Realme yf it meane not to returne to former olde meanes and basenes, but to stande in present and late former honour glorye and force, and not negligently and sleep-

ingly to slyde into beggery, to foresee and to plante at Norumbega or some like place, were it not for any thing els but for the hope of the vent of our woll indraped, the principall and in effecte the onely enrichinge contynueinge naturall commoditie of this Realme, And effectually pursueinge that course wee shall not onely finde on that tracte of lande, and especially in that firme northwarde (to whome warme clothe shalbe righte wellcome) an ample vente, but also shall from the northside of that firme finde oute knowen and unknowen Ilandes and domynions replenished with people that may fully vent the aboundance of that our commoditie that els will in fewe yeres waxe of none or of small valewe by forreine aboundaunce &c., So as by this enterprice wee shall shonne the ymmynent mischefe hanginge over our heades that els muste nedes fall upon the Realme without breache of peace or sworde drawen againste this Realme by any forreine state, and not offer our auncient riches to scornefull neighboures at home nor sell the same in effecte for nothinge as wee shall shortly, if presently it be not provided for. The increase of the wolles of Spaine and America is of highe pollicie with greate desire of our overthrowe indevoured, and the goodnes of the forren wolles our people will not enter into the consideration of, nor will not beleve oughte, they be so sotted with opinion of their owne, and yf it be not foresene and somme such place of vent provided, farewell the goodd state of all degrees in this Realme.

6. This enterprise may staye the spanishe kinge from flowinge over all the face of that waste firme of America, yf wee seate and plante there in time, in tyme I say, and wee by plantinge shall lett him from makinge more shorte and more safe returnes oute of the noble portes of the purposed places of our plantinge, then by any possibilitie he can from the parte of the firme that nowe his navies by ordinary courses come from, in this that there is no comparison betwene the portes of the coastes that the kinge of Spaine dothe nowe possesse and use, and the portes of the coastes that our nation is to possesse by plantinge at Norumbega, and on that tracte faste by more to the northe and northeaste, and in that there is from thence a moche shorter course, and a course of more temperature, and a course that possesseth more contynuance of ordinary windes then the present course of the spanishe Indian

navies nowe dothe. And England possessinge the purposed place of plantinge, her Majestie may by the benefete of the seate havinge wonne goodd and royall havens, have plentie of excellent trees for mastes, of goodly timber to builde shippes and to make greate navies, of pitche, tarr, hempe, and all thinges incident for a navie royall, and that for no price and withoute money or request. Howe easie a matter may yt be to this Realme swarminge at this day with valiant youthes rustinge and hurtfull by lacke of employment, and havinge goodd makers of cable and of all sortes of cordage, and the best and moste connynge shipwrightes of the worlde to be Lordes of all those Sees, and to spoile Phillipps Indian navye, and to deprive him of yerely passage of his Treasure into Europe, and consequently to abate the pride of Spaine and of the supporter of the greate Antechriste of Rome, and to pull him downe in equallitie to his neighbour princes, and consequently to cutt of the common mischefes that commes to all Europe by the peculiar aboundance of his Indian Treasure, and this withoute difficultie.

7. This voyadge albeit it may be accomplished by barke or smallest pynnesse for advise or for a necessitie, yet for the distaunce, for burden and gaine in trade, the marchant will not for profitts sake use it but by shippes of greate burden, so as this Realme shall have by that meane shippes of greate burden and of greate strengthe for the defence of this Realme, and for the defence of that newe seate, as nede shall require, and withall greate increase of perfecte seamen, which greate Princes in time of warres wante, and which kinde of men are neither nourished in fewe daies nor in fewe yeres.

8. This newe navie of mightie newe stronge shippes so in trade to that Norumbega and to the coastes there, shall never be subjecte to arreste of any prince or potentate, as the navie of this Realme from time to time hath bene in the portes of thempire, in the portes of the base Contries, in Spaine, Fraunce, Portingale &c., in the tymes of Charles the Emperour, Fraunces the Frenche kinge and others, but shall be alwayes free from that bitter mischeefe withoute grefe or hazarde to the marchaunte, or to the state, and so alwaies readie at the commaundement of the prince, with mariners, artillory, armor, and munition ready to offende and defende as shalbe required.

9. The greate masse of wealthe of the realme imbarqued in the marchantes shippes caried oute in this newe course, shall not lightly in so farr distant a course from the coaste of Europe be driven by windes and Tempestes into portes of any forren princes, as the spanishe shippes of late yeres have bene into our portes of the weste Contries &c. and so our marchantes in respecte of private state and of the Realme in respecte of a generall safetie from venture of losse, are by this voyadge oute of one greate mischefe.

10. No forren commoditie that commes into England commes withoute payment of custome once twise or thrise before it come into the Realme, and so all forren commodities become derer to the subjectes of this Realme, and by this course to Norumbega forren princes customes are avoided, and the forren commodities cheapely purchased, they become cheape to the subjectes of England to the common benefite of the people, and to the savinge of greate Treasure in the Realme, whereas nowe the Realme becommethe poore by the purchasinge of forreine commodities in so greate a masse at so excessive prices.

11. At the firste traficque with the people of those partes, the subjectes of this Realme for many yeres shall chaunge many cheape commodities of these partes, for thinges of highe valour there not estemed, and this to the greate inrichinge of the Realme, if common use faile not.

12. By the greate plentie of those Regions the marchantes and their factors shall lye there cheape, buye and repaire their shippes cheape, and shall returne at pleasure withoute staye or restrainte of forreine Prince, whereas upon staies and restraintes the marchaunte raiseth his chardge in sale over of his ware, and buyenge his wares cheape, he may mainteine trade with smalle stocke and withoute takinge upp money upon interest, and so he shalbe riche and not subjecte to many hazardes, but shalbe able to afforde the commodities for cheape prices to all subjectes of the Realme.

13. By makinge of shippes and by preparinge of thinges for the same: By makinge of Cables and Cordage, by plantinge of vines and olive trees, and by makinge of wyne and oyle, by husbandrie and by thousandes of thinges there to be don, infinite nombers of the english nation may be sett on worke to the unburdenynge of the Realme with many that nowe lyve chardgeable to the state at home.

14. If the sea coste serve for makinge of salte, and the Inland for wine, oiles, oranges, lymons, figges &c., and for makinge of yron, all which with moche more is hoped, withoute sworde drawen, wee shall cutt the combe of the frenche, of the spanishe, of the portingale, and of enemies, and of doubtfull frendes to the abatinge of their wealthe and force, and to the greater savinge of the wealthe of the Realme.

15. The substaunces servinge, wee may oute of those partes receave the masse of wrought wares that now wee receave out of Fraunce, Flaunders, Germanye &c. and so wee may daunte the pride of some enemies of this Realme, or at the leaste in parte purchase those wares, that nowe wee buye derely of the ffrenche and Flemynge, better cheape, and in the ende for the parte that this Realme was wonte to receave dryve them out of trade to idlenes for the setting of our people on worke.

16. Wee shall by plantinge there inlarge the glory of the gospell and from England plante sincere relligion, and provide a safe and a sure place to receave people from all partes of the worlde that are forced to flee for the truthe of gods worde.

17. If frontier warres there chaunce to aryse, and if thereupon wee shall fortifie, yt will occasion the trayninge upp of our youthe in the discipline of warr, and make a nomber fitt for the service of the warres and for the defence of our people there and at home.

18. The Spaniardes governe in the Indies with all pride and tyranie; and like as when people of contrarie nature at the sea enter into Gallies, where men are tied as slaves, all yell and crye with one voice *liberta*, *liberta*, as desirous of libertie or freedome, so no doubte whensoever the Queene of England, a prince of such clemencie, shall seate upon that firme of America, and shalbe reported throughoute all that tracte to use the naturall people there with all humanitie, curtesie, and freedome, they will yelde themselves to her governemente and revolte cleane from the Spaniarde, and specially, when they shall understande that she hath a noble navie, and that she aboundeth with a people most valiaunte for theyr defence, and her Majestie havinge Sir Fraunces Drake and other subjectes already in credite wth the Symerons, a people or greate multitude al-readye revolted from the spanishe governmente,

she may with them and a fewe hundrethes of this nation trayned upp in the late warres of Fraunce and Flaunders, bringe greate thinges to passe, and that wth greate ease: and this broughte so aboute, her Majestie and her subjectes may bothe enjoye the treasure of the mynes of golde and silver, and the whole trade and all the gaine of the trade of marchandize that nowe passeth thither by the Spaniardes onely hande of all the commodities of Europe, which trade of marchandize onely were of it selfe suffycient (withoute the benefite of the rich myne) to inriche the subjectes, and by Customes to fill her Majesties coffers to the full: and if it be highe pollicie to mayneteyne the poore people of this Realme in worke, I dare affirme that if the poore people of England were five times so many as they be, yet all mighte be sett on worke in and by workinge lynnen and suche other thinges of marchandize as the trade in the Indies dothe require.

19. The present shorte trades causeth the maryner to be cast of, and ofte to be idle and so by povertie to fall to piracie: But this course to Norumbega beinge longer and a contynuance of themploymente of the maryner dothe kepe the maryner from ydlenes and from necessitie, and so it cutteth of the principall actions of piracie, and the rather because no riche praye for them to take commeth directly in their course or any thing nere their course.

20. Many men of excellent wittes and of divers singuler giftes overthrowen by suertishippe, by sea or by some folly of youthe, that are not able to live in England may there be raised againe, and doo their Contrie goodd service: and many nedefull uses there may (to greate purpose) require the savinge of greate nombers that for trifles may otherwise be devoured by the gallowes.

21. Many souldiers and servitours in the ende of the warres that mighte be hurtfull to this Realme, may there be unladen, to the common profite and quiet of this Realme, and to our forreine benefite there as they may be employed.

22. The frye of the wandringe beggars of England that growe upp ydly and hurtefull and burdenous to this Realme, may there be unladen, better bredd upp, and may people waste Contries to the home and forreine benefite, and to their owne more happy state.

23. If Englande crie oute and affirme that there

is so many in all trades that one cannot live for another as in all places they doe, This Norumbega (yf it be thoughte so goodd) offreth the remedie.

21

A note of some thinges to be prepared for the voyadge, which is sett downe rather to drawe the takers of the voyadge in hande to the presente consideracion, then for any other reason for that divers thinges require preparation longe before the voyadge, withoute the which the voyadge is maymed.

Dead Victuall.

Hoggs fleshe barrelled & salted in greate quan-
   titie.
Befe barrelled in lesse quantitie.
Stockfishe Meale in Barrells.
Oatemeale in barrells, nere cowched.
Ryse. Sallett oile. Barrelled butter.
Cheese. Hony in Barrells.
Currans. Raisons of the sonne.
Dried prunes. Olives in Barrells.
Beanes, dryed on the killn.
Pease dried likewise.
Canary Wines. Hollocks.
Sacks racked.
Vinegar very stronge.
Aqua vitæ.
Syders of Fraunce, spaine, and England.
Bere brewed specially in speciall tyme.

Victuall by Rootes and Herbes.

Turnep seede.
Passeneape sede.
Radishe.
Cariott.
Naviewes.
Garlicke.
Onyons.
Leekes.
Melons.
Pompions.
Cowcombers.
Cabage cole.
Parseley.
Lettis.
Endiffe.
Alexander.
Orege.
Tyme.
Rosemary.

Mustard seede.
Fennell.
Anny seedes newe and freshe to be sowen.
The Encrease Renewe yᵉ Continewe of Victuall at the Plantinge Places, & Men and Thinges Incident and Tendinge to the Same.
Bores, Sowes.
Conies bucke & dowe.
Doves male & female.
Cockes. Hennes.
Duckes male & female for lowe soiles.
Turkies male and female.
Wheat. Rye. Barley. ⎞ To sowe, to
Bigge or burley bere. ⎟ vittell by
Oates. Beanes. ⎬ breade and
Pease. Facches. ⎟ drinke,
Three square graine. ⎠ &c.
Suger cane planters with the plantes.
Vyne planters.
Olyve planters.
Gardiners for herbes rootes, and for all earthe frutes.
Graffers for frute trees.
Hunters skilfull to kill wilde beasts for vittell.
Warryners to breede conies & to kill vermyn.
Fowlers.
Sea fisshers.
Freshwater fisshers.
Knytters of netts.
Butchers.
Salters and seasoners of vittell.
Saltemakers.
Cookes.
Bakers.
Brewers.
Greyhoundes to kill deere &c.
Mastives to kill heavie beastes of ravyne and for nighte watches.
Bloude houndes to recover hurte dere.

Provisions Tendinge to Force.

Men experte in the arte of fortification.
Platformes of many formes redied to carry with you by advise of the best.
Capitaines of longe and of greate experience.
Souldiers well trayned in Flaunders to joyne with the younger.
Harqubusshiers of skill.
Archers stronge bowmen.
Bowyers.
Fletchers.

Arrowheadmakers.

Bowstave preparers.

Glewmakers.

Morryce pikemakers and of halbert staves.

Makers of spades and shovells for pyoners, trentchers, and fortemakers.

Makers of basketts to cary earthe to fortes and Rampiers.

Pioners and spademen for fortificacion.

Salte peter makers.

Gonne powder makers.

Targett makers of hornes defensive againste Savages.

Oylethole doublett makers defensive lighte and gentle to lye in.

Turners of Targetts of elme and of other toughe wooods lighte.

Shippes, Pynesses, Barkes, Busses with flatt botoms furnished with experte seamen.

Swifte boates and barges to passe by winde & oare covered with quilted canvas of defence againste shott from the shoare to perce Ryvers for discoverie, and to passe to & froe offensive and defensive against savages devised by Master Bodenham of Spaine.

Shipwrightes in some nomber to be employed on the Timber.

Oaremakers, and makers of Cable and Cordage.

Provisions Incident to the Firste Traficque and Trade of Marchandize.

Grubbers and rooters upp of Cipres, Cedars, and of all other faire trees for to be employed in coffers deskes &c. for traficque.

Mattocks narrowe and longe of yron to that purpose.

Millwrightes to make milles for spedy and cheape sawinge of timber and boordes for trade and firste traficque of suertie.

Millwrightes for corne milles.

Sawyers for common use.

Carpinters for buildinges.

Joyners to cutt oute the boordes into chestes to be imbarqued for England.

Blacksmithes to many greate and nedefull uses.

Pitche makers.

Tarr makers.

Burners of asshes for the trade of sope asshes.

Cowpers for barrells to inclose those asshes.

Tallowchandlers to prepare the Tallowe to be incasked for England.

Waxechandlers to prepare waxe in like sorte.

Diers to seeke in that firme that riche Cochinilio and other thinges for that trade.

Mynerall men.

Artesanes Servinge Our Firste Planters Not in Traficque But For Buildinges.

Brickmakers.

Tilemakers.

Lyme makers.

Bricklayers.

Tilers.

Thackers wth reede, russhes, broome or strawe.

Synkers of welles and finders of springes.

Quarrellers to digge Tile.

Roughe Masons.

Carpinters.

Lathmakers.

Artesanes Servinge Our Firste Planters and in Parte Servinge for Traficque.

Barbors.

Launders.

Tailors.

Botchers.

Pailemakers.

Burrachiomakers.

Bottlemakers of London.

Shoemakers. Coblers.

Tanners. White tawyers.

Buffe skynne dressers.

Shamew skynne dressers.

A Present Provision for Raisinge a Notable Trade for the Time to Come.

The knitt wollen cappe of Toledo in Spaine called *bonetto rugio collerado* so infinitely solde to the Moores in Barbarie and Affricke, is to be prepared in London, Hereforde, and Rosse, and to be vented to the people, and may become a notable trade of gaine to the marchaunte, and a greate reliefe to oure poore people, and a sale of our woll & of our labour, and beinge suche a cappe that every particuler person will buye and may easelie compasse, the sale wilbe greate in shorte time, especially if our people weare them at their first arryvall there.

Thinges Forgotten May Here Be Noted as They Come to Mynde and After Be Placed with the Rest, and After That in All Be Reduced into the Best Order.

That there be appointed one or twoo preachers for the voyadge that God may be honoured, the people instructed, mutinies the better avoided, and obedience the better used, that the voyadge may have the better successe.

That the voyadge be furnished with Bibles and with bookes of service.

That the bookes of the discoveries and conquestes of the easte Indies be carried with you.

That the bookes of the discoveries of the West Indies and the conquestes of the same be also caried to kepe men occupied from worse cogitations, and to raise their myndes to courage and highe enterprizes and to make them lesse careles for the better shonnynge of common daungers in suche cases arisinge.

And because men are more apte to make themselves subjecte in obedience to prescribed lawes sett downe and signed by a prince, then to the changeable will of any Capitaine be he never so wise or temperate, never so free from desire of revenge, it is wisshed that it were learned oute what course bothe the Spaniardes and Portingales tooke in their discoveries for government, and that the same were delivered to learned men, that had perused moste of the lawes of thempire and of other princes Lawes, and that thereupon some speciall orders fitt for voyadges and begynnynges, mighte upon deliberation be sett downe and allowed by the Quenes moste excellent majestie and her wise counsell and faire ingrossed mighte in a Table be sett before the eyes of suche as goe in the voyadge, that no man poonished or executed may justly complaine of manifeste and open wronge offred.

That some phisition be provided to minister by counsell and by phisicke to kepe and preserve from sicknes, or by skill to cure suche, as fall into disease and destemperature.

A Surgeon to lett bloude and for such as may chaunce by warres or otherwise to be hurte is more nedefull for the voyadge.

An Apothecarye to serve the phisition is requisite, and the phisition dienge, he may chaunce (well chosen) to stande in steede of the one and thother, and to sende into the Realme by seede and roote herbes and plantes of rare excellencie.

If suche plentie of honye be in these Regions as is saied, yt were to goodd purpose to cary in the voyadge, suche of the servauntes of the Russia Companie as have the skill to make the drincke called meth, which they use in Russia and Poland, and nerer as in North Wales for their wine, and if you cannot cary any suche, to cary the order of the makinge of yt in writinge that it may be made for a nede.

And before many thinges this one thinge is to be called as yt were with spede to mynde, that the prisons and corners of London are full of decayed marchantes overthrowen by losse at sea, by usuerers, suertishippe and by sondry other suche meanes, and dare or cannott for their debtes shewe their faces, and in truthe many excellent giftes be in many of these men, and their goodd giftes are not ymployed to any manner of use, nor are not like of themselves to procure libertie to employe themselves. But are withoute some speciall meane used to starve by wante, or to shorten their tymes by thoughte, and for that these men, schooled in the house of adversitie, are drawen to a degree higher in excellencye, and may be employed to greate uses in this purposed voyadge, yt were to greate purpose to use meanes by aucthoritie for suche as maliciously, wrongfully or for triflinge causes are deteyned, and to take of them and of others that hide their heades and to employe them, for so they may be relieved and the enterprice furthered in many respectes.

And in choice of all Artesanes for the voyadge this generall rule were goodd to be observed that no man be chosen that is knowen to be a papiste for the speciall inclynation they have of favour to the kinge of Spaine.[86]

That also of those Artesanes which are protestantes, that where you may have chaunge and choice; that suche as be moste stronge and lusty men be chosen, and suche as can best handle his Bowe or his harquebushe; for the more goodd giftes that the goers in the voyadge have, the more ys the voyadge benefited. And therefore (many goinge) yf every mans giftes and goodd qualities be entred into a Booke before they be receaved, they may be employed upon any necessitie in the voyadge in this or in that, accordinge as occasion of nede shall require.

86. Sidenote: "A moste nedefule Note."

Chapter Forty-six
Edward Hayes's Plans for English Control of Newfoundland, 1586

EDWARD HAYES returned from Gilbert's second and fatal expedition in September, 1583, determined in some way to capitalize on his belief that Newfoundland offered considerable possibilities to English investors and settlers. He approached Lord Burghley with his plan in May, 1585, or 1586. The covering letter, abstract, and project (a second descriptive section on Newfoundland is not present) are all badly damaged. The last figure of the year date is imperfect, but internal evidence indicates it is 1586. Much of the expanded material is in greater or lesser degree conjectural and must be treated, in this its first publication, with caution. Possibly the material was called forth by Bernard Drake's successful raid on Portuguese and Spanish shipping at Newfoundland in 1585 (Vol. IV, nos. 541–545), reviving interest in an area that had been overshadowed by Ralegh's Virginia ventures of 1584–1585, but that was brought into prominence by Drake's achievement for which he had been knighted shortly before his death. The papers (362–364) have been divided. The covering letter is B.L., Lansdowne MS 37, fols. 166–167 and the two parts of the project Lansdowne MS 100, fols. 83–87v., the abstract being on fol. 83; the Newfoundland description fols. 84–87v. and the proposals for exploiting the fishery and the island fols. 88v.–94v., the latter dated February 12, 1585/6.

---

362. 10 May 158[6]. Edward Hayes to Lord Burghley.

[T]he infinit of waygthy cawses whearwith your honour is combred [t]he evyll handling besyds, & worse success of former dyscoveries have made me unwylling to offer agayn a discourse of the [Ne]wfoundland. Nevertheles considryng your honorabell mynd [unto] all mens honest indevors, never refusing to gyve eare [unto s]uch as pretend benifit unto our Contry: And how with [all these] thyngs are measured not by events but by reasons: [being en]couraged hear unto: and putt in Comfort by summe [that are] held wyse (whose judgements I have fyrst craved) [I trust th]ys bref discoorse wylbe accepted of your honor which [thus] may fynd so happy success: I wyll not utterly [den]ye but that it may work the desyred effect.

[Whence] I have framed two platts of the Newfoundland. The First [she]wing the Contries & commodities: the other shewyng a [mean]es how with easy charges the conquest may be made, and a trade mayntayned to doobell benefit of our weale publyke [an]d of pryvat men by erecting a corporation of the Newland [trades as] hath ben of others not upon so just occasion. A [travay]ll a[tt]ea[mpted] more plausibill then any heretofore [made] dyscoveries. But bicawse both Platts were [labor]iouse for your honor to reade: I have made an Abstract [of the] fyrst which humbly I present unto your honor. The second [I rese]rve untyll I may see how thys wylbe taken. Besechyng [God alm]yghty Such success to gyve unto my travayls, that hys [cause] may be advanced, our Contry benefited, and your honor [encourage]d by so much as thys Action may be made happy to thys [the] present and to the posterity. The state of that land & [o]thers adjoyning, he that shall obtayn it, as no dowt he shall [th]erby possess great ritches: So doo I wysh it myght be layed [upon so]m worth[y] personage your honor doth beare favor unto. [He sha]lbe assured then generally to be assisted, in expectation [of ritches as] heartofore, that thys Action shalbe followed with resolution [maintain]ed with Justice, & supported with authority.

[For] my own part I have already in thys cause made ventrer [of my] lyfe and substance: and am resolved to serve [the s]ame to the uttermost of both, yf by your honor it maybe [done], & sett forward. In the mean season humbly I crave [p]ardon for thus farr presumyng. from Charyng Cross. 10th of May. [ann]o 158[6]

Your honors most humbell in all service to comand:

[signed:] Edward: Haye[s]

[Addressed:] To the ryght honoralbell Lord hygh Threasurer of England.

363. "An abstract of this discourse [of the Newfounde lande]."

The Newfounde lande is an Ilande or many Ilandes and broken la[nds in 46. to 52.] degrees of Septentrionall latytude: Conteyneth in lengthe abov[e] 300 miles, warm in the southe, though could in the Northe: hath greate vary[ance] of seas[ons.]

Consideracions to induce her Majestie to take & annex it unto her dominions.

1. It moste rightely appertayneth unto the Crowne of Englande, being [found by ships] under the Conducte of Sebastian Cabot, and by the Comm[aun]dement of kin[g Henry the seventh.]

2. It lyeth fitt and neere unto her majesties Domynyons of Ireland especially.

3. It hathe varyetie of Commodyties and wanteth people. England h[ath many that] wanteth wherein to imploye them which convenyently may be sent with them that goe thether yearely.

4. It shalbe hable with the Countries adacient to furnishe the Navy [with all those] necessary provysions, which hetherto are only brought out of an [enemy] Princes jurisdiccions with great charges, and some hasard to o[ur shipping.]

5. It shall mynister as greate oportunytie to prejudice the French [((which every] where can be taken) as they maie take advauntage over us in the [fishing.]

6. It shalbe for the glorye of god and her majesties honor to inlarge her D[ominions] more then any her predecessors have done.

364. "Consideracions to induce some noble [persons] to conquer & possesse the New foun[de lande]."

1. It shalbe honorable to wynne and possesse so riche a Terrytory as [it shalbe to convert] Infydells and plante Religion, which hathe not ben done in this later ag[e by Englishmen.]

2. It shalbe easy because the people of the Countrye and Ilandes [are but a naked people] and have not ben founde hurtefull. Item the Christians which [do wont to use] harbors and their forces are by that meanes broken. Item En[glishmen do] commaunde alreddy in euery Harbor where they come. Item many [of] the Harbors mighte be fortefyed and garded, and have offred to [the fisherman that] they mighte stande assured to enjoye thies commodyties follo[wing.]

1. Namely to be defended from Pyrates and other oppressi[ors.]

2. To have stages buylte to their handes and groundes dressed for [drying fish.]

3. To have all their Pynnaces and small Boates (in which they goe out [of their] harbors reserved and kepte euery yere for the proper owners, which ot[herwise leave] them behynde.

4. Consideracions to move private & or[dinarie]

sorte of men that here live in wante to [adventure] thither to inhabit:

The Countrye is temperate, the soyle goode, The Sea and R[iver]s ab[ound in fish] and bothe lande and water with fowle.

Also fewe people to moles[t them.]

The Sea and lande will yeilde great varyetie of Commodyties togay[ther. Such as] can be devysed (being merchauntable) wilbe uttered and soulde in the [Harbor of Saint Johns] a famous mart, Marchauntes resorte thether with greate store of shippin[g. The] Lande alonge the harbors sydes wilbe deare lett to such as drye fishe [on land] and utter their wares speedely. Vittaylers above all others shalbe [needed. On the] harbor guestes shalbe buylte. Last of all every thinge that En[gland requireth is there] plentyfully.

Of the New Founde Lande:

That which we doe call the Newfoundelande and the Frenchemen the Baccalaos is an Ilande or rather by the opynyon of some, consisteth of sundry Ilandes and broken landes, Scituated in the Norwest of America upon the gulfe or entraunce into the greate Ryver of St. Lawrence or Canada, and by the same Ryver devyded from the Mayne, Whereinto navigacion maie be made bothe on the southe and northe syde of the lande./

The Lande lyeth Southe and Northe, And conteyneth in lengthe betwene 3 and 400 myles from Cape Rase (which is in .46. degrees 20 mynutes) unto the Grand Baye in .52. or 53 of Septentrionall latytude. Yt hathe very many goodly Bayes and Harbors, the lyke (in my opynyon) not to be seene in any place. Amonge which some by naturall Scite are stronge, and by fortificacion mighte be made invincibell./ The Common opynyon that is had of the intemperature and extreame Coulde that shuld be in this Countrye, As of some partes it maie be verefyed namely the Northe (where I graunte it is much coulder then in Countryes of Europe answerable unto the same heighte. So is it moste untrewe if the lyke be conceaved of the southe, Which as they doe lye under Clymes of Britiayne, A[ni]ou, Poictou and Orleans in Fraunce, betwene .46. and .49. degrees: So can they not much differ from the temperature of the same Countries. Unless upon the Coaste & outwarde partes, which lye open unto the Ocean and sharpe wyndes, Yt must by reason be subjecte to more [co]ulde then further within lande where the Mountaynes doe serve as walls and Bulwarkes to

defende [us] from the Asperytie and Rigor of the sea and wyndes./ And wheras it hathe ben objected that the Newfounde lande mighte be subjecte to more Coulde, [S]owmuch it lyeth high and neare unto the Middle Region. I doe graunte that not alone in the Newfoundelande but in Germany, Italy, and Affricke, the Mountaynes are extreame coulde, by the same reason that they extend towards the Middle Region, yet in the Countryes lyinge beneathe them, the contrarye is founde: So all hills havinge their discentes, the valleys and lower groundes in the Newefounde lande muste lykewise be hoatt and temperate as the Clyme doth [seeme]. Wherefore all doubtes may be removed, that by reason of the intemperature, the Newfoundlande shuld be unhabytable throughout, or in any parte that lyeth under so temperate Clymes as in .48. 47. and .46. degrees./ [t]owchinge the Commodyties of this Countrye servinge either for sustentacion of the Inhabytaunts or for [ma]yntenance of trade: there are and maie be made dyvers. That it seemeth nature hathe recompensed [t]hat only defecte and incommodytie of some sharpe Cowlde many wayes and with sundry benefittes, As [f]irste with the infynit and incredyble quantytie of Fishe in that Coaste. Which albeit they are in greate [va]ryette of kyndes and every one keepinge their seasons. Yet the fishinge of the Codd and whale [ha]the ben hetherto only in use, and so greate profitt is made thereby, That as unto a famouse [ma]rt the Marchauntes from the most partes of Christendome doe yearely repayre thither with [gre]ate store of shippinge only for the benefitt of Fishe and Trayne Oyles, To either of which the [catc]hinge of herrings mighte be made little inferyor (if the season were observed) which I have [see]ne there of exceedinge greatnes, larger then the Malstrond herringe in Norwaye.

Concernynge the Inlande Commodyties aswell of this Newefounde lande as Countryes adjacent There is nothinge that our Easte and Northerly Countries of Europe doe yeilde, but maie as plentyfully by tyme and industrye be made in them, Namely Rosen, Pitch, Tarre, Soape ashes, Deale boord Mastes for Shippes hydes Furrs Flaxe, Hempe, Corne Cabulls Cordage, Lynnen Clothe Mettalls of sortes and happely some ritche, All which thies Countries will afforde, and the soyle is apte to yeilde.

Consideracions that [would move her]

Majestie [to the] benefite of this Realme [and people] and [of] the enterprise for the peopling and inhabiting of the Newfound Lande with English men and to annex it unto the Domyn[ion] of Englan[d].

Firste it more rightely appertayneth vnto the Crowne of Engla[nde],[1] The same beinge firste founde and discovered by Sebastion Cabot by th[e commaundement of her Majesties Grandfather of worthy memory kinge Henry the vii[th].

Item it lyeth fitt and neare vnto her Majesties Domynyons of Irelande[2] especial[ly] servinge well) it is not above tenne dayes saylinge and beinge th[e queens] subjectes maie safe[ly] and freely trade thither without danger or re[striction.]

Item for asmuch as this Realme of Englande is growne [to popu]lus[3] and to [deare] whereby many dayly perishe and too many [rem]ayne lyv[ing] loose and Ide[ll] fall into unlawfull and dishonest practyzes, The ende [whe]rof by [example] (as wee daylie see) to the losse of their lyves in this worlde, and h[urtful and] lamentable to be suffered in a Christian Common weale, and dange[rous. It would] therefore be a greate ease unto the Common weale, to be discharged [of] them to be well ymployed in some other Countrye, wheras co[lonies] are wantinge, which a[c?]t wilbe a singuler benefitt to the one and the other [and the Newfound] lande the moste conve[ni]ent place in the worlde to serve that purpose,[4] [as well full] of Commodyties to sett people a worke of all sortes and Condicions, as [easy for the] transportacion of them, [by] the Shippes which yearely are sent from [England carrying] outwarde nothinge but vittayle and salte in Balas[t.[5] Ships of a certain] burden mighte be appoyncted to carry certayne men with the[m so that the] Newefounde lande in fewe yeres wulde be well peopled, and [they might] be there maynteyned, (without charginge her majestie or su[ch as to whom] occasion mighte be mynistered.)

Item wheras the moste necessary [provysions for the] shipping of this Realme,[6] have [ben]

broughte out of the [jurisdiccions of enemy] Princes with greate charges some hazarde, yet many tymes [it goes for] noughtc[. Here it] may be made plentyfully and sufficyent to serve all Europe in her [lands] borderinge upon the Newfoundelande, whereby this Realme may th[roughout] be furnished of all thinges necessary for the Navye And also be [able to supply] all the weste Countryes of Europe[7] with the same Comodyties For which [the Newfound lande is] very convenyent, and beinge alreddy so much traded for the only benefitt of [fishermen both may] herafter be had under one voyage, the greatest trade of the worlde may [grow] into the Newfoundelande, which wilbe as a keye unto the Countries ad[joyninge to the] mouthe of the greate Ryver St. Lawrence that stretcheth [into the] lande of Ameryca.

Item whereas the Kinges of Fraunce and Spayne may g[ain much] by surprysinge as it were at [an] instant our men and shippes [to their ad]vantage: The lyke or greater advauntage may her majest[ie gain in the Newfoundlande duringe the Fishinge.[8] Whether doe rep[air ships of] Spayne, (namely the Biskayes) and a multytude [of French men so that] pretendinge warres agaynste any the same kinges, she [may hurt] and distresse their Countryes (S[payne] chiefly of vittay[ll] and] ladinges belonginge to those Coun[tryes th]at are every Fis[hing tide there] which in no other place can be don[ne] and [the] facylytie more at large may appeare.

Last of all but not the leaste, it shalbe bothe glory to god, and [to her Majesties] Domynyons of Englande more then her predecessors ha[d by] converting Infydells unto Christyan[y]tie which [is of godly] Princes to be expected.[9] Bothe in respecte of the Convenyent Site and [in the] plasinge of her kingedomee upon the Occyan neare unto the Norwest of America (which seemeth to fall [unto] her majesties lott) And also of her highe callinge beinge Patrones and defendor of the Ch[ri]stian faithe. That thereby the prehemynence which the Romishe Churche doth challenge affirmynge that as a Note and badge of

1. Sidenote: "The Newland rightly apertayneth to the Crowne of England."
2. Sidenote: "It lyeth not farre from Irelande."
3. Sidenote: "England to Populus."
4. Sidenote: "Newfound Land hath commodities and wanteth People."
5. Sidenote: "Newfound lande most fitt for our spare people in respect of the comodities and that our shipps goo *thither yerely.*"
6. Sidenote: "Provision for the Navy may be had for the Newfound Lande."

7. Sidenote: "Newfoundland may be made the greatest trade of the World being a key and may be able to command all the Countries lying wityin it."
8. Sidenote: "The Newfound. may mynister as greate opportunytie to prejudice the french & Spanish Kynges as they may take advantage over us every vyntage."
9. Sidenote: "It is at her Majesties handes expected to plant religion in the Norwest of America which fall[eth] unto her Lott."

theirs to be true Churche, They alone have converted Infidells, and broughte Nacyons unto the faithe of Jesus Christe: Maie bee suppressed or made not so peculyar unto them: And that the defecte which to them seemeth to be in our Churche for not doinge the lyke, maie be supplyed, and the controversie betwene us in that poyncte maie be decyded.

[And] for conclusyon of this parte wherin I have produced reasons to move her Majestie to lykinge of the Cawse. What enterpryse in the worlde can sownde more plawsibell then this? whereby God shalbe glorified, here majestie reape honor, and her Countrye and people inestymable benefitt.

Consideractions which may induce some honorable Personage of sufficient credite to undertake the conquest and inhabiting of the Newfound Land with English men.

It shalbe   Honorable
              Profytable
              Easye

Honorable to gayne and possess so riche a Terrytory as that will fall out to bee, But chiefly beinge for the lo[v]e of God to make him knowne and rightly to be worshipped amonge Heathens, Which [is] the highest and moste excellent worke of all others that can be taken in hande So mu[ch m]ore for his honor and Comendacion that shall bringe it to passe, by howmuch the examp[le mo]re and not before accomplished by any of our professyon in this later age.

Profytable many wayes, but amyttinge all others, I will only at this present rely upon the greate benefite that presently maie be raysed by ymposinge a Custome upon the Comodyties alreddy in use, and yearely broughte from thence: as also upon such as shalbe [taken] out hereafter.

Towchinge the present, thoughe hetherto they only consiste in Fishe and Trayne Oyles, Yet it [doth] appeare by the computacion I have made according to the judgement of others so well as [my]self, that there come not fewer then 400 sayle of Shippes to this Fishinge every yeare [unto] the Banck (which lyeth on thissyde in the trade waie, somewhere .40. or .50. leagues [fr]om the Newefoundelande) and togither upon the Coaste. And in consideracion the shippes [gener]ally are of greate burden, Some of .400. 300 Tunnes (namely the Biskayes which bothe in the grand Baye on the Northe, and in the Baye of Placentia in the sowthe, use to [fi]she the whale to make

trayne Oyles). In lyke sorte many are of .200. 100. and few [or] none under .60 or 80. Tunnes: So valewinge the ladinge of one with an other to [be] worthe but VC^{li} [£500] a shipp which maie be the pryce of the leaste, for the best are worthe [2]000 and 1000^{li} a ladinge. I maie certaynely conclude, the summe in grosse being [200] thowsande pow[nde]s, The tenthe parte being paide for Custome will amounte unto [XX]^{tie} thowsande powndes of yearely and certayne Revenewe. which for a tyme maie be [r]eceaved in Comodytie, But when wee are growne stronge it maie be paide in golde and silver, as the kinge of Denmarke doth levye his Custome at Malstronde in Norwaye and ells where.

The Fishinge of Herringes if it mighte be broughte also unto perfection, or] any Comodytie servinge for vittayle: by reason those nacions [lack supply] of all [sorts] thereof in their owne Countryes, and are dryven [to seek] it in [such sort as] others do by sea.[10] And] nothinge is so much in requeaste as vittayle, Neither is any [countrie able] more plentyfully [to] afforde it them, then this Newefoundlande, w[here of God hath] fully endewed it to works (as maie be thoughte) some greate ma[rvel which] wolde greately increase the Revenewe./.

As hetherto I have only spoken of the benefitt that maie presently [be] are and maye be made of the Sea. So by the Inlande I [do see] more gayne maie be made in proces of tyme.[11] What they are [that] this Country will produce: I have before na[med to] begyn [with the best] Comodyties. How riche, by the greate wealthe our Easterly [trades will rise] unto by reason only of the same, which ells where have not ben [of so great effect.]

Then the same beinge as well to be had in the Newfoundeland [and there] to be vented, by reason it lyketh more convenyent for the west [where there] is alreddy a greate trade established. I cannot see but [how that] Lande shall drawe unto it the trade from the Easte, and the [shipping that] Europe hetherto have ymployed that waie.[12] Upon C[ommerce] kinges and greate

10. Sidenote: "Greate Varieties and plenty of fish abowt the Newfound[lande] which being dryed and provided accordingly wilbe in great request with the Spanyardes, Portingalls and Countries within the Streightes."

11. Sidenote: "Custome of the Inlande comoditie in tyme wilbe greate."

12. Sidenote: "Easterly comodities of Europe may be had in and neare unto the Newfound[lande] and spedily uttered. by reason the West parts of Europe lye neare it and have traffik there already."

states doe chiefly depende; which must [grow that] trade shalbe advaunced, and so [mu]ch it shalbe advaunced [before] any possible meanes be made [or] founde, within or ner[eby, the] benefitt whereof growinge [un]to our na[tion] shall [be such] and the Custome of the whole rysinge u[nto a great sum to] advaunce his Rev[enues].[13]

So for profite I knowe no Co[untrie or places] that can yeilde the lyke pro[fit once] there setled, and nature of those Co[mmodyties found there] And whatsoever can be made in the New[foundlande] boughte upp. So on the other syde every [Commodyty that] Europe dothe yealde wilbe broughte thither to togeather.[14]

Easie to be atchieved beinge the thirde consi[stinge] in attaynynge it without any greate assistaunce [from the Soveraign.] The last beinge a matter not difficult, the firs[t more so].

Towchinge resistaunce it must be by the [natur]rall Inha[bitants against the] Christians that trade thither.[15] Whereof the firste are naked [, of force] none at all (havinge as it is lyke abandoned the places [where the Christians come)] unhurtefull, and therefore are not to be [a danger to] any [they] beinge well entreated. The other, (the Christi[ans] dispersed with their Companyes at sundry harbors,[16] whereby their [will be no] greate resistaunce, neither is it lyke they will [risk] or hasarde their Shippes, their lyves and g[ood]s to w[hom we should not be] unreasonable, nor urge them further then wee have power [to make them] yeilde unto. Moreover our Englishemen beinge commen[ly Admyralles] in every Harbor wheresoever they come and doe comm[aund.[17] All (] our beinge there) will obey and assist him that shalbe [Admyral and] none other resist in the sam[e h]arbors where they [are wont to come.]

[L]aste of all wheras hetherto I doe admytt the worste, That all shulde be unwillinge and so farre as they durste wolde resiste this attempte to plante people, fortefye, and exacte Custome of

their Commodyties. I will upon my owne knowledge and Credite delyver the offer which many strangers did make unto us; Namely that they wolde repayre generally into those harbors which we shuld possesse, Paye Custome of all their Comodyties unto her majestes Deputes, and further encrease the gayne and yearely profittes of such as shuld there inhabite for thies and such lyke Consideracions followinge.

That they mighte be defended from Pyrates (by whome they have ben many tymes distressed) freed from all oppressions and wronge often layde upon them by the stronger, and mighte followe their labor without molestacion./

That they mighte have provyded unto their handes and certaynely enjoye every yeare standinges or stages (so called) and convenyent groundes within and alonge the harbor sydes to dresse and drye their Fishe, which often tymes wantinge, their voyages have ben much hindered, beinge compelled to make their Fishe abourde their shippes to their great [tro]uble. For as the weaker sorte doe all Covett to fishe under the Englishe mens proteccion so are they made subjecte with all to this inconvenyence, that they can gett noe stages nor [co]nvenyent groundes wherof to be certayne, and in places of securytie, They wolde only [re]payre thither.

[T]hat in lyke sorte, all their Pinnaces and small boates (in which they goe out to Sea to [Fishe and returne] into the Harbors where their Shippes lye still) mighte be reserved [from years to ye]ers, For somuch as beinge compelled to leave them behynde in the [lande] [(from] whence they goe laden with fishe or oyles) they bringe every yeare [new boats at such ch]arges and trouble in that, to every shipp of C tunnes, there are [eight?] of thies small Pynnaces.

[This] and such lyke as unto us maie seeme of small moment, So of them they are so [very muche] desyred, beinge very necessary, that to enjoye the same, they will forsake all other [harbors a]nd resorte to us, In somuch as after wee shalbe quyetly possessed of one, two, or three, [harbors where] without any lett wee maie fortefie, Chusinge such places wherein the Shippes [may safelie lye, t]he profittes of them will suffice the charges to plante in an other, and so by [degrees the w]hole or princypallest maie be obteyned, if meanes cannot be founde to [occupy all the] same at once. But good entreatye offred to all strangers, and experyence [of the buyinge] of

---

13. Sidenote: "In regard of the trade in Newfound[lande] Comodite must be raysed to the Lord. & inhabitantes."

14. Sidenote: "Nothing for profite or Pleasure can be wanting in the Newfound Land."

15. Sidenote: "In many Places of the Iland no people."

16. Sidenote: "Shipps that come for fysh are dispersed into divers places."

17. Sidenote: "English men are Admyralles [in eve]ry harbor they come into & doo already commande where it shalbe easy mater to fortifie."

their owne Commodytie by us will allure them more, then force shall [quell th]em. Nevertheles if any grow obstynate and wilfull, as it maie be the Biscayes [will, count]ynge upon their strengthe, their accustomed places to Fishe in, maie be taken [once they have] gone homewarde, without gaynesayinge, and the nexte yeare when they [returne] they shalbe compelled to order as the reste. Or otherwise their boates [and] Fishinge [stages being] without garde maie be taken from them, and by many wayes the[y] maie be soe [requi]ted as to purchase their quyetnes, they will rather yeilde unto reasonable condicions [than by] refusinge the same to bringe upon them so many dangers and inconvenyences as wee [shall be] able to inflicte upon them, havinge a princypall harbor or more to retyre unto.

[In th]em I have forecaste the worste, so stande I assured that if it once be made [certen her] majestie is bente to possesse the Newefounde-lande, None there dare resiste. [It would be mark]ed as madnes for pryvate men carryed with desyer of gayne, and not [stan]dinge [on] armes of honor, to sett them selves agaynste a Princes aucthorytie, her majestes especially. Who hathe there alreddy subjectes of great force, able to compell them and [upon] such as shall refuse obedyence to inflicte due ponishement with for-fecte of shipp and [this] they will not incurre for so small a dewtie as shalbe of them demaunded.

A collection of the former reasons

The premisses therefore considered, That the Naturall Inhab[itants are not] to be feared: That the Christians usinge this trade are dispersed [and] unable to make any greate resistaunce if they wolde: That Eng[lishmen] alreddy com-maunde wheresoever they come. That many of their harbors mighte be fortefyed and kepte, Laste of all that pryvate [men will] not hazard their state (which maie depende upon their shipp and goode[s) against] aucthorytie by withstand-inge it: I doute not it will appeare an en[courage-ment to get] the Newfounde lande in quyet pos-session without much resistaunce [from any.][18]

Howe with easye charges to compasse this so greate a matter: I [have put forward] seuerall to that effecte, wherein it maie appeare the easyest of all [of them][19] to be accomplished and maynteyned with gayne on all handes, and hinder

[none, would be] a Corporacion of the Newlande trade in Englande, which is proved [to be most] beneficyall for this Realme, to advaunce gods glorye, to bringe [into] vente our Course Clothes the better, and carry out nothing [else] thither, laste to increase our Navye, and nourishe men [therby.][20]

Thies Comodytie as they are incydent unto this act Corporacion besydes there shalbe lesse hasard of mens requyred for supplyes which never shalbe demaunded[21] in begonne and sett on foote shall stande of it self, and beinge made manyfest by reasons sufficyent in my other may be saide herein unto the same.

So to conclude this parte wherein it is proved an [important thing] and easye, to bringe the Newe founde lande into the quyet possession of the Personage, that will undertake it.[22] I can but pray [we do not delay lest] wee be prevented by an other nacyon, whom if expect[ed wars amongst them]selves doth not lett, they with some difficul-tie will attay[n to that] facylytie wee may come by. Reachinge furthe the hande [we shall have the] will [to conquer.]

Consideracions to induce euery private man
that lyveth he[re] in Wante, to goo and
inhabit the Newfound Lande.

Upon former Consideracions it maie be gathered howe beneficiall [possession of it] will be unto her Inhabytauntes Nevertheles I thincke it not [unmete to make a] colleccion of such thinges as maie serve to satisfie euery pryvate person who [maie goe there].

The Countrye in the southe is temperate, somewhat ho[t in summer]. The soyle is good, and beinge manured, will yeilde plentie [food for beaste and] man.

The Sea and Ryvers abounde in Fishe, the[re are beasts for food,] there is store of lande and waterfowl.

Fewe people are within the Lande to molest [our men and they may quickly be brought unto Civylytie.

The meanes to attay[ne] and gayne welthe (which are many) are easy] Namely by makinge

18. Sidenote: "Newfoundland may be possessed withowt resistance."
19. Sidenote: "It may be obtayned with easy charge."

20. Sidenote: "A Corporacion to be erected of the Newland trade is just and necessary."
21. Sidenote: "No supplies shalbe demanded of them that are free, yet the trade shalbe upholden."
22. Sidenote: "The French had determyned this yere to plant in New found Lande, But staye expecting warres at home."

Trayne Olyes, Provydinge [store of goods for trade, Fisshing] as herringes Codd, Salmons, and such lyke. By [labour Commodityes it will] yeilde, such as have alreddy ben named, as Rosen, Pitche, Tarre, Soape ashes, Deale boordes, Mastes for Shippes, Hempe, Flaxe, Lynnen, Cabells, Cordage, Hydes, Furre. Iron workers for Shippes of all sortes which is there to be had plentyfully. Also Chestes, Tables and such lyke of sweete woodes. To be shorte whatsoever thinge merchaunteable can be made by arte and industrye, Wilbe boughte upp every tyme when the Fleetes of shippes come./

As if a man shuld provyde wares that are greately in requeaste agaynste some famouse mart or faire; He standeth then in good assuraunce to utter them. So standeth it with Newefounde lande, whether at certayne seasons of the Yeare, doe repayre a multytude of merchauntes, with Shippinge, only for Fishe, and Trayne Cyles. Yet wilbe gladd of other Commodyties to mend their voyage. But a man maie make a sure recknynge of Fishe there, and money for Fishe, as any in Englande maie of his lande, and of Rente for his lande. Moreover all such lande as lyeth neare unto the Harbors alonge the Coaste, wilbe lett out for a rente at so deare a rate as the best grounde in Englande, beinge made reddy and stages buylte for to dresse and drye their Fishe; And the Boates belonginge to every shipp to be reserved in every mans severall grounde, and kepte for the owners.

In lyke sorte when howses shalbe buylte and furnished to entertayne guestes, What place in the worlde (duringe the Fishinge tymes) shalbe more frequented with Marchauntes and Saylors? who after their longe voyage by Sea and paynefull labor upon the lande will not a little rejoyce and liberally dispend to have unaccustomed rest and refreshinge within those howses to that use provyded. On the other syde what thinge servinge for necessatie or pleasure [t]hat Englande, Fraunce, Spayne, Italy, or Europe can yeilde, but wilbe broughte plentyfully into the Newefoundelande, when once it begynneth to be inhabyted with people of industrye to rayse Commodyties profytable for the merchaunte. Who in exchaunge will bringe to serve necessitie, and to please the delicate. Unto which speedy perfeccion no [n]ewe attempte or discoverie can be broughte, but will requyre firste a mans lyfe tyme [if on]ly by reason, That the lyke trade will not be setled in an unknowne lande in many [yere]s, as is at the presente in the Newefoundelande.

[To] make an ende of the Discourse, Althoughe I have largely commended this enterprise, & delyvered many reasons to perswade what promise of ampell benefittes to all generally: Yet I protest; as in reason they cannot be denyed. So in proufe I rest assured they shalbe founde trewe, yf so happie an enterprise for the State of Englande mighte with resolucion be taken in hande and executed by well disposed persons. First for the glorye of God, nexte for the weale [p]ublyke, and last for pryvate commodytie. which foundacion beinge laide, the sequele must be good, and for men of such myndes, such actions are only ordeyned, which ells will vanishe in[to] vapor.

But God the disposer of mens purposes, worke his will in this and all thinges ells.

[Endorsed:]

A Discours of Master Haies, of the Newe Lande discovered.

An extract of thys platt

Thys action intended into the Newfoundland, semyng to wayghty for one pryvat man to carry: It is thowght necessary to erect a Corporation of the Newland trade, whearby the easyer it may be accomplyshed.

By reason of certayn objections that have ben made agaynst thys co[u]rse to draw so comen a trade unto a Societie: It is proved. that it may be doone withowt injury to any man: more to the Commoditie of the Merchants then heartofoare hath ben: and to the great increase of our Navy. Item: that good vent may be fownd of Newland Comodities, Notwithstandyng our trade is left into Spayn and the strayghts whear our Merchants were wont for the most part to vent theyr fysh.

Thys Corporation (for sondry causes alleaged) is thowght necessary to be established in 5 chiefe Portes chosen owt of severall places within thys Realme. And to every of them by discreation shalbe lymited certayn Shyres, owt of them to receyve and to imploy all adventures that shalbe made withyn the precyncts of every Towne.

No man in thys Corporation shall at any tyme loose hys pryncipall or stock. Nether be urged to Supplyes, as in other Corporations they usually are.

All adventures wilbe of two Soarts.

Pryvate which wyll consist of great Merchants and owners of shipps, who wyll venter [thithe]r them selves.

[C]omen which wilbe of suche as have nether shypps nor perhapps abilitie to venter much: [w]ho nevertheles may be admitted for any small adventer, by joynynge many togither [choo]se an adventer which at least must be XXV^li. And the same beyrg entred in one [only] name, an other may be nominated when he shall dye. and in succession the [same as] longe as any remayn alyve of that nomber. The Survyvors alwayes payeng [fine at] every alienation.

The fynes at the admittance of pryvate Adventers. to be exacted of shypps rated by the Tunns.

[In] Prymis: for every tonn shalbe payed vi^s. viii^d: for every topp x^s.

[Ite]m for every xx^tie tonns. A man shalbe fornyshed with one yeares provysyon, and trans-[ported] into the Neufoundland. which shalbe no great charge nor inconvenience to the Merchant [as it] may at large appear.

[It]em yf any man hearafter wyll increase hys shypping: he shalbe fyned as afoare, for [ev]ery tonn only that shalbe increased.

[I]tem thoase that have not ben fyrst adventrers: shall paye doobell fyne in every thyng.

The fynes of Comen adventrers.

In the fyrst voyage no fyne shalbe exacted. but all the Adventers shalbe imployed to sett owt Men and shypps for the voyage. And at the retorne of the fleetes the Comodities shalbe devyded amongst the Adventrers ratably.

Item, yf any man hearafter wyll increase hys adventer or stock: hys fyne shalbe so muche only as a fyfth part of hys increase.

Item at every Alienation or death of a party nominated for a greater nomber; the survyvors shall paye so muche as a fyfth part of theyr Adventer at the entryng of an other mans name.

Item those that are not fyrst adventrers: shall paye doobell fyne in every thynge.

[Item] the fynes collected both of pryvate and Comen Adventers: shalbe kept withyn the threasure [ho]wses of the free Townes, to be imployed upon the Newfowndland by thassignment [of] the Generall with advyse of hys Assistants.

[The] rest of thys platt perswadeth unto a present exployt thowgh it shall extend but to the [fort]efyeng of two or thre Harbors in the meane tyme that ma[att]ers in thys corporation may [be est]ablyshed. Towards which smale begynnyng, a smale Sut[e is] intended, yet great [furtheran]ce of thys Action yf it may be obtayned of her Majestie.

Havinge in my other platt described the New-found[lande] Commodities incident unto the same. And further havinge [sett downe the] Considerations that may induce aswell her Majesties lykinge un[to the same] as also incourage somm Nobell personage to attempt a C[onquest upon the] sayd Contries, and thearyn to plant Englishmen: [I do think] it requisite to delyver a Course how the same may be a[chieved] for that it may seme a matter to wayghty for any pryv[ate person] to take the Charge upon him selfe, Which nevertheles by a mult[itude maye] easely be Caryed.

To drawe therefore many handes unto this worke: I judge it [necessarie] to erect a Corporation heare in England of the Newland trade[s and of those] suffred to use the same but those only of the Cocietie. Th[e means] whearof sithe now at the fyrst, (thowgh perhapps not so [greatlie] hearafter,) it may be with small Charges obtayned: I thin[k that it] wilbe generally imbrased, which have desyer ether to further [their Faith?] or to benefit theyr Contry, or to better theyr own estates. [And] for so much as objections have ben made agaynst this Course [namely:]

1. That to restrayn the Newland trade unto a Company, [every] man of the same beinge free for all Nations and the Contry su[bjected to a] Christian prince: Shalbe an injury and hindrance u[nto all those] which heartofore have used that Trade, As also ad[verse unto all those] of this Realme in which a great parte of the Ship[ping rests, the] West Chiefly) hath ben imployed into the Newfou[ndlande the same] being open. which will not be so when the same shalbe [a Corporation.]

2. That also by reason of late accidentes betwen us and [the Spanyards the] Newland Voyage wilbe altogither unproffitabell. For so[great a store] of fish and Trayn Oyles will not be fownd good now [that no waye] into Spayn and the Strayghtes is left. Whither for th[e moste parte] our Merchantes were

accustomed to Carry theyr Commoditie fro[m thence.]

To remove these dowtes I thinke it veary needefull Before [I end to set downe] the order I desyer to be observed in this Corporation, which [wilbe of] small effect unles that Merchantes (of whom it must Ch[iefely consist] may be induced first to think it both lawfull and Comod[ious] to have a Corporation erected of this trade.//

For answer therfore unto the first Objection. It Can[not be said that it is for] no man to draw the Newland trade unto a Societie. When as th[e Newfoundland is] ryghtly appertay[ni]nge unto the Crown of England since the [reign of our soveraign lord] King Henry the VII[th] when it was discovered and annex[ed unto the] Crown; her Majestie may lawfully dispose of the same to the [subject as parte] of her estate, So well as the King of Spayn may do of [his possessions in the Indies] and may restrayn this trade for Comon benefit (which to pryvate [persons is still] to be preserved) havinge doone the lyke in many others. N[ot only at the] Nerve [Narva] and Russia in Spayn and other Contries more late[ly Turkie. Where] as they have ben reduced unto Corporations for more pryvat[e and publike wealth.] So shall it be much more lawfull to doo the lyke in this [case of the Newfoundelande] sithe mo[r]e then in the rest matters may be accomplished [by this means (which otherwise can]not so well be doone:) greatly importinge Gods glory, as also both publike and pryvate wealth.

Moreover. It shalbe no hynd[eraunce] but Contrarywise more Comodious for the Merchantes which heartofoar have used the Newland trade, and shall procure unto them generally greater securitie in most of theyr other Trades.

For whearas our Merchantes have accustomed to goo emptie outwardes unto the Newfoundland, Caryenge only Salt and Vittayles (Which may be bestowe[d] for Balast:) And have made theyr Voyage upon the retorne only of fish. Whearby I may accownt half the voyage lost. In asmuch as in all other voyages they make gayn by Caryeng owt Commoditie or by takinge frayght so well as upon the retorne. Now when the Newfoundland shalbe peopled with Men of industry, thear wilbe Commodities raysed both of the Sea and Land: Then. for so much as the Newland Inhabiters shall alwayes have neede of our English Comodities: our Merchantes may serve them of the

same, and take in exchange the Newland Comodities Which they may fynd both ritche and of great variety, Yf strangers may be dryven to fetche and buy of us fishe and trayn. So our Merchantes may make doobell gayn of the Newland Voyage aswell owtward as inward more then heartofoare they have doone.

Item. Wheareas hitherto Shipps fornished for a New Land Voyage, [ha]ve ben doobell manned and vittayled, by reason that many Men [are] required, and a longe tyme is spent in the labor of fishinge: [he]rafter When the Contry shalbe peopled, our Merchantes may ether [find] theyr Ladinge made ready to theyr handes. or When they Come [unto the] Newfoundland, may hyer Men theare to labor in the fishinge [And by] either of which meanes theyr voyage shalbe shorter, and requir[e less] vittayll and feawer Men muche to the Merchantes benefit.

Ite[m] It must be of necessitie for our Merchantes Securitie [t]hat [t]he Newfoundland be possessed and Commanded by English men. [w]hearby the Shipps and Subjectes of forreyn princes repayrin[ge] thither, may be stayed at her Majesties pleasure. In lyke sort as her Majesties Subjectes have ben and may be at other tymes (of Vintage Chiefly) within the Dominions of other princes. For then no dowt the French and Spanish Nations, (Who Cannot forbear the Newland trade) Will hardly make staye of our Merchantes goodes When they shall perceyve that we may salve ourselves in doynge the like by them in the Newfowndland.

To Conclude the first Objection. That a Corporation Wold decaye our Navy: bryfly I may inferr, That as by a Corporation and generall Contribution of the Company the Newfoundland may soone be peopled. And the same beinge peopled, Varietie of Commoditie Wilbe found both theare and also browght thither: And by increase of Comoditie the trade also wilbe increased: And trade beinge increased more Men and Shipps must thearby be sett on Worke: So Consequently it must followe That our Corporation shalbe an increase not only unto our Navy, but also a strength unto our State, for so much as [the] Newfound land Within it sellf shall norish and trayn up a Multitude [of] men abell to serve her Majestie by Sea or Land in those partes or else [w]heare as occasion may hearafter be minist[er].

Now for answer unto the Second Objection. I

will [set out] reasons and probabilities. That Notwithstandinge our trafficke into [Spayne] and the Strayghtes is now Cutt of. Wheare our Merchantes for[merly] have usually vented theyr fish: Yet good uttrance therof [may be found] and the voyage made more beneficiall then ever it hath ben [heretofore.]

First I make no dowt but a veary great quantitie of [fish] may be uttered Within this Realme, When th'order hearafter [taken] in our Corporation, shalbe putt in execution. That fish ma[y be trans]ported and Convayed into all partes of the Realme from [the 5 chiefe Portes] as they doo lye most fitt and neare unto every quarter [of England] for albe[it] in somm places (of the West Chiefly) thear [alreadie be] to great plentie of fish browght from Newfoundland. expe[ciallie in the] last year, 1585: When Vent did fayle in other Contr[ies as] of my own experience I know, that at the same tyme [in other partes] of this Realme fish was much desyred but Cowld not [be had.] And further, the Wett or fish of the banke which is take[n upon] the Newland Coast, Was sowld in dyvers places after the [price of] iiii^{li} or V^{li} the hondred: Which I have sene usualle [solde in] the West for fyve, and somtymes under fower nobell[es the hondred, From which] I may inferr. That Yf pollecy and order may be tak[en to bring] the fish into all partes of the Realme: it shall be [of great benefite to the] Merchant and the Comonweale. Whearyn Vittayl[e hath of late come] to be more scarse and deare then in tymes past [it hath bene so] that we doo feede in manner altogither upon the [fruits of the soile] havinge less stoare of fish then in former ty[mes we have had in this] r[e]gard to feede thearon, becawse it is so scant[tie supplied.]

Item in tyme of Warr: fish beinge so necessa[ry unto our Navy] and for Howldes (especially the dry fish). It Can [be used] ether for our Navy of E[ng]land, or for the Townes and Howldes [of other frendly] Contries.

Moreover, for so much as the French Nation alonge th[e coastes of] Normandy and Brittayn even unto the borders of Spayn [(which is] a great tract of Land:) Also the Spaniardes on Bisk[aie have] the best Shipps and Mariners of Spayn: In lyke sort [too the] Portingalles. all doo mayntayn the greatest part of th[er Navy] by the Newland trade. Which withowt great decay of their S[hips and] Mariners. they Canot forgoo, but least of all the Spa[nyardes] for that the Newland fish doth serve to sustayn aswell th'inhab[itauntes of the] land, as to vittayle theyr fleetes abroad at Sea. The [consequence is that] When the Newfound land shalbe possessed: the Chief Harbors [along] the Sea Coast kept and garded by English forces: and that [Englishmen] doo kepe the fishinge unto themselves, and sell those Comm[odities] unto strangers: Thear is nothinge that ether Fran[ce or Spayne] or any Contry in Christendom doth yeld, but shalbe browght [thence] into the Newfoundland in exchange of our Newland Commodities [which now] doo only Consist in fish and Trayn: So hearafter When th[ose others] shalbe fownd out. viz. Rosen: pitche: Tarr: Cordage: and su[ch like] being Merchandise of veary great reckoninge in all our West[erne partes of] Europe: Then undowtedly the Newland trade shalbe Wonderfu[llie profitable.]

F[rom c]onsidringe the convenient Site of Newfoundland to serve the Westerly partes of Europe with such Commodities: reason leadeth me to think that in process of tyme we shall drawe the most part of wealth thither that hearafter shalbe imployed upon those Commodities Bicawse the Frenche, Spaniardes and Portingalles doo trade the Newfoundland themselves Wheare they will rather receyve the Commodities before mentioned, fresh and at the first and best hand, then (as in tymes past) to have them at second or thyrd hand yet many tymes veary insufficient.

Now weyenge thise reasons Well. That the Newland is so necessary a trade for the Frenche and Spanish Nations. Who in exchange of our Comodities theare will bringe thither unto us whatsoever theyr own or any Contryes besydes Can yeald: I demand. Which way may our English Merchantes [grou]nd theyr trade with greater safetie and gayn then unto the Newfoundland? Whear they may fynd gathered together into one place and Contry free from restraynt of forren princes, the same beynge governed and protected by her Majestie: all sortes of Comodities Which hitherto they have sowght and adventred for into forreyn Contryes not withowt great hasard and Loss to many.

Whearyn this is further to be noated. That the exactions and Customes which heartofore our Merchantes have payed unto forreyn princes by tradynge [to] theyr Contries: Shalbe eased, and Come into the handes of her Majestie or her Assignes, the Whole trade beynge thus drawn into her Majesties own Dominions, to the great advancement of this State, by so muche as forreyn princes [have heretofore] ben inriched by the same.

And truly seinge other our best trades doo grow so dangerouse both unto the Merchant [as unto the] State: I see no remedy but we shalbe Constrayned to leave of trade altogether, or to seke it somwheare else. Which as upon former [consid]erations, happely it may be translated into the Norwest partes of America: [And there] by the Newfoundland may become the richest Corner of the World. the [same] beynge endewed with most excellent Harbors for the securitie [of our] Shipps, and also abowndinge in variety of Comodities, Yf to Nature [ind]ustry may be joyned.

So to Conclude upon the second last Objection. This may suffice [us to] prove the Newland voyage Commodiouse Notwithstandinge the differences and dissentions breedinge betwen us and other Nations, doo hynder our trafficke [unt]o Spayn and the Contries Within the Strayghtes. Whearby Men of Capacitie and judgement may be induced to imbrace our Corporation, Which tendeth to the advancement of Christian religion, the benefit of our Realme, and Waranteth unto the Merchantes and whole Societie,: assured gayn with greater securitie then in any other trade Can be fownd.

And to th'intent no man shoold be discooraged from beynge a Member of our Societie, by greatnes of the Charge or fyne that must be paied for purchase of this fredome: I will delyver an order [thowghe not so exacte as tyme and experience hearafter may frame it) whearby every man according to the measure of his abilitie may be admitted into this Corporation. Leavinge it to theyr Choyse Whither they will adventer muche or little. for equale regard shalbe had th'imploymente of small as of the greatest adventures proportionable to th[ere] benefit. Bicawse (in my opinion) the most furtherance to begin the Action will grow by the Multitude of small adventers. Which others hear to foare upon my own Knowledge, have neglected to theyr great hyndrance admittinge only a Certayn rate of Adventures,

whearunto every [perso]ns abilitie wold not streatche.

> Orders Mete in this Corporation to be observed Our Corporation shalbe established in Sixe (at the leaste) principall Poartes Chosen out in severall places of the Realme. Viz.

{ London
Southampton }
Brystoa }
[Plymouth?]
Westchester
Newcastell
Harwiche

Unto every of thease Poartes shalbe appoynted Certayn Shyres to be [upon] the verges and lymites of every Poart Town: In Which Office[rs shall be] Chosen both to receyve and also imploye all adventures which sh[all be made] Within theyr own precinctes only. Whearby these Comodities [shall arise.]

1. First every man will the more willingly adventer his Stock in the Ch[arge of that] towne within or neare unto his own Contry, and will rather Comitt[e it] into the handes of men known to them to be of Credit, then unto a [stranger] to them unknown as the maner heartofoare in lyke attemptes [hath been.]

2. Item all sortes of peopell to be transported for habitation into [the Newfound] Land, may Conveniently be Conveyed unto these townes from all [partes of the] Realme. Whearunto the sympler sort wilbe easely drawn by th[e incouragement] and exampell of theyr Neyghbors.

3. Item fish browght from Newfoundland may the better be vented [from thence] into any part of this Realme owt of every of these Poartes [. As more] could be sayd hearyn which for brevity sake I omitt.

These selected townes for our Corporation to Consist[e of one Companie and] howld one Lawe and Custome in theyr trade of Newfoun[dland and shall] equally pertake of gayn or loss accordinge to the proporti[on of there] venture A somm whearof shalbe Collected and registred in every [the saide] Townes before the Fleete shall sett forth. At the returne w[hereof shalbe] deducted the principall of all the adventures from the whole [somm which for contyn]uance still of trade shalbe delyvered into every towne according [to the reckoning] kept to that ende as is before mentioned. The overplus sh[all be devided] ratably amongst th'adventrers.

By this meanes no man shall at any tyme Loose his Stock [and make it up] with supplyes as the Companies in other Corporations have be[en wont to do betwene] whom and us thear shalbe this difference. That they (bes[ides all the divers] Charges belonginge to the Shippinge) must provyde stockes in[wardes and out]wardes to buye or exchange for forreyn Commodities: Whearupon s[hould it be that a] loss shall happen Supplyes must be added or the former [Stock shall all be] made frustrate. But in our Newland voyage we nede in Stock [only that which suffices] to sett forth shippinge: sith fish and Trayn Cost mens Labors [only and they] allwayes in the retorne shall defray the Charges owtward. Notwithstan[ding no] loss shoold happen then may be expected in so safe a Course [of shipping as is] to Newfoundland.

Now the maner of adventures, and of Fynes to be exacted up[on every Adventure] for every mans fredome in this Corporation: may be as followeth:

All adventures wilbe made in two sortes.

In
Shypping which wilbe pryvate: Moneye which wilbe Commen.

[Pr]yvate adventers in shippinge will Consist of great Merchantes and Owners of [sh]ipps who (as heartofoare) may Continew still the trade to theyr own pryvate gayn or loss The fynes of Pryvate adventers to be exacted once and no more of every Shipp rated by the Tunn.

For every Tunn shalbe payed vi^s. viii^d. and for every Topp tenn shillinges.

Item. for every xx^{tie} Tuns: a man shalbe fornished of apparel, munition and vittaylles sufficient for one Whole yeare And with the sayd provisyon shalbe delyvered at place Convenient in the Newfoundland, unto the Generall or his Assygnes. Whatsoever shall excede tenn more then xx^{tie} tunns: Shalbe Charged with two Men as yf it were xl tunns Provyded alwaye. That Menn thus furnished and transported at the Merchantes Charges: shall labor in the fyshinge for the same merchantes untill they have theyr frayght: And further shall groe unto the same Merchantes theyr Shares in fysh otherwaye dew unto them, in recompence of the Merchantes Charges in furnishinge of them: Whearby the Merchant shall not

be greatly Charged, nor tyed to inconvenience [by] settynge out and transportinge these men. Inso muche as they Carry [un]to the Newfoundland more men then are requisite to sayle theyr Shipps [yet on]ly in respect of [the] labor in fishinge. Which beynge ended, it shalbe unto the Merchant a g[rea]t [ea]se to leave somm of his men behynd, and Somm gayn [be]sydes, to have th[e]r Shares.

Item Yf any hearafter upon good lykinge of the voyage; will increase [ther] Shippinge They shall pay for so many Tunns or Topps only [as they [sh]albe increased above theyr former adventure: accordyng to the above mentioned: That is to say: vi^s viii^d for every Tunn. [x^s] for every Topp: and a man furnished for every xx^{tie} tunns.

[Item]. The fynes shalbe doobell so muche as that above rehersed: of all men [tha]t will hearafter be admitted into this Societie, beynge not fyrst adventrers Suche I meane as in the fyrst Voyage that shalbe made by this Company have not adventred somwaht ether more or less.

So to Conclude of pryvate Adventrers: this is all that shalbe required of them. To paye

For every Tunn vi^s viii^d: and for every Topp: x^s.
For every xx^{tie} Tunns to furnish and transport a man.
For every Tun hearafter that shalbe increased, as muche.
For theyr fredome that are not fyrst Adventrers: doobell so muche.

Commen adventures in money Wilbe of suche as have no [shipping] nor perhapps abilitie to venter much. Whose port[ions how] small soever they are) may be accepted and imploed to[gether in] theyr proportion with the greatest. in manner as follo[weth.] Thear shalbe no somm of money admitted under the nam[e of any man f]or a Syngell share, Under xxv^{li}. But many may [lack abilitie enough] to rayse that Summ, entrynge the whole in one mans name, a[lbeit there will be] a register of the rest of theyr Names. That when the party [whose name is entered doth] dye: an other of the same nomber may enter his Name in pla[ce of him] deceased. and this Order may be held successyvely, so longe [as anye] are lyvinge Always payenge at every alienation or death [to have hymself] nominated: a fyne Which hearafter is sett downe.

This Order yf it may be observed, wilbe a great

ease unto parentes [and also to their] Children, to shom theyr fathers adventure beinge thus entayled, W[hich is a more] sewer staye then yf Landes were left unto them. Inasmuch [as thorough theyr] own follye and want of government theyr patrimony Maye be C[onsumed and nothing] left in theyr handes. But havinge Stockes in this Corporation [they] shalbe mayntayned whole and entier the same beyng deducted of [the profite at the] retorne of the Fleete every yeare: as already hath ben expressed[. And] further theyr Stockes beinge ordred and imployed to the most adva[untage to the] Body politike: the same shall yeald both greater and more C[ommodytie] then yf they were in the disposition of pryvat Owners w[ho shall have power over th'issues and increase thereof.

This Order also may greatly relieve the poorer sort of [men not] havinge any portion of money (be it veary small:) Which [they maye or] Can imploy to make unto them selves any Certayn stay of [Commodytie for] gayn: Maybe joyned many of them togither, and have [a share in the] Corporation. Whearunto this may incourage every [man to do it] That as the number of them shall dye and decrease [the value to them] shalbe increased which remayn alyve: and the longest [liver (which is what] man will hoape for) shall receyve the proffittes of th[e whole] in the ende.

The fynes that shalbe exacted at the admittance of Comen Adventrers.

In primis All the Comen adventrers the fyrst Voyage shalbe [admitted] Withowt payenge any fyne. In regard theyr first Adventure [(to be] imployed Wholly by good advise) to sett forth Men and Shipps [unto the] Newfoundland Wheare the Generall or his Assignes shall [determine what] Shipps the same be [(] beinge fyrst frayghted) so many Men from [every shipp with such] provision, as every shipp maye spare. Leavinge only so many [men on board] as may suffice to Carry those Shipps home.

Item yf any of these fyrst Adventrers hearafter Will incr[ease their shipping] they shall pay so much fyne, as a fyfth part of theyr incr[ease.]

Item upon every alienation happeninge by the decease [of any Adventrer] The survivors

shall paye so muche as a fyfth part of theyr [share.]

Item every Man beynge not a Fyrst adventrer: shall paye two [fyfths] for his admittance, and so for every increase.

All fynes to be Collected both of pryvat and Comen adventers [shalbe placed in the] treasuries of the free townes, and shalbe imployed by th'assignes [of the Generall] with advice of his Assistantes to mayntayn and Continew the Newfou[ndland trade] as also to pay stipends unto Officers, mete and Convenient f[or the use] of this Corporation towardes which also the xx^{tie} part of the yearly [overplus on each] adventure [m]ay be assigned to incorage Officers that must ta[ke risks for the] benefit of the whole Company.

[T]his is all I thinke nedefull to be spoken at this present Concerninge the [Corpo]ration: more then that I think it veary re[quis]ite to procure letters [from] Certayn Lords of the pryvy Cowncell in Commendation of the Newland [voy]age and of th'attempt to be made that waye. which letters being dyrected both unto the Magistrates of the free Townes before mentioned, as also to pryvat men within the same townes, and gentillmen abroade in the Contry best reputed amongst the Comon sorte: Will induce them to become members of this Societie, by whose perswasyon, or rather in beyng a presydent unto others themselves: A multitude wilbe drawn to doo the lyke. And every Man besydes to whom theyr honors letters shalbe dyrected will howld it an increase of his reputation by so many adventers as his Credit shalbe abell to procure unto this Action. A noate of which may be retorned unto theyr honors, that every Mans endevor may appeare by it sellf.

Whatsoever else shalbe thowght requisite to be doone yearyn: tyme will more perfectly delyver and minister occasions plentifully, When thease matters allready spoken of shall procede unto Action. Which woold not be deferred. Tyme servinge well now that other princes are occupied other wayes in expectation of great Matters at home. Who else perhaps woold take this attempt in hand (as it hath already ben determined in France) [that a]t least woold not suffer (yf they myght,) the same to be performed by the [En]glish Nacion. for that We may brydell the Frenche and Spanish [Fleet]es by possessinge the Newfoundland, more then W[ith] so slender Charge [her] Majestie Can doo in any other place.

[It is] therfore to be Wished. That this yeare two or thre at least of the principal [Harbors] in Newfoundland myght be fortefyed, Yf Charges so spedely Canot [be rai]sed to accomplish more. Which as it will require No great Matter [but t]hat maybe supplyed by Contribution of a feaw well willers unto the [same] so happely upon th[e] ret[ur]ne of they[r] shipps ho[me] theyr [char]ges may be Answered [and] with gay[n] sufficient.

Item. To help furnish this smale beginninge Which wilbe a good inducement unto the rest: [I] have thowght good to annex hearunto A small, yet a Charitabell and Christian lyke Sewt. Which yf it be obtayned of her Majestie (as only in this or suche lyke Case it is expedient:) Wilbe a great help and supply unto our Action, both of [money] and other necessaries appertayninge thearvnto. The effect whearof is:

That for so much as to plant and possess the Newfoundland with Englishmen wilbe a great benefit unto this Realme. And that to such an attempt nothinge is so requisite as to be fornished of sondry sortes of peopell, and of suche also as may be better spared then kept within the Realme: It may therefore please her Majestie, to grawnt unto the Generall that shalbe appoynted unto this Action The lyves and pardon of all manner of persones Within her Majesties Realme of England, that are already Condemned or by the Lawes of this Realme owght to suffer death or burninge in the hand, for former Offences already Committed before this pardon be sygned, Exceptinge only high treasons and willfull murders. And all person[es] to receyve benefit by this most gratiouse pardon under this Condition and not otherwayes, That they shalbe at the appoyntment of the Generall and his Assygnes to inhabit in the Newfoundland or to doo all manner of service that by the Generall or his Assygnes shalbe Commanded them. And furthermore that it may please [her] Majestie To give unto the sayd Generall at his descression to be imployed in any the services intended into the Newfoundland: all the landes and goodes Whearwith the same offenders were endowed, in such ampell manner as for

her Majestie the same owght to be fownd. Which may serve towardes the great Charges that must be spent to fornish and to transport those peopell, as also to mynister unto them all kynd of necessaries [fy]tt for habitation Withowt which they shall not be abell [th]ear to Continew alyve.

By this her Majesties gratiouse acte, the Lawes of this Realme shall [be upheld] nor any man beynge playntyfe be injured: for so much as the Lawes [takinge] theyr dew Course agaynst the offenders in Condemminge them to de[ath they] shalbe dead in effect to this Comonweale, from Which they shalbe [no more] members: Yet lyve in an other happely proffitabell Members.

Towchinge the benefit that may grow hearby unto this action inten[ded vnto the] Newfoundland: I will undertake by this Sewte (yf it may be obtayned [) the prisoners brought from the] Circuite of the Judges and Committed unto my orderinge: To transpor[te] more then 200 of all sortes of peopell with sufficient provision [unto] the Newfoundland Which with two thowsand powndes Charge Canot be a[tcheved] otherwayes. The service of these men shalbe most necessary [in the] Newfoundland both to rowe in Gallyes (which are fittest for the defence [of that] Contry:) and also to labor in Commen workes Whearyn Wilbe great use of [labor.]

So to make an ende. My prayer now to god shalbe to give good succes[se to the] travayle hearyn taken, and to rayse somm worthy person, Who undertakinge this Action in tyme, may be advanced thearby to wealth and honor, both [of which he shall] assuredly attayn unto in full Measure, by possessinge and obtayn[ing the Newfound] Land, Which reacheth forth the hand to him that first will take it [and wil yeeld] present rewardes more then by suche attemptes Can else whea[re be atchieved] by this reason Chiefly That in Newfoundland theare [is alredie a] great trade settled Which in any other Contry not yet [occupied by Christian?] or Civile peopell: Canot be browght to like perfection in [soe short a tyme.]

January: 10. 1585.

[Endorsed:] 12. februarie 1585 [–1586]. Master Ed: Hayes booke towching the Newe fownd land.

Chapter Forty-seven
Thomas Harriot's Report on Virginia

THOMAS HARRIOT'S SHORT BOOK was written, arguably, so that it could be published early in 1587, in time to encourage investors and speed settlers on their way before the summer (*see* D. B. Quinn "Thomas Harriot in the New World," J. W. Shirley, ed., *Thomas Harriot, Renaissance Scientist* (1974), pp. 38–40).

But circumstances were not ripe for it. Ralegh had cooled off the Virginia enterprise, and John White's City of Ralegh syndicate, which was ready to take the risk of a new venture, did not apparently need (or could not afford?) printed publicity. It was different by the opening of 1588. By then Ralegh and Grenville had joined forces and were ready to launch a large expedition that would need all the publicity it could get to attract investors and volunteers. *A briefe and true report* thus emerged early in 1588, not very long before the expedition was countermanded by the government for strategic reasons. Though ineffective for its immediate purpose, Harriot's tract was taken up by Hakluyt when completing his *Principall navigations* (1589) and was passed on to Theodor de Bry as the keystone of the first part of his illustrated series *America* (Frankfurt-am-Main, 1590), appearing in Latin, English, French, and German, and being thus assured of a long life in European libraries, although more for the information it contained than for its value as promotion literature. Hakluyt reprinted it for its original purpose for the last time in his *Principal navigations*, III (1600), 266–280, which version is reprinted here.

365. "A briefe and true report of the new found land of Virginia" (1588).

Rafe Lane one of her Majesties Esquiers, and Governour of the Colony in Virginia, above mentioned, for the time there resident, to the gentle Reader wisheth all happinesse in the Lord.

Albeit (gentle Reader) the credit of the reports in this Treatise contained can little be furthered by the testimony of one as my selfe, through affection judged partiall, though without desert: nevertheless, forsomuch as I have bene requested by some my particular friends, who conceive more rightly of me, to deliver freely my knowledge of the same, not onely for the satisfying of them, but also for the true information of any other whosoever, that comes not with a prejudicate minde to the reading thereof: thus much upon my credit I am to affirme, that things universally are so truely set downe in this Treatise by the authour thereof, an actor in the Colony, and a man no lesse for his honesty then learning commendable, as that I dare boldly avouch, it may very well passe with the credit of trueth even amongst the most true relations of this age. Which as for mine owne part I am ready any way with my word to acknowledge, so also (of the certaintie thereof assured by mine owne experience) with this my publique assertion I doe affirme the same. Farewell in the Lord.

To the Adventurers, Favourers, and Welwillers of the enterprise for the inhabiting and planting in Virginia.

Since the first undertaking by Sir Walter Ralegh to deale in the action of discovering of that countrey which is now called and knowen by the name of Virginia, many voyages having beene thither made at sundry times to his great charge; as first in the yere 1584, and afterwards in the yeres 1585, 1586, and now of late this last yeere 1587: there have bene divers and variable reports, with some slanderous and shamefull speeches bruted abroad by many that returned from thence: especially of that discovery which was made by the Colony transported by Sir Richard Grinvile in the yere 1585, being of all others the most principall, and as yet of most effect, the time of their abode in the countrey being a whole yere, when as in the other voyage before they stayed but sixe weeks, and the others after were onely for supply and transportation, nothing more being discovered then had bene before. Which reports have not done a little wrong to many that otherwise would have also favoured and adventured in the action, to the honour and benefit of our nation, besides the particular profit and credit which would redound to themselves the dealers therein, as I hope by the sequel of events, to the shame of those that have avouched the contrary, shall be manifest, if you the adventurers, favourers and welwillers doe but either increase in number, or in opinion continue, or having beene doubtfull, renew your good liking and furtherance to deale therein according to the woorthinesse thereof already found, and as you shall understand hereafter to be requisit. Touching which woorthinesse through cause of the diversity of relations and reports, many of your opinions could not be firme, nor the minds of some that are well disposed be setled in any certaintie.

I have therefore thought it good, being one that have beene in the discoverie, and in dealing with the naturall inhabitants specially imployed: and having therefore seene and knowen more then the ordinary, to impart so much unto you of the fruits of our labours, as that you may know how injuriously the enterprise is slandered, and that in publique maner at this present, chiefly for two respects.

First, that some of you which are yet ignorant or doubtfull of the state thereof, may see that there is sufficient cause why the chiefe enterpriser with the favour of her Majesty, notwithstanding such reports, hath not onely since continued the action by sending into the countrey againe, and replanting this last yeere a new Colony, but is also ready, according as the times and meanes will affoord, to follow and prosecute the same.

Secondly, that you seeing and knowing the continuance of the action, by the view hereof you may generally know and learne what the countrey is, and thereupon consider how your dealing therein, if it proceed, may returne you profit and gaine, be it either by inhabiting and planting, or otherwise in furthering thereof.

And least that the substance of my relation should be doubtfull unto you, as of others by reason of their diversitie, I will first open the cause in a few words, wherefore they are so different, referring my selfe to your favourable constructions, and to be adjudged of, as by good consideration you shall finde cause.

Of our company that returned, some for their misdemeanour and ill dealing in the countrey have bene there worthily punished, who by reason of their bad natures, have maliciously not onely spoken ill of their Governours, but for their sakes slandered the countrey it selfe. The like also have those done which were of their consort.

Some being ignorant of the state thereof, notwithstanding since their returne amongst their friends & acquaintance, and also others, especially if they were in company where they might not be gainsayd, would seeme to know so much as no men more, and make no men so great travellers as themselves. They stood so much, as it may seeme, upon their credit and reputation, that having bene a twelvemoneth in the countrey, it would have bene a great disgrace unto them, as they thought, if they could not have sayd much, whether it were true or false. Of which some have spoken of more then ever they saw, or otherwise knew to be there. Other some have not bene ashamed to make absolute deniall of that, which although not by them, yet by others is most certainly and there plentifully knowen, & other some make difficulties of those things they have no skill of.

The cause of their ignorance was, in that they

were of that many that were never out of the Island where we were seated, or not farre, or at the least wise in few places els, during the time of our abode in the country: or of that many, that after gold & silver was not so soone found, as it was by them looked for, had litle or no care of any other thing but to pamper their bellies: or of that many which had litle understanding, lesse discretion, and more tongue then was needfull or requisite.

Some also were of a nice bringing up, only in cities or townes, or such as never (as I may say) had seene the world before. Because there were not to be found any English cities, nor such faire houses, nor at their owne wish any of their old accustomed dainty food, nor any soft beds of downe or feathers, the countrey was to them miserable, and their reports thereof according.

Because my purpose was but in briefe to open the cause of the variety of such speeches, the particularities of them, and of many envious, malicious, and slanderous reports and devices els, by our owne countreymen besides, as trifles that are not worthy of wise men to be thought upon, I meane not to trouble you withall, but will passe to the commodities, the substance of that which I have to make relation of unto you.

The Treatise whereof, for your more ready view and easier understanding, I will divide into three speciall parts. In the first I will make declaration of such commodities there already found or to be raised, which will not onely serve the ordinary turnes of you which are and shall be the planters and inhabitants, but such an overplus sufficiently to be yeelded, or by men of skill to be provided, as by way of traffique and exchange with our owne nation of England, will inrich your selves the providers: those that shall deale with you, the enterprisers in generall, and greatly profit our owne countreymen, to supply them with most things which heretofore they have bene faine to provide either of strangers or of our enemies, which commodities, for distinction sake, I call Merchantable.

In the second I will set downe all the commodities which we know the countrey by our experience doth yeeld of it selfe for victuall and sustenance of mans life, such as are usually fed upon by the inhabitants of the countrey, as also by us during the time we were there.

In the last part I will make mention generally of such other commodities besides, as I am able to remember, and as I shall thinke behoovefull for those that shall inhabit, and plant there, to know of, which specially concerne building, as also some other necessary uses: with a briefe description of the nature and maners of the people of the countrey.

The first part of Merchantable commodities.

Silke of grasse, or Grasse silke. There is a kind of grasse in the country, upon the blades whereof there groweth very good silke in forme of a thin glittering skin to be stript off. It groweth two foot & an halfe high or better: the blades are about two foot in length, and halfe an inch broad. The like groweth in Persia, which is in the selfe same climate as Virginia, of which very many of the Silke works that come from thence into Europe are made. Hereof if it be planted and ordered as in Persia, it cannot in reason be otherwise, but that there will rise in short time great profit to the dealers therein, seeing there is so great use and vent thereof aswel in our countrey as elsewhere. And by the meanes of sowing and planting it in good ground, it will be farre greater, better, and more plentifull then it is. Although notwithstanding there is great store thereof in many places of the countrey growing naturally and wild, which also by proofe here in England, in making a piece of Silke grogran, we found to be excellent good.

Worme silke. In many of our journeys we found Silke-wormes faire and great, as bigge as our ordinary Walnuts. Although it hath not bene our hap to have found such plenty, as elswhere to be in the countrey we have heard of, yet seeing that the countrey doth naturally breed and nourish them, there is no doubt but if arte be added in planting of Mulberie trees, and others, fit for them in commodious places, for their feeding & nourishing, and some of them carefully gathered & husbanded in that sort, as by men of skil is knowen to be necessary: there wil rise as great profit in time to the Virginians, as thereof doth now to the Persians, Turks, Italians and Spanyards.

Flaxe and Hempe. The trueth is, that of Hempe and Flaxe there is no great store in any one place together, by reason it is not planted but as the soile doth yeeld of it selfe: and howsoever the leafe and stemme or stalke do differ from ours, the stuffe by judgement of men of skill is altogether as good as ours: and if not, as further proofe should finde otherwise, we have that experience of the soile, as that there cannot be shewed any reason to the contrary, but that it will grow there excellent well, and by planting will be yeelded plentifully, seeing there is so much ground whereof some may well be applied to such purposes. What benefit heereof may grow in cordage and linnens who cannot easily understand?

Allum. There is a veine of earth along the sea coast for the space of forty or fifty miles, whereof by the judgement of some that have made triall here in England, is made good Allum, of that kind which is called Roch allum. The richnesse of such a commodity is so well knowen, that I need not to say any thing thereof. The same earth doth also yeeld White coprasse, Nitrum, and Alumen plumeum, but nothing so plentifully as the common Allum, which be also of price, and profitable.

Wapeih. A kind of earth so called by the naturall inhabitants, very like to Terra sigillata, and having bene refined, it hath bene found by some of our Physicians and Chyrurgians, to be of the same kind of vertue, and more effectuall. The inhabitants use it very much for the cure of sores and wounds: there is in divers places great plenty, and in some places of a blew sort.

Pitch, Tarre, Rozen and Turpentine. There are those kinds of trees which yeeld them abundantly and great store. In the very same Island where we were seated, being fifteene miles of length, and five or six miles in breadth, there are few trees els but of the same kinde, the whole Island being full.

Sassafras, called by the inhabitants Winauk, a kind of wood of most pleasant and sweet smell, and of most rare vertues in physicke for the cure of many diseases. It is found by experience to be far better and of more uses then the wood which is called Guaiacum, or Lignum vitæ. For the description, the maner of using, and the manifold vertues therof, I refer you to the booke of Monardes, translated and entituled in English, The joyfull newes from the West Indies.

Cedar. A very sweet wood, and fine timber, whereof if nests of chests be there made, or timber thereof fitted for sweet and fine bedsteds, tables, desks, lutes, virginals, and many things els, (of which there hath bene proofe made already) to make up fraight with other principall commodities, will yeeld profit.

Wine. There are two kindes of grapes that the soile doth yeeld naturally, the one is small and sowre, of the ordinary bignesse as ours in England, the other farre greater and of himselfe lushious sweet. When they are planted and husbanded as they ought, a principall commodity of wines by them may be raised.

Oile. There are two sorts of Walnuts, both holding oile; but the one farre more plentifull then the other. When there are mils and other devices for the purpose, a commodity of them may be raised, because there are infinite store. There are also three severall kindes of berries in the forme of Oke-akornes, which also by the experience and use of the inhabitants, we find to yeeld very good and sweet oile. Furthermore, the beares of the countrey are commonly very fat, and in some places there are many. Their fatnesse, because it is so liquid, may well be termed oile, and hath many speciall uses.

Furres. All along the Sea coast there are great store of Otters, which being taken by weares and other engines made for the purpose, wil yeeld good profit. We hope also of Marterne furres, and make no doubt by the relation of the people, but that in some places of the countrey there are store, although there were but two skinnes that came to our hands. Luzernes also we have understanding of, although for the time we saw none.

Deers skinnes dressed after the maner of Chamoes, or undressed, are to be had of the naturall inhabitants thousands yerely by way of traffike for trifles, and no more waste or spoile of Deere then is and hath bene ordinarily in time before.

Civet-cats. In our travels there was found one to have bin killed by a Savage or inhabitant, & in another place the smel where one or more had lately bene before, whereby we gather, besides then by the relation of the people, that there are some in the country: good profit will rise by them.

Iron. In two places of the countrey specially, one about fourescore, & the other six score miles from the fort or place where we dwelt, we found nere the water side the ground to be rocky, which by the triall of a Minerall man was found to holde iron richly. It is found in many places of the country els: I know nothing to the contrary, but that it may be allowed for a good merchantable commodity, considering there the small charge for the labour & feeding or men, the infinite store of wood, the want of wood & deerenesse thereof in England, and the necessity of ballasting of ships.

Copper. An hundred and fifty miles into the maine in two townes we found with the inhabitants divers small plates of Copper, that had bene made as we understood by the inhabitants that dwell further into the country, where as they say are mountaines and rivers that yeeld also white graines of mettall, which is to be deemed Silver. For confirmation whereof, at the time of our first arrivall in the countrey, I saw, with some others with me, two small pieces of Silver grosly beaten, about the weight of a testron, hanging in the eares of a Wiroans or chiefe lord that dwelt about fourescore miles from us: of whom through inquiry, by the number of dayes and the way, I learned that it had come to his hands from the same place or neere, where I after understood the Copper was made, and the white graines of metall found. The aforesayd Copper we also found by triall to holde Silver.

Pearle. Sometimes in feeding on Muscles we found some Pearle: but it was our happe to meet with ragges, or of a pide colour: not having yet discovered those places where we heard of better and more plenty. One of our company, a man of skill in such matters, had gathered together from among the Savage people about five thousand:[1] of which number he chose so many as made a faire chaine, which for their likenesse and uniformity in roundnesse, orientnesse, and pidenesse of many excellent colours, with equality in greatnesse, were very faire and rare: and had therefore beene presented to her Majesty, had we not by casualty, and through extremity of a storme lost them, with many things els in comming away from the countrey.

Sweet gummes of divers kinds, and many other Apothecary drugges, of which we will make speciall mention, when we shall receive it from such men of skill in that kinde, that in taking reasonable paines shal discover them more particularly then we have done, and then now I can make relation of, for want of the examples I had provided and gathered, and are now lost, with other things by casualty before mentioned.

Dies of divers kinds: There is Shoemake well knowen, and used in England for blacke: the seed of an herbe called Wasebur, little small roots

called Chappacor, and the barke of the tree called by the inhabitants Tangomockonomindge: which dies are for divers sorts of red: their goodnesse for our English clothes remaine yet to be prooved. The inhabitants use them only for the dying of haire, and colouring of their faces, and mantles made of Deere skinnes: and also for the dying of rushes to make artificiall works withall in their mats and baskets: having no other thing besides that they account of, apt to use them for. If they will not proove merchantable, there is no doubt but the planters there shall finde apt uses for them, as also for other colours which we know to be there.

Woad: a thing of so great vent and uses amongst English Diers, which can not be yeelded sufficiently in our owne countrey for spare of ground, may be planted in Virginia, there being ground enough. The growth thereof need not to be doubted, when as in the Islands of the Açores it groweth plentifully, which are in the same climate. So likewise of Madder.

We caried thither Suger-canes to plant, which being not so well preserved as was requisite, and besides the time of the yeere being past for their setting when we arrived, we could not make that proofe of them as we desired. Notwithstanding, seeing that they grow in the same climate, in the South part of Spaine, and in Barbary, our hope in reason may yet continue. So likewise for Orenges and Limmons. There may be planted also Quinses. Whereby may grow in reasonable time, if the action be diligently prosecuted, no small commodities in Sugars, Suckets, and Marmelades.

Many other commodities by planting may there also be raised, which I leave to your discreet and gentle considerations: and many also may be there, which yet we have not discovered. Two more commodities of great value, one of certeinty, and the other in hope, not to be planted, but there to be raised and in short time to be provided, and prepared, I might have specified. So likewise of those commodities already set downe I might have sayd more: as of the particular places where they are found, and best to be planted and prepared: by what meanes, and in what reasonable space of time they might be raised to profit, and in what proportion: but because others then welwillers might be there withall acquainted, not to the good of the action, I have

---

1. Sidenote: "Five thousand pearles gathered."

wittingly omitted them: knowing that to those that are well disposed, I have uttered, according to my promise and purpose, for this part sufficient.

The second part of such commodities as Virginia is knowen to yeeld for victuall and sustenance of mans life, usually fed upon by the naturall inhabitants; as also by us, during the time of our abode: and first of such as are sowed and husbanded.

Pagatowr, a kinde of graine so called by the inhabitants: the same in the West Indies is called Mayz: English men call it Guiny-wheat or Turkey-wheat, according to the names of the countreys from whence the like hath beene brought. The graine is about the bignesse of our ordinary English peaze, and not much different in forme and shape: but of divers colours: some white, some red, some yellow, and some blew. All of them yeeld a very white and sweet flowre: being used according to his kinde, it maketh a very good bread. We made of the same in the countrey some Mault, whereof was brewed as good Ale as was to be desired. So likewise by the helpe of Hops, therof may be made as good Beere. It is a graine of marvellous great increase: of a thousand, fifteene hundred, and some two thousand folde. There are three sorts, of which two are ripe in eleven & twelve weeks at the most, sometimes in tenne, after the time they are set, and are then of height in stalke about six or seven foot. The other sort is ripe in foureteene, and is about tenne foot high, of the stalks some beare foure heads, some three, some one, and some two: every head conteining five, sixe, or seven hundred graines, within a few more or lesse. Of these graines, besides bread, the inhabitants make victuall, either by parching them, or seething them whole untill they be broken: or boiling the flowre with water into pap.

Okindgier, called by us Beanes, because in greatnesse and partly in shape they are like to the beanes in England, saving that they are flatter, of more divers colours, and some pide. The leafe also of the stemme is much different. In taste they are altogether as good as our English peaze.

Wickonzowr, called by us Peaze, in respect of the Beanes, for distinction sake, because they are much lesse, although in forme they litle differ: but in goodnesse of taste much like, and are far better then our English Peaze. Both the beanes and peaze are ripe in ten weeks after they are set. They make them victuall either by boiling them all to pieces into a broth, or boiling them whole untill they be soft, and beginne to breake, as is used in England, either by themselves, or mixtly together: sometime they mingle of the Wheat with them: sometime also, being whole sodden, they bruse or punne them in a morter, and therof make loaves or lumps of doughish bread, which they use to eat for variety.

Macocquer, according to their several formes, called by us Pompions, Melons, and Gourds, because they are of the like formes as those kinds in England. In Virginia such of severall formes are of one taste, and very good, and do also spring from one seed. There are of two sorts: one is ripe in the space of a moneth, and the other in two moneths.

There is an herbe which in Dutch is called Melden. Some of those that I describe it unto take it to be a kinde of Orage: it groweth about foure of five foot high: of the seed thereof they make a thicke broth, and pottage of a very good taste: of the stalke by burning into ashes they make a kinde of salt earth, wherewithall many use sometimes to season their broths: other salt they know not. We our selves used the leaves also for potherbs.

There is also another great herbe, in forme of a Marigolde, about sixe foot in height, the head with the floure is a spanne in breadth. Some take it to be Planta Solis: of the seeds hereof they make both a kinde of bread and broth.

All the aforesayd commodities for victuall are set or sowed, sometimes in grounds apart and severally by themselves, but for the most part together in one ground mixtly: the maner therof, with the dressing and preparing of the ground, because I will note unto you the fertility of the soile, I thinke good briefly to describe.

The ground they never fatten with mucke, dung, or any other thing, neither plow nor digge it as we in England, but onely prepare it in sort as followeth. A few dayes before they sowe or set, the men with wooden instruments made almost in forme of mattocks or hoes with long handles: the women with short pecker or parers, because they use them sitting, of a foot long, and about five inches in breadth, doe onely breake the upper part of the ground to raise up the weeds, grasse, and olde stubbes of corne stalks with their roots. The which after a day or two dayes drying in the

Sunne, being scrapt up into many small heaps, to save them labour for carying them away, they burne into ashes. And whereas some may thinke that they use the ashes for to better the ground, I say that then they would either disperse the ashes abroad, which wee observed they do not, except the heaps be too great, or els would take speciail care to set their corne where the ashes lie, which also wee finde they are carelesse of. And this is all the husbanding of their ground that they use.

Then their setting or sowing is after this maner. First for their corne, beginning in one corner of the plot, with a pecker they make a hole, wherein they put foure graines, with care that they touch not one another (about an inch asunder) & cover them with the molde againe: and so thorowout the whole plot making such holes, and using them after such maner, but with this regard, that they be made in ranks, every ranke differing from other halfe a fadome or a yard, and the holes also in every ranke as much. By this meanes there is a yard spare ground betweene every hole: where according to discretion here and there, they set as many Beanes and Peaze; in divers places also among the seeds of Macocquer, Melden, and Planta solis.

The ground being thus set according to the rate by us experimented, an English acre conteining forty pearches in length, and foure in breadth, doth there yeeld in croppe or ofcome of corne, Beanes and Peaze, at the least two hundred London bushels, besides the Macocquer, Melden, and Planta solis; when as in England forty bushels of our Wheat yeelded out of such an acre is thought to be much.

I thought also good to note this unto you, that you which shall inhabit, and plant there, may know how specially that countrey corne is there to be preferred before ours: besides, the manifold wayes in applying it to victual, the increase is so much, that small labor & paines is needful in respect of that which must be used for ours. For this I can assure you that according to the rate we have made proofe of, one man may prepare and husband so much ground (having once borne corne before) with lesse then foure and twenty houres labour, as shall yeeld him victual in a large proportion for a twelvemoneth, if he have nothing els but that which the same ground will yeeld, and of that kinde onely which I have before spoken of: the sayd ground being also but of five and twenty yards square. And if need require, but that there

is ground enough, there might be raised out of one and the selfesame ground two harvests or ofcomes: for they sow or set, and may at any time when they thinke good, from the midst of March untill the end of June: so that they also set when they have eaten of their first croppe. In some places of the countrey notwithstanding they have two harvests, as we have heard, out of one and the same ground.

For English corne neverthelesse, whether to use or not to use it, you that inhabit may doe as you shall have further cause to thinke best. Of the growth you need not to doubt: for Barley, Oats, and Peaze, we have seene proofe of, not being purposely sowen, but fallen casually in the woorst sort of ground, and yet to be as faire as any we have ever seene heere in England. But of Wheat, because it was musty, and had taken salt water, we could make no triall: and of Rie we had none. Thus much have I digressed, and I hope not unnecessarily: now will I returne againe to my course, and intreat of that which yet remaineth, apperteining to this chapter.

There is an herbe which is sowed apart by it selfe, and is called by the inhabitants Uppowoc: in the West Indies it hath divers names, according to the severall places and countreys where it groweth and is used: the Spanyards generally call it Tabacco.[2] The leaves thereof being dried and brought into pouder, they use to take the fume or smoake thereof, by sucking it thorow pipes made of clay, into their stomacke and head; from whence it purgeth superfluous fleame and other grosse humours, and openeth all the pores and passages of the body: by which meanes the use thereof not onely preserveth the body from obstructions, but also (if any be, so that they have not bene of too long continuance) in short time breaketh them: whereby their bodies are notably preserved in health, and know not many grievous diseases, wherewithall we in England are often times afflicted.

This Uppowoc is of so precious estimation amongst them, that they thinke their gods are marvellously delighted therewith: whereupon sometime they make hallowed fires, and cast some of the pouder therin for a sacrifice: being in a storme upon the waters, to pacifie their gods, they cast some up into the aire and into the water: so a weare for fish being newly set up, they cast

2. Sidenote: "Tabacco."

some therein and into the aire: also after an escape of danger, they cast some into the aire likewise: but all done with strange gestures, stamping, sometime dancing, clapping of hands, holding up of hands, and staring up into the heavens, uttering therewithall, and chattering strange words and noises.

We our selves, during the time we were there, used to sucke it after their maner, as also since our returne, and have found many rare and woonderfull experiments of the vertues thereof: of which the relation would require a volume by it selfe: the use of it by so many of late men and women of great calling, as els, and some learned Physicians also, is sufficient witnesse.

And these are all the commodities for sustenance of life, that I know and can remember, they use to husband: all els that follow, are found growing naturally or wilde.

Of Roots.

Openauk are a kinde of roots of round forme, some of the bignesse of Walnuts, some farre greater, which are found in moist and marish grounds growing many together one by another in ropes, as though they were fastened with a string. Being boiled or sodden, they are very good meat. Monardes calleth these roots, Beads or Pater nostri of Santa Helena.[3]

Okeepenauk are also of round shape found in dry grounds: some are of the bignesse of a mans head. They are to be eaten as they are taken out of the ground: for by reason of their drinesse they will neither rost nor seethe. Their taste is not so good as of the former roots: notwithstanding for want of bread, and sometimes for variety the inhabitants use to eat them with fish or flesh, and in my judgement they do as well as the housholde bread made of Rie here in England.

Kaishucpenauk, a white kinde of roots about the bignesse of hennes egges, and neere of that forme: their taste was not so good to our seeming as of the other, and therefore their place and maner of growing not so much cared for by us: the inhabitants notwithstanding used to boile and eat many.

Tsinaw, a kind of root much like unto that which in England is called the China root brought from the East Indies. And we know not any thing to the contrary but that it may be of the same kinde.

These roots grow many together in great clusters, and do bring foorth a brier stalke, but the leafe in shape farre unlike: which being supported by the trees it groweth neerest unto, will reach or climbe to the top of the highest. From these roots while they be new or fresh, being chopt into small pieces, and stampt, is strained with water a juice that maketh bread, and also being boiled, a very good spoonmeat in maner of a gelly, and is much better in taste, if it be tempered with oile. This Tsinaw is not of that sort, which by some was caused to be brought into England for the China root; for it was discovered since, and is in use as is aforesayd: but that which was brought hither is not yet knowen, neither by us nor by the inhabitants to serve for any use or purpose, although the roots in shape are very like.

Coscushaw some of our company tooke to be that kinde of root which the Spanyards in the West Indies call Cassavy, whereupon also many called it by that name: it groweth in very muddy pooles, and moist grounds. Being dressed according to the countrey maner, it maketh a good bread, and also a good spoonmeat, and is used very much by the inhabitants. The juice of this root is poison, & therefore heed must be taken before any thing be made therewithall[4]: either the roots must be first sliced and dried in the Sunne, or by the fire, and then being punned into floure, will make good bread: or els while they are greene they are to be pared, cut in pieces, and stampt: loaves of the same to be layd nere or over the fire untill it be sowre; and then being well punned againe, bread or spoonmeat very good in taste and holesome may be made thereof.

Habascon is a root of hote taste, almost of the forme and bignesse of a Parsnip: of it selfe it is no victuall, but onely a helpe, being boiled together with other meats.

There are also Leeks, differing little from ours in England, that grow in many places of the countrey; of which, when we came in places where they were, we gathered and eat many, but the naturall inhabitants never.

Of Fruits.

Chestnuts there are in divers places great store: some they use to eat raw, some they stampe and boile to make spoonmeat, and with some being sodden, they make such a maner of

---

3. Sidenote: "Monardes parte 2. lib. I. cap. 4."

4. Sidenote: "The juice of Coscushaw is poison."

dough bread as they use of their beanes before mentioned.

Walnuts. There are two kinds of Walnuts, and of them infinite store: in many places, where are very great woods for many miles together, the third part of trees are Walnut trees. The one kinde is of the same taste and forme, or little differing from ours of England, but that they are harder and thicker shelled: the other is greater, and hath a very ragged and hard shell: but the kernel great, very oily and sweet. Besides their eating of them after our ordinary maner, they breake them with stones, and punne them in morters with water, to make a milke which they use to put into some sorts of their spoonemeat: also among their sodde wheat, peaze, beanes and pompions, which maketh them have a farre more pleasant taste.

Medlars, a kinde of very good fruit: so called by us chiefly for these respects: first in that they are not good untill they be rotten, then in that they open at the head as our Medlars, and are about the same bignesse: otherwise in taste and colour they are farre different; for they are as red as cheries, and very sweet: but whereas the chery is sharpe sweet, they are lushious sweet.

Mutaquesunnauk, a kinde of pleasant fruit almost of the shape and bignesse of English peares, but that they are of a perfect red colour aswell within as without. They grow on a plant whose leaves are very thicke, and full of prickles as sharpe as needles. Some that have beene in the Indies, where they have seene that kind of red die of great price, which is called Cochinile, to grow, doe describe his plant right like unto this of Metaquesunnauk; but whether it be the true Cochinile, or a bastard or wilde kinde, it cannot yet be certified, seeing that also, as I heard, Cochinile is not of the fruit, but found on the leaves of the plant: which leaves for such matter we have not so specially observed.[5]

Grapes there are of two sorts, which I mentioned in the merchantable commodities.

Strawberies there are as good and as great as those which we have in our English gardens.

Mulberies, Applecrabs, Hurts or Hurtleberies, such as we have in England.

Sacquenummener, a kinde of berries almost like unto Capers, but somewhat greater, which grow together in clusters upon a plant or hearbe that is found in shallow waters: being boiled eight or nine houres according to their kinde, are very good meat and holesome; otherwise if they be eaten they will make a man for the time frantike or extremely sicke.

There is a kinde of Reed which beareth a seed almost like unto our Rie or Wheat; and being boiled is good meat.

In our travels in some places we found Wilde peaze like unto ours in England, but that they were lesse, which are also good meat.

Of a kinde of fruit or berry in forme of Acornes.

There is a kinde of berry or acorne, of which there are five sorts that grow on severall kindes of trees: the one is called Sagatemener, the second Osamener, the third Pummuckoner. These kinde of acornes they use to drie upon hurdles made of reeds, with fire underneath, almost after the maner as we dry Malt in England. When they are to be used, they first water them untill they be soft, and then being sod, they make a good victuall, either to eat so simply, or els being also punned to makes loaves or lumps of bread. These be also the three kinds, of which I sayd before the inhabitants used to make sweet oile.

Another sort is called Sapummener, which being boiled or parched, doth eat and taste like unto Chesnuts. They sometime also make bread of this sort.

The fift sort is called Mangummenauk, and is the acorne of their kinde of Oake, the which being dried after the maner of the first sorts, and afterward watered, they boile them, and their servants, or sometime the chiefe themselves, either for variety or for want of bread, do eat them with their fish or flesh.

Of Beasts.

Deere, in some places there are great store: neere unto the Sea coast they are of the ordinary bignesse of ours in England, and some lesse: but further up into the countrey, where there is better food, they are greater: they differ from ours onely in this, their tailes are longer, and the snags of their hornes looke backward.

Conies. Those that we have seene, and all that we can heare of are of a gray colour like unto Hares: in some places there are such plenty that all the people of some townes make them mantles

5. Sidenote: "There are iii. kinds of Tunas whereof that which beareth no fruith bringeth foorth the Cochinillo."

of the furre or flue of the skinnes of those which they usually take.

Sawuenuckot and Maquowoc, two kinds of small beasts greater then Conies, which are very good meat. We never tooke any of them our selves but sometime eat of such as the inhabitants had taken and brought unto us.

Squirels, which are of a grey colour, we have taken and eaten.

Beares, which are of blacke colour. The beares of this countrey are good meat. The inhabitants in time of Winter do use to take & eat many: so also sometime did we. They are taken commonly in this sort: In some Islands or places where they are, being hunted for, assoone as they have spiall of a man, they presently run away, and then being chased, they clime and get up the next tree they can: from whence with arrowes they are shot downe starke dead, or with those wounds that they may after easily be killed. We sometime shot them downe with our calievers.

I have the names of eight and twenty severall sorts of beasts, which I have heard of to be here and there dispersed in the countrey, especially in the maine: of which there are only twelve kinds that we have yet discovered; and of those that be good meat we know only them before mentioned. The inhabitants sometime kill the Lion, and eat him: and we sometime as they came to our hands of their Woolves or Woolvish dogs, which I have not set downe for good meat, least that some would understand my judgement therein to be more simple then needeth, although I could alleage the difference in taste of those kinds from ours, which by some of our company have bene experimented in both.

Of Fowle.

Turkie cocks and Turkie hennes, Stockdoves, Partridges, Cranes, Hernes, and in Winter great store of Swannes and Geese. Of all sorts of fowle I have the names in the countrey language of fourescore and sixe, of which number, besides those that be named, we have taken, eaten, & have the pictures as they were there drawn, with the names of the inhabitants, of severall strange sorts of water fowle eight, and seventeene kinds more of land fowle, although we have seene and eaten of many more, which for want of leasure there for the purpose, could not be pictured: and after we are better furnished and

stored upon further discovery with their strange beasts, fish, trees, plants, and herbs, they shalbe also published.

There are also Parrots, Faulcons, and Marlin hauks, which although with us they be not used for meat, yet for other causes I thought good to mention.

Of Fish.

For foure moneths of the yeere, February, March, Aprill and May, there are plenty of Sturgeons. And also in the same moneths of Herrings, some of the ordinary bignesse of ours in England, but the most part farre greater, of eighteene, twenty inches, and some two foot in length and better: both these kinds of fish in those moneths are most plentifull, and in best season, which we found to be most delicate and pleasant meat.

There are also Trouts, Porpoises, Rayes, Oldwives, Mullets, Plaice, and very many other sorts of excellent good fish, which we have taken and eaten, whose names I know not but in the countrey language: we have the pictures of twelve sorts more, as they were drawn in the countrey, with their names.

The inhabitants use to take them two maner of wayes; the one is by a kinde of weare made of reeds, which in that country are very strong[6]: the other way, which is more strange, is with poles made sharpe at one end, by shooting them into the fish after the maner as Irish men cast darts, either as they are rowing in their boats, or els as they are wading in the shallowes for the purpose.

There are also in many places plenty of these kinds which follow:

Sea-crabs, such as we have in England.

Oisters, some very great, and some small, some round, and some of a long shape: they are found both in salt water and brackish, and those that we had out of salt water are farre better then the other, as in our countrey.

Also Muscles, Scalops, Periwinkles, and Crevises.

Seekanauk, a kinde of crusty shel-fish, which is good meat, about a foot in bredth, having a crusty taile many legges like a crab, and her eyes in her backe. They are found in shallowes of waters, and sometime on the shore.

There are many Tortoises both of land and sea

---

6. Sidenote: "In the gulfe of Califormia they use the like fishing."

kinde, their backs and bellies are shelled very thicke; their head, feet, and taile, which are in appearance, seeme ougly, as though they were members of a serpent or venimous beasts; but notwithstanding they are very good meat, as also their eggs. Some have bene found of a yard in bredth and better.

And thus have I made relation of all sorts of victuall that we fed upon for the time we were in Virginia, as also the inhabitants themselves, as farre forth as I know and can remember, or that are specially woorthy to be remembred.

The third and last part of such other things as are behovefull for those which shall plant and inhabite to know of, with a description of the nature and maners of the people of the Countrey.

Of commodities for building and other necessary uses.

Those other things which I am more to make rehearsal of, are such as concerne building, & other mechanicall necessary uses, as divers sorts of trees for house and ship-timber, and other uses else: Also lime, stone, and bricke, least that being not mentioned some might have bene doubted of, or by some that are malitious the contrary reported.

Okes there are as faire, straight, tall, and as good timber as any can be, and also great store, and in some places very great.

Walnut trees, as I have said before very many, some have bene seene excellent faire timber of foure and five fadome, and above fourescore foote streight without bough.

Firre trees fit for masts of ships, some very tall and great.

Rakiock, a kinde of trees so called that are sweete wood, of which the inhabitants that were neere unto us doe commonly make their boates or Canoas of the forme of trowes, onely with the helpe of fire, hatchets of stones, and shels: we have knowen some so great being made in that sort of one tree, that they have caried well 20. men at once, besides much baggage: the timber being great, tall, streight, soft, light, and yet tough ynough I thinke (besides other uses) to be fit also for masts of ships.

Cedar, a sweete wood good for seelings, chests, boxes, bedsteads, lutes, virginals, and many things els, as I have also said before. Some of our

company which have wandered in some places where I have not bene, have made certaine affirmation of Cyprus, which for such and other excellent uses is also a wood of price and no small estimation.

Maple, and also Wich-hazle, whereof the inhabitants use to make their bowes.

Holly, a necessary thing for the making of birdlime.

Willowes good for the making of weares and weeles to take fish after the English maner, although the inhabitants use onely reedes, which because they are so strong as also flexible, doe serve for that turne very well and sufficiently.

Beech and Ashe, good for caske-hoopes, and if neede require, plowe worke, as also for many things els.

Elme.} {Sassafras trees.

Ascopo a kinde of tree very like unto Lawrell, the barke is hot in taste and spicie, it is very like to that tree which Monardes describeth to be Cassia Lignea of the West Indies.

There are many other strange trees whose names I know not but in the Virginian language, of which I am not now able, neither is it so convenient for the present to trouble you with particular relation: seeing that for timber and other necessary uses, I have named sufficient. And of many of the rest, but that they may be applied to good use, I know no cause to doubt.

Now for stone, bricke, and lime, thus it is. Neere unto the Sea coast where wee dwelt, there are no kinde of stones to be found (except a few small pebbles about foure miles off) but such as have bene brought from further out of the maine. In some of our voyages we have seene divers hard raggie stones, great pebbles, and a kinde of gray stone like unto marble of which the inhabitants make their hatchets to cleave wood. Upon inquirie wee heard that a little further up into the Countrey were of all sorts very many, although of quarries they are ignorant, neither have they use of any store whereupon they should have occasion to seeke any. For if every housholde have one or two to cracke nuts, grinde shels, whet copper, and sometimes other stones for hatchets, they have ynough: neither use they any digging, but onely for graves about three foote deepe: and therefore no marveile that they know neither quarries, nor lime-stones, which both may be in places neerer then they wot of.

In the meane time until there be discovery of sufficient store in some place or other convenient, the want of you which are & shalbe the planters therein may be as well supplied by bricke: for the making whereof in divers places of the Countrey there is clay both excellent good, and plentie, and also by lime made of oyster shels, and of others burnt, after the maner as they use in the Isles of Tenet and Shepy, and also in divers other places of England: Which kinde of lime is well knowen to be as good as any other. And of oyster shels there is plentie ynough: for besides divers other particular places where are abundance, there is one shallow Sound along the coast, where for the space of many miles together in length, and two or three miles in breadth, the ground is nothing els, being but halfe a foote or a foote under water for the most part.

Thus much can I say furthermore of stones, that about 120. miles from our fort neere the water in the side of a hill, was found by a Gentleman of our company, a great veine of hard ragge stones, which I thought good to remember unto you.

Of the nature and maners of the people.

It resteth I speake a word or two of the naturall inhabitants, their natures and maners, leaving large discourse thereof until time more convenient hereafter: nowe onely so farre foorth, as that you may know, how that they in respect of troubling our inhabiting and planting, are not to be feared, but that they shall have cause both to feare and love us, that shall inhabite with them.

They are a people clothed with loose mantles made of deere skinnes, and aprons of the same round about their middles, all els naked, of such a difference of statures only as wee in England, having no edge tooles or weapons of yron or steele to offend us withall, neither knowe they how to make any: those weapons that they have, are onely bowes made of Witch-hazle, and arrowes of reedes, flat edged truncheons also of wood about a yard long, neither have they any thing to defend themselves but targets made of barkes, and some armours made of sticks wickered together with thread.[7]

Their townes are but small, and neere the Sea coast but fewe, some contayning but tenne or twelve houses; some 20. the greatest that we have seene hath bene but of 30. houses: if they bee walled, it is onely done with barkes of trees made fast to stakes, or els with poles onely fixed upright, and close one by another.

Their houses are made of small poles, made fast at the tops in round forme after the maner as is used in many arbories in our gardens of England, in most townes covered with barkes, and in some with artificiall mats made of long rushes, from the tops of the houses downe to the ground. The length of them is commonly double to the breadth, in some places they are but 12. and 16. yards long, and in other some we have seene of foure and twentie.

In some places of the Countrey, one onely towne belongeth to the government of a Wiroans or chiefe Lord, in other some two or three, in some sixe, eight, and more: the greatest Wiroans that yet wee had dealing with, had but eighteene townes in his government, and able to make not above seven or eight hundreth fighting men at the most. The language of every government is different from any other, and the further they are distant, the greater is the difference.

Their maner of warres amongst themselves is either by sudden surprising one an other most commonly about the dawning of the day, or moone-light, or els by ambushes, or some subtile devises. Set battels are very rare, except it fall out where there are many trees, where either part may have some hope of defence, after the delivery of every arrow, in leaping behind some or other.

If there fall out any warres betweene us and them, what their fight is likely to bee, wee having advantages against them so many maner of wayes, as by our discipline, our strange weapons and devises else, especially Ordinance great and small, it may easily bee imagined: by the experience wee have had in some places, the turning up of their heeles against us in running away was their best defence.

In respect of us they are a people poore, and for want of skill and judgement in the knowledge and use of our things, doe esteeme our trifles before things of greater value: Notwithstanding, in their proper maner (considering the want of such meanes as we have), they seeme very ingenious. For although they have no such tooles, nor any such crafts, Sciences and Artes as wee, yet in

7. Sidenote: "Jaques Cartier, voyage 2. chap. 8."

those things they doe, they shew excellence of wit. And by how much they upon due consideration shall finde our maner of knowledges and crafts to exceede theirs in perfection, and speede for doing or execution, by so much the more is it probable that they should desire our friendship and love, and have the greater respect for pleasing and obeying us. Whereby may bee hoped, if meanes of good government be used, that they may in short time bee brought to civilitie, and the imbracing of true Religion.

Some religion they have already, which although it be farre from the trueth, yet being as it is, there is hope it may be the easier and sooner reformed.

They beleeve that there are many gods, which they call Mantoac, but of different sorts & degrees, one onely chiefe and great God, which hath bene from all eternitie. Who, as they affirme, when hee purposed to make the world, made first other gods of a principall order, to be as meanes and instruments to be used in the creation and government to follow, and after the Sunne, moone, and starres as pettie gods, and the instruments of the other order more principal. First (they say) were made waters, out of which by the gods was made all diversitie of creatures that are visible or invisible.

For mankinde they say a woman was made first, which by the working of one of the gods, conceived and brought foorth children: And in such sort they say they had their beginning. But how many yeeres or ages have passed since, they say they can make no relation, having no letters nor other such meanes as we to keepe Records of the particularities of times past, but only tradition from father to sonne.

They thinke that all the gods are of humane shape, and therefore they represent them by images in the formes of men, which they call Kewasowok, one alone is called Kewas: them they place in houses appropriate or temples, which they call Machicomuck, where they worship, pray, sing, and make many times offring unto them. In some Machicomuck we have seene but one Kewas, in some two, and in other some three. The common sort thinke them to be also gods.

They beleeve also the immortalitie of the soule, that after this life as soone as the soule is departed from the body, according to the workes it hath done, it is either caried to heaven the habitacle of gods, there to enjoy perpetuall blisse and happinesse, or els to a great pitte or hole, which they thinke to be in the furthest parts of their part of the world toward the Sunne set, there to burne continually: the place they call Popogusso.

For the confirmation of this opinion, they tolde me two stories of two men that had bene lately dead and revived againe, the one happened but few yeeres before our comming into the Countrey of a wicked man, which having bene dead and buried, the next day the earth of the grave being seene to move, was taken up againe, who made declaration where his soule had bene, that is to say, very neere entring into Popogusso, had not one of the gods saved him, and gave him leave to returne againe, and teach his friends what they should do to avoyd that terrible place of torment. The other happened in the same yeere we were there, but in a towne that was 60. miles from us, and it was told me for strange newes, that one being dead, buried, and taken up againe as the first, shewed that although his body had lien dead in the grave, yet his soule was alive, & had travailed farre in a long broad way, on both sides whereof grew most delicate and pleasant trees, bearing more rare and excellent fruits, then ever hee had seene before, or was able to expresse, and at length came to most brave and faire houses, neere which he met his father that had bene dead before, who gave him great charge to goe backe againe, and shew his friendes what good they were to doe to enjoy the pleasures of that place, which when he had done he should after come againe.

What subtiltie soever be in the Wiroances and priestes, this opinion worketh so much in many of the common and simple sort of people, that it maketh them have great respect to their Governours, and also great care what they doe, to avoyd torment after death, and to enjoy blisse, although notwithstanding there is punishment ordeined for malefactours, as stealers, whoremongers, and other sorts of wicked doers, some punished with death, some with forfeitures, some with beating, according to the greatnesse of the facts.

And this is the summe of their Religion, which I learned by having speciall familiaritie with some of their priests. Wherein they were not so sure grounded, nor gave such credite to their traditions and stories, but through conversing with us they were brought into great doubts of their owne, and no small admiration of ours, with earnest desire in many, to learne more then wee had meanes for want of perfect utterance in their language to expresse.

Most things they sawe with us, as Mathematicall instruments, sea Compasses, the vertue of the load-stone in drawing yron, a perspective glasse whereby was shewed many strange sights, burning glasses, wilde fireworkes, gunnes, hookes, writing and reading, springclockes that seeme to goe of themselves and many other things that wee had were so strange unto them, and so farre exceeded their capacities to comprehend the reason and meanes how they should be made and done, that they thought they were rather the workes of gods then of men, or at the leastwise they had bene given and taught us of the gods. Which made many of them to have such opinion of us, as that if they knew not the trueth of God and Religion already, it was rather to bee had from us whom God so specially loved, then from a people that were so simple, as they found themselves to be in comparison of us. Whereupon greater credite was given unto that wee spake of, concerning such matters.

Many times and in every towne where I came, according as I was able, I made declaration of the contents of the Bible, that therein was set foorth the true and onely God, and his mightie workes, that therein was conteined the true doctrine of salvation through Christ, with many particularities of Miracles and chiefe points of Religion, as I was able then to utter, and thought fit for the time. And although I told them the booke materially and of it selfe was not of any such vertue, as I thought they did conceive, but onely the doctrine therein conteined: yet would many be glad to touch it, to embrace it, to kisse it, to holde it to their breastes and heads, and stroke over all their body with it, to shew their hungry desire of that knowledge which was spoken of.

The Wiroans with whom we dwelt called Wingina, and many of his people would bee glad many times to be with us at our Prayers, and many times call upon us both in his owne towne, as also in others whither hee sometimes accompanied us, to pray and sing Psalmes, hoping thereby to be partaker of the same effects which we by that meanes also expected.

Twise this Wiroans was so grievously sicke that he was like to die, and as he lay languishing, doubting of any helpe by his owne priestes, and thinking hee was in such danger for offending us and thereby our God, sent for some of us to pray and bee a meanes to our God that it would please him either that he might live, or after death dwell with him in blisse, so likewise were the requests of many others in the like case.

On a time also when their corne began to wither by reason of a drought which happened extraordinarily, fearing that it had come to passe by reason that in some thing they had displeased us, many would come to us and desire us to pray to our God of England, that he would preserve their Corne, promising that when it was ripe we also should be partakers of the fruit.

There could at no time happen any strange sicknesse, losses, hurts, or any other crosse unto them, but that they would impute to us the cause or meanes thereof, for offending or not pleasing us. One other rare and strange accident, leaving others, wil I mention before I end, which moved the whole Countrey that either knew or heard of us, to have us in wonderfull admiration.

There was no towne where wee had any subtile devise practised against us, wee leaving it unpunished or not revenged (because we sought by all meanes possible to win them by gentlenesse) but that within a few dayes after our departure from every such Towne, the people began to die very fast, and many in short space, in some Townes about twentie, in some fourtie, and in one six score, which in trueth was very many in respect of their numbers. This happened in no place that we could learne, but where we had bin, where they used some practise against us, & after such time. The disease also was so strange, that they neither knewe what it was, nor how to cure it, the like by report of the oldest men in the Countrey never happened before, time out of minde. A thing specially observed by us, as also by the naturall inhabitants themselves. Insomuch that when some of the inhabitants which were our friends, and especially the Wiroans Wingina, had observed such effects in foure or five Townes to followe their wicked practises, they were perswaded that it was the worke of our God through our meanes, and that we by him might kill and slay whom we would without weapons, and not come neere them. And thereupon when it had happened that they had understanding that any of their enemies had abused us in our journeys, hearing that we had wrought no revenge with our weapons, and fearing upon some cause the matter should so rest: did come and intreate us that we would be a meanes to our God that they as others that had dealt ill with us might in like sort die, alleadging how much it would bee for our credite and profite, as also theirs, and hoping furthermore that we would doe so much at their requests in respect of the friendship we professed them.

Whose entreaties although wee shewed that they were ungodly, affirming that our God would not subject himselfe to any such prayers and requests of men: that indeede all things have bene and were to be done according to his good pleasure as he had ordeined: and that we to shewe our selves his true servants ought rather to make petition for the contrary, that they with them might live together with us, be made partakers of his trueth, and serve him in righteousnesse, but notwithstanding in such sort, that wee referre that, as all other things, to bee done according to his divine will and pleasure, and as by his wisedome he had ordeined to be best.

Yet because the effect fell out so suddenly and shortly after according to their desires, they thought nevertheless it came to passe by our meanes, & that we in using such speeches unto them, did but dissemble the matter, and therefore came unto us to give us thankes in their maner, that although we satisfied them not in promise, yet in deedes and effect we had fulfilled their desires.

This marveilous accident in all the Countrey wrought so strange opinions of us, that some people could not tell whether to thinke us gods or men, and the rather because that all the space of their sicknes, there was no man of ours knowen to die, or that was specially sicke: they noted also that we had no women amongst us, neither that we did care for any of theirs.

Some therefore were of opinion that we were not borne of women, and therefore not mortal, but that we were men of an old generation many yeeres past, then risen againe to immortalitie.

Some would likewise seeme to prophecie that there were more of our generation yet to come to kill theirs and take their places, as some thought the purpose was, by that which was already done.

Those that were immediatly to come after us they imagined to be in the aire, yet invisible and without bodies, and that they by our intreatie and for the love of us, did make the people to die in that sort as they did, by shooting invisible bullets into them.

To confirme this opinion, their Phisitions (to excuse their ignorance in curing the disease) would not be ashamed to say, but earnestly make the simple people beleeve, that the strings of blood that they sucked out of the sicke bodies, were the strings wherewithall the invisible bullets were tied and cast. Some also thought that wee shot them our selves out of our pieces, from the place where wee dwelt, and killed the people in any Towne that had offended us, as wee listed, howe farre distant from us soever it were. And other some said, that it was the speciall worke of God for our sakes, as we our selves have cause in some sort to thinke no lesse, whatsoever some doe, or may imagine to the contrary, specially some Astrologers, knowing of the Eclipse of the Sunne which we saw the same yeere before in our voyage thitherward, which unto them appeared very terrible. And also of a Comet which began to appeare but a fewe dayes before the beginning of the saide sicknesse. But to exclude them from being the speciall causes of so speciall an accident, there are further reasons then I thinke fit at this present to be alleadged. These their opinions I have set downe the more at large, that it may appeare unto you that there is good hope they may be brought through discreete dealing and government to the imbracing of the trueth, and consequently to honour, obey, feare and love us.

And although some of our company towards the end of the yeere, shewed themselves too fierce in slaying some of the people in some Townes, upon causes that on our part might easily ynough have bene borne withall: yet notwithstanding, because it was on their part justly deserved, the alteration of their opinions generally and for the most part concerning us is the lesse to be doubted. And whatsoever els they may be, by carefulnesse of our selves neede nothing at all to be feared.

The Conclusion.

Now I have (as I hope) made relation not of so few and small things, but that the Countrey (of men that are indifferent and well disposed) may bee sufficiently liked: If there were no more knowen then I have mentioned, which doubtlesse and in great reason is nothing to that which remaineth to be discovered, neither the soyle, nor commodities. As we have reason so to gather by the difference we found in our travailes, for although al which I have before spoken of, have bene discovered and experimented not farre from the Sea coast, where was our abode and most of our travailing: yet sometimes as we made our journeys further into the maine and Countrey; we found the soile to be fatter, the trees greater and to grow thinner, the ground more firme and deeper mould, more and larger champions, finer grasse, and as good as ever we saw any in England; in some places rockie and farre more high and hilly ground, more plentie of their fruites, more abundance of beastes, the more inhabited with people, and of greater pollicie and larger dominions, with greater townes and houses.

Why may wee not then looke for in good hope from the inner parts of more and greater plentie, as well of other things, as of those which wee have already discovered? Unto the Spaniards happened the like in discovering the maine of the West Indies. The maine also of this Countrey of Virginia, extending some wayes so many hundreds of leagues, as otherwise then by the relation of the inhabitants wee have most certaine knowledge of, where yet no Christian prince hath any possession or dealing, cannot but yeelde many kinds of excellent commodities, which we in our discovery have not yet seene.

What hope there is els to bee gathered of the nature of the Climate, being answerable to the Iland of Japan, the land of China, Persia, Jury, the Ilands of Cyprus and Candy, the South parts of Greece, Italy and Spaine, and of many other notable and famous Countreys, because I meane not to be tedious, I leave to your owne consideration.

Whereby also the excellent temperature of the aire there at all seasons, much warmer then in England, and never so vehemently hot, as sometimes is under and betweene the Tropikes, or neere them, cannot be knowen unto you without further relation.

For the holsomnesse thereof I neede to say but thus much: that for all the want of provision, as first of English victuall, excepting for twentie dayes, we lived onely by drinking water, and by the victuall of the Countrey, of which some sorts were very strange unto us, and might have been thought to have altered our temperatures in such sort, as to have brought us into some grievous and dangerous diseases: Secondly the want of English meanes, for the taking of beastes, fish and foule,[8] which by the helpe onely of the inhabitants and their meanes could not bee so suddenly and easily provided for us, nor in so great number and quantities, nor of that choise as otherwise might have bene to our better satisfaction and contentment. Some want also we had of clothes. Furthermore in al our travailes, which were most specially and often in the time of Winter, our lodging was in the open aire upon the ground. And yet I say for all this, there were but foure of our whole company (being one hundreth and eight) that died all the yeere, and that but at the latter ende thereof, and upon none of the aforesaide causes. For all foure, especially three, were feeble, weake, and sickly persons before ever they came thither, and those that knew them, much marveled that they lived so long being in that case, or had adventured to travaile.

Seeing therefore the aire there is so temperate and holsome, the soyle so fertile, and yeelding such commodities, as I have before mentioned, the voyage also thither to and fro being sufficiently experimented to be perfourmed twise a yeere with ease, and at any season thereof: And the dealing of Sir Walter Ralegh so liberall in large giving and granting lande there, as is already knowen, with many helpes and furtherances else: (The least that he hath granted hath bene five hundreth acres to a man onely for the adventure of his person) I hope there remaines no cause whereby the action should be misliked.

If that those which shall thither travaile to inhabite and plant bee but reasonably provided for the first yeere, as those are which were transported the last, and being there, doe use but that diligence and care, that is requisit, and as they may with ease: There is no doubt, but for the time following, they may have victuals that are excellent good and plentie ynough, some more English sorts of cattel also hereafter, as some have bene before, and are there yet remayning, may, and shall be (God willing) thither transported. So likewise, our kinde of fruites, rootes, and

8. Sidenote: "This want is hereafter to be supplied."

hearbes, may be there planted and sowed, as some have bene already, and prove well: And in short time also they may raise so much of those sorts of commodities which I have spoken of, as shall both enrich themselves, as also others that shall deale with them.

And this is all the fruit of our labours, that I have thought necessary to advertise you of at this present: What else concerneth the nature and maners of the inhabitants of Virginia, the number with the particularities of the voyages thither made, and of the actions of such as have bene by Sir Walter Ralegh therein, and there imployed, many worthy to be remembred, as of the first discoverers of the Countrey, of our Generall for the time Sir Richard Grinvil, and after his depar-ture of our Governour there Master Ralph Lane, with divers other directed and imployed under their government: Of the Captaines and Masters of the voyages made since for transportation, of the Governour and assistants of those already transported, as of many persons, accidents, and things els, I have ready in a discourse by it selfe in maner of a Chronicle, according to the course of times: which when time shall be thought conven-ient, shall be also published.

Thus referring my relation to your favourable constructions, expecting good success of the ac-tion, from him which is to be acknowledged the authour and governour, not onely of this, but of all things els, I take my leave of you, this moneth of February 1587.

Chapter Forty-eight
Plans for an English Colony
in New England and Acadia, 1592–1602

CHRISTOPHER CARLEILL took the personnel of his aborted venture in the summer of 1584 to man and settle a frontier post at Coleraine, on the fringes of the autonomous O'Neill territory in Ulster. Thereafter he continued to use Ireland as his base, performing various military tasks for the English administration there. He took a year off to accompany Sir Francis Drake on his West Indian voyage 1585–1586 but later returned to Ireland, although he came to England from time to time on visits. On one of these visits—probably after the death of his stepfather Sir Francis Walsingham in 1591—it appears that he teamed up for a time with Edward Hayes and together they produced a new treatise on the settlement of North America. The evidence on the authorship of the tract (which has remained unpublished) is so far completely internal evidence. That which links Hayes with its composition is convincing. Style, information, reference to previously held views leave no doubt that he was involved. The shorter version published in 1602 (368) is specifically attributed to him. The presentation is unpolished and the grammar at times imperfect—it has been given with very little change. It is notable that much of its information on French activities depends on material obtained by Hakluyt in France, 1583–1588. Much, though not all, is in the *Discourse of Western Planting*. Either Hakluyt passed the material to Hayes whom he knew, or else Carleill obtained it from Walsingham's papers where Hakluyt's *Discourse* and other papers could have been found. The association with Carleill is less explicit and rests largely in the reuse and development of ideas and statements already published by him in his *A breef and sommarie discourse* in 1583. But nothing came of the plan. Carleill was reported to have died in November, 1593. Printed from Cambridge University Library, MS Dc. 3.85, no. 4.

366. [Edward Hayes and Christopher Carleill]." "A discourse Concerning a voyage intended for the planting of Chrystyan religion and people in the North west regions of America in places most apt for the Constitution of our boddies, and the spedy advauncement of a state."

The Contents are followyng.

1. Of her Majesties Ryght unto all the Contries of America extended Northward from the Cape of Florida. Chapter. 1.

2. That our Churche & fayth shall receyve great advancement & propagation by perfourmance of thys Action. Chapter. 2.

3. Of the Scituation & temperature of those places we choose fyrst to inhabit and of the diversities of Comodities to be raysed there. Chapter. 3.

4. Of the inestimable benifit that we shall fynd, by planting ourselves neare unto the Newfoundlan[d] in regard of the yearly trade & concourse unto the fyshing. By meanes whearof we

shall readely vent our Comodities, and be Supplyed of our wants. And shall after a whyle remove the trade from Newfoundland unto us. Chapter. 4.

5. A Confutation of theyr error which hould those Contries of no value, unles that Meyns of goold and Sylver may there be found. And which doo Contein these gross Comodities before mentioned. The same being nevertheless most needfull for the State of England, to imploye our people & Shypps. And Shall procure unto us both goold & Sylver and also preciouse wares. Chapter. 5.

6. That thys Action shalbe accomplished with easy charges, and Continued wythowt just cause of dowt to be by any other Nation Supplanted. Chapter. 6.

7. Of a passage certaynly to be found (at least by Som part overland) from the places we intend (by gods assistance) to inhabit, into the South Sea or back Sea of those lands. By meanes whearof, all soarts of ryche comodities of the East world, shall Conveniently be brought unto us thyther. From whence agayn, our Merchaunts of England may featche the same of us at all tymes of the yeare and make retourns comonly every 3. Monethes. Chapter. 7.

1

Of her Majesties Ryght unto all the Contries
of America extended Northward from the
Cape of Florida.

Forasmuche as we have intent (by gods assistance) to plant Christian Inhabitants & trew religion in a remote & heathen land: I thynk good to sheaw briefly, that th'English Nation hath ryght thearunto before any other amongst Chrystians. To the end that the Action being entred & begon upon a ryght, we may hoap of better success.

It hath ben observed & held for ryght amongst Christian prynces even to thys daye, that whatsoever lands have ben recovered by any kinge from Infidells. or being before unknown, have ben discovered: the same to be the proper dominions and Inheritance of that prynce & hys successors.

For by thys custome the kings of Portingall have enjoyed theyr so ample Territories and kyngdoms both of the Ilands & Continents of Affrycke, America & Asia called the East Indes.

In lyke sorte the kynges of Spayn have possessed theyrs in America called the West Indes. And by the same reason also is her Majestie the Successor & ryghtfull Inheritor unto all those ampell dominions of America extended from the 38. degres of Septentriall Latitude, unto the Cape of Labrador in 58. Which large tract of lands was fyrst discovered by thenglish Nation under the conduct of Gabott & hys Sonns in the tyme of kyng Henry the vij^th. And hath remayned ever since unpossessed, though often attempted by other Christian prynces. As yf God had deffended the ryght of England agaynst both the Spanyards & Frenche. And had reserved those Contries to be by us converted unto the fayth at hys appoynted tyme.

For the Spanyards veary prosperouse in theyr Southern discoveries have proved as infortunate in all theyr Northerly attempts. So have the Portingalls in seking a passage into the South Sea by the Northwest Regions of America.

Whearyn it may seme by theyr ill success reported in theyr own hystories, that god hath appoynted theyr lymytts not to excede North of Florida.

Lyke ill success hath happened unto the Frenche seking to intrude possession upo[n] the English ryght. Who, notwythstanding theyr many discoveries into these lands, and attempts to plant themselves: could never yet obtayn theare a settled possession & goverment, yet in theyr relations, have hyghly commended the Contries, Clymats & people.

The reason hearof to our seming was undowtedly want (both in the Spanyards & Frenche) of meanes which we have long had. Namly, peace & people.

For France hath ben long afflicted with Cyvyll warrs. And Spayn wanteth people to replenish theyr wyde & vaste Indes. Which lye subject to every small & souddayn invasion, by reason the Contries are veary thynnly inhabited of Portingalls & Spanyards.

But Seing that we have both ryght & meanes to possess these Contries before other Nations: We may be thought veary remiss in so long neglecting the benifyyts which God hath offred unto us. By meanes of our longe & happy peace, and multituds of spare people, to plant, and to possess those ample & most fertile Contries.

2

That our Churche & fayth shall receyve great advancement & propagation by perfourmance of thys Action.

Our adversaries have noted thys to be a veary great deffect in our Churche. that we have not Converted Infidells unto the fayth. And doe arrogat unto theyr Romish churche, the Conversion of pagans (in the East & West Indes) as a singuler preheminence & propper marck of the trew churche. It shalbe therfo[re] a great honor & advancement unto our Churche: lyke as the same hath doone in the fyrst & primative state: So now agayn in thys latter are to travayll in sowyng the Seed of pure Religion in those exceeding large & popolus Nations lyeng to the Northwest of America and to sett them free from the Captivetie of the dyvell. Who houldeth them under miserable Idolatry & paganisme being nevertheles found a people docible & veary capable of Christianitie.

And lyke as the Portingalls & Spaniards haue travaylled worthely in bryngyng many spatious Contries & kyngdoms in the East & west parts of the world into the fayth, yet not wythowt myxture of superstition & error whearyn never the less they have prospered, bycause they preache Christ: Even so, thys la[rge] portion of America (greater than Europe) falleth into the lott of our Nation to be converted unto the fayth. Because God dyd fyrst discover the same unto us which in Scituation & temperature is nearest unto, and seme[th] to be reserved for us. No Nation havyng the power hytherto (according to theyr sondry intents & attempts) to possess the same actually.

We must beleve by Chryst hys own prophesy that the gospell shalbe preached throughout the world: We may also beleve that the same shalbe carryed into these Northwest Regions of America, which are a veary great portion of the world and never yet preached vnto.

Onto thys infallible prediction of Christ, I wyll drawe a probable conjecture allso from the Revolution of Gods word, which hytherto hath moved Cyrcularly.

For lyke as the same begann in the East in paradice, And moved westwards in[to] Palestina, And at length into Europe. thear beginning in the East also proceded by South into the west, and spredd afterwards North: Even from Europe it hath contynewed hys Revolution west into America, wh[ile] it begann East: proceded South & west. And may happely more purely [be] preached also in the North by us. Unto which tyme (thys being the last of the last Age of the world:) we are now arryved. And therfore may ho[pe] by so muche the more, of our good success in thys Action now. Seing the last dayes are come upon us. And that now or never theyr conversion is to [be] expected.

Whearupon veary many zealouse men, are moved by the same Charitable Spyrit towards those paganish Americans. whearby holy men in elder tymes were styrred upp to the converting of us (in these North & than obscure regions of Europe) unto the Chrystyan fayth which we now enjoye by the same meanes. And withowt which we also had contynued Barbarouse unto thys daye.

Therfore doo desyer, Aswell for the saving of innumerable Soules amongst those Barbarians, As to supply that deffect in our churche (before noted by Our Adversar[ie]) to venter theyr Substance & persons in so honorable attempt as thys: to plant [or] to establish Religion in those remote lands. Which canot be doon without a habitation of Chrystians fyrst settled thear & Contynued.

3

Of the Scituation & temperature of those places we choose fyrst to inhabit. And of the dyversitie of comodities to be raysed there.

Those Contries which amongst others we chiefly respect doe lye under temperat Clymes. betwen 40. & 50. degres of latitude. in the veary same Scituation & parallels of Italy France and the most fertile & best inhabited Contries of Europe. Well agreing with the Constitution of our boddies. Which ought to be a specyall regard, in making choyse of new habitations.

And Albeit the Sonns heate is qualyfyed, by hys Course alltogither over the occean, After he leaveth the Coasts of Europe, untyll he arryveth upon the Coasts of America. Attracting aboundance of vapor from the Sea. By meanes wherof all the East & owter parts of America, are less hoatt than the Contries of Europ & Affryck answerable unto the same Clymats. Which have not the lyke accidens of Seas, to mynister vapor so aboundantly: Nevertheles unto us. that myttigation of heate shalbe benifycyall. Seing that the heat of Sommer in Italy and all placcs clsc of Europe under 40 degrie[s] (being not hyndred by accidentall causes) is unto our boddies offensyve, Which cannot prosper in dry and scalding heates. more naturall to the Spaniard than us.

Lyke as also the pearchyng heat of sommer there is qualifyed & tempered to the Consti[tution] of our boddies: Even so the rigor & continuance of wynter is also myttigated & Shortned, by reason of the Sonns propinquitie & nearnes unto them in 40.degres lyttle more or less. Wheare the Sonne in hys greatest declynation and progression into the South, in December, is elevated 27.degres almost above theyr orison. And is than but 15. degrees hygh with us at London. Which difference wyll produce a more tymely Spryng, Longer Sommer, & shorter wynter with them than with us in England by a Moneth at least.

Then forasmuche as the places intended of our habitations in America shalbe on the same parallels of Italy & France in 40. & 44. (or thearabowts:) It canot be that those clymes which in Europe are over hoatt for our boddies, shoold be over could in America, as some have surmised the same to be.

The Course from England thyther is not long, which may be accomplished comonly in 30 dayes or under. Is alltogither through the occean, apt for most wynds that can blowe, the trade aleways open & free from restraynt by forren prynces. which is a benifyt wanting in all our other trades, and hath ben no small anoyance unto our Marchaunts.

The Coasts along those contries are fayer, and in all respects Comodiouse for traffyck, havyng goodly Bayes, Roads, and harbors for shypps, with places apt to be fortefyed & made defensible agaynst any force that can be brought thyther.

Comodities are & wylbe: videlicet.

Fysh of exceding largeries and aboundance more vendible for England & France then the Newland fysh for the most part. Besyds that we may fysh upon those southern coasts at all tymes of the yeare. which we canot doe upon the Newfoundland & coulder regions.

Salt is found in some places so good (by relation of a Frenche man) as that of Bourage in France. otherwayes it may be made by Arte thear to fournish all the fyshyng ether by heat of the Sonn, or by fyer whear wood is so plentifull.

Whales & Seales in abundance. Whearof we may make oyles to serve all England Also of other fyshes in great varietie as herrings. Bonitas. Tunnis: Lobsters. Salmonds with infinite more. oysters havyng pearle. All which besyds tha[t] the same shall minister unto us (that shall inhabit theare) plenty of food: wylbe also in tyme proffitable for trade.

The Soyle is exceding good consisting both of woodlands, champions & pleasaunt Meadowes. But overstrong untill by manurance it be fyned. In the mean tyme it will beare aboundantly. Hemp. flax. Rape seeds. and whatsoever else that doo requyre suche strength of soyle as thys must have. which never was used from the beginning of the world hytherto so farr as is known.

Vynes grow there withowt industry. Bearing nevertheles good grapes. In lyke sort there grow peason. Roses. Respasses. Hemp. Besyds infinit kynds of plants. hearbs. fruits. and flowers. the great varietie. pleasaunt view and odoriferous savour of all which Simpells, produced by nature, withowt help of Arte: doo gyve argument sufficient, how dylectable & fruytfull Contries the same may be made by the industry of skyllfull & ingenuouse inhabitaunts.

Myneralls in many places appeare veary evydently. A ryche Moyne of Copper hath ben discovered by certayn Frenche men of late. The place is made known unto us by description, and of the Mettall hath ben brought some proofe into England. Not far from the same place is gyven us also great hoap of Syluer Allam is sayd to be there also. Quarries of stone most fayer and of Sondry Coullors for curiouse buyldings.

The Salvage people doe weare in Skynns & other theyr attyre, fayer coullors which gyve us hoap of ryche dyes & coullors for paynting.

There grow myghty trees of Fyrr, pyne & cedar. abell to Mast the greatest shypps of the world. And to make Tarr. pytche. Rosen. Soap Ashes. Tymberrs and excellent Board. There grow also Oakes. Ashes. and other trees servyng to all uses.

Beasts of sondry kynds. Somme of the Bygnes of an oxe. apt (no dowt) unto the yoake: and to other uses, not muche unlyke the Buffell. theyr Hydes make excellent Buff. Aboundance of Deare both redd and other soarts: Lucerns. Martins. Sabulls. Beares. Woolves. Beavers. foxes & Squyrylls which to the Northward are black and esteemed to be rycche furrs. There be other kynds of Beasts to us unknown. But generally. theyr hydes. Skynns & furrs wylbe ryche Comodities. As proofe hath been made by certayn Frenche men. Who have in secreat manner frequented those coasts. And by trucking with the Salvages. for theyr pettie wares they have retourned of the foarsayd comodities into France. wheare they have gayned 14. upon one.

Fowles. both of water and land. As Ducks. Bustards. Swanns. penguynns–which is a fowle of a great boddy and small wyngs, not abell to flye. And are therfore taken with great ease, by dryvyng them (as flocks of sheepe) into the strayght. they beare most excellent feathers, delycat for stuffing of Bedds. Also. Hawkes both short & long wynged. patridges. veary great & easily taken. Heathcocks. other fowles and Byrds great & of infinit varietie & nomber. whearof many are lyke. and others unlyke unto ours of Europe.

Ryvers. veary many descending from the Mowntayns. But how farr they extend into the land is unknown. They are all stoared aboundantly with fysh veary delicat. Amongst many other Ryvers yet unknown: Two are of most fame. One abowt 40 degrees. called (thowgh falsly) Norombega. Whose aboundant streame causeth the Sea whear it dischargeth to be in a maner fresh. Thother is of us comonly called St. Laurence. but of the Inhabitaunts whose name it beareth) Canada. which by sondry Frenche men hath ben searched and found navygable many leagues. But for Boates or vessells of good burden it is not found portable more than a thousand english myles into the land. It leadeth further (as hath ben gathered by intelligence from those inhabitaunts) unto a great Lake (which is fresh at the issue of the Ryver. but beyond is bytter or salt. and non[e] could gyve knowledge how farr the same extendeth. At the Mowth of thys ryver is scytuated the same Land which we call Newfoundland. being an Iland or Consisting of many Ilands or broken lands. Betwen Newfoundland and Cape Brytton in 46. or thearebowts, is one entrance into the sayd ryver. And at the grand

Bay in 52 de[gres] is an other by the north syde of Newfoundland. whear the Byskayes have a great whale fyshing. The ryver, from grand Baye, enclyneth to Sowth west by lyttell & lyttel, and is discovered unto 45 degres of latitude alongst the North-syde whearof lye veary goodly Contries of Canada. Saguenay. Hochelaga and others. The lyke or no dowt better, lye on the South Syde, and ar both sydes well peopled. the fyelds replenished with Corne or Maiz. pasture & vynes. besyds aboundance of fruits and other delyghts, which are brought forth more by the bowntie of Nature, then by help of Arte.

So as by consideration of the premisses. we shalbe abell by the industry and skyll of our people when they are planted, to rayse these comodities both of the Sea & land. Nam[ely] Fysh & Salt. Oyles of whales & Seales. pearles. Grapes. raysins wynes. Corne flax flaw. Hemp. lynen cloath. Sayll cloath. Cabulls Roapes. Tarr. pytche. Rose[n.] Turpentine. Soape ashes. Soap. Rape Seeds & oyles. Masts. tymbers & Boards of ceda[r] and pynes. Hydes. Skynns & furrs. Dyes. Coulors for paynting. Mettalls & other Myneralls. Besyds other manifold Comodities which are there to be found, Servyng both to mayntayn trade, and to sustayn armies of men wyth varietie of Beasts. fysh & fowle to content every tast.

4

Of the inestimable benifit that we shall fynd by planting our selves neare unto the Newfoundland. In regard of the yearly trade & concourse unto the fyshing. By meanes whearof we shall readely vent our Comodities. and be supplyed of our wants. And shall after a whyle remove the trade from Newfoundland unto us.

In all attempts of new discoveries and planting of people in places remote & unfrequented, the greatest difficultie is in the beginning to procure supplies in due tyme. which unto the Adventrers and setters foorth of suche actions, is a heavy and dead charge, untill comodities may be rayse[d] and a goverment established; whearby Merchaunts may be induced for a certayn gayn to repayr unto those places wyth shypping. and for the comodities of that place to bryng others in supply of the new Inhabitors.

When thys is brought to pass: all difficulties are

overcome, and those Contries may allwayes b[e] demed happy & flourishing states, wheare pollecy & industry are used to provyde Comoditie[s] and ready meanes to vent the same. for it is trade that inrycheth Contries and causeth the same to abound in wealth & prosperitie. Therfore have the founders of most famouse Cytties, had specyall regard to scituat the same in convenient places for traffyck. And framed all meanes possible to draw trade unto them.

Then in what forwardnes are our intended places of new habitation browght allready to the obtay[n]inng of great wealth & prosperitie. Seing that unto the fertilitie of the Soyle, and fytt matter of many vendible comodities: there is also added thys benifit of an exceding great trade & concourse of Merchaunts, which frequent the same Coasts yearly with 3 or 400. Sayles of Shypps at the least. only for the comoditie of fysh & whale oyles. So as nothing is wanting to perfect and make a state thear Compleat, But only to transport people thyther. ingeniouse & industriouse. Which also shalbe a matter of much facilitie Considring that in England we have a multitude of distressed people, both of Menn Women & chyldren, which the realme may happely spare: And that veary many shypps doo yearly goe from hence unto the same coasts (wythowt any frayght or other lading then vyttaylls & some quantitie of Salt.) by whom we shall have both people & provysyons conveniently transported.

These be reasons whearupon is ground an assurance of great & spedy success to follow in thys Action. which being once well entred and sett one foote: wyll stand and goe forward of it self. with incredible increase of honor & gayn unto the Actors. for what can be more avayling to advance a state. then A Contry Copiouse of Comodities by the bountie of Nature: people industriouse & skyllfull to prepare them: Shypps in readines to vent them, and to bryng others agayn.

Of these: two are allready effected before we begynn. And the thyrd shall not be hard to effect. Namely.

1. The Contries selected to plant upon: doe mynister the Subject & matter of many notable Comodities.

2. The trade unto Newfoundland adjoyning: shall fournish us of shypping sufficiente.

3. The spare & distressed people of England: as they shalbe happely rydd owt of the realme: So wyll they be wyllyng to goe thyther for gayn, and may conveniently be carryed by our shypps repayring yearly unto those coasts.

Then what Action of the world can be thought upon. of so great importaunce & ease for our Nation to accomplish, as thys. By carryeng only of people, which wyllyngly and conveniently may be carryed hense: to possess and enjoy most fertile Contries incomparable wealth.

Wyth farr greater difficulties, of long & daungerouse Navigations: of fair and unknown Coasts: of contagiouse & untemperat Regions: of armed Nations and walled Townes have the Portingalls & Spanyards with veary feaw people obtayned theyr most ample & ryche Domynions in bothe East & west Indes. Whear they have buylded Townes & fortresses. and made places (before obscure & desolate) to be frequented with trade. And these great attempts dyd they take in hand. upon a beare imagination of suche lands to be; and even when the wownds recyved in their warrs agaynst the Moores were grene or scarce healed.

How muche easier shall it be for us, that have enjoyed so long peace (whearby our people are increased exceedingly, and fayle of imployments:) to possess & injoye Contries so neare unto us: temperat: allready discovered & known: frequented with trade[:] fruytfull: the people unarmed and Townes weakly or not at all fensed: the inhabitaunts tractable. unto cyvilitie & obedience. which Contries & nearest parts after the same are possessed, Shall give us way unto greater & rycher kyngdoms and passage into the back and South Sea unto Cathay China the Molucces, and all the East Regions of the world, yealding most ryche & preciouse thyngs unto the possessing, and possession mayntayning of which Contries: we have thear allwa[yes] so great a trade of English: Frenche. Portingall & Spanish Merchaunts. as no other place or coast unfrequented, can scarce be procured in a mans Age, nor with expence of half a Myllyon. By meanes whearof, shall we have brought thyther in exchaunge of ours: all maner of comodities that Europe doth yeald. ether to Supply our wants, or to advaunce our wealth. And our habi[tacions] wylbe made A staple & receptacle both of Comodities deryved from the same Countr[ies] and also of English. Frenche & Spanysh wares.

For Considring that Marchaunts are curiouse inquisitors after gayn; and wyll leave one place and frequent another wearsoever they see advauntage unto theyr trade: It may not than be dowted. But all Men wyll leave to trade the Newfoundland, and remo[ve] unto us (near adjoyning:) when they shall understand that we have better, & greater varietie of comodities, and may better cheap affoord them, then they can provyde theyr lading of fysh & oyles at the Newfoundland.

For yf we conferr the nature & condition togither of the trade unto Newfoundland, wyth that they shall fynd with us: it shall appeare veary evydently. that Merchaunts shall with greater securitie & gayn have traffyck with us, than upon the Newland Coasts. Bycause unto the Newfoundland theyr voyage must be perfourmed in the Somer tyme only—in respect of could & aboundance of Ise brought down from the hygher contries in the wynter, at what tyme also, it is thought that the fysh doo forsake the coast. There are no places fortefyed to secure theyr shipps & goods. Which are many tymes therfore spoyled by pyrats. or they are dryven to kepe togither so many in a harbor, as the place canot affoord them convenient meanes to dres & make theyr fysh: They vyctuall and Mann theyr Shipps dooble in respect that the labor is great, and the tyme long of theyr fyshing for many tymes that voyage is of vi and 9. or 12. Monethes for the whale-fyshyng. Theyr provision of Salt is to many veary chargeable. They carry owtward no frayght to make benifit. And retourn nothyng but fysh & oyles after theyr tediouse & chargeable voyage. Add hearunto the charges of Netts. hookes & lynes. and Boates or pynnaces to goe owt to take theyr fysh at sea. which Boates they are dryven yearly to supply with new for the most part. and 8. of them for every shypp of a hondred tonns: these Conferred togither, shall gyve cause of wonder, how by fysh alone the Merchaunt can save hym self. yet is there good gayn dowtles gotten hearby. Or else it would not be so muche used.

On thother syde. The places we intend (by Gods permission) to inhabit: Are temporat and at all tymes to be occupyed. fysh never fayle there Harbors shalbe fortefied & guarded to secure the Merchaunts. and great regard to intertayn them with all humanitie Charges shalbe abridged of dooble vyttayling & manning theyr shypps. Bycause theyr lading shalbe all wayes prepared unto theyr hands, and no cause of staye above 10 dayes. No necessitie to bryng salt thyther. unles to sell. which we shall not nede in regard that by nature it is there found: or by industry we may conveniently make it. They shall then carry frayght owtward also. to Supply us and the Contries wyth in land of all thyngs needfull. And so make benifyt of that voyage both wayes. Other charges of theyr Neets. hookes. lynes. and Boates shalbe all cutt of. And for one comoditie of the Newfoundland: shalbe retourned 20. as vendible.

These reckonnings Merchaunts wyll soone grow into. And presently fall into traffyck with us. the sooner. in that we plant so neare unto theyr accustomed places of trade in the Newfoundland, and that one same course by sea, wyll serve in a maner for both. So as yf at the beginning they may be dowtfull to fynd lading wyth us: they wyll yet easely be induced to visit us under hoape of gayn. Which yf it shoold fayle: they may nevertheles fall unto the Newfoundland with lyttle loss of tyme. But after they shall fynd with us better fyshing, with so great increase of other Comodities: then wyll they be wonn unto us for ever.

Then lyke as the Frenche. Portingalls & Spanyards. wyll bryng unto us Wynes Sugars. Spyces. Swete oyles. goold & Sylver, in exchaunge of our fysh. Oyles of the whale & Seall. Corne. pytch & tarr. Cabulls. roapes. Masts. & cetera (of all which provisions, we shalbe able to furnish all comers thyther, at a farr easier rate, than the same are brought through the Sounds of Denmarck:) Even so for our goold & sylver. and all other our comodities deryved ether from our soyle theare, or from forren parts: our English Merchaunts wyll bryng unto us agayn: Cloath: Cattell for our stoare & brede: and all thyngs else that England may happe[n] spare for suche exchaunge. By which meanes our Cloath shall notable vent into all the Cold regions of America, lyeng North, and extended infinitly from thence As also by a trade we shall in tyme make way for into the South Sea, as shalbe proved in a chapter of that argument followyng.

These reasons doo brede in me an Assurance of wonderfull spedy success & advancement in thys, before any Action of lyke nature in the world.

Bycause that all places wheresoever, not allready frequented with trade: canot in many yeares, nor without muche expence have suche a trade brought unto them, as hath ben these many yeares established upon the coasts of Newfoundland.[1] which concourse wylbe easely & spedely removed unto our habitations, planted so neare unto them. for the reasons before mentioned. Besyds that. suche as doe repayr unto us, shalbe exempted from many exactions which shalbe imposed upon them that styll frequent the Newfoundland. which wyll the rather also bryng them unto us.

For Considring that the fletes Comyng to Newfoundland are sequestred and dispersed into sondry harbors: And that they must send owt theyr Boates to fysh in the open sea: It shalbe an easy matter ether to compell them to yeald unto our Impositions, or to disturb theyr fyshing so, as they shall not be abell to make theyr voyage. Yf only we mayntayn certayn Gallies upon the Coasts to such intent: But undowtedly they wyll yeald unto any reasonable imposition, rather then hasard theyr boddies & goods. Seing that fysher men and Men of theyr qualitie. doo seke for proffit, and stand not muche upon tearmes of honor, to hyndir theyr comoditie.

Thys also shalbe a meanes. to advance a great revenew by the Newland fyshing lyke as the kyng of Denmarcke useth to doe in all the fyshings & trades upon hys Domynions. Which is the greatest portion of hys revenewes.

5

A Confutation of theyr error. Which holde these Contries of no value onles that Moynes of goold & Sylver may theare be found. And which doo contem these gross comodities before mentioned. The same being nevertheles most needfull for the state of England to imploy our people & shipps. And shall procure unto us both goold and Sylver, and other preciouse wares.

Many veary inconsideratly doe holde thys error: and are persuaded that no remote land newly to be planted, is worthy regard & estimation:

1. Sidenote: "Yf the Colonie planted in Virginia, had chosen theyr habitation neare unto thys trade: they must have prospered beyond all mens expectations."

unles the same by ryche in goold & Sylver Moynes.

To whom I shape thys answer.

That we have hoape also of Sylver Moynes. And of other Mettalls assurance. Nevertheless goold & Syluer Moynes are found most plentifull in hoatt & untemperat Regions.

But. Seing that other gross (yet needfull) comodities, which our intended Countries of new habitation doe yeald aboundantly: and whearof those Contries stand in nede, which possess the fountayns of treasure: shall purchase unto us goold & sylver, dwelling under temperat & holesome clymats: Then how muche better shall it be for us there to possess goold & Sylver in health of boddy & delyght,: than for gredy desyer to possess the Moynes, to depryve our selves of all health & delight by dwelling in Contries wythyn the burning zoanes. whear the heate or Ayer shalbe unto our complexions intemperat & contagiouse. Nature hath framed the Spanyards apt to suche places. Who prosper in drye & burning habitations. But in us she abhorreth suche. And by proofe we know that the English Nation never thryved so well as in the Contries of Gascoign and Guienne in France. which are under the same parallels whear we intend to plant.

It is not Moynes of goold & Sylver which make a comonwealth & state to floorish. For than shoold the desart and obscure Regions of Affryck & America (abounding in Moyns) have ben most famous Nations. But A temperat & holesome land: well peopled: replenished with comodities albeit gross, yet needfull for mans use: Aptly scytuated for concourse & recourse of Nations to the mayntenaunce of trade: These be the matters & fytt foundations to reare & advance a state spedely.

The fower Monarchies of the world past. Namly. th'Assirians. Meads & Persians. Grekes & Romayns. were not raysed unto theyr greatnes by meanes of goold & Sylver Moynes, which were never found veary plentifull amongst any of those kingdoms.

Nether in France is found to thys daye any such Moynes. which nevertheles is the rychest & myghtiest Nation of Europe. howsoever the same is now wasted by cyvile warrs.

The states of the Low Contries and Antwerp.

which have overgone all Cytties of Europe (in thys age) in ryches & aboundance of all thyngs: hath had no dealings nor increase by goold or Sylver Moyns.

The same may be averred of the honorable state of Venice. of thys most happy & puissant kyngdom of England. And generally. Nether these mentioned, nor any states else of the known world, have obtayned theyr greatnes, by the meanes of goold & Sylver Moynes found wythyn, or neare unto any of them.

But by the valor of the Inhabitants & people in Conquering: theyr Arte & industry in raysing of comodities & drawyng traffyck unto them: and theyr pollecy in governing, they have ben fyrst advanced, and are continewed in theyr gretnes.

For. Whosoever dooth Comaund over a fraytfull soyle, and muche people: may soone be great.

Now touching owr gross comodities, how necessary the same shalbe both for the realm of England, and all the South & west Nations of Europe specyally: Lett it be considr[ed] by the particularities. Namly. Fysh. oyles. Soap Ashes & Soap. Rosen. turpentyne. Tarr. pytche. Masts. Boords & tymber of cedar fyrr & pynes for ex-quisit & curiouse buyldings. flax. Hemp. lynen cloat[h.] cloath for sayles. Cabulls & Roapes. grapes. raysins & wynes. fruits. Corne. rape Seeds & oyles. Hydes. Skynns. furrs. Dyes. Col-ours for paynting. Mettalls & other Myneralls. Besyds other comodities. All which dowtles may be drawn owt of those Regions of America, yf once it may be peopled with industriouse and Ingeniouse Inhabitants. for the Subject and Symples of the same Comodities are apparauntly known to be thear. So as people are only wanting, And we in England are overburdened, and as it were pestred with people. If therfore many, yea 20 thousand of our spare people, (not all men of servyce, but wemen & chyldren, and such also as can but serve to turne & dry a fysh:) were sent and imployed into those Contries there to in-habit,: as conveniently they mey be transporte[d] by shypps that doe yearly from hence unto the fyshyng at Newfoundland withowt frayght: It shoold both ease the realme of our superfluouse people, and bryng muche wealth & happines & honor unto the state; with increase of our shypps & Marryners, by so great increase of trade. the

want whearof hath caused our poarts to fall into decaye and dooth increase Idelnes & beggary wythyn the realme.

But amongst many other benifits: thys shalbe of veary great importaunce and Consequence for the Securitie & strength of thys Realme. That is to saye.–

All provisions needfull for the rygging & trymmyng of our Navyes: shalbe than made wythin her Majesties own Domynions of America: By her own subjects: and safely browght hyther wythowt molestation or restraynt of forren pow-ers. which shall not be feared in a course through the occean hyther. Whearas now we receyve the same provisions from & through many forren dominions. Whearby we canot so frely enjoy them. Seing that upon accidents occurryng in state affayrres, we may be barred from them, to the weakning of our puissant Nauyes, the royall defenses of thys noble Realme. The feare hearof dooth make our Merchants to indure many molestations & Injuries at the Easterlings hands & other prynces in the North. Whearof I have heard many complayn. with protestatio[n] that they woold forsake veary wyllingly the eastern trades (grown full of troobles & new impositions:) yf in these Norwest regions they myght be as-sured to fynd the same comodities.

Then yf upon so just occasion gyven unto our Merchaunts to forsake the East, and to remove theyr trade into the west, we shalbe abell to draw them unto us, when we shalbe planted: what great advancement shall grow thereby unto our new erected state, may well be conjectured, by the infynit wealth that the East States have ob-tayned by repayr of our Nation unto them. who have all wayes thys blissing followyng them: that unto what places soever they repayr to be theyr comon Marts, the same doo spedely grow unto rype[ness] of wealth & prosperitie. which also ceaseth, when our Nation forsaketh the pla[in] Examples. of the Low Contries. and all the Haunse Townes. also of all the tra[des] our Mer-chaunts have most frequented in Europe. But Antwerp above the [rest] gave confyrmation hearof. whan wyth solem precession & state with apparaunce of exceding joye in all degres and sexes: they brought our Merchants into theyr cyttie, who before had forsaken the same & were agayn reconcy[led] into theyr prystinat amytie & entercourse. Reknowledging thearyn that theyr happynes grew and decayed by entertayning or loosing suche amitie or enterco[urse] with our Nation.

By this I inferr. That. As by reason of late discontentments our Merchaunts haue received in our East trades: and also th'oportunitie of suche comodities in the Northwest, they wyll easely be induced to remove theyr east trade vnto us: Even so. our Nation shalbe not less happy to inryche [them]selves. Then the same hath ben to inryche other Nations. But more happy shall we be hearyn: both by qualifyeng the intollerable exactions by forren st[ates] imposed upon our Merchaunts: and also by conferryng the proffytts unto [them]selves. whearby we have hytherto inryched & exalted other Nations apt to requyte us but veary badly.

Therfore to Conclude thys chapter. Forasmuche as the Contries we intend (by Gods g[race]) to inhabit, are temperat & healthfull: fytt to brede & to nourish people of st[rong] & abell boddyes: Replenished with varietie & plentie of needfull comodities: scituated veary conveniently for concourse & recourse of Nations: hath allready a great & frequent trade upon the Newland Coasts adjoyning. Which may easely be removed unto us, and shall in the mean whyle furnish us of supply: shall also fournish England of all provisyons for our Navyes, with greater Securitie u[nto] the state, & comoditie unto our Merchaunts. By which meanes we may also draw that, or most part of the east trade unto us, And make our selves no less ha[ppy] thereby, then we have made forren Nations: These be reasons auayling to the erection & spedy advancement of a state & comon weale. which may induce every man (capable of hys good & preferment) to joyn with us in thi[s] Action. whose estate heare is not so well grounded & secure, as that in no place else it may be bettred.

6

That thys Action shalbe accomplished with easy charges and continewed withowt just cause of dowt to be by any other Nation Supplanted.

Twoo difficulties have ben chyfly objected agaynst thys Action. Namely: objections.

1. In respect of the charges it is thought to be an action fytt for a prynce of wealth & power, and not for pryvat men to attempt.

2. That we shalbe supplanted ether by the Salvages, or by Chrystians which challenge Interest, and have intent also to plant in the same contries.

Solution of the fyrst objection.

Touching the fyrst objection I answer. That all difficultie of charges and expence, is even in the entraunce into thys Action. Bycause they are veary feaw which have a ryght conceyt of the same. and the comon sort are to be ledd more by judgement of theyr sences, then by probable reasons and conjectures. Therfore the charges in the begynning must be drawn from veary feaw, whearby the burden to every Man wylbe the greater. But after one voyage or two perfourmed with gayn: there wylbe hands inough to the edefyeng of thys worke. For the English man by nature is slow to begynn a matter whearyn appeareth difficultie & dowbt: But is vehement in prosecuting & followyng. whearby I am persuaded, that we must have lawes devysed in England hearafter, to deteyn our people wythyn the realme, which otherwayes wyll goe to fast over into those parts, inflamed with the comon bruite of the pleasures & proffytts of the same contries as it happened in Spayn after the discovery of the West Indes.

And lyke as the charges in layeng the foundation only of thys honorable worke, shalbe deryved from feaw: Even so the honor unto them shalbe the more. Causing them as specyall starrs of note, to shyne above the rest. So lykewyse shall theyr proffyt be the greater. Whyle the disposing of all matters for goverment & trade shall rest in the hands of feaw. Being reason, that preferments be gyven unto the fyrst Attempters. Upon whose adventure is raysed assured gayn unto the followers. Therfore. in them must rest the power of admytting & disposing Adventures hearafter. Yet allwayes to the furtherance of the cause. Which must be governed by a boddy pollitike & incorporat. Most indifferent and requysit aboue other fourmes of goverment, to the erection & advancement of thys new state & comon weal.

Touching the charges so muche feared: Two thowsand pounds stocke shalbe sufficyent to transport & to leave there fortefyed 50 Menn. with one yeares provision of vyctualls. Which chyfly must be bread & Beverage. for Netts.

hookes & lynes. and lyme: wyll supply them aboundantly of fysh. fowles and Beasts.

Then for to remayn there. 50. Menn shalbe suffycyent also the fyrst tyme.[2] To gyve us proofe of every comoditie incident unto that place. Whearof (as in a plentifull garden) I wysh but one flower of every soart to be gathered. Which shall content us in England, yf only we know suche thyngs of worth to be there growyng.

Thys stocke also of 2000[li] shalbe happely re-tourned whole the fyrst voyage (yf we goe foorth accordingly, as by thys somme it shalbe under-taken compleat of all thyngs necessary:) by fysh which upon these coasts we shall have veary good, and rysing to better reckoning than the Newland fysh. In lyke maner by somm Inland comodities we shall fynd by trucking with the salvages. wherof the Frenche men never fayled to make great gayn.

Then by retourne of better fysh: we shalbe suer to draw thyther our Newfoundland Merchaunts the next voyage. For we have ben promised 20. sayles owt of the Ryver of Thames yf only they myght be assured of good fysh.

The retourn also of other comodities (in demon-stration only of that which may of the whole be expected) shall draw unto us many Adventrers & assistants, the next voyage. Who wyll sooner advente[r] a C[li] upon certayn grounds confyrmed with theyr eyes: than tenn shyllings upon a bare probabilitie of matters they have not seen. So as by our own stock retourned: and by Addition of Adventrers, our next supply and increase of Menn in the second voyage, shalbe more aboun-dant. But in the thyrd all defects wylbe supplyed. And we shalbe than both fournished of people, and stoared with all provisions by access of the Newland Merchants. Who wyll be wholly drawn unto us, all such as have gone owt of England: and many also of other Nations.

Every shypp than repayring unto us: shall ren-der an easy benevolence of theyr goods towards the mayntenaunce of the state. So owt of the proffytts & increase of every Aduenter and share, shalbe reserved som portion to the state. which none wyll refuse in so godly a cause. Besyds that every Mann there inhabiting. Lyke as he shall grow in we[alth] and abilitie, by sale of hys fysh prepared & layd upp in stoare howses, and of

other comodities, as the same shalbe found owt: Even so he wyll increase hys trayn retynew, to increase the more hys benifit, so shall the contry grow apace into st[rength] and the Inhabitaunts increase myghtely in wealth at the beginning especyally.

For the gayn is allwayes mervaylouse great: when but feaw men doe fynd owt & occupy a trade.

Therfore. If thys Action be once but sett one foote: it wyll presently goe and runn forward of it self. By reason of the place being fruitfull & copiouse of comodities: And that it is scytuated so neare a great trade & concourse of Merchaunts. By reason whearof we canot fayle of supply. which in such actions is most diffycult to con-tynew in the beginning. As we have known by proofe the Frenche men in Florida to be over-thrown by want only of supply in due tyme. And how it fareth with our Colon[ie] in Vyrginia we know not. which yf the same had ben planted neare unto thys trade of Newfoundland, and in convenient harbor: then had it ben an easy matter to have sent supply unto them. Which is now a dead & unproffitable cha[nce] discouraging the setters foorth. who yf they had but fysh & oyles retourned (which are the least of many comodities to be expected theare, yet certayn:) they myght have mayntayned styll theyr fyrst stocks, & mynistred supply unto theyr colonies. which with small charges had ben sent un[to] them, yf they had so ready meanes, as we shall have by opor-tunitie of shypps that goe year[ely] unto the New-foundland from hense.

Therfore I wyll fully resolve & refell thys objec-tion (that such an Action must requyre a pri[nces] purse) wyth thys Maxime & reason. That is to saye. No prynce with hys propper treasure hath at any tyme, nor can erect a new comon weale or state to make the same flourishe: unles the place be indued with needfull & vendible comodities, And aptly scytuated for trade.

But whear comodities by the bountie of nature: And convenient places of Concourse & recourse [are] discovered and made known: there may be made a flourishing state, and that soone withowt help of a prynces purse & treasure. or great disbursments of any particuler man.

For lyke as in England. our Brydges. hygh wayes. castells. walled townes. Colleg[es].

churches. hospitalls. Monasteries and suche lyke. were for the most part buylded by t[he] ayd & contribution of many devout persons. Which were works to somptuouse for any o[ther] prynce to accomplish: Even so. By the ayd & contribution of many. whom pietie. honor. or proffit wyll draw to assist thys cause: the same wylbe advanced [&] supported, in a short tyme. Seing that we have aboundance of spare people and Me[chan]icall men, which by a shorter course can effect greater matters, then in former Ages. When people were not so aboundant, nor rype in all maner of trades & faculties.

Nether the Spanyards had meanes so fully to perfect theyr attempts in the Indes at t[he] begynning as we have. By reason that they were occupyed else whear in warrs, and are not a Nation so popolus as we, nor had the benifyt of a perfect discovery, nor settled trade neare unto theyr Indes, nor suche aboundance of shypps vytt[ayles] nor Munition. So as in respect of our long peace: Multitude of people: shyp[pes] vyt-tayles & Munition: places allready discovered & known: trade settled upon the same. We of all other Nations are most fytt for thys enterpryse. whearyn we nede not be discouraged, havyng not the help of a prynces purse, and being but pryvat pe[rsons] Seing that veary mean persons amongst the Spanyards (for no better was Hern[ando] Curtes. mor many besyds:) have attempted to discover, and obtayned Conquest a[nd] posses-sion of many ample kingdoms, sensed cytties and states. to theyr perpetull fame in the west Indes. And the lyke have the portingalls atchieved in the East And we no dowt (more able to suche ex-ploytts,) may compass as great matters in th[e] infynit lands, left for us in the Northwest regions of America. which contayn m[any] regions so temperat, kyngdoms & cytties of great wealth & state by all lykelyhoo[d] further upp in the bowels of that large continent. whearby also there is gathered an assurance by infallible reasons, of a trade to be discovered into the South or back Sea, washing thother Shoar of thys land, which shall gyve us a veary short passage unto Cathay Chyna & other Contries of the East world. An Action of incomparable pryce which shall eternise the Names of the Dyscoverers.

And thys may suffice to remove the nedeles feare of charges growyng by inconsideration of the Nature of thys Action. which is not to be measured by other discoveries, wanting the grounds on which thys dooth consist. Touching the second objection. proceding of feare to be supplanted: I answer.

Solution of the second objection.

The naturall Inhabitants are salvage. Simple. naked & unarmed people. destitut of edge tooles an[d] weapon. Whearby they shalbe unable to defend themselvees, or to offend us. Nether is our intent to provoke. but to cherish and wynn them unto Chrystianitie by all fayer mean[s]. To pro-vyde yet agaynst occurrences, and not unad-vysedly to trust. Notwithstanding. both the Frenche men, and our Nation in Vyrginia have found the people kynd and tractable. In so muche as some both Frenche & English, have gone upp into land unto theyr habitations, and remayned with the people in great securitie, wythowt pledges gyven for the same. And at what tyme have we ever heard, that any Colony hath ben distressed or overthrown by those selly people? Unles amongst the Spanyards, whose tyrannie hath exceded towards them. Yet coold those un-armed wreatches never prevayll but agaynst the Spanyards stragglyng from theyr forces.

For the Chrystyans. No Nation hath so Just tytell unto those Contries, as the English. Whearof hath ben spoken suffycyent in the fyrst chapter. But those we most may dowt, are Spanyards or Frenchmen.

The kyng of Spayn is olde: Impotent: full of troubles & warrs abroad and at home, even hard at hys doores. Waneth people to fournish & garde hys ryche & vast Indes: Therfore unlyke. That he wyll or can spare people from home, or wyll unfurnish hys Indes, to imploy forces to supplant us, in places yet unknown. So remote & seperat both from Spayn & hys Indes.

The Frenche kyng is occupyed in recovering hys Crown of France. And wyll not be at leysure (for many yeares) to looke so farr as into America. there to undertake a Conquest agaynst hys Neyghbours, subjects of her Majestie hys best frend. And wythowt just tytell also.

But yf we gett the starte of Spanyards & Frenche men two yeares before them. And growe to be but 200, menn strong: we shall not feare to be removed by as many thousand of them.

For we have known by experience. That 200 men well fortefyed & vyctualled both in France and the Low Contries: have held theyr pece agaynst all such power, as the kyngs have bent agaynst them, albeit wythyn theyr own kyngdomes or neare home. How much less abell shall they be, to remove us well fortefyed & vyctualled in America so farr of. when as theyr power (with exceding charges, and hasard) must pass over th'occean—at the disposition of sea & wynds, by a long & tediouse course. And afterwards must continew a siege, against us. We being fresh and strong, they wearyed & feeble: we lodged in howses, they in the open field. So as they shall not be able to proulong a seige, throwgh want of vyctuall, harbor & relief. whom rygor of wynter shall constrayn ether to depart, or miserably to perish yf we lye styll, and make but easy defence.

Thys considred. Tyme it self cutteth awaye all fear of supplanting by Spanyards or Frenche men. It being certayn, that nether of them hath oportunitie nor meanes to molest u[s] yet. In Contries so remote And hearafter. We shalbe careles of any thyng they can do when we be once grown unto any indiffrent strength. Besyds that. Thys Action happely shall not displease the Spanyards hearafter, for reasons I wyll now omytt. Moore may be sayd, and reasons examplyfyed upon a subject so ample, as thys Cause mynistreth. But it may suffice that the intent of the Actors is, to ser[ve] god, our prynce & Contry, and to better our estats. By so godly, reasonable and honest meanes.

7

Of a passage certaynly to be found (at least by some part over land) from the parts we intend (by Gods assistance) to inhabit, into the South Sea or back sea of those lands. By meanes wherof all soarts of ryche comodities of the East world, shall conveniently be brought unto us thyther. From whence agayn our Merchants of England may fetche the same of us at all tymes of the yeare. And make retournes comonly every 3 Monethes.

Amongst the manifold Comodities incident unto thys Action of planting in the Northwest Regions of America: Thys benifit also unvaluable, shall most assuredly be attayned unto. That is to saye.

The fynding owt of a passage, or convenient waye for trade into the South & back sea which by interposition of thys same Land of America,

(lyeng as a barr overthwart from South to North:) is devyded from our occean. Yeat both seas, by secreat instinct of Nature, doe mutually desyer to assemble & mete togither. And therfore press with all theyr myght upon both sydes of the land. Into which they penitrate by so large extensions and bosoms, as that in the South angle they have inforced a passage through, called the Strayghts of Maggellane. Wheare fynding the same to strayght for both so myghty Seas frely to assemble: they ronne with vehement force, (and as it were repyning at the resistance in those uncapable strayghts) along the coasts to the Northward. Leaving no places, unassayed, apt to gyve them passage. So as they are only kept a sonder agayn in that Istmus and narrow land (placed betw[ene] Nome di Dios [Nombre de Dios] & Panama:) by the thycknes of certayn Mowntayns & rockes. Whose invincible hardnes & heyght, the seas being unable to overcume: doe pass from thence with a forcible currant making on our syde an other great Baye abowt 37 degrees Septentryall latitude, called of th'inhabitants the Gesepian Baye. And is unknown yet to us, how farr into the land, or which waye it extendeth most.

The Currant is Contynued alongst that Coast, and engulfeth agayn at Cape Bryttayn abowt 45. deg. breaking into the land by so many wayes from thence to the Northw[ard] As there remayneth great hoape of a passage through into thother Sea. Which fo[r] hys part agayn, being as wylling to mete: dooth by all lykelyhood assaye all place[s] on thother syde, apt to yeald them thys access. Whearby many great boso[ms] and Bayes are extended into the boddy of the Land, aswell on that South & west Syd[es] as on our North & east parts. In so muche as. they that have late trended tho[se] other back Coasts of America: have found the land to enclyne muche to the East from 44 degrees Northward, and not to be extended so farr west, as ignorantly it hath ben hytherto placed in most charts. Which error is somwhat reformed in som new drawghts. though not exactly, by reason there is no certayn discovery extant of that other syde from 44 degres Northward. Nevertheles, by the former re[ason] that both seas intend & indevor to Joyn. Pearcing by unknown passages and extensions into the bowells of both sydes the Mayns seking to come togither: w[hich] shall gather (most assuredly) thys proffit therby. That ether those seas make passage through the Land, and doe mete also in those Northerly Regions: or else they leave somwhear an Istmus or strayght of land, which betwen both se[as] shall contayn no suche space,[3] but as may conveniently be passed over with Comoditie[s] from one sea to another. Lyke as the maner is betwen Nome di Dios & Panama or betwen the Redd Sea & the ryver Nilus in Egipt.

Besyds the former probabilities, ether of a passage through into the South & back sea, or narrow spaces of land, whear the Seas on both sydes approache neare togither,: I wyll deryve an other infallible argument from Indraughts and Ryvers,[4] whose chanells, aswell by the flowyng and ebbing of the Seas, as by the aboundant streames of fresh waters, descending from the hygh or myddlands: are made navygable for shypps, and portable afterwards for Boates farr upp, and veary neare in the mydds of the Land, on both sydes respecting the South or North occean. Which must gyve us convenient waye of traffyck into the South Sea.

For thys we know allready, by late discoveries of the Frenche whose true plotts we have, conferred and agreing togither. That besyds other great Ryvers not yet searched into: that of S[t]. Laurence or Canada is found Navigable into the land aboue 100 leagues. And for Boates portable above 300 leagues or a thousand Myles English.[5] How much further it featcheth hys Course, they know not certaynly. But Jacques Noell a Frencheman. (Who passed beyond the Sauts or downfalls of waters, whear Chartyer left of to discover, judging the same impassable, notwithstanding that Noell hath proceded further by an other branche synce, and found the ryver portable:) understood by the Inhabitaunts thearabouts, (which travayll muche, and have intelligence of places farr of) that this Ryver leadeth into a huge lake, whose utter most bounds and ende was to th'inhabitaunts thear unknown. That also those people called the lake Tadoac,[6] which at the issue of the same ryver was fresh. But further beyond, bytter or salt.

What we may conjecture of thys lake or sea, (wherof no perfect discovery hath yet ben made.)

I wyll not heare muche rely on. Albeit we may be assured that there is suche a lake. Seing that in all discoveries and descriptions hytherto of those Regions, mention is made therof. Yet by many placed wrong more Northward than in dede it is. The truth hearof shalbe found in us. Who when we are planted and shalbe resident upon those Contries, shall have better oportunitie, intelligence and means to perfect our discoveries, than the Frenche could have in theyr long voyages from France thyther, and theyr short abode thear.

Then, lyke as that great Ryver of S[t]. Laurence (and other ryvers also, which at theyr falls into our occean appeare veary great:) dooth extend farr and even unto the Mydds at least of the same Continent.[7] Which also must be the more portable, by how muche it bryngeth hys course farr, through many Contries, receyvyng other streames in hys waye: Even so. beyond the head of thys ryver. (whyther the same descendeth from the Lake afoarsayd, or from Mowntaynes:) by reason & nature it standeth, that other Ryvers from thense doo lykewyse descend in the same maner into thother back Sea, as thys of S[t]. Laurence with many others doo fall into our occean.

For the Seas are the propper Mansions and rest of all waters from whence they are deryved. Whyther they procede or rayn or snowe or spryngs. And therfore (yf not otherwayes. constrayned) every part of water, be it never so lyttle, seketh waye home unto the Seas from all parts of the earth. In so muche as. We see no sea which from the Lands abowt it receyveth not streames and ryvers. Which ryvers are allwayes the greater, proceding from large continents.

Therfore yf from lakes, these Ryvers in our regions of America, take begynning: then doo the same lakes also send forth streames into the South occean.[8] Which hath as great interest in the same, as our North occean. and is as capable of them. And nature shoold dygress, yf she were not as kynd to the one, as to the other. The lyke we see in the great Lakes of Russia, Moscovia, and other parts of Europe and Asia. Which send owt large Ryvers into all the Seas invironning. Namely. the Caspian Sea. Meotis palus. the Livonian Sea. and Seas lyeng on the North regions.

3. Sidenote: "Probabilitie ether of a passage through: or of an Istmus whear both Seas aproache neare togither."
4. Sidenote: "Proofes of a way for trade into the South Sea by Indraughts & ryvers."
5. Sidenote: "The ryver of S[t]. Laurence a 1000 myles portable into the Mayn."
6. Sidenote: "Tadoac Sygnifyeth in the Salvages tounge a Sea."

7. Sidenote: "Ryvers fall down from the Mayn into both the North & South Seas."
8. Sidenote: "Lakes send foorth ryvers dyverse wayes."

In lyke sorte. yf the sayd ryvers deryve theyr heads from Mowntanes, (in which are Contayned waters as it were in cesternes, and from whence comonly both lakes & Ryvers are supplyed:) then also doe those Mowntayns cast from them streames every waye into the Seas[9] invyronning the lands. for Mowntayns have allwayes theyr descents, which doo respect and inclyne towards the Seas, which are the lowest places.

And waters which from the hygh Mowntayns doo naturally descend into the lowest places doo by all descents of the Mowntaynes by lyttle and lyttle assemble togither in places declyning. resorting styll unto the lower places, which at last by repay [of] many streames, become portable and great channells, (and so on all sydes of those Mowntaynes carrye[th] wyth them thother streames into those seas which ly m[ost] apt to receyve them. For Example.

The Alpes. which are Mowntayns confyning Germany. France & Italy: send foorthe eas[t] the myghtiest Ryver of Europe Danubius into the Sea Euxinus. In lyke sort [the] Ryver of Rhyne North into the Germane Sea. Rhosne by west & South into the Mediterrane Sea. And the Poo through the most fertile contries of Lombardy into [the] Adryatick Sea or gulf of Venice. Other instances to the same effect are produced in Affryck. Asia, yea at home amongst the Mowntayns in England.

Seing then in Nature thys must be graunted; and by experience is found in all plac[es] elsewheare trew, that Mowntayns and lakes doe send from them streames into all Seas invyronning: we wyll make no dowt, but that it houldeth trew in those regions of America. Wheare Ryvers are known to descend both into the South and North occean. albeit the back Coasts, opposit unto the places we mea[n] to inhabit, are not so well known unto us.

A recapitulation of the former reasons proving a convenient waye for trade into the South Sea.

And as we may certaynly Conclude of great ryvers through so large a continent bot[h] on the North & South Sydes: Even so the large extension of the land betw[een] both Seas shalbe lessened, and the Seas brought nearer togither by Bayes & boso[ms] penetrating into the land. from those Bayes.[10] the indraughts and flowys of the Seas on both Sydes, shall cause navigable chanells for shypps yet furth[er] into the land.[11] And from suche places wheare shypps can no further pass may Boates pass upp the fresh streames[12] even unto theyr heads veary neave comoditie of vessells and other inventions as they use in Germany, whear upon veary shallow streames, they transport infinit Masses of goods.

In which courses, it is to be noted, that in carrieng over of goods into the South or back [side], and retourning of other goods by the same wayes: we shall have the benif[it to] fall with the streames ever half the waye. besyds the help of indrawghts with t[he] flouds & ebbs from the North & South Seas.[13] Whearby the trade and excercis[e of] Merchaundise shalbe made veary easy & convenient. Upp and down those ryver[s] And that intervallum or space of land betwen the heads of the ryvers, as it s[hould] not be great, (which that honorable Counsayllor late deceased Master Secretary Wal[singham]. thought a happy discovery for England yf it myght be made over land but 200 leagues:)[14] Even so. by the help of the Salvages excersysed in carryeng burdens. and of the great soarts of beasts plentifull in those contries which serve to carry and draw as Elks or Buffells:) all soarts of Comodities, suche especyally as we shall receyve from the most ryche contries of the East: sh[albe] with muche ease and benifit transported over that portion of land, and afterwar[ds] imbarked.

It is furthermore to be noted, that all these Countries, (so farr as is known of them) yeald Cedar trees. fyrrs. pynes. oakes & such lyke. Whearby we shalbe abell [to] buyld, mast and rygg shypps, havyng hemp also.[15] Wherfore we may no[t] dowt to have shypping also one the South syde.

And for the better disposing of thys voyage, (after that the nearest waye overland [for] one sea unto an other shalbe found:) there may be erected

---

9. Sidenote: "Mountayns cast foorth ryvers into all Seas abowt them."

10. Sidenote: "Bayes."
11. Sidenote: "Indraughts."
12. Sidenote: "Ryvers."
13. Sidenote: "half waye with the Stream ebbs and fludds help besyds."
14. Sidenote: "Salvages and strong beasts of the contry. to carry goods over the land."
15. Sidenote: "Meanes to buyld shypps on the South or back Sea."

4 poarts & staple place[s][16] wheare goods must be laden and unladen. That is to saye.

Two upon the North Syde at the fall & head of the ryver: And two others on the [other] syde at the head & fall also of that other ryver.

The two outermost poarts, placed next the seas on both sydes: shall receyve and delyv[er] from and into shypps which can pass up no hygher into the land.

The other two Innermost staples, placed at the heads of the ryvers: shall receyve an[d] dely[ver] goods from and into the Boats, when they nether can pass further from these Inland staples, the goods brought in from both Seas, must be carryed o[ver].

By thys meanes. The order of traffyck wylbe veary Convenient & comodius.[17] Notwithstanding it may appear difficult at the fyrst. And these 4 poarts & staples, wyll become most famous Marts[18] of the world. whyther Merchaunts shall have free access, by the wayes of both the North & South oceans from all quarters of Europe. Affryck. Asia & America wythowt barr & restraynt through so large and wyde seas. Never touching nor approaching any lands untill they arryve at these our poarts. Whearby they shalbe exempted from all other customs and tolls.

The Comodities of greatest importance comyng by waye of the North occean unto us, wylbe English cloath & carsies[19] which shall have spedyer vent thys waye than by all the trades we use else wheare. for the shipps comyng from England shall discharge their fraight at the next poart placed upon the mouth of the ryver fallyng into our North occean. whear also they shall take in theyr lading of comodities both of those regions of America, and also suche as have ben brought thyther from the South Sea. So as theyr voyage shalbe perfourmed owt of England comonly in 3 Monthes, and at all tymes of the yeare. with short and exceding ryche retourns.[20]

The Comodities lykwyse comyng unto us by the waye of the South & back Sea from Cathay.[21] China. the Molucces and all regions of the East world: wylbe Spyces. Sugars. Druggs. Musk.

Sylks. Cloath of goold. goold. pearle. stones and all soarts of preciouse wares. Which by a short course shalbe brought unto our poart placed upon the mouth of that ryver falling into the South or back Sea. Whear shypps that occupy those seas, shall also discharge, and take in theyr lading of English cloath, carsies or whatsover else transported from the North occean and brought thyther by ryvers through the land.

Thus may we in England by fyndyng owt thys easy waye of trade; draw unto us the ryche & preciouse thyngs of the world. And fournish all Nations abowt us of the same, better cheap & better conditioned, then we and they doo now receyve them from Lisbone at the Portingalls & Spanyards hands. Who spoyle and greatly decay the vyrtue & strength of Spynces, in theyr long voyages from the East, by the Cape of Bona Speranza. And reservyng the most fresh: they sell theyr rotten wares dear unto us & other Nations.[22]

I call thys way of trade (which I persuade unto) easy. In respect of trades sought owt both un[to] those East parts, and elsewhear. for thys may be perfourmed by veary short & temperat courses indifferent betwen the extremities of both the burning & frosen zoanes. And may therfore by all ryght, preferr the same above the long & tediouse way of the Portingalls[23] who by 3 yeares voyage, cutting ofte the lyne and burning zoanes; doo hardly fynish theyr course from Lisbone, to theyr East Indes, and back agayn.

Or above the wayes. Supposed by the Northeast or Northwest passages into those Indes through greater extremities under the frosen zoanes.[24] yf the veary Moment of the tyme to pass, be omytted: then shall we be frosen in the seas or strayghts: or force[d] to wynter in extreme could, and uncomfortable obscuritie, by depryvation of the son[ne] for many Monethes. Or else in the best Season and mydds of Sommer, we shalbe in jeopardie to have our shypps overwhelmed, or crusht into peces, by hydeouse Mountayns of Ise, floating than upon those seas.

Voyages of wonderfull difficultie, have ben sought owt, to bryng the Comodities of these

16. Sidenote: "4 staples."
17. Sidenote: "A Comodiuse way for thys trade."
18. Sidenote: "famous Marts."
19. Sidenote: "Vent for our cloath & carses."
20. Sidenote: "short & ryche retournes."
21. Sidenote: "Preciouse wares of the East."

22. Sidenote: "Abuse of the Portingalls."
23. Sidenote: "The Portingalls trade by Cape de bona speranza into India."
24. Sidenote: "Incomodities in the Northeast & Northwest passages."

East Indes through the myghty Continent of Asia, by the fludd Indus.[25] Into the Caspain Sea [and] thense by other ryvers unto Moscovy. And thense into the Lyvonian Sea at the Town of Rye.

A daungerouse & most tediouse voyage was that, the Moores frequented from Fess & Marocko unto Cayro.[26] Through the Contynent & whole length of Affryck, passing over the Movab[le] Sands, often drenched in them. Allwayes distressed in the same of water and dryven to kyll and drynck water taken owt of theyr camells bellyes. Then they imbarked theyr goods and carryed the same agaynst the stream of the ryver Niger. disbarked agayn. And carryed the same by land unto Nilus. And from thense by Boat unto Cayro. Wheare they buy at Second and thyrd hand the same Indyan wares. And retourne by the wayes they came.

Comendable was the industry of our English Merchaunts: yet tediouse & peryllouse was the voyage they made & frequented into Persia.[27] by & through Sondry domynions of the Emperor of Russia and other Tartars. Upp and down ryvers into the Caspain Sea, and a[lso] unto Ormus in the Persian Gulf or Sea.

These and many other voyages have ben attempted, many perfourmed & used to thys day by Courses as longe as the whole circuit of the world & longer:[28] through burning and through freysing zoanes: through the long tracts of large Continents upp and downes great ryvers: often Imbarking and disbarking of goo[ds] abyding extremities somwheare of cold, of heate and of thyrsts: Incurr[ing] perylls of drowning in Seas in maner impassable, and upon la[nd] amongst the movyng Sands by dryfts of wynds: Subject to customes & tolls, passing by sondry domynions: And sustayning of infinit daunger and molestations.

These considred. We may thearby be incouraged to follow thys enterprise with a farr easyer Course, shall make waye unto us, for the obtayning of th[e] same Comodities of East India,: which in all the former voyages, have ben sought for with tolleration of great extremities & vyolences.

For as thys waye into the South Sea, and to the East Indes, is veary certayn.[29] If we cann be content to make the same by som part overland. (which lan[d] is washed on the back shoare by the South occean:) Even so th[e] same shalbe perfourmed by short retournes (as hath ben before declared:) through most temperat clymets passing over Seas or Land. betwen the extremes of heat & could.: through oceans free from barr or restraynt: over the best and most fertile lands of America (as the Scituation under 40 & 45 degrees dooth gyve:) The contry & people, to be commanded by us. And looke what happynes any action or indevor for godly or humayn respects may promise: the same may well be expected in thys whearby we may advance the churche & glory of God, enlarge the do[my]nions of her Majesty, and attayn unto the most ryche & preciouse thyng[s] that Nature dooth bryng foorth into the world. By making a waye for trade into the South Sea. Which shall never be known, (by th'opinio[n] of most judiciall Cosmographers) untill these Northwest region[s] of America be fyrst planted with Chrystyan Inhabitants. Who being resident and abyding theare, shall have oportunitie & meane[s] to search owt all wayes into the South Sea, aswell by inquisition & intelligence from those natife inhabitants, as by our own navigations and travaylls.

God graunt as happy success unto thys Action, as the same is honestly intended.

367. After 1592. Commentary on the Hayes-Carleill project.

An undated paper, a rather imperfect copy, P.R.O., State Papers, Colonial, CO 1/1, 9, appears to be a response to the Hayes-Carleill paper. It seems to belong to the period between 1593 and 1597 when the idea of sending nonconforming Brownists to America was raised since "the precise" are mentioned among the potential colonists. The author is skeptical about the evidence for a passage to the Pacific and about the peaceful acceptance of the intruders by the Amerindians. He realizes that in a cold country, without high-

---

25. Sidenote: "A trade for spyces unto Moscovy & Rye to be brought from India."
26. Sidenote: "The Moores trade to Cayro."
27. Sidenote: "Our Merchants trade into Persia."
28. Sidenote: "daungerous attempts."

29. Sidenote: "an easy & comodius trade into the South Sea."

value produce, returns would be slow and inves-
tors easily discouraged. But he thinks that with
foresight something could be done to plant col-
onists. When Captain Charles Leigh attempted,
unsuccessfully, to introduce Brownists to settle
the Magdalen Islands in 1597, it is probable that
he had some of these projects in mind. In his
narrative he gives details of the resources of the
islands. On his return he produced a plan for a
miniscule settlement on the islands that could
well have been influenced by these plans, al-
though it was not followed up (Vol. IV, no. 569).

Yt being a very noble action to inlarge a dominion, wheather yt be by a Conquest, wheare resistance is made or by plantinge upon plases nec-
lected thoroughe the barbarousnes of the inhabitantes or [ther] neyghbores[:] the most vertuous
mindes are easly taken with falseste hopes; ambe-
sion makinge a quicke sence of the good & casting
and conferminge the mind againste all difficulties,
& the for[ce] in this preposition of plantinge an
English Collonee in the northe weste of America:
conceavinge that the uttermoste argumentes
with the greatest hopes are expresse[d] for the
action, I thincke yt is intended that the difficult[ie] should be explained, thatt by the Comparison; the possibility or glory of the worke
mighte be forseen. Yt is graunted the strength
our navy gives us, the necessity of ther maintenaunce butt how owre state standes more
dangerous then ever is not proved; and as itt is to
bee wishte, that wee had plases of our owne to
furnishe soe necessary a Comoditye as aper-
tinentth to our shippinge, so muste yt be examined wheather our Contrey shoul[d] not bee as
muche wrested or more to recover them thence
then by the wayes they have them & to the
argument that God foresawe our necessities to
come of those provision[s] & therfore discovered
to Henry the 7th thes Cuntris, yt weare to be
Construed Largely butt heare this only God
foresaw from the beginninge, this purpose to
have love amongeste all men, & therefore gave
abondaunce and necessitie to Countries to mak[e]
trafficke, & expresse an[d] use one of another, by
which way of trafficke wee are furnishte plen-
tiouslye of all those Commodities nether is yt to
bee feared, that any tyme Canne bringe forth a
nutter bar of trade to us except all the world att

once should turne againste us, & then wee muste
keepe the new gotten by miracle & defend the
ould hardly, and many examples make plaine as
nowe with us wee see, that soe longe as a State
resiste the Sworde & Cane furnishe mony or
other matter for exchange, trafficke will bring the
enemies moste forbidden Comodities in sufficiency, soe as yf the only benefitt weare the
havinge a land fit from whence too fetche thinges
necessary for our shippinge yt weare like to bee
baughte to deere, since with the bringinge in of
those trades from the east, wee carry out our
aboundinge Commodities to the furnishinge of
our state which is sayde should likewyse be donne
this way, in two kindes, one by trafficke with
those nation[s] that Come thether for fishe, &
then over Land. Both which two wayes requi[re]
much tyme to bringe them to a ripenes, & in the
trade over Land theare riseth many difficulties,
first accordinge to the expedition made yt seemes
to be an infinite great mayne of Land & wheare
yt is sa[id] the inhabitants speake of a bitter water
which affection would understand for salte yt may
rightelie be Conceaved to be Some Lake which are
Common in waste Contries & of suche nature, the
watters of them, thorrowe the separament of the
earth, & the saleing in of leves havinge noe Cur-
rantes to cleanse that, they ever yeld a bitter
taste & all though at the first & upon the uttermoste skirte of a lande wee find butt a naked
people, & sutche as while wee stay not to give
them lawe but flatter them with toyes, & exchaunge to theyre advantage, & so departe, apear
well inclined & apte to reseve us; yett by the
Comparison of thes plasses with others that have
bene discovered yt may be conseaved that they
have more with in Land townes peopled, & will
when they shall see that wee attempte upon
them, as a people that, will perswade accordinge
to owre knowledges theyre had or forse yt, then
will they putt them selves into resistance, nothinge beyinge able to change the forme of religion
in the moste barberous but the spirite of revela-
tion or an absolute Conqueste; neyther is example
only in many ages able to alter the habite of a Lyfe
confirmed in Libertye and Idlenes to order and
industrye, especially in Could regions which
brings forth a dull inflexible people, obstinately
affectinge barbarous liberty & Jelous of all aucthority thoughe too much to theyre good, yf they
had sence of sivillity to examine yt by; so as I finde

little foundation for hope of trafficke into thes partts untell Longe tyme have made us masters of att least all the Convenient passages & those secured by fortifications or inhabitants subjecte to our Lawe which muste firste have a beginninge, & thatt is to bee examined how yt may rise from Commodities of the fishinge & exchange of trafficke & to invite us the rather Lett us admitte, the trafficke to Muscovia, is a hevey Jorney to our marchants, in respecte of the length of the voyage & Couldnes of the region which suffers butt one voyages in a yeare, & there owre merchants subjecte att pleasure of the prinse to arrestes of ther persons & goods and to passe by a st[r]aighte sea of the Denmarkes stronge in shippinge & of whome wee cane have no security, & thatt the Easterlings now increase in there mislike & in Juries towards us whear of they have given aparent marks & from hence Lett us conclude thatt a nother trade weare more Convenient for us & that this land of New Found Land, for the shortenes of the passage & openesse of the sea, & less intemperate Could then Muscovia, havinge the commodities necessary for shippinge & trade settled there is more Convenient, admittinge the necessities for owre navye to be theare in abundaunce Lett us examine how a trade may be settled there & whatt may bee the difficulties in their trade as well as in the settlinge; whearin wee muste somethinge [say of] the nature of that Cuntry with other new discoveries, peopled which peradventure att the first aprehension maks this worke seeme the easier: The Contrye seemes by the preposicion to bee cowlde, & to bringe forthe Commodities as coulde Cuntries doth which industery, our contry people havinge ever bene bred with plenty in a more temperate ayre, and naturally not very industrous, at home and lesse to seeke out plases, wheare ther Labours are present and their hopes a Littell differed, wheare of we have too good experience by Ireland whiche neere us, a temperate & fertile Contrye, subjecte to our owne Lawes and halfe civill, the portts and many places freindly inhabited, notwithstandinge many of good reputacion, became undertakers there in the tyme of pease, coulde not invite our people, neyther in any Competent numbers, nor constantly in ther action, the reason beinge cheefely thatt in climatts that bring forthe, butt yearely riches & that with Labour, a

stocke & industrie must bee adventured upon expectacion; our able men are in the same trade at home allreddy, & Love ease and securitie and the poore men wantts welthe to disburse any thinge, wants wisdome to foresee the good, & wants vertu to have patiens, & constantly to attend the reward of a good worke & industry: those new discoveries inhabited by the Portingalls & Spaniardes was in regions that althoughe they weare intemperately hotte, yett bringe forth by reason of theare heate and fertillity, gould, silver, pretious stones, spices, riche dies & drugges, which they have eyther for the gatheringe or by trafficke for small exchange which was such a profitable increase, as att there retorne both the prinses and people weare incurraged to inhabite not only theare butt upon all the passages & borders, that mighte eyther winne those cuntries to them, or serve to keepe out others or them in ther trade theather, the Contries for the moste parte all wheare they do inhabite yeldinge abundance of all thinges bothe for use and pleasure with small industry; and for the intemperatenes of the sonne for heate, by Caves & forme of ther howses they with a Little Labour and coste save them selves from that ayre, as wee in America are to do by stoves from the Could.

The generall discovery beinge made, a particuler discovery is to bee made, of the plase wheare our nation should settle, yf there bee hope eyther of mines or other good return that may drawe on a secondinge of the action, which is moste to bee doubted; for yf her Majestie shall only Cowntenaunce yt and recommend yt to her marchauntts whoe may have her incorragment: the difficultie of the [venture admitted?] & gratious [grant?] of the trafficke of America to bee only reserved to the firste adventurers, yett when soe great a Charge muste be firste Issued as the sendinge of a Competent nomber to inhabite, with all necessaries requisitt for new inhabitantes, and victualls for a hole yeare for them that ther retorne shall bringe home nothinge above the ordinarye freight of fish and a narration of the sighte of a Cuntrey and hope of better by the nexte adventure, yt is feared that the ordinary wayes of trade, beinge lesse chargeable, they will Content them selves & lokke upon the dangers and allteracions a farr of, and eyther slowlye or not at all give second; and wheare yt is propounded that our poore of England, may bee easly sent thether, by the shippes that goe to fishe yearely they beinge delivered un[to] the portts, with victualls for a yeere, our common people of England are not riche, & doe almoste repine att those most behovefull imposicions which are layed upon them, for Leveinge of souldiers & yett those willinge subsidies and payments they graunt to her Majestie for Juste reasons deputed in open parliment, then wee muste remember whatt pore they are thatt arre requisite to people a new Conqueste, not the impotente [lame and old?] they muste remaine burden to the parishes, and then what charge would bee requisite to every man, which is not onely Competent aparell for one yeare, money to bringe hime to the porte, & armes of defence and of offence, but victualls for a year[e] & [tools?] to plante & and build with all, for wantinge eyther sufficiensy untill the freute of there Labours shalbe reapte to them, or wantinge industry to make sufficiensy, & not havinge wheare with to exchange for victualls with the savadge people they shalbe forste to doe outrages which will shutt up all wayes of trafficke or intelligens with those people, and Cause them to stand upon force, before we[e] shalbe able to force them, or well to defend our selves; the number for the firste and second is like wyse to bee had in consideration, for the first ytt Cannot be Lesse then may bee thoughte Competent, to fortefye and secure the harboure, to plante and geather provision for the nexte yeare, & to defend what soever they shall take for theyrs without they bee Lodgings, and att the firste to avoyde the losse of time in the trade, there would bee builded Convenient Lodgings and storehowses, for the safe [guard?] keepinge and exchanginge of sutche Commodities, & should a trafficke betweene us and the people or others [arise?] toe fishe; and the second muste performe as muche with an increase further of a competent troope or troopes, to discover the rivers and the Lande, wheather with mines or other marchandise may be presently putt in use to give incorragement to the adventurers, for certaine charge & uncertaine retornes will quickly quaile an action thowghe well founded, and this may well bee lookte for,

thatt the inhabitants, will give us noe better way then wee Can forse, & will easly insulte upon our weakenes yf they can find an advantage, besides wee are to concerne, thatt the Frenche whoe have pretenses, & have a secreat trafficke thether; will repine & resiste yf they can or dare, all under the subjection of the Spaniards are declared opositts, & wee muste resolve that the kinge & thatt state will have his eyes open upon ower actions, & will yf hee Cane forse us from any benefite, att leaste wee muste looke that from all his partts or wheare his seas that hee can command lett us in any trafficks thatt plase will yeald us, since bothe the Easterlinges and Dutches whoe have a greeter trade into Muscovia then [we] will furnishe hime of all needfull things thence thatt are to bee had in the th[e] parte of America wee pretend toe.

Now thorowe all these difficulties, yf the prinse would assiste yt in parte & her marchants thatt are well affected goe Liberallye into yt, & that the Cuntries might bee stirred [to?] an assistance by men in some meate measure, & some gentelmen moved to bee venturers, that should fore see not only the undertakinge butt the secondinge: then I Conceave, that a worthye generall beinge chosen, thatt mighte have a Royall Commission, & weare quallified to Judge of the sighte of plases for strengthe & for Comodities, would exercise Justice by the [lawe?] to the presise the marchaunts adventurers & gentelmen or others thatt should [adventure?] ther persons woulde keepe thes troopes in obedience, and in industrie, and use clemensey & Justice to the inhabitants, yt mighte bee a glorious action, for our prinse and Cuntrie, honorable for the generall and adventurers and in tyme profitable, to the generall and particuler. & I doubte not an acceptab[le] service to God, the purpose and execution beinge to magnifie his name in the extendinge of his worde, thoughe the example of our saviour and hi[s] desiples is preachinge, butt not compellinge, unlesse wee may make use of this thatt the first tyme hee sente forthe his desiples hee willed them to Carry nothinge nor to Care for any thinge, & the nexte tyme hee Commaunded him that had a Coate to sell itt and buy a[nother].

[Endorsed:] Plantacion in America

A REVISED VERSION OF THE PLAN BY
EDWARD HAYES

WE CANNOT TELL if Edward Hayes was or was not directly connected with Bartholomew Gosnold's attempt to explore the shores of Norumbega (New England) and to establish (though he failed to do so) a fur-trading post. After his return, there appeared John Brereton's *A briefe and true relation of the discoverie of the north part of Virginia* (1602, two editions). It contained additional material, perhaps supplied by Richard Hakluyt, and a scaled down version of the Hayes-Carleill project of 1592 (366). Contributions to notes on potential resources of America point to Hayes's participation in the making of the collection, and it may be understood that he prepared the shorter version of his earlier plan. Sidenotes, in general, have been eliminated.

368. 1608. "A Treatise, conteining important inducements for the planting in these parts, and finding a passage that way to the South sea and China."

The voiage which we intend, is to plant Christian people and religion upon the Northwest countries of America, in places temperat and well agreeing with our constitution, which though the same doe lie betweene 40. and 44. degrees of latitude, under the Paralels of Italy and France, yet are not they so hot; by reason that the suns heat is qualified in his course over the Ocean, before he arriveth upon the coasts of America, attracting much vapour from the sea: which mitigation of his heat, we take for a benefit to us that intend to inhabit there; because under the Climat of 40 degrees, the same would be too vehement els for our bodies to endure.

These lands were never yet actually possessed by any Christian prince or people, yet often intended to be by the French nation, which long sithence had inhabited there, if domesticall warres had not withheld them: notwithstanding the same are the rightfull inheritance of her Majestie, being first discovered by our nation in the time of King Henrie the seventh, under the conduct of John Cabot and his sonnes: by which title of first discovery, the kings of Portugall and Spaine doe holde and enjoy their ample and rich kingdomes in their Indies East and West; and also lately planted in part by the Colonies sent thither by the honourable knight, Sir Walter Ralegh.

The course unto these countreys, is thorow the Ocean, altogether free from all restraint by forren princes to be made; whereunto other our accustomed trades are subject; apt for most winds that can blow, to be performed commonly in 30 or 35 daies. The coast faire, with safe roads and harbors for ships: Many rivers.

These lands be faire and pleasant, resembling France, intermedled with mountains, valleys, medowes, woodlands, and champians. The soile is exceeding strong, by reason it was never manured; and will be therefore most fit to beare at first, Rape-seeds, Hempe, Flax, and whatsoever els requireth such strong soile. Rape-oiles, and all sorts of oiles, will be very commodious for England, which spendeth oiles aboundantly about Clothing and Leather-dressing. In like sort, Hempe and Flax are profitable, whether the same be sent into England, or wrought there by our people; Oad also will grow there aswell or better then in Terçera.

The Salvages weare faire colours in some of their atire, whereby we hope to finde rich dies and colours for painting.

The trees are for the most part, Cedars, Pines, Spruse, Firre and Oaks to the Northward. Of these trees will be drawn Tarre and Pitch, Rosen, Turpentine, and Soapeashes: They will make masts for the greatest shippes of the world: Excellent timbers of Cedar, and boords for curious building.

The cliffes upon the coasts and mountaines every where shew great likelihood of Minerals. A very rich mine of Copper is found, whereof I have seene proofe; and the place described. Not farre from which there is great hope also of a Silver mine. There be faire quarries of stone, of beautifull colours, for buildings.

The ground bringeth forth, without industrie, Pease, Roses, Grapes, Hempe, besides other plants, fruits, herbs and flowers, whose pleasant view and delectable smelles doe demonstrate sufficiently the fertility and sweetnesse of that soile and aire.

Beasts of many kindes; some of the bignesse of an Oxe, whose hides make good buffe: Deere, both red and of other sorts in aboundance: Luzerns, Marterns, Sables, Beavers, Beares, Otters, Wolves, Foxes, and Squirrels, which to the Northward are blacke, and accounted very rich furres.

Fowles both of the water and land, infinit store and varietie; Hawks both short and long winged, Partriges in abundance, which are verie great, and easily taken. Birds great and small come like unto our Blacke-birds, others like Canarie-birds: And many (as well birds as other creatures) strange and differing from ours of Europe.

Fish, namely Cods, which as we encline more unto the South, are more large and vendible for England and France, then the Newland fish. Whales and Seales in great abundances. Oiles of them are rich commodities for England, whereof we now make Soape, besides many other uses. Item, Tunneys, Anchoves, Bonits, Salmons, Lobsters, Oisters having Pearle, and infinit other sorts of fish, which are more plentifull upon those Northwest coasts of America, then in any parts of the knowen world. Salt is reported to be found there, which els may be made there, to serve sufficiently for all fishing.

So as the commodities there to be raised both of the sea and land (after that we have planted our people skilfull and industrious) will be Fish, Whale and Seale oiles, Soape ashes and Soape, Tarre and Pitch, Rosen and Turpentine, Masts, Timber and boords of Cedars, Firres, and Pines, Hempe, Flaxe, Cables and Ropes, Saile-clothes, Grapes, and Raisens and Wines, Corne, Rape-seeds & oiles, Hides, Skinnes, Furres, Dies and Colours for painting, Pearle, Mettals, and other Minerals.

These commodities before rehearsed, albeit for the most part they be grosse, yet are the same profitable for the State of England specially, aswell in regard of the use of such commodities, as for the imploiment also of our people and ships; the want whereof, doth decay our townes and ports of England, and causeth the realme to swarme full with poore and idle people.

These commodities in like sort, are of great use and estimation in all the South and Westerne contreys of Europe; namely, Italie, France and Spaine: for the which all nations that have beene accustomed to repair unto the Newfound-land for the commoditie of fish and oiles alone, will henceforward forsake the Newfound-land, and trade with us, when once we have planted people in those parts:[1] by whose industrie shall be provided for all commers, both fish and oiles, and many commodities besides, of good importance & value.

Then will the Spaniards and Portugals bring unto us in exchange of such commodities before mentioned, Wines, Sweet oiles, Fruits, Spices, Sugars, Silks, Gold and Silver, or whatsoever that Europe yeeldeth, to supply our necessities, and to increase our delights.

For which Spanish commodities and other sorts likewise, our merchants of England will bring unto us againe, Cloth, Cattell, for our store and breed, and every thing els that we shall need, or that England shall haply exchange for such commodities.

By this intercourse, our habitations will be made a Staple of all vendible commodities of the world, and a meanes to vent a very great quantitie of our English cloth into all the cold regions of America extended very farre.

This intercourse also will be soone drawen together by this reason: That neere adjioining upon the same coasts of Newfound-land, is the greatest fishing of the world; whether doe yeerely repaire about 400 sailes of ships, for no other commoditie than Fish and Whale-oiles. Then forasmuch as merchants are diligent inquisitours after gaines, they will soone remoove their trade from Newfound-land unto us neere at hand, for so great increase of gaine as they shall make by trading with us. For whereas the voyage unto the Newfound-land is into a more cold and intemperate place, not to be traded nor frequented at all times, nor fortified for securitie of the ships and

---

1. Sidenote: "The trade to Newfoundland shalbe removed to us."

goods; oft spoiled by pirats or men of warre; the charges great for salt; double manning and double victualling their ships, in regard that the labor is great and the time long, before their lading can be made readie: they cary outwards no commodities for fraight; and after six moneths voyage, their returne is made but of Fish and Oiles.

Contrariwise, by trading with us at our intended place, the course shalbe in a maner as short; into a more temperate and healthfull climat; at all times of the yeere to be traded; harbors fortified to secure ships and goods; charges abridged of salt, victualling and manning ships double: because lading shall be provided unto their hands at a more easie rate than themselves could make it. They shall carry fraight also outward, to make exchange with us; and so get profit both waies: and then every foure moneths they may make a voyage and returne, of both fish and oiles, and many other commodities of good worth.

These reasons advisedly waighed, shall make our enterprise appeare easie, and the most profitable of the world, for our nation to undertake. The reasons we chiefly relie upon are these namely.

1. Those lands which we intend to inhabit, shall minister unto our people, the subject and matter of many notable commodities.

2. England shall affoord us people both men, women and children above 10000, which may very happily be spared from hence to worke those commodities there.

3. Newfound-land shall minister shipping to carrie away all our commodities and to bring others unto us againe for our supplie.

Now two of these reasons are already effected unto our hands: that is to say: The place where we shall finde rich commodities, and ships to vent them. It remaineth only for our parts, to carrie and transport people with their provisions from England, where the miserie and necessitie of manie crie out for such helpe and reliefe.

This considered, no nation of Christendom is so fit for this action as England, by reason of our superfluous people (as I may tearme them) and of our long domesticall peace. And after that we be once 200 men strong, victualled and fortified, we can not be removoed by as many thousands.

For besides that, we have seene both in France and the Low-countreys, where 200 men well fortified and victualled, have kept out the forces both of the French & Spanish kings, even within their owne kingdomes: it shall be also a matter of great difficulty, to transport an army over the Ocean with victuals and munition, and afterwards to abide long siege abroad, against us fortified within, where the very elements and famine shall fight for us, though we should lie still and defend onely.

The Salvages neither in this attempt shall hurt us, they being simple, naked and unarmed, destitute of edge-tooles or weapons; whereby they are unable either to defend themselves or to offend us: neither is it our intent to provoke, but to cherish and win them unto Christianitie by faire meanes; yet not to trust them too far, but to provide against all accidents.

Then to conclude, as we of all other nations are most fit for a discovery and planting in remote places, even so, under the heavens there is no place to be found so convenient for such a purpose; by reason of the temperature, commodities, apt site for trade, & repaire thither already of so many ships, which in any other frequented countrey, can not be procured in a mans age, nor with expense of halfe a million.

So as the only difficultie now, is in our first preparation to transport some few people at the beginning; the charges whereof shall be defraied by our first returne, of fish and some commodities of Sassafras, Hides, Skinnes and Furres, which we shall also have by trading with the Salvages. The proofe of which commodities shall incourage our merchants to venter largely in the next.[2] The supplie shall easily and continually be sent by ships, which yeerely goe from hence unto the Newfound-land and us; and the intercourse & exchange we shall have with all nations repairing thither, shall store us with aboundance of all things for our necessities and delightes. Which reasons if they had beene foreseene of them that planted in the South part of Virginia (which is a place destitute of good harbours, and farre from all trade) no doubt but if they had settled neerer unto this frequented trade in the Newfound-land, they had by this time beene a flourishing State,[3] and plentifull in all things; who also might then have made way into the bowels of that large

2. Sidenote: "This action but set on foot, will goe forward of it selfe."
3. Sidenote: "Oversight in choice of a new habitation."

continent, where asuredly we shall discover very goodly and rich kingdomes and cities.

It may also seeme a matter of great consequence for the good and securitie of England; that out of these Northerly regions we shall be able to furnish this realme of all maner of provisions for our navies; namely, Pitch, Rosen, Cables, Ropes, Masts, and such like; which shall be made within those her Majesties owne dominions, by her owne subjects, and brought hither thorow the Ocean, free from restraint of any other prince; whereby the customes and charges bestowed by our merchants (to the inriching of forren Estates) shall be lessened, and turned to the benefit of her Highnesse and her deputies in those parts: which also shall deliver our merchants from many troubles & molestations which they now unwillingly indure in our East trades; and shall make us the lesse to doubt the malice of those States whom now we may not offend, lest we should be intercepted of the same provisions, to the weakening of our navie, the most roiall defence of this noble realme.

Of a convenient passage and trade into the South Sea, under temperate regions part by rivers, and some part over land, in the continent of America.

I Will adde hereunto an assured hope (grounded upon infallible reasons) of a way to be made part overland, & part by rivers or lakes, into the South seas unto Cathay, China, and those passing rich countreys, lying in the East parts of the world: which way or passage (supposed to be beyond the uttermost bounds of America, under the frozen Zone) is neverthelesse, held by the opinion of many learned writers and men of judgement now living, to be in these more temperate rigions; and that the same shall never be made knowen, unlesse we plant first; whereby we shall learne as much by inquisition of the naturall inhabitants, as by our owne navigations. I will not herein relie upon reports made in the French mens discoveries; that the sea which giveth passage unto Cathay, extendeth from the North, neere unto the river of Canada, into 44 degrees, where the same of the Salvages is called Tadouac.

Neither upon the discoveries of Jaques Noel, who having passed beyond the three Saults, where Jaques Cartier left to discover, finding the river of S. Laurence passable on the other side or branch; and afterwards, understood of the inhabitants, that the same river did lead into a mighty lake, which at the entrance was fresh, but beyond, was bitter or salt; the end whereof was unknowen.

Omitting therefore these hopes, I will ground my opinion upon reason and nature, which will not faile.

For this we know alreadie, that great rivers have beene discovered a thousand English miles into that continent of America; namely, that of S. Laurence or Canada, But not regarding miles more or lesse, most assuredly, that and other knowen rivers there doe descend from the highest parts or mountaines, or middle of that continent, into our North sea. And like as those mountaines doe cast from them, streames into our North seas; even so the like they doe into the South sea, which is on the backe of that continent.[4]

For all mountaines have their descents toward the seas about them, which are the lowest places and proper mansions of water: and waters (which are contained in the mountaines, as it were in cisternes) descending naturally, doe alwaies resort unto the seas inviroing those lands: for example; From the Alps confining Germanie, France, and Italie, the mighty river Danubie doth take his course East, and dischargeth into the Pontique sea: the Rhine, North, and falleth into the Germane sea: the Rhosne, West, and goeth into the Mediterran sea: the Po, South, is emptied into the Adriatick or gulfe of Venice. Other instances may be produced to like effect in Africk; yea, at home amongst the mountaines in England.

Seeing then in nature this can not be denied, and by experience elsewhere is found to be so, I will shew how a trade may be disposed more commodiously into the South sea thorow these temperate and habitable regions, than by the frozen Zones in the supposed passages of Northwest or Northeast: where, if the very moment be omitted of the time to passe, then are we like to be frozen in the seas, or forced to Winter in extreame cold and darkenesse like unto hell: or in the midst of Summer, we shalbe in perill to have our ships overwhelmed or crusht in pieces by hideous and fearefull mountaines of yce floting upon those seas.

Therefore foure Staple-places must be erected,

---

4. Sidenote: "A large course of a river thorow a mightie continent, produceth a portable river."

when the most short and passable way is found: that is to say, two upon the North side, at the head and fall of the river; and two others on the South side, at the head and fall also of that other river.

Provided, that ships may passe up those rivers unto the Staples, so farre as the same be navigable into the land; and afterwards, that boats with flat bottomes may also passe so high and neere the heads of the rivers unto the Staples, as possibly they can, even with lesse than two foot water, which can not then be far from the heads; as in the river of Chagre.

That necke or space of land betweene the two heads of the said rivers, if it be 100 leagues (which is not like) the commodities from the North and from the South sea brought thither, may wel be carried over the same upon horses, mules or beasts of that countrey apt to labour (as the elke or buffel) or by the aid of many Salvages accustomed to burdens; who shall stead us greatly in these affaires.

It is moreover to be considered, that all these countreys do yeeld (so farre as is knowen) Cedars, Pines, Firre trees and Oaks, to build, mast, and yeard ships; wherefore we may not doubt, but that ships may be builded on the South sea.

Then as ships on the South side may goe and returne to and from Cathay, China, and other most rich regions of the East world in five moneths or thereabouts; even so the goods being carried over unto the North side, ships may come thither from England to fetch the same goods, and returne by a voyage of foure or five moneths usually.

So as in every foure moneths may be returned into England the greatest riches of Cathay, China, Japan, and the rest which will be Spices, Drugges, Muske, Pearle, Stones, Gold, Silver, Silks, Clothes of gold, & all maner of precious things, which shall recompense the time and labour of their transportation and carriage, if it were as farre and dangerous as the Moores trade is from Fess and Marocco (over the burning and moveable sands, in which they perish many times, and suffer commonly great distresses) unto the river called Niger in Africa, and from thence, up the said river manie hundred miles; afterwards over-land againe, unto the river Nilus; and so unto Cairo in Egypt, from whence they returne the way they came.

Or if it were a voyage so farre as our merchants have made into Persia, even to Ormus, by the way of the North, through Russia into the Caspian sea, and so foorth, with paiment of many tolles. But this passage over and thorow the continent of America, as the same shall be alwaies under temperate and habitable climats, and a pleasant passage after it hath beene a little frequented: even so it must fall out much shorter than it seemeth, by false description of that continent, which doth not extend so farre into the West, as by later navigations is found and described in more exquisit charts. Besides that, the sea extends it selfe into the land very farre in many places on the South side; whereby our accesse unto the South ocean, shall be by so much the shorter.

XI

Sir Humphrey Gilbert's American Enterprises, 1578–1583, and Their Immediate Successors

THE GILBERT ENTERPRISES are important in the development of English concern with North America rather than for their positive achievements, which were minimal. The first venture is significant because the wide-ranging patent of June, 1578 (370), was a basis for later, more significant attempts to establish an English presence. The confusion of alleged objectives during the period of preparation may reflect indecision on Gilbert's part or else a smoke screen to cover a design to reconnoiter the coast north of Spanish Florida with the aid of a Portuguese pilot, Simon Fernandez (Simão Fernandes), who had been in the Spanish service. The project evoked from the elder Richard Hakluyt the first plan for an English settlement in temperate North America, although for a region between 40° and 45° N (359). The voyage itself, with its division of interests between Gilbert and his partner Henry Knollys, showed that it was still almost impossible to disentangle a legitimate colonizing project, which this appears to have been, from the piratical activities of most armed English vessels once they left their home waters. The venture split on this, Knollys going for robbery and Gilbert being forced back to Ireland by a storm and breaking off his voyage at Kinsale. The *Falcon* alone, under Walter Ralegh and with the Portuguese pilot on board, aimed to go to Puerto Rico and thence to the North American mainland, but after a call at the Canaries (386–387) appears to have run into difficulty off the Cape Verde Islands and to have returned from there. The venture would be scarcely worth notice if it had not produced more significant consequences.

From 1580 onward Gilbert acted as if he had rights over the whole eastern seaboard, granting permission to explore north of 50° to Dr. John Dee and apparently granting a similar permission for the Gulf of St. Lawrence to Edward Cotton (Vol. IV, no. 538). Gilbert, himself, concentrated on Norumbega, the later New England. The first reconnaissance by his small vessel, the *Squirrel* (8 tons), under Fernandez, successfully reached this area, but whether it reached Narragansett Bay or elsewhere is not known. It returned safely (388–389, 391), while another ship under John Walker did some trade with the Indians of Penobscot Bay (391). Although threatened with loss of his patent, he retained the support of Sir Francis Walsingham, the secretary of state. Through him he made contact with Catholic gentlemen anxious to escape the fiscal effects of anti-Catholic legislation (394–395). He then commenced a great land-sales program among Catholic and non-Catholic gentlemen and townsmen. From the contracts he made to dispose of lands he had never seen (but some of which were located round Verrazzano's "Refugio," Narragansett Bay [400]), much can be learned of his objectives. These included the planting of great feudalized estates in North America and placing himself as lord proprietor at the pinnacle of a hierarchy of inferior landholders (397). His Catholic and non-Catholic gentry associates were to have comparable estates and authority under his general supervision (399). Towns might be offered special trading privileges in the new congeries of colonies, and Southampton was finally selected for a privileged position (398). In all, at least twenty million acres were disposed of in a fantastic land-disposal campaign.

In the background, the younger Richard Hakluyt was preparing a small volume, *Divers voyages touching the discoverie of America*, that came out in May, 1582, and was intended to be a handbook on what was known of eastern North America, while a Hungarian poet, Stephen Parmenius, sang Gilbert's praises in Latin for a more learned audience. In 1582 it was intended that several reconnaissance voyages should be undertaken by his associates, and a more ambitious one by Gilbert himself. One valuable document, a plan for a survey of resources on the spot, is now available (401). For reasons so far partly undisclosed, his associates failed to get any ships to sea. Gilbert's own fleet at Southampton was held up by failure in organization and by exceptionally bad weather, and so the season for a direct voyage passed. Gilbert held on to the notion of a winter voyage by way of the Caribbean as long as possible, although by the end of 1582, he was forced to disband his men for the winter (407–411).

During the spring of 1583 Gilbert revived his venture, but under changed circumstances. Most of the Catholic gentlemen, except Sir George Peckham, withdrew in face of Spanish threats and charges of disloyalty to their faith; other supporters, such as Sir Philip Sidney, retired. On the other hand, Christopher Carleill, Walsingham's stepson, came into the field, aiming to settle in Acadia (the Maritimes) and possibly to penetrate the St. Lawrence. It was probably with the prospect of a passage to Asia by this route that he enticed the Muscovy Company to give him some support. His pamphlet *A breefe and sommarie discourse* (1583) (357) apparently had a wide circulation because it went into two editions. His venture was aimed at raising Bristol support and was aided by the younger Richard Hakluyt. Gilbert's own resources when he left were meager enough. The *Delight* (120 tons), the *Bark Ralegh* (200 tons) which rapidly deserted the expedition, the *Golden Hind* (40 tons), the *Swallow* (40 tons), and the *Squirrel* made up his fleet, which was poorly manned and victualed. He decided not to sail directly to Norumbega. The advantages of a Newfoundland foothold had been suggested to him and he hoped to reconnoiter the island. His voyage thus becomes one to Newfoundland and is dealt with under that heading (Vol. IV, nos. 534–538). After leaving the island, his expedition turned back when the *Delight* was wrecked on Sable Island, and he himself was lost at sea in the *Squirrel* late in September, 1583.

Sir George Peckham, cheered by the return of the *Golden Hind,* if dubious about Gilbert's survival, rapidly put in print a generalized plea for English colonization in America. His *True reporte of the late discoveries* (358) came out before the end of 1583. It praised Gilbert's achievements in Newfoundland but continued to set its sights on a settlement of the mainland farther south. But the promotion wave had subsided; money failed in spite of intensive advertising to come in (421–426), so he retired. Carleill made some progress during the early part of 1584 and set out in June, but his expedition broke up at Cork, the causes unascertained, and he transferred to the service of the queen in Ireland.

The main importance of the Gilbert ventures and those connected with them was the massive promotion enterprises with which they were associated. Thousands of English people learned of the prospects of American settlement for the first time. But the ineffectiveness and ill-luck of Gilbert and his friends on the one hand discouraged many potential investors and settlers, and on the other created a band of enthusiasts whose support for further, more practical enterprises could be assured. By 1584 there was clearly a public in England for whom American ventures were of substantial interest and concern and some would possibly invest and venture in them.

The promotion documents and treatises of the period 1576–1602 have been assembled as a separate section (355–368). The narrative materials of the 1583 expedition have been placed with other Newfoundland materials of which they are the center (Vol. IV, nos. 534–538). What is left mainly illustrates the organizational aspects of the venture.

Documents on the Gilbert ventures are collected in D. B. Quinn, ed., *The Voyages and Colonising Enterprises of Sir Humphrey Gilbert,* 2 vols. (London, Hakluyt Society, 1940), supplemented in D. B. Quinn and N. M. Cheshire, *The New Found Land of Stephen Parmenius* (Toronto, 1972). Hakluyt's *Divers voyages* and the earlier *A short and briefe narration of the two navigations . . . to . . . Newe Fraunce* (1580) (see Vol. I, nos. 203–204) were published in facsimile in Amsterdam in 1967, with an introductory volume by D. B. Quinn, *Richard Hakluyt, Editor.*

Chapter Forty-nine
The 1578 Expedition and Its Aftermath

369. May 14, 1578. Dedication of Enciso's *Geography* by John Frampton to Sir Humphrey Gilbert.

Before Sir Humphrey Gilbert had formulated his plans, although after his preparations had begun, a small book was published whose dedication indicated that it was intended to act as propaganda for his voyage. John Frampton, who had in 1577 published Nicolas Monardés's book on American medicinal plants, Joyfull newes out of the newfounde world, *put out his translation of Martin Fernández de Enciso's* Suma de geographia *(1519) without alteration and with its very inadequate information on North America. Interestingly enough, its information on the Caribbean would have some continuing value for English navigators. This was* A briefe description of the portes, creekes, bayes, and havens, of the Weast India *(1578). Later in the year the printer Henry Bynneman also published Thomas Churchyard's poem,* A discourse... whereunto is adjoyned a commendation of Sir Humfrey Gilberts ventrous Journey, *so that the two items were evidently part of a propaganda campaign to obtain support for Gilbert. Frampton's translation [S.T.C. 10823] exists in only two copies, one in the Henry E. Huntington Library and the other in the John Carter Brown Library.*

To the right worshipfull Sir Humphrey Gilbert Knight.

There came to my hands of late (right woorshipfull) a notable peece of woorke, of the Portes, and of divers rare things bothe of the Easte and Weast Indians, written by Martin Fernandes Denciso, aboute *Anno.* 1518. then Dedicated to Don Charles King of Castile, and after called in aboute twentie yeares past, for that it revealed secretes that the Spanish nation was loth to have knowen to the worlde. And finding in the same worke the Longitudes and Altitudes of many Ilandes, and of the Portes of the tracte of the firme lande of America, I thought good to translate out of Spanish into English some parte of the same Calling to minde, that your worship was the firste man of our nation that gave light to our people for the finding out of the north-west straight, and that now you meane in proper person, and that at your owne charges, to take some noble voyage and discoverie in hande, to leave behind you renowne to your family, and honour and profite to your countrie: I could not but honour you in harte. And to make some shew of my good will, I desired much to present some thing to you, and was sory that I had no notable worke of matter of Navigation to Dedicate unto you, meete for your so great worthinesse. But yet such as this is, I dedicate it unto you, besechyng you most humbly to take the same in good parte, and to way the good will of the giver, as very great persons of highe honour have done, when little trifels have bene given them by others of low degree. And Sir, albeit this small gifte (in respect of ministring any knowledge to you your self) may seeme nothing, in that you doe under stande the tongues, wherein this and many other knowledges of high value, lie hid from our Seamen, although not from you: yet this may for our meere English seamen, Pilotes, Marriners, &c. not acquaynted with forrayne tongues, bring great pleasure (if it fortune our Mariners or any other of our Nation, to be driven by winde, tempeste, currents, or by other chaunce to any of the Ilandes, Portes, Havens, Bayes or Forelandes mencioned in this Pamphlet,) and so it may also in the voyage, be a meane to keepe them the more from ildenesse, the Nurce of villany, and to give them also right good occasion by way of example, upon any new Discoverie, to take the Altitude and Latitude, to set downe the tracte of the Ilandes, the natures of the soyles, and to note the qualitie of the ayre, the severall benefites that the Soyles and the Rivers yeelde, with all the discomodities and wantes that the same places have, and if our Countrie men fortune the rather to be awaked out of their heavy sleepe wherein they have long lien, and the rather hereby be occasioned to shunne bestiall ignoraunce, and with other nations rather late than never to make themselves shine with the brightnesse of knowledge, let them give Sir Humfrey Gilbert the thankes, for whose sake I translated the same. And thus committing your worship to the greate Neptune, the greate God of the Christians that ruleth lande and Sea, I leave you to your voyage, and to the government of that mightie God, who never planted in any man so his courage, with so much desire to greate attempts, but to some greate end, as heretofore in many hath bene seeene, and as the sequele in your happie successes no doubt shall be founde, as England and the whole world shall out of question witnesse. From London the xiiij. of May. 1578.

Your worships at commaundement

[signed:] John Frampton

370. June 11, 1578. Patent granted to Sir Humphrey Gilbert by Elizabeth I.

The letters patent are evidence that the queen and her advisers were impressed by the ability of Gilbert to organize a voyage for discovery and by his plans for establishing a colonial settlement. The terms of the patent could be said to embody the fruits of all his thinking and practical experience of the previous ten years, but they were cast in a form that was already conventional. Like the much earlier patent of 1496 to John Cabot, no precise location was specified but it was generally taken to refer to North America alone. All of Gilbert's subsequent actions were based on the assumption that it covered the whole of the eastern coastline of North America, north of Spanish Florida, and overlapped the northwest area over which the Muscovy Company considered itself to have prior rights. It was subsequently regarded as the basic charter for English enterprise in North America and from it was derived, with little alteration, that granted to Walter Ralegh in

1584 after Gilbert's death. Gilbert's patent was valid for six years and covered both the 1578 and 1583 voyages.

From P.R.O., Patent Roll, 21 Elizabeth I, part 4, m.8–9. C66/1178; printed in Hakluyt, Principall navigations (1589), pp. 677–679. and in Principal navigations, III (1600), 135–137, VIII (1904), 17–23; D. B. Quinn, Gilbert, I (1940), 188–194.

The Letters Patents graunted by her Majestie to Sir Humfrey Gilbert knight, for the inhabiting and planting of our people in America.

Elizabeth by the grace of God Queene of England, &c. To all people to whom these presents shall come, greeting. Know ye that of our especiall grace, certaine science and meere motion, we have given and granted, and by these presents for us, our heires and successours, doe give and graunt to our trustie and welbeloved servaunt Sir Humfrey Gilbert of Compton, in our Countie of Devonshire knight, and to his heires and assignes for ever, free libertie and licence from time to time and at all times for ever hereafter, to discover, finde, search out, and view such remote, heathen and barbarous lands, countreys and territories not actually possessed of any Christian prince or people, as to him, his heires & assignes, and to every or any of them, shall seeme good: and the same to have, hold, occupie and enjoy to him, his heires and assignes for ever, with all commodities, jurisdictions and royalties both by sea and land: and the sayd sir Humfrey and all such as from time to time by licence of us, our heires and successours, shall goe and travell thither, to inhabite or remaine there, to build and fortifie at the discretion of the sayde sir Humfrey, and of his heires and assignes, the statutes or actes of Parliament made against Fugitives, or against such as shall depart, remaine, or continue out of our Realme of England without licence, or any other acte, statute, lawe, or matter whatsoever to the contrary in any wise notwithstanding. And wee doe likewise by these presents, for us, our heires and successours, give full authoritie and power to the saide Sir Humfrey, his heires and assignes, and every of them, that hee and they, and every, or any of them, shall and may at all and every time and times hereafter, have, take, and lead in the same voyages, to travell thitherward, and to inhabite there with him, and every or any of them, such and so many of our subjects as shall willingly accompany him and them, and every or any of them, with sufficient shipping, and furniture for their transportations, so that none of the same persons, nor any of them be such as hereafter shall be specially restrained by us, our heires and successors. And further, that he the said Humfrey, his heires and assignes, and every or any of them shall have, hold, occupy & enjoy to him, his heires or assignes, and every of them for ever, all the soyle of all such lands, countries, & territories so to be discovered or possessed as aforesaid, and of all Cities, Castles, Townes and Villages, and places in the same, with the rites, royalties and jurisdictions, as well marine as other, within the sayd lands or countreys of the seas thereunto adjoyning, to be had or used with ful power to dispose thereof, & of every part thereof in fee simple or otherwise, according to the order of the laws of England, as nere as the same conveniently may be, at his, and their will & pleasure, to any person then being, or that shall remaine within the allegiance of us, our heires and successours, paying unto us for all services, dueties and demaunds, the fift part of all the oare of gold and silver, that from time to time, and at all times after such discoverie, subduing and possessing shall be there gotten: all which lands, countreys and territories, shall for ever bee holden by the sayd Sir Humfrey, his heires and assignes of us, our heires and successours by homage, and by the sayd payment of the sayd fift part before reserved onely for all services.

And moreover, we doe by these presents for us, our heires and successours, give and graunt licence to the sayde Sir Humfrey Gilbert, his heires or assignes, and to every of them, that hee and they, and every or any of them shall, and may from time to time, and all times for ever hereafter, for his and their defence, encounter, expulse, repell, and resist, as well by Sea as by land, and by all other wayes whatsoever, all, and every such person and persons whatsoever, as without the speciall licence and liking of the sayd sir Humfrey, and of his heires and assignes, shall attempt to inhabite within the sayd countreys, or any of them, or within the space of two hundreth leagues neere to the place or places within such

countreys as aforesayd, if they shall not bee before planted or inhabited within the limites aforesayd, with the subjects of any Christian prince, being in amitie with her Majesty, where the said sir Humfrey, his heires or assignes, or any of them, or his or their, or any of their associates or companies, shall within six yeeres next ensuing, make their dwellings and abidings, or that shall enterprise or attempt at any time hereafter unlawfully to annoy either by Sea or land, the said sir Humfrey, his heires or assignes, or any of them, or his or their, or any of their companies: giving and graunting by these presents, further power and authoritie to the sayd sir Humfrey, his heires and assignes, and every of them from time to time, and at all times for ever hereafter to take and surprise by all maner of meanes whatsoever, all and every person and persons, with their shippes, vessels, and other goods and furniture, which without the licence of the sayd sir Humfrey, or his heires or assignes as aforesayd, shall bee found traffiquing into any harborough or harboroughs, creeke or creekes within the limites aforesayde, (the subjects of our Realmes and dominions, and all other persons in amitie with us, being driven by force of tempest or shipwracke onely excepted) and those persons and every of them with their ships, vessels, goods, and furniture, to detaine and possesse, as of good and lawfull prize, according to the discretion of him the sayd sir Humfrey, his heires and assignes, and of every or any of them. And for uniting in more perfect league and amitie of such countreys, landes and territories so to bee possessed and inhabited as aforesayde, with our Realmes of England and Ireland, and for the better encouragement of men to this enterprise: wee doe by these presents graunt, and declare, that all such countreys so hereafter to bee possessed and inhabited as aforesayd, from thencefoorth shall bee of the allegiance of us, our heires, and successours. And wee doe graunt to the sayd sir Humfrey, his heires and assignes, and to all and every of them, and to all and every other person and persons, being of our allegiance, whose names shall be noted or entred in some of our courts of Record, within this our Realme of England, and that with the assent of the sayd sir Humfrey, his heires or assignes, shall nowe in this journey for discoverie, or in the second journey our heires or successours: and that upon such for conquest hereafter, travel to such lands, countries and territories as aforesaid, and to their and every of their heires: that they and every or any of them being either borne within our sayd Realmes of England or Ireland, or within any other place within our allegiance, and which hereafter shall be inhabiting within any the lands, countreys and territories, with such licence as aforesayd, shall, and may have, and enjoy all the privileges of free denizens and persons native of England, and within our allegiance: any law, custome, or usage to the contrary notwithstanding.

And forasmuch, as upon the finding out, discovering and inhabiting of such remote lands, countreys and territories, as aforesayd, it shall be necessarie for the safetie of all men that shall adventure themselves in those journeys or voiages, to determine to live together in Christian peace and civill quietnesse each with other, whereby every one may with more pleasure and profit, enjoy that whereunto they shall attaine with great paine and perill: wee for us, our heires and successours are likewise pleased and contented, and by these presents doe give and graunt to the sayd Sir Humfrey and his heires and assignes for ever, that he and they, and every or any of them, shall and may from time to time for ever hereafter within the sayd mentioned remote lands and countreys, and in the way by the Seas thither, and from thence, have full and meere power and authoritie to correct, punish, pardon, governe and rule by their, and every or any of their good discretions and pollicies, as well in causes capitall or criminall, as civill, both marine and other, all such our subjects and others, as shall from time to time hereafter adventure themselves in the sayd journeys or voyages habitative or possessive, or that shall at any time hereafter inhabite any such lands, countreys or territories as aforesayd, or that shall abide within two hundred leagues of any the sayd place or places, where the sayd sir Humfrey or his heires, or assignes, or any of them, or any of his or their associats or companies, shall inhabite within six yeeres next ensuing the date hereof, according to such statutes, lawes and ordinances, as shall be by him the said sir Humfrey, his heires and assignes, or every, or any of them devised or established for the better governement of the said people as aforesayd: so alwayes that the sayd statutes, lawes and ordinances may be as neere as

conveniently may, agreeable to the forme of the lawes & pollicy of England: and also, that they be not against the true Christian faith or religion now professed in the church of England, nor in any wise to withdraw any of the subjects or people of those lands or places from the allegiance of us, our heires or successours, as their immediate Soveraignes under God. And further we doe by these presents for us, our heires and successours, give and graunt full power and authority to our trustie and welbeloved counseller, sir William Cecill knight, lord Burleigh, our high treasurer of England, and to the lord treasurer of England of us, for the time being, and to the privie counsell of us, our heires and successours, or any foure of them for the time being, that he, they, or any foure of them, shall, and may from time to time and at all times hereafter, under his or their handes or seales by vertue of these presents, authorize and licence the sayd sir Humfrey Gilbert, his heires and assignes, and every or any of them by him and themselves, or by their or any of their sufficient atturneys, deputies officers, ministers, factors and servants, to imbarke and transport out of our Realmes of England and Ireland, all, or any of his or their goods, and all or any the goods of his or their associates and companies, and every or any of them, with such other necessaries and commodities of any our Realmes, as to the said lord treasurer or foure of the privie counsell of us, our heires, or successours for the time being, as aforesayd, shall be from time to time by his or their wisedoms or discretions thought meete and convenient for the better reliefe and supportation of him the sayd sir Humfrey, his heires and assignes, and every or any of them, and his and their, and every or any of their said associates and companies, any act, statute, lawe, or other thing to the contrary in any wise notwithstanding.

Provided alwayes, and our will and pleasure is, and wee doe hereby declare to all Christian Kings, princes and states, that if the said Sir Humfrey, his heires or assignes, or any of them, or any other by their licence or appointment, shall at any time or times hereafter robbe or spoile by Sea or by land, or doe any act of unjust and unlawfull hostilitie to any of the Subjects of us, our heires, or successours, or any of the Subjects of any King, prince, ruler, governour or state being then in perfect league and amitie with us, injurie, or upon just complaint of any such prince, ruler, governour or state, or their subjects, wee our heires or successors shall make open proclamation within any the portes of our Realme of England commodious, that the said Sir Humfrey, his heires or assignes, or any other to whom these our Letters patents may extend, shall within the terme to be limited by such proclamations, make full restitution and satisfaction of all such injuries done, so as both we and the saide Princes, or others so complayning, may holde us and themselves fully contended: And that if the saide Sir Humfrey, his heires and assignes, shall not make or cause to bee made satisfaction accordingly, within such time so to be limited: that then it shall bee lawfull to us, our heires and successors, to put the said Sir Humfrey, his heires and assignes, and adherents, and all the inhabitants of the said places to be discovered as is aforesaide, or any of them out of our allegiance and protection, and that from and after such time of putting out of protection the saide Sir Humfrey, and his heires, assignes, adherents and others so to be put out, and the said places within their habitation, possession and rule, shal be out of our protection and allegiance, and free for all Princes and others to pursue with hostilitie as being not our Subjects, nor by us any way to bee advowed, maintained or defended, nor to be holden as any of ours, nor to our protection, dominion or allegiance any way belonging, for that expresse mention, &c. In witnesse whereof, &c. Witnesse our selfe at Westminster the 11. day of June, the twentieth yeere of our raigne. Anno Dom. 1578.

Per ipsam Reginam, &c.

371. September 23, 1578. Letter from Sir Humphrey Gilbert to Sir Francis Walsingham.

Sir Francis Walsingham was secretary of state from 1573 until his death in 1590. He was an ardent Protestant, concerned with foreign affairs, and took an active interest in voyages of discovery and attempts to establish colonies on the North American mainland, undertaken partly as a means to limit the power of Spain. As this letter shows he was a patron of Gilbert, an interest that was transferred to Walter Ralegh after Gilbert's death. His official position enabled him to give considerable help to Richard Hakluyt in his preparation of the first edition of Principall navigations, *which Hakluyt dedicated to him.*

P.R.O., State Papers, Domestic, Elizabeth I, SP 12/125,70; printed in D. B. Quinn, Gilbert, *I, 199–200.*

Sir knowinge you to be my principall patron aswell in furtheringe and procuringe me her majestes favor and lycence for performaunce of this my sea voyage and also manye other wayes having fownd you my good and honorable frend. I thoughte it my duyty to signefye unto your honor the state and tyme of my present departure from this porte of Dartmowthe which was on the xxiiith of this instante September beinge accompanied with xi sayle well victualed for a yere and furnished with 500 choyse souldiers and saylers. our staye so longe in these partes proceeded by reason of my London shippin[g] not comminge downe, which throughe contrarye windes arryved not here till the 25 of Auguste—Howbeyt our longe taryinge I truste shalbe noe impeachement to our enterprises, the tyme and season of the yere servinge yet verie fyt for our travell. I have nothinge els whereof to advertise your honor, but to assure you that I am and wilbe ever redye to doe you anye service that shall lye in my power, prayinge your honor not onlye to contynue your favor towardes me. But also as occasion shall serve, to make me partaker of your good speeches to her majesty for the better supportacion of my poore credyt with her highnes, And so I commyt your honor to god, Grenewaye the xxiiith of September 1578

Your honors moste humble to commaund

[signed:] H. Gylberte

Addressed:—To the righte honorble Sir Frauciss Walsingham knighte her majestes principall Secretary

Endorsed in other hand:—23 Novemb 1578 From Sir H: Gylbert

The tyme and nomber of shippes men &c, that departed with him from Dartmouth. To keepe him in hir Majesties good favour and Creditt.

372. November 18–19, 1578. Shipping of the respective fleets of Sir Humphrey Gilbert and Henry Knollys at their final departure.

Sir Humphrey Gilbert's own fleet, which left Plymouth on November 19, comprised the flagship, Anne Ager (or Anne Aucher) "Admiral" (250 tons), the Hope of Greenway (160 tons), "Vice-admiral," the Falcon (100 tons), formerly the queen's ship but now belonging to William Hawkins (386), the Red Lion (110 tons), the Gallion (40 tons), the Swallow (40 tons), and the Squirrel (8 tons). The full complement of the fleet is given as 365 gentlemen, soldiers, and mariners but the separate numbers given in the document add up to 388. The armament amounted to 106 pieces.

Henry Knollys's fleet, which left Plymouth a day earlier, on November 18, comprised the flagship ("Admiral"), the Elephant (140 tons), the Bark Dennye, and the Francis [or Armyn] (70 tons). The full complement is given as 160 (161 if added item by item); and the total armament was 53 pieces. State Papers, Domestic, Elizabeth I, SP12/126, 49. Printed in Carlos Slafter, Sir Humfrey Gyilberte (1903), pp. 253–258, and in D.B. Quinn, Gilbert, I (1940), 209–213.

Sir Humphrey Gilbert's Fleet at his Departure.

The names of all the Shippes Officers and gentlemen with the peces of ordynances in them And the number of all the Solgiars and mariners gonne in the viage with sir Humfrye Gilbert knight, generall in the same, for a dyscoverye to be made by him, who Toke the Seas From Plymouthe with vii Sayles the xixth day of November 1578.

1. An Ager.[1] admirall of the Flete in Burden ccl Tunes havinge Caste peces 24. fowlers 4. one Brasse pece. sir Humfry Gylbart generall Henrye Pedly master his mates. Richard Smythe. Boteswane. John Inglishe mr Battes deputye of his ship.

Richard Wigmore esquie[r]
Thomas Hamonde gent.
Thomas Skivington gent.
Edward Ventris gent.
} The whole number of gentlemen solgiars and mariners are cxxv.

Jaques Harvye a frenche gentleman
Thomas Olyver } Wolton gent.
William Heringe gent.
Thomas Renoldes gent.
William Stonewell gent.
Edward Dethicke gent.
John Friar phisition
Surgeons ii.
Musitians vi.
Trumpiter i.
Drume i.
} The whole number of gentlemen solgiars and mariners are cxxv.

2. The Hope of Greneway[2] Vice Admirall of clx Tunnes havinge in hir of Caste peces—xviii fowlers fower.

Carye Rawlye brother to sir Humfrye Gilberte Capitayne
Jacobbe Whidon master his mate John Perdew
William Horselye master Goner
Henrye Noell esquier. an Ancient by lande
Robert Wray gent.
James Fulford gent.
James Hilsdon gent.
George Whetstone gent.
Anthonye Hamerton gent.
Henrye Barker gent.
Androw Piper gent.
Surgeon i. Trumpiter i.
} The whole number of gentlemen solgiars and marinars are 80.

3. The Falcon[3] which was the Quenes ship of c Tunes havinge in hir of Caste peces—15. / fowlers. 4. doble bases 12.

Capitayne Walter Rawlye brother to sir Humfrye Gilberte a capitayne of An Anciant by Lande.
Fardinando the Portugale his master
Edward Eltope esquier
Charles Champernewne gent.
John Robertes gent.
John Flere gent.
Thomas Holborne gent.
John Antoll gent.
William Hugford gent.
} The whole number of gentlemen soligars and mariners are 70.

---

1. Sidenote: "Quid non."

2. Sidenote: "meliora spero."
3. Sidenote: "Nec mortem peto nec finem fugio."

4. The Red Lyon[4] of a cx Tunnes havinge caste peces xii Doble bases vi.

Myles Morgayne of Tred-
gar in the Countye of
Mulmot [Monmouth?] esquier Capitayne
John Anthony. his master
his mates Risa Spar-
owe. black Robin
Edward Marvoyle bote-
swane.
Drew Tonne master Goner
George Harbart gent.
Edmond Mathew gent.
Charles Bucly gent.
Risa Lewes gent.
John Martin gent.
Thomas Nycholas gent.
John Amerideth gent.
Lewes Jones gent.

The whole number of gen-
tlemen soligiars and
mariners are liii.

5. The Gallion[5] of 40 Tunns havinge of Caste peces vi videlicet fower fawlconetes one mynien, one falcon.

Richard Udall Capitayne
Cowrte   Heykenborow
master   his   mate
Richard Nycols
Thomas Fowler master
Goner
Benjamin Butler gent.
Frances Rogers gent.
George Worselye gent.
Arthur Messinger gent.

The whole number of gen-
tlemen solgiars and
mariners are xxviii.

6. The Swallow[6] of 40
Tunnes   Capitayne
John Vernye gent.

The whole number in hir
of solgiars and mar-
iners xxiiii

7. The lytell Frigat or Squerrill of viii Tunes The whole number of Solgiars and mariners are viii.

The whole number of gentlemen solgiars and mariner in this Fleete are } ccclxv.

The sayd ships were vitaled at thear departure
with Beff for thre monethes. Item with
Fyshe and Byscate for a yeare at iii byscates
a day for a man. With pease and Benes for a
yeare. Besydes particuler provisions.

Memorandum that sir Humfri his ships came to
Darkemothe August 25.

Dyvers provisions for aparell stollen away by a
pynisse Sept.8.

Mr Knollis came to Dartemouth the xth of September

Item he departe to Plymouth the 22 of September

Item the 26 of September the sayd navy departed
out of Dartemoth & wear dyspersed by contrary wyndes, some to the yle of Wyte some
other wayes.

Item the sayd ships arived at Plymouth. the
15 of October

Item the 29 of october inbarked agayne from
thence, & by tempest inforced to take harborow, whear they remayned untill the 19 of
November.

Henry Knollys' fleet at his departure.

The names of the ships officers and gentlemen as accompaned mr Henrye Knollis in his viage begonne the xviiith of November 1578.

The Eliphante Admirall beinge in Burden cl Tunes havinge of Cast Brasse peces xii, of Caste Iorne peces 12, fowlers vi.

Henrye Knollis esquier
Capitayne.
Frances Knollis gent his
brother, leftenant.
Olde Morse his master his
mate Thomas Grene.
John Callis Pilot.
William More master
Goner
John More Boteswane.
Fardynando Feldinge
gent.
Henry Smythe gent.
Simond Digby gent.
Everad Digby gent.
Walter Spenlow gent.

The whole number of gen-
tlemen solgiars and
mariners, c.
Well vitaled for a whole
yeare.

Barke Denye[7] vice admirall called the same a Frigat in leangth by the kele lxxii foote having Castes peces 9. fowlers ii.

Edward Denye esquier
Capitayne
John Granger master his
mates Edward Cales
and Blacborne
Master   Goner   Steven
Houlingby
George Hopton gent.
Jeremye Turner gent.

The whole number of gen-
tlemen solgiars and
mariners are xxx.

The Frenche Barke called the Frances of 70 Tunns havinge of Castes peces 4. of doble dogges 6. portugale Bases of Brasse 2.

Gregory Fenton Capitayne
The whole number is xxxi.
The whole number of gentlemen solgiars and } clx.
maryners in this Flete

---

4. Sidenote: "Aut nunc aut nunquam."
5. Sidenote: "Metuo crucem eam."
6. Sidenote: "iora trasiit periculii. Concordia minima criseunt."

7. Sidenote: "Quis prohibet."

Captayne Sharpam and Master Foscue are also nere in a Redynes with v ships vittaled for a yeare for ccl persons bounde in a lyke viage.

Endorsed:—A note of the ships and persons gone with Sir Humfrey Gylbert.

CORRESPONDENCE ON THE DEPARTURE OF GILBERT'S EXPEDITION

AS THE FIRST major colonizing expedition, Gilbert's venture attracted considerable comment and correspondence. Its course was followed by the Spanish ambassador (376), and several English officials provide us with sidelights on its development (374–375). Thomas Radcliffe, earl of Sussex, was a member of the Privy Council, Edward Fiennes de Clinton, earl of Lincoln, was lord high admiral, William Cecil, Lord Burghley, was lord high treasurer; Edmund Tremayne as clerk of the Privy Council, Henry Killigrew, M.P. for Truro in Cornwall, and William Davison (later a privy councilor and secretary of state) would also be interested in Gilbert's voyage.

Gilbert's letter to Sussex is from BM, Cotton MS Otho E viii, f.67; Lincoln to Burghley from Hatfield House, Cecil MS 214/11, calendared in HMC, *Cecil MSS*, xiii, 164; Killigrew to Davison from State Papers, Domestic, Elizabeth I, Additional, SP 15/25, 116 (extract); Tremayne to Burghley from Hatfield House, Cecil MS 161/85, calendared in HMC, *Cecil MSS*, II, 218–219. All are printed in D. B. Quinn, *Gilbert*, I (1940), 200–203.

373. September 23, 1578. Sir Humphrey Gilbert to the Earl of Sussex.

[. . .] this [my sea voyage for the] performance of w[hich] there is in my syllye fleete [xi sayle] well victayled for a yeare, and [furnished with] five hundrethe choyse souldiers, si[gnifying unto your honour that] our longe staye in these partes pr[oceeded by reason of] the contrarye windes, which stayed m[y London] shippinge from comminge abowte hither u[ntill the] xxvth of Auguste, whereby alth[ough I] have bin dryven to a farther chardge os[tensiblie] then I loked for, yet dought not but [that] the time and season of the yere will se[rve yet] verie aptely for our travells. Thus mu[ch] have I thoughte good to signefye unto your [lordship] tochinge the state and tyme of my departur[e] from hence, besechinge you to contynue your fa[vour] towardes me, in sorte as I have here tofore fown[de in] you assuring your good Lordship that you shall ever

finde me ready to doe you anye service that shall lye in my power. And so prayinge your good Lordship to presente my humble duytie to my good Ladye your wief. I cease to troble you anye farther / Greinewaye this xxiiith of September 1578 /

your Honors moste humble to commaund

[signed:] H. Gylberte

Addressed:—To the righte honorable and my very good Lord Therle of Sussex. H G.

374. October 9, 1578. Earl of Lincoln to Lord Burghley.

My very good Lord

I do humbly thank your Lordship for your leter, wherby I perseve yow have had some knolayge of ye deling of Mr Pelam and others who take apon them to dele with pyrattes goods insomoch as they when the fynd ye goods stayd for her Majeste the convey it from thens to such plasis as they may dystrybut and convey it to ther owne use and dyseve her Majestie / and for y your Lordship may better know ther delynges as well in Sussex as in ye west countrey I send your Lordship herwith soch letters as I have resevyd from thens to thend your Lordship may take order for ye reformasyon of ther doinges / and your Lordship shall perseve how thes gentyllmen y^t ar gon to seke a voyage into ye Indya do behave themsellffes I have forder advartesments wych I wyll send your Lordship, bot presently I can not fynd my lettars I am sorry to hear y^t soch boldnes is takyn to do on the see y^t wych is not to be alowed nor lykyd whereof your Lordship shall hear more very shortly and thus I leve forder to troble your Lordship at this tym and wishe yow long lyffe in moch honor From ye Cort the ixth of Octobr, 1578.

Your Lordships assurd to command

[signed:] E. Lyncoln

Addressed:—To the right honorable and my verie good Lord the Lord High treasurer of Ingland.

Endorsed:—9 octob. 1578 The L. Admirall to my L. towching the wreke in Sussex. Sir Humfrey Gilberts demeanor.

375. October 17, 1578. Edmund Tremayne to Lord Burghley.

By letters from my good Lord therle of Bedford I here that Sir H. Gilbert hath but a badd begynninge of his voyage. For setting forth out of Dartmouth about thende of the last moneth, he was incountered with a contrarie winde, which dispersed all his shippes and beinge sore beatten with weather, were inforced, not without grete daungier, to come back againe to Dartmouth, where at verie grete chargies, they remained the xth of this present, being the date of his Lordships letters. Sir Humfrey himself being in the

admirall was driven to the Kowe [Cowes] by the Isle of Wieght, where he remained till the daie aforesaid, for want of winde to bringe him Westwardes. I am sorrie that so forwarde a mynde, hath so backwarde succease. And so prainge pardon of my boldenesse I most humblie take my leave, with desire of your Lordship's good helth and gretenesse to your hartes desire. From Ankerwik the xviith of October 1578.

[Holograph. Addressed:]—To the right Honorable my verie good Lord the Lord Thresorer of Englande

[Endorsed:]—17 octob. 1578. Mr Tremain to my L. with a letter from Sir Rich: Grenefeild.

376. June 3, 1578 to February 26, 1579. Spanish evidence on Gilbert's expedition.

The correspondence of Don Bernardino de Mendoza, Spanish ambassador in London, if not always reliable, provides additional evidence on Gilbert's 1578 voyage. The letters are taken from Navarette, Documentos inéditos para la historia de España, *XCI, 243–244, 249–250, 271, 394, 549, 557; translated and calendared in* C.S.P. Spanish 1568–79, *nos. 503, 510, 521, 549, 557, 580; printed in D. B. Quinn,* Gilbert, *I (1940), 187–188, 194, 199, 219, 223. Extracts.*

[a]   June 3, 1578.
Don Bernardino de Mendoza to Philip II.

On the 16th of last month I wrote to your Majesty about the ships that Onpegilberto [Humphrey Gilbert] has ready here and although they say that he will make a different course from the one that master Stuquel intends to take (who as I wrote to your Majesty is going with six ships), it is thought that once they get out to sea, they will join and make a course for the Indies, unless anything happens in Ireland or Scotland to make them change. And for this purpose they are taking with them one Simon Fernandez, a Portuguese, a thorough-paced scoundrel, who has given and is giving them much information about that coast, which he knows very well. As I am told, he has done no little damage to the king of Portugal by reason of the losses suffered in this kingdom by his subjects by reason of this man. When Champagni was here it was arranged with the Earl of Leicester in his own room—the Queen being present—that the way to insure themselves against your Majesty and put a stop to your good fortune was to make a course to the Indies and rob the fleets, unless they could establish a footing on the coast, for thus they would prevent so much money coming to your Majesty, a matter which is likewise continually urged by Orange, who is of the same way of thinking.

[b]   June 13, 1578.
Don Bernardino de Mendoza to Philip II.

After I wrote to your Majesty on the 3rd (duplicate sent on the 11th) there has arrived here one Coques [Cox] master of a ship which two and a half years ago sailed for the Indies in company of another ship, Bacar [Barker] being in command of both. He says they landed men on *terra firma* near the river Acha, where he has been a year and a half among the Camarones [Cimaroons], and that these are the men who plundered the son of Don Cristobal de Eraso and, according to what they say, along with this prize they put away 20,000 escudos taken from others. This Coques carried in his ship—which was the smaller—80 men, and only 14 have returned. They can give no news of Bacar or the rest, as they fled from the mainland in what they call a launch [lancha], taking with them a small boat, in which. they reached the island of Suie [Scilly?] on the west and Cornualla [Cornwall] coast. It is said that the Queen has ordered him to be arrested for having returned without the Captain and men. I suspect this will not be carried out, because he is trying to return with the ships Onpegilberto [Humphrey Gilbert] is taking out, urged by hopes of great gain, though things have gone badly with them. The Queen has given him [Gilbert] permission to start on his voyage as also to Jorvirger [Frobisher], as I wrote to your Majesty. I have men watching on this shipmaster to inform me if he sails on this voyage, and to know what is Onpegilberto's aim in taking him, and I have plans

well advanced for getting hold of Jorvirger's sailing chart.

[c]   August 14, 1578.
Don Bernardino de Mendoza to Gabriel de Zayas.

In the ships of Onofre Gilberto [Humphrey Gilbert] I have sent a special man to give a complete account of the voyage if he returns. It has been a good piece of luck finding a skilled man and trustworthy (since he is English). Make this known to His Majesty. I have given him orders, that if on the return, they touch at Spain he is to go straight to Madrid and see you in order to inform you as to what may have happened.

[d]   February 7, 1579.
Don Bernardino de Mendoza to Philip II.

The ships with which Onfre Gilberto [Humphrey Gilbert] and Conols [Knollys] had sailed, as I wrote to your Majesty on 8 December, have returned under stress of weather to Ireland, where they are revictualling in order to resume their voyage.

[e]   February 26, 1579.
Don Bernardino de Mendoza to Gabriel de Zayas.

Onfregilberto [Humphrey Gilbert] and Conoils [Knollys] have returned to this kingdom with all their ships, having contented themselves with having captured a French ship carrying merchandise. One of them is at Court. They have disarmed their ships. The man I sent in them has returned.

[f]   June 20, 1579.
Don Bernardino de Mendoza to Philip II.

The Queen has received news that Jaime Fenemoris [James Fitzmaurice], the Irishman, was off the coast of Cornualla [Cornwall] with a ship of 800 tons and two smaller ones with which he had taken an English ship of Bristol and thrown all the crew into the sea. For this reason Onfregilberto [Humphrey Gilbert], who was going about robbing, has been ordered to go out to deal with the Irishman, who, although he has not many ships, appears to have given them a fright.

GILBERT EXPLAINS WHY KNOLLYS SEPARATED
FROM THE EXPEDITION

BETWEEN SEPTEMBER 26, when the whole fleet left from Dartmouth, and the beginning of November, when the fleet, scattered by storms, reassembled, first at Dartmouth and then at Plymouth, relations between Gilbert and Knollys were so strained that Knollys decided to break with Gilbert and set out on his own. Anticipating this, Gilbert wrote to Walsingham to ensure that his version of the cause of friction reached Walsingham early. He also made a sworn statement before justices of the peace at Plymouth recording his account of the quarrel.

State Papers, Domestic, Elizabeth I, SP 12/44 and SP 12/46. Printed in Carlos Slafter, *Sir Humfrey Gylberte* (1903), pp. 245–252 (377–379) and D. B. Quinn, *Gilbert*, I (1940), 203–209. Gilbert's letter to Walsingham, November 18 (378), is also printed in E. G. R. Taylor, *Hakluyts* I (1935), 135–136.

377. November 12, 1578. Sir Humphrey Gilbert to Sir Francis Walsingham.

Sir as in all my occasions heretofore I have ever founde you my most honorable freinde, so in my gretest extremities I meane such as by false suggestions maye hazard my creditt, I will never dispaier to fynd lesse favour, duringe the longe contrarietie of the wyndes by what perswasions ledd god knoweth Master Knoles hathe forsaken my Companye in my pretended jorney and unto hyme drawen as many as either the longe tyme of staie by contrarie wyndes have tyred or his affeccion allured, which is noe otherwise then from the begynninge I douted for noe curtesie or patience of my parte could possiblie cause Master Knoles to thinke me either mete to direct or advise hym and yet to abide the hardiest construccons that maye be, I never offred such cause as might either be a discreditt unto him to susteyne, or any occasion to breke of so honest an enterprice, but once before this tyme he in like refused the jorney, wherin by meanes of Sir John Gilbert my brother he was once agayne reconciled and the brech by me omitted and forgotten. But still to be trobled with every smale surmised occasion I counte it a greater disturbaunce to me then my pretended jorney I hope shalbe. For without eny occasion ministred he often and openly persuaded my company and gentlemen to my disgrace howe much he embased and subjected himself to serve under me Consideringe his estimacion and creditt, accomptinge him self as he often and openlie saied equal in degree to the best knightes and better then the most in Englande, Farther he in my owne heringe not onely used me so disdaynfullie both in spech and countenaunce as my rashe and folish Condicion hath seldome bynne sene accustomed to endure, but also taken partes and boldened such of my companye as I throughe theire brech of pece and bloodshed with other intollerable disorders have admonished or found fault with all which I held my duetye both as a Justice and governer by comission over my companye, Farther in open presence of gentlemen of all sortes to my grete disgrace when I entretid him unto my table he answered me that he had money to paie for his dynner as well as I, and that he would leve my trencher for those beggers that were not able to paie for theire meles, which semed a bare thankes for my good will, besides in my absence he thretened to hange a captayne and gentleman of my company called Morgan in lyvinge litle or nothinge inferiour to hym self, And one that was not longe before shrife of the Shiere wherein he dwelt. Farther my Lord of Bedforde comaunded Master Lyeile a Justice of the pece to require Master Knoles in his behalf and all the rest of the Justices in the Quenes Majesties name to delyver two of his company which ymbrued theire handes in the blood of a gentleman called John Leonard that was of late wilfullie murdered in Plymouth, which Master Knoles utterlie refused to doe, the maiour of the towne

Sir John Gilbert and my self requiringe hym in like manner, Besids this his men had almost killed a constable, but they would not be delyvered to ponishment, Farther Master Knoles shippe toke Holbeame a notorious pyratt and did lett hym goe which bred me grete slaunder of suspicion of pyracie, Besides he fell in outragious termes of daringe of a Justice of peace which thinges together with his disdainfull usage of me gave me just cause to doute his tractablenes at see that carid so little for Justice counselours & Justices of the peace a shore. Whereuppon I told him privatlie by waye of counsell as my freind without quarell or wordes of offence, that he used me somewhat to disdainfullie consideringe the goodwill I bare hym and the place I held, and that if he used hym self in this sorte and uphold such as offended by his countenaunce, it would not onely kyndle dislike betwene him and me, but also brede faction and sedicion. uppon this onely it plesed him to take hold, sayeng that I called him proude & sedicious, and so haynouslie racked it, that he left my company and consorte, But unto willinge myndes there nedes no grete enforcementes, beyng as it semes, by some of his company persuaded to runne a shorter course, which I pray god, it maye turne to his advauncement and creditt, for he hath store of notorious evill men about hym as Loveles & Callice with others; Assuringe you that I am for strenght as well able to performe that which I undertoke as I desired havinge of my owne shipps seaven sayle well manned and victualled. So that my onely sute unto your honor is, that as you have bene allwayes the piller unto whome I lent, so I hope you will allwayes remayne in my juste occasions such a one as I in goodwill and service desier to deserve if god of his mercye doe but geve me leve and hapely to returne, I then hope you shall fynd that I will at last performe somewhat of that which I in thought and goodwill have with my self longe promised, desiringe onelye in this matter for the satisfaccion of the truth, herof and of my behaviour every waye that it maye plese your honor ether to send my lettres to the Maiour and towne of Plymouth to retourne there knowledge of theis my behaviour either els to write to my Lord of Bedford that by him you may be satisfied from them of the matter. And so to condemme me if I be found fautie, to my reproche wherin I desiere noe favour. And so I most humbly Committ your

honor to god. Plymouth this xiith of November 1578.

Your honors most humble to Commaunde
    [signed:] H. Gylberte.

Addressed:—To the Right honorable Sir Fraunces Walsingham knight principall Secretarie to her Majestie theis be delivered—H G.

Endorsed:—12. Novemb. 1578

From Sir H. Gylbert of Mr H: Knollys unkynd & yll dealyng towards him & others the best of the Countie of Devon: wheruppon their societie in the viage is broken of.

378. November 18, 1578. Sir Humphrey Gilbert to Sir Francis Walsingham.

Sir as in my former lettres (I advertised your honour) by what straunge accident, Master Knoles hathe left the service, he understooke with me, before her Majestie moved by such trifles or toyes / As (under your honors correction) were meter to breke amitie amongest children, rather than men. So bycause I doe waye; in equall ballance, with lif, your honors good opinion of me, I thoughte it good, to sende your honor this certificat, under the Maiours hand of Plymouthe; and other of her Majesties servauntes and captaynes, who were presente; when I publikely desired, Master Knoles, to declare all the causes, that moved hym to mislike. All which he did, or could allege are particulerly sett downe; in the said Certificat, Committinge my self upon the sight therof, to be judged, as the thynge it self shall gyve cause; but truely I can gesse noe other, but that his pretence was to breke of, from the begynning: and ranne this course thereby to have cullour to arme to see. And then withall, either to learne my enterprice, & so to undertake the discoverye of hym self, as one moved there unto, throught ambicion, and disdayne, either els to runne some shorter course, which I wishe to prove mete for his callinge. I most humbly beseche your honour to ymparte this certificat to the Quenes Majestie my Lord of Leceister, & Master Vicechamberlayne; with such other as to your honour shall seme good. But my principall care is, to satisfie you, above all others, bycause your honour was thonly meanes of my lycence. And therefore as my patrone I studie principallie next unto her Majestie, to mayntayne my self in your good opinion, Whome I my self will honor and serve duringe lif noe man more. And I trust god willinge to bringe althinge to good passe, theis Crosses and thwartes notwithstandinge. Moreover my cosen Deny doth accompany Master Knoles in this his brech & retire from our consorte the cause of my cosin Denys departure was only for that I blamed hym for striken of a sayler with his naked sworde, whoe had not his wepon drawen desiringe hym to leve quarellinge, for that it was a thinge verey unmete for this jorney. And if he left it not I judge hym not fitt for the voyage, whereuppon he verey outragiouslye and with very unsemely termes abused me in not only challenginge me, but also in dispitfull manner defyenge me which I thought to be hardly donne, consideringe I holde the places of a Justice of pece in the country. And thus your honours hath thoccasion also of this his speech, wherin if I have enformed your honour otherwise then trothe, then judge me a villayne and a knave. For better accompte I judge noe man worthe that shalbe founde unjust in word and dede. And this I hold for my best tryall And so I most humbly commit your honour to god with my duetifull comendacion to my good Ladye. Plymouth this xviiith of November 1578.

Your honours humble most assured to Commaunde

[signed:] H. Gylberte.

Sir I am sympully worthe the accomptynge of, but as I am, I am and ever wilbe your honours humbull and moste faythfull to commande and longer then I shall shewe my selffe worthe (in respecte of not beynge gylte of villany) of your favour, to be adjudged by the tochestone of every mans honeste I praye you leve and forsake me, as one not worthe of your protection.

Addressed:—To the Right honorable Sir Fraunces Walsingham knight principall secretary to her Majestie theis. H G.

Endorsed:—18. Novemb. 1578. From Sir H. Gilbert with a certificatte of the cawses of Mr Henrie Knollys departure from him in this viage: wherwith he desyrethe that hir Majestie & other of my L. may be made acquaynted. The cawse also of his cousen Dennyes departure from him.

379. November 5–[18], 1578. Certificate of the reasons why Henry Knollys separated from Sir Humphrey Gilbert.

A Certificat of the cawses of Master Knoles forsakinge the Jorney, and consorte of Sir Humfry Gilbert knighte, alleged before the Maiour of the towne of Plymouth Master John Hele Justice of pece, and dyvers other gentlemen, the fifte of November 1578 viz

1. Imprimis the causes of discurtesie, that Master Knoles could allege; why he would breke of the jorney, with sir Humfry Gilbert, and leve the voyage; were that sir Humfry Gilberte saied he was factious, sedicious, and proude; To which sir Humfry Gilbert gave answere, as followeth.

2. Item he saieth, he never called hym factious, or, sedicious, but said, that if he gave countenaunce to men of evill and disordered behaviour, then he should nourrice faction and sedicion, which woordes sir Humfry Gilbert spake privatlie to hym, and not to defame hym, or by way of quarell, but Master Knoles, with that his publike deniall, would not be satisfied. Except sir H. Gilbert would there openly swere upon a boke that he never spake it, which sir H. Gilbert refused, saienge othes oughte to be reserved for Judges. /

3. Item touchinge the accusinge hym of pride; sir Humfry Gilbert denied not, but that Master Knoles did esteme hym self to much and hym to litle, alleginge that Master Knoles had dyvers tymes spoken woordes to his disgrace and disdaine, as dispisinge his knighthoode, saienge he toke hym self to be a better man than xx knightes. And that he often tymes had refused that degree as a callinge he estemed not of.

4. Item moreover Master Knoles often openly reported that he had submitted & embased hym self, to serve under sir Humfry Gilbert, takinge hym self to be farre better in estimacion, then eny of the company. /

5. Item moreover when Sir Humfry Gilbert bad

Master Knoles to dynner, he answered that he had monye to paie for his dynner, aswell as he, And that he would leve his trencher, for those that were not able to paie for theire meles, which thinge made Sir Humfry Gilbert judge; that Master Knoles estemed of hym verey litle, consideringe the place he held, by her Majesties comission. All which wordes Master Knoles confessed he spake.

6. And yet not withstandinge Sir Humfry Gilbert toke not it, as eny quarell, but semed lothe to leve his Company, but noe curtesie or patience of his parte coulde perswade or content hym.

Wm Hawkyns
Jhon Robertes
W. Rauley: Myles Morgan
Edmond Eltoftes

Memorandum one the xiith of November Master Wigmore who was only presente; when sir Humfry Gilberte should call Master Knoles factious and sedicious denied the heringe therof, but that sir Humfry Gilbert saied to theffect as afore by hym self is confessed and not otherwise then is in the second Artic[le].

Myles Morgan
Henrie Noelles
W. Rauley: Jhon Robartes
Edmond Eltoftes

Endorsed:—Certificatt from diveres men of the towne of Plimmouthe what the cawses of Mr Henrie Knollys departure from Sir H. Gilbert in his viage.

Chapter Fifty
The Aftermath of Gilbert's 1578
Expedition

KNOLLYS WITH his three ships ventured only as far as Ireland, taking a Breton ship and disposing of her goods in Cork or Dungarvan. He returned to England without the *Bark Dennye* and sent the *Francis* on a privateering voyage to Spanish waters. The expedition under Gilbert, with seven vessels, also made for Ireland, subsequently returning to England except for the *Falcon*, which appears to have gone out into the Atlantic as far as the Cape Verde Islands (387). The orders from the Privy Council show that Gilbert had returned by April, 1579, was contemplating a further voyage, and that the piratical activities of his associates had come to the attention of the council.

Acts of the Privy Council, 1578–80, pp. 108, 142–143, 146; printed in D. B. Quinn, *Gilbert*, I (1940), 220–223.

380. April 20, 1579. The Privy Council revokes Sir Humphrey Gilbert's license to travel.

To Sir Humfrey Gilbert for revoking of him from his intended journey at the seas for seking of forreyne cuntries, or if he shall procede in it, that he putt in suerties, &c. according to the minute in the counsell Chest.

381. May 28, 1579. The Privy Council writes to Sir John Gilbert.

xxviii Maii 1579

A letter to Sir John Gilbert that wheras heretofore their Lordships wrote their letters to his brother, Sir Humfrey, that either he would in respecte of divers misfortunes wherwith he had been crossed forbeare to proceade any further in his intended voyage, or els put in good bandes and suerties to her Majesties use for his and his companyes good behaviour on the seas; by letters of his of the vith of this present and Sir Humfreyes of the viiith their Lordships understoode that haveing before the receipt therof repaired to the seas, and could not without great losse staie, did not performe the said order accordingly, in the meane time the said Sir John assured their Lordships that his brother and his companie were cleere of suche complaintes as were made of spoiles and injuries to be by them committed, and did undertake to be aunswerable for them; howbeit sith that time complaintes have been brought before their Lordships of the like disorders committed by his brother or his companie, and that sith the date of the said letters he hath a good whiles remained on that coast, and hath not put in bandes accordinglie; and amongst the rest it is complained by Gonzala de Levilia, a Spaniarde that the iiiith of this present his brother as it is said being at his house of Grenewaye, which was the verie same daie on which he writeth his brother to be departed to the seas, a certain barke laden with oranges and lemons lyinge at anker was, by some of his brother's companie, taken out of her Majesties streames at Walfled Bay within the Castell, he is required to see the said Spaniard restored to his barke and goodes or otherwise sufficientlie recompenced; and for that their Lordships are advertised that his brother, Sir Humfrey, is not yet departed and his brother, Walter Rawley retorned to Dartmouthe, like as their Lordships have written to the Sheriffe, Viceadmiral and Justices of that countie to commande them both to staie, so he is required frendlie to advise them to surcease from proceeding anie further, and to remaine at home and answer such as have been by their companie domaged.

382. May 28 and May 31, 1579. The Privy Council writes to the Sheriff, etc., of Devonshire.

[a] xxviii Maii 1579

A letter to the Sheriffe, Viceadmirall and Justices of Peace in the county of Devon, &c., requiringe them to assemble them selves together in some mete place, and there, with the assistaunce of the Maiour and other officers of priviledged townes, take order that no person or shipping passe to the seas in warlike manner, although the parties would put in bandes and suerties for their good behaviour, commanding them, upon paine of her Majesties indignacion, to desist from any such enterprise, and that forth-[with] they charge Sir Humfrey Gilbert and his companie, if he be not allreadie departed and maye convenientlie be sent unto, to repaire to lande, and Walter Rawley, his brother, Eltophe and other, who are retorned to Dartmouthe, to remaine on lande, in her Majesties name charginge everie of them to surcease to proceade in that their enterprised journeye, and to medle no further therin without expresse order from their Lordships; and where a certaine Spanishe vessell laden with lemons and orenges is found to have ben taken [out] of her Highnes' porte at Dartmouthe by some of Sir Humfrey Gilbertes men, and the persones afterwarde landed at Torbaye, they are required to make diligent enquirie

therof and to doe their best endevours for the apprehendinge and committinge of th'offendours to be aunswerable to lawe for their misdemeanours; and Sir John Gilbert who had undertaken to aunswer for his brother's doinges, is required to content the complainant so as he may departe satisfied and procure [sic] no further inconvenience, as their Lordships also have written in a letter aparte to him self.

[b] laste of May 1579

A letter to the Sheriff, Viceadmirall, Commissioners of Piracies and Justices of Peace in the county of Devon requiringe them to make diligent enquirie of all piracies by seas and robberies by lande committed by anye suche persons which heretofore pretended to accompanie Sir Humfrey Gilbert, knight, Walter Rawley, Fortescue and others in their voyages, and to either commit them to prison, or, if they shall so see cause, to take good bandes of them to be forthcominge to aunswer to such thinges as they shalbe charged with according to lawe; commaunding the rest of the mariners and companie, being of other countyes of the Realme, either to repaire home to the places of their former aboade, geving them their pasportes, or if they will remaine there, to be of such good behaviour as no complainte be made of their misdemeanors; and whereas it is enformed unto their Lordships that those disorded personnes make their aboade commonlye in the roade of Torbay, and having committed any piracies bring the spoile to lande, they are required all in generall, and especiallie the Commissioners for Piracies and the Justices of Peace dwelling thereabout, and principallie Mr. Carye of Cockington, to have diligent care for the safetie of the shippes that repaire thither, and for removing of the said pirates and apprehencion of them when they shall come to lande after any suche facte by them committed, and either to commit them to safe custodie or take bandes of them to be forthcoming to aunswer to lawe.

383. January, 1580. Examination of the crew of the *Francis* concerning piracy.

The records of the High Court of Admiralty have several cases relating to piracies committed by

Henry Knollys's ships, notably by the Francis, *whose master, Richard Derifall, was afterwards hanged for his part in these depredations. So far as is known Miles Morgan's ship, the* Red Lion, *was the only one of Sir Humphrey Gilbert's vessels to take part in this piratical activity, although vague charges were also leveled at Gilbert himself.*

The Articles (a) are from High Court of Admiralty, Libels. HCA 24/50, 10; the examination of Stephen Jackson (b) from High Court of Admiralty, Examinations, Instance and Prize. HCA 13/24. Both are printed in D. B. Quinn, Gilbert, *I (1940), 232–236.*

[a] Interrogatories to be administered to those who were on the Armyn alias the Frauncyes.

1. From whence are you? Where have you been on the seas during these last nine months?

2. Who was captain, owner, victualler of the ship? Where on the seas have you been, and by whom authorised?

3. Do you know the two French ships: the Margaret of the burden of about 100 ton, master Stephen Phichot of Normandy; the other of like burden, called the Marye, master William Malhearbe of Normandy; both laden with woollen cloth?

4. Were either of the two ships boarded by the Armyn of Brest, afterwards called the Fraunceys, their goods taken to the Isle of Bayon and there loaded on to the Armyn?

5. What was done with the ships, or either of them, their merchandise, munitions and tackle?

6. Was not parcel of the merchandise sold at Torbay in Cornwall or thereabouts?

7. Whether the surplus of the goods was not put in the Castle Cornet or other place in the Isle of Guernsey.

8. Was not part of the cloth uttered for sale in the said Isle? Who were the buyers?

9. What were the marks on the said merchandise?

10. Was part of the merchandise brought from the Isle in the ship called the Armyn? Where was it unladen and to whom assigned?

11 and 12. What were the names of the buyers, and also of the officers, soldiers and mariners on the said ship?

13. Do you not know that part of the said merchandise was put into hogsheads and other barrels to disguise and convey them away?

14. Who kept the account of the division of the merchandise?

15. Was division made at Torbay? Did Richard Aldersey or any other receive one half for the owner, Mr. Henry Knowles?

16. Did not Mr. Henry Knowles come to Guernsey?

17. Did you come from Guernsey in the said ship, Mr. Knowles being in her?

18. At the setting forth of the ship called the Armyn alias the Frauncyes at the Isle of Wight or thereabouts was not Mr. Henry Knowles present and also Mr. Frances Knowles his brother, or either of them? Did they not appoint Mr. Fenton captain, Walter Spindola lieutenant, Richard Derifall master, and Richard Aldersey purser or factor for the owners?

19. Were not the most part of the goods put into the castle at Guernsey? Was not Mr. Henry Knowles, at his coming thither, made privy of the same?

[b] 15 Jan. 1579. Eustacius Travachi, Ferdinandus de Zaratte and others v. Henricus Knollyz Esq. 'Stephen Jackson of Marleborowe in Wiltshire surgeon sworn and examined before Mr. Doctor Lewes Judge of Thadmiraltye uppon certen articles geven against him on the behalfe of Martine de Venero, John de Ratana, Eustace Travache, and other merchantes straungers deposethe and sayethe thereunto as followethe.

To the first he sayethe, That he ys of Marleborowe as before. And that aboute christmas was xii monethe he served on the seas with Mr. Henrye Knollyze in a shipp of his called the Frauncys. In which shipp he served untill aboute a sevenight before Easter followinge and bare thoffice of surgeon in the same.

To the seconde he sayethe, That their Capitayne was one Fenton, and the foresaid Mr. Knollyz was owner of the said shipp. And sayethe that first they departed from Bristowe and sayled to Plymouthe, and from thence to Dartmowthe, and soe back to Plymowthe agayne, from whence they sayled towardes Ireland where they remayned a certen space, and then sayled back towardes the Cowes under the Isle of Wight, where the foresaid Mr. Henrye Knolleze departed and went a lande, and left the foresaid Fenton Capitaigne of the same. Whoe iii or iiiiᵒʳ dayes after hoysed sayle and with the cumpanye thereof sayled to the Sowth Cape uppon the quoast of Spayne, And further sayethe that he was hyred and aucthorised to goe in the same by the foresaid Mr. Knollyz his Capitaigne, And other victualler then him he knewe none.

To the thirde he sayethe, That he knowethe suche a shipp called the Margarett laden with Lynnen clothe and other commodityes what the Masters name was he cannot specifye. And sayethe towchinge thother shipp specified in this article he never knewe ne sawe the same, ne yett the Master thereof soe farr as he remembrithe.

To the iiiith he sayethe, That the foresaid Fenton and his cumpanye beinge in the said shipp the Frauncys at the foresaid place called the Cape, did apprehend, take, and bourde the said shipp called the Margarett and the same they carryed to the Isle of Bayon, where they unladed the said shipp called the Margarett, and stowed and put the goodes that were in her in their owne shipp called the Frauncys.

To the vth he sayethe, That after thunladinge of the goodes furthe of the Margarett as before the same with all her tacle and furniture excepte one cable was all restored back to the master and cumpanye thereof, what became of the bills of ladinge and other writinges he cannot depose for that as he sayethe he sawe none.

To the vith he sayethe, That at Torbay there was division of the said goodes made vizt. thone halfe to their owner Mr. Knollyze which one Aldersey his man tooke chardge of, and thother halfe was devided betwixt the Capitaigne, Master, and cumpanye of the same shipp but noe parte thereof was sould at Torbay to his knowledge.

To the viith he sayethe. That after division made of the goodes as before they sayled to Garnesey where thowners parte beinge a moytye was unladen over against the Castell, but whether it were putt into the same he cannot depose. And sayethe that the moast parte of the cumpanye landed their shares at the keye in Garnesey.

To the viiith he sayethe, That this examinantes parte beinge ten peeces he soulde (as others of his cumpanye did) to diverse of the Towne and countreye but what their names are he cannot declare.

To the ixth he sayethe, That marckes there was uppon the said goodes but what the same were he cannot specifye.

To the xth he cannot depose, For that as he sayethe he forsooke and departed from the said shippe at Garnesey and came for Newporte in Thisle of Wight by passage and from thence to Sowthampton and soe home to Marleborowe where he dwellethe.

To the xith and xiith he cannot depose, Savinge he sayethe the Capitaignes name was Fenton, the Master Richard Derifall, one Tho: Grove of Bristowe the Masters mate, one Walter Spindola was Lieftenaunte being Sir Christofer Hattons man, James Fleminge the Master gonner Raphe Johnson his mate, John Lawe a Sommerset shire man the Boateswayne, Richard Aldersey Master Knollyz his man was Corporall, one [blank] Webstar an other, Roger Silver alsoe an other corporall, and one Frauncys Greene was one of the cumpanye thereof but what office he had he cannot depose. All which aforesaid with diverse others were at the takinge of the said shippe and goodes and had their shares accordinge to their offices some more, sume lesse.

To the xiiith he cannot depose.

To the xiiith he sayethe, That Richard Aldersey kepte thaccompte for thowner Master Knollyze, and Derifall the Master kepte thaccompte for the cumpanye. Whoe alsoe delivered them their shares.

To the xvth he deposethe and sayethe as before he hathe to the vith article.

To the xvith he sayethe, That at their beinge at Garnesey Master Knollyze came thither, and lodged at the Castell, unto whome repayred and went diverse and sundrye tymes tharticulate Fenton, Spendola and Aldersey, but whether Derifall were with him he cannot say, But sayethe all the rest he sawe with him in his cumpanye.

To the xviith he saye nothinge. For that as he sayethe he departed from Garnesey and left the shipp there as in the xth article.

To the xviiith he deposethe, That tharticulate Mr. Frauncys Knollyze was abourd the morninge before the departure of the said shipp from the Isle of Wight, but whether Mr. Henrye Knollyze were on bourde he cannot depose. And further sayethe that Fenton, Spendola, Derifall, and Aldersey had & bare the severall offices specified in this article but whether they were thereunto appoynted by the said Mr. Henrye Knollyze he cannot depose.

To the xixth he sayethe, that the moytye of the goodes was landed over against the Castell as before he hathe deposed in the viith article. And that Mr. Knollyze was privey thereunto as he thinckethe. And otherwyse he cannot depose'.

[signed:] Stephen Jackson

384. [1579]. Piracies by Henry Knollys and Miles Morgan.

State Papers, Domestic, Elizabeth I, Additional. SP 15/27A, 42. Extracts. Printed in D. B. Quinn, Gilbert, I (1940), 226.

A note of suche goodes appertaininge to Spaniardes whiche was laden at Newehavon uppon a Shipp named the Margarett whereof was Master Stephen Fischott, whiche ship was taken by a Shipp named the Ermyn alias the Frauncis apptayninge to Mr Harrie Knowles whereof was Captaine, Fenton, and his lyfetenaunte Walter Spendola and Master, Richard Derifall and Purser, Richard Aldersey Mr Knowles his man.

[Details of 39 fardels and a chest of linen cloth worth £1600. They claim £200 for legal costs.]

Item besides this there was likewise one other Shipp taken named the [*Marie*]. whereof was Master Malerve [Guillaume Malhearbe] by Myles Morgan which was in consorte with the Shippes of Master Knowlles wherein the foresaid merchauntes Spaniardes had threescore and sixe Fardelles and one Cheste of lynnen clothe which was woorthe twoe Thowsande and seaven hundred pounde / Wherof Master Knowles Companie had parte of the same afore the aforesaid Master Morgan with the shipp and goodes were cast awaie / which by equitie and Conscience he ought likewise to aunswere for that he did receave parte of the goodes as aforesaid /

385. May, 1579. The fate of two of Henry Knollys's ships, 1578-1579.

Proceedings in the High Court of Admiralty against some of Henry Knollys's ships followed their return from Gilbert's abortive expedition. The Francis, *herself a French prize earlier taken by Knollys, and her crew were specifically charged with robbery, and her master Richard Derifall was eventually hanged for piracy. Answers by certain members of the crew throw some light on the course followed by the* Elephant (Oliphant) *and* Francis (Frauncys). *Extracts are from P.R.O., HCA 13/23, fols. 315-316v.*

[a] 20 May 1579. John Webster, gentleman.

To the first Interrogatory he saythe That on Friday last was fortnight he came from Southampton and so to this Cittye [London] before whose cominge to Southampton he was on the seas in a Shippe of Master Knolles callyd the Frauncys wherein he was abowt x weekes space. And before that he was in another Ship of the said Master Knollys called the Oliphaunt certen weekes the tyme well he remembreth not.

To the seond he sayth That at Mighellmas last the foresaid Oliphaunt began her vyage from Bristowe to passe in the seas with Sir Humfrey Gilbert. Of which Olipaunt the said Master Frauncys Knolles was Capitaine and owner. Which Shippe after her settinge furth with force of wether was browth to Corcke Havon in Ireland where she remayned from abowte Martillmas to Candlemas And then she was carryed to Bristowe where she hathe contynued ever since. But nyther the said Master Knollys nor this examinate went thither in the same, but came home in the foresaid Frauncys from Corck Havon aforesaid. This examinate was allowed (as he sayth) by the said Master Knollys to passe on the viage with him.

[b] 20 May 1579. Frauncys Greene, servant to Master Henry Carye.

To the first Interrogatorye he sayethe that aboute two monthes past he came from Corke in Irelonde in a shipp of Master Henry Knollyz called the Frauncys unto the Isle of Wight beinge sore brused in the same shipp with a fall. In which shipp he was and servid aboute viii weekes; and before that in an other shipp of his called the Oliphant from St James tyde untill a fortenighte before Christmas last.

To the second he sayethe that the foresaid Master Knollz was Capitayne and owner of boathe the said shipps, In which shipp called the Oliphant he was and toke shippinge from Bristowe aboute St James tyde and thence sayled in her to Dartmowthe, with which shipp by the waye they putt into Hayleford [Helford] where they founde iii men of war, which had with them a prize beinge a Frenchman as he this deponent tooke yt havinge in her a certen quantitye of wynes, which ship this examinate with his cumpanye apprehended and tooke, and the same they brought to Dartmouthe as before, and soe they sayled from Dartmouthe to Plymouthe where they continued by the space of ix weekes and then putt unto the seas, where they were saylinge to and froe by the space of iii weeckes and afterwardes putt into Corck Havon by a storme of weather, where they said Oliphant had a great leake on her, which shipp the said Master Knollyz there left to be sent unto Bristowe, And himselfe with his cumpanye went on bourde the said Frenche shipp which as before he had taken and named the Frauncys, and in her saylid from the said river of Corck to the Isle of Wight. And sayethe that he was aucthorized & allowed by Master Frauncys Knollyz whome he served in the said shipp. And victualler he knowethe none more then the said Master Henrye Knollyz whoe was Capitaigne and owner of the same as before.

386. February 3 to July 10, 1580. A Chancery case arising out of Sir Humphrey Gilbert's 1578 voyage.

Since we have no narrative account of the 1578 voyage, the evidence of a case in the Court of Chancery (P.R.O., Court of Chancery, Town Bundles, C24/150), which gives some information on his ship the Falcon, *is helpful. This evidence is all that remains of a suit by Sir Humphrey Gilbert against William Hawkins of Plymouth, brother of Sir John Hawkins, and consists of questions (interrogatories) and answers (depositions) by Walter Ralegh and by the pilot Simon Fernandez (or Simão Fernandes) concerning the poor condition of the ship* Falcon, *chartered from William Hawkins for the voyage. Hawkins had, he said, supplied the ship in poor condition and was, he claimed, in part responsible for its poor performance on the voyage. Much detail is given on the ship's guns and equipment, particularly the trinkets carried for disposal, one assumes, to the North American Indians, although the ship never reached there. The depositions contain valuable information on the dis-persal of the fleet and on the call at Grand Canary on the outward voyage.*

The reference to this document was given to me by Agnes Latham; it has not previously been published.

February 3–July 10, 1580. Simão Fernandes and Walter Ralegh are examined on Sir Humphrey Gilbert's 1578 voyage.

Ex parte Humfri Jylbert militis defendentis versus William Hawkyns armigerem qui est examinatus per Henricum Jhones in cancellarum Examinatorem iuratum.

[a] Interrogatoreies to be exhibited in the behalf of Sir Humfrey Gilbert Knight concerninge a suit dependinge in the highe courte of Chauncery between hym and William Hawkins of Plymmouth, esquier.

1. Item whether doo youe knowe Sir Humfrey Gilbert Knight and William Hawkins of Plymmouth gent. yea or no? and if yee knowe theim, what was the cheifest occasion that youe had of their acquaintaunce.

Symon Fernandus of London servant to the right honorable Sir Francis Walsingham Knight Principall Secreatarye to ower sovereing Ladye Queene Elizabeth of the age of xxxix years of thereabouts sworn and examyned the tenthe daie of Julye in the xxiiith yere of her majestys Reigne, by vertue of his othe deposeth and saith to the first Interrogatory that he doth knowe bothe the parties plaintiff and defendent, And saith that he bene Acquaintyd with Sir Humfrey Jylbert the defendent by reason he was in his company in the Shippe called the Fawcone in the Jorney of his Discoverye and with the now complaintiff by reason he hath had dealinges with him.

2. Item whether do youe knowe that Sir Humfrey Gilbert and William Hawkins had any dealinges together for and concerninge the settinge forth of any shipp or shipps to the sea? and if yee doo, how or by what occasion came youe to the knowledge of the same?

To the 2. that he cannot certinly trulye depose what dealinges have bene between the said complaintiff and defendent but by their own report, that is that they were persuurs of the foresaid shippe called the Fawcone, that is to saye that the complaintiff had ii parts of her and the defendent had one, with all her furniture and munycon vittelling and merchaundise as moch as was receyved by the said complaintiff towards setting fourth of the same shippe to the sea, this he saith he did understand for twardes the said voyage he this deponent was made Master of the said Shippe.

3. Item whether do you know a shipp that was latelie of the said William Hawkins called the Faucken? and if youe doo know her, whether is shee an olde shipp or a newe and of what Burden is shee, as youe thincke?

To the 3. that he doth knowe that the said Shippe called the Fawcon wherof the said complaintiff and defendant were parteners was an old shippe and very greatlye shaken with see voyages, and saith that she is of the burden of lxxx tonne of merchaunts poides or therabouts.

4. Item what Ordinance, tacklinge or other furniture had she of Master William Hawkins, when she was delivered to Master Walter Raleigh as Captaine, and youer seelf as master, and to what valewe doo youe esteeme the saide shipp with all her saide furniture, at the tyme of her Deliverie as afore saide.

To the 4. that the said shippe called the Fawcone when she was delivered to Walter Raleighe as Capten and this deponant as Master towards the said voyadge had in her . . . Masts yards topps and top masts one Cheyne pompe three ducors ii new cables one old cable and no hawssars; all for sayles suche as they were, with one skyffe with vii oars and no boate, with all her tackling fitt for the said Shippe, the certen value of the same Shippe and of her said tackling and furniture in that tyme belonging to the same he saith he could not estymate. And further saith that the said Shippe had in her at the tyme of Ordinaunce xii cast peces of Iron, foure fowlers with ther Chambres and some bases how many he cannot tell. And as he did heare the overseer saye there wer in her also three sacres, foure mynions and fyve fawcones all of iron with ther cariadge and applyaunces with certen round shott and crosbarres the certen store of nombre he knoweth not, but as he heard the said Overseer saye, that he shuld have for everye peace, x round shott and two crosbarres. And saith that ther were in her also at the same tyme, Bowes, Arrowes in Sheaffe, billes pykes, but what nombre he knoweth not. And saith also that ther were certen Calyvers Targatt, Moryans

and hedpieces to what nombre he knoweth not, the which Calyvers Targatt Moryons and hedpieces he saith he heard the capten of the said shippe saye, that they were his and not the ships. And further remembreth that ther was in the same Shippe more at the same tyme ii little peeces of brasse the which he heard the said Capten saye he bought of the said complaintiff for his own use; And more Ordynaunce and Artillarye he saith he knoweth came not into the said shippe at that tyme.

5. Item with what quantitie of Victuall was shee furnished with all at the saide tyme, and what occasion had youe to knowe the same.

To the 5. that ther was in the said Shippe at the delivery these as is aforesaide, three thowsand of Biskett one hundreth bushells of flower packt in xv barrells of Plymmouth measure as this deponant was informed and no other or more bread or flower, for he saith that the said Flower made the quantytie of eight thowsand biskett with the three thowsand of biskett beforenamed which was the proporcion of bread for the said voyage. Six hogshedes of beof two hogshedes of pork two thowsand fyve hundreth or thereabouts of newland fishe two hundreth Dry Cod Ling and Congre, two great barrells of Candles how many in nombre he knoweth not xvii tonne of byer, one pype of Canarye Wyne, four tonnes of water caske, viii byrrycos of water, three stepe tubbes, four Bucketts, vi lanternes, one thowsand of nayles or therabouts of all sorts, threescore pounde of spyke, two thowsand of scoop nayles, fyve or vi boats lading of Norway Billett the boat of ii tunes Burden or thereabouts, two hog skulles of Beanes, and ii of pease, halfe a Buschell of mustard seeds, one Kettle and one peasepott, two or three dosen of Platters ii or iii dosen of cannes, iii or four trayes ii hogshedes of vynagre ii hogshedes of Sault. And nether oyle, Butter nor chese for the shipps store. All which provision of vitell and no more of the ships own store he saith was full and whole in the said shippe whan they went on seeboard on ther voyage this he knoweth to be true for he was pryvie of the lading therof.

6. Item what quantitie of powder, shot, or municion had shee of William Hawkins at the tyme of her settinge forth, and by what meanes doo youe knowe the same.

To the 6. that ther was also in the same shippe at the delivery thereof vi kilderkins of Powther, and as the Overseer told this deponant ther was no more, and as for Shott and munycion he hath sayd afore the 4. Interrogation.

7. Item what spare store had youe delivered at the saide tyme of ropes, methesiches, poldavies, picks or other furniture, and by what meanes doo youe knowe the same?

To the 7. that ther was put into the same shippe by the commaundes of the same complaintiff for the same ships store fyve quyle of small ropes that weyed about fyve hundreth weights, Twelf bolts of Poll Davies to make new Sailes, as mayn sayle A foresayle and A mayne topp sayll, for the ould ones were not shrincable, and no other Canvas was there in her for store; lx pounde weight or therabout of lead, two founding leades as one for the deepes, and three deesye lynes; viii peces of lynes for latchet lynes, Fyve Dosen of Saill needles, viii or x pounde weight of twyne, fyfty pounde weight or therabouts of Ratlyn, Fyftie pounde weight or therabouts of Marlyn and twoe hundreth or one hundreth de pounde weight of Ocone, three Compasses, vi running glasses. And no more store of any other thing that he remembreth.

8. Item what sortes of merchandise and to what valewe were they, as you thincke that the saide William Hawkins did at the foresaide tyme put into the saide Fauken of hisown for the foresaide pretended voyage, and by what meanes youe doo knowe the same?

To the 8. that he remembreth of no merchaundice that was in the said Shippe at her setting fourthe, but of A certen quantitye of hollande of xxd. the ellne or therabouts, to the nombre of cc yards by the report of the Capten and of viii silke dobletts embrothered and not fynished, ii peces of Callycow clothe, and certen Manylios of brasse, certen Morys bells which Manylios and Belles came into ii furkins, six belts of Canves for clothes for the maryners and souldyers, certen shirts to the nombre of 4 dosen, certen dosens of hose and shoes how many he knoweth not, the certentye of which thinges he knoweth not nor then knew, but by the report of the said Capten. And further saith that this was at the same tyme in the said shippe one firkin of gray sope and A quantitie of cake soap as the stuard of the said shippe informed this deponant which drew to an hundreth weight, the value of all the which premisses he knoweth not. And for any other Marchaundise he saith he doth knowen this came none into the said

shippe at or against ther setting forth towards the said voyage.

9. Item who was the principall overseer of the rigginge, and furnishinge of the saide shipp, and by what meanes doo you knowe the same?

To the 9. that he this deponant was the principall overseer of the Rigging and furnishing of the said shipp being the Master of the same.

10. Item who was the cheifest overseer for the ladinge, bestowinge, and receavinge of the victuels municion, merchandise, and other store of the said shipp at the tyme of her settinge forth as aforesaide.

To the 10. that as touching the victuells put into the said shippe at the same tyme, the Stuarde receyved it, and this deponant did oversee it and tooke ordre for the stowing of it, and the Gunnar for the overseeing and ordring of his ordinaunce and municion. And as for the merchaundyse the Capten had the recept and order therof.

11. Item where is the said Fauken at this tyme, as you thincke and who with the same?

To the 11. that he knoweth no other but that the said shippe is at this tyme in Plymmouthe, and for any thing that is knoweth the complaintiff with her, for that (as this deponant hath heard him saye) that he wold new build her againe.

12. Item whether had hee, or hath hee her, in his possession or disposition, sythens or before the firste of marche last past yea, or no?

To the 12. that he doth know that the servants of the now complaintive by his commaunde as he verelye thinketh did laye uppe the saide shippe before one Jo. Beryes Doctor and in his key in Plymmouthe aforesaid about Candlemas last was twelf month, to build her new againe, as it was then said. And doth know no other but that the complaintive hathe her in his private possession. And saith that as touching the said shippe and all her furniture, provision store and merchaundyce aforesaid which she had in her at her setting fourthe towards the foresaid voyage, he never could not yet cann make any estimate of the value therof either in particular, or in generall. And further he saith not to the Interrogations, nor more doth say in this matter.

[signed:] Simão Fernandez.

[b] Walter Rawley one of the extraordinarye Esquires of the Body of the Queen's majestie of the age of xxvi yeres or therabouts sworn and

examined the 3rd daye of February in the yere aforesaid etc. To the first Interrogation that he doth knowe both the parties plaintiff and defendant. And th'occasion of his Acquaintaunces knowledge of them is by reason Sir Humfrey Gilberte is his brother on the mothers syde and Master Hawkyns is his country man and his familiar acquaintaunce.

1. Item whether Doe youe knowe Sir Humfrey Gylbert, knight and William Hawkins Hawkins of Plymouth gent. yea or no and yf yee knowe them what was the cheyfest occasion that you had of the Acquaintaunce.

2. Item whether doe youe knowe that Sir Humfrey Gylbert, and Wylliam Hawkins had any dealinge together for and concerning the setting forth of any shippe or shippes to the sea? and yf yee doe knowe or by what occasion came youe to the knowledge of the same.

To the [1 and] 2. that he doth know that the said Sir Humfrey Jylberte and the said Master Hawkyns had Dealings together about the setting fourthe of one Shippe to the Sea towards his pretended journey in sommer last was twelfmonethe. And the occasion of his knowledge therof was bicause he this was A partye to the same journey.

3. Item whether doe youe knowe a shippe that was lately of the saide Wylliam Hawkins called the Fawcken, and yf youe doo knowe how, whether ys she an olde shipp or a newe and of what burden ys she as you thincke?

To the 3. that he did know the Shippe called the falcome which was the said Master Hawkyns. And saith that she is an old Shippe for she was A shippe in the tyme of King Henrye th'eight, and of xx.iiii tonne burden or therabouts.

4. Item what Ordynaunce, Municion, tacklinge, Vyctuales, Marchandyze or other Furniture had shee of Mr Wyllyam Hawkins when she was delivered to you as Captaine and to Farnande as master and to what valewe doe you esteme the sayd shipp with all her said furnyture at the settyng forth of her Sir Humfry Gylberts later pretended voyadge?

To the 4. that the said shippe whan this deponant was capten of her and one Fernando was Master had in her and about her all suche and so moch ordinaunce, munycion, tackling, and Victualls and other furnyture and provision as is conteyned and specyfyed in A certen Inventary

or note in paper now showed to this deponant at this his examinacion. wherunto the examyner hath put his hand and wherunto also he doth refere him self. But what the said Shippe was worth with all the said furniture and provision longing unto her and within her at the tyme she was delivered to this deponant and to the said Fernando to the said pretended voyadge he saith he cannot Depose, nor esteme it.

5. Item whether ys the Inventorie nowe by youe presented a trewe Inventorie of the vttermoste chardges that the said William Hawkins was at the setting forthe of the fore said shippe both for Victuales, marchaundize, Ordinaunce, munission and other furnyture yea or not?

To the 5. that the said Inventary or note of the said perticulars of the said Shippe conteyneth A true and perfyte Inventarye or note of the uttermost value and charges for any thing that he knoweth that the said Master Hawkyns was at, for the setting fourthe of the said shippe towards the said voyage, both for ordinaunce, Municion Victualls merchaundyce and other furnyture anyewaye.

6. Item whoe was the principall overseer of the rigging and furnishing of the shipp and by what meanes doe youe knowe the same?

To the 6. that the said Fardinando who was Master of the said Shippe was principall Pursar and overseer of the Rigging and furnishing of the said Shippe.

7. Item who was the cheyfest overseer for the lading, bestowing and receaving of the victualle, muniscion, marchaundyze, and other store of the sayd shipp at the tyme of her setting forth as aforesayde?

To the 7. that the said Fardinando and one of the said Master Hawkyns menn that was appoynted to be purser of the said Shippe and shuld have gone in her, were the principall oversears for the lading, bestowing and receyving of all the Victualls Ordinaunce Munycion merchaundyce and all other furniture and store of the said shippe at the timeof her setting fourthe.

8. Item where is the sayd Fawcken at this tyme as youe thincke and who with the same?

To the 8. that at this deponants reterne from the said voyage he delivered the said Shippe to the said Master Hawkyns, and as he thinketh she remayneth still with him or is or was at his disposicion, and otherwayse to this Interrogation he cannot depose.

9. Item whether had hee or hath hee her in his possession or disposytion sythens or before the firste of marche last past yea or no?

To the 9. that the said Master Hawkyns had her in his possession for any thing he knoweth before the first of Marche last past, for before that he this deponant delivered her unto him, but what because of her sins the first of Marche last he saith he cannot certenlye tell.

10. Item whether did the sayd William Hawkins adventure with the said Sir Humfrey in his late pretended Dyscoverie any other shippe uppon his one chardge other than his only adventure of and in a shippe callyd the Fawcken yea or no?

To the 10. that to his knowledge the said Master Hawkyns did not adventure with the said Sir Humfrey Jilbert in the said voyage any other Shippe upon his owne charge, than the Shippe aforesaid called the Faucone.

11. Item whether did the sayd William Hawkins warrant vnto you before yower going to the sea in her at the tyme of the foresayd pretended dyscoverie that she was a good strong and able shippe for the iourney yea or not?

To the 11. that he cannot expressely depose that the said Master Hawkyns did warraunt the said Shippe to this deponant to be A strong and able Shippe for that Journey, but said and affirmed that she was a Good Shippe and fitt for the said Journey.

12. Item whether dyd you fynde her in yower visadge so strong and sounde a shipp as the said Hawkins warranted yea or not?

To the 12. that for any thing that he founde by the said Shippe, she served the terrme in that voyadge although with some daunger by reason of her age and leakying.

13. Item how many tymes was Sir Humfrey dryven to come backe from the seas into Ireland and Syllye with his fleght by the only occasion of the weaknes, and leaknes of the said shipp.

14. Item whether was not his coming backe thoroughe the foresayde Occasions, a great hyndraunce and chardge to the sayd Sir Humfrey and his company and thereby a great hyndraunce to hys Visadge yea or no?

To the 13 and 14. that as he remembreth the said Sir Humfrey Jilbert was dryven backe in his said voyage partlie into the coste of Ireland, and partlie into Sillye with his Flete but ones by occasion of the leake of the said Shippe to his no small hinderaunce and theirs that were in his company both in charges, and losse of season.

15. Item whether was the sayd Sir Humfrey and you bounde to the sayd William Hawkins in an obligacioun of an hundred pounds for the supplyeing of certeyne wantes of Victuales and other things for the setting forth of the foresaid Fawcken in the said vyoadge yea, or no?

To the 15. that true it is that the said Sir Humfrey Jilberte and this deponant were bounde by obligacion in an hundreth poundes to the said Master Hawkins for the supplye or want of certen shippe stuffe, and as he thinketh it was for the said Shippe and for no other towards the said voyage.

16. Item whether did youe at yower owne chardges or by the healp of any of yower frendes bestowe any other somes of money for the better victoualing and setting forth of the foresayde fawcken in the sayd voyadge yea, or not, and yf you dyd to what valewe was the same to yower remembraunce?

To the 16. that he for his own part in the setting fourth of the voyage in the said Shippe did charge himselfe for the better furniture of her with Dyvers furniture and thinges besydes the perticulers of the said Inventarye to the value as he Doth verelie think of one hundreth marks.

17. Item whether had you any supply of Gascoyne Wynes in Plymmouth before you went yower vioadge for yower Victuale of the said Faucon vnder and above the store laide in by the sayd Hawkins and yf you had how many tunnes was thereof to yower remembraunce?

To the 17. that he lade into the said Shippe besydes the content of the said Inventary, which he had in plymmouth for the better suppliy in the said voyage to the nombre of vi tonne of gascoyne wyne, before the said Shippe took her Journey in that voyage.

18. Item whether did Sir Humfrey Gilberte make any more supplie in Ireland to the fawcken of Breade, Wynes, Beyfe, Fishe together with other victuales yea, or no? and whether was sutche supply uppon sawse ye or no?

To the 18. that he doth well remember the said Sir Humfrey Jilbert did make A certen new supplye of Victuells of Dyvers kynds in Ireland, whann he was dryven to take that coast, as is aforesaid, which supplye as it was not superfluous, so was it not upon any great necessitye.

19. Item whether wer not you supplyed with other vyctuales at an other tyme in the same Jorney yea or no? and to what Quantytie of them and of what sortes.

To the 19. that true it is they Did take A new supplye of canarye wyne at the graund Canaries with some relief of swete meats, which wyne was about the nombre of xiiii or xv tonnes, and that was not without great nede. bicause ther drink was all nere spent.

20. Item whether was all the sayde provysion and revictualing uppon want or necessorie suplie of victualle yea or no?

To the 20. that he can say no more than he hath before said to the ii last formes Interrogations.

21. Item whether did you and yower good and dilligent Indevours for the good government in saving of yower vyctuals to drawe the same in as great lenght as convenyentlie you might to have served you for the hole vyoadge yea or no?

To the 21. that in troth he this deponant and the Master of the said Shippe dyd ther best and diligence both for the good governement of the said Vyctualles and provision, and also to Draw the same to as convenient lenght, as possiblye they could for the service of that voyage. And this is all that he can saye to this Interrogation.

[signed:] W. Rauley.

387. 1587. The voyages of Gilbert and Ralegh, 1578–1579, as seen by contemporary historians.

These two accounts, the first by John Hooker (a) and the second by either Hooker or John Stow (b), both contemporary historians, summarize the attempts by Gilbert and Ralegh to establish colonies in North America. They are useful in giving information on Ralegh's voyage in the Falcon *in 1578–1579.*

They are printed in Raphael Holinshed, Chronicles, *2nd ed., 3 vols. (London, 1587), II, sig. 3–3v., and III, 1369; D. B. Quinn,* Gilbert, I *(1940), 236–238.*

[a] For after that you had seasoned your primer yeares at Oxford in knowledge and learning… you travelled into France, and spent there a good part of your youth in the warres and martiall services. And having some sufficient knowledge and experience therin, then after your return from thense, to the end you might everie waie be able to serve your prince and commonweale, you were desirous to be acquainted in maritimall affaires. Then you, togither with your brother sir Humfreie Gilbert, travelled the seas, for the search of such countries, as which if they had beene then discovered, infinite commodities in sundrie respects would have insued, and whereof there was no doubt, if the fleet then accompanieng you had according to appointment followed you, or your selfe had escaped the dangerous sea fight, when manie of your companie were slaine, and your ships therewith also sore battered and disabled. And albeit this hard beginning (after which followed the death of the said woorthie knight your brother) was a matter sufficient to have discouraged a man of right good stomach and value from anie like seas attempts; yet you, more respecting the good ends, wherunto you levelled your line for the good of your countrie, did not give over, untill you had recovered a land, and had made a plantation of your owne English nation in Virginia.

[b] This countrie of Norembega aforesaid (and the land on this side of it) sir Humfrie Gilbert, brother to sir Walter Raleigh, a man both valiant and well experienced in martiall affaires, did attempt to discover, with intention to settle an English colonie there, in the yeare 1578: having in his companie his two brethren, Walter and Carew Raleighs, Henrie Knolles, George Carew, William Careie, Edward Dennie, Henrie Nowell, Miles Morgan, Francis Knolles, Henrie North, and divers other gentlemen of good calling,[1] and ten sailes of all sorts of shipping, well and sufficientlie furnished for such an enterprise, weighed anchor in the west countrie, & set to the sea. But God not favoring his attempt, the journeie tooke no good successe:[2] for all his ships inforced by some occasion or mischance, made

1. Sidenote: "Gentlemen that associated sir Humfreie Gilbert in his viage to Norembega 1578."
2. Sidenote: "The viage hath not wished successe."

their present returne againe; that onelie excepted, wherein his brother Walter Raleigh was capteine, who being desirous to doo somewhat woorthie honor, tooke his course for the west Indies, but for want of vittels and other necessaries (needfull in so long a viage) when he had sailed as far as the Ilands of Cape de Verde upon the coast of Affrica, was inforced to set saile and returne for England. In this his viage he passed manie dangerous adventures, as well by tempests as fights on the sea; but lastlie he arrived safelie at Plimouth in the west countrie in Maie next following.[3] Sir Humfreie Gilbert notwithstanding this unfortunate successe of his first attempt, enterprised the said viage the second time and set to the sea with three ships and pinesses, in the yeare 1584, in the which journeie he lost his life; but in what sort no man can witnesse. For being by force of foule weather separated from his companie, he was never heard of afterwards.[4]

3. Sidenote: "Maister Walter Raleigh sailed as far as Cape Verde, &c. and arriveth in safetie at Plimouth."
4. Sidenote: "Sir Humfrie Gilberd severed from his companie, dead, and never heard of."

Chapter Fifty-one
A Reconnaissance in 1580 and
Its Aftermath

388. December, 1579. Preparations for the reconnaissance voyage of the *Squirrel*.

Sir Humphrey Gilbert served the queen with the Anne Aucher, the Relief, and the Squirrel between July and October, 1579. His sailors made off with the first two ships late in 1579. The letter following shows that in recovering the Relief he got back charts and books on navigation that he had collected for his voyage of 1578. By the time it was written, he had the Squirrel ready for her voyage of reconnaissance.
British Library, Lansdowne MS 144, fol. 384.

After myne harty comendacions I am geven to understand by the reporte of my very frind Sir Humfry Gibert Knight, of your good dealing towardes him, & carefull dilligence used in accomplishing his request, touchinge the recovery of his barck called the Reliefe, wherin as youe have given great hope of good service to be expected at your handes hereafter in greater matters. So Sir Humfry hath at large made relacion therof to the Lordes of her Maiesties Councill, to their great good likinges and your comfort hereafter, as occasion shall serve, & for his owne part remaineth most thanckfully affected towardes youe for the same. I am likewyse verye gladd to hear so good report of youe, hoping that such your sound dealing shall growe hereafter to the generall benefit of our prince & Contrey. And wheras Sir Humfrey doth also tell me, that the capitaine of the said shipp, named Frier, hath in his custody, certaine bookes of navigacyon and other Sea ryters belonging to the same Sir Humfrye, whatsoever he shall alledg to the contrary; wherof twoe ar written with Friers owne hand. Theis ar most earnestly to pray you to deal in somme effectuall & secrett manner with the same Frier, for the obteyninge of the same bookes into your owne pos-

session, and so as he may not in any wise discrye your entent, The which assone as youe have gotten, I pray youe send the same unto me well packed or sealed by somm trustye messenger, And if after ward for the answeringe of Frier youe shall thinke it good, youe may shew him this mye lettre, and if Frier shall seeme to refuse the same then to put hym a land & commytt you to safe kepinge to some of her Maiestes officers till the Lordes pleasures be knowne. As ever youe will pleasure me or looke for a good turne at my handes faile not hereof, and after your first seasure of the Books lett not Fryer or any other have the use or sight of them. At the court 10 of April 1580.

Your very assured lovyng frend

[signed:] Tho: Wylson

[Addressed:] To my verie lovyng frynd Augustine Clark

[Endorsed:] Master Secretory Wylsons letter wrytten to Asten Clarke Captayn of the Seabryte with a comeshon grauntyd to the sayd clark uder the hands of the Lord Tresorer and Master Secretory Wylson.

389. April 7, 1580. Sir Humphrey Gilbert's bond for the good behavior of the *Squirrel*'s crew.

In the spring of 1580 Gilbert was ready to take the first steps to launch a new venture. Under the influence of Dr. John Dee, he was determined to make Verrazzano's "Refugio" (400), which Dee called the Bay of the Five Islands, his objective. His small frigate, the Squirrel, under Simão Fernandes, was to make the reconnaissance. On April 7, 1580, he entered into bond in the High

Court of Admiralty for £500, to be paid by June 1 for the good behavior of the vessel and her crew while on the voyage. The ship reached and returned from New England, but there are no details of the voyage (391).

P. R. O., High Court of Admiralty, Book of Acts 1578–1583. HCA3/18. Printed in D. B. Quinn, Gilbert, II (1940), 239–240.

Die Jovis vii⁰ die predicti mensis Aprilis Coram D: Davido Lewes legum doctore Judice &c. in edibus suis &c. Presente me William Harewarde Registore comparuit D: Humfridus Gilbert miles ac recognovit[1] se debere Serenissimo Domino nostre Regine summam quingentarum librarum monete Anglie solvendum eidem domino nostre Regine heredibus vel successoribus suis primo die futuri mensis Junii Et nisi &c.

The condicion of this Recognizance is suche That where the said Sir Humfreye hath equipped and sett unto the seas a certen Frigott of his called the Squirrell of the burthen of viii tonnes or thereaboutes under the conduction of Simon Fernandes having with him the number of tenn men or thereaboutes to sayle uppon a viadge for a discoverye to be made bye the said Fernandes, whereunto the said Sir Humfreye is aucthorised by her Majestes lettres patentes / Yf the said Simon Fernandes and cumpanye be in all his said viadge of good behaviour towardes her Majestes subjectes, and the subjectes of other Princes with whom her Majestye is in league and amitye, and doe not robbe nor spoile eanye duringe the said viadge The &c. Or else &c.

[signed:] H. Gilbertes

Recognovit coram D: Lewes Jwdice die et anno suprascriptis

[signed:] D: Lewes

390. 1582. Interrogation of David Ingram on his American experiences.

David Ingram claimed to have been marooned by John Hawkins on the shores of the Gulf of Mexico

in 1568 and to have walked to Cape Breton where he was rescued by a French ship. If he ever made this journey, he must have been picked up on the Gulf shore by a French privateer that may have made one or two calls at North American harbors on its way to France. After the Squirrel voyage of 1580 his tales (even if they had little contact with reality) began to be listened to. In 1582 he was interrogated and his answers compared with the information brought by Sir Humphrey Gilbert's man Simon Fernandez. This led to (a) "Certayne questions to be demaunded of Davy Ingram," P.R.O., State Papers, Domestic, Elizabeth I, SP 12/175, 95, printed in D. B. Quinn, Gilbert, II, 281–283 (390); (b) "Reportes of the Contrie Sir Humfrey Gilbert goes to discover," P.R.O., State Papers, Colonial, CO 1/1, ff. 3–10, printed in Quinn, Gilbert, II, 296–310 (brief extract relating to expeditions of Simon Fernandez and John Walker in 1580 (391); (c) "The Relation of David Ingram," known to have been printed in 1583, but no copy so far found, reprinted by R. Hakluyt, Principall navigations (1589), pp. 557–562, reprinted in Quinn, Gilbert, II, 283–296.

1582. Examination of David Ingram.

Certeyne questions to be demaunded of Davy Ingram, sayler, dwellinge at Barkinge in the countye of Essex / what he observed in his travell one the Northe side of the ryver of May where he remayned three monethes or there aboutes

1. Imprimis howe longe the sayed Ingram travyled one ye North side of the Ryver of May,

He hath confessed that he travelled there three monethes

2. Item whether that country be frutfull, and what kinde of frutes there be

He hath confessed that it is excedinge frutefull and that there is a tre as he called it a planten tree, which of the leaves thereof beinge pressed will come a very excellent lycor as pleasant to drincke and as good, as any kinde of winne. /

3. Item what kinde of beastes and cattell he sawe there. /

He hath confessed, that he sawe a beast in all pointes like unto a horse, savinge he had two longe tuskes, of which beast he was put in great dawnger of his lyfe, but he escaped by clyminge a tree Also that there be wyld horses of goodly

---

1. Sidenote: "Recognitio D: Humfridi Gilberte militis."

shape, but the people of the country have not the use of them Further that there, be shepe, which beareth redde woole, sume thinge course. / there flesh good to eat, but is very redde. /

4. Item what kind of people there be, and how they be apparrelled

He hath confessed that farre into the land there be many people, and that he sawe a towne halfe a myle longe, and hath many streates farre broader then any streat in London. /

Further that the men gooe naked savinge only the myddell part of them covered, with skynnes of beastes, and with leaves, And that genirallye all men weare about there armes dyvers hoopes of gold and silver which are of good thicknes. / and lykwyse they weare the lyke about the samle [= small] of there legges. / which hoopes are garnished with pearle, dyvers of them as bigge as ones thume. /

That the womenne of the countrye, gooe aparyled, with plates of gold over there body much lyke unto an armor, about the myddest of there bodye they weare, leafes, which hath growinge there one very long much lyke unto heare. / and lykwyse a bout there armes and the smale of there legges they weare hoppes of gold and sylver, garnyshed with fayer pearle. 5. Item what kind of buyldinges, and howses they have.

He hath confessed that they buyld there howses round lyke a dowhouse and hath in like manner a lover on the toppes of there howses / and that there be many pillors that upholdeth many thinges, of gold and silver very massye and great, and lykewise many pyllors of Cristall /

Sir Humfrye Gylbertes man which he sent to discover that land reporteth there howses to be buylt in lyke mannor rounde. /

6. Item whether there is any quantitye of gold, silver and pearle, and of other jewelles in that country. /

He hath confessed that there is great aboundaunce of gold sylver and pearle, and that he hath seanne at the heades of dyvers springes and in smale rounninge broukes dyvers peaces of gold some as bigge as his fynger, others as bigge as his fyst and peaces of dyvers bignes. /

Further that he hath seanne greate aboundaunce of pearle and dyvers straunge stones of what sort or valewe he knewe not. /

7. Item whether he sawe a beaste farre exceydinge an ox in bignes. /

He hath confessed that there be in that country great aboundaunce of a kinde of beast almost as bigge agayne as an oxe, in shape of body not much differinge from an oxe, savinge that he hath eares of a great bignes, that are in fashone much like unto the eares of a bloudhound having there on very longe heare, and lykwyse on his breast, and other partes of his bodye longe heare. /

Sir H: Gylbertes man brought of the hydes of this beast from the place he discovered. /

Further he hath reported of dyvers kindes of wyld beastes whose skynnes are very rich furres / lykwyse of dyvers kindes of frutes, and trees, of great eastimatione.

That there is a tree which beareth a frute lyke an aple, but is poyson to eate for the aple beinge broken there is a blacke lycor in the mydest thereof / Also that there is a tree that the barcke thereof tasteth lyke pepper.

Divers other matters of great importaunce he hath confessed (yf they be true) which he sayeth that upon his lyfe, he offereth to goe to the place, to approve the same true. / [Endorsed:]—Questions to be demanded of David Ingram concerning his knowledge of a discovery.

391. 1582. Extract from "Reportes of the Contrie Sir Humfrey Gilbert goes to discover."

D. B. Quinn, Gilbert, *II, 310.*

1579. Simon Ferdinando mr. Secretary Walsinghams man went and came to and from the said coast within three monethes in the little Frigatt without any other consort, and arryved at Dartmouth where he ymbarkd when he beganne his viage.

Note.
1580

John Walker Englishman and his Company did discover, a silver mine within the River of Norumbega, on the North shore upon a hill not farre from the river side about ix leagues from the mouth thereof where he founde the said river vii leagues or thereabout over and xviii fadome and haulf deepe. The river at the mouth beinge about x leagues broade, and xxv. fadome deepe withoute barre.

And the said river to holde that his breadthe so much farther then he was as he coulde possibly kenne. beinge by estimacion about xx miles. The Country was most excellent both for the soyle, diversity of sweete woodes and other trees. Who also founde at the same time in an Indian house vii miles within the lande from the ryvere side above iii C. drye hides, whereof the most parte of them were eighteene foote by the squire.

Both he and his Company sayled from the said cost into Englande in xvii. dayes.

Endorsed:—Sondrie reports of the contrie which Sir Humfry Gilbert goeth to discover.

392. October 22, 1581. Sir Humphrey Gilbert ordered by the Privy Council to deliver up his patent.

Gilbert's good faith was still in doubt in 1581, and he was ordered in October, 1581, to surrender his patent. He somehow managed to persuade the Privy Council (probably with the support of Sir Francis Walsingham) not to insist on enforcing this decision.
Acts of the Privy Council 1581–82 (1896), p. 240; printed in D. B. Quinn, Gilbert, II, 242.

Uppon informacion delivered unto the Lordes that Sir Humfrey Gilbert, knight, had made certen deputacions for the transporting of vyctuell oute of the Realme into the partes beyond the seas, grounding the same his deputacions uppon the authoritye of her Majesties Letters Patentes graunted unto him certen yeres paste in consideracion of some discoveries and concquestes of contryes which he pretended then to enterprise, the benefitt of which his Letters Patentes for transporting of vyctuell was intended for such contryes which he should concquer and inhabite as aforesaid; forasmuche as his intended vyoges and discoveries, &c., have taken no effecte, and that therefore he cannot justlie clayme the benefitt and commodytie of her Majesties said Letters Patentes, their Lordships dyd this daye order that the said Sir Humfrey should be sent for and caused to deliver in the said Letters Pattentes, and further to deliver a note unto Mr Secretarie of the names of such persones unto whome he hathe made the aforesaid deputacions, that lyke order maie be taken for the staie and revoking of them accordingly.

393. April 19, 1582. P.H. to [Lord Burghley].

The first report that Catholics were interested in Gilbert's preparations comes in this extract. P.R.O., State Papers, Domestic, Elizabeth I, SP 12/153, 14.

There is a mutteryng among the Papystes that sir Humfraye Gylberde goithe to seeke a new founde lande, syr George Peckham, & Syr Thomas Gerarde goyth with hym.

I have harde it saide among the Papystes, that they hipe it wyll prove the beste Journeye for England that was made these fortie yeres. /

[Endorsed:] 19 April 1582 secret advertisements.

Chapter Fifty-two
The Emergence of Gilbert's Project,
1582–1583

394. May or June, 1582. Petition of Sir George Peckham and Sir Thomas Gerrard to Sir Francis Walsingham.

P.R.O. State Papers, Domestic, Elizabeth I, SP 12/146, 40; printed in D. B. Quinn, Gilbert, II, 255–256.

Articles of petition to the righte Honnorable Sir Francis Wallsinghame knighte Principall Secretarrie unto the Quens Majestie by Sir Thomas Gerrarde, and Sir George Peckeham knightes as followeth viz.

That where Sir Humferie Gylberte knighte, hath graunted and assigned to the saide Sir Thomas, and Sir George authoritie by vertue of the Quens Majestes lettres patentes to discover and pocesse &c. certaine heathen Landes &c. /

Their humble peticion is /

Firste that it wolde please her Majestie that all souche parsons whose names shall be sett downe in a booke Indented made for that purpose thone parte remayninge with some one of her Majestes pryvie Councell, thother with the saide Sir Thomas and Sir George, Maye have lycens to travell into those Counteris at the nexte viaige for conqueste withall manner of necessarie provision for them selves and their families, their to remaine or retorn backe to Englande at their will and pleasure, when and as often as nede shall requier.

Item the recusances of abillitie that will travell as aforesaide maie have libertie uppon discharge of the penallties dewe to her Majestie in that behallffe to prepare them selves for the said voiage /

Item that other recusances not havinge to satisfie the saide penaltie maie not withstandinge have lyke libertie to provide as aforesaide, and to

sta[nd] charged for the paiement of the saide penallties untill such tyme as god shall make them able to paie the same.

Item that none under Colour of the saide Lycence shall departe owte of this Realme unto any other foren Christian Realme /

Item that they nor anye of them shall doo any acte tendinge to the breache of the leage betwene her Majestie and any other Prince, in amytie with her highnes, neither to the prejudice of her Majestie or this Realme /

Item that the xth person which they shall carrie with them shalbe souche as have not any certaintie whereuppon to lyve or maintaine them selves in Englande.

[Endorsed:]—Petitions of sir Tho: Gerard and sir George Peckham.

395. June, 1582. Terms agreed between Sir George Peckham and two further groups of adventurers under which they would go to America.

The document summarized below was printed in this form in D. B. Quinn, Gilbert, II (1940), 257–260, when it was among the Brudenell MSS, Deane, Northamptonshire, although the collection has been dispersed and its present whereabouts are unknown. It gives the fullest early conspectus of the terms under which adventurers were being recruited for the Gilbert-Peckham-Gerrard venture, and is closely linked with the type of agreement worked out later by Gilbert himself (398) when he had elaborated his venture still further. Nothing is known to have come of this particular arrangement; it may not even have been formally executed.

Articles concluded [blank] June 1582 between (1) Sir Thomas Gerrarde and Sir George Peckham, (2) Sir Edmond Brudnell, Sir William Catesbye, William Shelley and Phillipp Basset, and (3) Sir William Standley of Storton, Cheshire, Richarde Bingham and Martyn Furbusher.

1. Sir Thomas and Sir George, by authority from Sir Humfrye Gylbert, at their charges and those of the Adventurers named in a schedule or entered in a register of which two copies shall remain with them and one be deposited with Sir Fraunces Walsingham, intend to furnish certain vessels with men, etc., for the next intended voyage for possession or conquest of parts of America, and set them to sea before the last day of March next by the conduct of Standley, Bingam or Forbusher or one of them authorised as General by sea.

2. They grant that all the Adventurers entered in the schedule or register book before the vessels sail shall have the privileges following:

3. Every Adventurer going at his own costs on the voyage shall have, according to his share, out of the third part of the commodities got on the voyage.

4. Every Adventurer shall have according to the property of his adventure.

5. Every person adventuring £100, with ten men for the first voyage and forty men for the subsequent voyage, provisioned for a year, to be an Associate, and have a seignory of 10,000 acres, with as large privileges as any in England, paying Sir Thomas and Sir George ten shillings a year for every thousand acres possessed, reserving precious stones and metals.

6. Every person adventuring £50 and twenty men to be an Assistant and have a lordship of 1000 acres on the same terms.

7. Every person adventuring between £30 and £50 to have five hundred acres for each £5, with liberty to keep court leet and court baron, on the same terms.

8. Persons adventuring under £30 to be Adventurers only and to have five hundred acres for each £5 on the same terms.

9. Associates and Assistants to be free of tortures, martial law and attachment of their persons for actions real and personal.

10. Sums adventured with Anthony Brigham "in his late intended voyage" to be allowed as adventures in this second voyage, if the persons are "not satisfied therof in the first jurney."

11. The General and Admiral to rank as an Associate.

12. The Lieutenant and Vice-admiral as an Assistant.

13. Captains and masters of ships as Adventurers of £25.

14. Masters, mates, master gunners and master carpenters as Adventurers of £15.

15. Gunners, carpenters' mates, stewards, boatswains and pursers as Adventurers of £10.

16. Inferior officers and artificers, having their necessary instruments and tools, as Adventurers of £5.

17, 18, 19. Associates to hold of Sir Thomas and Sir George, as lords paramount, by free socage; Assistants by homage and fealty; Adventurers by knight service, all paying as above.

20. Persons holding of any other shall do so by tenures agreed between their lord and them.

21. These "rewardes" to extend only to those who adventure in the next two voyages and who are entered in the schedule or register book before 1 March next.

22. One-thirteenth part of the lands to be reserved for the maintenance of soldiers and persons maimed in the wars.

23. Lands to be allotted as near the place to be inhabited as possible.

24. Adventurers to have choice of lands in order [of the entry] of their adventures.

25. Associates entered before 1 March to have authority to determine cases concerning Associates, Assistants and gentlemen entered before 1 March. Those entered subsequently to have ordinary trial as common persons.

26. Assistants entered before 1 March to have the same regarding inferior Adventurers.

27. Judgment to be as near as they can according to the laws of England: Associates and Assistants to be tried by twenty-four of their equals and every other by twelve honest men.

28. Associates and Assistants to be "of Counseyle" in matters of state and importance. Associates to be elected to the chief offices in government, and to be parties to these indentures.

29. Adventurers and others may hold their lands of Associates or Assistants and shall have them near to theirs.

30. The Lord Paramount shall ratify all grants and agreements made in England and elsewhere.

31. Adventurers to be free of all trades with the said countries and their apprentices and servants after seven years' service.

32. Standley, Bingham and Forbusher agree to be ready for the seas before 31 March [1583], and undertake to discover four islands and 4,000,000 acres on the adjoining mainland, without any action unjustifiable in England.

33. The general at sea shall fortify a fit place on the mainland or on an island, leaving [blank] persons, provisioned for a year to hold it in the name of all the land granted by Sir Humfrye to Sir Thomas and Sir George.

34. Gentlemen wintering there to have four times the land due to them and others double.

35. Mutinous and disobedient persons convicted to lose all benefits.

36. Stanley, Byngham and Forbusher agree to cause all the commodities got in the voyage to be entered in a journal, which shall be delivered to Sir Thomas and Sir George, with "mappes cardes observacions and notes": the commodities to be distributed to the adventurers according to their shares.

37. A speedy supply to be sent to those who winter there.

38. Sir Thomas and Sir George will confirm their lands, etc., to such Adventurers as will pay the charges, under the conditions agreed between Sir Humfry, Sir Thomas and Sir George in indentures of 9 June.

[Added:] A covenant is necessary for the Adventurers to give such assistance in war to Sir Thomas and Sir George as they are covenanted to give Sir Humfry.

There must be special privileges to encourage women to go on the voyage.

BUSINESS ARRANGEMENTS BY SIR HUMPHREY GILBERT AND HIS ASSOCIATES RELATING TO LANDS AND PRIVILEGES IN AMERICA, JUNE, 1582 TO JULY, 1583

THE ARRANGEMENTS for taking up land in North America which Sir Humphrey Gilbert made in 1582–1583 are of considerable interest, but they are in formal language and are necessarily repetitive. Only those of particular interest are given in full, but brief indications are given of each item in the series:

(a) June 6, 1582, agreement to transfer 500,000 acres to Sir George Peckham and Sir Thomas Gerrard. P.R.O., Close Roll, 24 Elizabeth I, part 6, C 54/1126, mm. 5–6; printed in D. B. Quinn, *Gilbert*, II, 245–250 (396).

(b) June 6, 1582, agreement to transfer 500,000 acres to Sir George Peckham. P.R.O., C 54/1126, mm. 6–8; printed in Quinn, *Gilbert*, II, 250–254.

(c) June 9, 1582, agreement to transfer 1,500,000 acres to Sir George Peckham and Sir Thomas Gerrard. Formerly Brudenell MS O.i.9; abstract printed in Quinn, *Gilbert*, II, 256–257.

(d) June, 1582, agreement between Sir Thomas Gerrard and Sir George Peckham with Sir Edmund Brudenell, Sir William Catesby, William Shelley, and Philip Basset, and they in turn with Sir William Stanley, Richard Bingham, and Martin Frobisher. Peckham and Gerrard will transfer lands to Brudenell, etc. while Stanley, etc. will "discover" some four million acres which they may exploit. Formerly Brudenell MS O.i.11; abstract printed in Quinn, *Gilbert*, II, 257–260 (395).

(e) July 7, 1582, transfer from Gilbert to Philip Sidney of 3,000,000 acres. P.R.O., C 54/1153, mm. 13–14; printed in Quinn, *Gilbert*, II, 260–266.

(f) July 8, 1582, assignment of authority, in case of his death, to his brother Sir John Gilbert, Sir George Peckham, and William Aucher, his brother-in-law. P.R.O., C 54/1127, mm. 1–4; printed in Quinn, *Gilbert*, II, 266–278 (397).

(g) November 2, 1582, agreement between Gilbert and the Merchant Adventurers of Southampton who are associated with him. P.R.O., State Papers, Domestic, Elizabeth I, SP 12/155, 86; printed in Quinn, *Gilbert*, II, 313–326 (398).

(h) December 12, 1582, draft of additional articles by which Gilbert associates other persons and groups with the Merchant Adventurers, and leaves some instructions in the event of his departure. P.R.O., SP 12/156, 13; printed in Quinn, *Gilbert*, II, 326–355 (399).

(i) February 28, 1583, agreement between Gilbert, Sir George Peckham, and George Peckham his son to assign to him the Bay of the Five Islands (Narragansett Bay) and 1,500,000 acres adjoining. P.R.O., C 54/1154, mm. 2–3; printed in Quinn, *Gilbert*, II, 341–346 (400).

(j) May 15, 1583, agreement between Sir George Peckham and William Rosewell, the latter to have 500,000 acres. P.R.O., C 54/1154, mm. 31–32; printed in Quinn, *Gilbert*, II, 369–373.

(k) July, 1583, agreement between Sir Philip Sidney and Sir George Peckham, transferring 30,000 or (more probably) 3,000,000 acres to the latter. P.R.O., SP 12/161, 44 (a draft); printed in Quinn, *Gilbert*, II, 376–378 (421).

396. June 6, 1582. Agreement between Sir Humphrey Gilbert, Sir George Peckham, and Sir Thomas Gerrard.

Articles tripartite[1] Indented of Agreament made concluded and agreed upon the sixte daye of June in the foure and twentith yere of the reygne of our soveraigne ladye Elizabeth by the grace of god Quene of England Fraunce and Ireland defendor of the faythe &c. Betwene Sir Humfrey Gilbert of Compton in the countye of Devon knighte on the first partye And Sir Thomas Gerrard of the Brynne in the Countye of lancaster knighte on the second partie And Sir George Peckham of Denham in the Countye of Buckingham knight on the third partie as followeth videlicet

1. Sidenote: "Scriptum inter Gilbert Militem & Gerrard Militem & alios."

Inprimis whereas our saide Soveragne ladye the Quenes Majestie by her graces lettres patentes under the greate Seale of England bearinge date at Westminster the eleaventh day of June in the twentith yere of her Majesties reigne hathe gyven and graunted unto the said Sir Humfrey Gilberte his heires and assignes forever free libertie from tyme to tyme and at all tymes hereafter forever to discover serche fynde out and vewe suche Remote heathen and Barbarous landes Countryes and Territories not actuallye possessed of any christen prince or people as to hym hys heires and assignes and to every or any of them shall seme good And the same to have holde occupye and enjoy to hym hys heires and assignes forever withall comodities Jurisdiccions and realties both by sea and lande And did lykewyse by the said lettres pattentes for her Majestye her heires and successors gyve full power and aucthoritie to the said Sir Humfrey hys heires and assignes and every of them that he and they and every or any of them shall and maye at every tyme and tymes hereafter have take and leade in the saide voiage to travill thetherward or to inhabitc thcirc wyth hym and thcm and cvcry or any of them suche and so many of her majestes subjectes as shall willingly accompany hym and them and every or any of them with sufficient shippinge and furniture for theire transportacions So that none of the saide persons or any of them be suche as after the makinge of the saide lettres pattentes shoulde be speciallye restrayned by our saide soveraigne ladye her heires and successors The statutes or actes of Parliamente made agaynst fugityves or agaynst suche as shall departe remayne or contynue out of her Majesties Realme of England without licence or any other acte statute lawe or matter whatsoever to the contrarye in any wyse notwithstandinge as by the saide lettres pattentes amonge other grauntes articles and liberties therin conteyned more at large appeareth Nowe the saide Sir Humfrey Gilbert as well for the more spedye executinge of her Majesties saide graunte and the Inlargemente of her Majesties Domynions and goverment and also for the better incoragement of the saide Sir Thomas and Sir George and theire Assosiates in so worthie and comendable an enterprise And for theire sure warrant to prosecute the same orderlye accordinge to the lawes and statutes of this realme And in consideracion that the said Sir Thomas and Sir George have disbursed divers sommes of money and adventured the same as principall adventurers with the said Sir Humfrey towardes his nowe intended vyoge for discoverye and habytinge of certeyne partes of America so ment by hym or hys assignes to be discovered As also for dyvers other waightye and good consideracions hym the saide Sir Humfrey especially movinge for hym hys heires successors and assignes and every of them doth covenaunte promyse and graunte to and with the saide Sir Thomas Gerrarde and Sir George Peckham theire heires executors admynistrators and assignes and to and with the heires executors admynistrators and assignes of every and eyther of them by theis presentes That they the saide Sir Thomas and Sir George and every or eyther of them theire or eyther of theire heires executors admynistrators or assignes Assosiates Adventurers and people and every of them shall and maye at all tymes hereafter and from tyme to tyme forever have and enjoye full power and free libertie and

aucthoritye by vertue of the saide lettres pattentes to discover serche fynde out and vewe all those landea and Islea lyinge or beinge upon that parte of America betwene the Cape of Florida and Cape Bryton and the Seas thereunto adjoynynge And the same landes and Isles so by the said Sir Thomas and Sir George or eyther of them theire or eyther of theire heires executors admynistrators or assignes or by theire or eyther of theire Assosiates Adventurers or people serched vewed discovered and founde out as aforesaide that yt shall and may be lawfull to and for the said Sir Thomas and Sir George and every or eyther of them theire and every of theire heires assignes adventurers and assosiates and every of them to have holde occupye use and enjoye to theire and every of theire owne onlye use and uses forever two Isles or Islandes of any foure by them to be taken or named beinge noe parte of the nowe supposed contynent at theire choise out of the landes and Seas so discovered within three monethes nexte after the Aryvall of the saide Sir Thomas or Sir George or any of theire assignes or pryncipall Assosiates into those Remote heathen Countryes or Territories or att any convenyent tyme before or after suche tyme as the saide Sir Humfrey his heires successors or assignes shall make hys or theire first choise of two of the said Foure Islandes And also so moche and suche quantetye of the said landes within the supposed contynent lyinge as nere unto the saide two Islandes as conveniently maye be as shall amounte to the nomber and quantetye of fyftene hundreth thowsand acres of grounde every acre to conteyne foure pole in bredth fortye pole in length and to allowe twentye foure foote to every pole with full power and aucthoritie to inhabite people and manure the same Islandes landes and Countries togeather withall Jurisdiccons privyleges liberties benyfittes comodities and emolumentes whatsoever for the governynge inhabiting disposinge peopleinge and manuringe the premysses and every parte and parcell therof holdinge the saide two Islandes and fyftene hundreth thowsand acres of lande of the saide Sir Humfrey his heyres successors and assignes by fealtye in free soccage and not otherwyse To have holde and enjoye the saide two Isles and all the saide fyftene hundreth thowsande acres of grounde comodities Jurisdiccions and liberties and all other the premysses and every parte thereof with theire appurtenaunces unto the saide Sir Thomas and Sir George theire heires and assignes to the onelye use of them and every of them forever yeldinge and payinge unto the saide Sir Humfrey hys heires successors or assignes for every of the saide two Isles yerelye after they shalbe possessed and manured by the saide Sir Thomas or Sir George theire heires or assignes ten poundes sterlinge and two fifte partes of all the golde sylver perle and precyous stones theire growinge founde and gotten out of which the Quenes Majesties parte reserved by the saide lettres pattentes is to be aunswered and allowed for all dutyes servyces and demandes whatsoever And yealdinge and payinge to the saide Sir Humfrey Gilbert hys heires successors or assignes yerelye for every thowsand acres of grounde of the saide nowe supposed contynent mencioned as aforesaide after the first seaven yeres which the same shalbe actuallye possessed and manured by the saide Sir Thomas or Sir George theire heires assygnes or Assosiates fyftene pence and two fyfte partes all the golde sylver pearle and precious stones there growinge founde and gotten out of the which the Quenes Majesties parte reserved by the said lettres patentes to be allowed for all dutyes servyces and demaundes. Item the said Sir Humfrey for the consideracion aforesaide doth further covenaunte promyse and graunte for hym selfe hys heires successors and assignes and every of them to and with the saide Sir Thomas and Sir George their heires and assignes and every of them by theis presentes that they the saide Sir Thomas and Sir George theire heires assignes Assosiates Adventurers and people and every of them shall or may have and enjoy free libertie to trade and traffique into all the landes Isles and Countries and every parte thereof which the saide Sir Humfrey hys heires successors or assignes shall possesse by vertue of the Quenes Majesties saide lettres patentes or hys graunte thereof And also that they the saide Sir Thomas and Sir George theire heires and assignes and every of them shall have the execucion of all lawes Ecclesiasticall temporall politique marshall and Civell both Maryn and others and of every of them as well within the saide two Islandes and the precynct of the saide fyftene hundreth thowsand acres of the said supposed contynente and also upon the Sea costes so far as the saide landes and

Isles shall extend. Item the said Sir Humfrey for hym selfe hys heires successors assignes and every of them dothe further covenaunte promyse and graunte to and with the saide Sir Thomas and Sir George theire heires assignes and Assosiates and every of them by theis presentes That he the saide Sir Humfrey shall doe hys best endevor to procure and obteyne her Majesties leave and good lykinge that all those whoe hath or shall adventure with the saide Sir Humfrey Sir Thomas Sir George or any of them and whose names shalbe entred into a Register booke for that purpose to be made and kepte and shalbe willinge to travell into any of the saide remote Countryes maye freelye passe into those Countries theire to remayne or Retorne backe at his or theire or any of theire will and pleasure And also that he the saide Sir Humfrey hys heires successors or assignes shall and will from tyme to tyme exonerate and discharge or sufficiently save harmeles the saide Sir Thomas and Sir George theire heires Assosiates Adventurers and assignes and every of them of and from the Quenes Majestye her heires successors and assignes for and concernynge the payment of the Ewer of golde and silver and other duities services and demaundes to her Majestie her heires and successors by the saide lettres pattentes payable and reserved And lykewyse shall and will make and fynishe suche further and better assurance and assurances of the premysses unto the saide Sir Thomas and Sir George theire heires and assignes forever within three monethes nexte after the first and nexte retorne of the saide Sir Humfrey or hys assignes or consortes Adventurers or Assosiates from the saide vyoge of discoverye by the saide Sir Humfrey nowe Intended in suche manner and sorte as by the saide Sir Thomas and Sir George their heires or assignes or any of them or the learned counsell of them or any of them shalbe reasonablie and laufully devised and required In witnes whereof the saide parties to theis presente Articles Interchaungeablie have sett theire Seales yeven the daye and yere first above written.

397. July 8, 1582. Grant of authority by Sir Humphrey Gilbert, of his rights in

America, to Sir John Gilbert, Sir
George Peckham, and William Aucher.

To all Christian people to whome this presente
writinge indented shall come, Sir Humfrey Gilbert of Compton in the Countie of Devon knighte
sendeth greetinge in our lord God everlastinge,
whereas our soveraigne ladie Elizabeth the
Quenes Majestie that nowe is by her graces
lettres pattentes under her greate seale of England bearinge date at Westminster the
eleventh daye of July in the twentith yeare of her
Majesties raigne of her graces especiall certen
science and mere mocion, hath given and
graunted to me the said Sir Humfrey by the name
of her trustie and welbeloved servaunte Sir Humfrey Gilberte of Compton in her Countye of Devon
knighte and to my heires and assignes forever
free libertie and licence from tyme to tyme and at
all tymes forever there after to discover serche
fynde oute and viewe such remote heathen and
barbarous landes countries and terrytories not
actually possessed of any Christian prince or
people as to me my heires and assignes and to
every or anye of us shall seeme good And the
same to have hold occupie and injoye to me my
heires and assignes forever with all commodities
jurisdiccions and royalties both by sea and lande
And I the Said Sir Humfrey and all suche as from
tyme to tyme by licence of her Majestie her heires
and successors shall goe or travell thither to
inhabit or remayne there to buyld and fortefie at
the discretion of me the said Sir Humfrey my
heires and assignes the statute or act of Parliament made agaynste fugetives or agaynste suche
as shall departe remayne or contynue out of her
Realme of England withoute her licence or anye
other acte statute lawe or matter whatsoever to
the contrarye in any wise notwithstandinge And
her Majestie did likewise by the saide lettres
pattentes for her her heires and successors give
full power and auctoritie to me the saide Sir
Humfrey my heires and assignes and every of
them that wee and every or any of us shall and
maye at all and every tyme and tymes thereafter
have take and leade in to the said voyages to
travell thetherwarde or to inhabite there with me
and them and every or anye of them suche and soe

manye of her subjectes as shall willingly accompanye me and them and every or anye of them
with sufficiente shipping and furniture for our
transportacions soe that none of the same persons
nor any of them be suche as thereafter shoulde be
speciallie restrayned by her Majestye her heires
or successors And further that I the said Sir
Humfrey my heirs and assignes and every or anye
of them shall have holde occupie and enjoye to me
my heires and assignes and everye of them
forever all the soyle and all such landes countries
and territories soe to be discovered or possessed
as aforesaid And of all citties castells townes
villages and places in the same with the right
royalties and jurisdiccions as well maryne as
other within the said landes or countries or the
seas thereunto adjoyninge to be had or used with
full power to dispose thereof and of every parte
thereof in fee symple or otherwise accordinge to
the order of the lawes of England as neere as the
same convenyently may be att myne and their will
and pleasure to any persone then beyinge or that
shall remayne within the allegiaunce of her
Majestie her heires and successors reservynge
always to her highnes her heires and successors
for all services duties and demaundes the fifte
parte of all the owre of golde and silver that from
tyme to tyme and at all tymes after such discoverye subduynge and possessinge shalbe there
gotten All which landes countries and territories
shall forever be holden by me the saide Sir Humfrey my heires and successors by homage and by
the payement of the said fifte parte in the said
lettres pattentes reserved only for all services,
And moreover her Majestie did by the said lettres
patentes for her heires and successors give and
graunte licence to me the said Sir Humfrey Gilbert my heires and assignes and every of them
that wee and every of us shall and maye from
tyme to tyme and at all tymes thereafter forever
for defence encounter expulse repell and resist as
well by sea as by land and by all other waies
whatsoever all and every such persone and persones whatsoever as withoute the speciall licence
and likeinge of me the said Sir Humfrey and of my
heires and assignes shall attempts to inhabite
within the space of twoe hundreth leagues nere to
the place or places within suche countries as
aforesaid yf they shall not be before planted or
inhabited within the lymytt aforesaid with the

subjectes of any Christian Prince beinge in amytie with her Majestie where I the said Sir Humfrey my heires or assignes or anye of them or any of our assosiates or companyes shall with[in] <u>sixe</u> yeres then nexte ensuynge make their dwellinges and abidinges or shall enterprize or attempte at any tyme thereafter unlawfullye to annoye either by sea or lande me the said Sir Humfrey my heires or assignes or any of them or any of our companyes goinge and grauntynge by the said lettres patentes power and aucthoritie to me the said Sir Humfrey my heires and assignes and every of them from tyme to tyme and at all tymes then after forever to take and surprize by almanner of meanes whatsoever all and every those persone and persones with their shippes vesselles and other goodes and furnyture which withoute the licence of me the said Sir Humfrey my heires or assignes as aforesaid shalbe founde traffakinge into any harborough or harboroughes creke or creekes within lymyttes aforesaid the subjectes of her Majesties realmes and domynyons and all other persones in amytie with her highnes beinge driven by tempeste or shippwracke only excepted and those persones and every of them with their shippes vesselles goodes and furniture to detayne and possesse as of good and lawfull prize accordinge to the discretion of me the said Sir Humfrey my heires and assignes and every or any of them And for unitinge in more perfecte league and amytie of such countries landes and territories soe the[re] possessed and inhabited as aforesaid within her Majesties realmes of England and Ireland And for the better encouragemente of men to this enterprize her highnes did by the said lettres patentes graunte and declare that all such countries soe thereafter to be possessed and inhabited as aforesaid from thensforthe shalbe of the allegeiaunce of her Majestye her heires and successors And her Majestye did graunte to me the said Sir Humfrey my heires and assignes and to all and every of them and to all and every other persone and persones beinge of her highnes allegeaunce whose names shalbe noted or entred in somme of her Majesties Courtes of record within this her realme of England and that with thassent of me the said Sir Humfrey my heires and assignes shall nowe in this jorney for discoverye or in the second jorney for conqueste hereafter travell to such

landes countries and territories as aforesaid and their and every of their heires that they and every of them beinge either borne within her Majesties said realmes of England or Ireland or in any other place within her highnes allegeaunces and which thereafter should be inhabitinge within anye the landes countries and territories with such licence as aforesaid should and myghte have and enjoye all the priveleges of free denizens and persones native of England and within her Majesties allegeaunce the such like ample manner and forme as yf they were borne and personallie resiant within her hyghnes said realme of England any lawe custome or usage to the contrarie not with standinge, And for as muche as uppon the fyndinge oute discoverynge and inhabitinge of such remote landes countries and territories as aforesaid it shalbe necessarye for the safetie of all men that shall adventure them selves in those voyages or jorneys to determyne to live togethers in Christian peace and civill quietnes eache with other whereby every one may with more pleasure and profitt enjoy that whereunto they shall attayne with paine and perill, her majestie for her her heires and successors was likewise pleased and contented and by the said lettres pattentes did give and graunte to me the said Sir Humfrey and my heires and assignes forever that wee and every or any of us shall and maye from tyme to tyme forever thereafter within the said mencioned remote landes and countries and in the waye by the seas thether and from thence have full and mere power and aucthority to correcte punyshe pardone governe and rule by oure and every of oure good discretions and pollicies as well in Causes capitall or crimynall as civill both maryne and other, All suche her subjectes and others as shall from tyme to tyme thereafter adventure them selves in the said jorneys and voyages habitative or possessive or that shall at any tyme thereafter inhabite any suche landes countries or territories as aforesaid or that shall abide within twoe hundreth leagues of any of the said place or places where I the said sir Humfrey my heires and assignes and everye or any of them or any of oure assosiates or companyes shall inhabite within six yeares nexte ensuyinge the date of the same lettres patentes accordinge to such statutes lawes and ordinaunces as shalbe by me the said Sir Humfrey my heires and assignes and every or any of them devised or establieshed for the better governement of the saide people as aforesaid soe alwayes as the said statutes lawes and ordinaunces may be as nere as convenyently may be agreable to the forme of the lawes and pollicie of England, And also so as they be not agaynst the true Christian faythe or relegion nowe professed in the Church of England nor in anye wise to with drawe any of the subjectes or people of those landes or places from the allegeaunce of her Majestie her heires and successors as theire ymediate soveraigne under God as by the said lettres pattentes amongeste divers other thinges therin contayned more at large it doth and may appeare, knowe ye nowe that I the said Sir Humfrey Gilbert knighte callinge to mynde the mortalities of mankynd and the uncertene event of longe voyages in maryne and martiall affaires and carefullie foreseeinge leaste thorowe my death captivitye or other myshappe this intended enterprize myghte quaell throwe the mysfortunes aforesaid and the mynoritye of my nexte heire for the avoydinge of such enconvenyences as myghte thereby ensue to the hinderaunce of so godlye and honorable an enterprize, have assigned deputed and appointed and by theis presentes doe assigne depute and appoynte give and graunte unto my welbeloved brother Sir John Gilberte of Grenewaye in the Counte of Devon knighte Sir George Peckham of Denham in the Countie of Buckingham knighte and William Aucher of Borne in the Countie of Kent Esquyre all suche estate righte title power and aucthoritie as I have maye myghte shoulde or oughte to have in and to the premysses by force and vertue of the said lettres patentes to me made and graunted by our said soveraign ladie the Quene as aforesaide together with the same lettres pattentes, To have and to holde the premysses to the saide Sir John Gilbert Sir George Peckham and William Archer their executors and assignes to the uses intentes and purposes and in such manner and forme to be used ymployd and ordered so farre forth as they convenyently may as are declared appointed lymyted and sett downe in a scedule indented hereunto annexed and to no other use intente and purpose, In witnes whereof to either parte of this my presente writing I the said Sir Humfrey Gilbert have putt my hande and seale, yeven the eighte day of July in the foure

and twentith yere of the Raigne of our soveraigne ladie Elizabeth by the grace of God Quene of England Fraunce and Ireland defendor of the fayth &c, 1582 /.

The Aucthoritie to be to Sir John Gilberte Sir George Peckham knightes and William Archer Esquire jointly or any two of them yf they shalbe lyvinge or the survivor of them after my death or other ympedymentes in my lyfe tyme whereby I shall not be hable in persone to followe the same to performe and confyrme and ratefie all the grauntes for landes and territories to any of my adventurers in such sorte and manner as I have covenaunted to graunte the same. Also that after my death or such ympediament as aforesaid to dispose of all offices duringe life countries territories landes and tenementes within the said countries nowe to be discovered vewed searched and possessed and to governe the same and to dispose of almanner the revennewes thereof to the beste behoof of my wief and children as hereafter is specified reservynge in all their giftes and grauntes all customes chief rentes royaltis jurisdiccions and services to the heires males of my bodie lawfullie begotten And reservynge to dame Anne my wief duringe the mynoritie or mynorities of my eldest sonne sonnes or heire the third parte of all the whole revennews before specified And after his or their full age then shee to have the fyveth parte thereof duringe her naturall lyef shee also to have during her lyfe of landes in one entire seinorie or lordeshippe fiftye english myles square to be placid in neare or aboute the beste and safeste place of the Countrie and territorie at her choise or by her good likinge to be appoynted which parcell of lande to be forever the joynture of the wief of the cheif lord and governor of those Countries under the crowne of England with aucthoritie to appoynte twoe such other seignories to be likewise to the behoof of such other wives of the said governors from tyme to tyme lyvinge togethere as maye happen hereafter to survive their husbandes And to give also to every one of my sonnes the like seniories in goodnes and quantitie at the leaste to them and their heires and to every of my daughters that I have or shall have twentie miles square in like manner as aforesaid to them and their heires in fee symple, And my wief and every of my children to have execucion of Justice within every of their seniories payeinge unto the cheif lord of those countries under the Crowne of England and his successors for ever yerely after the firste seaven yeres that they shall possesse and manure the same or any parte thereof be it more or lesse for every thowsand acres foure pence with one fiveth parte of the gold silver pearle and precious stones that theare shalbe gotten holdinge the same in fre soccage only duynge hym his heires and successors in his or their warres by land fourtie dayes in the yere att their own charges with one soldyar sufficiently furnished for the warres yf they shalbe thereunto requyred for every five thowsand acres that shalbe inhabited and manured in manner as aforesaid whereof hereafter from tyme to tyme as many of them to be horsed and furnished for the warres as they may convenyently, Also my principall assignes joyntly or any twoe of them or the survivor of them to have aucthoritie to dispose of all the soyle in those partes in fee farme to any persone and their heires in such sorte as herein is expressed with good consideracion had to reserve in the beste places for the buyldinge of townes and fortes with sufficiente for their commons of pasture And for the provision of the captaynes or governors together with sufficient demesnes to be annexed rente free for ever to every such charge And alsoe for somme smale porcion not excedinge tenn acres or thereaboutes to be alowed for every particuler house that shalbe buylte in such places for the better mayntenaunce of the poore inhabitauntes reservynge some smalle rentes for the said tenantes and landes as to their discrecions shalbe thoughte mete Also every one that shalbe sent over by the generall charge of the Realme with such provisions as is hereafter mencioned shall have in lease for three lives sixtie acres of land besides common for soe much cattell in somer as they maye kepe uppon their severalles in wynter with allowaunce for housebote hedgebote and ploughboote as the Countrye may serve and shall paye for the same per annum beinge possessed and manured after the firste three yeres twoe shillinges together with twoe fiveth partes of all the gold silver pearle and precious stones that shalbe therin gotten founde or hadd And the tenth parte of all other mettalles and submyneralles by the name of a toalle And after every death or alienacion a best beaste for a herriott and one yeres rente for a

relief The provision that every of the poore muste bringe to have the foresaid allowaunce. Inprimis of wheate seavies or quarter one prize, twentie shillings, of Barley busshelles, four prize, sixe shillinges eighte pence, of oates busshelles, foure, prize, three shillinges foure pence, of beanes busshelles, twoe prize, five shillinges, of pease bushelles, twoe, prize, foure shillinges, one hatchet, prize, twelve pence, one Pickaxe, prize, twelve pence, one hande sawe, prize, twelve pence, one spade, priz, twelve pence, / which amounteth unto. in the whoale, fouretie three shillinges, besides somme allowaunce to be had for their transportacions and apparell, All which to be receaved uppon their firste arivall by an officer to be appoynted for the same purpose and to be redelyvered them agayne when they shalbe appoynted their dwellinges whiche shalbe at the fartheste forever within fortie daies nexte after their arivall theare. And for such store as shalbe soe sente over, for boyes or wentches not able to take charge of household their porcons to be ymployed at the discrecion of the Officers to be appoynted for the same purpose and the like in goodes to be redelyvered them with their landes and dwellinge places when they shalbe Maried or become hable to take charge of household. Provided alwaies that the Realme of England shalbe alwaies repaied the said charge for theis poore every third yere for the charges of the firste yere yf they shall requyre the same and so successively one after an other the whole Countrie standinge charged for ye same which can be noe losse to the Realme of England, And all other that shall come thus furnished at their owne charges with a sworde dagger and hargabusse of encrease shall have for the like terme sixscore acres payenge for the same after the before specified rates All the poore people and voluntaries that shall come over uppon the generall provision of the Realme of England or at their owne proper charges as aforesaid and not broughte over at the charges of other adventurers shalbe tenauntes to Sir Humfrey Gilberte and his heires successors / or / Children and to the heires and successors of them and to noe others. Provided nevertheles yf any man shall either bringe or sende over at his or their charges any persone to be an Adventurer tenaunte or servaunte with or under hym, or yf any other persone that shall voluntarily come over at their owne charges shall before their arivall in those partes enrolle themselves in the Masters or Pursors bookes of the shippe wherin they shalbe then ymbarkd that they mynde to be adventurers tenauntes or servauntes to any one man by them to be named. Then every such persone shall and maye have free libertie after his or their arivall thether to become a venturer tenaunte or servaunte with or to hym in such sorte as aforesaide for which persones neither sir Humfrey Gilbert his heires or successors shalbe chargid to give any landes or territories to any of them But they to be lefte to seke satisfaccion at their handes that they shall soe become Adventurers tenauntes servauntes or followers unto, Item every gentleman or suche persone as shalbe soe theare allowed that shall bringe five men theare to dwell and enhabite at his owne proper charges and furnished as is aforesaide shall have for hym selfe in fee symple twoe thowsand acres of land And he that shall send the like nomber in like sorte shall have one thowsand acres And for every one of their men theare so brought sente and planted to have sixscore acres in fee symple payeinge at their admyttaunce unto the said landes for a fyne after the rate of tenne shillinges for every one hundred acres that shalbe soe allotted for the Master or land lordes demeanes and yerely after the firste three yeres twentie shillinges rente for every thowsand acres to be allotted to hym selfe in sorte as before saide And noe man to be capable of those benefyttes of theise Rates unlesse he be an Adventurer in the twoe nexte voyages withoute speciall allowance by the said Sir Humfrey or his assignes uppon speciall consideracion And for every one of their men to have alowed in fee symple sixscore acres payenge for a fyne at the assuraunce thereof twentie shillinges and yerely after the first thre yeres twoe shillinges sixe pence, together with twoe fiveth partes of all the golde silver pearle and precious stones that shalbe gotten in and uppon the same And the tenth parte of all the mettalles and submyneralls by the name of a toall and after every death of the cheif lord of that soile or alienacion of the landes a best beast and one yeres rente holdinge the same in fealtie only And every man that shall bringe thyther ten men shall have for his owne persone foure thowsand acres in fee symple And he that shall but sende the like nomber shall have but the halfe thereof And they to be alowed for every follower adventurer tenaunte or servaunte accordinge to the rentes and rates abovesaide with this generall provision nexte ensuynge to be sett downe for all men to clayme by videlicet every man that shall bringe above the nomber of tenne men to be allowed for his owne persone for every ten men above the other firste ten men so broughte thether one thousand acres of lande, and soe more or less accordinge to the nomber that he shall then bringe, And to have for every of his men tenauntes followers or adventurers sixscore acres doynge and payenge for the same accordinge to the rates and rentes above specified and every wief of any of those that shall bringe thither five men or upward which shall goe in any the nexte twoe voyages to be allowed also duringe their naturall lives for supply of their Joyntures a third parte of asmutch as their husbandes hadd heretofore sette downe in respect of them alone and every one of their children that shall soe come thether in persone to have to every one of them in like manner duringe their lives a fourth parte of asmutch as their fathers should have done for the like porcions of landes every tenaunte to sixtie acres of land shall maynteyne for his defence a longe bowe and a sheff of Arrowes together with a sworde dagger and a wooden targett Alsoe every man that shall have sixscore acres shall doe the like with encrease of a Caliver furnished Also every man that shall have twoe hundreth and fortie acres shall keepe in his house one hable man besides hym self furnished for a hargabyzier to serve in the warres every man encreasinge or demyshinge [sic] his martiall provision and charge accordinge to the quantitie of the grounde that he shall manure and everye gentleman or such as shall bringe thither and maynteyne theare five men or more as is aforesaid and shall have in his demaynes twoe thowsand acres or upwardes shall keepe a lighte horsse furnyshed for the warres after such tyme as god shall send sufficient horses in those partes And in the meane tyme to keepe twoe men for shotte in lewe of every such horse. And every man that shalbe alowed foure thowsand acres or more in respecte of his owne persone besides his people and followers shall keepe accordinge to the like rates answerable to his porcion and shalbe bound to buylde a dwellinge house for hym selfe in the cheif Cittie of the province or in such other apte place as by the cheif officers shalbe thoughte mete accordinge to suche plattes as shalbe sett downe and agreid on for that purpose by my assignes or any twoe of them answerable to every mans callinge, payenge for the same seate per Annum, foure pence, And alsoe their shalbe yerely one halfe pennye sterlinge levied forever oute of every acre of lande and woode within all the foresaide Countries Ilandes territories or domynyons the saide paymentes to begyn after the first and nexte tenn yeres that any of the same shalbe possessed and manured which money shalbe only ymployed towardes the maynetenaunce of an Navy and soldyars for the generall defence of those Countries territories Ilandes and domynyons as a treasuer of the peoples to the uses aforesaid the which money to be yerely payed and kepte in a treasure house for the state to be appoynted for that purpose and the same to be ymployed by the consente of the cheif governor of the said Countries with the consente of the more parte of thirtene such as shalbe chosen by the consente of the people to be Counsellors for Marshall and maryne causes, every Mynyster of what degree soever to give yerely forever oute of their porcions the full twentith parte of their whoalye lyvinge, And every landlorde beinge a temporall man to give forever the fortith parte of his landes to be indyfferently appoynted towardes the mayntenaunces of mayned soldiars and of learninge, lectures, scholers and other good and godlye uses in such sorte as shalbe from tyme to tyme thoughte moste mete by the consente of the cheif Majestrates and lawe makers of those Countries not ymployenge the same to any other ende then as is hereby mente And every Countrie parishe through the whole domynyons to conteyne in bignes neither more nor lesse then juste three English myles square And the Church to be alwayes placed in the Middeste thereof And every persone or Mynyster shall have to his benefice beside all his tithes three hundreth acres of good landes lyenge togethers as neare unto the Church as it convenyently maye bee fitt for hym to dwell on And to have and occupie the said glebe landes in severall at his will and pleasure and to be alowed comon of pasture in the waste of the same parishe rateablie for his porcion as others shalbe the said rates before specified to be establieshed forever withoute alteracion for the Mynysters the lorde of the parishe beinge alwaies charged to alott oute of his owne landes in sorte as is aforesaid the glebe landes before specified at the fyrste devidinge of the parishes which beinge so appoynted shall always remayne in fee symple to the Church subjecte to noe mans alteracion neither yett shall the Clergy have power to lease any of the same other then for the present Incumbent his lief at the furthest nor soe neither to be good in lawe but with reservacion of soe mutch rent as it shalbe adjudged worth by the judgemente of twelve of the beste sorte of his parishoners And no Mynyster to have at one tyme above one benefice nor any at all excepte he be resident thereon at the leaste sixe whole monethes in the yere. Item every Bisshoppe to have tenn thowsand acres of lande in one Senyorie and to have alowed hym of the same tithe free for his demeanes twoe thowsand acres Alsoe every Archebisshoppe to have twentie thowsand acres to be devided into twoe seniories of tenne thowsand acres the peice and to have of the same alowed hym in each lordshippe or seigniory twoe thowsand acres of grounde for his demeane tithe free in respecte of which tithes they shall encrease the livinge of the parsone of every the said parishes where their landes shalbe soe freid with as mutch glebe landes as may countervaile the same. Provided always and my meanynge is that my saide assignes shall not have to doe in disposinge of anye of the premysses any longer then duringe the mynoritie of my heires.

398. November 2, 1582. Agreement between Sir Humphrey Gilbert and the Merchant Adventurers.

Articles Bipartite Indented made the secunde daye of November In the yeere of our Lorde god from the Incarnation of Crist 1582 And in the xxiiiith yeere of the Raigne of our Soveraingne Lady Elizabethe by the grace of god Queene of England Fraunce and Ireland Defender of the fayethe &c: Betwene the right worshipfull Sir Humfrey Gilbert Knight of the one party, And the merchant Adventurers with the sayde Sir Humfry gilbert and the societie And company of them whose names surnames and somes adventured be

Inscribed particulerly in the cedull unto these presentes annexed of thother party, And of eyther the same parties to be fulfilled and performed in manner and forme heer ensuinge viz:

1. First That all the saied merchant Adventurers with the sayed Sir Humfry Gilbert and all and every theire Children heyres and posteryty for ever shalbe wholie free of and in bloode and also they and every of them, And theire apprenteces servinge seaven yeeres shalbe wholy free of and in all and all manner trade and trades of entercourse buinge sellinge occupyinge and merchandizinge, Whatsoever in all and every those contries Territories and dominions whatsoever and whersoever with the sayde sir Humfrey Gilbert or his heires his successors or Assignes or the Heyres successors or Assignes of any of them at any tyme hereafter by vertue and aucthority of her Majestes Lettres patentes bearing date at Westmonaster the Eleventh of June in the xxth yeere of her Majesties raingne &c. or by Conquest relinquishment of composicion or otherwise whatsoever. And that ye same societie and company of Marchant Adventurers aforesaide shall beare the name and also sue and be sued by ye name of the Merchant adventurers with Sir Humfry Gilbert untill suche tyme as it shall please God that ye Quenes Majestie or Sir Humfry Gilbert theire heyres or successors or The heyres or Successors of eyther of them shall geve the Contries and company of Marchant adventurers aforesayd some other name or names therby to be incorporated and to Sue and be sued as is aforesaide Provided neverthelese that all the sayde merchant Adventurers, and every of them theire children heyres and theyre posterity afforesaide shall well and truely from time to time content and paie or cause to be contentid and payde unto the sayde Sir Humfry Gilbert his heyres Successors or Assignes but onely the half custome, And theire Aprentices afforesayde the whole custome and customes ther due and to be due for all and singuler theire goodes and Marchandizes hereafter brought thether or at any time after this first voiage Laden or brought from thence all fishes and fishinge there or theraboutes excepted. And unto them and every of them wholy freed and freely discharged for ever without any custome toll or Imposicion or demand therfore whatsoever.

2. Item That the sayde Sir Humfry Gilbert his heyres Successors and assignes and the heyres Successors and assignes and every of them and theire assignes shall from tyme to tyme and for ever ordaine make keep and establishe onely in the Towne of Southhampton within the sayde kingdome of England and no wher els within the sayde kingdome a perpetuall staple receipt and repository for all and all manner theire goodes wares and merchandizes whatsoever at any tyme heereafter in the sayed countries territories or dominions Aforesaid or the precinctes therof or of any of them In anie manner of shipp boat Creyer or other vessell or vessels whatsoever in the trade of marchandis or marchandizinge for and unto the Realme of Englande afforesaied laden or caused to be laden. And also that all and every other person and persons whatsoever that shall hereafter by waye of merchandizinge lade or cawse to be laden within the sayde cuntries, Territories or dominions or the precinctes therof or anie of them for and into the realme of Englande aforesaide any manner of fishes goodes Bullian wares or marchandizes whatsoever shall bring or cawse to be brought the same and everie part therof unto the porte of the Towne of Southampton afforesaide and ther onely and no where else within the kingdome of England, shall discharge and laie on lande the same, Except that by the governer Officers and the Assistantes of the sayde societie of the most parte of them in open courte it shalbe otherwyse ordered and disposed and shall not transport or carry from thence any of the sayde Fishes goodes bullian wares or marchandizes without the speciall licence of the Governor Tresorer Agent, and Secretarie Assistantes and the Society afforesayde for the tyme beinge or the moste parte of them.

3. Item That ye saied Sir Humfry Gilbert shall nowe before his present departure owt of England Nominate elect and place owt of the sayde Society and company of the sayed merchant Adventurers resiant within the towne of Southampton or the precinctes therof fower Principall officers that is to saye a Governor, Treasurer, Agent, and a Secretary to continewe in the sayde offices accordinge to his Election will and pleasures eyther untill they and every of them dyeth or resigneth or be by the same society and company or the most part thereof fownde and lawfullie proved insufficient or defective And then after the Death or resignation of any of the same offi-

cers or after any insufficiency so by them fownd and proved the sayde Sir Humfry gilbert yf he be then within the Realme of England shall in his and theire steedes and places so deade resigninge or fownde insufficient or Defective nominate elect and place owt of the sayde Societie and company so many others to supply his and theyre roome and roomes and in the same office & offices to continewe and indure accordinge to his owne good will and pleasure. But yf it happen the sayde Sir Humfry Gilbert then to be absent owt of the Realme of England aforesayde at the tyme of anie suche deathe resignacion or insufficiencie or defecte proved as aforesayde, That then and in those cases it shalbe at all tymes lawfull to the rest of the said officers not Dying or resigning nor fownde insufficient or defective and to theyre Assistantes Society and company aforesayde or to the most part of them utterly to remove and displace all and every suche officer and officers afforesayde and in his and in every of their places so Dying resigning or removed to nominate elect and chuse three others of the most wyse and gravest men of the same Society and company ther dwelling in Southampton aforesayde in their writinge testefying and declaring the cause and causes therof to presente unto the Honnorable Sir Fraunces Walsingham Knight one of her Majestes Privie counsaill and Highe Secretarie, as unto theyr in this respect under her Majestie and ye sayde Sir Humfry Gilbert in his absence by him appointed cheif and principall Patron and gouvernor, The names and Surnames of all and every the sayd three other men so at any tyme or tymes hereafter In all and every suche presentment and presentmentes aforesayde it shalbe Lawfull unto the sayde Sir Fraunces Walsingham at his onely will and good pleasure so that he doe it within the space of xx^{ty} Dayes then next ensuing to prick one of them so nominated and presented And by prickinge to ratefy and confirme the same man to be the lawfull officer for that tyme in the steed and place of thother late officer so deade resigning or removed as aforesayde.

And The same person and persons so by him pricked ratefied and confirmed, untill his or theyre naturell Death resignacion or remocion shall keep have and enjoie all ye place proffites and preheminences incident thereunto whollie and in as ample manner and forme as his predecessors in that office or anie of them before that

tyme ever kept had and injoyed, But yf it shall happen the sayed Sir Fraunces Walsingham upon the said presentmentes of the thre other names and surnames aforesayde at anie tyme not to prick ratefye and confirme one of them as aforesayde within the space of xx^{tie} Dayes as aforesayed, That then and for that tyme it shalbe lawfull for the rest of thofficers Assistance, Society and company aforesayde or to the most part of them to all intentes constructions and purposes to name place and confirme in the cases aforesayde and to theffect aforesayde all and every suche officer and officers aforesayde as they or the most of them shall best lyke and agree upon for that tyme Provided alwaies that all and every of the saied Officer officers shall once in every yeere that is to saye within vii Dayes next Ensuing the feast of all Sainctes yeerly make and yeelde up in their sufficient writtinge unto the rest of the officers Assistantes and Society aforesayd or to the most parte of them for the tyme being within theyre place of common Assemblies theire severall True just and lawfull Accomptes and reckeninges of all and singuller suche receiptes and paymentes whatsoever by them or anie of them or theire assignes at anie tyme in the yeere before that tyme to the use and behoof of the sayed society and company of merchant Adventurers aforesayd theyre successors or Assignes or anie of them received had and imbursed

4. Item that the sayde Gouvernor and other the officers and society and company aforesayde dwellinge in Southampton and elswher within the Realme of England that conveniently may come theither shall in and upon the first daye of August next ensuinge ye date heereof or before yf they or the most parte of them shall thincke it necessary and convenient shall in some open and comodious place by the same officers apointed in good manner meet and assemble them selves toghether about Eyght of the clock in the Morninge and after some devine Service or sermon had and heard shall freely nominate elect and chuse and place owt of the sayed company and society aforesayde Eyght of the most wysest and Discreatest persons for one wholle yeer then next followinge to be Assistantes And to theyre uttermost power dilligently to assist the same officers and society and company aforesayde And also shall then and there in open court for the better gouverment and commodyty of the whole

society and company aforesayde according unto theyre wisdomes and good discretions Effectuallie make ordaine and establishe for them and every of them and theyre Successors all and all maner good necessary and convenient orders Decrees and statutes And that ye wholle Society and company aforesayde and everie of them and theyre successors and assignes shalbe unto the same orders decrees and statutes and to every of them In all respectes obedient and the same and every of them shall fulfill and performe upon suche payn and paines as the sayde Gouverner, Treasurer Agent secretarie Assistantes and the Society and company aforesayde or the most parte of them for the tyme beinge shall in ye same orders decrees and statutes and every of them specefie and set downe in due order and true meaning of the same to be inflicted and imposed upon all and every offender and offenders doing to ye contrary. And also that to the same good effectes and purposes the sayed officers Assistances and The whole Society and company aforesayde and every of them yf they maie Conveniently shall in like sorte at the tyme and place aforesaid upon the firste Daye of Marche then next followinge meet togeather and keep their generall lyke Court or Assembly And so forth also after that tyme the sayde officers all and singuler and the society and companie aforesayde In like manner and to the good intentes and purposes aforesayde In and upon every of the sayed two first Dayes of August and March aforesayd at the place and tyme aforesayde yeerely and in every yeere for ever shall duetefullie meet togeather and keepe their generall Sessions and solempne Assemblies and courtes as aforesaide, Provided neverthles that it shalbe Lawfull unto the saide officers and Assistances aforesaide and the most part of them wherof the Governer or Tresorer to be alwaies one at theire pleasurers to Assemble themselves togeather wher otherwise and as often as they or the most part of them wherof the sayed Governor or Treasuror alwaies to be one shall for the direction of newe or newely emergent causes or busines think it meet and convenient. Provided farder that yf it happen in those meane and speciall meetinges and assemblies or any of them any person or persones to be wronged or hardly dealt with all every party so greved maie lawfully apeale from the saied officers and the speciall assemblies aforesaide unto the next court

and generall Sessions to be holden and kept, And ther upon due excaminacion and tryall of the cause to receive a fynall order and determinacion therin from the saied officers Assistance and the whole Society and company aforesaied or the most part therof Provided Also farder that every of the sayde generall courtes Sessions and Assemblies aforesayd at the Dayes tymes and places afforesaid yerely and in every yeere for ever to be kept holden and solempnized in manner and forme aforesayde shall yf need require be holden and continewe by the space of Eyght daies or els longer or shorter as unto the saide officers and society aforesayd or to the most part of them ther shalbe thought most meet and convenient And yf it happen any of the saied two first Dayes of August or Marche aforesayde to fall upon the Sondaie or dominicall daye that then and in all those cases the sayed generall Courtes and assemblies and every of them to be kept holden and celebrated the secunde daye of those Moneths and of every of them in manner and forme aforesayde

5. Item That it shalbe lawfull unto the sayed gouvernor officers Assistances Society and companie aforesaide and the most part of and their successors from tyme to tyme and as they or the most part of them shall thinck it meet and convenient onely in the generall courtes and assemblies aforesayde upon suche fyne and fynes as shalbe by them or the most part of them for the tyme being Seased taxed and agreed upon to admitte and receive into the saied Society and company suche and as many redemptionary and redemptionaries as they or the most part of them shall well like of Provided Alwaies that as every some of five powndes in monny or comodities nowe first adventured is called ment and intended to be a single adventure so it shall not be Lawfull unto the sayde society and company at anie tyme to admit anie redemptionary to purchase and have for his fyne any more or above fower single adventures after the rate of the fyve powndes aforesayde as the same shall rise and fall And the fyne and fynes of the saide redemptionaries for the space of fifty yeeres now next ensuing shall lawfully imploie and convert to theyre owne uses and comodities and to the comodity of theyre heyres and assignes Rate for rate and according to the vallewe of their particuler somme and somes adventured and in the cedule indented specefied and contained Saving allwaies and re-

served unto ye sayde Sir Humfry Gilbert his heyres sucessors and Assignes and to every of them the fifte parte of every suche fyne and fynes to the onely use of the saide Sir Humfry Gilbert his heyres successors and Assignes by the sayd governor Assistance society and companie aforesayd for the tyme being to be well and truely contented and payed Provided alwaies that all and every the sayd redemptionary and redemptionaries theyr children and Apprentices serving seaven yeeres and theyre posterity and every of them shall from tyme to tyme well and truely paye or cause to be payed unto the sayd Sir Humfry Gilbert his heyres and assignes the whole custome and customes there in those contries territories and Dominions aforesayd at anie tyme due or to be due for all And every their goodes wares and Marchandizes brought thether or laden from thence Fishes and fishing onely excepted and forepryzed, And that neyther they the saide redemptionaryes nor any of them nor their children nor heyres nor apprenteces nor posterity aforesaide shalbe by reason of anie their adventures eyther in person or in goodes priveledged to have within any of the saide contryes, Territories or Dominions anie manner of Land or inherritance of lande or suche other prerogatives as the Merchant adventurers specified and contained in the cedull indented or infreed of and in consideracion of their first adventures ought to have.

6. Item That every man adventuring in this first voiadg whose knowen name and surname and some adventured shalbe sett downe in the sayd indented cedull of the Adventurers heerunto annexed and signed with the hand and seale of the said Sir Humfry Gilbert by the Assignement and allowance of the saide Sir Humfry Gilbert his heyres his successors or Assignes shall have to him and to his heires for ever in those countries Territories or Dominions or some one of them so by him the sayde Sir Humfry Gilbert his heyres Successors or Assignes or any of them at any tyme after The Date hereof discovered conquered or any wayes possessed, for every fyve powndes in mony or comodities Adventured one thousand acres of grownd over and above the retourne of his Adventure as the same shall fall owt to gayne or losses and so forth proportionably according to the rate of every severall adventure aforesaide.

7. Item that every adventurer in person and not in goodes in this first voiadg and theyre heyres shalbe for ever free of and in all trades and traffickes of and in all those contries territoris And Dominions and every of them paying unto the sayde Sir Humfry Gilbert his heyres successors and assignes the half custome and customes of and for theyre wares goodes And merchandizes, fishe and fishing onely Excepted as aforesaide brought frome hence thether or from thence hither unto England aforesayde and that it shalbe lawfull hereafter for those that have not nowe adventured in goodes putting in theyre mony for their adventures onely into the banke for every officer and gentilman in respect of the Adventure of his person to be admitted an adventurer of a Doble adventure and for every privat person of a single adventure, yf they so will doe.

8. Item That every man that shall nowe in this first voiage adventure in stock and also goe in person shall have a Doble proporcion of land ther in those countries territories or Dominions aforesayd aswell for his person as also for his Adventure in goodes that anie other hathe that shall venture onely in goodes and not in person.

And that every Gentelman In this sort Adventuring yf at any tyme he will put so much mony into the comon bancke or purse after the rate of a single adventure aforesayde maye have and shalbe admited unto four single Adventures and every pryvat mann unto two single Adventures, Doing and paying in his mony therefore ratably as aforesayde.

9. Item That every man that shall in this first voiadge tarry with the saide Sir Humfry Gilbert in the sayde countries territories or Dominions or any part therof nowe intended to be discovered conquered seased or possessed therwith him to remaine by the space of Eyght Monethes next after his first arryvall ther as a possession taker and holder to the onely use and behoof of the sayed Sir Humfrey Gilbert his heyres and assignes shall have double the proporcion in and of Lande ther as well for his person as also for his other adventure over and above all those proporcions and Acres of Landes which he shall have that goeth thether in person and remainethe not ther so long tyme with the sayed Sir Humfry gilbert but retourneth from thence againe before thende of the sayde space of Eyght monethes aforsaid Except allwaies suche person and persons as it shall please the sayd Sir Humfry Gilbert to use and employe in message or otherwyse in

this next retourne from thence into England which person and persons so used and Imploied shall have the same proporcion of Land ther as others as is aforesaide remaininge ther so long tyme shall have.

10. Item That every person and persons so adventuring in this first voiadge in person or in goodes or in both person and goodes shall hold all and singuler their sayd proporcion and nombers of Acres of Land aforesaide to him and to them and to his and to their heyres for ever in free Soccage tenure onely and not in Capite of and from the saide Sir Humfry Gilbert his heyres Assignes and Successors for ever yielding and paying therfore yeerly unto the sayde Sir Humfry Gilbert his heyres Assignes and successors After the ende of the first Seaven yeeres Exspired that the same nomber of Acres shalbe by him or them be possessed and Manured in Signe of a Chyvage or quitt rent for every thousand Acres ten shillinges and so ratablye and yeerely for ever.

11. Item That in farther reward and for perpetuall Memory of all those which nowe in this voiage dothe adventure thither with the saide Sir Humfry Gilbert eyther in person or in goodes or in bothe as is before specefied and their heyres children and successors shalbe for ever free and freely Discharged from all tortures Marshall lawes and from all arrestes and atachmentes of all and singuler their bodies and goodes whatsoever for all and every accion and accions personalls Realls and mixt, both in those countryes territories and Dominions and in every of them and every of theyr precinctes, and also at all tymes in all and singuler their passag and passages both by water and Land thither and from thence heyther notwithstanding any power and auctority or preheminence whatsoever heretofore geven and granted or hereafter to be geven and granted to the Sayde Sir Humfry Gilbert his heyres successors and assignes or the heyres successors or assignes of any of them by the sayde Lettres patentes from our soveraigne Lady Elizabeth Quene of England aforesayd or anie otherwyse.

12. Item that all and every of the kindred in bloude and consanginuity of the sayd Sir Humfry gilbert and his wyf and of everie of them shalbe in all those contries territories and Dominions and every of them for ever free and injoye all and every the aforesaide liberties freedomes immunities and priviledges and every of them without any fyne or fines whatsoever in as ample and as large manner as any of the saide Society and company by anie waies or meanes hath or maie or ought to have and injoie, Anie thing or thinges in those articles or anie of them specified or contayned to ye contrary in any wyse notwithstanding. Provided Alwaies and it is straightly charged and comanded And expresly inhibited and forbid unto the sayde Society and company aforesaide and every of them by the saide Sir Humfry Gilbert that none of the nowe Marchantes of the Moscovy company nor none of their children or issues nor none of the nowe inhabitantes of the Towne of Southampton or within the freedome therof nor none of their children or issues of Anie of them which neyther adventured with the sayde Sir Humfry Gilbert in his first pretence of Discovery nor nowe in this last voiage shall at any time heere after be capable of the freedomes or of anie part of the liberties imunities or priviledges aforesayde by redemption grant gifte consent or by anie other waies or meanes whatsoever, And in consideracion therof the saide Sir Humfry Gilbert his heyres Successors and assignes covenanteth and granteth to and with the saide Society and companie by those presentes that he the saide Sir Humfry Gilbert his heires successors and assignes or some of them shall at all times hereafter confiscate and sease uppon as forfeited all and all manner their fishes wares and marchandizes there in those countries Territories or Dominions or anie of their precinctes aforesaid at anie time heereafter fownd or Laden there or from thence and also all and all manner the fishes goodes and wares and marchandizes of all other person or persons whatsoever not being free of this Society and companie inhabiting within this Realme of England or the Isles of Guernsey or Jersey or the Isles lying theraboutes ther in those countries territories or Dominions or within the precinctes of anie of them at anie time fownd and taken shalbe confiscated and forfeited the one half to himself his heyres Successors and assignes and thother half unto the saide society and companie of the nowe marchant Adventurers with the sayed Sir Humfry Gilbert By him the sayd Sir Humfry Gilbert his heyres Successors and assignes well and truely to be contented and paied And in Lyke sort all and all manner Seasure And seasures forfect and forfectures of anie and all manner of goodes wares and marchandizes of any

and of every the person and persons aforesaide so as aforesaide restrained Inhibited and not free of the saide society and company made taken or donne by ye saied company thier successors and Assignes within the porte or Towne of South Hampton or within anie port or place of the Realme of Englande shalbe in Lyke sort made and taken to the onely use and profitt of the saide Sir Humfry Gilbert his heires successors and as-signes, And alsoe to the use and behoof of the saide societie and company aforesaide their suc-cessors and assignes by Equall half porcions to be devided That is to saie the one half therof to ye saide Sir Humfry Gilbert his heyres Successors and Assignes, And thother half to the saide soci-ety and company Their successors and Assignes for ever.

13. Item that all those which shall apeere to be certefied unto the officers and Society aforesayd under the hande and seale of the sayde Sir Hum-fry Gilbert to have ben adventurers in the Last pretence of discovery with him and also al those which continewed with him in the voiage untill the breaking up therof at Kinsaell in Ireland in those Countries territories and Dominions and every of them shalbe as free to all intentes and purposes as the nowe Adventurers ar or ought to be in any manner and respect aforesaide.

14. Item That the saide Sir Humfry Gilbert of his special and meere mocion towardes the com-fort and relief of the poore travelers and decaied persons of the society aforesaid And other good uses to be bestowed and imployed within the saide towne of South Hampton aforesayd geveth and granteth unto the saide Society and company of the marchant adventurers aforesaide and to their successors and assignes for ever tenne Thowsande Acres of Lande to be holden of him his heyres Successors and assignes unto the saide Society and company aforesayde And unto their successors and assignes for ever in those contries Territories and Dominions aforesayde or some of them In Socage tenure aforesayd and also one pownde owt of every his hundreth pownds that shall hereafter ryse and come unto him owt of and upon his fift part of the fynes of the Redemp-tionaries aforesayde during the terme of the fifty yeeres aforesayde And the saide Society and company also and their successors in like sort and to those goode workes and intentes shall and will yeerly geve graunt and distribute in monny one pound of everie hundreth powndes that by godes providence and their goode industry shall heere after happen to be gotten and gained or growen unto the same society and company aforesaide, owt of and by all the yeerelye gaines and profittes of all the whole company aforesaide for ever by reason of their trade and traffick theyther and from thence as aforesaide.

15. Item That he the saide Sir Humfry Gilbert his heyres and successors after his first Arrivall in the saide countries Territories or Dominions or anie of them and as soone as he or they can doe the same to good effect in Lawe shall effectualy ratefie confirme and assure to all intentes and purposes unto all and every the saide Adventur-ers their heyres children posterity and others aforesayd in manner and forme aforesaide all and every the saide Landes Liberties freedomes im-munities and commodities and every other thing and thinges requisitt and incident therunto and to every part therof in suche manner and sort as by and from her Majestie her heyres and successors for the further confirmacion And strenghtning of the premisses and every part therof unto the said Governor officers Assistantes society and com-pany afforesaid and unto every of th[em their] heyres [children] successors and others aforesayd in anie respect shalbe at anie tyme heerafter needful or necessary And that all and every the grauntes Articles clauses and sentences concern-ing eyther the said Sir Humfry Gilbert his heirs or successors or any of the saide Society or company of Marchant Adventurers or any other person or persons aforesaide shalbe at all times construed interpreted and understoode according to the most true plaine And usuall sence and construc-tion in all thinges and no otherwyse And that yf ther shall happen any difference betwene the sayde Sir Humfry Gilbert his heires and assignes and the saide society and company or any of them their heires children or posterity or any other aforesayde abowt any ambiguous construccion of any Article or articles clause or sentence what-soever heerin contained the exposition and finall determinacion of all and every suche controver-sies and differences shall rest and abide in the handes Judgment and finall determinacion of the Lorde Chaunncellor of England for the tyme be-inge In witnes wherof unto the one part of the sayde Articles Indented Remayning with the saide society and company aforesayde the saide Sir Humfry Gilbert hathe putt his hande and seale and to the other part remaining with the saide Sir

Humfry Gilbert the saide society and company aforesayd have cawsed the seale of the Office of the Maioralty of the Towne of Southampton aforesayde to be sett unto Yeven the Daye and yeere first above written.

[*Endorsed:*] Articles of agreement indented between Sir Humfry Gilbert and such of Hampton as adventure with him: as also between him and all other Adventurers with him.

399. December 12, 1582. Draft of additional articles between Sir Humphrey Gilbert and those individuals and groups who adventured with him, with instructions in the event of his departure.

Addicons to the Articles

[1] And further that all and every person and persons that shall heerafter intend to goe into the remote Countries Territories or Dominions aforsaid or anie of them shall first enter into bande unto ye Governer, Tresorer, Agent and Secretary assistances And the Society aforesaide by the discrecion of the said Governor, Tresorer Agent Secretary Assistantes and the Society aforesaid or the most of them to runne and goe suche course (as neere as he or they maye) as shalbe sett downe by the dirreccion of the said governer Tresorer Agent Secretary Assistances and Society aforesaid or the most part of them, And that they nor anie of them so entring into bande as aforsaid shall attempt or doe anie thing directly or indirectly that shalbe contrary to theffect And true meaning of her Majesties Comission graunted to the said Sir Humfry Gilbert And also upon their arrivall there in those Countries Territories or dominions they and everie of them to doe everie thing and thinges to the use of the said Sir Humfry his heyres and Successors In suche manner and forme as the nowe Adventerers in person with the said Sir Humfry Gilbert doth or ought to doe According to the tennor and forme of the Articles aforsaid and none otherwise.

And further that the said Governer, Tresorer, Agent Secretaire Assistances and Society shall have full power and lawfull auctoritie to Admitte into this forsaid accion for Discoverie anie person and persons that upon the condicions aforsaid or suche other condicions as the said Governor Tresorer Agent Secretary Assistances and Society aforsaid or the most part of them by the consent of the aforsaid Sir Fraunces Walsingham knight shalbe thought meet, so that everie suche person so to be admitted do imbark himself and depart from the coast of England to the intentes aforsaid before the ende of Aprill next, And that all suche persons so Auctorised by the governor tresorer Agent secretary Assistances and Society or the most part of them Inrold in the recordes of Suthampton So that he depart before the last of Aprill as aforsaid shall have and injoye the like priviledges liberties and fredomes as the nowe adventerers in person with the said Sir Humfry hath or ought to have by vertue of thesse present Articles.

Provided Alwaies and nevertheless it is concluded condiscended and agreed that yf anie person as is aforesaid Auctorised shall at anie tyme or tymes heereafter willingly wittingly and maliciously pretend do or goe about to doe or willinglie suffer to be don anie manner of act thing or thinges whatsoever tending to the distruccon or subvercion of the said Sir Humfry his heyres Successors or cheef Assignes or principall governor or doe comitte piracy or open hostility against anie Cristian prince or people wherby the lettres pattentes of the said Sir Humfry shall or maye be made voide or frustrat contrary to the true meaning purpoce and effect of the said lettres pattentes graunted to the said Sir Humfry, or yf he or they do publiquely notoriously and maliciously mainteyn anie suche person or persons as shall publiquely or openly goe about to distroye or overthrowe the right tytle or person of the said Sir Humfry his heyres Successors or cheef and principall Assigne in principall government, or the subvercion of the common Wealth of the said Sir Humfry his heyres or Successors, their Countries or Territories That then And from thenceforth thes present Addicions and the Covenantes aforsaid to become voide and of none effect to all intentes and purposes as yf the same Addicions hadd never ben had nor made anie thing heerin contained to the contrary heerof In anie wayse notwithstandinge.

And by these presentes I the said Sir Humfry Gilbert for me my heires successors and Assignes do geve full power and Auctority unto the said governor, Tresorer Agent Secretary Assistances Society and Company to arme and sett out from time to tyme as my Assignes anie and as many shipp and shipps to discover Searche and find out all and every suche remote heathen miscreant and barberous landes Countries and Territories whatsoever not nowe actuallie possessed by anie Cristian Prince or people as to them it shalbe thought meet and convenient in anie part of the Worlde whatsoever, by and under the Auctority of her Majestes graunt made to me the said Sir Humfrey Gilbert, All which Countries Territories or dominions the said Governor, Treasorer Agent Secretary and Company aforsaid shal conquer have holde occupy and injoye Inhabitt and governe by and under me the Said Sir Humfry Gilbert my Successors and Assignes In suche manner and forme as the Acres of land in the Articles afore mentioned or occupied and Injoyed And to Injoye as large liberties priveledges and freedoms In all and every the said Countries And Territories as aforsaid as they maie do or ought to doe by vertue of anie graunt liberties or freedoms heertofore geven or graunted to them by me the said Sir Humfry Gilbert, so that they neither willingly do nor cause to be done anie thing or thinges contrarie to the true meaning of the Queenes Majestes graunt to me the saide Sir Humfry graunted, anie thing or Thinges heertofore graunted or heerafter to be graunted to the contrary In any wise notwithstanding.

Memorandum that these Addicions to the Articles and all rasures And Interlininges of these presentes weere don with the good liking And consent of the said Sir Humfry Gilbert and company before the delivery of thes present bookes in the presence of thes persons whose names ar heer under written.

[2]   These Highe and Honnorable personadges heer underwritten And their heires for ever by the free gift and full consent and asent of the said Sir Humfry Gilbert knight and the Society and Companie of the nowe Marchant Adventerers aforesaid, after their severall adventures heerin entred ratably as is in these Articles expressed shall have lawfull freedome and free trade or traffike of marchandize and marchandizing in all and singuler the Countries territories And Dominions within written nowe intended to be discovered in as ample manner and forme as the

saide nowe Marchant Adventurers by vertue heerof hathe or ought to have in the same trade or trafficques viz.

  Sir Thomas Bromley knight Lord Chanceler of England.
  William Lord Burgley highe tresorer of England.
  Lord Earle of Sussex highe chamberlain of England.
  Lord Erle of Warwick.
  Robert Lord erle of Lecester.
  Sir Cristopher Hatton knight vice chamberlain to her majestes
  Sir Fraunces Knowles knight
  Sir James acroft [Croft] knight
  Sir Walter Milemaye knight
  Sir Henry Sidney knight

And Also dyvers other knightes Esquiers And gentlemen viz.

  Phillip Sidney Esqr.
  Sir George Peake knight.
  Sir Henry Knevett knight.
  Thomas Knevett Esqr.
  William Archer Esqr.
  William Archer Jun. his sonne gent.
  John Dee gent.
  Anthony Packhurst Esqr.
  James Parkinson esqr.
  Richard Bingham esqr.
  John Mawle gent.
  Androwe Mallery esqr.
  Lawrance Tompson gent.
  Edward Cordell esqr.
  William Parry esqr.

[3]   The names and Surnames of suche persons with their severall Somes of monny and comodities Adventured with the said Sir Humfry gilbert In this present voiadge of discovery heere insueth viz.

Sir Fraunces Walsingham knight	1 li.
William Barwick Maior of Southampton	x li.
Mr. Edward Cotton of Suthampton esqr.	1 li.
Nicolas Caplin of Suthampton marchant	xx li.
Robert Knaplock of the towne of Hampton	xx li.
William Knaplock of Clementes Inn gent	xxx li.
Richard Goddard of Suthampton Marchant	xl li.
John Knight of Suthampton Ironmunger	x li.
Robert Moore of Suthampton Marchant	xx li.
John Errnighton of Suthampton marchant	x li.

John Smith of the Towne of Hampton gent — xx li.
Thomas Homes of Suthampton esqr. — i li.
Fraunces Mills of Suthampton gent — x li.
Edmund Stafford of Suthampton gent — x li.
John Eyles of Suthampton Mercer — v li.
Barnard Courtnill of Suthampton Marchant — x li.
John Hopton of Suthampton draper — v li.
Androwe Studley of Suthampton Mercer — xv li.
Richard Waterton of Suthampton gent — x li.
Edmund Capelin of Suthampton gent — x li.
Thomas Demaresk of Suthampton marchant — v li.
Robert Russell of Suthampton beer-bruer — v li.
Henry Moore of the Towne of Hampton gent — v li.
William Grose of Suthampton Mercer — v li.
Thomas Courtnill of Suthampton baker — v li.
Thomas Haward of Suthampton draper — v li.
John Sedgwick of Suthampton marchant — xx li.
Paule Elliot of Suthampton mercer — v li.
Laurance Grosse of Suthampton mercer — v li.
Thomas Griston of Southampton shipmaster — v li.
John Greni of Suthampton Yeoman — v li.
Hughe Dervall the yonger of Suthampton mercer — v li.
Mr. Christopher Kenn Esqr. — x li.
William Eling of the Towne of Suthampton — v li.
Sampson Thomas of Suthampton beer-bruer — v li.
Sir William Winter knight
William Winter gent
Helleni Edmondes of Suthampton widowe — v li.
Harry Edmundes of Suthampton Yoman — v li.
Thomas Clark thelder of Burton in Dorset gent — v li.
Nicolas Roche of Suthampton Marchant — v li.
Robert Mawle of Chalock in Kent gent — xx li.
John Elsey of Suthampton Marchant — v li.
John Deslile of Suthampton Marchant — v li.
John Smith of Suthampton taylor — v li.
Robert Studley of Suthampton baker — v li.

[4] These heer underwritten ar free alsoo of the said traffique and trade of marchandize by the gift and consent aforesaide According to the proporcion of a single Adventure. but not to injoye the Division of anie gains untill hereafter they shall putt in their stokes According unto thes Articles.

Henry Hopkins of Suthampton Clerk.
John Calvert of Suthampton Clerk.
Emery Lakes of Suthampton marchant.
Thomas Dickenson of Suthampton Yoman.
John Riges of Suthampton Yoman.
Robert Kenninges of Suthampton Yoman.
Richard Jackson of Suthampton Yoman.
Richard Mudford of Suthampton Yoman.
Georg Dalton of Suthampton Yoman.
Augusteni Reynolds of Southampton.
John Favor of Suthampton Clerk marchant.
Dionis Brett of Sale in the Conty of Norfolk.

[5] These Also whose names ar here Written which Adventured with Sir Humfry gilbert in his First voiadge in monny or comodities not Inhabiting within the Towne of Suthampton aforsaid shall in like sorte be free of trade And traffick as aforesaid.

The Lord Northe
Mr. Edmondes of the privie chamber.
Sir Mathew Arrundell.
Sir Edward Horsey.
Sir William Morgan
Sir John Gilbert.
Sir george Peckham.
Charles Arrundell esqr.
Mr. Mackwilliam esqr.
Mr. Walter Rawley esqr.
Mr. Carrowe Rawley esqr.
Mr. Cotton esqr.
Mr. Edward
Henry Nowell esqr.
Mr. Wigmore esqr.
John Dudley esqr.
William Moham esqr.
Edward Bartley esqr.
Thomas Smith Customer of London.
Edmund Eltoft esqr.
Georg Carrowe of okington esqr.
Mr. Rudgwaye esqr.
Mr. Laurance Radford esqr.
Adrian Gilbert esqr.
Charles Champernowne esqr.
Robert Wraye gent.
Thomas Hamond gent.
Mr. Whetstone gent.
Edward snelling gent.
Mr. Haies gent. of Leerpolle
John Upton [Unton] esqr.
Mr. William hawkins gent.
Mr. James Hilston gent.
Barnard Smith marchant

John Periam Marchant
William Weymouth Marchant
William Martin Marchant
Lawrance Barckham marchant
John Rodford
Simon Bowiar esqr.
Georg Maydo gent.
John Amerrideth gent.
John Robertes gent.
Mr. Warckhope esqr.

[6]   Allso all those persons whose names ar heer under written that in person Adventured with the sayde Sir Humfry gilbert knight in his first voiage About this discovery within written and continewed with him untill the breaking up therof At kinsaell in Ireland After their severall Adventures heerin entrend ratably as aforsaid shall have freedom in the trade and traffick of Marchandizes as is aforesaide. [Blank.]

[7]   Allso all and singuler other the Adventurers with The said Sir Humfry Gilbert of the Townes of Tottnes and Darkmouth and all others adventuring with the said Sir Humfry Gilbert under the name of Sir John Gilbert knight thelder brother of the said Sir Humfry Gilbert and Also all others Adventuring to theffectes aforsaid under the name Barnard Drake esquire or Anthony brigham gent, After the certificat In writting under the handes and seales of the said Sir Jo: gilbert, Sir Humfry gilbert Sir georg peckhame or of anie of them of the true severall adventures of every suche adventurer made and delivered unto the Governor Tresorer Agent Secretary Assistantes And Society aforsaid shall in the next generall Court or Assembly then after the delivery of every of the said certificates to be holden within the Towne of Suthampton aforsaid In like sort be heerin entrd and also be free of traffick in the places aforsaid In suche manner As the nowe adventerers with Sir Humfry gilbert by vertu of these Articles be or ought to be And no otherwise, And so that the said certificates be made and delivered within the space of three Yeeres next ensuing the Date of these Articles. [Blank.]

[8]   The names and surnames of all suche as nowe in this present discovery adventureth in person with the said Sir Humfry Gilbert. [Blank.]

[9]   The names and surnames of the four principall Officers of the said Society, that is to saie of the Governor, tresurer, Agent And Secretary, named elected and chosen by the said Sir Humfry gilbert before his nowe departure out of Englande as heer followethe viz— [Blank.]

[10]   Instructions Left by Sir Humfry Gilbert unchangably to be observéd.
1. The Yellowe wax is to be broken at the Landes ende of Englande and not before for that it is for their Course onely—
2. The redde wax is not to be broken up before they come upon the Coast of America or within a hundreth Leagues thereof—
3. The parties to whom the same ar delivered ar to give their faithes not to do anie thing contrary to this Direction—

Ther ar xii of the same bales for direccion delivered upon the Delivery of the Articles of our Aggreement and one littell rolle with a labell wraped up in redd wax and Sealed as the other this xiith of December 1582

Also I woulde have these writes the lettres pattentes the graunt to the Towne and the Sea Carde and all other thinges touching this matter putt into an Iron chest with Three lockes And not to forgett to speak with Iron Simcottes marchant of London at his retorne from Barbery for this graunt for I hadd conference with him about the same before his departure.—

And those three keyes aforsayd to be kept the one by the Maior of Suthampton th'other by Richard goddard And the thirde by robart Moore. Untill the officers be knowen—

H: G:

[Endorsed:] Additions to the former articles between Sir Humfrey Gilbert and the adventurers with him.

400. February 28, 1583. Agreement between Sir Humphrey Gilbert, Sir George Peckham, and George Peckham.

Articles Indented of agreemente made concluded and agreed upon the laste daye of Februarie in the fyve and twentith yere of the raigne of oure soveraigne ladye Elizabeth by the grace of god Queene of Englande Fraunce and Irelande defendor of the faithe &c. Betwene Syr Humfrey Gilbert of Compton in the Countie of Devon knighte on the one partie and Sir George Peckham of Denham in the Countie of Bucks knighte and George Peckham his second sonne on the other partie as followeth viz.

Inprimis Whereas oure saide Soveraigne ladye the Queenes majestie by her graces lettres Patentes under the greate seale of Englande bearinge date at Westminster the eleventh daye of June in the twentith yere of her majesties raigne hath geven and graunted unto the saide Syr Humfrey Gilberte his heires and assignes forever free libertye from tyme to tyme and at all tymes hereafter forever to discover searche finde oute and vewe suche remote heathen and barborous landes countries and territories not actuallie possessed of any Christian Prince or people as to hym and his heires or assignes and to every or any of them shall seme good and the same to have holde occupie and enjoy to hym and his heires forever with all commodities Jurisdiccions and rialties both by sea and lande and did likewise by the saide lettres patentes for her majestie her heires and Successors geve full power and aucthoritie to the saide Sir Humfrey his heires and assignes and every of them that he and they and every or any of them shall or maye at every tyme and tymes hereafter have take and leade in the saide voyage to travell thitherwardes or to inhabitt there with hym or them and every or any of them suche and so many of her majestyes subjectes as shall willinglie accompanye him and them and every or any of them with sufficiente shippinge and furniture for their transportacons so that none of the saide persons or any of them be suche as after the makinge of the saide lettres patentes shoulde be speciallie restrayned by oure saide soveraigne her heires or successors the statutes or actes of Parliamente made againste fugitives or againste suche as shall departe remaine or contynue oute of her majesties realme of Englande withoute licence or any other acte statute lawe or matter whatsoever to the contrarie in anywise notwithstandinge as by the saide lettres patentes amongeste other grauntes articles and libertyes therein conteyned more at large appeareth. Nowe the saide Sir Humfrey Gilberte as well for the more spedye execucion of her majesties saide grauntes and thenlargmente of her

majesties Domynions and govermente and also for the better encouragemente of the saide Sir George Peckham and George hys sonne and their associates in so worthie and comendable an enterprise as also for his and their sure warrante to prosecute the same orderlie accordinge to the lawes and statutes of this realme. And in consideracion that the saide Sir George hath disbursed diverse sommes of money and adventured the same as a principall adventurer with the saide Sir Humfrey as also for divers other weightie and good consideracions him the saide Sir Humfrey speciallie movinge for hym his heires executors administrators and assignes and every of them doth covenante promise and graunte to and with the saide Sir George Peckham knighte and George hys sonne their heires executors administrators and assignes by theis presentes that the saide Sir George Peckham and George his sonne his and their assignes and associates adventurers and people and every of them shall and may at all tymes hereafter and from tyme to tyme forever have and enjoy full power and free libertie and aucthoritie by vertue of the saide lettres patentes to discover searche fynde oute and vewe any landes Countries or Islandes heretofore not discovered searched and inhabited by any Christian Prince or people by the assignemente of the saide Sir Humfrye his heires and successors and allso to enjoye to his and their owne use all that ryver or porte called by Master John Dee, Dee Ryver which Ryver by the discripcion of John Verarzanus a Florentyne lyeth in Septontrionall latitude about fortye twoo degrees and hath his mouth lyinge open to the South halfe a league brode or there aboute and enteringe within the saide Baye betwene the Easte and the Northe encreaseth his breadith and contynueth twelve leagues or there aboutes and then maketh a gulfe of twentie leagues compasse or thereaboutes and conteyneth in it selfe five small Islandes newlie named the Cinque Isles. And the saide gulfe and the fyve Isles therein and all other Isles lyinge within the saide Ryver or gulfe together with fyfteene hundred thousande acres of ground within the supposed contynent lyinge nexte adjoininge upon the saide ryver gulfe and fyve Isles at the choyce of the saide Sir George and George his yongeste sonne their heires deputies or asignes or any of them. To have holde and enjoye the saide Isle and Islande together with the saide fyfteene hundred thousande acres of landes to the saide Sir George Peckham and George Peckham their heires and assignes to hys and their onlie uses forever by Soccage tenure of the same Sir Humfrye his heyres and assignes so as the uttermoste partes or lymyttes of the saide Fyftene hundred thousande acres of grounde extende not alongst the sea coaste westwarde towardes the ryver of Norunnbedge above threescore englishe myles in length at the moste with full powre and aucthoritie to inhabite people and manure the saide Islandes landes countries and territories with all Jurisdiccions priviledges liberties and royallties both by lande and by sea alongest all the costes of the saide countries and territories as is aforesaide yeldinge and payinge unto the saide Sir Humfrye his heires successors or assignes for every thousande acres of grounde after the firste seaven yeres proporcianallie which the same shalbe actuallie possessed and manured by the saide Sir George Peckham or George his sonne their heires or assignes five shillinges and twoo fyfte partes of all the golde silver pearle and precious stones there growinge founde and gotten oute of the which too fyfte parts the Queenes majesties parte reserved by the lettres patentes ys to be allowed and deducted. Item that they the saide Sir George nor George his sonne their heires nor assignes shalbe charged with any contribucion towardes any Warres other then defencis and that onlie by acte of Parliamente of whiche assemblie the saide Sir George and all those which shall beare the name of an Associate with hym shalbe as principall members in every suche Sessions and assemblie. Item the saide Sir Humfrye for the consideracions aforesaide doth covenante and graunte for him selfe his heires successors and assignes and every of them to and with the saide Sir George Peckham and George his sonne their heires and assignes and every of them by theis presentes that he the saide Sir George and George his sonne their heires assignes and people and every of them shall and maye have and enjoye free liberties to trade and traffique into all suche Countries Islandes Isles and territories and into every and any parte of them which the saide Sir Humfrye his heires successors or assignes shall possesse by vertue of the Queene majesties saide lettres patentes and his graunte thereof and also that he the saide Sir George and George hys sonne their heires and assignes and every of them shall

have thexecucion of all lawes Ecclesiasticall temporall politique marshall and Civill both marine and others and every of them aswell within the precincte of the saide fyfteene hundred thousande acres of grounde as also uppon the sea coste thereof so farr as the said landes shall extende it selfe as aforesaid Item the saide Sir Humfrye Gilberte for him his heires successors and assignes doth covenante from tyme to tyme upon performance of the covenantes in this booke conteyned to exonerate discharge and sufficientlie to save harmeles the saide Sir George and George his sonne theire heires and assignes and everie of them of and from the Quenes majesties her heyres successors and assignes for and concernynge the payment of the Ewer of golde and silver and other duties services and demaundes to her majestie her heires and successors by the saide lettres patentes payable and reserved and likewise shall and will fynishe suche further and better assuraunce and assuraunces of the premysses unto the saide Sir George and George hys sonne their heyres and assignes forever within three monethes nexte after the first and nexte retorne of the saide Sir Humfrye or hys assignes consortes adventurers or associates from the saide voyage of discoverye by the saide Sir Humfrye nowe intended in suche manner and sorte as by the saide Sir George and George hys sonne their heyres or assignes or any of them or the learned counsell of them or any of them shalbe reasonablie and lawfullye devised and required. And the same Sir George and George hys sonne for them selfes their heires and assignes and every of them doe covenaunte promyse and graunt to and with the said Sir Humfrey his heires successors and assignes and every of them by theise presents that they the said Sir George and George hys sonne shall doe their best indevor to procure and obteyne her majesties leave and good lykeinge that all those whoe have or shall adventure with the saide Sir Humfrye Sir George or George hys sonne or eyther of them into the saide Countries and whose names shalbe entered into a register booke for that purpose to be made and kepte and shalbe willinge to travaile into anye of the saide remote Countries maye freelye passe into those countries there to remayne or to retorne backe at hys or their, or any of their will and pleasure And the said Sir George Peckham and George hys sonne doe further covenaunt and graunte for them selves their heires executors and assignes to and with the said Sir Humfrey Gilbert hys heyres successors and assignes by theis presentes that he nor they nor any of them their heires or assignes shall deferre thexecucion of Justice within their liberties beinge thereunto required by the saide Sir Humfrey hys heyres successors or assignes against any suche as shall conspire against the person of the saide Sir Humfrey hys heyres successors or principall assignes or commytt any capitall offence or shall deteyne or protecte from Justice any person hys landes or goodes contrarie to the lawes to be established in the before mencioned remote countries and territories nowe ment to be discovered which the saide Sir Humfrey Gilbert hys heyres successors or assignes shall have holde occupie or enjoye by right or tytle under or by vertue of the Quenes majesties lettres patentes to hym graunted as before is mencioned provided alwaies and nevertheles yt is concluded condiscended and agreed by and betwene the saide parties that yf the saide Sir George or George hys sonne their heyres or assignes shall at any tyme or tymes hereafter willinglye wittinglye and maliciouslye pretend doe or goe about to doe or willinglye suffer to be done any manner of acte thinge or thinges Whatsoever tendinge to the distruccion or subvercion of the said Sir Humfrey hys heyres successors or chief assigne or principall governor or doe or willinglye commytt any acte whereby the saide Sir Humfrye hys heyres successors or assignes shall lose the benefitt of the graunt of the said lettres patentes or he or hys heyres successors or assignes to be by the Quenes Majestie or her successors dissavowed forever or yf he or they doe publiquelye or notoriouslye maynteyne any suche person or persones as shall publiquely or openlye goe about to distroye or overthrowe the right tytle or person of the said Sir Humfrye hys heyres successors or hys chief and principall assigne in princypall government or the subversion of the common wealth of the said Sir Humfrey hys heires or successors their Countreys or Terrytoryes that then and from thensfourth this present graunte and all covenauntes therein conteyned to be come voide and of none effecte to all ententes and purposes as yf the same hadd never ben had nor made anythinge in these presentes conteyned to the contrarye hereof in any wise notwithstandinge In wittnes wherof the parties

abovesaid to theise present articles Indented Interchaungeablie have hereunto putt their handes and Seales yeoven the daye and yere first above written.

401. Instructions for a voyage of reconnaissance to North America in 1582 or 1583.

This document, which has not appeared complete in print before, is of considerable importance. It is a set of instructions, lacking the first page, which was copied by Sir Edward Hoby into his commonplace book (British Library, Additional Manuscript 38823, ff. 1–8) for a voyage to America, clearly associated with the plans of Sir Humphrey Gilbert (whom Hoby knew) in 1582 or 1583. It is most probably connected with the expedition planned for 1583 by Sir George Peckham, Sir Thomas Gerrard, and their associates. The expedition, which, in fact, never took place, was to depart sometime between June, 1582, and March, 1583, under the joint or several command of Sir William Stanley, Richard Bingham, and Martin Frobisher. They were to be required to furnish, on their return, information acquired according to these instructions (see D. B. Quinn, Gilbert, II, 260). Sir George Peckham and Martin Frobisher could have been responsible for some of the suggestions made in the instructions; so could Gilbert himself and also one or both of the Richard Hakluyts—the elder, Hakluyt the lawyer of the Middle Temple, and the younger, a clergyman and fellow of an Oxford College. The late Eva G. R. Taylor believed that William Borough may well have had something to do with them ("Instructions to a colonial surveyor in 1582," The Mariner's Mirror, XXXVII (1951), 48–62). Thomas Bavin, the surveyor and artist named in them, may have been the son of Thomas Bavand of Liverpool or else may have come from a Chester family of this name (see D. B. Quinn, England and the Discovery of America (1974), pp. 374–375).

The document probably began with one or two general paragraphs and then continued with "Instructions for the captain" who may or may not have been named.

[a]   [Instructions for the captain.]

[1]... And springes togither with ther diversyties in Colour or Tasty nothing distinctly the particular place where every suche thinge shalbe fownde to be sett downe bothe in the Jornall and drawen plottes./

[2] Also another to note all the Islandes their bignes Commodityes and havens and the elevacion of every Isle and to sett downe thesame bothe in your mappes & Jornalles./

[3] Also another to note & learne all kinde of Fishes bothe shell fishes and other setting downe the particuler places where every suche thing shalbe founde in the Jornall & Drawne plottes./

[4] Another to note the resemblances of all sortes of beastes & their differences either in kinde or colour with or from ours in Europe./ noting distinctly the particuler places where every suche thing shel be fownde as aforesayd in the Jornall & plottes./

[5] Another to note the like of birdes & Flyes but chiefly for bees wax honnye and Cohoniell Noting distinctly the particular places where every suche thing shalbe founde as aforesayd in the Jornall and plottes./

[6] Another to note their manner of taking byrdes fowles Fyshes and beastes in those Contryes./ Another to note all sortes of earthes with their differences in colour & Taste and the fertilitye, & barrennes thereof. Noting precisely the distinct places where every such thing shalbe fownd both in the Jornall or plott./

[7] Another to note the like of Trees fruictes and Gummes noting precisely the particuler places where every suche thing shalbe founde bothe in the Jornall & plott./

[8] Another to note all sortes of metalls & submyneralls togither with the places where they shalbe fownde. Noting distinctly the particuler places where every suche thing shalbe fownde both in the Jornall & plott./

[9] Another to note the like of hearbes seede and appotycary drogues noting precisely the particuler places where eny suche thing shalbe fownd bothe in the Jornall & plott./

[10] Another to note what plentye of pytche Tarre & Rozen there may be fownd noting precisely the particuler places where every suche shalbe fownde both in the Jornall & plott./

[11] Another to note the manner of their planting & manuring of the earthe./

[12] Another to note the statures Conditions apparell and manner of foode, which of them be men eaters with the thinges that they in every particuler place shall most esteme either of their owne Contrye commodyties or of ours. Noting also the greatnes and quantetie of every distinct Kinges Contryes people and forces and in What manner they arme and order them selfes in Warres and who are Freindes or enemies to eache other of them noting preciselye the particuler places where every suche observacions are to be made as well in the Jornall as platt./

[13] Another to note the dyversitie of their languages and in what places their speache beginnethe to alter as nere as you can both in the Jornall & platt. And the same man to Carry with him an Englishe dictionarie with the Englishe wordes before therin to sett downe their language./

[14] Another to see that the fyer be always putt out after the Kettle is soe that no candles be occupyed and Carryed on shippeboord but in Lanthornes./

[15] Another to consyder precysely wether the ryver of Norramberge may be defended att or nere the mouthe therof either by dispersed Islandes or by the Channells running nere them or the maine./ Yf not then observe the Just place of the Ryver where the same may be defended either by thone or thother or by any other good meanes whatsoeuer. And yf yt may not be well defended att the mouth then consyder well whether there be any good Roades for shippes to ride or landing places for men or munition betwene the Sea and the place

[16] Where you may defend the ryver as aforesayde./ And yf there be any suche rodes may serve and for Shippes of what burther and for how many of them./ Another to note their severall kinde of boates their burther & usage./

[17] Another to observe Bayes Havens Rivers & landing places And for what windes they serve with their flattes rockes and for what nomber and burden of shippes they will serve And howe farre the ryvers do flowe up and to what height./

[18] Another to observe Convenient places to make Salt./

[19] Another to attend always, Baven with penne onck paper & pensill with black leade and Ephimerides or with somme other Calculated Tables to observe the latitude./

Another to attend him alweis with an uneversall Dyall a Crosse staffe and A Sayling Compasse.[1]

[20] Another to attend him alweis with an Instrument for the varyation of The Compasse and with the Instrument for the Declynation of the nedle. Another to attend him alweis when he draweth with all his marckes written in parchment to oversee him that he mistakes not any of the sayd marckes in his plottes which are sett downe as follethe./

[b] Instructions for the master.

[1] Before you put out of Harborowe slinge your Pynneses with a Junke of a Cable or a strong Lasew Lest in storme by gyving them a Towe you teare out the steme./

[2] Also delyver to every shippe a note in writing before you put out of harborowe where to meete yf you should be dispersed with storme or miste before you comme to your ordynary bayse which is about .30. or 40. leages to the Southward of the elevacion of the Canaries./

[3] Also Delyver to every Shippe A Token how to knowe each other when they meete after they be dispersed./

[4] Also yf any Shippe be in danger to be lost in the night thorowe leake or otherwise and cannot recover her consortes then lett her shewe foorthe 2 lightes to give the rest knowledge of her danger contynewing those lightes untill some of her consortes comme to her ayde./

Note

And lett him that shall first descrye those lightes answere them by like lightes to contynewe for a smale tyme only to signefye unto them that they have seene their signe./

[5] Also yf like perill happen by day then signefye the same either by showting a peese of ordynance or by hanging out a flagge in the shrowdes or by somme other token to be agreed on betwene you./

[6] Also yf theire happen any storme or contrary windes amongst you in tyme of your discovery then the shippes to repayre alweis to the last haven from whens you departed./

[7] Also lett the master never goe without a payer of writing tables and one always to attend him with penne ynck & paper./

[8] Also to observe any fishing banck with their depthes and elevations how farre they are from the Shoare./

[9] Discover only with your Pynneses and boates in dyvers bayes and havens & in doubtful weather alongest the Sea coaste./ Also lieving there your shippes in somme haven to fishe or traffique untill you have found with the Pynneses somme other good haven forwards in your viage and in that order procede to the ende of your discovery./

[10] Also dowble in effect every Rock and goe with your Pynneses harde aboorde the shore searching every place that openeth into the land thoughe yt seme never so litle,/ For otherwise you may over passe the best havens of strengthe./ For Dartmouth haven Corke haven Bere haven Baltmore haven and Castle haven with dyvers other seme nothing as you do saile by them./ And yet are most excellent bothe for strengthe and goodnes./

[11] Also in your discovery searche every Ryver that is navigable so farre as you may passe with your Pynneses & boates and learne of the Inhabitantes how muche farther every ryver shall extend yt self and do the like in every notable Baye and haven observing the daungers depthes of waters & soundinges togither with the hightes [and] Fawles of Flowdes, ebbes and also how farre yt shall flowe up into any ryver and in which of them you may ride, land lockett and which Shippes of what burthen and with what number of Sayles.

[12] And for the rest of the harbours to observe for what windes they may give you safe roades setting by the Compasse how they do open into the Sea and with what winde you may put into the sea out of them setting them all downe in your journall as they shalbe worthie of note./

[13] Also yf it be possible lett not your Shippes or Pynnesses ryde in ose or faste grounde for the wormes will soonest and most increase there./

[14] Also in your discovery lett alweis your great shippes in the morning yf yt be clere & fayer weather put of from the coast almost a Kenne for the better discryeing of Islandes and especially be carefull for Claudini and Saint Johns Isles when you shall comme nere those partes where they are thought to [be] bring alweis in the evening towardes the shoare to meet with the pynneses./

[15] Also yt is necessary that one of the Pyneses

---

1. This is followed by a series of "characteristic signs," marks to be used to indicate fixtures on a map such as are indicated in section [c], 17, p. 243 below.

do in the evening beare out into the Sea from the highe landes that the Shippe may knowe the better where to finde them for that they cannot be descryed under land aboarde the shore./

[16] Also when you have perfectly discovered all the coste then in your retorne as you put of from Cape Breton lett one of your shippes saile two leages in sorte as followeth to finde the Isle of Sablon which is very full of cattell and swyne which may supplye your wantes with greate gaine./

[17] And for the more certaine finding of the sayd Isle of Sablon direct your course from Cape Briton with one of your shippes south & by west./ And another Shippe to go Sowthe
And another shippe to go Sowthe and by East. And sett of from the foresayd cape a watche before day./

[18] And yf any of your shippes do discrye the sayd Island by day then lett him lay his shippe twice uppon the See to give his consortes knowledge therof./

[19] And yf you discover not the Island by day then att night to Sommon & speake with the admyrall uppon newe conference for farther search therof./

[20] The like order to be observed in searching for the Isles of Claudia and Saint John./

[c] Instructions to be observed by Thomas Bavin.

[1] Lett Bavin carry with him good store of parchments, Paper Ryall, Quills, and Inck, black powder to make yncke, and of all sortes of colours to drawe all thinges to life, gumme, pensyll, a stone to grinde Colours, mouth glue, black leade, 2 payres of brazen Compasses, And other Instrumentes to drawe cardes and plottes./

[2] Also lett him carry with him your Sea Instrumentes, a flate watch clock, which dothe shewe or devide the howers by the minutes, and such a one as will runne 24 howers or .40. howers without any winding up and lett the Wheles be glyded or silvered, for yt will preserve them from ruste./

[3] Also lett him carry with him .2. Instrumentes thone for the variacion of the Compasse, the other for declyning of the nedle, noting in every destinct place and elevacion, the declyning of the needle and the variacion of the Compasse./

[4] Also yf you have with you .3. good Clockes made, as is aforesayd with your uniuversall dyall you may with them precisely observe the longetude of every place bothe by Sea and land duly observing those instructions I gave you for the same./

[5] Also lett Bavin never go att any tyme without a payer of writing Tables.

[6] And one alweis to attend him with penne Inck and paper and somme others to attend him with an universall Dyall a Crosse staffe and Ephimerides or somme other Calculation Tables to observe the latitude. The instrument for variation of the Compasse the instrument for the Declynacion of the nedle and a sailling Compasse.

[7] Also lett him carry a universall Dyall And by that Dyall sett your Clock precisely from tyme to tyme by the Sonne and kepe your clock in suche precise sort going .3. or .4. days before the 19. day of June next to thend you may thereby observe the Juste mynute of the hower of the day when the eclipse of the Sonne shall then and there appear unto you.

[8] And note the same exactly the which eclipse will appeare to use att London att .4. of the clocke and .5. mynutes in the morning the same 19. day of June as the Almanack of this yeare .1582. will shewe./

[9] By which observacion you may certainly knowe the true longitude and the place where you shall make this observacion yf the same eclipse shall than and there appeare unto you./

[10] Also sett downe the sayd eclipse by paincture in the very place of your plott where you shall observe the same taking the elevacion of the pole att the same place noting the same downe in figures in the self same place and even there observe bothe the variacion of the Compasse and declyning of the nedle./

[11] And for the more certentie therof note all the observations of the same eclipse together with the latitude of the place in the captaines Jornall./

[12] Also by your universell dyall you may alweis finde the variacion of the Compasse att noonetyde by observing how fare your Compasse dothe differ from your Just meridian which difference sett downe in the same place of your Corde where you shall observe the same by drawing a double flye Noting also the juste observacion of the same pole in the same place./

[13] Also lett Bavin in the discovery drawe to lief one of each kinde of thing that is strange to us in England by the which he may alweis garnishe his plott as he shall so course upon his retourne. As by the portraiture of one Cedar Tree he may drawe all the woodes of that sorte and as in this so[rte] may he doe the like in all thinges ells./

[14] Also you shall not neede to sett downe any lyne for devision of degrees in any of your first draftes in paper before all your plottes be perfectlye fynished for losse of tyme./

[15] Also sett downe in your plottes the places where any oysters mustells with pearle or any other shell fishe shalbe founde./

[16] Also drawe and sett downe the distinct places and countries by drawen plott as also by writing and observe with their juste latitudes where you Shall fynde any thing worth the noting either like our thinges in Europe or differing from them in any manner of way. Noting alweis the differences in Colour or quantetie although they be of one sorte As the Newlandes herring ys farre bigger then ours being bothe of one kinde.

[17] And lett Bavin in his first plottes use severall marckes for severall thinges to be sett downe without alteration, As one for Woodes, another for hills, Another for Rockes, another for shelfes, another for the Channell of a Ryver not altering his marckes untill he shall perfectly fynishe his whole discovery Noting the depthe of the Shelfes by the foote and the depthe of the Channells with fathoms / As in figures the nomber of the foote or fathoms./

Here followe the particuler marckes of every thing to be sett downe in the first draughtes of this plottes. [See Plate 111a.].

Woodes   [oblique lines, 10, 3, 2, 1]

Hills [3 vertical interlinked curvedshapes—bare; two interlinked curved shapes with shading—hills with woods; two interlinked curved shapes with crosses—hills with rocks]

Rockes   [crosses, the horizontal longer than the vertical]

Ryvers   [no mark]

Shelfes in Ryvers   fo.3.fo.6. [references to folios in original not now extant]

Channells in Ryvers   fo.6.fo.8.fo.9. [references to folios in original not now extant]

Rockes in ryvers above water   [no sign]

Rockes lying under water   [no sign]

A Foote   fo.3.fo.5.fo.7 [references to folios in original not now extant]

A Faddamme   fo.4.fo.6.fo.8. [references to original not now extant]

The elevation of the pole   La. 24. La. 43. La. 65.

The marckes of the varyacion of the Compasse./ [arrow pointing upright, attached to sign, line with circle imposed on it, making an angle to right]

The flie of your Sea compasse   [arrow pointing almost upright]

The rectified flye by the instrument of variacion./ [circle with stroke across it, off vertical]

The declynacion   De

The Longitude./   Lon. 24. Lo. 240. Lo. 3. 40.

[18] Adding also to every marck the name of that kinde of thing that it betokineth as under his marck of woodes which serveth for all sortes of Trees without alteration write the name of that kinde of Tree as the same wood ys of A Cedar yf the wood be of Cedar Trees and Firre yf yt be of Firre trees and of all the rest./

[19] Also divide your plattes of the Countrye into sondrye particuler Cardes of .4. shetes of paper Royall alongest by the Sea coste according to the biggnes of the Table of your Instrument or as you shall see cawse for your best devision of the bondes either by ryvers headlandes etc.

[20] In making of your boundes make princypall choise of your marckes uppon the Cost for your better devision by Sea./

[21] Also becawse you may the better knowe how theise cardes should be rightly Joyned togither you may note them uppon the Sea costes begynning the first towardes Cape Florida with a great .A. and the next Carde with .B. and so to the end of the Crosse river./ And then begynne againe in the same order with the rest of your Cardes with a dowble .A. and a dowble .B. Multeplying your letters as occasyon shall requier Till your whole discovery be perfectly fynished & sitt downe in platt which I wold not have sett down with figures least yt might prove mistaking of the latitude formalye appointed to be noted in them./

[22] Also in the making of this particuler Cardes specially sett down in figures the just latitude of every Notations place to be there. Noted as you shall observe the same and especially note yt on the particuler Carde Aswell within land as uppon the Sea Cost. And also in any case Omitt not to

sett downe the same many places where you shall finde any difference of latitude Be yt never so litle./

[23] Also observe alweis one proportion in your skele without alteration by yt of never so smale an Island or thing worthye the mesuring. For yf you alter your skele you shall never make your plottes.

[24] Also by your Instrumentes justly mesure and sett downe the distances of Capes hedlandes and hilles the depth & bredthe of havens & bayes & ryvers placing uppon eache of them in figures their severall elevacions and to use the like order within lande for Champions woodes hills dales Lakes pooles & ryvers. Noting distinctly the diversitye of the nature of every kinde of grownde by yt self./

[25] Also note how the Soyle ys compassed or furnished with hills medowes woodes or Champions or whether they be garnished with ryvers freshe water springes or bogges Setting down their height bredthe or distances./

[26] Also sett downe in your plottes the dyvers sortes of Trees in eache of their particuler places be yt in woodes or otherwise dispersed naming the woodes by those kinde of Trees that shall most growe there./

[27] Also drawe to life all strange birdes beastes fishes plantes hearbes Trees and fruictes and bring home of eache sorte as nere as you may./

[28] Also drawe the figures and shapes of men and women in their apparell as also of their manner of wepons in every place as you shall finde them differing.

[d]   Thinges knowen by experyence to be in the countryes about the Ryver of Norrinberge which is one of the greatest ryveres in the world The cosmographie .fo.1008 [André Thevet, *La cosmographie universelle* (1575)]. As also by Verarzanus the discouverer of those coastes and certaine other mens opiniones of the saved partes of the world By inhabiting of which ryver and fortefyeng the mouthe therof only you may Injoye a soyle to yelde you by nature culture and Industrye all the commodyties that do or may growe betwene 00 and 23 degrees of latitude besides yt offereth assurances to keepe shipping in the gulfe of Mexico and to hopes of traffique by Marii de Sur And thoroughe which ryver and the branches therof you [may go] by bate [= boat] about 2000 leagues And all this by fresh ryvers and lakes

wherby no prince can possibly impeache your traffique./

The soyle ys most excellent plesaunt fertill and of champyon replenished with pastures and meadowes interlarded with woodes most plesaunt to behould as may be imagined of Cedars Cidorus Pynes Firre and Spruce trees Gwacon Figge Almond Orrenge Damysson Apple Baytrees and Goosbery trees white and red with nutt trees of all sortes also Oke Ashe Elme Walnutt Maple Beche Willowe Ewe Boxe and White Thorne that carryes berryes as bigge as damsons with many other sortes of trees unknowen to us of Europe which yelde most sweet savores the most of them all growing in rowes as yf they had bynne sett arteficially by hand, making therby most delicate walkes, there are also grapes of sondrye sortes there is also graynes of the kind of the guine pepper. You may make and prepare there plenty of Oyle pytche Tarre and rozen Francensence Turpentine and sondry other gummes and Appotycary Drugues Also ther is great plenty of Scruchinella waxe and hony and also spices as Verarsanus thought / There are also pease hempe strawberyes blackberyes red and white roses damaske roses parsley rosemary with sondry other good hearbes & flowers Also muske myllion Pompines gourdes Cocombers Violettes Lyllies and sondrye sortes of oderyferous flowers differing from ours. There is also a wilde Corne like our rye also oates There ys also Thrushes Stork doves pigeons turtles Cranes Swannes Ducks Geese Fesauntes partheriges black birdes goldfynches robynreadbrestes Nitingalles sparrowes Lynnettes Cranes margulls which ys a fowle as bigge as geese Aponates Goddettes and sondry kinde of hawkes. There are also beares Libbardes Bevars Wolfes Foxes red dere Fallowe Deere Martens and a beast that hathe a skynne like a martene Hares Conyes Otters Weasells Badgers Also a great beast like a bull with a long shagge heares called a Buffall. Also another beast as bigge as he, which hath 2 teethe like an elyfante and liveth most in the Sea Also water mise as bigge as conyes which are very good meate. Besides sondry sortes of riche Furres & other beastes which I cannot name. There are also good havens and sondry navigable ryvers The coste shore deepe with great plenty of freshe water fishe As Eles Sammons Cod Hake Maquerells Soles Porposes Whales Seahorses which are headed like greyhoundes and as white as snowe and 100 of that Corfishe or Drye fishe of that countrye are more worth the 1000 of the best Newland fishe of those sorte. There ys also a Banck alongest the coste where you may fishe all the yeare./ There is also plenty of Salt to be made./

There is also plenty of copper Sylver and somme gold which they accompt the besest metall. They have also rubies, jaspers, marble, allablaster Freestone and other sondry sortes of Stones of dyvers colours that the place ys like to be most riche and plesaunt./

Yt was told Sir Humfrye Gylbart by 2 or 3 of the best sort bothe by office skill and judgment that accompanied Sir Francis Drake in his viage about the world that the most excellentest place that they sawe in all their Vyage bothe for fertilitie pleasure and profytt every kinde of way as well mynnerall as otherwayes was about 45 Degrees of Latitude./ And as one of his Quarter masters told him they sawe an Island in Marii de Sur called de Malco which lay in 46 degrees of Latitude which excelled every kinde of waye all the rest or att the least was Second to no other place that ever they sawe in that their Travaill and Navigation./

402. April 26, 1582 to March 17, 1583. The Spanish ambassador reports on Gilbert's preparations.

Don Bernardino de Mendoza, the Spanish ambassador in London, kept careful watch over Gilbert's preparations, although his information was not always accurate. His most important action was to threaten the Catholics who were involved with Gilbert that they were betraying their church and would be attacked by Spaniards if they settled in North America. He also promised to get Father William Allen, the leading English Catholic on the Continent, to send warnings (see D. B. Quinn, England and the Discovery of America *(1974), pp. 376–377), which were apparently sent, discouraging the Catholic gentry from the American enterprise. The following extracts from letters between the ambassador and Philip II provide illustrations of what went on:*

(a) April 26, 1582. Documentos inéditos para la historia de España, *XCII (1888), 358, extract, translated.*

(b) July 11, 1582. Ibid., pp. 396–397.

(c) July 25, 1582. Ibid., p. 280.

(d) March 17, 1583. Ibid., p. 476.

They are printed in D. B. Quinn, Gilbert, *II, 278–279, 280, 349.*

[a] April 26, 1582.

I have had news today that the ships [under Edward Fenton], which I wrote to your Majesty were ready to sail for the Malucos, have now left, and also that Onxiginberto [Humphrey Gilbert] is fitting out three more with which to go to Florida and settle there in the place where Estucle [Stukeley] was and Juan Robero [Jean Ribault], (the man whom Pero Melendez beheaded), with the French. When he asked for the Queen's assistance he was answered in council that he might go, and, that when he had landed and fortified, the Queen would send 10,000 men to conquer the territory and safeguard the port.

[b] July 11, 1582.

As I wrote to your Majesty some days since, Ongi Gilberto [Humphrey Gilbert] was fitting out several ships for a settlement in Florida and as this was not only prejudicial to your Majesty but also to the English Catholics as giving advantage to heretics, Walsingham put it secretly to two spendthrift Catholic gentlemen who have some land that if they helped Ongi Gilberto in his expedition, they would escape losing life and property, by asking the Queen to allow them, in consideration for this service, to live in those parts with freedom of conscience and enjoy the use of their property in England—for which purpose they might rely on Phelippe Sideney. As these men were anxious to live as Catholics without risking their lives, they thought it a good plan, and informed other Catholics of it. These also have approved and offered to help with money, petitioning the Queen on the subject. She has given them a patent under the Great Seal of England to settle in Florida on the coast of Noromberga and live there with freedom of conscience, enjoying the use of their English properties—this not only for those who leave the realm for the purpose but other English abroad, although declared rebels. The Queen restores them to her favour and accepts them as loyal subjects and vassals—this for no other motive that, in spite of persecution, imprisonment and the bloodshed of martyrs,

Catholics were increasing. These it was expedient to weaken and destroy in some way. When this was done, there would be no maintaining of seminaries abroad nor would priests living here be able to continue their preaching if there were no one to receive and shelter them. In this way once and for all the small remnant of good blood in this sick body would be drained away. Through the clergy here I made known to the Catholics the purpose of the Queen and Council in admitting them to favour—and that these lands belonged to your Majesty, that you had garrisons and fortresses there, and that they would immediately have their throats cut as happened to the French who went with Juan Ribao [Jean Ribault], that further they were imperilling their consciences by engaging in an enterprise prejudicial to His Holiness and that it would be well for them to report the matter to him through Dr. Alano [Allen] and learn if they could justifiable make the voyage.

Some have withdrawn on this, but others who are spendthrifts persist in wishing to make the voyage, convincing themselves that there is nothing in it against your Majesty because in the map it is marked as Nueva Francia, which proves it was discovered by the French, and that since

Cartier fitted out ships at his own expense to make conquests—and he was a Catholic—they could do the same. At the same time I have notified the Abbot Briceño in Rome and have written to Alano how necessary it is for the reduction of this kingdom that he make every effort to prevent the expedition.

[c]   July 25, 1582.

As to the ships which as I previously wrote to your majesty the Catholics were getting ready here, it turns out that not more than two are going this year with Hongigilberto [Humphrey Gilbert] to reconnoitre the place where they can land next year. These ships are already riding in Sotamton [Southampton] harbour, only waiting for the weather to set sail, and with them a pinnace.

[d]   March 17, 1583.

The ships, which I wrote to your majesty that Hongi Gilberto [Humphrey Gilbert] was fitting out on behalf of the Catholics to go to the Florida coast, are now getting ready to start, as they think that the two which they sent to reconnoitre last summer are delaying too long.

LETTERS FROM MAURICE BROWNE TO
JOHN THYNNE ON GILBERT'S PREPARATIONS

The personal letters of Maurice Browne, son of a London merchant, to John Thynne the younger of Longleat, throw considerable light on Sir Humphrey Gilbert's preparations, and, particularly, on the reasons for his delays in 1582 and the revival of his plans in 1583. They enable us to see something of what was going on from the point of view of one of the men who was drawn by his geographical interests into the venture. Browne commanded the *Swallow* on the outward voyage to Newfoundland and was captain of the *Delight* when she and he were lost off Sable Island.

The letters are in the collection of the Marquess of Bath, Longleat, Thynne Papers, V, fols. 204–205, 212–213, 231–239, 252–253. These and other extracts were first published in D. B. Quinn and N. M. Cheshire, *The New Found Land of Stephen Parmenius* (1972), pp. 189–208.

403. August 20, 1582. Maurice Browne to John Thynne.

Good master Thynne:

I receyved your frindly letter sent by your boye also my geldinge and old broke your nagge for that I am uncerteyne of my cominge doune to yow which wilbe I trust now within this fower dayes. I have bin stayed here sence sir Rowlandes [Sir Rowland Heyward's] departure from london, by A matter that happyned within three dayes after which I thought of as much as of the Pope of Rome, as the proverbe. I had thought veryly the next day after Sir Rowlandes departure from London to have Ryden into Essex and within two dayes after to have begonne my jorny towardes yow. But what man determyneth god disposeth at his goodwill and pleasure and I trust all for the beast. But godes will be donne. Master Smith and I beinge together it was told us that Sir Humfry Gylbert was at his house in London, who I assure yow I had thought had bin at sea towardes his voyage of A newe discovery a moneth before as it was certeynly told me his was. And I thought veryly he was not in London, bu[t] beinge cer-tyfed of the certeyntie thereof by one who desco[vered?] Master Smythes and my good worde unto Sir Humfry in his behalf, where upon Master Smithe and I went to Sir H. Gylbertes howse where we found hym. And after we had dis-spached with him for that we came. We fell to discoursinge with Sir H. of his voyage. and in that discourse kept o[n] so longe, that he wolde neades have us staye to supper, a[t] which tyme we were with hym we had noe other talke, but of the frutfullnes and great riches that was in that coun-try where he intendeth by godes assistance to goe unto. We both lykede so well of his discourses, and of the large Awthoritie that the Queene hath graunted hym for the furtheraunce of his voyage that our awnswere was we were sory that we had not knowledge of those matters in tyme for if we had we wold have made provysion to have accom-panyed hym, and so we departed from hym, not thinckinge to have senne hym any more before his departure. The next morninge Sir Humfry sent his man very early unto our lodginge, very ear-nestly desiring us to suppe with hym that nyght. Within A whyle after our cominge to hym we fell

into oure former discour[s]es, where upon he shewed us his graunt from her majestie under the great seale of England, further he shewed us the card of the whole cuntry where he ment to settill hym self, which country was the last yeere with great commodities there in discovered by A cun-ning Navigator which Sir Humfry sent thether, which man goeth as chefe pylat for his voyage, and offereth to bringe Sir Humfry and his com-pany (by godes good assistaunce) into that parte of the country, (which lyeth in the North west of America) which is the most richest place for gold, silver, and pearle, as also for all frutefulnes of the soyle, and a boundannce of all kind of wylde cattell and beastes necessary for meannes use for victuall as also for great profitt and in lyke sort for other frutes trees, and woodes, in which countrye are aboundannce of goodly freshe ryvers re-plenyshed aboundantly with all kinde of freshe fyshe. But which is the greatest he is veryly of opynion, that there is A passage that way by the west in to the sowth sea, which will prove the greatest matter of importaunce for the wealth of the state of England that can be in the world. For the wealth, and fructfulnes of the country aforesayd he offereth to aprove true upon the losse of his lyfe, and for the passage there is as great lyklyhode as can be. All which is confirmed by one Davy Ingram, who was left seven yere sence, by master Hawkinges with above three score more in the gowlfe of Mexico & there set a land in the sowth part of America. This Davy Ingram with two more in his company only de-termyned to travell towardes the North of America, hopinge that way to have come to newe found land, where in the tyme of the yere he hopped to have found englyshe shipes there, and so to have come into England, they traveled throwght all the West of America, and travel-lynge toward the north, he had passage over A great ryver above twentie leages over, in A kind of bote of that country called a *Canoas*. It is thought this is the Ryver of May one the North side whereof he travelled in that country above Three monethes, in which country he found most Aboundannce of all the wealth frutes beastes and commodities aforesayed, in more aboundannce then in all the travell he passed throught the country which laye one the west side of that Ryver of May, where he travelled eyght monethes. In the hole his travell one foote was eleven monethes. This man hath lykwyse confessed as aforesayed first to Sir Humfry and next unto my Master who hath his confessione in writinge, And offereth, with godes assistaunce sending hym lyfve to bringe Sir Humfry to these places of wealth and all other commodities upon ye losse of his lyfve, if they prove not true when [he] comes to lande.

The particularyes of all theise matters I am throwghly instructed. Sir Humfry performes this voyage at his owen charge saving three or fower of his frindes which in all, beinge but certeyne comodities of smale price, in all their venture is not A Hundreth pound. Sir Humfry hath two shippes & three pynesses; he caryeth About A eleven score men with him, and meaneth to plant hym self there, and to contynewe there this yeere. But After he hath bin there a whyle and had understandinge of the wealth and state thereof: He intendeth to send backe one pynyse (by godes grace) into England frayt with the comodities of the country, as also one to declare the state of the country unto the Qweenes Maiestie, and her Pryvy counsell. My Master is the only counsellour in England that Sir Humfery hath made acquanted with his voyage, and he is the only man Sir Humfry doth relye hym self one. The Qweene hath promysed Sir Humfry At what tyme he doth retourne newes of his landinge and of the commoditie of the country her Maiestie will send hym as much shippinge and men, and other necessary thinges for his strenngh and furtheraunce of his intentes as he will write unto her Maiestie for to send hym. My Master hath protested by his honor to further the same and to se it performed. Here upon Sir Humfry told my master that he wanted, A sufficient man to be the messenger (as he trusted in god) of the good newes that should send to her Majestie, and his honour. And desired my master to healp hym with A man for that purpose. In this meanne tyme not knowinge of this matte[r] Sir Humfry very earnestly moti[o]ned me of this voyage and to undertake this matter. I lyked very well of the voyage, as also of his most frindly offer, only relyuing my self upon the good liking and perswatione of my Master thereunto. Where upon Sir Humfry presently wrote unto my master requestinge my masters lawfull favore if he thought me sufficien[t] to discharge such A matter to goe with hym to be the man to retorne (as he trusted in god) with happye newes. My master presently talked with me and showed me of his lykinge of this voyage and of his likinge for me to goe this voyage and of the profitte in divers respectes that might there[by] redound unto me. I told my master that I holy relyed my self upon the lyki[ng] of his honor, and that I was very glad to undertake the voyage in r[es]pect his honor did favore the same. Here upon my master used me with very honorable wordes and countinaunce and presently my master wrote A letter to Sir Humfry in my behalf. I wold I were such A one as he commended me unto Sir Humfry for and howe well he liked of and therewithall desired hym to have an especiall care of me—so yow se how I am disposed of. We are ready and shall take shippinge at Sowthamton or else I thincke rather at Plymoughe in Devonshire. So that within this fower dayes (god will[inge]) I will beginnge my jorny towardes Longleat to se yow before my departure. And if [you wi]ll be A venturer, ether in mony or corne, as wheat especially or whyt pease, I will be your factor for them to your commoditie I trust in god. I pray yow let me request of yow A crasbowe and arrowes. Thus Have I declared unto yow how unlooked for, god I trust to somme good ende hath stayed me from yow all that while. Wherein the old proverbe is verified that many thinges chaunce betwene the cuppe and the lyppe, but godes will be donne, and I trust in god that he hath appointed this for the best, A meanne for me After ward to lyve with yow quietly, to enjoye your frindship and company which I protest before god I wyshe only. . . .

And so hartely I committ yow to god. Tower streat this xxth of August

Your faithfull lovinge frinde

[signed:] M. Browne

404. [September] 21, 1582. Maurice Browne to John Thynne.

Good master Thynne:

I am Apon further occation offered me to use your friendship and credit, at this present, which at my last departure from yow upon your most frindly offere, I told yow that if occation where that myght be for my profitt I wold carve your frindship, of which I never dowbted. So it is that for my better adventure and credit, I wold request your letter of credit unto William Staveley to whom I did your commendations, And told him yow thought your self much beholdinge unto hym for the wynne he sent yow of credit, and that A bout Mychelmas yow wold se hym satisfied. The man is an Alderman of Sowthampton of great wealth And A very honest man And the best howse keeper in the citie of A comminer. He told me he alwayes was much beholdinge to Sir John Thynne, And did alwayes serve hym of wynne. He told me that my Lady Thynne and master Rawley deales hardly hym about wynne they had longe sence. Thus having speach with hym I told hym I was to use your frindship and credit, About Sowthampton to the Valewe of twentye poundes, for provysion of corne about Sowthamton for this my Voyage. And I told hym he myght shewe me great pleasure if he wold shewe me so much favore as to take your bill for twentie poundes for half A yeere, to the which he awnswered me very frindly that he wold accept of your bill or letter for as much as he was worth very honestly. Wherefore in respect aforesayde I desire your bill or letter creditt for twentie poundes, for half a yere or till oure lady day. And god willinge accordingly I will take order for the savinge of yow harmeles. And as yow shall here by greatly benefitte me so will I if, god make me able, as I trust in god he will requit it assuredly, in the meanne tyme contynewe as thanckfull and lovinge A mynde towardes yow as yow can wyshe A frind to bearere yow. And Thus desiring god to prosper your procedinges and myne to his honor, with my hartye commendations to my good Governes litill Tom & lastly your self I committ yow all to god. This xxj^th day At nyght 1582

Your faythfull lovinge frind ever

[signed:] M. Browne

Postscript. The shipp which Sir Humfry Gylbert loked for to come from the Dounes hath bin by most contrary wyndes kept backe, but At this present the wynd serves very well beinge all this day easterly but nowe flatt east so that if god contynewe this wynd but two dayes the ship will Aryve in Hampton roode, by the grace of god.

405. [September], 1582. Maurice Browne to John Thynne.

I doe not here but that master Norrice most wonderfully scaped withowt any great hurt his soldyers had A very great spoyle of the eneymy, And Master Norrice so gallan[t]ly did gather his men together and did behave hymself in so good order, that after the conflict and all ended, Monshire and the Prince of Orrannge and the chefe of the citie did receyve hym with all the honor that might be, Monshire gave hym for rewarde A Thowsand poundes, which presently Master Norrice gave his gentilmen a soldyers. All theise ill successes that happens towardes the Kinge of Spayne, makes the most for oure voyage & for oure quietnes that may be which make Sir H. Gylbert glad and all his company, godes will be donne.

The plage increseth in London there died the last weake 160 of the plage god of his mercye seace it, The terme is adjorned. I have letters from London since my cominge from yow that the plage is very hott in fraunce, and that they make tentes in the feyldes for the sicke. god be mercifull unto us & them to. Thus have yow all the newes I here And my self yow shall have ever your fayfull and lovinge freind

[signed:] M. Browne

I send my man to Bristowe to cause all my thinges I have there to be brought to Sowthamton.

[Addressed:] To the worshipfull assured good freind Master John Thynnes Esquier

[Endorsed:] M. Browne to M^r. 1582.

406. November 1, 1582. Maurice Browne to John Thynne.

Good Master Thynne,

I had thought longe sence to have written unto yow could I had A messenger to my mynde, to have signified unto yow of the recept of your letter to Master Staveley in my behalf. The same nyght I receyved your letter Master Staveley fell sicke sodenly being by the water side of A deade palsey, and within fower dayes after died, so that I never delyvered your letter and I made fension of my desire. Yow have lost the best frind of A townnesman in Southampton, where he lyved with the love and likinge of all that knewe hym and his death greatly lamented. Sence the death of this man I have dealt with one master Richard Godarde one of the substantialest marchauntes in Southamton, who maryed one master Heyers dawghter of Wilshire. And she doth knowe yow. Master Godard is willinge to pleasure me in supplyinge my wannt if yow will write your letter or credit unto hym wherfore I pray yow in such sort as yow wrote your letter unto master Staveley (which by this bearer I send yow). Write the like to master Godard in my behalf addinge not only corne but also any other necessarye thinge which I shall wannt to that somme which yow please to set doune for the which god willinge I will take order yow shall be noe loser if yow can increase the somme to twentie poundes. Sence the cominge of Sir Humfry Gylbertes ship to Sowthampton, which was fortnyght sence there hath bin such foule weather till this fyve dayes past that men could not worke on her nether could she take any of her ladinge. The maior of Sowthampton and the Burgesses doe venture with Sir Humfry about 300^{li} such good likinge have they of his proceidinges And he doth incorporate the company of adventurers with hym the staple for ever to be kept at Sowthampton. I trust in god we shalbe redye to depart within this 8. or 9. dayes. I wold have bin with yow or this but oure departure hath bin so often tymes deferred and all for the betteringe of oure voyage. And I trust in god yeat will have good successe to the benifitt of all Englande.

Yow shall understand of oure procedinge as often as I can fynd A messenger to send to yow. After our departure from Sowthampton we shall touche at Dartmouth and I thincke we shall stay senyght there so that I judge it will be 3 weakes before we shall depart from England. We are almost pursse penilesse, but I dowte not the lowe ebbe will have as hye a flowde, which god graunt if it be his will. I pray yow let me intreat yow to perswade your mane Lowe to goe with me in the company of Sir Humfry, And shall retornne with me, I dowt not by godes grace, to his very great profit and he shall after be more able to lyve in your service with conntynaunce. Yf yow speake but A worde to hym I knowe he will goe, and for

such matters as he hath in lawe or in controversy by your good meannes there may be good order taken notwithstandinge Lowes absence, and also his wyfe may be by your frindship provyded for in his absence. In sendinge hym with me I veryly thincke that yow cannot doe A thinge more for his benifit, and here after more inablyed every way to do you service. If he come to Dartmouth to Sir John Gylbertes in Devonshire, he shall there have Sir Humfry Gylbert, which is the best place for hym to come to, and whether he shalbe very welcome. I have written to Lowe to perswade hym (with your good likinge) to goe this voyage. If he be here within this 7 or 8 dayes he shall have Sir H. here at Sowthampton. If you can healp Sir H. with A good fremason he will gyve hym interteynment to his contentment. . . .

Thus desiringe yow ever to account me most myndfull of all your frindship with my most harty commendations to your self and good mistris Thynne my only good Governes and litell Tom. I comite yow to god. Sowthampton this first of November 1582

Your assured faithfull frind

[signed:] M. Browne

[Addressed:] To the worshipfull his very good frind Master John Thynne esquier at Longleat in Wilshire dd/this

[Endorsed:] Mr. Brownes lettre 1⁰ Novembris 1582

407. December 17, 1582. Maurice Browne to John Thynne.

Good Master Thynne

I receyved your most freindly letter wherby I understand how greatly yow have bin mysinformed of the proceydinges intent & dealinges of Sir Humfrey Gylbert & his company. The Lyngeringe here yow write of, god hath bin the only cause of, as All those which hath had occation to marke the wyndes can to their great charge to well testify the same, the lyke tempestious and stormy weather contynewinge this fower monethes Sowthwest hath not by the moste Auntiauntes men of this Towne heretofore bin seen.

But at this present Sir H. is ready to set sayle, & I trust god hathe cleared the heavens of All stormes and now will send us large wyndes in the North, & east to bringe us to the place we desire to Aryve at wherein godes will be donne to his honour & glory. There was never greater expectations and good hope conceyved of this voyage by her Majestie and those of her counsell which deale therein then At this present. There is great preparation of A present supply to be sent After Sir H. by certen consortes gentilmen of great account. Of all matters here, And of all the proceydinges of this voyage, this gentilman Master Stowghton A master of Art and A very learned preacher who doth gooe with Sir H. can at a large asserteyne yow. he is my very frend of whose company I take great comfort. I pray yow let hym be very welcome to yow. Thus beinge redy to goe A ship borde, and to hawsth sayle towardes Dartmought. I ever pray to god for your prosperous eastate. I wold longe sence have certyfyed yow how master Richard Godard hath accepted of your letter very freindly and I have as it doth apeare, under my hand tha[t] I have receyved Tenne poundes in lynine cloth of his credit. If yow have occation to deale with any marchaunt of Sowthampto[n] yow cannot deale with a more honester & A substantiall marchaunt. Thus commendinge my self holye to your frendship and to my good governes, And Tom. I committ yow to god, desiringe all to pray to god to blesse us And send us mery meetinge. Sowtha[m]ton this 17th of December. 1582.

Your assured faythfull freind, noe man more
  [signed:] M. Browne

I pray yow send Lowe your Trumpyter to Sir John Gylberte by Dartmought.

[Addressed:] To the worshipfull my estemed good freind Master John Thynne esquier at Longleat, Wilshire.
[Endorsed:] Mr Browne. 17º Dec' 1582

408. December 19, 1582. Maurice Browne to John Thynne.

Good Master Thynne I pray yow pardon me for the stay of your boy Edward, for this two dayes

hath him so extreme fowle weather, as Sir Humfrey Gylbert hath not bin able to goe aborde his ship till this day, and of purposse I stayed hym to bringe the certeynty, of Sir H. intent to depart from hence (god willinge) with the wynd to carry his shipes to Dartmought. Untill which tyme Sir H. is determyned not to come, or at the lest lye owt of his ship a shore, so that we only depart when it shall please god with a good wynd to carry us from hence. This last nyght Sir H had a messenger from Sir George Peckham and others of his good freindes that there is dyvers good shipes preparinge to follow Sir H, As A newe supply to assist hym in this Action. My master with all the meannes possible doth advaunce the same, Sir H. will not stay for any, but I doubt not but within one moneth after our arryvall on that cost where we (god willinge) determyne to land to have A eyght or nyne sayle of very good ship[s] well appoynted for defence. In the meanne tyme we will commit oure selves to god, and ever after . . .

Further the cause of stay of your footeman was to conduct master Stowghton to your howse, who told me at his departure he wold ryde to or three myles owt of the way From this town is cominge to your howse. The boy was here on sonnday at dynner. Thus desiringe yow contynually and in lyke manner my good Governes to pray for my good successe as for hym who doth wyshe yow both all happynes & felycitie. And so I commend my self howly to yow both and us all to god. desiringe hym to send us a joyfull meetinge to our comfortes, makinge me able (if it be his will) accordinge to my mynd to requite all frendshipes receyved of yow in the meane tyme except as thanckful A mynd as may be. From Sowthampton this 19th of December 1582.

Your Assured faithfull freind
  [signed:] M. Browne

[Addressed:] To the worshipfull my very good freind master John Thynne esquier
[Endorsed:] Mr Browne. 19º Decembris 1582.

409. [April–May, 1583]. Maurice Browne to John Thynne.

Good Master Thynne one day this weake I ryde

to Sowth[amp]ton where Sir Humfry Gylbert is redy with all his shipes very excellently appointed to depart on his voyage. I trust god hath appointed this his stay for Sir Humfreys most good, for he was never half so well appointed for excellent shipes of streanthe & conntinaunce as nowe he is. Sir Humfreys brother Water Rawley (who at this present hath her majestes favore above all men in the court) hath at his owne cost and charges bought a newe ship of Master Owttred at Hampton: she is of bourden twelfe score tonnes, redy furnyshed of all thinges belonginge to her & victuled for .60. men. The settinge owt of this ship will cost Master Rawley two thowsande marckes. Sir Humfrey doth goe in her and is the Admyrall. Also Sir Humfrey hath another ship of seven score tonnes as good A ship as any is in England of that bourden which Master William Wintter goeth in for that he is at half the charge in settinge owt that ship. [*crossed out:* Further my Lord Vycount Byndon doth send A ship with Sir Humfry of six score tonnes. A very excellent ship as any is of that bourden and A newe ship, throughly appoynted, wherein my selfe doth goe and have charge of her. I wo[ld not] wyshe I assure yow to goe in a better ship.] Sence the writing of this letter I have receyved intelligence that my Lord Vicount according to his old humor of fantasticalines hath disappointed Sir Humfrey and my self of his ship. But I hope to be shipped to my contentment.

Besides theise [Sir] Humfrey hath three pynasses, of good bourden, In A present supply divers of the cheife marchauntes of London, and the marchauntes of Bristowe dooe joyne in consort, and doth send fyve sayle more of good shipes with provision and men to Sir Humfrey my Master, and Master Rawley doth joyne together to further this Actione by all the meannes they can, so that Sir Humfrey havinge two good supporters (at this time provided of god) I hope it will have great good successe. The Qweenes majestie hath used Sir Humfrey with very great favore, with promyse unto hym that upon awnswere from hym, he shall not want any thinge that may be for his assistaunce in this action, After Sir Humfrey had taken his leave of her majestie and gon doune to Hampton, the Qweene sent Sir Humfrey as A token of her especiall good favore A very excellent Jewell. The device was An Anckor of gold set with .29. diamondes with the Portracture of A

Qweene holdinge the ringe of the Ancor in one hand the flux of the Ancor in The other hand. In the breast of which picture there is set A very greate poynted Diamonde, and in the Crowne that standes on the head is set A very greate ruby and at eache end of the ankor A great peare. On the back side of the ankor is written as followeth, *Tuemur sub sacra ancora.* Which Jewell doth hange at two smale cheynes devised with roses set with rubyes and diamondes which was tyed with two pointes of heare couler tagged with gold and inamile and A scarffe of white silke Ciperous egged with A fayer lace of Gold and silver. And here with receyved A letter of very great favore, so that I Assure yow I hope god hath sent all theise former delayes as a meannes for the better performaunce of this Actione for Sir Humfrey never had her majesties favore more hyghly nor ever had so great meannes to contynewe the same, for the bringinge of his Actione to good effect, which god graunt if it be his will. . . .

410. May, 1583. Maurice Browne to John Thynne.

Sir as I was writing hereof I receyved A letter from yow which yow sent to Hampton dated the xiij[th] of Aprill, and receyved it the 25[th] of the same, wherefore I though[t]e good to deferre the sending of this letter unto you [un]till my cominge to Sowthampton which was one Maye Day last. I underst[and] by Sir Humfrey Gylbert that yow are well contented [that] your man Syssell should goe one this voyage with hym. I wold your busines wold by any meannes suffer yow to come to Sowthampton. . . .

I pray do my most harty commendations to my good Governes with thanckes A Thowsand fold for my butter and marmylade and to my litell [master] great suertye, wishinge to you all three as to my owne soule. With my commendations I committ yow to God who send us all good successe and joyful meeting. this [ ] of May 1583.

Your assured fayfull friend

[signed:] M. Browne

411. December 17, 1582. Sir Humphrey
Gilbert to John Thynne.

*A hasty note, printed as it is written, shows how
touchy Gilbert was about the delays to his expedition. MSS of the Marquess of Bath, Longleat,
Thynne Papers, V, fol. 231v.; printed in D. B.
Quinn and N. M. Cheshire,* The New Found
Land of Stephen Parmenius *(1972), p. 202. (Enclosed in document 407.)*

good master thyn I commend me moste hartely
unto yow and to your wyeffe as to the daster of a
deyd mother that I lovyed and honerid mytche,
for your soundery commendations I dow moste
hartely thancke yow. for soundery mens folishe
opineons either of my Jorne, or of my longe abode
in Hampton, or of my gevynge over of the Jorne,
or of any dyshonest course that I shoulde mean to
rune. I answer yow as my freynde, to tell them
from me, that I nether caer for ther lykynges nor
myslykynge but if any of them shall daer to Injure
me at my retorne, I will answer them or sonner if
that they will saye it to my faese whom am boeth
as honest and as worshipfull as the beste in this
land of my callynge and lesse I esteym not of my
selffe.

and so faer yow well as my good Frend. Hampton
the 17 of desember 1582.

Yours hoelly

[signed:] H. Gylberte

Chapter Fifty-three
Last Preparations

412. February 7, 1583. Sir Humphrey
Gilbert to Sir Francis Walsingham.

*Queen Elizabeth has had doubts whether Gilbert's
delays meant he was too unlucky to be allowed to
revive his project. Here he pleads (successfully as
it proved) to be allowed to do so. P.R.O., State
Papers, Domestic, Elizabeth I, SP 12/158, 59;
printed in D. B. Quinn, Gilbert, II, 339-340.*

Right honorable, wheras it hath pleased your
honour to let mee understande that her majestie
of her especiall care had of my well doinge, &
prosperous success, hath wished my stay att
home from the personall execution of my intended
discovery as a man noted of not good happ by sea:
for the which I acknowledge my selfe so much
bounde unto her majestie, as I know not how to
deserve the leaste parte therof, otherwise then
with my continuall prayer, and most faythfull and
forwarde service during lyfe: And now to excuse
my selfe, and satisfye your honor touching the
objections made of my staye, it may please yow to
be advertised that in my first enterprise I retorned with great losse, because I would not my
selfe, nor suffer any of my companye to doe any
thinge contrarye to my worde given to her majestie and your selfe: for yf I had not farr preferred
my credit before my gayne, I needed not to have
retorned so poore as then I did. / And touching
this my last stay at Hampton, it hath proceeded
by Southwest wyndes of godes making and sending: and therefore not my faulte or negligence.
But yf I wear giltye of delaye, the principall
charge is my owne, and noe losse to any other, for
my adventures as I had them for the most parte in
wares, so I have them still without any losse to
anye of them. And in truthe the outerage of this
winter hath ben a common hyndrance to all men of
this realme southwarde bounde. Yea and the
wyndes so contrarye as that it hath droven shippes from the yles of the Asores uppon this coste
without spreading any sayle at all. A thinge I
thinke never harde of before. And the king of
Portingale beeing at the Tercera coulde not in all
this tyme recover the Maderaes, How farr impossible then hadd it ben for mee to have performed
my jorney this winter? Your honour can judge
dwelling soe farr to the northewardes of the place
intended to bee discovered. And seeing the
Queenes majestie so to have a fyfthe of all the
golde & sylver there to bee gotten without any
charge to her majestie, I truste her hyghnes of
her accustomed favour will not denye mee libertye to execute that which resteth in hope so
profitable to her majestie & crowne. The great
desyre I have to performe the same hath coste
mee first & last the selling and spending of a
thowsand marke land a yeere of my owne getting
besydes the scorne of the worlde, for conceaving
so well of a matter that others held so ridiculous,
although now by my meanes better thought of.
Yff the dowbte bee my wante of skill to execute
the same I will offer my selfe to bee opposed, by
all the best navigatoures, and Cosmographeres
within this realme. Yff it bee cowardlines, I seeke
noe other purgation therof then my former service don to her majestie. Yf it bee the suspition of
daynitines of dyett or sea sicknes in those both I
will yeeld my selfe seccond to noe man lyving,
because that comparison is rather of hardines of
bodye, then a boste of vertue. But how little
accomte soever is made ether of the matter or of
mee, I truste her majestie with her favour for my
xxviii^tie yeares service will alowe mee to gett my
livinge as well as I may honestly (which is every
subjectes righte), and not to constrayne mee by
my idle aboade at home to begg my bredd with my
wife and children, especially seeing I have her
majestyes graunte and lycense under the great
seale of Englande for my departure, withoute the

which I would not have spent a penny in this action. wherin I am most bounde to her majestie for her great favour, which of all thinges I most desyre: and take comforte in: protesting that noe man lyving shall serve her majestie more faythfully and dutifully during my life sith all the good fortune that god shall bestowe on mee. And thus I truste I have satisfyed your honour of all my intentes and proceedinges, Leaving your honour

to the tuition of the almightye, From my howse in Red Crosse streat the 7th of February. 1582.

Your honores most humble
  [signed:] H. Gylberte

[Addressed:]—To the right honorable Sir Frauncis Walsyngham Knight Principall Secretarye to her majestie.
  [Endorsed:]—1582. 7 Feb: Sir H. Gilbert that he may be suffered to continewe his voyage.

ATTEMPTS TO GET BRISTOL AID FOR CHRISTOPHER CARLEILL'S EXPEDITION, MARCH, 1583

CHRISTOPHER CARLEILL, step-son of Sir Francis Walsingham, entered the picture as an associate of Gilbert. His task was to persuade the Muscovy Company merchants in London and the merchants of Bristol to take part in a parallel venture, which was focused rather farther north (Maritimes and St. Lawrence) and was concerned more with trade and with a possible passage to Asia than with colonization. The following letter shows how Bristol was involved with him through the agency of Sir Francis Walsingham and Richard Hakluyt the younger. It is not known what they contributed to Carleill's venture in the end. The letters were published by Hakluyt (a) March 11, 1583, Walsingham to Hakluyt, *Principal navigations*, III (1600), 181 (413); (b) March 11, 1583, Walsingham to Thomas Aldworth, Mayor of Bristol, Ibid., III, 182 (414); (c) March 27, 1583, Thomas Aldworth to Walsingham, *Principall navigations* (1589), p. 718, *Principal navigations*, III (1600), 182 (415).

413. March 11, 1583. Sir Francis Walsingham to Richard Hakluyt the younger.

A letter of Sir Francis Walsingham to M. Richard Hakluyt then of Christchurch in Oxford, incouraging him in the study of Cosmographie, and of furthering new discoveries, &c.

I understand aswel by a letter I long since received from the Maior of Bristoll, as by conference with Sir George Pekham, that you have endevoured, & given much light for the discovery of the Westerne partes yet unknowen: as your studie in these things is very commendable, so I thanke you much for the same; wishing you do continue your travell in these and like matters,

which are like to turne not only to your owne good in private, but to the publike benefite of this Realme. And so I bid you farewell. From the Court the 11. of March. 1582.

Your loving Friend,
  [signed:] Francis Walsingham

414. March 11, 1583. Sir Francis Walsingham to Thomas Aldworth, Mayor of Bristol.

A letter of Sir Francis Walsingham to Master Thomas Aldworth merchant, and at that time

Maior of the Citie of Bristoll, concerning their adventure in the Westerne discoverie.

After my heartie commendations, I have for certaine causes deferred the answere of your letter of November last till now, which I hope commeth all in good time. Your good inclination to the Westerne discoverie I cannot but much commend. And for that sir Humfrey Gilbert, as you have heard long since, hath bene preparing into those parts being readie to imbarke within these 10. dayes, who needeth some further supply of shipping then yet he hath, I am of opinion that you shall do well if the ship or 2. barkes you write of, be put in a readinesse to goe alongst with him, or so soone after as you may. I hope this travell wil proove profitable to the Adventurers and generally beneficiall to the whole realme: herein I pray you conferre with these bearers, M. Richard Hackluyt, and M. Thomas Steventon, to whome I referre you: And so bid you heartily farewell.

Richmond the 11. of March. 1582.

Your loving Friend,
    [signed:] Francis Walsingham.

415. March 27, 1583. Thomas Aldworth, Mayor of Bristol, to Sir Francis Walsingham.

A letter written from M. Thomas Aldworth merchant and Maior of the Citie of Bristoll, to the right honourable Sir Francis Walsingham principall Secretary to her Majestie, concerning a Westerne voyage intended for the discovery of the coast of America, lying to the Southwest of Cape Briton.

Right honourable, upon the receit of your letters directed unto me and delivered by the bearers hereof M. Richard Hakluyt and M. Steventon, bearing date the 11. of March, I presently conferred with my friends in private, whom I know most affectionate to this godly enterprise, especially with M. William Salterne deputie of our company of merchants: whereupon my selfe being as then sicke, with as convenient speede as he could, hee

caused an assembly of the merchants to be gathered: where after dutifull mention of your honourable disposition for the benefite of this citie, he by my appointment caused your letters being directed unto me privatly, to be read in publike, and after some good light given by M. Hakluyt unto them that were ignorant of the Countrey and enterprise, and were desirous to be resolved, the motion grew generally so well to be liked, that there was eftsoones set downe by mens owne hands than present. & apparently knowen by their own speach, and very willing offer, the summe of 1000. markes and upward: which summe if it should not suffice, we doubt not but otherwise to furnish out for this Westerne discovery, a ship of threescore, and a barke of 40. tunne, to bee left in the countrey under the direction and government of your sonne in law Master Carlile, of whom we have heard much good, if it shall stand with your honors good liking and his acceptation. In one of which barks we are also willing to have Master Steventon your honours messenger, and one well knowen to us, as captains. And here in humble maner, desiring your honour to vouchsafe us of your further direction by a generall letter to my selfe, my brethren, and the rest of the merchants of this city, at your honors best and most convenient leisure, because we meane not to deferre the finall proceeding in this voyage, any further then to the end of April next coming, I cease, beseeching God long to blesse and prosper your honourable estate. Bristoll. March 27. 1583.

416. March 16, 1583. Walter Ralegh to Sir Humphrey Gilbert.

This gave the queen's permission for the expedition to go ahead. Copies in P.R.O., State Papers, Miscellaneous, SP 9/55 (I), and B.L., Additional MS 4231, fol. 85, printed in D. B. Quinn, Gilbert, II, 348.

Brother—I have sent you a token from her Majesty an ancor guyded by a Lady as yow See, & farther her Highness willed me to send yow worde that She wished as great good hap and

safty to your Ship as if hersealf were ther in person desireing yow to have care of yowrsealf as of that which She tendereth and therefore for her Sace yow must provide for hit accordingly; farther She commandeth that yow leve your picture with me for the rest I leve till owr meeting or to the Report of this berer who would needs be the messengre of this good newses, So I commit yow to the will and protection of God who Send us such life or death as he shall please or hath appoynted. Richmonde this fryday morning
Your trew Brother
 [signed:] W. Rauley

 [Addressed:]—To my Brother Sir Humfry Gilbert Knight.
 [Endorsed:]—Reseived the 18th of Marche 1582.

417. May 9, 1583. Further American ventures indicated.

By May 9, 1583, Gilbert's venture had been revived and was well under way and Peckham's was understood to be also, while Carleill, too, had launched his enterprise. One version of the document on Carleill's dealings with the Muscovy Company is dated May 9 (D. B. Quinn, Gilbert, II, 365–369), and it was printed as A breef and sommarie discourse... *written by Captaine Carleill in Aprill 1583 (London, 1583) (357). On May 9, too, court news circulated on what was going on as in this extract from a letter from Nicholas Faunt to Anthony Bacon, Lambeth, Tenison MS 647, fol. 151 v.; printed in D. B. Quinn, Gilbert, II, 365.*

We have sondry voyages of Discoverye in hand and some alredy entred into; Sir Humfrey Gilbert is once againe Crossing sayle towards a part of America not yet perfectly discovered: with whom Mr Rawley our newe favorite hath made an Adventure of 2000 li. in a shippe and furniture

therto. / Sir Thomas [*sic*] Peckham is towardes some such Course and one Mr Carlisle a gentleman allyed to my Master wherby you may perceave y^t our long peace doth not breed in us all slothfull and abject myndes: but that this Island is of to streight boundes to conteyne some of us &c. . . .

From the Court at Grenewich the vith of Maie 1583.

Yours most unfaynedly & ever to Commande in the Lord:
 [signed:] Nich: Fant

418. May 26, 1583. Gilbert records additional subscribers.

As in this note to William Barwick, Mayor of Southampion, Gilbert continued to enroll a few subscribers, though not enough for his needs. Southampton Record Office, Stockwell Papers, Addenda; printed in D. B. Quinn, Gilbert, II, 374.

Mr. Anthony Cooke	66–13–4
Captin Jhon Allyne	5– 0–0
Mr. Giles Arkenshall	50– 0–0
Mr. Thomas Chapman	10– 0–0
Mr. Bartholemew Hoges	100– 0–0
Mr. Roger Hay	35– 0–0
Waynwryght	5– 0–0
Michell Bowles	5– 0–0
	210– 0–0
	[= £276-13-4]

Master Mayer
 I praye you enter thes men beynge eyghte men emongest them to be alloyd in seyll and previledge of adventurer as fre men in the discovery for all trades acordynge to the spesiall somes above wryte not excedynge the some of two hunderyd and ten poundes.

Hamble the 26. of Maye 1583.
 [signed:] H. Gylberte

CONTEMPORARY HISTORIANS ON GILBERT

419. 1586. John Hooker on Sir Humphrey Gilbert.

Raphael Holinshed, Chronicles, *3 vols. (London, 1587), II, 132–133.*

Sir Humfreie Gilbert, he was a second brother, and borne of a great parentage, whose ancestors came and descended from the earle of Cornewall, a man of higher stature than of the common sort, & of complexion cholerike; from his childhood of a verie pregnant wit and good disposition: his father died leaving him verie yoong, and he conceiving some great good thing to come of his towardnesse, provided some portion of living to mainteine and keepe him to schoole. And after his death, his mother, being no lesse carefull of him, did cause him to be sent to schoole to Eton college: from thense, after he had profited in the elements & principall points of grammer, he was sent to Oxford, & did there prosper & increase verie well in learning and knowledge. And being (as his friends thought) verie well furnished, they would have put him to the ins of court. But an aunt of his, named mistres Katharine Ashlie, who was attendant to the queenes majestie, after that she saw the yoong gentleman, and had had some conference with him, she fell in such liking with him, that she preferred him unto hir majesties service: and such was his countenance, forwardnesse, and behaviour, that hir majestie had a speciall good liking of him; and verie oftentimes would familiarlie discourse and conferre with him in matters of learning. After a few yeares spent in the court, he passed over into Ireland, being commended by hir highnesse to sir Henrie Sidneie then lord deputie: who gave him interteinement, and made him a capteine over an hundred horssemen: wherein he so well acquited himselfe, that he was also made coronell of Mounster and had appointed unto him, besides his owne band of hundred horssemen, foure hundred footemen, besides such Geraldines as Thomas of Desmond, brother to the erle of Desmond had procured, & upon his oth of loialtie and pledges had promised his faithfull service.

And albeit he were but yoong of yeares, which might seeme to hinder his credit: yet such was his devout mind to serve hir majestie, and so effectuallie to his great praise he followed the same; that with manie good gifts and excellent vertues he so supplied even as much as manie men of elder yeares & greater experience did not commonlie atteine unto. For in service upon the enimie he was as valiant and couragious as no man more; and so good was his hap to answer the same: for he alwaies for the most part daunted the enimie, and appalled their courage; as did appeare in the overthrow given neere Kilkennie in the Butlers warres, when he with twelve persons gave the onset upon a thousand men, of which six hundred were armed Gallowglasses, who then were overthrowne: and likewise in Mounster,[1] which was altogether up in rebellion: and he coronell, did not onelie in martiall affaires shew himselfe most valiant; and in short time reduced the whole troope of the rebels, and the proudest of them to obedience, having under him but five hundred against sundrie thousands; and inforced that proud earle of Clancart to follow him to Limerike, and there humblie upon his knees to aske pardon and mercie: but also, after that he had subdued and overcome them, did most uprightlie order and direct his governement, and with all indifferencie would heare, decide, and determine the complaints & griefs, and compound all the causes of everie sutor. Which was so rare a thing in one of his yeares, as scarse was credible, had not eiewitnesses and dailie experience prooved and justified the same.

After that he had established peace and tranquillitie in that countrie, he went to Dublin: where when he had recounted all his services, and the good successe thereof; and in what quiet state he had left the countrie, he desired leave to passe over into England, for and about certeine matters of great importance, which he had to follow, which he did obteine: as also in reward of his service, and for his good deserts he (as is before said) was honored and dubbed a knight; and with letters in his praise and commendation to hir majestie, and the lords of the councell, he departed. As sone as he had presented himselfe

1. Sidenote: "The valiantnes in service, and the wisedome in governement of sir Humfreie Gilbert."

before hir highnesse, hir good countenance and favour, in respect of his good service to hir majestie was increased and doubled; and he speciallie above all others magnified and well accepted. Not long after, he was maried to a yoong gentlewoman, and an inheritrix: and thense foorth he gave himselfe to studies perteining to the state of government, and to navigations. He had an excellent and readie wit, and therewith a toong at libertie to utter what he thought. Which being adorned with learning and knowledge, he both did and could notablie discourse anie matter in question concerning either of these, as he made good proofe thereof, as well in familiar conference with the noble, wise and learned: as also in the open assemblies of the parlements, both in England and in Ireland: in which he shewes the great value of knowledge, wisedome, and learning which was in him, and the great zeale he had to the commonwealth of his countrie. He had a great delight in the studie of cosmographie, and especiallie in navigations: and finding out by his studies, certeine nations and unknowne lands, which being found, might redound to the greate benefite of his countrie: he made hir majestie acquainted therewith, and obtained of hir a licence to make a navigation, which he tooke in hand. But before he could compasse the same to effect, he was in a foule storme drowned at the seas. Onelie he of all his brethren had five sons and one daughter, children by their countenances giving a hope of a good towardnesse. And albeit he in person be deceassed, yet in their visages, and in the memoriall of his great vertues, and a life well spent, he shall live in fame immortall. Thus much without offense. and not altogither impertinent,

concerning this gentleman, and now to the historie.

420. William Camden on Gilbert's ventures.

William Camden, The history of... Princess Elizabeth (London, 1688), p. 287, translated from Annales (1615), p. 345.

Near the same time was swallowed by the Ocean Sir Humphrey Gilbert Knight, a quick and lively-spirited man, famous for his Knowledge in matters relating both to War & Peace, in his Return from the North part of America, which we call New-found-land, whither he had set sail a little before with five Ships, having sold his Patrimony, in hope to plant a Colony there. But after he had by an Herald or Crier proclaimed that Countrey to belong to the English Jurisdiction, (for Sebastion Cabot was the first that discovered it, in the year 1497, being employed therein by Henry the Seventh,) and had assigned Lands to every particular man of his Company: he suffered so much by Shipwrecks and want of necessary Provision, that he was constrained to give over his Enterprise, learning too late himself, and teaching others, that it is a difficulter thing to carry over Colonies into remote Countries upon private mens Purses, than he and others in an erroneous Credulity had perswaded themselves, to their own Cost and Detriment.

Chapter Fifty-four
The Aftermath of Gilbert's Fatal
Newfoundland Voyage

421. July, 1583. Draft arrangement between Sir Philip Sidney and Sir George Peckham.

If this agreement was implemented, it would seem that Sidney put his 3,000,000 acres obtained from Gilbert in July, 1582 at the disposal of Sir George Peckham. The proceeds from the sale of this would go to help finance Peckham's venture. P.R.O., State Papers, Domestic, Elizabeth I, SP 12/161, 44; printed in D. B. Quinn, Gilbert, II, 276-278.

Articles Endented concluded and agreed upon the [blank] daye of Julye in the xxvth yere of the Reigne of our Sovereigne ladye Elizabeth by the grace of god Quene [of] England Fraunce and Ireland defender of the faith &c. Betwene syr Philipp [Syd]ney of Penthurst in the county of Kent knight on the thone partye And Sir George Peckham of Denham in the countie of Kent [Buckinghamshire] knight on thother partye

Imprimis wheras the said syr Philipp Sydney by good and sufficient assuraunce in the Lawe fromme and under her majestes lettres patentes knowledged and enrolled in the Chauncerye is licenced and aughtorized to discover search Find out vew & inhabit certene partes of America not yet discovered And out of those contries by him his heires factours or assignes to have and enjoye to him his heires and assignes forever such and so much quantytye of ground as shall amount to t[he nu]mber of Thirtye hundred thousand acres of ground and wood with all commodyties Jurisdiccions and Royalties both by sea and land with full power and auchtorytys That yt shall & may be Lauffull to and for the said syr Philipp Sydney his heires and assignes at all tymes therafter to have take and leade in the said voyage to travaill thitherwards or to inhabit there with him or them & every or any them such and so

meny her majestes subjectes as shall willinglye accompanye him and them and every or any of them with sufficient shipping and furniture for theire transportacions as by the said lettres patentes & assurances amongst divers others Articles and liberties therin conteined more at large appereth Now the said sir Philipp Sydney as well for the more spedye execucion of her majestes said graunt & the enlargemente of her majestes domynions & govermentes & for the better incoragemente of the said Sir Georg Peckham and his associates in so worthye and comendable an enterprese as also for divers other causes & consideracions him speciallye movinge for him his heires executours [a]dministrators & assignes doth covenaunte & promise and graunte to & with the said Sir Georg Peckham his heires & assignes by theis presentes That he the same Sir Philipp Sydney his heires & assignes shall & will at all tymes hereafter upon the Lauffull request of the same Sir Georg his heires or assignes make or cause to be made such good & sufficient assuraunce in the Lawe of the said xxx^m [for xxx^cM = 300,000?] Acres of Land lyinge within the same contries unto all & every such person & persons Guyld mysterys body pollytiques or corporate his heires or assignes shall nominate and [ap]ppointe In such larg and ample maner and forme to the same person or persones Guyld misterye bodye pollytique or corporate so to be nominated or Appointed his or their heires successours or assignes and every of them As the said Sir Philipp his heires or assignes can or may convey or assure the said xxx^m acres of Land together withall Royalties titles prehemynences privileges liberties and Dignyties therunto belonging to any person or persons or to any uses whatsoever by vertue of the said assuraunces or the said lettres patentes

Item the said syr Philipp Sydney for the consideracion aforesaid is contented & agreed that all and every such some [or] somes of money and

260

other commodyties whatsoever which by th[is] assignemente shalbe procured gotten & received of any ther persone or persones Guyld mysterye bodye pollytique [or] corporate aforesaid adventurers for & Towardes the said discovery shalbe paid to the same Syr Georg his heires or assignes for & Towardes his and their charges in Fu[r]n[i]shing & setting forth a supplye of shippinge & victuell men municion & other necessaries unto the said contres without an accompte to be yelden therfore by the same Syr Georg his heirs or Assignes unto the said Syr Philip Syneye his heyres

In wytnes

[Endorsed:]—The right worshipfull syr Phillip Sydney knight.

herken unto suche offers as Sir Philipp Sidney & Sir George Peckham will make unto you who have sufficient Aucthoritie by & under her Majestes Lettres patentes to performe theffect of your Desire. No whit mystrusteng but that this voiage will prove proffitable to thadventurers in particler & generallie beneficiall to the whole realme, So expecteing your answere I bidd you hartelie farewell the [blank] daie of [blank] 1583

Your loveing freind

[Endorsed:] The mynnute of a lettre for Mr Secretary. Minute of a Letter touching the discovery in America 1583.

422. [After July, 1583]. Sir Francis Walsingham supports the Peckham-Sidney drive for subscribers.

After Gilbert's departure Peckham attempted to rally his supporters to advance the project for his settlement on the "Bay of the Five Islands" (Narragansett Bay). Christopher Carleill also went ahead trying to collect subscriptions from other groups. The Peckham-Sidney appeal was sponsored in this draft letter from Sir Francis Walsingham, and it is evident that Carleill had similar documents. The Peckham campaign seems to have come to an end about January, 1584, but that of Carleill was continued until April, 1584, at least. Both men were no doubt assisted by the printed tracts, which they had published.

The draft is from P.R.O., State Papers, Domestic, Elizabeth I, SP 12/165, 35; printed in D. B. Quinn, Gilbert, II, 375–376.

After my Hartie Commendacions whereas I am enformed by Mr Anthonie Brigham that upon some conference he findeth in you a verie good enclynacion to the western discoveries so as you maie be sufficientlie aucthorised so to doe and have a Societie by yourselves without joigneing with anie gentleman or anie other Citties or Townes other then suche as yourself shall make choise of I am of opinion you shall doe well to

423. December, 1583 to January, 1584. Sir George Peckham appeals for support at Exeter.

The Merchant Adventurers of Exeter was the trading guild of the City of Exeter. They had been approached on Gilbert's behalf by Walsingham in a letter of December 8, 1582 (though we do not know with what precise result), and again by Sir George Peckham in a letter of December 13, 1583. His servant, Oliver Manwayringe, came before the Court of the Merchant Adventurers on January 11, 1584, and after a further meeting on January 30, subscriptions to the amount of £100 towards equipping a ship were put up. This is the latest document we have on Peckham's activities. They appear in the register of the Merchant Adventurers and were printed in D. B. Quinn, Gilbert, II 480–482.

The courte: kept and holden before the Governour, consulls and companye the fourth daye of January 1583: in the syx and twenteth yeare of the reigne of oure sovereigne Ladye queene Elizabeth etc.

Mr Michaell Germyn Governour Mr Nicholas Martyn Mr Thomas Martyn John Hoyell William Spicer consulls Mr George Smyth threaserer

At this courte ther is a lettre reade from the right worshipfull Sir Fraunces Walsingham knight chief Secretary to her Majestie dated the viiith daye of December 1582, directed to the maiour of Exeter towching the voyage pretended to the westren partes of America by Sir Humfrye Gilbert Knight and others. / Also ther is an other lettre reade from the right worshipfull Sir George Peckham knight dated the xiiiith of December 1583, directed also to the saide maiour of Exeter, towching the saide matter. /

And this Courte being especiallie called to understande what money everie one of this companye will disburse and adventure in and aboute the settinge forth of certen Shippinge to the saide parties of America. And the Governour movinge the companye thereunto, and declared the greate beneficte and commoditie thereof ensuyng. The whole generallitie doo lyke well of the saide voyage and wysse good successe thereunto, and woulde be glade to adventure and set forth Shipping thether: But considering the tyme of the yeare to be Farr spente for preparacion of Shippinge and provision for suche a voyage, They mynde to respecte thereupon this yeare, and the next yeare as they shall see success therein, they wilbe glade to adventure thether and doo any thinge for the furtherance thereof. /...

Memorandum: that the xith daye of January 1583 one Olyver Manwayringe sarvante to the right worshipfull Sir George Peckham Knight (being aucthorized for that purpose) came in and declared the pretence and order of a voyage pretended to the westren partes of America and the greate benefeicte and commoditie that maye ensue thereof aswell to the whole realme as to the adventurers that waye: And shewed forth certen lettres patent for the assuraunce of the benefeicte of the saide adventurers, and a booke towching the discription and order of the saide pretended voyage: whereupon the Governour moved the companye to set forth certen Shipping and to be adventurers that waye: But forasmoche as there is two lettres directed to the maiour of Exon: one from the right worshipfull Sir Fraunces Walsingham Knight. chief Secretary to her Majestie: and thother from the saide Sir George Peckham towching the saide matter. The Governour consulls and companye thought it good that the maiour and alderman his brethern shoulde conferr aswell for the aunswering of their saide worshipfull lettres: as also to take order for Shipping and adventuring in the saide voyage...

The courte: kept and holden before the Governour, consulls and companye the xxxth daye of January 1583: in the Syx and twenteth yeare of the reigne of oure Sovereyne Ladye queene Elizabeth etc. /

Mr Michaell Germyn Governour Mr. Nicholas Martyn John Hoyell consulls Mr. George Smyth threaserer

This courte being especiallie called to understand what everie one of this companye woulde adventure to the foresaide parties of America And the Governour moving theim thereunto (Olyver Manwayring being present) the parties whose names are hereunder writen dyd agree and promise to adventure everie of theim to the setting forth of a Shipp that waye as hereafter followeth viz. /

Mr Nicholas Martyn	xii li. xs.
Mr Thomas Martyn	xii li. xs.
Mr George Smyth	xii li. xs.
Mr Thomas Spicer	xii li. xs.
John Hoyle	xii li. xs.
Richarde Jordeyne	xii li. xs.
Myles Lambert	xii li. xs.

CHRISTOPHER CARLEILL CONTINUES HIS SEARCH FOR SUBSCRIPTIONS

IT SEEMS PROBABLE that it was at the end of 1583 or, more probably, early in 1584 when Christopher Carleill had the second edition of his pamphlet printed to assist his drive for subscribers, *A discourse upon the intended voyage to the hethermoste partes of America: written by a Captaine Carleill* (but this time without the date April, 1583); see (357) and (413–415).

Carleill's agent, Master Stevington (or Steventon), then went on tour, during the early months of 1584 to try to collect money for an expedition to the coast north of Peckham's objective. So far he has been traced only at Shrewsbury and Chester, and in neither case does he appear to have had much success. In Shrewsbury the town council wrote to Sir Henry Sidney, who had recommended Carleill, and we may suspect their answer was negative. In Chester a request for £100 was met by offers of £20 10s only and ultimately by a refusal directed probably to Carleill himself (though the entry of the letter does not say so). (a) Shrewsbury Assembly Book, 1553–1584, fol. 379v., Shrewsbury Guildhall (424). (b) Chester Assembly Book, 1539–1624, items 450, 453, 444, Chester City Record Office. Both are published for the first time (425).

424. February 5, 1584. Shrewsbury.

Tempore Georgeii Higgens Micahelis
Chambre ballivorum

Assemblacio aldermanorum et Communis consilii ville predicte viz. Jovis quinto die Februarii anno Regni Elizabethe &c. xxvj° [1584].

The most number of this assembly be agreed Master Bayliffes shale write there letteres to the lord presydent [of the Council of Wales and the Marches, Sir Henry Sidney] for the answering of his lordships lettre conserninge the vyadge into the land of America in suche sorte as the same is nowe written by the advice of master Prince [letter not given].

They be allso agreed that there shalbe geven to Master Stevington the messenger in this cause in respecte of my Lord presydents sayd lettres and his travell and paynes in this behalfe the some of iij[li.] vj[s] viij[d] and suche wine and other pleasures as master bayliffes shale thinke good.

425. February 18 to April 7, 1584. Chester.

[a] At an Assembly in the Inner Pentice within the Cittie of Chester, the Third day of Marche Anno Regine Elizabeth &c xxvj°[1584] before the saide Master Brerewood Maior.

At[1] which Assembly motion was made upon the readinge of a lettre, sente to the saide Maior and Citizens from one Master Xpofer Carlile towchinge his requeste to haue the Citizens to be Contributories to his procedinge, or his adventuringe to America a voyadge pretended / what annswere is thereunto Convenyent to be made but not determyned.

[b] At an Assembly houlden in the Commen Hall of the Cittie of Chester the Tenth daye of Aprill anno Regine Elizabeth &c xxvj° before the said Robert Brerewood Maiore. . . .

An[d] at the said Assembly[2] a lettre from Master Xpofer Carlill to the Maiour and Aldermen of this Cittie, to move the Cittizens to be Contributories to the adventuringe vnto America is read and considered of and euery man demaunded what they will adventure Where there were none of this Assembly that of them sellues wolde adventurie eny thinge to that enterprise Saving that Master William Massy saide he wolde be one of the xx[ie] for v[li] and Master Thomay Blynyall offered he wolde adventure v[li] if others woulde doe the like. One other saide he wolde Xs. but none of them sellues wolde adventure eny thinge excepe others wolde Ioyne with theym And therefore ordered that annswer of that lettre shoulde be made in denyall, to be Contributaries in respect of the decayed estate of this Cittie.

[c] Like as wee haue (right wurshippfull) received your lettre of the xviii[th] of February laste by Master Steventon therein namyd, Advertizinge vs and this Citie thereby of a pretended voyadge into the hethermoste partes of America, and that by our good meanes the[y] woulde be

---

1. advice upon answer to master Carlills lettre of his adventureing to America /

2. What answer is appointed to be made to master Carlill to his said requeste

brought to Contribute some small porcion for the better settinge forward of so godlie an enterprise. Soe haue wee aswell Conferred with the saide Master Steventon touchinge the same. As allso Called an Assembly of the wholle bodie of this City together, and to them haue made knowen theffect of your saide lettre And haue moved them, at the verie assemblie to Contribute to the saide proceedinges And albeit bothe wee and the reste of the Citizens of this Cittie, wolde wishe withall our harte that our habilities were answerable to our willinge myndes to accomplishe theffect of your saide lettre. Yet of our sellues, wee haue bene so overcharged with taxacions and paymentes in buildinge of a Newe Haven in the Porte of Chester and for a newe Conduit, to reduce freshe water into this Cittie to serve the same and otherwise as our habilities will not extende to Contribute to the Charge of the saide adventure, nether can wee bringe or perswade eny of the other Citizens of this Cittie of them sellues to contribute eny porcion in that behallf, by reason of theire disabilities to accomplish the same. Havinge bene alredie overcharged with the like burthens of payment as wee haue bene. As allso by great losses on the Seas. Wherefore wee humbly beseche your Consideracion of this our poore decayed estate. As allso to accepte in good parte this our vnfayned excuse and our willinge mynds to have performed your saide motion.

Thus prayinge god to preserve your wurshipp As allsoe prosper the saide proceedinges Comytt you to the blessed tuytion of thalmightie:

Chester this viith daye of Aprill 1584. /

426. July 21, 1584. Sir Philip Sidney to Sir Edward Stafford.

Although Philip Sidney had failed to assist Sir George Peckham's venture late in 1583 and early in 1584, it is clear that in the summer of 1584 he still hankered after making an American expedition. Instead, he involved himself, fatally, in the Netherlands.

*Printed by Arthur Collins (*Letters and memorials of state, *I [1746], 298) from an original then, but not now, extant among the State Papers (*Hist. MSS Comm., *De L'Isle and Dudley MSS, II, xxxvi); extract reprinted in D. B. Quinn,* Roanoke voyages, *I, 90.*

We are haulf perswaded to enter into the journey of Sir Humphrey Gilbert very eagerly whereunto your Master Hackluit hath served for a very good Trumpet.

XII

The Roanoke Voyages, 1584–1590

THE EXPEDITIONS of 1584, 1585 (with a colony), 1586 (with colonists), 1587 (with a colony), 1588 (with colonists who did not arrive) and 1590 (which was to search for those left in 1587), constitute a series that brought Englishmen into close and continuing contact with the realities of living on American soil for somewhat extended periods. Occupation was neither as continuous nor as fruitful as had been hoped for by those, such as Sir Walter Ralegh, Sir Richard Grenville, Sir Francis Walsingham, Ralph Lane, Thomas Harriot, John White, and a few others, who were or became optimistic about the prospects of settlement. The causes for their failure were partly ill chance (always an element where small vulnerable expeditions were concerned), partly because settlement was a slower, more painful, and expensive process than had been imagined by those who had written about it on the basis of no or very imperfect experience hitherto. It was also interfered with, fatally perhaps, by the exigencies of war, which interrupted a series of expeditions that might have produced a stable English colony by the 1590s. On the other side the Spanish plans to occupy the area where the English were, or had been, were also frustrated by the war, so that speculation on whether English colonies could have been maintained in the reign of Elizabeth I or would have been overlaid by Spanish ones as the French Florida ventures had been cannot be carried fruitfully very far.

The narratives bring to life the appearance of the Carolina Outer Banks and of the surrounding areas and show something of the people (especially if studied with P. H. Hulton and D. B. Quinn, *The American Drawings of John White*, 2 vols., [1964]). The advantage of the narratives is that they do bring the situation to life; their disadvantage is that only between the lines can the day-to-day problems of settlement be envisaged. The economic and social context is left largely unfilled, although a little can be gathered from Harriot's *Briefe and true report* (365), which should be read with the chronological material.

Chapter Fifty-five
The Reconnaissance Voyage of 1584

427. March 25, 1584. Letters Patent to Walter Ralegh.

This patent is modelled on that granted to Sir Humphrey Gilbert in 1578 (370), but excepts Newfoundland from Ralegh's wide-ranging authority, possibly because Gilbert's family were claiming rights there or because Newfoundland was an international fishery.

The original patent is not now extant, but Hakluyt's version, printed below, was taken from the original or a copy. Patent Roll, 26 Elizabeth, pt. I, mm. 38–40, P.R.O., C66/1237; printed in R. Hakluyt, Principall navigations (1589), pp. 725–728 and Principal navigations, III (1600), 243–245; D. B. Quinn, Roanoke voyages I, 82–89, prints from the patent roll.

The letters patents, granted by the Queenes Majestie to M. Walter Ralegh, now Knight, for the discovering and planting of new lands and Countries, to continue the space of 6. yeeres and no more.

Elizabeth by the grace of God of England, France and Ireland Queene, defender of the faith, &c. To all people to whom these presents shal come, greeting. Know ye that of our especial grace, certaine science, & meere motion, we have given and granted, and by these presents for us, our heires and successors doe give and grant to our trusty and welbeloved servant Walter Ralegh Esquire, and to his heires and assignes for ever, free liberty & licence from time to time, and at all times for ever hereafter, to discover, search, finde out, and view such remote, heathen and barbarous lands, countreis, and territories, not actually possessed of any Christian prince, nor inhabited by Christian people, as to him, his heires and assignes, and to every or any of them shall seeme good, and the same to have, holde,

occupy & enjoy to him, his heires and assignes for ever, with all prerogatives, commodities, jurisdictions, royalties, priviledges, franchises and preeminences, thereto or thereabouts both by sea and land, whatsoever we by our letters patents may grant, and as we or any of our noble progenitors have heretofore granted to any person or persons, bodies politique or corporate: and the saide Walter Ralegh, his heires and assignes, and all such as from time to time, by licence of us, our heires and successors, shal goe or travaile thither to inhabite or remaine, there to build and fortifie, at the discretion of the said Walter Ralegh, his heires & assignes, the statutes or act of Parliament made against fugitives, or against such as shall depart, remaine or continue out of our Realme of England without licence, or any other statute, act, law, or any ordinance whatsoever to the contrary in any wise notwithstanding.

And we do likewise by these presents, of our especial grace, meere motion, and certaine knowledge, for us, our heires and successors, give and graunt full authoritie, libertie and power to the said Walter Ralegh, his heires and assignes, and every of them, that he and they, and every or any of them, shall and may at all and every time and times hereafter, have, take, and leade in the sayde voyage, and travaile thitherward, or to inhabite there with him or them, and every or any of them, such, and so many of our subjects as shall willingly accompany him or them, and every or any of them: and to whom also we doe by these presents, give full libertie and authoritie in that behalfe, and also to have, take and employ, and use sufficient shipping and furniture for the transportations, and Navigations in that behalfe, so that none of the same persons or any of them be such as hereafter shall be restrained by us, our heires or successors.

And further that the said Walter Ralegh his heires and assignes, and every of them, shall have, holde, occupie and enjoy to him, his heires and assignes, and every of them for ever, all the soyle of all such landes, territories, and Countreis, so to be discovered and possessed as aforesayd, and of all such Cities, Castles, Townes, Villages, and places in the same, with the right, royalties, franchises, and jurisdictions, as well marine as other within the sayd landes, or Countreis, or the seas thereunto adjoyning, to be had, or used, with full power to dispose thereof, and of every part in fee simple or otherwise, according to the order of the lawes of England, as neere as the same conveniently may be, at his, and their wil and pleasure, to any persons then being, or that shall remaine within the allegiance of us, our heires and successors: reserving alwayes to us, our heires and successors, for all services, dueties, and demaunds, the fift part of all the oare of golde and silver, that from time to time, and at all times after such discoverie, subduing and possessing, shall be there gotten and obteined: All which lands, Countries, and territories shall for ever be holden of the sayd Walter Ralegh, his heires and assignes, of us, our heires and successors, by homage, and by the sayd payment of the sayd fift part, reserved onely for all services.

And moreover, we do by these presents, for us, our heires and successors, give and grant licence to the said Walter Ralegh, his heires, and assignes, and every of them, that he, and they, and every or any of them, shall and may from time to time, and at all times for ever hereafter, for his and their defence, encounter and expulse, repell and resist aswell by sea as by lande, and by all other wayes whatsoever, all and every such person and persons whatsoever, as without the especiall liking and licence of the sayd Walter Ralegh, and of his heires and assignes, shall attempt to inhabite within the sayde Countryes, or any of them, or within the space of two hundreth leagues neere to the place or places within such Countryes as aforesayde (if they shall not bee before planted or inhabited within the limits as aforesayd with the subjects of any Christian Prince being in amitie with us) where the sayd Walter Ralegh, his heires, or assignes, or any of them, or his, or their, or any of their associats or company, shall within six yeeres (next ensuing) make their dwellings or abidings, or that shall enterprise or attempt at any time hereafter unlawfully to annoy, eyther by Sea or Lande the

sayde Walter Ralegh, his heires or assignes, or any of them, or his or their, or any of his or their companies: giving, and graunting by these presents further power and authoritie to the sayd Walter Ralegh, his heires and assignes, and every of them from time to time, and at all times for ever hereafter, to take and surprise by all maner of meanes whatsoever, all and every those person or persons, with their Shippes, Vessels, and other goods and furniture, which without the licence of the sayde Walter Ralegh, or his heires, or assignes, as aforesayd, shalbe found traffiquing into any Harbour, or Harbours, Creeke, or Creekes, within the limits aforesayd, (the subjects of our Realmes and Dominions, and all other persons in amitie with us, trading to the Newfound lands for fishing as heretofore they have commonly used, or being driven by force of a tempest, or shipwracke onely excepted:) and those persons, and every of them, with their shippes, vessels, goods, and furniture to deteine and possesse as of good and lawfull prize, according to the discretion of him the sayd Walter Ralegh, his heires, and assignes, and every, or any of them. And for uniting in more perfect league and amitie, of such Countryes, landes, and territories so to be possessed and inhabited as aforesayd with our Realmes of England and Ireland, and the better incouragement of men to these enterprises: we doe by these presents, graunt and declare that all such Countries, so hereafter to be possessed and inhabited as is aforesayd, from thencefoorth shall be of the allegiance to us, our heires and successours. And wee doe graunt to the sayd Walter Ralegh, his heires, and assignes, and to all, and every of them, and to all, and every other person and persons, being of our allegiance, whose names shall be noted or entred in some of our Courts of recorde within our Realme of England, that with the assent of the sayd Walter Ralegh, his heires or assignes, shall in his journeis for discoverie, or in the journeis for conquest hereafter travaile to such lands, countreis and territories, as aforesayd, and to their, and to every of their heires, and they, and every or any of them, being eyther borne within our sayde Realmes of England or Irelande, or in any other place within our allegiance, and which hereafter shall be inhabiting within any the Lands, Countryes, and Territories, with such licence, (as aforesayd) shall and may have all the priviledges of free Denizens, and persons native of England, and within our allegiance in such like ample maner and forme, as if they were borne and personally resident within our said Realme of England, any law, custome, or usage to the contrary notwithstanding.

And forasmuch as upon the finding out, discovering, or inhabiting of such remote lands, countries, and territories as aforesaid, it shalbe necessary for the safety of all men, that shall adventure themselves in those journeyes or voyages, to determine to live together in Christian peace, and civill quietnesse eche with other, whereby every one may with more pleasure and profit enjoy that whereunto they shall atteine with great paine and perill, wee for us, our heires and successors, are likewise pleased and contented, and by these presents doe give & grant to the said Walter Ralegh, his heires and assignes for ever, that he and they, and every or any of them, shall and may from time to time for ever hereafter, within the said mentioned remote lands and countries, in the way by the seas thither, and from thence, have full and meere power and authoritie to correct, punish, pardon, governe, and rule by their and every or any of their good discretions and policies, aswell in causes capitall, or criminall, as civil, both marine and other, all such our subjects, as shal from time to time adventure themselves in the said journeis or voyages, or that shall at any time hereafter inhabite any such lands, countreis, or territories as aforesayd, or that shall abide with 200. leagues of any of the sayde place or places, where the sayde Walter Ralegh, his heires or assignes, or any of them, or any of his or their associats or companies, shall inhabite within 6. yeeres next ensuing the date hereof, according to such statutes, lawes and ordinances as shall be by him the sayd Walter Ralegh, his heires and assignes, and every or any of them devised, or established, for the better government of the said people as aforesaid. So alwayes as the said statutes, lawes, and ordinances may be, as nere as conveniently may bee, agreeable to the forme of the lawes, statutes, governement, or pollicie of England, and also so as they be not against the true Christian faith, nowe professed in the Church of England, nor in any wise to withdrawe any of the subjects or people of those lands or places from the alleagance of us, our heires and successours, as their immediate Soveraigne under God.

And further, we doe by these presents for us, our heires and successors, give and grant ful power and authoritie to our trustie and welbeloved Counsailour Sir William Cecill knight, Lorde Burghley, or high Treasourer of England, and to the Lorde Treasourer of England for us, our heires and successors for the time being, and to the privie Counsaile of us, our heires and successors, or any foure or more of them for the time being, that he, they, or any foure or more of them, shall and may from time to time, and at all times hereafter, under his or their handes or Seales by vertue of these presents, authorise and licence the saide Walter Ralegh, his heires and assignes, and every or any of them by him, & by themselves, or by their, or any of their sufficient Atturneis, Deputies, Officers, Ministers, Factors, and servants, to imbarke & transport out of our Realme of England and Ireland, and the Dominions thereof, all or any of his or their goods, and all or any the goods of his and their associats and companies, and every or any of them, with such other necessaries and commodities of any our Realmes, as to the sayde Lorde Treasurer, or foure or more of the privie Counsaiie, of us our heires and successors for the time being (as aforesaid) shalbe from time to time by his or their wisedomes, or discretions thought meete and convenient, for the better reliefe and supportation of him the sayde Walter Ralegh, his heires, and assignes, and every or any of them, and of his or their or any of their associats and companies, any act, statute, law, or any thing to the contrary in any wise notwithstanding.

Provided alwayes, and our wil and pleasure is, and we do hereby declare to all Christian kings, princes, and states, that if the sayde Walter Ralegh, his heires or assignes, or any of them, or any other by their licence or appointment, shall at any time or times hereafter robbe or spoile by sea or by land, or doe any acte of unjust or unlawfull hostilitie, to any of the subjects of us, our heires or successors, or to any of the subjects of any the kings, princes, rulers, Governours, or estates, being then in perfect league and amitie with us, our heires and successours, and that upon such injurie, or upon just complaint of any such Prince, Ruler, Governour or estate, or their subjects, wee, our heires and successors, shall make open Proclamation within any the portes of our Realme of England, that the saide Walter Ralegh, his heires and assignes, and adherents, or any to whom these our Letters patents may extende, shall within the termes to bee limited, by such Proclamation, make full restitution, and satisfaction of all such injuries done: so as both we and the said Princes, or other so complaining, may hold us and themselves fully contented: And that if the said Walter Ralegh, his heires and assignes, shall not make or cause to be made satisfaction accordingly within such time so to be limitted, that then it shal be lawful us, our heires and successors, to put the sayde Walter Ralegh, his heires and assignes, and adherents, and all the inhabitants of the saide places to be discovered (as is aforesaid) or any of them out of our allegeance and protection, and that from and after such time of putting out of protection of the saide Walter Ralegh, his heires, assignes and adherents, and others so to be put out, and the said places within their habitation, possession and rule, shall be out of our allegeance and protection, and free for all Princes and others to pursue with hostilitie, as being not our subjects, nor by us any way to be avouched, maintained, or defended, nor to be holden as any of ours, nor to our protection, or dominion, or allegeance any way belonging: for that expresse mention of the cleere yeerely value of the certaintie of the premisses, or any party thereof, or of any other gift, or grant by us, or any our progenitors, or predecessors to the said Walter Ralegh, before this time made in these presents, bee not expressed, or any other grant, ordinance, provision, proclamation, or restraint to the contrary thereof, before this time, given, ordained, or provided, or any other thing, cause, or matter whatsoever, in any wise notwithstanding. In witnesse whereof, wee have caused these our letters to be made Patents. Witnesse our selves, at Westminister the five and twentie day of March, in the sixe and twentith yeere of our Raigne [1584].

428. December, 1584. Parliamentary bill to confirm Ralegh's patent.

This bill was presented to the House of Commons for a first reading on December 14, 1584. After the preamble, ending videlecit, *the patent (427) was recited. Having passed through three readings and committee in the Commons, it went on December 19 to the House of Lords but was rejected by them. It is not clear why Ralegh went to the expense of introducing this bill as it did not add anything to the rights he already enjoyed under his patent.*

House of Lords MS (see Historical Manuscripts Commission, 3 Rep., app., p. 5); copy in P.R.O., S.P., Domestic, Elizabeth I, SP 12/169, 36. Printed in D. B. Quinn, Roanoke voyages, *I (1955), 126–129.*

An acte for the confermacion of the Quenes maiesties Lettres Patentes graunted to Walter Ralegh Esquire Touchinge the discoverie and Inhabitinge of certeyn Foreyne Landes & Cuntries

Wheras the Queenes most exelent Maiestie of her most gracious disposicion to the Benyfite and proffite of her Realme of Englande emongeste sondrie other the singuler frewtes of her goodnes towardes the same Hath by all good meanes endeavored, that the godspell of our saviour Iesus Christe might be trewlye and syncerelie sette forth, And Ignoraunce error and supersticion Abolished within her Majesties Domynions, And is also desirous that the knowledge of god and trewe religion might by her heighnes Labors be propagatyd Amongeste foreign Nacions, The people of this her heighnes Realme mainteyned and encresed And traficke to the most benefitte and Comodytie of her lovinge subiectes as otherwise shulde spende there tyme in Idellnes to the greate prejudice of the Common Welthe be trayned in vertuous and Commodyous Labor, And beynge enformed of some greate hope of a discoverie to be hadd by her trustie and well beloved servaunte Walter Raleigh Esquier of an unknowen Lande never hertofore possessed by anye Christian Prynce or Christian people The nerenes whereof and Infynite Comodities of the same mighte yelde unto this her Realme of Englande the benefittes before remembred and manye others, Her majestie for the consideracions aforesaid hath by her heighnes Letteres Patentes under her greate Seale of England graunted unto the said Walter Raleigh in manner and forme folowinge videlicet....

Sythence which Letters Patentes made &

graunted as aforesaid to the said Walter Rawleigh, There is discoverd by the meanes charge Labor & procurement of the said Walter Rawleigh a Land called Wyngandacoia, not inhabited by anye Christian Prince or Christian people And some of the people borne in those parties brought home into this our Realme of England by whose meanes & direccion & by suche of her maiesties subiectes as were sent thyther by the said Walter Rawleigh singuler great comodities of that Lande are revealed & made knowen unto us which discoverie hath byn heretofore attempted by dyverse persons & never brought to any suche perfection

It maye therfore please the Queenes most exelent maiestie with thassent of the Lordes spirituall & temporall And the Comons in this presente parliament assembled And by the aucthoritie of the same That it be enacted That the said Walter Rawleigh his heires & assignes shall & maye by the aucthoritie of this present parliament from henceforth for ever Have holde & enjoye the saide Land so discouerd with all realties previledges powers prehemynences & authorities menconed & conteyned in the said Lettres Patentes accordinge to the purport effect & true meanynge of the same Letters Patentes and that the said Lettres Patentes and all and singuler the grauntes Liberties priviledges & other thinges therin conteyned shalbe by aucthoritie aforesaid Established approved confirmed allowed and be effectuall unto the said Walter Rawleigh his heires & assignes accordinge

to the tenour & purport of the said Lettres Patentes

Provided allwayes that this Acte or anie thinge therein contayyned shall not in any wise be intended to geve any Licence power or Aucthority to any person or persons beinge in Prison either uppon Execucion at the sute of any person for debte or being imprisoned or under Arreste for any other cause whatsoever or the wife ward or apprentyce of any other person or persons to departe this Realme or to geve Any Lycence power or Aucthority to the said Walter Rawley hys heyres or assignes to enlardge any such person or to take or sende any such person or persons over Sea or [ ] or take any shippinge, or furnyture for shipping withowt the assent & good wylle of the person or persons this Acte or any thinge therein contaygned to the contrary hereof in any wyse notwithstandinge

[Endorsed:] [Act for t]he confermacion [of l]ettres patentes [grau]nted to Walter [Ral]eghe esquier

Lune xiij° decembris 1584 The fyrst Reading

post meridiem The secund Reading and commytted

Jouis xvij° decembris 1584 Ordered to be ingrossed

Veneris xviij° decembris 1584 The thirde Readinge and with a proviso added was passed upon the questyon

Novembris et Decembris 1584

Judicium

RICHARD HAKLUYT'S LETTERS TO
SIR FRANCIS WALSINGHAM, JANUARY TO APRIL, 1585

RICHARD HAKLUYT was secretary and chaplain to the English embassy in Paris from 1583 to 1588 when Sir Edward Stafford was ambassador. He frequently reported to Sir Francis Walsingham any information he picked up on overseas activities as well as other news from France. In 1584 (429) he urges that a voyage of discovery should be made before the expiry in June of Sir Humphrey Gilbert's patent, granted for six years in June, 1578, and expresses his willingness to make the voyage. As far as is known he never visited America at this time or later. He follows this (430) a few months later with a plea for the establishment of a lectureship for the training of masters and pilots in the new scientific navigation to ensure that England did not lag behind France and Spain in nautical expertise.

Document 429 is from P.R.O., State Papers, Domestic, Elizabeth I, S.P. 12/167, 7; printed in E. G. R. Taylor, *Hakluyts*, I, 205–207. Document 430 is from P.R.O., S.P., Domestic, Elizabeth I, S.P. 12/180, 1; printed in Taylor, *Hakluyts*, I, 208–210, extract.

429. January 7, 1584. Richard Hakluyt to Sir Francis Walsingham.

Right Honorable

I understand from your servant Curtis your good reception of my hastie letter, your special favour and good will towards me, as also your expectation of my diligent inquirie of such thinges as may yeld any light into our western discoveries. For the two former I yeld most humble thanks, and for the later I nether have nor wil omitte any possible diligence, expecting intelligenses thereof from Roan, Diepe and St. Malo very shortly.

In Paris I have seen in one mans house called Perosse the value of five thousand crowns worth of furres, as sables, bevers, otters and other sortes which he bought in August laste of the men of St Malo, and the yeare before, he tolde me, he bestowed four thousand crownes with them in the like commodities. He gave me further to understand that he sawe great quantities of buff hides which they brought home and sent into the Lowe Countrys to sell. Al which commodities with diverse other of noe lesse value are brought out of the most northerly partes of those countreys whereunto our voyage of inhabiting is intended.

And nowe because I knowe that this present enterprise is like soone to waxe colde and fall to the ground unlesse in this second voyage al diligence in serching out everie hope of gayne be used, And calling to mynd that your honor made a motion heretofore unto me, whether I could be contented to goe myselfe in the action, these are to put your honor out of doubte that for myne parte I am most willinge to goe now in the same this present setting forth and in the service of God and my country to employ al my simple observations readinges and conference whatsoever. For obtaining leave of my Lord Ambassador heere to departe I doubte not but to find meanes of myselfe, seeing he may have inough to supply my roome.

For leave of my colledg and entertaynment in this voyage I wil wholy referre yt unto your honor, who wish mee so well as you wil not see my poore estate impared. Because the tyme is exceeding shorte I wold desire your honors present answere, uppon sight whereof with wings of Pegasus I wold soone fly into England.

I have talked twise with Don Antonio of Portugal and with five or six of his best captaynes and pilotes, one of whom was borne in Easte India. They al wish al prosperitie to Her Majestie and yourselfe, and say that if the Queene of England will joyne with their Master, whose strength by sea they commende unto the skyes, that they know how the King of Spayne, our mortal enemy, might easily be met withal, and she much enriched. The number of Portingalls which hange uppon the poore King are about an hundred or sixe score. Divers of them are lately come unto him, among whom are one or two are come out of the East India overlande by Tripoly in Siria. They have a voyage in hand with five or six sayle of ships, which are in preparing at Newe Haven for the coste of Guinea and the castle of Mina, wherein most of the Portingals aforesayd are to be employed, being joyned in company with the french. They set forward as I heare within this monthe.

One Sinior Andreas borne in Savoy is nowe heere in Paris, which hath bin lately in the island of Japan, with whom by meanes of Mr. Doctor Pena, I shal have conference within a day or twoe. Diverse other intelligences tending toward the furtherance of our western planting and discoverie I looke for from sundrie places very shortly. In the meane season with my humble dutie to your honor and to your worthie and honorable sonne in lawe, I cease for the present and beseech the Almightie to hold you bothe in safe garde.

It was told me by Perosse of whom I spoke before, and by Andrewe Thevet the Kinges cosmographer, that Duke Joyeuse, Admiral of France, and the Cardinal of Burbon and their frendes, have had a meaning to send out certayne ships to inhabite some place for the north part of America, and to carry thither many friers and other religiouse persons, but I thinke they be not in haste to do yt.

Paris, from my Lord Ambassadours house, the vii of Januarie 1584.

Your honors most humble to command
    [signed:] Richard Hakluyt, Preacher

430. April 1, 1584. Richard Hakluyt to Sir Francis Walsingham.

Hakluyt did his best to maintain contact with the expeditions that were being prepared in England for North America by Christopher Carleill and under the auspices of Sir Walter Ralegh. As chaplain secretary to the English embassy in Paris (1583–1588) he was in the position of a modern attaché, concerned to report on general news to the secretary of state, but specially concerned with economic and intellectual information that might further the overseas activities in North America which he and his master Walsingham were concerned to assist.

Right Honorable,

The famouse disputations in al partes of the mathematikes which at this present are held in Paris, for the gayning of the lecture which was erected by the worthy scholer Petrus Ramus, to the great increase of those excellent sciences, put me in mynd to solicite your honour agayne and agayne for the erection of that lecture of the arte of navigation whereof I have had some speech with your honor, Sir Francis Drake and Alderman Barnes and other. And that you might meet with al inconveniences which might frustrate the expected profit which is hoped for by the erection of the same, I send your honour here the testament of Petrus Ramus, newly put out agayne in printe, and sent unto me by Monseer Bergeron,

Ramus his executor; whereby you may see first the exceeding sheale the man had to benefit his country in bestowing 500 livers, which (as your honour knoweth) is fiftie pounds sterling, uppon establishing of that lecture, bequething not halfe as much to al the kindred and frendes he had in the world. Secondly you may note that he being one of the most famouse clerkes of Europe, thought those sciences next after divinitie to be most necessarie for the commonwelth, in that he erected a new lecture of the same, whereas there was one before erected and endowed with fiftie pounds stipend by the kings of France. Thirdly that most provident order which the good man by his will hath taken is most requisite to be put in execution in England: which is that everie three yeeres, there shalbe publicke disputations signified to al men by publicke writing, wherein yt shalbe free for any man for three monethes space to dispute agaynst the reader for the tyme being, who yf he be found negligent, or yf any one of the competitors be found more worthy by the opinion of certayne indifferent men of lerninge chosen out of the purpose to be judges, that then the unworthie shall give place to the more sufficient; who soe being placed is bound in three yeeres space to read through the course of the mathematikes.

Yf by your honours instigation her Majestie might be enduced to erecte such a lecture in Oxford, and the like for the arte of navigation might by some other meanes be established at London, allowing to ech of them fiftie poundes yearly with the same conditions, in my simple judgement yt wold be the best hundred pounds that was bestowed this five hundred yeares in England. For yt is not unknowne unto your wisdome, how necessarie for the service of warres arithmeticke and geometrie are, and for our new discoveries and longer voyages by sea the arte of navigation is, which is compounded of many partes of the aforesayd sciences.

Understandinge hearetofore of your honours greate abundance of business, and your dangerouse sicknes, I thought it not meet to trouble your honour with such thinges as I had carefully sought out here in France concerning the furtherance of the westerne discoveries but chose rather to imparte the same with Master Carlile, which thing I also did. But being lately advertised of your recovery (for which I humblie thank almightie God) I was bold to signifie unto your honour my dealing with Horatio Palvasini to become an adventurer in those westerne voyages, and among other talke, alleaged your good disposition to the same, which he hearing of replyed very chearfully that yf he were moved thereunto by the least word from your honour, he would put in his hundred pound adventure or more. If Master Carlile be gone, yet yt might come in good time to serve Master Frobishers turne, yf your wisdome shold like wel of yt, seeing he setteth not forth as I understand, until the beginning of May. . . .

431. [1584–1585]. Notes, possibly by Sir Roger Williams, for the guidance of Ralegh and Cavendish.

These notes on establishing a settlement, mostly about its defense, are anonymous, but a probable author is Roger Williams since passages, especially those on fortifications, in his A briefe discourse of warre *(1590) closely resemble these notes. Thomas Cavendish is associated with Ralegh only on the 1585 expedition which firmly links these notes to that date. References to men with other skills such as geographers and painters connect with the earlier Bavin instructions (401) and the later partnership between Thomas Harriot and John White (365).*

Essex County Record Office, County Hall, Chelmsford, MS D/DRh, M1; printed in D. B. Quinn, Roanoke voyages, *I (1955), 130–139.*

For Master Rauleys Viage.

In to that cuntery I would have men geo armored of this sorte, for that they ar to deall with naked men, yett will I have furnytur to prevent the Invasion of the Spanyardes.

The Number being, 800, I would have them thus devided.

Fyrst 400. harqubusiers.

Then 100. swordes and lyght moddena targetes

Then 150. long bows,

Then 100, Armed men with millan corsseletes lyght

Then 50. Armed men with lyght Corsseletes with short weapons.

Of this nomber I would dayly have in the forte 100 in garde, and, so, nyghtly for the sentenels, all the rest should labor by turns tyll the forte be Ended.

Whylst the forte is a buldyng I would have, 200, that should continually geo a discoveryng, and returne every eyght or tenthe day, and then 200, mor to do the lyke and that Companys that Com from discovery to be iij days excempte from labor wache or ward after ther returne, so as yow shall have, 500, men to labor for the buldyng of your forte

I would not have any Company above, 50, bycause the mor Commaunders the better servis, and the Companys wilbe the fayrer and better

What maner of forte I woulde have I would have It a pentangell in this manner, with, v, large bulwarkes the Casemates of the Boulwarkes large and open, with a way out of the bulwarke and an other Into the Streat The Collionsides or ocrechons, large and longe, The Curtyns sumwhat slant, that the yearthe may lye the faster and the rampir of the Curtyns very braude, Every bulwarke shall have bye It a cavalir to beat the feald, or tow wer better, In the mydst I would have a markitt plase large, for assemblys, and to sytt in if neade be.

I would have Every streat strayt to every bulwarke, and to Every gatt and to the mydst of Every Curtyne, so as standyng In the market plase yow may see all the bulwarkes Curtyns and gates.

The diche I would have large with walles, beyound the diche a 20 foot from the diche I would have a wall of, 4. foot hyght with arayll on the tope so as the tope of this wall shouldbe within a 3 foot as hyght as the parrepett of my Curtyns or bulwarkes. Within the diche I would have a hyght pall of xv foot hyght by Cause It shall prevent any suddeyn Scallado, for that your forte is of yearthe, which yow know in tyme moulders. This forte with 500, men with the help and Incorragment of the Commander wilbe fenyshed In a monthe. bysydes the howses. which being fynyshed I know no reason but it is abell long to hould a gaynst all the forces of Indda. how I would have It seated, eyther uppon rocke, marrishe, an Iland or peninsulla, if this forte wer In an Iland then would I have on the next land to It a forte, wherby I would always be sure of a landyng assured, and of a retreat, for nothing would be so dangerus as to lande men In disorder, neyther any thing so eminent a distruction as Imbarkyn followd by the Enymy,

What men ar nessesary to Carry. I will leave the ministers and officers of war, which all men know what ar nessesary, but the choyse of them is a great matter, for a discreat vigelant temporat experimented and a vallient commander, acthiuethe all with honor, and the, undiscreat rashe, unexperimented and Necligent, is the utter over throw of all bothe army and honner, I leave this to his Jugment who chuses & [pays?] the officers I woulde have, an Ingenyr and Cunynge trevese Master whos Jugment wer abell to know the plases of Best advantages to buylde on, he to bulde, with Jugment that his forte be not to byge, that his men may not be abell to defend It, nor to littell for that is mor dangerus, and an ould maxime a monxt the men of war that nothing that is littell Is abell to hould longe. for divers reasons I could allege.

Then I would have a phisitien as well for the healthe of the souldier as to discover the simpels of earbs plantes trees roothes, and stons, [a] good geographer to make discription of the landes discoverd, and with hym an exilent paynter, potticaris and Surgiantes for low sycniss and woundes.

An alcamist is not Impertinent, to trye the mettaylls that maybe discoverd and an perfett lapidary not to be forgotten. Masons, Carpenters. makers. of mudwals, su[m] of myners of Cornwell, Sume exelent husband men, with all thinges appertayninge to husbandry, and all maner of Sead Corne. for all other [Sienus?] nessessaty will not spare them. at home,.

What manner of geovernement is to be used and what offics to geoverne.

The generall, to Commaund absolutely within the forte and without all matters marshall, to geve all offices In the geovernement, to punnyshe any man by his Commandment but not to prosead to deathe of any man but by order of law. To have autoryty to pardon all offences saving Treason to hir Maiestie and the Cuntrye.

Tow Justis one cauled hight Judge. who shall sett uppon all matters In Law and have autoryty to make an end definitive of all Causes, and from whos Jugment no appelation, nor no Contradiction no not at the Counsell tabell, for wher appeals ar contraversis never sease.

For the Collonell, the sergant maior, the marshall and Captens all know ther offices. and what by duty they ar to do,

The hyght Tresorir shall once every year yeald up his account unto the geoverneur and Counsell. he shall reseave all appertaynynge unto the Prince, and shall geve all officers appertaynyng to a hyght treserer which is petty treserers audites, Customers Conptrulers searches & suche lyke.

The Admirall shall once every. 3. monthes be accountabell unto the hyght Tresorir of all suche parte as shall appertayne to the Prince whiche shalbe the fyfte parte of all acquisted.

When the generall shall send out any Company of discovery ther shalbe over, 200, which is iiij Companys, and with them shall ever geo Sume great officer and a Tresorir to reseave the fyft for the Queens Maiestie, That the chefe officer shall aunswer for his Companyes and Every particuler Capten In his Company for Commyttyng any of thes disorders

First that no Souldier do violat any woman, 2 That no Souldier do take any mans goodes forcibly from hym. 3 That no Indian be forced to labor unwillyngly. 4. That no Souldier shall defraud Her Maieste of her fyfte. 5 That no Souldier abbandon his ensegne without leave, of his Capten, 6 That non shall stryke or mysuse any Indian. 7 That non shall Enter any Indians howse without his leave, 8 That non shall stryke within the forte nor fytt within a myll of It. 9 That non offer to draw any weapon uppon any Conseler or his Captain, 10 That no. Souldier sleep in sentenell or abbandon his sentenell or garde

To the fyrst deathe, To the second a dubbell restutution, if the souldier be not abell, to have a years Imprisonment the whype and bannishement or condemd to the gallys for vij years. and the party to have his restutition of the. Prince, To the, 3. iij monthes Imprisonment, to the .4. deathe or a perpetuall Condemnation to the gallys or myns. to the 5 deathe or vij yeres Slavery to the 6, to have xx blows with a cuggell In the presentz of the Indian strucken. To the .7. vj monthes imprisonment or slavery To the .8. lose of hand. To the .9. & 10th present deathe without remission.

[Endorsed across fold:] Notes geven to Master Candishe.

432. 1584. Arthur Barlowe on the first Virginia voyage.

This account of the reconnaissance voyage of 1584, based on the ship's journal, is smoothed out and edited to give an idyllic picture of Virginia. It was used by Ralegh in the promotion of his parliamentary bill (428). The ships are not named, but the "Admiral," Philip Amadas captain, could have been the Bark Raleigh, *which turned back on Gilbert's voyage of 1583, and the pinnace, Arthur Barlowe captain, the* Dorothy *(434), both owned by Ralegh.*

Printed in R. Hakluyt, Principall navigations *(1589), pp. 728–733;* Principal navigations, *III (1600), 246–251, VIII (1904), 297–310; D. B. Quinn,* Roanoke voyages, *I, (1955), 91–116. Document 433 from R. Holinshed,* Chronicles, *III (1587), 1369, is the first published account of this voyage.*

The first voyage made to the coastes of America, with two barkes, wherein were Captaines Master Philip Amadas, and Master Arthur Barlowe, who discovered part of the Countrey, now called Virginia, Anno 1584: Written by one of the said Captaines, and sent to sir Walter Raleigh, knight, at whose charge, and direction, the said voyage was set foorth.

The 27. day of Aprill, in the yeere of our redemption, 1584. we departed the west of England, with two barkes, well furnished with men and victuals, having receyved our last, and perfect directions by your letters, confirming the former instructions, and commandements delivered by your selfe at our leaving the river of Thames. And I thinke it a matter both unnecessarie, for the manifest discoverie of the Countrey, as also for tediousnes sake, to remember unto you the diurnall of our course, sailing thither, and returning: onely I have presumed to present unto you this brief discourse, by which you may judge how profitable this land is likely to succeede, as well to your selfe, (by whose direction and charge, and by whose servants this our discoverie hath beene performed) as also to her Highnes, and the Common wealth, in which we hope your wisedome will be satisfied, considering, that as much by us hath bene brought to light, as by those small meanes, and number of men we had, could any way have bene expected, or hoped for.

The tenth of May, we arrived at the Canaries, and the tenth of June in this present yeere, we were fallen with the Islands of the West Indies, keeping a more southeasterly course then was needefull, because we doubted that the current of the Baye of Mexico, disbogging betweene the Cape of Florida, and the Havana, had bene of greater force then afterwardes we found it to be. At which Islands we found the aire very unwholsome, and our men grewe for the most part ill disposed: so that having refreshed our selves with sweete water, and fresh victuall, we departed the twelfth daye after our arrivall there. These Islands, with the rest adjoynging, are so well knowen to your selfe, and to many others, as I will not trouble you, with the remembrance of them.

The second of July, we found shole water, which smelt so sweetely, and was so strong a smell, as if we had bene in the midst of some delicate garden, abounding with all kind of odoriferous flowers, by which we were assured, that the land could not be farre distant: and keeping good watch, and bearing but slacke saile, the fourth of the same moneth, we arrived upon the coast, which we supposed to be a continent, and firme lande, and wee sailed along the same, a hundred and twentie English miles, before we could finde any entrance, or river, issuing into the Sea. The first that appeared unto us, we entred, though not without some difficultie, and cast anker about three harquebushot within the havens mouth, on the left hande of the same: and after thankes given to God for our safe arrival thither, we manned our boates, and went to viewe the lande next adjoyning, and to "take possession of the same, in the right of the Queenes most excellent Majestie, as rightfull Queene, and Princesse of the same, and after delivered the same over to your use, according to her Majesties grant, and letters patents, under her Highnes great Seale. Which being performed, according to the ceremonies used in such enterprises, wee viewed the lande about us, being whereas we first landed, very sandie, and lowe towardes the water side, but so full of grapes, as the very beating, and surge of the Sea overflowed them, of which we founde such plentie, as well there, as in all places else, both on the sande, and on the greene soile on the hils, as in the plaines, as well on every little shrubbe, as also climing towardes the toppes of the high Cedars, that I thinke in all the world the like aboundance is not to be founde: and my selfe having seene those partes of Europe that most abound, finde such difference, as were incredible to be written.

We passed from the Sea side, towardes the toppes of those hils next adjoyning, being but of meane heighth, and from thence wee behelde the Sea on both sides to the North, and to the South, finding no ende any of both waies. This lande laye stretching it selfe to the West, which after wee founde to be but an Island of twentie leagues long, and not above sixe miles broade. Under the banke or hill, whereon we stoode, we behelde the vallies replenished with goodly Cedar trees, and having discharged our harquebushot, such a flocke of Cranes (the most part white) arose under us, with such a crye redoubled by many Ecchoes, as if an armie of men had showted all together.

This Island had many goodly woods, and full of Deere, Conies, Hares, and Fowle, even in the middest of Summer, in incredible aboundance. The woodes are not such as you finde in Bohemia, Moscovia, or Hyrcania, barren and fruitlesse, but the highest, and reddest Cedars of the world, farre bettering the Cedars of the Açores, of the Indias, or of Lybanus, Pynes, Cypres, Sassaphras, the Lentisk, or the tree that beareth the Masticke, the tree that beareth the rinde of blacke Sinamon, of which Master Winter brought from the Streights of Magellane, and many other of excellent smell, and qualitie. We remained by the side of this Island two whole daies, before we sawe any people of the Countrey: the third daye we espied one small boate rowing towards us, having in it three persons: this boate came to the landes side, foure harquebushot from our shippes, and there two of the people remaining, the thirde came along the shoare side towardes us, and we being then all within boord, he walked up and downe uppon the point of the lande next to us: then the Master, and the Pilot of the Admirall, Simon Ferdinando, and the Captaine Philip Amadas, my selfe, and others, rowed to the lande, whose comming this fellowe attended, never making any shewe of feare, or doubt. And after he had spoken of many things not understoode by us, we brought him with his owne good liking, aboord the shippes, and gave him a shirt, a hatte, and some other things, and made him taste of our wine, and our meate, which he liked very well: and after having viewed both barkes, he departed, and went to his owne boate againe, which hee had left in a little Cove, or Creeke adjoyning: assoone as hee was two bowe shoote into the water, hee fell to fishing, and in lesse then halfe an howre, hee had laden his boate as deepe, as it could swimme, with which he came againe to the point of the lande, and there he devided his fishe into two partes, pointing one part to the shippe, and the other to the Pinnesse: which after he had (as much as he might,) requited the former benefits receaved, he departed out of our sight.

The next day there came unto us divers boates, and in one of them the Kings brother, accompanied with fortie or fiftie men, very handsome, and goodly people, and in their behaviour as mannerly, and civill, as any of Europe. His name was Granganimeo, and the King is called Wingina, the countrey Wingandacoa, (and nowe by her Majestie, Virginia,) the manner of his comming was in this sorte: hee left his boates altogether, as the first man did a little from the shippes by the shoare, and came along to the place over against the shippes, followed with fortie men. When hee came to the place, his servants spread a long matte uppon the grounde, on which he sate downe, and at the other ende of the matte, foure others of his companie did the like: the rest of his men stoode round about him, somewhat a farre off: when wee came to the shoare to him with our weapons, he never mooved from his place, nor any of the other foure, nor never mistrusted any harme to be offered from us, but sitting still, he beckoned us to come, and sitte by him, which wee perfourmed: and beeing sette, hee makes all signes of joy, and welcome, striking on his head, and his breast, and afterwardes on ours, to shewe we were all one, smiling, and making shewe the best hee could, of all love, and familiaritie. After hee had made a long speech unto us, wee presented him with divers thinges, which hee received very joyfully, and thankefully. None of his companye durst to speake one worde all the tyme: onely the foure which were at the other ende, spake one in the others eare very softly.

The King is greatly obeyed, and his brothers, and children reverenced: the King himselfe in person was at our beeing there sore wounded, in a fight which he had with the King of the next Countrey, called Wingina, and was shotte in two places through the bodye, and once cleane thorough the thigh, but yet he recovered: by reason whereof, and for that hee laye at the chiefe Towne of the Countrey, beeing six dayes journeye off, wee sawe him not at all.

After wee had presented this his brother, with such things as we thought he liked, we likewise gave somewhat to the other that sate with him on the matte: but presently he arose, and tooke all from them, and put it into his owne basket, making signes and tokens, that all things ought to be delivered unto him, and the rest were but his servants, and followers. A daye or two after this, we fell to trading with them, exchanging some thinges that we had for Chammoys, Buffe, and Deere skinnes: when we shewed him all our packet of merchandize, of all things that he saw, a bright tinne dishe most pleased him, which he presently tooke up, & clapt it before his breast, & after made a hole in the brimme thereof, & hung it about his necke, making signes, that it would defende him against his enemies arrowes: for those people maintaine a deadlie and terrible warre, with the people and King adjoyning. We exchanged our tinne dishe for twentie skinnes, woorth twentie Crownes, or twentie Nobles: and a copper kettle for fiftie skinnes woorth fiftie Crownes. They offered us very good exchange for our hatchets, and axes, and for knives, and would have given any thing for swordes: but we would not depart with any. After two or three daies, the Kings brother came aboord the shippes, and dranke wine, and ate of our meate, and of our bread, and liked exceedingly thereof: and after a few daies overpassed, he brought his wife with him to the shippes, his daughter, and two or three little children: his wife was very well favored, of meane stature, and very bashfull: she had on her backe a long cloke of leather, with the furre side next to her bodie, and before her a peece of the same: about her forehead, she had a broad bande

of white Corrall, and so had her husband many times: in her eares she had bracelets of pearles, hanging downe to her middle, (whereof we delivered your Worship a litle bracelet) and those were of the bignes of good pease. The rest of her women of the better sorte, had pendants of copper, hanging in every eare, and some of the children of the Kings brother, and other Noble men, have five or six in every eare: he himselfe had upon his head, a broad plate of golde, or copper, for being unpolished we knew not what metall it should be, neither would he by any meanes suffer us to take it off his head, but feeling it, it would bowe very easily. His apparell was as his wives, onely the women weare their haire long on both sides, and the men but on one. They are of colour yellowish, and their haire blacke for the most, and yet we sawe children that had very fine aburne, and chestnut colour haire.

After that these women had bene there, there came downe from all parts great store of people, bringing with them leather, corrall, divers kindes of dies very excellent, and exchanged with us: but when Granganimeo, the kings brother was present, none durst to trade but himselfe, except such as weare redde peeces of copper on their heades, like himselfe: for that is the difference betweene the Noble men, and Governours of Countries, and the meaner sort. And we both noted there, and you have understood since by these men, which we brought home, that no people in the worlde carry more respect to their King, Nobilitie, and Governours, then these doe. The Kings brothers wife, when she came to us, as she did many times, shee was followed with fortie or fiftie women alwaies: and when she came into the shippe, she left them all on lande, saving her two daughters, her nurce, and one or two more. The Kings brother alwaies kept this order, as many boates as he would come withall to the shippes, so many fires would he make on the shoare a farre off, to the ende wee might understand with what strength, and companie he approched. Their boates are made of one tree, either of Pine, or of Pitch trees: a wood not commonly knowen to our people, nor found growing in England. They have no edge tooles to make them withall: if they have any, they are very fewe, and those it seemes they had twentie yeeres since, which as those two men declared, was out of a wracke which happened upon their coast of some

Christian shippe, being beaten that way by some storme, and outragious weather, whereof none of the people were saved, but onely the shippe, or some part of her, being cast upon the sande, out of whose sides they drewe the nailes, and spikes, and with those they made their best instruments. Their manner of making their boates, is this: they burne downe some great tree, or take such as are winde fallen, and putting myrrhe, and rosen upon one side thereof, they sette fire into it, and when it hath burnt it hollowe, they cutte out the coale with their shells, and ever where they would burne it deeper or wider, they laye on their gummes, which burneth away the timber, and by this meanes they fashion very fine boates, and such as will transport twentie men. Their oares are like scoopes, and many times they sette with long poles, as the depth serveth.

The Kings brother had great liking of our armour, a sworde, and divers other things, which we had: and offered to laye a great boxe of pearle in gage for them: but wee refused it for this time, because we would not make them knowe, that wee esteemed thereof, untill we had understoode in what places of the Countrey the pearle grewe: which nowe your Worshippe doth very well understand.

He was very just of his promise: for many times wee delivered him merchandize uppon his worde, but ever he came within the daye, and performed his promise. Hee sent us every daye a brase or two of fatte Buckes, Conies, Hares, Fishe, the best of the worlde. Hee sent us divers kindes of fruites, Melons, Walnuts, Cucumbers, Gourdes, Pease, and divers rootes, and fruites very excellent good, and of their Countrey corne, which is very white, faire, and well tasted, and groweth three times in five monethes: in Maye they sowe, in July they reape: in June they sowe, in August they reape: in July they sowe, in September they reape: onely they cast the corne into the ground, breaking a little of the soft turfe with a wooddten mattocke, or pickeaxe: our selves prooved the soile, and put some of our Pease into the ground, and in tenne daies they were of foureteene ynches high: they have also Beanes very faire, of divers colours, and wonderfull plentie: some growing naturally, and some in their gardens, and so have they both wheat and oates.

The soile is the most plentifull, sweete, fruitfull, and wholsome of all the world: there are above foureteene severall sweete smelling timber trees, and the most part of their underwoods are Bayes, and such like: they have those Okes that we have, but farre greater and better. After they had bene divers times aboord our shippes, my selfe, with seven more, went twentie mile into the River, that runneth toward the Citie of Skicoake, which River they call Occam: and the evening following, we came to an Island, which they call Roanoak, distant from the harbour by which we entred, seven leagues: and at the North ende thereof, was a village of nine houses, built of Cedar, and fortified round about with sharpe trees, to keepe out their enemies, and the entrance into it made it like a turne pike very artificially: when we came towards it, standing neere unto the waters side, the wife of Grangyno, the Kings brother, came running out to meete us very cheerefully, and friendly, her husband was not then in the village: some of her people she commanded to drawe our boate on the shoare, for the beating of the billoe: others shee appointed to carry us on their backes to the dry ground, and others to bring our oares into the house, for feare of stealing. When we were come into the utter roome, having five roomes in her house, she caused us to sitte downe by a great fire, and after tooke off our clothes, and washed them, and dried them againe: some of the women pulled off our stockings, and washed them, some washed our feete in warme water, and shee her selfe tooke great paines to see all thinges ordered in the best manner shee coulde, making great haste to dresse some meate for us to eate.

After we had thus dried our selves, shee brought us into the inner roome, where shee set on the boord standing along the house, some wheate like furmentie, sodden Venison, and roasted, fishe sodden, boyled, and roasted, Melons rawe, and sodden, rootes of divers kindes, and divers fruites: their drinke is commonly water, but while the grape lasteth, they drinke wine, and for want of caskes to keepe it all the yeere after, they drinke water, but it is sodden with Ginger in it, and blacke Sinamon, and sometimes Sassaphras, and divers other wholesome, and medicinable hearbes and trees. We were entertained with all love, and kindnes, and with as much bountie, after their manner, as they could possibly devise. Wee found the people most gentle, loving, and faithfull, void of all guile, and treason, and such as lived after the manner of the golden age. The earth bringeth foorth all things in aboundance, as in the first creation, without toile or labour. The people onely care to defend them selves from the cold, in their short winter, and to feede themselves with such meate as the soile affoordeth: their meate is very well sodden, and they make broth very sweete, and savorie: their vessels are earthen pots, very large, white, and sweete: their dishes are woodden platters of sweete timber: within the place where they feede, was their lodging, and within that their Idoll, which they worship, of which they speake uncredible things. While we were at meate, there came in at the gates, two or three men with their bowes, and arrowes, from hunting, whome when we espied, we beganne to looke one towardes another, and offered to reach our weapons: but assoone as she espied our mistrust, she was very much mooved, and caused some of her men to runne out, and take away their bowes, and arrowes, and breake them, and withall beate the poore fellowes out of the gate againe. When we departed in the evening, and would not tarry all night, she was very sorie, and gave us into our boate our supper halfe dressed, pots, and all, and brought us to our boates side, in which wee laye all night, remooving the same a pretie distance from the shoare: shee perceiving our jealousie, was much grieved, and sent divers men, and thirtie women, to sitte all night on the bankes side by us, and sent us into our boates five mattes to cover us from the rayne, using very many wordes to intreate us to rest in their houses: but because wee were fewe men, and if wee had miscarried, the voyage had beene in very great daunger, wee durst not adventure any thing, although there was no cause of doubt: for a more kinde, and loving people, there can not be found in the world, as farre as we have hitherto had triall.

Beyonde this Islande, there is the maine lande, and over against this Islande falleth into this spatious water, the great river called Occam, by the Inhabitants, on which standeth a Towne called Pemeoke, and six daies journey further upon the same is situate their greatest citie, called Schycoake, which this people affirme to be very great: but the Savages were never at it, onely they speake of it, by the report of their Fathers, and other men, whome they have heard affirme it, to be above one daies journey about.

Into this river falleth another great river,

called Cipo, in which there is found great store of the Muscels, in which there are pearles: likewise there descendeth into this Occam, another river, called Nomopana, on the one side whereof standeth a great Towne, called Chowanoake, and the Lord of that Towne and Countrey, is called Pooneno: this Pooneno is not subject to the King of Wingandacoa, but is a free Lorde. Beyonde this Countrey, is there another King, whome they call Menatoan, and these three Kinges are in league with eache other. Towards the Sunne set, foure daies journey, is situate a Towne called Sequotan, which is the Westermost Towne of Wingandacoa, neere unto which, six and twentie yeeres past, there was a shippe cast away, whereof some of the people were saved, and those were white people, whom the Countrey people preserved.

And after ten daies, remaining in an out Island unhabited, called Wococan, they with the helpe of some of the dwellers of Sequotan, fastened two boates of the Countrey together, and made mastes unto them, and sailes of their shirtes, and having taken into them such victuals as the Countrey yeelded, they departed after they had remained in this out Island three weekes: but shortly after, it seemed they were cast away, for the boates were found uppon the coast, cast aland in another Island adjoyning: other then these, there was never any people apparelled, or white of colour, either seene, or heard of amongst these people, and these aforesaide were seene only of the inhabitants of Sequotan: which appeared to be very true, for they wondered mervelously when we were amongest them, at the whitenes of our skinnes, ever coveting to touch our breastes, and to view the same: besides they had our shippes in marvelous admiration, and all things els was so strange unto them, as it appeared that none of them had ever seene the like. When we discharged any peece, were it but a harquebush, they would tremble thereat for very feare, and for the strangenes of the same: for the weapons which themselves use, are bowes and arrowes: the arrowes are but of small canes, headed with a sharpe shell, or tooth of a fishe sufficient enough to kill a naked man. Their swordes are of wood hardened: likewise they use woodden breastplates for their defense. They have besides a kinde of clubbe, in the ende whereof they fasten the sharpe hornes of a stagge, or other beast. When they goe to warres, they carry with them their Idoll, of whome they aske counsell, as the

Romanes were woont of the Oracle of Apollo. They sing songs as they march towardes the battell, in steede of drummes, and trumpets: their warres are very cruell, and bloodie, by reason whereof, and of their civill dissentions, which have happened of late yeeres amongst them, the people are marvelously wasted, and in some places, the Countrey left desolate.

Adjoyning unto this Towne aforesaide, called Sequotan, beginneth a Countrey called Ponouike belonging to another King, whom they call Piemacum, and this King is in league with the next King, adjoyning towardes the setting of the Sunne, and the Countrey Neiosioke, situate uppon the side of a goodly River, called Neus: these Kings have mortall warre with Wingina, King of Wingandacoa, but about two yeeres past, there was a peace made betweene the King Piemacum, and the Lorde of Sequotan, as these men which we have brought with us into England, have made us understande: but there remaineth a mortall malice in the Sequotanes, for many injuries and slaughters done upon them by this Piemacum. They invited divers men, and thirtie women, of the best of his Countrey, to their Towne to a feast: and when they were altogether merrie, and praying before their Idoll, which is nothing else, but a meere illusion of the Devill: the Captaine or Lorde of the Towne came suddenly upon them, and slewe them every one, reserving the women, and children: and these two have oftentimes since perswaded us to surprise Piemacum his Towne, having promised, and assured us, that there will be founde in it great store of commodities. But whether their perswasion be to the ende they may be revenged of their enemies, or for the love they beare to us, we leave that to the triall hereafter.

Beyond this Island, called Croonoake, are many Islands, very plentifull of fruites and other naturall increases, together with many Townes, and villages, along the side of the continent, some bounding upon the Islands, and some stretching up further into the land.

When we first had sight of this Countrey, some thought the first lande we sawe, to be the continent: but after wee entred into the Haven, wee sawe before us another mightie long Sea: for there lieth along the coast a tracte of Islands, two hundreth miles in length, adjoyning to the Ocean sea, and betweene the Islands, two or three entrances: when you are entred betweene them (these Islands being very narrowe, for the most part, as in most places sixe miles broad, in some places lesse, in fewe more,) then there appeareth another great Sea, containing in bredth in some places, fortie, and in some fiftie, in some twentie miles over, before you come unto the continent: and in this inclosed Sea, there are about a hundreth Islands of divers bignesses, whereof one is sixteene miles long, at which we were, finding it to be a most pleasant, and fertile ground, replenished with goodly Cedars, and divers other sweete woods, full of Currans, of flaxe, and many other notable commodities, which we at that time had no leasure to view. Besides this Island, there are many, as I have saide, some of two, of three, of foure, of five miles, some more, some lesse, most beautifull, and pleasant to behold, replenished with Deere, Conies, Hares, and divers beastes, and about them the goodliest and best fishe in the world, and in greatest aboundance.

Thus Sir, we have acquainted you with the particulars of our discoverie, made this present voyage, as farre foorth, as the shortnes of the time we there continued, would affoord us to take viewe of: and so contenting our selves with this service at this time, which we hope hereafter to inlarge, as occasion and assistance shall be given, we resolved to leave the Countrey, and to apply our selves to returne for England, which we did accordingly, and arrived safely in the West of England, about the middest of September.

And whereas we have above certified you of the Countrey, taken in possession by us, to her Majesties use, and so to yours, by her Majesties grant, wee thought good for the better assurance thereof to recorde some of the particular Gentlemen, and men of accompt, who then were present, as witnesses of the same, that thereby all occasion of cavill to the title of the Countrey, in her Majesties behalfe, may be prevented, which other wise, such as like not the action may use, and pretend, whose names are:

Master Philip Amadas, ⎱ Captaines.
Master Arthur Barlowe, ⎰
William Greeneville,
John Wood,
James Browewich,
Henrie Greene,   ⎰ Of the companie.
Benjamin Wood,
Simon Ferdinando,
Nicholas Petman,
John Hewes,

We brought home also two of the Savages being lustie men, whose names were Wanchese and Manteo.

433. 1584. The Holinshed *Chronicle* account of the 1584 voyage.

The first published account of the 1584 voyage was in Raphael Holinshed, Chronicles, 2nd edition, 3 vols. (London, 1587), I, 90–91, and was compiled by Abraham Fleming out of material supplied by William Camden who was closely in touch with the voyagers (his sidenote reading "Abraham Fleming ex additionibus Guilelmi Camden").

In this yeare, 1584, even at the prime of the yeare, namelie in Aprill, maister Walter Raleigh[1] esquier, a gentleman from his infancie brought up and trained in martiall discipline, both by land and sea, and well inclined to all vertuous and honorable adventures, having built a ship and a pinesse, set them to the sea, furnished with all provisions necessarie for a long viage, and committed the charge of them to two gentlemen (his owne servants) the one called Philip Amadis; the other Arthur Barlow[2], with direction to discover that land which lieth betwéene Norembega and Florida in the west Indies; who according to their commission, made as sufficient a discoverie thereof as so short a time would permit: for they returned in August next following, and brought with them two savage men of that countrie[3], with sundrie other things, that did assure their maister of the goodnesse of the soile, and of great commodities that would arise to the realme of England, by traffique, if that the English had anie habitation, and were planted to live there. Whereupon, he immediatlie prepared for a second viage, which with all expedition (nothing at all regarding the charges that it would amount unto) did presentlie set in hand.[4]

1. Sidenote: "A.F. ex add. G.C. Maister Walter Raleigh his viage for the discoverie of that land which lieth betwéene Norembega and Florida."

2. Sidenote: "Philip Amadis, and Arthur Barlow."
3. Sidenote: "Two savage men and other things brought from the said land discovered."
4. Sidenote: "Maister Walter Raleigh prepareth for a second viage to the said land late discovered."

Chapter Fifty-six
The Virginia Voyage of 1585

434. 1585. The second voyage to Virginia—the *Tiger* journal.

This was prepared, like the account of the 1584 voyage, from a journal kept by a member of the Tiger's company, but the name of the author is not given. The Tiger *was the queen's ship and "Admiral" of the expedition, Richard Grenville general, Ralph Lane lieutenant, and Simon Fernandez pilot. The other ships were the* Roebuck, *"Vice-admiral," John Clarke captain; the* Lion, *George Raymond captain; the* Elizabeth, *Thomas Cavendish captain, and the* Dorothy. *The fleet carried 600 persons, sailors, soldiers, and settlers, taking the southerly route across the Atlantic by way of the Canary Islands to the West Indies before coasting northward to Virginia. Early in the voyage the ships were scattered by a storm in the Bay of Biscay. This journal records the meeting of the* Tiger *and the* Elizabeth *in the West Indies, but the arrival of the rest of the fleet is alluded to only indirectly. The Holinshed account (435) indicates that they had arrived at the Carolina Banks before the* Tiger *and the* Elizabeth. *This account also lists Arthur Barlowe as a member of the expedition, but he is not mentioned elsewhere.*

Printed in R. Hakluyt, Principall navigations *(1589), pp. 733–736;* Principal navigations, *III (1600), 251–253; VIII (1904), 310–317; D. B. Quinn,* Roanoke voyages, *I (1955), 178–193.*

The voyage made by Sir Richard Greenvile, for Sir Walter Ralegh, to Virginia, in the yeere, 1585.

The 19. day of Maye, in the yeere above saide, wee departed from Plymmouth, our fleete consisting of the number of seven sailes, to wit, the Tyger, of the burden of seven score tunnes: a Flie boate called the Roe Bucke, of the like burden: the Lyon of a hundred tunnes, or thereabouts: the Elizabeth, of fiftie tunnes, and the Dorothie, a small barke, whereunto were also adjoyned for speedie services, 2. small Panesses. The principall Gentlemen of our companie, were, Master Ralfe Lane, Master Thomas Candishe, Master John Arundell, Master Raimund, Master Stukely, Master Bremige, Master Vincent, and Master John Clarke, and divers others, whereof some were Captaines, and other some Assistants for counsell, and good directions in the voyage.

The 14. day of Aprill, we fell with Lançacota, and Forte Ventura, lakes of the Canaries, and from thence we continued our course for Dominica one of the Antiles, of the West India, wherewith we fell the 1 day of Maye, and the 10. day following, we came to an anker at Cotesa, a little Island situate neere to the Island of S. John, where wee landed, and refreshed our selves all that day.

The 15. day of Maye, we came to an anker, in the Baye of Muskito in the Island of S. John, within a Fawlcon shot of the shoare: where our Generall Sir Richard Greenvill, and the most part of our companie landed, and began to fortifie, very neere to the sea side: the over ranne by the one side of our forte, and the other two sides were environed with woods.

The 13. day we began to builde a new pinnesse within the Fort, with the timber that we then felled in the countrey, some part whereof we fet three myle up in the land, and brought it to our Fort upon trucks, the Spaniards not daring to make or offer resistance.

The 16. day, there appeared unto us out of the woods 8. horsemen of the Spaniards, about a quarter of a myle from our Fort, staying about halfe an hower in viewing our forces: but as soone as they saw x. of our shot marching towards them, they presently retyred into the woodes.

The 19. day, Master Candish, who had bene seperated from our fleete in a storme in the Bay of Portingal arrived at Cotesa, within the sight of the Tiger: we thinking him a farre off to have ben either a Spaniard or French man of warre thought it good to waigh ankers, and to goe roome with him, which the Tyger did, and discerned him at last to be one of our Consorts, for joy of whose comming our ships discharged their ordinance, and saluted him, according to the manner of the Seas.

The 22. day, 20. other Spanishe horsemen shewed them selves to us upon the other side of the river: who being seene, our General dispatched 20. footemen towards them, and two horsemen of ours, mounted upon Spanish horses, which wee before had taken in the time of our being on the Iland: they shewed to our men a flagge of truce, and made signes to have a parle with us: whereupon two of our men went halfe of the way upon the sands, and two of theirs came and met them: the two Spaniards offred very great salutations to our men, but began according to their Spanish proud humors, to expostulate with them, about their arrival, and fortifying in their countrie, who notwithstanding by our mens discrete answers were so cooled, that whereas they were told, that our principal intention was onely to furnish our selves with water, and victuals, and other necessaries whereof we stood in neede, which we craved might be yelded us with faire, and friendly means, otherwise our resolution was to practise force, and to releeve our selves by the sworde: the Spaniards in conclusion, seeing our men so resolute, yelded to our requestes with large promises of all curtesie, and great favor, and so our men and theirs departed.

The 23. day our pinnesse was finished, and lanched, which being done, our Generall with his Captaines, and Gentlemen, marched up into the Country about the space of 4. myles, where in a plaine marsh, they stayed expecting the comming of the Spanyards according to their promise, to furnish us with victuals: who keeping their old custome for perjurie and breache of promise came not, whereupon our General fired the woods thereabout, and so retired to our Fort, which the same day was fired also, and each man came aboord to be ready to set saile the next morning.

The 29. day we set saile from Saint Johns, being many of us stoong before upon shoare with the Muskitoes: but the same night we tooke a Spanish Frigat, which was forsaken by the Spanyards upon the sight of us, and the next day in the morning very early, wee tooke another Frigat, with good and rich fraight, and divers Spaniards of accompt in her, which afterwards we ransomed for good round summes, and landed them in Saint Johns.

The 26. day our Lieutenant Master Ralfe Lane, went in one of the Frigats which we had taken, to Roxo bay upon the Southwest side of Saint Johns, to fetch salt, being thither conducted by a Spanish Pilot: as soone as he arrived there, he landed with his men, to the number of 20. and intrenched him selfe upon the sandes immediatly, compassing one of their salt hils within the trench: who being seene of the Spanyards, there came downe towards him two or three troopes of horsemen, and footemen, who gave him the looking, and gazing on, but durst not come neere him to offer any resistance, so that Master Lane mauger their troopes, caried their salt aboord and laded his Frigat, and so returned againe to our fleete the 29. day, which road at Saint Germans Bay. The same day we all departed, and the next day arrived in the Iland of Hispaniola.

June.

The 1. day of June we ankered at Isabella, in the North side of Hispaniola.

The 3. day of June, the Governor of Isabella, and Captaine of the Port de Plata, beeing certifyed by the reports of sundry Spanyards, who had bene wel intertained aboord our shippes by our General, that in our fleete were many brave, and gallant Gentlemen, who greatly desired to see the Governor aforesaid, he thereupon sent gentle commendations to our Generall, promising within few daies to come to him in person, which he performed accordingly.

The 5. day the foresaid governor, accompanied with a lusty Frier, & xx. other Spaniards, with their servants, & Negroes, came downe to the sea side, where our ships road at anker, who being seene, our General manned immediatly the most part of his boats with the chiefe men of our fleete, every man appointed, and furnished in the best sort: at the landing of our Generall, the Spanishe Governor received him very curteously, and the

Spanish Gentlemen saluted our English Gentlemen, and their inferior sort did also salute our Souldiers and Sea men, liking our men, and likewise their qualities, although at the first, they seemed to stand in feare of us, and of so many of our boats, whereof they desired that all might not land their men, yet in the end, the curtesies that passed on both sides were so great, that all feare and mistrust on the Spanyardes part was abandoned.

In the meane time while our English Generall and the Spanish Governor discoursed betwixt them of divers matters, as of the state of the Country, the multitude of the Townes and people, and the commodities of the Iland, our men provided two banquetting houses covered with greene boughs, the one for the gentlemen, the other for the servants, and a sumptuous banquet was brought in served by us all in Plate, with the sound of trumpets, and consort of musick, wherewith the Spanyards were more than delighted. Which banquet being ended, the Spanyardes in recompense of our curtesie, caused a great heard of white buls, and kyne, to be brought together from the Mounteines, and appointed for every Gentlemen and Captaine that would ride, a horse ready sadled, and then singled out three of the best of them to be hunted by horsemen after their manner, so that the pastime grew very plesant for the space of three houres, wherein all three of the beasts were killed, whereof one tooke the sea, and there was slaine with a musket. After this sport, many rare presents and gifts were given and bestowed on both partes, and the next day wee plaied the Marchants in bargaining with them by way of trucke and exchange for divers of their commodities, as horses, mares, kyne, buls, goates, swine, sheepe, bul hydes, sugar, ginger, pearle, tabacco, and such like commodities of the Iland.

The 7. day we departed with great good will from the Spanyardes from the Island of Hispaniola: but the wiser sort do impute this greate shew of friendship, and curtesie used towardes us by the Spanyards rather to the force that we were of, and the vigilancie, and watchfulnes that was amongst us, then to any harty good will, or sure freindly intertainment: for doubtlesse if they had bene stronger then wee, we might have looked for no better curtesie at their handes, then Master

John Hawkins received at saint John de Ullua, or John Oxnam neere the streights of Dariene, and divers others of our Countrymen in other places.

The 8. day we ankred at a small Iland to take Seales which in that place wee understood to have bene in great quantitie, where the Generall and certaine others with him in the pinnesse, were in very great danger to have bene all cast away, but by the helpe of God they escaped the hazard, and returned aboord the Admirall in safetie.

The 9. day we arrived and landed in the Isle of Caycos, in which Islande we searched for salt pondes, upon the advertisement, and information of a Portingall: who in deede abused our General and us, deserving a halter for his hire, if it had so pleased us.

The 12. we ankered at Guanema, and landed.

The 15. and 16. we ankered and landed at Sygateo.

The 20. we fell with the mayne of Florida.

The 23. wee were in great danger of a Wracke on a breache called the Cape of Feare.

The 24. we came to anker in a harbor where we caught in one tyde so much fishe as woulde have yelded us xx. pounds in London: this was our first landing in Florida.

The 26. we came to anker at Wocokon.

The 29. wee waighed anker to bring the Tyger into the harbour, where through the unskilfulnesse of the Master whose name was Fernando, the Admirall strooke on grounde, and sunke.

July.

The 3. we sent word of our ariving at Wococon, to Wingino at Roanocke.

The 6. Master John Arundell was sent to the mayne, and Manteio with him: and Captayne Aubry and Captaine Boniten the same day were sent to Croatoan, where they found two of our men left there, with 30. other by Captaine Reymond, some 20. daies before.

The 8. Captaine Aubry, and Captaine Boniten returned with two of our men found by them to us at Wocokon.

The 11. day the Generall accompanied in his Tilt boate with Master John Arundell, Master Stukelye, and divers other Gentelmen, Master Lane, Master Candish, Master Harriot, and 20. others in the new pinnesse, Captaine Amadas, Captaine Clarke, with tenne others in a ship boate, Francis Brooke, and John White in another ship boate passed over the water from Ococon to the mayne land victualled for eight dayes, in which voyage we first discovered the townes of Pomioke, Aquascogoc and Secota, and also the great lake called by the Savages Paquype, with divers other places, and so returned with that discovery to our Fleete.

The 12. we came to the Towne of Pomeioke.

The 13. we passed by water to Aquascococke.

The 15. we came to Secotan and were well intertayned there of the Savages.

The 16. we returned thence, and one of our boates with the Admirall was sent to Aquascococke to demaund a silver cup which one of the Savages had stolen from us, and not receiving it according to his promise, we burnt, and spoyled their corne, and Towne, all the people beeing fledde.

The 18. we returned from the discovery of Secotan, and the same day came aboord our fleete ryding at Wocokon.

The 21. our fleete ankering at Wokocon, we wayed anker for Hatoraske.

The 27. our fleete ankered at Hatoraske, and there we rested.

The 29. Grangino, brother to King Wingino, came aboord the Admirall, and Manteo with him.

August.

The 2. The Admirall was sent to Weapemeoke.

The 5. Master John Arundell was sent for England.

The 25. our Generall wayed anker, and set saile for England.

About the 31. he tooke a Spanish ship of 300. tunne richly loaden, boording her with a boate made with boards of chests, which fell a sunder, and sunke at the shippes side, assoone as ever hee and his men were out of it.

September.

The 10. of September, by foule weather the Generall then shipped in the prise lost sight of the Tyger.

October.

The sixt the Tyger fell with the landes ende, and the same day came to an anker at Falmouth.

The 18. the Generall came with the prise to Plymmouth, and was courteously received by diverse of his worshipfull friends.

435. 1587. The Holinshed *Chronicle* account of the 1585 voyage.

The first published account of the 1585 Virginia voyage was in Raphael Holinshed, Chronicles, *2nd edition, 3 vols. (London, 1587), III, 1401–1402, which was compiled by Abraham Fleming from material apparently supplied to him by Sir Richard Grenville, whose personal narrative of the voyage would seem to be in part preserved here. A sidenote expanded reads: "Abraham Fleming ex chirographo Domini Grenville militis."*

In this yeare 1585, even in Aprill, at the pleasant prime, sir Walter Raleigh knight, being incouraged by the reports of his men of the goodnesse of the soile and the fertilitie of the countrie, which they had discovered this yeare last past, and now by her maiestie called Virginia, with knightlie courage countervaileable to his double desire of honour, by undertaking hard adventurs, furnished to his great charges eight sailes of all sortes, and immediatlie set them to the sea, ordeining sir Richard Greenfield his kinsman (a gentleman of verie good estimation both for his parentage and sundrie good vertues, who for love he bare unto sir Walter Raleigh, togither with a disposition that he had to attempt honorable actions worthie of honour, was willing to hazard himselfe in this voiage) his lieutenant, injoining him either to tarrie himselfe, or to leave some gentleman of good worth with a competent number of soldiers in the countrie of Virginia, to begin an English colonie there. Who with the ships aforesaid, having in his companie sir John Arundell, Thomas Candish, Rafe Lane, Edward Gorges, Iohn Stuklie, Edward Stafford, Philip Amadis, Arthur Barlow, Thomas Heriot, and diverse other gentlemen with a competent number of souldiers, departed from London in April aforesaid. But after they had sailed certeine numbers of leagues at the sea, by force and violence of fowle weather they were separated one from another; so that sir Richard Greenefield being singled from his fleet, all alone arrived in the Iland of Hispaniola in the west Indies, about the middest of June following, where he determined resolutelie to remaine, untill he had built a bote (for he had lost his owne bote in the tempests aforesaid.)

Whereupon immediatlie after his landing, finding a place to his liking, he esconsed himselfe in despite of the Spaniards, who by all possible means did there best indevour by proffering of sundrie skirmishes, to inforce him to retire to his ship: but he nothing appalled with their brags kept his ground. Twelve daies after his arrivall there, after Thomas Candish arrived at the same place, where sir Richard Greenfield was esconsing of himselfe, to the great rejoising both of themselves & their companies. The Spaniards finding it too hard for them (notwithstanding their multitudes) to remoove these few resolute Englishmen by violence, came to a parlee, and in the same concluded an amitie, that the one nation might in safetie traffike with the other. Now when sir Richard Greenfield had taried in that Iland almost a moneth, and had built his bote, revittled himselfe, and laden his ships with horsses, mares, kine, sheep, swine, &c: to transport with him to Virginia (bicause these sorts of cattell heretofore were not to be found in that countrie) he departed thense; and in his waie he made discoverie of manie Ilands and havens upon the continent adjoining, and arrived safelie in the new discovered countrie (where he met with the rest of his fleet that attended his comming thither) about the middest of Iulie next insuing, not without great danger of shipwracke. For at the verie entrance into the harborough, his ship strake on the ground, and did beat so manie strokes upon the sands, that if God had not miraculouslie delivered him, there had beene no waie to avoid present death. In this danger his ship was so brused, that the saltwater came so aboundantlie into hir, that the most part of his corne, salt, meale, rice, bisket, & other provisions that he should have left with them that remained behind him in the countrie was spoiled.

After he had remained there certeine daies, according to his commission from sir Walter Raleigh, he began to establish a colonie, appoint-

ing maister Rafe Lane (a gentleman of good account) generall of those English which were to remaine there, being in all to the number of an hundred and seaven persons, amongst whom diverse gentlemen remained; namelie, Philip Amadis, Edward Stafford, Mervin, Kendall, Prideaux, Acton, Heriot, and others. When he had taken sufficient order for the establishing of master Lane and his companie aforesaid, leaving with them as much of all provisions as his plentie would give him leave, he weighed anchor for England. But in his returne, not having sailed manie leagues from the coast of Virginia, he descried a tall ship of foure hundred tuns or thereabouts, making the same course that he did, unto whome he gave chase, and in few houres by goodnesse of saile overtooke, and by violence wan, richlie laden with sugar, hides, spices, and some quantitie of gold, silver, and pearle: she was the viceadmerall of the fleet of Sancto Domingo that yere for Spaine. After this good fortune, having a merie gale, not manie daies after he arrived at Plimmouth in October next insuing; where sir Walter Raleigh meeting with him, did presentlie resolve upon another voiage, to supplie Rafe Lane, and his companie that were left with him in Virginia, the next spring following: which accordinglie was performed with all expedition.[1]

436. 1585–1586. The first Virginia colonists at Roanoke Island.

This list, printed after the Tiger *journal, gives the names of those soldiers and others, carried by Grenville's fleet, who remained at Roanoke Island to form the first colony, 107 names in all. Thomas Harriot is listed but not John White who was a settler, unless John Twyt or William White represents him. Possibly the list was drawn up by White himself omitting his own name. There were no women in the first settlement.*

Printed in R. Hakluyt, Principall navigations *(1589), pp. 736–737;* Principal navigations, *III (1600), 254; VIII (1904), 317–318; D. B. Quinn,* Roanoke voyages, *I (1955), 194–197.*

1. Sidenote: "An other voiage resolved upon by sir Walter Raleigh for the supplie of those that were left in Virginia."

The names of all those as well Gentlemen as others, that remained one whole yeere in Virginia, under the Governement of Master Ralfe Lane.

Master Philip Amades,
  Admirall of the countrie.
Master Hariot.
Master Acton.
Master Edward Stafford.
Thomas Luddington.
Master Marvyn.
Master Gardyner.
Captaine Vaughan.
Master Kendall.
Master Prideox.
Robert Holecroft.
Rise Courtney.
Master Hugh Rogers.
Thomas Foxe.
Edward Nugen.
Darby Glande.
Edward Kelle.
John Gostigo.
Erasmus Clefs.
Edward Ketcheman.
John Linsey.
Thomas Rottenbury.
Roger Deane.
John Harris.

Master Thomas Harvie.
Master Snelling.
Master Anthony Russe.
Master Allyne.
Master Michel Polyson.
John Cage.
Thomas Parre.
William Randes.
Geffrey Churchman.
William Farthowe.
John Taylor.
Philppe Robyns.
Thomas Phillippes.
Valentine Beale.
James Skinner.
George Eseven.
John Chaundeler.
Philip Blunt.
Richard Poore.
Robert Yong.
Marmaduke Constable.
Thomas Hesket.
William Wasse.
John Fever.
Daniel.

Frauncis Norris.
Mathewe Lyne.
Edward Kettell.
Thomas Wisse.
Robert Biscombe.
William Backhouse.
William White.
Henry Potkin.
Dennis Barnes.
Joseph Borges.
Doughan Gannes.
William Tenche.
Randall Latham.
Thomas Hulme.
Walter Myll.
Richard Gilbert.
Steven Pomarie.
John Brocke.
Bennet Harrye.
James Stevenson.
Charles Stevenson.
Christopher Lowde.
Jeremie Man.
James Mason.
David Salter.
Richard Ireland.
Thomas Bookener.
William Philippes.
Randall Mayne.

Thomas Taylor.
Richard Humfrey.
John Wright.
Gabriell North.
Bennet Chappell.
Richard Sare.
James Lasie.
Smolkin.
Thomas Smart.
Robert.
John Evans.
Roger Large.
Humfrey Garden.
Frauncis Whitton.
Rowland Griffyn.
William Millard.
John Twyt.
Edwarde Seklemore.
John Anwike.
Christopher Marshall.
David Williams.
Nicholas Swabber.
Edward Chipping.
Sylvester Beching.
Vincent Cheyne.
Haunce Walters.
Edward Barecombe.
Thomas Skevelabs.
William Walters.

LETTERS FROM RALPH LANE IN VIRGINIA

THREE OF THESE LETTERS (437, 438, 440) are the first written by Lane from Virginia while he was still on Hatorask Island. They were sent by the *Tiger*, which sailed from Port Ferdinando on August 25, but the date of August 12 on the letters may indicate that she expected to sail earlier. Two letters (439, 441) are written from the fort on Roanoke Island indicating that it was sufficiently advanced in construction to be occupied at the beginning of September. They were probably sent by the *Roebuck*, which must have sailed after September 8.

The letters to Sir Francis Walsingham first hint at and then elaborate on friction with Grenville. They also give a most favorable description of the country with reservations only about the harbors on the Carolina Banks. The letter to Sir Philip Sidney appears to encourage Sidney to embark on some adventure in the West Indies, possibly with Drake. The letter to Richard Hakluyt of the Middle Temple, cousin of the compiler of *Principall navigations*, is a detailed report of the natural commodities of Virginia, probably at Hakluyt's request since this was his particular interest, as was the need to find new markets for English cloth. Master H. cannot be identified with certainty.

(437) is from State Papers, Colonial, CO 1/1, 4, printed in D. B. Quinn, *Roanoke voyages*, I (1955), 197–198. (438) is State Papers, Colonial, CO 1/1, 3, printed in *Roanoke voyages*, I, 199–204. (440) is State Papers, Colonial, CO 1/1, 6, printed in *Roanoke voyages*, I, 210–214. (439) is State Papers, Colonial, CO 1/1, 5, printed in *Roanoke voyages*, I, 204–206. (441) is printed in R. Hakluyt, *Principall navigations* (1589), p. 793; *Principal navigations*, III (1600), 254–255; VIII (1904), 319–320; *Roanoke voyages*, I, 207–210.

437. August 12, 1585. Ralph Lane to Sir Francis Walsingham.

Right honorable, The bearer hereof Master Attekynson your honours servante hathe carryed him selfe soo honestely, and soo industryousely in all occasyones and acciones of thys voyeage, that I canne not lesse doo havynge sume prynsypalle chardege in the same to note him by thys my bolde lettre to your honour, for one moost worthye of grete accompte emongest us, and with your honour, not to bee the lesse reckenned of in thys behalfe, havynge doonne your honour by suche hys honeste demeanours as myche honour as eny servante canne doo to soo honorable a master:/

I have also wrytten to your honour, by your servante Master Russelle to a lyke effecte, Who notwithstandynge the generales dysplesure towardes him; and his complayentes, wyll neverthelesse I am persuaded cleare him selfe very well to your honour of Every chardege or ymputacione whatsoever: And even soo sir, humbly comyttyng your honour to the mercyes of the Allmyghty, For thys tyme I take my leave of the same.

From the Porte FerdyNando, in Verginia, the 12ᵗʰ of Auguste: 1585

Your honours, humble and most assured,
[signed:] Rafe Lane

[Addressed:] To the Right honorable Sir Frances Wallsyngham Knight, prynsypall Secrettary to her maiesty and one of her highness most honorable pryvy Counselle: thys bee delivered at the courte, of ENglande./

[Endorsed:] 1585 12 Aug. Master Rafe Lane. from Virginia Virginia

438. August 12, 1585. Ralph Lane to Sir Francis Walsingham.

Right honorable, With humble Remembrance of all dewetye and most hartye affeccione unto you, accordynge as I acknowledge my selfe to have moost good cause: The Generalles returne in hys owene personne into Englande dothe presently cutte me of from usinge cyrcumstances in reporte of the partycularityes of thys countreye in thys my lettre unto your honor: / Only thys yt maye plese you by mee in generally to understande, that thys our presente arryvalle into thes partes, thoughe late in the yeare, (and that whoolly thoroughe the defalte of him that intendethe to accuse others) hathe neverthelesse dyscoverdde unto us soo many, soo rare, and soo singulare commodytyes (by the vnyversalle opynyone bothe of our Appotycaryes and all our merchantes here) of thys her Maiestes newe kingedom of Verginia, As all the kingedomes and states of Chrystendom theyere commodytyes joyegned in one together, doo not yealde ether more good, or more plentyfulle whatsooever for publyck use ys needefull, or pleasinge for delyghte. They partycularytyes whereof I leave to the generalles reporte, As also to the iudgementes of all your honores, your selfes, and that upon the vyewe, of a grete amasse of good thynges that hee bryngethe hys shippe presently frayegheted withall; to avoyde all suspycyone of fraude: / Theyre thynges that wee have had tyme as yeate to see, and to sende, are but suche as are fyrst cummen to hande with very smalle serche, and which doo presente them selfes upon the upper face of the Earthe: They barreneste, and

moost suncken plattes whereof, doo neverthelesse, every where yealde sumwhat that ether
for knowen Vertue ys of pryce in Chrystendom,
or sumwhat at leeste to the smelle plesinge; Not
havynge as yeate founde on all our serche one
stynckinge weede growynge in thys lande; (A
matter in all our opynyones here very straunge) /
Into the bowelles of the Earthe as yeate we have
not serched: And therefore not meanynge to advertyse your honor, of eny thinge that myne
owene eyes haue not seene, I leave to certefye
your honor of what lyckelyhuddes founde, or
what ye sauvages reporte of better matters: / The
mayene Terrytory As yt ys Vaste and huge, and
replenysshed as beeforesaid, Soo also all the entryes into the same are soo by Nature fortefyed to
the sea warde, by reason of a shoelle and moost
daungerouse coaste aboue 150 leagues lyinge all
alonge thys her maiestes domynyone allready
dyscoverdde, That yt ys not with grete Shippinge
at eny hande to bee delte with all: / There bee only
in all iij Entryes, and Portes; The one which wee
have named TryNytye harboroughe, The other
Ococan, in the Entry whereof all our Fleete
strucke agrounde, and the Tyger lyinge beatynge
uppon the shoalle for the space of ij houres by the
dyalle, wee were all in extreeme hasarde of beyng
casteawaye, but in the ende by the mere worck of
god flottynge of wee ranne her agrounde harde to
the shoare, and soo with grete spoyelle of our
prouysyones, saved our selfes and ye Noble
shippe also, with her backe whoolle, which all
they marryners aborde thoughte coolde not pos-
sybelly but have beene brooken in sunder;
havynge abydden by juste talle above ,89,
strockes agrounde: The iij^de Entry and beste harboroughe of all the reste, ys the Porte which is
called FerdyNando Dyscoverdde by the master
and Pylotte maggiore of our Fleete your honors
servante Symon FerdyNando who trewly hathe
carryed him selfe bothe with greate skylle, and
grete governement all thys voyeage, notwithstandyng thys grete crosse to us all; As the
whoolle gynge of masteres and marryners wyll
with one voyce affyrme: / The ij harboroghes
above mensyoned (Whereof Trynyty harboroughe ys one, and only of viij foote, Uppon the
barre at hyghe water) are as you may Judge: /
Thys other called the FerdyNando hathe a barre
also, but at xij foote uppon the same at hyghe
water: and the barre very shorte, beyng within

iij, iiij, and v, fathom water: Soo as thys Porte at
the poynte of the lande beyng fortefyed with a
skonse, yt ys not to bee enterdde by all ye force
that Spayne canne make, wee havyng the favure
of God. / The clymate ys soo whoollesom, yeate
somewhat tendying to heate, As that wee have
not had one sycke synce wee enterdde into ye
countrey; but sundry that came sycke, are re-
coverd of longe dyseases especially of Reumes.
My selfe have undertaken with the favoure of
God, and in hys feare, with a good compagnye
moore aswell of gentlemen as others, to remayene
here, the returne of a newe supply. As resolute
rather to loose our lyfes then to deferre a possessione to her Maieste, our Countrey, and that
our moost Noble Patrone Sir Water Rawelley, of
soo noble a kingedome, as by hys moost woorthy
endevoure and ynfynytte chardege, as also of
your honor and the rest of the mooste honorable
aduenturerres, our honorable entry ys made into
(by the mercy of God) to the conqueste of: And for
myne owne parte doo finde my selfe better contented to lyve with fysshe for my dayely foode,
and water for my dayelye dryncke, in the prose-
cucione of suche one Accione, then oute of the
same to lyve in the greateste plenty that the
Courte coolde gyve mee: Comforted cheefely
hereunto with an assuerance of her Maiestes gret-
enes hereby to growe by the Addycione of suche
a kingedom as thys ys to the reste of hir
Domynyones, by meane whereof lykewyse the
Churche of Chryste thoroughe Chrystendom,
may by the mercy of God in shorte tyme finde a
relyfe and freedom from the servytude, and
tyrannye that by Spayene (beynge the swoorde of
that Antychryste of Rome and hys secte) the
same hathe of longe tyme beene moost
myserabelly oppressed with; / Not doutyng in the
mercy of God, to bee suffycently provyded for by
hime, and most assuered by fayethe in Chryste
that rather then hee wyll sufferre hys ennemyes
the Papystes to tryumphe over the overthrowe,
ether of thys most Chrystyan Accione or of us hys
poore servantes in that thoroughe famyne or
other wante, beyng in a vaste Countrey yett
unmanuredde, (thoughe most apte for yt) that hee
wyll commaunde even the Ravennes to feede us,
As hee did by hys servante the Prophett Abacuc,
and that only for hys mercyes sake: To the which I
moost hartely comytt your honor, and with my
humble commendaciones to my lady your Wyffe,

for thys tyme I take my leave of the same: / From the Porte FerdyNandon, in Verginia: the 12ᵗʰ of Auguste: 1585

Your honors humble and most assuered duryng lyfe:

[signed:] RafeLane:///

[Addressed:] To yᵉ Right honorable Sir Frances Wallsingham, Knight, Prynsypalle Secrettary to her Maieste, and one of her highness, moost honorable pryvy Counselle: thys bee delivered att the Courte of ENgland.

[Endorsed:] 12 August 1585. From Master Ralphe Lane. Virginia.

439. September 8, 1585. Ralph Lane to Sir Francis Walsingham.

Right Honorable,

Sythence Sir Richard Greenefeelde, by the tyme of the arryvalle of thys my lettre ys to delyver unto your honor as also to Sir Walter Rawlley our lorde, sundry complayntes, against sundry gentlemen, of thys servyce; and partycularely against our hyghe Marsshell Master Candysshe, Master Edward Gorge Master Frances Brooke our Threasurer, and Captain Clerck, captain of the flee boate, I thoughte good thus muche to advertyse your honor and that moost trewly concernynge them: That yt ys not possyble for men to beehave them selfes moore fayethefully, and moore Industryousely in an Accione, (the same by the generalles only grete defalte havynge beene made bothe moost payenefulle and moost perellouse) then every of thes gentlemen, but especially Master Candysshe our high Marsshall, and Master Frances Broke our Threasurer have donne and that even since the fyrste to the laste: / Contrarywyse how Sir Richard Greenefeelde Generalle, hathe demeaned him selfe, from the fyrst daye of hys entry into governement at Plymmouth, untyll the daye of hys departure from hence ouer the barre in the Porte Ferdinando, farre otherwyse then my hoope of him, thoughe very agreeable to the expectaciones, and predycciones of sundry wyse and

godly personnes of hys owene Countreye, that knewe hym better then my selfe, and partycularely how tyrannouse an Execucione withoute eny occasyone of my parte offered, hee not only purposed, but even propounded the same, to have broughte mee, by indyrecte meanes, and moost untrewe surmyses, to the questione for my lyfe, and that only for an advyse, in a publycke consultacione by mee gyven, which yf yt had beene executed had beene for the grete good of us all, but moost cheefely of him selfe, I am therefore to referre your honor to an ample dyscourse of the whoolle voyeage in a booke to Sir Walter Rawley dedycated of the same, wherein hys used manner of proceedynge towardes all men in the Accione in generally, and partycularely towardes my selfe (the same to bee approoved by the testymonyes and deposycyones of Master Canndysshe, Master Edward Gorge, and Captain Clercke) ys playenely and trewly sette doune; which gentlemen hee aparte and together at dyvers tymes sounded, by all meanes to have drawen theyere [con]sentes to have joyegned with him uppon a mmost untrewe surmyse of hys owne, to have broughte my hedde in questione: Soo as for myne owene parte I have had soo muche experyence of hys governement, as I am humbelly to desyre your honor and the reste of my honorablest frendes, to gyve mee theyere favoures to bee freedde from that place where sir Richard Greenefeelde ys to carry eny authorytye in chyeffe. Assueringe you sir, with all that the Lorde hathe myraculosely bleste thys accione, that in the tyme of hys beeynge emongest us, even thoroughe hys intollerable pryede, and unsaciable ambycione, hyt hathe not at iij severalle tymes taken a fynalle overthrowe, the which had bene gretely to have beene pyttyed, not only in respecte of the losse of soo many subjectes, but cheefely for the ruyne of soo honorable an Accione, which the Lord to hys glory dothe dayely blesse here with a dayely dyscoverye of sumwhat rare growynge that Chrystendom wantethe, (as even iij dayes before ye date hereof a kinde of Gynneye wheate founde here growynge and usualle, that yealdethe bothe corne, and suger, whereof our Physycyan here hath sente an assaye to our Lord Sir Walter Rawlleye) or elles of sume fertylle and plesante provynces in the mayene fytte to bee cyvylly, and Chrystyanly inhabyted, as at the presente yt ys inhabyted only with savages, but most populousely, specially, towardes the weste; where there are towene[s] of theyere fasshyone, scytuated upon moost delycate plattes of grounde, dystant the one from the other not above 3 Englysshe myelles: Soo as uppon one of theyere holly dayes there hathe beene of my compagnye in the mayene that hathe seene aboove 700 personnes, yonge and [olde to]gether on a playene. I meane with the favoure of the Allmyghtye to vysytte that provynce and summe parte of the wynter to passe there, beynge 140 myelles within the mayene; In the meane whylle and durynge lyfe, I am to praye to the Allmyghty to blesse you and yours: / From the Newe Forte in Verginia, the 8th daye of September: 1585

Your honours and most assuered durynge lyfe
    [signed:] Rafe Lane

Postscript—Sir the bearer hereof our Threasurer Master Brooke shall delyver to your honor a trewe copye of the whoolle dyscoursse of the voyeage, dyrected to Sir Walter Rawlley: and subscrybed, and to bee confyrmed with sundry credyble deposyciones: /

[Addressed:] To the Right honorable Sir Frances Wallsingham, Knight, prynsypalle Secrettary to the Queenes Maieste, and one [of] her highness moost honorable pryvy Counselle, thys bee delevered at Courte.

[Endorsed:] 1585. 8th September 1585. Master Rafe Lane. Virginia.

440. August 12, 1585. Ralph Lane to Sir Philip Sidney.

My moost Noble Generalle. Albeyt in the myddest of infynytt busynesses, As havyng, emungst sauvages, the chardege of wylde menn of myne owene nacione, Whose unrulynes ys suche as not to gyve leasure to the goovernour to bee all most at eny tyme from them. Neuerthelesse I wolde not omytte, to wryte thes fewe lynes of dewety, and affeccione unto you; In the which I am to leave you to the letre which I wrotte to your most honorable father in lawe Master Secrettary, touchyng the advertysementes of thys her Maiestes newe kingedom of Verginia, and the

singularityes thereof, and to advertyese you alltogether (but bryefely) of sume such matter as in our coursse hytherwardes wee have found worthye of your partycpacione: Which in fewe wordes ys thys, that yf her maieste shal at eny tyme finde her selfe burthened with the King of Spayene, wee have by our dwellyng vppon the Ilande of St Ihon and Hyspagniola for the space of 5, weekes, soo dyscoveredde the forces thereof with the infynytt ryches of the same, As that I find yt an attempt most honorable and fesible, and proffytable, and only fytte for your selfe to bee cheeffe commaunder in. / Thys entry wolde soo gaulle the king of Spayene, as yt wolde dyverte hys forces that hee troublethe these partes of Chrystendom with, into thos partes where hee canne not gretely annoye us with them. And how gretely a small force woulde garboyelle hym here, when ij of hys most rychest and strongest Ilandes St Iohn, and Hyspagnyola, tooke suche allarmes of us not only landyng but dwellyng upon them with only 120, menn, I referre yt to your Iudgement. To conclude, findynge by myne owene vyewe, hys forces at Lande to bee soo meane, and hys terror made soo grete emongeste us in ENgland, consyderyng that the reputacione thereof dothe alltogeather growe from the mynes of hys threasor and the same in places which wee see here are soo easye bothe to bee taken and kepte by eny small force sent by hyr Maieste, I colde not but wryte these ylle fasshyoned lynes unto you, and to exhorte you my Noble Generalle by occasyone not to refuse the good oportunyty of suche a servyce, to the churche of Chryste, of greate releyffe from many callamytyes that thys threasor in Spanyardes handes, dothe inflycte unto ye members thereof, veary honorable and proffytable for her maieste and our countrey, and moost commendable and fytte for yourselfe to bee the Enterpryser of: / And even soo for thys tyme ceasyng further to trouble you, with my humble commendacyones to my lady your wyffe, I commytt you, my Noble Generalle, to the mercie of the Allmyghty.

From the Porte FerdyNando in Verginia, the 12th of Auguste: 1585

Your poore soldyoure, and assured at Commandement,
    [signed:] Rafe Lane

[Addressed:] To my moost honorable Frende, Sir Phyllyppe Sydney Knight thys bee delyvered at the Courte of ENglande.

441. September 3, 1585. Ralph Lane to Richard Hakluyt the elder and Master H——— of the Middle Temple.

An extract of Master Lanes letter, to Master
Richard Hakluyt Esquire, and another gentleman of the middle Temple, from Virginia:

In the meane while you shall understand that
since sir Richard Greenvils departure from us, as
also before, we have discovered the maine to bee
the goodliest soile under the cope of heaven, so
abounding with sweete trees, that bring such
sundry rich and most pleasant gummes, grapes of
such greatnes, yet wild, as France, Spaine nor
Italy hath no greater, so many sortes of
Apothecarie drugs, such severall kindes of flaxe,
and one kind like silke, the same gathered of a
grasse, as common there as grasse is here. And
now within these few dayes we have found here a
Guinie wheate, whose eare yeeldeth corne for
bread, 400. upon one eare, and the Cane maketh
very good and perfect suger, also Terra Samia,
otherwise Terra sigillata. Besides that, it is the
goodliest and most pleasing territorie of the world
(for the soile is of an huge unknowen greatnesse,
and very wel peopled and towned, though
savagelie) and the climate so wholesome, that we
have not had one sicke, since we touched land
here. To conclude, if Virginia had but Horses and
Kine in some reasonable proportion, I dare assure
my selfe being inhabited with English, no realme
in Christendome were comparable to it. For this
alreadie we find, that what commodities soever
Spaine, France, Italy, or the East parts do yeeld
unto us in wines of all sortes, in oiles, in flaxe, in
rosens, pitch, frankenscence, currans, sugers, &
such like, these parts do abound with ye growth of
them all, but being Savages that possesse the
land, they know no use of the same. And sundry
other rich commodities, that no parts of the
world, be they West or East Indies, have, here
we finde great abundance of. The people naturally most curteous, & very desirous to have

clothes, but especially of course cloth rather than
silke, course canvas they also like wel of, but
copper carieth ye price of all, so it be made red.
Thus good Master Hakluyt and master H. I have
joyned you both in one letter of remembrance, as
two that I love dearely well, and commending me
most hartily to you both, I commit you to y^e
tuition of the almighty. From the new Fort in
Virginia, this 3 September 1585.

Your most assured friend, Rafe Lane.

442. October 29, 1585. Sir Richard Grenville reports to Sir Francis Walsingham.

*Enough time had elapsed between Grenville's
arrival at Plymouth on October 18 in the prize,
Santa Maria de San Vicente (443), for rumors of
her value, no doubt conflicting, to have reached
London. For the Spanish account of the capture
and the value of her cargo see I.A. Wright,
Further English Voyages, (1951), pp. 12–15.
Here Grenville gives only a factual report of his
mission to Virginia with no comments on Lane or
others.*

*P.R.O., State Papers, Colonial, CO 1/1, 7.
Printed in D. B. Quinn, Roanoke voyages, I
(1955), 218–221.*

Remembringe my dutie to your honor, Beinge
by the hande of god delyvered from the daungers
on the seas, and aryved in Inglonde I may not
forgette to acquainte your honor with the successe of my voiadge, wherin I am perswaded that
god hath bene the rather favorable unto me for
that your honour hath bene an adventurer therin /
I have god be thanked performed the action
wherunto I was directed as fullye as the tyme
wherin I have bene absente from hense and all
possibilities wolde permitte me. I have possessed
and peopled the same to her Maiesties use, And
planted it with suche cattell & beastes as are fitte
and necessary for manuringe the Countrey and in
tyme to geve reliefe with victuall, as also with
such fruites and plantes as by my travaile by the
waie thetherwardes I mighte procure / And as the
Countrey of hit selfe, as never bene labored with
mannes hande, so I hope that hit being once by
our industrie manured will prove moste fertill

The Comodites that are founde there are suche as my cousen Raleighe hathe advertized you of, your honor shall hereafter have the reporte of suche as I have broughte with me /

In my waie homewardes I was encountred by a spanishe shippe whome assaultinge me and offeringe me violence god be thanked with defence and safetie of my selfe and all my companye after some fighte I overcame and brought into Inglonde with me her landinge is gynger & Suger, And whereas by the ignoraunce of such as have come before me a large reporte hathe bene made of great quantitie of pearle and mettall of golde and sylver, I do assure your honour that [we] have founde but lytell nether dothe ony suche quantitie passe from St Domingo from whence they came unto Spayne, That which was heere belonged only to pryvate persons who were passengers into Spaine from St Domingo, And the same when the Shippe yelded was imbesiled by the company. The whole estimate of the shippe by the Confession of the Spanierdes and viewe of their bookes amountethe only to 40000 or 50000 Ducates The same beinge sufficiente to awnswer the charges of eache adventurer, wherein I am gladde that my happe is to yealde your honor the retorne of your adventure with some gagne / the acounte wherof with other relacions of the whole course of the voiadge at my repaire to the Courte which god willinge shalbe shortly I will my self imparte unto you And so restinge alwaies moste bownde to your honour I humbly take my leave

Plymouth this 29 of October 1585.
Your honours alwaies at Your comaundement
    [unsigned]

[Addressed:] To the Righte honorable Sir Frauncys Walsingham knighte principall Secretary to the Queenes Maiestie

[Endorsed:] 1585, 29 Oct. Sir Ric: Grenvile

443. October 16, 1585. Henry Talbot to the Earl of Shrewsbury.

This letter is in the Ralegh Collection in the Library of the University of North Carolina. The year-date and the writer's name are not contained in the text but appear to be correct. Professor William P. Powell, when he was Director of the North Carolina Collection, brought it to my attention and considered it appropriate that it should be published.

I Receaved you Lordships Letters by Thomson the xvjth of this instante, and Intend to goe tomorowe to the Courte, and to doe all thinges accordinge to your Lordships direction. I have dilivered the venison accordinge to the note, and it was by all moste thankefully received, but especially, by the Lord Treasurer who caled for me into his chamber & asked me many questions touchinge your Lordships goute and was verie glad, to understande of your good health: whereas your lordship in your letter did say, that I mighte dedoucte oute of the nommber to bestowe on theme whome you had forgotten, I coulde not doe soe without bretch of credyt for in your letter to master wade it was sette doune, howe many he shoulde receave. Conserninge your wife, I have not harde any thinge of her, since the courte came to Ritchmounde.

Heare is noe other speeche but of killinge the Spaniardes, both at sea and lande, for Sir Ritcharde Grinfilde, hath taken a spaniarde verie ritchely laden, both with pearle, goulde, and spices, the barke is of CCC. tonne, and there are CC Spaniardes aborde her, the which I thinke by this tyme, are all comme to Plimouthe, soe that, it is thought, this shippe, will make Sir Water Rauley a saver by his voiage.

There are letters comme from master Lane whoe reameneth in Wingandecoia, wherin he declareth, the fertiletie of the soile, not to bee inferior to Englande, and beinge of the same temperature, but for goulde, or pearle, there canne none be founde, only this, the earth is good, but wantes both cattell, & manuringe, and therfore it is thought the voiage will have bad sowccesse.

Touchinge my Lord Lecesters gooinge into Flanders, there are divers speeches, but this is certaine, he hath not as yet bestowed one pennie.

Chapter Fifty-seven
The First Virginia Colony, 1585–1586

444. 1585–1586. Ralph Lane's narrative of the Roanoke Island colony.

Lane arrived back in England on July 27, 1586, and prepared this report for Ralegh. It is not very detailed and is often confusing both about relations with the Indians and areas explored. The report may well have been edited and censored for publication to prevent Spain from knowing precisely where the site of the colony was and to play down hostility shown by the indigenous people and Lane's treatment of them. It records exploration of the Chowan and Roanoke rivers and of an area to the south of Chesapeake Bay, the site for future settlement.

Printed in R. Hakluyt, Principall navigations *(1589), pp. 737–747;* Principal navigations, *III (1600), 255–264; VIII (1904), 320–345. D. B. Quinn,* Roanoke voyages, *I (1955), 255–303.

An account of the particularities of the imployments of the English men left in Virginia by Sir Richard Greenevill under the charge of Master Ralfe Lane Generall of the same, from the 17. of August, 1585. untill the 18. of June 1586. at which time they departed the Countrie: sent, and directed to Sir Walter Ralegh.

That I may proceed with order in this discourse, I thinke it requisite to devide it into two partes. The first shall declare the particularities of such partes of the Country within the mayne, as our weake number, and supply of things necessary did inable us to enter into the discovery thereof.

The second part, shall set downe the reasons generally moving us to resolve on our departure at the instant with the General Sir Frauncis Drake, and our common request for passage with him, when the barkes, pinnesses, and boates with the Masters and Mariners ment by him to bee left in the Countrie for the supply of such, as for a further time ment to have stayed there were caried away with tempest, and foule weather: In the beginning whereof shalbe declared the conspiracie of Pemisapan, with the Savages of the mayne to have cutt us off, &c.

The first part declaring the particularities of the Countrey of Virginia.

First therefore touching the particularities of the Countrey, you shall understand our discovery of the same hath bene extended from the Iland of Roanoak, (the same having bene the place of our settlement or inhabitation) into the South, into the North, into the Northwest, and into the West.

The uttermost place to the Southward of any discoverie was Secotan, being by estimation foure score miles distant from Roanoak. The passage from thence was thorowe a broad sound within the mayne, the same being without kenning of land, and yet full of flats and shoales: we had but one boate with foure oares to passe through the same, which boat could not carry above fifteene men with their furniture, baggage, and victuall for seven dayes at the most: and as for our Pinnesse, besides that she drewe too deepe water for that shalow sound, she would not stirre for an oare: for these and other reasons (winter also being at hand) we thought good wholy to leave the discovery of those partes untill our stronger supplie.

To the Northwarde our furthest discoverie was to the Chesepians, distant from Roanoak about 130. miles, the passage to it was very shalow and most dangerous, by reason of the breadth of the sound, and the litle succour that upon any flawe was there to be had.

But the Territorie and soyle of the Chesepians (being distant fifteene miles from the shoare) was for pleasantnes of seate, for temperature of Climate, for fertilitie of soyle, and for the commoditie of the Sea, besides multitude of beares (being an excellent good victuall, with great woods of Sassafras, and Wall nut trees) is not to be excelled by any other whatsoever.

There be sundry Kings, whom they call Weroances, and Countries of great fertilitie adjoyning to the same, as the Mandoages, Tripanicks, and Opossians, which all came to visit the Colonie of the English, which I had for a time appointed to be resident there.

To the Northwest the farthest place of our discoverie was to Choanoke distant from Roanoak about 130. miles. Our passage thither lyeth through a broad sound, but all fresh water, and the chanell of great depth, navigable for good shipping, but out of the chanell full of shoales.

The Townes about the water side situated by the way, are these following: Pysshokonnok, The womans Towne, Chipanum, Weopomiok, Muscamunge, and Mattaquen: all these being under the jurisdiction of the king of Weopomiok, called Okisco: from Muscamunge we enter into the River, and jurisdiction of Choanoke: There the River beginneth to straighten untill it comes to Choanoke, and then groweth to be as narrowe as the Thames betweene Westminster, and Lambeth.

Betweene Muscamunge and Choanoke upon the left hand as we passe thither, is a goodly high land, and there is a Towne which we called the blinde Towne, but the Savages called it Ooanoke, and hath a very goodly corne field belonging unto it: it is subject to Choanoke.

Choanoke it selfe is the greatest Province and Seigniorie lying upon that River, and the very Towne it selfe is able to put 700. fighting men into the fielde, besides the forces of the Province it selfe.

The King of the sayd Province is called Menatonon, a man impotent in his lims, but otherwise for a Savage, a very grave and wise man, and of very singular good discourse in matters concerning the state, not onely of his owne Countrey, and the disposition of his owne men, but also of his neighbours round about him as wel farre as neere, and of the commodities that eche Countrey yeeldeth. When I had him prisoner with me, for two dayes that we were together, he gave me more understanding and light of the Countrey then I had received by all the searches and salvages that before I or any of my companie had had

conference with: it was in March last past 1586. Amongst other things he tolde me, that going three dayes journey in a canoa up his River of Choanoke, and then descending to the land, you are within foure dayes journey to passe over land Northeast to a certaine Kings countrey, whose Province lyeth upon the Sea, but his place of greatest strength is an Iland situate as he described unto me in a Bay, the water round about the Iland very deepe.

Out of this Bay hee signified unto mee, that this King had so great quantitie of Pearle, and doeth so ordinarily take the same, as that not onely his owne skins that he weareth, and the better sort of his gentlemen and followers, are full set with the sayd Pearle, but also his beds, and houses are garnished with them, and that hee hath such quantitie of them, that it is a wonder to see.

He shewed me that the sayd King was with him at Choanoak two yeeres before, and brought him certaine Pearle, but the same of the worst sort, yet was he faine to buy them of him for copper at a deere rate, as he thought: He gave me a rope of the same Pearle, but they were blacke, and naught, yet many of them were very great, and a fewe amongst a number very orient and round, all which I lost with other things of mine, comming aborde Sir Francis Drake his Fleete: yet he tolde me that the sayd King had great store of Pearle that were white, great, and round, and that his blacke Pearle his men did take out of shalowe water, but the white Pearle his men fished for in very deepe water.

It seemed to mee by his speech, that the sayde king had traffike with white men that had clothes as we have for these white Pearle, and that was the reason that he would not depart with other then with blacke Pearles, to those of the same Countrey.

The king of Choanoak promised to give me guides to goe over land into that kings Countrey whensoever I would: but he advised me to take good store of men with mee, and good store of victuall, for he sayd, that king would be loth to suffer any strangers to enter into his Countrey, and especially to meddle with the fishing for any Pearle there, and that hee was able to make a great many of men into the fielde, which he sayd would fight very well.

Hereupon I resolved with my selfe, that if your supplie had come before the end of April, and that you had sent any store of boats, or men, to have had them made in any reasonable time, with a sufficient number of men, and victuals to have found us untill the new corne were come in, I woulde have sent a small Barke with two Pinnesses about by Sea to the Northwarde to have found out the Bay he spake of, and to have sounded the barre if there were any, which shoulde have ridden there in the sayd Bay about that Iland, while I with all the small boats I could make, and with two hundreth men would have gone up to the head of the River of Choanoak, with the guides that Menatonon would have given, which I would have bene assured should have bene of his best men, (for I had his best beloved sonne prisoner with me) who also should have kept me companie in an handlocke with the rest foote by foote all the voyage over land.

My meaning was further at the head of the River in the place of my descent where I would have left my boates to have raysed a sconse with a small trench, and a pallisado upon the top of it, in the which, and in the garde of my boates I would have left five and twentie, or thirtie men, with the rest would I have marched with as much victuall as every man could have carried, with their furniture, mattocks, spades and axes, two dayes journey. In the ende of my marche upon some convenient plot would I have raysed another sconse according to the former, where I would have left 15. or 20. And if it would have fallen out conveniently, in the way I woulde have raised my sayd sconse upon some corne fielde, that my companie might have lived upon it.

And so I would have holden this course of insconsing every two dayes march, untill I had bene arrived at the Bay or Porte he spake of: which finding to be worth the possession, I would there have raised a mayne forte, both for the defence of the harboroughs, and our shipping also, and would have reduced our whole habitation from Roanoak and from the harborough and port there (which by proofe is very naught) unto this other before mentioned, from whence, in the foure dayes march before specified could I at all times returne with my companie backe unto my boats ryding under my sconse, very neere whereunto directly from the West runneth a most notable River, and in all those partes most famous, called the River of Morotico. This River openeth into the broad sound of Weopomiok: And whereas the River of Choanoak, and all the other sounds, and Bayes, salt and fresh, shewe no currant in the world in calme weather, but are mooved altogether with the winde: This River of Morotico hath so violent a currant from the West and Southwest, that it made me almost of opinion that with oares it would scarse be navigable: it passeth with many creeks and turnings, and for the space of thirtie miles rowing, and more, it is as broad as the Thames betwixt Greenwich, and the Ile of dogges, in some place more, and in some lesse: the currant runneth as strong being entred so high into the River, as at London bridge upon a vale water.

And for that not onely Menatonon, but also the Savages of Morotico themselves doe report strange things of the head of that River, and that from Morotico it selfe, which is a principall Towne upon that River, it is thirtie dayes as some of them say, and some say fourtie dayes voyage to the head thereof, which head they say springeth out of a maine rocke in that abundance, that forthwith it maketh a most violent streame: and further, that this huge rocke standeth nere unto a Sea, that many times in stormes (the winde comming outwardly from ye Sea) the waves thereof are beaten into the said fresh streame, so that the fresh water for a certaine space, groweth salt and brackish:

I tooke a resolution with my selfe, having dismissed Menatonon upon a ransome agreed for, and sent his sonne into the Pinnesse to Roanoak, to enter presently so farre into that River with two double whirries, and fourtie persons one or other, as I could have victuall to carrie us, untill we could meete with more either of the Moratiks, or of the Mangoaks which is another kinde of Savages, dwelling more to the Westwarde of the sayd River: but the hope of recovering more victuall from the Savages made me and my company as narowly to escape starving in that discoverie before our returne, as ever men did that missed the same.

For Pemisapan, who had changed his name of Wingina upon the death of his brother Granganimo, had given both the Choanists, & Mangoaks word of my purpose touching them, I having bin inforced to make him privie to ye same, to be served by him of a guide to the Mangoaks, and yet he did never rest to solicite continually my going upon them, certifying me of a generall assembly even at that time made by Menatonon at Choanoak of all his Weroances, & allyes to the number of 3000. bowes preparing to come upon us at Roanoak, and that the Mangoaks also were joyned in the same confederacie, who were able of themselves to bring as many more to the enterprise: And true it was, that at that time the assembly was holden at Choanoak about us, as I found at my comming thither, which being unlooked for did so dismay them, as it made us have the better hand at them. But this confederacie against us of the Choanists and Mangoaks was altogether and wholly procured by Pemisapan himselfe, as Menatonon confessed unto me, who sent them continuall worde that our purpose was fully bent to destroy them: on the other side he tolde me that they had the like meaning towards us.

Hee in like sort having sent worde to the Mangoaks of mine intention to passe up into their River, and to kill them (as he sayd) both they and the Moratiks, with whome before we were entred into a league, and they had ever dealt kindely with us, abandoned their Townes along the River, and retyred themselves with their Crenepoes, and their corne within the mayne: insomuch as having passed three dayes voyage up the River, we could not meete a man, nor find a graine of corne in any their Townes: whereupon considering with my selfe, that wee had but two dayes victuall left, and that wee were then 160. miles from home, besides casualtie of contrarie windes or stormes, and suspecting treason of our owne Savages in the discoverie of our voyage intended, though we had no intention to be hurtfull to any of them, otherwise then for our copper to have had corne of them: I at night upon the corps of garde, before the putting foorth of centinels, advertised the whole companie of the case wee stoode in for victuall, and of mine opinion that we were betrayed by our owne Savages, and of purpose drawen foorth by them, upon vaine hope to be in the ende starved, seeing all the Countrey fledde before us, and therefore while we had those two dayes victuall left, I thought it good for us to make our returne homewarde, and that it were necessarie for us to get the other side of the sound of Weopomiok in time, where we might be relieved upon the weares of Chypanum, and the womans Towne, although the people were fled.

Thus much I signified unto them, as the safest

way: neverthelesse, I did referre it to the greatest number of voyces, whether we should adventure the spending of our whole victuall in some further viewe of that most goodly River in hope to meete with some better hap, or otherwise to retyre our selves backe againe.: And for that they might be the better advised, I willed them to deliberate all night upon the matter, and in the morning at our going aborde to set our course according to the desires of the greatest part. Their resolution fully and wholly was (and not three found to be of the contrary opinion) that whiles there was left one halfe pinte of corne for a man, that we should not leave the search of that River, and that there were in the companie two mastives, upon the pottage of which with sassafras leaves (if the worst fell out) the companie would make shift to live two dayes, which time would bring them downe the currant to the mouth of the River, and to the entrie of the sound, and in two dayes more at the farthest they hoped to crosse the sounde and to bee relieved by the weares, which two dayes they would fast rather then be drawen backe a foote till they had seene the Mangoaks, either as friends or foes. This resolution of theirs did not a little please mee; since it came of themselves, although for mistrust of that which afterwards did happen, I pretended to have bene rather of the contrary opinion.

And that which made me most desirous to have some doings with the Mangoaks either in friendship or otherwise to have had one or two of them prisoners, was, for y[t] it is a thing most notorious to all y[e] countrey, that there is a Province to the which the sayd Mangoaks have recourse and traffike up that River of Morattico, which hath a marveilous and most strange Minerall. This Mine is so notorious amongst them, as not onely to the Savages dwelling up the sayde river, and also to the Savages of Choanoke, and all them to the westward, but also to all them of the mayne: the countries name is of fame, and is called Chaunis Temoatan.

The mineral they say is Wassador, which is copper, but they call by the name of Wassador every mettall whatsoever: they say it is of the couler of our copper, but our copper is better then theirs: and the reason is for that it is redder and harder, whereas that of Chaunis Temoatan is very soft, and pale: they say that they take the sayd mettall out of a river that falleth very swift from hie rocks, and hyls, and they take it in shallowe water: the manner is this. They take a great bowle by their discription as great as one of our targets, and wrap a skinne over the hollowe part thereof, leaving one part open to receive in the minerall: that done, they watch the comming downe of the currant, and the change of the couler of the water, and then suddenly chop downe the said bowle with the skin, and receive into the same as much oare as will come in, which is ever as much as their bowle wil hold, which presently they cast into a fire, and forthwith it melteth, and doeth yeelde in 5. partes, at the first melting, two parts of metall for three partes of oare. Of this metall the Mangoaks have so great store, by report of all the savages adjoyning, that they beautifie their houses with great plates of the same: and this to be true, I received by report of all the country, and particularly by yong Skiko, the King of Choanokes sonne my prisoner, who also himselfe had bene prisoner with the Mangoaks, and set downe all the particularities to mee before mentioned: but hee had not bene at Chawnis Temoatan himselfe: for he sayd, it was twentie dayes journey overlande from the Mangoaks, to the saide minerall country, and that they passed through certaine other territories betweene them and the Mangoaks, before they came to the said country.

Upon reporte of the premisses, which I was very inquisitive in all places where I came to take very particular information of, by all the savages that dwelt towards those parts, and especially of Menatonon himselfe, who in every thing did very particularly informe mee, and promised mee guides of his owne men, who shoulde pass over with mee, even to the sayde country of Chaunis Temoatan, (for over lande from Choanok to the Mangoaks is but one dayes journey from sunne rysing to sunne setting, whereas by water it is 7. daies with the soonest:) These things I say, made me verie desirous by all meanes possible to recover the Mangoaks & to get some of that their copper for an assay, and therefore I willingly yeelded to their resolution: But it fell out very contrarie to all expectation, and likelyhood: for after two dayes travell, and our whole victual spent, lying on shoare all night, wee could never see man, onely fires wee might perceive made alongst the shoare where we were to passe, and up into the countrie untill the very last day. In the

evening whereof, about three of the clocke we heard certaine savages call as we thought, Manteo, who was also at that time with mee in boate, whereof we all being verie glad, hoping of some friendly conference with them, and making him to answere them, they presently began a song, as we thought in token of our welcome to them: but Manteo presently betooke him to his peece, and tolde mee that they ment to fight with us: which word was not so soone spoken by him, and the light horseman ready to put to shoare, but there lighted a vollie of their arrowes amongst them in the boate, but did no hurt God be thanked to any man. Immediatly, the other boate lying ready with their shot to skoure the place for our hand weapons to land upon, which was presently done, although the lande was very high and steepe, the Savages forthwith quitted the shoare, and betooke themselves to flight: we landed, and having fayre and easily followed for a smal time after them, who had wooded themselves we know not where: the sunne drawing then towards the setting, and being then assured that the next day, if wee would pursue them, though wee might happen to meete with them, yet we should bee assured to meete with none of their victuall, which we then had good cause to thinke of, therefore choosing for the companie a convenient grounde in safetie to lodge in for the night, making a strong corps of garde, and putting out good centinels, I determined the next morning before the rising of the sunne to be going backe againe, if possibly wee might recover the mouth of the river into the broade sownde, which at my first motion I found my whole companie ready to assent unto: for they were nowe come to their dogs porredge, that they had bespoken for themselves, if that befell them which did, and I before did mistrust we should hardly escape. The ende was, we came the next day by night to the rivers mouth within 4. or 5. miles of the same, having rowed in one day downe the currant, as much as in 4. dayes we had done against the same: we lodged upon an Islande, where wee had nothing in the worlde to eate but pottage of sassafras leaves, the like whereof for a meate was never used before as I thinke. The broad sownde wee had to passe, the next day all fresh and fasting: that day the winde blewe so strongly, and the billow so great, that there was no possibilitie of passage without sinking of our boates. This was upon Easter eve, which was fasted very trulie. Upon Easter day in the morning the wind comming very calme, wee entred the sownde, and by of the clocke we were at Chipanum, where all the Savages that wee had left there were fled, but their wears did yeelde us some fish, as God was pleased not utterly to suffer us to be lost: for some of our companie of the light horsemen were far spent. The next morning we arrived at our home Roanoake.

I have set downe this voyage somewhat particularly, to the ende it may appeare unto you (as true it is) that there wanted no great good will from the most to the least amongst us, to have perfited this discoverie of the mine: for that the discovery of a good mine, by the goodnesse of God, or a passage to the Southsea, or someway to it, and nothing els can bring this country in request to be inhabited by our nation. And with the discovery of any of the two above shewed, it wilbe the most sweete, and healthfullest climate, and therewithall the most fertile soyle, being manured in the world: and then will Sassafras, and many other rootes & gummes there found make good Marchandise and lading for shipping, which otherwise of themselves will not bee worth the fetching.

Provided also, that there be found out a better harborough then yet there is, which must bee to the Northward, if any there be, which was mine intention to have spent this summer in the search of, and of the mine of Chawnis Temoatan: the one I would have done, if the barks that I should have had of Sir Francis Drake, by his honorable curtesie, had not bene driven away by storme: the other if your supply of more men, and some other necessaries had come to us in any convenient sufficiencie. For this river of Moratico promiseth great things, and by the opinion of Master Harriots the heade of it by the description of the country, either riseth from the bay of Mexico, or els from very neere unto the same, that openeth out into the South sea.

And touching the Minerall, thus doth Master Yougham affirme, that though it be but copper, seeing the Savages are able to melt it, it is one of the richest Minerals in the worlde.

Wherefore a good harborough founde to the Northward, as before is sayd, and from thence foure dayes overland, to the river of Choanoak sconses being raysed, from whence againe overlande through the province of Choanoak one

dayes voyage to the first towne of the Mangoaks up the river of Moratico by the way, as also upon the sayd river for the defence of our boats like sconses being set, in this course of proceeding you shall cleare your selfe from all those dangers and broad shallowe sownds before mentioned, and gayne within foure dayes travell into the heart of the mayne 200. myles at the least, and so passe your discoverie into that most notable, and to the likeliest partes of the mayne, with farre greater felicitie then otherwise can bee performed.

Thus sir, I have though simply, yet truely set downe unto you, what my labour with the rest of the gentlemen, and poore men of our company, (not without both payne, and perill which the lorde in his mercy many wayes delivered us from) could yeelde unto you, which might have bene performed in some more perfection, if the lorde had bene pleased that onely that which you had provided for us had at the first bene left with us, or that he had not in his eternall providence now at the last set some other course in these things, then the wisedome of man could looke into, which truely the carying away, by a most strange, & unlooked for storme all our provision, with barks, master, Marryners, and sundrie also of mine owne company, all having bene so curteously supplyed by the Generall Sir Francis Drake, the same having bene most sufficient to have performed the greatest part of the premisses, must ever make me to thinke, the hand of God only, (for some his good purpose to my selfe yet unknowne), to have bene in the matter.

The second part touching the conspiracy of Pemisapan, the discoverie of the same, and at the last, of our request to depart with Sir Francis Drake for England.

Ensenore a savage father to Pemisapan being the only frend to our nation that we had amongst them, and about the king, dyed the 20. of April, 1586. hee alone, had before opposed himselfe in their consultations against al matters proposed against us, which both the king, and all the rest of them after Grangemoes death, were very willing to have preferred. And he was not onely by the meere providence of God during his life, a meane to save us from hurt, as poysonings and such like, but also to doe us very great good, and singulerly in this.

The king was advised and of himselfe disposed,

as a ready meane to have assuredly brought us to ruine in the moneth of March, 1586, himselfe also with all his Savages to have runne away from us, and to have left his ground in the Island unsowed, which if he had done, there had bene no possibilitie in common reason, (but by the immediate hand of God) that we could have bene preserved from starving out of hand. For at that time wee had no weares for fishe, neither could our men skill of the making of them, neither had wee one grayne of corne for seede to put into the ground.

In mine absence on my voyage that I had made against the Chaonists, and Mangoaks, they had raised a bruite among themselves, that I and my company were part slayne, and part starved by the Chaonists, and Mangoaks. One part of this tale was too true, that I and mine were like to be starved, but the other false.

Neverthelesse untill my returne, it tooke such effect in Pemisapans breast, and in those against us, that they grew not onely into contempt of us, but also (contrary to their former reverend opinion in shew, of the almightie God of heaven, and Jesus Christ, whome wee serve and worship, whome before they woulde acknowledge and confesse the onely God:) nowe they began to blaspheme, and flatly to say, that generall name, all the inhabitants of the whole mayne, of what province soever. Insomuch as olde Ensenore, neither any of his fellowes, coulde for his sake have no more credite for us: and it came so farre that the King was resolved to have presently gone away as is aforesaid.

But even in the beginning of this bruite I returned, which when hee sawe contrarie to his expectation, and the advertisement that he had received: that not only my selfe, and my company were al safe, but also by report of his owne 3. savages, which had bene with mee besides Manteo in that voyage, that is to say, Tetepano, his sisters husband Eracano, and Cossine, that the Chaonists, and Mangoaks, (whose name, and multitude besides their valour is terrible to al the rest of the provinces) durst not for the most part of them abide us, and that those that did abide us were killed, and that we had taken Menatonon prisoner, and brought his sonne that he best loved to Roanoak with me, it did not a little asswage all devises against us: on the other side, it made Ensenors opinions to be received againe with greater respects. For hee had often before tolde

them, and then renewed those his former speeches, both to the king and the rest, that wee were the servants of God, and that wee were not subject to be destroyed by them: but contrariwise, that they amongst them that sought our destruction, should finde their owne, and not be able to worke ours, and that we being dead men were able to doe them more hurt, then now we coulde do being alive: an opinion very confidently at this day holden by the wisest amongst them, and of their olde men, as also, that they have bene in the night, beeing 100. myles from any of us in the ayre shot at, and stroken by some men of ours, that by sicknesse had dyed among them: and many of them holde opinion, that wee be dead men returned into the worlde againe, and that we doe not remayne dead but for a certaine time, and that then we returne againe.

All these speeches then againe grew in ful credite with them, the King and all touching us, when hee saw the small troupe returned againe, and in that sort from those whose very names were terrible unto them: but that which made up the matter on our side for that time, was an accident, yea rather, (as all the rest was) the good providence of the Almightie for the saving of us, which was this.

Within certaine dayes after my returne from the said journey, Menatonon sent a messengere to visite his sonne the prisoner with me, and sent me certaine pearle for a present, or rather as Pemisapan told me, for the ransome of his sonne, and therefore I refused them: but the greatest cause of his sending then, was to signifie unto me, that hee had commaunded Okisko king of Weopomick, to yelde himselfe servant, and homager, to the great Weroanza of England, and after her to Sir Walter Ralegh: to perfourme which commandement received from Menatonon, the sayd Okisko joyntly with this Menatonons messenger, sent foure and twentie of his principallest men to Roanoak to Pemisapan, to signifie that they were readie to perfourme the same, and so had sent those his men to let me knowe, that from that time forwarde hee, and his successours were to acknowledge her Majestie their onely Soveraigne, and next unto her, as is aforesayde.

All which being done, and acknowledged by them all, in the presence of Pemisapan his father, and all his Savages in counsel then with him, it did for the time, thorowly (as it seemed) change him in disposition towards us: Insomuch as forthwith Ensenore wan this resolution of him, that out of hand he should goe about, & withall, to cause his men to set up weares forthwith for us: both which he, at that present went in hand withal & did so labour the expedition of it, that in the end of April, he had sowed a good quantitie of ground, so much as had bene sufficient, to have fed our whole company (God blessing the grouth) and that by the belly for a whole yere: besides that he gave us a certaine plot of grounde for our selves to sowe. All which put us in marveilous comfort, if we could passe from Aprill, untill the beginning of July, (which was to have bene the beginning of their harvest,) that then a newe supplie out of Englande or els our owne store would well inough maintayne us: All our feare was of the two moneths betwixt, in which meane space, if the Savages should not helpe us with Cassada, and Chyna, and that our weares should fayle us, (as often they did) wee might very well starve, notwithstanding the growing corne, like the starving horse in the stable, with the growing grasse as the proverbe is, which we very hardlye had escaped but onely by the hande of God, as it pleased him to try us. For within few dayes after, as before is sayde Ensensore our friende dyed, who was no sooner dead, but certaine of our great enemies about Pemisapan, as Osocan a Weroance, Tanaquiny and Wanchese most principally, were in hand again to put their old practises in ure against us, which were readily imbraced, & al their former devises against us renewed, & new brought in question.

But that of starving us, by their forebearing to sowe, was broken by Ensenore in his life, by having made the king all at one instant to sowe his grounde not onely in the Islande but also at Addesmocopeia in the mayne, within two leagues over against us. Neverthelesse there wanted no store of mischevous practises among them, and of all they resolved principally of this following.

First that Okisko, king of Weopomick, with the Mandoages, should bee moved, and with great quantitie of copper intertayned to the number of seven, or 800 bowes to the enterprise the matter thus to be ordred. They of Weopomiok should be invited to a certaine kind of moneths minde which they do use to solemnise in their Savage manner for any great personage dead, and should have

bene for Ensenore. At this instant also should the Mandoaks, who were a great people with the Chesepians, and their friends to the number of 700. of them be armed at a day appoynted to the mayne of Addesmocopeio, and there lying close at the signe of fyers, which should interchangeably be made on both sides, when Pemisapan with his troup above named should have executed me, and some of our Weroances (as they called all our principall officers,) the mayne forces of the rest should have come over into the Iland where they ment to have dispatched the rest of the company, whome they did imagine to finde both dismayed and dispersed abroade in the Islande seeking of crabs, and fish to live withall. The manner of their enterprise was this.

Tarraquine and Andacon two principall men about Pemisapan, and very lustie fellowes with twentie more appointed to them had the charge of my person to see an order taken for the same, which they ment should in this sort have bene executed. In the dead time of the night they would have beset my house, and put fire in the reedes, that the same was covered with: meaning (as it was likelye) that my selfe woulde have come running out of a sudden amazed in my shirt without armes, upon the instant whereof they woulde have knocked out my braynes.

The same order was given to certaine of his fellowes, for Master Herriots: so for all the rest of our better sort, all our houses at one instant being set on fire as afore is sayde, and that as well for them of the forte, as for us at the towne. Now to the end that we might be the fewer in number together, and so be the more easilie dealt withall (for in deede ten of us with our armes prepared, were a terrour to a hundred of the best sort of them,) they agreed and did immediatly put it in practise, that they should not for any copper, sell us any victuals whatsoever: besides that in the night they should send to have our weares robbed, and also to cause them to be broken and once being broken never to be repayred againe by them. By this meanes the King stood assured, that I must bee enforced for lacke of sustenance, there to disband my company into sundry places to live upon shell fishe, for so the Savages themselves doe, going to Ottorasko, Crotoan, and other places fishing and hunting, while their grownds be in sowing, and their corne growing, which fayled not his expectation. For the famine grewe so extreeme among us, our weares fayling us of fish, that I was enforced to send captaine Stafford with 20. with him to Crotoan my lord Admirals Island to serve two turnes in one, that is to say to feede himselfe, and his company, and also to keepe watch, if any shipping came upon the coast to warne us of the same. I sent master Pridiox with the Pynnesse to Otterasco, and ten with him, with the Provost Marshal to live there, and also to wayte for shipping: also I sent every weeke 16. or 20. of the rest of the companie to the mayne over against us, to live of Casada, and oysters.

In the meane while Pemisapan went of purpose to Addesmocopeio for 3. causes, the one, to see his grounds there broken up, and sowed for a second croppe: the other to withdrawe himselfe from my dayly sending to him for supply of victuall for my company, for hee was afrayde to denye me any thing, neither durst he in my presence but by colour, and with excuses, which I was content to accept for the time, meaning in the ende as I had reason, to give him the jumpe once for all: but in the meane whiles, as I had ever done before, I and mine bare all wrongs, and accepted of all excuses.

My purpose was to have relyed my selfe with Menatonon, and the Chaonists, who in truth as they are more valiant people and in greater number then the rest, so are they more faithfull in their promises, and since my late being there, had given many tokens of earnest desire they had to joyne in perfect league with us, and therefore were greatly offended with Pemisapan and Weopomiok for making him to beleeve such tales of us.

The third cause of his going to Addesmacopeio was to dispatch his messengers to Weopomiok, and to the Mandoages, as aforesaid, al which he did with great impresse of copper in hand, making large promises to them of greater spoyle.

The answere within fewe dayes after, came from Weopomiok, which was devided into two parts. First for the King Okisko, who denyed to be of ye partie for himselfe, or any of his especial followers, and therefore did immediatly retyre himselfe with his force into the mayne: the other was concerning the rest of the sayd province who accepted of it: and in like sort the Mandoags received the imprest.

The day of their assembly aforesayd at Roanoak, was appointed the 10. of July: all which the premises were discovered by Skyco, the king Menatonon his sonne my prisoner, who having once attempted to run away, I laid him in the bylboes, threatning to cut off his head, whome I remitted at Pemisapans request: whereupon he being perswaded that he was our enemie to the death, he did not only feede him with himselfe, but also made him acquainted with all his practises. On the other side, the yong man finding himself as well used at my hand, as I had meanes to shew, and that all my companie made much of him, he flatly discovered all unto me, which also afterwards was revealed unto me by one of Pemisapans owne men, ye night before he was slaine.

These mischiefes being al instantly upon mee, and my companie to be put in execution, stood mee in hand to study how to prevent them, and also to save all others, which were at that time as aforesaid so farre from me: whereupon I sent to Pemisapan to put suspition out of his heade, that I ment presently to goe to Crotoan, for that I had heard of the arival of our fleete, (though I in trueth had neither heard nor hoped for so good adventure,) and that I meant to come by him, to borrow of his men to fish for my company, and to hunt for me at Crotoan, as also to buy some foure dayes provision to serve for my voyage.

He sent mee word that he would himselfe come over to Roanoak, but from day to day hee deferred, only to bring the Weopomioks with him, and the Mandoags, whose time appoynted was within 8. dayes after. It was the last of May, 1586. when all his owne savages began to make their assembly at Roanoak, at his commandement sent abroad unto them, and I resolved not to stay longer upon his comming over, since he ment to come with so good company, but thought good to go, and visite him with such as I had, which I resolved to do the next day: but that night I ment by the way to give them in the Island a Canuisado, and at the instant to sease upon all the Canoas about the Island to keepe him from advertisements.

But the towne tooke the allarum, before I ment it to them: the occasion was this. I had sent the Master of the light horsemen with a few with him, to gather up all the Canoas in the setting of the sunne, & to take as many as were going from us to Adesmocopeio, but to suffer any that came from thence to land: he met with a Canoa, going from the shoare, and overthrew the Canoa, and cut off 2. savages heads: this was not done so secretly but hee was discovered from the shoare, whereupon the cry arose: for in trueth they, privie to their owne villanous purposes against us, held as good espial upon us, both day and night, as we did upon them.

The allarum given, they took themselves to their bowes, and we to our armes: some three or foure of them at the first were slayne with our shot, the rest fled into yᵉ woods: The next morning with the light horseman, & one Canoa, taking 25. with the Colonel of the Chesepians, and the Serjeant major, went to Adesmocopeio, and being landed sent Pemisapan word by one of his owne savages that met me at the shore, that I was going to Crotoan, and ment to take him in the way to complaine unto him of Osocon, who the night past was conveying away my prisoner, whom I had there present tied in an handlocke: hereupon the king did abide my comming to him, and finding my selfe amidst 7. or 8. of his principal Weroances, & followers, (not regarding any of the common sort) I gave the watchword agreed upon, (which was Christ our victory,) and immediatly those his chiefe men, and himselfe, had by the mercie of God for our deliverance, that which they had purposed for us. The king himselfe being shot thorow by the Colonell with a pistoll lying on the ground for dead, & I looking as watchfully for the saving of Manteos friends, as others were busie that none of the rest should escape, suddenly he started up, and ran away as though he had not bene touched, insomuch as he overran all the companie, being by the way shot thwart the buttocks by mine Irish boy with my Petronell. In the end an Irish man serving me, one Nugent and the deputie provost undertooke him, and following him in the woods overtooke him, and I in some doubt least we had lost both the king, and my man by our owne negligence to have bene intercepted by the Savages, we met him returning out of the woods with Pemisapans head in his hand.

This fell out the first of June, 1586. and the 8. of the same came advertisement to me from captaine Stafford, lying at my lord Admirals Island, that he had discovered a great Fleete of 23. sailes: but whether they were friends or foes, he could not yet discerne, he advised me to stand upon as good gard as I could.

The 9. of the said moneth, he himselfe came unto me, having that night before, and that same day travelled by land 20. miles, and I must truly report of him from the first to the last, he was the gentleman that never spared labour or perill either by land or water, faire weather or fowle, to performe any service committed unto him.

He brought me a letter from the Generall sir Francis Drake, with a most bountifull and honourable offer for the supplie of our necessities to the performance of the action, we were entered into, and that not onely of victuals, munition and clothing, but also of barkes, pinnaces and boates, they also by him to be victualled, manned, and furnished to my contentation.

The 10. day hee arrived in the road of our bad harborough, and comming there to an anker, the 11. day I came to him, whom I found in deeds most honourably to performe that which in writing and message he had most curteously offered, he having aforehand propounded the matter to all the captains of his Fleete, and got their liking and consent thereto.

With such thanks unto him and his captaines for his care both of us and of our action, not as the matter deserved, but as I could both for my companie and my selfe, I (being aforehand) prepared what I would desire, craved at his hands that it would please him to take with him into England a number of weake, and unfit men for my good action, which I would deliver to him, and in place of them to supply me of his company, with oare men, artificers, and others.

That he would leave us so much shipping and victuall, as about August then next followyng, would cary me and all my companie into England, when we had discovered somwhat that for lacke of needfull provision in time left with us as yet remained undone.

That it would please him withall to leave some sufficient masters not onely to cary us into England, when time should be, but also to search the coast for some better harborow if there were any, and especially to helpe us to some small boats and oare men.

Also for a supplie of calievers, handweapons, match and lead, tooles, apparell, and such like.

He having received these my requests according to his usuall commendable manner of governement (as it was told me) calling his captaines to counsell, the resolution was that I should send such of my officers of my companie, as I used in such matters, with their notes to goe aboord with him, which were the master of the victuals, the keeper of the store, and the Vicetreasurer, to whom he appointed foorthwith for me the Francis, being a very proper barke of 70. tunnes, and tooke present order for bringing of victuall aboord her for 100 men. for foure moneths withall my other demaunds whatsoever, to the uttermost.

And further appointed for me two fine pinnaces, and 4. small boats, and that which was to performe all his former liberalitie towards us, was that he had gotten the full assents of two of as sufficient experimented masters as were any in his fleete, by judgement of them that knewe them, with very sufficient gings to tarie with mee, and to employ themselves most earnestly in the action, as I should appoynt them, untill the terme which I promised of our returne into England agayne. The names of one of those masters was Abraham Kendall, the other Griffith Herne.

While these things were in hand, the provision aforesayd being brought, and in bringing a boord, my sayd masters being also gone aboord, my sayd barkes having accepted of their charge, and mine owne officers with others in like sort of my company with them, all which was dispatched by the said Generall the 12. of the said moneth: the 13. of the same there arose such an unwonted storme, and continued foure dayes that had like to have driven all on shore, if the Lord had not held his holy hand over them, and the generall very providently foreseene the worst himselfe, then about my dispatch putting himselfe aboord: but in the ende having driven sundry of the Fleete to put to sea the Francis also with all my provisions, my two masters, and my company aboord, shee was seene to be free from the same, and to put cleare to sea.

This storme having continued from the 13. to the 16. of the moneth, and thus my barke put away as aforesayd, the Generall comming a shore, made a new proffer to me, which was a shippe of 170. tunnes, called the Barke Bonner, with a sufficient master and guide to tarie with mee the time appointed, and victualled sufficiently to carie mee and my companie into England with all provisions as before: but hee tolde mee that hee would not for any thing undertake to have her brought into our harbour, and therefore hee was to leave her in the roade, and to leave the care of the rest unto my selfe, and advised mee to consider with my companie of our case, and to deliver presently unto him in writing, what I would require him to doe for us: which being within his power, hee did assure me as well for his Captaines, as for himselfe should be most willingly performed.

Hereupon calling such Captaines and Gentlemen of my companie as then were at hand, who were all as privie as my selfe to the Generals offer, their whole request was to mee, that considering the case that we stood in, the weaknesse of our companie, the small number of the same, the carying away of our first appointed barke, with those two especiall masters, with our principall provisions in the same, by the very hand of God as it seemed, stretched out to take us from thence: considering also, that his second offer, though most honourable of his part, yet of ours not to be taken, insomuch as there was no possibilitie for her with any safetie to be brought into the harbour: Seeing furthermore our hope for supplie with sir Richard Greenvill so undoubtedly promised us before Easter, not yet come, neither then likely to come this yeere considering the doings in England for Flaunders, and also for America, that therefore I would resolve my selfe, with my companie to goe into England in that Fleete, and accordingly to make request to the Generall in all our names, that he would bee pleased to give us present passage with him. Which request of ours by my selfe delivered unto him, hee most readily assented unto, and so hee sending immediately his pinnaces unto our Island for the fetching away of fewe that there were left with our baggage, the weather was so boysterous, and the pinnaces so often on ground, that the most of all wee had, with all our Cardes, Bookes and writings, were by the Saylers cast over boord, the greater number of the Fleete being much agrieved with their long and daungerous abode in that miserable road.

From whence the Generall in the name of the Almightie, waying his ankers (having bestowed us among his Fleete) for the reliefe of whom hee had in that storme sustained more perill of wracke then in all his former most honourable actions against the Spaniards, with praises unto God for all, set saile the 19. of June, 1586. and arrived in Portesmouth, the 27. of Julie the same yeere.

445. 1586. The *Primrose* journal of Drake's voyage: Florida and Virginia.

Drake left Plymouth on September 14, 1585, with 29 ships and pinnaces to strike a blow against the centers of Spanish power in the West Indies. Drake commanded the Elizabeth Bonaventure *and Martin Frobisher the* Primrose. *This account of the expedition is signed* Henrey, *whose identity is unknown but who appears to have served on the* Primrose.

This extract takes up the story at the point when the fleet, having sacked Santo Domingo and Cartagena, collecting ransoms and with released slaves on board, Negroes and Turks mainly, approaches Florida.

From B.L., Royal MS 7.C.xvi, fols. 166–173. Printed in J. Corbett, The Spanish war 1585–87 *(1898), pp. 1–26; D. B. Quinn,* Roanoke voyages, *I (1955), 303–308.*

The discourse and description of the voyage of Sir Frawncis Drake & Master captaine Frobisher, set forward the 14 daie of September. 1585/....

The 23 of Maie wee put of into the sea for the Cape of florida, and the xxv^th daie wee gott sight therof & sealinge alonge the coast, the 27 daie wee fell with a Towne called Saint Awgustine, There wee went on shore in the morninge, but coulde not enter the Towne for they had warninge of our comminge, and made a castle of pur[pose] for there defence against us in suche order that wee must winne the castle before wee coulde get the Towne, and our s[hips] could not come neere the Towne to batter hit, the water w[as] shallow excepte it weare a v or 6 miles from hit, Yet there wa[s] a goodlie River runninge close by the towne into the countrie.

The 28 daie wee tooke ordinawnce on shore to batter the Castle which stoode on the one side of the river & wee were on the other yet when wee had shott ij peeces at them, like fainte harted Cowardes they ranne awaie, This was abowte midnight, Then came over the river to us a frenche man & a ducheman who tolde us they were all fledd,

Then the Admyrall & Vizadmirall went over with xx^ti men & Entringe there Castle fownde there woordes trew, Then on the other side where our men laie the savages & others came owte of the woodes & with a verie strawnge crie, assawlted our men.

But they weare soone driven backe and our men followinge them into the woodes by mischawnce on master Waterhouse the Captaines lieftenaunte Of our shipp was slaine,

The 29 daie of Maie wee entered the Towne & the Spaniardes gave us 3 or 4 small shott & Ranne awaie & in followinge of them Captaine Powell was slaine by a horsman & ij footmen spaniardes

The 30 daie after wee had taken the spoile of this Towne wee set it on fire & soe wente to the Castle where wee rested 3 daies

In this Castle wee fownde a Cheste with the kinges Treasure, and hard by the Castle wee fownde a small Carvell with certaine treasure in her and somme letters from the kinge of Spaine,

For Shee was newlie come thence and further Wee fownde a lit[tle] Childe in her which the Spaniardes had lefte behinde them for has[te] Wee sent them the childe and they tooke her but woulde not c[ome] to us for anie thinge wee coulde doe,

There was 9 of the savages set up a flagge of Truce abo[ut] ij miles from the Towne, which our men fownde and carried them another,

The seconde daie of June wee set fire on the Castle, w[ee then the] same night set saile from Thence,

Also In that nighte wee set fire on the Carvell [which wee] had taken by the Matacosse laden with salte / and tooke t[he other] Carvell along with us,

This Towne Saint Awgustine / standeth in florydaie [where is] as goodlie a soyle as maie bee, with so great abundance [of] sweete woodes &c' as is woonderfull with goodlie meadowes, [and] store of fisshe Oysters & mussels with deere & goodlie feeldes of Corne after there manner,

There was abowte 250 howses in this Towne, but wee left not one of them standinge,

Wee fownde 40 pipes of meale in this place & muche ba[rley] but wee fownde neither wine nor Oyle nor anie other vict[ual] to make accompte of

Wee had in this towne xij greate peeces of Brasse Ordinawnce

This Towne had v weekes warninge before, of our comminge, and had builded this castle onlie for us keepinge 90 sowldiers there in garrison, And There wee understoode that the Hyabans had burn[ed] there towne themselves, and had gotten 1200 men to helpe the[m] thinkinge that we woulde come to them,

The wilde people at first comminge of our men died verie fast and saide amongest themselves, It was the Inglisshe God that made them die so faste/

There ar divers kinges emongest them, and these kinges ar distaunte on from an other & they have manie wifes, They tolde our men of one kinge not far from thence that had 140 wives,

Oure men killed the kinge of that place wee were In for that hee with hys people in on nighte had determined to murther all the Inglishmen / And an Indian did Bewraie the[ir] cowncell, Soe wee gave the kinge that for his paines which hee woulde have geeven us,

The have a churche with 3 Images in hit, And the[y] speake with the Divell once everie yeere uppon an highe Mowntaine,

Also they ar cladd in Skins and they have a Copper myne emongest them, And for the tagge of a pointe, a bell a cownter, a pinne or suche like, They will geeve you anie thinge they have/

Then wee sailed alonge the coast of this lande untill wee Came to the place where those men did lyve that Sir Walter Raleghe had sente thither to Inhabit the yeere before

Those gentlemen and others, as soone as they s[aw vs, thin]kinge wee had bin a new supplie [came from the] shore & tarried certaine daies, & a[fterwards we brought]e thense all those men with us, except iij [who had gone furt]her into the countrie and the winde gre[we so that] wee coulde not staie for them/

[The 13th] of June iiij of our Shippes weare forced to [put to sea] the weather was so sore & the Storme so [great th]at our Ankers woulde not holde, and no shipp [of them all] but eyther brake or lost ther Ankers, And our [ship th]e Prymrose Brake an Anker of 250 li. waighte [All the] Time wee weare in thys countrie, We had thunder [lightning] and raigne with hailstormes as Bigge as hennes egges [There were] greate Spowtes at the seas as thoughe heaven & [earth] woulde have mett/

[This c]owntrie is Indifferent frewtfull and hathe good [store of] fisshe with land Turtles & nice Frewtes & saxafrage [which are] the best thinges in all the lande that wee know of: [the rest] after the reporte of the people woulde bee to longe [Let th]is suffice/

[The 18th] daie of June 1586 wee set saile directinge our course [to Ne]wfownd Lande & so homewardes/

[signed:] Henrey

446. August 1, 1586. A report on Drake's voyage and of the return of the Roanoke colonists.

An unidentified foreign gentleman, possibly a German, was in London when Drake and Lane returned. He made early contact with both of them and formed a high opinion of both men. He wrote in Latin to an unidentified correspondent from Richmond Palace, where he was visiting the court (on August 1 new style; August 11 English or old style). His letter was intercepted and copied and found its way into Spanish hands. Philip II and his ambassador corresponded on July 18, August 7, and September 5, about a report of a German captain who had been taken prisoner by the English and reached Spain (A. G., Simancas, Estado Francia, K1448, Philip to Mendoza, July 18; Mendoza to Philip, August 7; Philip to Mendoza, September 5), but the dates and circumstances do not fit so that "the German Captain" cannot be the author, unless another earlier report of his was sent to Spain.

The report is important because it gives a reason—an impending Spanish attack—for Drake's visit to the Roanoke colony.

The Latin copy (A. G., Simancas, Estado Francia, K.1564 [B57, nos. 100–168]) is somewhat corrupt, and gave considerable difficulty to the translator, Neil M. Cheshire. A few passages (notably that on Davis), remain obscure. It has remained unpublished.

After I had returned to the city of London yesterday, my dear friend, I happened to meet Francis Drake, the Knight, on the next day. He was accompanied by Martin Frobisher, Petro Semearo [Peter Seymour] and Rofsio [Richard] Hawkins, who are captains and associates of his voyages, and he filled the whole Palace with a very special joy. His friends and relatives are celebrating his safe return from such a long journey, with its difficulties and dangers overcome. But he replied to them that he was more effective in austere conditions, and that they were rejoicing in his return with much greater affection than he could have expected to restore or generate anew now that almost a year had passed since he set sail from Plymouth. For he went away on 12th September last, and came back to Court on the last day of July.

He sailed from England with twenty-two ships and brought eighteen back to Portsmouth; three have docked at Plymouth, and another four are awaited from day to day,—four which were driven away and separated from the rest of the fleet by a storm which blew up after they left the coast of Virginia (for here, after starting the voyage back to Britain, our heroes paid homage to that shore which lies between Florida and Norumbega, since a colony has been planted there by Sir Walter Raleigh). Edward Winter is astray among these four: son of Sir William Winter, the naval Commander ("*Propraefectus*"), who died of a fever on this expedition, and a young man of outstanding character. That fleet was composed of two thousand soldiers and sailors, apart from the young lads and those assigned to more menial duties. Four hundred of these succumbed to some disease which afflicted the fleet, the rest surviving; only thirty died in action, of whom ten were struck down in fierce engagement with the enemy and the rest died later from the wounds they had received. This must immediately seem miraculous to anyone who reflects how tiny was the number with which they fought innumerable enemies; for whatever they attempted they took by force of arms.

These are the main places which Francis Drake went for in this second expedition to the Indies, and which he overpowered. The delightful island of Bonona, where he set free some captured Englishmen, took the island from those in possession as a penalty, and sailed away toward the Cape Verdes (I shall employ here the usage of our own day and not that known to our ancestors), where he took over the island dedicated to St. James (Santiago) (the Spanish have no name for the place). From there he struck across to Hispaniola and took into his jurisdiction the city called Santo Domingo, a large place, very luxurious and graced with spendid buildings, where there were galleons fitted out for war, more than four hundred armed horsemen well equipped for battle, and up to six thousand armed soldiers and citizens ranged against Francis Drake.

These Drake outwitted with the following strategy. He drew off his troops from the emptied ships three miles from the city, so that the foot-soldiers might invade the city by land in a single assault. He himself gathered the whole fleet under short sail into the harbour, as if to attack the city on that side from the ships; the militia and citizens closed the defences and blocked the gates at the place where the enemy seemed to be at hand, in order to repel him there. Meanwhile the troops who were storming the town by land took them by surprise, since they were concentrating on the fleet and not taking enough precautions against them on that flank, but the Spanish cavalry withstood the first English charge in the conviction that they would immediately turn their minds to flight.

However, when the Spaniards found themselves being wounded here and there by musket fire, and being stabbed and gouged by pikemen, it was they who were the first to take to flight, and they retreated to the city gates; but when Drake's men pursued them, they encountered greater armament installed at the gates, which the enemy turned upon the English inflicting considerable casualties. But, while the San Domingans were hiding themselves away in the city, Drake went up to the gates with his extraordinary *panache* and struck unaccustomed alarm into the astonished inhabitants (for it was a long time since they had experienced a military reverse), so that they surrendered to his approach and relinquished the city.

This same Drake attacked three other towns on the island of Hispaniola (where the Spanish governor's headquarters were, and also the royal residence); and when he had been in possession of the island for the space of a month, he then set his course toward the mainland of Peru; for contrary winds prevented him from reaching Havana, and he consequently sailed for the coastal town of Cartagena, a very important port, and easily overcame the enemy forces. Having put to the test his admirable faith in his men, he recounts to people's surprise what he has achieved, and he now wonders himself how he dared to attack such a large enemy army with such a small band of soldiers. But, in his reverence for Almighty God, he attributes it all to the providence and goodwill of the Divinity, by which people both great and small were roused against the numberless enemy.

His boldness in large-scale villainy was certainly astonishing; and when he had lorded it over Cartagena, he turned towards that district which they have begun to call Florida, and there he gained entry to a city designated, equally grandly, Augusta [San Agustín] and invaded the harbour. The castle called San Juan which he beseiged was handed over to him. These are the chief and almost the only strongholds, apart from Havana and Mexico, which the Spanish king keeps garrisoned (*Plidiarto*) or attaches some value to, and which Drake throughly devastated, ransacked and burned; but he did leave untouched by fire a sixth part of the city Sandoma, [Santo Domingo], whose total size equals London, Trevolentum [Treves] and Augusta [Cologne] put together,—a part which had to be redeemed at huge expense by the city governors who had deserted it in flight.

Drake took away with him to Britain two hundred guns of brass and a hundred of iron from the places he captured; his soldiers deprived the inhabitants of all military equipment, gunpowder, lead and iron shot which they use for firearms, and he seized their swords, spears, battleaxes and any kind of weapon. Warships, galleons, small boats and all seaworthy vessels he either burned, sank or requisitioned to his own use. In some of the places he captured he stayed for a fortnight, but in other he remained for a whole month; and although he had amassed an enormous amount of booty there, he still arranged that the inhabitants should ransom themselves out at a high price. Hence his boast that the King of Spain could not repair and reconstruct, in twenty years of continuous peace and with the expense of tens of thousands or millions of gold pieces, what he personally had destroyed, burned and ravaged in such a very little time, quite apart

from the treasure which he plundered and brought home with him from the captured places,—for that was by no means insignificant.

It was reduced, however, by the fact that the King had despatched a ship to Peru in anticipation of Drake's arrival a month before he sailed into Cartagena; for the King proposed to his officers throughout Peru that they should help to make peace with certain Indian kings on specified terms lest they might perhaps ally themselves with Francis Drake and deprive the King himself of his Indian possessions. And he instructed that the treasuries be moved from Cartagena and Nombre de Dios, in case Drake should land and invade them. Consequently Francis Drake did not intercept them, but only because the King turned them to his own use, to prevent Drake from quickly smelling out where they are hidden when he returns to the Indies. He did indeed ransack various hiding-places, of the King and the Marques de Santa Cruz, which the noble companion of the Queen had made, and plundered everything that the King had consigned to these places over three years.

From all this it can clearly be seen how much the King feared for himself from Drake's enterprises of this kind. Indeed when he established the fact that Captain Marchio [Pedro Menéndez Marqués] had organised an expedition to Virginia, in order to root out utterly the British Colony which had not yet consolidated its settlement there, Drake followed suit by putting to sea himself and set course toward Virginia, with the object, commendable of course, of rescuing Ralph Lane (the undoubtedly distinguished leader of that colony) and his people from death, and of bringing them all back home with him safely. So he stayed on the shores of Virginia just four days and sailed off from there for 36 days to British ports; a return which he would have made before two months were up if he had not deviated from his proposed route.

Those who came back with him report that he was perturbed by various rumours to the effect that certain Frenchmen had invaded and taken over Porto Rico and also the shores of Port Caballino [Puerto Caballos?] situated on mainland Peru. Drake says nothing about this; but I have seen and studied some letters which Ralph Lane recently (sent) to a friend from the royal ship who also helped him (for she was standing by off

Portsmouth at the time) in which he remarks on the fact that plenty of precious metals and stones are to be found in Virginia, a region which he intends to make for again soon. As far as Richard Greenfield [Grenville] is concerned, the Knight who put to sea with seven ships some months previously, Drake learned nothing else for certain. The Papists here are boasting that he was captured and taken off to Spain, but for various reasons we can conclude that this is not so; his own friends are afraid that he may perhaps have encountered Marchio's fleet while sailing to Virginia or making an expedition from there.

The whole court, however, is resounding with praise for Drake; and although mine is rather more modest, I of course believe in the truth of what I have reported about him. I have met him, and if I am any judge of a man's character, he seems destined by the Good Lord to achieve great things: perceptive and intelligent by nature, his practical ability astonishing, his memory acute, his skill in managing a fleet virtually unique, his general manner moderate and restrained, so that individuals are won over and gripped by affection for him. He easily evokes obedience from soldiers and sailors, and consequently if he is compelled to be severe, such is the fairness with which he acts that all resentment or even hatred soon dies away. I say nothing about his magnanimity; and about his learning, experience and technique in navigation, which events themselves have made abundantly clear, I would only add that he is lavishing such careful attention and foresight on the Province which he asked for that he is taking on both the ministry of a bishop and the practice of a doctor for the sake of its birth.

At Portsmouth (a harbour which, with its adjacent town, her Gracious Majesty is currently encircling with new fortifications), the fleet has been awaiting his return from day to day with keen enthusiasm, so that the soldiers may be paid off, of course, with their 40-fold wages. But the third expedition to the Indies is a matter of the most serious discussion and deliberation, whether Drake is to be put in charge again and be associated with the fleet.

Lane even imputes to him in a letter something which I had almost forgotten to mention, namely that he has very little doubt that Davis is going to be strong enough to link up along that passage which is to be traced into the Southern Sea through northern and western waters. For this is what Davis ventured upon last year (when its exploration had been more than enough for Martin Frobisher seven years ago), wanting to penetrate further into that passage, so that, when he himself had continued up to 500 miles beyond where Frobisher had sailed, he would clearly see, as a result of the navigational skill which has been stimulated in our times by the English, how we can intercept the Spanish and Portuguese trade to the Moluccas, with great profit, by sailing a quicker route to those islands. But I have gathered, from conversation with Francis Drake, that the man is under obligation to his Majesty the King of Navarre, the hope of Europe.

He [Drake] is going to come to London on Wednesday, where he will stay at the house of Martin the London member of parliament. I thought to tell this so that the good news might inspire some fresh happiness in you, to the extent of reminding you to keep your eyes open for how you may arrange a position in London, from which you could take the opportunity of conducting the business of his Gracious Majesty your King with our Drake as well.

Goodbye, my dear and famous man.

from Richmond Palace; August 1st, old style.

Chapter Fifty-eight
The Unsuccessful Venture of 1586 and
Its Aftermath

447. June, 1586. Relief ships for the first Roanoke colony.

This summary of the activities on the coast of Virginia of Drake's fleet and the two supply voyages made for the relief of Ralph Lane's colony was written by Richard Hakluyt.

Printed in R. Hakluyt, Principall navigations (1589), pp. 747–748; Principal navigations III (1600), 265; VIII (1904), 346–348.

The third voyage made by a ship sent in the yeere 1586, to the reliefe of the Colony planted in Virginia, at the sole charges of Sir Walter Ralegh.

In the yeere of our Lord 1586 Sir Walter Ralegh at his owne charge prepared a ship of an hundred tunne, fraighted with all maner of things in most plentifull maner, for the supply and reliefe of his Colony then remaining in Virginia: but before they set saile from England it was after Easter, so that our Colony halfe despaired of the comming of any supply: wherefore every man prepared for himselfe, determining resolutely to spend the residue of their life time in that countrey. And for the better performance of this their determination, they sowed, planted, and set such things as were necessary for their reliefe in so plentifull a maner as might have sufficed them two yeeres without any further labour. Thus trusting to their owne harvest, they passed the Summer till the tenth of June: at which time their corne which they had sowed was within one fortnight of reaping: but then it happened that Sir Francis Drake in his prosperous returne from the sacking of Sant Domingo, Cartagena, and Saint Augustine, determined in his way homeward to visit his countreymen the English Colony then remaining in Virginia. So passing along the coasts of Florida,

he fell with the parts where our English Colony inhabited: and having espied some of that company, there he ankered and went aland, where hee conferred with them of their state and welfare, and how things had past with them. They answered him that they lived all; but hitherto in some scarsity: and as yet could heare of no supply out of England: therefore they requested him that hee would leave with them some two or three ships, that if in some reasonable time they heard not out of England, they might then returne themselves. Which hee agreed to. Whilest some were then writing their letters to send into England, and some others making reports of the accidents of their travels ech to other, some on land, some on boord, a great storme arose, and drove the most of their fleet from their ankers to Sea, in which ships at that instant were the chiefest of the English Colony: the rest on land perceiving this, hasted to those three sailes which were appointed to be left there; and for feare they should be left behinde they left all things confusedly, as if they had bene chased from thence by a mighty army: and no doubt so they were; for the hand of God came upon them for the cruelty and outrages committed by some of them against the native inhabitants of that countrey.

Immediately after the departing of our English Colony out of this paradise of the world, the ship abovementioned sent and set forth at the charges of Sir Walter Ralegh and his direction, arrived at Hatorask; who after some time spent in seeking our Colony up in the countrey, and not finding them, returned with all the aforesayd provision into England.

About foureteene or fifteene dayes after the departure of the aforesayd shippe, Sir Richard Grinvile Generall of Virginia, accompanied with three shippes well appointed for the same voyage, arrived there; who not finding the aforesayd shippe according to his expectation, nor hearing any newes of our English Colony there seated, and left by him anno 1585, himselfe travelling up into divers places of the countrey, aswell to see if he could heare any newes of the Colony left there by him the yeere before, under the charge of Master Lane his deputy, as also to discover some places of the countrey: but after some time spent therein, not hearing any newes of them, and finding the places which they inhabited desolate, yet unwilling to loose the possession of the countrey which Englishmen had so long held: after good deliberation, hee determined to leave some men behinde to reteine possession of the Countrey: whereupon he landed fifteene men in the Isle of Roanoak, furnished plentifully with all maner of provision for two yeeres, and so departed for England.

Not long after he fell with the Isles of Açores, on some of which Islands he landed, and spoiled the townes of all such things as were woorth cariage, where also he tooke divers Spanyards. With these and many other exploits done by him in this voyage, aswell outward as homeward, he returned into England.

448. October 12, 1586. Comments by John Hooker on the Virginia colony.

This extract is from John Hooker's dedication to Ralegh of "The Irish historie ... by Giraldus Cambrensis." It summarizes Ralegh's earlier involvement with Sir Humphrey Gilbert's voyages of discovery (416, 433) and goes on to contrast the English way of planting a colony with the Spanish, as anti-Spanish propaganda. The dedication is printed in R. Holinshed, Chronicles, II *(1587), 2nd numeration, sigs. A3–A4; this extract is printed in D. B. Quinn,* Roanoke voyages, I *(1955), 489–493.*

For after that you had seasoned your primer yeares at Oxford in knowledge and learning, a good ground and a sure foundation to build thereupon all your good actions, you travelled into France, and spent there a good part of your youth in the warres and martiall services. And having some sufficient knowledge and experience therein, then after your returne from thense, to the end you might everie waie be able to serve your prince and commonweale, you were desirous to be acquainted in maritimall affaires. Then you, togither with your brother sir Humfreie Gilbert, travelled the seas, for the search of such countries, as which if they had beene then discovered, infinit commodities in sundrie respects would have insued, and whereof there was no doubt, if the fleet then accompanieng you, had according to appointment followed you, or your self had escaped the dangerous sea fight, when manie of your companie were slaine, and your ships therewith also sore battered and disabled. And albeit this hard beginning (after which followed the death of the said woorthie knight your brother) was a matter sufficient to haue discouraged a man of a right good stomach and value from anie like seas attempts; yet you, more respecting the good ends, whereunto you levelled your line for the good of your countrie, did not give over, untill you had recovered a land, and made a plantation of the people of your owne English nation in *Virginia,* the first English colonie that ever was there planted, to the no little derogation of the glorie of the Spaniards, & an impeach to their vaunts; who bicause with all cruel immanitie, contrarie to all naturall humanitie, they subdued a naked and a yeelding people, whom they sought for gaine and not for anie religion or plantation of a commonwelth, over whome to satisfie their most greedie and insatiable covetousnesse, did most cruellie tyrannize, and most tyranicallie and against the course of all human nature did scorch and rost them to death, as by their owne histories dooth appeare. These (I saie) doo brag and vaunt, that they onelie have drawne strange nations and unknowne people, to the obedience of their kings, to the knowledge of christianitie, and to the inriching of their countrie, and thereby doo claime the honor to be due to themselues onelie and alone. But if these your actions were well looked into, which such due consideration as apperteineth, it shall be found much more honorable in sundrie respects, for the advancement of the name of God, the honour of the prince, and the benefit of the common wealth. For what can be more pleasant to God, than to gaine and reduce in all christianlike manner, a lost people to the knowledge of the gospell, and a true christian religion, than which cannot be a more pleasant and a sweet sacrifice, and a more acceptable service before God? And what can be more honorable to princes, than to inlarge the bounds of their kingdoms without iniurie, wrong, & bloudshed; and to frame them from a savage life to a civill government, neither of which the Spaniards in their conquests have performed? And what can be more beneficiall to a common weale, than to have a nation and a kingdome to transferre unto the superfluous multitude of frutelesse and idle people (heere at home dailie increasing) to travell, conquer, and manure another land, which by the due intercourses to be devised, may and will yeeld infinit commodities? And how well you doo deserve everie waie in following so honorable a course, not we our selves onelie can witnesse, but strange nations also doo honour you for the same: as dooth appeare by the epistle of *Bassimerus* of France, to the historie of Florida: and by *Julius Caesar* a citizen of Rome in his epistle to his book intituled *Cullombeados*. It is well knowne, that it had beene no lesse easie for you, than for such as have beene advanced by kings, to have builded great houses, purchased large circuits, and to have used the fruits of princes favours, as most men in all former and present ages have doone; had you not preferred the generall honour and commoditie of your prince and countrie before all privat gaine and commoditie: wherby you have beene rather a servant than a commander to your owne fortune. And no doubt the cause being so good, and the attempt so honorable, but that God will increase your talent, and blesse your dooings, and everie good man will commend and further the same. And albeit the more noble enterprises a man shall take in hand the more adversaries he shall have to deprave and hinder the same: yet I am persuaded, as no good man shall have just cause, so there is none so much carried with a corrupt mind, nor so envious of his countries honour, nor so bent against you, that he will derogate the praise and honour due to so worthie an enterprise; and that so much the sooner, bicause you haue indured so manie crosses, and have through so much enviengs and misfortunes persevered in your attempts, which no doubt shall at last by you be performed when it shall please him, who hath made you an instrument of so worthie a worke....Exon. October 12. 1586.

449. December 30, 1586. Letter from Richard Hakluyt to Sir Walter Ralegh.

This is the only surviving letter to Ralegh on the Roanoke enterprises. It is interesting as evidence that Lane's report on the suitability of the Chesapeake area for a colony had been circulated.
From Bodleian Library, Clarendon MSS, Addenda 307, fos. 2–3v. Printed in E. G. R. Taylor, Hakluyts, II (1935) 353–356; D. B. Quinn, Roanoke voyages, I (1955), 493–494. Extract.

I heare nothinge from you of the acceptation of my dedication of that noble historie of the eight decades of Peter Martyr, which wil cost mee fortie french crownes, and five monethes travayle with that which is to come before yt be finished, which wilbe aboute the beginninge of march. Yf her majestie have of late advanced you, I wold be gladde to be acquaynted with your titles, and if there be any thinge else that you wold have mentioned in the epistle dedicatorie, you shal doe wel to let mee understand of yt betymes.

Your mappe answerable unto the Spanish voyage of Antonio de Espejo, uppon occasion of business unlooked for, hath bin hitherto differred by andrewe Home the Portingale, the prince of the Cosmographers of this age. But within this moneth you shall not fayle of yt God willinge, and that in better sorte for the longer staying for yt.

Yf you proceed, which I longe much to knowe, in your enterprise of Virginia, your best planting wilbe aboute the bay of the Chesepians, to which latitude Peter Martyr, and Franciscus Lopez de Gomara the Spaniard confesse that our Gabot and the English did first discover: which the Spaniardes here after cannot deny us whensoever wee shalbe at Peace with them. And your voyage of Antonio de Espejo bringeth you to rich sylver mynes up in the countrye in the latitude of 37. ½. ... Paris the 30th of December. 1586.

R[ichard] H[akluyt].

Chapter Fifty-nine
The Colonizing Expedition of 1587

JOHN WHITE'S ACCOUNT OF THE VIRGINIA VOYAGE OF 1587 AND HIS LIST OF COLONISTS

THIS IS the first narrative of John White's voyages to Virginia written by him. Of the three ships only the *Lion*, the "Admirall," is known by name, John White captain and Simão Fernandes master. Edward Spicer was master of the "flie-boate" and Edward Stafford master of the pinnace. They took the West Indies or "privateering" route to Virginia, a possible cause of the friction that developed between White and Fernandes. Although this group of settlers whose names are listed in Document 451 is called the second colony, the party of men left by Grenville at Roanoke Island the previous year (447) should perhaps be regarded as the second and this group as the third. The list sets out the names of the governor and assistants of the City of Ralegh (the agreement, itself, has not survived). Three of the assistants, William Fullwood, John Nicholls, and James Platt, had remained in England to act as factors for the company. As this narrative shows, White and Fernandes did not remain in Virginia. As can be seen also from the list this colony contained women and children, two born in Virginia.

Printed in R. Hakluyt, *Principall navigations* (1589), pp. 764–771; *Principal navigations*, III (1600), 180–186, 287; VIII (1904), 386–402, 420–423. D. B. Quinn, *Roanoke voyages*, II (1955),515–538, 539–543.

450. 1587. John White's narrative of the fourth Virginia voyage.

The fourth voyage made to Virginia, with three shippes, in the yeere, 1587. Wherein was transported the second Colonie.

In the yeere of our Lorde, 1587. Sir Walter Ralegh intending to persevere in the planting of his Countrey of Virginia, prepared a newe Colonie of one hundred and fiftie men to be sent thither, under the charge of John White, whom he appointed Governour, and also appointed unto him twelve Assistants, unto whome he gave a Charter, and incorporated them by the name of Governour, and Assistants of the Citie of Ralegh in Virginia.

Our Fleete being in number three saile, viz. the Admirall, a shippe of one hundred and twentie tunnes: a Flie boate, and a Pinnesse, departed the sixe and twentieth of Aprill from Portesmouth, and the same day came to an anker at the Cowes, in the Isle of Wight, where wee staied eight daies.

Maye.

The 5. of Maye, at nine of the clocke at night, we came to Plymmouth, where we remained the space of two daies.

The 8. we waied anker at Plymmouth, and departed thence for Virginia.

The 16. Simon Ferdinando Master of our Admirall, lewdly forsooke our Flie boate, leaving her distressed in the Baye of Portingall.

June.

The 19. we fell with "Dominica,[1] and the same evening we sailed betweene it, and Guadalupe: the 21. the Flie boat also fell with Dominica.

1. Sidenote: "One of the Isles of the Indias, inhabited with Savages."

The 22. we came to an anker at an Isle, called Santa Cruz, where all the planters were set on land, staying there till the 25. of the same moneth. At our first landing on this Island, some of our women, and men, by eating a small fruite, like greene apples, were fearefully troubled with a sudden burning in their mouthes, and swelling of their tongues so bigge, that some of them could not speake. Also a child by sucking one of those womens breast[s], had at that instant his mouth set on such a burning, that it was strange to see how the infant was tormented for the time: but after 24. howres, it ware away of it selfe.

Also the first night of our being on this Island, we tooke five great Torteses, some of them of such bignes, that sixteene of our strongest men were tired with carrying of one of them but from the Sea side, to our cabbins. In this Island we found no watring place, but a standing ponde, the water whereof was so evill, that many of our companie fell sicke with drinking thereof: and as many as did but wash their faces with that water, in the morning before the Sunne had drawen away the corruption, their faces did so burne, and swell, that their eies were shut up, and could not see in five or six daies or longer.

The second day of our abode there, we sent foorth some of our men to search the Island for fresh water, three one way, and two another way. The Governour also, with six others, went up to the toppe of an high hill, to view the Island, but could perceave no signe of any men, or beastes, nor any goodnes, but Parots, and trees of Guiacum. Returning backe to our Cabbins another way, he found in the discent of a hill, certaine potsheards of savage making, made of the earth of that Island: whereupon it was judged, that this Island was inhabited with Savages, though Fernando had tolde us for certaine, the contrarie. The same day at night, the rest of our companie very late returned to the Governour. The one companie affirmed, that they had seene in a valley, eleven Savages, and divers houses halfe a mile distant from the steepe, or toppe of the hill where they staied. The other companie had found running out of a high rocke, a very faire spring of water, whereof they brought three bottles to the companie: for before that time, wee dranke the stinking water of the pond.

The same second day at night, Captaine Stafford, with the pinnesse, departed from our fleete, riding at Santa Cruz, to an Island, called Beake, lying neere S. Johns, being so directed by Ferdinando, who assured him he should there finde great plentie of sheepe. The next day at night, our planters left Santa Cruz, and came all aboord, and the next morning after, being the 25. of June, we waied anker, and departed from Santa Cruz.

The seven and twentieth we came to anker at Cottea, where we found the pinnesse riding, at our comming.

The 28. we waied anker at Cottea, and presently came to anker at S. Johns in Musketas Bay, where we spent three daies unprofitable in taking in freshe water, spending in the meane time more beere, then the quantitie of the water came unto.

Julie.

The first we waied anker at "Muskitoes Baye,[2] where were left behind two Irish men of our companie, Darbie Glaven, and Denice Carrell, bearing along the coast of S. Johns, till evening, at which time we fell with Rosse Baye. At this place Fernando had promised wee should take in salt, and had caused us before, to make and provide as many sackes for that purpose, as we could. The Governour also, for that he understoode there was a Towne in the bottome of the Baye, not farre from the salt hils, appointed thirtie shotte, ten pikes, and ten targets, to man the pinnesse, and to goe a land for salt. Fernando perceaving them in a readines, sent to the Governour, using great perswasions with him, not to take in salt there, saying that he knewe not well, whether the same were the place or not: also, that if the pinnesse went into the Bay, she could not without great danger come backe, till the next day at night, and that if in the meane time any storme should rise, the Admirall were in danger to be cast away. Whilest he was thus perswading, he caused the lead to be cast, and having craftily brought the shippe in three fathome, and a halfe water, he suddenly began to sweare, and teare God in peeces, dissembling great danger, crying to him at the helme, beare up hard, beare up hard: so we went off, and were disappointed of our salt, by his meanes.

The next day, sailing along the West ende of S. Johns, the Governour determined to goe a land in

---

2. Sidenote: "Musketas Baye, is a harbour upon the South side of S. Johns Island, where we take in fresh water."

S. Germans Baye,[3] to gather yong plants of Oringes, Pines, Mameas, and Platonos, to set at Virginia, which we knewe might easily be had, for that they growe neere the shoare, and the places where they grewe, well knowen to the Governour, and some of the planters: but our Simon denied it, saying: he would come to an anker at Hispaniola, and there lande the Governour, and some other of the Assistants, with the pinnesse, to see if he could speake with his friend Alanson, of whome he hoped to be furnished both of cattell, and all such thinges as wee woulde have taken in at S. Johns: but hee meant nothing lesse, as it plainely did appeare to us afterwards.

The next day after, being the third of Julie, wee sawe Hispaniola, and bare with the coast all that day, looking still when the pinnesse should be prepared to goe for the place where Fernando his friend Alanson was: but that day passed, and we sawe no preparation for landing in Hispaniola.

The 4. of Julie, sailing along the coast of Hispaniola, untill the next day at noone, and no preparation yet seene for the staying there, we having knowledge that we were past the place where Alanson dwelt, and were come with Isabella: hereupon Fernando was asked by the Governour, whether he meant to speake with Alanson, for the taking in of cattell, and other things, according to his promise, or not: but he answered, that he was now past the place, and that Sir Walter Ralegh tolde him, the French Ambassador certified him, that the king of Spaine had sent for Alanson into Spaine: wherefore he thought him dead, and that it was to no purpose to touch there in any place, at this voyage.

The next day, we left sight of Hispaniola, and haled off for Virginia, about 4. of the clocke in the afternoone.

The sixt of Julie, wee came to the Islande Caycos, wherein Fernando saide were two salt pondes, assuring us if they were drie, wee might find salt to shift with, untill the next supplie, but it prooved as true as the finding of sheepe at Beake. In this Island, whilest Ferdinando solaced himself a shoare, with one of the company, in part of the Island, others spent the latter part of that day in other parts of the Island, some to seeke the salt ponds, some fowling, some hunting Swannes, whereof we caught many. The next daye, earely in the morning we waied anker, leaving Caycos, with good hope, the first lande that wee sawe next, should be Virginia.

About the 16. of July, we fell with the maine of Virginia, which Simon Fernando tooke to be the Island of Croatoan, where we came to an anker, and rode there two or three daies: but finding himselfe deceaved, he waied, and bare along the coast, where in the night, had not Captaine Stafforde bene more carefull in looking out, then our Simon Fernando, wee had beene all cast away upon the breache, called the Cape of Feare, for wee were come within two cables length upon it: such was the carelesnes, and ignorance of our Master.

The two and twentieth of Julie, we arrived safe at Hatoraske, where our shippe and pinnesse ankered: the Governour went aboord the pinnesse, accompanied with fortie of his best men, intending to passe up to Roanoake foorthwith, hoping there to finde those fifteene Englishmen, which Sir Richard Greenvill had left there the yeere before, with whome he meant to have conference, concerning the state of the Countery, and Savages, meaning after he had so done, to returne againe to the fleete, and passe along the coast, to the Baye of Chesepiok, where we intended to make our seate and forte, according to the charge given us among other directions in writing, under the hande of Sir Walter Ralegh. but assoone as we were put with our pinnesse from the shippe, a Gentleman by the meanes of Fernando, who was appointed to returne for England, called to the sailers in the pinnesse, charging them not to bring any of the planters backe againe, but leave them in the Island, except the Governour, and two or three such as he approoved, saying that the Summer was farre spent, wherefore hee would land all the planters in no other place. Unto this were all the sailers, both in the pinnesse, and shippe, perswaded by the Master, wherefore it booted not the Governour to contend with them, but passed to Roanoake, and the same night, at Sunne set, went aland on the Island, in the place where our fifteene men were left, but we found none of them, nor any signe, that they had bene there, saving onely we found the bones of one of those fifteene, which the Savages had slaine long before.

3. Sidenote: "A pleasant and fruitfull Countrey, lying on the west ende of S. Johns Island where groweth plentie of Oringes, Lemmons, Plantyns, and Pynes."

The 23. of July, the Governour, with divers of his companie, walked to the North ende of the Island, where Master Ralfe Lane had his forte, with sundry necessarie and decent dwelling houses, made by his men about it the yeere before, where wee hoped to finde some signes, or certaine knowledge of our fifteene men. When we came thither, wee found the forte rased downe, but all the houses standing unhurt, saving the neather roomes of them, and also of the forte, were overgrowen with Melons of divers sortes, and Deere within them, feeding on those Mellons: so we returned to our companie, without hope of ever seeing any of the fifteene men living.

The same day order was given, that every man should be imploied for the repairing of those houses, which we found standing, and also to make other newe Cottages, for such as shoulde neede.

The 25. our Flie boate, and the rest of our planters, arrived all safe at Hatoraske, to the great joye, and comfort of the whole companie: but the Master of our Admirall, Fernando grieved greatly at their safe comming: for he purposely left them in the Baye of Portingall, and stole away from them in the night, hoping that the Master thereof, whose name was Edward Spicer, for that he never had beene in Virginia, would hardly finde the place, or els being left in so dangerous a place as that was, by meanes of so many men of warre, as at that time were aboord, they should surely be taken, or slaine: but God disappointed his wicked pretenses.

The eight and twentieth, George Howe, one of our twelve Assistants was slaine by divers Savages, which were come over to Roanoake, either of purpose to espie our companie, and what number we were, or els to hunt Deere, whereof were many in the Island. These Savages beeing secretly hidden among high reedes, where oftentimes they finde the Deere asleepe, and so kill them, espied our man wading in the water alone, almost naked, without any weapon, save onely a small forked sticke, catching Crabs therewithall, and also being strayed two miles from his companie, shotte at him in the water, where they gave him sixteene wounds with their arrowes: and after they had slaine him with their woodden swordes, beat his head in peeces, and fled over the water to the maine.

On the thirtieth of Julie, Master Stafford, and twentie of our men, passed by water to the Island of Croatoan, with Manteo, who had his mother, and many of his kinred, dwelling in that Island, of whome we hoped to understande some newes of our fifteene men, but especially to learne the disposition of the people of the Countrey towards us, and to renew our olde friendshippe with them. At our first landing, they seemed as though they would fight with us: but perceiving us begin to marche with our shot towards them, they turned their backes, and fled. Then Manteo their countreyman, called to them in their owne language, whom, assoone as they heard, they returned, and threwe away their bowes, and arrowes, and some of them came unto us, embracing and entertaining us friendly, desiring us not to gather or spill any of their corne, for that they had but little. We answered them, that neither their corne, nor any other thing of theirs, should be diminished by any of us, and that our comming was onely to renew the olde love, that was betweene us, and them, at the first, and to live with them as brethren, and friendes: which answere seemed to please them well, wherefore they requested us to walke up to their Towne, who there feasted us after their manner, and desired us earnestly, that there might be some token or badge given them of us, whereby we might know them to be our friendes, when we met them any where out of the Towne or Island. They tolde us further, that for want of some such badge, divers of them were hurt the yeere before, beeing founde out of the Island by Master Lane his companie, whereof they shewed us one, which at that very instant laye lame, and had lien of that hurt ever since: but they said, they knew our men mistooke them, and hurt them in steade of Winginoes men, wherefore they held us excused.

August.

The next day, we had conference further with them, concerning the people of Secota, Aquascogoc, & Pomiock, willing them of Croatoan, to certifie the people of those townes, that if they would accept our friendship, we would willingly receave them againe, and that all unfriendly dealings past on both partes, should be utterly forgiven, and forgotten. To this the chiefe men of Croatoan answered, that they would gladly doe the best they could, and within seven daies, bring the Weroances, and chiefe Governours of those townes with them, to our Governour at Roanoak, or their answere. We also understoode of the men of Croatoan, that our man Master Howe, was slaine by the remnant of Winginoes men, dwelling then at Dasamongueponke, with whom Winchese kept companie: and also we understood by them of Croatoan, how that the 15. Englishmen left at Roanoak the yeere before, by Sir Richard Greenvill, were suddenly set upon, by 30. of the men of Secota, Aquascogoc, and Dasamongueponke, in manner following. They conveied themselves secretly behind the trees, neere the houses, where our men carelesly lived: and having perceaved that of those 15. they could see but 11. onely, two of those Savages appeared to the 11. Englishmen, calling to them by friendly signes, that but two of their chiefest men should come unarmed to speake with those two Savages, who seemed also to be unarmed. Wherefore two of the chiefest of our Englishmen, went gladly to them: but whilest one of those Savages traitorously embraced one of our men, the other with his sword of wood, which he had secretly hidden under his mantell, stroke him on the head, and slewe him, and presently the other eight and twentie Savages shewed themselves: the other Englishman perceaving this, fled to his companie, whome the Savages pursued with their bowes, and arrowes, so fast, that the Englishmen were forced to take the house, wherein all their victuall, and weapons were: but the Savages foorthwith set the same on fire, by meanes whereof, our men were forced to take up such weapons as came first to hand, and without order to runne foorth among the Savages, with whome they skirmished above an howre. In this skirmish, another of our men was shotte into the mouth with an arrowe, whereof he died: and also one of the Savages was shot into the side by one of our men, with a wild fire arrowe, whereof he died presently. The place where they fought, was of great advantage to the Savages, by meanes of the thicke trees, behinde which the Savages through their nimblenes, defended themselves, and so offended our men with their arrowes, that our men being some of them hurt, retired fighting to the water side, where their boate lay, with which they fled towards Hatorask. By that time they had rowed but a quarter of a mile, they espied their foure fellowes comming from a creeke thereby, where they had bene to fetch Oysters: these foure they receaved into their boate, leav-

ing Roanoake, and landed on a little Island on the right hand of our entrance into the harbour of Hatorask, where they remained a while, but afterward departed, whither, as yet we knowe not.

Having nowe sufficiently dispatched our busines at Croatoan, the same day wee departed friendly, taking our leave, and came aboord the fleete at Hatoraske.

The eight of August, the Governour having long expected the comming of the Weroanses of Pomioake, Aquascoquoc, Secota, and Dasamongueponke, seeing that the seven daies were past, within which they promised to come in, or to send their answers by the men of Croatoan, and no tidings of them heard, being certainly also informed by those men of Croatoan, that the remnant of Wingino his men, which were left alive, who dwelt at Dasamongueponke, were they which had slaine George Howe, and were also at the driving of our eleven Englishmen from Roanoake, he thought to differre the revenging thereof no longer. Wherefore the same night, about midnight, he passed over the water, accompanied with Captaine Stafford, and 24. men, whereof Manteo was one, whome wee tooke with us to be our guide to the place where those Savages dwelt, where he behaved himselfe toward us as a most faithfull Englishman.

The next day, being the ninth of August, in the morning so earely, that it was yet darke, wee landed neere the dwelling place of our enemies, and very secretly conveyed our selves through the woods, to that side, where we had their houses betweene us and the water: and having espied their fire, and some sitting about it, we presently sette on them: the miserable soules herewith amased, fledde into a place of thicke reedes, growing fast by, where our men perceaving them, shotte one of them through the bodie with a bullet, and therewith wee entred the reedes, among which wee hoped to acquite their evill doing towards us, but wee were deceaved, for those Savages were our friendes, and were come from Croatoan, to gather the corne, and fruite of that place, because they understoode our enemies were fledde immediatly after they had slaine George Howe, and for haste had left all their corne, Tabacco, and Pompions standing in such sorte, that all had beene devoured of the birdes, and Deere, if it had not beene gathered in time: but they had like to have paide deerely for it:

for it was darke, that they beeing naked, and their men and women apparelled all so like others, we knewe not but that they were all men: and if that one of them, which was a Weroans wife, had not had her childe at her backe, she had beene slaine in steede of a man, and as happe was, another Savage knewe Master Stafford, and ranne to him, calling him by his name, whereby he was saved. Finding our selves thus disappointed of our purpose, wee gathered all the corne, Pease, Pumpions, and Tabacco, that we found ripe, leaving the rest unspoiled, and tooke Menatoan his wife, with the yong childe, and the other Savages with us over the water to Roanoak. Although the mistaking of these Savages somewhat grieved Manteo, yet he imputed their harme to their owne follie, saying to them, that if their Weroans had kept their promise in comming to the Governour, at the day appointed, they had not knowen that mischance.

The 13. of August, our Savage Manteo, by the commandement of Sir Walter Ralegh, was christened in Roanoak, and called Lord therof, and of Dasamongueponke, in reward of his faithfull service.

The 18. Elenora, daughter to the Governour, and wife to Ananias Dare, one of the Assistants, was delivered of a daughter in Roanoak, and the same was christened there the Sunday following, and because this childe was the first Christian borne in Virginia, she was named Virginia. By this time our shippes had unlanded the goods and victuals of the planters, and began to take in wood, and fresh water, and to newe calke and trimme them for England: the planters also prepared their letters, and tokens, to send backe into England.

Our two shippes, the Lyon, and the Flieboate, almost ready to depart, the 21. of August, there arose such a tempest at northeast, that our Admirall then riding out of the harbour, was forced to cut his cables, and put to Sea, where he laye beating off and on, six dayes before hee coulde come to us againe, so that wee feared hee had beene cast away, and the rather, for that at the tyme that the storme tooke them, the moste, and best of their Saylers, were left aland.

At this time some controversies rose betweene the Governour, and Assistants, about choosing two out of the twelve Assistants, which should goe backe as factors for the companie into England: for every one of them refused, save onely one, which all the other thought not sufficient: but at length, by much perswading of the Governour, Christopher Cooper onely agreed to goe for England: but the next day, through the perswasion of divers of his familiar friendes, he changed his minde, so that now the matter stoode as at the first.

The next day, the 22. of August, the whole companie, both of the Assistants, and planters, came to the Governour, and with one voice requested him to returne himselfe into England, for the better and sooner obtaining of supplies, and other necessaries for them: but he refused it, and alleaged many sufficient causes, why he would not: the one was, that he could not so suddenly returne backe againe, without his great discredite, leaving the action, and so many, whome he partly had procured through his perswasions to leave their native Countrey, and undertake that voyage, and that some enemies to him, and the action at his returne into England, would not spare to slander falsely both him, and the action, by saying he went to Virginia, but politikely, and to no other ende, but to leade so many into a Countrey, in which he never meant to stay himselfe, and there to leave them behind him. Also he alleaged, that seing they intended to remove 50. miles further up into the maine presently he being then absent, his stuffe and goods, might be both spoiled, and most of it pilfered away in the carriage, so that at his returne, hee should be either forced to provide himselfe of all such things againe, or els at his comming againe to Virginia, finde himselfe utterly unfurnished, whereof already he had found some proofe, beeing but once from them but three daies. Wherefore he concluded, that he would not goe himselfe.

The next day, not onely the Assistants, but divers others, as well women, as men, beganne to renewe their requests to the Governour againe, to take uppon him to returne into England for the supplie, and dispatch of all such thinges, as there were to be done, promising to make him their bonde under all their handes, and seales, for the safe preserving of all his goods for him at his returne to Virginia, so that if any part thereof were spoiled, or lost, they would see it restored to him, or his Assignes, whensoever the same should be missed, and demanded: which bonde, with a testimonie under their handes, and seales, they foorthwith made, and delivered into his hands. The copie of the testimonie, I thought good to set downe.

May it please you, her Majesties Subjects of England, wee your friendes and Countrey men, the planters in Virginia, doe by these presents let you, and every of you to understande, that for the present and speedie supplie of certaine our knowen, and apparent lackes, and needes, most requisite and necessarie for the good and happie planting of us, or any other in this lande of Virginia, wee all of one minde, and consent, have most earnestly intreated, and uncessantly requested John White, Governour of the planters in Virginia, to passe into England, for the better and more assured helpe, and setting forward of the foresayde supplies: and knowing assuredly that he both can best, and will labour, and take paines in that behalfe for us all, and hee not once, but often refusing it, for our sakes, and for the honour, and maintenance of the action, hath at last, though much against his will, through our importunacie, yeelded to leave his government, and all his goods among us, and himselfe in all our behalfes to passe into Englande, of whose knowledge, and fidelitie in handling this matter, as all others, wee doe assure our selves by these presents, and will you to give all credite thereunto. the five and twentieth of August.

The Governour beeing at the last, through their extreame intreating, constrayned to returne into England, having then but halfe a daies respit to prepare him selfe for the same, departed from Roanoake, the seven and twentieth of August in the morning: and the same daye about midnight, came aboord the Flie boate, who already had waied anker, and rode without the barre, the Admirall riding by them, who but the same morning was newly come thither againe. The same day, both the shippes waied anker, and sette saile for England: at this waying their ankers, twelve of the men which were in the Flieboate, were throwen from the Capestone, which by meanes of a barre that brake, came so fast about upon them, that the other two barres thereof stroke and hurt most of them so sore, that some of them never recovered it: neverthelesse they assaied presently againe to waigh their anker, but being so weakened with the first fling, they were not able to weigh it, but were throwen downe, and hurth the seconde time. Wherefore were not able to

weigh it, but were throwen downe, and hurt the seconde time. Wherefore having in all but fifteene men aboord and most of them by this infortunate beginning so bruised, and hurt, they were forced to cut their Cable, and leese their anker. Neverthelesse, they kept companie with the Admirall, untill the seventeenth of September, at which time wee fell with Corvo, and sawe Flores.

September.

The eighteenth, perceaving of all our fifteene men in the Flie boate, there remained but five, which by meanes of the former mischance, were able to stande to their labour: wherefore understanding that the Admirall meant not to make any haste for England, but linger about the Islande of Tercera for purchase, the Flie boate departed for Englande with letters, where we hoped by the helpe of God to arrive shortly: but by that time wee had continued our course homeward, about twentie dayes, having had sometimes scarse, and variable windes, our fresh water also by leaking almost consumed, there arose a storme at Northeast, which for 6. dayes ceased not to blowe so exceeding, that we were driven further in those 6. then wee could recover in thirteene daies: in which time others of our saylers began to fall very sicke, and two of them dyed, the weather also continued so close, that our Master sometimes in foure daies together could see neither Sunne nor starre, and all the beverage we could make, with stinking water, dregges of beere, and lees of wine which remained, was but 3. gallons, and therefore now we expected nothing but by famyne to perish at Sea.

October.

The 16. of October we made land, but we knew not what land it was, bearing in with the same land at that day: about Sunne set we put into a harbour, where we found a Hulke of Dublin, and a pynesse of Hampton ryding, but we knew not as yet what place this was, neither had we any boate to goe a shoare, untill the pinnesse sent off their boate to us with 6. or 8. men, of whom we understood we were in Smewicke in the west parts of Ireland: they also releeved us presently with fresh water, wyne, and other fresh meate.

The 18. the Governour, and the Master ryd to Dingen Cushe, 5. myles distant, to take order of the new victualling of our Flye boate for England,

and for reliefe of our sicke and hurt men, but with 4. dayes after the boatswane, the steward, and the boatswanes mate dyed aboord the flyeboate, and the 28. the Masters mate and two of our chiefe Saylers were brought sicke to Dingen.

November.

The first the Governour shipped him selfe in a ship called the Monkie, which at that time was readie to put to Sea from Dingen for England, leaving the Flyeboat and all his company in Ireland, the same day we set sayle, and on the third day we fel with the Northside of the lands end, and were shut up the Severne, but the next day we doubled the same, for Monts Bay.

The 5. the Governour landed in England at Martasew, neere Saint Michaels mount in Cornewall.

The 8. we arrived at Hampton, where we understood that our consort the Admirall was come to Portsmouth, and had bene there three weekes before: and also that Fernando the Master with all his company were not onely come home without any purchase, but also in such weaknesse by sicknes, and death of their cheefest men, that they were scarse able to bring their ship into the harbour, but were forced to let fall anker without, which they could not way againe, but might all have perished there, if a small barke by great hap had not come to them to helpe them. The names of the chiefe men that dyed are these, Roger Large, John Mathew, Thomas Smith, and some other saylers, whose names I know not at the writing hereof. Anno Domini 1587.

451. 1587. List of the men, women, and children who made up the third colony and who were to be lost in America.

Richard Hakluyt, Principall navigations (1589), pp. 770–771, Principal navigations, III (1600), 287; frequently reprinted (for example in D. B. Quinn, Roanoke voyages, II, 539–543).

The Names of the 1587 Virginia Colonists
The names of all the men, women and Children, which safely arrived in Virginia, and remained to inhabite there. 1587.

Anno Regni Reginae Elizabethae .29.

John White [Governor].	George Martyn.
Roger Bailie [Assistant].	Hugh Pattenson.
Ananias Dare [Assistant].	Martyn Sutton.
Christopher Cooper [Assistant].	John Farre.
	John Bridger.
Thomas Stevens [Assistant].	Griffen Jones.
	Richard Shaberdge.
John Sampson [Assistant].	Thomas Ellis.
	William Browne.
Dyonis Harvie [Assistant].	Michael Myllet.
	Thomas Smith.
Roger Prat [Assistant].	Richard Kemme.
George Howe [Assistant].	Thomas Harris.
Simon Fernando [Assistant].	Richard Taverner.
	John Earnest.
Nicholas Johnson.	Henry Johnson.
Thomas Warner.	John Starte.
Anthony Cage.	Richard Darige.
John Jones.	William Lucas.
John Tydway.	Arnold Archard.
Ambrose Viccars.	John Wright.
Edmond English.	William Dutton.
Thomas Topan.	Morris Allen.
Henry Berrye.	William Waters.
Richard Berrye.	Richard Arthur.
John Spendlove.	John Chapman.
John Hemmington.	William Clement.
Thomas Butler.	Robert Little.
Edward Powell.	Hugh Tayler.
John Burden.	Richard Wildye.
James Hynde.	Lewes Wotton.
William Willes.	Michael Bishop.
John Brooke.	Henry Browne.
Cutbert White.	Henry Rufoote.
John Bright.	Richard Tomkins.
	Henry Dorrell.
Clement Tayler.	Charles Florrie.
William Sole.	Henry Mylton.
John Cotsmur.	Henry Payne.
Humfrey Newton.	Thomas Harris.
Thomas Colman.	William Nicholes.
Thomas Gramme.	Thomas Phevens.
Marke Bennet.	John Borden.
John Gibbes.	Thomas Scot.
John Stilman.	James Lasie.
Robert Wilkinson.	John Cheven.
Peter Little.	Thomas Hewet.
John Wyles.	William Berde.
Brian Wyles.	

Women

Elyoner Dare.	Alis Chapman.
Margery Harvie.	Emme Merrimoth.
Agnes Wood.	Colman.

Wenefrid Powell.

Joyce Archard.

Jane Jones.

Elizabeth Glane.

Jane Pierce.

Audry Tappan.

Margaret Lawrence.

Joan Warren.

Jane Mannering.

Rose Payne.

Elizabeth Viccars.

Boyes and Children.

John Sampson.

Robert Ellis.

Ambrose Viccars.

Thomas Archard.

Thomas Humfrey.

Tomas Smart.

George Howe.

John Prat.

William Wythers.

Children born in Virginia.

Virginia Dare.   Harvye.

Savages.

Manteo.

Towaye.

That were in Englande and
returned home into
Virginia with them.

Chapter Sixty
Unsuccessful Ventures, 1588–1590:
A Lost Colony

452. 1588. John White's account of the attempted Virginia voyage in 1588.

Ralegh was unable to send any help to the colonists until 1588. He equipped two small ships, the Brave *(30 tons), Arthur Facey captain, and a pinnace, the* Roe *(25 tons), and despatched John White with the supplies. The two ships were all that could be released since all others were requisitioned for the defense of England against the imminent Spanish invasion. With them was Pedro Diaz, a Spanish pilot captured by Grenville in 1585. A deposition made by Diaz in Havana in 1589 (454) gives further details of the expedition and the fight with the French ship.*

Printed in Principall navigations *(1589), pp. 771–773; D. B. Quinn,* Roanoke voyages, *II (1955), 562–569.*

The first voyage intended for the supply of the Colonie planted in Virginia by John White which being undertaken in the yeere 1588 by casualtie tooke no effect.

After the Governors returne out of Virginia the 20. of November 1587. he delivered his letters and other advertisments concerning his last voyage and state of the planters to Sir Walter Ralegh: whereupon he foorthwith appointed a pinnesse to be sent thither with all such necessaries as he understood they stood in neede of: and also wrote his letters unto them, wherein among other matters he comforted them with promise, that with all convenient speede he would prepare a good supply of shipping and men with sufficience of all thinges needefull, which he intended, God willing, should be with them the Sommer following. Which pinnesse and fleete were accordingly prepared in the West Countrey at Bidiforde under the chardge of Sir Richard Greenevil. This fleete

being now in a reddinesse only staying but for a faire wind to put to Sea, at the same time there was spred throughout all England such report of the wonderfull preparation and invincible fleetes made by the king of Spaine joyned with the power of the Pope for the invading of England, that most of the ships of warre then in a readines in any haven in England were stayed for service at home: And sir Richard Greenevil was personally commanded not to depart out of Cornewall. The voyage of Virginia by these meanes for this yere thus disappointed, the Governour notwithstanding labored for the reliefe of the planters so earnestly, that he obtained two small pinnesses the one of them being of 30. tonnes called the Brave, the other of 25. called the Roe, wherein 15. planters and all their provision, with certaine reliefe for those that wintered in the Countrie was to be transported.

Thus the 22. of Aprill 1588. we put over the barre at Biddiford in the edge of the Northside of Cornewal, and the same night we came to an anker under the Isle of Lundy, where some of our company went on land: After we had roade there about the space of three howers we wayed anker againe and all that night we bare along the coast of Cornewall.

The next day being S. Georges day and the 23. of Aprill stil bearing along the coast we gave chase to 4. ships, & borded them & forced them all to come to anker by us in a smal bay at the lands end, out of these ships we tooke nothing but 3. men, & the same night we weighed & put to Sea.

The 24. day we gave chase to 2. ships, the one of them being a Scot the other a Breton. These we borded also & tooke from them whatsoever we could find worth the taking, & so let them goe.

The 26. of April we escried a ship on sterne of us, for whom we strooke our toppe sayle, and stayed for it. By that time he came with us we saw in his flagge a redd crosse: wereupon we helde him for an Englishman, & gave over our preparation to fight with him. But when he was come neere to us we perceived his flagge not to be a right S. George: whereupon we were somewhat amased having so farre mistaken, for it was a very tall ship, and excellently well appointed & now readie to clap us aboord. And it was not now neede to bid every man to bestirre himselfe, for each one prepared with all speed to fight. In the meane time we hayled them whence they were: They answered of Flushing, bound for Barbarie. And they perceiving us to be Englishmen of warre bare from us and gave us a piece, and we gave them two pieces and so departed.

The 27. day in the morning we were come with the heigth of cape Finister, the winde being still at Northeast.

The 28. day the wind shifted: about foure of the clocke in the afternoone the same day we escried a sayle to the weather of us, whom we kept so neere unto us as we could all that night.

The 29. in the morning we gave chase to the same ship being then to the wind of us almost as farre as we could ken. Assoone as our pinnes, came up to them, the pinnes fought with the ship, & it was an Hulke of 200. tonnes & more, but after a few great shot bestowed on both sides, the pinnesse perceiving her consort not able to come to ayd her left the Hulke & came roome with the Brave againe. At their comming they desired the Captaine & Master of the Brave to lend them some men and other things whereof they had neede. Which things put aboord them they returned againe to the chase of the Hulke earnestly, and with ful purpose to boord her. But the Hulke bare all night in with the coast of Spaine, and by morning were so neere land, that we fearing eyther change of wind or to be calmed gave over the fight and put off to Sea againe.

May

The first day of May being Wedensday the wind came large at Northeast.

The 3. being friday we gave chase to another tal ship, but it was night before we spake with her: and the night grew darke sodenly in such sort, that we lost sight both of the great ship & of our consort also, having thus in the darke lost our pinnesse, & knowing our barke so bad of sayle that we could neither take nor leve, but were rather to be taken or left of every ship we met, we

made our course for the Isle of Madera, hoping there to find our pinnesse abiding for us.

The same day following being the 5. of May we spake with a man of warre of Rochel of 60. tons, very wel manned & bravely appointed being bound, as he said for Peru: having hailed ech other, we parted frindly in outward shew, giving ech other a voley of shot & a great piece: but nevertheles we suspected y^t which followed: for this Rocheller having taken perfect view of our ship, men, & ordinance, towards evening fell on sterne of us: and assoone as it was darke left us, and returned to his consort which was a tal ship of 100. tonne lying then on hull to weather of us out of ken, having 84. men in her, whereof 50. were smal shot, and 12. muskets, and in the ship 10. peeces of ordinance. This ship being this night certified by her consort that viewed us, of what force we were and how bad of sayle, this greater ship tooke in 20. of the chiefest men that were in the smallest ship, and presently gave us chase.

The next morning being Monday and the 6. of May, we escried them in the weather of us, so that it was in vaine to seeke by flight, but rather by fight to helpe our selves. The same day about 2. of the clocke in the afternoone they were come with us. We hayled them, but they would not answere. Then we waved them to leewardes of us, and they waved us with a sword amayne, fitting their sailes to clappe us aboord, which we perceiving gave them one whole side: with one of our great shot their Master gonners shoolder was stroken away, and our Master gonner with a smal bullet was shot into the head. Being by this time grappled and aboord each of other the fight continued without ceasing one houre and a halfe. In which fight were hurt & slaine on both sides 23. of the chiefest men, having most of them some 6. or 8. woundes, and some 10. or 12. woundes. Being thus hurt and spoiled they robbed us of all our victuals, powder, weapons and provision, saving a smal quantity of biskuit to serve us scarce for England. Our Master and his Mate were deadly wounded, so that they were not able to come forth of their beds. I my selfe was wounded twise in the head, once with a sword, and another time with a pike, and hurt also in the side of the buttoke with a shot. Three of our passengers were hurt also, whereof one had 10. or 12. woundes our Master hurt in the face with a pike and thrust quite through the head. Being thus put to our close fights, and also much pestred with cabbens and unserviceable folkes we could not stirre to handle our weapons nor charge a piece: againe having spent all the powder in our flaskes and charges which we had present for our defence, they cut downe our netting and entred so many of their men as could stand upon our poope and forecastle, from whence they played extremely upon us with their shot. As thus we stood resolved to die in fight, the Captaine of the Frenchmen cried to us to yeld and no force should be offred. But after we had yelded, they knowing so many of their best men to be hurt and in danger of present death, began to grow into a new furie, in which they would have put us to the sword had not their Captaine charged them, and persuaded them to the contrary. Being at length pacified they fell on all handes to rifling and carying aboord all the next day until 4. of the clock: at which time by over greedy lading both their owne boate and ours, they sunke the one and split the other by the ships side: by meanes whereof they left us two cables and ankers, all our ordinance and most part of our sailes, which otherwise had ben taken away also. Furthermore they doubting the wind would arise, and night at hand, & a tal ship al that day by meanes of the calme in sight, they came aboord us with their ship, and tooke in their men that were in us, who left us not at their departing any thing worth the carying away. Being thus ransacked and used as is aforesaid in all sorts, we determined (as our best shift in so hard a case) to returne for England, and caused all our able and unhurt men, to fal to newe rigging & mending our sailes, tacklings, and such things as were spilled in our fight. By this occasion, God justly punishing our former theeverie of our evil desposed mariners, we were of force constrained to break of our voyage intended for the reliefe of our Colony left the yere before in Virginia, and the same night to set our course for England, being then about 50. leagues to the Northeast of Madera.

The 7. day of May being Wednesday in the forenoone the wind came large at East northeast and we haled off as farre west and by north as we could untill the 10. of May, fearing to meete with any more men of warre, for that we had no manner of weapons left us.

The 11. the wind larged more, and thence forth we continued our due course for England.

The 17. of May we thrust our selves west of Usshant, & sounded, but found no ground at 110 fathoms. The same day at night we sounded againe, and found ground at 80. fathoms.

The 20. being Sonday we fell with the coast of Ireland.

The 21. in the forenoone we saw the Northside of Cornewal at the lands end.

The 22. of May we came to an anker betweene Lunday and Harting point neere unto Chavell key, where we road untill the next tyde, and thence we put over the barre, and the same day landed at Biddeford.

Our other pinnesse whose company we had lost before the last cruell fight, returned also home into Cornwall within fewe weekes after our arrival, without performing our entended voyage for the reliefe of the planters in Virginia, which thereby were not a litle distressed.

453. July 12/22, 1588. Pedro de Araña to Juan de Ibarra.

This report of the interrogation of a Spanish sailor who was for a time in English hands shows that William Irish, as well as John White, visited the Outer Banks, or possibly Chesapeake Bay, in search of the English settlers. He probably had stores to give them. His finding of a stray mule might indicate he was near Hatarask Inlet (approximately modern Oregon Inlet), but it is possible that the mule might have been left over from the winter stay of Lane's party (1585-1586) near the southern shore of Chesapeake Bay.

A.G.I., Seville, Santo Domingo 118 (54.1.54); translated in Irene A. Wright, Further English Voyages to Spanish America *(London, Hakluyt Society, 1951), 233-235.*

July 22, 1588. Pedro de Arana to Juan de Ybarra

In June, 1587, off the entrance to Matanzas, the English captured Alonso Ruiz, seaman, native of Cartagena, in a frigate belonging to Captain Francisco de Avalos and, with others, they carried him to England, whence he returned to this port in the manner I will recount . . .

I understand they sailed... coasting along Florida as far as Santa Maria bay, in 37°, where they took in water. There they found signs of horned cattle and a branded mule. From these indications I infer that this is where the English had their settlement. I am informed that the natives proved poor friends to the English and that Francis Drake carried off those who survived.

I have desired to report this to your honour because I would like His Majesty to know where the English were established and what became of them.

This man says that they remained three days in that bay, at the end of which time they made sail, with a ship from Santo Domingo which they took off Matanzas. At Cayo Romano they waited for the fleet from Santo Domingo and there seized three frigates. One was an advice-boat and two were coastwise traders. They took two more off Matanzas, not counting that of Francisco de Avalos.

They sailed along the coast as far as Newfoundland Banks, from where they steered for Ireland, southern coast, entering a port called Vilar where they took in water and announced that they came from the Indies. From there they crossed to England in a day and a night to the city of Bristol, where they sold all their cargo.

The ships that committed these robberies were three in number and their pilot was a Portuguese mulatto pilot of this course named Domingo Diaz. He is a Lutheran, according to what this seaman tells me, and a native of Aveiro. He was born under the arcade. He is about 40 years old, greyish, heavy-set, broad faced, and says he came as pilot of the advice-boat which the Marqués de Santa Cruz despatched to Santo Domingo with news that Francis Drake was coming to these parts in the year 1586.

At the end of three months after he reached England this seaman regained his liberty, along with thirteen other Christians. They crossed to Havre and made their way by land to Brittany, to the city of Saint Malo, whence they sailed for San Lucar. There he shipped as a seaman on Domingo González's vessel which went ashore a league from this harbour in running from the English who were chasing it, as is being reported to His Majesty.

These English are the same who were here last year and have been waiting for the fleet from Santo Domingo, which escaped them because every vessel took its own course. It was very inadvisable for them to come up by the Old Channel. I reported last year that the enemy would lie in wait there for the fleet. I informed the *Audiencia*, but evidently they did not bear in mind what I told them. I had it from a Portuguese pilot whom the English captured, a man thoroughly acquainted with all this course. They told him their plans for the present year and did not keep him with them because he fell dangerously ill. They sent him to shore nearly dead in a small boat. I made friends with him and he told me everything and I reported fully to the *Audiencia*. God was pleased to keep the ships from Santo Domingo out of the hands of these thieves this time. Next year it would be well for His Majesty to command them to sail by way of Cape San Antonio, these galleys to await them there, those from Santo Domingo (if they are in condition) to escort them as far as Cape Tiburon.

The captain in command of the said English ships last year was named Irishe native of the Isle of Wight and they were sent out by George Carey Master of the Wight.

If anything else of importance occurs I will inform your honour, whom God preserve, etc.

Havana, July 22, 1588.
    Pedro de Arana

454. March 11/21, 1589. The relation of Pedro Diaz.

This document is important for the additional detail it gives on the voyages to Roanoke from Grenville's relief voyage of 1586 to White's supply voyage of 1588, thus including also the voyage of the 1587 colony. (447, 450, 452). It also gives some indication of what the Spaniards knew of the location and circumstances of the Roanoke colony. A.G.I., Seville, Santo Domingo 118 (54.1.54). Translated and printed in Irene A. Wright, Further English voyages to Spanish America 1583–1594 (1951), pp. 237–41; D. B. Quinn, Roanoke voyages, II (1955), 786–795.

At Havana on 21 March 1589 there was taken from Pero Diaz, a native of La Palma and a pilot on this route, the relation hereunder, as from one whom the English pirates imprisoned and took when he was going to Spain in the flag-ship of the Santo Domingo fleet, [Alonso Cornieles], general.

In the year 1585, off Bermuda, there was one of the queen's ships called the *Tiquere* of which a renowned English knight, called Sir Richarte Granfil, was captain—the same who was in that year at the island of Puerto Rico and at Ysavela where he bartered for cattle, horses and dogs and then set out to colonise the coast of Florida. Whence he [Grenville] sailed after leaving there 100 men, and the cattle, mules and dogs he had bought, and took him [Diaz], guarding him closely so that he could not escape from them until 1 May 1588, in the manner following.

After he was captured off Bermuda he was taken straight to England by way of the island of Flores and brought to the English port of Plemua on 26 November 1585. The said captain, who went on to London, has his house and a town at Biriforte, where he resides with his lady wife, and he returned to the river of Biriforte, which is at the mouth of Bistable, and there he fitted out six ships, one of 150 tons and the rest from 100 down to 60 tons. With them, and with 400 soldiers and sailors and provisions for a year, he put to sea on 2 May 1586. He sailed round Cape Finisterra where he encountered fourteen French ships on their way from San Lucár and Cadiz to France and Flanders. Of these he captured two and the rest fled; and thus he took much merchandise which he sent to his house and to his land in his own ships. Later, he met with a Flemish fly-boat on its way with merchandise to San Lucár; and he took it and distributed the cargo among the six vessels. Then he equipped the fly-boat as though for war, as it was an excellent sailing ship.

With these seven ships he reached the island of Puerto Santo, near Madera, where he sent a boat to the shore to find out what there was there; and to take in water, and bring away what they could find and could [carry off]. The inhabitants, although few in number, prepared to defend themselves and prevent the English coming ashore, offering them a tun of water for each ship if they would not land. The captain, angered by this, determined to disembark, intending to burn the island and destroy it with its inhabitants. To do this he armed his boats and placed men in them and sent them to land. The islanders, however, prevented them from coming ashore, and fought

so bravely that the English returned to their ships. The next day the ships were brought close to the land in order to sweep the shore with artillery-fire, from which the inhabitants received no harm owing to the precautions they took. They defended themselves until noon, when the English ships withdrew and continued their journey to Florida where they had left settlers (which is latitude 36¼°) and is situated further from the Bay of Santa Maria to the north-east, thirty leagues from Cape San Juan, from which the coast runs north and south for twelve leagues to where the said settlement is, being on an island very near to the mainland and some six leagues long, it being possible to pass on foot from the island to the mainland. There were Indians on the island which were at war with those on the mainland and for this reason they admitted the English, of whom the mainland Indians killed about four. And so Francisco Draque had brought the rest away with him, finding them in poor condition and greatly in need of provisions, for the land produces little to eat, having nothing but maize, and of that little, and the land wretchedly poor.

And so they found the said island deserted and discovered the bodies of one Englishman and one Indian hanged. Of the native inhabitants they did not find more than three Indians. When bringing them to the ships, two of them got away and they seized the third, from whom they got an account of how Francisco Draque had brought away the people who had been on that island. On the island they have a wooden fort of little strength and it is on the inside by the water. There is plenty of timber and the soil is sandy, liable to be inundated and marshy. Of the mainland the said Pero Diaz does not know the quality of the soil beyond that it appears fertile and well-wooded.

In the said fort he [Grenville] left eighteen men and did not allow the said Pero Diaz to go on shore or enter the fort. The said captain stayed there for fourteen days and left in the said fort four pieces of artillery of cast-iron and supplies for the eighteen men for a year. In charge of them he left a Master Cofar, an Englishman, and another called Chapeman.

The reason why the English have settled here is, he says, because on the mainland there is much gold and so that they may pass from the North to the South Sea, which they say and understand is nearby; thus making themselves strong through the discovery of great wealth.

After doing what has been described above the captain put to sea in his ships and sailed far out, hoping to encounter vessels from the Indies, as far south as the Açores. His men were very sick and some thirty-four persons died. The ships then made their way to Newfoundland, entering the Bay of San Francisco, where the crew went ashore to rest and caught fish to eat. Thence they again sailed to the Açores, some 400 leagues away, and they spent eight days among the islands. There they captured a vessel bound for Tercera from San Miguel with passengers— humble folk whom the English took with them, and of whom the greater part died. A lad told the English how there was a vessel laden with hides from Bahaya in a small island called Billa Franca, and how the hides had been put on shore in order to careen the ship which was leaking. The English went to the place and loaded the hides on their ships. While they were near San Miguel they sent a vessel to Tercera which found another English ship pursuing a frigate from Puerto Rico, and together they captured the frigate.

After this, the English continued their voyage to their country where they arrived on 26 December 1586. They kept Pedro Diaz captive, together with other honest fellows to the number of about forty, and under strict guard, saying that they would give to none other save Pero Diaz information of the said settlement. The captain went thence to London where he recruited people for the settlement, 210 in number, both men and women. He then despatched three ships in charge of a Portuguese called Simon Fernandez, who had married in England and was a skilful pilot and, further, was the author and promoter of the venture. This man left London for the settlement in March 1587, while Pero Diaz, who was injured, remained at the captain's house and estate.

These ships reached the settlement, but did not find the eighteen men who had been left there, nor any trace of them, and, after disembarking their people, the vessels returned to England. There the captain fitted out and prepared two pinnaces in which he embarked seven men and four women for the settlement, their provisions consisting of biscuit, meal and vegetables. They were sent in the charge of Captain Artefaz, and the pilot was Pero Diaz. The instructions given were that the pinnaces should not approach land lest Pero Diaz should escape.

They sailed thus to within thirty leagues of the island of Madera where, having sighted a ship, the swifter of the two pinnaces went in pursuit and was thus separated from the other. This second vessel, in which Pero Diaz was travelling, continuing its voyage, sighted a French ship which overtook it, and boarded it with thirty men who fought those in the pinnace until the greater part on both sides was killed or wounded, when the pinnace surrendered. The French then plundered it, taking what they wished, and left it with some of the English on board. These, on their knees, begged the French to leave them Pero Diaz, without whom they could not navigate their ship and would perish. But he, on his side, was equally urgent in his request to the French not to leave him with the English who had all but finished him off. The French, therefore, took him with them, promising to leave him at the Canaries.

When, however, they arrived there, they did not wish to put him on land. Excusing themselves on the pretext of heavy seas, they took him to the Cape Verde Islands, where he begged them to let him go ashore. But they were unwilling and promised to leave him in the Indies, and to give him the ship's pinnace and many clothes, after the ship had loaded cargo there. He, seeing their unwillingness to let him go, told them, in order to reassure them, that he would remain, and, pointing to a cape, pretended that, as a pilot, he knew it well and that there was good fishing to be had there. When the ship had reached the spot he pointed out to them he threw himself overboard and escaped from the French by swimming to the island of Mayo, on which he remained for four months until a ship from Biena called on its way to Brazil on which he sailed as far as Cape Verde. There, he arranged with Pedro de Santiago to take him to Cartajena, whence he came to Havana in March 1589, and at the moment he remains here, intending to return to Spain with the *flota*.

The said Pero Diaz is of the opinion that the people who remained in the settlement should have, by this time, died of hunger, or been exposed to great need and danger.

I have prepared this report from the answers received to questions I put to Pero Diaz, who will go to Spain with the *flota*, and will take with him a despatch from me to Madrid, where he will make himself known; and his majesty and the royal council of the Indies will then be able to give those instructions touching the settlement which most conduce to the royal service. This Pero Diaz knows how to navigate in the waters around the settlement, is young, hard-working, a good pilot, and a trustworthy person, whom I am assured will find favour with his majesty. However, even if this should not be so, I will pay out of my private purse his expenses from Seville to Madrid, the cost of his stay in Madrid, and of his return to Seville. Having made him this promise, I have his word that he will go to Madrid with the despatch that I shall give him.

Dated, Havana, 21 March 1589.
[signed and sealed:] Pedro de Arana

[Endorsed:] Havana. Relation which the paymaster sends concerning the place where the English are settling on the Florida coast at latitude 36¼°.

455. Deposition of Richard Butler, taken in Spain.

A.G., Simancas, Estado Inglaterra, E 1139 (unfoliated leaves at end) translated. Extract from undated deposition of Richard Butler who had landed from a ship of the Earl of Cumberland's in Spain in 1594 and was under suspicion of heresy and of being an English spy. The process dragged on for a very long time and can be followed in Calendar of State Papers, Spanish, 1587–1603 *(1899), pp. 599–601, although this deposition is not mentioned. Eventually, in 1596 he was condemned to death but was reprieved and sent to the galleys (Ibid., p. 643). He was finally released in 1608, having survived in the galleys for some twelve years.*

Although his dates and some of his facts are wrong, the light he throws on the Virginia voyage of 1584 is considerable. He seems to have confused the 1585 and 1587 expeditions.

On the said day Licenciate Valladares Sarmiento of his majesty's council ordered to appear before him a man, who said that he was named Ricardo Butiler [Richard Butler] and that he was Irish, being a native of the province of Guatreforlia [Waterford]; and before me, the said Juan Gallo de Andrada, he took and received the oath in the form required by law. The oath was also taken by the said Ricardo Estanihurst [Richard Stanyhurst], an Irish gentleman and a servant of his majesty, and by the said Guillermo Bodenam [William Bodenham], both being interpreters of the English language; without concealing anything they were to say neither more nor less than that which was said in English, and they were to keep secret all that was written and said before them. This was promised. And being questioned, Richard Butler said and declared the following:

When asked if he were a Christian, if he held and believed all that which was held and believed by the church of Rome, and if he regarded his Holiness as head of the Catholic church, he replied 'Yes'. He was asked to say the creed, and he recited it well in Latin. He said that he believed in all that he was saying, and that it was because he was a Christian that he [now] came [ready] to serve his majesty. Whilst in prison he was confessed by Fr. Celandia of the Society of Jesus and by Fr. Jacobo Archero [James Archer], an Irishman of the same Society, and when he was ill he received the sacrament, which was brought from the church of Santa Cruz:

When asked at what age he had left his country, he replied that it was at the age of ten, and that he went to London, where he remained for some five or six years. On arriving there he entered the service of Guater Raule [Walter Ralegh], the great favourite of the Queen of England, and he served him for the entire period of five or six years.

When asked where he had spent these five or six years, by whom he was sent and with what orders, he said that he left England with a captain called Amadis [Philip Amadas] who commanded two ships. With instructions from Walter Ralegh, the owner of the two ships, they went in search of Florida. They coasted along the whole of the Florida coast, and disembarked in the central part of Florida at a place called Ococa [Wococon], so named by the natives of the country. Twelve leagues further on towards the northern part, they disembarked again in another place, known to the English as Puerto Fernando [Port Ferdinando] and to the savages as Ataurras [Hatarask]. From there they moved twelve leagues to the north and found a port, with a depth of nine feet, which the savages called Cacho Peos [Chesapeake]; and these savages were enemies of those of Puerto Fernando. From there, in accordance with the instructions they were carrying, they set sail for Bermuda, but they were unable to reach it because a storm arose when they arrived in the passage to the north of the island [*en la altura della*]. From there they set their course for the Azores, where they remained, as long as their provisions lasted, in the hope of capturing a ship. They were there for six weeks, and then, having failed to take a prize and lacking provisions, they sailed for England. The voyage lasted nine months. In both ships there were about one hundred sailors and soldiers, and the pilot they carried was one Fernando [Simão Fernandes], a Portuguese, whose proper name he does not know. During the voyage the deponent served as corporal. He was in England for two months, living in Ralegh's house, until he was paid his wages for the voyage. He then returned to sea with captain Clinton, whose one ship, of about eighty tons, carried seventy men; he remained in the captain's company for three years, at times with two ships and at other times with three. They captured ships of all nations, and it was because of the great disorders, for which the said captain was responsible, that the Queen ordered the arming of one of her ships; the captain was imprisoned and hanged. A short time before the imprisonment of the captain, the deponent was recalled to London by Ralegh, who was then planning to send some ships to the Florida coast and, therefore, had need of him in view of his experience of those parts. He was instructed to make the voyage, and he went as corporal in the flagship, the captain of which was General Ricardo Grenfeld [Sir Richard Grenville]. There were seven ships, and in them there were seven or eight hundred men, sailors and soldiers. They left England in the year eighty-one or eighty-two (he could not remember which year), in the month of June [1585]. The pilot was Fernando, the Portuguese, who, he believes, was called Simon Fernando. They sailed directly to the Canaries, from whence they set sail for Puerto Rico. They harboured to the south of that port and were there for twenty days, during which time they constructed a small frigate. They then proceeded to Española, where they provided themselves

with meat and water, and it was whilst they were there that a Spaniard came to them on horseback; he was accompanied by eight or nine other persons who said that he was the governor. The deponent does not know what business he had, except that he saw him eating with his captain and that they both made a demonstration of affection towards each other. They were there for eight or nine days, and then they sailed for the island of Cuba, and thence they went to the coast of Florida and entered the port of Acoca [Wococon] with only three ships, as the other four had been separated from them in a storm. The deponent was ordered by his general to sail the length of the coast in a canoe [*canoa*], as far as Puerto Fernando, to see if he could find the four ships. In the port he discovered two of them and learnt that the other two had returned to England with a Spanish ship, which was loaded with gold, pearls and silver. The said captain proceeded with the three ships to Puerto Fernando and gave orders that the port, a large river mouth, should be reconnoitred, but owing to a strong current coming from the interior, they were unable to progress forward very much. The deponent disembarked, and having encountered the natives of the territory, he went inland to investigate, leaving the hundred and twenty men, who had left the ship with him, at the edge of the sea. He was in the company of the natives for about eight days and they treated him well. As he had had some communication with the two natives who had left with the English on the occasion of their first visit, he was able to understand a few words of what they were saying. He went inland for about twenty leagues and then returned to his companions, who, he discovered, had also explored the interior '*de diez en diez y de ocho en ocho*'. On his return they embarked and wished to pass, but were unable to do so because of the current. Seeing that they could not proceed owing to the strength of the current, they crossed the current to the northern side. They landed and met some of the natives of those parts; they are the enemies of those of Puerto Fernando. They killed about twenty of them and captured some of the women whom they gave to the other savages. They then returned to where their ships were, and having left some one hundred and forty men and ten English women, together with munitions, provisions, arms and artillery with which to fortify themselves, the general departed for England. The deponent accompanied him and the voyage lasted a year. They took with them a great deal of raw silk [*seda cruda*], grown on low bushes, and also pearls, which were given to them by the natives, and which were black due to the fact that they had been removed from the oysters by means of fire. As soon as he returned to England, the deponent embarked again in another ship, which his master had ready to be sent to sea. The captain of the ship was Arturo Barlo [Arthur Barlowe], and the deponent went on the voyage as his lieutenant. Another ship of Plymouth accompanied them, and together the two ships sailed to the Azores where they captured ten Spanish and Portuguese ships. Some of the ships had cargoes of sugar, Brazilwood, hides, silver, pearls, gold and silk, whilst others were empty, and amongst those there were three, of which Pédro Sarmiento was captain. From there they returned to England, taking Pedro Sarmiento with them. The voyage, lasting about three months, took place either at the end of eighty-four or at the beginning of eighty-five [actually 1586]; he does not remember which it was. On his return to England, Ralegh, his master, gave him a ship to captain; it was of seventy tons and carried seventy men. Amongst the latter there was Eduarte Roche, a native of Bristol and a friend of the deponent, although born in Bristol, for his parents were from the same country as the deponent. He had known him [Roche] for five or six years, and he took him on the voyage as his steward. The rest were soldiers and sailors, acquaintances of his. In ten weeks, during which time the ship sailed from the entrance to Lisbon as far as the Terceira islands, three ships were taken with quantities of silver, gold, pearls, hides and other merchandise, the total value of which amounted to more than one hundred thousand ducats. Two parts of this were given to Ralegh, whilst the third part was divided amongst the deponent and his companions. Out of his share, the deponent made gifts to certain persons, one of them being a friend called Guatero Copo [Walter Cope], secretary of Guillermo Cecilio [William Cecil, Lord Burghley], the Queen's treasurer; he gave him three boxes of sugar, some pearls and other things of a curious value. On this occasion he was in London for five or six months, living in the house of his master, Ralegh, who favoured him much more than before, because he was now a captain, and because he had brought back such a valuable prize. In all this time he never went to Ireland. Since it was late, the deposition was left in this state to be continued another day. It was signed by Ricardo Estanihurst [Stanyhurst], Guillermo Bodenam, Ricardo Butiler, and by the said Licentiate, before me, Juan Gallo.

456. February 4, 1593. John White writes to Richard Hakluyt.

Enclosed with this letter was White's narrative of the 1590 voyage to Virginia (457). In the letter he attempts to explain why the ships that left England in March did not arrive off the Carolina Banks until August, too late in the season to make a prolonged search for the colonists. He also feels it necessary to explain why he was embarked on what is clearly and primarily a privateering venture. John Watts, a well-known privateering entrepreneur, prepared the three ships mentioned for such a voyage. They were the Hopewell *(140–160 tons), Abraham Cocke captain, the* Little John *(100–120 tons), Christopher Newport captain, and the* John Evangelist, *a pinnace, William Lane captain. William Sanderson, Ralegh's man of business, was concerned with the bond mentioned by White for the release of these ships to make a supply voyage to Virginia. He also induced Watts to agree to include one of his own ships, the* Moonlight *(80 tons), Edward Spicer captain, which left England later along with a pinnace, the* Conclude, *Joseph Harris captain. White's narrative outlines the privateering progress of the fleet through the West Indies, the most important prize being the* Buen Jesus *from the Santo Domingo fleet. This capture later gave rise to a case in the High Court of Admiralty. Eventually, it is the* Hopewell *and Sanderson's* Moonlight *that sail to Virginia.*

Printed in R. Hakluyt, Principal navigations, *III (1600), 287–295; VIII (1904), 404–422. D. B. Quinn*, Roanoke voyages, *II (1955), 712–716 [Document 456] (letter), 598–622 [457] (narrative).*

To the Worshipful and my very friend Master Richard Hakluyt, much happinesse in the Lord.

Sir, as well for the satisfying of your earnest request, as the performance of my promise made unto you at my last being with you in England, I have sent you (although in a homely stile, especially for the contentation of a delicate eare) the true discourse of my last voyage into the West Indies, and partes of America called Virginia, taken in hand about the end of Februarie, in the yeere of our redemption 1590. And what events happened unto us in this our journey, you shall plainely perceive by the sequele of my discourse. There were at the time aforesaid three ships absolutely determined to goe for the West Indies, at the speciall charges of Master John Wattes of London Marchant. But when they were fully furnished, and in readinesse to make their departure, a generall stay was commanded of all ships thorowout England. Which so soone as I heard, I presently (as I thought it most requisite) acquainted Sir Walter Ralegh therewith, desiring him that as I had sundry times afore bene chargeable and troublesome unto him, for the supplies and reliefes of the planters in Virginia: so likewise, that by his endevour it would please him at that instant to procure license for those three ships to proceede on with their determined voyage, that thereby the people in Virginia (if it were Gods pleasure) might speedily be comforted and relieved without further charges unto him. Whereupon he by his good meanes obtained license of the Queenes Majestie, and order to be taken, that the owner of the 3 ships should be bound unto Sir Walter Ralegh or his assignes, in 3000 pounds, that those 3 ships in consideration of their releasement should take in, & transport a convenient number of passengers, with their furnitures and necessaries to be landed in Virginia. Nevertheless that order was not observed, neither was the bond taken according to the intention aforesaid. But rather in contempt of the aforesaid order, I was by the owner and Commanders of the ships denied to have any passengers, or any thing els transported in any of the said ships, saving only my selfe & my chest; no not so much as a boy to attend upon me, although I made great sute, & earnest intreatie aswell to the chiefe Commanders, as to the owner of the said ships. Which crosse and unkind dealing, although it very much discontented me, notwithstanding the scarsity of time was such, that I could have no

opportunity to go unto Sir Walter Ralegh with complaint: for the ships being then all in readinesse to goe to the Sea, would have bene departed before I could have made my returne. Thus both Governors, Masters, and sailers, regarding very smally the good of their countreymen in Virginia; determined nothing lesse then to touch at those places, but wholly disposed themselves to seeke after purchase & spoiles, spending so much time therein, that sommer was spent before we arrived at Virginia. And when we were come thither, the season was so unfit, & weather so foule, that we were constrained of force to forsake that coast, having not seene any of our planters, with losse of one of our shipboates, and 7 of our chiefest men: and also with losse of 3 of our ankers and cables, and most of our caskes with fresh water left on shore, not possible to be had aboord. Which evils & unfortunate events (as wel to their owne losse as to the hinderance of the planters in Virginia) had not chanced, if the order set downe by Sir Walter Ralegh had bene observed, or if my dayly & continuall petitions for the performance of the same might have taken any place. Thus may you plainely perceive the successe of my fift & last voiage to Virginia, which was no lesse unfortunately ended then frowardly begun, and as lucklesse to many, as sinister to my selfe. But I would to God it had bene as prosperous to all, as noysome to the planters; & as joyfull to me, as discomfortable to them. Yet seeing it is not my first crossed voyage, I remaine contented. And wanting my wishes, I leave off from prosecuting that whereunto I would to God my wealth were answerable to my will. Thus committing the reliefe of my discomfortable company the planters in Virginia, to the merciful help of the Almighty, whom I most humbly beseech to helpe & comfort them, according to his most holy will & their good desire, I take my leave from my house at Newtowne in Kylmore the 4 February, 1593.
Your most welwishing friend,
John White.

457. 1590. John White's account of the 1590 voyage in search of the 1587 colonists.

John White's account of his fifth and last voyage to Virginia, which he entrusted to Richard Hak-

luyt in 1593, is partly journal and partly apologia for his delays in arriving at Virginia. As materials in the High Court of Admiralty reveal (D. B. Quinn, Roanoke voyages, II, 624-712), he became entangled in a very complex sequence of privateering operations of which his account is scarcely comprehensive. He does not make it clear that the Moonlight was not basically involved in the privateering ventures but had been sent by William Sanderson, presumably with substantial stores, for the relief of the colony. White's picture of himself as the sole captive-passenger of a privateering crew is not correct, although there are some grounds for believing that he was never at any time his own master. The critically important part of the narrative is his unavailing search for the Lost Colonists and the slight clues he is able to give regarding their possible destination.

Printed in R. Hakluyt, Principal navigations, III (1600), 288-295; frequently reprinted (for example, in D. B. Quinn, Roanoke voyages, II, 598-622).

The fift voyage of Master John White into the West Indies and parts of America called Virginia, in the yeere 1590.

The 20 of March the three shippes the Hopewell, the John Evangelist, and the Little John, put to Sea from Plymmouth with two small Shallops.

The 25 at midnight both our Shallops were sunke being towed at the ships stearnes by the Boatswaines negligence.

On the 30 we saw a head us that part of the coast of Barbary, lying East of Cape Cantyn, and the Bay of Asaphi.

The next day we came to the Ile of Mogador, where rode, at our passing by, a Pinnesse of London called the Mooneshine.

Aprill.

On the first of Aprill we ankored in Santa Cruz rode, where we found two great shippes of London lading in Sugar, of whom we had 2 shipboats to supply the losse of our Shallops.

On the 2 we set sayle from the rode of Santa Cruz, for the Canaries.

On Saturday the 4 we saw Alegranza, the East Ile of the Canaries.

On Sunday the 5 of April we gave chase to a double flyboat, the which, we also the same day fought with, and tooke her, with losse of three of their men slaine, and one hurt.

On Munday the 6 we saw Grand Canarie, and the next day we landed and tooke in fresh water on the Southside thereof.

On the 9 we departed from Grand Canary, and framed our course for Dominica.

The last of Aprill we saw Dominica, and the same night we came to an anker on the Southside thereof.

May.

The first of May in the morning many of the Salvages came aboord our ships in their Canowes, and did traffique with us; we also the same day landed and entered their Towne from whence we returned the same day aboord without any resistance of the Salvages; or any offence done to them.

The 2 of May our Admirall and our Pinnesse departed from Dominica leaving the John our Viceadmirall playing off and on about Dominica, hoping to take some Spaniard outwardes bound to the Indies; the same night we had sight of three smal Ilands called Los Santos, leaving Guadalupe and them on our starboord.

The 3 we had sight of S. Christophers Iland, bearing Northeast and by East off us.

On the 4 we sayled by the Virgines, which are many broken Ilands, lying at the East ende of S. Johns Iland; and the same day towards evening we landed upon one of them called Blanca, where we killed an incredible number of foules: here we stayed but three houres, & from thence stood into the shore Northwest, and having brought this Iland Southeast off us, we put towards night thorow an opening or swatch, called The passage, lying betwene the Virgines, and the East end of S. John: here the Pinnesse left us and sayled on the South side of S. John.

The 5 and 6 the Admirall sayled along the Northside of S. John, so neere the shore that the Spaniards discerned us to be men of warre; and therefore made fires along the coast as we sailed by, for so their custome is, when they see any men of warre on their coasts.

The 7 we landed on the Northwest end of S. John, where we watered in a good river called Yaguana, and the same night following we tooke a Frigate of tenne Tunne comming from

Gwathanelo laden with hides and ginger. In this place Pedro a Mollato, who knewe all our state, ranne from us to the Spaniards.

On the 9 we departed from Yaguana.

The 13 we landed on an Iland called Mona, whereon were 10 or 12 houses inhabited of the Spaniards; these we burned & tooke from them a Pinnesse, which they had drawen a ground and sunke, and carried all her sayles, mastes, and rudders into the woods, because we should not take him away; we also chased the Spaniards over all the Iland; but they hid them in caves, hollow rockes, and bushes, so that we could not find them.

On the 14 we departed from Mona, and the next day after wee came to an Iland called Saona, about 5 leagues distant from Mona, lying on the Southside of Hispaniola neere the East end: betweene these two Ilands we lay off and on 4 or 5 days, hoping to take some of the Domingo fleete doubling this Iland, as a neerer way to Spaine then by Cape Tyburon, or by Cape S. Anthony.

On Thursday being the 19 our Viceadmirall, from whom we departed at Dominica, came to us at Saona, with whom we left a Spanish Frigate, and appointed him to lie off and on other five daies betweene Saona and Mona to the ende aforesaid; then we departed from them at Saona for Cape Tyburon. Here I was enformed that our men of the Viceadmirall, at their departure from Dominica brought away two young Salvages, which were the chiefe Casiques sonnes of that Countrey and part of Dominica, but they shortly after ran away from them at Santa Cruz Iland, where the Viceadmirall landed to take in ballast.

On the 21 the Admirall came to the Cape Tyburon, where we found the John Evangelist our Pinnesse staying for us: here we tooke in two Spaniards almost starved on the shore, who made a fire to our ships as we passed by. Those places for an 100 miles in length are nothing els but a desolate and meere wildernesse, without any habitation of people, and full of wilde Bulles and Bores, and great Serpents.

The 22 our Pinnesse came also to an anker in Aligato Bay at cape Tyburon. Here we understood of Master Lane, Captaine of the Pinnesse; how he was set upon with one of the kings Gallies belonging to Santo Domingo, which was manned with 400 men, who after he had fought with him 3 or 4 houres, gave over the fight & forsooke him, without any great hurt done in eyther part.

The 26 the John our Vizadmirall came to us to cape Tyburon, and the Frigat which we left with him at Saona. This was the appointed place where we should attend for the meeting with the Santo Domingo Fleete.

On Whitsunday Even at Cape Tyburon one of our boyes ranne away from us, and at ten dayes end returned to our ships almost starved for want of food. In sundry places about this part of Cape Tyburon we found the bones and carkases of divers men, who had perished (as wee thought) by famine in those woods, being either stragled from their company, or landed there by some men of warre.

June.

On the 14 of June we tooke a smal Spanish frigat which fell amongst us so suddenly, as he doubled the point at the Bay of Cape Tyburon, where we road, so that he could not escape us. This Frigat came from Santo Domingo, and had but 3 men in her, the one was an expert Pilot, the other a Mountainer, and the third a Vintener, who escaped all out of prison at Santo Domingo, purposing to fly to Yaguana which is a towne in the West parts of Hispaniola where many fugitive Spaniards are gathered together.

The 17 being Wednesday Captaine Lane was sent to Yaguana with his Pinnesse and a Frigat to take a shippe, which was there taking in fraight, as we understood by the old Pylot, whom we had taken three dayes before.

The 24 the Frigat returned from Captaine Lane at Yaguana, and brought us word to cape Tyburon, that Captaine Lane had taken the shippe, with many passengers and Negroes in the same; which proved not so rich a prize as we hoped for, for that Frenchman of warre had taken and spoyled her before we came. Neverthelesse her loading was thought worth 1000 or 1300 pounds, being hides, ginger, Cannafistula, Copperpannes, and Casavi.

July.

The second of July Edward Spicer whom we left in England came to us at Cape Tyburon, accompanied with a small Pinnesse, whereof one Master Harps [Harris] was Captaine. And the same day we had sight of a fleete of 14 saile all of Santo Domingo, to whom we presently gave chase, but they upon the first sight of us fled, and separating themselves scattered here and there:

Wherefore we were forced to divide our selves and so made after them untill 12 of the clocke at night. But then by reason of the darknesse we lost sight of ech other, yet in the end the Admirall and the Moonelight happened to be together the same night at the fetching up of the Vizadmirall of the Spanish fleete, against whom the next morning we fought and tooke him, with losse of one of our men and two hurt, and of theirs 4 slaine and 6 hurt. But what was become of our Viceadmirall, our Pinnesse, and Prize, and two Frigates, in all this time, we were ignorant.

The 3 of July we spent about rifling, romaging and fitting the Prize to be sailed with us.

The 6 of July we saw Jamayca the which we left on our larboord, keeping Cuba in sight on our starboord.

Upon the 8 of July we saw the Iland of Pinos, which lieth on the Southside of Cuba nigh unto the West end or Cape called Cape S. Anthony. And the same day we gave chase to a Frigat, but at night we lost sight of her, partly by the slow sayling of our Admirall, & lacke of the Moonelight our Pinnesse, whom Captaine Cooke had sent to the Cape the day before.

On the 11 we came to Cape S. Anthony, where we found our consort the Moonelight and her Pinnesse abiding for our comming, of whom we understood that the day before there passed by them 22 saile, some of them of the burden of 300 and some 400 tunnes loaden with the Kings treasure from the maine, bound for Havana; from this 11 of July untill 22 we were much becalmed: and the winde being scarse, and the weather exceeding hoat, we were much pestered with the Spaniards we had taken: wherefore we were driven to land all the Spaniards saving three, but the place where we landed them was of their owne choise on the Southside of Cuba neere unto the Organes and Rio de Puercos.

The 23 we had sight of the Cape of Florida, and the broken Ilands thereof called the Martires.

The 25 being S. James day in the morning, we fell with the Matanças a head-land 8 leagues towards the East of Havana, where we purposed to take fresh water in, and make our abode two or three dayes.

On Sunday the 26 of July plying too and fro betweene the Matanças, and Havana, we were espied of three small Pinnasses of S. John de Ullua bound for Havana, which were exceeding richly loaden. These 3 Pinnasses came very boldly up unto us, and so continued untill they came within musket shot of us. And we supposed them to be Captain Harps pinnesse, and two small Frigats taken by Captain Harpe: wherefore we shewed our flag. But they presently upon the sight of it turned about & made all the saile they could from us toward the shore, & kept themselves in so shallow water, that we were not able to follow them, and therefore gave them over with expence of shot & pouder to no purpose. But if we had not so rashly set out our flagge, we might have taken them all three, for they would not have knowen us before they had bene in our hands. This chase brought us so far to leeward as Havana: wherfore not finding any of our consorts at yᵉ Matanças, we put over again to the cape of Florida, & from thence thorow the chanel of Bahama.

On the 28 the Cape of Florida bare West of us.

The 30 we lost sight of the coast of Florida, and stood to Sea for to gaine the helpe of the current which runneth much swifter a farre off then in sight of the coast.[1] For from the Cape to Virginia all along the shore are none but eddie currents, setting to the South and Southwest.

The 31 our three ships were clearly disbocked, the great prize, the Admirall, and the Mooneshine, but our prize being thus disbocked departed from us without taking leave of our Admirall or consort, and sayled directly for England.

August.

On the first of August the winde scanted, and from thence forward we had very fowle weather with much raine, thundering, and great spouts, which fell round about us nigh unto our ships.

The 3 we stoode againe in for the shore, and at midday we tooke the height of the same. The height of that place we found to be 34 degrees of latitude. Towards night we were within three leagues of the Low sandie Ilands West of Wokokon.[2] But the weather continued so exceeding foule, that we could not come to an anker nye the coast: wherefore we stood off againe to Sea untill Monday the 9 of August.

On munday the storme ceased, and we had very great likelihood of faire weather: therefore we stood in againe for the shore: & came to an anker

---

1. The state of the currents from the cape of Florida to Virginia.
2. Sandie Ilands West of Wokokon.

at 11 fadome in 35 degrees[3] of latitude, within a mile of the shore, where we went on land on the narrow sandy Iland, being one of the Ilandes West of Wokokon: in this Iland we tooke in some fresh water and caught great store of fish in the shallow water. Betweene the maine (as we supposed) and that Iland it was but a mile over and three or foure foote deepe in most places.

On the 12 in the morning we departed from thence and toward night we came to an anker at the Northeast end of the Iland of Croatoan, by reason of a breach[4] which we perceived to lie out two or three leagues into the Sea: here we road all that night.

The 13 in the morning before we wayed our ankers, our boates were sent to sound over this breach: our ships riding on the side thereof at 5 fadome; and a ships length from us we found but 4 and a quarter, and then deeping and shallowing for the space of two miles, so that sometimes we found[5] 5 fadome, and by & by 7, and within two casts with the lead 9, & then 8, next cast 5, & then 6, & then 4, & then 9 againe, and deeper; but 3 fadome was the least, 2 leagues off from the shore. This breach is in 35 degr. & a halfe, & lyeth at the very Northeast point of Croatoan, wheras goeth a fret out of the maine Sea into the inner waters, which part the Ilandes and the maine land.

The 15 of August towards Evening we came to an anker at Hatorask, in 36 degr.[6] and one third, in five fadom water, three leagues from the shore. At our first comming to anker on this shore we saw a great smoke rise in the Ile Raonoake neere the place where I left our Colony in the yeere 1587, which smoake put us in good hope that some of the Colony were there expecting my returne out of England.

The 16 and next morning our 2 boates went a shore, & Captaine Cooke & Captain Spicer & their company with me, with intent to passe to the place at Raonoak where our countreymen were left. At our putting from the ship we commanded our Master gunner to make readie 2 Minions and a Falkon well loden, and to shoot them off with reasonable space betweene every shot, to the ende that their reportes might bee heard to the

place where wee hoped to finde some of our people. This was accordingly performed, & our twoe boats put off unto the shore, in the Admirals boat we sounded all the way and found from our shippe untill we came within a mile of the shore nine, eight, and seven fadome: but before we were halfe way betweene our ships and the shore we saw another great smoke to the Southwest of Kindrikers mountes: we therefore thought good to goe to that second smoke first: but it was much further from the harbour where we landed, then we supposed it to be, so that we were very sore tired before wee came to the smoke. But that which grieved us more was that when we came to the smoke, we found no man nor signe that any had bene there lately, nor yet any fresh water in all this way to drinke. Being thus wearied with this journey we returned to the harbour where we left our boates, who in our absence, had brought their caske a shore for fresh water, so we deferred our going to Roanoak untill the next morning, and caused some of those saylers to digge in those sandie hilles for fresh water whereof we found very sufficient. That night wee returned aboord with our boates and our whole company in safety.

The next morning being the 17 of August, our boates and company were prepared againe to goe up to Roanoak, but Captaine Spicer had then sent his boat ashore for fresh water, by meanes whereof it was ten of the clocke aforenoone before we put from our ships which were then come to an anker within two miles of the shore. The Admirals boat was halfe way toward the shore, when Captaine Spicer put off from his ship. The Admirals boat first passed the breach, but not without some danger of sinking, for we had a sea brake into our boat which filled us halfe full of water, but by the will of God and carefull styrage of Captaine Cooke we came safe ashore, saving onely that our furniture, victuals match and powder were much wet and spoyled. For at this time the winde blue at Northeast and direct into the harbour so great a gale, that the Sea brake extremely on the barre, and the tide went very forcibly at the entrance. By that time our Admirals boate was halled ashore, and most of our things taken out to dry, Captaine Spicer came to the entrance of the breach with his mast standing up, and was halfe passed over, but by the rash and undiscreet styrage of Ralph Skinner his Masters mate, a very dangerous Sea brake into their boate and overset

3. They land in 35 degrees.
4. Sidenote: "A breach 2 or 3 leagues into Sea."
5. Sidenote: "Great diversity of soundings."
6. Sidenote: "Hatorask in 36 degr. & a terce."

them quite, the men kept the boat some in it, and some hanging on it, but the next sea set the boat on ground, where it beat so, that some of them were forced to let goe their hold, hoping to wade ashore, but the Sea still beat them downe, so that they could neither stand nor swimme, and the boat twise or thrise was turned the keele upward; whereon Captaine Spicer and Skinner hung untill they sunke, & seene no more. But foure that could swimme a litle kept themselves in deeper water and were saved by Captain Cookes meanes, who so soone as he saw their oversetting, stripped himselfe, and foure other that could swimme very well, & with all haste possible rowed unto them, & saved foure. They were a 11 in all, & 7 of the chiefest were drowned, whose names were Edward Spicer, Ralph Skinner, Edward Kelley, Thomas Bevis, Hance the Surgion, Edward Kelborne, Robert Coleman. This mischance did so much discomfort the saylers, that they were all of one mind not to goe any further to seeke the planters. But in the end by the commandement & perswasion of me and Captaine Cooke, they prepared the boates: and seeing the Captaine and me so resolute, they seemed much more willing. Our boates and all things fitted againe, we put off from Hatorask, being the number of 19 persons in both boates: but before we could get to the place, where our planters were left, it was so exceeding darke, that we overshot the place a quarter of a mile: there we espied towards the North end of the Iland ye light of a great fire thorow the woods, to the which we presently rowed: when wee came right over against it, we let fall our Grapnel neere the shore, & sounded with a trumpet a Call, & afterwardes many familiar English tunes of Songs, and called to them friendly; but we had no answere, we therefore landed at day-breake, and comming to the fire, we found the grasse & sundry rotten trees burning about the place. From hence we went thorow the woods to that part of the Iland directly over against Dasamongwepeuk, & from thence we returned by the water side, round about the Northpoint of the Iland, untill we came to the place where I left our Colony in the yeere 1586. In all this way we saw in the sand the print of the Salvages feet of 2 or 3 sorts troaden that night, and as we entred up the sandybanke upon a tree, in the very browe thereof were curiously carved these faire Romane letters CRO: which letters presently we knew to

signifie the place, where I should find the planters seated, according to a secret token agreed upon betweene them & me at my last departure from them, which was, that in any wayes they should not faile to write or carve on the trees or posts of the dores the name of the place where they should be seated; for at my comming away they were prepared to remove from Roanoak 50 miles into the maine. Therefore at my departure from them in Anno 1587 I willed them, that if they should happen to be distressed in any of those places, that then they should carve over the letters or name, a Crosse ✠ in this forme, but we found no such signe of distresse. And having well considered of this, we passed toward the place where they were left in sundry houses, but we found the houses taken downe, and the place very strongly enclosed with a high palisado of great trees, with cortynes and flankers very Fort-like, and one of the chiefe trees or postes at the right side of the entrance had the barke taken off, and 5 foote from the ground in fayre Capitall letters was graven CROATOAN without any crosse or signe of distresse; this done, we entred into the palisado, where we found many barres of Iron, two pigges of Lead, foure yron fowlers, Iron sackershotte, and such like heavie things, throwen here and there, almost overgrowen with grasse and weedes. From thence wee went along by the water side, towards the poynt of the Creeke to see if we could find any of their botes or Pinnisse, but we could perceive no signe of them, nor any of the last Falkons and small Ordinance which were left with them, at my departure from them. At our returne from the Creeke, some of our Saylers meeting us, tolde us that they had found where divers chests had bene hidden, and long sithence digged up againe and broken up, and much of the goods in them spoyled and scattered about, but nothing left, of such things as the Savages knew any use of, undefaced. Presently Captaine Cooke and I went to the place, which was in the ende of an old trench, made two yeeres past by Captaine Amadas: where wee found five Chests, that had been carefully hidden of the Planters, and of the same chests three were my owne, and about the place many of my things spoyled and broken, and my bookes torne from the covers, the frames of some of my pictures and Mappes rotten and spoyled with rayne, and my armour almost eaten through with rust; this could bee no other but the deede of the Savages our enemies at Dasamongwepeuk, who had watched the departure of our men to Croatoan; and assoone as they were departed, digged up every place where they suspected any thing to be buried: but although it much grieved me to see such spoyle of my goods, yet on the other side I greatly joyed that I had safely found a certaine token of their safe being at Croatoan, which is the place where Manteo was borne, and the Savages of the Iland our friends.

When we had seene in this place so much as we could, we returned to our Boates, and departed from the shoare towards our Shippes, with as much speede as we could: For the weather beganne to overcast, and very likely that a foule and stormie night would ensue. Therefore the same Evening with much danger and labour, we got our selves aboard, by which time the winde and seas were so greatly risen, that wee doubted our Cables and Anchors would scarcely holde untill Morning; wherefore the Captaine caused the Boate to be manned with five lusty men, who could swimme all well, and sent them to the little Iland on the right hand of the Harbour, to bring aboard sixe of our men, who had filled our caske with fresh water: the Boate the same night returned aboard with our men, but all our Caske ready filled they left behinde, unpossible to bee had aboard without danger of casting away both men and Boates; for this night prooved very stormie and foule.

The next Morning it was agreed by the Captaine and my selfe, with the Master and others, to wey anchor, and goe for the place at Croatoan, where our planters were: for that then the winde was good for that place, and also to leave that Caske with fresh water on shoare in the Iland untill our returne. So then they brought the cable to the Capston, but when the anchor was almost apecke, the Cable broke, by meanes whereof we lost another Anchor, wherewith we drove so fast into the shoare, that wee were forced to let fall a third Anchor; which came so fast home that the Shippe was almost aground by Kenricks mounts: so that wee were forced to let slippe the Cable ende for ende. And if it had not chanced that wee had fallen into a chanell of deeper water, closer by the shoare then wee accompted of, wee could never have gone cleare of the poynt that lyeth to the Southwardes of Kenricks mounts. Being thus cleare of some dangers, and gotten into deeper waters, but not without some losse; for wee had

but one Cable and Anchor left us of foure, and the weather grew to be fouler and fouler; our victuals scarse, and our caske and fresh water lost: it was therefore determined that we should goe for Saint John or some other Iland to the Southward for fresh water. And it was further purposed, that if wee could any wayes supply our wants of victuals and other necessaries, either at Hispaniola, Sant John, or Trynidad, that then wee should continue in the Indies all the Winter following, with hope to make 2. rich voyages of one, and at our returne to visit our countrymen at Virginia. The captaine and the whole company in the Admirall (with my earnest petitions) thereunto agreed, so that it rested onely to knowe what the Master of the Moone-light our consort would doe herein. But when we demanded them if they would accompany us in that new determination, they alledged that their weake and leake Shippe was not able to continue it; wherefore the same night we parted,[7] leaving the Moone-light to goe directly for England, and the Admirall set his course for Trynidad, which course we kept two dayes.

On the 28. the winde changed, and it was sette on foule weather every way: but this storme brought the winde West and Northwest, and blewe so forcibly, that wee were able to beare no sayle, but our fore-course halfe mast high, wherewith wee ranne upon the winde perforce, the due course for England, for that wee were dryven to change our first determination for Trynidad, and stoode for the Ilands of Açores, where wee purposed to take in fresh water, and also there hoped to meete with some English men of warre about those Ilands, at whose hands wee might obtaine some supply of our wants. And thus continuing our course for the Açores, sometimes with calmes, and sometimes with very scarce windes, on the fifteenth of September the winde came South Southeast, and blew so exceedingly, that wee were forced to lye atry all that day. At this time by account we judged our selves to be about twentie leagues to the West of Cuervo and Flores, but about night the storme ceased, and fayre weather ensued.

On Thursday the seventeenth wee saw Cuervo and Flores, but we could not come to anker that night, by reason the winde shifted. The next Morning being the eighteenth, standing in againe with Cuervo, we escryed a sayle ahead us, to

---

7. Sidenote: "They leave the coast of Virginia."

whom we gave chase: but when wee came neere him, we knew him to be a Spanyard, and hoped to make sure purchase of him; but we understood at our speaking with him, that he was a prize, and of the Domingo fleete already taken by the John our consort, in the Indies. We learned also of this prize, that our Viceadmirall and Pinnisse had fought with the rest of the Domingo fleete, and had forced them with their Admirall to flee unto Jamaica under the Fort for succour, and some of them ran themselves aground, whereof one of them they brought away, and tooke out of some others so much as the time would permit. And further wee understood of them, that in their returne from Jamaica about the Organes neere Cape Saint Anthony, our Viceadmirall mette with two Shippes of the mayne land, come from Mexico, bound for Havana, with whom he fought: in which fight our Viceadmirals Lieutenant was slaine, and the Captaines right arme strooken off, with foure other of his men slaine, and sixteene hurt, But in the ende he entred, and tooke one of the Spanish shippes, which was so sore shot by us under water, that before they could take out her treasure, she sunke; so that we lost thirteene Pipes of silver[8] which sunke with her, besides much other rich marchandize. And in the meane time the other Spanish shippe being pearced with nine shotte under water, got away; whom our Viceadmirall intended to pursue: but some of their men in the toppe made certaine rockes, which they saw above water neere the shoare, to be Gallies of Havana and Cartagena, comming from Havana to rescue the two Ships; Wherefore they gave over their chase, and went for England. After this intelligence was given us by this our prize, he departed from us, and went for England.

On Saturday the 19. of September we came to an Ancre neere a small village on the North side of Flores, where we found ryding 5. English men of warre, of whom wee understood that our Viceadmirall and Prize were gone thence for England. One of these five was the Moonelight our consort, who upon the first sight of our comming into Flores, set sayle and went for England, not taking any leave of us.

On Sunday the 20. the Mary Rose, Admirall of the Queenes fleete, wherein was Generall Sir John Hawkins, stood in with Flores, and divers other of the Queenes ships, namely the Hope, the Nonpareilia, The Rainebow, the Swift-sure, the Foresight, with many other good merchants ships

of warre, as the Edward Bonaventure, the Marchant Royal, the Amitie, the Eagle, the Dainty of sir John Hawkins, and many other good ships and pinnisses, all attending to meete with the king of Spaines fleete, comming from Terra firma of the West Indies.

The 22. of September we went aboard the Raynebow, and towards night we spake with the Swift-sure, and gave him 3. pieces. The captaines desired our company; wherefore we willingly attended on them: who at this time with 10. other ships stood for Faial. But the Generall with the rest of the Fleete were separated from us, making two fleetes, for the surer meeting with the Spanish fleete.

On Wednesday the 23. we saw Gratiosa, where the Admiral and the rest of the Queens fleete were come together. The Admirall put forth a flag of counsel, in which was determined that the whole fleete should go for the mayne, and spred themselves on the coasts of Spaine and Portugal, so farre as conveniently they might, for the surer meeting of the Spanish fleete in those parts.

The 26. we came to Faial, where the Admiral with some other of the fleete ankred, othersome plyed up and downe betweene that and the Pico untill midnight, at which time the Antony shot off a piece and weyed, shewing his light: after whom the whole fleete stood to the East, the winde at Northeast by East.

On Sunday the 27. towards Evening wee tooke our leave of the Admirall and the whole fleete, who stood to the East. But our shippe accompanied with a Flyboate stoode in againe with S. George, where we purposed to take in more fresh water, and some other fresh victuals.

On Wednesday the 30. of September, seeing the winde hang so Northerly, that wee could not atteine the Iland of S. George, we gave over our purpose to water there, and the next day framed our due course for England.

October.

The 2. of October in the Morning we saw S. Michaels Iland on our Starre board quarter.

The 23. at 10. of the clocke afore noone, we saw Ushant in Britaigne.

On Sunday the 24. we came in safetie, God be thanked, to an anker at Plymmouth.

---

8. Sidenote: "Pipes of silver."

XIII

The English and the
Mainland Northeast, 1580–1612

IT APPEARS DESIRABLE at this point to give some general conspectus of the area we know as New England, the Maritimes, and the approaches to the St. Lawrence River. The documents relating to English enterprises will follow, but those of the French will be reserved for later treatment. Yet, if they are not seen in relationship with one another, confusion is liable to arise. The specific activities of the French will be dealt with thereafter in the narrower context of their activities in the Northeast.

From Verrazzano's "Refugio" (Narragansett Bay), along the shores of Norumbega (New England), and of Acadia (the Maritimes) to the mouth of Cartier's River of Canada (St. Lawrence River), European activity is, after the period from Verrazzano to Roberval (1524–1545) down to about 1580, virtually a blank picture so far as positive evidence is concerned and cannot be illustrated by any documents whatever so far as can be ascertained. But we know that the French had a center of activity at Cape Breton that was a summer base alike for codfishing and for dealings in furs with the adjoining Micmac people. It is difficult to doubt that trading and fishing voyages, by the French, possibly by the Portuguese and even by English vessels, were taking place, however intermittently during these dark years, between the Island of St. John (Nova Scotia) and southern Norumbega (Cape Cod Bay probably as a southern limit). Similarly, with Spanish Basques active in the Grand Bay, the Strait of Belle Isle, and some French Basques involved in that region also, it is scarcely possible to dismiss the likelihood that a fur trade and some whaling, too (for the beluga at least), were continuing on the shores northward and westward from Cape Breton, westward from the Strait of Belle Isle and into the St.

Lawrence River, at least as far as Tadoussac. But the historian cannot yet establish clearly any of these conjectures.

Around 1580 our evidence begins to become firm. At least two English ships were in New England in 1580, one making a reconnaissance for Sir Humphrey Gilbert, the other trading skins with Abenaki Indians in the Rio de Gamas (the Penobscot). Then, too, from 1581 onward there is evidence, most of it fairly firm, that Breton and later Norman vessels were going regularly each season to trade with the Montagnais Indians and their allies at Tadoussac and that the fur trade had finally joined the fishery as a major European seasonal industry in North America. They were later joined by Basques, Spanish, and French. As will be indicated in a subsequent volume, in 1583 the French were reconnoitering the Bay of Fundy and the Maine coast for possible trading and mission stations, although nothing firm came of this. As early as 1577, the French also had revived the skeleton framework of a government of New France, whatever precisely that might imply. The Marquis de la Roche, the nominal head of that ghostly administration, was expected at various times from 1578–1584 to take up his post at, presumably, one of the Cartier or Roberval sites, although in 1584 his ship was wrecked and he failed to emerge as a new pioneer for France in the New World. The English continued to write about the possibility of colonies along the coastline from Narragansett Bay to the St. Lawrence, as has been shown, but their only initiatives in the 1590s were in the Gulf of St. Lawrence and the Magdalen Islands. These were puny and ineffective efforts and led to nothing except, perhaps, a renewal of French determination to make this area wholly a French sphere.

La Roche revived his activities in 1597, began to take some initiatives himself, and also to license others to do so, and, as will appear in a later volume, he continued to do so for some six years. His direct contribution was a curious convict colony on Sable Island, not on the mainland, from 1598 to 1603, but the first mainland post at Tadoussac was created in 1600 under license from him. Yet we can say that by the opening of the new century France was ready, and possibly able, to take some permanent stake in the St. Lawrence area, although no firm establishments had been created. The position to the south of Cape Breton was still wholly undetermined.

We can see the opening of the new century as very much a turning point. The international situation was at last favorable, since the European wars ended for France in 1598 and for England in 1604. Something of a revolution had been taking place in the fur trade. Indians in New England and southward had long been able to supply European traders with dressed deerskins, but the demand for them was never very great. It was different with the furs of the north. Indians and Eskimo could supply, indeed, skins of bear, fox, lynx, and, above all, beaver, which were cured, but their production in quantity could only come about by the development of what we must regard as a major industry among the Indians, not only of the coast but of the interior. Moreover, mere curing was not sufficient in all cases; dressing was desirable, too, and part-worn beaver skins were found to be more effective for sale in Europe than ones that had simply been preserved. At the same time the demand for North American furs was growing in Europe. Fox and lynx were desirable exotics, but beaver was becoming a necessary part of European dress, in the form of the felted hats that were being worn by both sexes. The small hair of the beaver was the major constituent in the felt. Thus the mainland Northeast was in process of becoming the first major area of European-Amerindian exchange. The stages in this remarkable process of interaction are and will almost certainly remain almost wholly obscured, and can scarcely even be directly documented, but they were crucial in directing attention to the St. Lawrence Valley and focusing French attention there.

So far as the Maritimes and New England were concerned their economic value, from the aspect of Indian exchanges, was still questionable. The Micmacs were involved with the French at Cape Breton and, increasingly it would seem, farther south into the Nova Scotia peninsula. But though this was to remain a fur-producing area for some time, it could not be seen to be a base for southward expansion until further experiments had been made. The French were to make these experiments from 1604 onward. The English, meantime, had begun from the other end, for Verrazzano's "Refugio" continued to fascinate speculators even though it had not been rediscovered. Thus when Bartholomew Gosnold brought out a small prospecting expedition in 1602, he passed along the coasts of Maine and Massachusetts southward so as to locate his proposed fur-trading station on an island at the mouth of Buzzards Bay, which was, in fact, very close to Narragansett Bay, the true "Refugio," although he did not know it. In 1603 Martin Pring set his base a little farther north, on Cape Cod Bay, either near the site of Provincetown or of Plymouth, and traded peacefully and, it is suggested, profitably with the Nauset or Massachusetts tribe. But trade alone did not lead to any permanent bases: Gosnold abandoned his and Pring did not intend to stay. The chief result of these tentative explorations was that southern New England, seen in summer, was thought to be a highly desirable place for Englishmen to live. The voyages revived the almost wholly theoretically based plans of Gilbert, Carleill, Hayes, and others for English colonization in this part of North America. This impetus had more to do with the fishing now found available in the Gulf of Maine than with the fur trade. It was, therefore, with this objective that George Waymouth in 1605 turned to New England to find bases from which Plymouth merchants could carry on a fishery and Catholic gentlemen could come to establish estates (reviving old plans of the 1580s in doing so). But he was attracted by the lands farther north, and his picture of part of Maine was too highly colored to represent reality objectively. By 1606 something was known of French initiatives in the same area and so the Virginia Company, when it decided in 1606 to combine a northern colony with its major southern venture, compromised. The great rivers of Maine, the Kennebec system in particular, had been disclosed by the Hanham-Pring expedition of 1606 (of which we know little), and this evidently suggested that furs might prove of major importance after all. So Fort St. George, the Sagadahoc colony, was created to exploit land (which was not easily exploitable), to tap a fur trade (for which the Abenaki tribes of the area were not yet organized) and to provide bases for fishing vessels that could best serve their interests by purely seasonal voyages with little need for a colony to back them up. The result was that in 1608 the colony came to seem pointless and was withdrawn. Thereafter the English concentrated for some years on seasonal fishing and a little summer trading with the Indians, although the idea of occupying and living in some part or other of North Virginia (as New England was usually spoken of) remained in prospect.

It was the French, with their concentration farther north, who made in these years the most thorough and active investigation of the whole coastline southward from Cape Breton to southern New England. The documents concerned with this will appear in a later volume. The Sieur de Monts obtained a monopoly of exploitation for this region from the French crown in 1603, and in 1604 he came out, with Samuel Champlain as his lieutenant, to set up a base there. The choice of the island site Ste Croix on the St. Croix River was intended to bring French influence far enough inland to tap the fur trade of what was thought to be an important river system before it became dispersed along the lengthy coastlands. If a major river could be tapped in this way, as was happening along the St. Lawrence by the summer trade at Tadoussac, then the interior might provide fresh riches for France. Champlain had already made a very thorough survey of the St. Lawrence Valley down to the rapids beyond Montreal in 1603, and although he had found the region most attractive and described it as such in the little book he published after his return, he came to feel that for the time being at least the gathering point at Tadoussac, attracting larger numbers of Indians and French (and some Spanish Basques also) each year, was a sufficient focus for the fur trade. The first exploration of the Bay of Fundy did not reveal any major sites on the bay itself, and the experiment at Ste Croix was a brave but mistaken one. Apart from anything else (and it proved totally useless for the fur trade), the French were almost frozen out there (the English settlers at Sagadahoc in 1607–1608 had a comparable but not so severe experience). But already, in 1604, a beginning was made in exploration farther south and relations were established with the center of the Abenaki tribal grouping on the Penobscot, as well as with the Micmac of the Bay of Fundy. Clearly some potentially useful sources of furs were in sight when Champlain moved his base from Ste Croix to Port Royal on the other side of the Bay of Fundy in 1605, although the bay, rather than the Annapolis Basin, was thought of as the focus. The Micmac of Nova Scotia were to cooperate well with the French and to keep them supplied with some furs during the next two years, but clearly there were no major sources of supply to be found there or on the Penobscot—minor sources were not sufficient to keep the Sieur de Monts' enterprises in profit. More effort was therefore put into exploration still farther south both in 1605 and 1606. This provides us with much essential information about New England. Some of it came out in 1609 when Lescarbot's "History" appeared in Paris (and was eagerly translated into English), but most had to wait until 1613 when Champlain told his full story. The French found the coastlands southward from Casco Bay very attractive, but the Indians do not appear to have offered anything of any appreciable interest to them in trade. Seeing the coastlands in the summer season, too, the French formed an exaggerated idea of the density of Indian population (considerable as it was in fact) because so many at that time had come down to fish and gather on the shores. Their settled agriculture also drew favorable attention. The French, whatever their interest in the region might be, did not find it commercially attractive and indeed wrote it off for practical purposes.

This was to be of major importance to the English when they finally came to settle. By 1607 it was clear that only the area round and near the Bay of Fundy, extending to the Penobscot but not further, retained any commercial attractions for France, and in that year the Sieur de Monts lost his monopoly. The French moved away and in 1608 decided to concentrate their fur-trading efforts through a permanent station or stations on the St. Lawrence. Nonetheless, the Sieur de Poutrincourt obtained rights to Port Royal, and from 1610 onward he and his family made a determined attempt to use it as the center of a fur-trading and agricultural estate. France thus kept a small foothold on the Atlantic coastland south of Cape Breton, which was to prove one area of continuing interest and involvement for her after 1612.

The period that ends in 1612 thus sees the Northeast—New England and the Maritimes—still with a major question mark over them so far as European activity was concerned. There would clearly be continued seasonal trading voyages along the coasts, probably by both English and French. There would also be seasonal fishing ventures using offshore islands for summer camps; but the whole question of whether there would be a substantial European intrusion into an area that offered, or seemed to offer, potential land and suitable climate (even if it was in places rather too thickly settled by its Amerindian owners to make white intrusion easy) remained wholly undetermined.

Chapter Sixty-one
The English Voyage of 1602
to New England

THE ASSOCIATION under Bartholomew Gosnold, of Gabriel Archer, Bartholomew Gilbert (the last no relation of Sir Humphrey's but a London goldsmith), and the Reverend John Brereton in a small expedition to the coast of Norumbega or North Virginia (as it was henceforth customary to call it) has never been adequately explained. Warner F. Gookin and P. L. Barbour in *Bartholomew Gosnold* (Hamden, Conn., 1965) paid detailed attention to its origins. Sir Walter Ralegh was certainly not directly involved. Edward Hayes, even if he did not take part in the expedition, was almost certainly concerned in the venture. A suggestion made in the work just cited that Hayes had received an earlier grant from Ralegh to carry out the exploration of the more southern territories which he had come, in the early 1590s, to regard as the most promising site for English settlements (366) is circumstantially the most likely explanation. Hayes had come back from Ireland in 1601 while Gosnold had been active earlier in West Indies privateering ventures. We have no evidence that they had an earlier association, but it seems at least likely that Hayes inspired (or was one of the inspirators) of the voyage. Why the goldsmith Bartholomew Gilbert, the legally-minded (and perhaps legally-trained) Gabriel Archer and the clergyman John Brereton should have decided to involve themselves is not known.

The voyage is known from a brief (and almost certainly abbreviated) narrative by Brereton published after the return of their ship *Concord* in 1602, by a fuller account acquired by Richard Hakluyt that was published by Samuel Purchas in 1625 and by a letter written by Bartholomew Gosnold to his father some weeks after his return.

Gosnold's objectives were two-fold: to explore the North Virginia coast with the special objective of finding Verrazzano's ancient "Refugio" (Narragansett Bay), interest in which may again have been aroused by Hakluyt's further republication of the Verrazzano letter in 1600, and, secondly, to establish a small trading station on the coast, the main object of which would be to test the potentialities of the area for furs. It is just possible he was influenced by the French attempt to establish a fur-trading post on the St. Lawrence in 1600, which had failed, since an English experiment might bring to light more favorable conditions for carrying on such a trade some 400 to 500 miles farther south. He was well briefed on the commodities such as cedar wood and sassafras that had been stressed in the published materials on the Roanoke voyages.

Setting out on March 26, 1602, the *Concord* reached the Maine coast on May 14, and proceeded to reconnoiter the shoreline south into Cape Cod Bay and then, rounding the Cape and Monomoy Point, they found most of the islands which lay to the south and west. The precise course followed by the vessel in Nantucket Sound has aroused much speculation but has not yet been satisfactorily traced, largely because the Brereton narrative (as we have it) has been trimmed so as to make it hard for subsequent expeditions to follow the *Concord*'s course in this part of her voyage. Martha's Vineyard was found and the north coast explored. The Elizabeth Islands at the mouth of Buzzards Bay appeared to offer a possible location for a post and the construction of a small trading factory was begun on an island in a lake within an island (which is now represented by the two islands, Cuttyhunk and Nashaweena). Gosnold appears to have believed Buzzards Bay to be the "Refugio" but found it did not match Verrazzano's descriptions, although on his return from his search he was, ironically, within sight of Point Judith, which marks the entrance to Narragansett Bay.

Sassafras roots were excavated and cedar cut. The many Indians seen had a few skins to exchange, but appeared to welcome the possibility of producing more later in the year. Careful notes were taken of fauna and flora as the expedition advanced. When it came to the point of leaving a party behind, the twelve men designated to remain refused to do so, and the carefully constructed post was abandoned without being used. It appears that the great number of Indians (collected for their summer gathering and fishing) intimidated them, even though the winter population would have been much smaller. The *Concord* set out on her return on June 17 and reached Exmouth on July 23.

This small venture had larger results. Sir Walter Ralegh was at Weymouth early in August awaiting the return of one of his vessels from what we may now term South Virginia (458), when Bartholomew Gilbert appeared there trying to dispose of sassafras roots, acquired by the *Concord*. Ralegh at once declared Gilbert had been poaching on territory comprised within his patent and without permission. He sent a letter to the Lord Admiral, the Earl of Nottingham, on August 21, making clear he had the right to confiscate the sassafras and proceeded to do so. He next made an arrangement with the presumed interlopers, perhaps finding they had, after all, some delegated authority from himself to Hayes (or another). In any event Bartholomew Gilbert was taken into his service to make a voyage to South Virginia in 1603 (Vol. V, no. 782). Brereton was encouraged to set out a brief narrative of the voyage, which he addressed to Ralegh himself, and to add to it there was collected a quantity of earlier promotion material. Edward Hayes abbreviated his earlier treatise (368); a Hakluyt tract was revived and a good deal of summarized information from Harriot and other sources assembled to append to the narrative. The compiler is most likely to have been Hayes, but Richard Hakluyt almost certainly supplied some of the ancillary materials (and may possibly, rather than Hayes, have been responsible for its assembly). The result was the appearance, possibly as early as October, 1602, of *A briefe and true relation of the discoverie of the north part of Virginia . . . made this present yeere 1602* (459). The first edition was a very slim tract with only part of the promotion material appended. It evidently circulated rapidly as it was soon padded out with some more of the collected promotion material for a second edition. This may have appeared before the end of the calendar year, and certainly did so before March 25, 1603. The little book has a twofold importance. It is the first independent English publication on the later New England, and it marked the emergence of Sir Walter Ralegh as a sponsor of the exploration and exploitation of an area to which he had hitherto, so far as is known, given little or no attention.

458. August 21, 1602. Sir Walter Ralegh to Sir Robert Cecil.

Hatfield House, Cecil Papers 94,/160. Printed in Edward Edwards, The Life of Sir Walter Ralegh, 2 vols. (London, 1866), II 251-252.

Sir,

Wheras as I wrate unto yow in my last that I was gonn to Weymouth to speake with a pinnes of myne arived from Virginia I founde this bearer Captayne Gilbert ther also who went onn the same voyage Butt myne fell 40 leagues to the west of it and this bearer as much to the east so as neather of them spake with the peopell. Butt I do sende both the barks away agayne, having saved the charg in sarsephraze woode butt this bearer bringing sume 2200 waight to Hampton his adventurers have taken away their parts and brought it to London.

I do therfore humblie pray yow to deale withe my Lord Admirall for a letter to make seasure of all that which is cume to London ether by his Lordships octoretye or by the Judge because I have a patent that all shipps and goods are confescate that shall trade ther without my leve. And wheras sarsephraze was worth 10s 12s and 20s a pound before Gilbert returned his cloying of the markett will overthrow all myne and his owne also. Hee is contented to have all stayde, not only for this present butt being to go agayne others will also go and distroy the trade which otherwize would yeild 8 or 10 for one in certenty and a return in xx weekes.

I desire butt right herein and my Lord Admirall I hope will not be a hinderance to a matter of trade graunted by the Great Seale of Inglande, his Lordship haivinge also freedome and an interest in the countrye. A man of my Lords of Hampton arested part of Gilberts for the tenths. I hope my Lord will not take it belonging not unto hyme having also hyme sealf poure to trade ther by his interest. And it were pitty to overthrow the enterprize for I shall yet leve to see it an Inglishe nation.

Ther was also brought 26 sedar trees by Gilbert which on Staplyne of Dartmouthe hath. If my Lord will vouchsauf to write to C. Harris to seaze them we will part of them in three partes to seele cabineates and make bords and many other deli-cate things. I beseich yow vouchsauf to speak to my Lord. I know his Lordship will do mee right herein. I for hast have not written. For if a stay be not made it wilbe spent and sold into many hands.

This bearer captayne Gilbert who is my Lord Cobhames man wil find out wher it is. Hee came to me with your post letter. It is he by a good token that had the great diamonde.

I beseich yow favor our rights and yow shall see what a prety honorabell and sauf trade wee will make.

Yours to serve yow
[signed:] W. Ralegh

[Postscript:] I hope yow will excuse my cumbersome letters and sutes. It is your destiney to be trobled with your frinds and so must all men bee. Butt what yow thinck unfitt to be dun for mee shall never be a quarrell ether internall or externall. I thanck yow evermore for the good and what cannot be effected farewell hit. If wee cannot have what we would neethinck it is a great bonde to finde a frinde that will strayne hyme sealf in his frinds causes in whatsoever as this world fareth.

Wemouth this 21 of August

[Second Postscript:] Gilbert went without my leve & therfore all is confiscate & he shall have his part agayne.

[Addressed:] To the right honorabell Sir Robert Cecyll Knighte Principall Secritorye &c.

[Endorsed:] 1602 August 21 Sir Walter Raleigh to my Master.

459. March to July, 1602. John Brereton's narrative of Bartholomew Gosnold's voyage to North Virginia.

The narrative by the Reverend John Brereton is unchanged in both editions. The title-page of the second edition (which is not merely a new impression but is reset and greatly added to) is:

A Briefe and true Relation of the Discoverie of the North part of Virginia; being a most pleasant, fruitfull and commodious soile:

Made this present yeere 1602, by Captaine Bartholomew Gosnold, Captaine Bartholomew Gilbert, and divers other gentlemen, their associats, by the permission of the honourable knight, Sir Walter Ralegh, &c.

Written by M. John Brereton one of the voyage.

Whereunto is annexed a Treatise, of M. Edward Hayes, conteining important inducements for the planting in those parts, and finding a passage that way to the South sea, and China.

With divers instructions of speciall moment newly added in this second impression.

Londini, Impensis Geor. Bishop. 1602.

To the honourable, Sir Walter Ralegh, Knight, Captaine of her Majesties Guards, Lord Warden of the Stanneries, Lieutenant of Cornwall, and Governour of the Isle of Jersey.

Honourable sir, being earnestly requested by a deere friend, to put downe in writing, some true relation of our late performed voyage to the North parts of Virginia; at length I resolved to satisfie his request, who also imboldened me, to direct the same to your honourable consideration; to whom indeed of duetie it perteineth.

May it please your Lordship therefore to understand, that upon the sixe and twentieth of March 1602, being Friday, we went from Falmouth, being in all, two and thirtie persons, in a small barke of Dartmouth, called *The Concord*, holding a course for the North part of Virginia: and although by chance the winde favoured us not at first as we wished, but inforced us so farre to the Southward, as we fell with S. Marie, one of the islands of the Açores (which was not much out of our way) yet holding our course directly from thence, we made our journey shorter (than hitherto accustomed) by the better part of a thousand leagues, yet were wee longer in our passage than we expected; which happened, for that our barke being weake, we were loth to presse her with much saile; also, our sailers being few, and they none of the best, we bare (except in faire weather) but low saile; besides, our going upon an unknowen coast, made us not over-bolde to stand in with the shore, but in open weather; which caused us to be certeine daies in sounding, before we discovered the coast, the weather being by chance, somewhat foggie. But on Friday the fourteenth of May, early in the morning, we made the land, being full of faire trees, the land somewhat low, certeine hummocks or hilles lying into the land, the shore ful of white sand, but very stony or rocky. And standing faire alongst by the shore, about twelve of the clocke the same day, we came to an anker, where six Indians, in a Baske-shallop with mast and saile, an iron grapple, and a kettle of copper, came boldly aboord us, one of them apparelled with a waistcoat and breeches of blacke serdge, made after our sea-fashion, hose and shoes on his feet; all the rest (saving one that had a paire of breeches of blue cloth) were all naked. These people are of tall stature, broad and grim visage, of a blacke swart complexion, their eiebrowes painted white; their weapons are bowes and arrowes: it seemed by some words and signes they made, that some Basks or of S. John de Luz, have fished or traded in this place, being in the latitude of 43 degrees. But riding heere, in no very good harbour, and withall, doubting the weather, about three of the clocke the same day in the afternoone we weighed, and standing Southerly off into the sea the rest of that day and the night following, with a fresh gale of winde, in the morning we found our selves embayed with a mightie headland; but comming to an anker about nine of the clocke the same day, within a league of the shore, we hoised out the one halfe of our shallop, and captaine Bartholmew Gosnold, my selfe, and three others, went ashore, being a white sandie and very bolde shore; and marching all that afternoon with our muskets on our necks, on the highest hilles which we saw (the weather very hot) at length we perceived this headland to be a parcell of the maine, and sundrie Islands lying almost round about it: so returning (towards evening) to our shallop (for by that time, the other part was brought ashore and set together) we espied an Indian, a young man, of proper stature, and of a pleasing countenance; and after some familiaritie with him, we left him at the sea side, and returned to our ship, where, in five or sixe hours absence, we had pestered our ship so with Cod fish, that we threw numbers of them overboord againe: and surely, I am persuaded that in the moneths of March, April, and May, there is upon this coast, better fishing, and in as great plentie, as in Newfoundland: for the sculles of mackerell, herrings, Cod, and other fish, that we dayly saw as we went and came from the shore, were woonderfull; and besides, the places where we tooke these Cods (and might in a few daies have laden our ship) were but in seven faddome water, and within lesse than a league of the shore; where, in New-found-land they fish in fortie or fiftie fadome water, and farre off. From this place, we sailed round about this headland, almost all the points of the compasse, the shore very bolde: but as no coast is free from dangers, so I am persuaded, this is as free as any; the land somwhat lowe, full of goodly woods, but in some places plaine: at length we were come amongst many faire Islands, which we had partly discerned at our first landing; all lying within a league or two one of another, and the outermost not above sixe or seven leagues from the maine: but comming to an anker under one of the[m], which was about three or foure leagues from the maine, captaine Gosnold, my selfe, and some others, went ashore, and going round about it, we found it to be foure English miles in compasse, without house or inhabitant, saving a little old house made of boughs, covered with barke, an olde piece of a weare of the Indians, to catch fish, and one or two places, where they had made fires. The chiefest trees of this Island, are Beeches and Cedars; the outward parts all overgrowen with lowe bushie trees, three or foure foot in height, which beare some kinde of fruits, as appeared by their blossomes; Strawberies, red and white, as sweet and much bigger than ours in England, Rasberies, Gooseberies, Hurtleberies, and such; an incredible store of Vines, aswell in the woodie part of the Island, where they run upon every tree, as on the outward parts, that we could not goe for treading upon them: also, many springs of excellent sweet water, and a great standing lake of fresh water, neere the sea side, an English mile in compasse, which is mainteined with the springs running exceeding pleasantly thorow the woodie grounds which are very rockie. Here are also in this Island, great store of Deere, which we saw, and other beasts, as appeared by their tracks, as also divers fowles, as Cranes, Hernshawes, Bitters, Geese; Mallards, Teales, and other fowles, in great plenty; also, great store of Pease, which grow in certeine plots all the Island over. On the North side of this Island we found many huge bones and ribbes of Whales. This Island, as also all the rest of these Islands, are full of all sorts of

stones fit for building; the sea sides all covered with stones, many of them glistering and shining like minerall stones, and very rockie: also, the rest of these Islands are replenished with these commodities, and upon some of them, inhabitants; as upon an Island to the Northward, and within two leagues of this; yet wee found no townes, nor many of their houses, although we saw manie Indians, which are tall big boned men, all naked, saving they cover their privy parts with a blacke tewed skin, much like a Black-smithes apron, tied about their middle and betweene their legs behinde: they gave us of their fish readie boiled (which they carried in a basket made of twigges, not unlike our osier) whereof we did eat, and judged them to be fresh water fish: they gave us also of their Tabacco, which they drinke greene, but dried into powder, very strong and pleasant, and much better than any I have tasted in England: the necks of their pipes are made of clay hard dried (whereof in that Island is great store both red and white) the other part, is a piece of hollow copper, very finely closed and semented together: we gave unto them certeine trifles, as knives, points, and such like, which they much esteemed. From thence we went to another Island, to the Northwest of this, and within a league or two of the maine, which we found to be greater than before we imagined, being 16 English miles at the least in compasse; for it conteineth many pieces or necks of land, which differ nothing fro severall Islands, saving that certeine banks of small bredth do like bridges joyne them to this Island, on the outsides of this Island are many plaine places of grasse, abundance of Strawberies and other berries before mentioned: in mid May we did sowe in this Island (as for triall) in sundry places, Wheat, Barley, Oats, and Pease, which in foureteene daies were sprung up nine inches and more. the soile is fat and lustie; the upper crust, of gray colour; but a foot or lesse in depth, of the colour of our hempe-lands in England; and being thus apt for these and the like graines; the sowing or setting (after the ground is cleansed) is no greater labour, than if you should set or sowe in one of our best prepared gardens in England. This Island is full of high timbered Oaks, their leaves thrise so broad as ours; Cedars, strait and tall; Beech, Elme, Hollie, Walnut trees in abundance, the fruit as bigge as ours, as appeared by those we found under the trees, which had lien all the yeere ungathered; Haslenut trees, Cherry trees, the leafe, barke and bignesse not differing from ours in England, but the stalke beareth the blossomes or fruit at the end thereof, like a cluster of Grapes, forty or fifty in a bunch; Sassafras trees plentie all the Island over, a tree of high price and profit; also divers other fruit trees, some of them with strange barks, of an Orange colour, in feeling soft and smoothe like Velvet: in the thickest parts of the woods, you may see a furlong or more round about. On the Northwest side of this Island, neere to the sea side, is a standing Lake of fresh water, almost three English miles in compasse, in the middest whereof stands a plot of woodie ground, an acre in quantitie or not above: This Lake is full of small Tortoises, and exceedingly frequented with all sorts of fowles before rehearsed, which breed, some lowe on the banks, and others on lowe trees about this Lake in great abundance, whose young ones of all sorts we tooke and eat at our pleasure: but all these fowles are much bigger than ours in England. Also, in every Island, and almost in every part of every Island, are great store of Ground nuts, fortie together on a string, some of them as bigge as hennes egges; they grow not two inches under ground: the which nuts we found to be as good as Potatoes. Also, divers sorts of shell-fish, as Scallops, Muscles, Cockles, Lobsters, Crabs, Oisters, and Whilks, exceeding good and very great. But not to cloy you with particular rehearsall of such things as God and Nature hath bestowed on these places, in comparison wherof, the most fertil part of al England is (of it selfe) but barren; we went in our lighthorsman fro this Island to the maine, right against this Island some two leagues off, where comming ashore, we stood a while like men ravished at the beautie and delicacie of this sweet soile; for besides divers cleere Lakes of fresh water (whereof we saw no end) Medowes very large and full of greene grasse; even the most woody places (I speake onely of such as I saw) doe grow so distinct and apart, one tree from another, upon greene grassie ground, somewhat higher than the Plaines, as if Nature would shew herselfe above her power, artificiall. Hard by, we espied seven Indians; and comming up to them, at first they expressed some feare; but being emboldned by our courteous usage, and some trifles which we gave them, they followed us to a necke of land, which we imagined had beene severed from the

maine; but finding it otherwise, we perceived a broad harbour or rivers mouth, which ranne up into the maine: but because the day was farre spent, we were forced to returne to the Island from whence we came, leaving the discoverie of this harbour, for a time of better leasure: of the goodnesse of which harbour, as also of many others thereabouts, there is small doubt, considering that all the Islands, as also the maine (where we were) is all rockie grounds and broken lands. Now the next day, we determined to fortifie our selves in the little plot of ground in the midst of the Lake above mentioned, where we built an house, and covered it with sedge, which grew about this lake in great abundance; in building whereof, we spent three weeks and more: but the second day after our comming from the maine, we espied 9 canowes or boats, with fiftie Indians in them, comming towards us from this part of the maine, where we, two daies before, landed; and being loth they should discover our fortification, we went out on the sea side to meet them; and comming somewhat neere them, they all sat downe upon the stones, calling aloud to us (as we rightly ghessed) to doe the like, a little distance from them: having sat a while in this order, captaine Gosnold willed me to go unto them, to see what countenance they would make; but assoone as I came up unto them, one of them, to whom I had given a knife two daies before in the maine, knew me (whom I also very wel remembered) and smiling upon me, spake somewhat unto their lord or captaine, which sat in the midst of them, who presently rose up and tooke a large Beaver skin from one that stood about him, and gave it unto me, which I requited for that time the best I could: but I pointing towards captaine Gosnold, made signes unto him, that he was our captaine, and desirous to be his friend, and enter league with him, which (as I perceived) he understood, and made signes of joy: whereupon captaine Gosnold with the rest of his companie, being twentie in all, came up unto them; and after many signes of gratulations (captaine Gosnold presenting their L. with certeine trifles which they wondred at, and highly esteemed) we became very great friends, and sent for meat aboord our shallop, and gave them such meats as we had then readie dressed, whereof they misliked nothing but our mustard, whereat they made many a sowre face. While we were thus merry, one of them had conveied a target of ours into one of their canowes, which we suffered, onely to trie whether they were in subjection to this L. to whom we made signes (by shewing him another of the same likenesse, and pointing to the canowe) what one of his companie had done: who suddenly expressed some feare, and speaking angerly to one about him (as we perceived by his countenance) caused it presently to be brought backe againe. So the rest of the day we spent in trading with them for Furres, which are Beavers, Luzernes, Marterns, Otters, Wild-cat skinnes very large and deepe Furre, blacke Foxes, Conie skinnes, of the colour of our Hares, but somewhat lesse, Deere skinnes very large, Seale skinnes, and other beasts skinnes to us unknowen. They have also great store of Copper, some very redde, and some of a paler colour; none of them but have chaines, earrings or collars of this mettall: they head some of their arrows herewith, much like our broad arrow heads, very workmanly made. Their chaines are many hollow pieces semented together, ech piece of the bignesse of one of our reeds, a finger in length, ten or twelve of them together on a string, which they weare about their necks: their collars they weare about their bodies like bandelieres a handfull broad, all hollow pieces, like the other, but somewhat shorter, foure hundred pieces in a collar, very fine and evenly set together. Besides these, they have large drinking cups, made like sculles, and other thinne plates of Copper, made much like our boarespeare blades, all which they so little esteeme, as they offered their fairest collars or chaines, for a knife or such like trifle, but we seemed little to regard it; yet I was desirous to understand where they had such store of this mettall, and made signes to one of them (with whom I was verie familiar) who taking a piece of Copper in his hand, made a hole with his finger in the ground, and withall, pointed to the maine from whence they came. They strike fire in this maner; every one carrieth about him in a purse of tewed leather, a Minerall stone (which I take to be their Copper) and with a flat Emerie stone (wherewith Glasiers cut glasse, and Cutlers glase blades) tied fast to the end of a little sticke, gently he striketh upon the Minerall stone, and within a stroke or two, a sparke falleth upon a piece of Touchwood (much like our Spunge in England) and with the least sparke he maketh a fire presently. We had also of their Flaxe, wherewith they make many strings and cords, but it is not so bright of colour as ours in England: I am persuaded they have great store growing upon the maine, as also Mines and many other rich commodities, which we, wanting both time and meanes, could not possibly discover. Thus they continued with us three daies, every night retiring themselves to the furthermost part of our Island two or three miles from our fort: but the fourth day they returned to the maine, pointing five or six times to the Sun, and once to the maine, which we understood, that within five or six daies they would come from the maine to us againe: but being in their canowes a little from the shore, they made huge cries and shouts of joy unto us; and we with our trumpet and cornet, and casting up our cappes into the aire, made them the best farewell we could: yet sixe or seven of them remained with us behinde, bearing us company every day into the woods, and helpt us to cut and carie our Sassafras, and some of them lay aboord our ship. These people, as they are exceeding courteous, gentle of disposition, and well conditioned, excelling all others that we have seene; so for shape of bodie and lovely favour, I thinke they excell all the people of America; of stature much higher than we; of complexion or colour, much like a darke Olive; their eie-browes and haire blacke, which they weare long, tied up behinde in knots, whereon they pricke feathers of fowles, in fashion of a crownet: some of them are blacke thin bearded; they make beards of the haire of beasts: and one of them offered a beard of their making to one of our sailers, for his that grew on his face, which because it was of a red colour, they judged to be none of his owne. They are quicke eied, and stedfast in their looks, fearleasse of others harmes, as intending noen themselves; some of the meaner sort given to filching, which the very name of Salvages (not weighing their ignorance in good or evill) may easily excuse: their garments are of Deere skins, and some of them weare Furres round and close about their necks. They pronounce our language with great facilitie; for one of them one day sitting by me, upon occasion I spake smiling to him these words: How now (sirha) are you so saucie with my Tabacco? which words (without any further repetition) he suddenly spake so plaine and distinctly, as if he had beene a long scholar in the language. Many other such trials we had, which are here needlesse to repeat. Their women (such as we saw) which were but three in all, were but lowe of stature, their eie-browes, haire, apparell, and maner of wearing, like to the men, fat, and very well favoured, and much delighted in our compane; the men are very dutifull towards them. And truely, the holsomnesse and temperature of this Climat, doth not onely argue this people to be answerable to this description, but also of a perfect constitution of body, active, strong, healthfull, and very wittie, as the sundry toies of theirs cunningly wrought, may easily witnes. For the agreeing of this Climat with us (I speake of my selfe, and so I may justly do for the rest of our companie) that we found our health and strength all the while we remained there, so to renew and increase, as notwithstanding our diet and lodging was none of the best, yet not one of our company (God be thanked) felt the least grudging or inclination to any disease or sicknesse, but were much fatter and in better health than when we went out of England. But after our barke had taken in so much Sassafras, Cedar, Furres, Skinnes, and other commodities, as were thought convenient; some of our company that had promised captaine Gosnold to stay, having nothing but a saving voyage in their minds, made our company of inhabitants (which was small enough before) much smaller; so as captaine Gosnold seeing his whole strength to consist but of twelve men, and they but meanly provided, determined to returne for England, leaving this Island (which he called Elizabeths Island) with as many true sorrowfull eies, as were before desirous to see it. So the 18 of June, being Friday, we weighed, and with indifferent faire winde and weather came to anker the 23 of July, being also Friday (in all, bare five weeks) before Exmouth.

Your Lordships to command, John Brereton.

460. 1602. Gabriel Archer's narrative of Gosnold's North Virginia voyage.

Printed in Samuel Purchas, Pilgrimes, IV (1625), 1647-1650 (XIX [1903], 302-313).

The Relation of Captaine Gosnols Voyage to the North part of Virginia, begunne the sixe and twentieth of March, Anno 42. Elizabethæ Reginæ 1602. and delivered by Gabriel Archer, a Gentleman in the said Voyage.

The said Captaine did set sayle from Falmouth, the day and yeere above written accompanied with thirtie two persons, whereof eight Mariners and Saylers, twelve purposing upon the Discovery to returne with the ship for England, the rest remayne there for population. The fourteenth of Aprill following, wee had sight of Saint Maries an Iland of the Assoris.

The three and twentieth of the same, beeing two hundred leagues Westwards from the said Iland in the latitude of 37. degrees, the water in the mayne Ocean appeared yellow, the space of two leagues North and South, where sounding with thirtie fadome Line, wee found no ground, and taking up some of the said water in a bucket, it altered not either in colour or taste from the Sea Azure.

The seventh of May following, we first saw many Birds in bignesse of Cliffe Pidgeons, and after divers other as Pettrels, Cootes, Hagbuts, Pengwins, Murres, Gannets, Cormorants, Guls, with many else in our English Tongue of no name. The eight of the same the water changed to a yellowish greene, where at seventie fadome we had ground. The ninth, wee had two and twentie fadome in faire sandie ground, having upon our Lead many glittering Stones, somewhat heavie, which might promise some Minerall matter in the bottome, we held our selves by computation, well neere the latitude of 43. degrees.

The tenth wee sounded in 27. 30. 37. 43. fadome, and then came to 108. some thought it to be the sounding of the Westermost end of Saint Johns Iland, upon this banke we saw sculs of fish in great numbers. The twelfth we hoysed out halfe of our shallop, and sounding had then eightie fadome without any current perceived by William Strete the Master, one hundred leagues Westward from Saint Maries til we came to the foresaid soundings continually passed fleeting by us Sea-oare, which seemed to have thier moveable course towards the North-east, a matter to set some subtle invention on worke, for comprehending the true cause thereof. The thirteenth, wee sounded in seventie fadome, and observed great beds of weeds, much woode and divers things else floating by us, when as we had smelling of the shoare, such as from the Southerne Cape and Andulazia in Spaine.

The fourteenth, about six in the morning we descried Land that lay North, &c. the Northerly part we called the North Land, which to another Rocke upon the same lying twelve leagues West, that wee called Savage Rocke, because the Savages first shewed themselves there, five leagues towards the said Rocke is an out Point of woodie ground, the Trees thereof very high and straight, from the Rocke East North-east. From the said Rocke, came towards us a Biscay shallop with saile and Oares, having eight persons in it, whom we supposed at first to bee Christians distressed. But approching us neere, wee perceived them to bee Savages. These comming within call hayled us, and wee answered. Then after signes of peace, and a long speech by one of them made, they came boldly aboord us being all naked, saving about their shoulders certaine loose Deere-skinnes, and neere their wastes Seale-skinnes tyed fast like to Irish Dimmie Trouses. One that seemed to be their Commander wore a Waste-coate of blacke worke, a paire of Breeches, cloth Stockings, Shooes, Hat, and Band, one or two more had also a few things made by some Christians, these with a piece of Chalke described the Coast thereabouts, and could name Placentia of the Newfound-land, they spake divers Christian words, and seemed to understand much more then we, for want of Language could comprehend. These people are in colour swart, their haire long up tyed with a knot in the part of behind the head. They paint their bodies, which are strong and well proportioned. These much desired our longer stay, but finding our selves short of our purposed place, we set saile Westwards, leaving them and their Coast. About sixteene leagues Southwest from thence, wee perceived in that course two small Ilands, the one lying Eastward from Savage Rock, the other to the Southwards of it, the Coast we left was full of goodly Woods, faire Plaines, with little greene round Hils above the Cliffes appearing unto us, which are indifferently raised, but all Rockie, and of shining stones, which might have perswaded us a longer stay there.

The fifteenth day we had againe sight of the Land, which made a head being as wee thought an Iland, by reason of a large sound that appeared Westward betweene it and the Mayne, for comming to the West end thereof, we did perceive a large opening, we called it Shole-hope: Neere this Cape we came to Anchor in fifteene fadome, where wee tooke great store of Cod-fish, for which we altered the name, and called it Cape Cod. Here wee saw sculs of Herrings, Mackerels and other small fish in great abundance. This is a low sandie shoare, but without danger, also wee came to Anchor againe in sixteene fadome, faire by the Land in the latitude of 42. degrees. This Cape is well neere a mile broad, and lieth Northeast by East. The Captaine went here ashoare and found the ground to be full of Pease, Strawberies, Hurtberies, &c. as then unripe, the sand also by the shoare somewhat deepe, the fire-wood there by us taken in was of Cypresse, Birch, Wich-hazell and Beech. A young Indian came here to the Captaine, armed with his Bow and Arrowes, and had certaine plates of Copper hanging at his Eares, hee shewed a willingnesse to helpe us in our occasions.

The sixteenth, we trended the Coast Southerly, which was all champaine and full of grasse, but the Ilands somewhat wooddie. Twelve leagues from Cape Cod, we descried a point, with some breach a good distance off, and keeping our loffe to double it, wee came on the sudden into shoale water, yet well quitted our selves thereof. This breach wee called Tuckers Terror, upon his expressed feare. The Point we named Point Care, having passed it wee bore up againe with the Land, and in the night came with it anchoring in eight fadome, the ground good. The seventeenth, appeared many breaches round about us, so as wee continued that day without remoove.

The eighteenth, being faire we sent forth the Boat, to sound over a Breach, that in our course lay of another Point, by us called Gilberts Point; who returned us foure, five, sixe and seven fadome over. Also a Discovery of divers Ilands which after prooved to bee Hils and Hummocks, distinct within the Land. This day there came unto the ships side divers Canoas; the Indians apparelled as aforesaid, with Tobacco and Pipes steeled with Copper, Skins, artificiall strings and other trifles to barter, one had hanging about his necke a plate of rich Copper in length a foot, in breadth halfe a foot for a brest-plate, the Eares of all the rest had Pendants of Copper. Also one of them had his face over painted, and his head stucke with feathers in manner of a Turkey Cocks traine: These are more timerous then those of the Savage Rocke, yet very theevish.

The nineteenth, we passed over the breach of

Gilberts Point in foure or five fadome, and anchored a league or somewhat more beyond it; betweene the last two Points are two leagues, the interim, along shoale water, the latitude here is 41. degrees two third parts.

The twentieth, by the ships side we there killed Pengwins, and saw many sculs of fish. The Coast from Gilberts Point to the supposed Iles lyeth East and by South. Here also we discovered two Inlets which might promise fresh water, inwardly whereof we perceived much smoake, as though some population had there beene: This Coast is very full of people, for that as we trended the same Savages still runne along the shoare, as men much admiring at us.

The one and twentieth, we went coasting from Gilberts Point to the supposed Iles, in tenne, nine, eight, seven, and sixe fadome close aboord the shoare, and that depth lyeth a league off. A little from the supposed Iles appeared unto us an opening, with which we stood judging it to bee the end of that which Captaine Gosnoll descrieth from Cape Cod, and as hee thought to extend some thirtie or more miles in length, and finding there but three fadomes a league off, we omitted to make further discoverie of the same, calling it Shole-hope.

From this opening the Mayne lyeth Southwest, which coasting along we saw a disinhabited Iland which so afterwards appeared unto us: we bore with it, and named it Marthaes Vineyard, from Shole-hope it is eight leagues in circuit, the Iland is five miles, and hath 41. degrees and one quarter of latitude: the place most pleasant; for the two and twentieth, we went ashoare, and found it full of Wood, Vines, Gooseberie bushes, Hurtberies, Raspices, Eglentine, &c. Heere we had Cranes, Hearnes, Shoulers Geese, and divers other Birds which there at that time upon the Cliffes being sandie with some Rockie stones, did breed and had young. In this place we saw Deere, heere we rode in eight fathome neere the shoare, where wee tooke breat store of Cod, as before at Cape Cod, but much better.

The three and twentieth wee weyed, and towards night came to Anchor at the Northwest part of this Iland, where the next morning offered unto us fast running thirteene Savages apparelled as aforesaid, and armed with Bowes and Arrowes without any feare. They brought Tobacco, Deere skins and some sodden fish. These offered themselves unto us in great familiaritie, who seemed to be well conditioned. They came more rich in Copper then any before. This Iland is sound, and hath no danger about it.

The foure and twentieth, we set saile and doubled the Cape of another Iland next unto it, which wee called Dover Cliffe, and then came into a faire Sound, where wee roade all night, the next morning wee sent off our Boate to discover another Cape, that lay betweene us and the Mayne, from which were a ledge of Rockes a mile into the Sea, but all above water, and without danger, we went about them, and came to Anchor in eight fadome, a quarter of a mile from the shoare in one of the stateliest Sounds that ever I was in. This called wee Gosnolls Hope; the North banke whereof is the Mayne, which stretcheth East and West. This Iland Captaine Gosnoll called Elizabeths Ile, where we determined our abode: the distance betweene every of these Ilands is, viz. from Marthaes Vineyard to Dover Cliffe, halfe a league over the Sound, thence to Elizabeths Ile one league distant. From Elizabeths Ile unto the Mayne is foure leagues. On the North side neere adjoyning unto the Iland Elizabeth, is an Ilet in compasse halfe a myle full of Cedars, by me called Hills Hap, to the Northward of which in the mouth of an opening on the Mayne appeareth another the like, that I called Haps Hill, for that I hope much hap may be expected from it.

The five and twentieth, it was that we came from Gosnolls Hope. The six and twentieth, we trimmed and fitted up our Shallop. The seven and twenteith, there came unto us an Indian and two women; the one we supposed to be his Wife, the other his Daughter, both cleane and straite bodied, with countenance sweet and pleasant. To these the Indian gave heedfull attendance for that they shewed them in much familiaritie with our men, although they would not admit of any immodest touch.

The eight and twentieth we entred counsell about our abode and plantation, which was concluded to be in the West part of Elizabeths Iland. The North-east thereof running from out our ken. The South and North standeth in an equall Parallel. This Iland in the Westerside admitteth some Increekes, or sandie Coves, so girded, as the water in some places of each side meeteth, to which the Indians from the Mayne doe oftentimes resort for fishing of Crabs. There is eight fadome very neere the shoare, and the latitude here is 41. degrees 10. minutes, the breadth from Sound to Sound in the Wester part is not passing a mile at most, altogether unpeopled and disinhabited. It is over-growne with Wood and Rubbish, viz. Okes, Ashes, Beech, Wal-nut, Weech-halfe, Sassa-frage, and Cedars, with divers other of unknowne names. The Rubbish is wild Peaze, young Sassa-frage, Cherie trees, Vines, Eglentine, Goose-berie bushes, Hawthorne, Honisuckles, with oth-ers of like qualitie. The herbs and Roots are Strawberies, Raspis, Ground Nuts, Alexander, Surrin, Tansie, &c. without count. Touching the fertilitie of the soyle by our owne experience made, we found it to be excellent for sowing some English pulse it sprowted out in one fortnight almost halfe a foot. In this Iland is a stage or Pond of fresh water, in circuit two miles, on the one side not distant from the Sea thirtie yards, in the Centre whereof is a Rockie Islet, contayning neere an Acre of ground full of wood, on which wee beganne our Fort and place of abode, dispos-ing it selfe so fit for the same. These Indians call Gold Wassador, which argueth there is thereof in the Countrey.

The nine and twentieth, we laboured in getting of Sassafrage, rubbishing our little Fort or Ilet, new keeling our shallop; and making a Punt or Flat bottome Boate to passe to and fro our Fort over the fresh water, the powder of Sassafrage in twelve houres cured one of our Company that had taken a great Surfet by eating the bellies of Dog-fish, a very delicious meate.

The thirtieth, Captaine Gosnoll with divers of his company went upon pleasure in the shallop towards Hills Hap to view it, and the Sandie Cove, and returning brought with him a Canoa that foure Indians had there left being fled away for feare of our English, which we brought into England.

The one and thirtieth, Captaine Gosnoll desir-ous to see the Maine, because of the distance, hee set sayle over; where comming to anchor, went ashoare with certaine of his companie, and im-mediately there presented unto him men women and children, who with all curteous kindnesse entertayned him, giving him certaine skinnes of wilde beasts, which may be rich Furres, Tobacco, Turtles, Hempe, artificiall Strings coloured, Chaines, and such like things as at the instant they had about them. These are a faire con-

ditioned people. On all the Sea coast along we found Mussell shells that in colour did represent Mother-of-pearle, but not having meanes to dredge, could not apprehend further knowledge thereof. This Maine is the goodliest Continent that ever we saw, promising more by farre then we any way did expect: for it is replenished with faire fields, and in them fragrant Flowers, also Medowes, and hedged in with stately Groves, being furnished also with pleasant Brookes, and beautified with two maine Rivers that (as wee judge) may haply become good Harbours, and conduct us to the hopes men so greedily doe thirst after. In the mouth of one of these Inlets or Rivers lieth that little Ile before mentioned, called Happes Hill, from which unto the Westermost end of the Maine, appearing where the other Inlet is, I account some five leagues, and the Coast be-tweene bendeth like a Bow, and lyeth East and by North. Beyond these two Inlets we might per-ceive the Mayne to beare up Southwest, and more Southerly. Thus with this taste of Discovery, we now contented our selves, and the same day made returne unto our Fort, time not permitting more sparing delay.

The first of June, we employed our selves in getting Sassafrage, and the building of our Fort. The second, third and fourth, we wrought hard to make readie our house for the provision to bee had ashore to sustaine us till our ships returne. This day from the Mayne came to our ships side a Canoa, with their Lord or chiefe Commander, for that they made little stay only pointing to the Sunne, as in signe that the next day hee would come and visit us, which hee did accordingly.

The fifth, wee continued our labour, when there came unto us ashoare from the Mayne fiftie Savages, stout and lustie men with their Bowes and Arrowes, amongst them there seemed to be one of authoritie, because the rest made an inclin-ing respect unto him. The ship was at their com-ming a league off, and Captaine Gosnoll aboord and so likewise Captaine Gilbert, who almost never went ashoare, the company with me only eight persons. These Indians in hastie manner came towards us, so as we thought fit to make a stand at an angle betweene the Sea and a fresh water, I mooved my selfe towards him seven or eight steps, and clapt my hands first on the sides of mine head, then on my breast, and after pre-sented my Musket with a threatning countenance, thereby to signifie unto them, either a choice of Peace or Warre, whereupon hee using mee with mine owne signes of Peace, I stept forth and imbraced him, his company then all sate downe in manner like Grey-hounds upon their heeles, with whom my company fell a bartering. But this time Captaine Gosnoll was come with twelve men more from aboord, and to shew the Savage Seignior that he was our Captaine, we received him in a guard, which he passing thorow, saluted the Seignior with ceremonies of our salutations, whereat he nothing mooved or altered himselfe. Our Captaine gave him a straw Hat and a paire of Knives, the Hat awhiles hee wore, but the Knives he beheld with great marvelling, being very bright and sharpe, this our courtesie made them all in love with us.

The sixt being raine, we spent idlely aboord. The seventh, the Seignior came againe with all his troupe as before, and continued with us the most part of the day, we going to dinner about noone, they sate with us and did eate of our Bacaleure and Mustard, dranke of our Beere, but the Mustard nipping them in their noses they could not indure: it was a sport to behold their faces made being bitten therewith. In time of Dinner the Savages had stolne a Target wherewith acquainting the Seignior, with feare and great trembling they restored it againe, thinking perhaps we would have beene revenged for it, but seeing our familiaritie to continue, they fell a fresh to roasting of Crabs, Red Herrings, which were exceeding great, ground Nuts, &c. as before. Our Dinner ended, the Seignior first tooke leave and departed, next all the rest saving foure that stayed and went into the Wood to helpe us digge Sassafrage, whom we desired to goe aboord us, which they refused and so departed.

The eighth wee divided the victuals, viz. the ships store for England, and that of the Planters, which by Captaine Gilberts allowance could be but six weekes for six moneths, whereby there fell out a controversie, the rather, for that some seemed secretly to understand of a purpose Captaine Gilbert had not to returne with supplie of the issue, those goods should make by him to be carried home. Besides, there wanted not ambitious conceits in the mindes of some wrangling and ill disposed persons that overthrew the stay there at that time, which upon consultation thereof had, about five dayes after was fully resolved all for

England againe. There came in this interim aboord unto us, that stayed all night, an Indian, whom wee used kindly, and the next day sent ashoare hee shewed himselfe the most sober of all the rest, wee held him sent as a Spie. In the morning he filched away our Pot-hookes, thinking he had not done any ill therein; being ashoare wee bid him strike fire, which with an Emerald stone (such as the Glasiers use, to cut Glasse) he did. I take it to be the very same that in Latine is called Smiris, for striking therewith upon Touch-wood that of purpose hee had, by meane of a mynerall stone used therein, sparkles proceeded and forth with kindled with making of flame. The ninth, wee continued working on our Store-house for as yet remayned in us a desired resolution of making stay. The tenth, Captaine Gosnoll fell downe with the ship to the little Ilet of Cedars, called Hills happe, to take in Cedar wood, leaving mee and nine more in the Fort, onely with three meales meate, upon promise to returne the next day.

The eleventh, he came not, neither sent, whereupon I commanded foure of my companie to seeke out for Crabbes, Lobsters, Turtles, &c. for sustayning us till the ships returne, which was gone cleane out of sight, and had the winde chopt up at South-west, with much difficulty would shee have beene able in short time to have made returne. These foure Purveyers, whom I counselled to keepe together for their better safety divided themselves, two going one wayes and two another, in search as aforesaid. One of these petie companies was assaulted by foure Indians, who with Arrowes did shoot and hurt one of the two in his side, the other a lusty and nimble fellow, leapt in and cut their Bow-strings whereupon they fled. Being late in the evening, they were driven to lie all night in the Woods, not knowing the way home thorow the thicke rubbish, as also the weather somewhat stormie. The want of these sorrowed us much, as not able to conjecture any thing of them unlesse very evill.

The twelfth, those two came unto us againe, whereat our joy was encreased, yet the want of our Captaine, that promised to returne, as aforesaid, strooke us in a dumpish terrour, for that hee performed not the same in the space of almost three dayes. In the meane wee sustayned our selves with Alexander and Sorrell pottage, Ground-nuts and Tobacco, which gave nature a reasonable content. Wee heard at last, our Captaine to lewre unto us, which made such musike as sweeter never came unto poore men.

The thirteenth, beganne some of our companie that before vowed to stay, to make revolt: where-upon the planters diminishing, all was given over. The fourteenth, fifteenth, and sixteenth wee spent in getting Sasafrage and fire-wood of Cedar, leaving House and little Fort by ten men in nineteene dayes sufficient made to harbour twenty persons at least with their necessary pro-vision.

The seventeenth, we set sayle, doubling the Rockes of Elizabeths Iland, and passing by Dover Cliffe, came to anchor at Marthaes Vineyard being five leagues distant from our Fort, where we went ashoare, and had young Cranes, Herne-showes, and Geese, which now were growne to pretie bignesse.

The eighteenth, we set sayle and bore for En-gland, cutting off our Shalop, that was well able to land five and twenty men, or more, a Boate very necessary for the like occasions. The winds doe raigne most commonly upon this coast in the Summer time, Westerly. In our homeward course wee observed the foresaid fleeting weeds to con-tinue till we came within two hundred leagues of Europe.

The three and twentieth of July we came to anchor before Exmouth.

461. September 7, 1602. Letter of Bartholomew Gosnold on his North Virginia voyage.

Printed in S. Purchas, Pilgrimes, *IV (1625), 1646 (XIX [1907], 300–302).*

Master Bartholomew Gosnolds Letter to his Father, touching his first Voyage to Virginia, 1602.

My duetie remembred, &c. Sir, I was in good hope that my occasions would have allowed mee so much libertie, as to have come unto you before this time; otherwise I would have written more at large concerning the Countrie from whence we lately came, then I did: but not well remembring

what I have already written (though I am assured that there is nothing set downe disagreeing with the truth) I thought it fittest not to goe about to adde any thing in writing, but rather to leave the report of the rest till I come my selfe; which now I hope shall be shortly, and so soone as with conve-niency I may. In the meane time, notwithstand-ing whereas you seeme not to be satisfied by that which I have already written concerning some especiall matters. I have here briefely (and as well as I can) added these few lines for your further satisfaction: and first as touching that place where we were most resident, it is in the Latitude of 41. degrees, and one third part; which albeit it be so much to the Southward, yet is it more cold then those parts of Europe, which are scituated under the same paralell: but one thing is worth the noting, that notwithstanding the place is not so much subject to cold as England is, yet did we finde the Spring to be later there, then it is with us here, by almost a moneth: this whether it hapned accidentally this last Spring to be so, or whether it be so of course, I am not very certaine; the latter seemes most likely, whereof also there may be given some sufficient reason, which now I omit: as for the Acornes we saw gathered on heapes, they were of the last yeare, but doubtlesse their Summer continues longer then ours. We cannot gather by any thing we could observe in the people, or by any triall we had thereof our selves; but that it is as healthfull a Climate as any can be. The Inhabitants there, as I wrote before, being of tall stature, comely pro-portion, strong, active, and some of good yeares, and as it should seeme very healthfull, are suffi-cient proofe of the healthfulnesse of the place. First, for our selves (thankes be to God) we had not a man sicke two dayes together in all our Voyage; whereas others that went out with us, or about that time on other Voyages (especially such as went upon reprisall) were most of them in-fected with sicknesse, whereof they lost some of their men, and brought home a many sicke, re-turning notwithstanding long before us. But Ver-azzano, and others (as I take it, you may reade in the Booke of Discoveries) doe more particularly intreate of the Age of the people in that coast. The Sassafras which we brought we had upon the Ilands: where though we had little disturbance, and reasonable plenty: yet for that the greatest part of our people were imployed about the fitting of our house, and such like affaires, and a few (and those but easie labourers) undertooke this worke, the rather because we were informed before our going forth, that a tunne was sufficient to cloy England and further, for that we had resolved upon our returne, and taken view of our victuall, we judged it then needefull to use expedition; which afterward we had more certaine proofe of; for when we came to an anker before Portsmouth, which was some foure dayes after we made the land, we had not one Cake of Bread, nor any drinke, but a little Vinegar, left: for these and other reasons, we returned no otherwise laden then you have heard. And thus much I hope shall suffice till I can my selfe come to give you further notice, which though it be not so soone as I could have wisht, yet I hope it shall be in convenient time. In the meane time craving your pardon, for which the urgent occasions of my stay will pleade, I humbly take my leave. 7. Septemb. 1602.

Your dutifull Sonne,
    Barth. Gosnold.

Chapter Sixty-two
The Voyage of 1603

462. April 10 to October 2, 1603. Martin Pring's voyage to North Virginia with the *Speedwell* and the *Discoverer*.

Sir Walter Ralegh's sponsorship of the Brereton pamphlet provided publicity for further voyages under his auspices. The first (and only) one was set in motion by the Reverend Richard Hakluyt who, among his other preferments, was a prebendary of Bristol Cathedral, and who had many merchant connections in Bristol. Leaving Bristol in March, the Speedwell *and the* Discoverer *were held up by contrary winds at Milford Haven and arrived in June on the coast of Maine, apparently off some of the islands at the mouth of the Penobscot, then made their way down the coast, most of which had previously been traversed by Gosnold. They did not aim to explore or to settle but merely to trade and observe. They established a camp near the site of modern Provincetown on Cape Cod (the older preferred site of Plymouth Harbor appears less likely), which they protected by a palisade and by the use of mastiffs to keep at bay the many curious Indians who visited them. They found it possible to obtain sassafras roots and took samples of other trees and plants. They found the Indians willing to trade in furs, although they appear to have had few available, but promised more on other occasions. The* Discoverer *was sent home with a cargo of sassafras at the end of July, and the* Speedwell *soon followed. Her voyage homeward took from about August 8 to October 2. A six months' voyage was shown to be reasonably easy, profitable (it might appear), and worth repeating. The reports on the country confirmed the favorable impression obtained by Gosnold. However, by October, Ralegh was disgraced, his patent resumed by the crown, and North Virginia voyages of the future a matter ultimately for the king to decide.*

Printed in S. Purchas, Pilgrimes, *IV (1625), 1654–1656 (XIX [1907], 322–329).*

A Voyage set out from the Citie of Bristoll at the charge of the chiefest Merchants and Inhabitants of the said Citie with a small Ship and a Barke for the discoverie of the North part of Virginia, in the yeere 1603. under the command of me Martin Pringe.

Upon many probable and reasonable inducements, used unto sundry of the chiefest Merchants of Bristoll, by Master Richard Hakluyt Prebendary of Saint Augustines the Cathedrall Church of the said Citie, after divers meetings and due consultation they resolved to set forth a Voyage for the farther Discoverie of the North part of Virginia. And first they sent the said Master Hakluyt accompanied with one Master John Angell, and Master Robert Saltern (which had beene in the said Discoverie the yeere before with Captaine Bartholomew Gosnold)[1] to obtaine permission of Sir Walter Raleigh (which had a most ample Patent of all those parts from Queene Elizabeth) to entermeddle and deale in that action. Leave being obtained of him under his hand and Seale, they speedily prepared a small ship called the Speed-well in burthen about fiftie tunnes, manning the same with some thirtie men and Boyes, wherein went for Master and chiefe Commander in the Voyage one Martin Pring, a man very sufficient for his place, and Edmund Jones his Mate, and Robert Salterne above mentioned, as their chiefe Agent, with a Barke called the Discoverer, of six and twentie tunnes or thereabout, wherein went for Master William Browne, and Samuell Kirkland his Mate, both good and skilfull Mariners, being thirteene men and a Boy in all in that Barke. The aforesaid ship and Barke were plentifully victualled for eight monethes, and furnished with slight Merchandizes thought

---

1. Sidenote: "M. Salterne yet liveth neither is his zeale dead to this action. He is now a Minister and hath both by word and writing to mee testified his affection to Virginia. M. Pring whose Voyage to the East Indies are in the former Tome."

fit to trade with the people of the Countrey, as Hats of divers colours, greene, blue and yellow, apparell of coarse Kersie and Canvasse readie made, Stockings and Shooes, Sawes, Pick-axes, Spades and Shovels, Axes, Hatchets, Hookes, Knives, Sizzers, Hammers, Nailes, Chissels, Fish-hookes, Bels, Beades, Bugles, Looking-glasses, Thimbles, Pinnes, Needles, Threed, and such like. They set saile from Kingrode the twentieth day of March.

We set saile from Milford Haven (where the winds had stayed us a fortnight, in which space we heard of Queene Elizabeths death) the tenth of Aprill 1603. In our course we passed by the Iles of the Açores, had first sight of the Pike, and afterward of the Iland of Cnerno and Flores, and after we had runne some five hundred leagues, we fell with a multitude of small Ilands on the North Coast of Virginia, in the latitude of 43. degrees, the [ ] of June, which Ilands wee found very pleasant to behold, adorned with goodly grasse and sundry sorts of Trees, as Cedars, Spruce, Pines, and Firre-trees. Heere wee found an excellent fishing for Cods, which are better then those of New-found-land, and withall we saw good and Rockie ground fit to drie them upon: also we see no reason to the contrary, but that Salt may bee made in these parts, a matter of no small importance. We sayled to the Southwest end of these Ilands, and there rode with our ships under one of the greatest. One of them we named Foxe Iland, because we found those kind of beasts thereon. So passing through the rest with our Boates to the mayne Land, which lieth for a good space Northeast and South-west, we found very safe riding among them, in sixe, seven, eight, ten and twelve fathomes. At length comming to the Mayne in the latitude of 43. degrees and an halfe, we ranged the same to the South-west. In which course we found foure Inlets, the most Easterly whereof was barred at the mouth, but having passed over the barre, wee ranne up into it five miles, and for a certaine space found very good depth, and comming out againe, as we sailed South-westward, wee lighted upon two other Inlets, which upon our search we found to pierce not farre into the Land, the fourth and most Westerly was the best, which we rowed up ten or twelve miles.

In all these places we found no people, but signes of fires where they had beene. Howbeit we beheld very goodly Groves and Woods replenished with tall Okes, Beeches, Pine-trees, Firre-trees, Hasels, Wich-hasels and Maples. We saw here also sundry sorts of Beasts, as Stags, Deere, Beares, Wolves, Foxes, Lusernes, and Dogges with sharpe noses. But meeting with no Sassafras, we left these places with all the foresaid Ilands, shaping our course for Savage Rocke, discovered the yeere before by Captaine Gosnold, where going upon the Mayne we found people, with whom we had no long conversation, because here also we could find no Sassafras. Departing hence we bare into that great Gulfe which Captaine Gosnold over-shot the yeere before, coasting and finding people on the North side thereof. Not yet satisfied in our expectation, we left them and sailed over, and came to an Anchor on the South side in the latitude of 41. degrees and odde minutes: where we went on Land in a certaine Bay, which we called Whitson Bay, by the name of the Worshipfull Master John Whitson then Maior of the Citie of Bristoll, and one of the chiefe Adventurers, and finding a pleasant Hill thereunto adjoyning, wee called it Mount Aldworth, for Master Robert Aldworths sake a chiefe furtherer of the Voyage, aswell with his Purse as with his travell. Here we had sufficient quantitie of Sassafras.

At our going on shore, upon view of the people and sight of the place, wee thought it convenient to make a small baricado to keepe diligent watch and ward in, for the advertizement and succour of our men, while they should worke in the Woods. During our abode on shore, the people of the Countrey came to our men sometimes ten, twentie, fortie or threescore, and at one time one hundred and twentie at once. We used them kindly, and gave them divers sorts of our meanest Merchandize. They did eat Pease and Beanes with our men. Their owne victuals were most of fish.

We had a youth in our company that could play upon a Gitterne, in whose homely Musicke[2] they tooke great delight, and would give him many things, as Tobacco, Tobacco-pipes, Snakes skinnes of sixe foot long, which they use for Girdles, Fawnes skinnes, and such like, and danced twentie in a Ring, and the Gitterne in the middest of them, using many Savage gestures, singing Jo, Ja, Jo, Ja, Ja, Jo: him that first brake the ring, the

---

2. Sidenote: "The Savages take great delight in musick."

rest would knocke and cry out upon. Some few of them had plates of Brasse a foot long, and halfe a foote broad before their breasts. Their weapons are Bowes of five or sixe foot long of Wich-hasell, painted blacke and yellow, the strings of three twists of sinewes, bigger then our Bow-strings. Their Arrowes are of a yard and an handfull long not made of Reeds, but of a fine light wood very smooth and round with three long and deepe blacke feathers of some Eagle, Vulture, or Kite, as closely fastened with some binding matter, as any Fletcher of ours can glue them on. Their Quivers are full a yard long, made of long dried Rushes wrought about two handfuls broad above, and one handfull beneath with prettie workes and compartiments, Diamant wise of red and other colours.

We carried with us from Bristoll two excellent Mastives, of whom the Indians were more afraid, then of twentie of our men. One of these Mastives would carrie a halfe Pike in his mouth. And one Master Thomas Bridges a Gentleman of our company accompanied only with one of these Dogs, and passed six miles alone in the Countrey having lost his fellowes, and returned safely. And when we would be rid of the Savages company wee would let loose the Mastives, and suddenly with out-cryes they would flee away. These people in colour are inclined to a swart, tawnie, or Chestnut colour, not by nature but accidentally, and doe weare their haire brayded in foure parts, and trussed up about their heads with a small knot behind: in which haire of theirs they sticke many feathers and toyes for braverie and pleasure. They cover their privities only with a piece of leather drawne betwixt their twists and fastened to their Girdles behind and before: whereunto they hang their bags of Tobacco. They seeme to bee somewhat jealous of their women, for we saw not past two of them, who weare Aprons of Leather skins before them downe to the knees, and a Beares skinne like an Irish Mantle over one shoulder. The men are of stature somewhat taller then our ordinary people, strong, swift, well proportioned, and given to treacherie, as in the end we perceived.

Their Boats, whereof we brought one to Bristoll, were in proportion like a Wherrie of the River of Thames, seventeene foot long and foure foot broad, made of the Barke of a Birch-tree, farre exceeding in bignesse those of England: it was sowed together with strong and tough Oziers or twigs, and the seames covered over with Rozen or Turpentine little inferiour in sweetnesse to Frankincense, as we made triall by burning a little thereof on the coales at sundry times after our comming home: it was also open like a Wherrie, and sharpe at both ends, saving that the beake was a little bending roundly upward. And though it carried nine men standing upright, yet it weighed not at the most above sixtie pounds in weight, a thing almost incredible in regard of the largenesse and capacitie thereof. Their Oares were flat at the end like an Oven peele, made of Ash or Maple very light and strong, about two yards long, wherewith they row very swiftly: Passing up a River we saw certaine Cottages together, abandoned by the Savages, and not farre off we beheld their Gardens and one among the rest of an Acre of ground, and in the same was sowne Tobacco, Pompions, Cowcumbers and such like; and some of the people had Maiz or Indian Wheate among them. In the fields we found wild Pease, Strawberries very faire and bigge, Goose-berries, Raspices, Hurts, and other wild fruites.

Having spent three Weekes upon the Coast before we came to this place where we meant to stay & take in our lading, according to our instructions given us in charge before our setting forth, we pared and digged up the Earth with shovels, and sowed Wheate, Barley, Oates, Pease, and sundry sorts of Garden Seeds, which for the time of our abode there, being about seven Weeks, although they were late sowne, came up very well, giving certaine testimonie of the goodnesse of the Climate and of the Soyle. And it seemeth that Oate, Hempe, Flaxe, Rape-seed and such like which require a rich and fat ground, would prosper excellently in these parts. For in divers places here we found grasse above knee deepe.

As for Trees the Country yeeldeth Sassafras a plant of sovereigne vertue for the French Poxe, and as some of late have learnedly written good against the Plague and many other Maladies; Vines, Cedars, Okes, Ashes, Beeches, Birch trees, Cherie trees bearing fruit whereof wee did eate, Hasels, Wich-hasels, the best wood of all other to make Sope-ashes withall, Walnut-trees, Maples, Holy to make Bird-lime with, and a kinde of tree bearing a fruit like a small red Peare-plum with a crowne or knop on the top (a plant whereof carefully wrapped up in earth, Master Robert Salterne brought to Bristoll.) We found also low trees bearing faire Cheries. There were likewise a white kind of Plums which were not growne to their perfect ripenesse. With divers other sorts of trees to us unknowne.

The Beasts here are Stags, fallow Deere in abundance, Beares, Wolves, Foxes, Lusernes, and (some say) Tygres, Porcupines, and Dogges with sharpe and long noses, with many other sorts of wild beasts, whose Cases and Furres being hereafter purchased by exchange may yeeld no smal gaine to us. Since as we are certainly informed, the Frenchmen brought from Canada the value of thirtie thousand Crownes in the yeere 1604. almost in Bevers and Otters skinnes only. The most usuall Fowles are Eagles, Vultures, Hawkes, Cranes, Herons, Crowes, Gulls, and great store of other River and Seafowles. And as the Land is full of Gods good blessings, so is the Sea replenished with great abundance of excellent fish, as Cods sufficient to lade many ships, which we found upon the Coast in the moneth of June, Seales to make Oile withall, Mullets, Turbuts, Mackerels, Herrings, Crabs, Lobsters, Crevises, and Muscles with ragged Pearles in them.

By the end of July we had laded our small Barke called the Discoverer, with as much Sassafras as we thought sufficient, and sent her home into England before, to give some speedie contentment to the Adventurers: who arrived safely in Kingrode above a fortnight before us. After their departure we so bestirred our selves, that our shippe also had gotten in her lading, during which time there fell out this accident. On a day about noone tide while our men which used to cut downe Sassafras in the Woods were asleepe, as they used to doe for two houres in the heat of the day, there came downe about seven score Savages armed with their Bowes and Arrowes, and environed our House or Barricado, wherein were foure of our men alone with their Muskets to keepe Centinell, whom they sought to have come downe unto them, which they utterly refused, and stood upon their guard. Our Master likewise being very carefull and circumspect having not past two with him in the shippe put the same in

the best defence he could, lest they should have invaded the same, and caused a piece of great Ordnance to bee shot off, to give terrour to the Indians, and warning to our men which were fast asleepe in the Woods: at the noyse of which Peece they were a little awaked, and beganne a little to call for Foole and Gallant, their great and fearefull Mastives, and full quietly laid themselves downe againe, but beeing quickned up eftsoones againe with a second shot they rowsed up themselves, betooke them to their weapons and with their Mastives, great Foole with an halfe Pike in his mouth drew downe to their ship: whom when the Indians beheld afarre off, with the Mastive which they most feared, in dissembling manner they turned all to a jest and sport, and departed away in friendly manner: yet not long after, even the day before our departure, they set fire on the Woods where wee wrought, which wee did behold to burne for a mile space, and the very same day that wee weighed Anchor, they came downe to the shoare in greater number, to wit, very neere two hundred by our estimation, and some of them came in their Boates to our ship, and would have had us come in againe: but we sent them backe, and would none of their entertainment.

About the eighth or ninth of August, wee left this excellent Haven at the entrance whereof we found twentie fathomes water, and rode at our ease in seven fathomes being Land-locked, the Haven winding in compasse like the shell of a Snaile, and it is in latitude of one and forty degrees and five and twentie minutes.

This by the way is not to be forgotten, that our Captaine fell so much to the Northward because he would find high grounds, where commonly the best Havens are: which also fell out to his expectation. We also observed that we could find no Sassafras but in sandie ground. In our returne we brought our selves into the latitude of eight and thirtie degrees about the Açores for certaine causes, and within five weekes space came from our Port of Virginia, into the Soundings of England, but there being long encountred with Easterly winds, we came at length into Kingrode, the second of October 1603. The Discoverer was out five moneths and an halfe. The Speedwell was out six moneths upon the Voyage.

Chapter Sixty-three
The Arundell Project and the Waymouth Voyage, 1605

IT IS PROBABLE that before the end of 1604 Sir Thomas Arundell was engaged in a plan to send English Catholics to America, since Brereton's 1602 pamphlet (459) had revealed the attractiveness of the area north and south of Cape Cod. James I had made peace with Spain, so it was thought that neither he nor the Spaniards would stand in the way of such a project. Many English Catholic refugees on the Continent of Europe, some of them soldiers in the Spanish service and perhaps due to be discharged, wished to come to terms with their homeland. It was somehow proposed that the new colony should be composed of both English Catholic gentlemen and their tenants and also such refugees as cared to risk coming back under the English crown (albeit several thousand miles from England). Tristram Winslade, an English Catholic refugee of some standing, on receiving some promotion material for such a plan, took the advice of Father Robert Persons, S.J. (better known as Robert Parsons), a prominent, and very pro-Spanish, English clerical leader. Persons's reply to Winslade (463) has survived and is hostile to the whole idea. Catholics would be betraying the faith in England and would be killed by the Spaniards: the only good that could come from the venture was conversion of the Indians. This, though scarcely a final verdict, appears to have killed the idea of a refugee element, as much depended on Spanish goodwill.

Arundell went ahead. He made an agreement with Captain George Waymouth, who also involved himself with a group of Plymouth merchants, to prospect the coast a little to the north of that explored by Gosnold. The voyage of the *Archangel* was rapid and successful. Waymouth explored a group of islands off the coast of Maine (St. Georges Islands and Monhegan), which offered good fishing bases for his merchant backers, and the St. George's River, which appeared to offer excellent land for settlement by Arundell's colonists. Setting out on March 5, Waymouth was back at Dartmouth on July 18, although he found Arundell, now Lord Arundell of Wardour, had left for the Spanish Low Countries. Waymouth set out to look for fresh associates. James Rosier, who kept the journal of the voyage, was to publicize it in print. Rosier's *A true relation*, appeared in London well before the end of the year, quite possibly before Waymouth's agreement with Sir John Zouche on October 30 (466). Besides the printed version, Samuel Purchas had a manuscript version that contained some interesting variants, and most of this he printed in his *Pilgrimes*, IV (1625), 1659–1667. Both versions are given here, for the first time printed in one place. Henry Burrage several times edited Rosier's 1605 book. The most accessible version is in Henry S. Burrage, ed., *English and French Voyages, 1534–1608* (1906), pp. 357–394.

463. March 8/18, 1605. Father Robert Persons, S.J. to Tristram Winslade.

Contemporary copy in Stonyhurst College Library, MS Anglia III, no. 53 (courtesy Miss P. Renold); partly printed in J. G. Shea, The Church in the Colonies 1531–1763 (New York, 1886), pp. 24–28.

My judgement about transferringe Englishe Catholiques to the Northern partes of America for inhabitinge those partes and convertinge those barbarous people to Christianitie.

The intention of the author and the good and godly endes proposed by hime and diverse good particularities of meanes and helpes wherby to arive to those endes discreetly and piously put downe, I like very well, but yet for the execution and puttinge in ure the enterpriz it self I find many great difficultyes which seeme to me scarsly to be superable as amonge others these that folowe.

First for England it self it is very likely that the kinge and his counsel will never allowe of it apprehendinge the same as not onely dishonorable to them but dangerous also, dishonorable in that they should force so many of thire naturall subjects to flie and abandon theire owne countrey in respect of persecutione: dangerous in that those men goinge abroad with averted minde might joyne together ether before theire goinge to the Indies or after and returne uppon them havinge theire kinsfolk and frends at home to joyne with them and then the kinge and counsell being against it, yt moste needs folowe that nonn shall have license to goe forth, nonn to sell theire lands, nonn to make over money, and the like. All which the Author himself doth graunt; and owt of this one head will growe many and great difficulties or rather impossibilities.

Secondly for the Catholiques to be drawne to the enterpriz will be a very hard matter for that the better and richer sort in respecte of theire wealth and commodities at home and of the love of the countrey and feare of the state will disdayne commonly to heare of such a motione, and the poore sort without the riche will be of smal importance, besides that they doe depende wholy of the riche and of thire counsell, and the difficultie of gettinge out will be common to all.

Thirdly I doe persuade myself that if this proposition should be begune or imparted to any Prince abroad without communicatinge the same first in England it would be verie ill taken by the Catholicks generally as a matter soundinge to thier discredite and contempte to have as it were theire exportation to barbarous people treated with Princes in thire name without theire knowledge and consent, the Hereticks also would laughe and exprobrate the same unto them as they did when Sir George Peckhame and Sir Thomas Gerrarde about XX yeares gone should have made the same viage to Nerembrage by the Queene and counsells consent with some evacuatione of Papistes as then they called them which attempte became presently most odiouse to the Catholicke partie.

Fourthly it may be more then probablie thought that this attempt may be very prejudiciall to the increase of Catholicke religione in England not onely by decresinge the number of Catholicks there and thireby discouraginge the rest, and makinge them more contemptible to thire adversaryes but also by exasperatinge the kinge and estate against them as unquiet and practizing people, and so by restrayninge there goinge out and in, the entrance of Priests and comminge of scholars to the Seminaries would be more narrowly looked unto under that pretence Priests also could not find sufficient harbour in England and other such like things would probable folowe.

Fifthly for foren partes princes and kingdome there doe offer themselves no lesse or fewer difficulties, for first wither and to what place or porte shall they come that first come out of England, to witt the first 1000 of diverse sorts of husband men laborers and craftesmen required by the Author, and so supposinge they might gette forth freely how shall they be mantayned and where untill thire passaige be redy, for noe prince will easely admitte 1000 strangers into his countrey together without jelosy especially if they shall offende also thereby the king and state of England.

Sixthly I doe see a mighty difficultie in behalfe of the Kinge of Spaine and his counsell who are soe jelouse that noe straunge nation take footinge in any part of the Indyes, as not any particular man lightly though he have lived never so longe in Spayne canne gette licence once to goe thither but by great sute and surties and then may we imagine what they will thinke of the going thither of a whole natione, which may in time uppon many occasions of state or otherwise being [overwritten, but not crossed out: "become"] thire enimyes though they be Catholicke, nether is it sufficient to say that those partes are not presently occupied by the Spaynairds for they will answere, they may be in time and that it is noe reason if a man have a pallace with a hundred chambers and doe occupie but 10 for the presente that a strainger enter uppon the rest and say that the other useth them not, the care of the Spaniards is that noe other European natione have footing in that continent beside them selves where a fleet may reste and refreshe or fortifie her self againste the rest of the Indies possessed by them and for this course they made such haste and put them selves to such laboure and charges to extinguishe the Frenchmen that were in Nova Francia, and the like noe doubt would they doe to the Englishe if they should goe thither without theire licence the which to obtaine I hould it for impossible yet may it be attempted if any man will take it in hand.

And hereupon seventhly it followeth that wee shall have very litle hope to deale with his heighnes or withe the Archeduke of Flanders or any other Prince of Italy that is frend to the Kinge of Spaine except firste the saide Kinge be delt withall.

The collections also to be made aboute the world for furnishinge the enterprice would have very doubtfull eventes in my opinione and perhapps offende not onely the Kinge of England but the Catholicks also to be spoken of in pulpitte for such a jorney for that the people would not soe much looke into the laste end of converting those barbarouse people as into the first apprehensione of thire flight.

Finally what thire successe would be amongst those wilde people wilde beasts unexperienced ayre unprovided lande God only knoweth, yet as I sayd the intention of converEtinge those people liketh me soe well and in soe high a degree as for that onely I would desire my self to goe in the jorny shutting my eyes to all other difficulties if it were possible to obtayne it but yet for others also wee moste looke to all other necessary cir-

cumstances whereof the first of moste importance are in my opinion that the matter be broken in England and Spaine wherein for many reasons I may not be the broaker but if those ii were once optayned I would then be willing to doe in Rome what lieth in me and this is all that I canne say in this matter. Christ Jesus keepe you in health this 18th of March 1605.

[Endorsed:] A Copye of F. Persons answere to Mr. Winslade touching Norimbega.

464. 1605. James Rosier, *A true relation of the most prosperous voyage made in this present yeere 1605, by Captaine George Waymouth* (London, 1605).

A True Relation of the most prosperous voyage made this present yeere 1605, by Captaine George Waymouth, in the Discovery of the Land of Virginia:

Where he discovered 60 miles up a most excellent River; together with a most fertile land.

Written by James Rosier, a Gentleman employed in the voyage. Londini, Impensis Geor. Bishop, 1605.

TO THE READER

Being employed in this Voyage by the right honourable Thomas Arundell Baron of Warder, to take due notice, and make true report of the discovery therein performed: I became very diligent to observe (as much as I could) whatsoever was materiall or of consequence in the businesse which I collected into this briefe summe, intending upon our returne to publish the same. But he soone changed the course of his intendments; and long before our arrivall in England had so farre engaged himselfe with the Archduke, that he was constrained to relinquish this action. But the commodities and profits of the countrey, together with the fitnesse of plantation, being by some honourable Gentlemen of good woorth and qualitie, and Merchants of good sufficiency and judgment duly considered, have at their owne charge (intending both their private and the common

benefit of their countrey) undertaken the transporting of a Colony for the plantation thereof; being much encouraged thereunto by the gracious favour of the Kings Majesty himselfe, and divers Lords of his Highnesse most Honourable Privie Councell. After these purposed designes were concluded, I was animated to publish this briefe Relation, and not before; because some forrein Nation (being fully assured of the fruitfulnesse of the countrie) have hoped hereby to gaine some knowledge of the place, seeing they could not allure our Captaine or any speciall man of our Company to combine with them for their direction, nor obtaine their purpose, in conveying away our Salvages, which was busily in practise. And this is the cause that I have neither written of the latitude or variation most exactly observed by our Captaine with sundrie instruments, which together with his perfect Geographicall Map of the countrey, he entendeth hereafter to set forth. I have likewise purposedly omitted here to adde a collection of many words in their language to the number of foure or five hundred, as also the names of divers of their governours, as well their friends as their enemies: being reserved to be made knowen for the benefit of those that shal goe in the next Voyage. But our particular proceedings in the whole Discoverie, the commodious situation of the River, the fertilitie of the land, with the profits there to be had, and here reported, I refer to be verified by the whole Company, as being eye-witnesses of my words, and most of them neere inhabitants upon the Thames. So with my prayers to God for the conversion of so ingenious and well-disposed people, and for the prosperous successive events of the noble intenders the prosecution thereof, I rest
Your friend

J. R.

A True Relation of Captaine George Waymouth his Voyage, made this present yeere 1605; in the Discoverie of the North part of Virginia.

Upon Tuesday the 5 day of March, about ten a clocke afore noone, we set saile from Ratcliffe, and came to an anker that tide about two a clocke before Gravesend.

From thence the 10 of March being Sunday at night we ankered in the Downes: and there rode till the next day about three a clocke after noone, when with a scant winde we set saile; and by reason the winde continued Southwardly, we were beaten up and doune: but on Saturday the 16 day about foure a clocke after noon we put into Dartmouth Haven where the continuance of the winde at South and Southwest constrained us to ride till the last of this moneth. There we shipped some of our men and supplied necessaries for our Ship and Voyage.

Upon Easter day, being the last of March, the winde comming at North-North-East, about five a clocke after noone we wayed anker, and put to sea, In the name of God, being well victualled and furnished with munition and all necessaries: Our whole Company being but 29 persons; of whom I may boldly say, few voyages have beene manned forth with better Sea-men generally in respect of our small number.

Munday the next day, being the first of Aprill, by sixe a clocke in the morning we were sixe leagues South-South-East from the Lizarde.

At two a clocke in the afternoone this day, the weather being very faire, our Captaine for his owne experience and others with him sounded, and had sixe and fiftie fathoms and a halfe. The sounding was some small blacke perrie sand, some reddish sand, a match or two, with small shels called Saint James his Shels.

The foureteenth of Aprill being Sunday, betweene nine and ten of the clocke in the morning our Captaine descried the Iland Cuervo: which bare South-west and by West, about seven leagues from us: by eleven of the clocke we descried Flores to the Southward of Cuervo, as it lieth: by foure a clocke in the afternoone we brought Cuervo due South from us within two leagues of the shore, but we touched not, because the winde was faire, and we thought our selves sufficiently watered and wooded.

Heere our Captaine observed the Sunne, and found himselfe in the latitude of 40 degrees and 7 minutes: so he judged the North part of Cuervo to be in 40 degrees. After we had kept our course about a hundred leagues from the Ilands, by continuall Southerly windes we were forced and driven from the Southward, whither we first intended. And when our Captaine by long beating saw it was but in vaine to strive with windes, not knowing Gods purposes heerein to our further blessing, (which after by his especiall direction wee found) he thought best to stand as nigh as he could by the winde to recover what land we might first discover.

Munday, the 6 of May, being in the latitude of 39 and a halfe about ten a clocke afore noone, we came to a riplin, which we discerned a head our ship, which is a breach of water caused either by a fall, or by some meeting of currents, which we judged this to be; for the weather being very faire, and a small gale of winde, we sounded and found no ground in a hundred fathoms.

Munday, the 13 of May, about eleven a clocke afore noone, our Captaine, judging we were not farre from land, sounded, and had a soft oaze in a hundred and sixty fathomes. At fowre a clocke after noone we sounded againe, and had the same oaze in a hundred fathoms.

From ten a clocke that night till three a clocke in the morning, our Captaine tooke in all sailes and lay at hull, being desirous to fall with the land in the day time, because it was an unknowen coast, which it pleased God in his mercy to grant us, otherwise we had run our ship upon the hidden rockes and perished all. For when we set saile we sounded in 100 fathoms: and by eight a clock, having not made above five or six leagues, our Captaine upon a sudden change of water (supposing verily he saw the sand) presently sounded, and had but five fathoms. Much marvelling because we saw no land, he sent one to the top, who thence descried a whitish sandy cliffe, which bare West-North-West about six leagues off from us: but comming neerer within three or fowre leagues, we saw many breaches still neerer the land: at last we espied a great breach a head us al along the shore, into which before we should enter, our Captaine thought best to hoist out his ship boate and sound it. Which if he had not done, we had beene in great danger: for he bare up the ship, as neere as he durst after the boate: untill Thomas Cam, his mate, being in the boat, called to him to tacke about and stand off, for in this breach he had very showld water, two fathoms and lesse upon rockes, and sometime they supposed they saw the rocke within three or fowre foote, whereon the sea made a very strong breach: which we might discerne (from the top) to run along as we sailed by it 6 or 7 leagues to the Southward. This was in the latitude of 41 degrees, 20 minuts: wherefore we were constrained to put backe againe from the land: and sounding, (the

weather being very faire and a small winde) we found our selves embaied with continuall showldes and rockes in a most uncertaine ground, from five or sixe fathoms, at the next cast of the lead we should have 15 and 18 fathoms. Over many which we passed, and God so blessed us, that we had wind and weather as faire as poore men in this distress could wish: whereby we both perfectly discerned every breach, and with the winde were able to turne, where we saw most hope of safest passage. Thus we parted from the land, which we had not so much before desired, and at the first sight rejoiced, as now we all joifully praised God, that it had pleased him to deliver us from so imminent danger.

Heere we found great store of excellent Cod fish, and saw many Whales, as we had done two or three daies before.

We stood off all that night, and the next day being Wednesday; but the wind still continuing between the points of South-South-West, and West-South-West: so as we could not make any way to the Southward, in regard of our great want of water and wood (which was now spent) we much desired land and therefore sought for it, where the wind would best suffer us to refresh our selves.

Thursday, the 16 of May, we stood in directly with the land, and much marvelled we descried it not, wherein we found our sea charts very false, putting land where none is.

Friday the 17 of May, about six a clocke at night we descried the land, which bare from us North-North-East; but because it blew a great gale of winde, the sea very high and neere night, not fit to come upon an unknowen coast, we stood off till two a clocke in the morning, being Saturday: then standing in with it againe, we descried it by eight a clocke in the morning, bearing North-East from us. It appeared a meane high land, as we after found it, being but an Iland of some six miles in compasse, but I hope the most fortunate ever yet discovred. About twelve a clocke that day, we came to an anker on the North side of this Iland, about a league from the shore. About two a clocke our Captaine with twelve men rowed in his ship boat to the shore, where we made no long stay, but laded our boat with dry wood of olde trees upon the shore side, and returned to our ship, where we rode that night.

This Iland is woody, grouen with Firre, Birch,

Oke and Beech, as farre as we saw along the shore; and so likely to be within. On the verge grow Gooseberries, Strawberries, Wild pease, and Wild rose bushes. The water issued foorth downe the Rocky cliffes in many places: and much fowle of divers kinds breed upon the shore and rocks.

While we were at shore, our men aboord with a few hooks got above thirty great Cods and Hadocks, which gave us a taste of the great plenty of fish which we found afterward wheresoever we went upon the coast.

From hence we might discerne the maine land from the West-South-West to the East-North-East, and a great way (as it then seemed, and as we after found it) up into the maine we might discerne very high mountaines, though the maine seemed but low land; which gave us a hope it would please God to direct us to the discoverie of some good; although wee were driven by winds farre from that place, whither (both by our direction and desire) we ever intended to shape the course of our voyage.

The next day being Whit-Sunday; because we rode too much open to the sea and windes, we weyed anker about twelve a clocke, and came along to the other Ilands more adjoyning to the maine, and in the rode directly with the mountaines, about three leagues from the first Iland where we had ankered.

When we came neere unto them (sounding all along in a good depth) our Captaine manned his ship-boat and sent her before with Thomas Cam one of his Mates, whom he knew to be of good experience, to sound and search betweene the Ilands for a place safe for our shippe to ride in; in the meane while we kept aloofe at sea, having given them in the boat a token to weffe in the ship, if he found a convenient Harbour; which it pleased God to send us, farre beyond our expectation, in a most safe birth defended from all windes, in an excellent depth of water for ships of any burthen, in six, seven, eight, nine and ten fathoms upon a clay oaze very tough.

We all with great joy praised God for his unspeakable goodnesse, who had from so apparent danger delivered us, and directed us upon this day into so secure an Harbour: in remembrance whereof we named it Pentecost harbor, we arriving there that day out of our last Harbour in England, from whence we set saile upon Easter-day.

About foure a clocke, after we were ankered and well mored, our Captaine with halfe a dozen of our Company went on shore to seeke fresh watering, and a convenient place to set together a pinnesse, which we brought in pieces out of England; both which we found very fitting.

Upon this Iland, as also upon the former, we found (at our first comming to shore) where fire had beene made: and about the place were very great egge shelles bigger than goose egges, fish bones, and as we judged, the bones of some beast.

Here we espied Cranes stalking on the shore of a little Iland adjoyning; where we after saw they used to breed.

Whitsun-munday, the 20 day of May, very early in the morning, our Captaine caused the pieces of the pinnesse to be carried a shore, where while some were busied about her, others digged welles to receive the fresh water, which we found issuing downe out of the land in many places. Heere I cannot omit (for foolish feare of imputation of flattery) the painfull industry of our Captaine, who as at sea he is always most carefull and vigilant, so at land he refuseth no paines; but his labour was ever as much or rather more than any mans: which not only encourageth others with better content, but also effecteth much with great expedition.

In digging we found excellent clay for bricke or tile.

The next day we finished a well of good and holesome cleere water in a great empty caske, which we left there. We cut yards, waste trees, and many necessaries for our ship, while our Carpenter and Cooper laboured to fit and furnish forth the shallop.

This day our boat went out about a mile from our ship, and in small time with two or three hooks was fished sufficiently for our whole Company three dayes, with great Cod, Haddocke, and Thornebacke.

And towards night we drew with a small net of twenty fathoms very nigh the shore: we got about thirty very good and great Lobsters, many Rockfish, some Plaise, and other small fishes, and fishes called Lumpes, verie pleasant to the taste: and we generally observed, that all the fish, of what kinde soever we tooke, were well fed, fat, and sweet in taste.

Wednesday, the 22 of May, we felled and cut wood for our ships use, cleansed and scoured our wels, and digged a plot of ground, wherein, amongst some garden seeds, we sowed peaze and barley, which in sixteen dayes grew eight inches above ground; and so continued growing every day halfe an inch, although this was but the crust of the ground, and much inferior to the mould we after found in the maine.

Friday, the 24 of May, after we had made an end of cutting wood, and carying water aboord our shippe, with fourteene Shot and Pikes we marched about and thorow part of two of the Ilands; the bigger of which we judged to be foure or five miles in compasse, and a mile broad.

The profits and fruits which are naturally on these Ilands are these:

All along the shore and some space within, where
    the wood hindereth not, grow plentifully
Rasberries.
Gooseberries.
Strawberries.
Roses.
Currants.
Wild-Vines.
Angelica.
    Within the Ilands growe wood of sundry sorts,
        some very great, and all tall:
Birch.
Beech.
Ash.
Maple.
Spruce.
Cherry-tree.
Yew.
Oke very great and good.
Firre-tree, out of which

issueth Turpentine in so marvellous plenty, and so sweet, as our Chirurgeon and others affirmed they never saw so good in England. We pulled off much Gumme congealed on the outside of the barke, which smelled like Frankincense. This would be a great benefit for making Tarre and Pitch.

We stayed the longer in this place, not only because of our good Harbour, (which is an excellent comfort) but because every day we did more and more discover the pleasant fruitfulnesse; insomuch as many of our Companie wished themselves settled heere, not expecting any further hopes, or better discovery to be made.

Heere our men found abundance of great muscels among the rocks; and in some of them many small Pearls: and in one muscell (which we drew up in our net) was found foureteene Pearles, whereof one of pretty bignesse and orient; in

another above fiftie small Pearles; and if we had had a Drag, no doubt we had found some of great valew, seeing these did certainly shew, that heere they were bred: the shels all glistering with mother of Pearle.

Wednesday, the 29 day, our shallop being now finished, and our Captaine and men furnished to depart with hir from the ship: we set up a crosse on the shore side upon the rockes.

Thursday, the 30 of May, about ten a clock afore noon, our Captaine with 13 men more, in the name of God, and with all our praiers for their prosperous discoverie, and safe returne, departed in the shallop; leaving the ship in a good harbour, which before I mentioned, well mored, and manned with 14 men.

This day, about five a clocke in the afternoone, we in the shippe espied three Canoas comming towards us, which went to the iland adjoining, where they went a shore, and very quickly had made a fire, about which they stood beholding our ships: to whom we made signes with our hands and hats, weffing unto them to come unto us, because we had not seene any of the people yet. They sent one Canoa with three men, one of which, when they came neere unto us, spake in his language very lowd and very boldly: seeming as though he would know why we were there, and by pointing with his oare towards the sea, we conjectured he ment we should be gone. But when we shewed them knives and their use, by cutting of stickes and other trifles, as combs and glasses, they came close aboard our ship, as desirous to entertaine our friendship. To these we gave such things as we perceived they liked, when wee shewed them the use: bracelets, rings, peacocke feathers, which they stucke in their haire, and Tabacco pipes. After their departure to their company on the shore, presently came foure other in another Canoa: to whom we gave as to the former, using them with as much kindnes as we could.

The shape of their body is very proportionable, they are wel countenanced, not very tal nor big, but in stature like to us: they paint their bodies with blacke, their faces, some with red, some with blacke, and some with blew.

Their clothing is Beavers skins, or Deares skins, cast over them like a mantle, and hanging downe to their knees, made fast together upon the shoulder with leather; some of them had sleeves, most had none; some had buskins of such leather tewed: they have besides a peece of Beavers skin betweene their legs, made fast about their waste, to cover their privities.

They suffer no haire to grow on their faces, but on their head very long and very blacke, which those that have wives, binde up behinde with a leather string, in a long round knot.

They seemed all very civill and merrie: shewing tokens of much thankefulnesse, for those things we gave them. We found them then (as after) a people of exceeding good invention, quicke understanding and readie capacitie.

Their Canoas are made without any iron, of the bark of a birch tree, strengthened within with ribs and hoops of wood, in so good fashion, with such excellent ingenious art, as they are able to beare seven or eight persons, far exceeding any in the Indies.

One of their Canoas came not to us, wherein we imagined their women were: of whom they are (as all Salvages) very jealous.

When I signed unto them they should goe sleepe, because it was night, they understood presently, and pointed that at the shore, right against our ship, they would stay all night: as they did.

The next morning very early, came one Canoa abord us againe with three Salvages, whom we easily then enticed into our ship, and under the decke: where we gave them porke, fish, bread and pease, all which they did eat; and this I noted, they would eat nothing raw, either fish or flesh. They marvelled much and much looked upon the making of our canne and kettle, so they did at a head-peece and at our guns, of which they are most fearefull, and would fall flat downe at the report of them. At their departure I signed unto them, that if they would bring me such skins as they ware I would give them knives, and such things as I saw they most liked, which the chiefe of them promised to do by that time the Sunne should be beyond the middest of the firmament; this I did to bring them to an understanding of exchange, and that they might conceive the intent of our comming to them to be for no other end.

About 10 a clocke this day we descried our Shallop returning toward us, which so soone as we espied, we certainly conjectured our Captaine had found some unexpected harbour, further up towards the maine to bring the ship into, or some river; knowing his determination and resolution,

not so suddenly else to make returne: which when they came neerer they expressed by shooting volleies of shot; and when they were come within Musket shot, they gave us a volley and haled us, then we in the shippe gave them a great peece and haled them.

Thus we welcomed them; who gladded us exceedingly with their joifull relation of their happie discoverie, which shall appeare in the sequele. And we likewise gave them cause of mutuall joy with us, in discoursing of the kinde civility we found in a people, where we little expected any sparke of humanity.

Our Captaine had in this small time discovered up a great river, trending alongst into the maine about forty miles. The pleasantnesse whereof, with the safety of harbour for shipping, together with the fertility of ground and other fruits, which were generally by his whole company related, I omit, till I report of the whole discovery therein after performed. For by the breadth, depth and strong flood, imagining it to run far up into the land, he with speed returned, intending to flanke his light horsman for arrowes, least it might happen that the further part of the river should be narrow, and by that meanes subject to the volley of Salvages on either side out of the woods.

Untill his returne, our Captaine left on shore where he landed in a path (which seemed to be frequented) a pipe, a brooch and a knife, thereby to know if the Salvages had recourse that way, because they could at that time see none of them, but they were taken away before our returne thither.

I returne now to our Salvages, who according to their appointment about one a clocke, came with 4 Canoas to the shoare of the iland right over against us, where they had lodged the last night, and sent one Canoa to us with two of those Salvages, who had beene a bord, and another, who then seemed to have command of them; for though we perceived their willingnesse, yet he would not permit them to come abord; but he having viewed us and our ship, signed that he would go to the rest of the company and returne againe. Presently after their departure it began to raine, and continued all that afternoone, so as they could not come to us with their skins and furs, nor we go to them. But after an houre or there about, the three which had beene with us before came againe, whom we had to our fire and covered them with our gownes. Our Captaine bestowed a shirt upon him, whom we thought to be their chiefe, who seemed never to have seene any before; we gave him a brooch to hang about his necke, a great knife, and lesser knives to the two other, and to every one of them a combe and glasse, the use whereof we shewed them: whereat they laughed and tooke gladly; we victualled them, and gave them aqua vitæ, which they tasted, but would by no meanes drinke; our beveridge they liked well, we gave them Sugar Candy, which after they had tasted they liked and desired more, and raisons which were given them; and some of every thing they would reserve to carry to their company. Wherefore we pittying their being in the raine, and therefore not able to get themselves victuall (as we thought) we gave them bread and fish.

Thus because we found the land a place answereable to the intent of our discovery, viz. fit for any nation to inhabit, we used the people with as great kindnes as we could devise, or found them capable of.

The next day, being Saturday and the first of June, I traded with the Salvages all the fore noone upon the shore, where were eight and twenty of them: and because our ship rode nigh, we were but five or sixe: where for knives, glasses, combes and other trifles to the valew of foure or five shillings, we had 40 good Beavers skins, Otters skins, Sables, and other small skins, which we knewe not how to call. Our trade being ended, many of them came abord us, and did eat by our fire, and would be verie merrie and bold, in regard of our kinde usage of them. Towards night our Captaine went on shore, to have a draught with the Sein or Net. And we carried two of them with us, who marvelled to see us catch fish with a net. Most of that we caught we gave them and their company. Then on the shore I learned the names of divers things of them: and when they perceived me to note them downe, they would of themselves, fetch fishes, and fruit bushes, and stand by me to see me write their names.

Our Captaine shewed them a strange thing which they woondred at. His sword and mine having beene touched with the Loadstone, tooke up a knife, and held it fast when they plucked it away, made the knife turne, being laid on a blocke, and touching it with his sword, made that take up a needle, whereat they much marvelled.

This we did to cause them to imagine some great power in us: and for that to love and feare us.

When we went on shore to trade with them, in one of their Canoas I saw their bowes and arrowes, which I tooke up and drew an arrow in one of them, which I found to be of strength able to carry an arrow five or sixe score stronglie; and one of them tooke it and drew as we draw our bowes, not like the Indians. Their bow is made of Wich Hazell, and some of Beech in fashion much like our bowes, but they want nocks, onely a string of leather put through a hole at one end, and made fast with a knot at the other. Their arrowes are made of the same wood, some of Ash, big and long, with three feathers tied on, and nocked very artificiallie: headed with the long shanke bone of a Deere, made very sharpe with two fangs in manner of a harping iron. They have likewise Darts, headed with like bone, one of which I darted among the rockes, and it brake not. These they use very cunningly, to kill fish, fowle and beasts.

Our Captaine had two of them at supper with us in his cabbin to see their demeanure, and had them in presence at service: who behaved themselves very civilly, neither laughing nor talking all the time, and at supper fed not like men of rude education, neither would they eat or drinke more than seemed to content nature; they desired pease to carry a shore to their women, which we gave them, with fish and bread, and lent them pewter dishes, which they carefully brought againe.

In the evening another boat came to them on the shore, and because they had some Tabacco, which they brought for their owne use, the other came for us, making signe what they had, and offered to carry some of us in their boat, but foure or five of us went with them in our owne boat: when we came on shore they gave us the best welcome they could, spreading fallow Deeres skins for us to sit on the ground by their fire, and gave us of their Tabacco in our pipes, which was excellent, and so generally commended of us all to be as good as any we ever tooke, being the simple leafe without any composition, strong, and of sweet taste; they gave us some to carry to our Captaine, whom they called our Bashabes; neither did they require any thing for it, but we would not receive any thing from them without remuneration.

Heere we saw foure of their women, who stood behind them, as desirous to see us, but not willing to be seene; for before, whensoever we came on shore, they retired into the woods, whether it were in regard of their owne naturall modestie, being covered only as the men with the foresaid Beavers skins, or by the commanding jealousy of their husbands, which we rather suspected, because it is an inclination much noted to be in Salvages; wherefore we would by no meanes seeme to take any speciall notice of them. They were very well favoured in proportion of countenance, though coloured blacke, low of stature, and fat, bare headed as the men, wearing their haire long: they had two little male children of a yeere and half old, as we judged, very fat and of good countenances, which they love tenderly, all naked, except their legs, which were covered with thin leather buskins tewed, fastened with strops to a girdle about their waste, which they girde very streight, and is decked round about with little round peeces of red Copper; to these I gave chaines and bracelets, glasses, and other trifles, which the Salvages seemed to accept in great kindnesse.

At our comming away, we would have had those two that supped with us, to go abord and sleepe, as they had promised; but it appeared their company would not suffer them. Whereat we might easily perceive they were much greeved; but not long after our departure, they came with three more to our ship, signing to us, that if one of our company would go lie on shore with them, they would stay with us. Then Owen Griffin (one of the two we were to leave in the Country, if we had thought it needfull or convenient) went with them in their Canoa, and 3 of them staied aborde us, whom our whole company very kindly used. Our Captaine saw their lodging provided, and them lodged in an old saile upon the Orlop; and because they much feared our dogs, they were tied up whensoever any of them came abord us.

Owen Griffin, which lay on the shore, reported unto me their maner, and (as I may terme them) the ceremonies of their idolatry; which they performe thus. One among them (the eldest of the Company, as he judged) riseth right up, the other sitting still, and looking about, suddenly cried with a loud voice, Baugh, Waugh: then the women fall downe, and lie upon the ground, and the men all together answering the same, fall a stamping round about the fire with both feet, as hard as they can, making the ground shake, with sundry out-cries, and change of voice and sound. Many take the fire-sticks and thrust them into the earth, and then rest awhile: of a sudden beginning as before, they continue so stamping, till the yonger sort fetched from the shore many stones, of which every man tooke one, and first beat upon them with their fire sticks, then with the stones beat the earth with all their strength. And in this maner (as he reported) they continued above two houres.

After this ended, they which have wives take them apart, and withdraw themselves severally into the wood all night.

The next morning, assoone as they saw the Sunne rise, they pointed to him to come with them to our shippe: and having received their men from us, they came with five or sixe of their Canoas and Company hovering about our ship; to whom (because it was the Sabbath day) I signed they should depart, and at the next Sun rising we would goe along with them to their houses; which they understood (as we thought) and departed, some of their Canoas coursing about the Iland, and the other directly towards the maine.

This day, about five a clocke after noone, came three other Canoas from the maine, of which some had beene with us before; and they came aboord us, and brought us Tabacco, which we tooke with them in their pipes, which were made of earth, very strong, blacke, and short, containing a great quantity: some Tabacco they gave unto our Captaine, and some to me, in very civill kind maner. We requited them with bread and peaze, which they caried to their Company on shore, seeming very thankefull. After supper they returned with their Canoa to fetch us a shore to take Tabacco with them there: with whom six or seven of us went, and caried some trifles, if peradventure they had any trucke, among which I caried some few biskets, to try if they would exchange for them, seeing they so well liked to eat them. When we came at shore, they most kindly entertained us, taking us by the hands, as they had observed we did to them aboord, in token of welcome, and brought us to sit doune by their fire, where sat together thirteene of them. They filled their Tabacco pipe, which was then the short claw of a Lobster, which will hold ten of our pipes full, and we dranke of their excellent Tabacco as much as we would with them; but we saw not any great quantity to trucke for; and it seemed they had not much left of old, for they spend a great quantity yeerely by their continuall drinking: and they would signe unto us that it was growen yet but a foot above ground, and would be above a yard high, with a leafe as broad as both their hands. They often would (by pointing to one part of the maine Eastward) signe unto us, that their Bashabes (that is, their King) had great plenty of Furres, and much Tabacco. When we had sufficiently taken Tabacco with them, I shewed some of our trifles for trade; but they made signe that they had there nothing to exchange; for (as I after conceived) they had beene fishing and fowling, and so came thither to lodge that night by us: for when we were ready to come away, they shewed us great cups made very wittily of barke, in forme almost square, full of a red berry about the bignesse of a bullis, which they did eat, and gave us by handfuls; of which (though I liked not the taste) yet I kept some, because I would by no meanes but accept their kindnesse. They shewed me likewise a great piece of fish, whereof I tasted, and it was fat like Porpoise; and another kinde of great scaly fish, broiled on the coales, much like white Salmon, which the French-men call Aloza, for these they would have had bread; which I refused, because in manner of exchange, I would alwayes make the greatest esteeme I could of our commodities whatsoever; although they saw aboord our Captaine was liberall to give them, to the end we might allure them still to frequent us. Then they shewed me foure yoong Goslings, for which they required foure biskets, but I offered them two; which they tooke and were well content.

At our departure they made signe, that if any of us would stay there on shore, some of them would go lie aboord us: at which motion two of our Company stayed with them, and three of the Salvages lodged with us in maner as the night before.

Early the next morning, being Munday the third of June, when they had brought our men aboord, they came about our ship, earnestly by signes desiring that we would go with them along to the maine, for that there they had Furres and Tabacco to traffique with us. Wherefore our Captaine manned the light-horseman with as many

men as he could well, which were about fifteene with rowers and all; and we went along with them. Two of their Canoas they sent away before, and they which lay aboord us all night, kept company with us to direct us.

This we noted as we went along, they in their Canoa with three oares, would at their will go ahead of us and about us, when we rowed with eight oares strong; such was their swiftnesse, by reason of the lightnesse and artificiall composition of their Canoa and oares.

When we came neere the point where we saw their fires, where they intended to land, and where they imagined some few of us would come on shore with our merchandize, as we had accustomed before; when they had often numbered our men very diligently, they scoured away to their Company, not doubting we would have followed them. But when we perceived this, and knew not either their intents, or number of Salvages on the shore, our Captaine, after consultation, stood off, and wefted them to us, determining that I should go on shore first to take a view of them and what they had to traffique: if he, whom at our first sight of them seemed to be of most respect among them, and being then in the Canoa, would stay as a pawne for me. When they came to us (notwithstanding all our former courtesies) he utterly refused; but would leave a yoong Salvage: and for him our Captaine sent Griffin in their Canoa, while we lay hulling a little off. Griffin at his returne reported, thay had there assembled together, as he numbered them, two hundred eighty three Salvages, every one his bowe and arrowes, with their dogges, and wolves which they keepe tame at command, and not anything to exchange at all; but would have drawen us further up into a little narrow nooke of a river, for their Furres, as they pretended.

These things considered, we began to joyne them in the ranke of other Salvages, who have beene by travellers in most discoveries found very trecherous; never attempting mischiefe, untill by some remisnesse, fit opportunity affoordeth them certaine ability to execute the same. Wherefore after good advice taken, we determined so soone as we could to take some of them, least (being suspitious we had discovered their plots) they should absent themselves from us.

Tuesday, the fourth of June, our men tooke Cod and Hadocke with hooks by our ship side, and

Lobsters very great; which before we had not tried.

About eight a clocke this day we went on shore with our boats, to fetch aboord water and wood, our Captaine leaving word with the Gunner in the shippe, by discharging a musket, to give notice if they espied any Canoa comming; which they did about ten a clocke. He therefore being carefull they should be kindly entreated, requested me to go aboord, intending with dispatch to make what haste after he possibly could. When I came to the ship, there were two Canoas, and in either of them three Salvages; of whom two were below at the fire, the other staied in their Canoas about the ship; and because we could not entice them abord, we gave them a Canne of pease and bread, which they carried to the shore to eat. But one of them brought backe our Canne presently and staid abord with the other two; for he being yoong, of a ready capacity, and one we most desired to bring with us into England, had received exceeding kinde usage at our hands, and was therefore much delighted in our company. When our Captaine was come, we consulted how to catch the other three at shore which we performed thus.

We manned the light horseman with 7 or 8 men, one standing before carried our box of Marchandise, as we were woont when I went to traffique with them, and a platter of pease, which meat they loved: but before we were landed, one of them (being too suspitiously feareful of his owne good) withdrew himselfe into the wood. The other two met us on the shore side, to receive the pease, with whom we went up the Cliffe to their fire and sate downe with them, and whiles we were discussing how to catch the third man who was gone, I opened the box, and shewed them trifles to exchange, thinking thereby to have banisht feare from the other, and drawen him to returne: but when we could not, we used little delay, but suddenly laid hands upon them. And it was as much as five or sixe of us could doe to get them into the light horseman. For they were strong and so naked as our best hold was by their long haire on their heads; and we would have beene very loath to have done them any hurt, which of necessity we had beene constrained to have done if we had attempted them in a multitude, which we must and would, rather than have wanted them, being a matter of great importance for the full accomplement of our voyage.

Thus we shipped five Salvages, two Canoas, with all their bowes and arrowes.

The next day we made an end of getting our wood aboord, and filled our empty caske with water.

Thursday, the 6 of June, we spent in bestowing the Canoas upon the orlop safe from hurt, because they were subject to breaking, which our Captaine was carefull to prevent.

Saturday the eight of June (our Captaine being desirous to finish all businesse about this harbour) very early in the morning, with the light horseman, coasted five or sixe leagues about the Ilands adjoining, and sounded all along wheresoever we went. He likewise diligently searched the mouth of the Harbour, and about the rocks which shew themselves at all times, and are an excellent breach of the water, so as no Sea can come in to offend the Harbour. This he did to instruct himselfe, and thereby able to direct others that shall happen to come to this place. For every where both neere the rocks, and in all soundings about the Ilands, we never found lesse water than foure and five fathoms, which was seldome; but seven, eight, nine and ten fathoms is the continuall sounding by the shore. In some places much deeper upon clay oaze or soft sand: so that if any bound for this place, should be either driven or scanted with winds, he shall be able (with his directions) to recover safely his harbour most securely in water enough by foure severall passages, more than which I thinke no man of judgement will desire as necessarie.

Upon one of the Ilands (because it had a pleasant sandy Cove for small barks to ride in) we landed, and found hard by the shore a pond of fresh water, which flowed over the banks, somewhat over growen with little shrub trees, and searching up in the Iland, we saw it fed with a strong run, which with small labour, and little time, might be made to drive a mill. In this Iland, as in the other, were spruce trees of excellent timber and height, able to mast ships of great burthen.

While we thus sounded from one place to another in so good deepes, our Captaine to make some triall of the fishing himselfe, caused a hooke or two to be cast out at the mouth of the harbour, not above halfe a league from our ship, where in small time only, with the baits which they cut from the fish and three hooks, we got fish enough for our whole Company (though now augmented) for three daies. Which I omit not to report, because it sheweth how great a profit the fishing would be, they being so plentifull, so great and so good, with such convenient drying as can be wished, neere at hand upon the Rocks.

This day, about one a clocke after noone, came from the Eastward, two Canoas abord us, wherein was he that refused to stay with us for a pawne, and with him six other Salvages which we had not seene before, who had beautified themselves after their manner very gallantly, though their clothing was not differing from the former, yet they had newly painted their faces very deep, some all blacke, some red, with stripes of excellent blew over their upper lips, nose and chin. One of them ware a kinde of Coronet about his head, made very cunningly, of a substance like stiffe haire coloured red, broad, and more than a handfull in depth, which we imagined to be some ensigne of superioritie; for he so much esteemed it as he would not for anything exchange the same. Other ware the white feathered skins of some fowle, round about their head, jewels in their ears, and bracelets of little white round bone, fastened together upon a leather string. These made not any shew that they had notice of the other before taken, but we understood them by their speech and signes, that they came sent from the Bashabes, and that his desire was that we would bring up our ship (which they call as their owne boats, a Quiden) to his house, being, as they pointed, upon the main towards the East, from whence they came, and that he would exchange with us for Furres and Tabacco. But because our Company was but small, and now our desire was with speed to discover up the river, we let them understand, that if their Bashabes would come to us, he should be welcome, but we would not remove to him. Which when they understood (receiving of us bread and fish, and every of them a knife) they departed; for we had then no will to stay them long abord, least they should discover the other Salvages which we had stowed below.

Tuesday, the 11 of June, we passed up into the river with our ship, about six and twenty miles. Of which I had rather not write, then by my relation to detract from the worthinesse thereof. For the River, besides that it is subject by shipping to bring in all traffiques of Marchandise, a benefit alwaies accounted the richest treasury to

any land: for which cause our Thames hath that due denomination, and France by her navigable Rivers receiveth hir greatest wealth; yet this place of itselfe from God and nature affoordeth as much diversitie of good commodities, as any reasonable man can wish, for present habitation and planting.

The first and chiefest thing required, is a bold coast and faire land to fall with; the next, a safe harbour for ships to ride in.

The first is a speciall attribute to this shore, being most free from sands or dangerous rocks in a continuall good depth, with a most excellent land-fall, which is the first Iland we fell with, named by us, Saint Georges Iland. For the second, by judgement of our Captaine, who knoweth most of the coast of England, and most of other Countries, (having beene experienced by imployments in discoveries and travels from his childhood) and by opinion of others of good judgement in our shippe, heere are more good harbours for ships of all burthens, than England can affoord, and far more secure from all winds and weathers than any in England, Scotland, France or Spaine. For besides without the River in the channell, and sounds about the ilands adjoining to the mouth thereof, no better riding can be desired for an infinite number of ships. The River it selfe as it runneth up into the main very nigh forty miles toward the great mountaines, beareth in bredth a mile, sometime three quarters, and halfe a mile is the narrowest, where you shall never have under 4 and 5 fathoms water hard by the shore, but 6, 7, 8, 9, and 10 fathoms all along, and on both sides every halfe mile very gallant Coves, some able to conteine almost a hundred saile, where the ground is excellent soft oaze with a tough clay under for anker hold, and where ships may ly without either Cable or Anker, only mored to the shore with a Hauser.

It floweth by their judgement eighteen or twenty foot at high water.

Heere are made by nature most excellent places, as Docks to grave or Carine ships of all burthens; secured from all windes, which is such a necessary incomparable benefit, that in few places in England, or in any parts of Christendome, art, with great charges, can make the like.

Besides, the bordering land is a most rich neighbour trending all along on both sides, in an equall plaine, neither mountainous nor rocky, but verged with a greene bordure of grasse, doth make tender unto the beholder of hir pleasant fertility, if by clensing away the woods she were converted into meddow.

The wood she beareth is not shrubbish fit only for fewell, but goodly tall Firre, Spruce, Birch, Beech, Oke, which in many places is not so thicke, but may with small labour be made feeding ground, being plentifull like the outward Ilands with fresh water, which streameth doune in many places.

As we passed with a gentle winde up with our ship in this River, any man may conceive with what admiration we all consented in joy. Many of our Company who had beene travellers in sundry countries, and in the most famous Rivers, yet affirmed them not comparable to this they now beheld. Some that were with Sir Walter Ralegh in his voyage to Guiana, in the discovery of the River Orenoque, which echoed fame to the worlds eares, gave reasons why it was not to be compared with this, which wanteth the dangers of many Shoules, and broken ground, wherewith that was incombred. Others before that notable River in the West Indies called Rio Grande; some before the River of Loyer, the River Seine, and of Burdeaux in France, which, although they be great and goodly Rivers, yet it is no detraction from them to be accounted inferiour to this, which not only yeeldeth all the foresaid pleasant profits, but also appeared infallibly to us free from all inconveniences.

I will not prefer it before our river of Thames, because it is Englands richest treasure; but we all did wish those excellent Harbours, good deeps in a continuall convenient breadth and small tide-gates, to be as well therein for our countries good, as we found them here (beyond our hopes) in certaine, for those to whom it shall please God to grant this land for habitation; which if it had, with the other inseparable adherent commodities here to be found; then I would boldly affirme it to be the most rich, beautifull, large and secure harbouring river that the world affoordeth.

Wednesday, the twelfth of June, our Captaine manned his light-horseman with 17 men, and ranne up from the ship riding in the river up to the codde thereof, where we landed, leaving six to keepe the light-horseman till our returne. Ten of us with our shot, and some armed, with a boy to carry powder and match, marched up into the

countrey towards the mountaines, which we descried at our first falling with the land. Unto some of them the river brought us so neere, as we judged our selves when we landed to have beene within a league of them; but we marched up about foure miles in the maine, and passed over three hilles: and because the weather was parching hot, and our men in their armour not able to travel farre and returne that night to our ship, we resolved not to passe any further, being all very weary of so tedious and laboursom a travell.

In this march we passed over very good ground, pleasant and fertile, fit for pasture, for the space of some three miles, having but little wood, and that Oke like stands left in our pastures in England, good and great, fit timber for any use. Some small Birch, Hazle and Brake, which might in small time with few men be cleansed and made good arable land: but as it now is will feed cattell of all kindes with fodder enough for Summer and Winter. The soile is blacke, bearing sundry hearbs, grasse, and strawberries bigger than ours in England. In many places are lowe Thicks like our Copisses of small yoong wood. And surely it did all resemble a stately Parke, wherein appeare some old trees with high withered tops, and other flourishing with living greene boughs. Upon the hilles grow notable high timber trees, masts for ships of 400 tun: and at the bottome of every hill, a little run of fresh water; but the furthest and last we passed, ranne with a great streame able to drive a mill.

We might see in some places where fallow Deere and Hares had beene, and by the rooting of ground we supposed wilde Hogs had ranged there, but we could descrie no beast, because our noise still chased them from us.

We were no sooner come aboord our light-horseman, returning towards our ship, but we espied a Canoa comming from the further part of the Cod of the river Eastward, which hasted to us: wherein, with two others, was he who refused to stay for a pawne: and his comming was very earnestly importing to have one of our men to go lie on shore with their Bashabes (who was there on shore, as they signed) and then the next morning he would come to our ship with many Furres and Tabacco. This we perceived to be only a meere device to get possession of any of our men, to ransome all those which we had taken, which their naturall policy could not so shadow, but we did easily discover and prevent. These meanes were by this Salvage practised, because we had one of his kinsemen prisoner, as we judged by his most kinde usage of him being aboord us together.

Thursday, the 13 of June, by two a clocke in the morning (because our Captaine would take the helpe and advantage of the tide) in the light-horseman with our Company well provided and furnished with armour and shot both to defend and offend; we went from our ship up to that part of the river which trended westward into the maine, to search that: and we carried with us a Crosse, to erect at that point, which (because it was not daylight) we left on the shore untill our returne backe; when we set it up in maner as the former. For this (by the way) we diligently observed, that in no place, either about the Ilands, or up in the maine, or alongst the river, we could discerne any token or signe, that ever any Christian had beene before; of which either by cutting wood, digging for water, or setting up Crosses (a thing never omitted by any Christian travellers) we should have perceived some mention left.

But to returne to our river, further up into which we then rowed by estimation twenty miles, the beauty and goodnesse whereof I can not by relation sufficiently demonstrate. That which I can say in generall is this: What profit or pleasure soever is described and truly verified in the former part of the river, is wholly doubled in this; for the bredth and depth is such, that any ship drawing 17 or 18 foot water, might have passed as farre as we went with our light-horsman, and by all our mens judgement much further, because we left it in so good depth and bredth; which is so much the more to be esteemed of greater woorth, by how much it trendeth further up into the maine: for from the place of our ships riding in the Harbour at the entrance into the Sound, to the furthest part we were in this river, by our estimation was not much lesse than threescore miles.

From ech banke of this river are divers branching streames into the maine, whereby is affoorded an unspeakable profit by the conveniency of transportation from place to place, which in some countries is both chargeable; and not so fit, by cariages on waine, or horse backe.

Heere we saw great store of fish, some great, leaping above water, which we judged to be Salmons. All along is an excellent mould of ground.

The wood in most places, especially on the East side, very thinne, chiefly oke and some small young birch, bordering low upon the river; all fit for medow and pasture ground: and in that space we went, we had on both sides the river many plaine plots of medow, some of three or foure acres, some of eight or nine: so as we judged in the whole to be betweene thirty and forty acres of good grasse, and where the armes run out into the Maine, there likewise went a space on both sides of cleere grasse, how far we know not, in many places we might see paths made to come downe to the watering.

The excellencie of this part of the River, for his good breadth, depth, and fertile bordering ground, did so ravish us all with variety of pleasantnesse, as we could not tell what to commend, but only admired; some compared it to the River Severne, (but in a higher degree) and we all concluded (as I verily thinke we might rightly) that we should never see the like River in every degree equall, untill it pleased God we beheld the same againe. For the farther we went, the more pleasing it was to every man, alluring us still with expectation of better, so as our men, although they had with great labour rowed long and eat nothing (for we carried with us no victuall, but a little cheese and bread) yet they were so refreshed with the pleasant beholding thereof, and so loath to forsake it, as some of them affirmed, they would have continued willingly with that onely fare and labour 2 daies; but the tide not suffering us to make any longer stay (because we were to come backe with the tide) and our Captaine better knowing what was fit then we, and better what they in labour were able to endure, being verie loath to make any desperate hazard, where so little necessitie required, thought it best to make returne, because whither we had discovered was sufficient to conceive that the River ran very far into the land. For we passed six or seven miles, altogether fresh water (whereof we all dranke) forced up by the flowing of the Salt: which after a great while eb, where we left it, by breadth of channell and depth of water was likely to run by estimation of our whole company an unknowen way farther: the search whereof our Captaine hath left till his returne, if it shall so please God to dispose of him and us.

For we having now by the direction of the omnipotent disposer of all good intents (far beyond the period of our hopes) fallen with so bold a coast, found so excellent and secure harbour, for as many ships as any nation professing Christ is able to set forth to Sea, discovered a River, which the Allcreating God, with his most liberall hand, hath made above report notable with his foresaid blessings, bordered with a land, whose pleasant fertility bewraieth it selfe to be the garden of nature, wherein she only intended to delight hir selfe, having hitherto obscured it to any, except to a purblind generation, whose understanding it hath pleased God so to darken, as they can neither discerne, use, or rightly esteeme the unvaluable riches in middest whereof they live sensually content with the barke and outward rinds, as neither knowing the sweetnes of the inward marrow, nor acknowledging the Deity of the Almighty giver: having I say thus far proceeded, and having some of the inhabitant nation (of best understanding we saw among them) who (learning our language) may be able to give us further instruction, concerning all the premised particulars, as also of their governours, and government, situation of townes, and what else shall be convenient, which by no meanes otherwise we could by any observation of our selves learne in a long time: our Captaine now wholy intended his provision for speedy returne. For although the time of yeere and our victuall were not so spent, but we could have made a longer voyage, in searching farther and trading for very good commodities, yet as they might have beene much profitable, so (our company being small) much more prejudiciall to the whole state of our voyage, which we were most regardfull now not to hazard. For we supposing not a little present private profit, but a publique good, and true zeale of promulgating Gods holy Church, by planting Christianity, to be the sole intent of the Honourable setters foorth of this discovery; thought it generally most expedient, by our speedy returne, to give the longer space of time to make provision for so weighty an enterprise.

Friday, the 14 day of June, early by foure a clocke in the morning, with the tide, our two boats, and a little helpe of the winde, we rowed downe to the rivers mouth and there came to an anker about eleven a clocke. Afterward our Captaine in the light horseman searched the sounding all about the mouth and comming to the River, for his certaine instruction of a perfect description.

The next day, being Saturday, we wayed anker, and with a briese from the land, we sailed up to our watering place, and there stopped, went on shore and filled all our empty caske with fresh water.

Our Captaine upon the Rocke in the middest of the harbour observed the height, latitude, and variation exactly upon his instruments.

1. Astrolabe.
2. Semisphere.
3. Ringe instrument.
4. Crosse Staffe.
5. And an excellent compasse made for the variation.

The certainty whereof, together with the particularities of every depth and sounding, as well at our falling with the land, as in the discovery, and at our departure from the coast; I refer to his owne relation in the Map of his Geographicall description, which for the benefit of others he intendeth most exactly to publish.

The temperature of the Climate (albeit a very important matter) I had almost passed without mentioning, because it affoorded to us no great alteration from our disposition in England; somewhat hotter up into the Maine, because it lieth open to the South; the aire so wholesome, as I suppose not any of us found our selves at any time more healthfull, more able to labour, nor with better stomacks to such good fare, as we partly brought, and partly found.

Sunday, the 16 of June, the winde being faire, and because we had set out of England upon a Sunday, made the Ilands upon a Sunday, and as we doubt not (by Gods appointment) happily fell into our harbour upon a Sunday; so now (beseeching him still with like prosperity to blesse our returne into England our country, and from thence with his good will and pleasure to hasten our next arrivall there) we waied Anker and quit the Land upon a Sunday.

Tuesday, the 18 day, being not run above 30 leagues from land, and our Captaine for his certaine knowledge how to fall with the coast, having sounded every watch, and from 40 fathoms had come into good deeping, to 70, and so to an hundred: this day the weather being faire, after the foure a clocke watch, when we supposed not to have found ground so farre from land, and before sounded in about 100 fathoms, we had ground in 24 fathomes. Wherefore our sailes being downe,

Thomas King boatswaine, presently cast out a hooke, and before he judged it at ground, was fished and haled up an exceeding great and well fed Cod: then there were cast out 3 or 4 more, and the fish was so plentifull and so great, as when our Captaine would have set saile, we all desired him to suffer them to take fish a while, because we were so delighted to see them catch so great fish, so fast as the hooke came down: some with playing with the hooke they tooke by the backe, and one of the Mates with two hookes at a lead at five draughts together haled up tenne fishes; all were generally very great, some they measured to be five foot long, and three foot about.

This caused our Captaine not to marvell at the shoulding for he perceived it was a fish banke, which (for our farewell from the land) it pleased God in continuance of his blessings to give us knowledge of: the abundant profit whereof should be alone sufficient cause to draw men againe, if there were no other good both in present certaine, and in hope probable to be discovered. To amplifie this with words, were to adde light to the Sunne: for every one in the shippe could easily account this present commodity; much more those of judgement, which knew what belonged to fishing, would warrant (by the helpe of God) in a short voyage with few good fishers to make a more profitable returne from hence than from Newfoundland: the fish being so much greater, better fed, and abundant with traine; of which some they desired, and did bring into England to bestow among their friends, and to testifie the true report.

After, we kept our course directly for England and with ordinary winds, and sometime calmes, upon Sunday the 14 of July about six a clocke at night, we were come into sounding in our channell, but with darke weather and contrary winds, we were constrained to beat up and downe till Tuesday the 16 of July, when by five a clocke in the morning we made Sylly; from whence, hindered with calmes and small winds, upon Thursday the 18 of July about foure a clocke after noone, we came into Dartmouth: which Haven happily (with Gods gracious assistance) we made our last and first harbour in England.

Further, I have thought fit here to adde some things worthy to be regarded, which we have observed from the Salvages since we tooke them.

First, although at the time when we surprised them, they made their best resistance, not knowing our purpose, nor what we were, nor how we meant to use them; yet after perceiving by their kinde usage we intended them no harme, they have never since seemed discontented with us, but very tractable, loving, and willing by their best meanes to satisfie us in any thing we demand of them, by words or signes for their understanding: neither have they at any time beene at the least discord among themselves; insomuch as we have not seene them angry but merry; and so kinde, as if you give any thing to one of them, he will distribute part to every one of the rest.

We have brought them to understand some English, and we understand much of their language; so as we are able to aske them many things. And this we have observed, that if we shew them anything, and aske them if they have it in their countrey, they will tell you if they have it, and the use of it, the difference from ours in bignesse, colour, or forme; but if they have it not, be it a thing never so precious, they wil denie the knowledge of it.

They have names for many starres, which they will shew in the firmament.

They shew great reverence to their King, and are in great subjection to their Governours: and they will shew a great respect to any we tell them are our Commanders.

They shew the maner how they make bread of their Indian wheat, and how they make butter and cheese of the milke they have of the Rain-Deere and Fallo-Deere, which they have tame as we have Cowes.

They have excellent colours. And having seene our Indico, they make shew of it, or of some other like thing which maketh as good a blew.

One especiall thing is their maner of killing the Whale, which they call Powdawe; and will describe his forme; how he bloweth up the water; and that he is 12 fathoms long; and that they go in company of their King with a multitude of their boats, and strike him with a bone made in fashion of a harping iron fastened to a rope, which they make great and strong of the barke of trees, which they veare out after him; then all their boats come about him, and as he riseth above water, with their arrowes they shoot him to death; when they have killed him and dragged him to shore, they call all their chiefe lords together, and sing a song of joy: and those chiefe lords, whom they call Sagamos, divide the spoile, and give to every man a share, which pieces so distributed they hang up about their houses for provision: and when they boile them, they blow off the fat, and put to their peaze, maiz, and other pulse, which they eat.

A Briefe Note of what Profits we saw the Country yeeld in the small time of our stay there.

Trees

Oke of an excellent graine, strait, and great timber.
Elme.
Beech.
Birch, very tall and great; of whose barke they make their Canoas.
Wich-Hazell.
Hazell
Alder.
Cherry-tree.
Ash.
Maple.
Yew.
Spruce.
Aspe.
Firre.
Many fruit trees, which we knew not.

Fowles

Eagles.
Hernshawes.
Cranes.
Ducks great.
Geese.
Swannes.
Penguins.
Crowes.
Sharks.
Ravens.
Mewes.
Turtle-doves.
Many birds of sundrie colours.
Many other fowls in flocks, unknown.

Beasts

Reine-Deere.
Stagges.
Fallow-Deere.
Beares.
Wolves.
Beaver.
Otter.
Hare.
Cony.
Hedge-Hoggs.
Polcats.

Wilde great Cats.
Dogges; some like Wolves, some like Spaniels.

Fishes

Whales
Seales.
Cod very great.
Haddocke great.
Herring great.
Plaise.
Thornebacke.
Rockefish.
Lobstar great.
Crabs.
Muscles great, with pearles in them.
Cockles.
Wilks.
Cunner-fish.
Lumps.
Whiting.
Soales.
Tortoises.
Oisters.

Fruits, Plants and Herbs

Tobacco, excellent sweet and strong.
Wild-Vines.
Strawberries
Raspberries
Gooseberries   } abundance.
Hurtleberries
Currant trees
Rose-bushes.
Peaze.
Ground-nuts.
Angelica, a most soveraigne herbe.
An hearbe that spreadeth the ground and smelleth like Sweet Marjoram, great plenty.
Very good Dies, which appeare by their painting; which they carrie with them in bladders.

The names of the five Salvages which we brought home into England, which are all yet alive, are these.

1. Tahanedo, a Sagamo or Commander.
2. Amoret
3. Skicowaros } Gentlemen.
4. Maneddo
5. Saffacomoit, a servant.

465. 1605. Extracts from James Rosier's manuscript account of George Waymouth's voyage.

The manuscript of Rosier's account of the 1605 Waymouth voyage came into Hakluyt's hands and from there went to Purchas. What he published was an abbreviated version (how abbreviated we cannot tell) but differing in some particulars from what was printed in 1605, particularly in the clues it provides on the links between Sir Thomas Arundell and the project through the presence of several of his servants on the voyage and the indications of a Catholic colonial objective in the naming of one of the Allen Islands, Insula Sanctae Crucis. It also adds a valuable Abenaki vocabulary.

Samuel Purchas, Pilgrimes, *IV (1625), 1659–1667.*

Extracts of a Virginian Voyage made Anno 1605. by Captaine George Waymouth, in the Archangell. Set forth by the Right Honorable Henry Earle of South-hampton, and the Lord Thomas Arundel, written by James Rosier.

Upon Easter day, the last of March, the winde comming at North North-east: about five of the clocke after noone, we weighed anchor and put to Sea from the Downes, [in the Name of God] being very well victualled, and furnished with Munition and all necessaries; our whole companie being nine and twenty persons, of whom I dare boldly say, few Voyages have beene manned forth with better Sea-men generally, in respect of our small number.

Munday the thirteenth of May, about eleven of the clocke in the fore-noone, our Captaine judging we were not farre from Land, sounded; and we had soft oze in an hundred and sixty fathome: at foure of the clocke after noone wee sounded againe, and had the like oze in an hundred fathome.

From ten a clocke that night till three a clocke in the morning, our Captain tooke in all Sayles and lay at hull, being desirous to fall with the Land in the day time, because it was an unknown Coast, which it pleased God in his mercy to grant us, otherwise surely we had runne our Shippe upon the hidden Rockes, and perished all: for when we set sayle, we sounded in an hundred fathom: and by eight a clocke, having not made above five or six leagues, our Captaine upon a sudden change of water supposing verily he saw the sand: presently sounded, and had but five fathome: much marvelling because we saw no

Land, he sent one to the top, who descried a whitish sandy Cliffe, which bare West Northwest about sixe leagues off: but comming neerer within three or foure leagues, we saw many breaches still neerer the Land. At last we espied a great breach ahead us right along the shoare, into which, before we entred, our Captaine thought best to hoise out his Ship-boat and sound it: which if hee had not done, wee had there ended our Voyage, together with our lives: for he bare up the Ship as neere as he could after the Boate, untill Master Cam his Mate being in the Boat, weffed and called to him to winde about and stand off, for in this breach he had very shoald water, two fathome upon Rockes, and sometime they supposed they saw the Rocke within three or foure foot, whereon the Sea made a very high strong breach, which we might discerne (from the top) to runne along as wee sayled by it, sixe or seven leagues to the Southward: and we saw no end thereof. Wherefore we were constrained to put backe againe from the Land; and sounding (the weather being faire) wee found our selves embayed with continuall Shoalds and Rocks, in a most uncertaine ground[1]; as by judgement of our Captaine and whole companie, they had never knowne the like; from five and sixe fathome, at the next cast of the Lead wee should have fifteene and eighteene fathome all hard Rocke over many which (by the unspeakable goodnesse and mercy of God towards us) wee passed. For if we had bare in with it but the day before (which was exceeding tempestuous) or in the night, we could by no meanes have escaped the danger. But God so blessed us, that we had weather and winde as faire as poore men could wish, in this distresse, whereby we both perfectly discerned every breach, and with the winde were able to turne, where wee saw most hope of safest passage. Thus we parted from the Land, which wee had not so much before desired: and at the first sight rejoyced: as now wee all joyfully praised God, that it had pleased him so miraculously to deliver us from so imminent danger of death before our eyes. Our Captaine found himselfe in the latitude of 41. degrees and an halfe. Here we found great store of fish, and saw many Whales, as we had done two or three dayes before.

Wee stood off that night and all the next day, being Wednesday: but the winde still continuing

---

1. Sidenote: "A dangerous place of rocks and shoalds."

for many dayes betweene the points of South South-west and West South-west, so as we could not by any possible meanes make any way to the Southward in regard of our great want of water and Wood (which was now spent) wee much desired Land, and therefore sought for it, where the winde would best suffer us to refresh our selves.

Thursday the sixteenth day of May, we stood directly in with the Land: and we much marvelled that we descried it not: wherein wee found our Sea Charts very false laying out Land where none was, for though we bare in directly with it according to them: yet in almost fifty leagues running we found none.

Friday the seventeenth of May, about six a clocke at night, wee descried Land, which bare from us North North-east: but because it blew a great gale of winde, the Sea very high and neere night, not fit to come upon an unknowne coast, our Captaine stood off till two of the clocke in the morning being Saturday and Whitson Eve: then standing with it againe, wee descried it by eight a clocke in the morning, bearing North-east from us. It appeared a meane high Land, as we after found it, being but an Iland of no great compasse: but I hope the most fortunate that ever men discovered, as shall appeare by the sequell. About twelve a clocke that day, wee came to an anchor on the North side of this Iland in forty fathome water, about a league from shoare.[2] This Iland is woody, growne over with Firre, Birch, and Beech, as farre as we saw along the shoare, and so likely to be within. On the Verge growe Gooseberries, Strawberries, wilde Pease, and wilde Rose bushes. The fresh water issued down the rocky Cliffes in many places; and much fowle of sundry kindes breed upon the shoare and Rockes. While wee were at shoare, our men aboord with a few hookes got above thirty great Cod and Haddocke, which gave us a taste of the great plenty of fish which we found afterward, wheresoever we went upon the coast.

From hence we might discerne many Ilands, and the maine Land, from the West South-west to the East North-east; and North North-east from us a great way as it then seemed (and as we after found it) up into the Maine, we might discerne very high Mountaines, although the Maine seemed but lowe Land, which gave us a hope, that it might please God, to direct us to the Discovery of some good, although wee were driven by windes farre from that place, whether both by our direction and desire, we ever intended to shape the course of our Voyage.

The next day being Whitsunday,[3] because we rode too much open to the Sea, and windes, wee wayed anchor about twelve a clocke, and came along to the other Ilands more adjoyning to the Maine, and in the Road directly with the Mountaines, about three leagues from the first Iland where we anchored. When we came neere unto them (sounding all along in a good depth) our Captaine manned his Ship-boat, and sent her before with Thomas Cam one of his Mates, whom he knew to be of good experience, to search and sound about and between the Ilands, for a place safe for our ship to ride in. In the meane while we kept aloofe at Sea, having given order to them in the Boat, by a token to weffe in the ship if he found a convenient Harbour, which it pleased God to send us, farre beyond our expectation in a most safe birth, defended from all windes in an excellent depth of water for ships of any burthens in six, seven, eight, nine and ten fathome upon a clay oze, very tough, where is good moring, even on the Rocks upon the Cliffe side.

We all with great admiration praised God, who had from so apparent danger miraculously delivered us, and directed us upon this day (upon which he sent the chiefe promised Director of all goodnesse unto his Apostles and Disciples) into such a place, wherof here before we reade none to have made either description or relation, and then which neither our selves could wish, or Nature affoord more secure. In remembrance whereof, our Captaine named it Pentecost Harbour.

Whitsun Munday the twentieth day of May, by three a clocke in the morning, our Captaine caused the Shalop to be carried ashoare: where while some were busied about her, himselfe set others to worke in digging Wels to receive the water, which we found issuing downe out of the Land in many places, and rising amidst the rocky Cliffes. In digging (amongst other things) we found in some places (and not deepe) clay ground, blue, red and white, to make Bricke or Tile, fit for building. This day our Pinnace was fitted together and lanched; in small time with two or three hookes were fished sufficiently for our whole companie three dayes, with great Cod.

---

2. Sidenote: "Our Captaine named this S. Georges Iland."

3. Sidenote: "Upon Whitsunday wee came into an excellent Harbour."

Hadocke, and some Thornbacke.[4] Towards night we drew with a small Same of 20. fathom just by the shoare, where we got about 30. very good Lobsters, many Rockfish, some Plaise, and other small fishes very good; and fishes called Lumpes, very pleasant to taste. And this wee generally observed, that all the fish of what kind soever we tooke, were well fed, fat, and in tast very sweet.

Wednesday the two and twentieth of May, our Captaine went ashoare with our men, where wee felled and cut wood for our ships use, cleansed and scoured our Wells. Wee likewise digged a small plot of ground, where in among some Garden seeds (which most the birds destroyed) we set Pease and Barley, which in sixteene dayes grew eight inches, and so continued every day growing more than halfe an inch: although this was but the crust of the ground, and farre inferiour to the mould we after found in the Maine.

All the next day we labored hard to make up our wood, because our Captaine intended not to spare, or spend any more time in that of our Voyage. This day our Boat fished againe as before, because wee still were much refreshed with the fresh fish.

Friday the foure and twentieth of May, after we had made an end of cutting wood, and carrying some water aboord our ship. Our Captaine with fourteene shot and Pike marched about, and thorow part of two of the Ilands, one of which we ghessed to be foure or five miles in compasse, and a mile broad.

Along the shoare, and some space within where the wood hindereth not, growe plentifully, Rashberries, Gooseberries, Strawberries, Corant trees, Rose bushes, wilde Vines, Angelica a soveraine herbe, many other fruits wee knew not. All within the Ilands, growe wood of sundry sorts, some very great, and generally all tall: Beech, Birch, Ash, Maple, Spruce, Cherrie tree, Ewe, Oake great and firme, with so fine graine and colour, as our Captaine, and men of best experience, had never seene the like. But the Firre trees great and small are most abundant, which I name last, as not the least of excellent profit: for from it issueth Turpentine in marvellous plenty,[5] and so sweet as our Chirurgeon and others affirmed they never saw so good in England. Wee pulled off much Gumme congealed on the outside of the Barke which gave an odour like Frankincense. This would be a very great benefit for making Tarre and Pitch.

We staied the longer in this place, not onely because of our good Harbour (which is an excellent comfort) but also because every day we found the Iland, more and more to discover unto us his pleasant fruitfulnesse, insomuch, as many of our company wished themselves settled here.

Also our men found abundance of great Mussels among the Rockes; and in some of them many small Pearles. In one Mussell (which we drew up in our Same) was found foureteene Pearles, whereof one was of pretty bignesse and orient, in another above fifty small Pearles; and if one had had a Dragge, no doubt we had found some of great value, seeing these did certainely shew that here they were bred: the shels within all glistering with mother of Pearle.

Thursday the thirtieth of May, the Captaine with thirteene departed in the Shallop, leaving the Ship in a good harbour.

Divers Canoas of Savages came to us. The shape of their body is very proportionable, and well countenanced, not very tall, nor bigge, but in stature like to us; they paint their bodies with blacke, their faces some with red, some with blacke, and some with blew. Their cloathing is Bever skins, and Deere skins, hanging downe to their knees before and behinde, made fast together upon the shoulder with a leather string; some of them weare sleeves, some buskins of leather tewed very thin and soft. Some weare the haire of their skins outward, some inward; they have besides a peece of skin, which they binde about their waste, and betweene their legges to cover their privities. They suffer no haire to grow upon their faces, but upon their head very long and very blacke, which behinde they binde up with a string on a long round knot, some of them have haire all curled naturally. They seemed all very civill and very merry, shewing tokens of much thankfulnesse for those things we gave them; which they expresse in their language by these words, oh, ho, often repeated. We found them then (as after) a people of very good invention, quicke understanding, and ready capacity.

Their Canoas are made of the barke of Beech, strengthned within with ribbes and hoopes of wood, in so good fashion and with such excellent ingenious art, as our men that had beene often in the Indies, said they farre exceeded any that ever

---

4. Sidenote: "Varietie of fishes."
5. Sidenote: "Turpentine plentifull, for Tarre and Pitch."

they had seene.[6] The chiefe of them told me by signes, that they would goe fetch Furres and Skins, and pointed to be with us againe by that time the Sunne should come somewhat beyond the midst of the firmament.

About ten a clocke this day we descried our Pinnace returning towards us. Our Captaine had in this small time discovered up a great River, trending all almost into the Maine. Untill his returne our Captaine left on shoare where they landed, in a path (which seemed to be frequented) a Pipe, a Brooch, and a Knife, thereby to know if the Savages had recourse that way, because they could at that time see none of them, onely a Beast a farre of, which they thought to be a Deere.

The next day being Saturday, and the first of June, wee traded with the Savages all the forenoone upon the Shoare, where were eight and twenty Savages, and because our Ship rode nigh, we were but five or sixe, where for Knives and other trifles, to the value of foure or five shillings, we had forty good Skins, Bevers, Otter, and other which we knew not what to call them. Our trade being ended, many of them came aboord us, and eate by our fire, and would be very merry and bold, in regard of our kinde usage of them. Our Captaine shewed them a strange thing, which they wondered; His Sword and mine having beene touched with the Loadstone, tooke up their Knife and held it fast when they plucked it away[7]: and made their Knife turne being laid on a blocke: and giving their Knife a touch with his Sword, made that take up a Needle, which they much marveiled at. This we did to cause them to imagine some great power in us, and for that to love and feare us.

When we went a Shoare to trade with them in one of their Canoas, I saw their Bowes and Arrowes, which in their sight I tooke up and drew an Arrow in one of them, which I found to be of a reasonable strength, able to carry an Arrow five or six score strongly; and one of them tooke it and drew as we draw our Bowes, not like the Indians. Their Bowe is made of Beech in fashion of our Bowes, but they want nocks, onely a string of leather put through a hole at one end, and made fast with a knot at the other. Their Arrowes are of a much greater size then our and longer, feath-

ered with three feathers tyed on, and nocked very artificially, headed with a long shanke bone of a Deere, made very sharpe, and some Iron heads, with two fangs in manner of a harping Iron. They have likewise Darts headed with sharpe bone, one of which I darted among the Stones and it brake not. These they use very cunningly to kill Fish, Fowle, and Beasts.

They gave us the best welcome they could, spreading Deere skins for us to sit on the ground by their fire, and gave us of their Tobacco in our Pipes, which was most excellent, and so generally commended of us all to be as good as any we ever tooke, being the simple Leafe without any composition, very strong and of a pleasant sweete taste: they gave us some to carry to our Captaine, whom they called our Bashabe, neither did they require any thing for it; but we would receive nothing from them without remuneration.

Here we saw their women, who stood behinde them, as desirous to see us, but not willing to be seene, for before whensoever we came a Shoare, they retired into the woods; whether it were in regard of their owne naturall modesty being naked, or by the commanding jelousie of their husbands, which we rather suspected; for it hath beene an inclination noted always generally in Savages, wherefore we would by no meanes seeme to take any speciall notice of them. They were very well favoured, low of stature, and exceeding fat; they had two little children very fat, and of good countenance, which they love tenderly, all naked, except their legges, which were covered with thin leather buskins, fastned with straps to a Girdle about their waste, which they gird very streight, and is decked round about with little round peeces of Copper. To these we gave Chaines, Bracelets, and other trifles, which the Savages seemed to accept with great kindnesse.

At our comming away, we would have had those two that supped with us to goe aboord and sleepe, as they had promised our Captaine; but it appeared their company would not suffer them, whereat we might easily perceive they were much grieved: but not long after our departure they came with three more to our Ship, signing to us, if one of our Company would goe lye a Shoare with them, they would stay with us. Our Captaine would command none: but Griffin, one of them we were to leave in the Countrey, by their agree-

---

6. Sidenote: "Their Canoas very artificiall."
7. Sidenote: "They woundred at the effect of the Loadstone."

ment with my Lord the Right Honorable Count Arundell (if it should be thought needefull or convenient) went with them in their Canoa; and three of them stayed aboord us.[8] Whom our Captaine and whole Company very kindely used, himselfe saw their lodging provided, and them lodged in an old Saile upon the Orlop, and because they most feared our Dogs, they were tyed up whensoever any of them came aboord us.

Griffin which lay on Shoare, reported unto me their manner, and (as I may tearme them) the Ceremonies of their Idolatry, which they performe thus. One among them (the eldest of the company as he judged) riseth right up, the rest sitting still, and sodainely cryed, Bowh, waugh; then the women fall downe, and lye upon the ground, and the men altogether answering the same, fall a stamping round about with both feete as hard as they can, making the ground shake, with sundry loud outcries, and change of voyce and sound; many take the fire stickes and thrust them into the earth, and then rest silent a while, of a sudden beginning as before, they looke round about, as though they expected the comming of something (as hee verily supposed) and continue stamping till the yonger sort fetch from the Shoare Stones, of which every man take one, and first beate upon them with the fire sticks, then with the Stones beate the ground with all their strength: and in this sort (as he reported) they continued above two houres. In the time of their Pavose, our watch aboord were singing, and they signed to him to doe so, which he did, looking and lifting up his hands to heaven: then they pointed to the Moone, as if they imagined hee worshipped that, which when he with signes denied, they pointed to the Sunne rising, which he likewise disliked, lifting up his hands againe, then they looked about, as though they would see what Starre it might be, laughing one to another. After this ended, they which have wives take them a part, and withdraw themselves severally into the wood all night.[9]

The next morning, as soone as they saw the Sunne rise, they pointed to him to come with them to our Ship, and having received their men from us, they came with all their Canoas and company hovering about our Ship, to whom (because it was

the Sabbath day,) I signed they should depart, and at the next Sunne rising wee would goe along with them to their houses, which they understood (as we thought) and departed: three of their Canoas coursing about the Iland, and the others towards the Maine. This day about five a clocke afternoone, came three other Canoas from the Maine, of which some had beene with us before, and they came directly aboord us, and brought us Tobacco, which we tooke with them in their Pipe, which was made of earth very strong, but blacke and short, containing a great quantity. Some Tobacco they gave to our Captaine, and some to me, in very civill kinde manner: we requited them with Bread and Pease. When we came at Shoare, they all most kindely entertained us, taking us by the hands, as they had observed we did to them aboord in token of welcome, and brought us to sit downe by their fire, where sat together thirteene of them. They filled their Tobacco Pipe, which was then the short claw of a Lobster, which will hold ten of our Pipes full, and we dranke of their excellent Tobacco as much as we would with them; but wee saw not any great quantity to trucke for, and it seemed they had not much left of old, for they spend a great quantity yearely by their continuall drinking: they would signe unto us that it was growne yet but a little above ground, but it would be high, with a leafe as broad as both their hands; and often would (by pointing to one part of the Maine Eastward) signe unto us that the Bashabe (whom wee take to be their King, or some great Commander) had plenty of Furres and much Tobacco.

At our departure they made signe, if any of us would stay there a shoare, some of them would goe lye aboord with us: at which motion Master Booles, servant to the Right Honorable Count Arundell, being desirous to see the manner of the foresaid Ceremonies, staied with them, and had Griffin with him: and three of the Savages lodged with us, in manner as the night before.

Early the next morning being Munday, the third of June, when they had brought our men a boord, they came about our Shippe, earnestly by signes desiring we would goe with them along to the Maine, for there they had Furres and Tobacco to traffique with us. Wherefore our Captaine manned the Shallop, with as many men as he could well, which was but fifteene with the Rowers, and we went along with them: two of their

8. Sidenote: "We brought them home againe."
9. Sidenote: "They lye with their wives secretly."

Canoas they sent away before, and they which were aboord us all night kept company with us to direct us. This we noted as we went along, they in the Canoa with three Oares, would at their will goe a head of us and about us, when we rowed with eight Oares strong: such was the swiftnesse by reason of the lightnesse, and exquisite composition of their Canoa and Oares.

When we came neere the point, where we saw their fires, where they intended to land, and where they imagined some few of us should come on Shoare with our merchandise, as wee had accustomed before: when they had often numbred our men very diligently, they scoured away to their company, not doubting we would have followed them. But when wee perceived this, and knew not either their intents, or number of Savages on the Shoare, our Captain after consultation stood of and weffed them to us, determining that I should goe a Shoare first to take a view of them, and what they had to traffique, if he whom at our first sight of them seemed to be of most respect, and being then in the Canoa, would stay as a pawne for me. When they came to us (notwithstanding all our former courtesies) he utterly refused, but would leave a yong Savage, and for him our Captaine sent Griffin in their Canoa, while we lay hulling a little of. He at his returne reported, they had there assembled together, as he numbred them, two hundred fourescore and three Savages, every one his Bowe and Arrowes, with their Dogges, and Wolves which they keepe tame at command[10]: and not any thing to exchange at all, but would have drawne us farther up into a little narrow nooke of a River, for their Furres as they pretended.

We began to alter our opinion of them, and to joyne them in the ranke of all Savages, who have beene by all travailers and in all discoveries found very treacherous, never attempting mischiefe, untill (by some remisnesse) fit opportunity affordeth them certaine ability to execute the same.[11] Wherefore we humbly gave God thankes, who had given us understanding to prevent this, and thereby warning to foresee and prepare our selves against the like danger. And after good advise taken, our Captaine determined, so soone as we could to Ship some of them, least (being

suspicious we had discovered their plots) they should absent themselves from us, which surely they had done, if we had not laid hold of the next occasion.

Tuesday came to the Ship, there were two Canoas, and in either of them three Savages, of whom two were below at the fire, the other staied about the Ship for victuall: and because we could by no meanes entice them aboord, we gave them a Can of Pease and Bread, which they carried to the shoare to eate, but one of them brought backe our Can againe presently, and staied aboord with the other two, for he being yong of a ready capacitie, and one wee most desired to bring with us into England, had received exceeding kinde usage at our hands, and therefore was much delighted in our company: we shipped him, and foure others, two Canoas, with all their Bowes and Arrowes, which is the chiefe substance they possesse.

Saturday the eight of June, our Captaine being desirous to finish all businesse about this Harbour, very early in the morning with the Pinnace coasted five or six leagues about the Ilands adjoyning, and sounded all along wheresoever he went: he likewise diligently searched and sounded along before the mouth of the Harbour, about the Rocks which shew themselves at all times, and are an excellent breach of the water, so as no Sea can come in to offend the Harbour. This he did to instruct himselfe, and thereby able to direct others that shall happen to come to this place: for every where both neere the Rockes and in all sounding about the Ilands, wee never found lesse water then foure or five fathome, which was very seldome, but seven, eight, nine, and ten fathome, is the continuall sounding by the shoare, in some places much deeper, upon clay Oaze or soft Sand.

This day about one a clocke afternoone, came from the Eastward two Canoas aboord us[12], wherein was he that refused to stay with us for a Pawne, and with him six other Savages, whom we had not seene, who had beautified themselves after their manner very gallantly, though their cloathing was not different from the former, yet they had newly painted their faces very deepe, some all blacke, some red, with stripes of blew over their upper lip, nose, and chin. One of them ware a kinde of Coronet about his head,[13] made very cunningly of a substance like stiffe haire,

10. Sidenote: "283. Savages assembled in a trecherie."
11. Sidenote: "Disposition of Savages in the Virginian Masacre, & other their dealings found too true."

12. Sidenote: "Two Canoas came aboord us from the Bashabe."
13. Sidenote: "Their Ornaments of gallantnesse."

coloured red, broad, and more then a handfull in depth, which he so much esteemed, as he would not for any trucke exchange the same: other weare the white feathered skins of some Fowle round about their head, Jewels in their eares, & Bracelets of little white round bone, fastened together upon a leather string. These made not any shew that they had notice of the other before taken, but we understood them by their speech & signes, that they came sent from the Bashabe, and that his desire was, we would bring up our Ship (which they call a Quiden) to his house, being as they pointed upon the Maine towards the East, from whence they came, and that hee would exchange with us for Furres and Tobacco: but because we had no desire to discover any further that way, and now making what speede we could up the River; wee let them understand, that if their Bashabe would come to us, hee should be very welcome, but wee would not remove to him.

Tuesday, the eleventh of June, we passed up into the River with our Ship about six and twenty miles; of which (were it not of necessitie I must report somewhat) I had much rather not to write, then by my relation to detract from the worthinesse thereof, not being sufficient in words to expresse the abundant utilitie and sweete pleasantnesse it yeeldeth. For the River besides that it is subject hereafter by Shipping to bring in all traffiques of Merchandise.

The first and chiefest thing required for a Plantation, is a bold Coast, and faire Land to fall with. The next, a safe Harbour for Ships to ride in.[14]

The first is a speciall attribute to this Shoare, being most free from Sands or dangerous Rockes, in a continuall good depth, with a most excellent Landfall as can be desired; which is the first Iland, named Saint Georges Iland.[15] For the second, by judgement of our Captaine, who knoweth most of the Coast of England, and most of other Countries (having beene experienced by impliments in discoveries and travailes from his childehood) and by opinion of others of good judgement in our Ship. Here are more good Harbours for Ships of all burthens, then all England can afoord: And farre more secure from all windes and weathers, then any in England, Scotland, Ireland, France, Spaine, or any other part hitherto discovered, whereof we have received any relation: for (be-

sides without the River in the channell and Sounds about the Ilands adjoyning to the Mouth thereof, no better riding can be desired for an infinite number of ships) the River it selfe, as it runneth up into the Maine very nigh fortie miles towards the great Mountaines, beareth in breadth a mile, sometimes three quarters, and halfe a mile is the narrowest, where you shall never have under foure or five fathom water hard by the Shoare, but six, seven, eight, nine, and ten fathom at a low water. And on both sides, every halfe mile, verie gallant Coves, some able to containe almost a hundred Sayle, where the ground is excellent soft oaze with a tough clay under for Anker hold; and where Ships may lye without either Anker or Cable onely mored to the Shoare with a Hazur. It floweth, by their judgement, sixteene or eighteene foote at a high water. Here are made by nature most excellent places, as Dockes to grave and Carine Ships of all burthens, secured from all windes, which is such a necessary incomparable benefit, that in few places in England, or in any other parts of Christendome, Art with great charges can make the like.

It yeeldeth plentie of Salmons, and other fishes of great bignesse, and assuredly great probabilitie of better things therin to be found, seeing about the Ilands wee had such certaine hope of Pearle and Oare. Besides all these commodities innative to this River, the bordering Land is a most rich neighbour trending all along on both sides, in an equall Plaine, neither Mountainous nor Rockie, but verged with a greene bordure of grasse, doth make tender unto the beholder of her pleasant fertility, if by clensing away the woods, shee were converted into Medow. The Wood it beareth is no shrubbish, fit onely for fewell, but good tall Firre, Spruce, Birds, Beech, and Oake, which in many places is not so thicke, but may with small labour be made feeding ground, being plentifull like the outward Ilands with fresh water, which streameth downe in many places.

As we passed with a gentle winde up with our Ship in this River, any man may conceive with what admiration wee all consented in joy; many who had beene travellers in sundry Countries, and in the most famous Rivers, yet affirmed them not comparable to this they now beheld. Some that were with Sir Walter Raleigh, in his Voyage to Guiana, in the Discovery of the River Orienoque, which ecceed fame to the worlds

14. Sidenote: "The profits of the River."
15. Sidenote: "Saint Georges Iland the Land fall."

eares;[16] gave reasons why it was not to be compared with this, which wanteth the dangers of many Shoalds and broken grounds, wherewith that was encombred. Others preferred it farre before that notable River in the West Indias, called Rio Grande:[17] some before the Rivers of Burduna, Orleance, and Brest in France, Naunce, and the River of Rhoane: which although they be great and goodly Rivers, yet it is no detraction from them to be accounted inferiour to this, which not onely yeeldeth all the aforesaid pleasant profits, but also appeared infallibly to us free from all imagined inconveniences. I will not preferre it before our River of Thames, because it is Natale solum,[18] Englands richest treasure, but wee all did wish those excellent Harbours, good Deepes, in a continuall convenient breadth, and small tide gates, to be as well therein for our Countrie good, as wee found them here (beyond our hopes) in certaine for those to whom it shall please God to grant this Land for habitation: which if it had with the other inseperable adherent Commodities here to be found; then I would boldly affirme it to be the most rich, beautifull, large, and secure harbouring River that the world affordeth; for if man should wish, or Art invent, a River subject to all conveniencies, and free from all dangers, here they may take a view in a Plat-forme framed by Nature, who in her perfection farre exceedeth all Arts invention.

Wednesday the twelfth of June, our Captaine manned his Shallop with seventeene men, and ran up to the Codde of the River, where we landed, leaving six to keepe the Shallop till our returne. Ten of us with our Shot, and some armed, with a Boy to carry Powder and Match, marched up into the Countrie towards the Mountaines, which we descried at our first falling with the Land, and were continually in our view. Unto some of them the river brought us so neere, as we judged our selves when we landed, to have beene within a league of them, but we found them not, having marched well nigh foure miles up in the Maine, and passed three great hils; wherefore because the weather was parching hot, and our men in their Armour not able to travell farre and returne to our Pinnasse that night, we resolved not to passe any further, being all very weary of so tedious and laboursome a travell.

In this march we passed over very good ground, pleasant and fertile, fit for pasture, having but little wood, and that Oake, like stands left in our Pastures in England, good and great fit timber for any use; some small Birch, Hazell and Brake, which might in small time be clensed with few men, and made good errable Land; but as it is now will feede Cattell of all kindes with Fodder enough for Summer and Winter. The soyle is good, bearing sundry Hearbes, Grasse, and Strawberries, in many places are low thickets, like our Copisses of small Wood: And it doth all resemble a stately Parke, wherein appeare some old trees with high withered tops, and other flourishing with living greene boughes: till we came to the Hils upon which doe grow exceeding tall, streight, and excellent great timber of sundry kindes, mast for Ships of foure hundred tunnes, and at the bottome of every hill, a little run of fresh water; but the furthest and last we came unto ran with a great streame able to drive a small Mill. Wee might see in some places, where Deere and Hares had beene; and by the rooting of ground we supposed wilde Hogs had ranged there, but we could descry no Beast, because our noise still chased them from us.

We were no sooner come aboord our Pinnasse, returning towards our Ship, but wee espied a Canoa comming from the further part of the Cod of the River Eastward, which hasted to us; wherein with two others was he whom we accounted chiefe of his Company: and his comming was very earnestly importuning to have one of our men to goe lye with their Bashabe or Captaine (as they now tearmed him) who was there ashoare (as they signed) and then the next morning he would come to our Ship with Furres and Tobacco. This we perceived to be onely a meere device to get possession of any of our men, to ransome all those we had taken[19]; which their naturall pollicy could not so shaddow, but we did easily discover and prevent.

These meanes were by this Savage practised, because we had one of his kinsmen prisoner, as we judged by his most kinde usage of him, being aboord us together.

Thursday, the thirteenth of June, by two a

16. Sidenote: "This River preferred before Oriensoque."
17. Sidenote: "Before the River Rio Grande."
18. Sidenote: *Nescio qua Natale solum &c.*

19. Sidenote: "A plot of the Savages."

clocke in the morning (because our Captain would take the helpe and advantage of the Tide) in the Pinnace with our Company well provided and furnished with Armour and Shot both to defend and offend: we went from our Ship up to that part of the River which trended West into the Maine, to search that[20], and wee carried with us a Crosse to erect at that point; which, because it was not day-light, we left on shoare untill our returne backe, when we set it up in manner as the former. And this we diligently observed, that in no place either about the Ilands, or up in the Maine, or along the River, wee could discerne any token or signe that ever any Christian had beene before; which either by cutting wood, digging for water, or setting up Crosses (a thing never omitted by any Christian travailours) wee should have perceived some mention left.

But to returne to our River, up into which we then rowed by estimation twenty miles. What profit or pleasure is described and truely verified in the former part of the River, is wholly doubled in this; for the breadth and depth is such, that any Ship drawing seventeene or eighteene foote water might have passed as farre as we went with our Shallop, and by all our judgements much further, because we left it in so good depth; which is so much the more to be esteemed of greater worth, by how much it trendeth further up into the Maine: for from the place of our Ships riding in the Harbour, at the entrance into the Sound, to the furthest point wee were in this River, by our estimation was not much lesse then threescore miles. From each Banke of this River, are divers branching streames running into the Maine, whereby is afforded an unspeakeable profit, by the conveniency of easie transportation from place to place, which in some Countries is both very chargeable, and not so fit, by Carriages on Wane or Horsebacke. Here wee saw store of Fish, some leaping above water, which we judged to be Salmon, for they were great. All along is an excellent mould of ground, the wood in most places, especially on the Easterne side, very thin, chiefely Oake and small Birch, bordering low upon the River, all fit for Meddow and pleasant Pasture ground. And in that space wee went, wee had on both sides the River many plaine places of cleere Meddow, some of three or foure acres, some eight or nine, so as we judged in the whole to be betweene thirty and forty acres of good grasse, and where the Armes runne into the Maine, there likewise went a space on both sides of the cleare grasse, how farre we knew not. In many places we might see pathes Beasts had made to come downe to watering. And we all concluded (as I verily thinke we might rightly) that we should never see the like River in every degree equall, untill it pleased God we beheld the same againe: for the further we went, the more pleasing it was to every man, alluring us still with expectation of better; so as our men (although they had with great labour rowed long; and eate nothing) for we carried with us no victuall but a little Cheese and Bread, yet they were so refreshed with the pleasant beholding thereof, and so loath to forsake it, as some of them affirmed, they would have continued willingly with that onely fare and labour two dayes; but the Tide not suffering us to make any longer stay (because we were to come backe with the ebbe) and our Captaine better knowing what was fit, then we; and better what they in labour were able to endure, being very loath to make any desperate hazard, where so little necessitie required, thought it best to make returne, because whether we had discovered, was sufficient to conceive that the River ranne very farre into the Land: for we passed sixe or seven miles altogether fresh water (whereof we all dranke) forced up by the flowing of the Salt, which after a great while ebbe where we left it, by bredth and depth of Channell was likely to runne by estimation of our whole companie an unknowne way further. And as our Captaine verily thought (although hee then concealed it) might possibly make a passage into (or very nigh) the South Sea: which hee neither had commission nor time now to search, but hath left that till his next returne: if it shall so please God to dispose of him and us.

Friday the fourteenth of June early, by foure a clocke in the morning with the Tide, our two Boats, and a little helpe of the winde, we warped our shippe downe to the Rivers mouth: and there came to an anchor about eleven a clocke. Afterward our Captaine in the Pinnace, searched the sounding all about the mouth and comming into the River, for his certaine instruction of a perfect description.

The next day being Saturday, we weighed an-

20. Sidenote: "We searched the Westerne part of the River. We set up another Crosse."

chor, and with a briefe from the Land, we sayled up to our watering place, and there stopped, went ashoare, and filled all our empty caske with fresh water[21].

Our Captaine upon the Rocke in the middest of the Harbour made his certaine observation by the Sunne, of the height, latitude, and variation exactly upon all his Instruments: 1. Astrolabe. 2. Semisphere. 3. Ring-instrument. 4. Crosse staffe. 5. And an excellent Compas, made for the variation. The latitude he found to be 43. degrees 20. minutes, North. The variation, 11. degrees 15. minutes, viz. one point of the Compas Westward. And it is so much in England at Lime-house by London, Eastward. The temperature affoorded to us no speciall alteration from our disposition in England: somewhat hotter up into the Maine, because it lieth open to the South, but scarse yeelding a sensible difference to any of us. The aire so wholsome, as I suppose, not any of us found our selves at any time more healthfull, more able to labour, nor with better stomachs to such good fare, as we partly brought, and partly found.

Sunday the sixteenth of June, the winde being faire, and because wee had set out of England upon a Sunday, descried the Ilands upon a Sunday, and (as we doubted not) by Gods appointment, happily fallen into our Harbour upon a Sunday: so now beseeching him with like prosperitie to blesse our returne into England: and from thence (with his good-will and pleasure) to hasten and fortunate our next arrivall here. Wee set sayle and quit the Land upon a Sunday.

Tuesday the eighteenth day of June, being not runne above five and thirty leagues from Land, and our Captaine for his certaine knowledge how to fall with the Coast, having sounded every watch, and from fifty fathom had come in good deeping to seventy, and so to an hundred. This day, the weather being faire, after the foure a clocke watch, when he thought not to have found ground, before sounding in above a hundred fathom, we had ground in foure and twenty fathom. Wherefore our Sayles being downe, one of our men presently cast out a hooke, and before hee judged it at ground was fished and haled up an exceeding great and well fed Cod: then there

were cast out three or foure hookes more, the fish was so plentifull and so great, as when our Captaine would have set sayle, we desired him to suffer them to take fish a while, because wee were so delighted to see them catch fish so great, so fast as the hooke came downe, some playing with the hooke they tooke by the backe.[22] And one of the Mates, with two hookes at a Lead, at five draughts together haled up ten fishes all were generally very great, some were measured. This caused our Captaine not to marvell at the shoalding: for he perceived it was a fish-banke, which (for our farewell from the Land) it pleased God in the continuance of his blessings to give us knowledge of.

Sunday the fourteenth of July about six a clocke at night we were come into sounding in our Channell: but for want of sight of the Sunne and Starre, to make a true observation: and with contrary windes we were constrained to beate up and downe till Tuesday the sixteenth of July, when by five a clocke in the morning wee made Sylly: from whence hindred with calmes and small windes. Upon Thursday the eighteenth of July about foure a clocke wee came to anchor safely in Dartmouth, which Haven haply (with Gods assistance) wee made the last and first Harbour in England, as the Termini of our Voyage.

A briefe Note of what profits we found the Countrie yeeld: in the small time of our stay there.

Trees. Oake, of an excellent graine, straight, and great timber; Elme, Beech, Birch, very tall and great, of whose Barque they make their Canoas; Nut-hasle, Hasle, Alder, Cherry tree, Ash, Maple, Ewe, Spruce, Asp, Fir in great abundance; many other fruit trees which we know not.

Fowles. Eagles, Hernshawes, Cranes, Duks great; Geese, Swans, Penguins, Shark, Crow, Raven, Kite, Soga, Mewes, Doves, Turtles, birds of sundry colours; and many other fowles unknown.

Beasts. Deere red and fallow, Beare, Wolfe, Beaver, Otter, Hare, Conie, Marterns, Sables, Hogs, Porkespines, Polcats, Cats, wilde great, Dogs some like Foxes, some like our other beasts the Savages signe unto us with hornes and broad eares; which we take to be Olkes or Loshes.

---

21. Sidenote: "The Iland where we watered is named Insula Sanctae Crucis, because there wee set our first Crosse." And "Our Captaine made his perfect observation on the Rocke."

22. Sidenote: "A fishy banke."

Fishes. Whales, Porpoise, Seales, Cod, very great; Haddocke, great; Herring, Plaise, Thornbacke, Rockfish, Lobster, great; Crabbe, Mussels, Cockles, Wilks, Cunner-fish, Lumpe-fish, Whiting: the Savages signe unto us that they have Tortoise very great.

Plants, Fruits, Herbs. Tobacco, excellent, sweet and strong; Vine, wilde; Strawberries, Raspberries, Gooseberries, Hurtleberries, Cor-ant trees, in abundance; Rose bushes; Pease, which the Savages signe to be very great in the Maine; Ground-nuts; Angelica, a most soveraigne herbe; and an herbe that spreadeth like Camomell, and smelleth like sweet Marjoram, great plenty. Good Dies, which appeare by their painting, which they carrie with them in blad-ders.

Words which I learned of the Savages, in their Language.

Sunne or Moone, Kesus. Cod-fish, Biskeiore. A fish with hornes, Manedo. Lobster, Shoggah. Rock-fish, Shagatocke. Cockle-fish, Hesucke. Muskell, Shoorocke. Cunner-fish, Tattaucke. Crabbe, Wussorasha. Porpoise, Muscopeiuck. Plaise, Anego. Tortoise, Romcaneeke. Pease, Ushcomono. Tobacco, Tomoch. A leafe, Mebeere. A weed, Cashterush. A Firre tree, Seteock. A stone, Nabscurr. A Bowe, Shoanor. An Arrow, Tobood. Barke of a tree, Mashquere. Water, Shamogoon. Sand, Cheemuck. Crowe, Cagagoose. Haire, Messer or Meris. A beard, Nicowur. A Beare, Rogsoo. Beaver, Paneah. Ot-ter, Nymemano. Rat, Sanuke. Polcat, Pocamka. Cat, Pushuck. Fallow Deere, Coribo. Hogge, Madoso. Red Deere, Moosurr. They tell us of other beasts, which they call, Tasquus, Pisho, Narsim. Teeth, Ibider. A hand and finger, Breeche. A Naile of the hand, Cushe. A legge, Codd. A foot, Musseete. Plum-tree, Epsegan. Strawberry, Pishoa. Gooseberry, Shewanor. Cherry tree, Espegononino. Corant tree, Asheemena. Rashberrie, Kiskeemy. A lippe, Me-toan. Fire, Squida. The maine Land, Be-moquiducke. Sea, Shoubbe. Father, Wado. Sonne, Usto. Wane of the Sea, Tobodgg. Pitch and Tallow, Poco. Wilde Rose, Minusheck. Birch, Pasquar. Sword, Edagawancke. Mountaine, Machoucke. Winde, Puckchawsen. Bloud, Pagâgocun. Red Paint, Woroman. Blacke Paint, Cogosho. A Dogge, Remoose. A Ship or Boat, Quiden. An Oare, Wuttohoganor. A Garnepo Fly,

Chussuah. Bread, Paune. Raine, Soogoran. A nose, Peech-ten. An Axe or Hatchet, To-maheegon. A Knife, Quodogon. Oake, As-kabesse. White Bone, whereof they have Chaines, Girdles, Bracelets, Speesone. The Cheeke, Canoah. A Shirt or Coat, Tenoganuke. The Chinne, Queh. An Eye, Sheesuck. Eylid, Momon. Forehead, Scottoquah. An Eare, Faw-wucke. A fish-hooke, Makeecon. A Rainbow, Shomogon.

The Names of their chiefe Governours, whom they call Sagomoh. 1. Bashabez. 2. Abatuck-quishe. 3. Bdahanedo, one of them we have. 4. Abokeesussick. 5. Shurokinit. 6. Psaheno. 7. Mentoelmet. 8. Ageemohuck. 9. Mawer-met. 10. Chanacoboin. 11. Amilquin. 12. Muasacoromoneete. These dwell upon the Maine, and weare an ornament of white bone upon their head; and Chaines, and Bracelets, and Girdles, and have their skinne garments laced with them.

The Names of our Virginians. Bdahanedo, Brother to the Bashabes. Amooret, his Brother. Satacomoah. Maneduck. Scikaworrowse.

466. October 30, 1605. Agreement for a Vir-ginia voyage between George Waymouth and Sir John Zouche.

After Waymouth returned from his discovery of Mawooshen (the area around and to the south of Penobscot Bay), he found that Lord Arundell of Wardour was no longer interested in bringing Catholics to America, but had involved himself in the creation of an English Catholic regiment in the service of the Archdukes in the Spanish Netherlands. Instead, he found backing from Sir John Zouche of Codnor in Derbyshire, a member of the collateral branch of the family of Lord Zouche, who also concerned himself with the venture, while the publication of James Rosier's A true relation *(464) was expected to bring in other supporters. Sir John Zouche promised to as-sociate himself with the merchant group at Plymouth, which Waymouth already repre-sented. What appears to have happened was that the Plymouth group was gradually diverted by Sir John Popham into taking part, as a separate division, in a chartered company responsible for Virginia as a whole (created in April, 1606 as the*

Virginia Company). Waymouth may then have turned for mercantile support to the London group headed by Lewes Owen, William Angell, and others who set out the Triall *for Virginia by an agreement in March, 1606, though their venture failed (471–472). Sir John Zouche was to have two ships and 200 men ready by April 30, 1606, and may have had them about that time. He was held back, perhaps, by doubt whether he was infringing on the Virginia Company charter, or, perhaps, because in June fresh plans for bringing Catholics to some part of Virginia were again being discussed (467–468). Zouche finally got his passport on August 14 (469–470), but by that time his shipping and men may have dispersed since he disappears from the scene. The Zouche project and the* Triall *episode are the only activities, with official sanction outside the dual Virginia Company, in North America south of 45° N. before 1620.*

Formerly P.R.O., Gifts and Deposits, Manchester Papers, P.R.O. 30/15, 2, 203; now Manchester Papers, Alderman Library, University of Virginia, Charlottesville. Printed in Alexander Brown, The Genesis of the United States, *2 vols. (Boston, 1890), I, 32–35.*

Articles of Agreement Indented made and agreed upon the Thirtiethe daie of October In the yeeres of the Reigne of our Sovereigne Lord James by the grace of God kinge of England Scotland Fraunce and Ireland defender of the faith &c. That is to saie of England Fraunce and Ireland the third and of Scotland the Nyne and thirtieth Betweene the Righte worshipfull Sir John Zouche of Codnor in the County of Darby knight on the one parte, and Captayne George Waynmouth [*sic*] of Cockington in the County of Devon gentleman on the other parte For and Concerninge a voiage, intended to be made unto the land commonly called by the name of Virginia upon the Continent of America.

Firste on the parte and behalfe of the said Sir John Zouche. It is Covenaunted and agreed, That he shall at his owne proper Costes and Charges, sett forth two shipps fitted, prepared and furnished with all necessaries of victuall provision munition, and two hundreth able and sufficient men, that is to saie of such trades and artes as are fittinge for a plantation and Colonie, before the last daie of Aprill nexte cominge after the date

hereof. Item it is covenaunted and agreed that he, the said Sir John, shall in present paymente give and deliver unto the said Captayne George Waymouthe the somme of one hundreth poundes of lawfull English money within twenty one dayes next after the date of theis presentes in Consideration of his travell and paynes to be taken in and about the saide voyage and for his owne Charge defrayringe. Item that whereas the said Captayne George Waymouth hath heretofore ingaged himself by band and Covenauntes, made betweene him and William Parker, Thomas Love, [Thomas?] Came, and William Morgan of Plymouth marchauntes to carry them with their shippinge and provision (accordinge to the Tenour of such Covenauntes of Agreementes as are made between him and them) to the saide lande of Virginia, there to fishe, traffick and to doe what els shalbe fittinge for a Marchantes voyage. He, the said Sir John Zouche, shall suffer and by all meanes permitt the said Merchauntes to make their trade for what Commodities soever without anie hindraunce or disturbance of his parte or any of his followers under his Commaund for the space of one wholle yeere nowe next Comminge, and not after. Item it is Covenaunted and agreed that he, the said Sir John Zouche, beinge Cheife Commaunder shall allowe and give unto the said Captaine George Waymouth the next place of Commaunde unto himselfe aswell at sea as at land. Item, if it soe please God to prosper and blisse the said intended voiage and the actions of the same, that thereby the lande aforesaid shalbe inhabited with our English Nation and according to polliticque estate of Goverment proportion of lande be allotted to such as shalbe transported thither to inhabit That then after the said Sir John shall have made his choise and assumed unto his possession in manner of Inheritaunce such quantitie of lande as the said Sir John shall thinck good Then he the said Captayne George Waymouth and his Assignes shall and maie make his or their next choise of lande for his or their possession and plantacion. To holde the same in tenure of him the said Sir John as Lorde Paramount which said lande soe by the said Captayne George Waynmouth to be chosen shall discend to his heires or assignes, or shalbe upon reasonable Consideracions to his or their uses imployed or disposed. And in like manner on the behalfe of the said Captayne George Waymouth it is agreed that he shall with his best indeavours

Councell and advise, be helpinge aydinge and assistinge to the said Sir John for the furnishinge and settinge forth of the said voyage. Item that hee the said Captaine George Waymouth shalbe readye to goe with him the said Sir John in the said voiage at such tyme as is lymitted or before, if conveniency shall require and all thinges necessary fitted in readines, unlesse he shalbe by sicknes or other such visitation hindred And that when they shalbe arrived uppon the land aforesaid, he shall with his best arte furtheraunce and indeavour, be assistinge to the said Sir John for his plantation and fortification, and what els shalbe thought fittinge and necessary *by the said Sir John.*[1] And that the said Captayne George Waymouth shall not be aydinge and assistinge by person or direction to any other in or for the said pretended lande or voiage without the Consent or allowance of the said Sir John.

In Witness whereof the parties abovenamed to theis present Articles Indented interchangeably have sett their handes and seales the daye and yeare first above wrytten.

John Zouche

Memorandum. Theise words by the said Sir John Zouche were interlyned before the Sealynge.

Sealed and delivered in the presence of
William Rigges, Robert Frayt, James Rosier, Jnno [John] Sanger

467. June 19, 1606. William Udall to the Earl of Salisbury.

Hatfield House, Cecil Papers 192/96 (Historical Manuscripts Commission, Calendar of Cecil MSS, XVIII, 13), extract.

At this tyme I am to acquaynt your Honor, before Hand with ij offers to be presented to his majestie by the secular priests and Lay Catholics. The first is contanyed in the enclosed paper [not present], which is intended (as they protest) not in that they thinke the Can prevayle therein but to make known Howe fre themselves are, and that the world may knowe that this Late treason [the

1. These four words are those mentioned in the "Memorandum" below Zouche's signature.

Gunpowder Plot] was done by a Generall Consent of the Jesuits otherwise they would before this tyme have procured some Censure from the pope which the Archpriest promised in his lettres Divulged within thre dayes after discovery of the Late treason. Besides that by this offer they entend the utter banishment of Jesuits and Archpriest whom they Hate.

The other offer, by way of Suite is That his Majestye may be pleased to Graunt Licence to three Hundred Catholic Housholds at theyre owne cost & Charges, to depart this Land to inHabit Virginia to hold such part as shalbe allotted to them, for his Majestie and his Successors, with and uppon such Conditions as his Majestye with the Advice of his Counsell shall sett downe, so that they be not agaynst theyre Consciences, with this proviso that no one Houshold shalbe admitted into that viage which is Convicted and might thereby Hinder any Commoditye due to his Majestye.... This 19 of June.

Your Honors most Devoted
William Udall

468. June 28, 1606. William Udall to the Earl of Salisbury.

Hatfield House, Cecil Papers 116/123 (Calendar of Cecil MSS, XVIII, 181–182), extracts.

My Singular Good Lord in my Last lettres I delivered to your Honor certayne propositions which being with such particularityes uppon which your Honor might be pleased to give further direction at this time....

The offer which the priestes and Lay Catholics made in the paper which I enclosed to your Honor was and is to be presented to his Majestye by Master Jhon Digby One of his Majestyes Carvers. That businesse is negotiated by his uncle [Sir Edward Digby?] who wrate that which I sent to your Honor. Yonge Digbyes place person and disposition is much applauded by some discontented Humores til I Heere more Certaynlye I will passe this observation but easyle.... This 28 of June.

Your Honors most Devoted
William Udall

PERMISSION TO SIR JOHN ZOUCHE
TO MAKE A VOYAGE TO VIRGINIA,
AUGUST 13–14, 1606

SIR JOHN ZOUCHE'S plan to make a Virginia voyage in March, 1606 was not prevented by the issue of the Virginia Company charter in April, but it was delayed by it. The whole question of permitting an expedition in which Catholics would take part (even though Zouche was not one) was a sensitive one after November 5, 1605. Consequently, permission was withheld so long that he was not able to make use of it—or at least we do not know that his vessels sailed.

See the letter printed by J. F. Jameson, "Notes and Queries," *Virginia Magazine*, XIX (1911), 195–196 (from what was then P.R.O., HCA, Miscellaneous 1140) (469): there is a copy of a draft of the Bond and Obligation in HCA 14/39, 239, the following document 470.

469. August 13, 1606. Charles Howard, Earl of Nottingham, to Sir Thomas Crompton.

Sir John Zouche his companye and shipps bound for Virginea with the band taken here inclosed.

Sir,

I have bene much laboured to geve Sir John Zouch leave to passe away with his shippes in his intended voyage for Virginea, whome for some private reasons knowne to myself I have thought good to staye. And now being sattisfied in some things whereof I stood before jelous, I am content to geve him power to passe, so that my Lord Zouch will become bound in a bond of a thousand pounds, uppon this condicion that Sir John Zouch shall not in the whole discourse of his voiage comitt any act ether prejudicial to the State of England or dishonorable to the peace and amitie which His Majestie hath now with forrain Princes: Thus having delivered unto you my pleasure herein I pray you to hasten his dispatching according to these direccions. And so I rest your very loving frend,

NOTTINGHAM.

at Grenewich
this 13th. of Aug., 1606.

[Addressed:] To my very loving friend Sir Thomas Crompton Knight, Judge of the Admiralty.

[Endorsed:] My Lord Admirall for takinge band of my Lord Zouche for the good behaviour of

470. August 14, 1606. Bond and Obligation by Lord Zouche in £1000 for the good behavior of Sir John Zouche in his voyage to Virginia.

Noverint universi per presentes me Edwardum dominum Zouch de Harningworth in comitatu Northampton teneri et firmiter obligari illustri ac prenobili viro Carolo comiti Notingham domino Magno Admirallo Anglie in mille libris monete Anglie Solvendis eiden domino Magno Admirallo aut suo certo atturnato heredibus vel successoribus suis ad quam quidem solutionem bene et fideliter faciendam obligo me heredesque et executores meos firmiter per presentes sigillo meo sigilatos Datum decimo quarto die mensis Augusti anno domini 1606 regnique serenissimi domini nostri Jacobi Dei gratia Anglie Scotie Francie et Hibernie Regis videlicet Anglie Frauncie et Hibernie quarto et Scotie quadragesimo.

E. ZOUCH.

The Condition of this obligation is suche That whereas Sir John Zouche knight is licensed to passe uppon an intended voyadge for Virginea with two shippes and a Pinnace and their Captaynes, Masters and Companyes Yf therefore the said Sir John Zouche and company or any of them shall not duringe the said voyadge Comitt any act eyther prejudiciall to the state of England or dishonorable to the peace and amytye which his Majestie nowe hath with forraine princes in any sort or condition That then this present Obligation to be voyde and of none effect or els to stand and remayne in full force strengthe and vertue.

Sigillatum et deliberatum
in presentia William Hereward
Hugh Pryce.

Chapter Sixty-four
The Voyage of the *Triall* from March,
1606 to September, 1607

THE STORY of the arrangement between a group of London merchants, certain of them members of the Fishmongers' Company of London, to send a ship to Virginia (evidently to North Virginia, approximately to where Waymouth had been in 1605) is obscure. It might appear that this was to parallel and be associated with the venture placed under Sir John Zouche (470). Arthur Chambers contracted by charter party to take the ship *Triall* to Virginia in March, 1606 and to return it to the Thames in December of the same year. Later the owners arranged that *Triall* would act in consort with ships preparing in Ireland to go to Virginia, and that Sir Ralph Bingley, who was already there, should become commander of the expedition. Bingley and Chambers received passports for Virginia on May 28. The voyage did not begin until June 1, 1606 and was wholly mismanaged, Chambers taking until late July to reach Dublin. Then, under Bingley's orders, he attempted to bring her round to the south coast but she was partly dismasted in a storm, put in at Waterford and so lost all hope of making an American voyage. Repaired, she reached Kinsale toward the end of the year, where Bingley took command. After stealing a pinnace at Cork, *Triall* got to sea and made a voyage off the Spanish coast, causing, it was alleged, damage and loss to Spanish and other ships, although Bingley denied it, and claimed he was only prevented from going to Virginia by a storm. By November, 1606 *Triall's* owners had already issued a writ for the arrest of both Bingley and Chambers but could not catch up with either of them. By June, 1607 Bingley's episode was denounced in the House of Commons as imperilling the safety of the Virginia enterprise (484). By September Chambers was in custody and was being charged with breaking his contract (among other things), and in September we get the evidence of Roger Bamford against him. Bingley got off scot free and in April, 1608 made lame excuses to Lord Salisbury (472), which were apparently accepted. The movement toward Virginia in 1606 was clearly a complex one and involved pirates and unreliable agents, as well as competent and reliable commanders like Christopher Newport. See D. B. Quinn, "The voyage of *Triall*, 1606–1607," *American Neptune*, XXXI (1971), 85–103.

471. September, 1607. Case in the High Court of Admiralty against Arthur Chambers for his dealings with the *Triall*.

The core of the action, brought by the owners of the Triall *for breach of contract and damages against*

Arthur Chambers, master of the Triall, *is found in the Interrogatories and the Deposition of Roger Bamford, which are given in question and answer form.*

P.R.O. HCA 24/72, 97 (Interrogatories); HCA 13/9, September 3, 1607 (Deposition of Roger Bamford), combined.

Articles ministred in his Majestes high Court of the Admiralty in the behaulf of Lewes Owne & William Lancaster Esquires William Angell and John Halsey of London Fishemongers late owners of the *Triall of London* against Arthure Chambers late Master of the same

1. In primis whether doe you knowe that in the monethes of May June July August September October November December January February & March in the yeare of our Lord god 1606 the said Lewes Owne William Lancastre William Angell & John Halsey were lawfull owners possessors & proprietors of the good shipp called the *Triall of London* of the burthen of one hundreth and sixty tones or thereaboutes, this so knowen reputed & accompted.

Die Jovis tertio die Septembris 1607

Roger Bamford servant to Master William Angell of London Fishemonger aged xxviij yeares or thereaboutes sworne & examined before Master Doctor Creake Deputy to the right worshipfull Sir Thomas Crompton knighte Judge of his Majestes high Courte of the Admiraltie and upon certaine articles ministred on the behaulf of Lewes Owen & William Lancaster Esquiers William Angell & John Halseye of London Fishmongers late owners of the *Triall of London* against Arthure Chambers late Master of the said shipp.

To the first article he certenly knoweth that in the monethes articulate the articulate Lewes Owen William Lancaster William Angell & John Halsey were lawfull owners possessors & proprietoures of the articulate shipp the *Triall* beinge of the burthen of one hundreth and sixty tonnes or thereaboutes and as owners did furnish and prepare the said shippe with all thinges necessary for such a shipp of his knowledge.

2. Item whether doe you knowe beleve & have hearde say that George Kennithorpe & others intending a viadge for Virginia by lawfull aucthoritye did hire & take to fraighte the said shippe the *Triall* of the said owners for nine Monethes after the rate of xxxli per monethe.

3. Item Whether doe you knowe that accordinge to the chartre party made betwixte the said parties the said owners did furnishe & prepare the said shipp with ordinaunce tacle apparell and other necessaries fit for such a viadge & delivered the said shippe so furnished & fitted to the said

George Kennithorpe & Arthur Chambers appointed Master for that viadge in the River of Thames.

To the second & third he knoweth that the articulate George Kennethorpe and others intendinge a viadge for Virginea did give & take to frayght the said shipp of the said owners by the monethe for nyne monethes and covenanted by the party made betwixte them for the said viadge to [pay] xxxli per moneth for the said shippe And there uppon the said [owners] did furnishe fitt and make ready the said shipp and delivered the [said shipp] to the said Kennithorpe in the River of Thames of this examinates kn[ow]ledge who was appointed to goe purser of the said shipp & sawe the thre party & other covenantes passed betwixte the owners & the said Kennithorpe & his partners, & therfore the articles doe conteyne truth.

4. Item Whether doe you knowe beleve or have hearde say that the said George Kennithorpe [and] Arthure Chambers did covenante to & with the said owners to bringe the said shipp into the River of Thames within the space of nine monethes nexte after the tenth of March 1605 [-1606] and there rediliver to the said owners or theire assinges the said shipp with her tacle furniture & apparell in as good case as they were delivered reasonable Wearinge & perills of the sea excepted, & that the said shipp should not be broughte into harbor or place likely to hurte & indomage the said shipp or eny of her tacle & apparell: And also gave theire bandes for performance of the same coventantes.

To the iiij[th] he certenly knoweth that the said George Kennithorpe Arthure Chambers & partners did covenant to & with the said owners to bringe backe againse the said shipp the *Triall* into the River of Thames and deliver the same to the said owners or theire assignes within nyne monethes after the tenth of March 1605[-1606] in as good estate as the said shipp was receaved reasonable wearinge & perills of the sea excepted And that the said shipp should not be brought into eany harbor or other place where the said shipp or the furniture thereof should be in daunger of spoile or hurte. Or that eany unlawfull acte should be don with the said shipp against eany his Majestes subjectes confederates or frendes Which he knoweth to be true For that he was privy to the said conitions & covenantes to be aggreed uppon & hath seene them in writinge under the parties handes & seales.

5. Item whether doe you knowe beleve or have hearde that the said Arthure Chambers of London Fishemonger by their Writinges under theire handes & seales covenant promise & graunte to & with the said Lewes Owen William Lancaster William Angell & John Halsey & every of them that the said Arthure Chambers should in & duringe the said pretended viadge well truly diligently & carefully use beare behave & imploy himself as a good just honest & diligente Master of a shipp ought to doe And that the said Arthure shold not in & duringe the said viadge pretended nor in the returne of the said shippe from the said viadge willingly doe, cause procure or suffer to be done eany acte cause or thing by meanes whereof the said shipp or eany of her furniture shall or may be lost or spoyled otherwise then by the perills & dangers of the seas or whereby the said owners maybe dampnified, but shall to his uttermost power hinder & lett the same.

To the vth he knoweth that the articulate Arthure Chambers & George Chambers did by theire writinges under theire handes & seales promise covenant & graunte to & with the said owners & every of them that he the said Arthur Chambers should in & during the said viadge well truly diligently & carefully use beare behave & imploy him self as a good just honeste & diligent Master of a shipp ought to doe And that he the saide Arthure should not in & duringe the said viadge pretended, nor in the returne of the said shipp from the said viadge willingly doe, cause promise or suffer to be don eany acte cause or thinge by meanes whereof the saide shipp or eany of her furniture should or mighte be lost or spoyled otherwise then by the perills of the seas, Whereby the said owners might be damnified but should to his uttermost endevor & power hinder & lett the same. Which he also knowth to be true for that he hath seen & reade the said covenantes and was appointed purser of the said shipp to looke to the same that no dammadge might happen to the owners which might be prevented.

6. Item Whether doe you knowe beleve or have hearde that the said Arthur Chambers contrary to the duty of an honest & carefull Master, and contrary to his covenantes & promises made to & with the said owners, upon the said ships departure from Wulwich to Gravesende stay behind

thre dayes the winde then beinge faire and the weather good to have caried the shipp to Waymouth their nexte porte, And whether by losinge that oportunity by the faulte and negligence of the said Master ther were not fyve weekes spent before the said shippe could gett to Waymouth and two anchors lost and many other damadges done the shipp by that occasion.

To the vjth he knoweth that the said Arthur Chambers contrary to the duty & care of an honest and carefull Master and contrary to his covenantes made with the said owners did absente him self from the said shipp aboute the first of June 1601. When as the said shipp was upon her departure from Wulwich to Gravesende & stayed thre dayes after the shipp was at Gravesend the winde being there verey faire to proceede, before he came thither And by reason of his stay the shipp could not proceede in her viadg when the winde & weather well served, & loosing that oportunity the winde & weather altered, & the shipp came not to Waymouth in fyve weekes after whereas in his conscience he beleveth she had gott thither in verey fewe dayes had the Master bin on borde at the ships comminge to Gravesende & taken the winde which then was verey good. And sayth before the shipp gott to Waymouth there were two ankers lost and other damadges don to the shipp by reason of the windes that hapened in that passage which he thinketh had byn avoided had the said shipp taken her first winde from Gravesend as aforesaid which could not be don by reasons of the Masters absence of this examinates certaine knowledg then being in the said shipp & Purser of the same.

7. Item Whether the said Arthur Chambers in the Downes conveyed out of the shipp two coile of newe ropes & a boulte of canvas to the valewe of iiij or vli. beinge the shipps provision & sould the same to mainteyne his idle & unnecessary expences a shore, & howe longe did he there ly ashore & what his usadge there.

To the vijth he sayth yt is true that in the Downes the said Arthur Chambers conveyed out of the said shipp the *Triall* two coile of newe rope & a bolte of canvas worth iiij or fyve poundes beinge parte of the shipps provision & sould the same to maintaine his vaine & lavish expenses on shore. For as he sayth the said Master would not come on bord in the foure or fyve dayes togeather excepte yt were to imbesle the shipps furniture or to borrow money of this examinate which this examinate thought better to furnish him with then that he should sell the ships provision to the lesse of the shipp or overthrowe of the viadge when there should be use & neede thereof.

8. Item Whether did not the said Arthur Chambers as the said shipp rode in Dover roade invite many of the towne on borde & whether did not the mariners seeing the masters prodigality invite there mates on borde And Whether was not there a hogshead of stronge beere wastfully consumed at one tyme in drinkinge of healthes, & xj shott of ordinaunce by the Masters commaundement shott of at theire departure to the damadge & hinderaunce of the viadge.

To the viij^th he sayth yt is true that whiles the said shipp lay in Dover Roade the said Arthure Chambers invited many of the towne on borde to drincke & make merry, & the mariners takinge example by the Masters prodigality and seeing his slender governement invited likewise many of their mates & acquaintances and made them drinck so liberally that there was drawn out above a hogshead of stronge beere at that tyme as the Stewarde affirmed & this examinate beleveth yt was not lesse, for theere were upwardes of xxx guestes on borde besides the ships company who dranck so many healthes that many of them were drunk and in the feasting & quaffing of healthes there were shott off by the Masters commaundemente elleeven peeces of ordinance of this examinates certaine knowledge then beinge presente.

9. Item Whether the nexte day there came not thre women or mayde servantes on borde whom the Master interteyned & at his goinge on shore with them whether did not he commaund a pece to be shott of, & whether in the dischardging did not the pece break & tere downe the deck of the shipp to the dammadge of the owners.

To the ix^th he sayth yt is most true that the nexte day beinge Munday there came on borde thre maide servantes as yt seemed by theire habett, whom the said Master interteyned & at his goinge on shore with them he would have a pece geven him which was donn, & in dischardging the peece, yt brake & tore downe the deck where yt stode of this examinates sight & knowledge to the greate hurte of the shipp & dammadge of the owners.

10. Item Whether in Waymouth havon did not

the said Arthur Chambers in the nighte tyme convey out of the said ship xvj barrells of salte belonging to the said owners being reproved by the owners servant then purser of the said shipp for wastinge his masters goodes whether did not the said Chambers answere he was sole Comaunder their, and would not be interrupted in eany thinge he did for that he & his frendes were bound to the owner for the shipp & goodes, that he would doe what please him, & unshipp the purser if he tooke eany thinge uppon him towchinge the shipp or goodes or to that effecte.

To the xth he knoweth that in the havon of Waymouthe as this examinate togeather with the Master ley one mighte ashore in one chamber there were in the nighte tyme xvj barrells of the owners salte conveyed on shore by the Masters commaundemente and sould by him and specially order geven by the Master to kepe yt from the knowledge of this examinate And when this examinate understood thereof he reproved the said Arthur Chambers the Master for makinge such spoile of the owners goodes, and he answered that this examinate had nothinge to doe with the shipp nor ought to her belonging, and that he avouched with a grevous oathe For that as he sayd he and his frendes were bound for the shippe and he would be s[ole] commaunder in her both of men and goodes, and therefore w[arned] this examina to not to interrupte him in eany thinge he did, for yf he [did] he would unship hym.

11. Item Whether was not their some controversy betwixte the said Arthur Chambers & the purser as the shipp rode in the Poole of Glantath (Clontarf) in Dublin Water where uppon frewe the same & what speeches did the said Chambers then use & howe demeayned him self there & declare the truth thereof & circumstances of the same.

To the xj^th he sayth yt is true that as the said shipp rode in the Poole of Glamtath in Dublin Water the said Arthur Chambers gave occasion of difference by reason he would be sole Captaine and Commaunder of the shipp, and he came to this examinate and willed him to be silente and not to meddle with eany thinge he did, and sayd that this examinate should not have eany thinge to doe with eany thinge in the shippe, and this examinate answered he would have as much to doe & commaund in his place beinge purser and with that belonged unto him as he should in his place,

And yf he the said Master had don that which belonged unto him and as he oughte to have done, he mighte have had more to doe then this examinate where uppon the said Chambers would have sente one William Crowe to Sir Raph Bingley to sertify him that this examinate denied Sir Raphe his authority in the shippe, but the said Crowe refused to goe knowinge the messadge was ridiculous & false, yet sente he others, & affirmed him self to Sir Raph that if he had not byn carefull to prevente yt with his diligent watchfulnes over this examinate, this examinate would have ron away with the shipp before Sir Raphes arrivall in Ireland.

12. Item Whether did not the said Arthur Chambers intend to have gon away from the shipp in a pinnace of Rowland Buckleye, & did not the said Chambers in the nighte tyme convey out of the *Triall* into the said Pinnace rossen, brimston, nayles, spikes & thrumes to grave & fitt her to sea, & would have victualed her out of the *Triall* & gon in her to the West Indies as you knowe beleve or have heard.

To the xijth he sayth he is verey persuaded the said Arthure Chambers did intende to have gon away from the shipp in a Pinnace of Rowland Buckleyes then beinge in Ireland For that the said Chambers did in the nighte tyme convey out of the *Triall* both rossen, brimston, nayles, spikes & thrumes to grave & fitt her to sea, and intended to have victualed the said Pinnace out of the *Triall* & to have gon in her to the West Indies as he himself confessed.

13. Item whether was not the *Triall* by storme putt from Ireland into Studwalles, And whether did not the said Chambers goe there ashore into the Cuntrey & there continued, the winde being faire to passe over again to Ireland, and whether was not the said Chambers sente for to come on borde by reason the wind was faire and when he returned did not he bring gentlemen aborde with him to feast them And whether by reason of his stay and loosinge that oportunity did there not happen a greate Storme wherein the shipps mastes were spente and the shipp in greate danger of perishinge by the only fault and carelesnes of the said Master to the greate damadge of the owners, and declare the manner thereof.

To the thirtene he sayth Yt is true that the said shipp the *Triall* passinge from Dublyn to Kinsale was by storme driven over to Studwalles in North Walles nere Pothelly being a wilde & open roade where the saide Chambers gott him a shore and into the Cuntrey, the winde comminge faire and so continuenge all nighte, And in the morninge when this examinate & company sawe that the winde continued faire & he came not, they sente a shore to looke for him, for in regarde he was Master no man would take uppon him to carry the shipp away without him beinge bound for her with his frendes. So about noone he came & brought aborde with him one Master Mondre & other gentlemen of the Cuntrey to see the shipp & to feast them, which was don all that afternoone untyll yt was nighte & to late as he sayd to sett saile beinge winter and the nightes longe, and beinge also to late for these gentlemen to goo home that nighte they at the request of the master stayed on borde all nighte, the winde continuenge still faire and blowinge hard at east north east and still increasinge more & more in the nighte untill Yt grew to a greate tempest in so much that althoughe the maine topp mast was striken and the shipp moved with two of her best ankers & cables, Yet grewe the storme so grevois that had not the bowe spritt and foremast gone by the boorde & close by the deck doubtlesse without the greate mercy of god the shipp had perished with this examinate and all the rest theron And yet after the bowespritt & mast were gon by the boorde one of the cables brake and yt so pleased god that presently after the winde began to abate, otherwise he verily thinketh they had perished.

14. Item whether that after the said storme ceassed were there not Jury mastes made and the shipp thereby brought over to Waterford, And whether was not the purser there committed & kept prisoner on borde the *Triall* for that he intended to have stayed the ship there the IX monthes beinge ended, & no hope of procedinge on the intended viadge, but rather on piracy as he feared and declare the maner of the same.

To the xiiijth he sayth yt is true that after the said storme ceassed, they fitted the shipp with jury mastes and sett saile for Ireland & putt into Waterford, Whither shortly after Sir Raph Bingley came, and committed this examinate prisoner in the shipp and sett watch men to kepe him and threatened to ponnish him for that he had sent a petition to the Lord Deputy of Ireland and therein shewed howe the said shipp was hired for nyne monethes only of his Master & partners to make a viadge for Virginea and that the nyne monethes were expired and noe hope to proceede on the viadge, & fearinge the shipp would be caried away uppon unlawfull adventures prayed the Lord Deputy his aide to make stay of the shippe for the good of the owners which he affirmeth to be most true.

15. Item whether the said Chambers fell not out with one Captaine Farmer because he might not be Captaine of the shipp & there uppon forsooke the shippe for a tyme & howe came he againe to the shipp & uppon what occasion.

To the xv[th] he sayth yt is true That at Waterford Captain Farmer and the said Chambers fell out aboute superiority of commaundinge in the said shippe & there uppon the said Arthur Chambers wente to Sir Raph Bingley & told him his promise was that the said Chambers shuld be Captaine in the shipp and nexte in aucthority under him, & excepte he woulde so aucthorize him he would not stay eany longer in the shipp. To whom Sir Raph answered his viadge had not bin so good to make him in love with him, & therefore if he would be gon he should, for he woulde neyther entrete him to stay or goe but for his leudnes he should never goe Master whiles he had the shipp, & so the said Chambers of his owne accord departed & went to Waterford Where he stayed some foure or fyve dayes, and by reason of this accident the saylers were much discontented and sayd they would not goe to sea under the command of eany other Master but the said Arthur Chambers, so as Sir Raph seeinge the inconvenience that was like to happen sente to the said Chambers, and made him Captaine, and they wente to sea one viadge & returned to Baltimore where the shipp was layd upp, & so the said Chambers beinge dismissed of his Captainshipp would not goe to sea againe with Sir Raffe in another shipp, nor stay with this examinate on the shipp aforesaid called the *Triall* to helpe to preserve her for the owners use, but suffered her furniture to be layd to paune & made away & shipped in [-him]self with one Captaine Isaack a pirate and went to sea with him about the midst of Aprill last of this examinates knowledge.

16. Item whether did the said Arthur Chambers eyther before the expiration of the IX monethes or after understand and perceive that the viadge intended for Virginia could not be

performed And whether did he accordinge to his covenantes endevor to bring back the said shipp into the River of Thames or complayne or protest against the courses intended with the said shipp, or did he ever goe aboute to make stay of the said shipp or to hinder her from unlawfull Viadges, but either willingly yelded thereunto.

To the xvj[th] he sayth the said Arthur Chambers both [before] the expiration of the nine monethes & after did well knowe that the viadge intended for Virginea could not be performed Fo-[rasmuch] that there was not victualls & other provision for the viad[ge which] could not be provided, And notwithstandinge he knoweth the said Chambers accordinge to his covenantes did not endevor or goe aboute to make stay of the said shipp, or to bringe her backe into the River of Thames, or to hinder her goinge to the quost of Spaine But wente him self in her and was Captaine of the same shippe as ys before sayd one viadge to the quost of Spaine of this examinates knowledge.

17. Item whether might not the said Arthur Chambers have procured the Maior of Waterford to have made pleg of the said shipp the *Triall* then being within comaund of the Kinges Castells at Waterford, When he saw the viadge intended for Virginia was overthrown & that they mente to goe to the cost of Spayne in the way of piracy: Yf he had had listed, or had regarded his covenantes & the good of his owners.

To the xvij[th] he sayth the said Chambers mighte have endevored to procure the Maior of Waterford to have made stay of the said shipp being under his commaund, and within the command of the kinges Castle there When he sawe the viadge for Virginea was overthrowne, & that a viadge was intended for the Quost of Spaine. Howe be it this examinate knoweth he never wente about or attempted eany such thinge, but willingly yelded to the viadge for the coast of Spaine after Sir Raffe was by occasions aforesaid driven to make him Captaine of the shippe as is aforesaid.

[18] Item what sailes cables ropes and other furniture of the *Triall* were pawned or sold & to whom.

To the xviij[th] he sayth that a mainesaile a maine top saile, a spritt saile, a cable of xj ynches, a shete anker with many small ropes of the furniture of the said shipp the *Triall* was pawned to

Thomas Crooke a gentleman in Baltimore for xxxij^li by the said Sir Raph Bingley and a bill of sale made that if the money were not paid by the first of this instant moneth of September, then the said furniture to be lost.

[signed:] per me Roger Bamford

472. April 5, 1608. Sir Ralph Bingley to Lord Salisbury.

P.R.O., State Papers, Ireland, James I, SP 63/ 223,64, extract.

Right honorable

.... I knowe that my doinges at sea have bein lykwyse made verie odious to your lordship good my lord geive me leave to set them downe unto you fullie, and trulie, for a more honorable Judge I cannot fynde.

First when throughe a most terrible storme I had beine tossd for vj weekes together uppon the coast of Spaine, all my lower Tyce of bere, and vj Tonne of water was leakt out, almost vij score men aboarde mee, & not above three buttes of drinke lefte in the whole ship, with a badd winde for England, In this distress I met with a smale barke that had in her some litle quantitie of Syder & water, which I tooke and gave the owners my bill for. of this if anie on complayne I knowe he had neither Comission nor Cawse to doe it. Another time I was forced for Savinge of my selfe & Companie when wee weare readie to sinke in the seas/ to possess a Frenche ship that I met with by chaunce, close aboarde the shoare of Spaine,

wheare wee weare seekinge out a habour after a great storme to save our lyves in, to them of this ship because the men desyrd to be set on shoare. I gave directions where they sholde fynde me out, and receave back boethe ship & such goodes (which was onlie wheate) that was in hir, which I after performd as the honorable Deputie can certefie your lordship which I doe here most earnestlie protest on my fayethe and credit was all & everie jott of harme that in all my voyadg I did at sea. Which if anie man can amplefie with a larger relacion (most honorable lord) I am well content to lose my lyffe.

When I intended first my voyadge to sea my thoughtes did soare to highe to stoope at those base & forbidden baytes that Pyrates oft are wont to byte at, And at my beinge at Sea. When that men did see how my buisines was bruisde, & my voyadge broken, woulde I then have changd my mynde, as my fortunes did change, I lackt no offers that weare daylie presented mee by men of that qualletie whoe with their shippes & them selves proffered mee their service, with whome if ever I acted or plotted anie thinge save that tooke on of them in Baltemore by order & warrant from Sir Hamy Brunnkern the Lord President then let no man spare to speake, nor Justice prolonge to punishe, ...

Your Lordships servant if I weare worthie to be Comaunded.

[signed:] Ra: Byngley

[*Addressed:*] To the right honorable my verie good Lord the Earle of Salsburie Principall Secretarie to the Kinges most excellent Majestie

[*Endorsed:*] 5° Aprilis 1608 Sir Ralph Bingley to my Lord in his justification.

Chapter Sixty-five
The Fate of the *Richard*, Henry Challons
Captain, on Her Voyage to Mawooshen, 1606

FOUR MONTHS after the Virginia Company charter constituted the Plymouth Company as the division of the Company concerned with what is now usually known as North Virginia, but known as Mawooshen by Indians brought to England the previous year, the ship *Richard* (55 tons), Henry Challons captain with thirty-one men (including the Indians Mannido and Assacomoit), left Plymouth. She was equipped with a pass to indicate that she was permitted by the crown (probably a passport from the Lord High Admiral) to make a voyage to Virginia. Between August 12 and (approximately) October 19, 1606, they crossed the Atlantic to the Caribbean, and early in November, entered the Florida Strait on their way north along the American coast. On November 10, by chance, they found themselves in the middle of the Spanish *flota*, returning to Spain. When they were fired on, they sought out the flagship galleon and offered to show credentials. They were attacked as enemies and their ship captured, the men being dispersed between a number of vessels. A gale scattered them and one was so damaged that she put into Bordeaux on December 23, 1606/January 2, 1607, where eventually the four Englishmen on her were released by the French and promptly had the ship arrested (she was ultimately released). The vessel, carrying the pilot John Stoneman, reached San Lúcar on December 24, 1606/January 3, 1607. The Englishmen were imprisoned, and the *Richard* confiscated.

The next eighteen months saw a long series of incidents in connection with the men. Some were given bail and eventually forfeited it by leaving Spain. Those who were kept in prison were harshly treated, and constant remonstrances by the English ambassador, Sir Charles Cornwallis, produced only increasingly hostile pronouncements from the Conde de Lemos to the effect that Spain would keep all the Indies intact and that the English must give up all voyaging to Virginia. This placed Lord Salisbury, who was a principal backer of the Virginia ventures, in a dilemma, since King James was negotiating to obtain a closer relationship with Spain. The temporizing policy that was evolved meant that the English representations were based on the right of free passage on the seas, the need for clemency where no hostile acts had been done by the *Richard's* men, and an unwillingness to face up to the questions of English rights to settle in Virginia. The Spanish pressure gradually increased to the point of blackmail when a number of the men were sent to the galleys. This led to a hardening of English attitudes, while Spain wished for English support in the complex negotiations over the Netherlands. In 1608, in a bid to obtain it, the prisoners were suddenly released although in the diplomatic sphere this did not have the desired effect. But the result of Spanish pressures was to place royal support much more firmly behind the Virginia Company and to lead to the alterations in the charter of 1609 and the great expedition to Jamestown in that year which effectively aligned English authority behind North American colonization.

The Challons incident is thus important in the wider sphere of international politics concerning America. In the short run it damaged the prospects of the Plymouth Company. Their initial advantage in establishing a settlement somewhat ahead of Newport's arrival at Chesapeake Bay, which would have attracted public interest and money, was lost; the inability of the Hanham-Pring expedition (486) to create a settlement, since it was equipped only to reinforce Challons, and the small resources with which the Sagahadoc colony could be established later in 1607 all combined, together with the failure of the latter to make a profitable beginning, to lead to the ending of the colonizing activities of the Plymouth Company after 1608. Whether it would have done better if Challons had not been intercepted is problematical.

See D. B. Quinn, "James I and the beginnings of empire in America," *Journal of Imperial and Commonwealth History*, II (1972), 1–19.

473. November, 1606. Relation of John Stoneman on the voyage of the *Richard* and the fate of her men.

Printed in S. Purchas, Pilgrimes, *IV (1625), 1833–1836 (XIX [1907] 284–295), extract.*

The Voyage of Master Henry Challons intended for the North Plantation of Virginia, 1606. taken by the way, and ill used by Spaniards: written by John Stoneman Pilot.

On Tuesday the twelfth of August, 1606. M Henry Challons Gentleman set forth from Plimouth, in our small Ship of the burthen of fiftie five Tunnes or there-about, called the Richard of Plimouth. Wherein went twentie nine Englishmen, and two of the five Savages (whose names were Mannido and Assacomoit) which were brought into England the yeere before out of the North parts of Virginia, from our goodly River by him thrice discovered, called [   ] in the Latitude of 43. degrees, 20. minutes were imployed for a farther discovery of these Coasts: And if any good occasion were offered, to leave as many men as wee could spare in the Country. Being victualled for eleven or twelve moneths, at the charges of the Honourable Sir John Popham Knight, Lord chiefe Justice of England, Sir Fardinando Gorges Knight, Captaine of the Fort of Plimouth, together with divers other worshipfull Knights, Gentlemen and Merchants of the West Countrye: John Stoneman of Plimouth being Pilot, who had

beene in the foresaid parts of Virginia the yeere before, with George Waymouth: The Masters name was Nicholas Hine of Cockington, neere Dartmouth;

The last day of August wee fell with the Ile of Madera, where we watered and refreshed our selves, and stayed three dayes, being very kindly used by the Inhabitants. The third day of September wee departed from thence, passing betweene Gomora and Palma, two of the Canary Iles, and from thence were driven by contrary winds, to take a more Southerly course then we intended, and so spent more then six weekes before wee could recover any of the Ant-Iles. The first that wee could recover, was the Ile of Saint Lucia, in the Latitude of 14. degrees, 20. minutes, where we refreshed our selves with Wood and Water. And saw certaine of the Savages there, about fortie or fiftie, came unto us at our Ship in one of their Cannoas, bringing unto us Tobacco, Potatos, Plantins, and Cassavi Bread, the which Savages had slaine more then fortie of our Nation, the yeere before, 1605. as after wee understood by Philip Glasco, and Miles Pett, being two of Captaine Nicholas Saint Johns company, which was there treacherously slaine among the rest.

Having stayed heare three dayes, about the two and twentieth of October we departed thence to the Northward. And in passing by the Ile of Dominica, wee chanced to see a white Flag put forth on the shoare, whereat marvelling, wee supposed that some Christians had sustained shipwrack their. And forthwith a Cannoa came off from the shoare towards us, which when they came neere, being very little wind, we layed our Ship by the lee and stayed for them a little, and when they were come within a little distance of the Ship, wee perceived in the Cannoa a Friar, who cried aloud in the Latine tongue, saying, I beseech, as you are Christians, for Christ his sake to shew some mercy and compassion on mee, I am a Preacher of the Word of God, a Friar of the Order of Franciscus in Sivill, by name Friar Blasius. And that hee had beene there sixteene moneths a Slave unto those Savages; and that other two Friars which were of his company they had murthered and throwne into the Sea. We demanded of him then, how he got so much favour to preserve his life, his Brethren being murthered: Hee answered, because hee did shew the Savages how to fit them Sayles for their Cannoas, and so to ease them of much labour often in rowing, which greatly pleased the Savages as appeared, for wee saw them to use sayles in their Cannoas, which hath not beene seene before.

Then we demanded of him where they had this Linnen Cloth to make those Sayles: hee answered, That about two yeeres before that, three Gallions comming to the West Indies were cast away on the Ile of Gwadalopa, where abundance of Linnen Cloth and other Merchandise was cast on shoare. We demanded farther, what was the cause of his being in this place, and how he came thither: he answered, That the King of Spaine did every yeere, send out of every great Monastery certaine Friars into the remote parts of the Indies, both to seeke to convert the Savages, as also to seeke out what benefits or commodities might be had in those parts, and also of what force the Savages were of, and what number of them were in the seven Ant-Iles, viz. Saint Vincent Granado, Saint Lucia, Mattalina, Dominica, Gwadalopa, Aisey. The which the said Friar Blaseus said he had diligently noted and observed, and did hope to make perfect relation of such great benefits and riches as was to be drawne from thence, as he doubted not but would bee greatly accepted of his King, if hee might live to returne to declare it: For, said hee, I have seene in one River discending from the Mountaines in the Ile of Dominica, the Sand to glitter like Gold or find Copper, whereupon I tooke some of it, and chewed it betweene my teeth, and found it perfect Mettall, the Savages noting me, began to have some jealousie of me, so as I durst not take any farther notice of it, neither would they suffer him forward to come neere to that place. And farther hee said, That if the great plentie of divers Fruits and Roots fit for mans sustenance were perfectly knowne, together with the Sugar-canes that they have in those Iles, and the fertilitie of the soyle he thought it would be very shortly inhabited; and as for the number of Savages there, as neere as we could understand, was scarce one thousand of all sorts of men, women, and children in all the said seven Iles.

Now, being moved with pittie at the lamentable complaint, and humble suit of this distressed Friar, wee tooke him into our Ship, and sent away the Savages much discontented. And from thence wee sayled to the Ile of Saint John De-port-rico, where on the nine and twentieth of October, wee arrived on the Southside, and forthwith sent the Friar on shoare, and delivered him to two Heardsmen, which most thankfully received him, and of their courtesie brought us a fat Cow, and proferred us more with Hogs, Calves, or any thing else that they could procure us in recompence of the good deed done to the Friar.

Wee departed from thence, and sayled out betweene the Iles of Saint John De-portrico, and Hispaniola standing away to the Northward. And leaving the great shoalds called Abrioio, on our Larboord side, being in the Latitude of 21. and 22. degrees, from thence Westward, our course North North-west, and North-west and by North, untill wee were in the Latitude of 27. degrees or better, and about one hundred and eightie leagues from Saint John de Port Rico.

In this place having had a very great storme of Wind and Raine continuing fiftie six houres and more before on the tenth day of November, about ten of the clocke in the morning, suddenly we found our selves in the middest of a Fleet of eight Sayle of ships in a very thicke fogge of mist and raine, so as we could not see them before they were very neere, and within shot of them, wherein three of them were on the wind-ward of us, on a third and fourth more to lee-ward: those at the wind-ward came rome unto us, and shot at us, requiring us to speake with their Admirall. When we saw that by no meanes we could avoid them, but that they would speake with us, we put abroad our Colours, and went toward the Admirall, before wee came unto him, he likewise strooke downe our Sayle, and came under his lee, demanding his pleasure: the other ship which first shot us, all our Sayles being downe, and shot our mayne Sayle in pieces lying on the Decke.

And forthwith the Admirall came on boord of us, with two and twentie men in their ships Boate with Rapiers, Swords, and halfe-pikes. We being all in peace stood readie to entertayne them in peace. But assoone as they were entred on boord of us, they did most cruelly beate us all, and wounded two of our Company in the heads with their Swords, not sparing our Captayne nor any. Also they wounded Assacomoit, one of the Savages aforesaid, most cruelly in severall places in the bodie, and thrust quite through the arme, the poore creature creeping under a Cabbin for feare of their rigour: and as they thrust at him, wounding him, he cried still. King James, King James, King James his ship, King James his ship[1]. Thus having beaten us all downe under the Deckes, presently they beat us up againe, and thrust us over-boord into their Boate, and so sent us on boord of the Admirall ship. Neither would they suffer any of us to speake a word, to shew the cause of our passing the Seas in these parts. Neyther regarded they any thing, our Commission which the Captayne held forth unto them in his hand: untill that the Admirall with the Company of foure other of the ships, had rifled, spoyled, and delivered all the Merchandize and goods of the ship among them: which beeing done, they also divided us beeing thirtie persons in all into the said five ships, by seven, six, five, and foure to a ship.

Three of the former eight Sayle made Sayle away, and never came neere us, neither were partakers of our spoyle. Then they also repayred our Maine Sayle which was torne with the shot aforesaid, and put their men into her. And after because they could not make her to sayle well, they tooke two of our men, and put into her to helpe them, the other five ships and our ship kept company two or three dayes together. After this they separated themselves either from other, not through any tempest or storme, but through wilfull negligence or simple Ignorance, by shaping contrary courses the one from the other. So as not two of them kept company together. My selfe and six more of our company in the Vice-Admirall (of the burthen of one hundred and eightie tunnes;

called the Peter of Sivill, the Captaynes name was Andreas Barbear) beeing alone, and having lost the company of the Fleet, continued our course untill the middle of December: at which time being about twentie leagues off from the Ile of Santa Maria, one of the Iles of the Azores, the Vice-Admiral and the whole company disliking the great Ignorance of the Pilot, because he had told them ten dayes before that he was very neere the Ilands, and had waited all this time, and could find any of them, entreated me very earnestly to shew my skill. And the Pilot himselfe brought mee his Instruments, and besought mee most earnestly to assist him, and to appease the company. Whereunto by there much importunitie I yeelded. And by Gods assistance on Christmasse Eeve, after our English account, I brought them safe to the Barre of Saint Lucas, being the first ship of the whole Fleet that arrived there.

One of the ships of this Fleet, by the great Ignorance of the Spanish Masters, Pilots, and Mariners was driven beyond all the Coast of Spaine, into Burdeaux in Gascoyne, In which shippe the Officers of the Admiraltie of France[2], finding foure of our Englishmen prisoners under the Deckes in hold; to wit, Master Daniell Tucker, who was our Cape Merchant, Pierce Gliddon and two others, did very friendly set them at libertie; and the said Daniel Tucker presently arrested the Spanish ship and goods beeing of great value, which of long time remayneth under arrest.

The good Duke of Medina hearing of the arrivall of certaine English prisoners taken here, the Coast of the West Indies, sent command to the Captaynes of the Spanish ships, to bring foure of the chiefest to be brought before him. Whereupon my selfe, Master Thomas Saint John, John Walrond our Steward, and William Stone our Carpenter were brought before him. The ship wherein Master Challons was, was not yet come.

Master David Nevill an Englishman dwelling in Saint Lucas, was appointed our Interpretor. And then the Duke required me upon my oath to yeeld a true and faithfull answere, according to the whole state and manner of our Voyage and proceedings, which I did, according to the former Relation afore written, whereupon his Excellencie replyed unto the Spanish Captaynes which had brought us, saying, if this bee true which this

---

1. Side note: "King James his name little respected by Spaniards."

2. Side note: "French courtesie."

Englishman affirmeth, you have greatly wronged these men. And so commanded them to provide meate, drinke, and fit lodging for us, and to bring us againe the next day before him. They sent us neverthelesse to Sivill, where wee were brought to a Dutchmans house, called Signior Petro, where we were reasonably lodged, and entertayned that night.

The next morning being New yeeres day we were brought before the President of Sivill, at the Contractation, who hearing of our comming, and not vouchsafing to speake with us, sent foure Officers to us, and cast us into Prison. Where for the space of five dayes wee had publike allowance, but such as poore men which were there Prisoners, also did of their mercie bestow on us. At length after many humble Sutes, and earnest Petitions exhibited to the President, we had a Riall of Plate allowed to each man a day, which is six pence English, which by reason of the dearth of all sorts of victuall in those parts, will not goe so far as three pence in England.

And so at severall times, within one moneth after eleven more of our Company were committed to Prison, as they came home, whereof our Captaine was one. Notwithstanding that the good Duke of Medina had discharged both him and all those of his Company, which came into Spaine with him, and willed him to goe home to the Court of England, or to the Court of Spaine where he thought to have best reliefe for his poore imprisoned Company. Whereupon Nicholas Hine our Master, and two more of our men wisely foreseeing what was like to bee the Issue, made haste away out of the Citie, and so got passage and escaped into England.

Before the comming of our Captaine to Sivill, my selfe and eleven more of my Company were examined before the President of the Contractation: who finding no just cause of offence in us, did often earnestly examine me of the manner and situation of the Countrie of Virginia, together with the Commodities and benefit thereof. And after the comming of our Captaine, they likewise examined him to the same purpose. We answered both to one purpose, according to our Commission in writing, which the Spaniards at our taking at Sea, had preserved and delivered up unto the hands of the President. Within few dayes after, they gave our Captaine and Master Thomas Saint John, libertie of mayne Prison, upon the securitie

of two English Merchants, which were Master William Rapier, and Master John Peckeford, whereof the later is dwelling and maried in Sivill. The rest of the Company being one and twentie in Prison, continued still in miserable estate. And about two moneths after, Robert Cooke of London one of our Company fell sick of a Fluxe, whereof he languished three moneths and more, and by no meanes that wee could make, could get him forth to bee cured. although wee spent more then sixtie Rials in Supplicaves and Sutes to get him out. At length being dead, they caused his bodie to bee drawne up and downe the Prison by the heeles, naked, in most contemptible manner[3], crying, Behold the Lutheran, as five others of our Company beeing then in close Prison beheld: and so laid him under the Conduit, and powred water into his dead bodie. This done, they cut off his Eares, Nose and Members, as the Spaniards themselves confessed unto us, and so conveyed his bodie wee could never learne whether, although we proffered them money to have his dead corps to burie it.

Shortly after Nathaniel Humfrie our Boatswaine was stabbed into the belly with a Knife by a Spaniard, which was a slave in the Prison, and fourteene dayes after dyed, who beeing dead I went unto the Keeper of the Prison, desiring to buy his dead bodie to burie it, and so for twenty Rials I bought his bodie, and buried it in the field. Then we besought the President for Justice on this slave which had slaine our Boatswaine: he demanded what we would have of the slave. And we requested, that as he had slaine an honest and worthy man of ours causelesse, that hee might die for it according to the Law. The President answered no, but if we would have him condemned for two or three yeares more to the Gallies he should. For said hee, The King of Spaine will not give the life of the worst Slave that he hath, for the best Subject the King of England hath, and so sent us away with this answere. Whereupon being out of all hope of Justice with the President, we repaired unto the Regent being an Ecclesiasticall man, one of the chiefest Judges of the Citie, desiring likewise Justice on the Murtherer aforesaid: who in kind tearmes promised us Justice, and so willed us to retaine counsell and Atturnies to prosecute our Sute; which wee

---

3. Side notes: "Hard hearted Spaniard," and "Cruell immanitie."

did accordingly, and so after two moneths Sute, and the cost of more then two hundred Rials on Lawyers, Scribes and other Officers at length we had him hanged by the favour of the Regent, which otherwise we had never obtained.

And now I may not omit to shew how I got the libertie to have the scope of the Citie for my Race to come, and go. Having beene three moneths in close Prison with our poore company as aforesaid. At length I got the favour of two Englishmen inhabiting in Sivill named Constantine Collins, and Henry Roberts who did ingage themselves for me. The Spaniards were very desirous to have me to serve their State, and proffered me great wages, which I refused to doe, affirming, that this imployment which I had in hand, was not yet ended untill which time I would not determine any.

Then the Alcadie major of the Contractation House and divers other Merchants perswaded me to make them some descriptions and Maps of the Coast and parts of Virginia, which I also refused to doe. They being discontent with me, sent mee againe to Prison, where I continued two and twentie dayes, and then I making meanes unto my good friends borrowed money, and so gave divers bribes unto the keepers of the Prison, whereupon they gave mee libertie to goe abroad againe into the Citie at my pleasure. And wayting every day for some order from the Court of Spaine of our discharge, there came none but delayes and prolonging of our troubles and miseries. So as we began almost to despaire of libertie.

At length an honest Dutch Merchant dwelling in Sivill, named Hanse Eloyse, sent unto mee to speake with me, which when I came unto him, signified unto me what he had learned of one of the Judges of the Contractation: who told him as he reported unto me, that the Spaniards had a great hate unto me above all others, because they understood that I had beene a former Discoverer in Virginia, at the bringing into England of those Savages; and that they thought it was by my instigation to perswade our State to inhabit those parts. And because they had received so small knowledge of those parts by my confession: and that they could not perswade mee to serve that State, neither would make them any note draught, or descriptions of the Countrie. They resolved to bring to the Racke and torment me,

whereby to draw some further knowledge by confession from me, before any discharge might come for us. The which this honest Merchant considering, and the Innocencie of our case, gave me to understand. And wished mee rather to flie and preserve my selfe, then to stand to their mercie on the Racke, I hearing this the next morning, being the three and twentieth of October, suddenly fled from Sivill, and with me Master Thomas Saint John aforesaid, and one other of our Company named James Stoneman my Brother, whom through great cost and charges bestowed on the Keepers of the Prison a little before I had got forth to bee cured of a Callenture. Thus wee fled from Sivill, leaving Master Henry Challons our Captaine at libertie upon sureties, and sixteene more of our Company in close Prison.

474. January 25/February 4, 1607. Nevill Davis to Sir John Popham.

Hatfield House, Cecil Papers 120/53; printed in Baxter, Gorges, III, 134–135.

Right Honnorable my humble duetie Remembred, May yt please your honor that at present Occasion beinge offereid whereby I am imboldned to send these fewe lines unto your lordshipp:

Thereby to signifye the misserye of dyvers poore men here pryssoners, that were taken in a small shippe of Plymouth called the *Richard* where of was Captaine one Henry Challines; And as yt appereth were set forth by Sir Fardenando Joorge, and dyvers other gentlemen and they Report your honor to be one of the Cheiffest adventurars in this there pretended voyage, beinge for a newe discovery in the norweast partes, under the Lattetude of 41 and 42 degrees. They were surprysed by seven marchant shippes, which did come from Santa Domingo; mettinge them some 150 leages to the norward of Porto Rico, in the height of 27 degrees or thereaboutes, here are 18 of them and 2 salvages of the country they went unto; The Captaine and one master Thomas St. John we have released under suerties. The Relation of there prosedinges, from the time they departed from Plymouth, I refer to there wryttinges, and report of some that have escaped, all there examynacions are taken and sent to the court ye last weeke; by there confessions yt appereth they have comytted noe offence against anie of this kinges subjectes, only to doe good to a Spanishe fryer, and preservynge his life was cause they fell into these trobles, I will doe my indevor to assyst them in what I may, beinge sorrye there pretence should so unfortunaytly be overthrowne, and discovered I have advertysed my Lord Embassedor hereof, who I hope will seeke remedye for there inlargment:

The Spaniardes here seme nothinge pleased with this attempt, and I doe thincke they will endevor to prevent us from goeing into those partes, if by anie meaines they can, wherefore in the attemptinge yt againe, those which are to manidge the fame, must deall very surcumspectlie for beinge enterseptted, I hope that god will oppen those Remoot and unknowen places unto us whereby in tyme our country may fynde a more saffer and proffetabler trade then we have donne here since the peace; for I doe asure your Lordshipp: what thorough the soundry molestacions by dyvers offycers here and the excessyve imposyssions we pay which inward and outward uppon our goods, we are, and shalbe consumed by this trade, as I referr me to ye gennerall report of those which doe adventer hether, and fell the losse, and I am sure yf a true Calcolation were taken yt would be found his Majestes subjectes have lost near Eyghtie thousand poundes by the trad of Spaine: All our woollen comodyties for the most part are in noe estimacion here, as before the warrs and daylie wilbe lese and lese, by reason of the great store of cloth made here, and for this hoot country, farr better then ours, wherefore yt is requysit we seeke other places for the venting of our cloth, Thus refferinge my self to the good consytheracion of your honor and craving pardon for my boldnes I rest contynewally prayinge for your Lordshipps happie Estayt ettc'a

Your honnor in all dutie:/
[signed:] Nevill Davis

[Endorsed:] 4 February. 1607: stillo Nova. 1607 Nevil Davis to my lo: cheef Justice concerning the men that went to Virginea.

475. February 4, 1607. The relation of Daniel Tucker on the fate of the *Richard*.

Hatfield House, Cecil Papers 115/89; printed in James P. Baxter, ed., Sir Ferdinando Gorges and his Province of Maine, *3 vols. (Boston, Prince Society, 1890) III, 129–131.*

The Relasion of Daniell Tucker merchant beinge Implyed by divers Advententerars of Plimmothe to goe as Facttor of a shipe bownd for Floredae wrytten by him selfe the 4th of February *1606*.

The wind beinge faer we departed from Plimmothe the 12th of Auguste, which winde contenued tell we came within 80 Leages of the westward Ilandes, and then the wind westerd with a grete storme, where by we waer put for the Iland of Maderes, where we wattered with the Governers Licence one the 4th of Septtember and there staed tell the 8th daye/

And from thens we stude owr Corse for the coste of Floredae, but after we had saled some 100 Leges we waer be Calmed 14 daes together, and by Reson of the exstrem hete owr freshe water scanted upon us so as we awer forsed to the outter moste Ilandes of the weste Inges.

And about the Laste of october we a Rived at a niland Called Margethanta, wher we wattered and Refresshed owr selves with suche Frutes as the Iland did afford, and staed ther 4 daes, from thens we wente by a Niland called Domeneca, wher a Spanishe Frier Came a bord owr shipe, in a small Cannoe with 5 Ingens which brought Frutes with them. The saed Frier desired us for Godes Caes to geve him passage for some parte of Christendom, whos shipe had bene Caste a waye some 13 monthes befoer and all his Company drownned and slaned by the Engians, only hee saved a Live.

Whiche saed Frier we tooke into owr shipe, and some 4 daes after we sete him a shoer at the Estward of Portarecca, and ther delevered him unto two Spanniardes which waer herdes men of Cattell, wher we staed two daes, and goinge from thens owr shipe Came a grownd, but with out anye harme we got Cleer, and so stude owr Corse to Floredae.

And beinge at see in the hithe of 26 degres & some 60 Leges from the shoer we mete with a Flete of a 11 shipes (all Spanniardes) merchant men, on the 10th of November in the morninge we waer in the middeste of the saed Flete, we standinge owr Corse, one of the windward shipes shot at us, wher uppone we wente to the Admerall, and Comminge under his Lee, the Admerall shot at us two shot, and came a borde of owr shipe in most veyholent manner, and disposeste us of owr shipe and goodes, and sent us a bowrde of his one shipe, and the nexte day parted us some 4 & 5 in a shipe and put Spanniardes a borde of owr shipe and stud for Sevell in Spane But by Resen the Admerall had a grete Lecke the Reste of the shipes Lefte him onlye with owr shipe and soe parted from the Admerall, and 6 daes after we Loste all owr Flete in a grete storme with moer winde then we Cowlde well stere afoer, and by Resen of exstreme fowle wether and havinge a bad Pilote who Cowld not tacke his Juste hither we Continued at see two monthes in grete meserie & exstremetie, and soe not knowinge where we waer, we arived at the Rever of Burdes the second of Januarye/

And the Master and the Reste of the Spanniardes knoinge theme selves to bee in Burdes, thaye Commanded my selfe with the three other of my Companye, to bee put into the shipes howld and there thaye kepte us Five daes and Five nites, in that manner, tell the Juge of the Admerralte Came a borde of the shipe Riddinge aganste the Towne of Burdex and Exsamened my selfe, And the Juge understandinge the truthe of owr Caues Carried me and the three other a shoer to Burdex.

And when I was at Lebertie I wente to one of the Cheffeste Counseller and sertefied him of owr veyage & howe the Spanniardes had used us and in what manner thay had tacken us. I desired his Cownsell what Course was beste to tacke a ganste the Spanniardes, who advised me to see a Procter, and macke a petesion to the Parlemente and to the Admerall to have the Master of the Spanishe shipe & the rest of my Company exsammened, which I did, and shoed the Copie of all owr exsammenasions to my Cownseller, who advised me to macke a Letter of a Turnie to my Procter and to some other whome I thought good, and thaye to folloe the Caues a ganste the Spaniardes in my Absence, and my selfe to Repaer for England with all spede, and to Returne with serteficate to Conferme owr exsammenasion to bee truthe.

Where uppone I made a Letter of a Turnye to my Procter and to a nother my solester which hathe order to areste the saed Spanishe ship and goodes, tell furder profe Commethe out of England.

This beinge Finnesshed I departed from Burdex and at my departtuer my Cownseller and my Procter saed ther was no dowt but the worthe of the shipe and gudes with all dammages wold bee Recovered of them/

By me/

[signed:] Daniell Tucker

[Endorsed:] 4 Feb 1606/1607 The Relation of Daniell Tucker going to Terra Florida.

476. February 19, 1607. Draft commission by the Lord High Admiral, Charles Howard, Earl of Nottingham, including interrogatories relating to the taking of the _Richard_ and the deposition of Nicholas Hind, February 16, 1607.

P.R.O., HCA 14/38, 118. Latin. Abstract.

[a] Commission from the Lord Admiral for making interrogatories and taking depositions in the case of the Richard.

[b] Interrogatories in the case of the Richard:

1. Whether the _Richard_ left Plymouth in the months of June, July or August 1606 and who set her out?

2. Whither was the _Richard_ bound? And did she carry in her two persons of that land of America or Virginia?

3. Whether the _Richard_ followed her course towards America or Virginia without any violence offered towards any?

4. In what circumstances did the _Richard_ encounter the Spanish fleet?

5. In what circumstances did the Spanish fleet take the _Richard?_

6. What did the commander of the Spanish fleet do when he was shown that the _Richard_ was going with the king's leave to Mayowshon in Virginia?

7. What did the commander of the Spanish fleet do with regard to the master, sailors, goods and merchandises of the *Richard* when she was taken?

8. In which ships was Henry Challenge taken and in which the two natives of America or Virginia?

9. Whether those of the *Richard* intimated to the Spaniards that the king of England was in amity with the king of Spain, and whether they showed their pass from the king and council, and whether they voluntarily submitted themselves to the Spaniards?

[c] Intimation that under the interrogatories the deposition of Nicholas Hind was taken 16 Feb. 1606[–7] and the deposition given

[d] The document authenticated and dated 19 February 1606 [–1607]

477. February 16, 1607. Deposition of Nicholas Hind, master of the *Richard*.

P.R.O., HCA 13/38, February 16, 1607.

xvj Februarij 1606 [–1607] Nicholes Hind de Cockenton in Comitatu Devonie nauta et nuper magister navis cuiusdum vocate the Richard portus Plymuthe etatis 44 annorum aut circiter testis in hac parte productus juretus, et examinatus dicit et deponit prout sequitur.

To the first article he sayth that he doth nowe know that the said shipp the Richard did in the moneth of August last past & in the xij[th] day thereof as he remembreth did sett sayle from the porte of Plymouth & was sett out on that voyadg by Sir Ferdinando Gorge, [   ] Waddon merchant[1] of Plymouth captaine Morgan & captaine Thomas Love of Plymouth merchantes together & others & was bound for the coast of Virginia called Pama Quidda in Mayaushon in trade of marchandizes by sufficient authority from the kinges Majesty of England & the Lordes of his

Majestes privy counsell, which he knoweth to be true being master of the said shipp the said voyadge.

Ad secundam articulatum dicit et deponit that the said shipp the Richard was bound for Pama Quidda in Mayashon in Virginia aforesaid & that there were two men borne in that Cuntry of Virginia on boord the said shipp the Richard at her going from Plymouth & xxviij Englishemen & none els of this examinates knowledg being master thereof the said voyadg.

Ad 3 affirmat that the said shipp the Richard & the company thereof after their departure from Plymouth aforesaid did with as much speed as they could (as wind & weather would suffer them) sayle towards the foresaid port of their discharge whither they had directions to goe being Mayoushon & to no other port & being on their said voyadg were driven by force of wether & stormes to an Island called Andozia[2] being an Island which doth border on the West Indies, where they remayned three dayes & did theire take in some wood & water & so departed to sea againe towardes Mayowshen aforesaid & sayled along by St John de Porterico where there was a certen Friar which was amongst the Salvages & this examinate & company sett him on shore at Porterico & saved his life from the Salvages & with all the speed, & with the winde & weather they might they made for the port of Mayaushen aforesaid which he knoweth to be true being master of the said shipp as aforesaid

Ad 4 affirmat that the company of the said shipp the Richard being on their course as aforesaid did uppon the high seas & about xxv degrees & a half meete with a fleet of Spanishe shippes comming from Santo Domingo & bound for Spaine being all merchantes shipps & the company of the said shipp the Richard as soone as they descried the said Spanishe fleet did sett out theyr colors being an Englishe flagge to the intent that the said Spaniardes shall see from whence they came, & notwithstanding the said flagg sett out the said Spaniardes in the said fleete did shoot at the said shipp the Richard & the said company of the Richard seeing the Spaniardes did offer them violence did offer them selves voluntaryly to show what they were and whence they were & did

---

1. Clerk unsure of name. It may be intended for William Parker.

2. In the Latin version "Andelozia," apparently a mistake of the clerk for "Dominica."

beare upp to the Admirall of the Fleete which he knoweth to be true as aforesaid.

Ad quintum affirmat verum esse that notwithstanding the voluntary submission & bearing uppe to the Admirall of the said Fleete, yet the shipps still shott of att the said shipp the Richard & Shot her throwghe & throughe & laid her violently on boord & toke the possession thereof & after they came on boord the Richard they did beset the company with their naked rapiers & thrust one of the two Indiens which were on boord the Richard at least six inches into the body & throughe & throughe the Arme & cutt one Robert Cooke an Englisheman in the head with a rapier & abused & beate every man in the shipp & took from them all that ever they had & made them go barefoote & almost naked & kept this examinate & the capten in one of their shipps with Cassatha being the pithe of the tree & water & ferkin beefe once a week which was full of maggottes & they would creepe uppon the spitt for the space of ix weekes & had water but once a day & then they went two to a pint, And so he hard the rest of the Company being in other of the Spanishe shippes were used which he knoweth to be true giving his resons of his knowledg as aforesaid.

Ad sextum affirmat verum esse that before the said Spaniardes came on boord the said shipp the Richard the master & company of the Richard did certyfy & declare to them that they were englishmen bound for the partes of Virginea to a place called Mayowshen & had nothing on boord of them but what they brought from England neither had they touched anywhere since theyr cominge from England & wished them to come on boord quietly and after theyr comynge on boord wished them to search their shipp without any resistance at all & tould them they were bound for Mayoushen aforesaid & theyr commodytyes were fitt for no other place but that & that they were bound for no place els but that, which he knoweth to be true as aforesaid

Ad septimum affirmat that the captens & company of the said Spanishe Fleete notwithstanding the premisses did presently uppon the company of them on board the said shipp the Richard did dispossewse the captaine & company thereof & greatly abused them as aforesaid & putt some into one shipp & some into another, & master Henry Challenns being capten of the Richard & this examinate were put into one shipp & they arived

at St Lucar in Spaine, and most of the rest of the company of the Englishemen are in prison in Sivill in Spaine with the capten saving some which were left in the Richard, & what is become of them on the shipp & goodes he knoweth not

Ad octavum affirmat ut supra that master Challen & this examinate & one of the two Indians were putt into one shipp & caried for Spayne, where both master Challenge & those two Indians & some xx^{ty} more of theyr company remayned prisoners.

Ad 9 et ultimum dicit that the capten & company of the Richard did voluntarily subiect them selves to the said Fleet for that theyr was peace & league betwixte England & Spayne at that tyme they mistrusted nothing especially no mercy to be offered to them by any Spaniardes showing theyr passe from the King of England & his counseile & for that they had bine kindly used before at Madares uppon the sight of that passe And he sayth that if they had mistrusted they would have offered them any violence they might haue escaped them being that they were of farr better sayle then they were

[signed:] Nicholas Hyns

478. March 13, 1607, Sir Ferdinando Gorges to Henry Challons.

P.R.O., State Papers, Colonial, CO1/1/115; printed in Baxter, Gorges III, 144–145.

Master Chalinge I received your lettres sent me by the Master Nicholas Hines by whom I rest satisfied for your parte of the proceedings of the voyadge and I doubte not but you wilbe able to aunswere the expectacion of all your freinds. I hoope you shall receive verie shortlie if alreadie you have not an Attestation out of the highe Courte of Admiraltie to give satisfaccion of the truthe of our intent that sett you out let me advise you to take heede that you be not overhott in acceptinge recompence for our wronges receivd for you knowe that the jorney hath bene noe smale Chardge unto us that first sent to the Coast and had for our returne but the five salvadges whereof two of the principall you had with you and since with in two monthes after your departure we sent out another shippe to come to your supplie and now againe we have made a nue preparacion of divers others all which throughe your misfortune is likelie to be frustrate and our time and Chardge lost, therefore your demandes must be Aunswerable hereunto and accordinglie seeke for satisfaccion which cannot be lesse then five thousande poundes and therefore before you conclude for losse attende to receive for resolucion from hence if they Aunswere you not thereafter for if their condicions be not such as shalbe reasonable we doe knowe how to right our selves for rather then we wilbe loosers a penny by them we will attende a fitter time to gett us our Content and in the meane time leave all in their handes therefore be you carefull herein and remember that it is not the buisines of Merchants or rovers, but as you knowe of men of another ranke and such as will not preferre manie Complayntes nor exhibite divers petitions, for that they understande a shorter way to the woode, soe Commendinge you to god and Continnuinge my selfe

Your most assured and lovinge Freinde/
[signed:] Ferdinando Gorges.
　　　　　Plimothe 13th of Marche 1606.

Postcript. I pray you use the meanes that the Salvadges and the Companie be sent over with as muche speede as is possible and that you hasten your selfe away, if you see not likelihoode of a prefent ende to be had for we will not be tired with their delaies and endlesse sutes suche as commonlie they use but leave all to time and god the just revenger of wronges.
　　　[signed:] Ferdinando Gorges

[Endorsed:] 1606. The Copie of Sir Ferdinando Gorges, his lettre to Master Chalens. Received ye 6 day.

479. June 16/26, 1607. Captain Henry Challons to Sir John Popham.

Hatfield House, Cecil Papers 121/113; printed in Baxter, Gorges, *III, 145–146. Copy.*

Right Honorable what I wrote your Lordship in my Last as dispearinge to be releved by our Ambassador here, experience hath ever sithens continewally approved, for I weekely solicitinge him with my lettres could never obtayne any materiall answere untill the 5 of June which was that the Conde de Leamos who is president of the Councell for the Indias, answered him that rather then such as wear taken in those parts should want an exicutioner, he wold serve for hangmen him selfe, and farther writes in an other that the Condi de Leamos had writen to the Contractacion here but writs not whether to hang us or discharge us. I repearinge to the president of the Contractacion here as desirous to knowe my paynes acquainted him that I understod that he had receaved Letters as concerninge our businis who answered not a word and that we wear merely forgotten. And that no man spake for us else could we not but have bin delivered long sithence We Increase disseases and debts six pence in England is not a peny heare Robert Cooke is already dead. The boteson in prison stabd in the belly In Judgment not like to recover. The Indians ar taken from me and made slaves. Our ship is sonke in the river not Like to be recovered. We Indure all the Indignities and extreamities that is possible as to hire hes Majestie her Majestie and especially Certayne of there honours of our privie Concell most untruly and vilely reproched. Most humbly besechinge your Lordship to Conceave herof and relive us before it be to late. We pray god Lengthen your honorable days who must shorten our miseris or else we perishe all.

　　　　　June 26 stilo nova (1607).

　　[unsigned]

480. June 23/July 3, 1607. Henry Challons to Sir John Popham.

Hatfield House, Cecil Papers 121/114; printed in Baxter, Gorges, *III, 146–148. Copy.*

My humblest dutie. Sithence my last unto your Lordship, Master Davice hath Receaved from our Ambassadors Secretary a Line or two as concerninge us, the Contrarietie wherof to his former writings, approves his Carelesnis of us, and the veritie of the presedents speeche heare, which was that we weare mearely forgotton, and that nobody spake for us, else coulde we not but have had libertie longe sithens. I most humbly beseche your Lordship not to be disceaved by the Ambassidors letters, for I doubt not but whiles he servs the Spaniards torne in suffringe us to perishe by loathsome and tedious Imprisonments, whome there lawes cannot touche for offence he furnisheth your Hounour with many glosinge writinges From which his delusions good Lord deliver us. My boteson that I wrote to your Lordship was stabde, is dead, sithence. And I was faine, though they had murthered him in prison to pay the fees of the house er I could have him out, to burie him, in the Fields. All those that have Died in prison, have bin most unchristianlike used. Some of them have had there brains beaten out after they weare dead, there noses ears and privie members Cutt of. And Robert Cooke, the first that died had a Stringe tied to on of his Legs and was Draged downe a peare of Stairs of thirtie steps affirminge they wold teach the Lutarane the way to hell. they forced his mouth open and puttinge a gag into it powred into his dead mouth three potts of water. Sayinge the *Boracha* should have drinke Inough. These extremities they use with us as I conceave to Inforce our men to there Religion, it doth much terrifie them. The god of all Strength strengthen and Comforte us all, there tiranies & Injustices ar Intollorable. I am commanded on paine of .300. Ducats and castigation. not to speake with the naturalls, for the[y] Conceave that by my means they Cannot make them Christians. They will eyther Convert them, or by Famine Confounde them for they ar almost Starved already. There is three of my Company more not Like to Live, and I Judge the on of them Cannot Recover. I beseech your Honour in Christianitie consider of us, and Let us with Speede have some Comforte, else will it Com to late for most of us, for there hath bin a Speach generally spread throughout all this Cittie, that the Inglishe Captaine Cominge to his Company in prison was slaine, But I thanke God I mist the hower, if there weare any Intention of such an action, as is much to be suspected by reason of such a Speach spread and howe Littell they value the Life of a Lutarane, as they terme us God and our Kinge value our Religion better, and suffer not his subjects miseries and Contempt of our Religion to be there Contents. Prayinge for your Lordship I most Humbly Implore reliefe in Season for our Extremities Cannot indure Delais.

More likely to die then live in your Lordships service/

  [signed:] Henry Challons

      Julie 3 stilo nova

[Endorsement to this and preceding letter:] The Coppies of my two Last Letters sent to my Lord Chiefe Justice.

481. August 7, 1607. Sir Ferdinando Gorges to the Earl of Salisbury.

Hatfield House, Cecil Papers 121/172; printed in Baxter, Gorges, *III, 148–150.*

Right Honorable my humble duty remembred. Master Newport (unto whome these lettres were directed) did set sayle from hence on Fryday, beinge the laste of July; I was not at home when hee came firste into the harbor, but I understoode so much by him since, as I conceave a possibility of great good to bee don in the place where they ar; the Harbor beinge commodiouse, the Contry fertel, the Clime healthfull, but the people daungerouse to bee dealt with, beinge by nature valiante and in number many. Wherfor in my poor opinion, it were necessary that all the haste possible were used for the supply of those that bee there; for if any disaster happen unto them, it wilbee a great discouragement and discountenance to the attempte; but if they bee royally seconded, there is no doubte of successe, so industry and good goverment be not wantinge.

I have understoode of your Lordshipps most honorable care had for the release of our poore men that ar Prysoners in Spayne, whose names I have sent to Captayne Barlee to be delivered to your Honors handes, yealdinge all possible thankes to your good Lordshipp in theyr behalfe, whose estate without your Lordshipps favour is desperate, for that they ar in the handes of such who delighte themselves in doinge wronges to all and right to none, unles forsed by necessity, contrary to theyr naturall custom. I forbeare to speake of them what I thinke, bycause I do not desire, it should bee thought I am delighted in the controversyes of Princes, but I pray god, common experience do not make to manifest our daunger procured by the word Peace, purchassed (as themselves confesse) for theyr necessity, not of love to our Prince or Nation. I cannot as yet give any ashurance to your Lordshipp of the particulars of the estate of the Contry where wee have sent our Colony. But (if I bee not much deceaved) it will prove it selfe to bee such, as there wilbee great reason to induce som noble nature to undertake throughly the protection for accomplishment therof; it beinge a designe for the aeternizinge of an honerable memory. The which (if I durste bee so boulde) I would rather wish your worthy selfe to undertake then any subject whatsoever, both in respect of your wisdom to understand thinges of this nature, as also your eminent favor and great authority in the Commonwealth (all matters of high consequence). For myne owne parte if our Nation may bee so fortunate as to finde your exception therof, I wilbee reddy and thinke myselfe moste happy, if you shall vouchsafe, to make use, or commaunde my best indeavors, to go my selfe thither in such fashion as you shall thinke mee able to doe his Majesty and my Contry service. Howsoever I beseech your good Lordshipp to rest undoubtedly perswaded that my life, and all I have shalbee for ever,

[signed:] Fard: Gorges

Plymouth this 7th of August 1607.

[Addressed:] To the Right Honorable my very good Lord the Erle of Salisbury: these.

[Endorsed:] 7, August, 1607. Sir Ferdinando Gorges to my Lord.

482. May 14/May 24, 1607. Sir Charles Cornwallis to the Earl of Salisbury.

P.R.O., SP 94/14, fols. 27-29, copy.

Madrid 24th Maij 1607. Cornwaleys

The Conde de Lemos, president of the Counsell of the Indies, Coming upon Sunday last to visit me (upon an occasion of a motion made to him, that after soe long a penance, improporcionable to soe light a fault, the poore men imprisoned at Lisbon, and Sivill (the first for Traffiquing in the Indies, the second for being found upon those seas, out of their way whether they had been enforced by Tempest) might receive absolution, and Libertie, entered into a great discourse with me, saying how much this state in generall and himselfe in particular disireth to give Contentment to the King my Master and to me for what I require for his Majesties service; But withall soe great is their zeale of their Indies (which they behold, with noe lesse watchfull eyes, then the governement of their owne wives) as notwithstanding his owne desire to serve the King, to satisfy me & give not distast to our nation (from which he saith, he holdeth it an Honour to be descended) yet he must be playn with me, In Coertions, & punishment, to restrayn Accesse to those Countries, he had an Inclination rather to Crueltie, then Clemency.

I replyed, that I much marvayled, that soe wise a nation, should not discerne, two such stones of scandall as they give to all other princes, and Countries, their neighbours. The one, in not taking some mean way, agreeable with their safety, and honour, to have ther pursuite of the absolute dominion, and possession of the Islandes united, whereby they seem to adde soe inistimable a power, to their already overgrown greatnesse. The other in the prohibition of all nations, to have navigation, and Commerce into the Indies.

Of the first I told him, they had already made a wofull experience, as whom those contende (with a people in their owne nature, soe unwarlike) had discovered to be other, then their victorious progresses, in all their former Attempts, had made them to be deemed. That it had been a meanes to dispeople their Countries, to exhaust their Treasury, To stop their proceedinges, in eyther acquiringe or setling their new discoveries; To distemper their Counsells and (by all probability) in time would draw their estate, into the depth of Danger.

The second (I sayd) was not only against the ordinance of God, but the Lawes of Nature and Nations. Caelum caeli domino, terras autem dedit filiis hominum.

Although necessary it was for Cohabitation, that the Earth was devided, and a knowne propriety in the parts of it, yet was it ever with a natural Caution, that the same should not be held in a Closed hand, and exempt from the generall use of Men, for whom God had created it. I told him, that Jure naturali, Communia sic omnium, et Aqua profluens, et Mare, Item flumina et portus. That our nation might with good Right use to them the verse of the poet, viz. Quod genus hoc hominum, quere hunc tam barbara monitur permittit patria, hospitio prohibemas arena.

Here he interrupted me, saying that for the first (viz that of the Low Countries) I had great Reason; But for the second, very strange it was I would undertake to perswade that, which was in such extremity opposite, both to their Religion, and State, whereof it became them (as well in christianity, as wisedome) to have a most especiall Consideration. That by Experience they had found that the Accesse of French, Germans, Hollanders, & English in those parts, had sowne amongst that people (being but newly seasoned with the Catholic fayth) such a mixture, and Confusion of diversity of sects, and opinions, as being once tasted, were hardly possible to be rooted out of them.

Besides I was to consider, that the Case for Traffique, and Navigation thither, was farre different from that of other parts of the world. That it was unto them, Regnum Novum, and therefore untill their being better setled, and fortifyed therein, they were with great Reason Jealous, and fearfull to object eyther to hungry, or Curious eyes soe pretious, & desirable a Jewell, Lastly that the Dominion, Right, and possession, was theirs, and therefore Lawfull, both by rule of nature, and nations, to appropriate it to themselves, and exclude others.

I answered, that for sowing of diversity of opinion in Religion, there was noe more danger there then here, for sure I was, that in all their ports there, they have the same Lawes, and the Like officers of the Inquisition, that they use in all other their Dominions; That although their soveraignty, and possession there were not soe well setled, as in other their Kingdomes, yet from Merchants (subject to their Confederates, and friendes, and coming only furnished for Trade, not for hostility or offence) they could not in Reason, expect violence or other prejudice; And as for sight of the Country, which might draw them to covet it, I tould him, that much more naturall it is to men to desire what is covered, and

restrayned, then what is open, and allowed, and thereof (meerely) I sayd I could give him, many evident, and familiar examples.

He replyed, that this State was resolved, never to take them for friendes, or allow them for Traders, that should resort into those parts, Concluding that it was not fit for them to suffer any use of Navigation thither, whereby to acquaynt other nations with that way which they intended should be only knowne, and accessible unto themselves, and sayd, that for that purpose by Gods Grace they would hereafter, never be without 12 Gallyons, continually to attend that service only.

I sayd, I was sorry, to find such a Resolution, which I feared would breed much more unrist unto them, and lesse benefit, then with permitting a quiet, and peaceable Traffique, with some Reasonable Conditions, as of returning by his Majesties ports here, and paying the Customs, and of some other orders, for removing of all suspition, of evill Intention. And as for the way thither (soe long as Bookes, & Cards should remayn) Impossible it was to keepe it from knowledge; And therewithall Company Coming into the place, where we were (the Earle saying, that he must have another time with me to debate, more largely of that, and other matters) we ended, this being the substance of what (concerning that matter) passed between us.

[Endorsed:] Spayn. Property of the Indies. Conference between yᵉ Conde de Lemos & Sir Charles Cornwallis, the latter shewing that other Nations ought not to be hindered to trade thither. 1607. Spain 24 May 1607

483. 1606–1607. "Opinion relative to the term 'Indies' at the Treaty with Spain & whether Virginia bee considered in them."

Hatfield House, Cecil Papers 119/149; printed in Baxter, Gorges, III, 132–133. In the hand of Levinus Munck, a secretary to the Earl of Salisbury.

It seemeth by the journal of the Treaty, that the Adventurers into any partes of the Indias, should be leaft unto the perill which they should incurr thereby. Hereupon groweth this question, what is to be done with the Marryners that are taken in Spaine, (being 18 or 20 in number) as they were goeing from the West partes of England to a discovery into Virginia; and what course is to be taken with the Spanish ship dryven into Bourdeaux, which ship was a principall actor in taking the English ship. First it must be considered, that although it is disputeable, whether Virginia be part of the Indias though it be situate upon the same continent of the West Indies; yet for avoiding of the occasion thereby to fall into the generall question of the Indias and our trading thereinto, it might be advised that it were better to leave these prisoners to their fortune, then by bringing it in question to stirr up some greater inconveniences that might ensue of it.

Secondly, yf it be alleadged, that they went but to a place formerly discovered by us, and never possessed by Spaine; it may be answered that this allegation altereth not the state of the question but only the forme, whether wee may trade into any partes of the Indias that are not possessed by Spaine which point was then at the handling of the Treaty directly denyed by the Spanish Commissioners.

All which considered, it may be more aptly stood upon, that these prisoners having not yet offended unless it be an offense, to be in those seas (which by the law of nations ought to be free quoad navigationem) but were only goeing, towards a place, which is yet disputable whether it be allowable or not by the Treaty, that in regard thereof, howsoever it may not seeme unjust to have stayd them and diverted them from their journey; yet it seemes to be unjust so rigourously to punish them for it, as to committ their bodys to prison, and to take away their goodes. And therefore it may be concluded (under humble correction) that his Majesty may write in their favour, upon the termes aforesaid, to the king of Spaine, or to his Ambassador there: and may geve order to his Ambassador in France, to insist to demand Justice against the Spanish Ship at Bourdeaux that tooke and robbed our men at sea, as Pyrats doe.

[Endorsed:] 1606 Concerning the ship taken at sea goeing to Virginia.

1606. Opinion relative to the term "Indies" at the Treaty with Spain & whether Virginia bee considered in them.

484. June 7, 1607. Sir Francis Bacon's report to the Commons of the Earl of Salisbury's speech to the Conference of Lords and Commons on the merchants' petition for redress against Spain, June 15, 1607.

B.L., Harleian MS 6792, fol. 162; printed in J. Spedding, Letters and life of Francis Bacon, *III (1868), 353–354.*

For the trade to the Indies, his Lordship did discover unto us the state of it to be thus: The policy of Spain doth keep that treasury of theirs under such lock and key, as both confederates, yea and subjects, are excluded of trade into those countries; insomuch as the French king, who hath reason to stand upon equal terms with Spain, yet nevertheless is by express capitulation debarred. The subjects of Portugal, whom the state of Spain hath studied by all means to content, are likewise debarred; such a vigilant dragon is there that keepeth this golden fleece. Yet nevertheless such was his Majesty's magnanimity in the debate and conclusion of the last treaty, as he would never condescend to any article, importing the exclusion of his subjects from that trade: as a prince that would not acknowledge that any such right could grow to the crown of Spain by the donative of the Pope, whose authority he disclaimeth; or by the title of a dispersed and punctual occupation of certain territories in the name of the rest; but stood firm to reserve that point in full question to further times and occasions. So as it is left by the treaty in suspense, neither debarred nor permitted. The tenderness and point of honour whereof was such, as they that went thither must run their own peril. Nay further his Lordship affirmed, that if yet at this time his Majesty would descend to a course of intreaty for the release of the arrests in those parts, and so confess an exclusion, and quit the point of honour, his Majesty mought [sic] have them forthwith released: And yet his Lordship added, that the offences and scandals of some had made this point worse than it was; in regard that this very last voyage to Virginia, intended for trade and plantation where the Spaniard hath no people nor possession, is already become infamed for piracy: Witness Bingley, who first insinuating his purpose to be an actor in that worthy action of enlarging trades and plantation, is become a pirate, and hath been so pursued as his ship is taken in Ireland, though his person is not yet in hold.[1]

485. 1607. "A Justification for Planting in Virginia."

This rough draft (which has been tidied up slightly to make it more readable) represents notes of a discussion inside the ruling group in the Virginia Company sometime between the late summer of 1607 and the early summer of 1608. As such it falls into the Virginia Company material in Volume V, but it is most clearly relevant to the discussions that were going on, as we have seen from the preceding documents about whether King James would take a firm line in backing the Virginia Company against Spanish threats to Jamestown, and whether a statement of the English case, publicly, would be politic. The arguments are extremely interesting, showing that until perhaps well into 1608 there was no real assurance that the king would not repudiate the Charter of 1606. The balance of opinion was that to lie low was most politic. But besides a pro-Spanish element in England, there appears to be identifiable an anti-colonial one, one objecting to the intrusion of Europeans into native society in North America. If this did exist, perhaps it helps to explain why the Virginia Company relied so much on sermons, advocating bringing Christianity to the Amerindians, for its publicity from 1609 onward.
Bodleian Library, Tanner MS 93, fol. 200; printed in S. M. Kingsbury, ed., Records of the Virginia Company of London, *4 vols. (Washington, D.C., 1906–1935), III, 1–3.*

A Justification for planting in Virginia

It was proposed [by master   ] that some forme of writinge in way of Justification of our plantation might be conceived and pass, (though not by publique authorytye) into many handes. The motion seemed to have these inducements.

1. First that it mought give adventurers, a clearnes and satisfaction, for yᵉ Justice of yᵉ Justice of yᵉ action, and so encourage them, and draw on others.

2. That yᵉ Spaniard might out of this intimation reasonably collect that wee understand our owne case to be such, that the state would neyther feare, nore be ashamed to proceed in that persecutuion ther of, if any Course should bee held agaynst yt: and that this Justification of our owne title, would deterr, or at least retard yᵉ Spaniard from suddayne attempting us.

And though it were sayd then; that this was a lowe and impotent way to convey it by such a close scedule; yet seemt, not to want example of other things carried in that manner: and yet to have wrought yᵉ same effect. as a more publique declaration of yᵉ state could doe.

They which differed from him had these motives;

1. That it conduc'd not to his first hope of encouraging, or inciting adventurers: for, they in this poynt needed it not, nor require yt. That there is much of a Confession, in every unnecessary Apology: that to move scruple, especially of Conscience, wher ther is afore quiettnes and no doubting rather shakes and deterrs, the settles, or confirmes. And that already some of best Judgement, startle upon yᵉ first noyse of yt.[1]

2. That yᵉ Spaniard hath already seene more publique, and authentique testemonyes, of yᵉ States good affection to yᵉ Journy, by establishing it under yᵉ great seale: and by yᵉ seconding, and Iterating supplyes, then this way can give him:

Besides it is more then probable that his Ambassador will forthwith expostulate with his Majestie about this writing, and then it is not conceav'd how far his Majestie wilbe pleased to avow yt, which may intimate disavowing: Besides that it seemed not to worke these good effects which were pretended, it hath these evident dangers in yt.

1. It will rather hasten yᵉ Spaniards rage, then retard yt; because we will see it, to grow every day harder for him to defeat us.

2. It will rayse undisputably, two penadversaries of divers sortes: The first are perfect

---

1. A reference to the activities of the "Triall."

1. In margin "if yᵉ first way fayle (because I doubt not of overthrowing yᵉ Donation) then this will follow, which if we could mayntayne yet with such subtelty of distinction as yᵉ merchant wilbe uncapable of satisfaction therby."

Spaniards, who will defend that title upon yᵉ Donation of Alexander, which is so grounded upon the principles of theyr religion that some of their best authors have pronounced yt Heresy to doubt yt. And we, (though wee want not inducinge and Convenient arguments from God, and Nature, and Nations) yet have no such convincinge and obligatory [ground such as (?) the]irs, especially towards them, and their ground.

The second sort wilbe neutrall writers, but of Spanish affections: who because they cannott therby hurt yᵉ Spaniard already established there, but may slacken us, if they can cast scruples into our Conscience will wright agaynst yᵉ lawfullnes of plantation in these, as well by yᵉ Spaniard, as by us, or any, which must necessaryly grow to dispututuon of so much intricasy, perlexity, and replication, as shall conduce unto theyr end of slackning us, if no farther. For when at first discovery of these partes yᵉ Spaniard did subject yᵉ Consideration of yt to Casuists, and Confessors, it became so indeterminable, that he was forced to resolve roundly upon yᵉ worst way, least he should have none, to prosecute yᵉ Indians as Barbar's, and therby Naturally slaves. When after 50 years his Fryars declyn'd him from that severe and unJust course, and he labourd by men of all learninge to provide himselfe of a more acceptable title, all yᵉ reasons, which were prepared to him, by men of discourse, from yᵉ Indians transagressing yᵉ Law of Nature; from his civilians for their denying commerce: from his Canonists by yᵉ Donation: and from his Devines, by preparation of religion, were so incohoeent and so resisted by one another, as many bookes written in his defence, were suppressed in his owne Kyngdome, and at this day; from all yᵉ authors extant, in that pointe, (though they admitt yᵉ purpose of yᵉ donation yet departing from yᵉ very letre) can be gathered for him no title, of Dominion or property, but only a Magistracy, and Empire, by which he is allowed to remove such impediments, as they had agaynst yᵉ knowledge of Religion.

Because there, we shalbe putt to defend out title, not yet publiquely quarreled, not only comparatively to be as good as yᵉ Spaniards (which we doubt not is easy enough, when it shalbe impugned), (agaynst which not notwithstandinge to governe them, ther arise yᵉ Donation, and that wee seek Dominion) but absolutely to be good agaynst yᵉ Naturall people: some though it better to abstayne from thus unnessisary way of provication, and reserve ourselves to yᵉ defensive part, when they shall offer any thing agaynst us: which will more easyly and satisfactoryly be donne, and we are like enough to bee too soone putt to yt by them, when they see yᵉ proportion and forwardness of this present supply.

Chapter Sixty-six
Further Preliminaries to Settlement

486. The Thomas Hanham-Martin Pring expedition to North Virginia.

This is the least-known expedition of the period and clearly a very important one. It provided the initial data that led to the selection of the Sagadahoc River, rather than the St. George, as the objective for the colony. Although intended merely as a supply vessel for the Challons pioneer settlement, their ship conducted a survey, brought back maps and reports, and generally occupied a most significant part in the preparations for the Plymouth Company venture. The major source, Thomas Hanham's journal (see 490) has proved impossible to trace.

A briefe relation of the discovery and plantation of New-England. Published by the presedent and council, *London, 1622, has a brief account, reprinted by S. Purchas*, Pilgrimes, *IV (1625), 1827.* (XIX [1907], 270).

.... but immediately upon his [Thomas Challons's] departure, it pleased the Noble Lorde Chiefe Justice, Sir John Popham knight, to send out another shippe, wherein Captayne Thomas Haman[1] went Commander, & Martin Prinne of Bristow Master, with all necessary supplies, for the seconding of Captayne Challons and his people; who arriving at the place appointed, and not finding that Captaine there, after they had made some Discovery, and found the Coasts, Havens, and Harbors answerable to our desires, they returned. Upon whose relation the Lord Chiefe Justice, and wee all waxed so confident of the businesse, that the yeere following everie man of any worth, formerly interested in it, was willing to joyne in the charge for the sending over a competent number of people to lay the ground of an hopefull Plantation.

487. 1606. The Hanham-Pring voyage.

Purchas had a journal of Thomas Hanham but did not print it, and it is lost. He used it in a brief reference.

Samuel Purchas, Pilgrimage, *2nd edition (London, 1614), pp. 755–756 (see 486).*

Captain Thomas Hanham sayled to the River of Sagadahoc 1606.[1] He relateth of their beasts, doggs like wolves, of colours blacke, white, red, and grisled: red Deere, and a beast bigger, called the Mus, &c. of their fowles, fishes, trees: of some Oare proved to be silver.

---

1. Purchas adds the side-note "Captain Hanam sent by Lord Chiefe Justice Popham."

1. Sidenote: "Thomas Hanham." "Master Chalenge made a voyage hitherward the same yeere, but was taken by the Spaniards."

THE DESCRIPTIONS OF THE COUNTRY OF MAWOOSHEN, *CIRCA* 1606

THE NAME MAWOOSHEN was clearly derived from the Indians brought back by Waymouth in 1605, as they learned English. It was the objective of Challons in 1606 and continued to be used as the Amerindian name for the region comprised within the effective Plymouth Company area over the next three years or more. It would appear to be the region occupied by the Abenaki group of tribes. Bashabees, the Abenaki chief located on the Penobscot, considered himself, or was considered, to be the high chief of this whole area (little evidence on the range of his effectiveness is available). In terms of space the distance southwest to northeast along the coast might be thought to correspond very roughly with that from Casco Bay to Machias Bay (though this would be merely a guess), while the inland area southeast to northwest would correspond roughly with the inland limits of modern Maine (a very improbable range of hunting grounds). Extensive study will prove necessary before the description is made fully intelligible.

The first reference to the description is in Samuel Purchas, *Pilgrimage* (1614), pp. 755–756 (488); he printed it in full in his *Pilgrimes*, IV (1625), 1873–1874 (XIX [1907], 400–405) (489), where his head note is to the effect that it covered the country known to the English between 1602 and 1609. This is more likely to mean it was composed in 1606, or, at latest, 1607, but remained available after the latter date until 1609.

488. 1606–1609. Mawooshen and its parts.

Samuel Purchas, Pilgrimage, *2nd edition (London, 1614), pp. 755–756 (3rd edition [1617], pp. 938–939; 4th edition [1626], p. 829), used some materials he did not employ in his* Pilgrimes, *4 vols. (1625), though they are fragmentary in nature. What follows is from the 1614 edition.*

Mawooshen was many yeeres together visited by our men, extending betweene 43. and 45. degrees, 40. league in bredth, and 50. in length. They found therein nine Rivers, Quibiquesson, Pemaquid, Ramassoc, Apanawapaske, Apaumensek, Aponeg, Sagadahoc, Ashamahaga, Shawokotoc. Sagadahoc is in 43. degrees, it is a mile and halfe at the mouth holding the same bredth a dayes journey,[1] and makes a sound three dayes journey broad, in which are six Ilands: it hath two branches, the one from the Northeast 24. dayes journey, the other North-west 30 dayes journey. At the heads are two Lakes the Westermost 8. dayes journey long and foure wide, the Eastermost halfe so large. This is Bashabaes his dominion. The Tarentines country[2] is in 44. degrees two third parts, where the Savages tell of a Rock of Allum, neere the River of Sasnowa....[3]

1. Sidenote: "The Savages reckon thus by dayes journey."
2. Sidenote: "Christopher Fortescue." His voyage (mentioned) is otherwise undated and unknown.
3. Omitted is the Hanham-Pring material given as (486).

Bashabes hath many under-Captaines, called Sagamos: their houses built with Withs, and covered over with Mats, six or seven paces long. He expresseth also the names of their twelve Moones or moneths: as January Mussekeshos, February Gignokiakeshos, &c.

489. "The description of the Countrey of Mawooshen, discovered by the English in the yeere 1602. 3. 5. 7. 8. and 9."[1]

Mawooshen is a Countrey lying to the North and by East of Virginia, betweene the degrees of 43. and 45. It is fortie leagues broad, and fiftie in length, lying in breadth East and West, and in length North and South. It is bordered on the East side with a Countrey, the people, whereof they call Tarrantines[2]: on the West with Epistoman, on the North with a great Wood called Senaglecounc, and on the South with the mayne Ocean Sea, and many Ilands.

In Mawooshen it seemeth there are nine Rivers, whereof the first to the East is called

1. Sidenote: This description of Mawooshen I had amongst Master Hakluyts papers."
2. Sidenote: "Tarantines are said to be the same with the Souriquois."

Quibiquesson; on which there is one Towne, wherein dwell two Sagamos or Lords, the one called Asticon, the other Abermot. In this Towne are fiftie houses, and 150. men. The name of which Towne is Precante; this River runneth farre up into the Mayne, at the head thereof there is a Lake of a great length and breadth; it is at the fall into the Sea tenne fathoms deepe, and halfe a mile over.

The next is Pemaquid, a goodly River and very commodious all things considered; it is ten fathoms water at the entrance, and fortie miles up there are two fathoms and a halfe at low water; it is halfe a mile broad, and runneth into the Land North many daies journey: where is a great Lake of 18. leagues long and foure broad. In this Lake are seven great Ilands: toward the farthest end there falleth in a River, which they call Acaconstomed, where they passe with their Boates thirtie daies jouney up, and from thence they goe over Land twentie daies journey more, and then come to another River, where they have a trade with Anadabis or Anadebiion, with whom the Frenchmen have had commerce for a long time. Neere to the North of this River of Pemaquid are three Townes: the first is Upsegon, where Bashabes their chiefe Lord doth dwell. And in this Towne are sixtie houses, and 250. men, it is three daies journey within the Land. The second is Caiocame; the third Shasheekeing. These two last Townes are apposite one to the other, the River dividing them both, and they are two daies journey from the Towne of Bashabes. In Caiocame dwelleth Maiesquis, and in Shasheokeing Bowant, two Sagamos, subjects to Bashabes. Upon both sides of this River up to the very Lake, for a good distance the ground is plaine, without Trees or Bushes, but full of long Grasse, like unto a pleasant meadow, which the Inhabitants doe burne once a yeere to have fresh feed for their Deere. Beyond this Meadow are great Woods, whereof more shall bee spoken hereafter. The River of Pemaquid is foure dayes journey from the mouth of Quibiquesson.

The third River is called Ramassoc, and is distant from the mouth of Pemaquid foure daies journey; it is twentie fathoms at the entrance, and hath a mile over; it runneth into the Land three daies journey, and within lesse then a daies journey of the dwelling of Bashabes: upon this River there is a Towne named Panobscot, the Lord whereof is called Sibatahood; who hath in his Town fiftie houses, and eightie men.

The fourth River Apanawapeske, lying West and by South of Ramassoc, at the entrance whereof there is twentie fathoms water, and it is a mile broad it runneth up into the Countrey five daies journey; and within three daies of the mouth are two Townes, the one called Meecombe, where dwelleth Aramasoga, who hath in his Towne fiftie houses, and eightie men. The other is Chebegnadose, whose Lord is Skanke, and hath thirtie houses and ninetie men. The mouth of Apanawapeske is distant from Ramassoc three daies journey.

To the South-west foure daies journey, there is another excellent River; in the entrance whereof is twentie fathoms water, and it is a quarter of a mile broad, it runneth into the Land two daies journey, and then there is a great fall, at the head whereof there is a Lake of a daies journey long and as much in breadth. On the side of this Lake there is a Strait, and at the end of that Strait there is another Lake of foure daies journey long, and two daies journey broad; wherin there are two Ilands, one at the one end, and another at the other end. I should have told you that both these Lakes, as also the rest formerly spoken of, doe infinitely abound with fresh water fish of all sorts, as also with divers sorts of Creatures, as Otters, Beeves, sweete Rats, and such like.

The sixt River is called Apponick, on which there are three Townes; the first is called Appisham, where dwelleth Abochigishic. The second is Mesaqueegamic, where dwelleth Aniquin, in which there is seventie houses and eightie men; the third is Matammiscowte, in which are eightie houses and ninetie men, and there dwelleth Narracomique.

To the Westward of this there is another River called Aponeg: it hath at the entrance ten fathoms water, and is a mile broad: it runneth up into a great Sound of fresh water. Upon the East side of this River there are two Townes, the one called Nebamocago, the other called Asshawe. In the first dwelleth Mentaurmet, and hath in his Towne 160. housholds, and some 300. men. In the second dwelleth Hamerhaw, and hath in his Towne eightie housholds and seventie men. On the West side there is another Towne called Neredoshan, where are 120. housholds, and 100. men. There is a Sagamo or Lord called Sabenaw.

Three daies journey from Aponeg to the Westward, there is a goodly River called Sagadohoc[3] the entrance whereof is a mile and a halfe over, holding that breadth a daies journey, and then it maketh a great Sound of three daies journey broad: in which Sound are six Ilands, foure great and full of Woods, and two lesse without Woods: The greater are called Sowaghcoc, Neguiwo, Neiwoc. And in the verie entrance of this River there is another small Iland: from the West of which Iland to the Maine, there is a Sand that maketh as it were a bar, so that that way is not passable for shipping: but to the Eastward there is two fathoms water. This Sound divideth it selfe into two branches or armes, the one running North-east twentie foure daies journey, the other North-west thirtie daies journey into the Maine: At the heads whereof there are two Lakes, the Westermost being eight daies journey long, and foure daies journey broad; and the Eastermost foure daies journey long, and two daies broad. The River of Aponeg runneth up into this Sound, and so maketh as it were a great Iland between Sagadahoc and it. From the Iland upward the water is fresh, abounding in Salmons, and other fresh-water fish. Some thirteene or fourteen daies journey from the entrance in the North-east branch, there is a little arme of a River that runneth East some daies journey, which hath at the entrance foure fathoms water. Upon this arme there is one over fall, which standeth halfe a daies journey above this branch: upon this arme there are foure Townes: The first is called Kenebeke, which hath eightie houses, and one hundred men. The Lord whereof is Apomhamen. The second is Ketangheanycke, and the Sagamos name is Octoworthe, who hath in his Towne ninetie housholds, and three hundred and thirtie men. This Towne is foure dayes journey from Kenebeke, and eight dayes journey from [   ]. To the Northward is the third Towne, which they call Naragooc; where there are fiftie housholds, and one hundred and fiftie men. The chiefe Sagamo of that place is Cocockohamas. And on the small branch that runneth East

standeth the fourth Towne, named by Massakiga; where there are but eight housholds, and fortie men. Upon the Northwest branch of this Sound stand two Townes more: The first is called Amereangan, and is distant from Kenebeke six dayes journey. In this place are ninetie housholdes, and two hundred and sixtie men, with two Sagamoes; the one called Sasuoa, the other Scawas. Seven daies journey hence there is another Sagamo, whose name is Octoworokin, and his Townes name Namercante, wherein are fortie housholds, and one hundred and twentie men. A dayes journey above Namercante there is a downefall, where they cannot passe with their Cannoes, but are inforced to carrie them by Land for the space of a quarter of a mile, and then they put them into the River againe: And twelve dayes journey above this Downfall there is another, where they carrie their Boates as at the first; and six dayes journey more to the North is the head of this River, where is the Lake that is of eight dayes journey long, and foure dayes broad before mentioned. In this Lake there is one Iland; and three dayes journey from this Lake there is a Towne which is called Buccawganecants, wherein are threescore housholds, and foure hundred men: And the Sagamo thereof is called Baccatusshe. This man and his people are subjects to the Bashabez of Mawooshen, and in his Countrey is the farthest limit of his Dominion, where he hath any that doe him homage.

To the Westward of Sagadahoc, foure dayes journey there is another River called Ashamahaga, which hath at the entrance six fathoms water, and is halfe a quarter of a mile broad: it runneth into the Land two dayes journey: and on the East side there is one Towne called Agnagebcoc, wherein are seventie houses, and two hundred and fortie men, with two Sagamos, the one called Maurmet, the other Casherokenit.

Seven dayes journey to the South-west of Ashamahaga there is another River, that is six fathoms to the entrance: This River is named Shawakotoc, and is halfe a myle broad; it runneth into the Land fiftie dayes journey: but foure dayes from the entrance it is so narrow, that the Trees growing on each side doe so crosse with their boughes and bodies on the other, as it permitteth not any meanes to passe with Boates that way: for which cause the Inhabitants that on any occasion

---

3. Sidenote: "Here Captain Popham built S Georges Fort, and planted."

are to travell to the head, are forced to goe by Land, taking their way upon the West side. At the end of this River there is a Lake of foure dayes journey long, and two dayes broad, wherein are two Ilands. To the North-West foure daies journey from this Lake, at the head of this River Shawakatoc there is a small Province, which they call Crokemago, wherein is one Towne. This is the Westermost River of the Dominions of Basshabez, and Quibiquisson the Westermost.

490. 1606–1611. Materials on New England formerly available but now lost.

S. Purchas, Pilgrimes, *IV, 1837 (XIX, 296), confessing to having omitted much New England material.*

Reader, I had by me the Voyage of Captaine Thomas Hanham (written by himselfe) unto Sagadahoc: also the written Journals of Master Raleigh Gilbert which stayed and fortified there in that unseasonable Winter (fit to freeze the heart of a Plantation) of James Davies, John Eliot, &c. but our voluminousnesse makes me afraid of offending nicer and queasier stomackes: for which cause I have omitted them, even after I had with great labour fitted them to the Presse: as I have also done a written large Tractate of Mawaushen,[1] and the Voyage of Master Edward Harlie (one of the first Planters with Captain Popham) and Nicholas Hobson to those parts 1611. with divers Letters from Captain Popham and others.

1. This would suggest that the treatise on Mawooshen he did print was another or a shorter version of the treatise he refers to here.

Chapter Sixty-seven
The Sagadahoc Colony of the Plymouth
Company, 1607–1608

THE EXPEDITIONS of Challons and of Hanham and Pring were set out under the pressure and inspiration of the Lord Chief Justice of King's Bench, Sir John Popham. His death in the summer of 1607 was a major blow to the Plymouth enterprise which he had made very much his own. The expedition of June, 1607, under Captains George Popham and Raleigh Gilbert, was prepared with very limited resources by Sir Francis Popham, Sir John's son and heir, and by Sir Ferdinando Gorges. The loss of the ship, lading and complement of the *Richard* damaged them, they reckoned, to the extent of some £5000 (478), though this was almost certainly much more than the sum they spent on her. The *Gift* and the *Mary and John* made efficient voyages across the ocean (June 10–July 27), but it took some time for them to decide to enter and locate their settlement on the Kennebec River, which they did not enter until August 17. The period from August 17 to early October was partly taken up by exploring the Kennebec basin and partly in constructing their Sagadahoc settlement, Fort St. George, on a peninsula some way upstream. The *Mary and John* set out on her return early in August and reached Plymouth on December 1. Her report was very mixed: the site and the prospects were promising but there were no goods and only a few specimens of plant products to show, while stores had proved inadequate (through both lack of money and some bad dealing it would appear), and George Popham and Raleigh Gilbert were on poor terms, Gilbert raising a party, it was said, to assert his own right to the ownership and control of the whole settlement. Nothing more was learned until the *Gift*, which had been intended to stay with the colonists, appeared at Plymouth on February 6 or 7, 1608. Her men reported the colonists to be seriously short of food, the weather to have become very bad (so that the ship was sent away for fear of being broken up by ice coming downstream). There seemed to be little of value to report except the work being done on building the pinnace, *Virginia*. Too little food was provided for the ship to bring her home, and she was forced to put into the Azores and there for lack of money she was forced to dispose of her cargo of masts (possibly the only products of value she carried) and even to pawn a gun to buy food. (Her master was afterwards sued by Lady Popham and her son Sir Francis for misappropriating their property by doing so, but he was acquitted [502–510].)

Sir Ferdinando Gorges was now left with most of the responsibility for maintaining the colony on his hands. He sent out two small ships and then a larger one which did not reach them until late summer 1608, by which time the 65 original settlers had been reduced by men sent home (twenty it would appear) and then through deaths. Moreover, George Popham had died in February, Gilbert was in command, and news came with the ship that his elder brother, Sir John Gilbert, had died, and that he was now heir to the family property. From the beginning the colonists' relations with the Indians had been ambiguous: each was somewhat suspicious of the other. Furs had been traded, including some valuable beaver pelts, but not in quantities which promised to make the Company profitable. The colonists had been discouraged by the harshness of the winter and again, most probably, by the meager support Gorges had contrived to send them. Gilbert was more interested in claiming his inheritance than in maintaining the settlement, and no other individual with a desire to rule came forward. The result was a decision to abandon the settlement on September 30, 1608 (496). The *Virginia*, now an effective 30-ton bark, was ready to take her place alongside the relief ship (whose name we do not know). The vessels returned to Plymouth late in 1608. Gorges had been hoping for some royal assistance in the project, on the pretext of keeping out the French. When he did not get it, the return of the settlers must have been something of a relief. The London Virginia Company treated the return of the colonists as an indication of the end of the Plymouth Company (they were almost right, though seasonal fishing and trading voyages continued under its auspices) and tried to enlist its members in an all-out drive in 1609 for the enlargement of the southern colony, now seated, if precariously, at Jamestown (520).

The Plymouth Company's activity fizzled out in a series of lawsuits (511–519), the chief importance of which is to show that, after the death of Sir John Popham, far too little money was invested in the project, and far too short a time allowed to ascertain whether it could provide at least a fur-trading post. There was misfortune, too, but on a much smaller scale than plagued the Jamestown colony. John Smith finally decided (521) that this part of the coast was simply not viable for human occupation.

491. May 31, 1607. George Popham accepts command of the Plymouth Company colony.

Hatfield House, Cecil Papers 121/65; James P. Baxter, Sir Ferdinando Gorges and his Province of Maine, 3 vols. (Boston, 1890), III, 144–145, extract.

Remembringe my self in all humble dutifulnes unto my righte honorable good lord, doe by theis make bolde to advertize, that I directed my late lettres unto your Lordshipp concerninge a commaunde I had from my Lord Cheife Justice of England, to appointe my self unto the discoverye and populacion of the western Colony in Virginia. I wishe my desire mighte goe accompanyed with any of the leaste acceptable service therein, yet durste I promise by due endevours to give my beste addicion unto the same. I sente alsoe a lettre in that of myne enclosed, concerninge the passage of our merchantes aboute theire occasions in Spaine, & Portugall, wherof I thoughte fytt to acquainte your honor. . . .

From Plymouth this Laste of Maye 1607:

Your honors moste humble to Commaund/
[signed:] George Popham

[Addressed:] To the righte honorable my verie good lord the Earle of Salisburye principall Seacretary to his moste excellente Majesty and of his highnes moste Honorable Privye Counfaile.

492. 1607–1608. Samuel Purchas's account of the Sagadahoc colony.

Purchas used sources for the second (1614) and subsequent editions of his Pilgrimage *which are not now available and which he did not print in his* Pilgrimes *(1625). He indicates his sources in the margins (often by initials), though they are not always identifiable. They are set in square brackets in the text.*
S. Purchas, Pilgrimage, *2nd ed. (1614), p. 830; 3rd ed. (1617), 4th ed. (1626), p. 830. The 1617 edition is used here.*

Anno 1607. was settled a Plantation in the River Sagadahoc, the ships called the *Gift*, and the *Mary and John* [k. James Davies] being sent thither by that famous English Justicier Sir John Popham and others. They found this coast of Virginia full of Ilands, but safe. They chose the place of their Plantation at the mouth of Sagadahoc, in a Westerly Peninsula: there heard a Sermon, read their Patent and Lawes, and built a Fort. They sailed up to discover the River and Countrey, and encountered with an Iland where there was a great fall of water, over which they haled their Boat with a Rope, and came to another fall, shallow, swift, and unpassable. They found the Countrey stored with Grapes white and red, good Hops, Onions, Garlicke, Okes, Walnuts, the soile good.

The head of the River is in forty five and odde minutes. Cape Sinis-amis is 43. degrees 30. minutes, a good place to fortifie. Their Fort bare the name of Saint George. Fortie five remained there, [1. John Eliot, George Popham to Sir John Gilbert and E(dward?) S(corie?).] Captaine George Popham being President, Raleigh Gilbert Admirall. The people seemed affected with our mens devotions, and would say, King James is a good King, his God a good God, and Tanto nought. So they call an evill spirit which haunts them every Moone, and makes them worship him for feare. Hee commanded them not to dwell neere, or come among the English, threatning to kill some and inflict sicknesse on others, beginning with two of their Sagamos children, saying he had power, and would do the like to the English the next Moone, to wit, in December.

The people [m. Raleigh Gilbert] told our men of Canibals, [n. These seem to be the deformed Armouchiquois made in the telling more dreadfull.] neere Sagadahoc, with teeth three inches long, but they saw them not. In the River of Tamescot they found Oysters nine inches in length: and were told that on the other side there were twice as great. On the 18. of January they had in seven houres space, thunder, lightning, raine, frost, snow, all in aboundance, the last continuing. On February the 5. the President died. The Savages remove their dwellings in Winter neerest the Deere. They have a kinde of shooes a yard long, fourteene inches broad, made like a Racket, with strong twine or sinewes of a Deere; the midst is a hole wherein they put their

foot, buckling it fast. When a Sagamos dyeth, they blacke themselves, and at the same time yerely renue their mourning with great howling: as they did for Kashurakeng who died the yeere before. They found a Bath two miles about, so hote that they could not drinke it. Master Patteson was slaine by the Savages of Nanhoc, a River of the Tarentines. Their short Commons [o. Edward Hartley (1614, Harley).] caused fear of mutiny. One of the savages, called Aminquin, for a straw hat and knife given him, stript himselfe of his cloathing to [of, 1614] Bevers skinnes, worth in England 50. shillings, or three pound to present them to the President, leaving only a flap to cover his privities. He would also have come with them for England. In winter they are poore [p. Other notes *apud* Hakluyt.] and weake, and do not then company with their wives, but in Summer when they are fat and lusty. But your eyes wearied with this Northerne view, which in that Winter communicated with us in the extremitie of cold, looke now for greater hopes in the Southerne Plantation, as the right arme of his Virginian body, with greater costs and numbers furnished from here.

493. March 27, 1607. Exeter City Council refuses Sir John Popham a contribution to the Plymouth Company.

The attempt to spread more widely the small net of subscribers who made up the Plymouth Company had little success. A laconic entry in the Exeter City records indicates that Sir John Popham, for all his prestige and influence, was unable to induce the city to subscribe. It is also significant that Popham, so soon before his death, was making personal attempts to raise further sums for what he clearly considered to be his own venture.

Exeter Public Library, Exeter City Records, Exeter Chamber Act Book, 1601–1611, p. 208.

xxvij die Martii Anno Jacobi Quarto

And they agree where my Lord Cheefe Justice hathe by his Lettres mocioned to the Cittie to have an Adventure from them to Terra Virginia to be borne. That an answer shalbe made therunto that the merchantes of this Cittie have bene Charged in former tymes with such Adventures very much to ther Losse & hinderans That they are not mynded to adventure to the seme. And that Master Recorder, Master Periam, Master Howell & Master Dorchester shall in ther descrecon [write to the same?].

494. April 7, 1607. Sir Ferdinando Gorges to the Earl of Salisbury.

Gorges refers to the continued sufferings of Challons's men in Spain and urges Salisbury to persuade the king to take up the Virginia venture.
Hatfield House, Cecil Papers 120/154; printed in J. P. Baxter, Gorges, III, 166–168, extract.

I have written to their Lordshipps shewinge the state and defects of this place wherin I have indeavoured with my best understanding to discharge my publike duty, humbly praying your Lordship to vouchsafe it what furtherance your wisdome shall think fitt, beseeching yow to Continue your Honors disposition in advancinge the relief of those pore wretches that we sent for the discovery of *Virginea*, dobting nothing, notwithstandinge the mallice of the Divell, that so unhappely hath wrought our Loss of tyme, but that the event will prove better then in truth your Lordship hath reason yet to expect it should, and I verely believe when it shall once be discovered, and the Commodetyes knowne, yt wilbe thought fitt by your Lordship and the rest of the Lords that his Majesty undertake yt as his proper designe, making it an enterprise and imployment fitt for some such Noble and generous spirite as his Highnes shall vouchsafe to thinke worthie to be sent his Lieftenant for the government and orderinge of those affaires. Even soe the god of heaven bless your Lordship and make you happie in all your Honourable desires beseeching you to commaund me during my lief as him that is

Your Lordships most humbly to be Commaunded
[signed] Fard. Gorges
From Plymouth the 7th of Aprill 1607.

[*Addressed:*] To the Right Honorable my verie good Lord the Erle of Salisburie these.

495. June 11, 1606. Town of Plymouth to Sir John Popham.

Plymouth was willing to be the seat of the Plymouth Company, the western branch of the Virginia Company, but was not satisfied that any of the ships should sail from Bristol (on the Severn), so that Plymouth (though cooperating with Bristol) would continue to monopolize the activities of the Company.
Plymouth Public Library, Plymouth Archives W360/18, draft.

Right Honorable our humble dueties remembred We have receaved two letters from your Lordshipp the one being dated the 21 of Maye the other the 29 [?] of the same in boath there seemeth to be some contrarietie that gave occasion of some distraction for in the firste itt pleased your Lordship to resolve that all thinges should be performed from this place according wherunto we have made our resolution giving order for the performance thereof as by our former letters in annswer of your Lordships itt doth appeare But this devision hath disjoynted itt more for nowe we neither do knowe What the particulars are that shalbe necessarie to be provided out of Severne nor can they tell what may be convenientlie had here and before theise thinges cann be resolved on the tyme wilbe spent And the Confusion withall wilbe infinite Wherefore itt may please your Lordship to hold your first determynation that We may build altogeather uppon a Certentie with one mynde and one order so shall we be sure neither to staye one for the other att places unsawfe nor one to surchardge or confounde the other by unnecessarie provisions neither be subject to the unconstancie of Wyndes and weather which may be good for us here when itt is evill for theym there And to the end we may be the better understood in this behalf we have appoynted this gentleman master Challange more particularlie to give your Lordship our reasons herein Withall we have made an estimate of the whole voyage the which we have likewise sent to your Lordship to thend you may perceave what we conceave is necessarie for the present out of the particuler understanding We have of the place Wherof more att large your Lordship shall receave farther advertisement from Sir Fardinando Gorge hereafter. And Whereas there are diverse gentlemen of Somersett willing to adventure some necessarie provisions If we may but knowe what itt is wee shall easilie take order by whatt meanes it may convenientlie be brought hither, And as for any quicke Cattell the[y] will with great ease com by lande. Farther we are to crave of your Lordship that if case we shall not be able voluntarilie to git men willing to goe fitt for the service that you wilbe pleased to be a meanes We may obteyne some letters from the Lordes to Certaine Justices for their assistance in that behalf

Thus much under your Lordships favor We are bold to recomend to your Wisdome and withall to remember you that the firste establishing of an uniforme order in all thinges wilbe occasion to the Contynewan[c]e hereof the better besides there wilbe taken away all occasion of envie or disgrise howe sorie we are that this occasion of protraction is falne out is needeles here to write notwithstanding We cannot but infinitelie acknowledg our selves bound unto your Lordshipp for the Contynewance of your Honores favour towards us humblie beseeching you to thinke us worthie to hold theym and to register us among those you have most power of. Even so with acknowledgement of our duetie we humblie take our leave

Plymouth the xjth of June 1606

Your Lordships most humblie to comaunde &c.

[Endorsed:] A lettre from the Town ye 11 of June 1606 to ye Lord Chief Justice of England

496. 1607–1608. "The relation of the Whole Voyage to Virginia."

The narrative of the Sagadahoc voyage and settlement from June 1 to September 26, 1607, is extant in a copy made after 1647 by a certain William Griffith. It was available to William Strachey when he was compiling "The historie of travaile into Virginia Britannia," in or about 1612. He reproduced the greater part of the earlier portion and continued it from September 26 to October 2. It might also appear that it is the material attributed by Samuel Purchas in his Pilgrimage *in the 1614 and subsequent editions (492) to James Davies, even though Davies is referred to in the third person.*

The two portions were put together by Henry Thayer in The Sagadahoc Colony *(Gorges Society, Portland, Me., 1892), and were reprinted in Henry Burrage,* English and French Voyages, 1534–1608 *(1906), pp. 399–407. The William Griffith copy is Lambeth Palace Library, MS 850; the British Library, Sloane MS 1622, addition in Strachey was first published in William Strachey,* The Historie of Travaile to Virginia Britannia, *edited by R. H. Major (London, Hakluyt Society, 1849), pp. 178–180, and from the Princeton University Library copy in Louis B. Wright and Virginia Freund, eds.,* The Historie of Travell into Virginia Britania *(London, Hakluyt Society, 1953), pp. 170–173.*

In the nam of God, Amen.

The Relation of a Voyage, unto New England. Began from the Lizard, the first of June 1607, By Captain Popham in the ship the Gift, and Captain Gilbert in the Mary and John:

Written by [   ] and found amongst the Papers of the truly Worshipfull Sir Ferdinando Gorges, Knight by me William Griffith.

Departed from the Lyzard the firste daye of June Ano Domini 1607, beinge Mundaye about 6 of the Cloke in the afternoon and ytt bore of me then Northeste and by North eyght Leags of.

from thence Directed our Course for the Illands of flowers and Corve in the which we wear 24 dayes attainynge of ytt. All which time we still kept the Sea and never Saw but on Saill beinge a ship of Salcom bound for the New Foundland whearin was on Tosser of Dartmoth Master in her.

The 25th daye of June we fell with the Illand of Gersea on of The Illands of the Assores and ytt bore of us then South and by est ten Leags of, our Master and his matts makinge ytt to be flowers but my Selffe with stood them and reprooved them in thear errour as afterward ytt appeared manyfestly and then stood Roome for flowers.

The 26th of June we had Seight of Flowers and Corvo and the 27th in the mornynge early we wear hard abord Flowers and stod in for to fynd a good rod for to anker Whearby to take in wood and watter. the 28th we Descryed to Sailles, standinge in for flowers Whearby we presently Wayed Anker and stood towards the rod of Sainta Cruse beinge near three Leags from the place. Whear we wattered. thear Captain Popham ankered to take in wood and watter but ytt was So calme that we Could nott recover or gett unto hem beffor the daye cam on.

The 29th of June beinge Mundaye early in the morning those to Sailles we had seen the nyght beffore Wear neare unto us and beinge Calme they Sent thear bots beinge full of men towards us. And after the orders of the Sea they hailled us demandynge us of whense we wear the which we told them: and found them to be Flemens and the Stats shipes. on of our Company named John Goyett of plymoth knew the Captain of on of the shipes for that he had ben att Sea with hem. Havinge aquainted Captain Gilbert of this and beinge all frinds he desyered the Captain of the Dutch to com near and take a can of bear the which hee thankfully excepted we still keepinge our Selves in a redynesse both of our small shott and greatt; the Dutch Captain beinge Com to our ships syde Captain Gilbert desyered hem to com abord hem and entertand hem in the beste Sort he Could. this don they to requytt his kind entertainment desyered hem that he wold go abord with them. And uppon thear earnest intreaty he went with them takinge three or 4 gentell with hem, but when they had hem abord of them they thear kept hem per Forse charginge him that he was a pyratt and still threatnynge hemselffe and his gentellmen with hem to throw them all overbord and to take our ship from us. in this Sort they kept them from ten of the Clok mornynge untill eyght of the Clok nyght ussinge Som of his gent in most wild maner as Settinge Som of them in the bibowes and buffettinge of others and other most wyld and shamffull abusses but in the end havinge Seene our Comission the which was proffered unto them att the firste but they reffused to See yt and the greatest Cause doutinge of the Inglyshe men beinge of thear owne Company who had promist Captain Gilbert that yf they proffered to perfform that which they still threatned hem that then they all woold Rysse with hem and either end thear Lyves in his deffence or Suppresse the shipe, the which the Dutch perseavinge presently Sett them att Lyberty and Sent them abord unto us aggain to our no small Joye. Captain Popham all this tyme beinge in the Wind of us never woold Com roome unto us not withstandinge we makinge all the Seignes that possybell we myght by strykinge on topsaill and hoissinge ytt aggain three tymes and makinge towards hem all that ever we possybell could. So

hear we lost Company of hem beinge the 29th daye of June about 8 of the Clok att nyght beinge 6 Leags from Flowers West norwest wee standinge our Course for Vyrgenia the 30th wee laye in Seight of the Illand.

The firste Daye of Jully beinge Wesdaye wee departed from the Illand of Flowers beinge ten Leags South weste from ytt.

From hence we allwayes kept our Course to the Westward as much as wind and weather woold permytt untill the 27th daye of Jully duringe which time wee often times Sounded but could never fynd grounde. this 27th early in the mornynge we Sounded and had ground but 18 fetham beinge then in the Lattitud of 43 degrees and ⅔ hear w[ee] fysht three howers and tooke near to hundred of Cods very great and large fyshe bigger and larger fyshe then that which coms from the bancke of the New Found Land. Hear wee myght have lodden our shipe in Lesse time then a moneth.

From hence the Wynd beinge att South west wee sett our Saills and stood by the wind west nor west towards the Land allwayes Soundinge for our better knowledg as we ran towarde the main Land from this bancke.

From this bancke we kept our Course west nor west 36 Leags which ys from the 27th of July untill the 30th of July in which tyme we ran 36 Leags as ys beffore sayed and then we Saw the Land about 10 of the Clok in the mornynge bearinge norweste from us About 10 Leags and then we Sounded and had a hundred fethams blacke oze. Hear as we Cam in towards the Land from this bancke we still found deepe watter. The deepest within the bancke ys 160 fethams and in 100 fetham you shall See the Land yf ytt be Clear weather after you passe the bancke the ground ys still black oze untill yo Com near the shore. This daye wee stood in for the Land but Could nott recover ytt beffor the night tooke us so we stood a Lyttell from ytt and thear strok a hull untill the next daye beinge the Laste of July. Hear Lyeinge at hull we tooke great stor of cod fyshes the bigeste and largest that I ever Saw or any man in our ship. This daye beinge the Last of July about 3 of the Clok in the after noon we recovered the shor and cam to an anker under an Illand for all this Cost ys full of Illands and broken Land but very Sound and good for shipinge to go by them the watter deepe. 18 and 20 fetham hard abord them.

This Illand standeth in the lattitud of 44 degrees and ½ and hear we had nott ben att an anker past to howers beffore we espyed a Bisken shallop Cominge towards us havinge in her eyght Sallvages and a Lyttell salvage boye they cam near unto us and spoke unto us in thear Language. and we makinge Seignes to them that they should com abord of us showinge unto them knyves glasses beads and throwinge into thear bott Som bisket but for all this they wold nott com abord of us but makinge show to go from us, we suffered them. So when they wear a Lyttell from us and Seeinge we proffered them no wronge of thear owne accord retorned and cam abord of us and three of them stayed all that nyght with us the rest depted in the shallope to the shore makinge Seignes unto us that they wold retorn unto us aggain the next daye.

The next daye the Sam Salvages with three Salvage wemen beinge the fryst daye of Auguste retorned unto us bringinge with them Som feow skines of bever in an other bisken shallop and propheringe thear skines to trook with us but they demanded over muche for them and we Seemed to make Lyght of them So then the other three which had stayed with us all ngyht went into the shallop and So they departed. ytt Seemeth that the french hath trad with them for they use many French words. the Cheeff Comander of these parts ys called Messamott and the ryver or harbor ys called Emannett. we take these peopell to be the Tarentyns and these peopell as we have Learned sence do make wars with Sasanoa the Cheeffe Comander to the westward whea[r] we have planted and this Somer they kild his Sonne. So the Salvages departed from us and cam no mor unto us. After they wear departed from us we hoyssed out our bot whearin my Selffe was with 12 others and rowed to the shore and landed on this Illand that we rod under the which we found to be a gallant Illand full of heigh and myghty trees of Sundry Sorts. hear we allso found aboundance of gusberyes, strawberyes, rasberyes and whorts. So we retorned and Cam abord.

Sondaye beinge the second of Auguste after dyner our bott went to the shore again to fille freshe watter whear after they had filled thear watter thear cam fower Salvages unto them havinge thear bowes and arowes in thear hands makinge show unto them to have them Com to the shore but our Saillers havinge filled thear watter wold nott go to the shore unto them but retorned and cam abord beinge about 5 of the Clock in the afternoon. So the bott went presently from the ship unto a point of an Illand and thear att Lo watter in on hower kild near .50. great Lopsters. you shall See them Whear they Ly in shold Watter nott past a yeard deep and with a great hooke mad faste to a staffe you shall hitch them up. Thear ar great store of them you may near Lad a Ship with them, and they are of greatt bignesse. I have nott Seen the Lyke in Ingland. So the bott retorned a bord and wee toke our bott in and about myd nyght the wynd cam faier att northest we Sett Saill and departed from thence keepinge our Course South west for So the Cost Lyeth.

Mundaye being the third of Auguste in the morninge we wear faier by the shore and So Sailled alongste the Coste. we Saw many Illands all alonge the Cost and great Sounds, goinge betwyxt them. but We could make prooffe of non for want of a penyshe. Hear we found fyshe still all alonge the Cost as we Sailled.

Tusdaye being the 4th of Auguste in the morninge 5 of the Clok we wear theawart of a Cape or head Land Lyeing in the Latitud of 43 degrees and cam very near unto ytt. Ytt ys very Low Land showinge Whytt Lyke sand but ytt ys Whytt Rocks and very stronge tides goeth hear from the place we stopt att beinge in 44 degrees and ½. Untill this Cape or head land ytt ys all broken Land and full of Illands and Large Sounds betwixt them and hear we found fyshe aboundance so large and great as I never Saw the Lyke Cods beffor nether any man in our shipe.

After we paste this Cape or head Land the Land falleth awaye and Lyeth in norwest and by north into a greatt deep baye. We kept our course from this head Land West and Weste and by South 7 Leags and cam to thre Illands whear cominge near unto them we found on the Southest Syd of them a great Leadge of Rocks Lyeinge near a Leage into the Sea the which we perseavinge tackt our ship and the wynde being Large att northest Cleared our Selves of them kepinge still our course to the westward west and by South and west Southwest untill mydnyght. Then after we hald in more northerly.

Wensdaye being the 5th of Auguste from after mydnyght we hald in West norwest untill 3 of the Clok afternoon of the Sam and then we Saw the Land aggain bearinge from us north weste and by

north and ytt Risseth in this forme hear under.[1]
Ten or 12 Leags from yo they ar three heigh
mountains that Lye in upon the main Land near
unto the ryver of Penobskot in which ryver the
Bashabe makes his abod the cheeffe Comander of
those parts and streatcheth unto the ryver of
Sagadehock under his Comand. Yo shall see
theise heigh mountains when yo shall not per-
seave the main Land under ytt they ar of shutch
an exceedinge heygts: And note, that from the
Cape or head Land beffor spoken of untill these
heigh mountains we never Saw any Land except
those three Illands also beffor mesyoned. We stood
in Right with these mountains untill the next daye.

Thursdaye beinge the 6th of Auguste we stood
in with this heigh Land untill 12 of the Cloke noon
and then I found the shipe to be in 43 degrees and
½ by my observation from thence we Sett Our
Course and stood awaye dew weste and Saw
three other Illands Lyenge together beinge Lo
and flatt by the watter showinge whytt as yff ytt
wear Sand but ytt ys whytt Rocks makinge show
a far of allmoste Lyke unto Dover Cleeves and
these three Illands Lye dew est and west on of the
other. So we Cam faier by them and as we Cam to
the Westward the heygh Land beffor spoken of
shewed ytt selffe in this form as followith.[2]

From hence we kept still our Course West and
Weste by North towards three other Illands that
we Sawe Lyenge from these Illands beffor spoken
of 8 Leags and about ten of the Clok att nyght we
recovered them and havinge Sent in our bott
beffor nyght to vew ytt for that ytt was Calme
a[nd] to Sound ytt and See whatt good ankoringe
was under ytt we bor in with on of them the which
as we cam in by we still sounded and founde very
deep watter 40 fetham hard abord of yt. So we
stood in into a Cove In ytt and had 12 fetham
watter and theare we ankored untill the
mornynge. And when the daye appeared We saw
we weare environed Round about with Illands.
Yo myght have told neare thirty Illands round
about us from abord our shipe. this Illand we Call
St. Georges Illand for that we hear found a Crosse
Sett up the which we Suposse was Sett up by
George Wayman [Waymouth].

Frydaye beinge the 7th of Auguste we wayed

our Ankor whereby to bringe our shipe in mor
better Safty how Soever the wynd should happen
to blow and about ten of the Cloke in the
mornynge as we weare standinge of a Lyttell
from the Illand we descried a saill standinge in
towards this Illand and we presently mad towards her and found ytt to be the *Gyfte* our
Consort So beinge all Joye full of our happy
meetinge we both stood in again for the Illand we
ryd under beffor and theare anckored both together.

This night followinge about myd nyght Captain
Gilbert caussed his ships bott to be maned and
took to hemselffe 13 other my Selffe beinge on,
beinge 14 persons in all, and tooke the Indyan
skidwarres with us the weather beinge faier and
the wynd Calme we rowed to the Weste in
amongst many gallant Illands and found the ryver
of Pemaquyd to be but 4 Leags weste from the
Illand we Call St Georges whear our ships remained still att anckor. hear we Landed in a
Lyttell Cove by Skydwarres Direction and
marched over a necke of the Land near three
mills. So the Indyan Skidwarres brought us to the
Salvages housses whear they did inhabitt although much against his will for that he told us
that they wear all removed and gon from the place
they wear wont to inhabitt. But we answered hem
again that we wold nott retorn backe untill shutch
time as we had spoken with Som of them. At
length he brought us whear they did inhabytt
whear we found near a hundreth of them men
wemen and Children. And the Cheeffe Comander
of them ys Nahanada. Att our fryste Seight of
them upon a howlinge or Cry that they mad they
all presently Isued forth towards us with thear
bowes and arrows and we presently mad a stand
and Suffered them to Com near unto us. Then our
Indyan Skidwarres spoke unto them in thear
language showinge them what we wear which
when Nahanada thear Comander perseaved what
we wear he Caussed them all to laye assyd thear
bowes and arrowes and cam unto us and imbrassed
us and we did the lyke to them aggain. So we
remained with them near to howers and wear in
thear housses. Then we tooke our Leave of them
and retorned with our Indyan Skidwarres with us
towards our ships the 8th Daye of August being
Satterdaye in the after noon.

Sondaye being the 9th of Auguste in the
morninge the most part of our holl company of

---

1. Profile in the manuscript not reproduced.
2. Ibid.

both our shipes Landed on this Illand the which we call St. Georges Illand whear the Crosse standeth and thear we heard a Sermon delyvred unto us by our preacher gyvinge god thanks for our happy metinge and Saffe aryvall into the Contry and So retorned abord aggain.

Mundaye beinge the Xth of Auguste early in the morninge Captain Popham in his shallope with thirty others and Captain Gilbert in his ships bott with twenty others Acompanede Departed from thear shipes and sailled towards the ryver of Pemaquyd and Caryed with us the Indyan Skidwarres and Cam to the ryver ryght beffore thear housses whear they no Sooner espyed us but presently Nahanada with all his Indians with thear bowes and arrows in thear hands Cam forth upon the Sands. So we Caussed Skidwarres to speak unto hem and we our Selves spok unto hem in Inglyshe givinge hem to understand our Cominge tended to no yvell towards hem Selffe nor any of his peopell. He told us again he wold nott thatt all our peopell should Land. So beccause we woold in no sort offend them, hearuppon Som ten or twelffe of the Cheeff gent Landed and had Some parle together and then afterward they wear well contented that all should Land. So all landed we ussinge them with all the kindnesse that possibell we Could. Nevertheless after an hower or to they all Soddainly withdrew them Selves from us into the woods and Lefte us. We perseavinge this presently imbarked our Selves all except Skidwarres who was nott Desyerous to retorn with us. We Seeinge this woold in no Sort proffer any Violence unto hem by drawing hem perfforce Suffered hem to remain, and staye behinde us, he promyssinge to retorn unto us the next Daye followinge but he heald not his promysse. So we imbarked our Selves and went unto the other Syd of the ryver and thear remained uppon the shore the nyght followinge.

Tuesdaye beinge the xi[th] of Auguste we retorned and cam to our ships whear they still remained att ankor under the Illand we call St. Georges.

Wensdaye being the xii[th] of Auguste we wayed our anckors and Sett our saills to go for the ryver of Sagadehock. we kept our Course from thence dew Weste until 12 of the Clok mydnyght of the Sam. then we stroke our Saills and layed a hyll untill the mornynge Doutinge for to over shoot ytt.

Thursdaye in the mornynge breacke of the daye beinge the xiii[th] of Auguste the Illand of Sutquin bore north of us nott past halff a leage from us and ytt rysseth in this form hear under followinge[3] the which Illand Lyeth ryght beffore the mouth of the ryver of Sagadehocke South from ytt near 2 Leags but we did not make ytt to be Sutquin so we Sett our saills and stood to the westward for to Seeke yt 2 Leags farther and nott fyndinge the ryver of Sagadehocke we knew that we had overshott the place. Then we wold have retorned but Could nott and the nyght in hand the *Gifte* Sent in her shallop and mad ytt and went into the ryver this nyght but we wear constrained to remain att Sea all this nyght and about mydnight thear arosse a great storme and tempest upon us the which putt us in great daunger and hassard of castinge awaye of our ship and our Lyves by reason we wear so near the shore. The wynd blew very hard att South right in upon the shore so that by no means we could nott gett of. Hear we sought all means and did what possybell was to be don for that our Lyves depended on ytt. Hear we plyed ytt with our ship of and on all the nyght often times espyeinge many soonken rocks and breatches hard by us enforsynge us to put our ship about and stand from them bearinge saill when ytt was mor fytter to have taken ytt in but that ytt stood uppon our Lyves to do ytt and our bott Soonk att our stern yet woold we nott cut her from us in hope of the appearinge of the daye. Thus we Contynued untill the daye cam. Then we perseaved our Selves to be hard abord the Lee shore and no waye to escape ytt but by Seekinge the Shore. then we espyed 2 Lyttell Illands Lyeinge under our lee. So we bore up the healme and steerd in our shipe in betwyxt them whear the Lord be praised for ytt we found good and sauffe ankkoringe and thear anckored the storme still contynuinge untill the next daye followynge.

Frydaye beinge the xiiii[th] of August that we anckored under these Illands thear we repaired our bott being very múche torren and spoilled. Then after we Landed on this Illand and found 4 salvages and an old woman. This Illand ys full of pyne trees and ocke and abundance of whorts of fower Sorts of them.

Satterdaye beinge the 15th of Auguste the storme ended and the wind Cam faier for us to go

3. Ibid.

for Sagadehock. So we wayed our anckors and Sett Saill and stood to the estward and cam to the Illand of Sutquin which was 2 Leags from those Illands we rod att anker beffor, and hear we anckored under the Illand of Sutqin in the ester-syd of ytt for that the wynd was of the shore that wee could no gett into the ryver of Sagadehock and hear Captain Pophams ships bott cam abord of us and gave us xx freshe Cods that they had taken beinge Sent out a fyshinge.

Sondaye beinge the 16th of Auguste Captain Popham Sent his Shallop unto us for to healp us in. So we wayed our anckors and beinge Calme we towed in our ship and Cam into the Ryver of Sagadehocke and anckored by the *Gyfts* Syd about xi of the Cloke the Same daye.

Mundaye beinge the 17th Auguste Captain Popham in his shallop with 30 others and Captain Gilbert in his shipes bott accompaned with 18 other persons depted early in the morninge from thear ships and sailled up the Ryver of Sagadehock for to vew the Ryver and allso to See whear they myght fynd the most Convenyent place for thear plantation my Selffe beinge with Captain Gilbert. So we Sailled up into this ryver near 14 Leags and found ytt to be a most gallant ryver very brod and of a good depth. we never had Lesse Watter then 3 fetham when we had Least and abundance of greatt fyshe in yt Leap-ing above the Watter on eatch Syd of us as we Sailled. So the nyght aprochinge after a whill we had refreshed our Selves upon the shore about 9 of the Cloke we sett backward to retorn and Cam abourd our shipes the next day followinge about 2 of the Clok in the afternoon. We fynd this ryver to be very pleasant with many goodly Illands in ytt and to be both Large and deepe Watter havinge many branches in ytt. that which we tooke ben-deth ytt Selffe towards the northest.

Tuesdaye beinge the 18th after our retorn we all went to the shore and thear mad Choies of a place for our plantation which ys at the very mouth or entry of the Ryver of Sagadehocke on the West Syd of the Ryver beinge almoste an Illand of a good bygness. Whylst we wear upon the shore thear Cam in three Cannoos by us but they wold not Com near us but rowed up the Ryver and so past away.

Wensday beinge the 19th Auguste we all went to the shore whear we mad Choise for our planta-tion and thear we had a Sermon delyvred unto us by our precher and after the Sermon our pattent was red with the orders and Lawes thearin pre-scrybed and then we retorned abord our ships again.

Thursdaye beinge the 20th of Auguste all our Companyes Landed and thear began to fortefye. Our presedent Captain Popham Sett the fryst spytt of ground unto ytt and after hem all the rest followed and Labored hard in the trenches about ytt.

Frydaye the 21th of Auguste all hands Labored hard about the fort Som in the trentch Som for fagetts and our ship Carpenters about the build-inge of a small penis or shallop.

Satterdaye the 22th Auguste Captain Popham early in the morninge depted in his shallop to go for the ryver of Pashipskoke. thear they had parle with the Salvages again who delyvred unto them that they had ben att wars with Sasanoa and had slain his Soone in fyght. Skidwares and Dehanada wear in this fyght.

Sondaye the 23th our presedent Captain Popham retorned unto us from the ryver of Pashipscoke.

The 24th all Labored about the fort.

Tuesdaye the 25th Captain Gilbert imbarked hem Selffe with 15 other with hem to go to the Westward uppon Som Discovery but the Wynd was contrary and forsed hem backe again the Same daye.

The 26th and 27th all Labored hard about the fort.

Frydaye the 28th Captain Gilbert with 14 others my Selffe beinge on Imbarked hem to go to the westward again. So the wynd Servinge we Sailled by many gallant Illands and towards nyght the winde Cam Contrary against us So that we wear Constrained to remain that nyght under the head Land called Semeamis whear we found the Land to be most fertill. the trees growinge thear doth exceed for goodnesse and Length being the most part of them ocke and wallnutt growinge a greatt space assoonder on from the other as our parks in Ingland and no thickett growinge under them. Hear wee also found a gallant place to fortefye whom Nattuer ytt Selffe hath already framed with out the hand of man with a runynge stream of watter hard adjoyninge under the foott of ytt.

Satterdaye the 29th Auguste early in the mornynge we depted from thence and rowed to the westward for that the wind was againste us.

but the wynd blew so hard that forsed us to remain under an Illand 2 Leags from the place we remayned the night beffore. Whilst we remayned under this Illand thear passed to Cannoos by us but they wold nott Com neare us. After mydnyght we put from this Illand in hope to have gotten the place we dessyered but the wind arose and blew so hard at Southwest Contrary for us that forsed us to retorn.

Sondaye beinge the 30th Auguste retornynge beffore the wynd we sailled by many goo[d]ly Illands for betwixt this head Land called Semeamis and the ryver of Sagadehock ys a great baye in the which Lyeth So many Illands and so thicke and neare together that yo Cannott well desern to Nomber them. Yet may yo go in betwixt them in a good ship for yo shall have never Lesse Watter the[n] 8 fethams. These Illands ar all overgrowen with woods very thicke as ocks wallnut pyne trees and many other things growinge as Sarsaperilla hassell nuts and whorts in aboundance. So this day we retorned to our fort all Sagadehock.

Munday being the Last of Auguste nothinge hapened but all Labored for the buildinge of the fort and for the storhouse to reseave our vyttuall.

Tuesday the first of September thear Cam a Canooa unto us in the which was 2 greatt kettells of brasse. Som of our Company did parle with them but they did rest very doutfull of us and wold nott Suffer mor then on att a tyme to Com near unto them. So he departed. The Second daye third and 4th nothinge hapened worth the wryttinge but that eatch man did his beste endevour for the buildinge of the fort.

Satterdaye beinge the 5th of September thear Cam into the entraunce of the ryver of Sagadehocke nine Canoos in the which was Dehanada and Skidwarres with many others in the wholl near fortye persons men women and Children. They Cam and parled with us and we aggain ussed them in all frindly maner We Could and gave them vyttaills for to eatt. So skidwarres and on more of them stayed with us untill nyght the rest of them withdrew them in thear Canooas to the farther Syd of the ryver. But when nyght Cam for that Skidwares woold needs go to the rest of his Company Captain Gilbert accompaned with James Davis and Captain Ellis best took them into our bott and Caryed them to thear Company on the farther syd the ryver and thear

remained amongst them all the nyght and early in the mornynge the Sallvages departed in thear Canooas for the ryver of Pemaquid promyssinge Captain Gilbert to accompany hem in thear Canooas to the ryver of Penobskott whear the Bashabe remayneth.

The 6th nothinge happened. the 7th our ship the *Mary and John* began to discharge her vyttualls.

Tuesday beinge the 8th September Captain Gilbert acompaned with xxii others my Selffe beinge on of them depted from the fort to go for the ryver of Penobskott takinge with hem divers Sorts of Merchandise for to trad with the Bashabe who ys the Cheeffe Comander of those parts but the wind was Contrary againste hem so that he could nott Com to Dehanada and Skidwares at the time apointed for ytt was the xith daye beffor he Could gett to the ryver of Pemaquid Whear they do make thear abbod.

Frydaye beinge the xith in the mornynge early we Cam into the ryver of Pemaquyd thear to Call Nahanada and Skidwares as we had promyste them. But beinge thear aryved we found no Lyvinge Creatuer. They all wear gon from thence. the which we perseavinge presently departed towards the ryver of Penobskott Saillinge all this daye and the xiith and xiiith the Lyke yett by no means Could we fynd ytt. So our vitall beinge spent we hasted to retorn. So the wynd Cam faier for us and we Sailled all the 14th and 15th dayes in retornynge the Wind blowinge very hard att north and this mornynge the 15th daye we perseaved a blassing star in the northest of us.

The 16th 17th 18th 19th 20th 21th 22th nothinge hapened but all Labored hard about the fort and the store house for to Land our wyttaills.

The 23th beinge Wensdaye Captain Gilbert acompaned with 19 others my Selffe on of them departed from the fort to go for the head of the ryver of Sagadehock. We Sailled all this daye. So did we the Lyke the 24th untill the evenynge. Then we Landed thear to remain that Nyght. Hear we found a gallant Champion Land and exceeddinge fertill. So hear we remayned all nyght.

The 25th beinge frydaye early in the mornynge we departed from hence and sailled up the ryver about eyght Leags farther untill we Cam unto an Illand beinge Lo Land and flatt. att this Illand ys a great down Fall of watter the which runeth by both Sydes of this Illand very swyfte and shallow.

In this Illand we found greatt store of grapes exceedinge good and sweett of to Sorts both red butt the on of them ys a mervellous deepe red. by both the syds of this ryver the grapes grow in aboundance and allso very good Hoppes and also Chebolls and garleck. and for the goodnesse of the Land ytt doth so far abound that I Cannott allmost expresse the Sam. Hear we all went ashore and with a stronge Rope made fast to our bott and on man in her to gyde her aggainst the Swyfte stream we pluckt her up throwe ytt perforce. after we had past this down-Fall we all went into our bott again and rowed near a Leage farther up into the ryver and nyght beinge att hand we hear stayed all nyght, and in the fryst of the night about ten of the Cloke thear Cam on the farther syd of the ryver sartain Salvages Callinge unto us in broken Inglyshe. We answered them aggain. So for this time they departed.

The 26ᵗʰ beinge Satterdaye thear Cam a Canooa unto us and in hear fower salvages those that had spoken unto us in the nyght beffore. His name that Came unto us ys Sabenoa. He macks hemselffe unto us to be Lord of the ryver of Sagadehock.

[*Endorsed:*] The relation of Whole Voyage to Virginia, New England, 1607.

They entertayned him friendly, and tooke him into their boat and presented him with some triffling things, which he accepted; howbeyt, he desired some one of our men to be put into his canoa as a pawne of his safety, whereupon Captain Gilbert sent in a man of his, when presently the canoa rowed away from them with all the speed they could make up the river. They followed with the shallop, having great care that the Sagamo should not leape overbourd. The canoa quickly rowed from them and landed, and the men made to their howses, being neere a league on the land from the river's side, and carried our man with them. The shallop making good waye, at length came to another downefall, which was so shallowe and soe swift, that by noe meanes they could passe any further, for which, Captain Gilbert, with nine others, landed and tooke their fare, the salvadge Sagamo, with them, and went in search after those other salvages, whose howses, the Sagamo told Captain Gilbert, were not farr off; and after a good tedious march, they came indeed at length unto those salvages howses

wheere found neere fifty able men very strong and tall, such as their like before they had not seene; all newly painted and armed with their bowes and arrowes. Howbeyt, after that the Sagamo had talked with them, they delivered back again the man, and used all the rest very friendly, as did ours the like by them, who shewed them their comodities of beads, knives, and some copper, of which they seemed very fond; and by waye of trade, made shew that they would come downe to the boat and there bring such things as they had to exchange them for ours. Soe Captain Gilbert departed from them, and within half an howre after he had gotten to his boat, there came three canoas down unto them, and in them some sixteen salvages, and brought with them some tobacco and certayne small skynes, which where of no value; which Captain Gilbert perceaving, and that they had nothing ells wherewith to trade, he caused all his men to come abourd, and as he would have putt from the shore; the salvadges perceiving so much, subtilely devised how they might put out the fier in the shallop, by which meanes they sawe they should be free from the danger of our men's pieces, and to performe the same, one of the salvadges came into the shallop and taking the fier brand which one of our company held in his hand thereby to light the matches, as if he would

3. There came a canoa unto some of the people of the fort as they were fishing on the sand, in which was Skidwares, who badd them tell their president that Nahanada, with the Bashabaes [or Basshabae's] brother, and others, were on the further side of the river, and the next daie would come and visitt him.

4. There came two canoas to the fort, in which were Nahanada and his wife, and Skidwares, and the Basshabaes brother, and one other called Amenquin, a Sagamo; all whome the president feasted and entertayned with all kindnes, both that day and the next, which being Sondaye, the president carried them with him to the place of publike prayers, which they were at both morning and evening, attending yt with great reverence and silence.

6. The salvadges departed all except Amenquin the Sagamo, who would needes staye amongst our people a longer tyme. Upon the departure of the others, the president gave unto every one of them copper beades, or knives, which contented

them not a little, as also delivered a present unto the Basshabaes brother, and another for his wife, giving him to understand that he would come unto his court in the river of Penobscot, and see him very shortly, bringing many such like of his country commodityes with him.

You maie please to understand how, whilst this busines was thus followed here, soone after their first arrivall, that had dispatch't away Captain Robert Davies, in the *Mary and John*, to advertise of their safe arrival and forwardness of their plantacion within this river of Sachadehoc, with letters to the Lord Chief Justice, ymportuninge a supply for the most necessary wants to the subsisting of a colony, to be sent unto them betymes the next yeare.

After Captain Davies departure they fully finished the fort, trencht and fortefied yt with twelve pieces of ordinaunce, and built fifty howses, therein, besides a church and a storehowse; and the carpenters framed a pretty Pynnace of about some thirty tonne, which they called the *Virginia;* the chief ship wright beinge one Digby [or Digbye] of London.

Many discoveries likewise had been made both to the mayne and unto the neghbour rivers, and the frontier nations fully discovered by the diligence of Captain Gilbert, had not the wynter proved soe extreame unseasonable and frosty; for yt being in the yeare 1607, when the extraordinary frost was felt in most parts of Europe, yt was here likewise as vehement, by which noe boat could stir upon any busines. Howbeyt, as tyme and occasyon gave leave, there was nothing omitted which could add unto the benefitt or knowledg of the planters, for which when Captain Davies arrived there in the yeare following (sett out from Topsam, the port towne of Exciter, with a shipp laden full of vitualls, armes, instruments and tooles, etc.,) albeyt he found Master George Popham, the president, and some other dead, yet he found all things in good forwardness, and many kinds of furrs obteyned from the Indians by way of trade; good store of sarsaparilla gathered, and the new pynnace all finished. But by reason that Captain Gilbert received letters that his brother was newly dead, and a faire portion of land fallen unto his share, which required his repaier home, and noe mynes discovered, nor hope thereof, being the mayne intended benefit expected to uphold the charge of this plantacion, and the feare

that all other wynters would prove like the first, the company by no means would stay any longer in the country, especyally Captain Gilbert being to leave them and Master Popham, as aforesaid, dead; wherefore they all ymbarqued in this new arrived shipp, and in the new pynnace, the *Virginia*, and sett saile for England. And this was the end of that northerne colony uppon the river [of] Sachadehoc.

497. December 1, 1607. Sir Ferdinando Gorges reports the first news of the Sagadahoc colony.

The ship Mary and John, *which left the Kennebec on October 6, reached Plymouth on December 1, 1607, when Sir Ferdinando Gorges hurried to report its not very good tidings to Lord Salisbury.*

Hatfield House, Cecil Papers, 123/77; printed in J. P. Baxter, Gorges, *III, 154–156.*

Right Honorable.

This present day, heere is arived on of our shipps out of the Partes of Virginia, with greate newes of a fertill Contry, gallant Rivers, stately Harbors, and a people tractable, (so discreete Courses bee taken with them,) but no returne, to satisfy the expectation of the Adventureres, the which may bee an occasion, to blemish the reputacion of the designe, although in reason it could not bee otherwayes, both bycause of the shortnes of theyr aboad there (which was but two monethes) as also, theyr want of meanes to follow theyr directions, theyr number being so small, and theyr busines so great, beside in very truthe, the defect and wante of understandinge of som of those imployed, to performe what they weare directed unto, from whense, there did not only proceede confusion, but thorough pride and arrogansay, faction, and privat resolution, as more at large your Lordshipp shall perceave, by my next, which the particulars therof, in the meane time, I have sente this inclosed, humbly beseeching, it may bee delivered to Sir Fransis Popham, whome I doubt not, but will at large accquaynte your Lordshipp what he receaveth, although I beleeve hee will not heare of all, that hath paste.

For my owne opinion, I am confident, there will bee divers reasons to perswade a constant resolution, to persue this place, as firste the bouldnes of the Coaste, the easines of the navigation, the fertility of the soyle, and the severall sortes of Commodityes, that they ar ashured, the contry do yealde, as namely fish in the season, in great plenty, all the Coste alonge mastidge for shipps, goodly Oakes, and Ceaders, with infinit other sortes of trees, Rasom, hempe, grapes very fayre and excellent good, wherof they have already make wine, much like to the Claret wine that comes out of France, rich Furrs if they can keepe the Frenchmen from the trade, as for mettals, they can say nothinge, but they ar confidente there is in the Contry, if they had meanes to seeke for it, neither could they go so high, as the Allom mines ar, which the Savages doth ashure them there is great plenty of. Thus mouch I humbly desire may satisfy your Lordshipp at this present, untill I bee better able to furnish your Lordshipp with the rest that they can say. I have likewise sent your Lordshipp Mr Challoones his letter, brought mee out of Spayne, wherby it may appeare unto your Honour what hopes hee had at the writinges thereof; howsoever for my particular I do infinitely thinke myselfe bounde to your Lordshipp in theyr behalfe, and do yealde humble thankes for your Honours favour, shewed towardes them; theyr Case is miserable, and the wronges profered them infinite. I know not how to helpe it, but humbly to implore for theyr releases Those who ar beste able to do them good and to ease theyr necessityes in what I may, all the rest of the adventurers having given them over. Even so recommending your Lordshipp to Gods protection I humbly take my leave resting in all servise during my life.

Your Lordshipps humbly to bee Commaunded/ [signed:] Fard: Gorges.

I should have remembred your Lordshipp that the Contry doth yealde Sauceparelia in a great aboundance and a certayne silke that doth grow in small Codds, a sample wherof I will send this night or to morrow.

Plymouth this 1 of December late at night 1607.

[Addressed:] To the Right Honorable my very good Lord the Earle of Salisbury theise.

498. December 3, 1607. Gorges reports further to Salisbury on the Sagadahoc colony.

Hatfield House, Cecil Papers 123/81; printed in J. P. Baxter, Gorges, III, 158–160.

Right Honorable:

It seemes to bee moste certayne, that ther is no enterprise, (how well so ever intended,) but hath his particular impedimentes meeting with many oppositions, and infinite Crosses, as in this small attempt, (begun by my Lord Cheefe Justice out of a noble zeale to his prince and Contry, (amongst many others,) it is experiensed) for firste as hee was honorable himselfe, so hee thought all others weare, beleeving what they toulde him, and trustinge to what, they promised, by which meanes, his Lordshipp was not a litle deceaved of what hee expected, for neither were his provisions answerable to his Charge bestowed, nor the persons imployed such as they ought; in as much as the wantes of the on was cause of inabilety, to performe what was hoped; & the Childish factions, ignorant timerous, and ambitiouse persons, (for of that nature I founde the commposition to bee) hath bread an unstable resolution, and a generall confusion, in all theyr affayres. For firste the President himselfe is an honest man, but ould, and of an unwildy body, and timerously fearfull to offende, or contest with others that will or do oppose him, but otherwayes a discreete carefull man. Captayne Gilberte is described to mee from thense to bee desirous of supremasy, and rule, a loose life, prompte to sensuality, litle zeale in Religion, humerouse, head stronge, and of small judgment and experiense, other wayes valiant inough, but hee houldes that the kinge could not give away that, by Pattent, to others, which his Father had an Act of Parliament for, and that hee will not bee put out of it in haste, with many such like idle speeches, which (allthough hee bee powrlesse to performe oughte) weare not unfit to bee taken notice of bycause it weare good in my opinion that all such occasion were taken away, as may hinder the publique proceedinge, and let the cause of sedicion bee plucked up by the Roote, before it do more harme; besides hee hath sent (as I am farther informed) into England for divers of his freindes, to com to him, for the strenghning of his party on all occasions (as hee termes it) with much more that I have receaved notis of to this effect; which I thought it my duety to advertise your Lordshipp in time, that som course may bee taken, to prevent mischiffe. which must bee don by immediate authority from thense, taking no farther notise heerof, then your wisdom shall thinke good, but the better to manifest, and to bringe all to light, without callinge the authors in Quaestion, your Lordshipp mey bee pleased to sende downe present commaunde, to intercept all letters whatsoever, and to whomesoever, and to cause them to bee sent up, (for I know in whose possession these letters ar yet, and I thinke I shall finde the meanes to keepe them from being delivered in haste. As for the reste of the Persons imployed, they ar either fit for theyr Places or tolerable, But the Preacher is moste to bee commended, both for his Paynes in his place, and his honest indevors; as also is Captayne Robert Daves, and likewise Mr Turner theyr Phisition, who is com over, to sollicite theyr supplyes, and to informe the state of every Particular. I have sayde in ny laste to your Lordshipp what I thinke how necessary it is, this busines shoulde bee thoroughly followed, but if I should tell your Honour how much I am affected unto it in my owne nature, it may bee that my commendations therof, would bee of the lesse credit, but I desire in my soule, that it would please God, his Majesty would take it into his owne handes, unto whome (of right) the conquest of kingdoms doth appertayne, and then should I thinke my selfe moste happy to receave such imployment in it, as his highnes should thinke mee fit for, and I woulde not doubte, but with a very litle charges, to bringe to passe infinite thinges; I will say no more of it, at this present, only I make no quaestion but that your Lordshipp will finde it to bee of greater moment, then it can easily bee beleeved to bee; I have sent unto your Lordshipp the Journalls that were taken by on of the Shippes, as I receaved it from theyr going out, untill theyr returne, by which the navigation will appeare to bee as easy as to Newfound lande, but much more hopefull. Even so commending your Lordshipp to Gods holy protection I will ever rest during life.

Your Lordshipps humbly to bee commaunded/
[signed:] Fard: Gorges.

Plymouth 3 of December.

[Addressed:] To the Right Honorable my very good Lord the Earle of Salisbury.

499. December 13, 1607. George Popham to James I.

P.R.O., CO 1/1/16; printed in Edward Ballard, Popham Memorial Volume *(Portland, Me., 1863), pp. 220–226, Latin, with English translation; reprinted in Charles H. Levermore,* Forerunners and Competitors of the Pilgrims, *2 vols. (Brooklyn, N.Y., 1912), I, 381–384.*

At the feet of his most serene King humbly prostrates himself George Popham, President of the second colony of Virginia. If it may please the patience of your divine Majesty to receive a few words from your most observant and devoted tho unworthy servant, I trust it will derogate nothing from the luster of your Highness, since they seem to redound to the glory of God, the greatness of your Majesty and the usefulness of the Britons. I have thought it, therefore, very just that it should be made known to your Majesty that among the Virginians and Moassons there is no one in the world more admired than King James, Sovereign Lord of the Britons, on account of his admirable justice and incredible constancy, which gives no small pleasure to the natives of these regions; who say, moreover, that there is no God to be truly worshipped but the God of King James; under whose rule and reign they would gladly fight. Tahanida, one of the natives who was in Britain, has here proclaimed to them your praises and virtues.

What and how much I may avail in transacting these affairs and in confirming their minds, let those judge who are well versed in these matters at home; while I wittingly avow that all my endeavors are as nothing when considered in comparison with my duty towards my Prince. My well considered opinion is that in these regions the glory of God my be easily evidenced, the empire of your Majesty enlarged, and the public welfare of the Britons speedily augmented.

So far as relates to commerce all the natives constantly affirm that in these parts there are nutmegs, mace and cinnamon, besides pitch, Brazil wood, cochineal and amberggis, with many other products of great importance and value; and these, too, in the greatest abundance.

Besides they positively assure me that there is a certain sea in the opposite or western part of this province, distant not more than seven days' journey from our fort of St. George in Sagadehoc; a sea large, wide and deep, of the boundaries of which they are wholly ignorant; which cannot be any other than the southern ocean, reaching to the regions of China, which unquestionably cannot be far from these parts.

If, therefore, it may please you to keep open your divine eyes on this matter of my report, I doubt not that your Highness will perform a work most pleasing to God, honorable to your greatnesse, and most conducive to the weal of your kingdom, which with most ardent prayers I vehemently desire; and I beg of God, the best and the greatest, that He will preserve the glorious majesty of my Sovereign James for ages to come.

At the Fort of St. George in Sagadahoc of Virginia, the thirteenth of December, 1607. In all things your Majesty's most devoted servant.

George Popham

[Addressed:] To the most heigh and mightie my gratious Sovereign Lord James of Great Brittain, France and Ireland, Virginia and Moasson [=Mawooshen], Kinge.

500. February 7, 1608. Gorges reports the return of a further ship from the Sagadahoc colony.

The Gift of God *left the Kennebec on December 16, 1607, and arrived in Plymouth on February 6 or 7, 1608, after a difficult voyage (502-510). Gorges conveys to Salisbury his general impression of the news of the colony they brought.*

Hatfield House, Cecil Papers, 120/66; printed in J. P. Baxter, Gorges, III, 161-164.

Right Honorable:

Our second shipp is returned out of the partes of Virginia, but with advertisement of nothinge more, then wee receaved at the first, only the extremity of the winter, hath ben great, and hath sorely pinched our People, notwithstanding (thankes bee unto God) they have had theyr healthes exceedingly well, although theyr Cloathes were but thinne and theyr Dyets poore, for they have not had on sicke from the time they came thither, to the instant of theyr comminge away. Ye President, and his People, feedes us still with hopes of wonders that wilbee had from thence in time, but I feare mee, ther must go other manner of spiritts, to settle those busines, before it wilbe brought to passe, for I finde the continuance of theyr idle proceedinges, to have mutch prejudicialld the publique good, devidinge themselves into factions, each disgracing the other, even to the Savages, the on emulatinge the others reputation amongst those brutish people; whose conversation, & familiarity they have most frequented, which is on of the cheefest reason, wee have to hope in time, to gayne that which presently cannot bee had, they shew themselves exceeding subtill and conninge, concealing from us the places, wheare they have the commodityes wee seeke for, and if they finde any, that hath promised to bringe us to it, those that came out of England instantly carry them away, and will not suffer them to com neere us any more.

These often returnes without any commodity, hath much discouraged our adventurers, in espetiall in these partyes, although in common reason, it bee not to bee looked for, that from a savage wildernes, any great matters of moment can presently bee gotten, for it is arte, and industry, that produceth those thinges, even from the farthest places of the worlde, and therfor I am afrayde, wee shall have much a doo, to go forwardes as wee ought, wherfor it weare to bee wished, that som furtherance might bee had (if it weare possible) from the cheefe springe of our happines, I meane his Majesty who at the laste, must reape the benefit of all our travell, as of right it belonges unto him; besides if it please your Lordshipp to looke into it with those eyes, with the which you pearce the greatest, and most obscure conjectures, you will finde it most necessary, it should bee so, both for many publique, and private reasons as first the certaynty of the commodityes, that may bee had from so fertill a soyle, as that is, when it shalbee peopeled, as well for buildinge of shippinge, havinge althinges risinge in the place, wherwith to do it, as also may other hopes therof to insew, as the increase of the Kinges Navy, the breedinge of marriners, the imployment of his People, fillinge the world with expectation, and satisfyinge his subjectes with hopes who now ar sicke in despayre, and in time will growe desperate through necessity, also hee shall sease that to himselfe, & to his posterity, the which hee shall no sooner quite, but his nighbors will enter into, and therby make themselves greate, as hee might have don, for at this instant, the French ar in hande with the natives, to practise upon us, promisinge them, if they will put us out of the Contry, and not trade with none of oures, they will com unto them, and give the succors, agaynst theyr Enemyes, and as our People heares, they have ben this yeare with fowre shippes to the Southwardes of them, som 50 Leagues and the truthe is, this place is so stored with excellent harbors, and so boulde a coaste, as it is able to invite any actively minded, to indevor the possessinge therof, if it weare only to keepe it out of the handes of others. I could say much more in this, but I am loathe to bee over troblesom to your Lordshipp and therfor I will thus conclude under your Lordshipps Favor, that I with his highnes would bee pleased, to adventer but on of his middle sorte of shippes, with a small pinnace, and with all to give his letters, and commission, to countenance and authoresy, the worthy enterpriser, and I durste my selfe, to undertake, to procure them to bee victualld by the Adventurers, of these partes, for the discovery of the whole coaste alonge, from the firste to the Seconde Colony, espetially to spende the moste parte of the time in the search of those places allready possessed, and for myne owne parte, I should bee proude, if I might bee thought worthy to bee the man, commaunded to the accomplishment heerof, by his Highnes, and should thinke it a season well spente, wherin I should have so many hopes, to serve my Contry, wherof the least would bee in this sleepy season, the inablinge of my owne judgment, and experience, in these Maren causes, therby, the better heerafter on all occasion, to discharge my duty to my Soverayne. Alwhich I humbly recommend to your Honors wisdom, to bee so handled as you shall vouchsafe to thinke good, for the reputation of him, whome

you have tyed to you, by many obligations, and even so I will humbly commend your Lordshipp to Gods holy protection, restinge ever

Your Lordshipps humbly to bee commaunded
[signed:] Fard: Gorges.
Plymouth this 7 of February.

[Addressed:] To the Right Honorable my very good Lord the Earle of Salisbury/

---

501. March 20, 1608. Sir Ferdinando Gorges to Lord Salisbury.

Hatfield House, Cecil Papers 120/130; printed in J. P. Baxter, Gorges, *III, 164–165.*

Right Honorable: This enclosed I thought it fit to send unto your Lordshipp, that by it your honor might perceave what effecte your noble favoure hath wrought, that soe worthilye endevored the libertie of those poore distressed soules that have this longe indured afflixcion contrary to common reason: but by theire proceedinges it is manifeste in how base esteeme they houlde our people, beinge carelesse what indignityes, or outrages they offer us, but I wish it might but please his Majestie to give his servantes leave to use theire best meanes to right them selves of this theire insupportable wrongs, provided that they violate noe article of peace, farther than they them selves have done in this: Neather doe I see, in my poore understandinge, whye his Highnesse may not make it free by his proclamation, for all his subjectes to make the warre in the Indes wher he hath concluded noe peace, nor whether his subjectes cannot goe, but to their losse, & ruen. It is reported, that the French Kinge hath taken this course, & that his people ar now in preparation to goe thether on all handes. But I cease farther to speake hereof, unlease it may be thought, I urge more then is fitt at this tyme. As concerninge our Plantation, we have found the meanes to encowrage our selves a newe, and have sent two shippes from Tapsome for the supplies of those that be there, with victualles & other necessaryes, havinge sett downe the meanes how we shalbe able, by Maye next, to send one more of 200 tunnes. We frame unto our selves many reasons of infinite good, that is likely to befall our countrye, if our meanes fayle us not to accomplish it. But we hope, before Summer be past, to give such satisfaction to the world and here of, as none that ar lovers of their Nation, but will (for one cause or other) be willinge to wish it well at the least, what crosses soever we have receaved heretofore. Yet I am verely perswaded, that ye end will make amendes for all; For it is sure, it is a very excellent countrye both in respecte of the clyme, as also the multitude of goodlye Rivers & harboures it doth abound with all; besides the severall commodityes that a fertile soyle will yeelde; when arte, and industrye shalbe used for the ease of Nature, the which seemes to shewe her selfe exceedinge bountifull in that place. But, here of to trowble your Lordshipp: noe more at this present. I humbly commend your Honour to Godes holye protection, & rest during lyfe

Your Lordshippes in all service to be commaunded/
[signed:] Fard: Gorges.
Plymouth March 20, 1607.

[Addressed:] To the right honourable my very good Lord the Earle of Salisbury these/
[Endorsed:] 20 Martii 1607. Sir Far: Gorges to my Lord.

CASE ARISING FROM INCIDENTS DURING THE RETURN OF THE *GIFT OF GOD* IN 1607–1608

SIR JOHN POPHAM'S death left his widow, Lady Anne Popham, and his son and heir, Sir Francis Popham, in control of the Popham interests in the Plymouth Company. The *Gift of God*, having gone to the Azores and disposed of masts and a cannon in return for foodstuffs before returning to England, had in their opinion dissipated the assets (the masts) belonging to the estate of Sir John. A lawsuit in the High Court of Admiralty ensued. Formal proceedings in the case are recorded in P.R.O., HCA 3/27, May 12, 23, 31, and June 8, 17, 23, 1608 (502), the most interesting aspect of which is the creation of a commission to take depositions at Topsham, which brought prominent Devonshire figures, Sir Amias Damfield, Sir William Pole, Sir Bartholomew Mitchell, Matthew Sutcliffe, Dean of Exeter, and a man named Ward, into the case, though we do not have their report. Sutcliffe and perhaps others were involved in the Plymouth Company. Havercombe's personal answer, HCA 13/104, June 7, 1608, has not hitherto been printed and is given in full (503). The formal reply to the charges of misappropriation, based on (504) was given by Havercombe's lawyer on his behalf on June 8. It is in S. M. Kingsbury, *Records of the Virginia Company of London*, III (Washington, D.C., 1933), 7–10: below, the Latin parts are summarily given and the English reproduced) (504). It is now HCA 24/73, no. 449. Depositions by Lancelot Booker, John Deaman, Timothy Savage, and John Fletcher, on June 10, and John Elliott, on June 23, on behalf of the complainants, are in HCA 13/29, under date. Four are in favor of Havercombe and one in favor of the Pophams (505–509). Substantial extracts have already been given from them in C. E. Banks, "New documents relating to the Popham expedition, 1607," *Proceedings of the American Antiquarian Society*, xxxix (1929), 307–333. Final sentence, given on June 23, 1608, is summarized briefly from Kingsbury, *Records*, III, 10–12. (510)

502. May 12, 1608 to June 23, 1608. Formal proceedings in the High Court of Admiralty in the case of Sir Francis Popham and Lady Anne Popham against John Havercombe.

P.R.O., H.C.A. Book of Acts, 1608–1610, folios 56, 59v., 63, 67v., 75v., 79. We are indebted to Dr. David Ransome's summary of proceedings given in Virginia Colonial Records Project, Survey Report no. 3993. Research Library, Colonial Williamsburg Inc.

May 12, 1608. Popham and Popham against Havercom; Forman appearing for the plaintiffs, the defendant being unrepresented.

[f. 56r.] On this day Forman showed his proctorship and produced as bailors for the Pophams Nicholas Tippet of Marberton, co. Devon, gentleman, and Edward Taylor, of St.-Martins-le-Grand, merchant tailor, who bound themselves in £30 for the carrying on of the case, the payment of expenses, and the standing by of the judgment. Forman then introduced the libel with the schedule annexed to it, which he sought to have admitted, in the presence of Havercom protesting. The judge admitted it. Forman then produced Havercom whom the judge put on oath and bade undergo his examination next law day on pain of a penalty of £5, assigning him a day for the "proving" of the libel. Havercom protested, stating that he was in gaol and was so poor that he was not worth £5 nor was he able to support himself in gaol. He therefore asked that a "Cautio juratoria" should be taken from him since he was unable to produce any bailors. Then the judge, having taken an oath of Havercom, with a proviso that Havercom should be obliged to produce bailors if it was later thought necessary, took the "Cautio juratoria" of Havercom that he would personally appear on the last law of next term and would not absent himself without the court's permission. This done, the judge then ordered his release from gaol.

On Forman's petition that his party had witnesses for the proving of the libel whom he could not produce in court, the judge ordered a commission to be made out to Sir Amias Bamfield, Sir William Pole, Sir Bartholomew Michell, Mathew Suckliffe the Dean of Exeter, and [blank] Ward gentleman. They were to meet with Havercom's representatives in the parish church of "Alsam" [?Topsham] on the Thursday, Friday and Saturday after next Trinity Sunday; and, with powers of pronouncing contumacious, of prorogation and of removal, and taking unto themselves an impartial notary public, they were to take the plaintiff's evidence, which they were to return into Court on 17 June next.

[f. 59v.]
May 23, 1608: Popham and Popham against Havercom; Browne for the plaintiffs, the defendant unrepresented.

Havercom had been bidden to give his evidence by this day, but came not; and on Browne's accusation, was declared contumacious by the judge, who stood the case over until Tuesday of the following week.

[f. 63r.]
May 31, 1608: Popham and Popham against Havercom; Browne for the plaintiffs, Williamson for the defendant.

Havercom still having failed to appear, Browne accused him of contumacy and asked for the penalty against him, and that he should be arrested and held until he had undergone his examination. The judge stood the case over until the Wednesday of the following week.

[f. 67v.]
June 8, 1608: as in the preceding entry.

Williamson showed his proctorship for Havercom and sought to have his allegation admitted, Browne protesting. The judge admitted it, and ordered Sir Francis Popham to appear personally to answer "ad decimum post". Williamson then produced as witnesses to the allegation Timothy Savadge, John Dyman, Michael Fernall, Lancelot Buckar and John Fletcher, of whom the judge took oaths to give evidence truthfully by next law day on pain of a fine of forty shillings.

[f. 75v]
June 17, 1608: as in the preceding entry.

By this day witnesses were ordered to give their testimony; the libel was to be proved; the commission was to be returned; and Havercom was personally to appear.

Browne produced John Elliott as a witness to the libel, and the judge took his oath to give his testimony by next law day on pain of a fine of forty shillings, Williamson with the usual reservations accepting the production of Elliott. Havercom then appeared, and Browne sought to have him committed. The judge then took a "Cautio juratoria" from Havercom not to depart from the city without the court's permission. Lear, for the commissioners, then presented the process of the examination of the witnesses (by virtue of the court's commission, which Browne exhibited); and the judge released the testimonies thus far of the witnesses, both elsewhere and in court, and ordered copies to be given to each party. Finally, he assigned the following Thursday for the hearing of his judgment in the hall of the College of Advocates.

[f. 79r.]
June 23, 1608: Sentence was pronounced in favour of Havercom.

503. June 7, 1608. Personal answer of John Havercombe in *Popham and Popham* v. *Havercombe.*

P.R.O., HCA 13/91, June 7, 1608.

Die martis vij Junij 1608

Responsa personalia Johannis Havercome facta propositionibus Libellae et scedulatie eidem annexae ex parte domini Francisci Popham militis et Dominae Annae Popham viduae contra eidem datis et oblatis sequntur.

Ad primam propositionem et scedulam annexam respondet quod credit that the articulate Sir John Popham knighte was [at] the tyme articulate owner and proprietary of the shipp articulate, & of all & singuler her tacle and furniture & of all the goodes specified in the said sced[u]le.

Ad secundam propositionem et scedulam respondet quod credit eundem esse veram.

Ad tertiam propositionem respondet quod credit eundem esse veram.

Ad quartam propositionem respondet that this respondent was appointed by the Counsell articulate to saile from Virginea unto the Islandes of Assoriz there to furnishe him selfe & company with victualls to returne for England with sale of mastes sparres & such other thinges as were in the shipp & appointed to be solde by Captaine Elliot & this respondent. And he beleveth that he had victualls sufficient to carry him & company to the Islandes aforesaid, & two hogsheades of beefe and two hogsheades of bread lefte unspente with two dayes provision of meale at his arrivall at the said Islandes Et aliter non credit hanc propositionem esse veram in aliquo.

Ad quintam propositionem respondet quod non credit eundem esse veram in aliquo. Saving he beleveth that according to the commaundemente & direction of George Popham president & others of the Counsels articulate he this respondent for that the said Governor Counsell and cuntrey could not sufficiently victuall and furnish this respondent with necessaries fitt to cary the said shipp articulate and company home into England did sayle with his said shipp unto the places articulate, there to releve him self and companye, & there stayd to make provision of victualls for the space of nyne dayes & not above as he belevethe. And he further beleeveth that xxxiij mastes & thre spars & one cable specified in the sced[u]le articulate were with this respondentes privitye and consente sould, and one sacre was pawned by the said Captaine Elliot at the places articulate for the some of thirtie one pound furtene shillinges sixpence & no more as he beleveth. Et aliter non credit huius propositionem sut scedulam esse veram in aliquo.

Ad sextam propositionem et scedulam annexam respondet quod credit that thirtythree mastes were sould at the Islandes aforesaid & delivered for custome for seaven pound ten shillinges & no more. And thre sparres for foure shillinges six pence, one cable for fourscore pound and a sacre pawned for ten pound & no more. Et aliter non credit hanc propositionem aut scedulam esse veram in aliquo.

Ad septimam propositionem respondet that the wind and weather was faire to have come for England when he put into the said Islandes & he might have come for England if he this respondent had byn furnished with sufficient victualles for England which he had not & had not byn appointed to have sayled to the said Islandes to provide the same. Ac aliter quam prius responsum est non credit hanc propositionem esse veram in aliquo.

Ad octavam novam et decimam propositiones respondet quod credit eiusdem esse veras.

Ad undecimam propositionem respondet quod salvis responsis suis predictis non credit hanc propositionem aut scedulam esse veram in aliquo.

Ad xij respondet quod credit se esse subditum et subjectum jurisdictionis huius Curie sed non ratione huius libellis/

Ad xiijᵃᵐ respondet quod credit esse querelentum minus tamen legitime ut credit.

Ad ultimam respondet et credit credita et negat negata.

[signed:] John Havarcom

504. June 8, 1608. Allegation by John Havercombe in reply to the libel in the case by Sir Francis Popham and Lady Anne Popham.

P.R.O., HCA, Libels, HCA 24/73/449. Records of the Virginia Company, edited by S. M. Kingsbury, III (1933), 7–10. Here printed from the original.

Dominus Franciscus Popham miles filius naturalis et legitimus ac Domina Anna Popham vidua relicta et executrix nominata in Testamento sue ultima voluntate honorandi viri domini Johnanis Popham militis Capitalis Justiciarii domini nostri Regis ad placita coram eo tenta contra et adversus Johannem Havercombe nuper magister navis vocatis the Guift of God.

Browne [for the plantiffs], Williamson [for the defendant].

Quo die Williamson nomine procurio et ut procuratur legitimus dicti Johannis Havercome ad omnem Juris effectum exinde quovismodo sequi valen' omnibus melioribus et efficatoribus via modo ac Juris forma quibus melius aut efficatius de Jure poterit aut potest debuitve aut debet allegavit articulatim prout sequitur.

1. Imprimis vizt. quod Anno domino 1600 [=1606] in mensibus eodem anno Concurrente ac etiam mensibus Martii, Aprilis, Maii, Junii, Julii,

Augusti, Septembris, Octobris, Novembris, Decembris, Januarii, et Februarii, anno domini 1607 Johannes Havercome fuit et erat per honorandum virum dominum Johannem Popham militem decessus pro quodam viagio maritimmo a partibus Angliae ad partibus ultramarinus vocatis et cognitis per nomen Virginiae faciendum ac ab alliis partibus secundum directionem et mandatum Georgii Popham presidentis et aliorum consiliarum per domini nostri Regis in partibus borealibus regionis predictis existentes ad hoc Regnum Angliae reddeunda magister navarchus sive gubernator navis praedictae vocatis the Guift of God rite et legitime constitutus. Et ponit Consilium et dandum et de quolibet.

2. Item quod annis et mensibus predictis dictus Johannes Havercome officium sive manus magistrum navis vocat the Guift of God pro viagio predicto in se suscepit et ut magister sive navarchus dicti navis the Guift of God durante viagio predicto in serviebat ac pro toto viagio predicto fuit et erat communiter dictus tentus habitus nominatus ac reputatus palam publice et notorium. Et ponit ut supra.

3. Item quod dictus Johannes Havercome anno et mensibus predictis seu eroum aliquo cum navi sua predicta cui profuit a partibus Angliae predictae decessit ac versus partes ultramarinas vocat et cogniter per nomen Virginiae predicta navigabat ibidemque salvo et ponit ut supra.

4. Item quod tempore apulsus dictae navis in partibus Virginiae predictus Georgius Popham fuit et erat in illis partibus borealibus regionis predictis rite et legitime constitutus et allocatus. Et ponit ut supra.

5. Item that presently uppon the arrivall of the said shipp the Guift of God in the North partes of Virginia aforesaid the said John Havercome master of the said shipp the Guift of God did Comitte himselfe his shippe and Companie and her ladeing unto the Comaund and governmente of the said President and others of the Counsaile aforesaid and did serve him and others of the Consaile boath with their boat and men and did all such service and labor as the said President and Counsaile did direct and appoint them: Hocque fuit et esse verum publicum notorium manifestum periter ac famosum. Et ponit ut supra.

6. Item that shortly after the premisses vizt. about the ninth of October the Mary and John (wherewith the said Havercombe and the Guift of

God was consorted) did departe from the said Havercombe out of the harbor of Sakadahoc in the North partes of Verginia before such tyme as the said Havercombe had discharged the said Guift of God either of her victualls or salte and presently after the unladeing of the salt and victuall aforesaid the said governor and others of the Counesaile aforesaid did determine to send the said Havercombe and his said shipp presently for England but by reason of some spech of the people of that Countrie that gave intelligence to the governor and others of the Counsaile that the French would come and besiege them the said governor and Counsaile Commaunded the said Havercombe and Companie to stay thither in the said Countrie and not to departe. Hocque fuit et est verum publicum notorium et manifestum periter ac famosum. Et ponit ut supra.

7. Item that by reason of the premisses in the next precedent articles menconed the said Havercombe and Companie with the Guifte of God aforesaid were by Comaundement of the President aforesaid and others of the Counsaile aforesaid Comanded to stay in the harbor of Sakadahoc aforesaid and there did by the appointment of the said governor and Counsaile remaine with the said shipp and Company and kept watch and ward for the space of 8, 7, 6, 5, 4, 3, or at least two monethes together. Hocque fuit et esse verum notorium publicum periter ac famosum. Et ponit ut supra.

8. Item that dureing the aboad of the said Havercombe and Companie with the Guifte of God aforesaid in the harbor aforesaid there happened much fowle weather and Ice in the said Countrie the extremitie whereof did much indanger and hurt the said shipp the Guifte of God whereuppon the President and others perceaving it did give directions unto the said Havercombe to ballast the said shipp and delivered unto the said Havercombe such store of victuall as they could well spare: Hocque fuit et verum publicum notorium manifestum periter ac famosum. Et ponit ut supra.

9. Item that the said President and Counsaile had not sufficient provision of victualls and other things to furnishe the said shipp to send for England when the said shipp the Mary and John were gone for England but were forced by reson therof as alsoe for that the said shipp would have bine utterly spoiled by the Ice and fowlnes of

weather aforesaid to send the said shipp for England. Et ponit ut supra.

10. Item that the said President and Counsaile did appoint one Captain Elliott Captain of the said shipp the Guifte of God in her return towardes England and did give commaundment and directions unto him and to the said Havercombe and Company to depart with their said shipp the Guift of God towards England with such smal provision of victualls as they could spare and appointed him the said Havercombe and Eliot to dispose of and sell 30 mastes, a peece of ordinance and any other thing of goods they had aboard the said shipp at the Island of the Asseraes and appointed them to stay and victuall themselves and Company there and fitt the said shipp the Guift of God with such necessaries as she wanted. Et ponit ut supra and at their arrival at the Assorez he had but twoo hogsheads of beere, twoo hogsheads of bread and two daies provision of meate left unspent, and then [   ].

11. Item that the said Havercombe and Company of the said shipp the Guifte of God after their departure forom [=from] Sakadahoc aforesaid towards England were for need and distresse of victualls and for want thereof by the appointment of the said Elliott forced to put into the said Islands of Assareos where the said Elliot did by Commaundement of the Governor and Councaile aforesaid sell certeine goods belonging to the said shipp to furnishe the said ship and Companie with victualls for the releife of the said Companie which otherwise would have perished for want thereof. Et ponit ut supra.

12. Item that before such tyme as the said Havercombe did put into the Assorroes with his said ship the Guifte of God he and his Company were for want of drinke forced to drinke water and endured such penutý and want that divers of the said Company died for lack of food and others for want thereof (yf they had not bine spedely relieved) would have likewise perished. Hocque fuit est verum notorium manifestum periter ac famosum. Et ponit ut supra.

Item quod premissa omnia et singula fuerunt et sunt vera publica notoria manifesta periter ac famosa atque de et super laborarant et in presenti laborant publica vox et fama unde facta fide de jure in hac parte requisito predicto petit ista proponens jus et justiciam etc.

[signed:] H. Byrdy

505. June 10, 1608. Examination of Lancelot Booker on behalf of John Havercombe.

P.R.O., HCA 13/39.

Lancelotus Booker Civitatis London vietor ubi per xv annos moram fecit, natus in vice de Rotherom on Comitatu Eboracum annos agens xxxiij vel circiter. Testis in hoc parte prodactus juratus et examinatus dicit quod Johannem Havercom a quinto Julij ultimi & Franciscum Popham ex visu respective noverit Annam Popham non novit.

Ad primum articulum allegationiis ex parter dicti Havercom in hac causa data ac ad secundum et tertium articulos euisdem affirmat that on the vth of July last this examinate being in a shipp of London called the Penelope belonginge to Master Richard Hall homeward bound from the West Indies mett with the articulate shipp called the Gifte of God about thre score leages from the Island of Flowers bound for Virginia, whereof the articulate John Havercom was master and George Popham Captain. And they wantinge a Cooper havinge lost there consorte intreated this examinate to leave the Penelope & to goe with them for Virginea, & made wages with him for xxxiiij^s the monethes. And so this examinate wente for Cooper with the said Havercom and knoweth that the said shipp arrived in savety in the North partes of Virginea. And that the said Havercom was master of the said shipp all the viadge, & as Master behaved himself very painfully & carfully untill the ships returne into England.

Ad quartum affirmat verum esse that the said George Popham wente in the said shipp to Virginia to be President of the Counsell in those partes & at his arrivall there he was accepted & allowed for president & so he continueth there of this examinates knowledge.

Ad quintum affirmat verum esse that after the arrivall of the said shipp the Gifte of God at Virginea the said John Havercom with the shipp & company were under the commaund of the said President & counsell there & did serve them with theire boate & persons in such labor & services as they were appointed unto from tyme to tyme by the said president & counsell of this examinates knowledge beinge one of the company & cooper of the said shipp ut prius dictum ejus.

Ad sextum et septimum affirmat verum esse that the articulate shipp the Mary & John consorted with the Gifte of God about the beinninge of October last was by order of the said President & counsell sente backe for England, & the Gifte of God was stayed by there order also to be senete away when yt shuld seme good unto them. And shortly after the departure of the Mary & John, the Salvages of the countrey gave intelligence to the said President and counsell, that the Frenche men would come & beseege them. And thereuppon the said Havercom with the said shipp & company were commaunded to stay longer in the harbor of Sakadahoc & to kepe watch & warde both a shipp bord & a shore so longe as they continued there which was by the space of viij or ix weekes as he remembreth. For this examinate was presente a shipp bord & a shore all the said tyme & knoweth that the said shipp the Mary & John was sente away from Virginea by the said President & Counsell before the Gifte of God was discharged of such salte and victualls as were brought thither from England.

Ad octavum et novum affirmat verum esse that dureing such tyme as the said shipp the Gifte of God remayned in the said harbor of Sakadahoc by appointement of the said President & Counsel there hapened much fowle weather & great floes of Ise wherewith the said shipp was much endangered and hurte for as he sayethe the force of the Ise one nighte struck in a pece of a planck of the said shippe of a foote & a halfe longe so as if the same had [not] byn presently spied and repayred the shypp had byn in greate danger of sinkinge, and thereuppon the said President & counsell gave directions to the said Havercom to ballast the said shipp & furnishe her to returne for England and delivered him such victuall as they could spare of this examinates certaine knowledge.

Ad decimum affirmat verum esse that the articulate Captaine Elliott was by the said President & Counsell appointed Captaine of the said shipp the Gifte of God in her returne for England and for that they were not able to furnishe the said shipp with victualls to bring the company for England the said President and Counsell gave commaundment & directions to the said Elliott & Havercom to return for England & gave them such victualls as they coud spare and gave them directions in writing to saile to the Islands of

Assores or such other Island as they could get to & there to dispose & sell certaine mastes and a pece of ordinance & such other thinges as they has & to furnishe themselves with victualls & repaire the shippe & fitt here with such necessaries as she wanted and this he knoweth to be true for he was present in the house of Captaine Gilbert, when as they said directions were given in writinge by the said President and Counsell to the said Captaine Elliott & John Havercom & this examinate then reade the same and saw that the said President gave the Captaine a letter in Spanish & Lattin which he willed him to deliver to the officers of the Island at his arrival there.

Ad xj affirmat verum esse that the said Havercom & company of the said shipp the Gift of God after there departure from the harbor of Sakadahoc towardes England were for wante of victualls enforced to putt into the Island of Assores by the appointment of the said Captaine Elliott and according to the directions of the said President and Counsell & there the said Captaine Elliott did sell xxxiij mastes & a cable and layd to pawne a gun belonginge to the said shipp to provide victualls & furnishe the shipp for the reliefe of the company and this he knoweth to be true for that he tasted of the said want & saw the said mastes and cable sold & the gun pawned to victuall the said shipp to come to England otherwise the company must have perished for wante of his knowledge.

Ad xij affirmat verum esse that the said Havercom & company before they putt into the Assores were by reason of wante inforced to drink [sea] water, and endured such pennury & wante that one the company died before they came to the Islandes & two more died before they came into England of his sight knowledge & many others had perished also if they had not byn releeved at the Islandes.

Ad ultimum dicat predeposita prout esse verum.

Ad Interrogatoria

Ad primum respondet that comminge from the West Indies in the Penelope & meeetinge with the said shipp the Gifte bound for Virginea he was hired by Captaine Popham & John Havercomb at sea to serve as Cooper in the Gifte of God for Virginea and promised to have xxiiij^s per month

so longe as he should serve in the said shipp whereof he hathe had as yet no parte.

Ad secundum respondet that this respondent came into the said shipp the Gifte of God at sea on the vth of July last & knoweth that the Gifte of God arrived in Virginea in August followinge & came these on the xvj of December last bound for England & arrived at Opsam [Topsham] about the last of February last.

Ac aliter respondent ut supra.

Ad tertium respondet that the Gifte of God was not comminge home above six weekes as remembrethe.

Ac aliter respondet se nescine.

Ad quartum respondet he was present when as Captaine Elliott & John Havercom had commission & directions from the said President & Counsell to sail to the Islandes & sell the mastes sparrs & other thinges to buy victualls. And the same was don in the house of Captaine Gilbert in the towne newe builte there called St George. And there were present George Popham president, Rawleigh Gilbert, Gawyn Cary, Robert Seaman, James Davies, Edward Harley, John Elliott of the counsell, master Foscue, John Havercom, this examinate & who else the remembreth not. And the said directions were given in writinge, & were firmed by the president & some of the counsell howe many he remembreth not. And yet as he saith he had the commission in his handes & reade yt.

Ad quintum respondet he doth not knowe what the mastes were worth but thinketh they were solde for the most valewe. Articulo respondet se nescire For that the had no experience in the valewe of the such thinges.

Ad sextum reddat causas sciente sue ut supra.

[signed:] By me Lanclet Bowker

506. June 10, 1608. Examination of John Deamen in *Popham and Popham* v. *Havercombe.*

P.R.O., HCA 13/39.

Johnanes Deamen of Stoke Gaverill [Gabriel] in Comitatu Devon sailor annos agends Lv aut eo circa, Testis in hac parte preductus juratus et examinatus dicit quod Johannem Havercome per duodecim annos bene noverit, de Franciscus Popham a mense Maij ad annum elapsum ex visum tantum noverit, Domina Annam Popham non novit.

Ad primum articulum allegationis ex parte dicti Havercome affirmat verissimum esse, That in the yeres & monethes articulate the articulate John Havercombe was master of the articulate shippe called the Guifte of God for a viadge to be made from the partes of England to Virginia articulate and that he was soe hired by the articulate Sir John Popham Knighte deceased and as master duringe the whole viadge articulate well and orderlye behaveing himselfe, and Sir George Popham articulate went Captaine outwardes bounde of the said shippe, which he knowethe to be true beinge quarter master of the said shippe the said viadge.

Ad secundum articulum affirmat verum esse, That the articulate John Havercome did take uppon him the place & office of master of the said shippe the Guifte of God dureinge the viadge articulate & soe was generallye accompted & taken reddendo rationem scientie sue ut supra.

Ad tertium articulum affirmat verum esse That aboute the beginging of Maye or June laste was xij moneth the said John Havercombe this examinate and company with the said shippe the Guifte of God sett saile from the Sounde of Plimouth for Virginia & arrived there in good safetie aboute Auguste followinge.

Ad quartum affirmat verum esse that the articulate George Popham wente in the said shipp from Plimouth to Virginia to be president of the Counsel there, and at his arrival at Virginia he was admitted & allowed for President & so held & accompted there of this examinates certaine knowledge.

Ad quintum affirmat verum esse ex huius testis visu et noticia beinge a quarter master of the said shippe and presente in her at Virginia under the command of the said President & counsell.

Ad sextum et septimum affirmat verum esse that the articulate shipp the Mary & John being consorted with the Gifte of God was by order of the said President & counsell sente from Virginia for England before the victualls salte & other provisions were unladen out of the Gifte of God &

yt was determined that the Gifte of God should be sente after verrey shortly. But uppon a reporte that the Frenche men would come & make spoile of them, the said president & counsell stayed the said shippe the Gifte of God & her company for a longer tyme, who by commaundemente aforesaid kepte watche & warde continuallye for the space of thre monethes during there continuance there of this examinates certane knowledge.

Ad octavum et nonum affirmat verum esse that the winter was verey foule & the Ise greate whiles the said shipp remayned in the harbor of Sakadahoc in the north partes of Virginia, For as he sayth the extreemity of the Ise was such that yt bruke a planck of the said shipp as she rode in the harbor to the indaungeringe of the said shipp if yt had not byn espied and amended of this examinates knowledge then beinge in the said shippe. And by reason thereof the said President & counsell gave directions to the said Havercom to provide his shippe & take in his ballaste for England & delivered him such victualls as they could spare at that presente. Ac aliter nescit.

Ad X^{um} affirmat verum esse that the said president & counsell appointed the articulate Captaine Elliott to be Captaine of the said shipp the Gifte of God for England & gave directions in writinge to the said Captaine Elliott & John Havercom the master to departe with the said shipp the Gifte of God for England with such victualls as they had, and to putt in to the Islandes to refreshe them selves of victualls with the sale of such thinges as were in the shipp. Which he knoweth to be true For that he was present when as the said Havercom receaved the said commission of the said President in presence of others of the counsel & hearde it reade Affirming that the victualls were little & shorte at the said ships arrivall at the Islandes as namely there was not a hogsheade of beare then lefte to his knowledge & about a hundreth wayght of breade & verey little other provision of his knowledge.

Ad xj affirmat verum esse that the said Captayne Elliott John Havercom & company accordinge to the said commission & directions of the said president & Counsell being in greate wante of victualls did putt into the Island of Tresares & there the said Captaine sould a cable about xxxij or xxxiij mastes & spares to the Spaniardes to buy victualls & pawned also a gun for that purpose accordinge as was he directed by the said President & counsell of this examinates certeine knowledge then being presente when as the said thinges were sold & pawned & victualls bought therewith otherwise the company must needes have perished by the wante thereof as he thinketh.

Ad xij affirmat verum esse that two of the company of the said shipp by reason of the wante of victualles to bring them home were sterved & died at sea & a thirde died also a little before the ships arrivall in England of this examinates certaine knowledge. Besides many others must of force have perished if they had not byn releeved in the Islandes with victualls as aforesaid as he beleveth.

Ad ultimum dicit predesposita prout esse verum.

Ad Interrogatorium

Ad primum respondet he was quarter master in the Gifte of God in the said viadge to Virginia & backe again & was to have xxv^s per moneth duringe the viadge. Whereof he hath not receved as yet eany penny.

Ad secundum respondent the said shipe the Gifte of God wente out of England uppon the said viadge about the beginninge of May was xij monethes, and arrived at Virginia in August as he remembreth & stayed there aboute three monethes & came from thence in December last as he remembreth and arrived at Opsam about the viij^{yj} of March last to his best remembrance.

Ad tertium respondet that the said shipp was coming home seven or viij weekes, & she could not have come home much soner as he thinketh.

Ac aliter respondet se nescire.

Ad quartum respondet he was present when the said president sayd openly to the company that they should have commission to goe to the Islandes to victuall them selves with the sale of such thinges as they had in the shipp, & he afterwardes saw the commission and was present when yt was delivered to the Master in presence of sondry of the consell & others.

Ad quintum respondet se nescire.

Ad ultimum reddat causas scientie sue ut supra.

[Signed with his mark]

507. June 10, 1608. Deposition of Timothy Savage for Havercombe in *Popham and Popham* v. *Havercombe*.

P.R.O., HCA 13/39.

Timotheus Savidge ex Precinctu Sancte Katherine nauta ubi per et annum et antea apud Horsey Downe per tres annos moram fecit natus in Parochie Sancte Brigitte London annos agends quadraginta quinque aut circiter testis in hac causa productus juratus et examinatus dicit quod Johammem Havercom a primo Aprilis ad annum elapsum et Sir Franciscus Popham militem a mense Martii ad annum prespective noverit et Annam Popham non novit.

Ad primum et secundum et tertium articulos allegationibus affirmat eosdem esse verum Et reddat rationem scientie That this examinate was one of the quarter masters of the articulate shipp the Gifte of God in the articulate viadge to Virginia & was hired and appointed to goe on the same viadge by Sir John Popham late Lord cheife Justice of England & knoweth that the articulate John Havercomb was master of the said shipp by the appointment of the said Sir John Popham & so continued all the viadge.

Ad quartum affirmat verum esse that the articulate George Popham was president of the Counsell in the north partes of Virginia, and wente over in the said shippe the Gifte of God to take uppon him the said place, and at his going thither he was accepted and taken for President of the said counsell of this examinates certaine knowledge who wente with him in the said shippe.

Ad quintum affirmat verum esse ex huius testis certa noticia who was a quarter master of the said shipp & an ey witnes there upon the arrivall of the said shipp in Virginea, the said Havercom committed himself the shipp and company to the said President & counsell, & all was at there disposinge & what they appointed & commaunded was don by the said master & his company.

Ad sextum affirmat verum esse that the articulate shipp the Mary & John was sente backe for England by the said President & counsell before the salte & victualls were dischardged out of the said shipp the Gifte of God. And yt was intended by the said President & counsell articulate that the Gifte of God should be sente after very shortly. How be it a rumor raysed by the cuntrey people that the Frenche men would come & beseege them the said shipp the Gifte of God & the company thereof were stayed for a longer tyme by the said President & counsell of this examinates certaine knowledge.

Ad septimum affirmat verum esse that uppon the said rumor the said Havercom was commaunded by the said President & counsell to stay in the harbor of Sakadahoc with the said shipp the Gifte of God & company & to keepe watch and warde all the tyme they continued there of this examinates certaine knowledge.

Ad octavum affirmat verum esse that there hapned verey foule weather & much ise whiles the said shippe the Gifte of God continued in the said harbor if Sakadahoc, whereby the said shipp was greately indaungered & hurte. For as he sayth a pece of Ise withe the extremity of the frost bruke in a plancke in the said shipp whereby such abaundance of water came into the shipp that if yt had not byn presently espied & remedied the shipp had byn in perill of singkinge. And thereuppon the said President & counsell gave order that the shipp should be balasted & senete away for England & delivered him such victualls as they could spare to bring them home of this examinates certaine knowledge.

Ad novum et decimum affirmat verum esse that the said President & Counsell had not sufficient store of victualls to spare to furnish the said ship with all to cary her for England & therefore gave commission and commaundment to Captaine Elliott who was sent home in the Gifte of God & to the said John Havercom the Master to putt ino the Islandes of Tresorees & there to sell such thinges as they had on bord & to furnish them selves with victualls to bringe them home. And this he knowethe to be true for that he was presente in the house of Captaine Gilbert in Virginea when as the commission was writte & made & signed & sealed by the President & counsell and openly spoken what the effecte thereof was, but he cannot remember that the said commission was given to the said Master at that tyme ac aliter nescit Saving he sayth that at their arrivall at the Islandes there was none of verey little beere left unspente and only a hogshead of breade lefte that he knows of.

Ad undecimum affirmat verum esse that the said Master by the appointemente of the said Captaine Elliott, in his journey towardes England putt into the Island of Treseres & there sold xxxiij mastes and a cable and pawned a gun & therewith bought victualles accordinge to their commission aforesaid, otherways they had perished at sea for want of victualls of his knowledg.

Ad xij affirmat verum esse that theire wante of victualls was so greate that one of the company died for wante of victualls before they came to the Islands, & two others were so weakened also that they died before they come into England & many others had perished likewise if they had not byn releived with victualls at the Islands as he verily beleveth.

Ad ultimum respondent predeposita prout esse verum.

Ad Interrogatoria

Ad primum respondent he went quartermaster in the Gifte of God interrogated the viadge aforesaid, and was soe placed by appointment of John Havercom Master of the said Shippe the said viadge. And he was to have xxiij^s per moneth and did receave one moneths wadges of the Lord Popham deceased and received of Sir Francis Popham iij^{li} more in parte of his wadges for the said viadge.

Ad secundum respondet the said shippe went forth on her viadge aboute the firste of Maie was xij moneths & arrived in Virginia in August following, & staied there aboute fower moneths, & arrived backe againe for England at Helford in Cornewall in Februarie last past. And saith that he was in the Guifte dureinge all the viadge both outwards & homewards untill her comeinge to Topsham upon the xth of Marche laste, and there the said Sir Francis promised to paie this respondent & the rest theire wadge which was unpaide, but as yet hath not paid this respondent nor anie of the rest to his knowledge, ac aliter respondet se nescire.

Ad tertium respondet they came from Virginia the xvth of December & arrived at Helford aboute the viij of Februarie & might have come sooner if they had not wanted victualls. And came as directlye & as fast as they coud & as winde and weather dide give them leave. Ac aliter respondet se nescire.

Ad quartum respondet that Captaine Elliott & the Master had order by writeinge from the President & Counsell at Virginia to go to the Treseras & to sell anie thinge in the shippe to buy victualls to bringe them home, for this respondent was in Captaine Gilbert Chamber in Virginia when the said order was a writinge & sawe Captaine Gilbert write the same togeather with the Counsell & saw it sealed. Ac aliter respondet se nescire.

Ad quintum respondent se nescire.

Ad sextum reddit causas scientie sue ut supra.

[signed:] Thimothye Savege

508. June 10, 1608. Examination of John Fletcher on behalf of Havercombe in *Popham and Popham* v. *Havercombe*.

P.R.O., HCA 13/39. Brief abstract.

John Fletcher, 27 years, was hired by Lord Popham to serve of the *Gift of God*. He knows Havercombe was master on the voyage outward. He remained in Virginia under Captain George Popham whom he saw "execute the place as Presidente & Governor there," and submitted the ship to his orders there. After the *Mary and John* had left the *Gift of God* was stayed to complete her unlading and then on "there was a speeche that certaine Frenchmen woulde beseidge the Englishe companie at Sakadahoc" and thereupon the *Gifte of God* was stayed to keep watch until "greate ice" endangered her. The president and council therefore caused Havercombe to ballast the ship and gave such victuals as they could spare, commissioning them to go "the Islands" to get more food. "The President and Counsell had not sufficient store of victualls to furnishe the Guifte of God" for England, and gave Captain Elliott commision to sell masts etc. in the Islands to buy food to bring them to England. He saw the commission. The masts etc. were sold and food bought at the Islands. Three men died and others would have done so if they had not bought provisions. On interrogation he said he was hired by Lord Popham at xx^s a month as "a comon man". He has received only six pounds so far, and is due six pounds ten shillings more. The ship arrived

back at Topsham about the 8th of March last. He says "he was presente in the old Storehouse at Sakadahoc when as the President appointed the master to sell mastes and thinges" and the president and council afterwards gave commision to do so.

[signed:] John Fletcher

509. June 23, 1608. Examination of John Elliott on behalf of Sir Francis Popham and Lady Popham in *Popham and Popham* v. *Havercombe*.

P.R.O., HCA 13/39.

Johannes Elliott de Newland Fee in comitatu Essex generosus annos agens xxiiij eo circiter, Testis in hac parte productus, juratus et examinatus dicit quod Franciscus Popham militem per apacium unius anni et Johannes Havercombe per idem tempus respective noverit ac Annam Popham non novit/

Ad primum articulatum libelli ex parte dicit Fransciscus Popham in hac causa datum affirmat, That the articulate Lord Popham deceased in the yeres & moneths articulate was accompted owner of the articulate shippe the Guifte of God & of her tackle apparrell & furniture, and was sett out for Virginia by the said late lord chiefe Justice & the rest of the Adventurers in that action. Ac aliter nescit/

Ad secundum dicit he knoweth the said shipp was sufficiently furnished with all things necessary for the viadge outwardes of his knowledge who wente from England in the said shippe to Virginia. And the cable & sacre & a roule of canvas mentioned in the sedula articulate were in the said shipp outwards bound of his knowledge/

Ad tertium affirmat he knoweth that the articulate John Havercom was appointed Master of the said shipp the Gifte of God for the said viadge by the said Sir John Popham, And according to his directions the said Havercomb wente Master of the said shipp in the said viadge of this examinates certaine knowledge/

Ad quartum affirmat verum esse that after the arrivall of the said shipp at Virginea the said shipp stayed there from the xiiijth of August to the xvith of December following & then the President & counsell there gave directions to the said Havercom to sayle directly for England with the said shipp & fifty men & boyes and a proportion of victualls for six weekes according to the said number of men by haverdepois waighte was allowed to the said Havercom to bringe the said shipp & company for England And this examinate being appointed to returne home in the said shipp told the said President that the said shipp was coming from England ten weekes & od dayes, & he feared the said proportion of victualls would be little to bringe them for England, & he answered that they had the sea, the Banks for fisheing & the Islandes to frende if they were scanted of victualls, & appointed him to sell anything in the shipp rather then they should be in want in theire returne which he affirmeth to be true/

Ad quintum affirmat verum esse that the said Havercomb havinge his directions to come for England came from Virginea, and kepte his directe course towardes England, untill he & company were come on the heighte of the Islandes or thereaboutes and then there was a generall mutiny in the shipp amongst the company that they wanted victualls & should be starved if they had not supply / Wherewith this examinate beinge appointed Captaine of the shipp, was made acquainted therewith and tould the Master & company that they were appointed to goe directly for England, & that if they should goe for the Islandes & make any stay there, they should greatly wrong the company left in Virginea for that theire want of victualls there required all hast that could be made for England to send them supply, and the company of the shipp answered that theire wante being at sea was more desperate, & that they should perishe if they were not releeved. Whereuppon this examinate consented they should goe for the Islandes of Treserues & sayled thither accordingly & stayed there viij dayes, & in that tyme there was sould by the consente of this examinate, the said Havercom & the officers of the shipp one cable one sacre xxx spars that this examinate knewe of one roule of canvas & some ropes belonginge to the said sacre & nothinge else to his knowledge, & xxxij^{li} sterling made thereof as he remembreth & bestowed all in victualls togeather also with thre pound of this examinates money for the use of the said

shipp & company. Ac aliter nescit. Savinge he thinketh that they mighte have come for England with the victualls that they brought out of Virginea if the Master & company had byn spareinge & would have dealte honestly with the said victualls, & the rather for that they had thre barrels of breade & a busshel of pease in the shipp as he hath heard, more then this examinate had knowledge of & [swore] them selves with drinkinge of whole cans of beere not to confesse yt as he hath byn tould by Peter Grislinge of Plymouth Masters mate & John Diamand one of the quarter Masters/

[He denied that he had anything to answer to the subsequent articles.]

Ad Interrogatoria

Ad primum respondet he hath knowen Sir Francys Popham knighte aboute a yeare & comethe to speake his knowledge in this cause by the meanes of the said Sir Francys. Ac aliter respondent negative.

Ad secundum respondet he was appointed by the late Lord cheife Justice to goe on the said viadge, & knoweth that the said Lord cheife Justice, Sir Ferdinando Gorge, Sir Francis Popham, Sir Bartholomew Michell & others are Adventurers in the said viadge /

Ad tertium respondet the said shipp arrived at Sakadahoc in the north partes of Virginea & a president & counsell were sente over to continue there, And uppon the arrival of the said shipp there the said Havercom submitted him self to the commaundemente & directions of the said President & counsell & he & the company served them with the boat and theire persons in such service & labor as they were appointed to /

Ad quartum respondet he knoweth not whether the Mary & John was sent backe for England before the Gifte of God was unladen of all her ladinge for as he remembreth the salte for the most part & the beere was unladen out of the Gifte with some bread after the Mary & John was gone. And sayth yt is true the Gifte & company thereof were stayed in the cuntrey for a longe tyme uppon a rumor spread that the French would come and beseedge them /

Ad quintum respondet yt is trew that the said Havercom & his company were commaunded to kepe watch duringe the tyme they stayed in the river of Sakadahoc and in that tyme there hapened greate store of Ise which did harm the said shipp as the said Havercom complayned. And uppon consideration had by the President & counsell the said Havercom was sente away for England with the said shipp & had such victualls as ys before declared.

Ad sextum resondet he hath answered his knowledge before to this interrogatory whereunto he referreth himself.

Ad septimum respondet verum esse that the saylors in the said shipp under hand as he beleeveth consumed and spilte more victuals then were necessary to bee so in excesse, and by reason thereof the rest were in wante and a mutiny grew amongst them when they perceved they were come unto the height of the Islandes & thereuppon they putt into the Islandes with this respondents consent to make supply of victualls /

Ad octavum respondet there was no salte water droncke in the viadge to his knowledge neyther doth he knowe what victualls were lefte when they arrived at the Islandes. And sayth that one for wante of victualls & partly by his owne beastlines in not cleneinge him selfe of lise &

vermyn, & two others died afterwards in the like maner /

Ad nonum respondet he thynketh that many more mighte have died if they had not byn releeved at the Islandes for that they had wastefully spent there victualls before /

Ad ultimum respondet causas scientie sue ut supra.

[signed:] per me John Eliott.

510. June 23, 1608. Sentence in *Popham and Popham* v. *Havercombe.*

P.R.O., HCA 24/73, no. 443; printed in Records of the Virginia Company, *edited by S. M. Kingsbury, III (1935), 10–12, Latin, abstract only.*

Sir Thomas Crompton, judge of the Admiralty, gives sentence in the case of Sir Francis Popham and Lady Anne Popham *versus* John Havercombe in favor of the defendant John Havercombe.

SERIES OF DOCUMENTS IN CHANCERY CASES BETWEEN ABRAHAM JENNINGS AND FERDINANDO GORGES, 1608–1615

THE RAMBLING and repetitive documents in the records of the Court of Chancery throw some light on the activities of the Plymouth Company during its short effective existence. Gorges was clearly an inefficient businessman and easily involved himself in legal, political, and social difficulties with those he dealt with. The earliest document, the bill by Abraham Jenninges of May 22, 1608 (511), does not appear to have been followed up. The case proper began on May 4, 1611 with the Informal Bill of Sir Ferdinando Gorges against Jennings (512), followed by the Formal Bill (515), the Writ, November 8 (not given) and the Demurrer (514) and Answer (516) (the latter of January 14, 1612, received in Chancery on January 28), with the Replication of Gorges following. No conclusion to the case is known. Jennings revived it against Sir Ferdinando Gorges and Sir Francis Popham in 1615, Gorges' Answer being dated October 2, 1615. Once again no issue is known.

The matters at issue appear trivial for so much time and paper, but they throw some light on the Plymouth Company: Francis Popham worked at Plymouth as his father's agent in the early, formative stages of the Company's activity. Sir Ferdinando Gorges took an intimate part in the

1607 preparations, personally helping to select objects to be taken on board the *Gift of God* and the *Mary and John* (Jennings did not know the latter's name), and the goods themselves, iron pots, boxes, chafing dishes, and locks, indicate something of the small scale of the venture. Sir Edward Seymour and Matthew Sutcliffe, Dean of Exeter, are named as subscribers and the amount of their subscriptions (£20 each) also stress the limited investment available. Abraham Jennings, a Plymouth general merchant, was himself a subscriber and goods were brought from his warehouse for the 1607 voyage. Gorges also mentions subscriptions received for a voyage other than that of 1607, possibly one of the relief expeditions of 1608, which brought the colonists home.

P.R.O., Chancery Proceedings, James I, C2, James I, G1/26.

511. May 22, 1608. Bill of complaint by Abraham Jennings against Sir Ferdinando Gorges to the Lord Chancellor.

22 May 1608, Clapham
To the Righte honorable Thomas Lord Ellesmere lord Chanceller of England

In most humble wise sheweth and Complayneth to your honor your dayly Orator Abraham Jennens of Plymouth in the countie of Devon merchant That whereas in or aboute the moneth of May in the yere of our lord god one Thousand six hundred and seven Sir Fardynando Gorge knighte and Sir Fraunces Popham knighte with dyvers others intended and purposed to set forth two shipps one called the Gifte & the other the [blank] from the port and haven of Plymoth in yᵉ Countie of Devon to Virginya beyond the seas and for the furnishing and setting forth of the said shipps in the said vyage the said Sir Fardinando Gorge and Sir Fraunces Popham boughte & tooke up dyvers wares and marchandice necessarie for the said intended vyage and the said Sir Fardinando being accompanyed with yᵉ said Sir Fraunces Popham came to your Orator in Plymouth aforesaid and boughte of him dyvers wares and merchandice as Iron pottes boxes Chafyng disshes lockes & divers other wares & marchandyse for the said intended vyage amounting to the some of Thirtie six poundes nyneteene shillinges & eleven pence which wares were sorted out by the said Sir Fardinando Gorge or by his appoyntment [and] were delyvered to the said

Sir Fardynando Gorge or to some other whome he appoynted to Receave the same to his use and were afterward Caryed abord the said shipps to be imployed in the said vyage and a trew note of the particulars of the said wares and marchandice was taken and delivered by John Garwde your Orators servant to the said Sir Fardynando Gorge or to Robert Edye his servant which note came to the handes of the said Sir Fardynando Gorge & yet Remayneth in his custody. And also the said Sir Fardynando Gorge Receaved of dyvers adventurers in the said vyage dyvers somes of mony as namely of Sir Edward Seymer late Barronet decessed the some of Twentie poundes of Mathew Sutclife Deane of Exon [Exerter] Twentie poundes and of dyvers others dyvers somes of mony which mony so by him Receaved was by agrement betwixte him and the said Sir Fraunces Pophame who as your Orator verely thinketh were joynte adventurers in the vyage to be disposed by the said Sir Fardynando Gorge for the payment of the wares boughte for the said vyage after which wares and marchandice so boughte the said Sir Fardynando Gorge having Receaved divers somes of mony upon adventure in the said vyage of the said Sir Edward Seymer Barronet Master sutcliffe and dyvers other for which he was either indebted as himselfe confessed to you in [debted] to the said Sir Fraunces Popham in the some of fortie poundes or accomptable to him for the same it was afterward agreed betwixte your said Orator & the said Sir Fardynando Gorge that the said Sir Fardynando Gorge should give a Bill of Exchange for the payment of a hundred poundes to one Ambrose Jennens your Orators brother then in London to the use of your Orator. And that your Orator should paye to the said Sir Fardynando Gorge threscore poundes in discharge of so much of the said hundred poundes. And it was then also further agreed betwixte them That if the said Sir Fraunces Popham would abate out of the said debte which he the said Sir Fardynando Gorge did owe him or for which he was accomptable to the said Sir Fraunces Popham the some of Thirtie sixe poundes nyne shillinges and Tennpence that then your Orator payinge to the said Sir Fardynando Gorge Three poundes Tenn shillinges and a pennye should be discharged of the said hundred poundes for which the said Bill of Exchange was made And the said Sir Fardynando would rest satisfied of the said some of a hundred poundes but if the said Sir Fraunces Popham would not abate the said Thirtie sixe poundes nyne shillinges and Tenn pence as aforesaid Then it was agreed that your orator should pay to the said Sir Fraunces Popham the foresaid some of fortie poundes and upon the payment thereof should be discharged againste the said Sir Fardynando Gorge of the said hundred poundes. And accordingly to his agrement afterward in or aboute the Eleventhe day of June in the sixth yere of his majestes Raigne the said Sir Fardynando Gorge did make a Bill of Exchange for the payment of the said hundred poundes to the said Ambrose Jennens to your orators use And your Orator did forthwith pay to the said Sir Fardynando Gorge the some of threscore poundes according to there foresaid agrement & aboute a quarter of a yere after the said agrement your orator Rode from Plymothe to Wellington to the said Sir Fraunces Popham to understand whether he would be contented that your Orator should Retayne ye said Thirtie sixe poundes ix^s and xj^d for the wares so boughte of him as aforesaid & acqayntyng him with the foresaid agrement made betwixte your Orator and the said Sir Fardynando Gorge the said Sir Fraunces Popham was contented and did agree that your orator should retayne ye said some of xvj^{li} ix^s xj^d to his awne vse in satisfaccion of ye said xxxvj^{li} ix^s xj^d due to him for ye said ware so boughte of him as aforesaid and upon his Retorne made ye same [request?] to ye said Sir Fardynando hereupon your oratour did paye to one William Catchmay to & for ye use of ye said Sir Fardenando Gorge ye some of iij^{li} x^s j^d in full satisfaccion of ye said C^{li} for which ye said bill of Exchange was made accordinge to the foresaid agrement which ye said Sir Fardynando Gorge hath receaved or allowed for which iij^{li} x^s j^d ye said Catchmey gave your orator a note in writing of ye receate thereof to ye use of ye said Sir Fardynando Gorge which note the said Sir Fardynando hath seenne & did alowe the same, but so it is of it may please your honour that notwithstanding ye agrement aforemencioned ye said Fardynando purposing unjustly to charge your said orator with ye said x^{li} [xl^{li}?] hath of late demaundede the said xl^{li} of hym & hath exhibited a bill into this honorable court against your oratour setting forth thereby that in or about ye xjth day of June in ye sixth yere of his Majestes Raigne he delivered to your orator a bill of exchange where by he appoynted one William Bell & in his absens James Bell Resident then in London to pay to the foresaid Abraham Iennens your orators brother or to ye bringer of ye said Bill ye some of a hundred poundes to ye use of your orator, that ye same was payed accordingly, [and] that your oratour in consideracion of ye said Bill of exchange & payment thereupon to be made promysed to pay to ye said Sir Fardynando Gorge ye said hundred poundes & payed threscore poundes towardes ye satisfaccion thereof & that your orator understanding that ye said Sir Fardynando Gorge was to pay to the foresaid Sir Fraunces Popham at Exon [Exeter] ye some of xl^{li} desired that he might pay ye xl^{li} Resting due to the said Sir Fardynando as he alleged to the said Sir Frauncys Popham in law & satisfaccion of ye said xl^{li} due to be payed as also allowd to hym the said Sir Fardynando Gorge alleging that ye said Sir Fraunces Popham did owe him some mony & that his payment of ye said Sir Fraunces Popham myghte be a meanes that he mighte be payed of ye mony due to him from the said Sir Fraunces Popham & ye said Sir Fardynando Gorge consented here unto & that your oratour faithfully promysed to ye said Sir Fardynando Gorge & also to ye foresaid William Cutchmay to pay ye said xl^{li} to ye said Sir Fraunces Popham in ye behalfe of him ye said Sir Fardynando Gorge & bring from ye said Sir Fraunces Popham a note in writing under his hand of ye Receate thereof or otherwise that he would pay ye same to ye said Sir Fardynando and further thereof that your orator did not pay to ye said Sir Fraunces Popham ye said xl^{li} nor bring from him to the said Sir Fardynando Gorge a note in writing of ye payment hereof nor payed to him yᵉ said Sir Fardynando the said xlˡⁱ as by yᵉ said bill appeareth and yᵉ said Sir Fardynando Gorge now denyeth that there was any such agrement betwixte him & your said orator as is before shewed & also denyeth that your oratour did paye to yᵉ said Catchmey yᵉ said iijˡⁱ xˢ jᵈ or that yᵉ same came to his use or that he was indebted to yᵉ said Sir Fraunces Popham or that he receaved any mony of yᵉ said Sir Edward Seymer or of yᵉ said Mathew Sutcliffe or of any others for which he was either indebted or accomptable for to yᵉ said Fraunces Popham or that he hath or retayned any such mony in his hand alleaging that yᵉ wares which were boughte of your orator as aforesaid were boughte aswell to & for yᵉ use & behoufe of yᵉ said Sir Fraunces Popham as of him yᵉ said Sir Fardynando Gorge & refuseth to satisfie your orator of the said xxxvjˡⁱ ixˢ xjᵈ for yᵉ said wares so boughte as aforesaid & also yᵉ said iijˡⁱ xˢ jᵈ which your orator payed to yᵉ said Catchmey to his use. And yᵉ said Sir Fraunces Popham also denyeth that any such mony as is before shewed was due to him from yᵉ said Sir Fardynando Gorge or that yᵉ said Sir Fardynando Gorge was accomptable to him for any such mony or that he did agree or condissend that your orator should Retayne yᵉ some of xxxvjˡⁱ lxˢ xlᵈ as satisfaccion of yᵉ said xxxvjˡⁱ ixˢ xjᵈ due for yᵉ wares sold as aforesaid And for asmuch as your said Orator is not able to make such direct profe as by yᵉ Comon lawes of this Realme is required of yᵉ foresaid Contracte for yᵉ said wares nor of yᵉ foresaid agrement betwixte him & yᵉ said Sir Fardynando Gorge nor what was due from yᵉ said Sir Fardenando to yᵉ said Sir Fraunces Popham nor what mony he yᵉ said Sir Fardynando had receaved or was accomptable for to yᵉ foresaid Sir Fraunces Popham nor is able to make such sufficcyent profe that yᵉ said Sir Fraunces Popham gave consent & did fully agree that your orator should retayne xxxvjˡⁱ ixˢ xjᵈ in satisfaccion of the mony due to him for the said wares as before is shewed for all which causes your orator hath not any meanes by yᵉ comon lawes of this realme to Free & discharge himselfe against yᵉ said Sir Fardenando Gorge of yᵉ foresaid xlˡⁱ which he now demandeth nor hath any meanes to recover yᵉ said xxxvjˡⁱ ixˢ xjᵈ due for his said wares nor for the foresaid iijˡⁱ xˢ jᵈ which he payed to the foresaid William Catchmey to yᵉ use of yᵉ foresaid Sir Fardenando Gorge by the comon lawes of this realme. May hit therefore please your honor the premisses considered to graunt his Majestes write of subpena to be dyrected to the said Sir Fardynando Gorge & Sir Fraunces Popham comanding them hereby personally to appeare before your honour in his Majestes highnes Courte of Chancery in some day therein to be lemitted then and answere the premisses and sett upon there othes by whome the said wares were boughte and to whose use and the truth of all the foresaid agrementes and whether your orator be satisfied or payed for the said wares or not and further to stand to and abide such further order herein as to your honor [then] shalbe thoughte to stand with equitie and concynce & your orator shall dayly pray to God to send your lordship long life with increase of honour.

[signed:] William Vastand

512. May 4, 1611. Bill on behalf of Sir Ferdinando Gorges against Abraham Jennings presented to the Lord Chancellor.

Quarto die May 1611, Saunders To the right honourable lord Ellesmer Lord Chaunceller of England.

I humbly complaininge sheweth unto your Lord your Orator Master Ferdinando Gorges of Plimouth in the County of Devon Knight That wheras your Orator In or aboute the eleventh day of June in the sixt yeare of his majestes Reigne that now is made and delivered unto one Abraham Jennens of Plimouth aforesaid merchant a certein bill of Exchaunce subscribed by your Orators hand bearing date at Plimouth as aforesaid wherby your orator appointed one William Bell gentleman then remayninge in London, And in his absence one James Bell Gentleman then also residinge in London to pay unto one Ambrose Jennens then also remayninge in London or to the bringer of the said Bill of Exchaunge upon two dayes sight therof at London the soumme of one hundred poundes of current Englishe money for and to the use of the said Abraham Jennens whiche said soumme of one hundred poundes was paid in London accordingely as by the said bill of Eschaunge redie to be shewen in this honorable courte it doth and may appere. And your orator further sheweth that the said Abraham Jennens in consideracion of the said bill of Exchaunge and of the said paiment therupon to be made promised to pay unto your Orator or to such as your Orator should appoint the soumme of one hundred poundes of current Englishe money and towards satisfaccion of the same did pay the soumme of three score poundes. And the said Abraham Jennens understanding that your Orator intended to pay fortie poundes unto Sir Francis Popham knight at the citty of Exon. [Exeter] desired that he the said Abraham Jennens might in lieu-of the said fortie poundes by him the said Abraham restinge due to your orator as is aforesaid pay the said forty poundes to Sir Francis affirminge that the said Sir Francis did owe unto him the said Abraham Jennens some monies and that his payinge of the said forty poundes might be a good meanes that he might be paid therof. Wherunto your Orator to doe the said Abraham Iennens a plesure and out of the trust and confidence your Orator reposed in the said Abraham Jennens willingely condiscended And therupon the said Abraham Jennens faithfully promised and Agreed to and with your said Orator and also to one William Catchmay Gentleman deceased for and in behalfe of your Orator that he the said Abraham Jennens would pay and deliver unto the said Sir Francis Popham for and in the [behalf of the] said Abraham Jennens the said soumme of forty poundes beinge the remainder of the said soumme of one hundred poundes whiche [the . . .] that the said Abraham Jennens [has to paye to your] Orator in consideration of the said Bill of Exchaunge And your Orator further sheweth [unto your good lordshipp that the said Abraham Jenninges did] further faithfully promise and assume unto your Orator And also unto the said William Catchmay for and in the behalfe of your Orator that he the said Abraham Jennens would not onely forthwith paie the said forty poundes to the said Sir Francis Popham as aforesaid but also bringe unto your Orator a note in wrightinge [vnder the hand of the said Sir Francis Popham mentioninge the receipt therof, or otherwise that he the said Abraham Jennens would pay the said fortie poundes unto your Orator. Now so it is if it may please your Lordship that the said Abraham Jennens did not pay unto the said Sir Francis Popham the said fortie poundes nor bringe unto your Orator a note under the hande of the said Sir

Francis Popham mentioninge his receipte therof as from your orator nether hath he the said Abraham Jennens paid unto your Orator the said soumme of forty poundes but hath and still doth deteine the same contrary to all equity or good concience. And to the great prejudice of your Orator havinge forborne the same almost three yeeres. Notwithstandinge all whiche the said Abraham Jennens doth still refuse to pay unto your Orator the said forty poundes though he well knoweth in his owne conscience the same to be due unto your Orator for the space of these three yeeres as is aforesaid, In consideracion wherof and for that your Orator is without remedy at the common lawe for the said fortie poundes by reason of the late deceasse of the said William Catchmay wherby your [orator] is deprived of his proffe of the said premisses May it please your good lordshippe to graunt unto your Orator his majestes most gracious writt of Sepena unto the said Abraham Jennens to be directed commandinge him therby at a certein day and under a certein paine to appere before your good Lordship in his majestes highe courte of chauncery then and ther to answer to the premisses and to abide suche further order as to your good Lordship shall seeme to stand with equity and good conscience.

[signed:] Ja: Brydgeman

513. November 8, James I, 1611. Writ in the case of *Gorges* v. *Jenninges* in Chancery, formally making the accusations contained in the bills.

This is not printed.

514. January, 1612? Demurrer of Abraham Jennings against the bill of Sir Ferdinando Gorges.

Clapham

The Demurrer and plea of Abraham Jenninges defendant to the bill of Complaynt of Sir Fardinando Gorges knight Complaynante

The said defendant not confessing any matter or thing in the said bill of Complaint to be true, dothe demurre upon the insufficiencie of the said bill, for that yt appeareth by the said bill that yf the matters therin contayned be true, yet the said complayment may by course of Common Lawe in an accion upon the Case have his remedie against this said defendant for the self same matters, as are in the said bill Contayned: And alsoe this defendant for plea to the said bill saieth, that the said Complaynante hath heretofore in his highnes Court of Kinges benche brought his accion of the Case against this defendant for the said 40ˡⁱ which the said Complaynante demaundeth against the said defendant by the same bill setting fourth therby in substancé the self same premisses, matter, and thinges as in the said bill are Contayned, wherunto this defendant appeared and pleaded to yssue: By reason wherof the same cawse being as yet depending in the said Court ys readie to Comme to tryall as by the said declaracion, and other the said proceedinges in the said Court may appeare. And therfore this defendant demaundeth judgement of this honorable Court yf he this defendant shalbe enforced to make any other, or further anseere to the said bill of Complaint and prayeth to be dismissed with his Costes and Charges in this Cause wrongfullie sustayned.

[signed:] Staplete

515. Sir Ferdinando Gorges's bill of complaint against Abraham Jennings to the Lord Chancellor.

This bill is almost identical in form and wording to that already printed. It bears no date and it is signed by a different lawyer, John Gidgman, on behalf of Sir Ferdinando Gorges. It is not printed.

516. January 14, 1612. Answer of Abraham Jennings to Sir Ferdinando Gorges.

Clapham

The Aunsweare of Abraham Jennens defendant to the Bill of Complaynt of Sir Fardinando Gorges knight Complaynaunt

The said defendant saving to himself nowe and att all tymes hereafter all advantages of Exception to the Faultes untruethes incertaynties insufficiencye & ymperfeccions of the said Bill of Complaint for aunsweare thereunto saieth that the said Complaynaunt in or about the moneth of Maye in the yeare of our lord god one thousand six hundred and seaven was indebted unto this defendant in the somme of thirtie six poundes nyne shillinges and eleven pence or thereaboutes for dyvers wares and goodes delivered by this defendant for the Complaynaunt and others by the Complaynauntes appoyntment towardes the setting forth of a Shipp or shippes to Virginia in the partes beyond the Seas, in which Shipp or ships and voyage the said Complaynaunt and Sir Frances Popham knight with dyvers others as this defendant was enformed were adventurers. And this defendant further saieth that hee this defendant did afterwardes oftentymes demaund of the said Complaynaunt the said thirtie sixe poundes nyne shillinges and eleven pence And this defendant also saieth that the said Complaynaunt did owe to the said Sir Frauncis Popham fortie poundes as the said Complaynaunt affirmed which Fortie poundes was to be disbursed and paid out to Marryners for the behooffe of the said Sir Frauncis Popham as the Complaynaunt also affirmed, whereuppon the said Complaynaunt and defendant did conclude and agree that the said Complaynaunt should geue a bill of Exchaunge to this defendant for the payment of one hundred poundes to Ambrose Jennens this defendantes Brother then resident in London and that he this defendant should geue and paie to the said Complaynaunt three score poundes in hand and that if the said Sir Francis Popham would allowe and holde himself satisfied of the said Fortie poundes by the said Complaynaunt due as aforesaid then the said Complaynaunt would allowe unto the said defendant the said thirtie sixe poundes nyne shillinges and eleven pence and that the said defendant should paie to the said Complaynaunt three poundes tenne shillinges and one penny in full payment of the said hundred poundes to be paid by Byll of Exchaunge as aforesaid, But if the said Sir Francis Popham would not allowe of the said Fortie poundes as aforesaid then this defendant was to paie to the said Sir Francis Popham the said

Fortie poundes And this defendant further saieth that the said Complaynaunt afterwardes in or about the Eleventh daie of June in the Sixth yeare of his Majestes Raigne that nowe is according to the said agreement made a Byll of Exchaung for the payment of one hundred poundes as in the said Bill of Complaynt is expressed. And that this defendant did paie and deliver the said three score poundes to the said Complaynaunt according to the agreement aforesaid and afterwardes about three monethes then next following this defendant travelled to the said Sir Francis Popham att his house in Wellington in the Countie of Somerset and was readie to have paid to the said Sir Francis Popham the said fortie poundes as he would not haue byn contented to have allowed the same fortie poundes to the Complaynaunt And this defendant saieth that the said Sir Francis Popham was then contented to allowe to the said Complaynaunt the said fortie poundes and thereof held himself satisfied as he then tolde this defendant. And this defendant doth verielie beleeve the same to be true and that the Complaynaunt is thereof discharged by the said Sir Francis Popham as he lykewise beleeveth. And that the said defendant did paie to the said William Catchmaye in the said Bill named the said somme of three poundes Tenn shillinges and one penny for the said Complaynaunt in full satisfaccion and allowance of the said Fortie poundes without that this defendant faithfullie promised and agreed to and which the said Complaynaunt and the said William Catchmay or either of them that he this defendant would paie and deliver to the said Sir Francis Popham for and in the behalfe of the said Complaynaunt the said somme of Fortie poundes as in the said Bill of Complaynt is alleaged in anye other manner then is before declared And without that that this defendant did promise unto the said Complaynaunt and to the said Catchmay or to eyther of them that hee this defendant would bring unto the said Complaynaunt a noate in writing under the hand of the said Sir Francis Popham mencioning the Receipt thereof as in the said Bill of Complaynt is moste untruelie alleaged but well remembreth that the Complaynaunt willed this defendant to bring a note from the said Sir Francis Popham concernyng the said receipt And without that that anye other matter or thing in the said Bill of Complaynt contayned touching or concerning this defendant

materiall or effectuall in the lawe to be answeared unto and herein not sufficientlie answeared confessed and avoyded traversed or denyed is true. All which matters this defendant is readie to averr and prove as this honorable Courte shall awarde and praieth to be dismissed out of the same with his reasonable Costes by him wrongfullie and without just cause sustayned.

Captum apud Plymouth in Comitatu Devon xiiij° die Januarij domino regni domini nostri Jacobi nunc regis Anglie &c. Nono, Coram nobis

> Wiliam Maynard
> John Stringe
> John Brooking

Traditur in Curia Cancellarie domini nostri regis Jacobi.

Pro Jenninges retorna Sancti Hillarii 28 Januarii

Per sacramenta Jonas Pincent, Mat Carew

517. 1612. The replication of Sir Ferdinando Gorges against Abraham Jennings.

                                    Saunders

The Replication of Sir Ferdenando Gorges Knight Complainant to the severall answers of Abraham Jennens defendant.

The said Complainant savinge to him selfe all advantages of exception to the incertenties and insufficiencies of the said Answers saieth that the said Answers of the defendant are in some thinges very untrue and in other some very uncertein to be replied unto, And that all the matters set forth in this Complaynantes Bill of Complaint are very true Certein and suffisient in the Lawe to be answered. And this Complainant wilbe redie to averre and prove the same as this honorable Courte shall awarde. And this Complainant further sayeth that this Complainant was never indebted unto the defendant in the soumme of thirtie six poundes nyne shillinges and eleven pence for wares delivered for a voyage as in the said answers is most untruly sett forth or that the defendant ever demanded the same as debt due from this Complaynant untill this Complainant demanded of the defendant the said fortie poundes in the Bill mencioned, whiche this Complaynant Conceved the defendent had paid to Sir Francis Popham in the Bill named accordinge to the trust by the Complaynant in the defendant reposed. And further sayeth that William Catchmay in the said Bill and answers mentioned did never paye to this Complaynant any penny in full satisfaction of the said fortie poundes in the said Bill and answers mentioned, nether did the said William Catchmay to this defendantes knowledge or by his appointment receve any penny of the said Abraham Jenninges to be paid to this Complaynant in discharge and satisfaction of the said fortie poundes as is in the defendantes answers very untruly sett forthe. And this Complaynant further sayeth that he the Complaynant was not Contented and satisfied with what Jenninges had donne for the spase of one whole yeare after the said fortie poundes left (as in the said Bill is expressed) in the defendantes handes to be by him (for and in the behalfe of the Complaynant) paid unto Sir Francis Popham in the said Bill & answers mentioned, and untill unkindnes grewe betwene this Complaynant and Sir Francis Popham as in the said Answers is untruly sett forthe, Because the defendant should have brought to this Complaynant a sufficient receipt under the hand of the said Sir Francis Popham touchinge the same, And this Complaynant sayeth that if any unkindnes grewe betwene this Complaynant and the said Sir Francis the defendant was the onely Cause thereof. For this Complaynant sayeth that the fortie poundes left in the defendantes handes to be Carried to Sir Francis Popham was not to be paid him in this Complaynantes behalfe as for a debte owinge by the Complaynant to Sir F[r]ancis Popham (for this Complaynant never ought the said Sir Francis any per.ny). But the said fortie poundes was money sent from the Complaynant by the defendant to Sir Francis Popham to be adventured in some jornies undertaken by Sir Francis Popham into partes beyonde the seas accordinge to former speches had betwene the said Sir Francis and this Complaynant to that purpose. And the said defendant not payinge the said fortie poundes to the said Sir Francis Popham accordinge to the trust reposed in him the defendant by the Complaynant was the Cause that Sir Francis tooke it not well at

this Complaynantes handes, Conceavinge this Complaynant had never sent the money to be adventured with him as aforesaid. As also that this Complaynant did loose a greate gaine whiche he should have had in that voyage, Because Sir Francis Popham would not suffer this Complaynant to partake in the benifite of that voyage, affirminge that he never receaved forty poundes or any penny from this Complaynant to be adventured in that voyage. So that both the unkindnes (if any were) and certeine damage to this Complaynant hath happened in that the defendant very unconscionable deteined this Complaynantes money in his the defendantes handes, And yet by speches assured this Complaynant that he had paid Sir Francis Popham the said fortie poundes in suche manner as this Complaynant always exspected parte in the adventure untill suche time as Sir Francis Popham denied to have receved the fortie poundes as from this Complaynant is redie to avere & prove as this honorable Courte shall awarde, without that that ther is any other matter or thinges in the defendantes said answers not herein sufficiently replied traversed or avoyded is true, And therfore payeth as In his said Bill of Complaint he hath prayed.

Receptus Jennings defendant adversus Gorges miles

518. October 2, 1615. Further answer of Sir Ferdinando Gorges against the complaint of Abraham Jennings.

Pennyman

The answere of Sir Ferdinando Gorges knight one of the defendants to the bill of Complaint of Abraham Jennens Complaynant.

The defendant saveing unto himselfe nowe and att all times hereafter all advantages of exception to the faults untruths incertainties insufficiencie and imperfection of the said bill of Complaint for Answere thereunto saith [that whereas Sir John] Popham knight late Lord Cheife Justice of England being in his lifetyme desirous to advance thestablishing of a Plantacion in the North partes

of Virginia beyound the Seas procured this defendant with others to [adventure with them (?)]
therein, to whom this defendant promised thirtie
poundes in money or commodities to that value,
towardes the accomplishement thereof which he
delivered in accordinglie, and a hundred poundes
more or thereabouts or to that [effect with Sir
John Popham (?)] and his Freindes. And the said
Sir Francis Popham in the bill mentioned sonne of
the said Sir John Popham being by his said father
sent to Plymmouth for the effecting of the said
busines was entertained by the [said Abraham
Jennings] att his house, whom also this defendant
(in courtesie he being a stranger) did sometime
accompannie aswell to the Celler or ware-house of
the Complainant as elswere that he the said Sir
Francis might view thinges necessa[ry] for the
said intended voiage as also that this defendant
might give his best advise and assistance therein,
being a Counsellour chosen and allowed by his
Majestie in that behalfe and no otherwise. And
this defendant denyeth that the [. . . did] buy of
the said Complainant for the said voyage annie of
the wares in the bill specifficed nor doth remember by whom they were bought, Neither
doth he knowe whether the said complainant be
satisfied for the same. But this defendant
acknoweleidgeth that neere about that tyme he
bought of the Complainant certaine other wares
for his owne particular use for which the Complainant was in short time after satisfied and paid.
But the particulars thereof or to what value they
amounted this defendant doth not nowe perfectlie
remember. Neither doth this defendant knowe
whether the wares in the bill mentioned were
carried a borde the said shipps or not nor by
whose appointement. neither were the said wares
delivered to this defendant or to anie other to his
use as farre as this defendant knoweth. Neither
was the said Robert Edye (to whom the Complainant alleageth the deliverie of the bills of
Accompt of the said wares to be made) ever anie
servant of this defendant as the Complainant in
his bill most falslie avoucheth. But this defendant
confesseth that he sawe brought into his house
(att the time of Sir Francis Pophams lodgeinge
there) certaine bills of accompt for wares of such
nature as are in the bill of Complaynt expressed,
whereof the defendant tooke notice as well for the
satisfaction of himselfe as other adventurers his
private freindes. And it manifestlie appeareth by

the notes of the said wares given in, by the
Complainant or his servaunt that they were delivered to one William Sprate who as this defendant thinketh was then servaunt to the said Sir
Francis Popham, the Coppies whereof are yet
remaineing under the same title with this defendant readie to be showne to this honourable
Courte when he shalbe thereunto required. And
this defendant denyeth to have received of the
said Sir Edward Seymor late barronet deceassed
or of the said Mathew Suttclife Deane of Exon
[Exeter] anie sume or summes of money to be
imployed for that intended voiage but the fortie
poundes in the bill mentioned was after received
and to be imployed in an other voiage, and was not
by any agreement between this defendant and the
said Sir Francis Popham to be disbursed for the
wares in the bill mentioned. Neither was this
defendant ever debtor to the said Sir Francis for
the said fortie pounds, nor did he att any time so
confesse unto the Complainant as he untruelie
suggesteth. And this defendant further saith that
he haveing occasion to retourne a hundred
poundes from London and desirous to receive the
same att Plymmouth he sent his servant to effect
the same, who acquainteing the now Complainant
therewith he undertooke to retorne the same (as
formerlie att severall times he had donne for this
defendant for other Summes of good value. But he
being not then (as this defendant thinketh) furnished with somuch money he paid to the defendantes servaunte but three score poundes and
desired a shorte time to be given for the payement
of the other fortie poundes which (as the defendant remembreth) was for some fourteen daies or
thereabouts. And the Complainant received from
this defendant a bill of exchange unto one Ambrose Jennens the Complaynants brother for the
receipt of an hundred pounds in London which the
Complainant confesseth to have byn received accordinglie. And this defendant denyeth the said
bill of exchange to have byn made by him uppon
any such condicions and Agreements as the Complainant suggesteth but that the Complainant
afterward understanding by the defendants servant that the defendant would send fortie pounds
unto the said Sir Francis Popham, and the Complainant haveing fortie pounds residue of the said
hundred poundes remaineing in his hands as
aforesaid, he became earnest Suitor to this defendant that he might be the messenger to deliver

the said fortie pounds unto the said Sir Francis hopeing (as he said) to be thereby the rather satisfied for his said wares which he pretended to be unpaid for, and for which he did then and ever before repute the said Sir Francis his sole debtor as this defendant understood him, and desired this defendant to write unto the said Sir Francis in his behalfe. And the defendant willing to pleasure him therein did agree that he should deliver the said fortie poundes unto the said Sir Francis Popham so that he brought backe unto this defendant a note of the receipt thereof under the hand of the said Sir Francis, or otherwise to make payement of the said fortie poundes unto this defendant which he promised accordinglie to doe, but he performed neither of the said Condicions, but ungratefullie and dishonestlie practised (the said William Catchmaie in the bill mentioned this defendants onlie wittnes of the condicions as aforesaid being dead) wrongefullie and deceiptfullie to detaine the said fortie pounds, and to impose the said dett of thirtie six poundes nyneteen shillinges and an eleven pence (due as he saith for the wares in the bill mentioned) uppon this defendant whereas before he never seemed to this defendants knoweleidge to take or repute him any waie engaged for the same, but did maunie times desier this defendants patience untill he brought him an receipt from the said Sir Francis of the said fortie poundes. And this defendant verilie beleiveth that yf the said Sir Francis Popham had agreed that the Complainant should have retained somuch of the said fortie poundes as should satisfie his supposed dett, that then the said Sir Francis would have given a Receipt for the same, and the Complainant would also have delivered unto the said Sir Francis the residue of the said fortie poundes. Also this defendant doth not beleive that the Complainant ever paid unto the said William Catchmaie three poundes x^s and a pennie as he alleageth (neither did the Complainant ever make mention of any such payement to this defendants knowleidge) in the life time of the said Catchmaie, and yet this defendant had then depending an accion att the Comon lawe against the nowe Complainant for the said fortie pounds. Neither did this defendant att any time allowe of the said supposed bill of receipt made by the said Catchmaie unto the Complainant neither to this defendants best remembrance did he ever see any such bill of receipt as the Complainant falslie

alleageth. And without that this defendant did agree with the Complainant to receive three pounds tenn shillinges and a pennie in full satisfaction of the said hundred poundes and discharge of the said bill of exchange. And without that the defendant did att any tyme sett forth, or purpose to sett forth from the porte or haven of Plymmouth joyntelie with the said Sir Francis Popham the said shippe called the Gifte & the said shippe called the [blank] otherwise then by adventureing therein as aforesaid. And without that any other matter or thinge in the said bill of Complaint matteriall or effectuall in the Lawe to be answered unto, and herein not sufficientlie traversed, denied, confessed or avoided is trewe. All which matters the defendant is readie to Averre and prove as this honourable Court shall awarde and praieth to be dismissed with his reasonable Costes and Charges wrongefullie susteined herein.

[signed:] Fard. Gorges Elize Hele

Capta fuit hac responsio apud Plymouth secundo die Octobris Anno Regis domini nostri Jacobi dei gratia Anglie Francie et Hibernia Regis fidei defensor &c. decimo tercio et Scotie quadragesimo nono Coram nobis Lavyngton [?], Lampson [?], Charles Crooke.

Receptus Jenninges versus Gorges miles Cl' pasche ultime in titulo Popham

519. [1615?] Further complaint by Abraham Jennings against Sir Ferdinando Gorges.

This is almost identical verbally with the first Bill of May 22, 1608 (511) above, although Sir Ferdinando Gorges's servant's name is given as Robert Cage (for Edye elsewhere) and that it is unsigned. It is not printed.

520. February 17, 1609. Council of the Virginia Company of London to the Town of Plymouth.

The return of the Sagadahoc colony late in 1608 appeared to mark the end of the Plymouth Com-

pany's venture. The London Company, engaged in getting a new charter for itself and preparing a major enterprise in Virginia, decided to assume that the northern venture was dead after consultation with other leading members of the Plymouth Company, Gorges and Sutcliffe, and invited the mayor and aldermen of the Town of Plymouth to abandon their separate colony and join the southern venture.

Plymouth Public Library, Plymouth Archives W 359/54.

After our hartie Comendacions. Having understood of your generall good disposition towardes your advancing of an intended plantacion in *Virginia* begun by divers gentlemen and Marchauntes of the Westerne partes which since for want of good supplies and secondes here, and that the place which was possessed there by you: annswered not those Comodities which meight keepe lief in your good beggyninges, it hath not so well succeeded as soe worthy intentions and labours did meritt But by the Coldenes of the Clymate and other Connaturall necessities your Colonie was enforced to retorne:/: We have thought fitt (nothing doubting that this one ill successe hath quenched your affections for soe hopefull and godlye an action) to acquaynt you briefely with the Progresse of our Colonie the fitness of the place for habitation and the Comodities that through gods blessing our industries have discovered unto us. Which though perhapps you have heard at large Yet uppon lesse assurednes and Creaditt, then this our informacion: We having sente 3: yeres past and foun[d a] safe and navigable River, beginn to builde and plante 50 myles from the m[outh] [th]ereof, have since yerelie supplyed and sent 100 men from whome we have ass[uraun]ce of a most frutefull countrey for the maytenaunce of mans lief and aboundant in rich commodities safe from any danger of the Salvages or other ruyn that maye threaten us, yf we joyne freelie togeather and with one Common and patient purse mayneteyne and perfecte our foundations: The staple and certayne Comodities we have are Sope Asshes, Pytch, Tarre, dyes of soundry sortes and rich valves, Tymber for all uses, Fyshing for Sturgeon and divers other sortes, which is in that Baye more aboundant then in any parte of the world knowen to us, making of

Glasse and Iron, and noe unprobable hope of Richer mynes, the assurednes of these besides many other good and publicque endes have made us resolve to send in the month of March a lardge supplye of 800 men under the goverment of the Lord Dela Warr accompan[ied] with divers knyhtes and gentlemen of extraordinarye rancke and sufficienc[ie. And] because the greate Chardge in furnishing such a nomber [of men can be] hardly drawne from our single adventures we have tho[ught good to ask] your Corporacion of Plymouth to joyne your indeavors w[ith our own] which if you please to do, we will uppon your Lettres incert you[r]se[lves into] our Patent and admytt and receive so many of you as shall adventure 25[li] i[n] [this] Corporacion Of which to all priviledges and liberties he shalbe as free, as if he hadd begun with us at the first difficultie. And whereas we have intreated the Right ho[nourable] the Earle of Pembrooke to adress his lettres to his officers in the Staneries, for providing us 100 Mynerall and laboring men We do not desire that such adventures as shalbe consented to amonge you mayebe disbursed by some officer, chosen among yourselves for the providing a Shipp marryners and victualls for 6 monethes for such a nomber, and to be readie by the last of **March,** About which tyme we purpose with our fleete to put in at your Haven, or where els you shall appoynt us to take them in our Companye./ It wilbe to lardge to discourse more perticularities of this business by lettre or to promote with many reasons so good and forward inclinations as we hope and receive yours to be, And therefore desiring onelie your speedie annswere of this, and that you will please to conferr with Sir Ferdinando Gorge and Master doctor Sutcliffe Dean of Exon to whome we have written to assist you and us herein. We bid you hartelie farewell, London the 17th of February 1608

your verie loving freindes

 [signed:] W. Waad, Tho. Smythe, Edwyn Sandys, Tho. Roe, William Romeny

[Addressed:] To the Right Worshipfull our verie loving freindes the Mayour and Aldermen of the Towne of Plymouth/

[Endorsed:] A lettre from y[e] Councell of Virginia to the Corporation of Plymouth y[e] xvij[th] of Februarie 1608. And an Annswere to y[e] same from y[e] Corporation [not extant]

521. 1607–1608. John Smith on the Sagahadoc colony.

John Smith, The generall historie of Virginia *(1624), pp. 203–204; reprinted* Works, *edited by E. Arber (Birmingham, 1884), p. 696.*

Now this part of America hath formerly beene called Norumbega, Virginia, Nuskoncus, Penaquida, Cannada, and such other names as those that ranged the Coast pleased.

But because it was so mountainous, rocky and full of Iles, few have adventured much to trouble it, but as is formerly related; nothwithstanding, that honourable Patron of vertue, Sir John Popham, Lord chiefe Justice of England, in the yeere 1606, procured meanes and men to possesse it, and sent Captaine George Popham for President, Captaine Rawley Gilbert for Admirall, Captaine Edward Harlow master of the Ordnance, Captaine Robert Davis Sargeant-Major, Captaine Elis Best Marshall, Master Seaman, Secretary, Captaine James Davis to be Captaine of the Fort, Master Gome Carew chiefe Searcher: all those were of the Councell, who with some hundred more were to staye in the Country: they set saile from Plimoth the last of May, and fell with Monahigan the eleventh of August.

At Sagahadahoc 9. or 10. leagues southward, they planted themselves at the mouth of a faire navigable River, but the coast thereabouts most extreme stony and rocky: that extreme frozen Winter was so cold they could not range nor search the Country, and their provision so small, they were glad to send all but 45. of their companye backe againe. Their noble President Captaine Popham died, and not long after arrived two ships well provided of all necessities to supply them; and some small time after another, by whom understanding of the death of the Lorde chiefe Justice, and also of Sir John Gilbert: whose lands there the President Rawley Gilbert was to possesse according to the adventurers directions, finding nothing but extreme extremities, they all returned for England in the yeere 1608. and thus this Plantation was begunne and ended in one yeere, and the Country esteemed as a cold, barren, mountainous, rocky Desart.

XIV

The Establishment of a Dutch Presence in North America

As EARLY AS the 1580s there were rumors that the Dutch were willing to join with the English in the attempted colonization of North America, though it remained merely a rumor. Sir Walter Ralegh claimed in 1593, on what grounds we do not yet know, that the Dutch were already active in the Newfoundland fishery. There were certainly some Dutch voyages to Newfoundland from about 1600 onward, though mainly with sack ships, to buy rather than to catch fish. In the 1590s they were preoccupied with the Northeast Passage, and in the early 1600s were turning their attention to possibilities of transpolar voyages up the East Greenland coast and to the Northwest Passage. In 1605 they planned to intervene in the St. Lawrence fur trade, and in 1606 sent in vessels to the river that managed, in spite of attempts to enforce the Sieur de Monts' patent, to buy many of the beaver pelts acquired by the French traders who had themselves succeeded in trading illegally (from the French point of view) for them. The Dutch did not apparently make further attempts to do this in subsequent years, but it was only a matter of time before they would try to gain a footing in the fur trade farther south.

Many Dutch merchants believed that there was another prize to be found in these waters, namely a passage through to the East that would give them easier access to the valuable markets of China. Therefore, from the beginning the Dutch saw America more as a center for trade than as a land ripe for colonization. Among those with an interest in the trade was Emanuel Van Meteren, the Dutch consul in London, who became well acquainted with the efforts of men like Martin Frobisher, John Davis, and Henry Hudson to discover a sea route to the East. In 1607 Hudson, acting for the Muscovy Company, attempted to find a northeast passage and sailed as far as the northern end of Spitzbergen. The following year he was employed by the Company on a second voyage, during which he landed on the coast of Novaya Zemlya, but was prevented from going farther by a frightened and potentially mutinous crew. On his return to England the directors of the East India Company, following the recommendation of Van Meteren, sent for him. Hudson impressed them with his theory that it was possible to sail right across the North Pole and with his view that the climate became warmer as one got closer to the pole. Hudson also believed that there was a passage just to the north of Virginia. This idea had been fostered by letters and maps he had received from Captain John Smith, who had been led to the same conclusion by his exploration of the Chesapeake Bay and his discussion with the Indians. Hudson knew that the coast between 37° and 41° 30′ had not been properly explored since 1524, and was more inclined to go for the westerly passage but was ordered by the Company to find one to the East.

Therefore, in 1609, he steered his way up the west coast of Norway but once more was threatened by a mutiny of the sailors who refused to go farther north. Hudson retraced his course and then decided to head west to the area north of the Chesapeake. The ship encountered the American coast at Newfoundland and then sailed south to the region of Cape Hatteras, where Hudson turned north to explore the coast in more detail in the hope of finding his passage. After investigating Delaware Bay, the *Halve Maen* sailed north and anchored in New York harbor on September 11. The ship then went up the Hudson River as far as the site of modern Albany, which was reached on September 19. Here some of the crew were sent upstream in a small boat. On their return they reported that the river became more narrow and shallow. By now Hudson was convinced that this was not the passage he sought. Ignoring suggestions that they winter in Newfoundland and resume the search the following year, he returned to England and sent a proposal to the Dutch that he should go out again to search for a northwest passage, but the English authorities refused to let him leave for Holland. Since it obviously did not lead to the East, Hudson regarded his journey up the river as a failure, and it was some years before the importance of his discovery was appreciated.

The Dutch made another attempt at finding the elusive passage and in 1611–1612 Captain Jan Corneliszoon May sailed along the coast but with no success. However, rumors that Hudson traded for furs with the Indians led several Dutch ships to visit the Hudson River in the next few years. It was soon realized by the merchants that the river was an easy route to the lands of the Iroquois Indians who were willing to supply the Europeans with furs. In 1614 the New Netherland Company was formed, and shortly afterwards the Dutch established trading posts at Fort Orange (Albany) and at New Amsterdam (New York). However, the aim of the New Netherland Company (later assimilated into the West India Company) remained essentially trade. Colonies, it was argued, would disturb the Indians and the commercial intercourse which had been established with them. Thus it was relatively easy for the English to remove the Dutch from the New Netherlands in the 1660s.

Documentary evidence for Hudson's voyages of 1609 and 1610 is scarce and generally of a piecemeal nature. The logs or journals kept by Hudson have disappeared, and only abstracts have survived. The chief source for the 1609 expedition is the journal kept by Robert Juet, a man who had been on one of Hudson's previous voyages (522). It is uncertain what position he held in 1609, but he must have been an officer of some kind. He also went on the ill-fated voyage of 1610–1611 and, after surviving the mutiny, the Indian attack, and other deprivations, died in

September, 1611 when the *Discovery* was nearing the coast of Ireland. There is also some uncertainty as to the nature of the account. Was it an official log or a personal diary? There are gaps in the journal. For example, Juet makes no mention of the mutiny in May, 1609 which forced Hudson to turn south. He gives bad weather as the reason for changing course. It is possible that Juet was one of the mutineers. If so, his journal, which gives few details up to the date of the mutiny, could have been a means of keeping his own record of events in case the mutiny was discovered and the participants brought to trial. Nevertheless, it is the most detailed account of the voyage. For example, he alone describes the voyage as far south as Cape Hatteras. The journal was preserved by Richard Hakluyt and first published in 1625 by Samuel Purchas in *Pilgrimes*, III (1625), 581–595 (XIII [1906], 333–377). It also appeared in G. M. Asher (ed.), *Henry Hudson the Navigator* (London, Hakluyt Society, 1860), pp. 45–93, and in 1959 under the title *Juet's Journal*, edited by Robert H. Lunny for the New Jersey Historical Society (Newark, N.J.). Additional information can be found in two other works, both Dutch.

The first published account of the voyage appeared in the third edition of Emanuel Van Meteren, *Commentarien Ofte Memorien Van-den Nederlandtschen Staet Handel Oorloghen ende Gheschiedenissen van-Onsen tyden etc.* (1611), fols. 337–375. Van Meteren breaks off in the middle of an account of the English colony in Virginia to describe Hudson's voyage (523). Unfortunately, he gives no clue as to the source of his information, although there is little positive evidence to support the view that it was Hudson himself. The precision in the matter of dates and degrees of latitude suggests that the information must have come from someone in authority, possibly the mate who was almost certainly Dutch. Van Meteren is the only source to describe events between May 5 and 19, including the mutiny and later controversy over where to spend the winter of 1609. His account is also very careful to note the aims and ideas of Hudson as evidence for the decision to go west and search for a passage. A reprint of the Dutch account together with a translation appeared in Asher, *Henry Hudson*, pp. 147–153, and in Henry C. Murphy, *Henry Hudson in Holland* (The Hague, 1909). The translation also appears in J. F. Jameson, *Narratives of the New Netherlands* (New York, 1909), and in Philip L. Barbour, *Jamestown Voyages* (1969).

The third source for the 1609 voyage is provided by Johann de Laet who published a description of America called *Nieuwe Wereldt* (Leiden, 1625). De Laet was a director of the Dutch West India Company. Later, he became a partner in the Dutch settlements in the Delaware Bay area. He was eager to collect all possible information on the geographical discoveries, both printed and in manuscript. It is thought that in compiling the account of the 1609 voyage he used Hudson's journal, which he later destroyed (524). De Laet's account adds accurate detail and is particularly valuable in containing Hudson's own description of his visit to the Indians along the Hudson River. The work of De Laet was reprinted by Asher, *Henry Hudson*, and by Murphy, *Henry Hudson in Holland*, both of whom also include a translation.

Chapter Sixty-eight
Hudson's Voyage

522. 1609. Robert Juet's journal of Hudson's voyage.

The third Voyage of Master Henrie Hudson toward Nova Zembla, and at his returne, his passing from Farre Ilands, to New-found Land, and along to fortie foure degrees and ten minutes, and thence to Capte Cod, and so to thirtie three degrees; and along the Coast to the Northward, to fortie two degrees and a half, and up the River neere to fortie three degrees. Written by Robert Juet of Lime-house.

On Saturday the five and twentieth of March, 1609. after the old Account, we set sayle from Amsterdam; and by the seven and twentieth day, we were downe at the Texel: and by twelve of the clocke we were off the Land, it being East of us two leagues off. And because it is a journey usually knowne, I omit to put downe what passed, till we came to the height of The North Cape of Finmarke, which we did performe by the fift of May (stilo novo) being Tuesday. On which day we observed the height of the Pole, and found it to bee 71. degrees and 46. minutes; and found our Compasse to vary six degrees to the West: and at twelve of the clocke, the North Cape did beare South-west and by South, tenne leagues off, and wee steered away East and by South, and East.

After much trouble with fogges, sometimes, and more dangerous of Ice. The nineteenth, being Tuesday, was close stormie weather, with much wind and snow, and very cold: the wind variable betweene the North Northwest, and North-east. We made our way West and by North till noone. Then we observed the Sunne having a slake, and found our heigth to bee 70. degrees 30. minutes. And the ship had out-runne us twentie leagues, by reason of the set of the streame of The White Sea: and we had sight of Wardhouse. Then at two of the clocke wee tackt to the Eastward: for we could not get about the North Cape, the wind was so scant; and at eight of the clocke at night, on the one and twentieth, the North Cape did beare South-east and by South seven leagues off. And at mid-night Assumption Point did beare South and by East, five leagues off us.

The two and twentieth, gusting weather with haile and snow, the Sunne breaking out sometimes: we continued our course along the Land West South-west. And at tenne of the clocke at night we were thwart off Zenam. The bodie of it did beare East off us five leagues: and the course from the North Cape to Zenam, is for the most part West and by South, and West South-west, fiftie foure leagues.

The three and twentieth, faire Sun-shining weather; the wind at East and by South, and East South-east, wee steered along the Land South-west, and South-west and by West, eight leagues a Watch, for so we found the Land to lye from Zenam to Lofoote. And the distance is fiftie leagues from the bodie of Zenam, to the Westermost Land of Lofoote. And from the one to the other, the course is South-west and by West. For the Needle of our Compasse was set right to the North. At twelve of the clocke at night, the bodie of Lofoote did beare South-east, sixe leagues off.

The foure and twentieth, faire cleere Sunshining weather: the wind variable upon all points of the Compasse, but most upon the South-east, and sometimes calme. We continued our course West South-west as before. And at eight of the clocke at night, the Souther part of Lofoote did beare South-east ten leagues off us.

The five and twentieth, much wind at Northeast, with some snow and haile. The first watch the wind came to the East a fine gale, and so came to the North-east, the second watch at foure of the clocke, and freshed in: And at eight of the clocke it grew to a storme, and so continued. At noone we observed, and made the ship to be in 67. degrees 58. minutes. Wee continued our course South-west, twelve leagues a watch. At nine of the clocke, Lofoote did beare East of us 15. leagues off. And we found the Compasse to have no variation. The wind increased to a storme.

The six and twentieth, was a great storme at the North North-east, and North-east. Wee steered away South-west afore the wind with our fore-course abroad: for wee were able to maintayne no more sayles, it blew so vehemently, and the Sea went so high, and brake withall, that it would have dangered a small ship to lye under the Sea. So we skudded seventy leagues in foure and twentie houres. The storme began to cease at foure of the clocke.

The seven and twentieth, indifferent faire weather, but a good stiffe gale of wind at North, and North North-east, wee held on our course as before. At noone wee observed and found our heigth to be 64. degrees 10. minutes. And wee perceived, that the Current had hindred us in fortie eight houres to the number of 16. leagues to our best judgement. We set our mayne-sayle, sprit-sayle, and our mayne-top-sayle, and held on our course all night, having faire weather.

The eight and twentieth, faire weather and little wind at North-east, we held on our course South-west. At noone wee observed the heigth, and were in 62. degrees and 30. minutes. The after-noone was little wind at North North-west. The second watch it fell calme. At foure of the clocke wee had sight of the Iles called Farre, and found them to lye out of their place in the Sea Chart fourteene leagues to farre Westerly. For in running South-west from Lofoote, wee had a good care to our steerage and observations; and counted our selves thirtie leagues off by our course and observation: and had sight of them sixteene or eighteene leagues off.

The nine and twentieth, faire weather sometimes calme, and sometimes a gale with the wind varying at South-west, and so to the North-east. Wee got to the Ilands, but could not get in. So we stood along the Ilands. The ebbe being come, we durst not put in.

The thirtieth faire weather; the wind at South-east and East South-east. In the morning we turned into a Road in Stromo, one of the Ilands of Farre, betweene Stromo and Mugge-nes, and got in by nine of the clocke: for it flowed so there that day. And assoone as we came in, we went to Romage, and sent our Boat for water, and filled all our emptie Caskes with fresh water. Wee made an end of our Romaging this night by ten of the clocke.

The one and thirtieth, faire Sun-shining weather, the wind at East South-east. In the forenoone our Master with most of his Company went on shoare to walke, and at one of the clocke they returned aboord. Then we set sayle.

The first of June, stilo novo, faire Sun-shining weather, the wind at East South-east. We continued on our course South-west and by West. At noone wee observed the Sunne, and found our heigth to be 60. degrees 58. minutes: and so continued on our course all night with faire weather. This night we lighted Candles in the Bittacle againe.

The second mystie weather, the wind at North-east. At noone we steered away West South-west, to find Busse Iland, discovered in the yeere 1578. by one of the ships of Sir Martin Frobisher, to see if it lay in her true latitude in the Chart or no: wee continued our course as before all night, with a faire gale of wind: this night we had sight of the first stars, and our water was changed colour to a white greene. The Compasse had no variation.

The third, faire Sun-shining weather; the wind at North-east. We stered on our course South-west and by West, with a stiffe gale of wind. At noone we observed and found our heigth to bee 58. degrees 48. minutes. And I was before the ship 16. leagues, by reason of the Current that held us so strong out of the South-west. For it is eight leagues in foure and twentie houres. We accounted our selves neere Busse Iland: by midnight we looked out for it, but could not see it.

The fourth, in the morning was much wind with fogge and raine. Wee steered away South-west by west all the fore-noone, the wind so increasing, that wee were enforced to take in our top-sayle: the winde continuing so all the after-noone. Wee steered away South-west all the fore-part of the night; and at ten of the clocke at night it was little wind; and that was at South, and so came up to the South South-east.

The fift, stormie weather, and much wind at South, and South by East, so that at foure of the clocke in the morning, we tooke in our fore-sayle, and lay a try with our mayne corse, and tryed away West North-west foure leagues. But at noone it was lesse wind, and the Sunne shewed forth; and we observed, and found our heigth to be 56. degrees 21. minutes. In the after-noone the wind vered to and fro betweene the South-west and the South-east, with raine and fogge, and so continued all night. Wee found that our ship had gone to the Westward of our course. The sixth, thicke hasie weather with gusts of wind, and showers of raine. The wind varied betweene East South-East and South-west, wee steered on many courses a West South-west way. The after-noone watch the wind was at East South-east, a stiffe gale with myst and raine. Wee steered away South-west, by West eight leagues. At noone the Sunne shone forth, and we found the heigth to bee 56. degrees 8. minutes. The seventh, faire sun-shining weather all the fore-noone, and calme untill twelve of the clocke. In the after-noone the wind came to the North-west, a stiffe gale. We steered South-west by West, and made a South-west way. At noone we found the height to be 56. degrees one minute, and it continued all night a hard gale. The eight, stormy weather, the wind variable, betweene West and North-west much wind: at eight of the clocke wee tooke off our Bonnets. At noone the Sunne shewed forth, and wee observed, and our height was 54. degrees 30. minutes. The ninth, faire sun-shining weather, and little wind all the fore-part of the day untill eleven of the clocke. Then the wind came to the South South-east, and we steered away West South-west. At noone we found our height to bee 53. degrees and 45. minutes, and we had made our way South by West ten leagues. In the after-noone the wind increased and continued all night at East North-east and East.

The twelfth, faire weather, the wind variable betweene East North-east and South-east, wee steered on our course as before. At foure of the clock in the afternoon the wind came up at South-east. And we held our course as before. At noone wee observed and found our height to be 52. degrees 35. minutes.

The eleventh, in the morning was thicke and foggie, the winde varying betweene South South-west, and North-west. At foure of the clocke in the morning, wee tackt about to the Southward: At eleven of the clocke the winde came to the North-west, and so to the West North-west. This day we had change of water, of a whitish greene, like to the Ice water to the North-west. At noone it cleered up, and became very faire weather: wee put out our mayne top-sayle: then we observed the Sunne, and found our height to be 51. degrees 24. minutes. We had sayled many courses and found our ship gone to the Southward of our account ten leagues, by reason of a current from the North-ward. The Compasse varied on point to the East.

The twelfth, faire Sun-shining weather, but much wind at the West: we stood to the South-ward all day, the wind shifting betweene the South-west and the West and by North. Wee made our way South halfe a point West, eight and twentie leagues. Our height at noone was 50. degrees 9. minutes. At eight of the clock at night we took off our Bonets, the wind increasing.

The thirteenth, faire Sun-shining weather: the wind variable betweene the West, and North North-west. We made our way South South-west seven and twentie leagues. At noone we observed, and found our heigth to be 48. degrees 45. minutes. But not to be trusted, the Sea went so high. In the after-noone the winde was calmer, and wee brought to our Bonets, and stood to the Southward all night with a stiffe gale.

The fourteenth, faire and cleere Sun-shining weather: the winde variable betweene the North-west and South-west by West. At mid-night I observed the North starre at a North-west by West Guarde; a good observation 49. degrees 30. minutes. And at noone wee observed the Sunne, and our heigth was 48. degrees 6. min-utes. And I made account we ranne betweene the two observations twelve leagues. At one of the clocke in the after-noone, wee cast about to the Westward, and stood so all night: the winde increased to a storme, and was very much winde with Raine.

The fifteenth, we had a great storme, and spent over-boord our fore-mast, bearing our fore corse low set. The sixteenth, we were forced to trie with our mayne sayle, by reason of the unconstant weather. So wee tried foure watches South-east and by South eight leagues and an halfe, and two watches six leagues. The seventeenth, reason-able faire weather: the wind variable betweene West South-west, and West North-west. And a stiffe gale of wind, and so great a swelling Sea out of the West South-west, that wee could doe nothing. So one watch and an halfe wee drove North foure leagues and an halfe, and foure watches and an halfe South and by East halfe a point East twelve leagues. The eighteenth, reasonable weather but close and cloudie, and an hard gale of wind, and a great Sea. The winde being at the North-west, wee lay to the Southward, and made our drift South and by West, five leagues. The after-noone prooved little wind, and the night part calme. The nineteenth, in the fore-noone faire weather and calme. In the morning we set the piece of our fore mast, and set our fore corse.

The one and twentieth, faire Sun-shining weather, but much wind and a great Sea. We split our fore saile at ten of the clocke; then we laid it a trie with our mayne sayle, and continued so all day. In the night it fell to be little wind. This day our heigth was 45. degrees 48. minutes.

The two and twentieth, very faire Sun-shining weather, and calme all the after-noone. At noone we made a very good observation, and found our height 44. degrees 58. minutes. At eight of the clocke at night wee had a small gale of winde at South-east. And wee steered away West for Newfound Land. The true Compasse varied one point East.

The three and twentieth, thicke weather with much wind and some raine. At eight of the clocke in the morning, the wind came to the West South-west, and West so stiffe a gale, that we were forced to take our top-sayle, and steered away North North-west untill foure of the clock in the after-noone. Then we tact to the Southward the winde at West North-west. At eight of the clocke at night wee tooke in our top-sayles, and laid it a trie with our mayne sayle, the winde at West.

The foure and twentieth, a stiffe gale of wind, varying betweene the West and North North-west, we tried till sixe of the clocke: at which time we set our foresaile, and steered way West and by South by our Compasse eight leagues in foure watches: and wee tried away South in one watch and an halfe.

The five and twentieth, faire Sun-shining weather, the wind at North North-west and North, we steered away West by South by our Compasse till twelve of the clocke: at which time we had sight of a sayle, and gave her chase but could not speake with her. She stood to the East-ward; and we stood after her till sixe of the clocke in the after-noone. Then wee tact to the West-ward againe, and stood on our course. It was faire all night, and little wind sometimes.

The six and twentieth, all the fore-part of the day very faire weather and hot, but at foure of the clocke in the after-noone it grew to bee much winde and raine: the winde was at South South-east. At noone wee observed and found our heigth to bee 44. degrees 33. minutes. At eight of the clocke at night, the wind came to South-west, and West South-west. Wee steered North-west, one Watch, and at twelve in the night, to the West, and West and by South, very much wind. So we could lye but North North-west.

The seven and twentieth, very much winde and a soare storme, the wind Westerly. In the morning at foure of the clocke, wee tooke in our fore-corse, and layd it a trie with our mayne-corse low set; and so continued all the day and night, two watches to the Northward. At eight of the clocke at night, we tackt to the Southward.

The eight and twentieth, faire sun-shining weather, the wind at West and by South; we lay a trie to the Southward till eight of the clocke in the morning. Then wee set our fore-corse, and stood to the Southward a stiffe gale of wind, but faire weather and a great Sea, out of the Wester-boord, and so continued all night.

The nine and twentieth, faire sun-shining weather, the wind at West and by South; we stood to the Southward untill sixe of the clocke at night, and made our way South and by East, foure leagues. Then the winde came to the South-west, and wee cast about to the Westward, and made our way West North-west all night. At noone, I found the height 43. degrees 6. minutes. The variation one point West.

The thirtieth, faire sun-shining weather, the winde at South-west and by West, we steered North-west and by West. And made our way so, by reason of the variation of the Compasse. At noone, I found the height to bee 43. degrees 18. minutes; wee continued our course all night, and made our way North-west and by West, halfe a point Westerly, five and twentie leagues.

The first of July, close, mystie and thicke weather, but a faire gale of wind at South-west, and South-west by South. We steered away North-west and by West, Westerly, and made our way so, by reason of the variation of the

Compasse. At eight of the clocke at night, wee sounded for the Banke of New-found Land, but could get no ground.

The second, thicke mystie weather, but little wind, and that at West, and West and by South. At eight of the clocke in the morning, we cast about to the Southward, and when our ship was on stayes, we sounded for the Banke, and had ground in thirtie fathoms, white sand and shells, and presently it cleered: and we had sight of a sayle, but spake not with her. In the night we had much Rayne, Thunder and Lightning, and wind shifting.

The third, faire Sun-shining weather, with a faire gale of wind at East North-east, and wee steered away West South-west by our Compasse, which varyed 17. degrees Westward. This morning we were among a great Fleet of French-men, which lay Fishing on the Banke; but we spake with none of them. At noone wee found our heighth to bee 43. degrees 41. minutes. And we sounded at ten of the clocke, and had thirtie fathoms gray sand. At two of the clocke wee sounded, and had five and thirtie fathoms gray sand. At eight of the clocke at night, we sounded againe, and had eight and thirtie fathoms gray sand, as before.

The fourth, at the fore-part of the day cleere, with a faire gale of wind, but variable betweene the East North-east, and South and by East, wee held on our course as before. The after-noone was mystie, the wind shifting betweene the South and the West, till foure of the clocke. Then we tooke in our top-sayle and sprit-sayle, and sounded and had no ground in seventie fathoms. The winde shifted still untill eight of the clocke, then it came to the North North-east, and North-east and by North, and we steered away West North-west, by our varyed Compasse, which made a West way halfe point North. The Compasse varyed 15. degrees from the North to the West.

The fift, faire sun-shining weather, the wind at North-east and by North, we steered away West North-west, which was West halfe a point North. At noone we found our heighth to be 44. degrees 10. minutes, and sounded, and had no ground in one hundred fathoms. The after-noone proved calme sometimes, and somtimes little wind, untill nine of the clocke in the night. Then the wind came to the East, and we held on our course. At mid-night I observed and found the height to bee 44. degrees 10. minutes, by the North Starre and the Scorpions heart. The Compasse varyed 13. degrees.

The sixth, the fore-part of the day faire weather, and a stiffe gale of wind, betweene South South-east, and South-west, wee steered West and by North, and West North-west. The after-part of the day from two of the clocke, was all foggie and thicke weather; the wind a hard gale, varying betweene South-west and by South, and West and by North, we made our way North-west halfe a point Northerly, nineteene leagues, upon many points foure Watches. At night at eight of the clocke, we sounded and had no ground at one hundred fathoms.

The seventh, faire sun-shining weather, the wind varying betweene West and by North, and West and by South. At foure of the clocke in the morning, we cast about to the Southward, and stood so till one in the after-noone. At noone we found our height to be 44. degrees 26. minutes. At seven of the clocke, we tackt to the Northward. At eight at night, we tackt to the Southward, and sounded, and had nine and fiftie fathoms, white sand.

The eight, in the fore-noone faire weather, but the morning foggie till seven of the clocke. At foure of the clocke in the morning we sounded, and had five & fortie fathoms, fine white sand, and we had runne five leagues South and by West. Then wee stood along one Glasse, and went one league as before. Then we stood one Glasse and sounded, and had sixtie fathoms. Then wee takt and stood backe to the Banke, and had five and twentie fathoms; and tryed for Fish, and it fell calme, and we caught one hundred and eighteene great Coddes, from eight a clocke till one, and after Dinner wee tooke twelve, and saw many great Scoales of Herrings. Then wee had a gale of wind at South, and it shifted to the West North-west, and we stood three Glasses and sounded and had sixtie fathomes, and stood two Glasses, and had two and fortie fathoms, red stones and shells. So wee sounded every Glasse and had severall soundings 35. 33. 30. 31. 32. 33. and 34. fathoms.

The ninth, faire calme weather, we lay becalmed all day and caught some Fish, but not much, because we had small store of salt. At three of the clocke in the after-noone, wee had a gale at South-east, and South South-east, and we steered away Westerly, our Compasse was West and by South halfe a point South. At foure of the clocke, we sounded and had but fifteene, seventeene, and nineteene fathoms on a fishing Banke; and we sounded every Glasse. Then we could get no ground in five and twentie fathoms, and had sight of a sayle on head off us. At noone our height was 44. degrees 27. minutes. We stood to the Westward all night, and spake with a Frenchman, which lay Fishing on the Banke of Sablen, in thirtie fathoms, and we saw two or three more.

The tenth, very mystie and thicke weather, the wind at South-west, a faire gale. We stood to the South-ward, and made our way South-east and by East. At twelve of the clocke we sounded, and had eight and fortie fathoms: againe at two we sounded, and had fiftie fathoms. And at six of the clocke we sounded: and had eight and fortie fathoms on the end of the Banke. Againe, at eight of the clocke at night wee sounded, and had no ground in eightie fathomes, and were over the Banke. So wee stood along till mid-night. The Compasse varyed 17. degrees to the Westward.

The eleventh, very thicke and mystie weather. At twelve of the clocke at night, we cast about to the Westward, and stood so all day, and made our way West North-west. We sounded at twelve of the clocke, but had no ground; so we stood to the Westward all the fore-part of the night, and sounded but could get no ground in fiftie or sixtie fathoms till mid-night. Then I sounded and had ground at fifteene fathoms, white sand.

The twelfth, was very foggie, we stood our course all the morning till eleven of the clocke; at which time we had sight of the Land, which is low white sandie ground, right on head off us; and had ten fathoms. Then we tackt to the Southward, and stood off foure Glasses: then we tackt to the Land againe, thinking to have rode under it, and as we came neere it, the fog was so thicke that we could not see; so wee stood off againe. From mid-night to two of the clocke, we came sounding in twelve, thirteene, and foureteene fathoms off the shoare. At foure of the clocke, we had 20. fathoms. At eight of the clocke at night 30. fathoms. At twelve of the clocke 65. fathoms, and but little winde, for it deeped apace, but the neerer the shoare the fairer shoalding.

The thirteenth, faire sun-shining weather, from eight of the clocke in the fore-noone all day after, but in the morning it was foggie. Then at eight of the clocke we cast about for the shoare, but could not see it; the wind being at South by our true Compasse, wee steered West and by North. At noone we observed, and found our height to bee 43. degrees 25. minutes; so we steered away West and by North all the after-noone. At foure of the clocke in the after-noone, we sounded and had five and thirtie fathoms. And at six of the clocke, wee had sight of the Land, and saw two sayles on head off us. The land by the waters side is low Land, and white sandie Bankes rising full of little Hils. Our soundings were 35. 33. 30. 28. 32. 37. 33. & 32. fathoms.

The foureteenth, full of mysts flying and vading, the wind betweene South and South-west, we steered away West North-west, and North-west and by West. Our soundings were 29. 25. 24. 25. 22. 25. 27. 30. 28. 30. 35. 43. 50. 70. 90. 70. 64. 86. 100. fathoms, and no ground.

The fifteenth, very mystie, the winde varying betweene South and South-west, wee steered West and by North, and West North-west. In the morning we sounded, and had one hundred fathoms, till foure of the clocke in the after-noone. Then we sounded againe, and had seventie five fathoms. Then in two Glasses running, which was not above two English miles, we sounded and had sixtie fathoms, and it shoalded a great pace untill we came to twentie fathoms. Then we made account we were neere the Ilands that lie off the shoare. So we came to an Anchor, the Sea being very smooth and little wind, at nine of the clocke at night. After supper, we tryed for Fish, and I caught fifteene Cods, some the greatest that I have seene, and so we rode all night.

The sixteenth, in the morning it cleered up, and wee had sight of five Ilands lying North, and North and by West from us, two leagues. Then wee made ready to set sayle, but the myst came so thicke, that we durst not enter in among them.

The seventeenth, was all mystie, so that wee could not get into the Harbour. At ten of the clocke two Boates came off to us, with six of the Savages of the Countrey, seeming glad of our comming. We gave them trifles, and they eate and dranke with us; and told us, that there were Gold, Silver, and Copper mynes hard by us; and that the French-men doe Trade with them; which is very likely, for one of them spake some words of French. So wee rode still all day and all night, the weather continuing mystie.

The eighteenth, faire weather, wee went into a very good Harbour, and rode hard by the shoare in foure fathoms water. The River runneth up a great way, but there is but two fathoms hard by us. We went on shoare and cut us a fore Mast, then at noone we came aboord againe, and found the height of the place to bee in 44. degrees 1. minute; and the Sunne to fall at a South Southwest Sunne. We mended our sayles, and fell to make our fore-Mast. The Harbour lyeth South and North, a mile in where we rode.

The nineteenth, we had faire sun-shining weather, we rode still. In the after-noone wee went with our Boate to looke for fresh water, and found some; and found a shoald with many Lobsters on it, and caught one and thirtie. The people comming aboord, shewed us great friendship, but we could not trust them. The twentieth, faire sunne-shining weather, the winde at South-west. In the morning, our Scute went out to catch fresh Fish halfe an houre before day, and returned in two houres, bringing seven and twentie great Coddes, with two hookes and lines. In the after-noone wee went for more Lobsters, and caught fortie, and returned aboord. Then wee espied two French Shallops full of the Countrey people come into the Harbour, but they offered us no wrong, seeing we stood upon our guard. They brought many Beaver skinnes, and other fine Furres, which they would have changed for redde Gownes. For the French trade with them for red Cassockes, Knives, Hatchets, Copper, Kettles, Trevits, Beades, and other trifles.

The one and twentieth, all mystie, the wind Easterly, wee rode still and did nothing, but about our Mast. The two and twentieth, faire Sun-shining weather, the winde all Northerly, we rode still all the day. In the after-noone our Scute went to catch more Lobsters, and brought with them nine and fiftie. The night was cleere weather.

The three and twentieth, faire sun-shining weather and very hot. At eleven of the clocke, our fore Mast was finished, and we brought it aboord, and set it into the step, and in the after-noone we rigged it. This night we had some little myst and rayne.

The foure and twentieth, very hot weather, the winde at South out of the sea. The fore-part of the day wee brought to our sayles. In the morning, our Scute went to take Fish, and in two houres they brought with them twentie great Coddes, and a great Holibut, the night was faire also. We kept good watch for feare of being betrayed by the people, and perceived where they layd their Shallops.

The five and twentieth, very faire weather and hot. In the morning wee manned our Scute with foure Muskets, and sixe men, and tooke one of their Shallops and brought it aboord. Then we manned our Boat & Scute with twelve men and Muskets, and two stone Pieces or Murderers, and drave the Salvages from their Houses, and tooke the spoyle of them, as they would have done of us. Then wee set sayle, and came downe to the Harbours mouth, and rode there all night, because the winde blew right in, and the night grew mystie with much rayne till mid-night. Then it fell calme, and the wind came off the Land at West North-west, and it began to cleere. The Compasse varyed 10. degrees North-west.

The sixe and twentieth, faire and cleere sunne-shining weather. At five of the clocke in the morning, the winde being off the shoare at North North-west, we set sayle and came to sea, and by noone we counted our ship had gone fourteene leagues South-west. In the after-noone, the winde shifted variably betweene West Southwest, and North-west. At noone, I found the height to bee 43. degrees 56. minutes. This Eevening being very faire weather, wee observed the variation of our Compasse at the Sunnes going downe, and found it to bee 10. degrees from the North to the Westward.

The seven and twentieth, faire sun-shining weather, the winde shifting betweene the South-west, and West and by North, a stiffe gale, we stood to the Southward all day, and made our way South and by West, seven and twentie leagues. At noone, our height was 42. degrees 50. minuts. At foure of the clocke in the after-noone, wee cast about to the Northward. At eight of the clocke, we tooke in our top-sayles and our fore-bonnet, and went with a short sayle all night.

The eight and twentieth, very thicke and mystie, and a stiffe gale of wind, varying betweene South South-west, and South-west and by West; we made our way North-west and by West, seven and twentie leagues, wee sounded many times and could get no ground. At five of the clocke, we cast about to the Southward, the wind at Southwest and by West. At which time we sounded, and had ground at seventie five fathoms. At eight, wee had sixtie five fathoms. At ten, sixtie. At twelve of the clocke at mid-night, fiftie sixe fathoms, gray sand. The Compasse varyed 6. degrees the North point to the West.

The nine and twentieth, faire weather, we stood to the Southward, and made our way South and by West a point South, eighteene leagues. At noone, we found our height to bee 42. degrees 56. minutes, wee sounded oft, and had these 60. 64. 65. 67. 65. 65. 70. and 75. fathoms. At night, wee tryed the variation of our Compasse by the setting of the Sunne, and found that it went downe 37. degrees to the North-ward of the West, and should have gone downe but 31. degrees. The Compasse varyed 5. ½ degrees.

The thirtieth, very hot, all the fore-part of the day calme, the wind at South South-east, wee steered away West South-west and sounded many times, and could find no ground at one hundred and seventie fathomes. We found a great current and many over-falls. Our current had deceived us. For at noone we found our height to be 41. degrees 34. minutes. And the current had heaved us to the Southward fourteene leagues. At eight of the clocke at night, I sounded and had ground in fiftie two fathomes. In the end of the mid-night watch, wee had fiftie three fathomes. This last observation is not to be trusted.

The one and thirtieth, very thicke and mystie all day, untill tenne of the clocke. At night the wind came to the South, and South-west and South. We made our way West North-west nineteene leagues. Wee sounded many times, and had difference of soundings, sometimes little stones, and sometimes grosse gray sand, fiftie six, fiftie foure, fortie eight, fortie seven, fortie foure, fortie six, fiftie fathomes; and at eight of the clocke at night it fell calme, and we had fiftie fathomes. And at ten of the clocke we heard a great Rut, like the Rut of the shoare. Then I sounded and found the former Depths; and mistrusting a current, seeing it so still that the ship made no way, I let the lead lie on the ground, and found a tide set to the South-west, and South-west by West, so fast, that I could hardly vere the Line so fast, and presently came an hurling current, or tyde with over-fals, which cast our ship round; and the Lead was so fast in the ground, that I feared the Lines breaking, and we had no more but that. At mid-night I sounded againe, and we had seventie five fathomes; and the strong streame had left us.

The first of August, all the fore-part of the day was mystie, and at noone it cleered up. We found that our height was 41. degrees 45. minutes, and we had gone nineteene leagues. The after-noon was reasonable cleere. We found a rustling tide or current, with many over-fals to continue still, and our water to change colour, and our sea to bee very deepe, for wee found no ground in one hundred fathomes. The night was cleere, and the winde came to the North, and North North-east, we steered West.

The second, very faire weather and hot: from the morning till noone we had a gale of wind, but in the after-noone little wind. At noone I sounded and had one hundred and ten fathomes; and our height was 41. degrees 56. minutes. And wee had runne foure and twentie leagues and an halfe. At the Sun-setting we observed the variation of the Compasse, and found that it was come to his true place. At eight of the clocke the gale increased, so wee ranne sixe leagues that watch, and had a very faire and cleere night.

The third, very hot weather. In the morning, we had sight of the Land, and steered in with it, thinking to goe to the North-ward of it. So we sent our shallop with five men, to sound in by the shore: and they found it deepe five fathomes within a Bow-shot of the shoare; and they went on Land, and found goodly Grapes, and Rose trees, and brought them aboord with them, at five of the clocke in the Eevening. We had seven and twentie fathomes within two miles of the shoare; and we found a floud come from the South-east, and an ebbe from the North-west, with a very strong streame, and a great hurling and noyses. At eight of the clocke at night, the wind began to blow a fresh gale, and continued all night but variable. Our sounding that wee had to the Land, was one hundred, eightie, seventie foure, fiftie two, fortie sixe, twentie nine, twentie seven, twentie foure, nineteene, seventeene, sometimes Oze, and sometimes gray sand.

The fourth, was very hot: we stood to the North-west two watches, and one South in for the Land, and came to an Anchor at the Norther end of the Headland, and heard the voyce of men call. Then we sent our Boat on shoare, thinking they had beene some Christians left on the Land: but wee found them to bee Savages, which seemed very glad of our comming. So wee brought one aboord with us, and gave him meate, and he did eate and drinke with us. Our Master gave him three or foure glasse Buttons, and sent him on Land with our shallop againe. And at our Boats comming from the shoare he leapt and danced, and held up his hands, and pointed us to a river on the other side: for we had made signes that we came to fish there. The bodie of this Headland lyeth in 41. degrees 45. minutes. We set sayle againe after dinner, thinking to have got to the Westward of this Headland, but could not; so we beare up to the Southward of it, & made a South-east way; and the Souther point did beare West at eight of the clocke at night. Our soundings about the Easter and Norther part of this Headland, a league from the shoare are these: at the Easter-side thirtie, twentie seven, twentie seven, twentie foure, twentie five, twentie. The North-east point 17. degrees 18. minutes, and so deeper. The North-end of this Headland, hard by the shoare thirtie fathomes: and three leagues off North North-west, one hundred fathomes. At the South-east part a league off, fifteene, sixteene, and seventeene fathomes. The people have greene Tabacco, and pipes, the boles whereof are made of Earth, and the pipes of red Copper. The Land is very sweet.

The fift, all mystie. At eight of the clocke in the morning, wee tact about to the Westward, and stood in till foure of the clocke in the after-noone; at which time it cleered, and wee had sight of the Head-land againe five leagues from us. The Souther point of it did beare West off us: and we sounded many times, and had no ground. And at foure of the clocke we cast about, and at our staying wee had seventie fathomes. Wee steered away South and South by East all night, and could get no ground at seventie and eightie fathomes. For wee feared a great Riffe, that lyeth off the Land, and steered away South and by East.

The sixth, faire weather, but many times mysting. Wee steered away South South-east, till eight of the clocke in the morning; Then it cleered a little, and wee cast about to the Westward. Then we sounded and had thirtie fathomes, grosse sand, and were come to the Riffe. Then wee kept our Lead, and had quicke shoalding, from thirtie, twentie nine, twentie seven, twentie foure, twentie two, twentie and an halfe, twentie, twentie, nineteene, nineteene, nineteene,

eighteene, eighteene, seventeene; and so deeping againe as proportionally as it shoalded. For we steered South and South-east till we came to twentie sixe fathomes. Then we steered South-west for so the tyde doth set. By and by it being calme we tryed by our Lead; for you shall have sixteene or seventeene fathomes, and the next cast but seven or six fathomes. And farther to the Westward you shall have foure and five foot water, and see Rockes under you; and you shall see the Land in the top. Upon this Riffe we had an observation, and found that it lyeth in 40. degrees 10. minutes. And this is that Headland which Captaine Bartholomew Gosnold discovered in the yeere 1602. and called Cape Cod; because of the store of Cod-fish that hee found thereabout. So we steered South-west three leagues, and had twentie, and twentie foure fathomes. Then we steered West two Glasses halfe a league, and came to fifteene fathomes. Then we steered off South-east foure Glasses, but could not get deepe water; for there the tyde of ebbe laid us on; and the streame did hurle so, that it laid us so neere the breach of a shoald, that wee were forced to Anchor. So at seven of the clocke at night, wee were at an Anchor in tenne fathomes: And, I give God most heartie thankes, the least water wee had was seven fathomes and an halfe. We rode still all night, and at a still water I sounded so farre round about our ship as we could see a light; and had no lesse then eight, nine, ten, and eleven fathomes: The myst continued being very thicke.

The seventh, faire weather and hot, but mystie. Wee rode still hoping it would cleere, but on the floud it fell calme and thicke. So we rode still all day and all night. The floud commeth from the South-west, and riseth not above one fathome and an halfe in nepe streames. Toward night it cleered, and I went with our shallop and sounded, and found no lesse water then eight fathomes to the South-east off us: but we saw to the North-west off us great Breaches.

The eight, faire and cleere weather. In the morning, by six of the clocke at slake water wee weighed; the wind at North-east, and set our fore-sayle and mayne top-sayle, and got a mile over the Flats. Then the tyde of ebbe came, so we anchored againe till the floud came. Then wee set sayle againe, and by the great mercie of God, wee got cleere off them by one of the clocke this after-noone. And wee had sight of the Land from the West North-west, to the North North-west. So we steered away South South-east all night; and had ground untill the middle of the third watch. Then we had fortie five fathomes, white sand, and little stones. So all our soundings are twentie, twentie, twentie two, twentie seven, thirtie two, fortie three, fortie three, fortie five. Then no ground in seventie fathomes.

The ninth, very faire and hot weather, the wind a very stiffe gale. In the morning, at foure of the clocke, our shallop came running up against our sterne, and split in all her stemme; So we were faine to cut her away. Then wee tooke in our mayne sayle, and lay atrie under our fore-sayle untill twelve of the clocke at mid-day. Then the wind ceased to a faire gale, so wee stood away South-west. Then we lay close by, on many courses a South by West way fifteene leagues; and three watches South-east by East, ten leagues. At eight of the clocke at night, wee tooke in our top-sayles, and went with a low sayle; because we were in an unknowne sea. At noone we observed and found our heigth to be 38. degrees 39. minutes.

The tenth, in the morning some raine and cloudie weather: the winde at South-west, wee made our way South-east by East, ten leagues. At noone, wee observed and found our heigth to bee 38. degrees 39. minutes. Then wee tackt about to the Westward, the wind being at South and by East, little wind. At foure of the clocke it fell calme, and we had two Dolphines about our ship, and many small fishes. At eight of the clocke at night, wee had a small lingring gale. All night we had a great Sea out of the South-west, and another great Sea out of the North-east.

The eleventh, all the fore-part of the day faire weather, and very hot. Wee stood to the West South-west till noone. Then the wind shorted, and we could lye but South-west and by South. At noone, wee found our heigth to be 39. degrees 11. minutes. And that the current had laid us to the Northward thirtie two minutes contrary to our expectation. At foure of the clocke in the after-noone there came a myst, which endured two houres. But wee had it faire and cleere all night after. The Compasse varied the North point to the West one whole point.

The twelfth, faire weather, the wind variable betweene the South-west and by South, and the North little wind. In the morning we killed an extraordinary fish, and stood to the Westward all day and all night. At noone we found our heigth to be 38. degrees 13. minutes. And the observation the day before was not good. This noone, we found the Compasse to vary from the North to the West ten degrees.

The thirteenth, faire weather and hot: the wind at North-east. Wee steered away West and by our Compasse two and twentie leagues. At noone wee found our height to bee 37. degrees 45. minutes, and that our way from noone to noone was West South-west, halfe a point Southerly. The Compasse was 7. degrees and a halfe variation, from the North point to the West.

The fourteenth, faire weather, but cloudie, and a stiffe gale of wind, variable betweene North-east and South-west, wee steered away West by South, a point South all day untill nine of the clocke at night; then it began to Thunder and Lighten, whereupon we tooke in all our sayles, and layd it a hull, and hulled away North till mid-night, a league and a halfe.

The fifteenth, very faire and hot weather, the winde at North by East. At foure of the clocke in the morning we set sayle, and stood on our course to the Westward. At noone wee found our height to bee 37. degrees 25. minutes. The after-noone proved little wind. At eight of the clocke at night, the winde came to the North, and wee steered West by North, and West North-west, and made our way West. The Compasse varyed 7. degrees from the North to the West.

The sixteenth, faire shining weather, and very hot, the wind variable betweene the North and the West, wee steered away West by North. At noone wee found our height to bee 37. degrees 6. minutes. This morning we sounded and had ground in ninetie fathomes, and in six Glasses running it shoalded to fiftie fathoms, and so to eight and twentie fathoms, at foure of the clocke in the after-noone. Then wee came to an Anchor, and rode till eight of the clocke at night, the wind being at South and Moone-light, we resolved to goe to the Northward to finde deeper water. So we weighed and stood to the Northward, and found the water to shoald and deepe, from eight and twentie to twentie fathomes.

The seventeenth, faire and cleere Sun-shining weather, the winde at South by West, wee steered to the Northward till foure of the clocke in the morning, then wee came to eighteene fathomes. So we Anchored untill the Sunne arose to looke abroad for Land, for wee judged there could not but be Land neere us, but we could see none. Then we weighed and stood to the Westward till noone. And at eleven of the clocke wee had sight of a low Land, with a white sandie shoare. By twelve of the clocke we were come into five fathomes, and Anchored; and the Land was foure leagues from us, and wee had sight of it from the West, to the North-west by North. Our height was 37. degrees 26. minutes. Then the wind blew so stiffe a gale, and such a Sea went, that we could not weigh; so we rode there all night an hard rode.

The eighteenth, in the morning faire weather, and little winde at North North-east and Northeast. At foure of the clocke in the morning, we weighed and stood into the shoare to see the deeping or shoalding of it, and finding it too deepe, we stood in to get a rode; for wee saw as it were three Ilands. So wee turned to windward to get into a Bay, as it shewed to us to the Westward of an Iland. For the three Ilands did beare North off us. But toward noone the wind blew Northerly with gusts of wind and rayne. So we stood off into the Sea againe all night; and running off we found a Channell, wherein we had no lesse then eight, nine, ten, eleven, and twelve fathomes water. For in comming over the Barre, wee had five, and foure fathomes and a halfe, and it lyeth five leagues from the shoare, and it is the Barre of Virginia. At the North end of it, it is ten leagues broad, and South and North, but deepe water from ninetie fathoms to five, and foure and a halfe. The Land lyeth South and North. This is the entrance into the Kings River in Virginia, where our English-men are. The North side of it lyeth in 37. degrees 26. minutes, you shall know when you come to shoald water or sounding; for the water will looke Greene or thicke, you shall have ninetie and eightie fathomes, and shoalding a pace till you come to ten, eleven, nine, eight, seven, ten, and nine fathomes, and so to five, and foure fathomes and a halfe.

The nineteenth, faire weather, but an hard gale of winde at the North-east, wee stood off till noone, and made our way South-east by East, two and twentie leagues. At noone wee cast about to the Westward, and stood till six of the clocke in the after-noone, and went five leagues and a halfe North-west by North. Then wee cast about

againe to the Eastward, and stood that way till foure the next morning.

The twentieth, faire and cleere weather, the winde variable betweene East North-east, and North-east. At foure of the clocke in the morning, wee cast about to the Westward, and stood till noone; at which time I sounded; and had two and thirtie fathomes. Then we takt to the Eastward againe; wee found our height to bee 37. degrees 22. minutes. We stood to the Eastward all night, and had very much wind. At eight of the clocke at night we tooke off our Bonnets, and stood with small sayle.

The one and twentieth, was a sore storme of winde and rayne all day and all night, wherefore wee stood to the Eastward with a small sayle till one of the clocke in the after-noone. Then a great Sea brake into our fore-corse and split it; so we were forced to take it from the yard and mend it; wee lay a trie with our mayne-corse all night. This night our Cat ranne crying from one side of the ship to the other, looking over-boord, which made us to wonder; but we saw nothing.

The two and twentieth, stormy weather, with gusts of rayne and wind. In the morning at eight of the clocke we set our fore-corse, and stood to the Eastward under our fore-sayle, mayne-sayle and misen, and from noone to noone, we made our way East South-east, fourteene leagues. The night reasonable drie but cloudie, the winde variable all day and night. Our Compasse was varyed 4. degrees Westward.

The three and twentieth, very faire weather, but some Thunder in the morning, the winde variable betweene East by North. At noone wee tackt about to the Northward, the winde at East by North. The after-noone very faire, the wind variable, and continued so all night. Our way we made East South-east, till noone the next day.

The foure and twentieth, faire and hot weather, with the wind variable betweene the North and the East. The after-noone variable winde. But at foure of the clocke, the wind came to the East and South-east; so wee steered away North by West, and in three Watches wee went thirteene leagues. At noone our height was 35. degrees 41. minutes, being farre off at Sea from the Land.

The five and twentieth, faire weather and very hot. All the morning was very calme untill eleven of the clocke; the wind came to South-east, and South South-east; so wee steered away Northwest by North, two Watches and a halfe, and one Watch North-west by West, and went eighteene leagues. At noone I found our height to bee 36. degrees 20. minutes, being without sight of Land.

The six and twentieth, faire and hot weather, the winde variable upon all the points of the Compasse. From two of the clocke in the morning untill noone, wee made our way North by East, seven leagues. In the after-noone the wind came to the North-east, and vering to the East South-east, wee steered away North-west fifteene leagues, from noone till ten of the clocke at night. At eight of the clocke at night wee sounded, and had eighteene fathomes, and were come to the Banke of Virginia, and could not see the Land. Wee kept sounding, and steered away North, and came to eight fathomes, and Anchored there; for the wind was at East South-east, so that wee could not get off. For the Coast lyeth along South South-west, and North North-east. At noone our height was 37. degrees 15. minutes. And wee found that we were returned to the same place, from whence we were put off at our first seeing Land.

The seven and twentieth, faire weather and very hot, the winde at East South-east. In the morning as soone as the Sunne was up, wee looked out and had sight of the Land. Then wee weighed, and stood in North-west two Glasses, and found the Land to bee the place, from whence wee put off first. So wee kept our loofe, and steered along the Land, and had the Banke lye all along the shoare; and wee had in two leagues off the shoare, five, sixe, seven, eight, nine, and ten fathomes. The Coast lyeth South South-west, and is a white Sandie shoare, and sheweth full of Bayes and Points. The streame setteth West South-west, and East North-east. At sixe of the clocke at night, wee were thwart of an Harbour or River, but we saw a Barre lye before it; and all within the Land to the Northward, the water ranne with many Ilands in it. At sixe of the clocke we Anchored, and sent our Boate to sound to the shoare-ward, and found no lesse then foure and a halfe, five, sixe, and seven fathomes.

The eight and twentieth, faire and hot weather, the winde at South South-west. In the morning at sixe of the clocke wee weighed, and steered away North twelve leagues till noone, and came to the Point of the Land; and being hard by the Land in five fathomes, on a sudden wee came into three fathomes; then we beare up and had but ten foote water, and joyned to the Point. Then as soone as wee were over, wee had five, sixe, seven, eight, nine, ten, twelve, and thirteene fathomes. Then wee found the Land to trend away North-west, with a great Bay and Rivers. But the Bay wee found shoald; and in the offing wee had ten fathomes, and had sight of Breaches and drie Sand. Then wee were forced to stand backe againe; so we stood backe South-east by South, three leagues. And at seven of the clocke wee Anchored in eight fathomes water; and found a Tide set to the North-west, and North North-west, and it riseth one fathome, and floweth South South-east. And hee that will throughly Discover this great Bay, must have a small Pinnasse, that must draw but foure or five foote water, to sound before him. At five in the morning wee weighed, and steered away to the Eastward on many courses, for the Norther Land is full of shoalds. Wee were among them, and once wee strooke, and wee went away; and steered away to the South-east. So wee had two, three, foure, five, sixe, and seven fathomes, and so deeper and deeper.

The nine and twentieth, faire weather, with some Thunder and showers, the winde shifting betweene the South South-west, and the North North-west. In the morning wee weighed at the breake of day, and stood toward the Norther Land, which we found to bee all Ilands to our sight, and great stormes from them, and are shoald three leagues off. For we comming by them, had but seven, sixe, five, foure, three, and two fathoms and a halfe, and strooke ground with our Rudder, we steered off South-west, one Glasse, and had five fathoms. Then wee steered South-east three Glasses, then wee found seven fathomes, and steered North-east by East, foure leagues, and came to twelve and thirteene fathomes. At one of the clocke, I went to the top-mast head, and set the Land, and the bodie of the Ilands did beare North-west by North. And at foure of the clocke, wee had gone foure leagues East South-east, and North-east by East, and found but seven fathoms, and it was calme, so we Anchored. Then I went againe to the top-mast head, to see how farre I could see Land about us, and could see no more but the Ilands. And the Souther point of them did beare North-west by West, eight leagues off. So wee rode till mid-night. Then the winde came to the North North-west, so wee waighed and set sayle.

The thirtieth, in the morning betweene twelve and one, we weighed, and stood to the Eastward, the winde at North North-west, wee steered away and made our way East South-east. From our weighing till noone, eleven leagues. Our soundings were eight, nine, ten, eleven, twelve, and thirteene fathomes till day. Then we came to eighteene, nineteene, twentie, and to sixe and twentie fathoms by noone. Then I observed the Sunne, and found the height to bee 39. degrees 5. minutes, and saw no Land. In the after-noone, the winde came to North by West; So wee lay close by with our fore-sayle: and our mayne-sayle, and it was little winde untill twelve of the clocke at mid-night, then wee had a gale a little while. Then I sounded, and all the night our soundings were thirtie, and sixe and thirtie fathomes, and wee went little.

The one and thirtieth, faire weather and little wind. At sixe of the clocke in the morning we cast about to the Northward, the wind being at the North-east, little wind. At noone it fell calme, and I found the height to bee 38. degrees 39. minutes. And the streames had deceived us, and our sounding was eight and thirtie fathoms. In the after-noone I sounded againe, and had but thirtie fathoms. So we found that we were heaved too and fro with the streames of the Tide, both by our observations and our depths. From noone till foure of the clocke in the after-noone, it was calme. At sixe of the clocke wee had a little gale Southerly, and it continued all night, sometimes calme, and sometimes a gale; wee went eight leagues from noone to noone, North by East.

The first of September, faire weather, the wind variable betweene East and South, we steered away North North-west. At noone we found our height to bee 39. degrees 3. minutes. Wee had soundings thirtie, twentie seven, twentie foure, and twentie two fathomes, as wee went to the Northward. At sixe of the clocke wee had one and twentie fathomes. And all the third watch till twelve of the clocke at mid-night, we had soundings one and twentie, two and twentie, eighteene, two and twentie, one and twentie, eighteene, and two and twentie fathoms, and went sixe leagues neere hand North North-west.

The second, in the morning close weather, the winde at South in the morning; from twelve untill two of the clocke we steered North North-west, and had sounding one and twentie fathoms, and in running one Glasse we had but sixteene fathoms, then seventeene, and so shoalder and shoalder untill it came to twelve fathoms. We saw a great Fire, but could not see the Land, then we came to ten fathoms, whereupon we brought our tackes aboord, and stood to the Eastward East South-east, foure Glasses. Then the Sunne arose, and we steered away North againe, and saw the Land from the West by North, to the North-west by North, all like broken Ilands, and our soundings were eleven and ten fathoms. Then wee looft in for the shoare, and faire by the shoare, we had seven fathoms. The course along the Land we found to be North-east by North. From the Land which we had first sight of, untill we came to a great Lake of water, as wee could judge it to bee, being drowned Land, which made it to rise like Ilands, which was in length ten leagues. The mouth of that Lake hath many shoalds, and the Sea breaketh on them as it is cast out of the mouth of it. And from that Lake or Bay, the Land lyeth North by East, and wee had a great streame out of the Bay; and from thence our sounding was ten fathoms, two leagues from the Land. At five of the clocke we Anchored, being little winde, and rode in eight fathoms water, the night was faire. This night I found the Land to hall the Compasse 8. degrees. For to the Northward off us we saw high Hils. For the day before we found not above 2. degrees of Variation. This is a very good Land to fall with, and a pleasant Land to see.

The third, the morning mystie untill ten of the clocke, then it cleered, and the wind came to the South South-east, so wee weighed and stood to the Northward. The Land is very pleasant and high, and bold to fall withall. At three of the clocke in the after-noone, wee came to three great Rivers. So we stood along to the Northermost, thinking to have gone into it, but we found it to have a very shoald barre before it, for we had but ten foot water. Then wee cast about to the Southward, and found two fathoms, three fathoms, and three and a quarter, till we came to the Souther side of them, then we had five and sixe fathoms, and Anchored. So wee sent in our Boate to sound, and they found no lesse water then foure, five, sixe, and seven fathoms, and returned in an houre and a halfe. So wee weighed and went in, and rode in five fathoms, Ozie ground, and saw many Salmons, and Mullets, and Rayes very great. The height is 40. degrees 30. minutes.

The fourth, in the morning as soone as the day was light, wee saw that it was good riding farther up. So we sent our Boate to sound, and found that it was a very good Harbour; and foure and five fathoms, two Cables length from the shoare. Then we weighed and went in with our ship. Then our Boate went on Land with our Net to Fish, and caught ten great Mullets, of a foot and a halfe long a peece, and a Ray as great as foure men could hale into the ship. So wee trimmed our Boate and rode still all day. At night the wind blew hard at the North-west, and our Anchor came home, and wee drove on shoare, but tooke no hurt, thanked bee God, for the ground is soft sand and Oze. This day the people of the Countrey came aboord of us, seeming very glad of our comming, and brought greene Tabacco, and gave us of it for Knives and Beads. They goe in Deere skins loose, well dressed. They have yellow Copper. They desire Cloathes, and are very civill. They have great store of Maiz or Indian Wheate, whereof they make good Bread. The Countrey is full of great and tall Oakes.

The fifth, in the morning as soone as the day was light, the wind ceased and the Flood came. So we heaved off our ship againe into five fathoms water, and sent our Boate to sound the Bay, and we found that there was three fathoms hard by the Souther shoare. Our men went on Land there, and saw great store of Men, Women and Children, who gave them Tabacco at their comming on Land. So they went up into the Woods, and saw great store of very goodly Oakes, and some Currants. For one of them came aboord and brought some dryed, and gave me some, which were sweet and good. This day many of the people came aboord, some in Mantles of Feathers, and some in Skinnes of divers sorts of good Furres. Some women also came to us with Hempe. They had red Copper Tabacco pipes, and other things of Copper they did weare about their neckes. At night they went on Land againe, so wee rode very quiet, but durst not trust them.

The sixth, in the morning was faire weather, and our Master sent John Colman, with foure other men in our Boate over to the North-side, to sound the other River, being foure leagues from us. They found by the way shoald water two

fathoms; but at the North of the River eighteen, and twentie fathoms, and very good riding for Ships; and a narrow River to the Westward betweene two Ilands. The Lands they told us were as pleasant with Grasse and Flowers, and goodly Trees, as ever they had seene, and very sweet smells came from them. So they went in two leagues and saw an open Sea, and returned; and as they came backe, they were set upon by two Canoes, the one having twelve, the other fourteene men. The night came on, and it began to rayne, so that their Match went out; and they had one man slaine in the fight, which was an English-man, named John Colman, with an Arrow shot into his throat, and two more hurt. It grew so darke that they could not find the ship that night, but labored too and fro on their Oares. They had so great a streame, that their grapnell would not hold them.

The seventh, was faire, and by ten of the clocke they returned aboord the ship, and brought our dead man with them, whom we carryed on Land and buryed, and named the point after his name, Colmans Point. Then we hoysed in our Boate, and raised her side with waste boords for defence of our men. So we rode still all night, having good regard to our Watch.

The eight, was very faire weather, wee rode still very quietly. The people came aboord us, and brought Tabacco and Indian Wheate, to exchange for Knives and Beades, and offered us no violence. So we fitting up our Boate did marke them, to see if they would make any shew of the Death of our man; which they did not.

The ninth, faire weather. In the morning, two great Canoes came aboord full of men; the one with their Bowes and Arrowes, and the other in shew of buying of Knives, to betray us; but we perceived their intent. Wee tooke two of them to have kept them, and put red Coates on them, and would not suffer the other to come neere us. So they went on Land and two other came aboord in a Canoe: we tooke the one and let the other goe; but hee which wee had taken, got up and leapt overboord. Then we weighed and went off into the channell of the River, and Anchored there all night.

The tenth, faire weather, we rode still till twelve of the clocke. Then we weighed and went over, and found it shoald all the middle of the River, for wee could finde but two fathoms and a halfe, and three fathomes for the space of a league; then wee came to three fathomes, and foure fathomes, and so to seven fathomes, and Anchored, and rode all night in soft Ozie ground. The banke is Sand.

The eleventh, was faire and very hot weather. At one of the clocke in the after-noone, wee weighed and went into the River, the wind at South South-west, little winde. Our soundings were seven, sixe, five, sixe, seven, eight, nine, ten, twelve, thirteene, and fourteene fathomes. Then it shoalded againe, and came to five fathomes. Then wee Anchored, and saw that it was a very good Harbour for all windes, and rode all night. The people of the Countrey came aboord of us, making shew of love, and gave us Tabacco and Indian Wheat, and departed for that night; but we durst not trust them.

The twelfth, very faire and hot. In the after-noone at two of the clocke wee weighed, the winde being variable, betweene the North and the North-west. So we turned into the River two leagues and Anchored. This morning at our first rode in the River, there came eight and twentie Canoes full of men, women and children to betray us: but we saw their intent, and suffered none of them to come aboord of us. At twelve of the clocke they departed. They brought with them Oysters and Beanes, whereof wee bought some. They have great Tabacco pipes of yellow Copper, and Pots of Earth to dresse their meate in. It floweth South-east by South within.

The thirteenth, faire weather, the wind Northerly. At seven of the clocke in the morning, as the floud came we weighed, and turned foure miles into the River. The tide being done wee anchored. Then there came foure Canoes aboord: but we suffered none of them to come into our ship. They brought great store of very good Oysters aboord, which we bought for trifles. In the night I set the variation of the Compasse, and found it to be 13. degrees. In the after-noone we weighed, and turned in with the floud, two leagues and a halfe further, and anchored all night, and had five fathoms soft Ozie ground, and had an high point of Land, which shewed out to us, bearing North by East five leagues off us.

The fourteenth, in the morning being very faire weather, the wind South-east, we sayled up the River twelve leagues, and had five fathoms, and five fathoms and a quarter lesse; and came to a Streight betweene two Points, and had eight, nine, and ten fathoms: and it trended North-east by North, one league: and wee had twelve, thirteene and fourteene fathoms. The River is a mile broad: there is very high Land on both sides. Then wee went up North-west, a league and an halfe deepe water. Then North-east by North five miles; then North-west by North two leagues, and anchored. The Land grew very high and Mountainous. The River is full of fish.

The fifteenth, in the morning was misty untill the Sunne arose: then it cleered. So wee weighed with the wind at South, and ran up into the River twentie leagues, passing by high Mountaines. Wee had a very good depth, as sixe, seven, eight, nine, ten, twelve, and thirteene fathoms, and great store of Salmons in the River. This morning our two Savages got out of a Port and swam away. After we were under sayle, they called to us in scorne. At night we came to other Mountaines, which lie from the Rivers side. There wee found very loving people, and very old men: where wee were well used. Our Boat went to fish, and caught great store of very good fish.

The sixteenth, faire and very hot weather. In the morning our Boat went againe to fishing, but could catch but few, by reason their Canoes had beene there all night. This morning the people came aboord, and brought us eares of Indian Corne, and Pompions, and Tabacco: which wee bought for trifles. Wee rode still all day, and filled fresh water; at night wee weighed and went two leagues higher, and had shoald water: so wee anchored till day.

The seventeenth, faire Sun-shining weather, and very hot. In the morning as soone as the Sun was up, we set sayle, and ran up six leagues higher, and found shoalds in the middle of the channell, and small Ilands, but seven fathoms water on both sides. Toward night we borrowed so neere the shoare, that we grounded: so we layed out our small anchor, and heaved off againe. Then we borrowed on the banke in the channell, and came aground againe; while the floud ran we heaved off againe, and anchored all night.

The eighteenth, in the morning was faire weather, and we rode still. In the after-noone our Masters Mate went on land with an old Savage, a Governour of the Countrey; who carried him to his house, and made him good cheere. The nineteenth, was faire and hot weather: at the floud being neere eleven of the clocke, wee weighed, and ran higher up two leagues above the Shoalds, and had no lesse water then five fathoms: wee anchored, and rode in eight fathomes. The people of the Countrie came flocking aboord, and brought us Grapes, and Pompions, which wee bought for trifles. And many brought us Bevers skinnes, and Otters skinnes, which wee bought for Beades, Knives, and Hatchets. So we rode there all night.

The twentieth, in the morning was faire weather. Our Masters Mate with foure men more went up with our Boat to sound the River, and found two leagues above us but two fathomes water, and the channell very narrow; and above that place seven or eight fathomes. Toward night they returned: and we rode still all night. The one and twentieth, was faire weather, and the wind all Southerly: we determined yet once more to goe farther up into the River, to trie what depth and breadth it did beare; but much people resorted aboord, so wee went not this day. Our Carpenter went on land, and made a Fore-yard. And our Master and his Mate determined to trie some of the chiefe men of the Countrey, whether they had any treacherie in them. So they tooke them downe into the Cabbin, and gave them so much Wine and Aqua vitæ, that they were all merrie: and one of them had his wife with him, which sate so modestly, as any of our Countrey women would doe in a strange place. In the end one of them was drunke, which had beene aboord of our ship all the time that we had beene there: and that was strange to them; for they could not tell how to take it. The Canoes and folke went all on shoare: but some of them came againe, and brought stropes of Beades: some had sixe, seven, eight, nine, ten; and gave him. So he slept all night quietly.

The two and twentieth, was faire weather: in the morning our Masters Mate and foure more of the companie went up with our Boat to sound the River higher up. The people of the Countrey came not aboord till noone: but when they came, and saw the Savages well, they were glad. So at three of the clocke in the after-noone they came aboord, and brought Tabacco, and more Beades, and gave them to our Master, and made an Oration, and shewed him all the Countrey round about. Then they sent one of their companie on land, who presently returned, and brought a great Platter full of Venison, dressed by themselves; and they caused him to eate with them: then they made him reverence, and departed all save the old man that lay aboord. This night at ten of the clocke, our Boat returned in a showre of raine from sounding of the River; and found it to bee at an end for shipping to goe in. For they had beene up eight or nine leagues, and found but seven foot water, and unconstant soundings.

The three and twentieth, faire weather. At twelve of the clocke wee weighed, and went downe two leagues to a shoald that had two channels, one on the one side, and another on the other, and had little wind, whereby the tide layed us upon it. So, there wee sate on ground the space of an houre till the floud came. Then we had a little gale of wind at the West. So wee got our ship into deepe water, and rode all night very well.

The foure and twentieth was faire weather: the winde at the North-west, wee weighed, and went downe the River seven or eight leagues; and at halfe ebbe wee came on ground on a banke of Oze in the middle of the River, and sate there till the floud. Then wee went on Land, and gathered good store of Chest-nuts. At ten of the clocke wee came off into deepe water, and anchored.

The five and twentieth was faire weather, and the wind at South a stiffe gale. We rode still, and went on Land to walke on the West side of the River, and found good ground for Corne, and other Garden herbs, with great store of goodly Oakes, and Wal-nut trees, and Chest-nut trees, Ewe trees, and trees of sweet wood in great abundance, and great store of Slate for houses, and other good stones.

The sixe and twentieth was faire weather, and the wind at South a stiffe gale, wee rode still. In the morning our Carpenter went on Land with our Masters Mate, and foure more of our companie to cut wood. This morning, two Canoes came up the River from the place where we first found loving people, and in one of them was the old man that had lyen aboord of us at the other place. He brought another old man with him, which brought more stropes of Beades, and gave them to our Master, and shewed him all the Countrey there about, as though it were at his command. So he made the two old men dine with him, and the old mans wife: for they brought two old women, and two young maidens of the age of sixteene or seventeene yeeres with them, who behaved themselves very modestly. Our Master gave one of the old men a Knife, and they gave him and us Tabacco. And at one of the clocke they departed downe the River, making signes that wee should come downe to them; for wee were within two leagues of the place where they dwelt.

The seven and twentieth, in the morning was faire weather, but much wind at the North, we weighed and set our fore top-sayle, and our ship would not flat, but ran on the Ozie banke at halfe ebbe. Wee layed out anchor to heave her off, but could not. So wee sate from halfe ebbe to halfe floud: then wee set our fore-sayle and mayne top-sayle, and got downe sixe leagues. The old man came aboord, and would have had us anchor, and goe on Land to eate with him: but the wind being faire, we would not yeeld to his request; So hee left us, being very sorrowfull for our departure. At five of the clocke in the after-noone, the wind came to the South South-west. So wee made a boord or two, and anchored in fourteene fathomes water. Then our Boat went on shoare to fish right against the ship. Our Masters Mate and Boat-swaine, and three more of the companie went on land to fish, but could not finde a good place. They tooke foure or five and twentie Mullets, Breames, Bases, and Barbils; and returned in an houre. We rode still all night.

The eight and twentieth, being faire weather, as soone as the day was light, wee weighed at halfe ebbe, and turned downe two leagues belowe water; for, the streame doth runne the last quarter ebbe: then we anchored till high water. At three of the clocke in the after-noone we weighed, and turned downe three leagues, untill it was darke: then wee anchored.

The nine and twentieth was drie close weather: the wind at South, and South and by West, we weighed early in the morning, and turned downe three leagues by a lowe water, and anchored at the lower end of the long Reach; for it is six leagues long. Then there came certaine Indians in a Canoe to us, but would not come aboord. After dinner there came the Canoe with other men, whereof three came aboord us. They brought Indian Wheat, which wee bought for trifles. At three of the clocke in the after-noone wee weighed, as soone as the ebbe came, and turned downe to the edge of the Mountaines, or the Northermost of the Mountaines, and anchored: because the high Land hath many Points, and a narrow channell, and hath many eddie winds. So we rode quietly all night in seven fathoms water.

The thirtieth was faire weather, and the wind at South-east a stiffe gale betweene the Mountaynes. We rode still the after-noone. The people of the Countrey came aboord us, and brought some small skinnes with them, which we bought for Knives and Trifles. This a very pleasant place to build a Towne on. The Road is very neere, and very good for all winds, save an East North-east wind. The Mountaynes looke as if some Metall or Minerall were in them. For the Trees that grow on them were all blasted, and some of them barren with few or no Trees on them. The people brought a stone aboord like to Emery (a stone used by Glasiers to cut Glasse) it would cut Iron or Steele: Yet being bruised small, and water put to it, it made a colour like blacke Lead glistering; It is also good for Painters Colours. At three of the clocke they departed, and we rode still all night.

The first of October, faire weather, the wind variable betweene the West and the North. In the morning we weighed at seven of the clocke with the ebbe, and got downe below the Mountaynes, which was seven leagues. Then it fell calme and the floud was come, and wee anchored at twelve of the clocke. The people of the Mountaynes came aboord us, wondring at our ship and weapons. We bought some small skinnes of them for Trifles. This after-noone, one Canoe kept hanging under our sterne with one man in it, which we could not keepe from thence, who got up by our Rudder to the Cabin window, and stole out my Pillow, and two Shirts, and two Bandeleeres. Our Masters Mate shot at him, and strooke him on the brest, and killed him. Whereupon all the rest fled away, some in their Canoes, and so leapt out of them into the water. We manned our Boat, and got our things againe. Then one of them that swamme got hold of our Boat, thinking to overthrow it. But our Cooke tooke a Sword, and cut off one of his hands, and he was drowned. By this time the ebbe was come, and we weighed and got downe two leagues, by that time it was darke. So we anchored in foure fathomes water, and rode well.

The second, faire weather. At breake of day wee weighed, the wind being at North-west, and got downe seven leagues; then the floud was come strong, so we anchored. Then came one of the Savages that swamme away from us at our going up the River with many other, thinking to betray us. But wee perceived their intent, and suffered none of them to enter our ship. Whereupon two Canoes full of men, with their Bowes and Arrowes shot at us after our sterne: in recompence whereof we discharged six Muskets, and killed two or three of them. Then above an hundred of them came to a point of Land to shoot at us. There I shot a Falcon at them, and killed two of them: whereupon the rest fled into the Woods. Yet they manned off another Canoe with nine or ten men, which came to meet us. So I shot at it also a Falcon, and shot it through, and killed one of them. Then our men with their Muskets, killed three or foure more of them. So they went their way, within a while after, wee got downe two leagues beyond that place, and anchored in a Bay, cleere from all danger of them on the other side of the River, where we saw a very good piece of ground: and hard by it there was a Cliffe, that looked of the colour of a white greene, as though it were either Copper, or Silver Myne: and I thinke it to be one of them, by the Trees that grow upon it. For they be all burned, and the other places are greene as grasse, it is on that side of the River that is called Manna-hata. There we saw no people to trouble us: and rode quietly all night, but had much wind and raine.

The third, was very stormie; the wind at East North-east. In the morning, in a gust of wind and raine our Anchor came home, and we drove on ground, but it was Ozie. Then as we were about to have out an Anchor, the wind came to the North North-west, and drove us off againe. Then we shot an Anchor, and let it fall in foure fathomes water, and weighed the other. Wee had much wind and raine, with thicke weather: so we roade still all night.

The fourth, was faire weather, and the wind at North North-west, wee weighed and came out of the River, into which we had runne so farre. Within a while after, wee came out also of The great mouth of the great River, that runneth up to the North-west, borrowing upon the Norther side of the same, thinking to have deepe water: for wee had sounded a great way with our Boat at our first going in, and found seven, six, and five fathomes. So we came out that way, but we were deceived, for we had but eight foot & an halfe water: and so to three, five, three, and two fathomes and an halfe. And then three, foure,

five, sixe, seven, eight, nine and ten fathomes. And by twelve of the clocke we were cleere of all the Inlet. Then we tooke in our Boat, and set our mayne-sayle and sprit-sayle, and our top-sayles, and steered away East South-east, and South-east by East off into the mayne sea: and the Land on the Souther-side of the Bay or Inlet, did beare at noone West and by South foure leagues from us.

The fift, was faire weather, and the wind variable betweene the North and the East. Wee held on our course South-east by East. At noone I observed and found our height to bee 39. degrees 30. minutes. Our Compasse varied sixe degrees to the West.

We continued our course toward England, without seeing any Land by the way, all the rest of this moneth of October: and on the seventh day of November, stilo novo, being Saturday: by the Grace of God we safely arrived in the Range of Dartmouth in Devonshire, in the yeare 1609.

523. 1609. Emanuel Van Meteren's description of Hudson's 1609 voyage.

E. Van Meteren, Commentarien (Amsterdam, 1611), fol. 327: a translation by Henry Murphy in 1859 was reprinted in Henry Murphy, Henry Hudson in Holland (The Hague, 1909) pp. 64–68, and followed here.

We have said in the preceding book that the Directors of the East India Company in Holland had sent, in the month of March last past, in order to seek a passage to China by the North-West or North-East, a brave English pilot named Henry Hudson, with a Vlie-boat, and about eighteen or twenty men, part English and part Dutch, well provided. This Henry Hudson sailed from Texel on the 6th of April 1609, and doubled the Cape of Norway on the 5th of May: he laid his course towards Nova Zembla, along the Northern coast, but found the sea as full of ice there, as he had found it the preceding year, so that he was compelled to abandon all hope for that year; whereupon, owing to the cold which some who had been in the East Indies could not support, the English and Dutch fell into disputes among themselves.

Whereupon the Master, Hudson, gave them their choice between two things, the first was, to go to the coast of America in the fortieth degree of latitude, mostly incited to this by letters and maps wich a certain Captain Smith had sent him from Virginia and on which he showed him a sea wherein he might circumnavigate their Southern Colony from the North, and from thence pass into a Western sea. If this had been true, (which experience up to the present time has shown to the contrary), it would have been very advantageous and a short route to sail to the Indies. The other proposition was, to search for the passage by Davis' Straits, to which at last they generally agreed; and on the fourteenth they set sail and, with favorable winds, arrived the last of May at the isle of Faro, where they stopped only twenty-four hours to take in fresh water. Leaving there they reached, on the eighteenth of July, the coast of new France in latitude forty-four, where they were obliged to make a stay to replace their *fore-mast* which they had lost, and where they obtained and rigged one. They found this a good place for catching codfish, and also for carrying on a traffic for good skins and furs which they could obtain for mere trifles; but the sailors behaved very badly towards the people of the country, taking things by force, which was the cause of a strife between them. *The English*, thinking they would be overpowered and worsted, were afraid to enter further into the country; so they sailed from there on the twenty-sixth of July and continued at sea until the third of August, when they approached the land in latitude forty-two. From thence they sailed again until the twelfth of August, when they again approached the land at latitude thirty-seven and three quarters, and kept their course thence along it until they reached the latitude of forty degrees and three quarters, where they found a good entrance between two headlands. Here they entered on the twelfth of September and discovered as beautiful a river as could be found, very large and deep, with good anchorage on both shores. They ascended it with their large vessel as high as latitude forty-two degrees and forty minutes, and went still higher on with the ship's boat. At the entrance of the river they had found the natives brave and warlike; but inside, and up to the highest point of the river, they found them friendly and civil, having an abundance of skins

and furs, such as marters and foxes, and many other commodities, birds, fruits and even white and blue grapes. They treated these people very civilly and brought away a little of what ever they found among them. After they had gone about fifty leagues up the river they returned on the fourth of October and again put to sea. More could have been accomplished there if there had been a good feeling among the sailors and had not the want of provisions prevented them.

At sea there was a consultation held at which there was a diversity of opinion. The mate, who was a Dutchman, thought that they ought to go and winter in Newfoundland, and seek for the Northwest passage through Davis' Straits. The master, Hudson, was opposed to this; he feared his crew would mutiny, because at times they had boldly menaced him, and also because they would be entirely evercome by the cold of winter and be, after all, obliged to return with many of the crew weak and sickly. No one, however spoke of returning home to Holland, which gave cause of further suspicion to the master. Consequently he proposed that they should go and winter in Ireland, to which they all agreed, and at length arrived, November 7th., at Dartmouth in England. From this place they sent an account of their voyage to their masters in Holland, proposing to go in search of a passage to the North West if they were furnished with fifteen hundred guilders in money to buy provisions, in addition to their wages and what they had in the ship. He wished to have some six or seven of his crew changed, making the number up to twenty men etc., and to sail from Dartmouth about the first of March in order to be at the North West by the end of that month and there pass the month of April and half of May in killing whales and other animals in the neighborhood of the isle of Panar; from there to go towards the North West and remain there till the middle of September, and afterwards to return, by the North East of Scotland, again to Holland. Thus was the voyage finished; but before the Directors could be informed of their arrival in England a long time elapsed by reason of contrary winds, when at last they sent orders for the ship and crew to return at once to Holland. And when this was about to be done, the Master, Henry Hudson, was ordered by the authorities there not to depart, but remain and do service for his own country, which was also required of the other Englishmen in the ship. Many however, thought it very strange that *the Masters*, who had been sent out for the common benefit of all kinds of navigation, should not be permitted to return in order to render an account and make a report of their doings and affairs to their employers. This took place in January 1610. It was supposed that the English wished to send the same persons with some vessels to Virginia to explore further the before mentioned river.

524. 1609. Johan de Laet on Hudson's voyage and the beginnings of Dutch interest in North America.

These extracts are from Johan [Jan] de Laet, Nieuwe Wereldt (Leyden, 1625), pp. 83–84, 88–89. The translation in Henry Murphy, Hudson in Holland (1909), pp. 146–150, is given here, having the Dutch miles converted into English miles.

As to the first discovery, the Directors of the authorized East India Company, in the year 1609, dispatched the yacht, Half-Moon, under the command of Henry Hudson, captain and supercargo, to seek a passage to China by the northeast. But he changed his course and stood over towards New France, and having passed the banks of New Foundland in latitude 43° 23', he made the land in latitude 44° 15', with a west-north-west and north-west course, and went on shore at a place where there were many of the natives with whom, as he understood, the French came every year to trade. Sailing hence, he bent his course to the south, until running south-south-west and south-west by south, he again made land in latitude 41° 43', which he supposed to be an island, and gave it the name of New Holland, but afterwards discovered that it was Cape Cod, and that according to his observation, it lay two hundred and twenty-five miles to the west of its place on all the charts. Pursuing his course to the south, he again saw land in latitude 37° 15'; the coast was low, running north and south, and opposite to it lay a bank or shoal, within which there was a depth of eight, nine, ten,

eleven, seven, and six and a half fathoms, with a sandy bottom. Hudson called this place Dry Cape.

Changing his course to the northward, he again discovered land in lat. 38° 9', where there was a white sandy shore, and within appeared a thick grove of trees full of green foliage. The direction of the coast was north-north-east and south-south-west for about twenty-four miles; then north and south for twenty-one miles, and afterwards south-east and north-west for fifteen miles. They continued to run along the coast to the north, until they reached a point from which the land stretches to the west and north-west, where several rivers discharge into an open bay. Land was seen to the east-north-east, which Hudson at first took to be an island, but it proved to be the main land, and the second point of the bay, in latitude 38° 54'. Standing in upon a course north-west by east, they soon found themselves embayed, and encountering many breakers, stood out again to the south-south-east. Hudson suspected that a large river discharged into the bay, from the strength of the current that set out and caused the accumulation of sands and shoals.

Continuing their course along the shore to the north, they observed a white sandy beach and drowned land within, beyond which there appeared a grove of wood; the coast running north-east by east and south-west by south. Afterwards the direction of the coast changed to north by east, and was higher land than they had yet seen. They at length reached a lofty promontory or head-land, behind which was situated a bay, which they entered and run up into a road-stead near a low sandy point, in lat. 40° 18'. There they were visited by two savages clothed in elk-skins, who showed them every sign of friendship. On the land they found an abundance of blue plums and magnificent oaks, of a height and thickness that one seldom beholds; together with poplars, linden trees, and various other kinds of wood useful in ship-building. Sailing hence in a northeasterly direction, they ascended a river to nearly 43° north latitude, where it became so narrow and of so little depth, that they found it necessary to return.

From all that they could learn, there had never been any ship or Christians in that quarter before, and they were the first to discover the river and ascend it so far. Henry Hudson returned to Amsterdam with this report; and in the following year, 1610, some merchants again sent a ship thither, that is to say, to the second river discovered, which was called Manhattes, from the savage nation that dwelt at its mouth. And subsequently their High Mightinesses the States General granted to these merchants the exclusive privilege of navigating this river and trading there; whereupon, in the year 1615, a redoubt or fort was erected on the river, and occupied by a small garrison, of wich we shall hereafter speak. Our countrymen have continued to make voyages thither from year to year for the purpose of trafficking with the natives, and on this account the country has very justly received the name of New-Netherlands. . . .

Henry Hudson, who first discovered this river, and all that have since visited it, express their admiration of the noble trees growing upon its banks; and Hudson has himself described the manners and appearance of the people that he found dwelling within the bay, in the following terms: —

"When I came on shore, the swarthy natives all stood around, and sung in their fashion; their clothing consisted of the skins of foxes and other animals, wich they dress and make the skins into garments of various sorts. Their food is Turkish wheat, (maize or Indian corn), which they cook by baking, and it is excellent eating. They all came on board one after another in their canoes, which are made of a single hollowed tree; their weapons are bows and arrows, pointed with sharp stones, which they fasten with hard resin. They had no houses, but slept under the blue heavens, sometimes on mats of bulrushes interwoven, and sometimes on the leaves of trees. They always carry with them all their goods, such as their food and green tobacco, which is strong and good for use. They appear to be a friendly people, but have a great propensity to steal, and are exceedingly adroit in carrying away whatever they take a fancy to."

In latitude 40° 48', where the savages brought very fine oysters to the ship, Hudson describes the country in the following manner:—"It is as pleasant a land as one need tread upon; very abundant in all kinds of timber suitable for ship-building, and for making large casks or vats. The people had copper tobacco pipes, from which I inferred that copper might naturally exist there; and iron likewise according to the testimony of the natives, who, however, do not understand preparing it for use.

Hudson also states that they caught in the river all kinds of fresh-water fish with seines, and young salmon and sturgeon. In latitude 42° 18' he landed:—"I sailed to the shore," he says, "in one of their canoes, with an old man, who was the chief of a tribe, consisting of forty men and seventeen women; these I saw there in a house well constructed of oak-bark, and circular in shape, so that it had the appearance of being well built, with an arched roof. It contained a great quantity of maize or Indian corn, and beans of the last year's growth, and there lay near the house for the purpose of drying, enough to load three ships, besides what was growing in the fields. On our coming into the house, two mats were spread out to sit upon, and immediately some food was served in well made red wooden bowls; two men were also despatched at once with bows and arrows in quest of game, who soon after brought in a pair of pigeons which they had shot. They likewise killed a fat dog, and skinned it in great haste with shells which they had got out of the water. They supposed that I would remain with them for the night, but I returned after a short time on board the ship. The land is the finest for cultivation that I ever in my life set foot upon, and it also abounds in trees of every description. The natives are a very good people, for when they saw that I would not remain, they supposed that I was afraid of their bows, and taking the arrows, they broke them in pieces, and threw them into the fire, etc."

He found there also vines and grapes, pumpkins, and other fruits; from all of which there is sufficient reason to conclude that it is a pleasant and fruitful country and that the natives are well disposed, if they are only well treated; although they are very changeable, and of the same general character as all the savages in the north.

NOTES ON THE MAPS

88. 1581. André Thevet's Printed Map of the Americas.
Library of Congress, Division of Geography and Maps, Lessing Rosenwald Collection.
This unique copy of the map printed in Paris in 1581 gives a very full picture of North America. It is most significant for its information on the Northeast, where it adds a little to earlier maps on the Cartier explorations. It is skeptical of the existence of a Northwest Passage. Although it shows the Strait of Anian and is well informed on the California Peninsula, it is surprisingly poor on Florida. Its systematic coverage of the interior is somewhat misleading, since many of the names appear to have been invented. The placing of "Terre Neufue" well to the north of New France is puzzling, while the Iberian name of "Bacalaos" is retained for Newfoundland.

89. 1580. An Earlier Spanish Map Copied by Simão Fernandes for Dr. John Dee.
London, British Library, Division of Manuscripts, Cotton Roll XIII, 48.
This probably derived from a Spanish map of the 1560s. It makes Cape Cod (or, rather, Monomoy Point), discovered by Estevão Gomes in 1525 into Cabo de las Arenas but does not carry it as far south as some Spanish cartographers. It influenced Dee in compiling his great map for Queen Elizabeth in 1580.

90. 1582. Map of America, Based on the Arctic; Made by John Dee for Sir Humphrey Gilbert.
The Free Library of Philadelphia, William M. Elkins Collection, no. 42. "Sir Humfrey Gylbert Knight his charte."
This map was part of the propaganda Sir Humphrey Gilbert used to persuade subscribers to his ventures that besides free land, there were numerous passages through and around North America which would be to their advantage as colonists. See Quinn, *Gilbert* (1940), I, 67–71, II, 347.

91. 1591. Map of Eastern North America, based on Earlier Spanish Maps, by Thomas Hood.
F. Kunstmann, *Atlas zur Entdeckungsgeschichte Amerikas* (Berlin, 1859), Plate XIII. Its present location is unknown. Courtesy of Division of Geography and Maps, Library of Congress.
This map carries an inscription: "Thomas Hood made this platt 1591." It is clearly derived from Spanish sources and shows no evidence of the influence of the Roanoke Voyages of 1584–1590. It has interesting materials on the offshore islands on the Florida-Georgia coast but, like the Le Moyne Map of the same year, shows the St. Johns River flowing from N.W. to S.E. The details of the Spanish profile clearly distinguish the Bahía de Santa Maria (Chesapeake Bay) from the New England discoveries of Estevão Gomes, Monomoy Point being indicated as Cabo do las Arenas, though Cape Cod appears (somewhat confusingly) as C. de Pero (Arenas)." We know that the Roanoke colonists in 1585 had a Spanish map with them and it could well have been of this type, which shows some significant differences from the Spanish map copied by Simão Fernandes in 1580 for John Dee (Plate 89).

92. 1584. Engraving of John White's Sketch of the Arrival of the English at Roanoke Island.
Engraved in Theodor de Bry, *America*, part i (Frankfurt-am-Main 1590), plate 2.

93. 1585. A Sketch made in September, Showing English Knowledge of the Roanoke Island Region.
London, Public Record Office, Maps, MPF 584.
Sent to England in 1585, the sketch represents a version of the earliest activities of John White and Thomas Harriot in surveying the coast and surroundings of Roanoke Island where the fort and settlement were being built. It was crudely copied, possibly by or for Ralph Lane, the governor. It is the earliest, surviving direct sketch of the North American coast by an English observer. See Quinn, *Roanoke Voyages*, I (1955), 215–217.

94. 1586. John White's Detailed Map of Ralegh's Virginia, 1584–1586.
London, British Museum, Department of Prints and Drawings 1906-5-9-1(3).
This map represents the work of John White the artist and Thomas Harriot the scientific observer in the region surrounding Roanoke Island during the period between July, 1585 and June, 1586. It is the first regional map of any part of North America to be based on an actual survey of the ground. Although White drew the map as we have it, it is thought that Thomas Harriot was largely responsible for its planning and construction. It remained the basis of European knowledge for much of this area into the middle of the seventeenth century. See P. Hulton and D. B. Quinn, *The American Drawings of John White*, 2 vols. (London and Chapel Hill, 1964), I, 136–137, and Plate 59.

95. 1590. Ralegh's Virginia, Engraved after John White.
    Engraved in Theodor de Bry, *America*, part i (Frankfurt-am-Main, 1590).
96. 1587. John White's General Map of Eastern North America.
    London, British Museum, Department of Prints and Drawings, 1906-5-9-1(2).
    The northern part of this map shows the area surveyed in 1585–1586; the southern part shows a copy of a French map of the 1562–1565 Florida enterprises. The attempt to link the two was notably unsuccessful. See Hulton and Quinn, *The American Drawings of John White*, I, 135–136, and Plate 58.
97. 1589. Baptista Boazio's Map of Sir Francis Drake's West Indian Voyage, 1585–1586.
    From the Collection of Mr. and Mrs. Paul Mellon, Upperville, Virginia.
    This map displayed in color the expedition by Sir Francis Drake, begun in September, 1585 and followed through by attacks on Vigo, Santiago, Santo Domingo, Cartagena, and San Agustín and a visit to the new English colony of Virginia, which led to Drake's removal of the first colonists there under Ralph Lane, the fleet arriving home in July, 1586. Boazio accompanied the expedition as its cartographer, and copperplate engravings after his drawings of Santo Domingo and Cartagena and San Agustín (with Latin inscriptions) were included in *Expeditio Francisci Draki equitis Angli in Indias occidentales A. M. D. LXXXV* (Leiden, 1588). The same plates were used, with the addition of this map with its captions in English, in Walter Bigges (and others), *A summarie and true discourse of Sir Frances Drakes West Indian voyage ... With geographical mappes* (London, 1589). The map was also issued, carefully colored, separately, both with and without a brief text relating to the voyage pasted below. A good example of the former type is in the John Carter Brown Library and a comparable one of the latter from the Mellon Collection is here reproduced.
98. 1593. Map of Eastern North America by Cornelis de Jode.
    Cornelis de Jode, *Speculum orbis terrae* (Antwerp, 1593).
    Along with his general map of North America from an Arctic angle, this map assimilates the new regional maps of Ralegh's Virginia and of French Florida from Theodor de Bry's *America*, parts i and ii (Frankfurt-am-Main, 1590–1591), and thus substantially modified earlier Spanish and French perspectives.
99. 1599. Edward Wright's Map of the Americas. State 1.
    This world map—"A true hydrographical description"—was added to the second volume of Richard Hakluyt's *Principal navigations*, 2nd issue, 3 vols. in 2 (London, 1599–1600). It owed much to material collected by Richard Hakluyt during his residence in France from 1583 to 1588. Some of this had already been incorporated in the first English globe produced by Emery Molyneux and others in 1592 (reissued with revisions in 1603). But Wright must have worked closely with Hakluyt in its compilation. It was one of the finest world maps of its time in its incorporation of detail of voyages made by English, Iberian, and French explorers, and it is of special interest for North America for its depiction of the Maritimes and of the Great Lakes (or at least one of them). There was evidence that the map was in demand in a separate version as well as a book illustration. A second issue contained an additional cartouche, dealing with the exploits of Sir Francis Drake, and this is represented in the reproduction in plate 100. See D. B. Quinn (ed.), *The Hakluyt Handbook*, 2 vols. (Cambridge, Eng., Hakluyt Society, 1974), I, 69–73, and Plates 5 (State 1) and 6 (State 2).
100. 1599. Edward Wright's Map of the Americas. State 2.
101. 1604. Samuel de Champlain's engraved Sketch of Port Mouton, Nova Scotia, May, 1604.
    Port Mouton, Nova Scotia, reached on May 8, 1604. This and the following sketches (101–105) in Champlain's *Les voyages* (1613), enabled his New England-Acadian voyages to be followed in detail.
102. 1604–1605. Samuel de Champlain's Engraved Sketch of the Settlement, 1604–1605, on Saint Croix Island.
    The settlement planned and built on Île Sainte-Croix on the St. Croix River in 1604 was the first mainland post occupied by the French during winter, since their abortive attempt to settle Tadoussac in 1600–1601.
103. 1605. Samuel de Champlain's Engraved Sketch of Mallebarre (Nauset Harbor), Visited in 1605.
    Mallebarre (Nauset Harbor) was visited in the summer of 1605. A poor impression of it was gained, as can be gathered from the sketch.
104. 1605. Samuel de Champlain's Engraved Sketch of St Louis (Plymouth Harbor), Visited July 18, 1605.
    Here the harbor entrance was shown to be a good one.
105. 1605–1607. Samuel de Champlain's Engraved Sketch of Port Royal (on Annapolis Basin, Nova Scotia), the *Habitacion* occupied 1605–1607.

Port Royal (on Annapolis Basin, Nova Scotia) proved, from 1605 onward, a much better location for their more modest *habitacion* than that which they had attempted to establish on Île Sainte-Croix in 1604.

106. 1607. Samuel de Champlain's Manuscript Map of His New England and Acadian Discoveries, 1604–1607.
Library of Congress, Division of Manuscripts; manuscript map "Description des costs... de la nouvelle france."
This is the earliest and only manuscript map of Champlain's to survive. He incorporated much of its material into his general maps of New France in 1612 and 1632. It represents a great addition to knowledge of the coasts from the head of the Bay of Fundy to the south of Cape Cod. His information on the Kennebec and Penobscot basins and on the Bay of Fundy was especially important. Some of his materials were, by some means, incorporated in the so-called Velasco map of 1610. It appears in Samuel de Champlain, *Works*, ed., H. P. Bigger, 6 vols. plus portfolio (Toronto: Champlain Society, 1922–1937), portfolio; reprinted, 7 vols. (Toronto, 1971), Vol VII.

107. 1607–1608. Plan of the English Fort St. George on the Kennebec (Sagadahoc) River.
Archivo General de Simancas.

108. 1610 or 1611. Part of the Velasco Map, Enlarged to Show the English and French Discoveries in New England, 1602–1607.
Archivo General de Simancas, M.P.y.D.I-1, Estado 2588-25. (See Vol. V, Plate 140.)
This map represents a valuable conflation of the materials obtained by English expeditions of the 1602–08 period with those of Champlain between 1604 and 1607, obtained by what means we do not know. Its interpretation is difficult, since it is now impossible to attribute precise discoveries to particular expeditions. For the English expeditions, it is the most comprehensive (indeed the only) valuable record. For the Champlain expeditions, it requires close comparison with the Library of Congress manuscript map of the Champlain expeditions, 1604–1607. Its view of Champlain's discovery of Lake Champlain in 1609 is also of considerable interest.

109. 1616. John Smith's Map of New England.
John Smith, *A description of New England* (London, 1616).
Although compiled as a result of Smith's 1614 exploration of the New England coasts and containing the nomenclature devised by Smith and by the young Prince Charles, this map throws light on the earlier English discoveries, which are virtually unrepresented on surviving English maps apart from the Velasco Map (Vol. V, Plate 140 with 108, 111). It also provided the area with a name for the old Norumbega, or the newer North Virginia, namely New England.

110. 1616. Map by Cornelis Hendrik, Showing the Delaware and Hudson River Valleys.
Gravenhage, Algemeen Rijksarchief; map by Cornelis Hendrick, no. 51g.
This map shows in great detail both the Delaware and Hudson Rivers as far as they had been explored by the Dutch. The upper bay is the entrance of what was to be the future New Amsterdam, and Manhattan Island may be seen at the mouth of the Hudson River.

111. 1610. Portion of the Velasco Map, Enlarged to Show the Hudson River and the Coastline Between Southern Maine and Cape Fear.
See Plate 108 and Vol. V, Plate 140.
Virginia, as shown, represents substantially the work done on this area by John Smith from 1607 to 1609, though still unpublished. It is also the earliest cartographic record of the Hudson River, discovered in 1609. The Hudson is shown linking up with a Great Lake (Ontario?). The Virginia material is of great value for comparison with the printed John Smith Map of 1612 (Vol. V, Plate 141).

111a. *Circa* 1582-1583. An early set of map symbols (with 401).

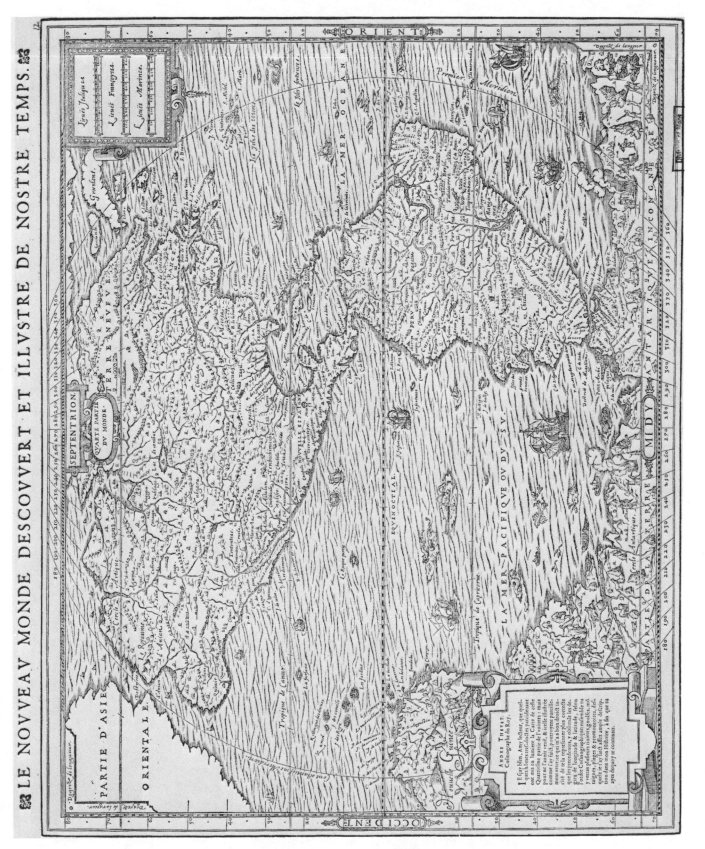

88. 1581. André Thevet's Printed Map of the Americas.

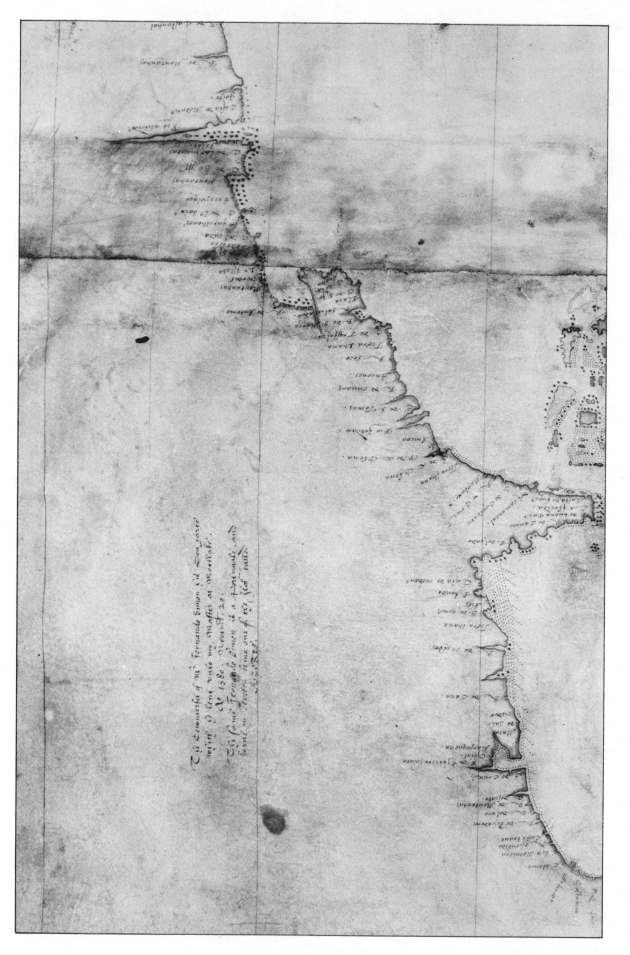

89. 1580. An Earlier Spanish Map Copied by Simão Fernandes for Dr. John Dee.

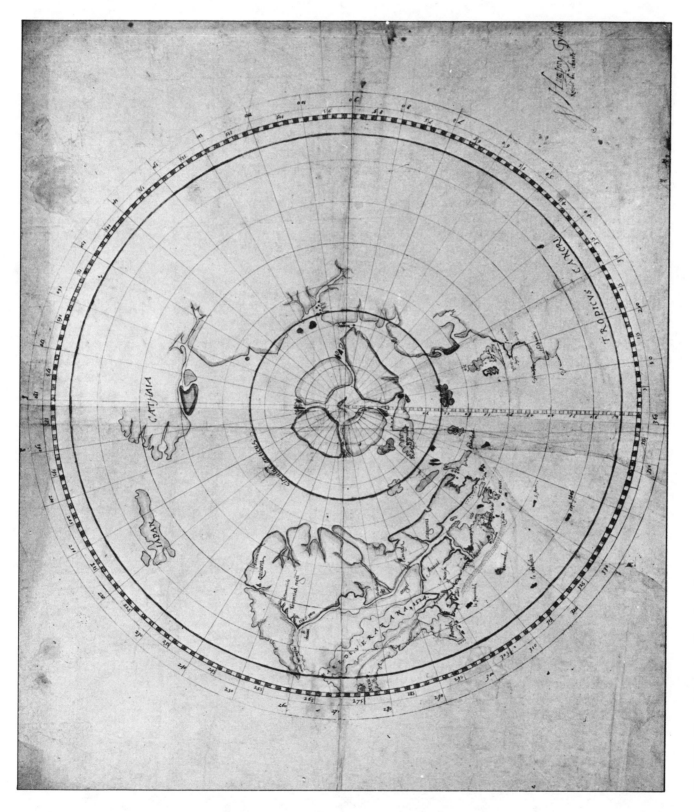

90. 1582. Map of America, Based on the Arctic; Made by John Dee for Sir Humphrey Gilbert.

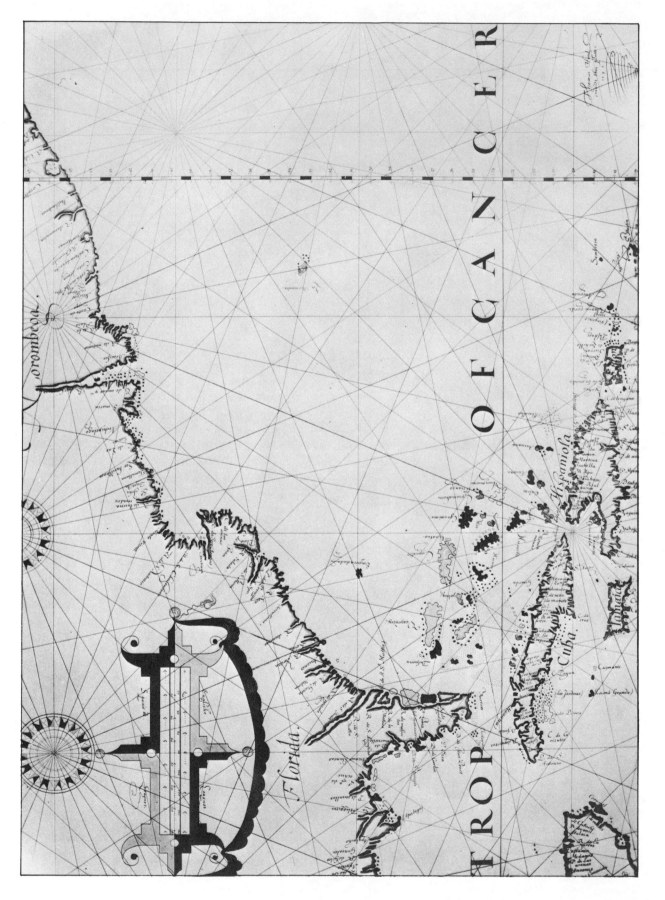

91. 1591. Map of Eastern North America, Based on Earlier Spanish Maps, by Thomas Hood.

92. 1584. Engraving of John White's Sketch of the Arrival of the English at Roanoke Island.

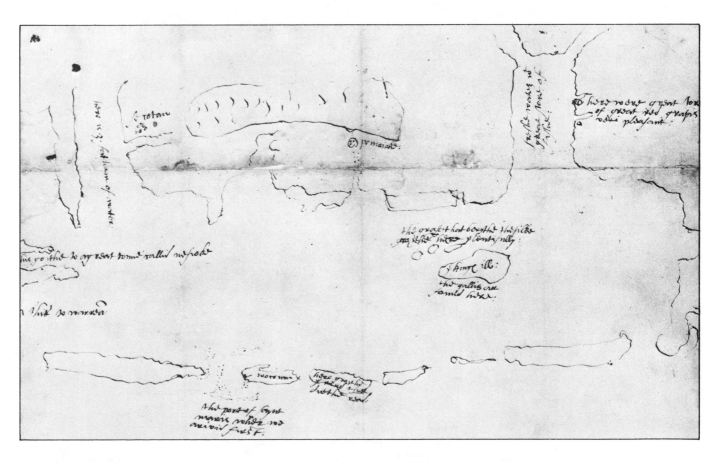

93. 1585. A Sketch Made in September, Showing English Knowledge of the Roanoke Island Region.

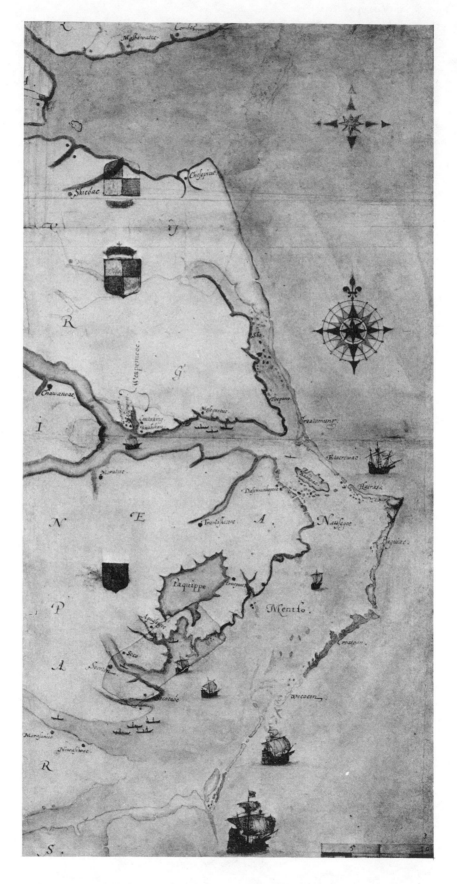

94. 1586. John White's Detailed Map of Ralegh's Virginia, 1584–1586.

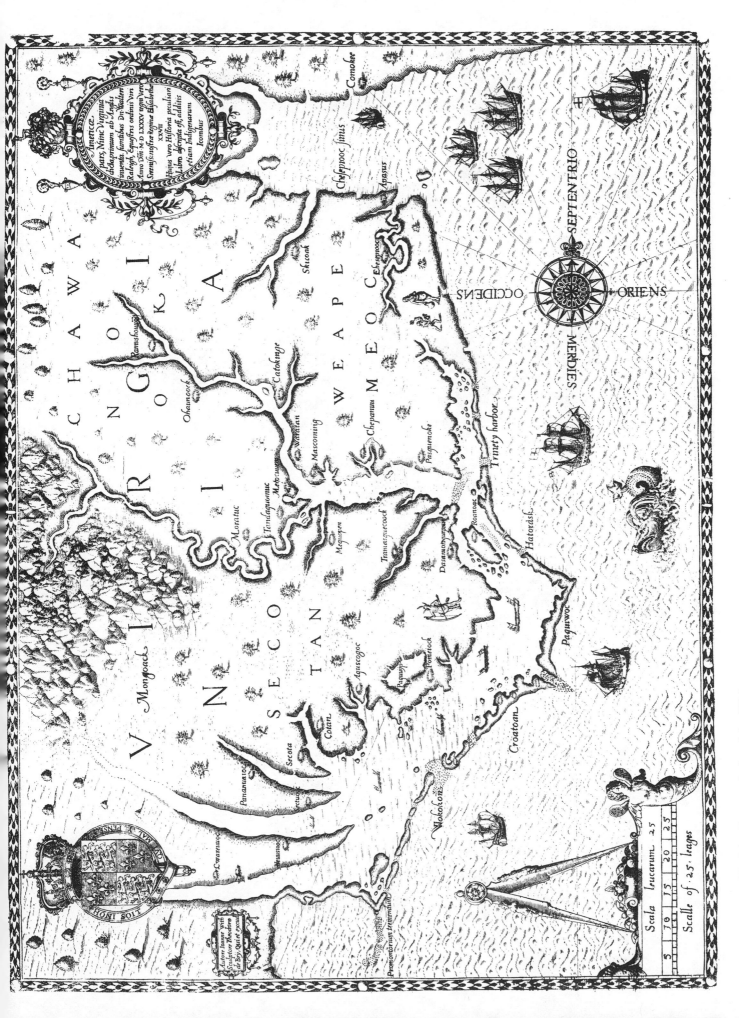

95. 1590. Ralegh's Virginia, Engraved after John White.

96. 1587. John White's General Map of Eastern North America.

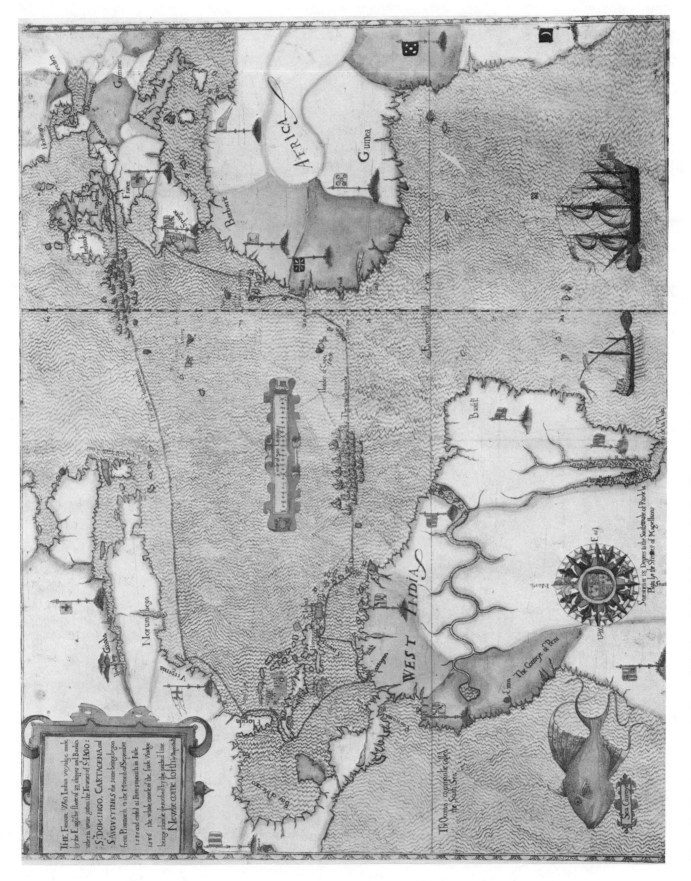

97. 1589. Baptista Boazio's Map of Sir Francis Drake's West Indian Voyage, 1585–1586.

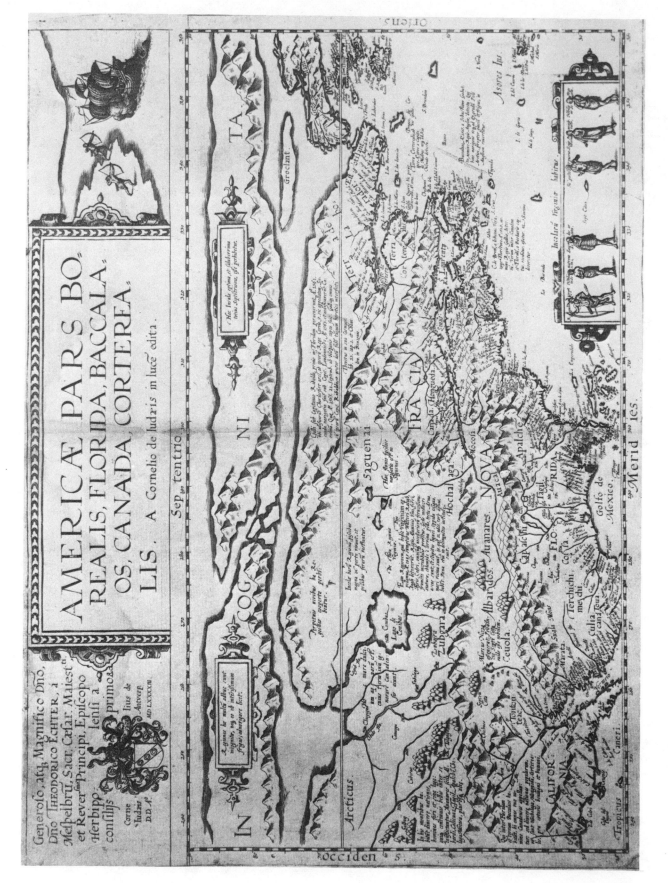

98. 1593. Map of Eastern North America by Cornelis de Jode.

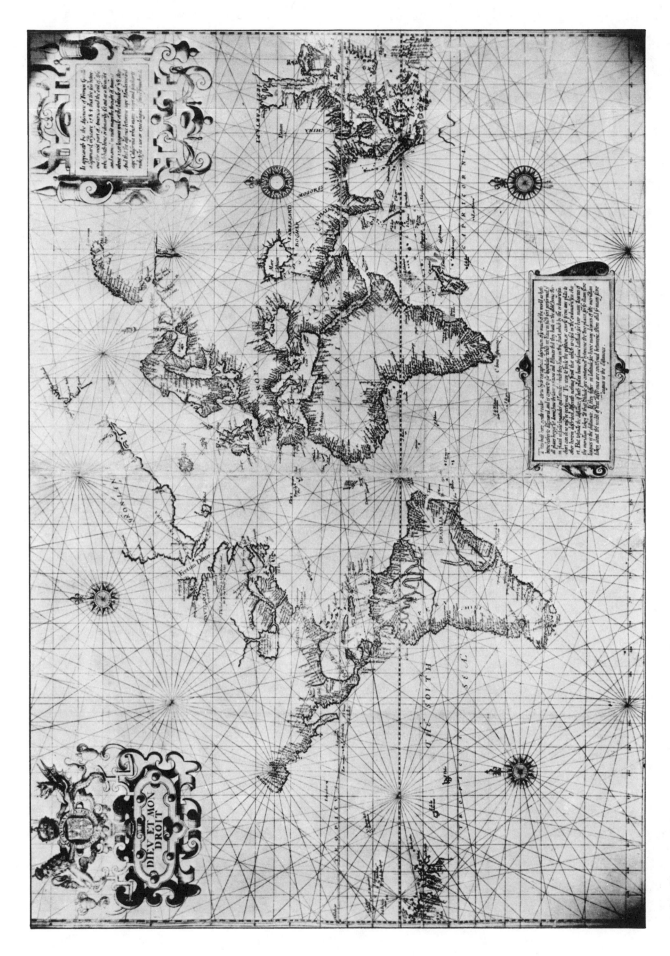

99. 1599. Edward Wright's Map of the Americas. State 1.

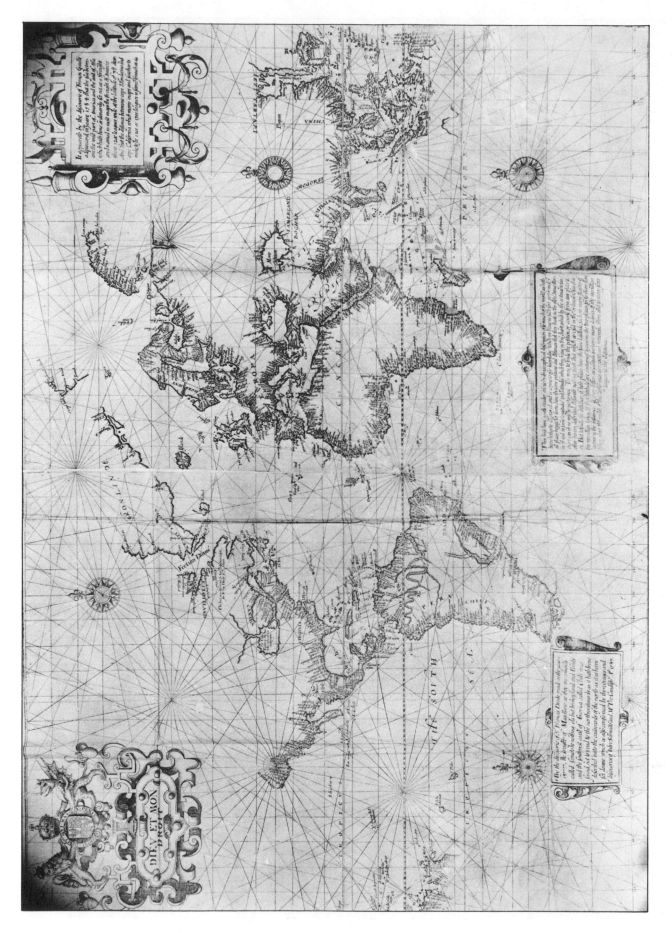

100. 1599. Edward Wright's Map of the Americas. State 2.

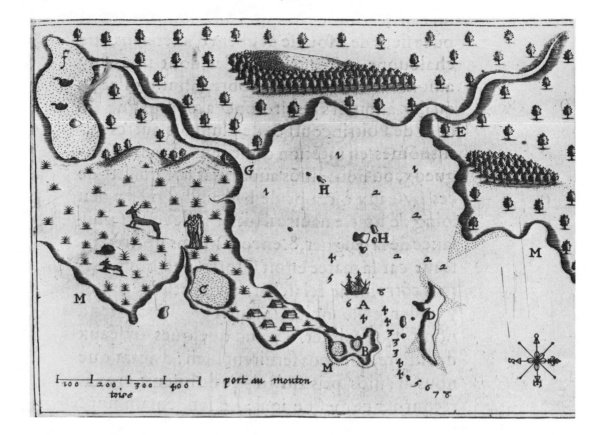

101. 1604. Samuel de Champlain's Engraved Sketch of Port Mouton, Nova Scotia, May, 1604.

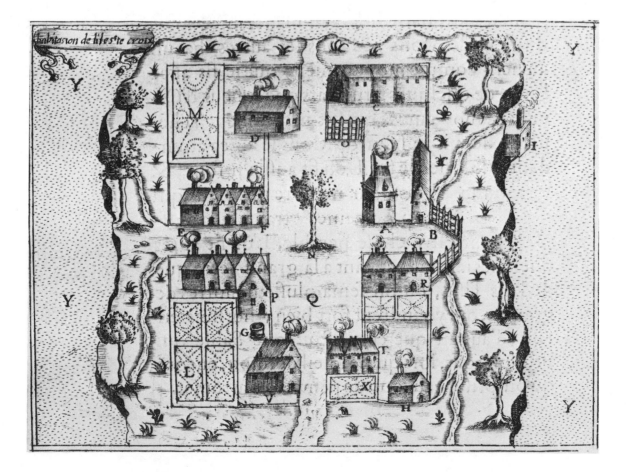

102. 1604-1605. Samuel de Champlain's Engraved Sketch of the Settlement, 1604-1605, on Saint Croix Island.

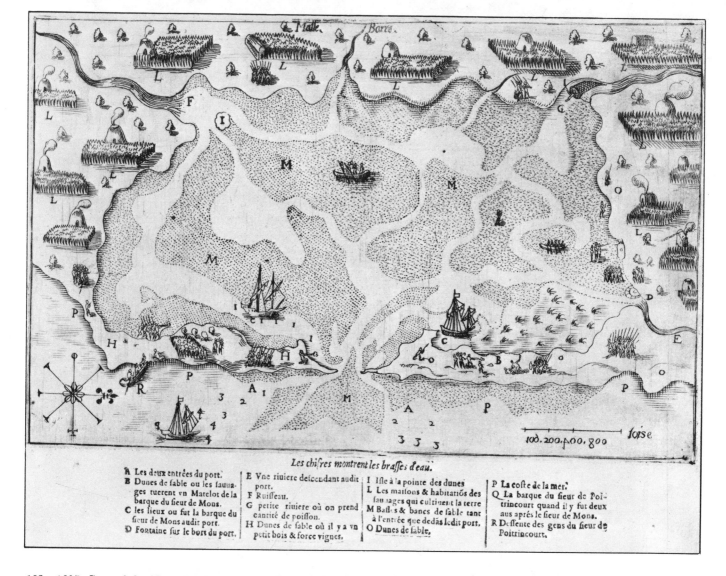

Les chifres montrent les brasses d'eau.

A Les deux entrées du port.
B Dunes de sable ou les sauvages tuerent vn Matelot de la barque du sieur de Mons.
C les lieux ou fut la barque du sieur de Mons audit port.
D Fontaine sur le bort du port.

E Vne riuiere descendant audit port.
F Ruisseau.
G petite riuiere où on prend cantité de poisson.
H Dunes de sable où il y a vn petit bois & force vignes.

I Isle à la pointe des dunes
L Les maisons & habitatiõs des sauuages qui cultiuent la terre
M Basses & bancs de sable tant à l'entrée que dedãs ledit port.
O Dunes de sable.

P La coste de la mer.
Q La barque du sieur de Poitrincourt quand il y fut deux aus après le sieur de Mons.
R Descente des gens du sieur de Poitrincourt.

103. 1605. Samuel de Champlain's Engraved Sketch of Mallebarre (Nauset Harbor), Visited in 1605.

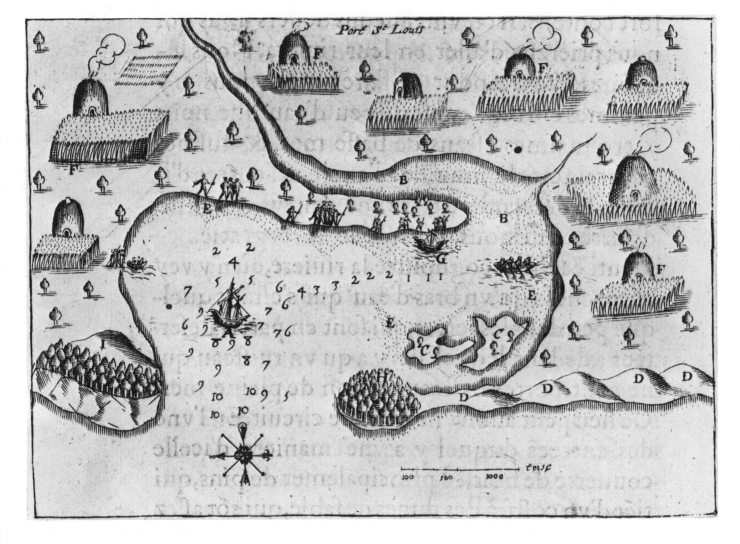

104. 1605. Samuel de Champlain's Engraved Sketch of St Louis (Plymouth Harbor), Visited July 18, 1605.

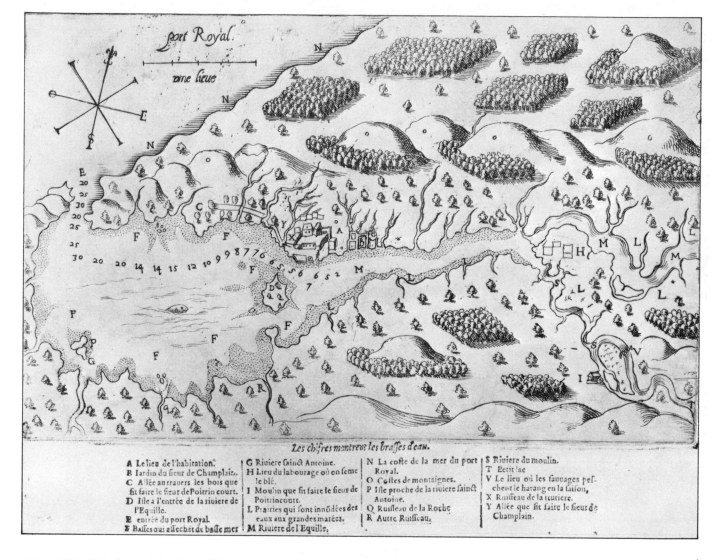

105. 1605–1607. Samuel de Champlain's Engraved Sketch of Port Royal (on Annapolis Basin, Nova Scotia), the *Habitacion* occupied 1605–1607.

106. 1607. Samuel de Champlain's Manuscript Map of His New England and Acadian Discoveries, 1604–1607.

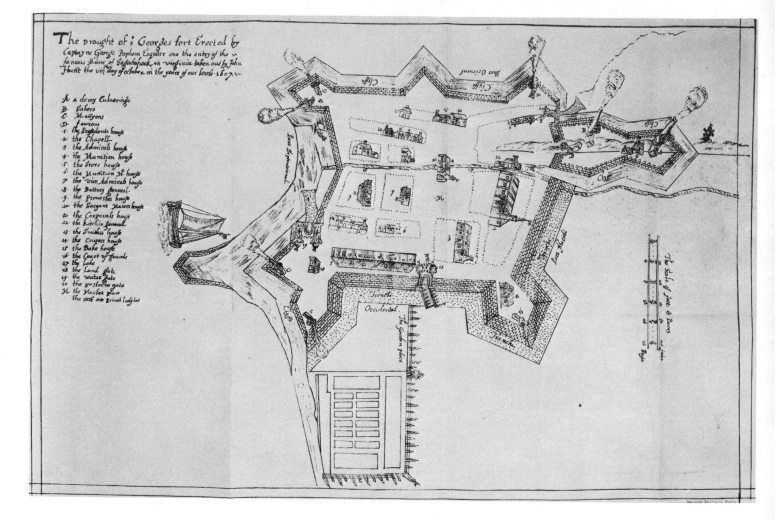

107. 1607–1608. Plan of the English Fort St. George on the Kennebec (Sagadahoc) River.

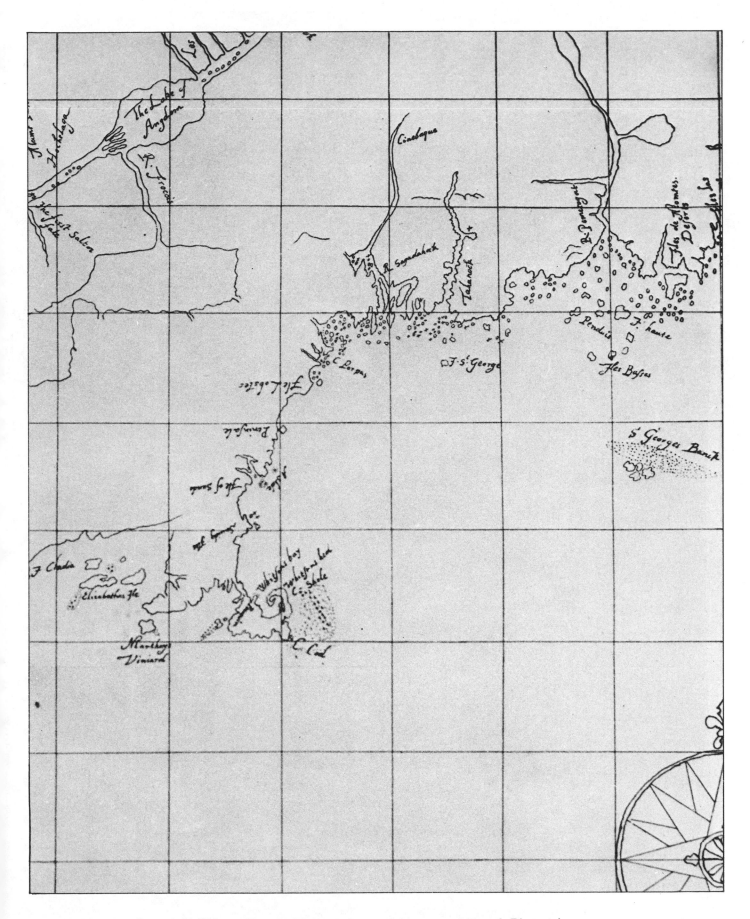

108. 1610 or 1611. Part of the Velasco Map, Enlarged to Show the English and French Discoveries
    in New England, 1602–1607.

109. 1616. John Smith's Map of New England.

110. 1616. Map by Cornelis Hendrik, Showing the
Delaware and Hudson River Valleys.

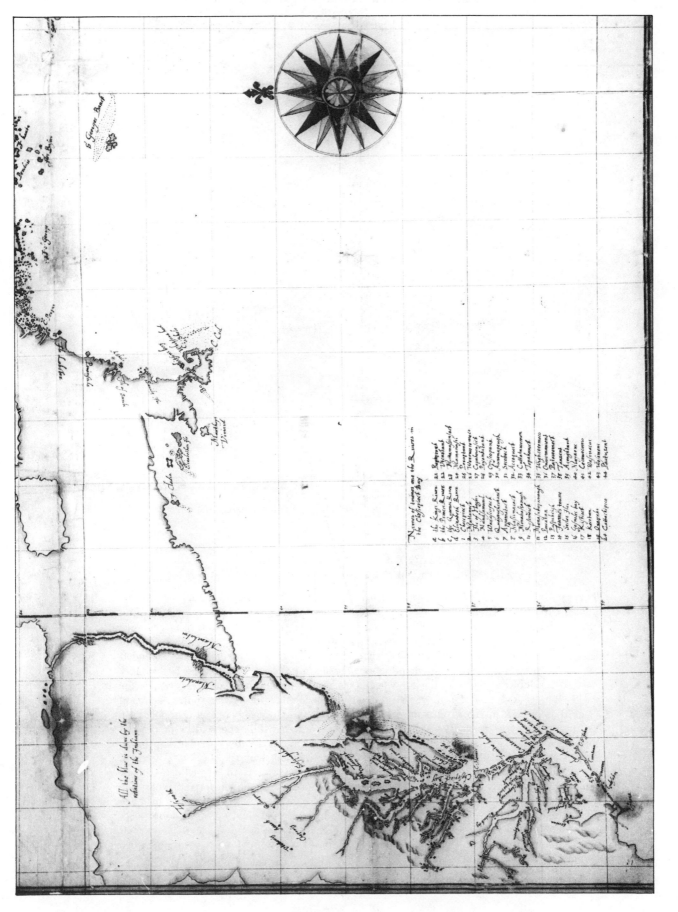

111. 1610. Portion of the Velasco Map, Enlarged to Show the Hudson River and the Coastline Between Southern Maine and Cape Fear.

111a. *Circa* 1582-1583. An early set of map symbols (with 401).

AN EARLY SET OF MAP SYMBOLS
(*circa* 1582–1583) FROM BRITISH LIBRARY MS 38823, fol. 2.

The set of instructions for the captain, master and surveyor of one of the expeditions planned by or for Sir Humphrey Gilbert in 1582 or 1583 contains what is probably the earliest list of map symbols (or "Characteristic Signs") set out in England for the guidance of chart and mapmakers. As the manuscript (401) lacks the first page, and is in any case a copy, we cannot be certain whether this representation is precisely that intended by the author, but it is repeated in identical terms on a later folio and so is probably not too inaccurate. The shading for woods, the elevations for hills and the crosses for rocks alone cover land features. We are left with a blank for rivers, but it is made clear that depths in rivers must be indicated in feet to show shelves and channels. We are left without a distinctive sign for rocks above water, while the scatter of crosses for rocks underwater could prove misleading. While the marks for a foot in depth are always clear, it is probably that those for "A fathame" should read "fa.3.fa.6.fa.8." and not "fo.3.fo.6.fo.8." Latitudes are to be indicated and an attempt is to be made to record longitudes (probably merely by dead reckoning). Directions are given for indicating the variation and "flie" (not "slie") of the compass and for certifying the "flie" by "the Instrument of variacyon," evidently a new type of instrument devised for this purpose, while declination is also to be indicated by a sign. The table still requires to be tested against surviving English charts of the period to show how far its prescriptions were common form at this time.